Understanding
Business Studies

...ham

...rt

...field

Stanley Thornes (Publishers) Ltd

First published in 1997 by
Stanley Thornes (Publishers) Ltd
Ellenborough House
Wellington Street
Cheltenham
GL50 1YW
UK

A catalogue record for this book is available from The British Library.

ISBN 0 7487 3346 9

97 98 99 00 01 / 10 9 8 7 6 5 4 3 2 1

Typeset by Northern Phototypesetting Co Ltd, Bolton and by Paul Manning
Printed and bound in Great Britain by Scotprint Limited, Musselburgh

Contents

Introduction

Understanding Business Studies is a new book about Business which has been written for students studying this field at the end of the 20th and start of the 21st century.

It is ten years since we first wrote a Business text for students at Advanced and Higher Levels and in that time great changes have taken place.

Business has now become established as an important field of study. Each year many thousands of students study Business in sixth forms, colleges and universities. This book has been written specifically for these students and is based on detailed research of current development.

Business is a continually changing and broad-based discipline. Students who follow the subject are studying a broad field encompassing areas as diverse as psychology, sociology, economics, history, mathematics, technology, geography and politics.

Critical thinkers

We believe that the strength of our text is that it encourages students to be critical thinkers with a concern for the place of individuals and organisations in society. Involvement in business should not be seen as a narrow technical exercise, although organisation members do at times need to work to technical constraints, develop detailed plans, create spreadsheets and charts and carry out other planning procedures in a detailed way.

Students need also to understand and explore broad perspectives on the nature of society, and the purpose of individuals and organisations in this society. They should have a good understanding of the political, economic and social environment in which business activity takes place.

An important charge often levelled at Business is that it is at times blinkered. It sets its sights too narrowly, focusing on a limited number of 'success criteria' related to such objectives as selling more products, becoming a market leader, making more profits. We hope that studying this text will help students to reject this approach. We stress the importance of viewing Business as part of a wider environment in which there is a range of stakeholders in the success or failure of the business. Such a stake might be employment for job holders, or freedom from disturbance for neighbours of a business organisation.

To be successful by modern standards businesses need to have a keen eye on ethics and an important part of ethical behaviour is acting as a custodian of the environment. Gro Haarlem Brundtland (the former Prime Minister of Norway) set out a pathway to sustainable development for our society: 'Development which meets the needs of the present without compromising the ability of future generations to meet their own needs.' Businesses which are short-sighted and fail to take these principles on board pose a threat to the structure and fabric of our society.

Progression

In creating this text we have followed the line of recent thinking articulated by the Dearing Report that students should be provided with avenues to progression in a field of study. All of us seek to move on from relatively simple to more complex ideas. We have therefore broken *Understanding Business Studies* down into two halves which could well represent distinct sections of a course, with say Part 1 for Year 1, and Part 2 for Year 2. The themes we have visited in the first part of the book are built on in the second half of the book in what we consider to be a logical way.

At the end of each part there are questions from past papers for students to try out to check on their understanding of what has come before. Some of these questions test discrete areas of business, for example finance, or organisational structure, but more commonly they will test integrated knowledge, that is a range of areas from across the course/book.

Changing times

Understanding Business Studies contains references to a range of modern materials not previously available to Advanced Level students. In a fluid field such as Business new ideas and practices are continually developing.

Today we have a Labour government with new ideas about creating a stakeholder economy; we have a United Kingdom which is more integrated into the European economy than at any time in previous history; we are moving towards using a common European Union currency, the Euro; we have different approaches to strategic planning in organisations; we have taken on board many Japanese working practices; we have organisations which are leaner and flatter; we have moved on to Human Resource Management and empowerment, and we have many other changes which are discussed in this book.

The importance of books

In these days of CD Roms and the Internet we would like to reaffirm our belief in the importance of books in the learning process. We believe that textbooks should not sit on shelves in neat dustcovers. They should be owned by students who take a delight in engaging in discourse with the text by writing their own views and notes all over them. A good book should be battle scarred and well thumbed through. In carrying out these actions you will be 'adding value' to the text. We want you to enjoy your studies.

Dave Needham
Rob Dransfield

The Nottingham Trent University
September 1997

Acknowledgements

The authors and publishers would like to thank the following individuals and organisations for help in the preparation of this book:

The Archbishop of Canterbury, General Accident, John Barnes, James Dyson, the Shell Education Service, Frank Hudson, Aubrey Nokes, Northern Examinations and Assessment Board, EdExcel – London Examinations, Nottingham Trent University, Oxford and Cambridge Examinations and Assessment Council, The Associated Examining Board, National Shoppers Survey, the National Extension College and United Biscuits plc.

The authors would also like to thank Andy Heming for creating the chapter on the importance of good management, Sarah Yeoman for the chapter on Europe, and Steph Howkins for the section on teamwork; Helen Robinson and Katie Lawson for providing case studies and Bryan Oakes for providing so many good ideas. Rob Dransfield would also like to thank Claire, Donald, Elspeth, Ken and Jean for many years of support. Dave Needham would like to thank his family, especially Alison, Alex and Graham both for their continued and enduring support for the writing and for developing a love of cricket. Both authors would also like especially to thank Sarah Wilman and Sandy Marshall at Stanley Thornes for their efforts to help us create a text which is more than just a book about Business Studies.

Photo credits:

JohnGiles/PA (page 5), Darlington Borough Council (page 17), Derek Tamea/Lambeth Palace (page 28), Shell Education Service (page 62), Dyson Appliances (page 65), Barclay Stratton/Pizza Hut (page 72), McDonald's Restaurants Ltd (page 114), the Ford Motor Company (page 233), British Airways (page 273), Roger D Smith/John Mowlem & Company plc (page 277), Corbis-Bettmann/UPI (pages 341 and 556), David Jones/PA News Photo Library (page 474), Fiona Hanson/PA News Photo Library (page 474), Marks and Spencer plc (page 553), Dave Kendall/PA News Photo Library (page 595), Tim Ockenden/PA News Photo Library (page 611).

Every effort has been made to contact copyright holders and we apologise if any have been overlooked.

Part 1

LEARNING ABOUT BUSINESS

1 *Business studies toolbox*

1 Meeting the demands of A/S and A level business studies courses

I think I know what I am doing!

Starting any new course at any level represents a new challenge. To some extent, how well you are able to adapt to the rigours of A and A/S Level courses in Business Studies might depend upon your previous experiences. For example, you may:

- have already taken some A/AS levels
- hold a GCSE in Business Studies
- have no experience of Business Studies at all
- have considerable experience of industry which you want to apply to an academic area by taking a course in Business Studies.

If you have already taken A or A/S Levels in different subjects and Business Studies is simply adding to your portfolio you would probably have fewer reservations about your own capabilities than if Business Studies at these levels is one of several new courses you are starting having just completed your GCSEs.

For nearly all of you, unless you are retaking the course, Business Studies at either A or A/S Level involves something new. In fact, it will involve a process transfer from either subjects or levels of learning which have a 'familiar context' to new areas and new levels of learning which present unfamiliar problems or are in an unfamiliar context. Though confidence is important and you may be sure that you 'know what you are doing', how well you cope with this depends upon how well you can transfer from the familiar to the unfamiliar.

For most of you education and training been presented to you in a familiar context with familiar problems. As many of you worked towards your GCSEs you may have understood what was required and may have been 'quietly confident' about what you were likely to achieve. Now that you are doing an A or A/S Level you are being placed in an unfamiliar situation. You need to ask yourself: 'What do I need to do to prepare myself for my new course?' Though you have mastered courses in the past, now you have no notes or track record to draw comfort from. There are no certainties in the things you do. Transferring from the familiar to the unfamiliar is a learning experience which will require you to find out more about your new context, learn new skills of analysis and move further forward to develop new skills and capabilities.

The business studies toolbox

The purpose for this opening section of the book is simply to help you to manage this process of change. Whether you are coming back to study or whether you are simply moving on from GCSEs to A Levels, there may be a number of learning issues with which you may feel that you need help, advice or simply the opportunity to read and reflect. Here we provide a practical focus for your course which we hope can be used as a source of reference. Though a lot of thought has gone into developing it we cannot offer off-the-shelf solutions for any learning issues in your A or A/S Level course. What we have tried to do, however, is to provide advice designed to improve your understanding of key issues involved in the process of studying for a Business Studies course at this level, so that you can think about how you can develop a pattern of learning which suits you best.

What am I studying?

The starting point for your course is to find out what you are studying. Though you may respond with 'Business Studies A Level', what does this mean? What is the rationale for the course and what are its aims? Have you read through the syllabus content? What skills might you require? Raising these issues in the early days of the course helps to set the context for your pattern of learning.

One way of understanding what Business Studies at A and A/S Level involves, as well as what you might be looking at and how you are going to study for it, is to use the acronym SPOEKS, which represents the three critical elements for all Business Studies courses at these levels. These are:

Element 1 The **Stakeholders** and their **Perspectives**
Element 2 The **Organisation** and its **Environment**
Element 3 The **Key Skills**

A and AS Level courses in Business Studies will help you to:

- **SP** Appreciate that businesses can be studied from the **perspectives** of a range of different types of **stakeholders** such as customers, managers, employees, owners and creditors. Business Studies draws upon a range of disciplines and you need to appreciate that these disciplines are interrelated.
- **OE** Develop a critical understanding of **organisations**, the markets they serve and the process of adding value. This will not just involve an understanding of the internal workings of an organisation but will also involve you developing an appreciation of the process of decision making in a dynamic external **environment**.
- **KS** Acquire a range of **key skills** such as communication, critical understanding, numeracy and problem solving which help you to make decisions when you are presented with a range of information.

The Northern Examinations and Assessment Board points out that the purpose of its Advanced Business Studies syllabus is:

> to enable centres to devise courses which will provide candidates with adequate knowledge and critical understanding of a wide variety of management problems within organisations in industry and commerce. The study should be firmly rooted in the current structure of business and business practice, and candidates should be aware of the uncertain and dynamic environment within which businesses operate.

NEAB then goes further and breaks this broad rationale into specific aims such as:

- to provide candidates with sound knowledge of the principles which govern business and management practice
- to develop a critical understanding of business concepts, theories and skills, and the ability to apply these to the definition, analysis and solution to business problems
- to provide the opportunity for candidates to acquire experience of practical decision making
- to develop the ability to communicate effectively in numerical, graphical and verbal form.

Find out which examination board you will be examined by. Ask you tutor for a copy of both the aims and syllabus rationale as well as a copy of the syllabus. Read the information you are provided with and fit it in to your programme of learning. Look at the syllabus periodically to find out what areas have been covered and what areas are to come. This may be particularly useful as:

- It helps you to appreciate that each part you cover builds up a picture which develops your understanding of business as a whole.
- It enables you to plan your work and fit the progression from one area to another area or one module to another into some form of order or perspective.
- It enables you to think about what you need to do for background reading and research not only regarding areas in which you have been taught but also areas that you will cover in the future.

Moral and ethical issues

Throughout the area of Business Studies you will come across moral and ethical issues. Ethics involve what you consider to be right as well as what you consider to be wrong. We all have thoughts about how other individuals and organisations behave. One of the most interesting aspects of Business Studies is being able to explore these moral and ethical areas as part of your process of learning in a way which helps you to develop your understanding about the nature, purpose and consequences of business activities.

These moral and ethical issues are an important part of learning about business. When you read the business news you will inevitably read about issues such as insider dealing, executive pay, share options, product testing on animals, corruption and bribery, as well as a host of other areas in which you are developing your views. As and when they relate to the process of learning in the classroom, find out more about them, discuss them with others and quote your findings. Exploration of these issues not only helps to improve your understanding of key areas of study, it also helps you to build skills while at the same time developing an appreciation that Business Studies is about real people in real situations where everyday decisions made in the world of business affect us all in one way or another.

Assessment

In a perfect world you might question the need for some form of assessment. Assessment in a number of different ways affects everybody at some stage during their lives, not just in education but also in the workplace. The process however is probably at its most formal when you are either at school or at college.

There is no doubt that any form of assessment can be stressful. It would be unwise for us to say that you have to take this in your stride. Inevitably, some of you will find the whole process of assessment easier than others.

One way of thinking about assessment is to compare it as a process to some form of sporting activity. What makes really good sportsmen or sportswomen? How can we tell how good they are? For example, is playing for a hockey team simply about being fit and having the necessary skills or is there more to it? If you think of some of the great performers of recent times, such as Sally Gunnell and Linford Christie, what factors have characterised these individuals to set them apart from other performers? There is no doubt that they have a determination and positive approach to their activities which has meant that they have had to sacrifice so much in order achieve their ambitions. The process must have been painful. In relative terms there must have been many failures which they probably think of as learning experiences.

In the world of education, examinations, course work and other forms of assessment might be viewed with foreboding. Entering into a race and coming second is one thing but to take an examination or other form of assessment and to fail is another! For A Level and AS Level Business Studies you must try to develop a positive and analytical approach which goes beyond straightforward knowledge of the subject area. The days of regurgitation are in the past. As examiners mark papers they are genuinely looking beyond the factual dissemination of knowledge in answer to discrete questions towards the interpretation you provide from your learning process, such as your understanding of key problems and issues. This is particularly important. One way of understanding how important is to look at the assessment objectives for your course in the context of the skills and context prescribed.

For example, assessment objectives might include the following. Candidates should be able to:

● demonstrate knowledge and understanding of the specified content
● apply their knowledge and critical understanding to problems and issues arising from both familiar and unfamiliar situations
● analyse problems, issues and situations
● evaluate, to distinguish between fact and opinion, and assess information from a variety of sources.

What factors have characterised performers like Linford Christie to set them apart from others?

It is useful for you to look at the specific assessment objectives for the syllabus you are undertaking so that you can think how these objectives might apply during the assessment process. You may also wish to see how these objectives are weighted for each syllabus and it might be helpful to ask your tutor to take you through this process.

Another important issue is to understand how a Grade A might differ from a Grade E. Again this might be the sort of thing you wish to talk through with a tutor. For example, for AS Level:

Grade A
The candidate demonstrates detailed in-depth knowledge and critical understanding of a wide range of business theory and concepts. He or she will use this knowledge and critical understanding to analyse familiar and unfamiliar situations, contexts and issues, using appropriate numerical and non-numerical techniques. He or she will also evaluate evidence and arguments, make reasoned judgements and present appropriate and supported conclusions.

Compare this with:

Grade E
The candidate will demonstrate knowledge and understanding of a range of business theory and concepts. He or she will apply this knowledge and understanding in a attempt to analyse familiar and unfamiliar situations, problems and issues. He or she will attempt to use both numerical and non-numerical techniques. He or she may also attempt limited evaluation of evidence and argument.

Now that you understand something about the process of assessment it is particularly important that, even early on in a course, you also know what the assessment will involve and the timing for that assessment. Schemes of assessment vary widely from one examination board to another. The purpose of this chapter is not to list the various schemes. We can however make some comparisons.

The nature of learning and studying

It is not possible to provide you with an off-the-shelf package which enables you to pass your A or AS Level in Business Studies with flying colours. As we pointed out earlier in the chapter, you are moving from a familiar context and problems to more unfamiliar contexts often with completely different problems. There are probably few areas of study which involve so much change year-on-year. In the world of business the environment and context in which we look at organisations is influenced almost daily by events and circumstances which affect the world in which decision makers have to operate. As you learn and study in this area you will come across new ideas. It is up to you to make sense of such new ideas by thinking them through within the context of your course requirements. Though we cannot promise that it is easy, we can assure you that as you develop your interest in the area and get stuck into your course you will find the Business Studies both interesting and rewarding.

2 Creating your own personal action plan

You might think that studying is a fairly straightforward activity 'once you get into the swing of it'. All you have to do is to turn up at lessons, make some notes, write a few essays, pontificate around some case studies, and after two years you will get an A Level! If only life was quite as easy as that.

There will be times during your course when you know that you need to get something done but do not know how to start. At other times you may want to start a project or some course work and then find that time is running out. You also need to think about how to set out a pattern of work within which you wish to operate.

I will never forget an interview I had with a Business Studies student a few years ago. The student was part-time and worked on a farm. He had not produced any written work for the course. In class he actively contributed to discussion and intelligently presented his ideas. When approached his response was, 'I do not know how you expect me to do your essays and case studies, Mr Needham. I do not finish work until 6.30 p.m. By the time I have had a bath and eaten my tea it is 8.15 p.m. I then phone my girl friend and we talk for half an hour. This does not leave a lot of time because at 9.30 p.m. I go to the pub and I need that. And, you have to remember my job is seven days a week!'

Though I sympathised and recommended a good dose of personal action planning I realised that unless he used a mechanism which exerted some form of discipline he would probably not complete the course. His problem was extreme. Before taking the course he should really have thought about how much time he would have to spend working and what he would need to sacrifice in order to pass it. Most people's problems tend to be more methodological. They might be able to find the time to study and learn but they need something which helps them to become better organised.

What is personal action planning?

Planning is about having a method or scheme which enables you to create a more organised way of going about a task or activity. An **action plan** is a particular form of plan, because it involves the essential ingredient of being able to put a plan into action. A **personal action plan** helps you as you work to set out the steps between where you are now and where you want to be in the future.

You have to remember that the opposite of planning is not planning. Without a plan, whether it is written or in your mind, you are likely to be less organised. The phrase used for a lack of planning is running around like 'headless chickens'.

There are a number of reasons why planning may help you with your Business Studies course.

- Planning may help you to be clear about your objectives and what you want to achieve. For example, for the university of your choice you may require a specific grade. The process of planning will help you to target your efforts at getting that grade.
- Sometimes working logically does not always come easily. Planning will help you to organise your activities into a sequence and improve the timing of events. How many people having been given a fortnight to do an essay end up doing most of the work the day before it is due in?
- Planning helps you to check upon your progress. It provides an opportunity to appraise your progress and think, 'How am I doing?' This is particularly important. If you have a series of aims and objectives the process of planning does link these objectives with what you are actually doing.
- Priorities can be sorted out through planning. Planning makes sure that the important things to do are not left until last.
- When writing essays or revising you need to think about all of the materials you need. Planning helps you to organise resources and materials.
- Planning saves time.
- Planning reduces stress.

How could an action plan be laid out?

There are a variety of ways of laying out an action plan. To a large extent the layout you choose will be determined by what you want to do and how you view the task you are undertaking. We are going to suggest two alternative layouts. The first is an action plan for a piece of work which you wish to hand in. The second refers more generally to how you wish to use the planning process to help you to achieve your A or AS Level in Business Studies.

PLAN 1 Planning for a piece of work

1 Description of work

2 Timings for work

3 Resources required

4 Action steps

a
b
c
d
e

5 Review of progress and evaluation

PLAN 2 Passing your A or AS Level Business Studies
My objectives in Business Studies are:

Over the next year in Business Studies

I want to achieve	The steps I need to take are	Timing of action steps
…	1	1
	2	2
	3	3
…	1	1
	2	2
	3	3

Priorities over the next year

1

2

Evidence of my achievements

Action planning is not simply designed to be a paper exercise. It is important that you periodically review your plan to make sure the things that are happening are the events that you intended to happen. Try to generate a series of action steps which provides you with a sense of discipline and helps to create a pattern of working which generates effective personal learning and development.

3 Making sense of information

Managing the flow of information

Imagine the worst possible scenario. You have six weeks to go before your examinations. Your file burst its seams half way through the first year of your A Level course. It lies in a bedroom cupboard. Since its expiry date all other notes for Business Studies have been stacked on top. There is no order or sequence. Handouts, newspaper cuttings and newspapers, and all other pieces of work need to be sorted out. Instead of being able to get down to the process of revision, much of your time in the early phases of the revision process is spent simply sorting yourself out.

One of the problems with an area such as Business Studies is that it attracts information. In almost every area there are supporting materials useful to your course: cuttings from newspapers and magazines, information from companies, mailshots through the door and even electronic information such as computer disks and pages of corporate information printed from the internet. At the same time, you may have notes from your lessons and may also be obtaining information for a project or course work. It is easy to accumulate vast quantities of data. Your problem is simply to deal with such information flows by developing your own information system enabling you to sort data into areas where it can be summarised for revision purposes.

Your first step in an A or AS Level Business Studies course is to make sure that you have some method of storing data. If your tutor has encouraged you to buy newspapers, this does not mean that for the next two years a pile appears and develops in the corner of your bedroom. Undoubtedly in two years you will accumulate a lot of valuable information which could help you with your course, particularly your course work. But, how do you find such information? It is not as if you can refer to Yahoo or Alta Vista to search the pile in the corner of the room. Electronic search engines do not work with piles of newspapers. You must learn to take out the relevant pieces, even as you read them, rather than keep the whole paper. Similarly, course notes need to be properly and logically organised so that when you come to revise you can find what you need – and quickly.

In business, decision makers rarely have all of the information they require. No matter how much detail is available, there is always more information which may be relevant in helping to tackle a problem. By asking the right questions you will be able to make more sense of the data you have collected and also use the information to show a good understanding of each area of study.

For example, imagine that you were collecting materials and notes in the area of **financial accounting**. The questions you might ask are as follows:

- **How am I going to organise information?** You may wish to collect data according to each module or topic you undertake. This might mean either setting up a file or sub-dividing a file of information for financial accounting. You may have to make a decision about whether to keep notes and other materials with teaching notes or you may wish to keep them separate. Whichever method you choose you need to stick with it.
- **What information might this include?** For Business Studies you may have a series of class notes and handouts. Added to this you may have been asked to do some work and so will have some marked feedback or form of assessment. Having at least one or even several company annual reports can be particularly useful. Some newspapers have an accounting column or section (e.g. *The Times* on Thursday). Cutting these out each week and filing them will help you to set up an invaluable information resource. You may also have taken financial information from company home pages on the internet.
- **How do I find what I need?** If your filing system is kept neatly and you know where all of the information is, it will not take you long to find what you require. This method would be particularly useful for undertaking any form of integrated work such as a project or other form of study.

Working with numbers

We live in a world where a lot of information is communicated numerically. How many times are numbers used in a Business Studies lesson? Do you readily use numbers when describing something? For example, what is a 2 litre car? If it is $-2°C$, what does this mean? And, how is this information presented to you? Inevitably, a lot of numbers may appear in conversation or in a text. However, some may appear in charts, graphs and tables or simply on diagrams.

Numerical ability is very important in business. There are some areas of business, such as finance and accounts, in which accuracy and skill with the use of number is critical. However, numeracy is also a general skill which is of great importance in many spheres of business activity, for example in quantitative work in market and product research, business forecasting and economics, and in performance measurement in all aspects of business life.

In following an A or AS Level course you will have many opportunities to develop your number skills, particularly in areas such as:

- collecting and recording data
- tackling problems
- interpreting and presenting data.

Numbers can be difficult because they represent a wealth of information which is condensed in an abstract form. On its own any number probably means very little. However, you have to learn how to read them in a way which places meaning and value to the information they represent. Numbers might also represent specialist knowledge and skills. For example, if someone talks about detailed financial information which you do not understand, then clearly there is a gap between your knowledge and application of number in that context and their knowledge and application of number in the same context. Therefore, in order to be able to confidently use number in Business Studies, whatever the area of analysis you need to:

- know how the numbers are being used, and
- what the numbers are being used to represent in each situation.

It is not the purpose of this chapter to provide you with the skills necessary to tackle numerical data. Given the nature of your course and the level at which this book is targeted we are assuming that you will have a prescribed level of mathematical and numerical skills. We would however like to emphasise that you should:

- Be prepared to use numerical techniques, including presentation, in a range of different ways in order to suit the problem that you are working on.
- Add, subtract, divide and multiply numbers of any size and make calculations using fractions, percentages and ratios, as well as formulae.
- Be prepared to make calculations involving measures such as National Income and the Retail Price Index as well as a range of other measures.
- Handle data using scales and tables, and work out and use the mean, median, mode and interquartile range.
- Perform techniques in the right order and choose and use appropriate units.
- Work accurately and use mathematical terms correctly. Your calculations should be correct and you should check the procedures you have used.

TASK 3.1

Look at the information contained in each of the charts in Figure 3.1. Comment briefly upon the usefulness of each piece of information.

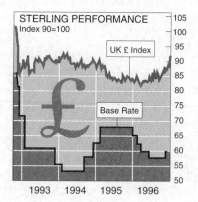

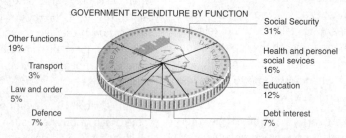

Figure 3.1

Figures, numbers and a range of different methods of using numbers appear throughout this book. It is important to remember that within your work, one of the best ways to describe your understanding of a key issue is to use numbers. Numbers add to the force of your description. They can be used to underpin your analysis in a way which emphasises the depth of your understanding. In doing this they add an extra dimension to your work.

4 Developing your case study techniques

Why are case studies used?

Business Studies is concerned with the dynamic world in which all organisations have to exist and in which all of you will have to work. By its very nature it is an area of constant change and we hear daily of events that have taken place in the business environment.

Case analysis is a learning mechanism that is used both in and out of the classroom. It helps you to look and appreciate how organisations act, make decisions and respond in different circumstances. It is a way of helping you to realise that Business Studies is not just about theory but also about application.

What is a case study?

A **case study** is a description of an actual organisation's situation or of a specific event effecting the business environment. Analysing the case therefore involves an element of realism that bridges the gap between the classroom and the commercial world, and enables you to apply your understanding to a practical situation. The purpose of case analysis is to:

- enable you to understand the forces underlying business activities
- appreciate the various factors that govern decision making
- provide a means by which you can develop problem-solving skills
- enable you to apply quantitative tools
- encourage you to recognise the significance of information
- provide an opportunity to work in groups
- encourage you to think about values, generate ideas and make practical suggestions.

Applying background theory to a case study will help you to become an active rather than a passive participant in the learning process. It will not only help to make Business Studies more practical, it will also generate greater realism and help you to develop a better understanding of the context in which issues and areas apply.

Real people, real problems

When looking at case studies it is possible for you to acquire knowledge of, and the need for, theoretical concepts by means of example, rather than by the more traditional method of being given a theory that is then supported or 'proved', by example. Though a lot of Business Studies involves the use of common sense, like any subject you might study, it possesses its own unique language. By using case studies you might see the common sense first, which can then be reinforced with theory afterwards. For example, look at the following extract:

Battle on the buses

A bus war has broken out around Grantham, giving villagers a super-service of six buses an hour.

Lincolnshire RoadCar has moved into Reliance's patch in Barrowby (a village on the edge of Grantham), slashed fares and given residents in the village a service they can hardly believe.

The long-established Reliance operation gave Barrowby people four buses an hour into town. Now Lincolnshire RoadCar has introduced a Road Runner service, upping the numbers by two an hour between Barrowby and Grantham.

It has set the scene for a battle between the established operator and the newcomer. In the Reliance corner is owner Joe Simmons, with 20 buses, while in the RoadCar corner, the company, which is part of Yorkshire traction, has more than 600 buses.

Joe Simmons has delivered 1000 leaflets to Barrowby homes stating that his service is reliable and well-known. RoadCar has chopped 5p off the 40p fare into town and Mr Simmons has matched the price cut. Mr Simmons is furious that the RoadCar schedule sees it Road Runner at bus stops just five minutes ahead of its service.

RoadCar is unrepentant and a spokesperson said, 'These changes are another step in the steady increase of our bus services. The introduction of the Barrowby route is just an extension of our success in other areas of the town.'

The above extract was used with a group of A Level students in order to help them to appreciate competitive forces in the business environment. Having presented them with the case illustrated, they were then asked to analyse the following questions:

- Why did RoadCar move into Barrowby?
- What were the company's short and long-term objectives?
- Explain the reaction of Reliance.
- What advantage might each company have?
- What factors would determine the likely outcome?

Students were then asked to write a newspaper report looking six months into the future and to comment upon the likely changes. They had to relate what they had learned about competition to other products and other sectors. Having looked at examples of competition, theory was then built into the course and students could immediately identify with its importance.

This case study helped students to analyse a current situation locally. By looking at it they learned not only to appreciate the nature and importance of events in their own local business environment but also their understanding of these events in such a way that they could intelligently rationalise outcomes as part of their learning.

Where do case studies come from and how might they be written?

Case studies may be taken from a wide variety of sources. For example, they may be extracted from magazines, newspapers or professional journals; they may relate to international events or nationally recognised organisations; they may even be fictitious. Some case studies may come from *The Times 100* while others may come from text books and workbooks. What is certain is that during your A or AS Level course you will come across literally hundreds of different case studies.

The types of case study you come across may vary enormously. Some may be fairly straightforward and require only a cursory analysis while others may be highly complex and require careful thought. Some case studies may simply be used by your tutors as the basis for discussion. Others will require considerable research and written analysis. Some case studies like the one illustrated above will simply be used to develop your understanding of a single theory or area of learning while others may be more generalised and provide a focus for learning across a range of areas of study. For example, you might get a case study which asks you questions which refer to areas of human resource management, finance and accounting and organisational theory.

What is certain is that case studies will appear as part of your assessment and will be an important part of your learning process. You must not be put off by this. They are designed to make learning more interesting by helping you to appreciate the dynamics of the business decision-making process.

Developing your own case study techniques

The following is a series of notes designed to help you develop your own case study techniques:

- **Read through the study carefully** before you attempt to answer any questions. If necessary read it several times to make sure that you understand key areas. It is sometimes useful to **make notes** to serve as a reminder of what has taken place and to help you to analyse the evolution of events.
- **Try to think about the sorts of questions you may be asked**. Consider the areas the study covers, the work you have covered in these areas, how the study relates to topical issues as well as other examples of similar issues.
- **Be aware of the nature of integration**. Think about the extent to which the study pulls together various elements of your course.
- **Read each question carefully**. Ask yourself: 'What does this question require?' If necessary, plan out your response in rough. If you do this it can be helpful to show rough notes with your response, particularly if you have undertaken a series of calculations.
- **If mark allocations are indicated, look at them and use them.** For example, if a question asks you to make a series of points and is allocated eight marks, you could expect a mark allocation for up to four good points, and then further allocation for application and synthesis. Similarly, if two marks are allocated for a definition, you must try to identify the two elements of the definition that will gain you the two marks.
- **Try to answer questions fully**. Do not list points. Think about how you expand and develop your answer within the context of your knowledge and understanding of the case. Providing lengthy analysis will add substance to your answer and enable you to pick up extra marks.
- **Wherever necessary, refer to the text**. Questions will vary in level of difficulty and some might require you to refer to specific parts of the case in order to assess your comprehension of it.
- **Think about the theory necessary to support your answer**. It would be a dreadful mistake to assume that all of the answers are in the study. Though this might happen if the study is being used inductively to introduce a specific area of study, in most cases you will be expected to support your answer by showing a broad understanding of what you have been taught as a whole, and how you can apply it to particular situations.
- **Do not be frightened to use common sense, ideas and practical suggestions**. The case study is intended to put you in a realistic situation and so a realistic and practical response is acceptable as long as it does not contradict existing theories.
- **Always read through your answer** at the end of each question and try to assess the value of your contribution. If you want to think further about your response and come back at a later stage leave a space or cross-reference your answer.

Case studies have become an exciting vehicle of learning and, in examinations, a creative means of assessment. In the real world, we rarely deal with business problems cold – we go and talk to the people concerned, we look at the problems with which they are faced and start with the details of their particular situation. Case analysis enables us to replicate the real world in this way in both the class and the examination room.

5 Writing essays for business studies

The importance of essay writing

Over recent years we have seen the introduction of an increasing variety of assessment techniques, including course work assignments, compulsory questions requiring short answers and case studies of different length. Though such changes of approach have led to less emphasis being placed on essay techniques, being able to write a good essay is still a crucial skill for many A and AS level students as essays provide an invaluable guide to a candidate's ability to tackle complex issues.

Few people would claim that essays are easy. They are not and, indeed, would lose their value as an assessment device if they were. Essays are designed to find out how you have responded to learning experiences. They allow you not just to describe something fully, but also provide an opportunity for you to show a depth of understanding and analysis through the written form.

Effective writing

We all come across situations in our professional or personal lives where we will be asked to make a statement, write a reference, send an article, make an assessment, write an appraisal or write a report. In each of these situations, we will be required to use our written skills based upon our knowledge, understanding and analysis or some research, event or belief. Though essay techniques are extremely useful in the school or college environment, their usefulness is not limited to this context. The skills developed can be transferred to any situation requiring a degree of written analysis.

An important point to note is that examination boards are concerned with 'Quality of Language' wherever candidates are required to produce continuous prose. This includes your use of grammar, punctuation and spelling as well as the structure and presentation of your ideas. This means that if candidates are guilty of errors in grammar, punctuation and spelling, or have specific weaknesses, they will be penalised. In fact around 4 or 5 per cent of marks could be lost. That might make the difference between one grade and another! It might even involve the difference between a pass grade and failure! It is critical that you work hard upon developing your skills and, if you have weaknesses, try to minimise their effect upon your work.

Levels of response

It is also important for you to realise that you are not only going to be marked for the information or hard facts you provide in your answer but also for the skills you use in answering each question. In the past, under traditional marking schemes, candidates were rewarded for the individual points they made. Under these circumstances insufficient focus was placed upon the overall quality of each candidate's answer. 'Levels of response' marking schemes search for the general qualities displayed by candidates as they interpret and answer questions.

The aim of a levels of response marking scheme is to reward quality so that where candidates provide high-level evaluative skills they will receive higher marks for a fuller analysis of a question. The Associated Examining Board identifies higher academic qualities as follows:

Analysis (breaking down)
- *Identification of cause, effect and interrelationships.*
- *The appropriate use of theory or business/cases to investigate the question set.*
- *Breaking the material down to show underlying causes or problems.*
- *Use of appropriate techniques to analyse data.*

Synthesis (bringing together)
- *Building the points/themes within the answer into a connected whole.*
- *Logical sequencing of argument.*
- *Clarity through summarising an argument.*

Evaluation (judgement)
- *Judgement shown in weighing up the relative importance of different points or side of an argument, in order to reach a conclusion.*
- *Informed comment on the reliability of evidence.*
- *Distinguishing between fact and opinion.*
- *Judgement of the wider issues and implications.*
- *Conclusions drawn from the evidence presented.*
- *Selectivity – ensuring material is all relevant to the question.*

Developing your essay techniques

Before writing an essay you must ask yourself: 'Do I fully understand this question?' Different types of question will require different degrees of thought and different types of response. Try to identify what it is that the question requires and remember to respond specifically to these requirements in your answer. Some essay titles are a little like a puzzle and so working out a solution may involve reading between the lines.

Look at the title

What are the key words in the title? Make sure that your answer responds specifically to these key words:
Discuss, Explain, What?, Contrast, Outline, Describe, Distinguish, Why?, How?, To what extent?

Plan your answer before you start to write your essay

Though you might think that planning may take up valuable time that could otherwise be spent writing, it will, in fact, help you to improve the structure, and therefore the quality, of your answer. How many times have you written an essay and then, towards the end of the answer remembered something that your should have put in at an earlier stage in your response? Planning:

- helps you to structure your answer so that it is presented in a logical sequence
- gives you a little time to think and rationalise before writing your response – it is sometimes easier to take a breathing space and think about the essay beforehand, than to try to think about your answer while you are actually writing
- can be used to make brief notes that you can then follow in your answer
- can be used as a revision device – looking at a series of essay titles and writing plans for them is a useful way of revising for an examination.

Writing an introduction

This helps you to bring your thoughts together. Try to show the marker that you understand the requirements of the question in your introduction. Respond directly to the question and, if necessary, make appropriate definitions by defining terms. The introduction provides a useful opportunity for you to explain to the marker how you intend to approach your answer.

Try to make your answer interesting

When writing your answer think about how it might be interpreted. One way in which you can do this is to refer to examples or analogies. There may be marks for such examples, particularly if used in context. By using them you are showing the marker the broad nature of your knowledge in the area and you ability to apply this knowledge to develop or support arguments and analysis.

Put your thoughts or ideas into your answer

An essay is an opportunity to show the marker that you can think, so it is perfectly acceptable to include your own ideas to support your response, as long as they are realistic and expressed within the context of the question. It is also acceptable to provide detailed analysis. Be careful, however, not to stray away from the question and not to spend too much time putting forward your own viewpoint at the expense of generally accepted theories. Remember to provide balance to your answer.

Make sure that your answer is relevant

Too often students spot a key word in an essay title and then fill the essay with everything they associate with that word. It is a bit like using a cannon to shoot a rabbit! Be specific in your answer and target it at the question. Remember to make points only within the specific context of the question. Do not put in irrelevant material as it just wastes time and does not win you any marks.

Try not to make lists in your answer

When you do this you are not providing synthesis and analysis. The only acceptable time for lists is if you are running out of time.

Sometimes the obvious is the most important

Try to see through each question and provide a full analysis of each point you make even though explaining the obvious might seem trivial.

Practise writing essays

Do this whenever you have an opportunity. Learning to write an essay in a given period of time is an important skill to develop. Many students, particularly those who have always written slowly, can find this extremely difficult. As all teachers will confirm, the announcement that there will be a timed essay next week will elicit the biggest groan from students. However, having to practise will prove invaluable.

Try to evidence wide-ranging knowledge in your answer

Remember that revision from just one source – either your notes or even just this text – is a little bit narrow. Try to use a variety of sources and then evidence the uses of these sources in your essays. During your course, you should, ideally, support your classroom notes with other notes taken from background reading. It is also sometimes useful to learn a few short but key quotes that you may have a variety of opportunities to apply. If you cannot remember them exactly, then paraphrase them rather than leave them out if they are particularly relevant.

Think about the various perspectives from which your answer comes

You may need to emphasise the relevance of your response in both the short- or long-term. Equally, you may try to develop your answer from a moral or ethical standpoint. Alternatively, there may be a pan-European or global view from which you can develop your answer. Remember to provide balance in your approach to answering a question. Look at it from all sides in a way which shows that you understand the complexities of the arguments.

Be prepared to integrate business disciplines

Many essays will require you to show knowledge across a range of areas within the answer. Be prepared to amalgamate information and use skills, knowledge and understanding from a variety of areas in your answer. For example, if an essay asks you to assess a particular change, you might be required to mention and develop within the context of the question the relevance of the process of decision making, investment appraisal, market research and current external factors within the same essay.

Show knowledge of concepts and theories

These are important in order to support your answer and develop your analysis. Concepts and theories help you to underpin your answer and show depth and breadth of understanding.

Try to make your essay stand out

This is easier said than done! Remember that what you are trying to do is to write something memorable. Being able to think out not just a rational answer but one which will show a tremendous capability to use your personal skills is important if you want to do very well.

Always conclude your answer

Provide a rational summary of the response you have developed in your essay. It is sometimes useful to relate your summary to the question to emphasise the nature of your approach.

Finally

If you have missed points out of your answer, put them underneath your essay and cross-reference them into the appropriate place with asterisks.

Always read through your answer after you have finished it and make corrections and amendments where necessary. Checking does not take long and may provide you with the opportunity to gain extra valuable marks.

The learning curve

Even if you remember all of this and put it into practice, writing essays will never be easy. Developing sound techniques such as these will, however, with some practice, help you to produce an end result which reflects your efforts.

6   The process of integration

What is integration?

In the world in which organisations operate, decision making does not just involve people from the top of the organisation. It is an everyday process which is carried out at all levels.

> **Decision making involves choosing a course of action from a series of alternatives.**

Within an organisation, different decisions lie within the province of different people within a hierarchy. These decisions broadly fall into two different categories:

- **Functional decisions** These decisions involve people in areas within the organisations such as marketing, personnel and finance. Decisions might have to be made about who to employ, some aspect of record keeping or the process of market research. To a large extent, but often not completely, functional decisions simply involve the analysis of problems relating to people operating within that functional area. Functional decisions tend to be more structured with set solutions and are more likely to be located in a specific operational area.

- **Integrated decisions** Though functional decisions may provide solutions to structured problems in specific operational areas, as problems become more complex, they not only become less structured, they also tend to require contributions from people around the organisation. In other words, in order to solve the problem there is a requirement to involve staff with different skills and levels of expertise. This is where integration takes place.

Many individuals within an organisation may have a range of skills relating to various functional areas. As managers move up the hierarchy there is an increasing requirement for them both to show and use skills and understanding from around their business environment as they make decisions.

As you work for your Business Studies qualification you may value the fact that you have an appreciation of various standpoints. At A and AS level, qualifications are designed to mirror the way that people in business have to think about problems as they become less structured. For this reason your work does not just involve structured functional problem solving, it also involves you looking at less structured problems so that you can develop an insight into the need to integrate your understanding of various parts of your course and use this understanding to replicate the way either a team of people or a senior manager might behave when dealing with a single business problem.

There are several ways in which you may come across integration through your course. These are:

- **Case analysis** Some Boards provide candidates with a long case study which attempts to integrate themes from various parts of their course. For example, for a non-modular course at A level, a paper may have a long case study followed by a number of questions based on the case. The case may be used to assess one or more areas of subject content in a way which integrates syllabus themes.

- **Project/course work**   This also allows candidates to blend together theory and practice from around their area of study. NEAB emphasise that their course work 'is intended to integrate the knowledge and understanding gained in Modules 1 to 5 and will form the basis of synoptic assessment.' London Examinations, or EDEXCEL as they now like to be called, provide a series of alternative routes for students taking a project, including 'a project which embraces several relevant areas of the syllabus yielding an opportunity for the student to inter-relate

these (e.g. it may deal with the performance and structure of a particular organisation and the strategies and policies necessary to resolve problems).'

- **Essays** These may require you to draw upon your knowledge of different parts of your course and use this all together in developing an argument as part of your analysis.

Integration helps you to draw skills and knowledge from different areas to help you to replicate the way people in the business world behave.

CASE STUDY CASE STUDY CASE STUDY CASE STUDY CASE STUDY CASE

EDUCATIONAL PROMOTIONS LTD

Educational Promotions Ltd (EPL) is a well-established company that has, until recently, specialised in providing a range of educational supplies to schools and colleges wholesale. The company has vast experience in the educational market and has generated considerable goodwill. Its services to this market have included:

- buying in goods, performing a wholesale function and then supplying goods to schools and colleges
- receiving a commission on sales by linking manufacturers with educational institutions
- providing a means whereby the educational services of large organisations may promote their wares.

Recently, the educational market has not been quite as profitable as EPL would have liked and so the company has been consciously changing the emphasis of its business. Though it wishes to retain its share of the educational market, it is looking to the future and to other changes in the external environment. It is also looking towards markets in Europe and is aiming to provide standard wholesaling facilities for a wide range of mail-order companies.

These moves are already testing its capacity. It has already proved necessary to take on a short-term lease for extra warehousing facilities close to the company's offices in Oldham and to have two pre-fabricated extensions added to the business premises. EPL employs more than 90 staff in the offices

and warehouse, and the lack of space is restricting the nature of its operations.

Senior managers are also becoming acutely aware that though at present they wish to retain their offices in the North West, that this is not the lowest-cost location. If they want more flexibility and costs, and improved access for European markets, they need to look at possible site locations on the eastern side of the country.

One area that particularly interests the directors of EPL is Darlington. The Operations Director has recently been to a seminar in the town and has come back with the following notes:

Darlington was the birthplace of the modern railway and today is the communications gateway to the North-East region. It has a thriving town centre supported by a strong industrial and commercial base. There are a large number of long-standing international companies based in the town and surrounding area, such as DSRM Group PLC, Cleveland Bridge, Whessoe, Millicom, Rothmans, Darchem and Rexam. In addition, there is land available for development North of the existing Faverdale Industrial Estate. Companies that locate in Darlington are able to appreciate the excellent links that Darlington provides to the northern region.

Darlington has excellent communications links, by rail, road, air or sea. The electrified East Coast main line runs directly through Darlington to London King's Cross, providing a high-speed rail link for freight and passengers, who can then change for international destinations.

The A1(M) Durham motorway lies a mile to the West of Darlington, providing superb road access to points throughout the northern region.

Teesside and Newcastle Airports have air links with numerous international destinations, providing regular services for commuters with business abroad.

The ports of Seaham and Teesside offer frequent freight services with facilities for both containers and conventional mixed cargo. Sailings to European ports are frequent and freight from world-wide destinations is regularly dealt with.

Darlington is situated in a government-defined intermediate area. The government, therefore, offers financial and other assistance to firms developing or expanding in Darlington. Assistance may also come from local government and may include relocation grants, rates equivalent grants or small business grants.

Darlington – a good distribution centre

Darlington

After lengthy deliberations, EPL has decided to consider seriously the Darlington option.

The company's main concerns at this early stage are:

- **Recruitment** From the 30 jobs created, at least four would have to supervisory and EPL would like to recruit these internally as it feels that it needs individuals with inside knowledge of how the company works. If it cannot persuade at least four experienced staff to move to Darlington, it might have to develop a detailed training programme.
- **Investment** The cost of the project, taking into consideration the grants offered, would be about £200,000 and, in return, EPL expects profits from the project to be: £75,000 in Year 1; £85,000 in Year 2; £90,000 in Year 3; £95,000 in Year 4; £120,000 in Year 5.
- **The economy** The directors are concerned about the economy. They are worried that rising interest rates and higher exchange rates might affect the company's ability to compete for overseas orders.
- **Overtrading** The Finance Director has pointed out that the proposed plans, which involve holding significantly larger stock levels, may create an imbalance in the working capital ratio.
- **Social costs** There are a number of minor considerations. Congestion on the A1(M) has been a problem in the past, but the site will require good access and will increase traffic locally, which might lead to some opposition. Depending on the orders taken, there might be considerable waste requirements, and these would have to be investigated beforehand.
- **Recent issues** The directors are concerned about a number of issues which they feel might have an affect on their proposals, including public disquiet about the nature of some junk mail, having to comply with new accounting standards, monetary union and political and economic changes.

CASE STUDY CASE STUDY CASE STUDY CASE STUDY CASE STUDY CASE

Integrated case analysis

This section is designed to build upon the earlier chapter on case analysis. When looking at a long case study:

- Be prepared to use information from various parts of your course.
- Try to think how this information might need to be

used, particularly when looking at the more unstructured questions.
- Even though the case study might be long, read through it several times beforehand. If necessary take notes.
- It is acceptable to use information from a range of areas, even for parts of a question.

- Sometimes integrated studies require you to use higher skills of analysis and synthesis.

In order to show you how this process works we have provided you with two examples of integrated case studies. The first comes complete with a model answer while the second is a long study extracted from an AEB Paper 2 at A Level.

TASK 6.1

1 Describe two functions of a wholesaler.
2 Explain how the Single Market and increasing economic integration might help EPL to develop into European markets.
3 EPL has decided to expand its business by diversifying its activities. What is diversification? What further research would you expect them to undertake before finalising their decision?
4 Why is EPL locating the second warehousing unit away from its centre of operations? Make a list of factors that are likely to influence its location decision. List four advantages of locating a warehouse in Darlington.
5 What inducements could EPL provide to encourage supervisory-level staff to move to Darlington? Compare and contrast the benefits of recruiting staff internally with those of external recruitment.
6 The cost of the project is £200,000:
   a What sources of finance could EPL use to obtain the necessary capital?
   b Using investment appraisal techniques, advise EPL on the financial merits of the project. Comment on the average rate of return, the payback period and the net present value discounted at 9 per cent.
   c What is overtrading?
   d How might these proposals affect EPL's working capital?
   e What actions could EPL take to maintain favourable liquidity ratios? (Figure 6.1)
7 Explain why rising interest rates and higher exchange rates might affect the company's ability to compete for overseas orders.
8 With such a project there are many social costs. Describe, what, if anything, EPL could do about the social costs mentioned in the case study.
9 Given the nature of decisions which EPL has to make, how might any of the recent issues identified affect its relocation proposals and why?

Future years										
	1	2	3	4	5	6	7	8	9	10
1	0.990	0.980	0.971	0.962	0.952	0.943	0.935	0.926	0.917	0.909
2	0.980	0.961	0.943	0.925	0.907	0.890	0.873	0.857	0.842	0.826
3	0.971	0.942	0.915	0.889	0.864	0.840	0.816	0.794	0.772	0.751
4	0.961	0.924	0.888	0.855	0.823	0.792	0.763	0.735	0.708	0.683
5	0.951	0.906	0.863	0.822	0.784	0.747	0.713	0.681	0.650	0.621
6	0.942	0.888	0.837	0.790	0.746	0.705	0.666	0.630	0.596	0.564

Figure 6.1

ANSWERS

1 This question is simply designed to help you to get to grips with the case. It is simple and factual. Functions might include:
   - breaking bulk – buying in volume from organisations and selling in smaller units
   - warehousing – manufacturers do not have to keep finished goods and they can respond quickly to the requirements of the market
   - transport costs – the system is simplified by using wholesalers and costs are cut
   - credit facilities – for business customers are either through trade credit or finance facilities.

2 It is important that you develop your answer to this question broadly. It is neither a simple question nor a straightforward factual one. You would have to link the process of European integration with the benefits for EPL. Points made might include:
   - size of the market and the number of potential consumers
   - the benefits of common policies such as standards and safety
   - the ability to tender for public work on the basis of fair competition
   - greater freedom to choose financial services from a larger market
   - no permits and restrictions on providing transport facilities.

3 The first part of this question requires a simple answer. Marks would be available for mentioning that this involves branching out into other activities. The second part would require more detail and structure. Answers might include:
   - primary research such as sampling of customers or potential customers. (The answer should show a detailed understanding of the process of primary research which is relevant and constantly referred to the case.)

- secondary research together with different types and sources which are again referred to in the context of the case.

4 Marks would simply be allocated for stating 'lowest cost location' for the first part of this question. You would then be expected to list factors influencing the location decision such as transport costs, labour, housing, market, raw materials, amenities, government grants, land availability, etc. The final part of the question would require further analysis which would involve you referring more specifically to the study by relating the factors influencing location to the case.

5 This is a straightforward question which would involve identifying a range of inducement which might encourage supervisory-level staff to move to Darlington (e.g. monetary rewards, non-monetary rewards, job satisfaction, or commission). The second part of the answer involves comparison. For example:
- internal candidates will understand the systems and will require a shorter training period
- the organisation will not be disrupted by a newcomer who might have unsuitable ideas
- internal promotion acts as a motivator
- outside appointments may be a risk.

6 The first part of this question requires a reference to be made to suitable sources of finance. These might include share issue, profit retention, bank loan, venture capital, etc. The second part of the question involves you making calculations which refer to the financial merits of the project using various forms of investment appraisal. Responses should be:
- 46.5 per cent
- Year 3
- £355,265.

For the third part you would have to describe, within the context of the study, what is meant by overtrading – undertaking operational activities without having the working capital to sustain such activities. The answer to **d** would involve an effect of the proposals on EPL's working capital. Your answer might include:

- holding large amounts of stock
- taking on more creditors
- cause a need to take on short-term debts
- cause EPL to deal with new creditors, whose reliability might be unknown.

The final part of the question involves a detailed analysis of how EPL could maintain a favourable liquidity position. For example, with improved management of the cash cycle, employment of a credit controller, constant review of stock levels, renting out the surplus area on the new site, use of budgeting, use of overdraft or factoring services, etc.

7 This is a particularly important question as it tries to probe your understanding of the dynamics of monetary policy and its effects upon business organisations. In response to your answer, marks would be allocated for explaining the effects of rising interest rates upon a business investment programme. Your answer might be along the lines that with higher interest rates a highly-geared business may find it both difficult to expand and also to compete on equal terms with organisations in low interest rate markets. Equally high exchange rates will make EPL's products expensive overseas. It may not then be competitive and may have to compete in parts of a market where it would have to compete on quality rather than volume sales.

8 It would be appropriate to explain what social costs are and relate this to the context of the case study. The answer should then refer more specifically to social costs mentioned in the case study. EPL can do little about congestion on the A1(M), though improvements are currently taking place with a number of three-lane sections being built. Waste requirements would have to be carefully researched and balanced against the costs of disposal, perhaps through incineration.

9 Answers to these questions would vary and relate to the prominence of these issues when looking at the case study. You would be expected to analyse each issue in turn with an appropriate degree of analysis.

CASE STUDY CASE STUDY CASE STUDY CASE STUDY CASE STUDY CASE

THE DRIVING RANGE

This case study is taken from an AEB A Level paper. You need to answer all parts of the question which has a total of 50 marks. Read the extract below and answer the questions which follow.

The driving range

Tricia's passion for golf started while at college. As she followed through her university and the legal career, the sport remained a constant source of enjoyment. Then, in 1992, her legal practice was bought out for an unexpectedly large sum (£360,000). Her thoughts immediately turned to golf. What business could she start up that would generate a good income, and give her regular contact with the game she loved?

After rejecting the idea of a golf shop and knowing that there were already too many courses locally, Tricia decided that an automated driving range was the answer. There were no others in her part of Birmingham even though there were six golf courses nearby. Over the following weeks she researched carefully into costs and location. She visited 15 different ranges from Bournemouth to Newcastle, to see exactly how they worked. An acquaintance came up with a marvellous site near to a road feeding onto the M6 motorway. It looked like a derelict industrial wasteland, but she had no doubt that clever landscaping could solve that. Her confidence was given a boost when the chairman of her golf club asked to come in as a 50/50 investor into the project.

The income from an automated driving range is generated by golfers buying basketfuls of balls which they take to a driving booth. There they stand and hit the balls towards their choice of target up to 320 yards away. This gives the golfer practice at striking perhaps 80 balls, but without walking around a whole course (with the time commitment that implies). The land itself is sculpted so that there are ridges and hills. This looks attractive and ensures that if a ball does not go down a hole, it will be channelled towards a conveyor belt that brings the balls back up to refill the basket automatically. The automation means that staff costs are minimal and that golfers can go on hitting balls without interruption.

Tricia's intention was to construct 60 driving booths and to keep the range open from 8.00 in the morning until 10.00 at night, 350 days a year. She knew that the average golfer would probably use two baskets of balls,

taking half an hour over each. Later on, further revenue-generating possibilities would include a golf equipment shop and cafe/bar.

It was a major setback to find that the asking price for the freehold of the M6 site was £1.4 million. However, by careful negotiation Tricia was able to get a ten-year lease for an initial sum of £100,000 plus an annual payment of £90,000. The work of clearing and then constructing the site and buildings was put out to tender with three local firms. Quotes of £580,000 and £620,000 seemed high enough but the third was for £825,000! All three firms stressed that the land needed to be reshaped, then given a layer of tarmac before laying Astroturf.

Knowing that she needed £770,000 just for the land and buildings, Tricia decided to aim for a total start-up capital of £1 million. She and her partner would each put in £300,000, leaving a £400,000 bank loan to be arranged. With this in view, Tricia prepared a cash flow forecast, profit and loss account and balance sheet for the first trading year – all based upon her estimate of customer demand. In the meantime she formed a limited company to operate the business.

The bank was quick to respond, providing a £400,000 loan at a fixed interest rate of 15 per cent. That gave Tricia the green light to sign contracts with the landlord and the lowest-priced building company. nine months later 'M6 Driving' opened its doors to an eager golfing public. At £2 per basket of balls it seemed very good value, when the local golf courses charged from £12 to £25 per round of golf.

Project Profit and Loss Account Year 1 (ending 30 July 1996)	
	£000s
Sales Revenue	784
Cost of sales	196
GROSS PROFIT	588
Expenses	160
Interest	60
Site rental	90
Depreciation	38
Launch advertising	80
NET PROFIT	160
Corporation tax	40
PROFIT AFTER TAX	120

Project Balance Sheet as at 30 July 1996	
	£000s
Land	90
Buildings	580
Stock	28
Debtors	7
Cash	465
less Creditors	50
ASSETS EMPLOYED	1120
Loans	400
Share Capital	600
Reserves	120
CAPITAL EMPLOYED	1120

FIGURE 6.2 Projected accounts for the first trading year

1 **a** Explain how Tricia might have decided upon her sales forecast. (6 marks)
   b Consider the reasons why it might prove inaccurate. (6 marks)
2 Tricia's profit forecast anticipates that the business will operate at two-thirds of its maximum capacity. Outline how she might try to increase the level of capacity utilisation. (6 marks)
3 **a** If the number of customers in year 2 is 240,000 paying £2.10 per basket of balls, what would be the profit? (Assume that variable costs per unit stay constant, while annual expenses rise 5 per cent.) (9 marks)
   b State your assumptions. (3 marks)
4 Six months after the range opened, Tricia heard that the three construction companies operated a market-sharing agreement that kept prices artificially high. Discuss why some firms operate in ways that are unethical. (8 marks)
5 Tricia is hoping that 'M6 Driving' will be the first of a chain of driving ranges to be opened by her firm. How realistic does this aim seem to be? (12 marks)

CASE STUDY CASE STUDY CASE STUDY CASE STUDY CASE STUDY CASE

Integrated project/course work

Different examination boards have different requirements for both project work or course work. It is important that you become familiar with such requirements. This is probably the easiest area in which to emphasise the nature of integration. Almost any issue will have some form of integration, though some may have more than others. The specifications for some boards, such as EDEXCEL, are specifically designed to encourage integration, which it then does by using the course work assessment for students to develop their own business plans. In the boards' guidelines they emphasise that through the process of planning and integration, candidates could actually try to put a plan into action, perhaps through Young Enterprise.

Integrated essays

When looking at essay titles it is sometimes possible to identify titles which will draw upon general areas of knowledge and those which simply draw upon one area of expertise. It is important that you carefully choose the essay questions you answer. By understanding about the nature of integration and the constraints it puts upon you as you answer a question, you are developing an important business methodology. The best way to understand this process of integration is to make quick comparisons of two essay titles which appeared on a recent AEB examination paper. The titles are as follows:

● *Title 1* Supply and demand supposedly determine price and yet firms employ an array of pricing strategies depending on circumstances.
  a Outline four such pricing strategies.
  b Examine the apparent contradiction in the quotation.

● *Title 2* Discuss the factors which a large retailing company would have to take into account when considering whether or not to open on Sundays.

Title 1 is clearly related to the process of pricing. Though it might be necessary to relate this to accounting policies as well as marketing and microeconomic theory, it is still very specific and narrow. There is therefore little integration. To answer this question you would require a good knowledge of the process of pricing. A good answer would involve providing some sort of view on the issue which balanced out or provided some form of analysis made upon what is declared to be a contradiction in the question. As long as the analysis is argued in a way which not only relates in some way to theory and the issues, but also shows a high degree of understanding, then the candidate will score well.

It is easy to contrast Title 2 with Title 1. There are many factors influencing whether a large retailing organisation might be able to open on Sundays. These might include profitability, making more efficient use of assets, marketing-related factors, providing a competitive advantage over other companies, the use of staff and the implications for their families, social costs for people in the local environment and so on.

There is clearly a lot to discuss but, as the title is very general, it is important to be careful about how the analysis is developed, i.e. the answer should not simply be a list of factors but be a clearly developed argument, together with appropriate analysis and synthesis, based upon a collection of factors.

7 Developing key skills through business studies

The importance of key skills

By undertaking a business course at A or AS Level you are not only learning a body of knowledge, you are also learning how to use knowledge across a range of situations. In doing so, you are developing skills which enable you to become an effective participant in business and social life.

Business knowledge is in itself of little value without the development of some form of skills. Though we do not necessarily view A or AS Level courses as vocational courses, it is important that whatever course you undertake as you move towards the next phase of either your education or professional life, skills of all kinds are important. Think of all the situations you might come across in your course. For example, you may have to research information for yourselves, argue and discuss important issues, use computers for simulations or make presentations. The message is that skills which are integrated within the education process provide a basis for you to develop your capabilities, have a better grasp of real-world issues and enable you to develop yourself to operate effectively in more situations.

For the purpose of your courses key skills are divided into: communication; application of number; and information technology.

Communication

It is easy to take the process of communication for granted. In your Business Studies course you should be able to use business terminology within your written materials. It has been said that when you talk about business it can be like talking a different language. For example, the word 'entrepreneur' is a word almost exclusively related to the world of business and economics.

Your written responses should be accurate and relevant to the subject and written within an appropriate context.

Grammar and spelling are important. As we emphasised in Chapter 5, you must use appropriate grammar. Marks on each paper will also be allocated for spelling. Paragraphs are also important and you must be prepared to present your work in a format which suits your audience.

Reading is an important skill. On your course you will be asked to select and summarise appropriate information and also to read reference materials such as newspapers and articles to clarify your understanding of key issues.

Speaking and listening involve you making contributions to topics within the context of discussions. You must remember to do this in a way which suits a target audience, taking the situation into account. Exchanging ideas in order to develop your understanding of issues and topics can be very interesting.

Application of number

In Chapter 3 we emphasised how important it is for you to feel confident about, and deal capably with, quantitative information. Application of number involves using fractions, decimal fractions, percentages, ratios, negative numbers, numbers of any size, estimations, approximate levels of accuracy, tolerances and appropriate units of measure as part of your study. In Business Studies this may also involve mathematical modelling, collection and selection of appropriate data and the manipulation, analysis and interpretation of data together with the presentation of results.

Though this seemingly exhaustive list sounds daunting, you should appreciate that it is important that you can analyse data and draw conclusions from such analysis.

Information technology

Computers are important aids for accessing, manipulating and using information in order to aid decision making within business situations. A key component of your course should involve the familiarity and use of hardware and software within the curriculum context.

It is important that you realise that knowledge, the development of your understanding and skills are all closely linked. You should use every opportunity to develop and demonstrate your key skills within the framework of your A/AS Level course. The opportunity for you to develop such skills is particularly relevant during course work, project work and investigations.

8 Undertaking research for a project or course work

What is project work?

Project work or course work places much more emphasis upon the need for you to organise yourself in a way which enables you to conduct penetrating and extensive investigations. This may involve:

- undertaking some form of research or investigation
- collecting evidence such as facts and opinions from a range of sources
- using your judgements in an informative and balanced way to produce some form of written work for assessment.

In order for you to undertake a project or coursework you have to:

- think about and develop a project idea
- select a topic that you are happy to work with
- decide what information you need
- plan how to complete the project
- present it in a written form.

Requirements for project work or course work vary from examination board to examination board. Inevitably, your first step is to find out what the work entails. For example, for some boards, course work involves the production of a business plan. The plan should include:

- an explanation of the purposes of the business plan
- the identification and explanation of the business objectives for a single product/service
- the feasibility of the objectives
- the legal and insurance implications of the objectives
- the details of the estimates of the marketing budget
- details of the production plan
- the identification of resource requirements for production, marketing, sales and the ability to meet these requirements
- the financial data and forecasts to support the plan
- the procedures for monitoring and the review of the plan
- details of potential support for the plan from external sources.

Almost in complete contrast to this is the EDEXCEL AS level syllabus. This is much more open for candidates to make key decisions about their project area. The process is designed for students to be adventurous and innovative and allows them to choose a topic which may:

- embrace several relevant areas of the syllabus, yielding an opportunity for them to inter-relate strategies and policies necessary to solve problems
- provide a specialist approach covering a narrower field

within a discipline, or

- be concerned with an aspect of the external business environment.

Note: Syllabuses are subject to constant changes and fine-tunings. Though statements are made here relating to specific course work requirements from specified examination boards, these requirements may have recently changed or been altered. Make sure that you find out about the requirements of the syllabuses you are taking from your tutor.

Getting started

The starting point for any project is for you to understand what you are doing. You need to think about what is required as an end product and how you are going to produce such a product. Make sure that you have been provided with the detailed requirements of the project. You must also understand the aims and purpose of the project and have a good idea of the process of assessment. If it is possible to glance at projects taken by former students then have a look at them. Think about issues such as:

- project length
- titles
- presentation.

Action planning, as shown in Chapter 2, is particularly important. Throughout the project process you need to set yourself action steps and targets and try to keep to the timings. Fitting your project work into all of the other work is not going to be easy, so try to set some time aside each week to reserve exclusively for your project.

A key decision you have to make at the start of the project or course work is making sure that the project title reflects what you want to do. Your tutor may have a list of titles which have been used in the past or a list of specimen titles provided by the examination board.

When undertaking a piece of research at university it is standard practice to encourage students to discuss their project titles with other students. Sometimes brainstorming in this way can help students to develop ideas and focus upon key issues. Find somebody that you can discuss your ideas with. It need not necessarily be your tutor and may be a parent, other student or friend of the family. Ask them what they think of your proposals. Remember that even though they may comment upon your ideas, essentially the project is yours. You must have 'ownership' of what you are doing – after all, the final result is a reflection upon *your* talents.

Working through the project

Rushing the project by writing it up a couple of weeks before it is due in is not really the purpose of the exercise. Make sure that as you work through the project you get things down on paper. Many of you will enjoy the process of research and, through your investigation, collect some invaluable data and materials. Though this is important the project does not just involve collection of materials but also involves writing the project up in a way which shows a good level of understanding and analysis of the issues involved.

Find out how long the project has to be. Project length is particularly important. Though the length might sound daunting the problem might be how to condense your materials and analysis into something limited by a word count. If it has to be 5,000 words, what does this include? Will it include appendices or any other material that you might like to attach to the project?

Another area is the requirements for presentation? There may be a specified structure which you have to follow. You tutor will provide you with the details. Will the project have to be word processed? You need to think about the issues of presentation. For example, how are you going to present graphs and other data?

Make sure that when you plan the project that you plan an appropriate and logical sequence of activities. Again, you may find it useful to talk your project plan through with your tutor.

If you make a direct quotation from a book, annual report or any other external source, it must be put in quotation marks and acknowledged. This is particularly important. The project is a reflection of your efforts and, though it is quite acceptable to use or mention other materials as part of your investigation, it is not if markers are put in a position whereby they have to question the project's validity or authenticity. According to EDEXCEL, 'whether from published or unpublished sources, direct quotation must be enclosed in quotation marks and clearly attributed.'

Your project will involve you in an investigation. From the early stage you will need to work out what information and materials you require to engage in some form of research. Looking at the market research pages in this book may help you to think about the nature of primary and secondary research as well as quantitative and quali-tative approaches to project work. Don't forget that given the nature and level of course that you are undertaking, you should be building upon the research skills you may have used for GCSE.

Your analysis is particularly important in your project. In fact the success of your project will largely depend not upon the material you gather but upon how you use that material as part of your analysis of a problem or issue. Terms, concepts, theories and your ability to apply this to a problem-related concept is particularly important. Don't forget that as part of your analysis it is useful to refer to work that you have undertaken as part of your business studies course. For example, if you were looking at how a business had been successful with a product launch it would be important to use terminology and theories relating to product life-cycle, product portfolios or any other form of product analysis. Theory is important as it helps to underpin things which happen in practice.

Evaluation of the processes undertaken through the project can also be useful. Try to evaluate what you are doing and how successful you have been. You may wish to provide some form of evaluation of the processes you have used within your research as part of your project. For example, you may wish to comment upon how the limitations of your techniques of analysis affect your conclusions.

At some stage in your project you will have to draw some conclusions or make some judgements. Make sure that these are fair and rational given the parameters of your project and the information you have available. Your judgements should be logical and relate to the issues within your project title.

Enjoy it!

It is probably easy to say this. No project is completed without some element of stress or concern at one stage or another. The beauty of project work or course work is that it provides you with a unique opportunity to be creative and use your research skills. Though the whole process is not as structured as classroom teaching and learning, it does provide you with the flexibility to determine your own pattern of learning. It also enables you to use your understanding of the world of business from the classroom to interact with someone in the business environment. It is a wonderful opportunity to show that business studies involves something which is tangible and real.

9 What next?

Making a decision

I remember meeting a psychologist many years ago who argued that one of the critical age ranges in anybody's lifetime is that between 16 and 19. In making this point he referred to the fact that during this period you have to make important decisions, the outcome of which you may have to live with for a very long time. From my point of view today, a (good) few years on, I am just grateful that the decisions I made all those years ago to go into higher education and to become a teacher were the right ones!

It could be argued that this short chapter could appear in any A Level text. Its purpose is simply to enable you to reflect upon the alternatives you face. The decision you make about your education beyond A and AS Level is one of the most important you make.

You may already have made a decision about what you want to do. In fact you may many years ago have thought about a career you want to follow and found out as much as you can about its requirements. Even though you could have done this you may want to think further about your intentions.

If you are undecided about your future you will benefit from further thought about the options available to you. The time you spend now thinking and talking as well as developing a plan is a worthwhile investment in time. At this stage it is always useful to talk to other people about your plans. You may wish to discuss what you want to do with friends with whom you could compare notes or with members of your family.

At this stage it is perfectly acceptable for you to go into one of the many fields of employment. However, don't just think 'I want a job'. A job is not the end product of the decision you make. The end product is the career path you create and the many years of enjoyment, pleasure and satisfaction you get from that career. You will also need to find out about professional and technical training, the opportunities to take further qualifications as well as other factors and influences within that organisation and industry, such as security and remuneration. If this appeals to you, talk to a careers adviser or anybody you know who works in that field.

The four routes

Roughly speaking there are four routes open to you:

- improve your grades
- higher education
- employment
- one-year break.

Improve your grades

Having set your sights upon either a career or a university of your choice, there is always a possibility, no matter how well you have performed during your course, that you do not get the grades you require. Facing this possibility, no matter how daunting the prospect, is important. If this does happen you then you have to ask yourself 'What do I do now?'

Throwing away your plans and doing something else is only realistic if you feel that you cannot improve upon the grades that you got the first time around. However, you may feel that, for one reason or another, the grades were not a serious reflection of your talents and that you can improve upon your examination performances. In that case, try to do so. In improving your grades you may not have to attend school or college full-time and may have the opportunity to undertake some work and save money before going on to higher education.

Alternatively, you may have started work without the grades you require to do the part-time courses you need to forward your career. Though this may be difficult, you need to create time to retake your A or AS Levels and improve upon your grades. This is a difficult option, but it is a situation that many people find themselves in. It requires a lot of planning and effort and a willingness to sacrifice time, often after a long day at work.

Higher education

Courses in higher education are those which lead to a qualification of a higher standard than those at A Level. It is usual for these courses to require one or more A Levels or comparable qualifications for entry.

There are so many courses in higher education, including those based in further education colleges, colleges of higher education and universities. Courses may be for degrees, HNDs and other diplomas, and also for professional qualifications. There are many key questions such as: How do you make a decision? What are you going to study? Where do you want to study?

It is certainly acceptable to look at courses outside your subject areas. Also try to avoid being influenced by the typecasting of certain courses as leading to careers for males or females. Look at the literature and discuss all of the possibilities with your teachers, careers officer, parents and friends.

There are, of course, different routes into higher education. You may wish to be full-time or to take some form of sandwich course. There are also an increasingly large number of summer courses, professional qualifications and part-time courses.

Prospectuses are a prime source of information about various colleges and universities. Some organisations have open days, which give you the opportunity to have a walk around the places you are considering, and to get the feel for each organisation.

Employment

You may wish to start work after your A or AS Level course. This is a perfectly acceptable route to a career. Try not, however, to think of the job as an end result. Look further ahead at what the job is providing for you and how it is going to help you to develop in years to come.

For example, how is the organisation you intend to join going to train you? What avenues is it going to provide for you to take other qualifications? You need to make sure that an employer is committed to providing you not just with the training opportunities you require but also with any support or help with professional or other qualifications.

One-year break

Life is not a race. You may not yet feel ready for further intensive study or for the formal employment market. You may wish to broaden your experience, for example, by doing voluntary work either within the UK or abroad. Such experiences could become an important part of your development and help you both to learn and develop your prospects. They may also serve to prepare you for higher education or employment and help you to get more out of the experience.

2 Business objectives

INTRODUCTION

In this unit we set out to examine the nature of business in the UK.

Organisations exist for many different purposes from the "night shelter" offering a roof over their head to homeless people to the multi-million pound business with a variety of units, sections and products throughout the globe. However, all of these organisations have a number of things in common and each can learn from how others operate.

Clearly, all organisations have objectives and purposes. The organisation therefore needs to be organised to achieve these objectives. This is often the difference between a successful organisation and a less successful one. The successful organisation knows where it is going and is well focused; it has strategies and systems which enable it to focus on its objectives. Other organisations are poorly managed and run with no clear sense of direction.

Organisations exist to serve their stakeholders. These are the people that have an interest in the affairs of the organisation and include shareholders, managers, employees, customers, suppliers and of course the community at large. Successfully managing an organisation involves enabling the wishes of stakeholders to be communicated to those with responsibility for making decisions. It involves giving stakeholders part-ownership of decision making whenever appropriate and practical.

Business planning is a key activity. It involves making preparation today for activities which are going to take place tomorrow and into the future. All organisations need to plan. In a small organisation the principal way of preparing for the future is to create a business plan. In larger organisations we talk about corporate planning. A key aspect of corporate planning is the creation of a strategy, i.e. an outline of the big decisions that the organisation must make, for example, what types of products or services to focus on or matching what the organisation intends to do to the resources available to it.

Today, organisations need to be flexible and to create flexible planning structures because they no longer operate in an environment of certainty. Businesses now operate in a dynamic environment. They therefore need to continually scan their environment in order to predict changes rather than follow others.

There are many types of businesses in the private and public sectors of the economy. The private sector is made up of companies which are owned by individual entrepreneurs and shareholders whereas public organisations are owned in part or entirely by the government on behalf of the people. In the 1980s and 1990s the emphasis in the UK has been very much on privatisation, i.e. the transfer of state-run industries to private ownership. In the private sector of the economy, there is a growing number of small businesses – a trend which is likely to continue into the next century. However, much of production in the UK is dominated by larger businesses such as Boots, Mars and BP. In recent years, these larger organisations have tended to cut down their size – a process known as downsizing.

10 What is business?

Business Studies is a very important subject. It is concerned with activities that affect all of us on a day-to-day basis. You have only to listen to the news or read the newspapers to find stories about business activity. Some of these stories can make us feel very optimistic about the place of business activity, for example, the creation of new goods and services which have helped to reduce disease and improve the living standards of people throughout the globe. At other times stories about business can make us gloomy and cynical, for example, when large companies have exploited weaker members of society by selling shoddy products, or have misled the public about safety standards. In studying business therefore it is important that you look carefully at business issues and make a balanced judgement based on available evidence about what it right and wrong. In this way you should be able to develop a view about the way in which business and organisational activity should be carried out.

CASE STUDY CASE STUDY CASE STUDY CASE STUDY CASE STUDY CASE

ARCHBISHOP QUESTIONS MORALITY OF BUSINESS – A CASE FOR TEAMWORK

Dr George Carey, Archbishop of Canterbury

In May 1992 the Archbishop of Canterbury, Dr George Carey, questioned the morality of some business practices at a sermon in Derby Cathedral to give thanks for the achievements of British industry.

He attacked greed and short-sightedness among industrialists and warned that God has hard things to say to those who wait for the 'trickle-down effect' to feed the poor. He said:

'When God sorts out the goats from the sheep, he tells them, "The curse is upon you ... for when I was hungry you gave me nothing to eat, when thirsty nothing to drink; when I was a stranger you gave me no home, when naked you did not clothe me; when I was ill, and in prison you did not come to my help."

'I doubt He would have been impressed by the argument that the goats had been waiting for those things to "trickle down" as a by-product of economic growth.'

Dr Carey said the purpose of trade and industry was to benefit humanity, 'not to make profits for shareholders, nor to create salaries and wages for the industrial community ... nor can the purpose of industry be to serve the market, as if the market was master instead of servant of human need. No, industry's purpose is surely to serve people by creating things of use and value to them.'

However, during the sermon the Archbishop praised British industry in general: 'It has excelled in creating things of use and value which have brought enormous benefits to many people's lives. I want to underline my admiration for many industrialists and industrial workers.'

But he had a great deal of specific criticism:

'Company law sometimes appears to enshrine an erroneous principle that companies exist to serve their shareholders. The other stakeholders in an enterprise and its fundamental purpose may not get a look in.

'Within our own society, our collective commitment to industrial enterprise will remain underpowered if the fruits of success appear to be concentrated too heavily in the pockets of shareholders and senior executives. For example, massive individual pay rises during a recession do not encourage public support for wealth creation.'

1 How does Dr Carey's speech indicate that industry and business has the power to do both good and evil?
2 What do you understand by a 'trickle-down effect'? How might such an effect work?
3 Why might 'trickle-down' be a poor model for a society to follow?

CASE STUDY CASE STUDY CASE STUDY CASE STUDY CASE STUDY CASE

What is business activity?

Business activity lies at the heart of modern societies. Business is concerned with meeting the wants and needs of people and groups in society through organised activity. The food, shelter, clothing, entertainment and other goods and services that we enjoy are not provided for us in a random and haphazard way. Usually, there is a highly-organised production and distribution process working to ensure that we have the goods and services that we want, where we want them, when we want them and how we want them. If this year fashion dictates that we want more green T-shirts and fewer blue ones then

IT'S A FACT

That there are many different views as to how business activity should be carried out. For example one point of view is put forward by Milton Friedman who argued that 'the business of business is business' by which he meant that business should focus on narrow business aims such as profitability without becoming distracted into wider social activities. Another perspective was that of Henry Ford who likened the Ford (automobile) business to a huge efficient machine which worked according to Ford's own plan. This view came to be termed Fordism. In contrast, Anita Roddick the founder of the Body Shop argues that the organisation consists of its people. She feels that everyone that works for Body Shop should be 'empowered' to make important decisions themselves. She also believes that the business should be based on 'ethical principles' so that it does not exploit people, for example, those in the South American rainforest where some of Body Shop's ingredients come from.

In the course of time, an organisation may change the way it operates and change its views. For example, in the mid-1990s Shell Nigeria was criticised for some of its activities in Nigeria where a pipeline was constructed through land belonging to the Ogoni people who were fiercely resistant to this development. In 1996, therefore, Shell developed a new set of principles which included a deeper commitment to human rights.

business organisations will make sure that this will happen. If next year we prefer pink ones, then businesses will make the decisions and carry out the organisational activities that set in chain the switch of resources to pink T-shirt manufacture.

There are a number of fundamental aspects of business. These are:

- economic activity
- producers and consumers
- organisation
- decision making.

Economic activity

Economic activity involves turning scarce resources into finished goods and services in such a way that they meet people's wants and needs. An individual person can carry out this economic activity. For example, primitive people living in this country were able to utilise flint and wood to make axes which could be used for hunting or cutting. At the time this seemed to be the most sensible way to use some of the wood and flint available. In a number of ways we have made considerable progress since the stone and flint ages.

Economic decision making involves making best use of a given basket of resources. In any society, resources will be scarce relative to the number of uses to which they could be put.

A resource is a means of support.

A resource can be regarded as any feature of our environment that helps to support our well-being.

There are two main types of resources:

- **Physical or natural resources** – for example, soil, climate, water, minerals, forests and fisheries.
- **Human resources** – people and their various skills.

If we were to take stock of the world's existing bundle of resources, we would find that there are severe limitations to its ability to meet our infinite wants.

A society's strategies for using resources to produce finished products should consider long-term as well as short-term objectives. Some resources such as mineral reserves cannot be replaced, i.e. they are non-renewable.

Producers and consumers

When early societies began to trade with each other they started to develop **the market**. A market exists in any situation in which goods are bought and sold. The people required to make up a market are the **buyers** and **sellers**. However, there are other important actors involved in the marketplace – these are the **producers** and **consumers**.

Producers are individual and organisations that actually make or provide goods and services, for example, a hairdresser, coal miner, insurance clerk and teacher are all producers. They make goods and services that help to provide **satisfaction** of **welfare** (well-being) for other people. They make goods and services because they are able to sell them in the marketplace. Through the income which they earn from their work they are able to earn a living.

Consumers are the end users of goods or services, for example, the person that consumes a sandwich or listens to a new CD or tape.

Producers will sell their goods and services either to final customers or to intermediaries, such as **wholesalers** who stock goods for further sale, or **retailers** who sell to the final customer.

Consumers do not necessarily buy products; they simply use them up. If I buy a sandwich and eat it myself then I am a customer and a consumer. However, if another member of my family buys a sandwich and then gives it to me to eat I am a consumer but not a customer.

Here is a summary of some definitions:

- *Producer*   *Provides or makes a good or service.*
- *Seller*   *Sells a good or service to someone else.*
- *Buyer*   *Purchases a good or service from someone else.*
- *Customer*   *Person who carries out the purchasing transaction.*
- *Consumer*   *Uses up the good or service.*
- *Manufacturer*   *Producer of a finished good (e.g. food production).*
- *Wholesaler*   *Buys and sells goods in stock; often an intermediary.*
- *Retailer*   *Breaks bulk, and sells goods to final consumer.*

Organisation

Business organisations take various forms, ranging from small, one-owner businesses to multinational corporations. Some are concerned with making goods and so we call these **industrial organisations**. Some are concerned

with buying and selling, so we call these **commercial organisations**. Some are concerned with banking and insurance, so we call these **financial organisations**. The features of a business or economic organisation are:

> *a group of people*
> **forming**
> *a structure with rules and authority*
> **pursuing**
> *an objective or set of objectives*
> **using**
> *economic resources*
> **to meet**
> *economic needs and wants for which people are prepared to sacrifice their own resources.*

An organisation is a unit that is set up by people to pursue certain aims and objectives. Many organisations set down guiding principles which can be used to check how successful they are. Most organisations have the following features:

- **A name** This can range from the Girl Guides or Crystal Palace Football Club to Barclays Bank PLC, Mars or Virgin Airways.
- **Objectives** These identify the directions in which you seek to move an organisation. Every organisation needs to have a clear idea of what it is seeking to achieve. By setting out a list of objectives, you make it possible to check how successful you are in moving in the right direction.
- **Rules and regulations** Some of these will be written down formally on paper. Other informal, codes of practice are not written down but are recognised and responded to. Some of the rules will be imposed externally in laws laid down by the government; every school or college, for example, will have a set of rules governing safety in the school.
- **Patterns and structures** Organisations are organised – they have set ways of doing things. In the army, for example, there is a distinct organisational structure comprising a hierarchy according to rank. Other organisations are more democratic; there will be many decision makers with similar status in, say, the Methodist Church.
- **Posts and offices** People within an organisation will have different positions of responsibility. In a football club, for example, there is a manager, trainer, coach, ticket seller, ground staff, etc.
- **Chain of command** In many organisations there will be a distinct chain of command, for example, from headteacher to deputy headteacher to head of department to class teacher. The responsibility of each of these will be set out in official and unofficial codes.
- **Power** Officers will have varying levels of power vested in them. These powers will often be set out in a written contract. For example, in a sports team the manager may select the team; the trainer may choose the training programme; the physiotherapist may set out a schedule for treating injuries, and so on.

- **Records** Organisations need to have systematic and well-organised records (e.g. patients' records in a doctors' surgery). Nowadays, many records are kept in computer files, but written records are also important. Most organisations will store records for several years.

TASK 10.1
Take an organisation that you know about and consider it in the light of each of the eight features outlined above. To what extent is the behaviour of members of the organisation governed by the features of the organisation outlined above?

Classifying organisations by their objectives
It is helpful to classify organisations according to their main objectives.

Pure business organisations
We shall see in Chapter 17 that business organisations take several forms, ranging from small, one-owner businesses to multinational corporations.

Government organisations
Government organisations operate at both a local and a national level. They are accountable to representatives elected by citizens. Examples include the Department for Education and the county councils. Increasingly we are looking to European Union wide organisations for making governmental decisions.

Public corporations
Public corporations are owned by the government on behalf of the people. An example is the British Broadcasting Corporation (BBC). They set out to produce goods and services to serve all the people of the country.

QUANGOS (quasi-autonomous non-government organisations)
These are unelected public bodies. They are run by boards of directors to manage a particular initiative. For example, local TECs (Training and Enterprise Councils) are responsible for providing training opportunities and schemes on behalf of local employees.

IT'S A FACT
That both the Labour and Conservative governments since the Second World War have been criticised for the number of QUANGOS which they have set up. People are highly critical of QUANGOS because they tend to be run by people who have been chosen by the government of the day – it is felt that they are not really accountable to 'the people'.

Economic interest groups
These are organisations representing groups of people with a shared interest. Examples are the Consumers' Association (representing consumers), the Confederation of British Industry (representing employers) and the Trades Union Congress (representing trade unionists).

Trade unions
Trade unions are economic interest groups. They are given a special status in law. They represent groups of employees in bargaining situations, both nationally and in individual plants.

Legal organisations
There are a number of legal organisations responsible for administering and supervising the legal process, for example, the courts, the Monopolies Commission and the European Court of Justice.

Political organisations
Many groups of people form themselves into political organisations. Some of these are highly organised (e.g. the Conservative Party); others are less organised, such as pressure groups campaigning on a particular issue (e.g. the destruction of the countryside).

Charities
Charitable organisations like OXFAM and the Spastics Society have a special status in law. In the past, charities were set up to provide for the helpless and the needy (the poor, the homeless). Nowadays, many organisations have adopted charitable status in order to gain tax and other advantages (e.g. public schools).

Mutual help organisations
Some organisations have been set up so that members can help each other rather than to make a profit. Co-operatives are a good example – any surpluses may be shared among members. Some labour organisations work on this basis – members club together to provide support for the sick and needy.

International and multinational organisations
Many organisations now have a membership in several nations, either at a government or private level. Examples are the Red Cross/Red Crescent and the European Union. Business organisations may have tentacles in many countries (e.g. IBM, Marks and Spencer, Shell, Laura Ashley or Virgin).

Decision making
Individuals, groups and organisations need to make new decisions continually. Decision making is a central feature of business activity. There are three main elements to business decision making:

- analysis
- choice
- implementation.

Analysis

This is concerned with making sense of information that will be required to make a decision. In order to analyse this information it is first necessary to collect and assemble a sufficient quantity of reliable information. For example, in making a decision as to whether to produce a new product or not you will need to gather information about likely demand patterns for the product, the cost of making and selling the product, etc.

Choice

Choice involves:

- setting out a menu of options (e.g. should we produce product A, B or C)
- comparing the options provided by the menu (e.g. comparing A with B and C)
- choosing the best option from the menu.

Implementation

This involves putting your choice into practice. For example, if you have chosen product A then you will need to secure the resources to produce it, the means to distribute it, the advertising campaign to promote it, etc.

Of course in implementing (carrying out) business decisions you will need to continually monitor and analyse what you are doing. By analysing your decisions and how they work out in practice you will be able to make more informed choices in the future.

Much of business activity is concerned with this decision-making cycle. Studying business should help you to build up a body of knowledge and decision-making skills which will enable you to become a more effective decision maker. However, to make informed decisions you will need to know a lot more about finance, about marketing, about human resource management and many of the other themes and issues that are covered in this book.

What is a good business?

A 'good business' has several distinguishing characteristics:

- It makes a profit by supplying products or services that people want to buy
- It contributes to its own and the community's long-term prosperity by making the best possible use of resources.
- It minimises waste of every kind and where possible promotes its reuse or recycling.
- It respects the environment, locally, nationally and globally.

- It sets performance standards for its suppliers – and helps in their achievement
- It offers its employees worthwhile career prospects, professional training, job satisfaction and a safe working environment.
- It expects the best from its employees and rewards them accordingly.
- It acts at all times as a good citizen, aware of its influence on the rest of society, including the local communities living near its factories and offices.

If a business is to remain a 'good business', all these characteristics are required.

For instance, no business can continue to earn a profit if it fails significantly to make the best possible use of available resources. It would simply be overtaken by competitors who do. In making the best possible use of resources – whether raw materials or human potential – it automatically contributes to the general prosperity.

Of course, 'best possible use' implies more than simply 'best possible use in the short-term'. If a company is short-sighted enough to exploit resources simply for immediate gain and at the expense of the environment or the customer's best, long-term interests, it will eventually encounter hostility, customer boycott and, possibly prosecution. A good business is ultimately a good citizen.

Since the most important resource available to any company is its people, they must be looked after, trained and generally enabled to fulfil their potential.

A good business will also remain aware of the 'knock-on' effects of its activities. Investment in a new factory may attract workers from outside the area and increase the local population significantly. It is not enough for the company simply to pay good wages and offer good 'at work' conditions. It must also help ensure that housing and other social facilities are in place, co-operating as necessary with the local authorities. Likewise, if a factory has to be closed and a significant proportion of the staff made redundant, the company will work with others to help the displaced staff find new employment.

Adding value

One of the most important terms in business is 'value added'. All businesses prosper in direct proportion to their ability to add value to their 'input' materials. The more value they add, especially in comparison with competitors, the better they do.

Value is added at each stage of production. A simple example is the carpenter converting relatively inexpensive materials into furniture. The difference between the cost of the wood and the price of the finished article is the wealth which he or she has created.

Businesses constantly seek ways of adding value to products. Value can be added to products by making them more desirable so that more people are prepared to buy them and at higher prices. For example, value is added to motor cars by creating additional features such as mobile phones, automatic route finders, increased safety features and economy fuel consumption.

A classic example of adding value to a product in a simple way is the sweet 'Love Hearts'. Children buy the sweets not just because of the taste but because they have messages written on them like 'Be mine', 'Big boy', and 'True love'!

One of the most important ways of adding value to products in today's competitive market conditions is through service – personal attention to customers' requirements, friendly relationships with customers, etc.

The value added by a business to its input materials is thus more than simply physical improvement – it also involves non-tangible considerations such as service and 'image'.

EXTENSION MATERIAL

Adam Smith and Karl Marx

Adam Smith and Karl Marx are two of the most celebrated thinkers of all time. They made substantial contributions to our understanding of the nature and purpose of economic and hence business activity.

Adam Smith

Adam Smith (1723–90) wrote his famous work *The Wealth of Nations* in 1776. In it he set out to answer a perplexing question: If people are driven by a desire to make money for themselves how then does society stop these individuals from holding us all to ransom? Smith believed that the answer to this was the 'market system' and competition. If we have a number of self-interested competitors working against each other then competition itself will serve to lead to the interest of all.

Smith argued that a manufacturer who tried to charge more than other manufacturers would not be able to find any buyers. Someone seeking work who sought a higher wage than others would not find a job. An employer who wants to pay lower wages than rivals would not be able to attract employees, etc.

Smith also believed that the market led producers to make those things that consumers wanted to buy. The manufacturer that tried to sell goods that people did not want would be left with unsold stocks on its hands. However, if people want more of a particular product its price will rise. This will lead more producers to make those goods that are in demand. The pressures of the marketplace direct the selfish activities as if by an 'invisible hand' (to use Smith's phrase) into socially responsible paths.

Smith argued that the market for goods and services is self-regulating. If anyone's prices, wages or profits stray from levels that are set for everyone, the force of competition will drive them back. The market thus proves to be a strict taskmaster that protects everyone. Because the market is its own regulator, Smith was opposed to government intervention that would interfere with the working of self-interest and competition.

Smith effectively provided a justification for capitalism and self-interest. His influence continues to this day. There are many people who continue to argue that competition should be the driving force behind business, and that although people may have selfish motives the results of their actions will be to lead to the greater good of all.

Smith believed that society went through a number of stages of development each of which was an improvement on previous ones. For example, earliest people relied on hunting and gathering before settling down to forms of farming. Eventually this led to trading and the growth of the industrial society. Smith saw capitalism (the industrial society) as being the finest achievement of civilisation.

Karl Marx

Marxist thinkers (people whose ideas have been influenced by Karl Marx) believe that capitalist society did not represent the final stage in society's development. Marx saw capitalism simply as the most recent stage of conflict in an ongoing series of conflicts.

Karl Marx (1818–83) argued that history develops in stages, determined by changes in the way people organise their lives. The move from one stage to another is brought about through the struggle between different social classes which results in revolutions.

Marx thought that the French revolution of 1789 marked the first change in modern Europe. It left behind the 'feudal stage', in which peasants were exploited by landlords. He believed that after the revolution society moved into a later, 'capitalist' stage of history: production shifted from the land to the city, from peasants to the urban working class (or 'proletariat'). Landlords were replaced by factory owners and investors (the 'bourgeoisie', literally the middle classes) as the leading class in society.

Marx stated that under capitalism employees are forced to sell their labour cheaply and thus lose control of the means of production (and of their working lives). He thought they could be freed through class struggles led by a revolutionary party which would rise up to defeat the bourgeoisie and take history into the next, 'socialist' stage, in which workers would gain control over the government and production.

This stage would eventually give way to the last historical stage; true communism. A 'communist' society would work according to the principle, 'from each according to his or her ability, to each according to his/her need'. The state would simply whither away.

Marx felt that the 'working class' is misled into being loyal and hard-working in a society in which it is exploited. The working class falsely accepts the ideology (ideas, values and justifications) of that society. He felt that a realisation of this position would inevitably lead to conflict.

Chapter summary

- Business is concerned with meeting the wants and needs of people and groups in society through organised activity.
- The fundamental aspects of business are economic activity, producers and consumers, organisation and decision making.
- Economic activity is concerned with using scarce resources to meet wants and needs.
- Producers are individuals and organisations that provide goods and services are designed to satisfy the end-user the consumer.
- An organisation is a group of people forming a structure with rules and authority pursuing an objective using economic resources to meet needs and wants.

- Organisations can be classified into a number of types according to their purposes and objectives, ranging from pure business organisations, government organisations, charities to international organisations.
- Decision making involves analysis, choice and implementation. Decisions will be most effective when they are based on detailed and balanced information.
- A good business takes on board a number of activities and objectives which go well beyond the bounds of just making a profit.
- Adding value is the improvement in a good or service that is made at each stage of the production process.

11 Stakeholders (priorities and conflicts)

Stakeholders are individuals and groups who have a stake in the running of an organisation and in the consequences of the organisation's activities. For example, stakeholders may include shareholders, managers, employees, suppliers, customers, creditors and the public at large.

Stakeholders appear both within an organisation (managers and employees) and outside the organisation (customers and shareholders). The expectations of stakeholders will influence how an organisation seeks to achieve its objectives.

For example, owners and managers may set objectives which bring them rewards for the effort and risks they undertake, customers will be concerned with value for money as well as a quality product. While most stakeholders will have common expectations, there may well be other areas over which disputes arise. For example, cus-

tomers may want lower prices whereas shareholders want higher profits. Furthermore, the expectations of each group of stakeholders may change over time.

Values, style and behaviour

All organisations consist of groups of individuals whose values, styles and behaviours are likely to be different in some ways while being similar in other ways. It is important to understand the beliefs and behaviours of stakeholders in an organisation. Our values affect the way in which we behave. It is possible to alter our behaviour, so that we act contrary to our values. But this creates a tension and we tend, in due course, to revert back to our natural behaviour. The most successful businesses are those where the staff share similar values and moral principles since these guide individual and corporate behaviour.

VALUES, STYLE AND BEHAVIOUR AT THE BODY SHOP

Central to the beliefs of Anita Roddick, the founder and chief executive of The Body Shop, is her concern that business should be carried on in a moral way, for example, in the areas of animal testing of products and 'green' environmental issues. Not a single decision is taken in the company without considering the environment and social impact.

Her approach is summed up by the following principles:

- no advertising
- minimal packaging
- emphasis on health rather than beauty
- no wild claims about products
- fair recruiting policy
- equal working conditions for all staff
- profit sharing
- working for and with the community.

1 To what extent are these principles likely to match those of the stakeholders in The Body Shop?
2 What do you see as being the business benefits of the values, styles, and behaviours of an organisation matching those of its stakeholders?
3 Contrast The Body Shop with an organisation where this matching does not appear to take place.

If the stakeholders in a business have very different values, tensions are likely to arise, leading to arguments and poor performance. If, on the other hand, stakeholders share the key values there is far greater chance of success.

It is easy to think of examples where tensions in values may occur. For example, you may have a group of innovative and creative employees wanting to help an organisation to make decisions but who are dominated by an autocratic and repressive manager. Another situation in which dissonance would occur would be one in which employees have a 'public service' motivation in which they want to serve the wider community but are constrained in their actions by the organisation's drive to make all of its activities concerned with maximising profits. Finally, imagine a situation in which you have a range of stakeholders with a deep concern for preserving the environment faced

by an organisation with poor waste management policies leading to pollution.

It is increasingly common these days for an organisation to try to encapsulate the shared values of its staff and other stakeholders into a 'values statement' which sets out its beliefs. These business values should help to determine the culture of the organisation. The **culture** of the organisation is the way in which things are done within the organisation. Values and behaviour are closely linked. If employees share the values of the organisation, this will be reflected in individual behaviour and consequently in the organisation's behaviour. It is therefore important for the organisation to create a values statement and vision which clearly matches that of its stakeholders, for example, the belief in serving the community, in working hard to create the best quality standards, in behaving in an ethical way or to consider the needs of individual customers. John Collins and Herry Porras, in their interesting book *Built to Last: Successful Habits of Visionary Companies* (Harper Business, 1994) state that values create 'a sense of purpose beyond making money that guides and inspires people throughout the organisation'.

Many modern organisations create a values statement which they publicise widely to employees and other stakeholders. For example, a recent values statement for British Telecom read:

> We put our customers first
> We are professional
> We respect each other
> We work as a team
> We are committed to continuous improvement.

It is essential that these values statements go well beyond simply being words on paper. They need to be represented in the reality of everything that an organisation does.

TASK 11.1

Find a values statement for each of three organisations. Compare these values statements and explain which you feel are the most effective and why.

The expectations of stakeholders may influence how an organisation seeks to achieve its objectives. While most stakeholders will have common expectations, there may well be other areas over which disputes arise. Furthermore, expectations may change with time.

The importance of power

Power is the key to how much influence stakeholders have over the way in which an organisation acts and behaves. At different times, different individuals or groups of stakeholders will have more or less influence. For example, in the 1950s environmental pressure groups had very little power or influence. As we move into the 21st century environmental groups have an increasing degree of power and influence in organisational decision making.

```
┌─ IT'S A FACT ──────────────────────────────┐
│                                            │
│  That in the last few years of the 20th    │
│  century, the Newbury by-pass has been     │
│  built by a consortium includ-ing the road │
│  construction company Costain. A number of │
│  environmentalists bought shares in the    │
│  company so that they could put pressure on│
│  the board to consider the environmental   │
│  impact of its activities through the medi-│
│  um of the Annual General Meeting of the   │
│  company.                                  │
│                                            │
└────────────────────────────────────────────┘
```

Few stakeholders are likely to hold sufficient power to influence the actions of an organisation on their own. Influence is more likely to come from stakeholders sharing expectations with other stakeholder groups.

Sources of power within organisations

The following are widely recognised sources of power.

Hierarchy or position power
Members of an organisation have power because of their position. For example, as Chief Executive of The Body Shop, Anita Roddick has considerable power within the organisation – considerably more power than a franchisee of one of her shops, an individual employee or a shopper.

Influence
Influence can also be an important source of power in that individuals or groups may for one reason or another be able to have a major input into decision making because of who they are (e.g. a close personal friend of someone with power or someone who is highly regarded by those with power).

Control of key resources
Particular groups or individuals may have considerable power because of the resources which they control. For example, the financial manager in a large organisation has considerable power because many people require access to finance within the organisation. A supplier of essential materials can also have considerable power to influence decision making, etc.

Specific knowledge or skills
Individuals can gain power as a result of their specific knowledge or skills. Some groups and individuals know how 'to get things done' which is important to an organisation. For example, they may know how to win an important order or how complex decisions are made.

Knowledge of the environment in which the organisation operates
Those with greatest understanding of how the environment in which the organisation is operating can have the greatest power.

Sources of power for external stakeholders

A useful distinction can be made between internal and external stakeholders of an organisation. The **internal stakeholders** are those who can be seen directly as being members of the organisation (e.g. its shareholders, managers or employees). **External stakeholders** are those that do not work directly within the organisation but have important dealings with it (e.g. suppliers, customers or the community within which it operates).

Sources of power for external stakeholders include the following.

Resource dependence
A number of external stakeholders will supply an organisation with resources. Some of these resources will be of central importance while others will be less significant. A supplier of an essential raw material or fuel for example might have considerable power.

Knowledge and skills critical to the success of an organisation
These provide another source of power. For example, a subcontractor may have considerable power if it provides a particularly important service.

The ability of external stakeholder to gain attention
In recent years, external stakeholders have been able to put considerable pressure on organisations to conform to certain standards particularly in relation to ethical and environmental standards by focusing the attention of the media on performances that fall short of expectations.

The relative powers of different stakeholders is no longer clear cut in many organisations. In the past, shareholders and managers had considerable power in top-down hierarchical organisations. Today there are many groups of influential stakeholders, for example, financial institutions with major shareholdings in organisations, groups of strategic managers, influential employees, work teams and groups, suppliers, contractors, pressure groups, and many others. Increasingly, organisations are empowering decentralised groups of employees to make more decisions for themselves.

If you want to understand how an organisation works and makes decisions it is helpful to look at various indicators of power within the organisation, for example, the position which someone has within an organisation, the sort of office he or she has (e.g. a large executive suite or cramped cubby hole), the size of the budget, etc.

Figure 11.1 provides a simplified picture of the relative power of the marketing department, production department, Nottingham department, and Lincoln department of a large retailing outlet.

Indicators of power	Marketing director	Production director	Nottingham director	Lincoln director
Status				
Position in company hierarchy	H	L	H	M
Salary of senior manager	H	L	H	L
Average grades of department members	H	M	H	L
Claims on resources				
Number of staff	M	H	M	M
Budget as % of total	H	M	H	L
Representation				
Number of directors	H	None	M	None
Symbols				
Quality of accommodation	H	L	H	L
Support services	H	L	H	M

H = High, M = Medium, L = Low

Figure 11.1 The relative power of stakeholders

A quick glance at Figure 11.1 indicates that Marketing and Nottingham have much more power and influence in decision making than Production and Lincoln.

TASK 11.2

Can you devise a chart of your own to indicate the relative power of a number of stakeholders in an organisation that you are familiar with?

Coalitions between stakeholders

Coalitions may develop between groups of stakeholders (e.g. between managers and shareholders). Most people associated with an organisation will be a member of more than one coalition. For example, there may be a coalition between departments in an organisation or between indi-

viduals in the management structure. In a large organisation or one which operates in international markets, these coalitions can be extremely complex.

Stakeholder conflict

There may be direct conflict between the expectations of groups of stakeholders. In some, but not all, conflicts a compromise will be reached between the various expectations which cannot all be achieved at the same time. The following are a few examples of the many situation where conflicts may arise:

- improved technology and efficiency may be at the expense of jobs
- management may choose short-term profits instead of awarding employees a pay rise
- in the public sector, increasing funding to education may be at the expense of decreasing funding to hospitals or vice versa
- opening a new business may create jobs and provide much needed income for a local community but, at the same time, it may create unacceptable noise levels and increased traffic to inconvenience local residents.

There is a wide range of issues where conflicts can occur between stakeholders because of differing expectations. It is important, therefore, that we look in turn at each of the major stakeholder groups so that we can understand and weigh up the power they exercise.

Shareholders and owners

The traditional view from a classical economist such as Adam Smith is that an organisation exists solely for the benefit of its owners, that the sole objective of owners is to maximise their wealth, and that this is achieved with the single objective of profit maximisation. It is assumed that profit maximisation is possible because the owner has total control over the business, makes all decisions and has perfect knowledge of organisational activities.

Although this is probably true of some small to medium-sized businesses today, it is unlikely to be the case with much larger organisations. In larger organisations, few shareholders will either work for the organisation or be in a strong position to influence its activities. Also, though profitability may be an overriding objective for many shareholders, they will also be concerned with other objectives which seek to develop the overall health of the business.

IT'S A FACT

That today there are a number of ethical unit trust institutions. Shareholders choose to invest in these trusts because they know that their money is being put into companies with ethical principles rather than ones which seek to maximise profits at all costs.

Managers

Research by William Baumol in the 1950s revealed that, in many organisations, top managers rather than owners have most control over activities and wealth generation. In many large organisations, ownership and control are divorced and do not go hand-in-hand. Many shareholders do not attend Annual General Meetings or take part in decision-making processes.

Many shareholders do not attend AGMs

Where there is a clear division between ownership and control, managers will have much more freedom to develop activities which meet their own aspirations, for example, developing brand or market leadership, the positions they hold within the organisation and the salaries they receive.

Though managers may reduce the influence of the owner/shareholders, it is still necessary for them to pursue objectives which seek also to satisfy the interests of shareholders. Baumol saw top managers pursuing aspirations through the maximisation of sales revenue rather than through profitability. Growing sales meant more prestige and better bargaining powers for managers.

Employees

Managers and workers at different levels are all employees but, within an organisation, managers may have objectives which are quite different from other groups of workers.

Senior managers may have the role of satisfying different groups of stakeholders. This can be difficult, particularly where conflict exists between groups. According to one view, decision makers have neither the time and resources, nor information and cognitive ability, to make maximising decisions. They simply try to provide accept-

able levels of satisfaction to everybody. Stakeholders amend their expectations according to how the business is performing, how they see environmental conditions affecting business performance, and how well other stakeholders are being treated.

Henry Mintzberg considers manager and the workforce as 'the internal coalition' within an organisation. Mintzberg then categorises them into six groups of influencers:

- top or general management (top strategist and aides)
- operators (involved in producing goods or providing services)
- line managers (these appear in the hierarchy between the chief executive and supervisors)
- analysts of the technostructure (staff specialists)
- support staff (those who provide indirect support for the operations such as accounting and legal staff)
- the ideology (i.e. the dominant set of ideas) of the organisation.

The last item in the list may seem curious, but Mintzberg suggests that though technically an organisation is inanimate, the beliefs shared by people who work for the organisation help to create a business culture which develop an identity of its own.

Suppliers

In providing goods and services for an organisation, suppliers hope that by winning contracts they are securing income and profitability for their own businesses. Suppliers will also have other interests. For example, they will also be concerned about discounts and payment periods being reluctant to wait for payment for credit sales for too long.

The organisation receiving supplies will want to make sure that supplies are regular, arrive on time and are of the right quality. Clearly then, conflicts of interest can arise between the supplier and the supplied. The suppliers have a stake in the organisation they supply, but their priorities may differ from those of organisations with which they trade.

Customers

Customers are perhaps the most powerful stakeholder group in organisations. If you cannot satisfy the needs and wants of your customers then your organisation has little chance of surviving for more than the shortest of periods.

Marketing orientation involves 'identifying, anticipating and satisfying customer requirements profitably'. It is for this reason that customers are high-priority stakeholders for the organisation. Customers will want something of value from their transaction. If organisations are not marketing oriented or do not provide customers with desired levels of satisfaction then this will lead to consumer frustration and dissatisfaction.

Creditors

Anybody owed money by an organisation, whether a bank or a supplier, is called a **creditor**. Creditors may be particularly interested in the success of the organisation, if this might affect its ability to make payments to them.

Society and the public

It is unacceptable for a modern organisation to ignore the impact of its activities on the wider community. People living in the society in which a business operates should be seen as important stakeholders. At the same time, the business should be seen as a key stakeholder in the wider community.

Today, many people recognise that development can only be beneficial if it takes into account community losses as well as profits. Organisations, therefore, have to work out how to strike a balance in order to become 'responsible corporate citizens'.

Stakeholder satisfaction/dissatisfaction cycles

An important objective for decision makers is the development of a stakeholder satisfaction cycle. By developing activities which satisfy external stakeholders – for example, prompt payments to creditors, satisfied customers, non-intervention by consumer groups, environmental pressure groups and government agencies – an organisation will improve its ability to carry out activities which earn rewards for internal stakeholders, such as employees, many of whom will have contributed to this planning process. Thus the organisation will have created mutual benefits in a cycle which has involved both internal and external stakeholders.

On the other hand, if the plans an organisation makes seriously disturb external stakeholders, a stakeholder dissatisfaction cycle may occur. For example, if the organisation provides environmentally unfriendly goods which are considered by consumers to be sub-standard and at the same time has a bad reputation for late payments and other business practices, it will reduce its ability to be profitable. Internal stakeholders will then not reap the rewards they might otherwise like.

Stakeholder analysis therefore helps us to appreciate, particularly when developing marketing objectives, the need to understand the power positions and expectations of various stakeholder groups. Balancing these responsibilities is difficult but far from impossible. In fact, organisations now realise that there is a synergy between the disciplined, innovative approaches needed to satisfy a purely commercial responsibility and those needed to satisfy, say, a problem of worker safety. The two aspects help each other.

CASE STUDY CASE STUDY CASE STUDY CASE STUDY CASE STUDY CASE

STAKEHOLDER CONFLICT

At the end of October 1996 a new wave of litigation was launched against pub landlord Inntrapreneur by disgruntled tenants.

The action representing 20 publicans, opened up a new stage in a long-running battle with the company, which was set up in the late 1980s by Grand Metropolitan and Foster's Brewing of Australia and has been locked in dispute more or less ever since with many of its tenants.

The dispute focused on an alleged refusal by Inntrapreneur to renew five-year leases that publicans had signed in the mid-1980s with their previous landlord, Courage. The tenants claimed that they were illegally forced by Inntrapreneur staff into signing much more onerous contracts that tied them in for 20 years, at much higher rents and with new obligations to repair and insure their pubs.

Tenants claimed they were persuaded to sign the harsher contracts after being told, wrongly, that changes in the law meant that old agreements could not be extended. Many believed they faced a choice between signing the replacement contract or being thrown out in the street.

A combination of the new leases and falling demand for beer in the pubs, due to the onset of recession in the early 1990s, forced many publicans into financial difficulties. It was estimated that 1500 tenants exchanged the renewable short leases, called five plus five agreements, for the longer Inntrapreneur contracts.

A number of actions were brought by tenants against Inntrapreneur arguing that it had acted illegally by tying tenants into restrictive contracts that offer them no commercial advantage. Claims have been commenced on this count, which runs counter to the European Union's Treaty of Rome, that may eventually total up to £300 million.

For Inntrapreneur, the recent increase in the volume of writs being filed against the company threatens to create financial problems. Dogged by differences between its owners – GrandMet was interested in running a property company while Foster's wanted to boost sales of its Courage subsidiary's beer – Inntrapreneur has never been a commercial success.

1 What does this case study tell you about the folly of failing to create shared values in an organisation?

2 Which stakeholders in the organisation are seen to be at odds in the case study?
3 How does the case study show that those who seem to have less power in an organisation may prove to have more power than expected?
4 What lessons can be learnt from the case study about finding out about stakeholder requirements and then creating a balance between stakeholder interests?

CASE STUDY CASE STUDY CASE STUDY CASE STUDY CASE STUDY CASE

Chapter summary

- An organisation has responsibilities to a range of interested parties, people who have a 'stake' in what the organisation does.
- All organisations consist of groups of individuals whose values, styles and behaviours will be both similar and different.
- Organisations can create values statements which enable them to run on a basis of consensus and co-operation rather than misunderstanding and disagreement. All stakeholders need to be considered in creating a values statement.
- Power is the key to how much influence stakeholders can have over the way in which an organisation acts and behaves.
- Power comes from a range of sources not just a per-

son's position within an organisation.
- Both internal and external stakeholders exercise power in the decision-making process.
- If you want to understand how an organisation works and makes decisions it is helpful to look at various indicators of power within the organisation.
- Coalitions frequently arise between groups of stakeholders.
- There may be direct and indirect conflict between the expectations of different groups of stakeholders. The sensible organisation will try to minimise conflict by involving all stakeholders in decision making.
- An important objective for decision makers is the development of a stakeholder satisfaction cycle.

12 Business goals and objectives

Businesses need to have a clear idea of what they are trying to achieve, in other words, they need clear goals and objectives. For example:

- an objective for Coca-Cola could be to continue to be the world's number one soft drink
- an objective for Newcastle United football club could be to become one of the top five clubs in Europe within five years

Today it is fashionable to talk about organisations having a mission, goals and objectives. The best way to explain these terms is to give examples (see Figure 12.1).

Organisations therefore need to decide what they are trying to achieve and then establish targets which enable them to measure the progress that they are making.

Term	Definition	Personal example	Organisational example
Mission	Overall purpose	Be healthy and look good	To be the best known name in confectionery
Goal	General statement	Lose weight	To be the market leader in confectionery sales
Objective	Quantification (if possible) or more precise statement of the goal	Lose 10 pounds by 1st November	To increase sales by 10% per year

Figure 12.1

IT'S A FACT

That the 3M Corporation set several specific targets in 1991:

- Generate half of its sales revenues outside America.
- Reduce the manufacturing cycle time by 50 per cent.
- Create $5 billion sales from products developed within the last five years.
- Maintain research and development at high levels (running at 6.9 per cent of sales which is double the US average).
- By 1995, cut by one-third the time taken to get innovations to market.
- By 1995, reduce unit costs by 10 per cent in real terms.

CASE STUDY CASE STUDY CASE

MIDLANDS COLLEGE OF FURTHER EDUCATION

Midlands College has been facing considerable competition from rival colleges in recent years. The College offers Advanced levels, GCSE re-sits, GNVQs and a range of vocational courses. Other colleges have been able to attract students away from the College prior to enrolment, and even after enrolment. What makes matters worse is that the College has a high drop out rate, lateness of students to lectures, and poor attendance. All this means that the College's revenues have been falling because students generate income. The College receives its funding according to the numbers of students on particular courses. Some courses bring in more funds than others.

1 What sorts of targets might the College set for the coming year?
2 Why should the college be realistic in setting these targets?

STUDY CASE STUDY CASE STUDY

A business organisation may decide that it wants to build up a competitive edge over its rivals. To do this it recognises that it needs to cut down on waste, increase customer demand and increase the quality of its products. Fortunately, all these objectives are measurable so that it becomes possible to set targets to achieve them (e.g. cut waste by 10 per cent per year, increase customer demand by 20 per cent per year, and improve quality in terms of measurable quality standards).

Having clear objectives therefore makes it possible for organisations to establish definite performance targets. The most common targets for businesses are ones for sales and profits to be achieved over time, usually in the third and fifth years. For example, a company may set twin targets of sales within three years of £40 million and within five years of £65 million with profits, respectively, of £3 million and £6 million.

EXAM TIP:

Confusion in terminology

The more books you study about business aims and objectives the more apparent it will become that different writers use terms like mission, goals, aims, objectives and targets in different ways. All of these terms are concerned with defining the **ends** which organisations are working towards, i.e. what it is that they want to achieve.

From the students' point of view it is best to work your way through these differences by remembering that there are a number of levels to establishing organisational direction.

At the first level it is necessary to ask? What is it that we are setting out to do, i.e. what is our mission?

At the second level you need to ask? What is the general aim or purpose of the organisation? Sometimes this is called a goal.

You can then start to break down the aim into a number of sub-sections. These are usually called objectives which are frequently measurable in the form of targets.

How do organisations set their measurable objectives?

These can be established using three different criteria.

Historical
This is where an organisation looks at it actual experience over the last few years as a guide to future performance. Establishing objectives therefore stems from analysing previous performance in order to see what will be feasible in the future.

Competitive
This involves examining the objectives of competitors and the ways in which competitors are operating in order to establish comparable objectives.

Normative

This involves adopting standards derived from literature surveys, rules of thumb or the opinions of outsiders, such as consultants, as well as internal management experts.

General aims of business organisations

Businesses are set up for many different reasons. Profit may be an important motive, but it is certainly not the only one. For example, many people are prepared to take a cut in earnings in exchange for the satisfaction and freedom of working for themselves, and many shareholders would prefer to be part owners of a company with high moral standards rather than one that goes all out for profits.

Businesses generally have a wide range of possible aims, including to:

- to make as much profit as possible
- to be the number one in a particular market or range of markets
- to maximise sales
- to grow quickly
- to operate in a wide range of markets
- to provide owners with a steady income
- to survive
- to provide the freedom for the owners to express themselves in the work they enjoy.

> **SYNTHESIS**
>
> *Can you think of organisations to which some of the aims outlined above apply? Can you explain why they have these different objectives?*

Profit maximisation

Unless a company makes a profit it cannot afford to modernise itself, install new technologies, or take commercial risks with, say, new product ranges. It can neither continue to fulfil its social responsibilities nor can it justify the investment of its owners – private individuals or institutions such as pension funds and insurance companies – who need to seek the best possible long-term return on their resources.

In a free competitive market, and in all but the shortest term, profit is the measure of how good a business is and how well-run and effectively it meets its responsibilities to all its stakeholders.

Profit maximisation occurs when there is the maximum difference between the total revenue (i.e. number of sales made × price) coming into a business and total cost being paid out (see point Q in Figure 12.2). However, in the real world, this process is a lot more complex than simply drawing up a diagram – it will involve a thorough programme of research, taking into account costings for different levels of outputs, the effects of charging different prices, calculations of potential sales and many other factors.

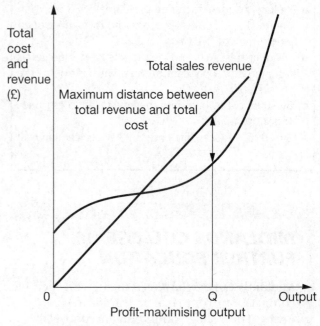

Figure 12.2 Profit maximisation

If we measured profit simply in money terms, then it would seem logical to assume that in the long term the rational business will seek to maximise the difference between its total revenue and its total cost. Accountants, for example, claim to be able to weigh up quickly the success of a business in terms of the financial profit – 'the bottom line'.

Profit is a major driving force. For example, at the end of the 20th century many business writers have recognised Coca-Cola as an object lesson in how to conduct a business well. Coca-Cola ploughs 60 per cent of its profits back into the business for product development and opening up new markets. It is able to make high profits on a very high sales figure. The company then puts these profits back into research and development, promotion and advertising, market research, opening up new distribution channels, etc. It is thus able to out-compete all its rivals. Profits yield higher sales and higher profits.

Why should a company avoid profit maximisation?
Companies should be careful about how they go about maximising. Maximising profits should be seen as a long-term rather than a short-term objective. Profitability should never involve short-term exploitation. Consumers, employees and communities who feel that they have been 'sold short' may quickly lose their loyalty to an organisation.

Market leadership

Many firms seek to be market leaders. They may want to sell more products than all rival brands combined, or simply want to sell more than the next best selling brand. The most reliable indicator of market share is relative to other brands – that is, the ratio of a company's market share to that of its largest competitor:

$$\text{Relative share of company A} = \frac{\text{Market share of Company A}}{\text{Market share of nearest competitor}}$$

A well-known study (by the Boston Consultancy Group) argued, on the basis of statistical information, that a ratio of 2:1 would give a 20 per cent cost advantage (i.e. you would be able to operate with costs 20 per cent lower than your nearest rival). If you dominate the market you can produce on a larger scale than your rivals. You can therefore spread your costs over a larger output. You can thus produce more cheaply than rivals. Profits can then be ploughed back into research, advertising and further expansion to maintain market leadership.

CASE STUDY CASE STUDY CASE

TAKING ADVANTAGE OF MARKET LEADERSHIP

In a recent statement to shareholders the Chairperson of a company producing the leading name in branded nappies made the following points:

'Over the last few years we have sought to drive our advantage home. Our product is recognised as being the most reliable, convenient and useful on the market. We currently have three times the sales of our nearest rival producer, and this has enabled us to pass the advantage of scale production on to consumers. We firmly believe that the road to success is to 'gain the lion's share of the market and then watch the profits flow in'. We will continue to find out what our consumers require in an ever changing marketplace in order to better meet their needs.'

1 How will the company benefit from making three times as many sales as the nearest rival? How will consumers benefit?

2 How will gaining the lion's share of the market lead to a flow of profits?

3 How can competitive advantage today lead to further competitive advantage tomorrow?

STUDY CASE STUDY CASE STUDY

Maximisation of sales

In some large companies the salaries earned by managers may depend on the size of the business. Thus, their objective may be to make the business as large as possible. Controlling a large business concern might also give individuals satisfaction derived from the power at their command. Increased sales might also mean reduced sales for competitors, which in the long term can be seen as being consistent with a policy of market leadership. In a college or school, a head teacher's or principal's salary will increase when the number of students goes over a certain threshold. This is of particular significance, as most senior managers will be relatively close to retirement age, and their pensions will be determined by their final few years' salary. Such managers have a big incentive to increase the number of students in their colleges. And, of course, they don't have to deal with the potential problems of over-expansion once they have retired.

A big incentive to increase sales is that the cost of making additional sales will often fall as sales rise. As a general rule, therefore, companies will be happier with higher sales figures.

Growth

Firms can benefit from growth. A firm that is growing will find it easier to attract investors and will be able to produce on a larger scale. However, one of the biggest mistakes that business people make in the early days is that of overtrading, or growing too quickly. Running a large business is very different from running a smaller one. Large businesses are managed differently and all sorts of problems arise from overtrading. For example, there might not be enough cash to pay bills in the short term, managing a large staff can be difficult, and so on.

It is surprising how many people fall into the trap of over-trading. Often someone will set up a new business and because of its early success believe that he or she is the new Richard Branson or Anita Roddick. The owner then decides to expand, but finds it difficult to manage a larger business, or to bring in the extra customers that are needed. A fairly common pattern is therefore for an entrepreneur to start with one business interest, expand to two or three business interests and then end up with no viable business interests.

Operating in a wide range of markets

Operating in several markets makes it possible to spread the risk. If one market fails, another may support the loss. However, opening into new markets also exposes a business to fresh risks. It may be better to operate in a small number of well-known markets than expose yourself to new risks.

Satisficing

Most of us at some time have had the word 'satisfactory' written on our school report or profile. This indicates that we have managed to do enough to get by without making a great success of the task in hand. The theory of business satisficing is that managers in given situations set minimum standards which they feel will establish a reasonable level of performance. They will seek to establish obtainable objectives which can be measured (although some information may be imperfect).

Management by objectives

Management by objectives (MBO) is a common business strategy which can be used to upgrade targets in the light of experience. It is a strategy that allows for the adjustment of objectives (see Figure 12.3).

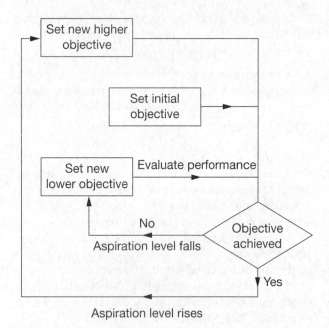

Figure 12.3   Management by objectives

Peter Drucker was particularly influential in stressing the importance of MBO. He set out to find out how best to manage a business to make sure that profits are made and that the enterprise is successful over time. He felt that business objectives help management to explain, predict and control activities. The business should establish a number of objectives in a small number of general statements. These statements can then be tested in the light of business experience. It then becomes possible to predict behaviour. The soundness of decisions can be examined while they are being made rather than by looking back on what has happened. Performance in the future can be improved in the light of previous and current experience.

Such objectives force the business to plan in detail what it is aiming at and to work out ways of achieving these aims. Management is the job of organising resources to achieve satisfactory performance.

In concrete terms, Drucker listed eight areas in which performance objectives need to be set out:

- market standing
- innovation
- productivity
- physical and financial resources
- profitability
- manager performance and development
- worker performance and attitude
- public responsibility.

Managers need to have information available to them which enables them to measure their own performance and the performance of their organisation.

Survival

As we approach the end of the 20th century it has become fashionable for a number of business writers to suggest that 'survival' has become the prime objective and motivator for organisations. The argument is that organisations, like species, have to adapt to their environments in order to survive. This is a Darwinian notion. Throughout the earth's long history species have adapted and changed in order to survive in a constantly changing environment. In the same way, business organisations operate in a chaotic environment of change. The primary driving force therefore is that of survival and this is best achieved by understanding the environment in which you operate and adjusting to changes that are taking place.

Freedom of expression

Many people set up a small business simply because it provides them with an opportunity to be creative and to be their own boss. Why work for someone else when you can work for yourself, make your own decisions and take the profits?

How important a priority is profit making?

In an important study carried out by Shipley in 1981 (*Journal of Industrial Economics*), the author concluded that only 15.9 per cent of a sample of 728 UK firms could be regarded as 'true' profit-maximisers. This conclusion was reached by cross-tabulating replies to two questions shown in Figure 12.4 below. Shipley considers as true maximisers only those firms that claimed both to maximise profits and to regard profits to be of overriding importance. Of course, there are a number of criticisms that can be levelled at any form of statistical analysis of motivations. However, there would appear to be a clear case for arguing that profit is only part of a set of business objectives.

Percentage of all respondents

1. Does your firm try to achieve:

   a. Maximum profits?   47.7
   b. Satisfactory profits?   52.3

2. Compared with your firm's other leading objectives, is the achievement of a target profit regarded as being:

   a. Of little importance   2.1
   b. Fairly important   12.9
   c. Very important   58.9
   d. Of overriding importance? 26.1

   Those responding both 1(a) and 2(d)   15.9

Figure 12.4   Responses from a sample of 728 firms

TASK 12.1

Fieldwork activity

The objectives of business firms are clearly of central importance to a course in Business Studies. We suggest that students carry out an applied piece of research, preferably by (a) talking to a small group of managers about their objectives, and (b) analysing the behaviour of a large number of businesses.

Chapter summary

- Business organisations need to have a clear focus or direction in the form of clear goals and objectives.
- A mission statement provides a generalised goal or aim; this then needs to be broken down into clearer objectives. If these objectives can be quantified then it makes it easier to measure and monitor performance against standards.
- Measurable objectives can be created by looking at the past (historical means), comparing an organisation with its competitors, or by using another measuring rod (norm).
- Businesses have a number of general aims depending on the type of business organisation, its history and the nature of competition in its operating environment. These aims are profit maximisation, market leadership, sales maximisation, growth, satisficing, management by objectives, survival and freedom of expression, as well as others.
- Although profit maximisation is important to the long-term survival of an organisation, there is considerable evidence that this is not the chief objective of many organisations.
- Some people argue that survival is the prime aim of most organisations. In the long term, organisations need to adapt and adjust to their environments in a Darwinian way.

13 The importance of business planning

A good business idea on its own does not create a good business. What is required in addition is the ability to organise and plan. Businesses require inputs of time, information, raw materials, capital, labour and paperwork. These inputs need to be put together in an organised way. However, that is not the end of the story. In addition, a business needs to create a public image to market and sell its products. It needs to consider channels of distribution, packaging, display and the many other details involved in getting goods to the final customer. All of this requires detailed planning.

A business plan is one of the key ingredients of any successful business, no matter how big or well established. It you want to start a business, it is vital. It helps you to anticipate problems and work out how to deal with them. It also gives essential information to the people whose support you need – particularly anyone lending you money.

In this chapter, we examine the ingredients that would need to go into a simple business plan. We then go on to discuss the key elements of a planning process for any organisation.

However, you will not be able to produce a detailed business plan until you have studied most of the content of this book. Before setting out a business plan, it is necessary to carry out some preliminary research to find out:

- whether people are prepared to buy the good or service
- what competition exists
- what premises and equipment are required
- whether planning permission is necessary

- how much money/capital is needed
- the cost of borrowing money
- what grants and other forms of assistance are available.

The contents of a simple business plan

Livewire has defined a business plan in the following way:

'A business plan is a complete description of a business and its plans for the next one to three years. It explains what the business does (or will do if it's a new business); it suggests who will buy the product or service and why; and, it provides financial forecasts demonstrating overall viability, indicates the finance available and explains the financial requirements.'

For most businesses, the business plan will be the main method of convincing prospective funders that the business proposal is viable and that the proprietor has the commitment and determination to succeed. The business plan should be presented in a form that can be quickly and easily understood. The main part of a business plan normally needs no more than eight to ten pages supported, if necessary, with more detailed appendices. The plan will then be manageable and is a working document in which the owner and potential funders can find the management information they need.

The business plan can be thought of as a marketing tool – for marketing the organisation to potential funders. It needs to be honest, but it should present the organisation in the best possible light. It should be easy for busy people, such as bankers, to read and assimilate quickly the required information.

A simple business plan should be clearly set out under the following headings:

- **Contents page** This is useful in any kind of report that is more than two or three pages long.
- **The owner** This section should give some information about the owner (or owners) including their educational background and work experience. It should also contain the names and addresses of two referees.
- **The business** This should first contain the name and address of the business and then go on to give a detailed description of the product or service being offered, how and where it will be produced, who is likely to buy it, and in what quantities.
- **The market** This section will describe the market research that has been carried out and what it has revealed. It should give details of prospective customers – how many there are and how much they would be prepared to pay. It should also give details of the competition.

- **Advertising and promotion** This should give information about how the business will be publicised to potential customers. It should give details of likely costs.
- **Premises and equipment** This section should show that the business has considered a range of locations and then chosen the best site. It should also give details of planning regulations (if appropriate). Costs of premises and the equipment needed should also be included.
- **Business organisation** This should state whether the enterprise will take the form of sole trader, partnership, company or co-operative.
- **Costings** The business should give some indication of the cost of producing the product or service, and the prices it proposes to charge. It is then possible to make profit calculations.
- **The finance** This should give details of how the finance for the business is going to be raised. How much will come from savings? How much will need to be borrowed?
- **Cash flow** This should list all expected incomings and outgoings over the first year. Cash flow calculations are important, but at this stage can only be approximate.
- **Expansion** Finally, the business should give an indication of future plans. Does it want to keep on producing a steady output or is a dramatic expansion possible? Does it intend to add to its product range? What kind of new competition is likely to emerge, and how will the business deal with it?

IT'S A FACT

That one of the most important reasons for business failure, particularly for start-up businesses is poor or no business planning. Sometimes the owners of new businesses have no idea of whether there is sufficient demand for their product, what prices competitors charge, the true cost of borrowing money, how to advertise and promote their business, and the importance of having a steady flow of new cash into the business.

Another way of starting a business plan is to start out the plan with a summary. The summary should briefly describe the business and highlight its purpose. It should explain how the purpose will be achieved and why the proprietor is the person to make it happen. The summary should highlight the strengths of the business and make it attractive to potential funders.

TASK 13.1

Create a five paragraph summary for a new business proposal of your choice. Focus on an idea which is practical, feasible and likely to interest providers of funds.

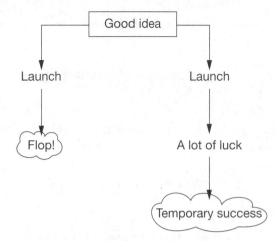

Figure 13.1

FAT FROG DESIGN

Study the following summary to a business plan. Assuming that you are a potential funder to the business, how helpful do you find it?

Fat Frog Design will provide a graphic design and desktop publishing service throughout the North East of England and other areas within the UK.

In providing this service, it is believed that Fat Frog Design will attract clients through the introduction of an annual design package, a competitive edge through pricing and attention to the detailed needs of each individual client through designer–client liaison.

Although the present market is extremely competitive, Fat Frog Design has found, through extensive market research, that there is a definite demand for Fat Frog Design's features and benefits, such as the annual design package, which none of its competitors offer.

Once Fat Frog Design has become established and has gained a reputation for quality and reliability within the North East, the business hopes to expand its range of services throughout the UK thereby increasing its client base, its turnover and ultimately its profits.

IT'S A FACT

That a common source of business failure is that of selling a large proportion of your output to a small group of customers who are then slow in paying up. Lack of cash flow can then force your business to wind up. Another cause of failure is poor paperwork. When records get in a mess then all sorts of problems start to surface (e.g. late payment for supplies or mix-ups in customer orders).

The key elements of the planning process

The planning process should be seen as a cyclical one based on continuous improvement. In other words, you don't simply create a single plan. Rather, you create a plan, then check on how well it is working, examine your performance against the plan in a critical way, and most likely adjust and develop your planning on an ongoing basis.

Within an organisation you will need to establish plans at a number of levels and you will need to create sub-plans for a range of key activities. For example, a large organisation may have an overall 'corporate plan', then a range of 'divisional plans' and then 'operational plans' for each of its operating units. At the same time it may have a 'marketing plan', a 'production plan', a 'financial plan', etc.

Planning makes it possible for managers to evaluate performance, and thus to keep control over organisational activities and to put things right as and when difficulties arise. Of course, plans are unlikely to be met in every detail. However, they establish guidelines against which performance can be checked and, if necessary, modified. A useful planning model is shown in Figure 13.2.

A detailed process

Business planning should therefore be seen as a detailed process, and one which will certainly pay off in the course of time. Without planning, the chances of business success are slim unless you have a 'very good idea' and a large slice of luck. For the unplanned, the chances of success will look like the scenario shown in Figure 13.1.

Even with a lot of luck you are only guaranteed temporary success for a product. In the long term you are going to have to put detailed plans into place, particularly as the complexity of your business increases.

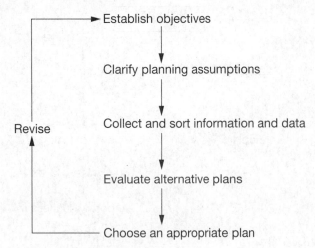

Figure 13.2   *A cyclical model of planning*

Planning for new product development

The major stages in new product development for a planned organisation are as follows:

Stage 1: Idea generation – coming up with a range of possible ideas. An idea is something that an organisation can see itself offering to the market.

Stage 2: Idea screening – looking at each of the ideas in turn to assess their strengths and weaknesses. Consider the feasibility of each for the organisation.

Stage 3: Concept development and testing – a concept is an elaborated definition of an idea expressed in meaningful consumer terms. For example, an idea might be for a business to produce a device for unfreezing frozen car locks. The concept may be for a keyring size solar energy charged rod that will inject a burst of heat into a frozen lock. An organisation may develop a range of such concepts and then test each concept out in writing on a group of potential target consumers.

Stage 4: Marketing strategy formulation – once a particular concept has been chosen, the organisation should develop an outline marketing plan to introduce the new program to the target audience. This should set out, for example, who the intended market for the new product will be and how customers will be informed about the new product.

Stage 5: Business analysis – the next stage is to carry out a detailed analysis of all the costs and revenues that will result from the product development to make sure that it will pay its way.

Stage 6: Offer development – having decided that the product is almost certain to be a success it then becomes possible to start designing brochures and promotional literature that will support the 'offer' of the new product to the market. Each of these materials should be consumer tested to check on their appeal.

Stage 7: Market testing – once the organisation is happy with its products and its promotional and advertising materials it can then do a test market. Rather than testing out the product and advertising it in the whole market a test market can be carried out in a much smaller test market (e.g. a particular supermarket, town, or a television region).

Stage 8: Commercialisation – if the test market is successful then it is time to prepare for the real launch. Important questions to be considered will include: When is the best time to launch? Where should the product be launched? Who should the launch be aimed at? How should the product be launched? Other important decisions will involve assigning responsibility for the launch to particular individuals and groups (e.g. a launch director or an advertising agency).

Stage 9: Launch

Suitability, acceptability and feasibility

All organisations need to know whether their plans and proposals are worth putting into practice. Therefore, they need to establish criteria to decide whether to go ahead with a plan or not.

There are three important techniques for evaluating options:

- suitability
- acceptability
- feasibility.

Suitability is concerned with whether plans and solutions fit the situation. For example, it would be unlikely to be suitable for an organisation to expand in a period of contracting markets and recession.

Acceptability is concerned with whether a plan will be acceptable to the organisation and to those with a significant interest in it (its stakeholders). For example, is the level of risk acceptable and are shareholders and other stakeholders prepared to agree to the plans? They may have reservations based on what they consider to be ethical, fair and reasonable.

Feasibility is concerned with whether plans can work in practice and primarily whether the organisation has adequate resources to carry out particular plans – for example, whether:

- the funds are available
- the organisation will be able to sustain the required level of output
- the organisation will be able to deal with the competition that it generates
- the organisation will be able to meet the required market share.

EXTENSION MATERIALS

You may find the following outline business plan useful. It is more detailed than the one given earlier in the chapter.

The business
Name of business
Address and location
History or background
Brief description of activities
Proposed date for trading or start-up
Legal identity – sole trader, partnership, company
Objectives
Professional advisers

Key personnel
Names of directors and managers
Background, experience, knowledge and expertise
Relevant work and business experience
Future personnel requirements
Recruitment proposals

The nature of the business
Description of product (including price)
Patents, trademarks, copyrights, etc.
Suppliers
Proposed developments of product
Market – size and potential
Trends in the marketplace
Needs of customers
Benefits offered to customers
Description of competitors' strengths and weaknesses
Unique features of product compared with competition
Projected turnover – three months, six months, 12 months, etc.
Break-even analysis
Production techniques
Reasons why proposals are achievable

Marketing plan
Marketing objectives
Environment
Market research
Marketing methods

– Product
– Price
– Distribution (place)
– Promotion

Future
Strengths, weaknesses, opportunities and threats (SWOT)
Socio-economic trends
Technological trends
Action plans
Timetable of activities

Resources
Premises, size and cost
Machines
Vehicles
Equipment
Overheads
Materials
Management salaries
Labour costs

Financial analysis
Start-up capital
Working capital
Grants
Own resources
Loans
Assets available as security
Cash flow forecast over three years
Profit and loss forecast over three years
Balance sheet

Other information
Address of accountant
Address of solicitor
Insurance arrangements
VAT registration
Summary

Chapter summary

- A good business idea does not create a good business, in addition detailed and effective planning is required.
- Before setting out a business plan it is necessary to carry out research into the market for your product, the competition, the cost of borrowing money and other details.
- A business plan is a complete description of a business and its plans for the next one to three years.
- A business plan may start with a summary of the

- business and its activities which is easy to read and simple to understand.
- Stages in planning new business ideas or products include: idea generation, idea screening, concept development and testing, marketing strategy formulation, business analysis, offer development, market testing, commercialisation and finally the launch.
- The planning process should be seen as an ongoing and cyclical one.

14 Using a business strategy to pursue corporate objectives

Business strategy is concerned with developing a clear picture of the direction an organisation needs to go in, coupled with a well thought out plan of how to steer the organisation in the chosen direction.

Two helpful definitions of business strategy are as follows:

> *'Strategy is the determination of the basic long-term goals and objectives of an enterprise, and the adoption of courses of action and the allocation of resources necessary for carrying out those goals.'*
> (A.E.Chandler, **Strategy and Structure: Chapters in the History of the American Industrial Enterprise**, *MIT Press, Cambridge, Mass.)*

> *'Strategy involves looking at the larger picture and developing major directions for an organisation to move in. It is concerned with the Generalship of business.'*
> (J. Kottler, **A Force for Change**, *1994, Macmillan Press)*

These definitions help us to divide the strategic process into two distinct areas:

- ends – setting the longer-term goals as well as the shorter-term objectives
- means – taking decisions and developing the ability to achieve the ends.

Many small businesses think of strategic or long-term planning as something that is only carried out by large businesses. However, the organisations that survive and prosper are those that meet their customers' needs by providing benefits to them at prices which cover the cost of provision and produce both sufficient profit for rein-

vestment and also a share of the profit or a dividend which satisfies the owners or the shareholders. To do this effectively, Peter Drucker argues that organisations need to focus on the external environment in order to create a customer. Similarly, Michael Porter argues that the way a business positions itself in the marketplace is of fundamental importance. Strategy therefore involves matching effectively the business' competences (knowledge, expertise and experience) and resources with the opportunities and threats created by the marketplace. Strategy is therefore as essential to the small as to the larger organisation. According to Drucker strategy is what converts plans into results. In Drucker's words, strategy 'converts what you want to do into accomplishment'.

The importance of strategic planning

Some organisations operate in a reactive way. In other words, they don't plan ahead they simply respond to changes as and when they occur. Enter strategic planning. Kerry Napuk (a management guru) defines strategic planning as:

> *'a management tool to deal with the commercial environment by thinking your way to the organisation you want.'*

Strategic planning is a powerful technique for leading from the top by marshalling all of the resources of an organisation behind an agreed plan. A strategic plan deals with the most fundamental questions in every organisation's life: Where do we go and how do we get there?

The organisation should start off by seeking answers to four basic questions:

- How did we get here? This involves reviewing the history and development of the organisation to identify what it currently does, and its current strengths and weaknesses.

- Where do we want to go?
- How will we get there?
- How can we make our plans work?

The end purpose of strategic planning is to gain a competitive edge over rivals by strategically positioning your organisation in the right markets at the right time; securing rapid and profitable growth during good times, or survival in bad times.

Where does strategic planning take place within the organisation?

Strategic planning is concerned with the big decisions that an organisation makes and focuses primarily on longer-term planning, i.e. over four or five years. However, this does not mean that strategic planning needs to be made at the centre or top of an organisation.

As Michael Goold of the Ashridge Strategic Management Centre said:

'In most large, multi-business companies, the trend today is towards decentralisation . . . the essence of decentralisation is to locate primary responsibility for proposing strategy and achieving results with the general managers of individual profit centres or businesses, not with central management. The purpose is to ensure that strategies are based on detailed knowledge of specific product-markets, to increase business level "ownership" of strategy and reduce the overload on the chief executive and his or her team ...'

We can highlight some of the key aspects of corporate strategy by taking a look at the case example of British Airways which appeared in the *Independent* newspaper in September 1996. We have added a commentary (in italics) to selected parts of this article.

IT'S A FACT

That major football clubs have developed detailed strategic plans. For example, in the mid-1990s Sir John Hall of Metro Centre fame created a strategy for Newcastle United which was aimed at making Newcastle United one of the major clubs in Europe – 'playing wise', 'business wise' and 'revenue wise'. This involved building a new stadium, with 'spin-off' leisure and recreation interests, and buying some of the best players and management staff in the world. At the heart of the success was the formulation and development of a clear-cut strategy targeted at a series of specific and attainable goals and objectives (e.g. to join the European elite), together with a series of practical actions taken to pursue this direction (e.g. new manager, players, ground facilities, results on the field of play).

CASE STUDY CASE STUDY CASE STUDY CASE STUDY CASE STUDY CASE

BRITISH AIRWAYS

British Airways (BA) is planning to shed at least 10,000 jobs and hive off large chunks of its operations, cutting down the airline to concentrate operations on little more than flying planes and dealing face to face with customers.

BA has taken a long hard look at its recent performance. It has decided to define what it does best – a narrow range of activities. Resources which are not needed for these purposes are surplus to requirements.

A whole raft of BA operations, including baggage and cargo handling, engineering and maintenance and information technology could be sold off.

The plan is part of a drive to cut costs by £1 billion by the year 2000.

It is therefore part of four to five year thinking.

A result of this strategy by BA, which employs more than 40,000 in Britain and is one of the country's flagship companies, would be an increase in profits to more than £1 billion by the end of the decade.

Strategies can be translated down into objectives and goals such as profit targets.

The company is also to switch work to 'cheaper locations'.

It has already set up computer-based functions in India to take advantage of a numerate English-speaking population, who will work for less than a tenth of the pay received by British staff.

Setting out scope and location of activities.

Such moves by a large blue-chip company could presage a wholesale export of jobs to the Third World elsewhere in British industry. If BA succeeds with such a policy, other companies, such as banks, could follow suit with serious implications for hundreds of thousands of jobs.

Knock-on effect on strategies of other companies.

It has long been a BA ambition to hive off its engineering function into a separate company, but the new strategy given the title 'Step Change' by senior managers will probably mean the sale to the baggage and cargo handling functions, crew support operations and other activities.

Far more radical, the strategy will mean that, within the next four years, BA will simply fly aircraft and provide the face-to face contact with customers.

All the rest will be sold or split away from the main company as part of management's plan to slash costs.

A cost-cutting strategy.

The British Airways case study therefore highlights the way in which an organisation needs to take a long-term strategic view in order to give clear direction for the future.

CASE STUDY CASE STUDY CASE STUDY CASE STUDY CASE STUDY CASE

Creating the direction – mission

It is very helpful to have a clear idea of where an organisation is going. A mission statement is a generalised form of objective, which sets out the overriding purpose of an organisation.

For example, in 1962 the American President John Fitzgerald Kennedy set out a mission for the space agency NASA to:

> 'Land a man on the moon and return him safely to earth.'

Before the decade was over NASA had succeeded in both these objectives.

The mission statement of the Automobile Association (AA) in the mid-1990s focused on people and service, i.e. to:

> 'Make AA membership truly irresistible and to be the UK's leading and most successful motoring and personal assistance organisation.'

The AA has proved to be highly successful in achieving this mission so that many people think of the AA as being 'the fourth emergency service', after the fire, police and ambulance services.

In its mission statement, Pedigree Petfoods, the leading producers of pet food in the UK, says:

> 'We work constantly towards identifying and satisfying consumer needs. It is the activity from which all else springs. We never forget that we cannot influence millions of consumer choices until we have convinced first one, then a second and a third consumer that our product is worthy of purchase. Our success is based on thorough research of the wide range of needs for pet

> animals and their owners. The knowledge which we gain is translated into a range of quality products which satisfy these needs better than any of our competitors.'

Clearly, then, Pedigree Petfoods describes itself as a market-driven organisation.

Today, it is fashionable for large organisations to place copies of their mission statement in prominent locations in the workplace so that employees are constantly reminded of its aims. Very often, part of the mission relates to creating quality working relationships.

IT'S A FACT

That a few years ago a Japanese motor cycle manufacturer set itself the mission statement: 'We will crush, squash, slaughter Yamaha.'

American companies are fond of creating mission statements. Some mission statements are useful if they successfully answer the following question: 'What are we, the management, trying to do for whom?'

Mission statements need to be readable. They need to make immediate sense to those that read them. They should also be brief.

Unfortunately, many mission statements are not clear, are often confusing and may be regarded with cynicism by those that read them.

A vision statement

An alternative to the mission statement is the vision statement. A **vision statement** is a clear declaration about where the managers of an organisation want to take it.

A vision therefore needs to be both inspirational and realistic. For example, Walt Disney's vision was simply 'to make people happy'.

TASK 14.1

If you were going to create a vision statement for an organisation that you are a member of, what would that vision be? Set it out in three or four brief lines.

Translating a vision or mission into aims and objectives

A mission statement is a generalised aim for a whole organisation. This then needs to be translated into practical objectives at each level within an organisation. The more specific these objectives can be the better.

We can see how a mission statement can be translated into objectives by means of a case study. Figure 14.1 shows how an educational organisation, Ashfield School, has decided on its mission. Having focused on this mission it is then able to create a series of general aims, and much more specific objectives to work towards.

Objectives are things that must be achieved in order to realise our vision so as to arrive at the chosen destination. An organisation sets objectives to break down the vision into parts that can be identified, measured and achieved.

Objectives therefore need to have a number of important characteristics. They should be:

- specific
- easily understood
- widely communicated
- challenging
- attainable
- measurable.

Developing strategic plans

Now that you know where you want to take an organisation, the emphasis should shift to getting there. How you get there depends on plans. These are called strategies and their purpose is to achieve the objectives.

Kerry Napuk has identified the characteristics of strategies as follows:

'1. They are rooted in the outside world which means you have to understand markets, opportunities, changes, trends and external threats.

2. Strategies are concerned with the product or service mix to be produced or offered and the markets in which the products or services will be sold.

MISSION STATEMENT

The mission of Ashfield School is to maximise the aspirations and attainments of all its students so that they develop into happy, caring and successful adults.

This will be achieved by the following:

AIMS

1. To provide equal opportunities for everyone.
2. To promote the highest academic standards.
3. To foster close links between home and school.
4. To help our pupils to develop the ability to make good relationships.
5. To encourage the fullest individual development through teaching and self-learning.

OBJECTIVES

- To deliver the National Curriculum.
- To help pupils to leave school with the best possible academic qualifications.

- To teach pupils to use language and numbers effectively.
- To help pupils develop lively and enquiring minds.
- To provide a balanced educational experience with equal opportunities for all.
- To help pupils develop their own personalities and be able to act independently whilst appreciating the value of teamwork.
- To help pupils develop a sense of self-discipline and a real sense of respect, courtesy and compassion.
- To help pupils to understand the multicultural society in which we live.
- To help pupils develop a respect for spiritual and moral values.
- To help prepare pupils for adult life and adult responsibilities particularly the world of work.
- To give guidance in health, fitness and sex education.
- To help pupils to become aware of and involved in the local community.

Figure 14.1 Ashfield School's mission statement

3. Strategies often involve complex decisions that deal with a high degree of uncertainty.

4. Strategies must be flexible, requiring you to be sensitive and responsive to market changes.

5. Strategy is not about making a single document but rather it is a continual process of adapting to an ever-changing environment.

6. Strategies usually result in ongoing improvements over time.

7. Strategy can also be defined as an action plan to deal with the commercial environment. For example, Ohmae say that "strategy is really no more than a plan of action for maximising one's strength against the forces at work in the business environment".'

It is helpful to make a distinction between strategic planning and strategic management.

Strategic planning is the process of making strategic choices while strategic managing is about producing the results from those choices.

The end point of strategic action is to create the right combination of new products, markets and technologies that produce the right results. You can create this combination by expanding successful existing products and businesses, adding new products or services, and by penetrating new markets while dropping less successful products and markets.

Key issues in strategic planning

In creating an effective strategic plan it is necessary to come up with detailed answers to the following questions:

- What are the changes that are taking place in your marketplace?
- What is happening to customers' tastes, attitudes and requirements?
- What changes are taking place in technology?
- What trends are emerging?
- Where will you compete?
- Which opportunities offer the best chances of success?
- What will your customers want in the future?
- How will you offer better products in the future?
- Can you build your business on any clear success factors?
- How will you generate the necessary resources?
- How will you out-compete your competitors?

SYNTHESIS

Consider a well-known consumer market, e.g. confectionery, soft drinks, or another. Choose a product in this market, and produce detailed answers to each of the questions outlined above. You will probably need to examine existing market research (e.g. from MINTEL consumer surveys) to provide you with key data.

CASE STUDY CASE STUDY CASE STUDY CASE STUDY CASE STUDY CASE

TAKING A STRATEGIC MOVE INTO EUROPE

This case study shows how and why Spillers Petfoods acquired Quaker European Petfoods for £465 million in April 1996 to create Europe's second largest petfood manufacturer.

Spillers + Quaker European Petfoods = Europe's Number Two

The European market is very important to many UK companies. Lifestyles and buying patterns in many European countries are similar to those in the UK.

Today, there can be no doubt that UK trade is closely tied to the EU, as over half of our exports by value go to EU countries. The bulk of the EU's trade with other countries is with the western industrialised countries (about 60 per cent), being made up mainly of manufactured products (65 per cent of imports and 83 per cent of exports in 1997).

In 1996, Dalgety put into effect a major strategic decision by focusing a key part of its activities on European petfoods. An important move in this direction was for the company to divest itself of its Golden Wonder and Homepride food businesses in order to acquire Quaker European Petfoods.

In addition, a rights issue was created to enable shareholders to put more capital into the business, which would as a result have the potential to yield much higher profit levels.

Spillers and Quaker have much to offer each other. Spillers was a major player in the UK but lacked a good continental presence, whilst Quaker had a well-developed European operation. This provided the opportunity to convert two medium-sized businesses into one good strong company, capable of playing a leading role in an industry which had considerable growth potential.

By creating a truly European branded business, Spillers was able to take advantage of a market which was at the time growing by about 3 per cent per year.

Spiller's flagship brand *Felix* provides an insight into how it is possible to maximise the benefits of European branding.

The current Felix concept was conceived in 1989 in the UK by creating a mischievous cat with whom pet owners would readily identify. The range was extended to seven varieties with an emphasis on high-quality cat food. Felix was used in national newspaper advertising for three years before appearing on the television in the early 1990s.

Five years later, Felix has surpassed any of the original predictions made. The brand is repeatedly found in the UK's list of top ten fastest growing brands, and its value even outstrips that of other household brand names such as Tango and Kleenex.

Since 1988, Felix has achieved an increase in UK market share from 6 per cent to over 25 per cent. This performance is doubly impressive considering most other brands remained static or lost market share. There is a strong potential for this performance to be repeated in other European markets. Felix has now come to play an increasingly important part in European Union markets, so that in 1997 it had around 15 per cent of the EU market.

1 Explain why the acquisition by Spillers of Quaker European Petfoods should be seen as a strategic move.
2 What elements of strategy can you identify in this move?
3 What do you understand by the term 'strategy'? Why is it such an important aspect of organisational management and planning?

CASE STUDY CASE STUDY CASE STUDY CASE STUDY CASE STUDY CASE

Chapter summary

- Strategy is concerned with developing a clear picture of the direction an organisation needs to go in coupled with a well thought out plan of how to steer the organisation in the chosen direction.
- Objectives are the ends which an organisation works towards; strategies are the means.
- Strategy is an essential activity for all businesses whether large or small.
- Strategic planning should start off by seeking answers to four key questions: How did we get here? Where do we want to go? How will we get there? How can we make our plans work?
- The end purpose of strategic planning is to gain a competitive edge over rivals.

- With the increasing trend towards decentralisation in organisations, strategic planning has increasingly become a function of general managers and profit centres within the organisation.
- A mission statement or vision should provide an organisation with a clear sense of overall direction or purpose.
- The vision should then be translated into clear and precise quantifiable objectives.
- Strategic plans are concerned with identifying the waysof achieving the mission, aims and objectives of the organisation.
- Without a clear strategy an organisation has no sense of purpose or direction.

15 Business as a dynamic activity

There is a saying that the only constant in organisational life is change. This is truer today than at any time in the past. Today, we are experiencing enormous changes in society, in organisations, in ways of doing things, and in our everyday lives. Business should therefore be seen as a dynamic activity.

Organisations make decisions which help them to cope in a changing world. The decisions that they make help to create new changes. For example, as standards of living rise consumers seek new goods and services to satisfy their growing demands.

Organisations come up with solutions to consumer requirements through new products. The new product can then alter people's lifestyles and way of doing things. For example, as standards of living have risen people have sought new forms of personal entertainment, for example, computers and sound systems. Business organisations have responded by producing a range of personal computers, CD-Roms, the Sony Walkman, etc. As more people have bought these products, others have begun to feel that they would like to have the products too, creating a mass demand for them. Producers are faced with a challenge and an opportunity – to create new and more sophisticated products to meet ongoing demands and expectations.

Organisations therefore respond to change, and create change. They are part of a two-way process (see Figure 15.1).

In this chapter we introduce just a few of the many changes that are taking place which have a dynamic impact on business.

Key changes that have taken place in recent times include: the decline of manufacturing, the development of the global marketplace, increased competition from developing economies, the influence of information technology and the changes associated with the arrival of the millennium.

The decline of manufacturing

The proportion of those employed in industry fell from 36 per cent to 28 per cent of the workforce between 1981 and 1991. In manufacturing, employment fell faster still and is now well below 20 per cent of the workforce. Work

carried out by the Institute for Employment Research in the mid-1990s led it to forecast that, over the 1994–2001 period as a whole, manufacturing is expected to lose 200,000 jobs from its total. This implies a significant slow down in the loss of jobs from manufacturing.

Between 1994 and 2001 the projected fall is 4 per cent. This is only around one-quarter of the rate of decline seen during most of the 1970s, 1980s and the first part of the 1990s. This situation of decline is typical of all modern industrial economies. In January 1994, Richard Brown and DeAnne Julius argued in the *Amex Bank Review* that employment in manufacturing could drop to 10 per cent of the total workforce or below in modern industrial countries during the next 30 years. Fortunately, the UK is well in advance of some of its rivals, such as Germany, in the restructuring process. However, it is important to remember that many of the organisations that have restructured are the larger well-known UK companies (e.g. BP, Shell, ICI) which for a long time offered secure employment to people, and produced many of the goods and services that the UK was famous for.

The development of the global marketplace

Today, business organisations increasingly operate in global markets. For example, the Coca-Cola trademark is recognised by 94 per cent of the earth's population and 'Coca-Cola' is the second most universally understood phrase after 'OK'.

Companies like Coca-Cola, Shell, Mars and Peugeot operate in global markets and are able to produce vast quantities of products at very low prices. Only the most successful can be sure of their long-term future. In recent

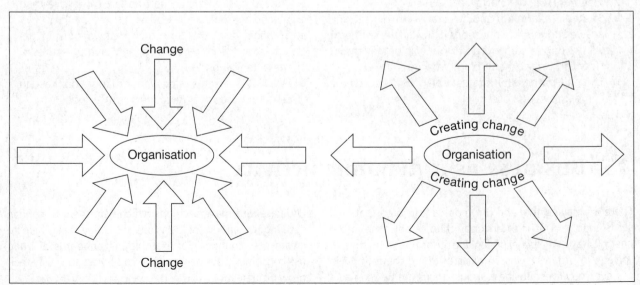

Figure 15.1 The two-way process

times, they have seen the need to be lean and fit with highly flexible people if they are to prevent rivals from stealing a march on them. Global corporations seek to reduce uncertainty in an age of uncertainty. The global economy has a potential for chaos because it involves so many simultaneous changes.

The life span of industries and organisations is constantly decreasing as they struggle to change quickly enough to survive. The restructuring of organisations has become intense, driven by more competitive global markets, and changes in technology which have led to faster and faster change.

The growth of the new economic powerhouses

The Japanese economy has been one of the great success stories of the post-Second World War world. Today, most of the fastest growing economies are in the Pacific Rim area and include countries such as South Korea, Malaysia and Thailand which are increasingly taking an important share of world trade.

The Pacific Rim is made up of millions of people whose incomes are increasing (particularly for people living in urban areas). Here, markets are developing for branded goods such as Johnny Walker whisky, Chanel No. 5 perfume, etc. However, these countries are also manufacturing and exporting their own high-quality branded products, such as motor vehicles. Increasingly, these economies are coming to develop a competitive edge in consumer product markets.

The key role of information technology

Information technology (IT) lies at the heart of modern organisations and also provides a driving force for change. IT makes it possible to empower project teams (groups of employees working together in relatively small groups to push a particular project through). IT applications are able to replace millions of routine tasks, so that many non-skilled and partly-skilled employees are no longer required.

There are two contrasting views on technology. One approach is that advanced technology makes it possible to do more tasks with fewer people, i.e. a drive towards greater efficiency. This leads to falling costs and prices, releasing increased spending power which helps to create new jobs in new growth sectors. An alternative view is what is known as the 'lump of labour theory', which assumes that there is a fixed amount of work to be done and, if fewer people are required to do it, this will lead to more unemployment.

IT has had a dramatic impact on the way in which businesses are organised today, and has led to massive increases in productivity. Twenty years ago, most large business organisations had a pyramid structure. People at the top made the big decisions. These flowed down to middle managers, who then passed their instructions down to operatives. These 'command and control' organisations are no longer desirable; they are slow and clumsy.

Today, we have new dynamic organisations in which there are far more decision-making points (see Figure 15.2).

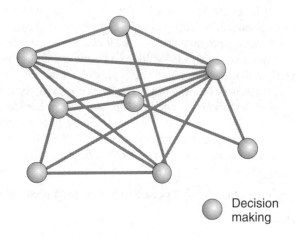

Figure 15.2   *Decision-making structure of the new dynamic organisation*

If we look at how big corporations are working, we can see that each operating company is broken down into a loose network of business units. The parts of these organisations only link up when they need to exchange information and work together on shared projects. The name of the game is 'flexibility'.

The development of IT has broken down a number of assumptions which in the past led to companies being large:

- Today, company databases are no longer the exclusive property of head office. Everyone with a lap-top or pocket-book computer has access to them and via the internet, to a world of information.
- Factory robots took over the routine and left people free to manage. Blue collar workers began to turn into white collar workers.
- Sales specialists could offer customers a complete range of personalised options and leave the computer to handle the detail: registering the order, requesting the item from store or, if it is to be specially made, from the factory, maintaining stock levels of standard products, organising delivery, preparing the invoice, controlling credit and recording payment. Armies of pen pushers or even button-pushers were no longer required.
- IT makes the world one small village. Financial markets, for instance, are fully global, with billions of pounds, dollars, marks, francs and yen chasing the sun round

the clock from Tokyo to London and New York and anywhere else in the globe.

- Routine accounting work can be contracted out globally wherever the skills exist to undertake it, with the results available instantly where they are needed. Major companies based in western Europe now have accounts departments thousands of miles from head office – sometimes in the Far East.
- Even highly-skilled work requiring close working contact with managers can be contracted out to sites hundreds or thousands of miles away. For instance, engineers in Aberdeen designing offshore oil platforms can work with qualified draughtsmen in India. The time difference enables the work to be done more cheaply.
- IT makes 'contracting out' much more feasible. Companies can now pick the best people and systems from anywhere in the world to carry out a particular task (which may be a one-off requirement or a long-term service) without communication difficulties. As a result, companies can concentrate on their core activities where they can operate at their most efficient.

The net result of the IT revolution is that small companies can compete with large companies on far more equitable terms. Large companies no longer have quite the same monopoly of the best and latest knowledge and know-how.

It has become almost a cliché that the unskilled in the West must now compete with the unskilled in the East. It is now becoming equally obvious that skilled personnel in the West will have to compete directly with skilled people in the East who now require less pay for equal quality and quantity of work.

Perhaps the West need not despair for too long. Its living standards are the envy of the East and it should not be too long before equalisation of income is approached by increases there rather than decreases here.

We are in a transitional period between the old, pre-IT, pre-Pacific Rim certainties when big companies had to act big to survive – and a new global equalisation when technology and its benefits will be found in most countries and not in a favoured few. Big companies have to accept the paradox that to stay big they have to act small. Small companies can stay small yet act with the efficiency and scope of a big company.

CASE STUDY CASE STUDY CASE STUDY CASE STUDY CASE STUDY CASE

CONTRACTING OUT WORK TO INDIA

In January 1997, Sir Brian Pitman, chief executive of Lloyds TSB told a group of business leaders that companies could benefit from 'much lower costs' by contracting out many of their activities. 'I don't think we have fully confronted the opportunities in outsourcing and what the consequences will mean for our business as we really grab the opportunities of much lower costs … by getting business done elsewhere,' he said.

Addressing a conference to launch 'Leading people', a study of leadership in the financial and business service sector, Sir Brian said that increasing competition would lead senior management to consider 'much more outsourcing than we have at the moment'.

In a reference to the whole of British industry, he said,'It is not a question of producing quality products at a high price, it is producing top quality products at the lowest price possible.'

Companies in widely different sectors such as British Airways and North West Water are already taking advantage of the low salaries earned by proficient and English-speaking Indians. Data-processing staff in the sub-continent generally earn around a tenth of the salaries received by British colleagues and so the burgeoning software industry in India can comfortably undercut in-house services in Britain.

A report by the Delhi-based National Association of Software and Service Companies pointed out that the sub-continent had 'the second-largest English-speaking scientific and trainable manpower pool in the world'.

While it started from a low base, the association calculated that the Indian software sector had grown 46 per cent annually between 1990 and 1995 – almost twice as fast as the business in the United States.

The author of the leadership report, Amin Rajan of the research consultancy Create, believes the resurgent interest in 'outsourcing' could mean banks farming out their cheque processing, insurance companies contracting out the payment of claims and securities dealers outsourcing settlements. Tens of thousands of jobs are involved in such activities. One chief executive of a banking group told Amin Rajan that 15 per cent of the company's costs could be saved by contracting out money transmission.

In the 1980s companies began by outsourcing in-house services such as catering and cleaning, then proceeded to farm out IT systems. It is likely that other activities will follow.

Some UK trade unionists are worried about such moves. For example, Ed Sweeney, general secretary of the Banking Insurance and Finance Union, expressed concern about the trend: 'There is nothing that can't be outsourced if they put their minds to it, but they can sacrifice quality and they can also lose control.'

He said that the cost saving could often be illusory. He detected that some companies were already taking back some activities which they had previously 'outsourced'.

1 What do you understand by the terms 'contracting out' and 'outsourcing'?
2 Why is outsourcing and contracting out such an attractive option for UK companies?
3 What are the main dangers of such a trend for people and organisations in the UK?

CASE STUDY CASE STUDY CASE STUDY CASE STUDY CASE STUDY CASE

IT'S A FACT

That if you book a holiday in the UK through a travel agent the processing of your reservations will almost certainly be done in India. India has a pool of highly skilled IT specialists who are able to handle such transactions at a fraction of the cost of similar specialists in the UK.

The importance of interdependence

Today, more than ever, interdependence lies at the heart of business relationships. Information is one of the greatest assets of an organisation. By sharing information efficiently, it can build a strong competitive advantage over its rivals.

But it is not just interdependence within a business that is important. Companies need to build excellent links with customers. The successful business of today and the future is the one that is able to identify, anticipate and meet customer needs.

Excellent links with suppliers are vital too. Businesses need to have quality raw materials and semi-finished products delivered 'just in time' to be made into final products.

The challenge of new markets

Today, many companies are moving into new markets. Large companies need to see the world as their marketplace. By doing so, they are able to spread their costs over a larger output. The costs of international communications and transport have been greatly reduced. Also, rather than transporting goods to other countries, companies are preferring to set up their own manufacturing plants overseas, either by building from scratch or setting up joint ventures.

The importance of new technologies

New technology has transformed our lives and will continue to do so in the future. Long-established technologies offer considerable scope for improvement. For example, the use of unleaded petrol has made the internal combustion engine much more environment-friendly, removing 90 per cent of harmful emissions such as carbon monoxide.

In spite of its phenomenal developments in recent years, IT still has immense potential. We quickly become frustrated with current technology, yet five years ago we would have been astounded at the speed of today's computers. IT will continue to astound us and to transform our lives.

SYNTHESIS

What recent examples of modern technology are you familiar with that have had a revolutionary impact on the way in which goods and services are produced?

Investing for the future

Business success involves a continual process of preparing for tomorrow. Businesses cannot rest on their past successes. They need to build for the future. For example, many companies famous for producing typewriters failed to respond to the word-processing revolution of the 1980s and disappeared. Others were eager to exploit the word-processing revolution, but failed to realise that the future lay with personal computers containing a WP package. They too disappeared.

The emphasis needs to be on making effective plans for the future and taking intelligent risks. P&O for example, realised that aircraft could deliver passengers to their destinations faster than their own cruise liners. Instead, they turned their attention to the ferry business, where journey times were longer, but passengers could take their own cars and enjoy the fun of a sea voyage.

The importance of the environment

Concern for the environment has become one of the most important business issues today. No company can survive and prosper if it neglects the developing needs of the customer and the increasingly insistent needs of the environment.

In practice, the two sets of needs go together. Customers will not want to buy products and services from companies with a bad environmental record. In addition, government regulation and taxation will put greater financial burdens on companies who do not meet agreed environmental standards. The net result is that business policies will have to become environmentally efficient to survive.

Smaller businesses

Today, there is more scope for small business than in the past. Because large organisations are 'downsizing' and streamlining, they need to buy in many of their 'non-core' requirements from outside. This is called outsourcing.

For example, in the past a large multinational company may have had its own photography department, perhaps employing a number of photographers with their own office. Today these companies will buy in professional photography services from outside the organisation. In the same way, a big company will outsource design work, advertising work, training work, cleaning of offices and many other jobs, leaving it free to concentrate on its core activities.

At the same time, people have more leisure and, as incomes increase, they want to buy in a wide range of personal services. There are therefore plenty of opportunities for people to set up small businesses providing hairdressing, massage, gardening, cleaning, ironing, etc.

The millennium

The millennium will have an enormous impact on organisational life in this country. It is likely to herald a major change in buying patterns, tastes, behaviours, and ways of doing things. It is likely to be a period of revolutionary change in which many new ideas will feed off each other creating a 'millennium approach'. Preparation for the millennium has already begun to take off (by 1996 most hotels and conference centres had been fully booked for the celebration of the New Year for the turn of the century). Major organisations such as political parties have realised the importance of riding the crest of the millennium wave. It will herald an era of extraordinary dynamic change. It is against this background of change that businesses need to operate and to think ahead.

The change process

We shall return to examine change in more detail in Part 2 where we explore ways in which organisations manage change and respond to the dynamic business environment in which they operate.

Change involves achieving a future desired state of affairs. This will involve crystal ball gazing, looking into the future to predict what will be the context in which organisations and individuals will operate in the future. Another part of the change process lies in the need for individuals to react and adapt to changed situations. Many organisations at some stage or another will find that their market share has dropped, or that a new product has been developed by a competitor. The organisation will need to change and adapt to these new pressures.

The first part of the change process, looking at the future, is called **planned change**. Targets are set, timetable for achieving intermediate goals are drawn up and the process is constantly monitored. The second element of change, adapting to an already changed situation, is called **reactive change**. Both elements are difficult to manage well in organisations.

Many writers have argued that organisations spend too much time in reactive change and not enough time in planning change programmes to cope with future contingencies. In order to minimise the disruptive and inefficient process of reacting, organisation should anticipate change and be proactive.

Throughout this book we constantly return to the idea of using strategy to manage change, i.e. by thinking ahead and creating well-constructed plans to manage change effectively.

IT'S A FACT

That the business guru Tom Peters brought out a book entitled *The Pursuit of Wow!* in 1995 in which he advocated that organisations and individuals need to be dynamic to be successful in a period of dynamic change. So what is 'Wow'? It's enthusiasm in your work, making your work count, taking risks. It's the intangible quality of a product. It's design, it's style, it's the extra little attention that the retailer gives. Wow is daring, wow is fresh, wow is what makes a particular product or service stand out!

Chapter summary

- The only constant in organisational life is change. This is truer today than ever before.
- Organisations respond to change, and they help to create changes.
- Key changes that have taken place in recent times include the decline of manufacturing, the development of the global marketplace, the influence of information technology (IT) and changes associated with the arrival of the millennium.
- The decline of manufacturing has slowed down in this country because we already have a substantial service base to the economy.
- Increasingly, business organisations are operating in a global marketplace rather than a regional or national marketplace.
- Asia and the Pacific Rim is an economic giant that is fast stirring, with unbelievable power, vitality and wealth. In time, Japan will be joined by Malaysia, Singapore, Taiwan, Korea and others, all teeming and pulsing with raw entrepreneurial energy. To ignore this and the developing China and Indonesia is to put one's own economy at risk.

- IT lies at the heart of modern organisations and has completely altered the structure of many organisations. IT has helped to change organisations from top–down, centralised hierarchies, to organisations in which there are teams of empowered workers making decisions at many points within the organisation.
- IT has given rise to an increasing emphasis on outsourcing and the contracting out of work particularly to countries which have skilled IT professionals who are prepared to work for less pay than Western IT professionals.
- Organisations are faced with a number of new challenges in today's dynamic business world including the development of new markets, new technologies, an increasing emphasis on the environment and other changes.
- In order to manage change effectively, organisations need to plan for change rather than simply respond to changes which are thrust upon them.

16 Starting a small business

Starting up your own business is a big step. It is always vital to carry out a lot of research and think things through carefully before rushing into it.

People start their own business for a variety of reasons. Some have a bright idea that they think will make them rich. Others find themselves unemployed and start their own business to survive. Some can only be themselves when they are their own boss. Others want to give some-

thing to their community and can see no other way of doing it except by setting up on their own.

Business ideas

Of course, an important starting point for a business is the business idea. Most people at some time or another have said things like: 'If only someone sold x here they could make a fortune …'; or 'I have a great idea for a new product.'

CASE STUDY

SPOTTING A BUSINESS OPPORTUNITY

In Europe today, we have surpluses of butter, grain and milk because more of these products are being produced than customers can buy. But other agricultural products are in comparatively short supply.

Jonathan Newell studied agriculture at university and found out, through studying the relevant trade statistics, that not enough snails are being produced to meet demand. In particular, the demand is not being fully met

in France. There is also a growing appetite for snails in the UK.

In recent years, most snails coming into France have come from Eastern Europe. However, because of the Chernobyl disaster, these snails still have excessive amounts of radioactivity and have been banned in France until recently.

Jonathan was convinced that if he could produce the product he could sell it to a ready market. He received a grant to do some more detailed marketing and found that Britain imported over 100,000 snails per year in the late 1980s and that the figure was rising in the early 1990s.

He then set up a private company which he called Escargot Anglais and he raised money by selling shares in the company to friends and relatives. The company had limited liability. This means that if it runs into difficulties Jonathan and the other shareholders will lose only the money they have actually put into the business. The idea of a limited company also appealed because limited companies must send a record of their accounts to Companies House every year. Jonathan felt that this would force him to keep records in an organised way.

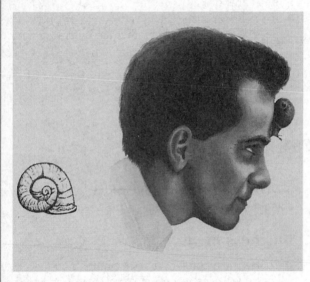

Spotting a business opportunity (Source: Shell Education Service)

The next step was for Escargot Anglais to hire a unit from the Kent Enterprise Agency in Ramsgate and to buy in a stock of 200 breeding snails from the Mediterranean. You will be glad to hear that edible snails are different from the ones you find in your garden. They grow more quickly and lay more eggs. They are also more tender.

Jonathan expects that his snails will produce an average of 10 clutches of eggs a year. Each clutch will hatch 60–70 snails. The eggs must be kept at a temperature of 21°C for about three weeks. It then takes between 100 and 120 days for the snails to build up to a marketable weight of 20–25 grammes.

The snails are kept in trays and are fed on animal feed. They can feed as soon as they start to move around.

Jonathan had been in business only a few months when the worst storm this century battered the Kent coast. Fortunately, the snails survived, and since then Jonathan has bought 200 more snails from Europe. Normally, during December and January, the snails are rested, but the remainder of the year they are expected to produce one clutch a month.

1 What is Jonathan's business idea?
2 Why is he taking a risk in setting out in business?
3 How can careful planning help him to reduce this risk?
4 What advantages will Jonathan gain from setting up in business?
5 What sorts of information would Jonathan require before setting up in business?
6 What evidence is given that Jonathan had researched and planned his business before setting up?
7 Apart from the ability to sell goods, what other criteria could be applied to measure the success of Escargot Anglais over a period of time?
8 What market is Escargot Anglais trying to sell to? What factors influence the choice of markets?

CASE STUDY CASE STUDY CASE STUDY CASE STUDY CASE STUDY CASE

Developing a business idea

With very few exceptions, every big company began as a small company, often with just one or two enterprising individuals at its head:

● William Morris began by mending bicycles in a back street garage in Oxford and went on to build up a major motor manufacturing company.

● Michael Marks arrived in this country from Russia in the 19th century speaking very little English. He set up as a door-to-door hawker of buttons, needles, ribbons and other small items. He progressed to selling from market stalls, setting up in partnership with Tom Spencer. Today Marks and Spencer is the best-known brand name in the UK.

● Anita Roddick set up her own small shop in the 1960s

to sell her preparations of cosmetics based on natural substances. Today, the Body Shop can be found on most major high streets.

Developing a business idea usually requires a combination of careful planning and good luck. It also requires careful attention to detail in a number of key areas, including production, finance and marketing.

IT'S A FACT

The Livewire organisation sponsored by Shell UK to support young people in business in this country has set out the following guidelines.

'The characteristics of self-employed people depend very much upon their business. A complicated, technical operation requires intelligent, well-qualified people – a straightforward business idea (e.g. one person and a delivery van) doesn't. There are businesses that suit brash, self-confident types and there are businesses run by people who are quiet and shy.

'There's no single stereotype, but experience has shown that there are some things that successful self-employed people often have in common. Here are some of them.

- Logical, perceptive, organised, realistic, responsible – good at getting things done.
- Out-going, confident, cocky.
- Communicator – able to get a point across.
- Sociable, good leader – can win people over instead of getting their backs up.
- Single-minded, decisive, independent.
- Open-minded – able to take advice.
- Flexible, adaptable.
- Opportunist, risk taker, ambitious.
- Hard working, committed, determined, "get up and go" type.
- Tough – often the best test of a successful person is their ability to handle failure.
- Individual – not afraid to stand out from a crowd, or of what others think.'

SYNTHESIS

Think about how you would rate yourself in terms of the characteristics outlined above.

The growing importance of small business

In recent years, small businesses have grown in importance in the UK. Statistical evidence supports the view that the 1980s in particular were the 'decade of the small firm'. Small businesses accounted for a substantial and developing proportion of total employment in the UK. As large organisations have shed labour and become more clumsy, small firms have grown in importance and have particularly benefited from flexibility.

Reasons for the growth of small businesses

Unemployment has been a key factor in the growing importance of small businesses. Redundancy, often with a golden handshake, encouraged many individuals to move into small business ownership. Another factor has been the growth of the service sector. Services have become more important in recent years and small firms frequently have a competitive edge in this sector. They are able to respond more flexibly to changes in market conditions as well as providing more personal attention to customer needs. As businesses began to downsize they increasingly sub-contracted out many of their activities to smaller enterprises. At the same time, politicians have recognised the need to help small businesses and many 'supply side' measures, such as state-funded help and advice agencies, increases in the VAT threshold and reductions in regulations, were made in the hope that a growing small business sector would generate employment, wealth, competition and choice. Such developments have helped to create an 'enterprise culture' which has encouraged small business activity and increased respect for the self-employed. While this focus on emphasis is most closely associated with the Conservative Party it is also something which New Labour has also taken to.

During the 1980s the small business sector experienced a 70 per cent expansion to a stage where it represented 17 per cent of the UK gross domestic product (GDP) and 35 per cent of private sector employment.

Small businesses reflect opportunities for profit and recognition within society. Many people with imagination, courage and belief in what they are doing start their own business with a determination to use hard work, skills and creative talents in order to succeed. A word of warning, however, the small business sector is extremely dynamic. Though 380,000 businesses started up in 1993, liquidations and bankruptcies were in excess of 62,000 and these figures do not reflect the businesses which simply withdrew from the marketplace. It is estimated that one in three small businesses cease trading in their first three years of operation.

SYNTHESIS

Think of two or three small businesses that you are familiar with. With these specific examples in mind see if you can come up with some more general principles which help to explain the advantages that give small businesses a competitive advantage over larger ones.

What is a Small Business Enterprise?

Small businesses clearly have features which make them different from large businesses. The problem with coming up with a clear-cut definition is that small businesses come in so many shapes, forms and sizes, from window-cleaners and buskers to publishers and professional business consultants. One definition of the term 'small business' is one which is independently operated and not dominant in its field of operations.

The first significant attempt to assess the small business sector was made under the chair of J.E. Bolton. In 1971 the *Bolton Report* was published. This report indicated that a small business has three essential characteristics:

- *it is managed by its owner(s) in a very personalised way*
- *in economic terms, it has a relatively small share of its market*
- *the owner is free from outside control in its principal decisions and it is independent in that it does not form any part of a larger enterprise.*

The *Bolton Report* also provided more specific measures of small business which were based upon the type of industry in which the business operated (see Figure 16.1).

Type of business	Definition
Manufacturing	200 employees or less
Construction	25 employees or less
Road Transport	5 vehicles or less
Retailing	£500,000 p.a. turnover or less
Miscellaneous Services	£500,000 p.a. turnover or less

Note that the turnover levels for the last two categories were £50,000 in 1971 but have been adjusted to 1994 prices.

Figure 16.1   The Bolton Committee definitions of small businesses

The first stage in setting up a business

The very first stage in setting up a business is to think of a good idea. Small businesses are often viewed as a 'hot bed' of creativity, where innovative products and new ideas abound. Many of the great entrepreneurs today came up with good ideas just a few years ago. For example, Anita Roddick at The Body Shop, Malcolm Walker and Peter Hinchcliffe at Iceland, and Virgin's Richard Branson.

Whether the idea the entrepreneur intends to implement involves a good or a service, the output for the business should be thought of as a product. A good idea should, however, not just stop at the product. It might include selling products to new markets, better methods of doing business or new marketing methods. For example, First Direct has been so successful in recent years because it saw ways of changing the face of banking using new communication links – to create telephone banking!

There are various sources of new ideas. For example:

- **A unique creation** Developing a new invention may provide a unique opportunity for a market. Surprisingly, however, very few businesses start with inventions and only about 2 per cent of patents come from private individuals.
- **Copying** This is another way of developing a good idea. Many entrepreneurs develop their ideas from the ideas of others who have been successful in different parts of the country.
- **Franchising** This is a useful way of starting a small business under the name of another business which allows the franchisee (the person using the franchise to start up a business) to use the franchisor's (the business giving the franchise) reputation and expertise.
- **Buying an existing business** This is a fairly easy way of developing a business idea and cuts out many of the difficulties involved in the start-up process.
- **Personal skills and experience** Personal experience, skills or expertise may help to develop the business idea. For example, knowledge of an industry, experience with crafts or involvement with a hobby may provide a useful background for setting up a business.

The important aspect of a business idea is to develop the product or the ways in which it is presented in a form which is different to that of competitors. By doing this a business can gain differential advantages over other businesses in the market and can also develop a unique selling proposition (USP) which will encourage customers to use that business.

Peter Drucker identifies seven sources for innovative opportunity. These are:

- **The unexpected** Unexpected success or failure may provide important indications about opportunity.
- **The incongruous.** This is the result of a difference between what everybody expects and what actually happens. Many business opportunities occur as a result of such an unpredictable sign.
- **Process need** An identified need in the market for new products and processes will lead to opportunities.
- **Industry and market structures** Sometimes industries or markets change after a considerable period of stability. This can provide real opportunities for innovators with new ideas.

- **Demographics** A study of the statistics of population may reveal important changes within society and may therefore become useful research in helping to identify small business opportunities.
- **Changes in perception** Trends, fashions and fads affect the ways in which consumers respond to products and provide a useful source of business opportunity.
- **New knowledge** Many new products arise from discoveries and inventions.

Analysing the opportunity

Having thought about an idea, the next step for the person intending to set up a small business is to analyse whether the business could be developed profitably. Small businesses are particularly vulnerable to a variety of unfavourable conditions, such as high interest rates, government regulations and recession, which make it difficult, no matter how brilliant an idea, for a small business to succeed.

Sources of information and advice for small businesses

There are a variety of sources of information and advice either for existing small businesses or those wishing to set up a small business. These include:

- **Local Enterprise Agencies** These are small advisory organisations such as South Lincolnshire Enterprise Agency, which act as a source of advice to small businesses on almost every issue.
- **Training and Enterprise Councils (TECs)** These have taken over the Small Firms Service and, today, most of their resources are directed at training.
- **The Enterprise Initiative** This is a package of advice, guidance, and help launched by the government.
- **Others** These include banks, local government and, for

businesses operating in rural areas, the Rural Development Commission.

The business plan

After investigating the idea and developing the proposals the small business owner should construct a detailed business plan, which includes an analysis of how much finance is required to start and run the business. For more information on writing a business plan, see chapter 13. One possible key to the success of a small business is the business plan. Many people with good ideas do not translate their ideas into a good business because they fail to plan properly.

Small business owners will need to plan so that they will have a direction to follow. They will want to know:

- where the business is likely to go
- how it is going to get there
- what resources are required
- whether they are going to be able to meet their objectives.

There are thus a number of steps involved in creating a successful small business including:

- an idea
- objectives
- analysis
- planning
- good fortune.

At the end of the day one of the most important ingredients in the success of a small business is good fortune. Even the best of ideas will be faced by considerable difficulties and pitfalls before it can be translated into a success story as the following case study illustrates.

CASE STUDY CASE STUDY CASE STUDY CASE STUDY CASE STUDY CASE

DIFFICULTIES IN MAKING A SMALL BUSINESS GROW

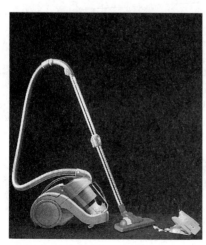

James Dyson's Dual Cyclone

Although the UK prides itself on the importance of its small business sector many small businesses feel that the dice are loaded against them on the road to success. James Dyson provides us with an example of a successful entrepreneur who has faced an uphill struggle in developing his ideas into a successful business organisation.

Dyson has looked bankruptcy in the eye on a number of occasions, struggled against the giant corporations that dominate the electrical appliance industry and fought off attempts to copy his designs. However, by 1996 he had built up a company with a turnover of over £100 million per year and tripling in size every 12 months.

Dyson is a former Royal College of Art student and one of Britain's most exciting designers in recent years. The Dual Cyclone Vacuum which he has become associated with is just one of a number of inventions, including the ball-barrow, that for a while dominated the wheelbarrow market.

In 1995 and 1996, his Dual Cyclone Vacuum Cleaner came to dominate the market as shown in Figure 16.2. Half a million consumers bought one in 1996 at twice the average price paid for other vacuum cleaners.

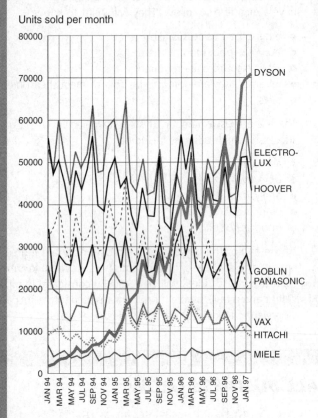

Units sold per month

Figure 16.2   Sales of Dyson Dual Cyclone compared with other cleaners

Like most successful inventions, the principle is simple. By filtering dust in a funnel of air spinning at up to 924 miles per hour, James Dyson has dispensed with the paper bags

that other cleaners use to catch the filth but which clog up in a matter of minutes. It is estimated that a traditional cleaner loses half its suction after cleaning just one room – the Dyson maintains 100 per cent efficiency 100 per cent of the time.

However, Dyson has always had an uphill struggle to raise the finance for his venture. Having sunk £4.5 million of his own money into the project, largely earned from overseas licensing of his patented design, the last £1 million to bring the Dual Cyclone to market should have been a stroll. It proved impossible, however, to raise the relatively modest sum in the private equity markets. Only a believer at Lloyds Bank, who overturned an original refusal to lend, allowed the cleaner to reach the shops at all. 'It was clear they were not backing me partly because I was a designer but also because they are not interested in backing new technology' said Dyson.

Dyson's problems are shared by many other smaller businesses. Generating enough capital to turn a good idea into a sound proposition is often difficult. However, with the injection from Lloyds the growth path has been tremendous. Launched in March 1993, sales reached £3 million in the first year, £10 million in the following, quadrupled to £40 million in 1995 (from which Dyson netted an £8 million profit), and reached £100 million in 1996.

During the mid-1990s Dyson left its competitors standing. Partly thanks to its £199 price tag the Dyson dominated the market by value. In unit terms it was also able to overtake Electrolux.

1 Why do you think the Dyson Dual Cyclone has been such a success?
2 What major obstacles did it have to cross on its path to success? Why do you think that these hurdles existed?
3 What lessons can be learnt from the Dyson case by people wanting to develop their own business ideas?

CASE STUDY CASE STUDY CASE STUDY CASE STUDY CASE STUDY CASE

IT'S A FACT

That recent research has indicated that only a small minority of family enterprises ever survives beyond the first generation in the hands of the founding family. Only 5–15 per cent continue into the third generation in the hands of the descendants. These figures compare unfavourably with the staying power of equivalent non-family controlled companies. Reasons given by Alden G Lank (a researcher) for such failure include:

- Failure to find capital for growth without diluting the family's equity (total ownership control being a sacrosanct principle for many families).
- Inability to balance optimally the family's needs for liquidity and the business's need for cash.
- Poor estate planning and the inability of the next generation to pay inheritance taxes.
- Lack of willingness of the older generation to 'let go' of ownership and management power at the appropriate moment.
- Inability to attract and retain competent and motivated family successors.
- Unchecked sibling rivalries with no consensus on the chosen successor.
- Inability to attract and retain competent senior non-family professional managers.
- Unmanaged conflict between the cultures of the family, the board and the business.

Chapter summary

- Starting up a small business is not something that should be taken lightly. To be successful the entrepreneur needs to have specific skills and aptitudes.
- The starting point for a small business is the idea. This may involve an original brainwave, adapting an existing idea, or a direct copy of something that already works.
- Nearly every large business has started from a small base.
- Success is based on careful planning coupled with a healthy dose of good luck.
- Small businesses grew in numbers particularly in the 1980s. They continue and will continue to grow in numbers as part of a longer-term trend, particularly as organisations downsize and contract out work. However, numbers will decline in periods of recession.
- It is difficult to define the term **small business**. One definition is that it is independent and not dominant in its field of operations.

- Other aspects of small business outlined by the Bolton Report were that:
  - they are managed in a personalised way
  - they have a small market share
  - the owner is an independent decision maker.
- Often a good starting point for a successful business will be an innovative opportunity. Coming up with the unexpected is only one source of such opportunities.
- Having identified opportunities it is necessary to make hard and careful decisions to ensure that there are clear profit opportunities.
- Prospective entrepreneurs should explore sources of help and information such as Local Enterprise Agencies.
- It is essential to create a well structured business plan.

17 Business organisations in the private sector

In the UK, the private sector plays a very important part in the creation of goods, employment and income for millions of people. The private sector is made up of hundreds of thousands of business organisations varying in size from small corner shops to billion pound enterprises like Shell and ICI. As we move towards the millennium, business has certainly established itself as a driving force for change and improvement in society.

As Peter Drucker has written in his book *The New Realities* (Butterworth Heinemann, 1994), 'Business has been the success story of the period since World War II – something very few people would have dreamed of in the 1930s or during the war. Thirty-five years ago "business" was still widely viewed as an anachronism to be engulfed everywhere in a rising socialist tide. But socialism has become the anachronism. Instead of capitalism being a transition stage on the socialist road, it now increasingly appears that socialism is a detour on the capitalist road.'

We therefore need to build up a picture of the sorts of organisations that exist in the private sector and their legal forms.

The sole trader

The sole trader is the most common form of business ownership and is found in a wide range of activities (e.g. window cleaning, plumbing, electrical work or busking).

Figure 17.1 shows a breakdown of sole proprietors into industrial groupings in the early 1990s.

Grouping	Percentage
Construction	20.3
Production	5.7
Agriculture	6.9
Other services	8.7
Motor trades	6.0
Business services	5.0
Catering	7.9
Finance	10.2
Retailing	18.6
Wholesaling/dealing	5.2
Transport	5.5

Figure 17.1   Percentage of the total for sole traders, broken down into industrial groupings (1993)

> **SYNTHESIS**
>
> *Why do you think sole traders tend to cluster into some groupings more than others?*

No complicated paperwork is required to set up a sole trader business. Decisions can be made quickly and close contact can be kept with customers and employees. All profits go to the sole trader, who also has the satisfaction of building up his or her own business.

But there are disadvantages. As a sole trader you have to make all the decisions yourself, and you may have to work long hours. (What do you do if you are ill or want a holiday?) You do not have limited liability, and you have to provide all the finance yourself. As a sole trader you need to be a jack-of-all trades, and just because you are a good hairdresser does not necessarily mean you have a head for business!

> *If a business with limited liability goes bankrupt because it is unable to meet its debts, the owners will not be liable (responsible by law) to lose their possessions to pay the money that is owed. The maximum amount that they could lose is the amount they have put into the business. Note that sole traders do not have limited liability.*

Legal implications of being a sole trader

As soon as one person starts to trade he or she becomes a sole trader. The sole trader business does not have a separate legal identity from that of the individual – i.e. they are one and the same. Sole traders trade in their own names and assume all of the responsibilities of being in business. Therefore, if the sole trader breaches a contract, he or she has to meet the claim from personal resources.

Sole traders have the minimum of formality and have the advantage of maximum flexibility. They have the advantage of being self-employed which enables them, for tax reasons, to offset legitimate business expenses against income tax.

The partnership

An ordinary partnership can have between two and 20 partners. Professional partnerships may have more. People in business partnerships can share skills and the workload, and it may be easier to raise the capital needed.

For example, a group of vets is able to pool knowledge about different diseases and groups of animals, and two or three vets working together may be able to operate a 24-hour service. When one of the vets is ill or goes on holiday, the business can cope. Figure 17.2 shows a breakdown of partnerships into industrial groupings.

Grouping	Percentage
Construction	11.2
Production	6.5
Agriculture	16.0
Other services	6.0
Motor trades	5.2
Business services	3.4
Catering	12.5
Finance	7.3
Retailing	24.0
Wholesaling/dealing	4.8
Transport	3.1

Figure 17.2   Percentage of the total for partnerships, broken down into industrial groupings

> **SYNTHESIS**
>
> *Are there any significant similarities or differences between the break down into industrial groupings of sole traders and partnerships? Perhaps you could present the two tables in the form of a pie chart using a desktop publishing package to make it easier to make comparisons.*

Partnerships are usually set up by writing out a deed of partnership which is witnessed by a solicitor. This sets out important details, such as how much each partner should put into the business, how the profits and losses will be shared, and the responsibilities of each partner.

Partnerships are particularly common in professional services (e.g. doctors, solicitors, accountants). A small business such as a corner shop may take the form of a husband-and-wife partnership.

The main disadvantages of partnerships are that people can fall out; ordinary partnerships do not have limited liability; and partnerships can rarely borrow or raise large amounts of capital. Business decisions may be more difficult to make (and slower) because of the need to consult all the partners. There may be disagreements about how things should be done. A final disadvantage is that profits will be shared.

There is also a special form of partnership called a limited partnership. **Limited partners** (sometimes called 'sleeping partners') can put money into a partnership and have the protection of limited liability. However, they play no part in the running of the business. The business will be run by at least one non-limited partner.

Legal aspects of a partnership

The relationships between partners are generally determined by a Deed of Partnership between the partners. Where no deed exists, the provisions of the Partnership Act of 1980 will specify the relationship between partners. Deeds normally cover areas such as capital, profit shares, responsibilities, salaries and procedures for dissolution.

Despite the Deed, partnerships in England and Wales do not have a legal personality and partners incur unlimited liability for the business. Partners are also responsible for the business debts of other partners. Partnerships may limit the flexibility of partners to sell or transfer their ownership as no partner may be able to transfer ownership without the consent of the other partners.

The company

A company is set up to run a business. It has to be registered before it can start to operate, but once all the paperwork is completed and approved the company becomes recognised as a legal body.

The owners of a company are its shareholders. However, other individuals and businesses do not deal with the shareholders – they deal with 'the company'.

Shareholders put funds into the company by buying shares. New shares are often sold in face values of £1 per share but this is not always the case. Some shareholders will only have a few hundred pounds' worth of shares, whereas others may have thousands of pounds' worth.

Company logos

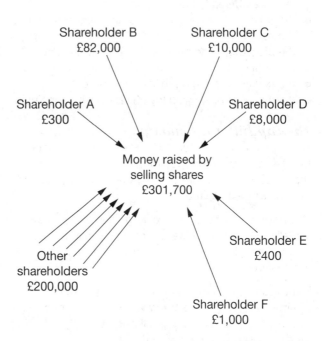

Figure 17.3   A company raises money from its shareholders

Legal aspects of companies

As a result of the court case *Salomon v Salomon & Co* (1897), a company exists as a separate legal identity from that of its owners. Assets such as property, as well as debts, belong to the company and not to individual members. To set up a limited company it is necessary to go through a number of legal procedures in order to gain recognition. This mainly involves the presentation of various documents and records to the Registrar of Companies. These documents are open to scrutiny.

All limited companies must present a Memorandum of Association and Articles of Association in order to receive a Certificate of Incorporation.

The Memorandum spells out the nature of the company when viewed from the outside. Someone reading the Memorandum would be able to obtain a general idea of what the company is and the business with which it is concerned. The Memorandum sets out:

- the name of the company
- the registered address of the company
- the objectives of the company
- the capital of the company.

Most companies will produce a fairly vague list of objectives in their Memorandum. This will give them the opportunity to alter their activities if market opportunities arise.

The Articles of Association set out the rules which governs the inside working of a company. They include:

- the rights attached to the holding of the various types of share offered by the company
- the rules and procedures for issuing and transferring shares
- the procedures and timings of company meetings
- the details of how accounts will be kept and recorded
- the powers and responsibilities of directors
- the details of how company officers will be appointed.

The capital of a company
The promoter or directors of the company can apply to the Registrar of Companies for permission to issue new shares. The amount that the Registrar agrees to is called the **authorised capital**.

The **issued capital** is the value of the shares that are actually sold to shareholders. A company may choose not to issue the full value of its authorised capital: it may hold back a certain amount for future issue.

Shares can be issued for payment in stages over a period of time. Each stage is then termed a 'call'. There may be three or four calls before the full price is finally paid. The **paid-up capital** is the money that has been received for these shares at a particular time.

Two types of company
There are two types of company – private companies and public companies.

Private companies
Private companies tend to be smaller than public ones and are often family businesses. There must be at least two shareholders but there is no maximum number. Shares in private companies cannot be traded on the Stock Exchange and often shares can only be bought with the permission of the board of directors.

The board of directors is a committee set up to protect the interests of shareholders. The members of the board choose the managing director, who is responsible for the day-to-day running of the business. The rules of the business set out when shareholders' meetings will take place and the rights of shareholders.

Private companies may find it possible to raise more cash (by selling shares) than unlimited liability businesses. The shareholders can also have the protection of limited liability. The main disadvantages, compared with unlimited liability businesses, are that they have to share out profits among shareholders and they cannot make decisions so quickly. They also cost more to set up.

Legal aspects of a private company
Once the Memorandum and Articles of Association have been accepted by the Registrar of Companies a private company will be granted a Certificate of Incorporation and can start to trade. The Certificate of Incorporation sets up the company as a legal body in its own right. The company (not individual shareholders) enters into contracts and can sue or be sued in court.

Public companies
A public company has its shares bought and sold on the Stock Exchange. Companies can go to the expense of having a 'full quotation' on the Stock Exchange so that their share prices appear on the share dealers' visual display screens.

The main advantage of selling shares through the Stock Exchange is that large amounts of capital can be raised very quickly. One disadvantage is that control of a business can be lost by the original shareholders if large quantities of shares are purchased as part of a 'takeover bid'. It is also costly to have shares quoted on the Stock Exchange.

In order to create a public company the directors must apply to the Stock Exchange Council, which will carefully check the accounts. A business wanting to 'go public' will then arrange for one of the merchant banks to handle the paperwork. Selling new shares is quite a risky business. The Stock Exchange has 'good days' (when a lot of people want to buy shares) and 'bad days' (when a lot of people want to sell). If the issue of new shares coincides with a bad day a company can find itself in difficulties. For example, if it hopes to sell a million new shares at £1 each and all goes well, it will raise the £1 million; but on a bad day it might only be able to sell half its shares at this price.

One way round this problem is to arrange a 'placing' with a merchant bank. The merchant bank recommends the company's shares to some of the share-buying institutions (e.g. pension funds and insurance companies) with which it deals. These may then agree to buy, say, one-tenth of the new shares. In this way the merchant bank makes sure that the shares are placed with large investors before the actual date of issue comes round. Then, even if its is a bad day on the Stock Exchange when the shares are issued, the company's money is secure.

Another common method by which public companies raise share capital is to offer new shares for sale to the general public. Very often the shares will be 'underwritten' by a merchant bank. The company's shares are advertised in leading newspapers and the public are invited to apply.

When a company is up and running, a cheaper way of selling is to contact existing shareholders inviting them to buy new shares. This is a 'rights issue'.

Legal aspects of a public company

A public company needs to take additional steps before being granted a certificate of trading. The Memorandum of a public company must state that the company is to be a public company, and it must abide by a legal minimum figure for allotted share capital. Before a Trading Certificate is granted, shares allotted must be paid up to at least 25 per cent of their nominal value plus the whole of any premium payable.

CASE STUDY CASE STUDY CASE STUDY CASE STUDY CASE STUDY CASE

THE GROWTH OF 'EXOTIC FASHIONS'

In 1976, Jenny Parsons set up her own dress shop selling her own designer dresses in a small shop in Nottingham. Over the years the shop gained in popularity and Jenny found that her dresses were being ordered by customers from all over the UK and even by other European customers.

Because Jenny was designing the dresses and selling them herself this created a lot of work pressure. Of course she was able to pay her own staff to make the dresses to her patterns. Initially they did this from a small workshop over the shop, but as orders built up Jenny hired a small factory unit on an industrial estate on the outskirts of Nottingham.

In the course of time Jenny realised that she was overstretching herself but was fortunate in 1985 to meet Sylvia Burns who had just graduated from the London School of Fashion. Sylvia had recently come into an inheritance and was looking to branch out into business for herself. As part of a research project she had met Jenny and she realised that they shared a common interest, had similar styles and a common flair for fashion. The two therefore decided to set up in partnership. With their combined capital they bought outright a new factory in Nottingham and a large shop in central London. The London site was to become the focus for retailing operations.

Within months they had a backlog of orders from all over Europe and they realised that they would need to expand again. They therefore decided to set up a private company in which they would be the major shareholders. However, they also needed extra share capital from a few wealthy individuals. They felt that the provision of limited liability would be a valuable

protection. They were now dealing with some major buyers – if one failed to pay up they could end up with serious cash flow problems. In addition, putting Ltd after the company name would give it extra status.

They filed a memorandum and articles of association with the Registrar of Companies and began trading as 'Exotic Fashions Ltd'.

However, expansion seemed to demand further expansion. They now had set up a chain of shops in ten major cities in the UK. But there seemed to be a never-ending demand for their products.

This time they decided to go public and sell shares on the Stock Exchange. They therefore produced a prospectus for potential share buyers and on the 15th August 1996 they went public. They sold £1 million of shares at £1 each. They could have sold over twice this number and on the day of issue share prices rocketed from £1.00 to £1.97.

1 Describe each of the forms of organisation that Exotic Fashions has been through since 1976?
2 Why has it been necessary for Exotic Fashions to change its form of organisation?
3 What problems might Exotic Fashions have encountered when it changed from being a sole trader into a partnership?
4 What are the advantages of being a private company rather than a partnership?
5 What sorts of details would you expect to find in the Memorandum and Articles of Association of Exotic Fashions?
6 What type of organisation is Exotic Fashions today? How would this be reflected in its name?
7 What are the disadvantages of having its current form of organisation?

CASE STUDY CASE STUDY CASE STUDY CASE STUDY CASE STUDY CASE

Franchising

In the USA, about one half of all retail sales are made through firms operating under the franchise system. It is a form of business organisation that has become increasingly popular in the UK, particularly in the 1980s and 1990s.

Franchising is really the 'hiring out' or licensing of the use of 'good ideas' to other companies. A franchise grants permission to sell a product and trade under a certain name in a particular area. If I have a good idea, I can sell you a licence to trade and carry out a business using my idea in your area. The person taking out the franchise puts down a sum of money as capital and is issued with equipment by the franchising company. The firm selling the franchise is called the **franchisor** and a person paying for the franchise is called the **franchisee**. The franchisee usually has the sole right of operating in a particular area.

This type of trading is common in the fast-food industry, examples being Spud-U-Like and Pizza Hut. Further examples are Dyno-Rod (in the plumbing business), Tumbletots, Body Shop and Prontaprint.

Pizza Hut: an example of a high street franchise operation

Where materials are an important part of the business (e.g. hamburgers, confectionery, hair salons) the franchisee must buy an agreed percentage of supplies from the franchisor, who thus makes a profit on these supplies as well as ensuring the quality of the final product. The franchisor also takes a percentage of the profits of the business, without having to risk capital or become involved in the day-to-day management.

The franchisee benefits from trading under a well-known name and enjoys a local monopoly. Training is usually arranged by the franchisor. The franchisee is his or her own boss and takes most of the profits.

Co-operatives

Co-operatives are increasingly popular as a means of business organisation. At one time they were only to be found in agriculture and retailing, but in recent years the biggest growth areas have been in service occupations and in small-scale manufacturing.

The basic idea behind a co-operative is that people join together to make decisions, work and share profits. There are many different types of co-operative; we consider here the three most commonly found in business.

Retail co-operatives

The first successful co-operative in this country was set up in the northern town of Rochdale in the 19th century. Twenty-eight weavers clubbed together to start their own retail shop, selling a few basic grocery items. The profits were to be shared according to the amount spent, and everyone would have an equal say in how the shop was run.

The basic ideas started in Rochdale continue in today's co-operatives. To become a shareholder in a 'co-op' you need only buy a £1 share; this entitles you to a vote at meetings and to elect the president and other officers of the local co-op society.

Retail co-operatives are organised on a regional basis. Over the years many of the smaller co-operatives have tended to be swallowed up by larger societies. The largest single retailing society is the CRS (Co-operative Retail Society), with its headquarters in Manchester. A small number of regional co-operatives give stamps to shoppers. These stamps can be collected and stuck in books which can be used in payment for goods. However, many co-operatives have stopped distributing their dividends in this way and simply use profits to improve their facilities and to make prices more competitive.

Some co-operatives not only provide supermarket services, but also have their own bank, milk delivery service, funeral service and libraries, and provide other benefits such as education courses for members.

In the later part of the 19th century the co-operatives flourished and societies sprang up all over Britain. It was the co-operatives that brought in some of the first supermarkets. However, in recent years they have had to face very severe competition from multiples like Tesco and Asda. In retaliation, many smaller co-operative societies have merged, and organisations like the CRS have for a number of years run their own hypermarkets. (CRS hypermarkets trade under the name 'Leo'.)

Producer co-operatives

Producer co-operatives are usually registered as companies 'limited by guarantee', which means that each member undertakes to fund any losses up to a certain amount. There are many types. A workers' co-operative, for example, is one that employs all or most of its members. In a workers' co-operative members:

- share responsibility for the success or failure of the business
- work together
- take decisions together
- share the profits.

Other examples of producer co-operatives are groups to grow tomatoes, to make furniture or to organise child-minding.

The main problems that such co-operatives face are finance and organisation. Co-operatives sometimes find it difficult to raise capital from banks and other bodies because they are not groups that seek primarily to make profits. A number of co-operatives in recent years have, however, been able to raise finance by selling shares. Some larger co-operatives have also found that it is necessary to set up a management structure in order to get decisions made.

IT'S A FACT

That in the South West of England there is a farmers' co-operative for marketing asparagus, in East Anglia there is a marketing co-operative for mustard growers, and in the Cevennes region of the South of France there is a marketing co-operative for 'oignon doux', i.e. gentle onions which are delicious to taste but don't make your eyes water.

Marketing co-operatives

Marketing co-operatives are most frequently found in farming areas. The farmers set up a marketing board to be responsible for, among other things, grading, packaging, distributing, advertising and selling their produce.

Chapter summary

- There are hundreds of thousands of organisations in the private sector which make a substantial contribution to the economy.
- Sole traders are the most common form of business ownership.
- Limited liability provides protection for owners of companies, only rarely to partners and never to sole traders.
- Partnerships are usually set up by a Deed and are commonly found in the professions or where the skills and capital of a sole trader are not sufficient on their own.
- A company is owned by shareholders.
- Before an organisation can become a company it must register a Memorandum of Association and Articles of Association with the Registrar of Companies.
- Part ownership of a private company is restricted to people approved by the board of the company. Public companies are open to the general public with their shares being traded on the Stock Exchange.
- Franchising has become a very important form of business ownership in this country and involves hiring out or licensing of a business name and a good idea to franchise outlets.
- There are three types of co-operatives – producer, retail, and marketing co-operatives. They are based on shared goals, ownership, and mutual co-operation.

18 Business organisations in the public sector

Some business organisations in this country are in the public sector, i.e. they are owned by the government for the people, and the government has some form of responsibility for the ways in which these organisations are run and managed.

In the 19th century the government played only a very limited part in running business organisations, its activities being restricted to specific state activities (e.g. the establishment of The Post Office) and, of course, running certain military concerns such as The Royal Docks, etc.

However, during the 20th century the control of government became more widespread as a result of the growing importance of the Bank of England in the financial sector and the development of a universal National Insurance Scheme, for example.

In particular, the two World Wars saw the government take over an increasing number of essential industries which were seen as 'the commanding heights' of the economy. After the First World War these were returned to private hands. However, after the Second World War the country returned a Labour government and increasingly industries were 'nationalised', i.e. taken over by the government. These included the coal, steel and railway industries. The 1960s and 1970s saw considerable parts of major industries being taken over by the government.

However, the return of the Conservative government in 1979 saw a complete turnaround in this policy. From 1979, the emphasis was on 'privatisation' with industries being returned to private shareholders. Indeed, Britain was to lead the world in this sphere and was increasingly copied by other countries. An extension of this movement was the privatisation of state industries as former communist countries in Eastern Europe turned to the market system in the late 1980s and the 1990s. The Labour Party today places more emphasis on a 'social market' framework but has committed itself to a number of the major tenets of privatisation and principles of competition.

Public sector involvement in UK industry

There are three major elements of public sector involvement in industry:

- direct state participation in industry through public corporations known as the nationalised industries and other Crown corporations
- industries in which there is public sector involvement, together with private investment (e.g. the government

held a 39 per cent share in BP from before the Second World War until the late 1980s when shares were sold to the public)
- industries in which there is a public sector involvement at local government level rather than at the level of national government.

A fourth group that can be identified is businesses that receive support from the government to establish new activities, such as research and development or product development in a particular field.

Public corporations

In the UK, the government still owns a number of industries and businesses on behalf of the people. Most of these take the form of public corporations. In recent years, however, there has been a sustained period of privatisation of government enterprises.

> *Privatisation means the de-nationalisation of state-controlled industries. We are all familiar with privatisations such as the sale of the Electricity Boards, the Water Boards, British Gas and British Rail. However, in addition, privatisation also includes the sale of council houses, the contracting out of local authority controlled services, such as street cleaning, and the introduction of private prisons.*

A public corporation is set up by an Act of Parliament. Examples of public corporations are few and far between today and include the Bank of England and the BBC.

Once a public corporation has been set up, the government appoints a chairperson to be responsible for the day-to-day running of the industry.

Reasons for setting up public corporations

There are a number of reasons why public corporations have been set up.

- **To avoid wasteful duplication**. In the 19th century, for example, there were three railway lines between Leeds and Harrogate. This is wasteful. Imagine the problems caused by having three electricity companies operating in your town.
- **To set up and run essential services that might not be profitable**. Would a private company supply post, electricity, gas and water to a small remote village if a lot of capital was needed to set up services that may not make a profit?
- **To gain the benefits of large-scale production**. It

may be more efficient to have one big firm producing a large amount of output than to have several smaller firms producing smaller amounts. When there is only one firm, the government as owner might be less inclined than a private firm to charge high prices.

- **To protect employment**. The government might take into consideration the need to create and keep jobs rather than just considering financial profits.
- **To control industries that are important to the country**, such as coal, steel and the railways. **Infrastructure** is the term used to describe the basic

backbone of an economic system including the transport network, energy and water supplies. Some people argue that the government has an important responsibility for the supervision and maintenance of the infrastructure.

During the 1980s and first half of the 1990s a number of public corporations were privatised. However, it has become successively more difficult to private industries as those most suited for privatisation have already been sold off. Privatisation involves turning the public corporations into companies owned by shareholders.

CASE STUDY CASE STUDY CASE STUDY CASE STUDY CASE STUDY CASE

CALLING A HALT TO PRIVATISATION?

In 1994, a government Bill to privatise the Post Office was rejected by the House of Lords after an outcry from the general public.

The Post Office had always been a popular national institution, owned on behalf of the people, to serve the people. The rejection was a significant defeat for the government. Many saw it as the final nail in the coffin of the Conservative policy of privatising state-owned industries.

Privatisation had been one of the major planks of Margaret Thatcher's economic strategy. There was little international precedent for it and, in the case of every major privatisation, a majority of the population was at first opposed. Despite this, Thatcher had pressed ahead with a programme of sell-offs which steadily changed the face of British industry.

Privatisation had caught on abroad, too. Overseas, it became an epidemic, spreading to

continental Europe and Russia, Asia, the Pacific and the developing world.

But as the rest of the world continued to steam ahead, with the defeat of the Post Office privatisation bill, the UK's programme of privatisation came to a shuddering halt. The Major government had little stomach for fresh privatisation. With the Labour government being returned in 1997 we are unlikely to see many more privatisations, or are we?

1 List four industries that were privatised between 1979 and 1997.
2 What were the main arguments put forward in favour of privatisation?
3 Why do you think that the British public were opposed to the privatisation of the Post Office?
4 What does the above extract tell you about privatisation in other countries?
5 Why do you think that the Major government had 'little stomach for privatisation' in the years 1994–97?

CASE STUDY CASE STUDY CASE STUDY CASE STUDY CASE STUDY CASE

Reasons for privatisation

There are a number of reasons for privatisation, including the following:

- Some people argue that state-run firms are not efficient because they do not have any real competition and do not risk going bankrupt as the government will always pay off their debts.
- It is argued that in a modern society as many people as possible should have shares in business. The idea is that everyone – not just the very rich – should become shareholders. People have therefore been encouraged

to buy, in some cases just a few hundred pounds' worth of shares, in enterprises like British Telecom and British Gas.

- It was argued that many public corporations were top heavy and slow to react in today's marketplace. People in these corporations had secure jobs because the state would pay for any losses they made. They could therefore carry high levels of inefficiency for a number of years. Employees did not feel obliged to provide a top quality service for people. The corporations were therefore product-oriented rather than consumer-oriented.

IT'S A FACT

That Margaret Thatcher believed firmly in a 'share owning democracy'. In a democracy, people are able to vote for the government they want to see in power in elections. She felt that by giving people shares they would then be able to influence companies to act in certain ways. They would be part-owners of a company. Lots of small part-owners could then influence the company in a democratic way. Unfortunately, this failed to happen. While many people initially bought shares in privatised companies – many sold these off for a profit not long after. Large parcels of shares were bought up by large financial institutions such as banks, pension funds and insurance companies.

Arguments against privatisation

A number of people have been opposed to the process of privatisation. They maintain that competition can be harmful in areas where standards need to be maintained, such as the National Health Service. Competition can lead to 'cutting corners' and to the deterioration of safety standards, for example, in maintaining track and signalling systems on the railways. There is also the strong argument that it is a nonsense to sell to the public shares in industries that are already owned by the people. Instead of an industry being owned by all citizens, it then become the property of shareholders.

When a public corporation is set up, an independent body is also formed to protect consumers' interests. Consumers can take their complaints to this body. For example, the Post Office Users' National Council will take up complaints made by users of the Post Office about the late delivery of letters or other matters.

The government keeps the power to make major decisions about how public corporations should run. For example, in the days when British Rail was a public corporation it could decide whether to close down large sections of the railway network. However, the chairperson and managers of the public corporation will decide on day-to-day issues such as wages and prices, timetables and industrial relations. The government does sometimes interfere even in these areas, leading to public argument and debate.

Whereas a limited company has to make an annual report to its shareholders, a public corporation must present its annual report to the appropriate government minister, who makes a verbal report to Parliament when Members of Parliament will make criticisms or voice support for the way the corporation is being run. A committee of MPs has the job of studying the running of each public corporation and of reporting on its operation. For example, there is a select committee of MPs acting as a watchdog over the BBC.

Figure 18.1 highlights some of the differences between public corporations and private corporations.

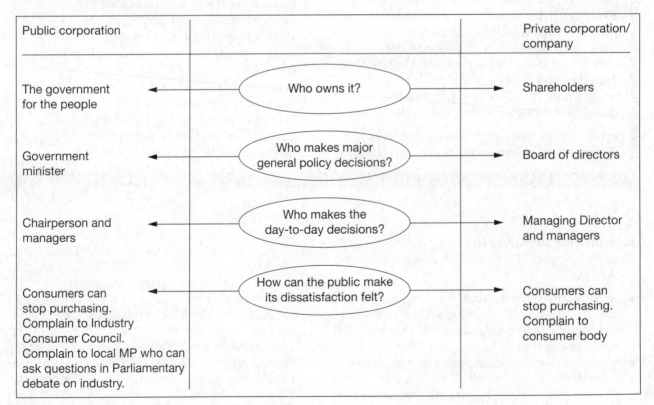

Figure 18.1   *Some comparisons of public and private corporations*

The declining importance of nationalised industries

One of the major criticisms of nationalised industries was that they used up a substantial part of national resources, which they did not utilise particularly well. In 1979, the combined turnover of the public corporations was £44 billion, nearly one-quarter of gross national output. Collectively, they employed nearly 2 million people and were responsible for 20 per cent of all investment in the economy. The argument was that money was being 'crowded out' of its best possible use, which in many cases would have been used for investment in the private sector. The critics felt that sluggish public sector organisations were wasting resources and holding the country back.

Despite large-scale privatisation, the turnover of public corporations was still nearly £40 billion in 1990 and they still accounted for 7.2 per cent of all investment. Corporations like British Rail which are today in the private sector were still major users of investment capital.

Figure 18.2 illustrates productivity growth in a number of industries between the early 1970s and the late 1980s. Study the measures of productivity and the performance of specific industries. What does Figure 18.2 show? Does it give an accurate measure of performance? What are the major weaknesses in the indicators shown?

EXAM TIP:

Make sure that you are clear about the difference between the public sector and the private sector; between public corporations and public companies; and between public and private companies.

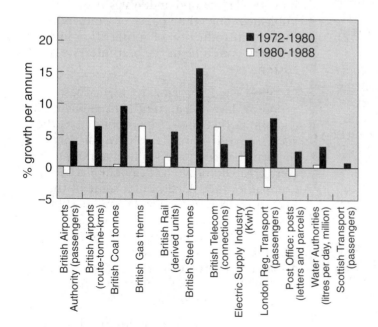

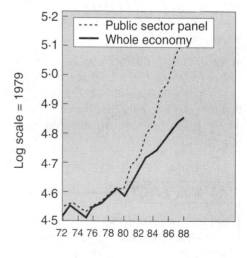

Figure 18.2   Focus: productivity growth of privatised industries, 1972–80 and 1980–88 (London Business School)

In 1948, the government set out that the nationalised industries were to meet the demand for their products at a reasonable price which would enable them to break even over a number of years. In the years that followed there was a lot of criticism about the way in which targets were set for public corporations. For example, under the break-even policy it was possible to charge some customers who could be supplied cheaply (e.g. gas consumers in cities) the same price as other customers who were far more expensive to supply (e.g. gas consumers in remote areas).

In 1961, the government set more precise financial targets for public corporations. Taking into account conditions in the market, the government set targets as a rate of return on the assets employed in a specific industry. In 1967, even more stringent rules were set, whereby the cross-subsidisation of one group of consumers by another was to be avoided. New investment was to be expected to yield a return equal to what the investment capital would earn in the private sector. It was, however, recognised that some activities of public corporations (e.g. supplying to rural areas and engaging in activities which were not profitable) were of a social rather than a commercial nature. These social contributions needed to be given a money value, and the government would provide a subsidy to meet these activities.

In 1979, the new Conservative government that came into power embraced a policy of privatisation. The emphasis was therefore on cutting out unprofitable operations in order to make these industries attractive to prospective shareholders. Over the years, this has meant cutting down loss-making operations such as some steel works, coal mines and shipyards.

A large number of nationalised industries were privatised during the 1980s. During the 1990s it has become increasingly difficult to sell off the remaining nationalised industries, as the government is now left with a smaller number of substantial corporations which are significant employers.

In the Acts of Parliament that have privatised industries, the government has set up regulatory bodies, such as OFTEL and OFGAS, with the responsibility for checking that the privatised industries keep to established rules governing prices, competition and the quality of service offered.

IT'S A FACT

That the Office of the Railway Regulator (ORR) was set up in 1993. It employs up to 91 people whose responsibilities include issuing licences to new railway operators and resolving disputes about access to the network by international services. ORR is also charged with protecting rail users interests and promoting the development of the network and competition for its use.

Today's remaining nationalised industries are expected to meet financial targets and to show a real rate of return on assets that indicate that resources are being used as effectively as if the capital was being employed in the private sector.

Public sector organisations, such as the National Health Service and the BBC, have been broken down into a number of independent sections. Each section (e.g. fundholding GPs and hospitals in the National Health Service) is expected to manage its own budget and to use resources efficiently. However in 1997 the Labour government announced that this practice will no longer continue in the NHS.

THE CHANGING FACE OF THE ELECTRICITY INDUSTRY

The publicly owned, co-ordinated electricity supply industry was first created in 1948. In each region of the country an area electricity board was introduced to be a retailer of electricity, taking supply at reduced voltage from the main grid and reducing it still further to distribute electricity to the customer.

In the 1950s, the Central Electricity Generating Board (CEGB) took responsibility for the generation of electricity and the nationwide transmission of power through the main grid system.

In 1988, a government white paper proposing the privatisation of the electricity industry in England and Wales was published. The white paper recommended that the introduction of competition into the industry would be in the best interests of customers.

In 1989, The Electricity Act made these proposals law and a number of public limited companies (PLCs) were incorporated as the successor to the previous Boards as part of the privatisation process. Twelve companies were created known as Regional Electricity Companies (RECs). Although some of the RECs now form subsidiary companies in larger organisations, by virtue of their Public Electricity Supply licence, each REC is responsible for the operation of its local distribution network and is obliged to meet reasonable requests for electricity from customers within its area.

In this newly-organised industry, the generation of electricity (power stations) was split from the transmission system (National Grid) and the supply and distribution (RECs). Regional Electricity Companies purchase electricity from the generators who supply electricity through the National Grid. The generators now sell their supplies to the RECs on a half hourly basis.

Since 1994, we have moved towards even greater competition. All customers nationally with an electrical demand over 100 kilowatts (half a million customers) can choose their electricity suppliers. Suppliers may include the generators as well as the RECs.

In 1998, this choice is being extended to the rest of the market – which includes domestic customers – who will for the first time have a choice. This is the largest operational change ever made to the electricity industry.

At the time of privatisation, the Office of Electricity Regulation (OFFER) was set up as an independent body to regulate the electricity industry and to protect customers' interests by controlling prices and setting customer service standards in monopoly areas. OFFER has set customer service standards for each of the RECs. These consist of:

- **Guaranteed standards** – which must be achieved on every occasion.
- **Overall standards** – which set targets for levels of performance.

STUDY CASE STUDY CASE STUDY

The Citizen's Charter

In July 1991, John Major introduced his Citizen's charter, which set out consumer rights as the 'central theme of public life' for the 1990s. The proposed consumer rights would extend throughout the National Health Service, education and transport, to the privatised gas, water, electricity and telecommunications utilities.

Officials with responsibility for supervising public utilities (the utility regulators) have new powers, including the option to award compensation for reasonable complaints by consumers. This means clear commitments to the quality of service, fixed appointment times and new means of seeing complaints through. There is a new charter standard for quality which entitles those who can prove they meet the high standards to use a 'charter mark'. In recent times, the Social Democratic and Labour Parties have developed their own Citizen's Charters.

The Social Market

In the late 1990s, many of the free-market principles of the Conservative government were toned down in recognition of the importance of the social market. Labour and Conservative policies became increasingly alike. The emphasis has been on creating a social market in which government exercises a regulating hand to constrain the activities of corporations whether they be in the public or private sectors.

Stakeholder economy

In the late 1990s, Tony Blair and 'New Labour' have placed increasing emphasis on the importance of organisations to be accountable to all their stakeholders. This means a greater involvements of consumers, employees, the community, etc. in decision-making processes. It also requires a greater accountability of organisations for all of their activities to shared and agreed standards and codes of behaviour.

Other central government enterprises

In addition to public corporations, the other two major areas of government control over economic activity occur where:

- an activity is run by a government department
- an activity is run by a public company in which the government has a shareholding.

When an activity is run by a government department, a government minister has overall charge for the department. The department is staffed and run by civil servants. A typical example of this would be the Customs and Excise Department which deals with the supervision and collection of some taxes. The major criticisms of such a form of organisation from the business point of view are that:

- Decisions are made slowly because there are many links in the chain of command, and government departments are usually wrapped up in rules and regulations.
- The organisation may appear to be inefficient because of lack of competition.
- There is no external agency to protect the public's interest by checking on how the department runs. While in many cases there will be a mechanism for making complaints, it may be so complex as to be inaccessible to the ordinary person.

In recent years, the government has reduced its shareholding in public companies as an extension of its policy of privatisation.

Local government enterprises

In the UK, certain services in local areas are supervised by locally elected councils. These councils usually run some forms of business organisations such as the municipal car parks, swimming baths, sports centres, bus services and toilets. However, in the late 1980s council activities were subjected to the policy of privatisation. In the late 1990s, many activities, such as road cleaning and refuse disposal, are contracted out to those firms that put in the lowest tender for a particular job. Council officials simply monitor the effectiveness with which the work is done, and can refuse to continue a contract if work fails to meet the required standards.

Local councils receive money from two main sources:

- a grant given to them by central government, and
- a local tax.

Local councils often subsidise loss-making activities such as local parks which provide benefits to the community.

TASK 18.1

Nigel Lawson (a Conservative Chancellor of the Exchequer, and more recently better known for writing books on dieting) famously said, 'The business of government is not the government of business'. What do you think he meant by this statement? Do you agree with him?

Chapter summary

- Parts of a number of industries in this country still remain in the public sector. However, there have been considerable privatisations of former state enterprises in this country since 1979.
- The UK blazed a trail for many other countries in its move to privatisation. Indeed some commentators have argued that the freeing of markets in the West was a major catalyst behind the revolutions that took place in Eastern Europe.
- Public sector involvement in industry can be in the form of public corporations, government shareholding in organisations, and local government ownership of all or parts of business organisations.
- Most of government ownership of industry in the UK this century was in the form of public corporations.
- Immediately after the Second World War we saw the biggest growth of nationalisation involving the utilities and many key industries.
- A public corporation is set up by Act of Parliament. The day-to-day running of the industry is then in the hands of a chair and board, although the corporation is closely accountable to Parliament.
- Privatisation should be seen as a political philosophy, i.e. the belief in individual freedom as well as a business proposition. Margaret Thatcher saw privatisation as being part of a move towards a 'share owning democracy'.
- A public corporation is accountable to the public in a number of ways, not only through Parliament but through a consumers' council.
- Privatised industries are accountable to a regulator who has a public duty to ensure that organisations within the industry meet prescribed standards and codes of behaviour. In addition to the regulators' office there is a consumers' watchdog.
- By 1979, nationalised industries accounted for a quarter of all output and 20 per cent of investment in the economy. Today public corporations are much smaller and are expected to work in many ways like public companies in order to ensure the best use of resources.
- However, a number of people in public corporations today, for example, the Post Office, argue that they are not able to make decisions about how best to use their own profits. Instead profits have to be handed over to the Treasury and then the organisation must plead for investment funds.
- In recent years, all major political parties have shown a commitment to a competitive state sector but with a commitment and accountability to 'stakeholders'.
- Government departments and local government enterprises are other important parts of the public sector. Like public corporations these have been subject to considerable privatisation in recent times.

3

The business environment

INTRODUCTION

In this unit we set out to examine some of the key features of the business environment in which organisations operate. Organisations are influenced by changes in the operating environment in many ways ranging from the changing tastes and fashions of consumers, to changes in rules and regulations about business practice made by governments, to the actions of competitors.

With each year that passes, most organisations are subjected to increasingly turbulent environments. The pace of change has accelerated at the end of the 20th century particularly with the growth of mass communications (including the media and transport) making people almost instantly aware of changes that are taking place, the rising speed of technological innovations, the increase in international competitiveness and internationalisation of business links.

One of the most important aspects of the business environment is the economic environment. Business activity takes place within a wider marketplace in which producers respond to the changing wants and needs of consumers. If consumers want more of a product they will vote for it by spending their money on that product. We call this *effective demand*. Should consumers lose interest in a good or service they will switch their demand away from them.

Suppliers respond to signals in the marketplace. If they see prices and profits rising for particular types of prod-

ucts they will move into that line in the hope of making an increased profit. Some organisations operate in highly competitive markets in which there are lots of similar producers making and selling highly similar products, while others operate in situations in which there is little or no competition.

Organisations are affected not only by the particular sector of the market which they operate in (e.g. the market for take-away food in South Swindon), they are also influenced by conditions in the wider economy. The economy goes through a cycle of activity. At some times conditions are booming so that there is generally a high level of demand for goods and services across the economy. At other times this economic activity may go into decline so that all organisations feel the pinch.

In the UK, the government plays an important part in trying to influence the level of economic activity. The government can seek to boost economic activity in times of slump, for example, by lowering interest rates and taxes in order to provide incentives to increase the level of business activity.

The business environment is highly complex. However, it is important for organisations to understand this environment and how changes in the environment will affect the organisation.

19 The nature of the business environment

A business organisation works within a wider system. Every day, people involved in business make decisions. These decisions are influenced by what is going on in the wider environment.

A good way of looking at the wider environment is to do a PEST analysis.

This is an analysis of changes which are taking place around organisations all the time involving:

- Political (P) changes
- Economic (E) changes
- Social (S) changes
- Technological (T) changes.

This complex environment exists outside of the organisation and can exert enormous pressure on the way in which it can operate. Although this environment does not exist as a clear physical presence its effects are often very powerful.

Political

The political environment is created by governments and powerful decision makers who are able to create laws, regulations and codes, as well as imposing taxes on organisations. Political changes are brought in by those with power to bring in new laws and regulations. For example, the UK government has the power to make anti-pollution laws even stricter or softer. The UK is part of the European Union (EU) that has the power to pass laws and regulations affecting all 15 Member States.

The way in which business is treated by government will vary from nation to nation. For example, in Russia and China business activity is heavily regulated by the state even despite recent changes in these countries.

Economic

Different countries have different economic systems ranging from highly-controlled and planned ones to others where the free market is given more importance. Economic changes are concerned with the wider economy of the country. For example, the UK may be experiencing a boom period or a slump, unemployment, rising or falling prices and so on.

Social

Society exerts an enormous pressure on the way in which individuals and organisations behave. Values and attitudes are particularly influential. This is why, for example, very few people pick their noses in public places, and why most businesses avoid highly unethical or immoral prac-

tices. Social changes are those which affect attitudes and values in society as a whole. For example, in recent years there has been a considerable reduction in smoking, as people have turned to healthier lifestyles and as smoking has increasingly come to be regarded as an 'unpleasant' and anti-social activity. There can also be changes in the make-up of society, such as an increase in the number of old people.

Technology

Technological characteristics include the level of advancement of knowledge and equipment in society (or in specific countries) and the rate of development and application of such knowledge. Technological changes are changes in the way we make things, and in the tools and equipment we use. Today, we live in an age of rapid technological change.

TASK 19.1

Can you classify the following into:

- Political
- Economic
- Social
- Technological

influences on an organisation. (Bear in mind that some of them could be listed under more than one heading.)

The new Labour government stops sponsorship of sport	European Monetary Union
An increase in the number of women going out to work	Development of a cure for the common cold
Rising inflation	Breaking up of the former Soviet Union
Increases in the number of people working from home	Massive development of public transport
The re-unification of Germany	Exchange rates are linked to the Deutschmark
Migration of labour to the South of France	An increase in the number of oil tanker disasters
The end of the Cold War	Peace in the former Yugoslavia

Ageing of the population	Growing competitiveness of the Pacific Rim
Rising numbers of divorces	Increased automation of industry

Organisations need to scan the environments in which they operate in order to understand the key changes which currently face them, as well as future changes. If they are going to be able to plan for change and to react to changes effectively then they need to be able to understand this change environment.

IT'S A FACT

That some organisations not only scan the business environment from the point of view of their own organisation, but also from that of rivals. They identify the strengths and weaknesses of their rivals to deal with change environments.

Figure 19.1 is derived from a simple model created by David Wilson and Robert Rosenfeld. It provides a useful picture of the major external factors which all organisations face.

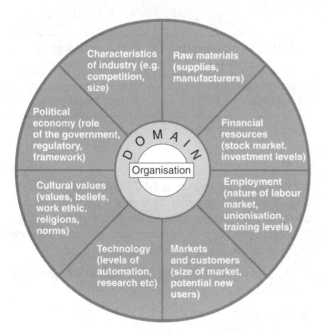

Figure 19.1   The organisational environment

The environment within which organisations operate is usually split into four broad categories:

- the general or societal environment – the society in which the organisation carries out its activities

- the inter-organisational environment – all organisations interact with a range of other organisations
- the political and economic environment
- the specific or task environment.

Managers are both concerned with the wider environment as outlined by the first three points above, and with the specific or task environment. The specific or task environment has a direct influence on their day-to-day 'brass tacks' work and is likely to take up most of their time and energy. The task environment is made up typically of customers, suppliers, trade unions, government agencies and competitors. This immediate environment is often referred to as the **organisational domain** and is shown in Figure 19.1 as being closest to the organisation. It is easy to imagine the variety of activities and contacts that take place within the specific or task environment: purchasing from suppliers, finding out what consumers require, dealing with customer complaints, trying to outcompete rivals, etc.

In terms of inter-organisational relations many writers today argue that organisations are increasingly dealing with networks of relationships with other organisations.

ENVIRONMENTAL AUDIT FOR DEEP PAN PIZZA

The UK pizza market is an extremely competitive one, although currently restaurant sales have become stagnant due to the increasing trend towards convenience foods and healthier diets. However, there has been a growth in home delivery/take away pizzas. In 1993, pizza sales were estimated at £655 million which represented 14 per cent of the UK fast-food market. Pizza restaurants are growing at 12 per cent per year whereas delivery units are growing at a rate of 30 per cent per year.

There is intense price competition among the leading chains (e.g. Pizza Land and Pizza Hut). To overcome this problem Deep Pan Pizza has introduced a number of new ideas to their restaurants such as salad/buffet lunches, value meals, family feasts, personal pizzas and special children's deals (e.g. boxes with a toy or Disney characters) to help generate larger sales.

The main development in recent years, in the larger chains, is the introduction of pizza slice outlets. This was to compete with the other 'quicker' fast-food stores such as

McDonald's, KFC and independent traders. These outlets are usually inside the restaurants and allow the customer to gain a slice of pizza immediately rather than waiting for waitress service, delivery or for the pizza to be prepared and cooked.

The market growth slowed during the early 1990s recession period, picking up again in the second half of the 1990s. In 1996/97 the sector comprised an estimated 3500 outlets:

	Number of outlets
Pizza Hut	390
Perfect Pizza	250
Pizzaland	123
Deep Pan Pizza	95
Domino Express	80
Pizza Express	75

The most significant factors that have an impact on the pizza industry are demographic shifts in the UK population as well as changes in eating habits/lifestyle (e.g. vegetarianism and worries about health.

As the number of women in employment increases, so does demand for convenience foods. The move towards less formal eating is increasing. Snacking or 'grazing' has become a way of eating for a significant proportion of the population, particularly the young.

The market size forecast for pizza at 1995 prices is as follows:

	Market size (£m)
1995	431.0
1996	455.6
1997	484.2
1998	508.6
1999	523.8

You have been asked to carry out an environmental audit for Deep Pan Pizza, examining the external environment for this organisation in October 1996. Identify the main political, economic, social and technological factors that are of relevance to the organisation. Set these factors out under each of the four headings:

- Political factors
- Social factors
- Economic factors
- Technological factors.

Recently, one problem for fast-food restaurants that has added to costs is implementing the increasingly stringent government health and safety regulations, and the penalties for non-compliance.

Carrying out a SWOT analysis of an organisation

A particularly important approach to examining the relationship between an organisation and its environment is to carry out a SWOT analysis.

A **SWOT analysis** sets out to focus on the **S**trengths, **W**eaknesses, **O**pportunities and **T**hreats facing a business at a given time. A SWOT includes an internal and an external element. The internal element looks at the current strengths of the organisation and its current weaknesses. The external element looks at the opportunities presented in the environment in which an organisation operates, and the threats.

Carrying out a SWOT requires research and analysis of the organisation's current and potential future position. The SWOT is used to match an organisation's strengths and weaknesses with the external forces in the business environment.

The internal audit element of SWOT analysis is the organisation's strengths and weaknesses; opportunities and threats reflect influences external to the organisation in the business environment.

Within the organisation (internal)	In the environment (external)
Strengths (positive) Weaknesses (negative)	Opportunities (positive) Threats (negative)

Figure 19.2 A SWOT analysis

As a result of carrying out a SWOT analysis, the organisation should then go on to develop the policies and practice that will enable it to build on its strengths, minimise its weaknesses, seize its opportunities, and take measures that will cancel out or minimise threats.

A simplified SWOT analysis of a business organisation might show that it has:

- **Strengths**
  A good product
  Good relationships with customers
  A good management team
- **Weaknesses**
  It operates on a very small scale
  It has regular cash flow problems
  Only deals in a very limited market

- **Opportunities**
  New and rapidly growing markets
  Changing tastes by consumers
  Diversifying into a number of product lines
- **Threats**
  Growing competition from rivals
  A recession leading to poor demand in the economy
  Development of foreign competitors in this country.

EXAM TIP:

Remember that **strengths and weaknesses are internal** to the organisation, and that **opportunities and threats relate to the external environment** in which the organisation operates.

Coping with a changing environment – scenario planning

Scenario planning is a very useful way of proactively planning to deal with changes in the external environment in which an organisation operates. It is a planning technique that was most influentially pioneered by Shell and which has since been copied by a number of other leading organisations.

Scenario planning involves thinking ahead over the next five, ten, 15 years to identify the sorts of changes which might take place in the environment in which you operate. Groups of managers and specialists identify all the possible changes which might take place in the environment in which they operate, for example: What would be the impact of having a new Labour government' What would be the impact of the dynamic increase in growth of the Chinese economy' What would be the impact of a major conflict in a sensitive part of the world economy' Scenario planning involves identify a range of scenarios in the environment in which the organisation operates and helps the organisation to think specifically about its position within the marketplace and within a change environment. For every scenario there needs to be a set of plans for efficiently managing the organisation through the change process.

Scenarios are not strictly forecasts, they simply reflect one possible way in which the future may emerge – i.e. they are 'What if'? situations. It makes sense to identify a range of possibilities – you never know what will emerge.

CASE STUDY CASE STUDY CASE STUDY CASE STUDY CASE STUDY CASE

SCENARIO PLANNING AT SHELL

Shell is particularly proud of one scenario, set out in 1984. The price of oil was $28 a barrel; one scenario envisaged oil falling to $16 a barrel by April 1986. With some pushing, Shell executives devised plans to deal with this possible scenario. In the event, the price of oil did fall: from $27 in January 1986 to $17 in February and just $10 in April. The fact that Shell had already considered what it would do helped it to successfully manage this period of difficulty.

Peter Schwartz, in his book *The Art of the Long View* (Century Business, 1991), tells another story of how scenario planning was used effectively at Shell. In 1983, there was still considerable tension between the Soviet Union and the West and it would have been difficult to imagine the changes that have taken place in Russia and its satellites. At the time, Shell was reviewing demand for North Sea gas and considering whether to develop the Troll gas field. The platform and its associated equipment was calculated to cost over $6 billion although it would make it possible to sell gas throughout Europe.

At the time, the other potential supplier of natural gas was the Soviet Union which could provide it far cheaper. The Western European states had agreed informally to limit supplies from the Soviet Union to 35 per cent of the market. Shell was concerned, however, that it would take a long time and cost a great deal of money to develop this new gas field. To be worthwhile, Shell needed a decent return on its investment, and to get that return it needed good sales. It therefore need to identify all the factors that would determine the size of those sales.

In particular, Shell were interested to identify factors which might lead to other European countries relaxing their 35 per cent limit of gas supplies from the Soviet Union. The planners felt that the failing Soviet economy might force the Soviet Union to abandon its existing communist system. They could see that it was possible that this failure would come about.

One of the scenarios the planners developed ('the Greening of Russia') was based on Gorbachev achieving power, massive economic and political changes, opening up to the West, declining tension in the West, and major shifts in international relationships. This scenario was one of a series of scenarios that Shell developed. However, it was invaluable in helping them to understand the environment in which they operated and for coping with these changes when they actually materialised.

1 What is scenario planning?
2 Explain why scenario planning is important to a large organisation like Shell?
3 Do you think that all organisations should analyse their environments in this way?

CASE STUDY CASE STUDY CASE STUDY CASE STUDY CASE STUDY CASE

Scenario planning and other methods of scanning the environment are invaluable in reducing uncertainty from the business planning process.

Oliver Sparrow, one of Shell's scenario planners, has set out in a book, *Management Options* (Routledge, 1993) that in using scenarios to help you to decide how you should help your organisation to respond to a change environment you need to:

- *Seek a shared understanding of the important features which influence the business and develop a model of how things work.*
- *Rank the features for their importance to the business.*
- *Distinguish between the factors over which the business can exercise choice.*
- *Build a map which defines the options open to the business.*
- *Define and prioritise the work needed in order to decide between those options.*
- *Set up a mechanism to deliver the chosen option.*

Analysing profit potential in a particular industry

Clearly, a major concern for all organisations is profitability. Without profits organisations cannot grow or compete. The environment in which an organisation operates will be a key determinant of profitability. For example, if the environment contains little competition, high and growing demand, and little regulation of business activity then it is possible that high profits are there for the taking. (Of course, however, this is likely to attract new competitors to the industry.)

The business writer, Michael Porter, has argued that the key aspect of the context in which a company operates is the industry or industries in which it competes. He refers to five basic forces which he calls 'the structural determinants of the intensity of competition'. These, he feels, determine the profit potential of the industry (and of companies working within it).

Porter's five forces are:

- rivalry among existing competitors
- the bargaining power of buyers
- the bargaining power of suppliers
- the threat of new competitors entering the industry
- the threat of substitute products.

Porter argues that the strength of these five forces will determine not only the sort of competition a company has to face but also the profitability of the whole industry.

Rivalry amongst existing competitors

This is the most obvious form of competition: the head-to-head rivalry between firms making similar products and selling them in the same market. Rivalry can be intense and cut-throat, or it may be governed by unwritten 'rules' – agreements which help the industry to avoid the damage that excessive price-cutting advertising and promotion expenses can inflict on profits. Competition may be over price or over a range of other factors such as advertising, service, quality, availability of outlets, etc.

The industry tends to be more competitive the greater the number of firms, and the slower the level of demand is increasing by. However, competition can also be intense when there is a small number of producers making and selling highly similar products.

Power of buyers

Powerful buyers can bargain away potential profits from the firms in the industry. They can cause firms to undercut each other in order to get the buyer's business, and they can use their power to extract other benefits from firms, like quality improvements, credit, etc. For example, Marks and Spencer (M&S) is a powerful buyer in that it purchases the total output of some factories, e.g. food factories producing 'ready meals' for M&S. M&S is in a strong buying position because it can switch the contract to an alternative factory should the existing one fall short of its price and quality specifications.

Buyers tend to be powerful when there are relatively few of them and they buy a lot of the total output, and often when there are a lot of quite small sellers.

Power of suppliers

In a similar way, suppliers of vital resources to the industry can exact high prices, leading to a squeeze on profits through higher input costs. Such suppliers would include suppliers of raw materials, power, skilled labour and components.

Threat of entry

If it is easy to get into an industry then, as soon as profits look attractive, new firms will enter. It is easier to move into industries where the capital costs of setting up are not excessive, and where there are no restrictions on entry, such a patents and detailed standards and restrictive legislation.

Threat of substitutes

A **substitute** is something that meets the same needs as the product produced in an industry. For example, it could be argued that going to the theatre is a substitute for going to the cinema. If a substitute becomes more attractive in terms of price, performance or both, then some buyers will be tempted to move their custom to the new substitutes.

The combined effect of the five forces

If all the five forces are strong, industry profitability would be expected to be low, regardless of the products or services being produced. Conversely, weak forces permit higher prices and above-average industry profitability.

TASK 19.2

Using the five forces model and the knowledge you have of one of the following industries assess the profit potential for firms in one of the following industries:

- tabloid newspapers
- fast-food outlets
- premier league football clubs.

(Clearly, this is a difficult task because you need to have a lot of specialist information about the industries concerned. However, while your analysis will lack a lot of detail, doing the exercise should help you to familiarise yourself with the model.)

An understanding of the business environment is very important to any business organisation. If you understand the dynamics of your industry, you can then think about how to change things or how best to manoeuvre the organisation to deal with the threats and take up the opportunities that may be emerging.

Chapter summary

- A business organisation operates within a wider system comprising overlapping environments.
- A PEST analysis is a useful way of assessing the political, economic, social and technological environment in which business activity takes place.
- It is important for business organisations to scan their environments to develop a good understanding of likely changes and how they will influence the organisation.
- Another approach is to split the environment into four categories – the general or societal environment, the inter-organisational environment, the political and economic environment, and the specific or task environment.
- Many managers focus a considerable amount of their attention on the task environment but it is important also to raise our sights to scan the wider picture.
- A SWOT analysis is a particularly useful way of looking at the relationship between the internal strengths and weaknesses of an organisation and the opportunities and threats that arise within the wider environment.
- Scenario planning is a very useful method of proactively planning to deal with changes in the external environment.
- Scenario planning involves thinking ahead over the next five, ten, 15 years to identify the sorts of changes which might take place in the environment in which an organisation operates. It involves developing plans to cope with a range of possible scenarios.
- Another useful way of analysing the organisational environment is to carry out a five forces analysis as suggested by Michael Porter. The five forces to be analysed are: rivalry among competitors, the bargaining power of buyers, the bargaining power of suppliers, the threat of new competitors entering the industry, and the threat of substitute products. Where these forces are strong then profitability in an industry is likely to be low. Where they are weak then there are better chances of profits.

20 Markets for goods and services

Today, most people live in societies in which the buying and selling of goods takes place in the marketplace. Buyers purchase those goods which best meet their requirements with a given income. Sellers set out to meet these needs in such a way that they are able to make profits.

The act of buying and selling is called a **transaction** and every day billions of transactions are made in local, regional, national and global markets. Most transactions involve face-to-face dealings, for example, when you purchase a newspaper or magazine in your local newsagent. However, buying and selling does not have to involve face-to-face transactions. For example, oil trading is nearly always done by telephone, with the traders accessing up-to-the-minute information from all over the world via their computer screens. So a market does not need to involve a physical trading place, it occurs whenever buyers and sellers engage in transacting business.

Markets determine:

- the price at which goods are bought and sold
- the quantity supplied to the market by producers and sellers
- the quantity demanded from the market by buyers.

It is this interaction between demand and supply which creates the market price. The market is a very important part of our lives. If people want goods badly enough and are prepared to back up their wants with purchasing power then they will create a great demand for a product. This demand will encourage suppliers to satisfy this demand with goods and services which are sold to the market in order to make profits.

Buyers	Sellers
Are **driven by** their wants and needs	Are **driven by** their desire to supply goods and services at a profit
Are **constrained by** the size of their disposable income	Are **constrained by** their ability to produce goods. Constraints include the cost of production and the extent of technical 'know-how'

In order to understand how markets operate it is essential to explore:

- the factors influencing demand
- the factors influencing supply.

Factors influencing demand

Price

The demand for a product means the actual amount of the product that will be bought at a given price. Common sense tells us that more of a product will be bought at a lower than at a higher price. For example, market research on the number of people who would use a new swimming pool produced the results shown in Figure 20.1.

Price for adults (£)	Demand per week (no. of people)
4.00	100
3.00	150
2.00	250
1.00	800
0.75	1200
0.50	1400
0.40	1500
0.30	1600

Figure 20.1

The demand for a product is commonly shown graphically by means of a demand curve. In Figure 20.2, a stationer has drawn out a demand curve, DD, for correcting fluid. By reading off the graph, you can see that by charging 90p per item, 2000 bottles will be sold in a month, whereas by charging 80p per bottle, 3000 will be sold in a month.

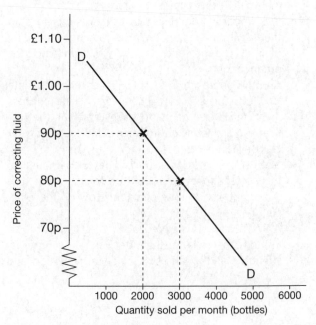

Figure 20.2   Demand for correcting fluid

An individual demand curve can be likened to a snapshot taken at a particular time showing how much of a product would be bought at different prices. At that time, price is seen to be the only variable that can be altered which will influence the quantity purchased.

Most demand curves drawn from real situations will have a shape that is more of a squiggle than a straight line. However, the common factor of nearly all demand curves is that they slope down to the right, indicating that – the conditions of demand remaining the same – more units will be bought at a lower price than at a higher price. In this book, therefore, we will draw demand curves as if they are always straight lines.

CASE STUDY CASE STUDY CASE STUDY CASE STUDY CASE STUDY CASE

CONSTRUCTING A DEMAND CURVE

John Richards has invented and developed a new piece of computer software for large companies. He has carried out some market research to find out how many units of the software he would be able to sell at different prices in a three-month period. If he charges a high price of £1000 per unit he will only be able to sell 500. If he goes for a much lower price of £200 he will be able to 14,000. There is a considerable difference between these two figures. He has also investigated intermediate prices. At £800 per unit of software he could sell 1000. At £600 he could sell 10,000, and at £400, 12,000 units.

1 Draw a demand curve to illustrate the figures set out above.
2 What do you think would be the best price to charge for units of the software? Explain.
3 What other information would you need to have to be able to decide on the most appropriate price to charge?

CASE STUDY CASE STUDY CASE STUDY CASE STUDY CASE STUDY CASE

Other factors influencing demand

There are a number of other factors that influence the demand for a product in addition to price. If one of these factors alters, **the conditions of demand** are said to have changed. These factors include tastes, income, population, the price of substitute products and the price of complementary products.

Changes in one or a combination of these factors will cause shifts in the demand curve. The demand curve can shift either to the left or to the right. A shift to the left indicates that smaller quantities are wanted than before at given prices.

These changes are illustrated in Figure 20.3.

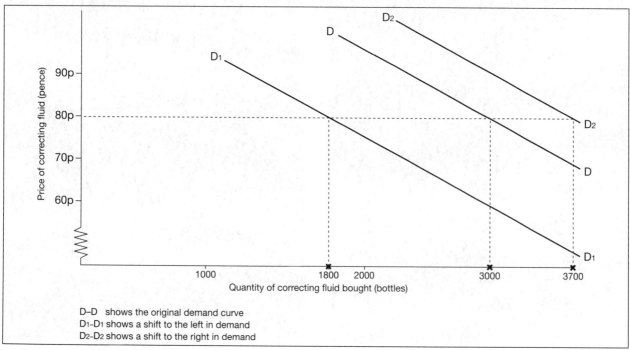

D–D   shows the original demand curve
D₁–D₁ shows a shift to the left in demand
D₂–D₂ shows a shift to the right in demand

Figure 20.3   Shifts in the position of a demand curve

The figure shows that in the original situation a quantity of 3000 would have been bought at 80p. When the conditions of demand move in favour of the product, more will be required at all prices so that, for example, at 80p, 3700 bottles of correcting fluid would now be demanded. Alternatively, if the conditions of demand move against a product, less will be required at all prices so that, for example, at 80p only 1800 bottles of correcting fluid would now be demanded.

Factors that can cause these shifts in demand are outlined below.

Tastes

As time moves on, new products become more fashionable and popular while others go into decline. For example, in 1993, 1994 and 1995 a number of book publishers started to produce CD-ROMs because of their growing popularity with the public. However, by 1996 and 1997 the public had become more interested in the Internet and so book publishers, like Dorling Kindersley, began to move out of CD-ROM publishing. In the 1990s, the public took an increasing interest in mobile phones and the demand for these rose considerably. In the early 1980s, Citizens' Band radios (CBs) were a popular craze. However, they don't have much demand today. The millennium is likely to bring with it a range of new tastes and fads so that new products will emerge with considerable demand for them while 'old fashioned' products and lines lose demand.

A pronounced example of a rapid shift to the left in the demand curve for a product occurred in 1996 with the BSE scare that led to a dramatic fall in demand for beef products. In the same period, the public developed a new demand for ostrich and venison steaks and burgers.

Population

Population statistics can be very helpful for forecasting changes in demand. Demographers (people who compile population statistics) frequently make predictions about future population trends based on existing statistics. Predictions based on the size of the population in different age groups are particularly easy to chart because, once a child has been born, he or she will become steadily older.

Populations can be classified in a number of ways including by age, sex, locality, race, educational background – or even by the newspaper they read.

Demand forecasters will often analyse population statistics according to clusters of relevant factors, for example, males in the 35–45 age group living in Hartlepool.

An increase in the relevant population will tend to move the demand curve for a product to the right. A decrease

The BSE scare led to a fall in demand for beef products ...

... while demand grew for ostrich products

in the relevant population will tend to move the demand curve to the left.

Income
The more money people have, the easier it is for them to buy products. The amount of money that people have to spend on goods is known as their **disposable income**, i.e. their pay minus taxes and other deductions.

Average incomes tend to rise over time and this will lead to a general increase in the level of demand for goods. The demand for individual items, however, will be related more to changes in the incomes of different groups, such as teenagers (for teenage magazines and fashions), pensioners (for retirement homes, winter sun holidays) and others.

The demand for most products will rise as a result of an increase in incomes for the relevant population. This will lead to a shift in the demand curve to the right. Rising incomes will tend to result from improved job opportunities and increases in the demand for goods.

Some products may become less popular as incomes rise. These are goods that come to be regarded as inferior when people's spending power increases. The consumer who was once happy to rent a flat, wear second-hand clothes and drive a second-hand, low-powered car may switch to buying a house, wearing designer labels and driving a status-symbol car when his or her income increases sufficiently.

We can thus state the relationship between income and demand in the following way:

> *For most products demand will shift to the right when income increases, and to the left when income falls. In the case of inferior items, however, demand would shift to the left when income rises.*

Inherited wealth
A number of studies have highlighted the level of inherited wealth that is coming the way of middle-aged households. The overall effect is that a sizeable number of middle-aged households inherit a considerable amount of wealth which is rapidly turned into spending power. An increase in inherited wealth in this way can have an important effect in raising the demand for products and thus shifting demand curves to the right.

The price of substitute products
The demand for products that have close substitutes will often be strongly influenced by the price of the substitutes. This would be the case, for example, with different brands of tinned fruit or different brands of petrol, because there are many brands to choose from.

The demand curve for a product is likely to shift to the right if a substitute product rises in price. The demand curve for a product is likely to shift to the left if a substitute product falls in price (assuming that other factors influencing demand do not alter at the same time).

IT'S A FACT

That during the middle part of the 1990s, *The Times* ran a sustained campaign of price cuts in order to win demand away from other substitute newspapers such as *The Independent* and *The Guardian*. By charging a very low price *The Times* was able to reduce the revenues of these newspapers giving them virtually no profits to plough back into their businesses.

The price of complementary products
Some products are used together so that the demand for one is linked to the price of another. An example of this might be a word processor and a floppy disc or CD-ROM. If a particular brand of word processor were to rise in price, then potential buyers might switch their purchases to an alternative brand. This would also reduce the demand for the floppy discs that are compatible with the original brand of word processor.

Factors influencing supply

Price
The supply of a product is the amount that suppliers will wish to produce at a given price. Commonsense tells us that more of a product will be supplied at a higher price than at a lower price. For example, a survey of tomato growers' intentions in a particular farming district revealed that the acreage that would be committed to tomato production would vary with the price of tomatoes, as shown in Figure 20.4. (It should be borne in mind that quantities produced would depend on the acreage planted, but also on weather conditions and other variables.)

Price of tomatoes (market price per lb)	Quantity of land committed to tomato production (acres)
15	800
20	2400
25	4400
30	10,000
35	14,000

Figure 20.4   Price and production

The supply of a product can be shown graphically by means of a supply curve. In Figure 20.5 a newspaper manufacturer has plotted the numbers of copies of papers that the company would be prepared to supply per day at different prices. By reading off the graph, you can see that at a price of 20p, 400,000 copies will be produced each day, whereas at a price of 25p, 800,000 copies will be produced.

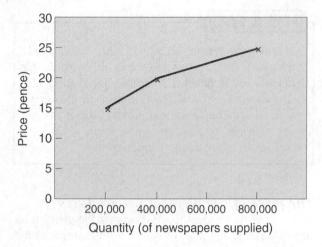

Figure 20.5   The supply curve of newspapers

The individual supplier (e.g. the newspaper manufacturer) will be prepared to purchase more capital and equipment and to employ more factors of production the higher the price of the product. The risk becomes more attractive and capital outlays (e.g. the cost of new equipment for an advanced printing process) can be recovered more quickly. In the market for national newspapers as a whole, more producers will be prepared to enter the market to supply at higher prices. More entrepreneurs will be prepared to risk capital if returns promise to be higher and even the less efficient producers will anticipate an excess of revenue over costs.

An individual supply curve can be likened to a snapshot taken at a particular time, showing how much of a product would be supplied at different prices. At that time, price is seen to be the only variable that can be altered which will influence the quantity supplied.

Most supply curves drawn from real situations will have a shape that is more of a squiggle than a straight line. However, the common factor of nearly all supply curves is that they slope up to the right, indicating that – conditions of supply remaining the same – more units will be supplied at a higher price than at a lower price. In this book, therefore, we will draw supply curves as if they are always straight lines.

Other factors

There are a number of factors that influence the supply of a product in addition to prices. If one of these factors alters, the **conditions of supply** are said to have changed. These factors include the price of factors of production, the price of other commodities, technology and the changing objectives of producers.

Changes in one or a combination of these factors will cause shifts in the supply curve. The supply curve can shift either to the left or to the right. A shift to the left indicates that smaller quantities will be supplied than before at given prices; a shift to the right indicates that larger quantities will be supplied than before at given prices.

These changes are illustrated in Figure 20.6.

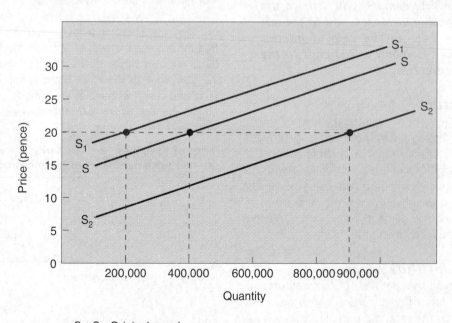

S—S= Original supply curve
S_1—S_1= Shift to left in supply curve
S_2—S_2= Shift to right in supply curve

Figure 20.6   Shifts in the supply curve for newspapers

Figure 20.6 shows that in the original situation a quantity of 400,000 papers a day would have been supplied at 20p. When the conditions of supply move in favour of the product, more will be supplied at all prices so that, for example, at 20p, 900,000 newspapers will be supplied. Alternatively, if the conditions of supply move against a product, less will be supplied at all prices so that, for example, at 20p only 200,000 newspapers will be supplied.

Factors that can cause these shifts in supply are outlined below.

Prices of factors of production

Production is based on the combination of factor inputs in order to produce outputs. If the cost of a factor input rises, then it will become more expensive to produce outputs. Factors of production will be used in the long term only if the value of their output is greater than the cost of their hire. As factor prices rise, fewer factors will be used in production and hence the supply of a product will fall.

For example, let us assume that an agricultural crop requires three main inputs: land, labour, and chemical fertiliser. If the cost of one or more of these inputs was to rise, then farmers might cut back on the acreage committed to this particular crop. Conversely, if the price of one or more factors of production was to fall, then supply conditions would move in favour of increased production and supply is likely to shift to the right.

Prices of other commodities

In a number of areas of production, it is possible to switch production from less profitable to more profitable lines. For example, many arable farmers have a certain degree of discretion over which crops to grow. A food factory can choose whether to focus mainly on Italian pasta dishes, such as cannelloni and ravioli, Indian dishes, such a Korma and Vindaloo, or traditional English dishes, such as Lancashire Hotpot and beef stew. If a particular line becomes relatively more profitable, then scarce resources, such as equipment, time and materials, can be switched into producing it and away from producing other products. A rise in the price of carrots may therefore lead to a shift to the left of the supply curve for cabbages and a fall in the price of carrots may lead to a shift to the right of the supply curve for cabbages.

Changes in the level of technology

An improvement in the level of technology means that more output can be produced with fewer resources. This means that the supply curve for a product will shift to the right. Modern technology based on computers and factory robots has enabled a wide range of producers to produce larger outputs at lower unit costs – for example, in car production, newspapers, modern breweries and the processing of cheques by banks.

Producers' objectives

Business-owners have a wide range of objectives. To some, expansion may be seen as a goal in itself. The firm might therefore decide to produce more to gain a higher profile, to take a larger share of a market or simply because the owner enjoys the cut and thrust of business life.

The weather

One of the major factors influencing the supply of a number of goods and services is the weather, for example, the appearance of umbrella sellers at the entrances to underground stations in rainy weather! The supply of agricultural products depends very much on changing weather conditions.

EXAM TIP:

Make sure you know the difference between changes in demand and supply, and changes in the conditions of demand and supply. A change in demand or supply occurs as the result of the change in the price of the good being considered. A change in the conditions of demand or supply results from changes other than the change in the price of the product being considered.

The formation of a market price

In the marketplace the forces of demand and supply will interact to create a market price. To illustrate this point, Figure 20.7 shows a fictional daily demand and supply schedule for fish at a small fishing village.

Price of fish (p)	Quantity demanded	Quantity supplied
35	800	350
40	700	400
45	600	450
50	500	500
55	400	550
60	300	600

Figure 20.7   Demand and supply in a daily fish market

When the price of fish is high, the owner of the only fishing boat will spend more time fishing than when prices are low. Conversely, consumers will want to purchase more fish at low than at high prices.

This information can then be plotted on a graph, as shown in Figure 20.8. If you study this graph, you can see that there is only one price at which the wishes of consumers and the supplier coincides, i.e. 50p. At this price the quantity that will be bought and sold is 500.

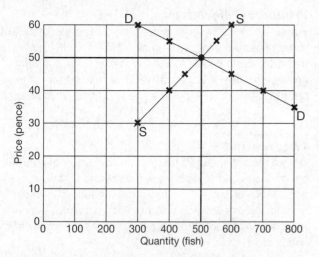

Figure 20.8   Graph showing demand and supply in a daily fish market

We can see that the market provides a mechanism for automatically bringing the decisions of consumers and producers into line, even though the two groups have different motives. (The producers will want to sell at the highest price possible, and the consumers will want to purchase at the lowest price possible.)

We can see how the process of forming an equilibrium price comes about by considering two disequilibrium situations (see Figure 20.9).

If for example, we consider the price of 60p, we will see that, at this price, consumers of fish would be prepared to buy only 300 fish – leaving a surplus stock of 300 fish which would go to waste. In this situation, the owner of the fishing boat would lower prices and resort to working fewer hours.

Alternatively, if the price of fish was pitched at 40p, consumers would be prepared to buy 700 fish. However, the owner of the fishing boat would be prepared to work long enough to catch only 400. There would now be a shortage of fish – stocks would rapidly sell out and customers would try to bid up the price. This would make it worthwhile for the owner of the fishing boat to work longer hours.

The net effect is that at prices above 50p, too much will be produced and so forces will interact to pull prices down to 50p. At prices below 50p, too little will be produced and so forces will interact to pull prices up to 50p. At 50p, prices are just right and there is no tendency to change.

The above analysis is a simplification. In the real world markets do not always move smoothly towards equilibrium. Consumers and producers frequently lack important market information which would help them to respond promptly to changes.

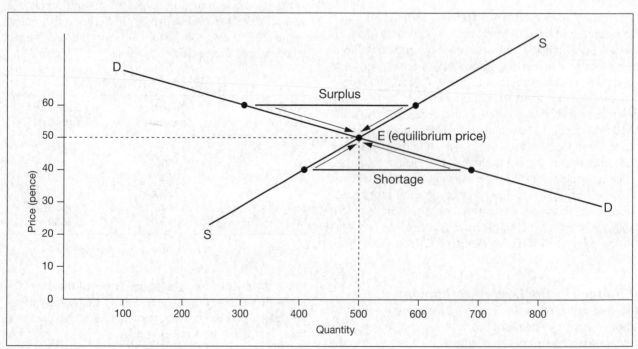

Figure 20.9   Creating the equilibrium price

Shifts in demand and supply

So far, we have analysed market prices solely in terms of the relationship between price and demand and supply. This has been like taking a snapshot under the assumption that factors other than price do not alter.

However, in our earlier analysis we saw that there are a number of factors influencing demand, and a number of factors influencing supply. Markets are constantly in motion, and combinations of factors will cause shifts in demand and supply.

For example, we can see that in Figure 20.10(a) a shift to the right of the demand curve has increased the equilibrium price and equilibrium quantity in the market; a shift to the left of the demand curve has had the reverse effects (see Figure 20.10(b)).

In Figure 20.11(a), we can see that a shift to the right of the supply curve has decreased the equilibrium price and increased the equilibrium quantity. Conversely, in Figure 20.11(b), a shift to the left of the supply curve has increased the equilibrium price and decreased the equilibrium quantity.

Real world situations will be complicated by the interaction of numerous demand and supply factors.

EXAM TIP:

Many students initially find it difficult to distinguish between factors causing movements up or down a demand or supply curve and factors causing shift to the left or right of demand or supply curves.

The golden rule is that movements along curves are caused solely by changes in the price of the item in question. Changes in factors other than price cause the whole curve to shift in position.

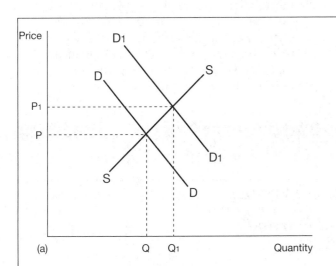

Figure 20.10 (a)   A shift to the right in demand

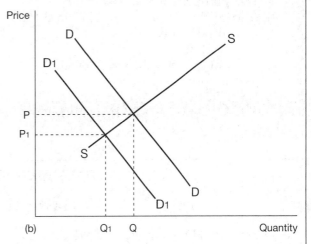

(b) A shift to the left in demand

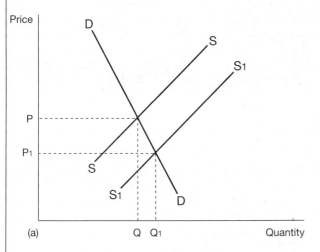

Figure 20.11(a)   A shift to the right in supply

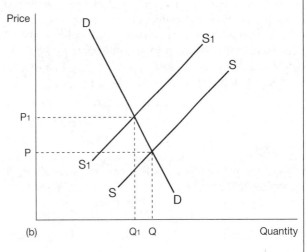

(b) A shift to the left in supply

CASE STUDY CASE STUDY CASE STUDY CASE STUDY CASE STUDY CASE

CHANGES IN THE MARKET CONDITIONS FOR BRITISH WINES

State whether the following situations would lead in the first instance to:

a A movement up the demand curve
b A movement down the demand curve
c A shift to the right of the demand curve
d A shift to the left of the demand curve
e A movement up the supply curve
f A movement down the supply curve
g A shift to the right of the supply curve
h A shift to the left of the supply curve.

All situations relate to the demand and supply of British wine:

1 Increased popularity of British wine.
2 Improved technology involved in British wine manufacture.
3 The falling price of British wine.
4 A scare about safety standards in British wine production
5 A general increase in incomes.
6 A fall in the relevant sector of the population.

7 Falling wine prices.
8 An increase in the price of a product that is produced on land similar to that used for growing wines.
9 Excellent weather for wine growing and harvesting.
10 An increase in European consumption of beer at the expense of wine.
11 Removal of a government subsidy to wine producers.
12 A general reduction in all price levels.

Of course, you need to bear in mind the dynamic nature of markets. For example, when there is an increase in demand this will be followed by an increase in price. This may then lead to an increase in supply, which may or may not help to modify the initial price increase. Markets will be constantly adjusting to a wide range of interdependent forces, such as changes in tastes, incomes, prices of complements/substitutes, etc.

CASE STUDY CASE STUDY CASE STUDY CASE STUDY CASE STUDY CASE

EXTENSION MATERIAL

Elasticity of demand

Elasticity of demand is a measure of 'the responsiveness of quantity demanded to a change in price'.

If quantity demanded is very responsive to price changes then a small change in price will lead to a relatively large change in quantity demanded. In this case, we would say that demand is **elastic**. For example, many popular fruits have an elastic demand at their existing market prices so that if say the price of apples rose by 2p or 3p then customers could easily switch to cheaper substitutes such as another type of apple or to pears.

Where quantity demanded is relatively unresponsive to price change we say that demand is **inelastic**. An example of this would be the case of someone addicted to smoking 40 cigarettes a day. Even though the price of cigarettes goes up they still continue to smoke 39 or 40 because their demand is highly inelastic (i.e. responds little to a price change). Of course, there are limits to this – if the price of cigarettes doubled or trebled then the cigarette smokers might have to look for substitute ways of feeding their habit.

To be precise, we can define elasticity of demand as:

the relationship between the proportionate change in price and the proportionate change in quantity demanded.

We can provide a numerical value for elasticity by using the formula:

$$\text{Elasticity of demand} = \frac{\% \text{ change in quantity demanded}}{\% \text{ change in price}}$$

Where this ratio is greater than 1, demand is said to be elastic. Where this ratio is less than 1, demand is said to be inelastic. Where this ratio is equal to 1, demand is said to have unitary elasticity.

For example, if a good fell in price by 50 per cent (say, from £1 to 50p) and the quantity demanded increased by 100 per cent (say, from 1000 to 2000), we could say that the elasticity of demand is 2:

$$\frac{100\%}{50\%} = 2$$

If a good fell in price by 50 per cent (say, from £1 to 50p) and the quantity demanded increased by 25 per cent (say, from 1000 to 1250), we could say that the elasticity of demand is one-half.

$$\frac{25\%}{50\%} = \frac{1}{2}$$

From a producer's point of view it is important to understand what will happen to demand if you raise or lower price. There are clearly many advantages to be gained if people buy a lot more of our goods when (as a producer) we lower price.

To producers or sellers it is important to know how much demand will change as a result of price changes so that they can calculate the effect on sales and on the amount of money they receive from sales. Money received from sales is called **revenue**.

- If a producer knows that demand for a product is elastic around the existing price:
  it may make sense to lower price – to increase sales and revenues
  it would be foolish to raise price – because sales and revenues will fall by a bigger percentage than the price rise.
- If a producer knows that demand for a product is inelastic around the existing price:
  it may make sense to raise price – because revenues would increase
  it would be foolish to lower price – because even though you are selling a few more items you are losing revenues on all of the units that you sell.
- If a producer knows that demand is unitary for a product around the existing price then there is no justification for raising or lowering price.

Chapter summary

- Markets bring together the interactions of buyers and sellers to create market prices.
- The most important factor affecting quantities demanded at a moment in time is price.
- A demand curve shows the relationship between price and quantity demanded. A typical demand curve slopes down from left to right.
- Factors which can cause a demand curve to shift to the left or right include changes in tastes, population, income, inherited wealth, the price of substitute products, and the price of complementary products.
- The most important factor influencing the supply of a product at any one time is its price.
- A supply curve shows the quantities of a product that will be supplied to the market at different prices.
- Factors leading to a shift to the left or right in the supply curve include changes in prices of factors of production, changes in the prices of other commodities, changes in the level of technology, the objectives of producers, and the weather.
- Market price is determined by the interaction of supply and demand.
- If prices are higher or lower than the equilibrium point for the market then buyers and sellers will adjust the quantities that they buy and sell until the equilibrium point is arrived at.
- The real world is characterised by a dynamic marketplace in which demand and supply is constantly changing and interacting so that prices and quantities frequently change.
- Market equilibrium is only a temporary state. The market is forever seeking new equilibrium situations.

21 Competition

Introduction

Competition is a very important part of business life. The dictionary provides us with some useful definitions of competition, for example:

> **A contest in which a winner is chosen from among two or more entrants.**

and:

> ***The opposition offered by competitors.***

The implication is that if five million people want to buy national newspapers on a Monday, then each individual newspaper publisher will not be able to sell five million copies. The *market* will be divided up between sellers. The competitor that proves to be most successful will be the one that is able to attract the most buyers.

A market is a situation in which buyers and sellers come

into contact. There are a great many markets for different products, for example, the market for jeans, the market for car phones, the market for perfume, etc.

Going back to the example of competition between national newspapers, we can see that companies will compete to have:

- the best stories
- the most attractive layout
- the best sports reports
- the most interesting pictures
- the most interesting gossip
- the best value for money

...and so on.

The above list identifies some of the most important features of competition in the national newspaper market.

SYNTHESIS

What do you think are the ten most important features of competition for the following products:

- **perfume?**
- **crisps?**
- **teenage magazines?**
- **computers?**

Being competitive

The famous American business writer Michael Porter suggests that there are two major ways to be competitive:

- low costs
- differentiation.

Low costs

A business needs to become the producer that produces at the lowest cost. This can be done by producing goods in a very efficient way using the best technology. It can also be done by producing and selling very large quantities of products. Companies like Coca-Cola and the soap powder manufacturers are able to produce individual items at very little cost because they produce literally millions of units. You will have lower costs than your rivals by winning a bigger share of the market than them.

Differentiation

Differentiation involves making your product 'better' than that of your rivals, while at the same time making sure that the product is bought by customers. A Rolls-Royce is different to other motor cars; it is also very expensive. It is a success because enough people are prepared to buy the product because of its special quality.

Choosing a market to compete in

Some products compete in a very broad market, for example supermarkets sell many types of groceries to a wide audience. Other products compete in a much narrower market, for example, specialist food shops such as delicatessens, sell a much narrower range of products to a more select group of customers.

So, as well as choosing whether to compete through low cost or differentiation, businesses must also choose whether to sell to a *mass market*, or to a *narrow market*. The alternatives are:

- *Mass market + low cost, for example, general purpose washing-up liquid, 'own brand' baked beans, most fish fingers*
- *Mass market + differentiation, for example, Mars Bars, Kellogg's Corn Flakes*
- *Narrow market + low cost, for example, revision guide textbooks, second-hand car sales*
- *Narrow market + differentiation, for example, Rolls Royce, Renault Twingo.*

Note: Firms that focus on low costs will set out to have the lion's share of the market, enabling them to produce more cheaply than rivals. Firms that focus on differentiation compete through providing goods that meet consumers' needs better than rival products.

TASK 21.1

How would you place the following products in terms of the four categories listed above:

a Milky Bars?
b Anais Anais perfume?
c the Ford Escort?
d Benetton clothes?
e Pritt Stick?
f Mighty White bread?
g Pringle jumpers?
h Harrods Christmas Hampers?
i this book?

The danger of getting stuck in the middle

There is a danger of trying to be the lowest cost producer and at the same time trying to differentiate your product from rivals. The danger is that by differentiating you are not able to produce at a low enough cost, and by trying to produce at a low cost you fail to make your product different enough because you don't make enough profits.

CASE STUDY CASE STUDY CASE

JAPANESE CARS: STUCK IN THE MIDDLE?

Kenichi Ohmae thinks that Japan's cars may be getting stuck in the middle. On the one side there are German companies like Mercedes and BMW selling their goods at very high prices. Because their prices are high they are able to cover their high costs. The Germans are able to concentrate on differentiation.

On the other side are the low–price, large quantity producers like Korea's Hyundai, who can make products for less than half of what it cost the Japanese.

Being caught in the middle leads to a painful squeeze for the Japanese.

1 What cars can you think of whose strength is differentiation?
2 What cars can you think of whose strength is low cost of production?
3 Is there a danger for some cars of being stuck in the middle' What do you think?
4 What goods can you think of that have become stuck in the middle of other markets?

STUDY CASE STUDY CASE STUDY

The influence of competition

Competition is a major influence on business. A company's prices and many other policies will be influenced by the level of competition it faces. It is common practice to classify markets according to the level of competition that exists within them. At one extreme we have highly competitive markets, at the other we have a monopoly situation in which there is only a single supplier to the market (see Figure 21.1).

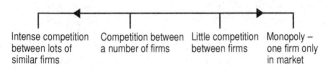

| Intense competition between lots of similar firms | Competition between a number of firms | Little competition between firms | Monopoly – one firm only in market |

Figure 21.1 The extremes of competition

The fact that there are many companies in a market does not necessarily mean that there is intense competition. Indeed, in the real world some of the most competitive situations occur when there is a relatively small number of companies, each of a similar size, each seeing the other as a competitor, and producing or selling a similar range of products or services to the same target audience.

Competitive markets

A competitive market is one in which there are a number of producers supplying goods which are considered to be highly similar. For example, if there were a number of small farmers producing apples which looked and tasted alike, then the products would be very close substitutes. In deciding whose apples to buy, a major consideration would be the price of the apples. The farmer who undercut the prices of rivals would be the one most likely to sell off his or her stock.

A highly competitive market exists when companies compete vigorously with each other. Features of intense competition might include:

- producers supplying highly similar products (for example, sliced white bread)
- consumers having detailed knowledge of the offers being made by different suppliers (for example, a shopper in a large supermarket who can check on the relative prices of different brands of products such as baked beans)
- ease for producers and suppliers to enter a market (for example, the ease with which a plumber can set up in business in a medium-sized town).

A good example of a competitive market is that of service stations. Service stations offer highly similar products and services:

- a similar range of petrol, diesel, and other fuels
- a similar range of customer services, for example, fast service, paper towels to wipe hands on after filling up, toilets, a range of extra products such as comics, newspapers, etc.
- light, flexible hoses
- a place to check air pressure, vacuum the car, etc.

The higher the level of competition, the greater the pressure on individual service stations to rival the products and services offered by competitors.

IT'S A FACT

A major way in which service stations compete is through location. The best location is the first available site on the left when motorists have just left a busy urban area. They don't need to concentrate on finding their way through busy traffic – they can just pull in at a convenient service station.

Direct and indirect competition

Competition occurs where two or more organisations act independently to supply their products to the same group of consumers. Some markets are characterised by an abundance of products and services so that customers have a considerable amount of choice. In other markets there may be little (if any) competition and consumers may only be able to make a limited choice from the range of goods and services on offer.

Direct competition exists where organisations produce similar products which appeal to the same group of consumers. For example, a pack of unsalted butter made by one manufacturer is in direct competition with a pack of unsalted butter of the same weight produced by a different manufacturer.

Even when an organisation provides a unique end-product with no direct competition, it will still have to consider **indirect competition**. This occurs where potential customers examine slightly different ways of meeting the same needs. For example, a family has the choice of going to see a Christmas pantomime in London, or going to watch their local premier division football club on the same day. An individual can save up for an expensive winter-break holiday or put a deposit down to buy a new car.

The degree of competition in a market is likely to influence the **level of sales and profits**. The company that is first to the market with a new product may be able to make large sales and profits. However, in the course of time other companies will enter the market, so that sales will be shared between a larger number of competitors. Each will compete for market share, so that price wars may result leading to falling profits.

Monopoly

A business that does not have direct competition is said to be a **monopoly**. It does not face outside pressure to be competitive. We must be careful, however, not to assume that monopolies are inefficient. Monopolies do not need to duplicate systems of administration, services and other processes. They can also put a lot of money into product development and research in order to keep up a long-term competitive advantage.

A **pure monopoly** exists if there is only one producer or seller. Because there is only one company in the market, it has considerable powers. For example, if you are not happy with the prices, quality or service, conditions of sale, etc., offered by the monopolist you cannot switch to a rival because there isn't one.

In the real world there are unlikely to be many examples of pure monopolies because most manufactured goods can be copied. Some minerals are restricted to a few geographical areas; for example, a large concentration of world gold reserves is found in Russia and its surrounding states and in southern Africa. When a new product is invented, the company that supplied it will initially have a monopoly. However, very soon other people will copy the product and provide close imitations. For example, it does not take long for an 'exclusive' perfume to be copied and to appear in a slightly modified form at a much lower price on market stalls and street corners throughout the country. Visit Oxford Street in December and you are almost certain to come across 'sales people' offering you three bottles of 'exclusive perfume' for £20 out of a suitcase.

An understanding of monopoly, however, is very important in business. Monopoly powers help to explain how companies are able to make more than the normal amount of profit. When a company can restrict competition it is in a position to raise prices, and perhaps to exploit consumers. For example, if I desperately needed a loaf of bread when shops were closed, I might be forced to buy an over-priced loaf of not-too-fresh bread from a garage.

Oligopoly

Whereas monopoly means that there is one seller, *oligopoly* means that there are a few major sellers. Oligopoly is typical of many markets in the UK where there are a few major sellers in national and local markets (although there may be additional smaller sellers).

Examples of oligopoly markets are:

- quality newspapers, for example, *The Times*, *The Independent*
- tabloid newspapers, for example, *The Mirror*, *The Sun*
- contraceptives manufacturers, for example, Mates (Virgin), Durex (London Rubber)
- soap powders, for example, Unilever, Procter & Gamble
- car manufacture, for example, Peugeot, Honda
- confectionery, for example, Cadbury, Nestle
- personal computers, for example, Apple Macintosh, IBM
- petrol, for example, Shell, BP, Esso.

Oligopoly markets have the potential for intense competition as well as the potential to restrict competition and act as monopolists.

Oligopolists could agree to share a market and to avoid potentially damaging competition, for example they could agree that Company A can dominate the North, Company B the South, Company C the West, and Company D the East. However, they would be unlikely to do this, because:

- business organisations tend to have a natural desire to expand and dominate. For example, Company A may also want to be the major player in the South, East and West

- it is against the law to carry out uncompetitive practices. Companies that collude are using their powers to exploit less powerful groups and individuals. In this country this will lead to legal penalties.

Oligopoly markets are therefore often characterised by **extensive competition**. Competition acts as a spur, encouraging individual companies to improve their performance in order to increase their market share, sales, receipts and profits.

- High-market-share companies are able to gain larger profits and plough this money back into research and development, which gives them a competitive edge.
- Companies with a high market share will continually be improving their products to keep them ahead of the market.
- Companies with a high market share are able to sell their products in bulk so that the cost per unit of transporting, advertising, and other aspects of marketing goods, falls considerably.

IT'S A FACT

For many years the London Rubber Company was the sole supplier of male contraceptives in the UK. In recent years Richard Branson broke this monopoly situation by introducing a low-cost, high-quality sheath called 'Mates'.

Methods of competition within markets

There are a number of important aspects of competition which we need to examine:

- competition for market share
- competition for customers
- competition for product superiority
- competition for sales
- price and image.

Different organisations will focus on these different aspects of competition at different times.

Competition for market share

Market share is often regarded by businesses as a key indicator of their current and future success. The argument is that if you gain market share, then the profits will follow.

A company will want to have a dominant market share in a particular market. In Figures 21.2 and 21.3, for example, you can see that SuperPC just has the lead in the personal computer market in 1980 over its nearest rival International PC. This gives it a slight competitive edge. However, by 1997 it has extended its lead, giving it a considerable advantage.

Research indicates that market share leads to **market power**. The advantages of having a large market share are striking:

- High-market-share companies are able to buy their ingredients and raw materials, or make them 'in-house', far more cheaply than their smaller rivals.

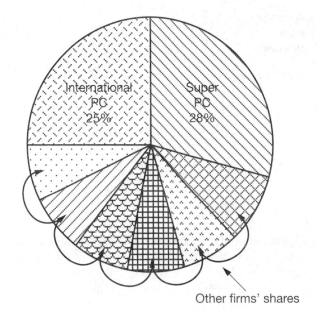

Figure 21.2   Market shares in the PC market, 1980

FIG 21.3

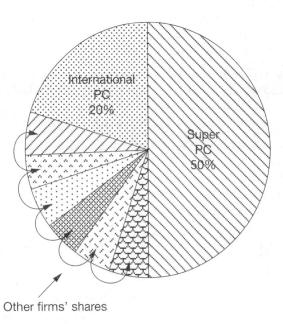

Figure 21.3   Market shares in the PC market, 1997

Consider, for example, the cases of Coca-Cola and Mars Bars. Both these products are shipped out to retailers in massive quantities at very low cost per unit. The message is simple – 'win the lion's share of the market if you wish to be successful'. In the short term, it may be worth sacrificing profit margins in order to 'hike up' market share.

The Boston Consultancy Group has shown how market share leads to falling costs through an 'experience curve', shown in Figure 21.4.

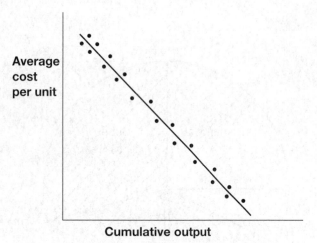

Figure 21.4   An experience curve

The cost of producing each unit will fall, as the total output that has been produced increases over time with experience. *Gains in efficiency stem from greater experience*. The Boston Consultancy Group argues that this is a general principle and that, as a rough rule, average cost per unit fell by 20 to 30 per cent with each doubling of experience. Greater experience stems from:

● economies of scale
● the elimination of less efficient factors of production
● increased productivity, stemming from technical changes and learning effects
● improvements in product design.

The key lesson to be learnt is that the benefits of experience do not just arise – they need to be worked at. Companies must take steps to ensure that these benefits are reaped, through deliberate management policies.

Companies which have a high market share should be able to accumulate more experience. Therefore companies should strive for a high market share. The best indicator of market share is relative – that is, the ratio of a company's market share to that of its largest competitor.

$$\text{Relative share of Company A} = \frac{\text{Market share of Company A}}{\text{Market share of nearest competitor}}$$

This indicator gives a clear measure of comparative strengths. The Boston Consultancy Group used statistical evidence to argue that a ratio of 2:1 would give a 20 per cent cost advantage.

Competition for customers

Competition for customers is perhaps the most important aspect of competition. You are most likely to be successful in attracting customers if you have a clear picture of who they are and what they want. Market research is an important way of finding out about customers and their requirements. Once you have found out what customers want it will be important to give them:

● what they want
● at the right place
● at the right price
● promoted and offered in an appropriate way.

Competition for product superiority

People buy those products which best meet their needs. Just listen to people who are buying a durable electrical good, such as a vacuum cleaner, freezer or dishwasher. They are essentially concerned with making sure that they buy the product which is just right for them. They will discuss relative price, reliability, additional features and many other factors. For example, the Dyson Dual Cyclone has a range of additional gadgets and features compared with rival models of vacuum cleaner.

Competition for sales

Competition for sales is an important aspect of rivalry between organisations. The volume of sales is vital in many business areas.

The **turnover** of a business is measured by multiplying the average price of items sold by the number of items sold:

Turnover = Average price of items × Number of items sold

The more items that a business can sell, the more it can spread its costs over a larger output. The supermarket chains have benefited for a long time from policies of selling large volumes of goods. A popular business saying in America in recent times has been 'pile them high and see them fly'. The implication is that high sales at low prices will lead to low buying-in costs and hence to profitability.

IT'S A FACT

There may come a point at which goods are sold too cheaply and consumers lose confidence in the value of an item. A good example of this was the jewellery chain Ratners. Gerald Ratner set up a highly successful chain of businesses selling low-price jewellery in the UK. However, in a speech to business people he let slip that now-famous remark that much of the jewellery was basically 'crap!' This remark contributed to the crash of the Ratners organisation as customers stopped buying the jewellery.

Price and image

For a detailed discussion of pricing policies you will need to look at Section 2 in Part 2 of this book. In some markets, a product's image is more important than its price. This is apparent in some car advertising. Cars do not just offer you a way of getting from A to B, they also reflect your lifestyle. A particular type of car may give you the image of being a cautious, family person, while another may present you as a risk-taking, exotic extrovert. Note how frequently rock stars and lottery winners trade in the car which they drove prior to 'stardom' for one or several very expensive cars. Imagery is therefore a very important ingredient in product competition.

SYNTHESIS

Do you think that it is possible to arrive at a situation in which the consumer has 'too much choice'?

EXTENSION MATERIAL

Competition between businesses to shift demand curves

Competitive edge gives a business an important advantage over rivals. Competitive edge will improve the position of an organisation's demand curve. This may mean, for example, that more of the product will be demanded at the same price as before, or that a higher price can be charged without losing a significant number of sales.

Figure 21.5 shows the effect on sales of two successful **advertising** campaigns for a product. At a market price of £0.80 it was originally possible to sell 1800 items; after the first advertising campaign demand rose to 3000 and after the second to 3700. Advertising is important in that it keeps products in the public eye. It also enables suppliers to describe the key benefits of their products.

Of course, advertising is not just concerned with shifting the demand curve in the way illustrated in Figure 21.5. It is also concerned with making the demand curve more inelastic so that if price of the product goes up there is only a small drop in sales. Brand loyalty and commitment to a product will develop when consumers are able to appreciate the relative strength of a product when compared with their rivals' products.

In Figure 21.6 we can see that as we move up from the previous market price, demand becomes relatively more inelastic as a result of an advertising campaign. **Merchandising** is another way of making products more attractive. For example, merchandising might be concerned with creating an attractive and appealing display of goods in a shop to gain the attention and interest of consumers. Because companies are able to compete to satisfy the wants and needs of consumers, they will produce a variety of similar but different products. Visit a sweet shop and count the hundreds of different types of chocolate bars and tubes of sweets on display – all meeting similar, but subtly different, tastes and requirements.

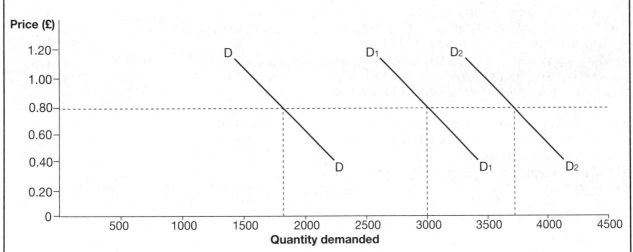

Figure 21.5 Shift in the position of a demand curve resulting from advertising

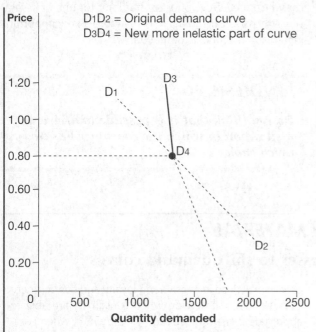

D1D2 = Original demand curve
D3D4 = New more inelastic part of curve

Figure 21.6   *Demand becomes more inelastic above the market price*

Competition also has the effect of acting as a spur to quality. If I am sold a poor quality good then I will switch to a better one. If a producer persists in supplying low-quality items, then they will quickly lose business as customers switch to rival producers. It only takes a small lapse in quality for people to choose not to buy a good. I used to buy my newspapers from a particular garage every day. Two days in a row the newspaper was dirty inside, where someone in the garage had spilled tea on it. I have never bought papers or petrol from that garage since. Recently my morning milk deliverer has left bottles on my doorstep late, so I am seriously thinking of changing to buying milk from supermarkets instead.

Some people argue that today we have gone over the top in providing customer choice. They argue that there is so much to choose from that it is impossible to make a rational choice.

Chapter summary

- Competition involves rivalry between two or more business organisations.
- Michael Porter suggests that the two principle means to being competitive are through low costs, or through differentiation.
- Organisations therefore have a choice of going for a mass market with low costs, a mass market with differentiation, a narrow market with low costs, or a narrow market with differentiation.
- It is suggested that there is a real danger of 'getting stuck in the middle'.
- Competition in the market place ranges through the spectrum from monopoly to intense competition.
- Just because there are only a few companies in the market this does not necessarily indicate lack of competition. Oligopoly situations can be intensely competitive.
- A competitive market is one in which there are a number of producers supplying goods which are considered to be highly similar, consumers are aware of prices being offered by various sellers, and there is ease of entry into the market.
- Even where there is little direct competition, indirect competition may be intense.
- A pure monopoly exists if there is only one seller in the market place. When a company can restrict competition it is in a position to raise prices, and perhaps to exploit consumers.
- Oligopoly involves competition between a few companies.
- Competing for market share is very important. By winning a lion's share of the market you can substantially reduce your costs relative to those of your rivals.
- Organisations also compete for customers, for product superiority, for sales, and through price and image.
- Price competition is one of the most important ingredients of competition, but forms of non-price competition are also important, for example, packaging, branding, image, free gifts, special offers, etc.

22 The economy

Earlier we identified the economy as providing a key part of the business environment in which organisations operate.

Anyone who wants to have an informed understanding of how businesses operate needs to understand the economy. Lack of this knowledge can lead to all sorts of problems for organisations and individuals, for example for:

- The business that borrowed a lot of money, at a high rate of interest at the height of an economic boom, soon went 'bust' when the boom evaporated.
- The trader that sold goods to a foreign importer on three months' credit who found that when asking for payment the money received was worth less than expected because of a fall in the value of sterling.
- The student who budgeted how much she was going to spend in a term, who was shocked to find that her expenditure was much higher than she planned because of 'inflation'.
- The trainee who had followed a training course to become a skilled engineer who found that there were no longer any jobs for engineers.

In all of the above cases more knowledge about how the economy operates would have helped.

The National Economy

In order to understand how the economy works it is helpful to draw up a simple model of the national economy. Of course, we should always remember that increasingly organisations operate in global rather than national markets. We can only begin to understand how the national economy works by simplifying it.

At the heart of this model we find:

- producers of goods and services, and
- consumers in households.

Producers will make goods and services, and employ the services of households in producing goods. Households are said to provide 'factor services'. For example, they might provide labour, for which they would be paid wages; they might provide land or buildings for which they would be paid rent; they might provide money capital for which they would be paid interest; or they might actually take a share in owning an enterprise for which they would be paid profits.

Households provide:

Factor service	Factor reward
Labour	Wages
Land	Rent
Capital	Interest
Enterprise	Profit

Once households have earned their factor rewards they will need to make a decision about what to do with the income they have earned. For many people the logical solution will be to spend their income on the millions of goods and services that are weekly produced by producers of goods and services.

We can therefore set out a simple economic model which shows the relationships we have described above (see Figure 22.1).

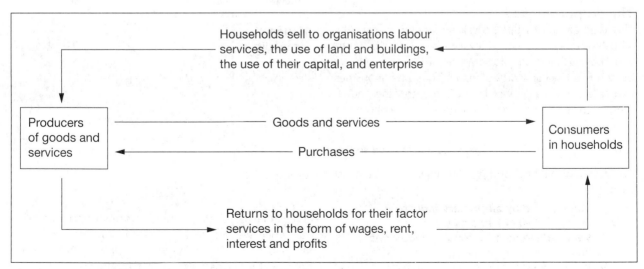

Figure 22.1   A simple model of the economy

The simple model that we have drawn below is sometimes described as the circular flow of income:

- Households earn income for helping to make goods and services.
- Households then spend this income by purchasing goods.
- The purchases provide revenue for producers.
- Producers are then able to make more goods and services.
- They hire the factor services of households to produce more.
- Households earn income for helping to make goods and services, etc.

The National Income

National Income is made up of the total flow of the goods and services produced by factors of production in a particular time period. When national income rises we talk about economic growth taking place in the system. This can lead to improved standards of living. Figures measuring national income can be used to assess living standards. They can also be broken down to show changes in the structure of the economy and to provide comparisons with other countries.

Measuring income generation

The national income accounts provide three methods of measuring income generation in a country.

The income approach

This involves counting up all the incomes received by citizens in a time period, for example:

> *Incomes from employment and self-employment*
> + *Interest*
> + *Business profits*
> + *Rents*

The output method

This method counts up the value of outputs made by industries in an economy. It involves summing the values added by each industry. For example, if the steel industry buys in £100 million worth of inputs from other industries and sells £200 million worth of outputs to other industries, then it will have added value to the economy of £100 million:

£200 m outputs – £100 m in inputs = £100 m value added.

In calculating national output, the following method is used:

> **Value added by all primary industries**
> (those involved in extracting raw materials)
> + **Value added by all secondary industries**
> (those involved in manufacturing goods)
> + **Value added by all tertiary industries**
> (those involved in providing services)

The expenditure method

This method measures all final expenditures on goods and services. It is important that only final expenditures are counted (to avoid what is called double-counting). If I buy a sandwich it is a final expenditure, likewise a litre of petrol. If a school buys chalk and exercise books those are final expenditures. However, if a business buys raw materials that is not a final expenditure, because the raw materials will go into making something else. These raw materials would not be counted under the final expenditure method (unless they are stockpiled for use in another year).

In a simple economic model we expect the three methods of calculating national income to produce the same result because when goods are produced, the factors of production that make the goods receive all the income from making goods in factor rewards. If they spend all the money they receive, it will then return to the producers of the output that households buy.

The relationship between output, income and expenditure

In an ideal world everyone who wanted a job would have one and people's incomes would steadily rise. With rising incomes people would be able to buy more goods. Because more goods would be demanded this would encourage employers to make more goods, and this would help to secure jobs and rising living standards.

We could illustrate rising output, incomes and expenditures as shown in Figure 22.2.

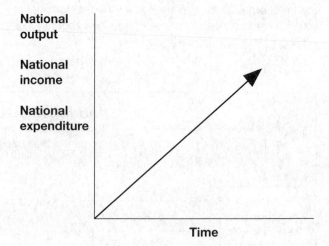

Figure 22.2

Unfortunately, when we study how things operate in the real world we find that this ideal picture does not exist. We find that periodically, and at fairly regular intervals, demand for goods falls, so that producers cut back on output, leading to a fall in incomes.

What happens in these periods of downturn in economic activity is that actual national output falls short of potential national output (see Figure 22.3).

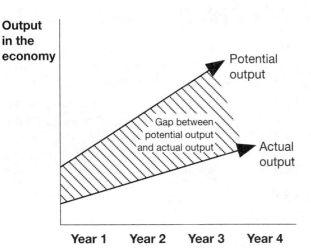

Figure 22.3

The trade cycle

The 20th century has seen regular cycles of booms and slumps in economic activity:

In a boom
- Output rises
- Firms take on more employees
- Wages and prices rise
- Prosperity rises
- Businesses boom

In a slump
- Output falls
- Firms lay off employees
- Wages and prices fall
- Prosperity falls
- Businesses do badly (some cease trading)

The trade cycle which is a feature of all industrialised and industrialising countries is made up of:

- A boom in which economic growth occurs at a steady rate.
- A recession in which economic activity starts to slow down.
- A slump in which economic growth may go into reverse.
- A recovery in which economic activity starts to pick up again.

The trade cycle is perhaps the most important economic

influence on business activity. When the 'good times roll' businesses generally do well. However, when the boom evaporates everyone (or nearly every one) 'feels the pinch'.

IT'S A FACT

That over the years there have been many different attempts to explain the causes of the trade cycle. One of the earliest theories was that they were related to the appearance of 'sun spots'.

What causes the trade cycle?

There are many different possible causes of the trade cycle. An important explanation relates to the general level of optimism that exists in a particular period. If business people are optimistic they will invest, often buying new plant and equipment. This generates new incomes as people who were previously unemployed are taken on to make the new goods. New incomes generate new expenditures which serve to feed a 'boom'.

If people are optimistic they will be prepared to take more risks. New inventions and innovations are likely to be tried out in the early part of a boom. Of course, as the boom continues it tends to use up all the best opportunities and inventions. Eventually, a point is arrived at where there arises a small downturn in economic activity. This tends to 'dent' people's confidence. Optimism may be replaced by a general feeling of 'pessimism'. Once a downturn sets in it will tend to feed on itself leading to recession and perhaps to an overall slump. Inventions and innovations will go on the 'back boiler' because they have become too risky.

The twin problems – unemployment and inflation

In any discussion about the economy it is not long before the two 'problems' unemployment and inflation are mentioned:

- Unemployment exists when productive resources are lying idle, for example, people that want to work can't find jobs, a piece of agricultural land that could be used for arable or dairy farming lies fallow without reason.
- Inflation occurs when there is a general rise in the level of prices.

Both of these 'problems' are closely associated with the trade cycle. In a period in which economic activity starts to rise then prices may also start to pick up, whereas in a recession of slump we may see increases in the level of unemployment.

Only the person that 'buries their head in the sand' would fail to realise the importance of unemployment and inflation for everyone. In a period of unemployment we have wasted resources which are not being used to produce the goods and services that we all want and need. And, of course, some unemployed people will become disaffected and alienated from society, perhaps turning to anti-social behaviour such as crime.

Inflation, or general increases in price levels, leads to a rising 'cost of living' for everyone.

Businesses are particularly affected by unemployment and inflation. Unemployment leads to a lack of demand in the economy, and hence a fall in demand for the goods and services of particular organisations. Inflation pushes up costs for most firms; this might force them in turn to push up their prices, making their goods less 'price competitive'.

Government and the economy

Throughout the 20th century, the government has played an important part in influencing and sometimes controlling economic activity in this country. Today, government influence works at a number of levels:

- At European Union wide level we are increasingly accountable to EU wide laws and regulations. For example, as we move beyond the millennium increasing importance is attached to countries abiding by the requirements of European Monetary Union, and European Union wide regulation of social and environmental policy. Each year the European Union sets a budget which involves raising revenues from Member States to spend on union wide expenditures.
- At national level the government plays a key role in establishing economic policy. In particular, it sets its annual budget and revenue plans in November. This sets out how government will spend its money in the year ahead (e.g. on education, health or roads), and how the money will be raised (e.g. from income tax or tax on wines and spirits).

- At local levels, local government bodies raise revenue through local taxes, and carry out their local expenditure programmes (e.g. for the maintenance of local roads, and other amenities).

Demand and supply management

Aggregate demand is the total level of demand in the whole economy. Aggregate demand is made up of:

- demand by consumers for goods and services – call this C
- demand by producers for goods that go into further production (e.g. machines and machine tools) – call this I, for investment demand
- government demand for goods and services (call this G).

IT'S A FACT

That in November 1996 the Chancellor's budget reduced the standard rate of income tax by 1p, and kept taxes on beer stable, while reducing taxes on spirits.

To many these moves were seen as being typical features of a pre-election budget. Traditionally, Chancellors reduce taxes when the government is trying to win popularity with the electorate. However, in 1997 the Conservatives lost the election by a 'landslide'.

Furthermore, we need to add the demand from foreigners for our goods and services (i.e. exports) – denoted by X – and subtract the demand (M) by our citizens for foreign goods and services (i.e. imports) because in this way money leaves the country. A useful measure of aggregate monetary demand is therefore:

$$\textit{Aggregate monetary demand} = \\ C + I + G + X - M$$

Figure 22.4 shows that this demand comes from many sources.

TASK 22.1

Types of aggregate demand

The following list includes items of consumer demand, investment demand, government demand, exports and imports. Classify each item as C, I, G, X or M.

a A car brought into this country from Japan by a car dealer.
b A sandwich bought from a coffee shop in Soho.
c Spending by the police on 'stingers' to slow cars down.
d Royalties paid to UK 'pop stars' by foreign record labels.
e The purchase by a factory of a new automated plant.
f Your most recent purchase of clothing.
g Expenditure by your school or college on textbooks.
h Your own expenditure on books.
i Purchases that you make when on holiday in France.
j The purchase by a company of spare parts for a photocopier.
k Insurance policies sold to foreigners by UK insurers.

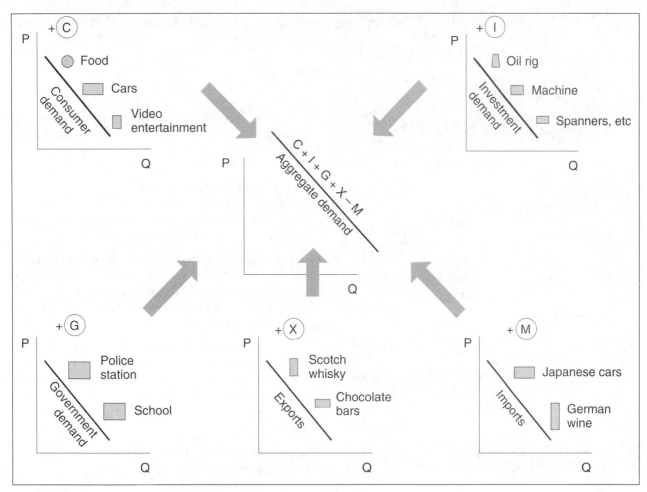

Figure 22.4   Sources of demand

The money that people spend in an economy will be received by the producers of goods and services. If we want to be absolutely accurate, however, in counting spending we should also account for indirect taxes and subsidies.

If you buy a packet of sandwiches in a bakery, the owner of the bakery will not be able to use all of this money in his or her business. Some of this revenue will be paid over to the government in VAT (valued added tax) and other indirect taxes. When measuring aggregate monetary demand, therefore, we should subtract indirect taxes. Furthermore, some sellers will receive more than the sales price of their goods, probably as a result of government subsidies. A subsidy should therefore be seen as an addition to consumer demand, provided by the government. A more comprehensive definition of aggregate money demand (AMD) is therefore:

$$AMD = C + I + G + X - M - indirect\ taxes + subsidies$$

Aggregate monetary demand goes into purchasing the goods produced in a country, i.e. the national output.

National output is another way of describing total supply (aggregate monetary supply).

When aggregate monetary demand (AMD) in the economy equals aggregate monetary supply (AMS), the economy is in temporary equilibrium (i.e. there is no reason why change in demand or supply should take place). If this state of equilibrium remains then prices will remain steady, and so too will the level of production (see Figure 22.5).

However, as we have already seen, in the real world economic forces are continually changing. Conditions of aggregate demand and aggregate supply frequently alter, and economies tend to go through a trade cycle.

EXAM TIP:

When we use the term investment in Business Studies we usually mean the purchase of an asset which goes into further production, for example, a tool, a machine or a motor vehicle that is used for business purposes.

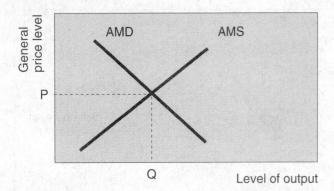

Figure 22.5   When AMD = AMS

Living with the economy

Our simple analysis of the marketplace should make it clear that businesses operate in a dynamic economy in which many changes are taking place. Organisations therefore need to be able to live with these changes. Particularly important changes that they have to live with are:

* changes in demand conditions
* changes in supply conditions
* changes in interest rates
* changes in taxes
* changes in exchange rates.

Changes in demand conditions

Every business has to cope with changes in demand conditions. If I produce fashion clothes, I will be all too aware that tastes are fickle and that demand for my product will be influenced by what the competition is offering, the available income of my customers, the seasons and of course the weather. However, on top of that I have to contend with the trade cycle. In a boom there will be an increase in demand for my clothes, just as there will be a boom in demand for new houses, meals out, travel, leisure and most other goods. In a slump I will need to be very careful about not overstretching my business and producing clothes that people feel are affordable in harder times.

Changes in supply conditions

Most business organisations have a fair amount of control over the conditions under which they supply goods and services. In this respect, their success or failure is in their own hands. However, businesses are all too painfully aware that there are many factors which are 'beyond their control'. For example, most businesses rely on inputs such as raw materials, and finished goods. If the cost of these inputs rises then the business will suffer. For example, if the price of potatoes or rice goes up this will have a significant impact on a restaurant's cost structure; if the price of paper or print goes up this will affect the cost structure of a publishing firm. In a similar way, if an industry is exposed to changes in technology, then a firm may find it necessary to invest in new technology in order to keep abreast of the market leaders in its industry. Failure to do so could lead to ruin – but the cost of change is often substantial.

Changes in interest rates

The interest rate can be seen as the price of borrowing money. Interest rates are a major cost for many business organisations.

If I borrow a small amount of money for a short period of time then the interest rate will be relatively low. If I borrow a large amount of money for a long period of time then the interest rate will be relatively high (because the lender is taking a bigger risk).

Business people borrow money because they need the cash in the short period, to enable them to provide goods and services at a profit. The borrower is working on the assumption that the profits they make with the borrowed money will outweigh the costs of borrowing.

However, life in the real economy can often be a painful business. For example, a small business owner might calculate that they could:

Now borrow	Pay interest in year 1	Pay interest in year 2	Pay back the original sum at the start of year 3
£12,000	£1200 (£100 per month)	£1200 (£100 per month)	Repayment from profits of £12,000

Everything looks rosy. In a short period of time the loan will be paid off.

Unfortunately, however, costs turn out to be higher than expected, and sales are less than expected. As a result the business finds it difficult to pay off the interest payments each month. At the start of the third year the debt including the original sum and unpaid interest has mounted up to, say, £18,000. This would mean that the firm is now having to pay £150 in interest per month. Instead of working for themselves the business is now working for 'the bank'.

And, of course a further problem is that interest rates do not stay at a constant figure. The government and lending institutions such as banks are able to change the interest rates they charge. In periods when prices are rising in the economy interest rates are also likely to rise – the government pushes interest rates up to try and discourage excess spending because it is inflationary. Business people who have borrowed large sums of money are likely to suffer from rising interest rates. Talk to any business person who will tell you how seriously a threat he or she regards high interest rates to be!

Changes in taxes

Changes in taxes also have an important impact on business activity. If the government raises taxes on particular businesses their costs rise; if the government lowers taxes on particular businesses their costs fall. Higher taxes reduce the profit potential of firms and industries.

Changes in exchange rates

The exchange rate is the rate at which one currency will exchange against other currencies. When your currency rises in value against other currencies this makes your goods more expensive when you export them.

It is important that your currency exchanges at a high enough rate to bring in proper revenues from selling goods overseas. However, if the value rises too much, foreigners will become reluctant to buy your products. If the value of your currency falls to much it will be easy to sell products abroad – but it may not be worth doing so if each product does not yield enough revenue.

International competitiveness is measured by comparing the relative prices of the goods from different countries when these are measured in a common currency. For example, at a constant exchange rate of dollars/sole (US and Peruvian currencies), Peruvian goods became 14 times as expensive in dollars in 1980 as they had been in 1970. Since American goods in dollars were only twice as expensive in 1980 as 1970, Peruvian competitiveness would have been reduced seven times.

The importance of exchange rates in the competitiveness equation cannot be overestimated. Business people often suffer from an ongoing fall in competitiveness caused by exchange rate changes either because the pound sterling is too strong or because it is too weak. The key is to secure just the right balance which makes our goods competition without being too cheap.

It is important that exchange rates remain stable over a period of time so that traders know what to expect when they exchange goods. In recent years, there has been a lot of emphasis on creating stable exchange rates within the European Union. The ideal is that at some stage in the (not too distant) future there will be a single currency for all Members States of the European Union. At the moment, it seems likely that this will be arrived at in a staged process with the UK lagging well behind countries like Germany, the Netherlands, Luxembourg and France.

CASE STUDY CASE STUDY CASE STUDY CASE STUDY CASE STUDY CASE

HIGHER TAXES ON ALCOPOPS, LOWER TAXES ON WHISKY

In the 1996 November budget, taxes on alcopops, the controversial fruit-flavoured alcoholic drinks, were hit with a 40 per cent tax increase designed to deter under-aged drinkers.

At the same time the Chancellor had good news for grown-up tipplers, cutting 26p off the duty on a bottle of spirits and freezing the level for beer and wine for the second year in a row.

Mr Clarke, who sipped malt whisky and water during his speech, also announced a Customs and Excise crackdown on

bootleggers illegally bringing in cheap drinks from Europe, where duties are still much lower.

The measures were aimed at helping the beleaguered British drinks industry cope with the flood of cheap alcohol arriving both illegally and legally from Europe.

1 Why do you think the Chancellor raised taxes on alcopops while lowering taxes on spirits and freezing taxes on beer and wine?
2 How might these changes have affected the producers of these products?

CASE STUDY CASE STUDY CASE STUDY CASE STUDY CASE STUDY CASE

EXTENSION MATERIAL

Keynesian Economics

Much of our understanding of the forces that govern the working of the UK economy is drawn from the writings of John Maynard Keynes. The key ingredients of his analysis are presented below.

An equilibrium state in the national economy is one in which there is balance, i.e. there is no tendency to change.

An equilibrium level of income for a country is one that does not change from one period to another. If all goods and services are bought and all incomes are spent, a country will be in equilibrium. A disturbance in the equilibrium position will occur if income, expenditure, or output increases or decreases for some reason.

In simple terms, we talk about a withdrawal from the circular flow when money is taken out; we talk about an injection when fresh money demand is put into the system.

We must now look at what happens when injections or leakages disturb the existing circular flow.

Keynes argued that demand and supply analysis can be applied when examining the whole economy. Before Keynes, economists had argued that the economy would sort itself out and that full employment was a natural state of affairs. These economists believed that if demand in the economy increased then producers would respond with increased supply; if demand fell then supply would fall. If supply fell workers would be laid off. These workers would seek new jobs. Because the

supply of labour would be increased, wages would fall. With cheaper labour employers would take on more people until full employment returned. The economists prior to Keynes were known as the classical economists. They believed that the economy, if left alone by government, was a self-righting system in which prices would restore full employment after a temporary period of recession.

Keynes however disagreed with the classical economists. He believed that full employment was not a natural state of affairs. He argued that the supply of goods in the economy and the demand for goods were determined by different groups of people. There was no guarantee that full employment would occur. The economy was therefore likely to go through periods of upturn and downturn. In some circumstances the economy could get stuck in a long period of depression, as in the 1930s.

Keynes showed that the level of output and employment of resources depended upon:

- total demand for goods and services in the economy (aggregate demand)
- total supply of goods and services in the economy (aggregate supply).

As with supply curves for individual products, the aggregate supply curve sloped upwards from the bottom left as the economy increases its output towards higher prices (see Figure 22.6).

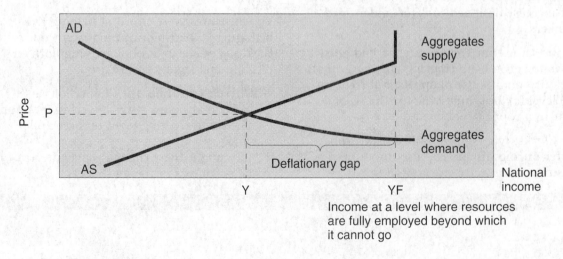

Figure 22.6   The deflationary gap

However, there will always be a limit to supply, and this is at the point where the factors of production are fully employed. At the full-employment point the supply curve will be vertical (given the current state of technology). The aggregate demand curve will slope downwards from the top left because as prices fall total demand for goods and services will increase.

The actual level of national income at any time will be established at the point where the aggregate demand curve intersects the aggregate supply curve. However, this will rarely be at full employment.

The difference between the equilibrium national income (where AD cuts AS) and the full employment point shows the extent to which it is possible to expand national income to increase the employment of resources. The difference between equilibrium national income and full employment is known as the **deflationary gap**.

However, it is also possible to have situations in which resources are already fully employed. Increases in aggregate demand cannot then be met by increases in output. Instead, increased demand will be met by increased prices.

In the figure below we can see that prices would be at P if aggregate demand were equal to aggregate supply at the full-employment point.

However, because there is excess demand in the economy, prices are pushed up to P1. We call this excess demand the **inflationary gap**.

If demand decreased we might fall back to the full-employment point with no inflation. If it decreased still further, then unemployment would occur and possible prices would fall as well.

Keynesian economists suggest that, by manipulating shifts in the aggregate demand curve, it is possible to change national income and price levels and work towards the full employment of resources.

Aggregate demand can be shifted upwards to the right by injecting fresh demand into the economy, or downwards to the left by withdrawing demand from the economy.

The government therefore has a key role to play:

- By encouraging injections of demand into the economy in a period of unemployment (or by reducing withdrawals).
- By encouraging the reduction of injections of demand into the economy in a period of inflation (or by increasing withdrawals).

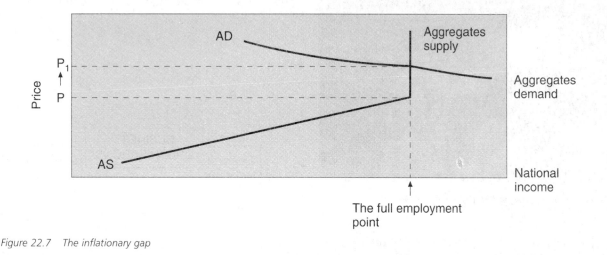

Figure 22.7   The inflationary gap

Chapter summary

- Anyone who wants to have an informed understanding of how business operates must have a good grasp of how the economy operates, and how it affects business activity.
- At the heart of the national economy we have a series of relationships between firms and households. Firms produce output which they sell to households. Household provide factor services to firms for which they receive rewards in the form of wages, interest, dividends and rent.
- National income can be measured by adding all incomes, all expenditures, or the value of all outputs.

- If national output falls below potential output we have a waste of resources in the economy.
- The real world economy is characterised by a series of booms, recessions, slumps and recoveries.
- Two of the major problems associated with the trade cycle are unemployment and inflation. Both of these have a direct impact on business people.
- The government can and should play a major part in trying to smooth out the difficulties caused by the trade cycle.
- One way the government can try and do this is by managing demand and supply in the economy.
- Aggregate demand consists of C + I + G + X − M.

- The government needs to encourage businesses and households to sustain enough aggregate demand in the economy to secure high levels of employment, low inflation rates, and a steady rate of growth.
- Businesses are directly affected by changes in the wider economy, particularly in relation to changes in:

  - demand conditions
  - supply conditions
  - interest rates
  - taxes
  - exchange rates.

23 Economic systems

McDonald's in Moscow: reflecting a change in an economic system

We can look at the effect of the economy on organisations at a number of levels. Organisations may be as directly affected by local changes as by national or international ones. For example, the closure of the collieries at Grimethorpe in South Yorkshire in the early 1990s hit local people harder than any effects of a world recession.

Macro-economics is the study of large-scale economic changes that tend to affect the whole of the nation's economy. However, we should always remember that 'macro' trends affect different groups and individuals in different ways.

The national economy can be viewed as a systems model (see Figure 23.1). Organisations use inputs such as labour and machinery to create goods and services. If the

demand for goods is higher than the stock available, then organisation will employ more inputs to increase production. Prices may start to rise (because of relative scarcity) and unemployment may start to fall (more jobs). On the other hand, if supply is greater than demand, there will be unsold stock and companies may begin to discard workers, to invest less in new machinery and to reduce prices. This is a **simple** model of the economy.

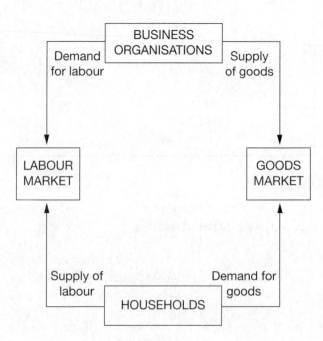

Figure 23.1   A simple systems model of a national economy

A more complex model of the economy

The simple model of the economy outlined above shows that it is made up of two basic groups: business organisations and households. Households supply labour and other factors of production to organisations (e.g. funds for investment). In return, households receive incomes for their services, which they then spend on the outputs produced by businesses. If the businesses supply products that households wish to purchase, this system works very well. Indeed, in a market economy led by market-conscious business units, firms supply goods and services to the market. They employ labour and other factors. They also purchase capital items (e.g. machinery, raw materials and partly finished goods) in the marketplace. Although some goods will be temporarily unsold, new products will be developed to replace those that are outmoded.

In the real world, economies are more complex. We need to add governments and international transactions to our model. The government buys and sells good; for example it buys armaments and health care in the marketplace and it sell products and services such as the outputs of the nationalised industries. The government is the major purchaser of goods in the UK.

Trading between nations is also significant. Finished goods, partly finished goods, raw materials and foodstuffs are imported and exported. The service sector (e.g. financial services) also accounts for a considerable volume of trade.

We therefore need a more complex diagram to represent government activities and international trade. This is shown in Figure 23.2.

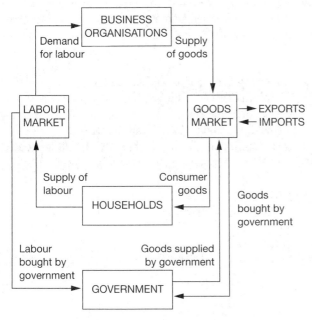

Figure 23.2   Labour and goods market in an open economy with government

Types of economic system

All societies must develop a system for dealing with three interrelated problems:

- What will be produced?
- How will it be produced?
- For whom will it be produced?

We can illustrate the wide differences in possible systems by looking at two imaginary island communities which are dependent on fishing and farming.

We shall call these two communities Sealand and Skyland. In Sealand all decisions are made by a small group of chieftains. The chieftains decide who will do the fishing and who will do the farming. They decide how many hours are to be put into each activity and how the necessary equipment will be made (e.g. the fishing boats, agricultural implements). They have also decided that everyone will receive an equal share of the produce – except for the chieftains, who will have a double portion of everything.

In Skyland there is no organising group. Individuals are left to their own devices. They decide individually what to make and they trade or store their surpluses. They decide how to produce their equipment, and how long to spend at particular activities. They consume the bulk of their own produce, except for what they can exchange.

TASK 23.1

1   Make a list of eight strengths and eight weaknesses of each of the economic systems described.
2   Devise a third system which you would regard as preferable to those of Sealand and Skyland. In what ways do you think that your system is preferable? Why might other people disagree with you? What would be the reasoning behind these objections?

In the past, the basic economic problems were solved by custom and tradition; for example, the way crops were grown and shared out was decided by folk tradition. In many parts of the world traditional economies are giving way to three major systems.

- the planned system
- the free-market system
- the mixed system.

Within these three basic models, there will be a wide range of variations and differences.

Planned systems

Planning involves some form of official co-ordination of activities. This can take place at either a local or a centralised level. Planning authorities will be responsible in some way for the creation of targets, systems, and procedures. The process of organised planning is most commonly associated with countries in the former Communist Bloc.

It is worth examining some of the common features associated with planned economies. However, it must be stressed that in recent years many communist countries have experienced substantial phases of economic reform such as *perestroika* in Russia. Such changes have involved a relaxation of price controls and of production control from the centre and a greater freedom to set up private enterprise.

In the customary division of the world into three parts – the West, the Communist bloc and the Third World – countries with planned economic systems (including Kampuchea, North Korea, Cuba and China) represent a large proportion of the world's population and industrial output. It is interesting to note that in recent times increasingly large parts of the Chinese economy have been liberalised. However, central authorities still play a major role. We should not underestimate the importance of the Chinese economy which is expected to take over early in the next century as the world's major economic super-power.

Although there are wide differences in the economic organisation of central planning economies and their respective stages of development, there are also a number of important similarities:

- The means of production are publicly owned. This takes the form of state, collective or co-operative ownership. However, decisions about their use can be made in a variety of ways ranging from collective decision making to decision making by a small committee of people.
- Planning is centralised and strategies to increase the quantity and/or quality of overall output are laid down by the planning authority.
- There is a market for consumer goods (although consumers will not necessarily have the freedom to spend money in the way they would wish) and a market for labour. Wages are paid, and a large proportion of consumer goods are exchanged in the market, via transactions using some form of money.
- Prices for all goods sold by the state are decided by planning authorities. They are not able to change spontaneously.
- Nearly all decisions relating to capital formation will be made and controlled by planning authorities. Capital formation is the production of those goods and equip-

ment that go into further production such as that of factory machinery.

The key feature of a planned, or **command**, economy is that it is planning committees that decide what will be produced, how it will be produced and how products will be distributed. Smaller groups, such as factories and other business units, submit their plans to a local committee, decide which resources will be made available to each local area, which in turn will allocate resources to each factory, farm or other productive unit.

Productive units are often set production targets, and are then given a set quantity of resources and a time constraint to meet set targets.

Advantages of a planned economy
- Effective long-term strategies can be developed taking into account the needs of the total system.
- Planning can be carried out according to the collective needs and wants of each of the individual parts of a system.
- Duplication of resources can be eliminated.
- Resources and products can be shared out more equitably according to the dominant value system prevailing in that society.
- Planning decisions can be made in a consistent manner.
- The system can be shaped in such a way as to reflect the social and political wishes of a group of people.

Disadvantages of a planned economy
- Heavy-handed planning and control may stifle individual enterprise.
- The process of planning itself uses up scarce resources for administration and supervision.
- The absence of the profit motive removes the spur to individual effort and enterprise. It is argued by some that people are more inclined to work harder and to make personal sacrifices if they can profit from doing so.
- The process of communication between consumers and producers can become distorted so that the goods that are produced fall far short of consumer requirements. If planning decisions are made well in advance of consumption decisions, then by the time goods appear in the marketplace tastes and fashions may have changed.
- Where price controls are established unofficial black markets may develop, leading to bribery and corruption.

The end of the Berlin Wall, 1989

CASE STUDY CASE STUDY CASE STUDY CASE STUDY CASE STUDY CASE

CHANGES IN ECONOMIC SYSTEMS

From the period 1945 until the end of the 1980s it looked as if the world economic system would continue to be divided between two sets of economic ideologies and principles – state planning and the market economies. In the socialist economies, decisions were made by central planners working to models of how resources should be utilised in the economy. At one stage, for example, planners in the Soviet Union had created a huge model of their system which they housed in an aircraft hangar. They used markers to represent flows of goods between industries. It was not surprising that while the model was effective in the confines of the hangar, it led to glaring inefficiencies in the real world. The Third World, or the Developing Countries as they were called at the time, was a battleground between the two ideologies.

Then, suddenly at the end of the 1980s, the whole house of cards came tumbling down, first with *perestroika* bringing an end to the Soviet Union and the Cold War, and other movements such as Solidarity in Poland. The re-unification of Germany saw an end to the old Cold War frontier between the Western and Eastern powers.

At first, there was a rush by countries like the Czech Republic, Hungary, East Germany, Poland, and so on to embrace market systems. However, these solutions have not always been successful, and it was not surprising that a few years later countries like Poland turned back partially towards the protection of Socialism. The free market solution is not an easy solution for economies which have been struggling to use their resources effectively for a number of years.

1 What do you see as being the five major points of difference between a centrally planned economy and a free market one. Set your answer out in the form of a table.
2 Why do you think that at the end of the 1980s citizens of Eastern European countries were so keen to embrace the market system?
3 Why do you think that accommodating to the free market was not an easy transition?
4 Why do you think that some countries stepped back towards socialism?

CASE STUDY CASE STUDY CASE STUDY CASE STUDY CASE STUDY CASE

The free-market system

In a free market the decisions about what, how and for whom are made by consumers and producers; the government does not intervene. Consumers in effect 'vote' for a certain pattern of output by the way in which they distribute their spending between the alternatives on offer. How much they are prepared to pay is thus a reflection of the strength of consumer preferences. (Some people think that it does not always work quite like this; they think that producers often decide what they would like to make and then persuade consumers to follow their wishes through advertising.) If a product sells well, firms will be inclined to produce it. The prices at which producers offer their goods for sale will depend on their production costs. The prices charged will thus reflect the relative scarcity of the various resources needed in order to produce that good for the market. If a product sells well, firms will be inclined to produce it, but if no one buys the product firms will stop making it, since under the market system firms seek to make profits from all the goods they sell. Producers are thus forced to pay attention to the wishes of consumers in order to survive.

The interests of consumers and producers conflict. Consumers want to pay low prices while producers would like to charge higher prices. The market serves to strike a balance, with profits settling at just those levels that match the strength of consumer preferences with the scarcity of resources. When prices change this acts as a signal for the pattern of production and consumption to alter. For example, when a new fashion style becomes popular, the producers are able to charge a higher price and to put more resources into producing more such garments, while for clothes that are no longer fashionable manufacturers may be forced to lower their price, put less resources into their production and eventually stop making them altogether.

Advantages of the free-market system

- Production reflects the wishes of the consumer.
- The system is flexible in the way it can respond to different conditions of demand and supply.
- Individuals have greater freedom to make their own demand and supply decisions.
- Scarce resources do not have to be wasted on administering and running (planning) the system.
- It is argued that the free market will lead to larger, better quality outputs at lower unit costs.

These arguments are succinct but extremely powerful. Their power is reflected in the way in which most economies in the world have moved towards freer market systems in recent years.

Disadvantages of the free-market system

- The free market system does not guarantee everyone what many would regard to be the minimum acceptable standard of living in a healthy society. The price mechanism, when it is freely operating, fails to provide a 'safety net' for citizens less able to compete, including the sick and elderly.
- There are some goods which by their very nature include elements of what is known as 'non-excludability'. For example, all ships using a particular seaway benefit from its lighthouse; all citizens could be seen to benefit from a national system of defence. If we take the example of bridges, it is immediately apparent why the price system could not always be effective as a means of provision. If people were made to pay to go over all bridges the traffic system would rapidly snarl up. (It is worth bearing in mind however that when new roads were being built and road traffic was less common many toll bridges were used in this country.)
- The free market can lead to great inequalities. Those with the means to purchase large quantities of goods can use their money to ensure that the goods and services they want are produced (hence taking away resources from other products). One way of looking at the opportunity cost to society of producing luxury goods (e.g. speedboats, expensive clothes) is to consider the inability of society to meet the needs of the less fortunate.
- Resources may not be able to move as freely as a pure market theory would suggest. Regarding human resources (labour), people may be resistant to moving to new areas and away from their established roots; they may be reluctant to learn new skills which offer high pay packets if they feel that the job does not meet their needs for such factors as self-respect, pride in the job or the ability to work at one's own pace.
- Many buying decisions are made by consumers with an imperfect knowledge of the market. Producers frequently change the details of their products including price, shape, size and packaging. This makes it very difficult for consumers to weigh up alternative purchases, and many buying decisions may be based on impressions rather than hard evidence. For example, a recent survey conducted by the authors reveals that, out of a sample of 400 shoppers, fewer than 10 per cent of them could remember the prices of five randomly-selected, commonly-used items in their shopping basket.
- In a free market, many resources can be wasted through the high failure rate of new businesses. A lot of time and money is spent on setting up a new business. When it closes down after a few months, many of its resources may end up as little more than scrap.

The mixed economy

In the real world, no economy relies exclusively on the free market, nor can we find examples of purely planned economies. A mixed economy combines elements of both the free market and planned systems; some decisions are made solely through the private sector while others are made by the government.

The UK is a good example of a mixed economy. Some parts of industry are owned and operated by the government but large chunks of the business world remain in private hands. The public sector is that part of the economy that is government-owned; the private sector is that part of the economy that is owned by private citizens.

Throughout much of the 20th century, government spending in the UK has made up a significant percentage of all spending (see Figure 23.3).

During the 1980s and up until 1997, steps were taken by the Conservative government to reduce the relative size of government spending. A major aim of the Conservative government since coming into office in May 1979 was the restoration of market forces throughout the economy.

With the return of a Labour government in 1997, the emphasis has moved towards the creation of a social market in which the government plays an important role in helping the market to work more efficiently, making sure that large organisations do not take advantage of less powerful individual organisations, and ensuring a measure of social justice.

In a mixed economy, one of the central issues of debate will be about the nature of the mix between the private and public sectors.

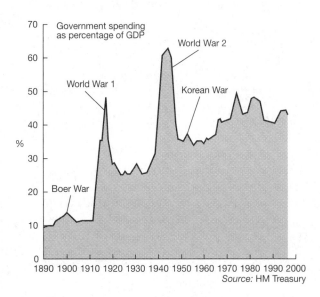

Figure 23.3   Changes in government spending as a percentage of national expenditure. (Source: HM Treasury) GDP = gross domestic product (the total value of a nation's output in a given time period)

Chapter summary

- Macro-economics is the study of large-scale economic changes that affect the whole of the nation's economy.
- The economy can be viewed as a system in which national output represents the supply of goods and national expenditure represents demand.
- In the real world, this model is more complex because it will also include, for example, international trade and the actions of governments.
- Different economies are set up in different ways to decide what to produce, how to produce, and how goods and incomes will be distributed between people in the economic system.
- The three main types of models are the planned economy, the free market economy and the mixed economy.
- The planned system involves some form of official co-ordination of activities. Planning authorities create targets, systems and procedures. This type of system is associated with socialism and was the model adopted by Eastern bloc countries, China,

Vietnam and many other countries in the world between 1945 and the late 1980s.
- Planned economies make it possible to make long-term decisions, and to make sure that everyone has employment, and receives a share of goods produced.
- However, heavy handed planning can stifle individual enterprise and lead to the waste of resources.
- In a free market system, decisions are made by consumers and suppliers interactions through the price system.
- Production in free markets reflects the wishes of consumers.
- However, the free market does not guarantee everyone a minimum acceptable standard of living.
- The mixed economy combines elements of these two systems. The government is able to facilitate the running of the market.

4 Marketing

INTRODUCTION

It is not so long ago that few people understood what was really meant by marketing. In fact, as you read through the first chapter in this unit you will learn that the marketing concept has largely evolved over the last 50 years through three distinct phases. Marketing today reflects a key approach to doing business. It reflects the importance of the customer as well as an acceptance of a complex business environment. It also is a dynamic area; one in which changing consumer needs and wants influence an organisation's strategies and plans.

Today, more and more organisations emphasise the marketing function. General Electric is often regarded as one of the first organisations to have recognised the importance of marketing. The General Electric view that marketing is not something that you 'bolt-on' to an organisation's activities, rather it is a key part of all activities – from product innovation and development, through to manufacture and delivery, and even to after-sales service. In fact, all decisions that an organisation makes should be based upon consumer requirements.

As you work through this unit you will learn to understand the importance of the marketing process. In Chapter 24 you will learn about the development of the marketing concept, find out what marketing is and then you can appreciate the complexity of the process and begin to think about what would be considered to be good marketing. In Chapter 24 we provide some extension material which is designed to help you to understand degrees of marketing orientation. Perceptions of good marketing are likely to change again in years to come as organisations develop different and winning strategies focused upon the changing requirements of their customers.

In Chapter 25 we look at many of the influences upon marketing decisions. In doing so we look at an organisation's external environment with the use of PEST analysis to analyse this environment. The chapter then proceeds to look at the differences between consumer markets and organisational markets as well as the distinctions between the different kinds of competition. The bulk of Chapter 25 centres upon the behaviour of consumers in consumer markets and organisations in their markets. This is a key area in marketing as it provides the basis for further research.

Chapter 26 is a key chapter which looks at the processes involved with market research. It identifies distinctions between different kinds of research and then, in some detail, looks at the nature of internal, external and primary information. As you read through this chapter it is important that you understand that market research helps to reduce the risks associated with decision making.

Up until this point, all of the marketing chapters refer to understanding the marketing process and the preparation for something to happen. It is marketing planning and strategy that makes the process work. Chapter 27 attempts to show how marketing operates as part of a business strategy. It introduces the concept of the marketing mix as well as the complexities of segmentation.

The unit concludes with Chapter 28 and a brief analysis of the operation of the marketing mix. The workings of the mix can be appreciated by looking at the product life-cycle. In this chapter there is some interesting extension material on alternative life-cycles. Finally, the chapter concludes with a description of consumer protection legislation.

24 Marketing: meeting customer needs

Business analysts frequently think about issues that influence the success of an organisation. Its management, innovation and the setting and achieving of performance standards are frequently cited as being of importance. At the same time, however, authors of such studies tend to agree that good marketing is an equally important factor in influencing business success.

So, what is marketing? If you go out into any street and ask a number of people what marketing is, they will probably come up with a variety of answers which might include selling, advertising, branding or researching. Yes, these are all right, and marketing does concern itself with these activities, but as a process it goes further. Marketing involves everything that an organisation has to make happen if customers are to be satisfied with its products. For this to be done effectively and successfully, an organisation has, therefore, to discover and assess customer needs.

The Chartered Institute of Marketing uses the following definition:

> *Marketing is the management process responsible for identifying, anticipating and satisfying consumer requirements profitably.*

The key feature of this definition is that it places the consumer at the centre of an organisation's activities.

> *Identifying consumer requirements*
> +
> *Anticipating consumer requirements*
> +
> *Satisfying consumer requirements*
> =
> *PROFITABILITY*

- **Identifying** – This will involve answering questions such as 'How do we find out what the consumer's requirements are'? and 'How do we keep in touch with their thoughts, feelings and perceptions of our good or service'?
- **Anticipating** – Consumer requirements change all the time. For example, as people become richer they may seek a greater variety of goods and services. Anticipating involves looking to the future as well as the present. What will be the Next Best Thing that consumers will require tomorrow?

BARBIE AND ACTION MAN: THE BATTLEFIELD FOR TOYS

In a toy market worth £1.6 billion a year, rivalry is intense. Hasbro's biggest UK seller is Action Man. Thirty years old in 1996, Action Man raked in around £45 million in 1996. Sales of the figure have doubled every year since 1992 when he was brought back to life in the toy battlefield after an eight year absence. Hasbro imported its GI Joe design from America and modified it for the UK market. The strategy worked well. Recently up to 5,000 Action Man devotees attended a convention at Wembley.

Hasbro's Action Man pales into insignificance next to Mattel's Barbie. Two Barbies are sold every second somewhere in the world. West End Barbie was a top-seller in the Christmas of 1996, outselling Sindy by 17 to one at Hamley's in Regent Street. Only Action Man's Street Car Racer rivalled her charms.

Average spending per head on toys at Christmas is estimated to be £70 for girls and £80 for boys. With many children wanting videos and computer games, toy companies fight hard for their slice of this budget. Increasingly, companies realise that it is not just the toy business that they are in but the toy entertainment business. Despite the stock shortages, toys or complementary products like Buzz Lightyear can be hugely successful. Companies like Mattel and Hasbro spend millions a year promoting their wares around the world, often pursuing product promotions of links with other companies and businesses.

While the show goes on the toy industry works hard to predict what items will do well for the forthcoming year. Though Action Man and Barbie were both ranked joint first by The British Association of Toy Retailers in 96, what will happen next year and how will good marketing help the leading players to develop other winners?

1 Both Action Man and Barbie have been hugely successful products. Why have they both been so successful?
2 Buzz Lightyear became a toy phenomenon in 1996. Shortages in shops soon developed. How difficult is it for toy manufacturers to anticipate the changing tastes of their customers?
3 Action Man has upset the leanings of anti-violence protesters. What ethical issues are involved in supplying toys?

CASE STUDY CASE STUDY CASE STUDY CASE STUDY CASE STUDY CASE

- **Satisfying** – If you do not satisfy consumers they will look to alternatives. Consumers want their requirements to be met. They will seek particular benefits. They will want the right goods or services, available at the right price, at the right time and in the right place.
- **Profitability** – The word 'profitability' is used simply to reflect that marketing is all about having a purpose which involves meeting organisational objectives. Whereas in the private sector profitability may be an overriding business objective, for public sector organisations this may not be the case. Profitability, therefore, for the purpose of this definition is best interpreted as achieving a series of business objectives. For an organisation to achieve these objectives it must find out in good time what its customers want to buy and then satisfy these requirements.

The process of planning

The American Marketing Association (AMA) identifies the importance of planning in the marketing process. It defines marketing as:

the process of planning and executing the conception, pricing, promotion, and distribu-
tion of ideas, goods and services to create exchanges that satisfy individual and organisational goals.

It is important that we appreciate that marketing is a process of planning. Every organisation needs to have clear **goals** and the major route to achieving organisational goals will depend on **strategy**. It is, therefore, important to be clear about the difference between strategy and **tactics**.

These terms originate from military use. Military strategy before and during a battle is the general policy overview of how to defeat the enemy. Developing a **strategy** involves establishing clear aims and objectives around which the framework for a policy for the whole organisation is created. Having developed a strategy, an organisation can then work out its day-to-day tools and **tactics** to meet objectives.

Marketing can thus be viewed as the process of developing and implementing a strategy to plan and co-ordinate ways of identifying, anticipating and satisfying consumer demands, in such a way as to make profits or satisfy a range of other marketing objectives. It is this strategic planning process that lies at the heart of marketing.

IT'S A FACT

That scary findings from a recent report by the research specialists DMS, reveal that the average company marketing director lasts less time in his or her job than the average football manager!

So, do companies believe that marketing is the key element in their strategy? In a recent Annual Report IBM's chairman and chief executive, Louis V. Gerstner Jr., stated that:

'The fact is, no company is going to succeed without a clear set of tough-minded strategies grounded in a clear understanding of what's happening in the marketplace. Some call it a mission. Some call it vision. I call it strategy. And strategy is particularly important for IBM because our industry is going through a period of fundamental change at breakneck speed. So are our customers.'

IT'S A FACT

That according to a survey recently published by the Economist Intelligence Unit called *Developing Leadership for the 21st Century*, marketing has overtaken finance as the fastest route up the corporate ladder to the top jobs. Organisations are increasingly looking to marketing experts to both protect and develop their market share. Of the 160 senior executives interviewed, some 37 per cent named marketing as the experience of choice, 30 per cent tipped international exposure and only 14 per cent tipped finance as the best qualification for future chief executives. Looking ahead at the next ten years, respondents expect customer satisfaction to replace profitability as the most important measure of a chief executive's success.

This statement emphasises the link between satisfying the needs of customers and making plans and decisions for the organisation. It is therefore essential to match the production and development of goods and services with the identification and anticipation of customer desires. The ability to meet customer needs and requirements may be identified in almost all areas of organisational activity from the original idea, through to design, including operational activities as well as in providing the product, through to the sale and exchange right up to the post-sale support.

The evolution of the marketing concept

The satisfaction of customer needs has not always spearheaded organisational strategies. In fact it is possible to map the development of marketing orientation into three distinct phases:

* production orientation
* sales orientation
* marketing orientation.

Production orientation

Where goods are scarce and in markets where very little competition exists, organisations do not really have to pay close attention to customer needs. Production orientation was based upon post-industrial revolution, massive changes in technology and strong consumer demand. At this time, emphasis was upon scientific management and structured work based on output. In terms of customer satisfaction, this whole era can best be understood by the statement made by Henry Ford that 'customers can have any colour they want as long as it is black'.

For many organisations this commitment towards production orientation lasted too long. The classic example comes from the motorcycle industry. The heavy, slow-revving, large-capacity machines with the names of BSA, Triumph, Ariel and Norton predominated. Imports from Italy, particularly from Ducatti, were hardly given a glance

'It's your job to listen to what your customers are saying!'

by British manufacturers. They did not make them so customer could not have them! Today the demise of much of that industry is history. Motorcycles are now associated with names such as Kawasaki, Honda and Suzuki. If the British manufacturers had listened to the marketing missionaries, the position might have been very different today.

Production orientation predominated in the UK in the 1930s and 40s when goods were in short supply. Lack of competition simply created a **sellers' market**. An important feature of production orientation was **monopoly power**. Where monopolies exist there is little need to improve products.

Sales orientation

After the Second World War the beginnings of the 'age of the consumer' was in its infancy. During the 1950s incomes began to rise faster than the cost of basic necessities of life and so standards of living began to rise. In the face of these changes organisations became sales orientated. Sales orientation led to more spending on advertising, selling and other promotional elements rather than upon satisfying customer needs. Businesses thought that by increasing sales profitability would follow. Sales orientation increased competitiveness but rarely helped to improve customer satisfaction. According to one expert, 'Selling focuses on the needs of the seller; marketing on the needs of the buyer.'

Marketing orientation

During the 1970s, marketing came to be recognised as an essential function within a successful organisation. However, even at that time, it usually took place within a department and only had a tactical responsibility. Increasing competition and developing consumer awareness during the 1980s and 1990s led marketing to be viewed as a strategic discipline which puts the customer at the centre of an organisation's activities.

The great benefit of marketing is that the needs of the customer are taken into account ahead of the production process. This approach has three major benefits:

- It identifies the difference between customer needs and the ability to satisfy such needs.
- It uses marketing to co-ordinate, organise and link production decisions with market needs and requirements.

- It places an onus on businesses to meet customer needs successfully if they wish to remain competitive.

Marketing is now well accepted in most well-run businesses as a strategic discipline that cares for the health of the organisation. Though profit today may be important, in the longer term it is important for organisations to develop their market shares and improve their brands in the search for brand leadership.

Marketing services

Marketing services are the tools used by the marketing department. The marketing department will set out to identify the most appropriate services to use such as public relations, trade and consumer promotions, point-of-sale materials, editorial, publicity and sales literature.

Any communication with consumers also comes under the responsibility of the marketing function. The traditional areas of advertising and market research are clearly marketing services. In addition, marketing services may include the production of statements, invoices and final demands, because the perception of the organisation by customers is too important to be neglected in any way. These services all constitute the tactical side of marketing.

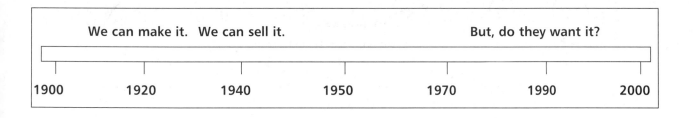

A cycle of marketing activities

The implementation of marketing policy can be viewed as an ongoing cyclical process.

- **Reconnaissance** involves carrying out market and product research to find out what customers want, how well the products are performing, and the strengths and weaknesses of competitors. This research should enable an organisation to make forecasts and predictions of likely future trends.
- **Strategy** involves deciding on objectives and priorities for an organisation as well as laying down clear plans for marketing activities (e.g. what range of products will be made, their prices, and how they will be delivered to customers).
- **Operations** involve tactics. This involves putting a strategy into practice. For example, organising advertising and selling campaigns, getting the goods to the right place, etc.
- **Control** involves checking on the effectiveness of the marketing plan in operation. For example, checking on the volume of sales made, measuring the effectiveness of an advertising campaign, gaining feedback from customers and analysing the profitability of operations. Once again, this feeds back into reconnaissance. If sales are falling, why is this so? Why has an advert been so effective? The information that stems from control activities should feed back into fresh research.

Good marketing

Very few organisations operate in a static situation. In fact, today, for many goods and services, we live in a global marketplace in which technology, purchasing power, tastes and many other factors are all changing at the same time. In adapting to these changes marketing is a key factor. Good marketing involves:

- looking outwards in order to respond to changes in markets, business conditions and competition
- looking inwards in order to develop the organisation so that it can meet all of those consumer needs which have been identified by the marketing process.

In other words, marketing ensures a good fit between the external environment in which the organisation operates and the resources of the organisation.

At the heart of good marketing is the process of planning. It enables an organisation to plan for the present and for the future and to learn from the past. Within the context of marketing the three main objectives of planning are:

- to assess how well the organisation is doing in the various markets in which it operates
- to identify the strengths and weaknesses of the organisation in each of these markets
- to establish goals and objectives, so that resources can be used in an appropriate way.

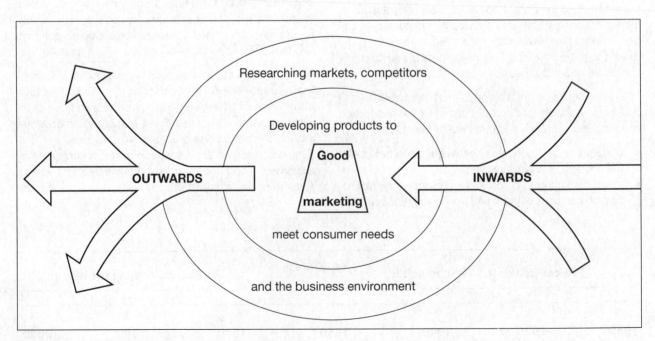

Figure 24.1   Good marketing

EXTENSION MATERIAL

Degrees of marketing orientation

Marketing is about being close to customers. But how close can an organisation get to its customers and what strategies can it use to serve this need in order to become market orientated? A number of approaches have been used to sharpen the focus upon the consumer. These include sur/petition, customer relationships, sensitivity to consumer issues and mass customisation.

Sur/petition

Edward de Bono used the term 'sur/petition' to signify a situation in which business organisations concentrate upon providing a range of integrated values for consumers. He argued that there have been three phases of business:

- **Phase 1** – Product driven, in which a firm simply provided a good or service.
- **Phase 2** Competition, in which the firm sought to beat rivals.
- **Phase 3** – Sur/petition based on integrated values. In this phase business creatively seeks to provide a range of integrated goods or services for consumers. For example, when someone purchases a car, he or she will need to drive the car, service the car, park the car and insure the car. De Bono talks about creating value monopolies resulting from valufacture, which is the creation and formation of values. Organisations that take sur/petition to heart will create value monopolies focused on the consumer that will be successful because they simply are the best.

Customer relationships

Don Peppers and Martha Rogers, in their book *The One Future: Building One Customer at a Time*, urge businesses to form impregnable relationships with individual customers. They argue that event the mass marketer can strike up these relationships. This involves gathering as much information as possible about individual customers and then developing the organisation to meet their individual needs. They refer to this as **customer segmentation**. Peppers and Rogers illustrate this point by reference to gift order catalogues:

- the customer may order gifts for friends and relatives many months in advance
- the company would then schedule delivery of the gift on the right day

- the customer would be charged for each gift two days before delivery
- the customer would receive a reminder postcard ten days before each gift is sent
- when the annual catalogue is sent out the customer would receive a reminder form of last year's gifts and addresses.

The main selling point would be the high quality relationship with the customer.

Sensitivity to consumer issues

Freedom of speech, reducing inequalities, improved educational standards and vastly improved communications in a rapidly-changing and more technological world have increased consumer awareness of issues and expectations. Increasingly, modern organisations are trying to balance internal and external expectations. Internally, they have to make profits for shareholders and monitor how the organisation is run. Externally, they have to contend with having to sell products in the face of competition, respond to regulatory influences exerted on them by governments and also respond to other interdependent consumer influences. Failure to listen to organised pressure groups may lead to the worst possible outcome – a consumer boycott.

Mass customisation

This is probably the ultimate in marketing orientation. It involves meeting the needs of each customer personally. Ron Westbrook and Peter Williamson, writing in the *European Management Journal*, identified this as the latest stage of an industrial revolution emerging from Japan. This involves finding out what customers need and coupling it with highly responsive and flexible production methods. They quote an example of the Melbo company which makes and supplies customised suits within just three days.

And so, what of marketing orientation in the future? Marketing orientation will help to provide market-led flexible factories with shorter lead times, catering for higher levels of demand change and optimised to provide maximum product variety and choice.

Chapter summary

- Marketing is the management process responsible for identifying, anticipating and satisfying consumer requirements profitably.
- When we talk about profitability, we are referring to how marketing can be used to achieve a series of business objectives.
- Planning lies at the heart of the marketing process.
- Strategy involves developing a framework for policy for the whole organisation.
- The evolution of the marketing concept has been developed from three phases from production orientation to sales orientation to marketing orientation.
- Marketing services are the tactical tools used by marketers.
- Marketing is a cyclical process.
- Good marketing involves looking outwards at the business environment and then matching the resources of the organisation to areas identified by the marketing process.
- There are various degrees of marketing orientation as signified by a number of approaches.

25   Influences on marketing decisions

Organisations today exist in a far more complex business environment than ever before and this places more emphasis upon the role of the marketing function. Influences outside an organisation may be friendly or hostile and pose either many threats or opportunities.

Marketing involves understanding this changing environment so that organisations can develop activities to deliver appropriate goods or services more effectively than their competitors. Such an understanding should be the driving force behind the decisions they take.

In this chapter we look at three broad influences external to an organisation within the broad business environment in which it markets its goods or services. These are:

- the external marketing environment
- the market
- changing customer behaviour.

The external marketing environment

The first stage in the marketing process is to develop an understanding of the business environment in which an organisation operates so that it can glean an idea about what it needs to deliver goods and services more effectively than its competitors. This sort of understanding underlies all subsequent decisions.

In Chapter 19 we looked at a PEST analysis. This approach is particularly useful when marketing products. A PEST analysis helps an organisation to be aware of the environment in which it operates by neatly grouping influential forces into four areas. These are the **P**olitical, **E**conomic, **S**ocial and **T**echnological.

For the purpose of marketing PEST analysis can inform the decision making process by focusing upon two key issues:

- the state of the market now
- the market as it may develop in the future.

For example, in relation to marketing activities, it is possible to identify clear areas of influence by these four forces.

Political factors

Conditions for business in every country and market are influenced by a political system. For example, a Government might wish to use tax, such as 'VAT on fish and chips', which affected the fast-food industry or introduce legislation, such as further hygiene regulations in butchers or food retailers, which increase costs or impose ethical standards for organisations using direct mail.

Economic factors

Although the economic environment is largely influenced by domestic politics, it is also affected by world economic trends. Rates of interest or exchange rates may seriously affect the profitability of a proposition. Other economic factors, such as rates of economic growth, may affect consumption patterns.

Social factors

The social environment provides a good idea of the structure and make-up of society which is particularly important for marketers. Demographic changes such as population growth, movements and age distribution will be important as will changes in cultural values and social trends such as family size and social behaviour.

Technological factors

In marketing goods or services, organisations must become aware of new materials as well as developments in manufacturing techniques and business processes. At the same time, they have to look at the nature of their products and, in particular, at their cost-effectiveness and performance.

The market

An organisation can use the picture of its external environment created by the PEST analysis to help it to identify marketing opportunities. Such opportunities exist in the marketplace.

> *A market exists when buyers and sellers come into contact.*

The key players in the marketplace are the buyers and sellers. When a buyer and a seller decide to undertake a transaction the sale will involve:

- communication
- an offer for sale
- an exchange (usually goods or services for money or credit).

IT'S A FACT

That the fastest growing market between 1994 and 1995 was 'Betting and Gaming'. The size of the market is defined by the stake less winnings. Over this period it grew by 55.6 per cent! The size of the beer market in 1995 at retail selling prices was more than £14,000 billion. Are we becoming a nation of gamblers and drinkers?

All organisations, whether in the public sector or the private sector, have **customers** (who may also be called users or clients). A customer may be either a person or another organisation. A customer in a newsagent's shop is clearly a person buying the goods on offer. In the public sector it might be an organisation asking for advice from a government department. You, yourself, in your capacity as a student, may be a customer of a college, school or other type of institution. So, customers (and therefore markets) may be roughly divided into two types: consumers and organisations.

Consumer markets

These markets are made up of individuals who purchase items for personal or domestic consumption, typically from retailers, most of which tend to be or relatively low value. They include:

- non-durable goods with a short-shelf life for immediate consumption such as food and confectionery
- durable goods with a longer life such as cars, washing machines and video recorders
- services providing intangible benefits such as education, a haircut or a bus ride.

Organisational markets

These markets largely consist of buyers who purchase goods or services for use in the production of other goods or services. They include:

- non-durable goods which have a pattern of frequent purchase such as chemicals or stationery
- durable goods such as machinery and equipment
- services such as those provided by a banker or an accountant.

Competition

Among the activities affecting an organisation within the marketplace is that of competition.

> *Competition occurs where two or more organisations act independently to supply their products to the same group of consumers.*

Some markets are signified by an abundance of products and services so that customers have a massive choice. In other markets there may be little competition (if any) and consumers may only be able to make a limited choice from the range of goods or services on offer.

Direct competition exists where organisations produce similar products which appeal to the same group of consumers. For example, the Ford Mondeo is in direct competition with the Vauxhall Vectra.

Even when an organisation provides a unique end-product with no direct competition, it will still have to consider **indirect competition**. This occurs where potential customers examine slightly different ways of meeting the same needs. For example, instead of going on holiday in St Ives they might go to Majorca; instead of buying a newspaper they might buy a magazine.

Changing customer behaviour

Irrespective of whether a business' customers are consumers or organisations, it is the job of marketers to understand the needs of their customers. In doing so they can develop goods or services which meet their needs more precisely than their competitors. The problem is that the process of buying a product is more complex than it might at first appear.

Customers do not usually make purchases without thinking carefully about their requirements. Wherever there is choice decisions are involved, and these may be influenced by constantly changing motives. The organisation that can understand why customers make decisions such as who buys, what they buy and how they buy will, by catering more closely for customers needs, become potentially more successful.

Consumers

If an organisation hopes to match products with consumer needs, it must have detailed knowledge of consumer behaviour. Marketers will wish to know about the economic, social and cultural differences of their target group of customers, as well as any reasons for changes in behaviour. The knowledge will help them to predict the answers to questions such as:

- What types of consumer can afford the products?
- What goods will they wish to purchase?
- How will they buy?
- How often will they buy?
- What loyalty will they show?

There are many influences on consumer behaviour which affect purchasing patterns. For example, by identifying the need of working families to organise meals quickly without taking the time and effort of having to prepare them from scratch, marketers were able to develop the market for ready-cooked meals.

Economic factors

One group of factors affecting consumer behaviour concerns the economic determinants of consumer demand. The most important factor is **real disposable incomes**, which are those incomes available for consumers for spending on goods and services. An increase in real incomes (i.e. after inflation has been taken into account) will generally increase the demand for goods and services.

A second economic determinant is the **relative price of a substitute product** whose purchase might be preferred or viewed as better value for money. A fall in the price of butter might switch some purchases away from butter substitutes such as Golden Crown.

CASE STUDY CASE STUDY CASE STUDY CASE STUDY CASE STUDY CASE

THE WORLD OF THEME RESTAURANTS

Make no mistake, this is the 'Theme Age'. Robert Earl, co-founder of Planet Hollywood and king of the 'eater-tainment industry' recently announced that he intends to create the largest and most successful leisure business in the world. Planet Hollywood is set to become a global empire to rival Disney. Meanwhile Fashion Café has just launched its London branch and the 25-year-old Hard Rock Café has opened a hotel and casino in Las Vegas. London has also seen the arrival of Football Football.

- **Planet Hollywood** One of the quartet of Arnie, Sly, Bruce and Demi always attends an opening which guarantees acres of space. Frequent parties of celebrities keep up appearances.
- **Hard Rock Café** At 25 years old, this is the godfather of theme. Memorabilia started with Pete Townshend donating a guitar. Bands have been fed backstage and other funky things have supported its image.
- **The Fashion Café** As an anagram of O Fatties Chafen, this also has some celebrity status, as long as wafer-thin models do not put customers off guzzling fast-food.

An extension of the theme restaurant – customers served by the stars?

- **Football Football** In here there is a real past and present hero potential, if only presented on television screens. Diners are 'tastefully' greeted with the roar of the crowd as they walk in from the tunnel!

So what do these restaurants provide? Is it an association with celebrity status or is it the glamour and 'buzz' or is it pure snobbery? Its a far cry from the days when the food was the important feature of a restaurant. Whatever the motives, themed restaurants have leaped across the bounds of

good taste to provide multi-dimensional entertainment in an area which is set to expand.

1 Why do themed restaurants appeal to customers?
2 What advantages do themed restaurants have over traditional restaurants which simply emphasise the quality of their food?
3 Why, therefore, it is important for organisations in the fast-food business to understand consumer behaviour?

CASE STUDY CASE STUDY CASE STUDY CASE STUDY CASE STUDY CASE

The **size and structure of the population** will affect demand for various products. A baby boom will clearly stimulate demand for infant products such as disposable nappies.

Tastes, fashions and habits will act as a constant influence on the patterns of demand for goods and services. We have already seen how the market for restaurants has changed over recent years, but think of how the market for beverages or electronic goods has changed!

Finally, **government measures** in many areas, such as credit controls or safety, may influence demand for goods and services.

TASK 25.1

How have the following markets been affected by changes in the economic determinants of consumer demand in recent years:

a fashion clothes?
b cars?
c magazines?

Self-image
The 'self' is an individual's image of himself or herself. Within this 'self' there are various ways to maintain and enhance this image. By discovering how customers wish themselves to be perceived in terms of an image, organisations can design, promote and retail goods which are consistent with those sought by prospective purchasers.

Individual motivation
A provider of goods or services must be interested in what inspires a customer's individual motivation to purchase a particular commodity. In Chapter 37 we look at the work of Abraham Maslow in developing a hierarchical picture of human needs. As well as relating such needs to motivation and behaviour at work, it is also possible to use them to help us to understand consumer purchasing

behaviour. Maslow identified five broad areas of human needs:

- **Physiological needs** are concerned with acquiring food, shelter and clothing. These are the most basic of consumer needs.
- **Safety and security needs** relate to well-being and the need for protection. Products that concern personal safety and protection fall into this category.
- **Love needs** centre upon purchases that are linked to being part of society and to goods and services that provide us with an element of acceptance – for example, socialising, or belonging to a football club.
- **Esteem needs** stem from a desire for status and for a sense of achievement. Lavish lifestyle products and prestigious items fall into this category.
- **Self-actualisation needs** relate to products that allow individuals to develop fully and creatively.

The implications of Maslow's work are easy to perceive. Different products and services are related to different needs. By identifying where consumer needs lie, it is possible to develop goods and services to relate directly to them. For example, in Western societies many more products and services are related to higher needs than in poorer countries.

SYNTHESIS

Identify the last five goods or services you have purchased. Using the work on consumer behaviour from this chapter, carefully relate your purchasing decision to the decisions to purchase these products. Think carefully about what this says about you, your lifestyle and pattern of personal consumption. How far do you think your pattern varies with any of your contemporaries?

Consumer personality

Many different customers have different personalities. It is possible to identify different parts of markets according to different personalities. Fashion products in particular reflect the personality traits of customers.

Lifestyles

Over recent years, organisations have paid increasing attention to the lifestyle of consumers. A **lifestyle** is a behaviour pattern adopted by a particular community or a sub-section of it. By understanding such as lifestyle, they can develop products and then target them at this group. For example, someone upwardly mobile and ambitious would seek an affluent lifestyle and a higher material standard of living. The British 'Yuppy' is reputed to be a young (24–35), well-educated and upwardly mobile professional.

Cultural factors

Culture encompasses standard patterns of behaviour and plays an important role in shaping our purchasing patterns. It stems from the traditions, beliefs and values of the community in which we live. For example, our attitudes towards alcohol, the food we eat and the relative importance of our families are all based upon our culture. Although a nation may be characterised by one dominant culture, there may be many sub-cultures within it – e.g. youth cultures, ethnic groups, or senior citizens.

Socio-economic factors

Perhaps the most frequently used way of classifying customers into groups so that products can be accurately targeted at them is to use socio-economic groupings or social stratification.

With social stratification, the assumption is that certain jobs have certain lifestyles attached. Whatever one may think of the correctness of socio-economic grouping, it does provide a reliable guide to the relationship between occupation and income and as such provides valuable information which can be used for marketing purposes. For example, members of each group are assumed to have certain priorities which will influence their needs. We would expect some members of groups A, B and possibly some C1 to spend some of their income on private health and education whereas members of groups D and E would spend more their incomes on necessities.

Socio-economic group	Social 'class'	Occupation types	Examples
A	Upper or upper-middle	High managerial, Administrative, Professional	Surgeon, Director of a large company
B	Middle	Intermediate managerial, Administrative, Professional	Bank manager, Headteacher, Architect
C1	Lower-middle	Supervisory, Junior managerial, Junior administrative, Clerical	Bank clerk, Nurse, Teacher
C2	Skilled working	Skilled manual workers	Joiner, Welder, Foreman
D	Working	Semi-skilled, Unskilled	Driver, Postman, Porter
E	Lowest subsistence level	Low-paid, unemployed	Casual worker, State pensioner

Figure 25.1   Socio-economic groupings

IT'S A FACT

So, how many people fall into each of these socio-economic categories by chief income earner? The data shown in Figure 25.2 were based upon a survey carried out in 1996.

Social Grade	All adults 15+ (000s)	%	Men (000s)	%	Women (000s)	%
A	1,312	2.9	732	3.3	580	2.5
B	8,690	18.9	4,575	20.5	4,115	17.4
C1	12,435	27.0	5,729	25.7	6,706	28.3
C2	10,404	22.6	5,498	24.6	4,906	20.7
D	7,758	16.9	3,736	16.7	4,023	17.0
E	5,400	11.7	2,052	9.2	3,348	14.1

Figure 25.2

Organisations

In the business market, organisations buy goods and services that are either used directly or indirectly in the production of other goods or services, or are stocked in order to be resold.

A complex manufactured product such as a car is made up of numerous parts obtained from many suppliers. What we tend to think of as a single product in fact represents the culmination of a process of assembly that has brought together around 12,000 parts, about half of which will have been bought in from other suppliers/producers. The organisations supplying such parts will also have suppliers from whom they will have purchased raw materials and components.

Perhaps the main difference between a consumer market and a business or organisational market lies in the total number of customers. A consumer market has a potential of 56 million domestic users; the total number of business organisations within the UK is fewer than 3 million. Furthermore, the likelihood is that the more specialised the product, the more limited will be its appeal.

The demand for organisational products is usually called **derived** because the amounts purchased are determined by the demand for the relevant goods and services that will be produced. Being dependent upon derived demand can have serious consequences for businesses, particularly during recession. Organisational markets are subject to **business cycles**, and the demand for industrial products may vary widely as the pace of industrial activity changes.

In organisational markets the smooth running of the purchasing function ensures that goods and services are provided by reliable suppliers. The **buying centre** refers to the group of people within an organisation involved in making a purchasing decision. It may also be called the **decision making unit (DMU)**.

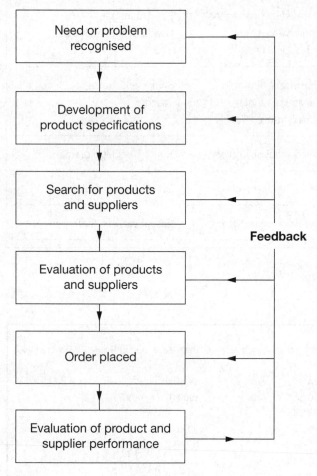

Figure 25.3   The organisational buying process

As the buying process takes place a number of factors might influence the decision makers. These might include:

- **Environmental considerations** These might involve 'uncontrollable' forces in the business environment such as regulations, politics, technological change and the actions of pressure groups.
- **Organisational initiatives** These might include **just-in-time production** which involves goods being delivered just in time for their inclusion in the manufacturing process rather than keeping large stocks in hand, **quality assurance** which places emphasis upon the seller to deliver goods of appropriate quality, the use of **ISO 9000** or other standards which impose specific requirements upon the quality of products provided by suppliers and b, used to speed up transaction time between suppliers and customers.

Companies supplying goods in organisational markets face changing circumstances which are often called **contingency factors**. For example, these might include:

- the supplier is usually expected to provide credit facilities for the customer
- there is always the risk of takeover by the customer
- buyers may influence buying power suppliers in areas such as discounts
- buyers may deliberately delay payment for goods or services received
- there is always the risk of the supplier becoming too dependent on the buyer.

Organisational markets are sometimes described as being either vertical or horizontal. Where a supplier provides for only a few customers, the market is **vertical** in nature. Where there are many customers from different industries, the market will be **horizontal**.

Chapter summary

- Organisations exist in a complex business environment. Understanding how this environment works helps decision-makers to supply better or more appropriate goods and services than their competitors.
- A PEST analysis is a useful way of analysing the marketing environment.
- Markets can be divided into consumer markets and organisational markets.

- The type and nature of competition will affect an organisation's activities.
- Organisations serving consumer markets need to understand the behaviour of consumers.
- As organisational markets have fewer customers than consumer markets, they require different strategies.

26 Market research

As we have seen, the first stage in the marketing process for any organisation is to thoroughly understand its business environment, the nature of the markets in which it operates as well as its customers. To find out about each of these areas, an organisation requires information. Though this information does not eliminate the risks associated with being in business, it will help to reduce them. As a tool of management, the purpose of market research is to provide this information, thereby enabling business organisations to use precise techniques which help them to plan ahead with certainty rather than to rely upon unsubstantiated guesswork and hunches.

Information requirements vary from one organisation to another. Some view market research simply as an ad hoc data gathering and analysis function, while others view market research as an information centre for decision making which provides meaningful information for planning and control. The benefit is that the information reduces areas in decision making and increases control over parts of the business in which planning developments may take place. Market research therefore provides the information which pulls together the activities of the organisation and focuses them upon the needs of customers in the marketplace.

What is market research?

Perhaps the most widely used definition of market research is that of the American Marketing Association:

> 'Market research is the systematic gathering, recording and analysing of data about problems relating to the marketing of goods and services.'

We can break this definition down into its various ingredients:

- **Systematic** – in other words, using an organised and clear method or system.
- **Gathering** – knowing what you are looking for, and collecting appropriate information.
- **Recording** – keeping clear and organised records of what you find out.
- **Analysing** – ordering and making sense of your information in order to draw out relevant trends and conclusions.
- **Problems relating to marketing** – finding out answers to questions which will help you to understand better your customers and other details about the workplace.

Market research should not be a one-off activity which takes place only as part of a new product development. It should be ongoing and continuous. Marketers are constantly collecting and analysing information and feeding it through for planning and control and decision-making purposes.

SYNTHESIS

In 1996, a former ice hockey international, Geoffrey Williams, opened his shop 'Willy's World of Football' in Plumstead in South East London. Though he thought about widening the scope of his shop to concentrate upon areas other than football, he wanted to become a specialist. His idea was to become established for the forthcoming season and Euro '96 helped his shop to gain a flying start.

Given the specialist nature of Geoffrey's shop what questions or issues would he have broached before engaging in this venture. Think about the information requirements he will have needed for his new business.

1. *How important would this information be?*
2. *From where might he have obtained this information?*
3. *How might it have helped him provide greater certainty for his venture and to develop and establish his business?*

Information requirements

Market research can be time-consuming and is not cheap. It is important to ensure that any research undertaken is relevant for an organisation's information requirements. For example, specific objectives of market research might be to:

- identify new markets
- monitor changes in customer needs and preferences
- identify new product opportunities
- improve the quality of decision-making
- improve the organisation's understanding of changes in the marketplace
- identify opportunities and threats
- monitor the effects of the external business environment.

Market research may be **basic** or **applied**. Basic research attempts to develop some aspect of the process of marketing goods or services. Information obtained may have limited influence upon management processes. Applied research, in contrast, is specifically directed at obtaining information to assist managers in making key business decisions.

Basic research v	**Applied research**
Proactive v	**Reactive**
Quantitative v	**Qualitative**

Figure 26.1

Research may also be **proactive** or **reactive**. Proactive research deals with the new ideas of tomorrow, while reactive research looks at what has happened in the past.

Information obtained from market research may be either **quantitative** or **qualitative**.

- **Quantitative information** involves amounts, such as the average number of customers who come into a shop at various times in a day. This is objective.
- **Qualitative data** involves descriptions which may be made be respondents in surveys, such as attitudes, opinions, reactions and suggestions. This sort of information is more difficult to categorise and measure and, because it is based on thoughts, it is subjective.

Sources of information

The first question decision makers within any organisation should ask is 'what information do we need'? This will largely depend upon their objectives. Remember the more accurate the information the more successful decision making is likely to be. There are three broad areas in which market research can take place:

- Existing organisations may already have **internal information** kept within their own systems.
- A lot of information may already be published as **external** or **secondary information**.
- The third source of information will not already exist in any identifiable form and will have to be collected first-hand. This is **primary information**.

Internal information

Much of the information an organisation requires will already be held within its various departments, although at least some of it will be out-of-date. The secret may be to know where to find it.

Most organisations accumulate vast quantities of data which may be of use in the market research process. Its usefulness may depend upon how well it has been organised and whether it is accessible for the market researcher. For example, in the past it was often difficult to get regular and reliable feedback from 'people in the field' such as sales representatives, because paperwork was kept in their vehicles, was haphazard, bulky and rarely filed. This information may have had enormous value as it represented first-hand experience of customers.

Databases have revolutionised the way information is stored, retrieved and analysed and created a basis for the efficient handling of information. Computers provide the means whereby information can be recorded in a simple manner, and contacts with each customer can be 'processed' so that information can be retrieved very quickly and then displayed in a way that is easy to understand. Techniques like this improve the quality of the market research process.

Internal data within an organisation may include:

- purchasing – stock levels, unit costs, usage rates
- production – output, materials, labour inventory
- personnel – wage costs, efficiency levels, staff absenteeism, production details
- marketing – promotional and administration expenditure, brand and market data
- finance – cost and accounting data, payment records, correspondence.

For example, think of the information which may be held by a bank on each customer. Each customer will have a unique account number with a branch which has a code number, and these clearly provide a means of identifying and sorting customer information. Information will undoubtedly cover the following points:

- date when account opened
- age, marital status and occupation
- address/area of habitation and (possibly) the type of property
- size of mortgage (if this is with the bank)
- pattern of use of banking services
- spending and consumption patterns as shown by bank statements
- credit rating.

This information can be used to place customers into different categories in order to target services. From such information it may also be possible to obtain answers to questions such as:

- What type of customers use different banking services?
- Who are the best, and possibly the most profitable, customers for the bank?
- How do customers use banking services?
- To what extent do customer requirements vary according to age and occupation?
- What type of customer is most likely to require services currently promoted by the bank?
- When do customers like to use the bank?

Internal information may also have a valuable second purpose, and that is to know as much as possible about an organisation's capability of fulfilling the demands within its main market as well as its potential outside that market.

IT'S A FACT

That 51.4 per cent of adults over 18 go on a major grocery shopping trip each week. The busiest day is a Friday when 19.6 per cent of trips occur.

The gender divide narrows! In 1982, 38 per cent of males 16+ smoked. By 1994, this has dropped to 28 per cent, a fall of 10 per cent. In 1982, 33 per cent of women over 16 smoked. In contrast, this has fallen to 26 per cent in 1994, a drop of 7 per cent. The average weekly consumption for a male smoker in 1994 is 114 cigarettes and for a women it is 97.

External sources of information

Internal information must be put into context, since on its own it simply provides a snapshot of an organisation and its customers. In particular, it tells an organisation nothing about how effective its performance is relative to that of its competitors, nor how the organisation could be threatened by its competitors.

External information is more commonly called 'secondary data' because it is often to be found in published materials such as reports, periodicals and books where it will have been collected by someone else. It can provide a broader dimension to data previously collected and can be used in two main ways.

Firstly, external information can enhance an organisation's existing knowledge. For example, postcodes help to group customers geographically. By identifying and labelling the characteristics of its customers, an organisation may be able to make assumptions about their needs. Two examples, of useful external sources are:

- **domestic socio-economic data** – certain assumptions can be made about lifestyles
- **industrial classification** – organisational customers may be classified according to the nature of their activities. Certain organisations can then be expected to have predictable demands for certain services.

Secondly, external information may complement an organisation's own information by providing useful comparisons with competitors. It may also help identify markets offering potential and put performances into context by relating them to the economy/industry as a whole.

Main advantage of collecting secondary data:	Main disadvantage of collecting secondary data:
savings in time and money	not specifically related to the project undertaken.

Sources of external data are:
- official statistics
- commercial agencies
- libraries
- electronic sources
- panels.

Official statistics

A wide variety of UK government statistics are available for use by marketers. The government's statistical services is co-ordinated by the Central Statistical Office (CSO) which publishes a booklet called *Government Statistics: A Brief Guide to Sources*. Government departments prepare statistics and the CSO publishes both a monthly and an annual analysis (*Annual Abstract of Statistics*). In addition, *Business Monitors*, published quarterly, provide detailed information about specific markets. Other information comes in the following publications:

- *Financial Statistics* (monthly)
- *Economic Trends* (monthly)
- *Department of Employment Gazette* (monthly)
- *British Business* (weekly)
- *Housing and Construction Statistics* (quarterly).

Government information on particular groups of industries is identified by a code which relates to a **Standard Industrial Classification (SIC)**. SIC codes run from division 0 to division 9 and within each division there are subdivisions into more specialised industries. As the codes are frequently used for classifying organisations and markets, they are frequently used in market research.

Another useful source of government information, particularly for organisations working in consumer markets, is **census data** published by the Office of Population, Censuses and Surveys. A full census is carried out every ten years, the last one being in 1991. This office also carries out two ongoing surveys which are published as *Family Expenditure and General Households*.

In addition to the UK government, many international organisations provide useful statistics and publications. Information comes from the United Nations (UN), the International Monetary Fund (IMF), the statistical offices of the European Union and the Organisation for Economic Cooperation and Development (OECD).

NUMBERS: FUN OR FICTION?

For many, numbers are nice. They are tangible, solid things you can quote in conversations and pub quizzes. They are useful in arguments and politicians use (or misuse) them all of the time. For example, 75 per cent of French people would not be shocked if the Queen had an affair; 76 per cent of Britons think that it is immoral to lie to their husband or wife, etc.

The people who provide these figures are market researchers. In the UK, market research is big business. In 1996, its revenues grew by almost 15 per cent. And why? Because it makes sense. A MORI survey revealing that two-thirds of teenage smokers considered that the risks from smoking were unimportant could trigger government action. A drinks company may spend half a million pounds before changing the shape of a bottle. A confectionery manufacturer may invest a considerable time, effort and money in researching changing tastes before even thinking about launching a new brand. The whole process makes sense not just for shareholders but also for senior managers. If they make mistakes such errors could cost their businesses millions of pounds each year.

In many ways market research is a bit like economics. It tries hard to be a science but human nature and the complexity of the world many it very difficult. Remember that it was market researchers that failed to predict John Major's second term of office and did not stop Coca-Cola investing millions in a drink that failed.

Qualitative researchers or 'Quallies' shun figures. They gather 'focus groups' of up to a dozen or so people and get them to discuss the shape of a new bottle or the features of a new motor car. They observe them, analyse their comments and then write a nice juicy report for their clients. Focus groups produce subtle, unquantified results.

In contrast the 'Quanties' are the boffins of market research. Quantitative researchers use figures to write complex computer models so that they can analyse the figures and produce a set of neat results. This type of research works well where there is an unambiguous choice. But it was this type of research that failed to predict the election victory in 1992. The commercial equivalent of a mistake was the launch of 'new Coke'. Despite being tested on 190,000 people it still flopped because they assumed that people just bought Coke because of the taste.

The research industry has tried to ensure in recent years that these types of mistakes can not take place. When interviewing respondents they have become aware of distortions that might arise from client's prejudices. And some subjects just cannot be measured properly. Ask most people how much they drink and they will underestimate!

Next time you read feedback from market research, think about not just the figures but how far they can be believed. Science is a precise area upon which it would be possible to make decisions and base a business plan. But, what about the Coke factor? Might they have make a mistake? Could there be an error?

1 Identify five issues about which it might be difficult to research with precision. In each case explain why.
2 Describe the difference between qualitative research and quantitative research.
3 How important is research for decision making? Why is it sometimes dangerous to rely upon it?

Commercial agencies

The supply of information is itself an important business. A number of agencies exist which collect information, compile it into reports and the sells such reports to anyone who requires them.

Mintel is a commercial research organisation which, in return for a fee, provides a monthly journal containing reports on a variety of consumer markets – for example, bread, alcoholic drinks and insurance. Mintel reports are about 20 pages long with information such as market size, main competitors, projected growth, market share of main producers, advertising spend of main brands and trends. Mintel also produces other in-depth reports on certain markets. Another similar research outfit is Euromonitor which provides monthly compilations and special reports. Key Note Reports produce detailed reports for business markets.

Research establishments may also provide useful information for specific market sectors. For example, for the food industry there are the Food Research Association and the Food Policy Research Unit.

A C Nielsen and Retail Audits are research organisations which collect data relating to sales figures through supermarkets and large chains and sell figures to organisations wishing to buy them. These figures help suppliers to work out their share of the market, the sales of different products, and the effects of any recent strategy such as a price change or a promotional campaign.

Specific data may often be obtained through trade associations. These relate to specific industries and can be identified using the *Directory of British Associations*.

Libraries

Libraries are a rich source of information. College, university and town and city libraries have a wide range of reference materials which may be put to use. Libraries subscribe to many major data sources and academic journals. They will usually have a variety of sources providing information about the media. For example, *Benn's Media Directory* provides details of TV and radio companies, newspapers and magazines. *British Rate and Data (BRAD)* provides coverage of virtually all the media that sells advertising space, together with rates. *Advertisers Annual* makes detailed comparisons of advertising agencies. Information about companies is available from many sources. *Kompass* publishes two volumes of products and services listed under the SIC codes mentioned earlier. *Extel* provides details extracted from the published accounts of all the public companies and many of the larger private companies.

Electronic sources

Changes in the electronic transmission of information are in the process of transforming traditional reference sources and the ways in which information is handled. The two basic forms are Teletext which transmits information through the broadcast media and Viewdata which sends information via the telephone network. Further developments are likely to include using the World Wide Web for customer surveys, i.e. converting a survey into an e-mail message and the use of ISDN lines and remote databases.

Panels

Another way of finding out what is happening in the marketplace is to buy information from panels. A panel is a group of consumers who record their purchases and/or media habits, usually in a diary. The purpose of this diary is not just to record purchases but also to provide research information which relates purchasing habits to social status, occupation, income, demographic details and neighbourhood. Audits of Great Britain (AGB) Ltd produces panel data across a variety of areas. Some panels, such as those set up by the Broadcasters' Audience Research Board (BARB) are designed simply to see how many people are watching various television programmes at different times of the day.

IT'S A FACT

That the top 10 brands in the UK in 1995 are as follows:

1. Coca-Cola
2. Nescafe
3. Walkers Crisps
4. Ariel
5. Persil
6. Andrex
7. Pampers
8. Whiskas
9. Robinsons Squash
10. Flora.

Primary sources of information

Internal and external data may not answer all the questions an organisation wants to ask. It may be out-of-date or it may not cover the right market sector. To meet an organisation's more specific needs primary or field research has to take place.

Primary research is first-hand knowledge, 'straight from the horse's mouth'. Information an organisation compiles from its own research is called primary. This type of research involves the collection of new data which is to be used for a specific purpose. For example, before a supermarket chain opens a new supermarket it will conduct a local shopping survey.

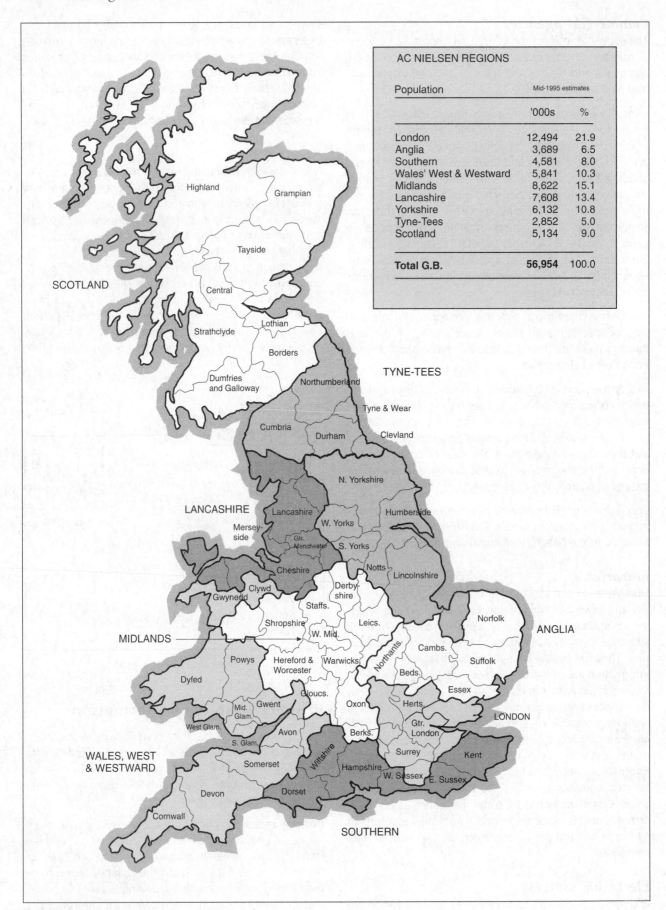

AC NIELSEN REGIONS		
Population	Mid-1995 estimates	
	'000s	%
London	12,494	21.9
Anglia	3,689	6.5
Southern	4,581	8.0
Wales' West & Westward	5,841	10.3
Midlands	8,622	15.1
Lancashire	7,608	13.4
Yorkshire	6,132	10.8
Tyne-Tees	2,852	5.0
Scotland	5,134	9.0
Total G.B.	**56,954**	**100.0**

A C Nielsen regions

THE MARKET RESEARCH SOCIETY

The Market Research Society (MRS) is the professional body for market researchers. All of the members of the MRS operate within the Data Protection Act, which means that any personal data supplied in a survey will be used only for statistical purposes. In addition to the Data Protection Act, all MRS members abide by a strict Code of Conduct which ensures that the research is carried out to the highest possible standards.

The leaflet illustrated in Figure 26.2 is representative of the sort that could be issued to survey respondents.

1 Give three reasons why an organisation may wish to employ an agency to undertake primary market research.
2 Why may a researcher wish to talk to a cross-section of the population?
3 How important is confidentiality in a survey, and how does the Data Protection Act protect respondents?
4 What alternative methods of delivering questionnaires are identified in Figure 26.2?

Market research

■ Why is market research important?

Market research is your opportunity to give your opinion on things that may affect you and your family. Manufacturers, retailers, service companies, political parties and the Government can only succeed if they please you the customer. so they need to find out what you need and what you want. Your opinion can influence a wide range of products from pension plans to washing powder and also have a bearing on issues that affect the quaiity of your life

It is the job of market researchers to ask questions – to find out what you, and people like you, think.

■ Why were you chosen?

For most research projects it is necessary to talk to a cross-section of the public-people from all walks of life and all ages. You have been asked to give your opinion as a representative of the population.

■ Why is it necessary to ask personal questions?

To make sure that we do achieve a cross-section of the population we do need to ask personal questions which may include details on occupation, income and age. This information is given in total confidence and is only asked to ensure that we have a representative sample of the population

■ The replies are confidential so why do we ask for your name and address?

This is a safety mechanism mainly for your benefit. To check that this interview has been carried out fairly and that the correct cross-section has been contacted, the Supervisor of the fieldwork company may contact you to confirm the accuracy of the interview. Nobody outside the fieldwork company will gain access to your name and address.

■ About The Market Research Society

The Market Research Society (MRS) is the professional body for market researchers, all MRS members have to operate under a Code of Conduct which includes certain guarantees for you, the interviewee. These guarantees state that you are entitled to remain anonymous it you wish, that you will suffer no adverse effects from being interviewed and that you may withdraw from the interview at any stage.

Answering questionnaires, in face-to-face interviews, via the post or on the telephone, gives you the opportunity to speak directly to those who can make the changes you want. As a safeguard for the public, the MRS has developed three schemes to check that you have been approached by authentic researchers and not by somebody trying to sell to you

■ Interviewer Identity Card

Carried by up to 65,000 interviewers across the country, giving the interviewer's name, photograph and the company they work for

■ Market Research Mark

For questionnaires sent out by post, this guarantees that the questionaire is for research purposes only and that your name is not being added to a mailing list.

■ Freefone Market Research Society

The Freefone is available seven days a week, 9am–11pm by dialling 100 and asking for Freefone Market Research Society. You can then check whether the company carrying out the research (either by telephone or face-to-face) Is recognised by The Market Research Society.

Figure 26.2   Market research

Surveys are the most common method used to collect primary data. They involve contacting respondents to find out how they react to a range of issues contained in a questionnaire.

There are two types of survey, a census and a sample. A **census** involves questioning everybody in a marketplace. Unless the market is very small, this is unlikely to be practicable. Taking a **sample** involves questioning a selection of respondents from the target market. In order to ensure that the results of a sample survey are accurate, the market research process must identify a representative cross-section of customers. If the selection of the sample is fair and accurate, then information should be **statistically reliable**. If the sample is incomplete and does not accurately represent a group of consumers, then misleading data is obtained and the sample is said to be **biased**.

Choosing a sample
Samples fall into either of two categories:

- **Probability samples** are so constructed that every customer or element has a known probability or chance or selection and the limits of possible error are known in advance. Included in this category are simple random sampling, systematic sampling, stratified random sampling, cluster sampling and multistage sampling.
- **Non-probability samples** are based simply on the choice of the selector and may be subject to error in sample selection. These include quota sampling, convenience sampling and judgement sampling.

Simple random sampling
With this method the researcher chooses the size of the sample required and then picks the sample on a random basis. The sample must be selected in such a way that every item in the 'sampling frame' has an equal chance of being selected.

Systematic sampling
Another way is to use systematic sampling, which involves selecting items from the list at regular intervals after choosing a random starting point. For example, if it is decided to select 20 names from 1,000, then every 50th name (1,000 divided by 20) should be selected, after a random start anywhere in the first 50. If 18 is chosen as the starting point, then the sample series would start: 18 …68 …118 …168 …, etc.

Stratified random sampling
If some customers are more important than others,

simple random sampling can distort the results. Stratified random sampling therefore weights the sample on the basis of the importance of each group of customers in the market.

Cluster sampling
With cluster sampling the population/customers are divided up into small areas, but instead of sampling from a random selection of these areas, sampling is carried out in a few areas which are considered to be typical of the market in question.

Multistage sampling
Multistage sampling cuts the field to be sampled into small units or segments in much the same way as cluster sampling. The purpose of multistage sampling is simply to cut down sampling and research costs.

Quota sampling
Although random sampling, if properly conducted, can produces the best results, it can be expensive and time consuming. In other situations quota sampling is used. Interviewers are given instructions as to the number of people to interview along with certain characteristics such as sex, age, socio-economic group, etc.

Convenience and judgement sampling
This involves gathering information from anybody available for the interviewer to survey, no matter what their background. This simply involves selection of a respondent based upon the judgement of the interviewer.

The importance of probability
At the heart of probability samples is the concept of the standard error. Estimates given by a large number of samples fit into a standard pattern, called the **normal distribution**. This is a bell-shaped curve in which most of the sample estimates bunch together around the centre while some tail off in either direction, above and below the central estimate. It is possible to determine how sample estimates form themselves into a normal distribution by calculating the **standard error**: two-thirds of all the estimates would be within plus or minus one standard error of the average (central) estimate, 95 per cent within two standard errors and 99 per cent within three standard errors (see Figure 26.3). Thus we know by calculation based on sampling theory, the probability that the true proportion for the population lies within a certain range of the estimate given by our sample.

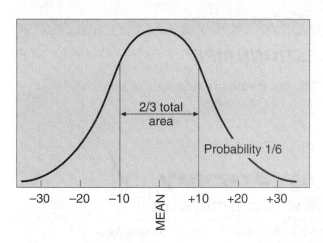

Figure 26.3   A normal distribution curve

Questionnaire

When the sampling issues have been decided, the market researcher must design a questionnaire. A questionnaire is a systematic list of questions designed to obtain information from respondents about:

● specific events
● their attitudes
● their values
● their beliefs.

Questionnaire design is probably the most crucial part of the survey. A badly designed questionnaire will lead to biased results and these could influence the decision-making process. For example, a badly constructed questionnaire may lead to respondents misinterpreting questions.

In designing a questionnaire, the following points are important:

● Questions should be simple, clear and unambiguous.
● Questions should relate directly to information requirements so that issues can be addressed from the responses.
● The questionnaire should not be too long or take too much of the respondent's time.
● Personal questions should not be asked.
● Questions should be arranged so that the respondents answer truthfully. They should not suggest or prompt the interviewee into making a preferred response.
● Questions should have been tested, possibly through trial interviews.

Another element to consider in questionnaire design is how to present questions to respondents and also how to record their responses. For example, questions in a questionnaire may be 'open' or 'closed'. **Open questions** allow the person answering to provide an opinion and may encourage them to talk at some length. **Closed questions** require an answer from a fixed list of responses which may simply be yes/no. Closed questionnaires can be analysed more quickly and efficiently.

In order to be able to quantify the various strengths of responses, some questionnaires have **rating scales**. Scales are a useful way of measuring attitudes or more subjective responses. A scale would offer a range of answers (see Figure 26.4).

Do you like our new product ranges?

(Tick one box)

Very good ☐	Good ☐	
Satisfactory ☐	Poor ☐	Very poor ☐

Figure 26.4

Prompt cards may be used to help respondents recall particular brands or items. For example, if respondents were asked where they did their shopping, a list of numbered supermarkets could be provided and the answers could be recorded as numbers (see Figure 26.5).

Asda	01
Tesco	02
Sainsbury's	03
Safeway	04
Morrisons	05
Aldi	06
Netto	07

Figure 26.5

Some questionnaires are designed so that respondents can concentrate on the questions of greatest relevance, and be able to skip over questions which do not relate to them. For example:

4   Have you shopped previously at this Centre?
   Yes   If yes go to question 5
   No   If no go to question 6

NATIONAL SHOPPING SURVEY QUESTIONNAIRE

Look at the NSS questionnaire (Figure 26.6) on the following pages.

The questionnaire was sent to households around the country.

National Shoppers Survey

Thank you for taking part in Britain's biggest Consumer Survey!

You are invited to take part in this new edition of the National Shoppers Survey. Your opinions are important to firms who provide the goods you use every day.

In return for your answers you will receive £100 worth of Savings Coupons .. plus Free Entry into our Grand Prize Draw.

Please spare a few minutes to tick the boxes in this survey. If you prefer not to answer some of the questions, just ignore them. Then mail it within 7 days in the envelope supplied. No stamp is needed. Thank you for taking part, your answers will help to make shopping better for everyone.

The information you provide will be held by CMT (Computerised Marketing Technologies) Ltd. and safeguarded under the Data Protection Act. CMT uses your answers to determine the contents of Reward Packs which you receive and for market analysis purposes. CMT may make your responses available to other reputable organisations who may wish to contact you with information about themselves and offers, products or services that you may find interesting. You can choose not to receive additional material by ticking the box on page 3 of your survey. Certain questions have been asked on behalf of: Sec 1 Q9 First Choice Holidays & Flights Ltd, Sec 1 Q19 AOL Ltd, Sec 1 Q21-22 Mercury Communications, Sec 1 Q25 Plantiflor Ltd, Sec 2 Q12-21 Procter & Gamble Ltd, Sec 4 Q1-8 Imperial Tobacco Ltd, Sec 7 Q8 Scholl Consumer Products Ltd, Sec 7 Q10-11 Procter & Gamble Ltd, Sec 9 Q12 Justice for Victims Ltd, Sec 9 Q21 RBS Advanta, Sec 9 Q23 First Direct, Sec 9 Q32 Zurich Insurance Company. They may use your answers for research and marketing purposes. Thank you for your valued help,

Linda Harrison

Linda Harrison, National Shoppers Survey

P.S. If you don't want to answer some of the questions, that's OK - just ignore them!

EXAMPLE: Do you drink tea? 1 ☑ Yes 9 ☐ No

1. HOBBIES & ACTIVITIES

1 Please tick ALL the leisure interests and activities you and your partner enjoy regularly:

01 ☐ Avid Book Reading	17 ☐ Grandchildren
02 ☐ Charities/Voluntary Work	18 ☐ Hiking/Walking
03 ☐ Coin/Stamp Collecting	19 ☐ Home Computing
04 ☐ Collectables	20 ☐ Active Sport/Exercise
05 ☐ Cooking	21 ☐ Knitting
06 ☐ Crosswords/Puzzles	22 ☐ National Trust
07 ☐ Current Affairs	23 ☐ Photography
08 ☐ Do-It-Yourself/DIY	24 ☐ Going to the Pub
09 ☐ Eating Out	25 ☐ Records/Tapes/CDs
10 ☐ Fashion Clothing	26 ☐ Religious Activities
11 ☐ Fine Art/Antiques	27 ☐ Self Improvement
12 ☐ Fishing	28 ☐ Sewing/Needlework
13 ☐ Foreign Travel	29 ☐ Snow Skiing
14 ☐ Gardening	30 ☐ Theatre/Cultural/Art Events
15 ☐ Playing Golf	31 ☐ Wildlife/Environment
16 ☐ Gourmet Foods/Wines	32 ☐ Wines by Mail Order

2 Please write the numbers of your four favourite activities from the list above:

You: 1 ☐ 2 ☐ 3 ☐ 4 ☐

Partner: 1 ☐ 2 ☐ 3 ☐ 4 ☐

3 On average how many hours TV do you watch in a day?
1 ☐ 0-1 2 ☐ 1-2 3 ☐ 2-3 4 ☐ 3-4 5 ☐ 4-5 6 ☐ 5+

4 How often do you eat at the following types of restaurants?

	Once a Week	Once a Month	3 Months	Once/Twice a Year
English/Steak House	01 ☐	04 ☐	07 ☐	10 ☐
Pub Meals	02 ☐	05 ☐	08 ☐	11 ☐
Other	03 ☐	06 ☐	09 ☐	12 ☐

5 Do either of you bet on: (Please tick all that apply)
1 ☐ Pools 2 ☐ Bingo 3 ☐ Horseracing 4 ☐ Other

6 How many prize draws, competitions or lotteries did you enter in the last year excluding the National Lottery? 9 ☐ None
1 ☐ 1-3 2 ☐ 4-6 3 ☐ 7-10 4 ☐ 11 plus

7 Where have you been on holiday in the last 3 years?
(Please tick all that apply)
1 ☐ UK 2 ☐ Europe 3 ☐ USA 4 ☐ Rest of World

8 What type of holiday(s) do you take?
1 ☐ Camping/Caravanning 4 ☐ Winter Sun
2 ☐ Hotel/Hotel Package 5 ☐ Weekend or City Breaks
3 ☐ Self Catering 6 ☐ Winter Snow

9 Do you own/part own a holiday property in:
1 ☐ Portugal 3 ☐ The Canaries 7 ☐ Malta
2 ☐ Florida 4 ☐ Italy 6 ☐ Spain (including Balearics)

10 Are you considering making any of the following long-haul trips within the next 12 months?
1 ☐ USA/Canada 3 ☐ Australia/New Zealand 5 ☐ Round the World
2 ☐ South Africa 4 ☐ Far East/Asia

11 Are you interested in Annual Travel Insurance?
1 ☐ Yes 2 ☐ Possibly 9 ☐ No

12 Have you or your partner travelled to the USA on business in the last 3 years? 1 ☐ Yes 9 ☐ No

13 Please tick all the newspapers that are REGULARLY read by your family: 99 ☐ None

	Daily	Sunday		Daily	Sunday
Express	01 ☐	21 ☐	Financial Times	10 ☐	
Independent	02 ☐	22 ☐	Guardian	11 ☐	
Mail	03 ☐	23 ☐	Star	12 ☐	
Mirror	04 ☐	24 ☐	Sun	13 ☐	
Sport	05 ☐	25 ☐	News of the World		29 ☐
Telegraph	06 ☐	26 ☐	Observer		30 ☐
Times	07 ☐	27 ☐	People		31 ☐
Other/Local	08 ☐	28 ☐	Post		32 ☐
Daily Record	09 ☐		Sunday Mail (Scotland)		33 ☐

14 From the list above, please write the number of your main newspaper: Daily: ☐ ☐ Sunday: ☐ ☐

15 Do you or would you consider purchasing romantic fiction from Mills & Boon? 1 ☐ Already do 2 ☐ Would consider

16 Does anyone in your household support any of the following football teams?
01 ☐ Manchester United 05 ☐ Tottenham 09 ☐ Aston Villa
02 ☐ Liverpool 06 ☐ Chelsea 10 ☐ Glasgow Rangers
03 ☐ Newcastle United 07 ☐ Middlesborough 11 ☐ Celtic
04 ☐ Arsenal 08 ☐ Leeds United 12 ☐ Other

17 How many times in the last year have you bought goods/services via the mail?
1 ☐ 1 2 ☐ 2-3 3 ☐ 4-5 4 ☐ 6 plus 9 ☐ None

18 Is anyone in your household considering buying or do they already have any of the following computer equipment?

	Consider	Have		Consider	Have
P.C.	01 ☐	07 ☐	Internet Connection	04 ☐	10 ☐
Apple Mac	02 ☐	08 ☐	Laser Printer	05 ☐	11 ☐
Lap Top	03 ☐	09 ☐	CD ROM	06 ☐	12 ☐

19 If you have a computer at home, do you own a modem?
1 ☐ Yes 2 ☐ Considering 9 ☐ No

20 Do you have an office at home? 1 ☐ Yes 9 ☐ No

21 How much is your usual quarterly phone bill?
1 ☐ Up to £99 2 ☐ £100 - £149 3 ☐ £150 +

22 Do you regularly make the following types of calls?
1 ☐ International 2 ☐ Long distance/Nationally 3 ☐ Local

23 If you have a mobile phone do you have voicemail/message retrieval facility? 1 ☐ Yes 9 ☐ No

24 Do you regularly purchase goods from a catalogue?
1 ☐ As a customer 2 ☐ As an agent

25 Would anyone in your family buy or consider buying any of the following through the mail: Buy Considering Buying
Bulbs/Plants — 1 ☐ 4 ☐
Roses/Shrubs — 2 ☐ 5 ☐
Books — 3 ☐ 6 ☐

26 Do you or would you consider saving for a Christmas Hamper?
1 ☐ Yes 2 ☐ Would consider 9 ☐ No

27 What causes have you contributed to in the past year?
01 ☐ Environmental 06 ☐ Disaster Relief
02 ☐ Health Research 07 ☐ Wildlife
03 ☐ Third World Causes 08 ☐ Animal Welfare
04 ☐ Children's Welfare 09 ☐ Disabled/Handicapped
05 ☐ Helping the Elderly 10 ☐ Other

28 How do you contribute? (Please tick all that apply)
1 ☐ By covenant 2 ☐ In street/at door 3 ☐ By post

29 Would you consider supporting any of the following charitable concerns?
1 ☐ AIDS 4 ☐ Blind
2 ☐ Deaf 5 ☐ Homeless
3 ☐ Human Rights 6 ☐ Medical
  7 ☐ Mental Health

30 Would you support a Christian charity working in any of the above areas? 1 ☐ Yes 9 ☐ No

31 Would you purchase Christian worship music on tape /CD by post? 1 ☐ Yes 9 ☐ No

32 Would you donate to any of the following charities?
1 ☐ RNIB (Royal National Institute for the Blind) 4 ☐ PDSA (Peoples Dispensary for Sick Animals)
2 ☐ RSPCA
3 ☐ Salvation Army 5 ☐ RSPB

33 Are you or your partner vegetarian You: 1 ☐ Yes Partner: 2 ☐ Yes

2. SHOPPING

1 Which of the following stores do you use for food and grocery shopping? (Please tick all that apply)
01 ☐ Aldi 14 ☐ Mace/Spar/VG
02 ☐ Alldays/Circle K 15 ☐ Marks & Spencer
03 ☐ Asda 16 ☐ Morrisons
04 ☐ Budgen 17 ☐ Netto
05 ☐ Co-op Leo's 18 ☐ Presto
06 ☐ Co-op Pioneer 19 ☐ Safeway
07 ☐ Co-op Others 20 ☐ Sainsbury
08 ☐ Food Giant 21 ☐ Savacentre
09 ☐ Gateway/Solo 22 ☐ Somerfield
10 ☐ Garage Shop 23 ☐ Tesco
11 ☐ Iceland 24 ☐ Tesco Metro
12 ☐ Kwik Save 25 ☐ Waitrose
13 ☐ Lo-Cost 26 ☐ Corner Shop/Other

2 Please write the number of the store where you do your main shopping: ☐☐

3 Where do you buy most of your tobacco products?
1 ☐ Corner Shop 3 ☐ Newsagent
2 ☐ Supermarket 4 ☐ Other
If Supermarket, please indicate from the list of stores above, the number of your store: ☐☐

4 Do you or your partner use any of the following supermarket club cards on a regular basis?

	You	Partner		You	Partner
Safeway - ABC	01 ☐	07 ☐	Tesco - Club Card Plus 04 ☐		10 ☐
Sainsbury - Reward	02 ☐	08 ☐	Asda - Club 05 ☐		11 ☐
Tesco - Club Card	03 ☐	09 ☐	Other 06 ☐		12 ☐

WHEN DOING YOUR MAIN SHOPPING:

5 Why do you buy where you do? (Please tick a maximum of 2)
1 ☐ Distance 5 ☐ Range of Products
2 ☐ Convenience 6 ☐ Prices
3 ☐ Quality of Products 7 ☐ Store Loyalty Card
4 ☐ Parking Facilities 8 ☐ Other

6 How far is your main grocery store from your home?
1 ☐ Less than 1 mile 3 ☐ 3-4 miles 5 ☐ 8-10 miles
2 ☐ 1-2 miles 4 ☐ 5-7 miles 6 ☐ more than 10 miles

7 What do you spend on groceries a week?

Main shopping
1 ☐ Under £15 3 ☐ £30-44 5 ☐ £60-74
2 ☐ £15-29 4 ☐ £45-59 6 ☐ £75+
Other Grocery shopping 7 ☐ Under £10 8 ☐ £10-19 9 ☐ £20+

8 How often have you bought the following products in the past 3 months?

	1	2-3	4+	None
Environmentally Friendly Products	1 ☐	3 ☐	5 ☐	7 ☐
Recycled Products	2 ☐	4 ☐	6 ☐	8 ☐

9 Do you/your household drink fizzy drinks every day?
1 ☐ Yes, sugared 2 ☐ Yes, Diet/light 9 ☐ No

10 Which diet fizzy drinks are drunk everyday?
1 ☐ Pepsi Diet 3 ☐ Supermarket's Own Diet Fizzy Drinks
2 ☐ Diet Coke 4 ☐ Other Diet drinks

11 How often do you buy the following pasta brands?

(Times bought in the past 3 months)	Once	2-3	4+	Never
Buitoni	01 ☐	06 ☐	11 ☐	16 ☐
Napolina	02 ☐	07 ☐	12 ☐	17 ☐
Barilla	03 ☐	08 ☐	13 ☐	18 ☐
Shop's Own	04 ☐	09 ☐	14 ☐	19 ☐
Other	05 ☐	10 ☐	15 ☐	20 ☐

12 Which washing powder or liquid do you use in your machine? (Please tick all that apply)

	Frequently	Sometimes	Never
Ariel	01 ☐	21 ☐	41 ☐
Bold Spring Fresh	02 ☐	22 ☐	42 ☐
Bold Summer Meadow Fresh	03 ☐	23 ☐	43 ☐
Daz	04 ☐	24 ☐	44 ☐
Fairy Non-Bio	05 ☐	25 ☐	45 ☐
Novon/Sainsbury's Own	06 ☐	26 ☐	46 ☐
Persil Bio/New Generation	07 ☐	27 ☐	47 ☐
Persil Non Bio	08 ☐	28 ☐	48 ☐
Radion	09 ☐	29 ☐	49 ☐
Surf	10 ☐	30 ☐	50 ☐
Safeway Cyclon	11 ☐	31 ☐	51 ☐
Tesco Advance	12 ☐	32 ☐	52 ☐
Other Shop's Own/Other	13 ☐	33 ☐	53 ☐

13 If you use Cyclon, Advance or Other Shop's Own, do you usually use:? 1 ☐ Bio 2 ☐ Non Bio

14 Which type of automatic washing powder/liquid do you usually purchase?
1 ☐ Regular/Auto Powder 4 ☐ Colour Liquid
2 ☐ Regular/Auto Liquid 5 ☐ Ultra/Concentrated/Future/Micro Powder
3 ☐ Colour Powder 6 ☐ Ultra/Concentrated/Future/Micro Liquid

15 Which separate fabric conditioner do you use in your washing machine? 9 ☐ Do not use
1 ☐ Comfort Blue 5 ☐ Lenor Spring/Summer
2 ☐ Comfort Pure/Country Garden 6 ☐ Sainsbury's Own
3 ☐ Comfort Silk 7 ☐ Other Shop's Own
4 ☐ Lenor Alpine/Tropical Fresh 8 ☐ Other

16 If you use a fabric conditioner which type is it?
1 ☐ Ultra or Concentrated 2 ☐ Regular 3 ☐ Refill

17 And how often do you use it?
1 ☐ All Washes 2 ☐ Most Washes 3 ☐ Rarely

18 Which of these washing-up liquids do you usually use? (Please tick all that apply)
01 ☐ Fairy 06 ☐ Persil (Other)
02 ☐ Fairy Lemon 07 ☐ Sunlight/Sqezy
03 ☐ Fairy Spring Fresh 08 ☐ Shop's Own Lemon
04 ☐ Morning Fresh 09 ☐ Other Shop's Own
05 ☐ Persil Lemon/Citrus

19 If you have an automatic dishwasher, which of these do you usually use?
1 ☐ Fairy 3 ☐ Sainsbury's Own 5 ☐ Sun
2 ☐ Finish 4 ☐ Other Shop's Own 6 ☐ Other

20 Which type do you usually purchase?
1 ☐ Traditional/Regular Powder/Granules 3 ☐ Liquid
2 ☐ Ultra/Concentrated/Micro Powder 4 ☐ Tablets

21 Which of these household cleaners do you usually use? (Please tick all that apply)
01 ☐ Domestos Multi Surface Cleaner 11 ☐ Jif Micro Liquid
02 ☐ Duck Mousse 12 ☐ Jif Mousse
03 ☐ Flash All Purpose 13 ☐ Mr Muscle Kitchen and Bathroom
04 ☐ Flash Bathroom Liquid 14 ☐ Shop's Own Bathroom Spray
05 ☐ Flash Bathroom Spray 15 ☐ Shop's Own Floor Cleaner
06 ☐ Flash Gel 16 ☐ Shop's Own Kitchen Spray
07 ☐ Flash Spray with Bleach 17 ☐ Shop's Own Liquid Kitchen Cleaner
08 ☐ Jif Bath Spray 18 ☐ Shop's Own Liquid Kitchen Cleaner
09 ☐ Jif Cream 19 ☐ Other Shop's Own
10 ☐ Jif Kitchen Spray 20 ☐ Other

3. ABOUT YOUR PETS

1 How many pets do you own? 9 ☐ None
Dogs ☐ Cats ☐ Others ☐

2 What are the ages of your pets?
Dogs: 1 Y Y M M 2 Y Y M M 3 Y Y M M
Cats: 1 Y Y M M 2 Y Y M M 3 Y Y M M

3 Which of the following pet foods do you feed your pet regularly? (Please tick all that apply)
DOG FOOD
01 ☐ Pal 03 ☐ Pedigree Chum 05 ☐ Chunky
02 ☐ Butcher's Tripe 04 ☐ Winalot Prime 06 ☐ Shop's Own/Other Cans
07 ☐ Bakers Complete 10 ☐ Hill's Science Diet 13 ☐ Eukanuba
08 ☐ Chum Complete 11 ☐ Beta 14 ☐ Chum Advance Formula
09 ☐ Winalot Complete 12 ☐ Omega 15 ☐ Shop's Own/Other Complete
CAT FOOD
16 ☐ Sheba 18 ☐ Whiskas 20 ☐ Felix
17 ☐ Purrfect 19 ☐ Arthur's 21 ☐ Shop's Own/Other Cans
22 ☐ Iams 23 ☐ Hill's Science Diet 24 ☐ Shop's Own/Other Complete
25 ☐ Felix Mix 27 ☐ Whiskas Crunch 29 ☐ Whiskas Cocktail
26 ☐ Brekkies 28 ☐ Friskies Go Cat 30 ☐ Shop's Own/Other Dry

4 Where do you usually buy your pet foods?
1 ☐ Corner Shop 3 ☐ Supermarket 5 ☐ Pet Shop
2 ☐ Vet 4 ☐ Breeder 6 ☐ Other

4. SMOKING

IMPORTANT	If you or your partner smoke, please sign to confirm that you are a smoker aged 18 or over:	YOUR SIGNATURE	PARTNER'S SIGNATURE

Each person must sign to qualify for special tobacco offers.

If you or your partner smoke CIGARETTES please indicate ALL brands smoked. (Please tick all that apply).

1 CIGARETTES

	You:	Partner:		You:	Partner:		You:	Partner:
Benson & Hedges	01 ☐	31 ☐	Berkeley	08 ☐	38 ☐	Kensitas	15 ☐	45 ☐
B&H Superkings	02 ☐	32 ☐	Embassy	09 ☐	39 ☐	Red Band	16 ☐	46 ☐
B&H Sovereign	03 ☐	33 ☐	Rothmans Royals	10 ☐	40 ☐	Mayfair	17 ☐	47 ☐
Regal	04 ☐	34 ☐	Rothmans	11 ☐	41 ☐	Craven A	18 ☐	48 ☐
Lambert & Butler	05 ☐	35 ☐	John Player Special	12 ☐	42 ☐	Dorchester	19 ☐	49 ☐
Silk Cut	06 ☐	36 ☐	Raffles	13 ☐	43 ☐	Dunhill	20 ☐	50 ☐
Superkings	07 ☐	37 ☐	Marlboro	14 ☐	44 ☐	Other: Under £2.55	21 ☐	51 ☐
						Other: Over £2.55	22 ☐	52 ☐

Please indicate which ONE cigarette brand you and/or your partner smoke MOST OFTEN by writing in the box number from the list above.   You: ☐   Partner: ☐
(Cigarette Brand smoked most often)

2 Is your/your partner's main brand:

	You:	Partner:	**3 HANDROLLING**	You:	Partner:	**4 Which Gift schemes do you/your partner collect for:**	You:	Partner:
Lights/mild version:	1 ☐	4 ☐	Golden Virginia	1 ☐	4 ☐	Focus:	1 ☐	3 ☐
Menthol:	2 ☐	5 ☐	Old Holborn	2 ☐	5 ☐	Gratis:	2 ☐	4 ☐
Longer than King size:	3 ☐	6 ☐	Other Handrolling	3 ☐	6 ☐			

5 CIGARS Do you or your partner smoke CIGARS?   1 ☐ Yes   9 ☐ No

If yes, how frequently?	You:	Partner:		You:	Partner:
Occasionally	1 ☐	5 ☐	2-4 packs per week	3 ☐	7 ☐
1 pack per week	2 ☐	6 ☐	1 pack per day	4 ☐	8 ☐

6 Which ONE brand is smoked MOST OFTEN?

	You:	Partner:		You:	Partner:
Hamlet	01 ☐	12 ☐	King Edward Coronets	07 ☐	18 ☐
Café Crème	02 ☐	13 ☐	Castella Panatella	08 ☐	19 ☐
Classic	03 ☐	14 ☐	King Six	09 ☐	20 ☐
Panama	04 ☐	15 ☐	Hamlet Reserve	10 ☐	21 ☐
Hamlet Miniature	05 ☐	16 ☐	Other Cigars	11 ☐	22 ☐
Henri Wintermans	06 ☐	17 ☐			

7 PIPE Do you or your partner smoke a PIPE?   1 ☐ Yes   9 ☐ No

8 If yes, which one brand is smoked MOST OFTEN?

	You:	Partner:		You:	Partner:
Clan	01 ☐	07 ☐			
Condor	02 ☐	08 ☐			
Dutch Blend	03 ☐	09 ☐			
Gold Block	04 ☐	10 ☐			
St Bruno	05 ☐	11 ☐			
Other Pipe	06 ☐	12 ☐			

Remember, each smoker must sign above.

5. MOTORING

What cars do you have?

	MAIN CAR	SECOND CAR
1 Make of Car? e.g. Ford	MAKE	MAKE
2 Model & Type? e.g. Escort/Ghia	MODEL TYPE	MODEL TYPE
3 Registration Letter? e.g. K	CC: CC	CC: CC
4 Who is the main driver?	1 ☐ You 2 ☐ Partner	1 ☐ You 2 ☐ Partner
5 Is the car owned?	1 ☐ Privately 2 ☐ Company	1 ☐ Privately 2 ☐ Company
6 Its yearly mileage?	☐,000	☐,000
7 Bought?	1 ☐ New 2 ☐ Used in 19 ☐	1 ☐ New 2 ☐ Used in 19 ☐
8 Is this car?	1 ☐ Diesel 2 ☐ Estate 3 ☐ 4WD	1 ☐ Diesel 2 ☐ Estate 3 ☐ 4WD
9 Plan to change it?	1 ☐ 0-6mths 2 ☐ 7-12 mths 3 ☐ 1-2 yrs	1 ☐ 0-6mths 2 ☐ 7-12 mths 3 ☐ 1-2 yrs
10 Who services your car?	1 ☐ Main Dealer 2 ☐ Independent 3 ☐ Yourself	1 ☐ Main Dealer 2 ☐ Independent 3 ☐ Yourself

11 When is your next service due?
1 ☐ 0-3 Months   2 ☐ 4-6 Months   3 ☐ 7-9 Months   4 ☐ 10-12 Months

12 If you have a company car, can you choose the make/model?
1 ☐ Yes   9 ☐ No

13 Number of cars in your household?
1 ☐ One   2 ☐ Two   3 ☐ Three plus   9 ☐ None

14 When does your current car insurance expire?
(If not sure of exact month, please tick nearest)

Main Car:	01 ☐ Jan	04 ☐ April	07 ☐ July	10 ☐ Oct
	02 ☐ Feb	05 ☐ May	08 ☐ Aug	11 ☐ Nov
	03 ☐ Mar	06 ☐ June	09 ☐ Sep	12 ☐ Dec
Second Car:	01 ☐ Jan	04 ☐ April	07 ☐ July	10 ☐ Oct
	02 ☐ Feb	05 ☐ May	08 ☐ Aug	11 ☐ Nov
	03 ☐ Mar	06 ☐ June	09 ☐ Sep	12 ☐ Dec

15 Please indicate if you renew your main car insurance:
1 ☐ In the first half of the month   2 ☐ In the second half of the month

16 Where do you keep your car(s)?

Main Car:	1 ☐ Garage	2 ☐ Driveway	3 ☐ Road
Second Car:	1 ☐ Garage	2 ☐ Driveway	3 ☐ Road

17 What is the main use of your car(s)?

Main Car	Second Car
1 ☐ Social/Domestic/Pleasure	4 ☐ Social/Domestic/Pleasure
2 ☐ Travel to work	5 ☐ Travel to work
3 ☐ Business	6 ☐ Business

18 Has anyone who drives your car had:

	Yes	No
An accident in the last 3 years?	1 ☐	3 ☐
A licence endorsement in the last 5 years? (Not parking/speeding)	2 ☐	4 ☐

19 How many years No Claims do you have?

You:	0 ☐ 0	1 ☐ 1	2 ☐ 2	3 ☐ 3	4 ☐ 4+	5 ☐ Unsure
Partner:	0 ☐ 0	1 ☐ 1	2 ☐ 2	3 ☐ 3	4 ☐ 4+	5 ☐ Unsure

20 How long have you been with your current motor insurer?
1 ☐ 1 year   3 ☐ 3 years   5 ☐ 5 years +
2 ☐ 2 years   4 ☐ 4 years   6 ☐ Unsure

21 Have you considered changing your current motor insurer in the last 12 months?   1 ☐ Yes   9 ☐ No

22 In which month will you renew your car MOT?

01 ☐ Jan	04 ☐ April	07 ☐ July	10 ☐ Oct
02 ☐ Feb	05 ☐ May	08 ☐ Aug	11 ☐ Nov
03 ☐ Mar	06 ☐ June	09 ☐ Sep	12 ☐ Dec

23 Which motoring organisation are you a member of?
1 ☐ Britannia Rescue   3 ☐ AA   5 ☐ Europ Assistance
2 ☐ Green Flag National Breakdown   4 ☐ RAC   6 ☐ Other

24 In which month did you join?

01 ☐ Jan	04 ☐ April	07 ☐ July	10 ☐ Oct
02 ☐ Feb	05 ☐ May	08 ☐ Aug	11 ☐ Nov
03 ☐ Mar	06 ☐ June	09 ☐ Sep	12 ☐ Dec

6. WINES & SPIRITS

1 Please tick all the whisky brands you buy to drink AT HOME:

	Often	Sometimes		Often	Sometimes
Bell's	01 ☐	21 ☐	Other American	10 ☐	30 ☐
Famous Grouse	02 ☐	22 ☐	Jameson	11 ☐	31 ☐
Johnnie Walker	03 ☐	23 ☐	Other Irish Whiskey	12 ☐	32 ☐
Teacher's	04 ☐	24 ☐	Glenfiddich	13 ☐	33 ☐
William Grant's	05 ☐	25 ☐	Glenmorangie	14 ☐	34 ☐
Whyte & Mackay	06 ☐	26 ☐	Glenlivet	15 ☐	35 ☐
White Horse	07 ☐	27 ☐	Macallan	16 ☐	36 ☐
Other Blended	08 ☐	28 ☐	Shop's Own Malt	17 ☐	37 ☐
Jack Daniels	09 ☐	29 ☐	Other Malt	18 ☐	38 ☐

2 From the above list please indicate the number of the whisky brand bought most often: ☐☐☐

3 How many bottles of THIS whisky do you buy in a year?
1 ☐ 1   2 ☐ 2   3 ☐ 3   4 ☐ 4   5 ☐ 5+

4 Please tick all the brands you buy to drink at home:

SHERRY
01 ☐ Croft Original
02 ☐ Croft Particular
03 ☐ Harvey's Bristol Cream
04 ☐ Harvey's Club Amontillado
05 ☐ Other Harvey's
06 ☐ Tio Pepe
07 ☐ Shop's Own Label
08 ☐ Other Sherry

BRANDY/COGNAC
09 ☐ Courvoisier
10 ☐ Hennessy
11 ☐ Martell
12 ☐ Remy Martin
13 ☐ Three Barrels
14 ☐ Hine
15 ☐ Shop's Own Brandy/Cognac
16 ☐ Other Brandy/Cognac

GIN
17 ☐ Beefeater
18 ☐ Gordon's
19 ☐ Bombay Sapphire
20 ☐ Shop's Own Label
21 ☐ Other Gin

VODKA
22 ☐ Smirnoff
23 ☐ Vladivar
24 ☐ Absolut
25 ☐ Virgin
26 ☐ Other Vodka

OTHER DRINKS
27 ☐ Archers
28 ☐ Bacardi
29 ☐ Bacardi Breezer
30 ☐ Pimm's
31 ☐ Taboo
32 ☐ Cointreau
33 ☐ Kahlua
34 ☐ Malibu
35 ☐ Pernod
36 ☐ Southern Comfort
37 ☐ Tequila
38 ☐ Drambuie
39 ☐ Tia Maria
40 ☐ Bailey's
41 ☐ Cadbury's Cream
42 ☐ Sheridan's
43 ☐ Smirnoff Mule
44 ☐ Metz
45 ☐ Shott's
46 ☐ Hoopers Hooch

5 How many bottles of the following are purchased by your household in one year?

	1	2-3	4-6	7+	None
Brandy/Cognac	01 ☐	07 ☐	13 ☐	19 ☐	25 ☐
Gin	02 ☐	08 ☐	14 ☐	20 ☐	26 ☐
Liqueurs	03 ☐	09 ☐	15 ☐	21 ☐	27 ☐
Sherry	04 ☐	10 ☐	16 ☐	22 ☐	28 ☐
Whisky	05 ☐	11 ☐	17 ☐	23 ☐	29 ☐
Vodka	06 ☐	12 ☐	18 ☐	24 ☐	30 ☐

6 Do you drink ready mixed spirits? 1 ☐ Yes   9 ☐ No

7 How many bottles of wine do you normally buy in a month?
1 ☐ None   3 ☐ One to Two   5 ☐ Six to Eleven
2 ☐ Less than one   4 ☐ Three to Five   6 ☐ Twelve Plus

8 Do you ever buy wine by the case? 1 ☐ Yes   9 ☐ No

9 Where do you buy your wines and spirits?

	Often	Occasionally		Often	Occasionally
Supermarket	01 ☐	13 ☐	Oddbins	07 ☐	19 ☐
Victoria Wine	02 ☐	14 ☐	Bottoms Up	08 ☐	20 ☐
Victoria Wine Cellars	03 ☐	15 ☐	Haddows	09 ☐	21 ☐
Greenall Cellars	04 ☐	16 ☐	Unwins	10 ☐	22 ☐
Berkeley Wines	05 ☐	17 ☐	Wine Rack	11 ☐	23 ☐
Threshers Food/Drink	06 ☐	18 ☐	Corner Shop	12 ☐	24 ☐

10 How often do you or your partner visit a pub/club or wine bar?

	Never	Once a month	Once a week	Several times a week	Every day
You:	01 ☐	03 ☐	05 ☐	07 ☐	09 ☐
Your Partner:	02 ☐	04 ☐	06 ☐	08 ☐	10 ☐

7. HEALTH

1 Does your family use:
2 ☐ Health Foods
1 ☐ Herbal remedies
3 ☐ Vitamin/Food Supplements

2 Does anyone in your home have:
1 ☐ Back Trouble
2 ☐ Arthritis/Rheumatism
3 ☐ Hayfever
4 ☐ Asthma
5 ☐ Spectacles
6 ☐ Contact Lenses
7 ☐ Tension Headaches

3 Where do you buy your toiletries?
1 ☐ Boots
2 ☐ Superdrug
3 ☐ Lloyds Chemist
4 ☐ Supermarket
5 ☐ Local Chemist
6 ☐ Other

4 Do you or your partner have:

	You	Partner
Hearing Difficulties	1 ☐	3 ☐
A Hearing Aid	2 ☐	4 ☐

5 Do you or your partner suffer from sensitive teeth?
1 ☐ Yes   9 ☐ No

6 If Yes, how often do you use a treatment toothpaste:
1 ☐ Once a day   3 ☐ When symptoms occur
2 ☐ Twice a day   9 ☐ Never

7 If you suffer from sensitive teeth and use a treatment toothpaste, which of the following toothpastes do you use?
1 ☐ Macleans Sensitive   3 ☐ Sensodyne Other
2 ☐ Sensodyne Mint   4 ☐ Other

8 How often are treatments purchased for anyone in your home with these conditions?

(Times per year)

	Less Than Once	1-2	3+		Less Than Once	1-2	3+
Varicose Veins	01 ☐	07 ☐	13 ☐	Bunions	04 ☐	10 ☐	16 ☐
Athlete's Foot	02 ☐	08 ☐	14 ☐	Corns	05 ☐	11 ☐	17 ☐
Blisters	03 ☐	09 ☐	15 ☐	Verrucae	06 ☐	12 ☐	18 ☐

9 If you are female, which best describes your dress size?
1 ☐ Under 8   2 ☐ 8-10   3 ☐ 12-14   4 ☐ 16 plus

10 Which sanitary protection products do you use?
(Please tick all that apply)
1 ☐ Thick/Normal Towels/Pads   3 ☐ Tampons   5 ☐ Others
2 ☐ Thin/Ultra Towels/Pads   4 ☐ Panty Liners

11 Which sanitary protection products do you usually buy?
01 ☐ Tampax Tampons
02 ☐ Shop's Own Tampons
03 ☐ Other Tampon Brand
04 ☐ Bodyform/Libra
05 ☐ Always Ultra
06 ☐ Always Normal
07 ☐ Vespré/Silhouettes
08 ☐ Kotex/Simplicity
09 ☐ Boots' Own
10 ☐ Other Shop's Own Towel
11 ☐ Other Towel Brand
99 ☐ None

8. YOU AND YOUR HOME

1 Do you? 1 ☐ Own your own home 2 ☐ Rent (Private) 3 ☐ Rent (Council)

2 Is your home a: 1 ☐ Flat   2 ☐ Maisonette   3 ☐ Terraced
4 ☐ Semi-Detached   5 ☐ Detached   6 ☐ Bungalow

3 When did you move to this address?
Year : 19 ☐☐   Month: ☐☐

4 How many people are in your home including yourself?
1 ☐ One   2 ☐ Two   3 ☐ Three   4 ☐ Four   5 ☐ Five   6 ☐ Six

5 How many bedrooms do you have?
1 ☐ One   2 ☐ Two   3 ☐ Three   4 ☐ Four   5 ☐ Five plus

6 Are you planning to move in the next year?   9 ☐ No
If Yes, when? 1 ☐ 1-3 mths   2 ☐ 4-6 mths   3 ☐ 7-12 mths

7 When was your home built?
1 ☐ Pre 1918   2 ☐ 1919 - 1944   3 ☐ 1945 - 1976   4 ☐ Post 1977

8 Which Council tax bracket applies to your home?
1 ☐ A   2 ☐ B   3 ☐ C   4 ☐ D   5 ☐ E   6 ☐ F   7 ☐ G   8 ☐ H

9 What is the approximate value of your home and mortgage?

	Home	Mortgage		Home	Mortgage
Up to £40,000	01 ☐	09 ☐	£100,001 - £120,000	05 ☐	13 ☐
£40,001 - £60,000	02 ☐	10 ☐	£120,001 - £200,000	06 ☐	14 ☐
£60,001 - £80,000	03 ☐	11 ☐	£200,001 - £500,000	07 ☐	15 ☐
£80,001 - £100,000	04 ☐	12 ☐	Over £500,001	08 ☐	16 ☐

10 How many years has your mortgage left to run ?
1 ☐ Under five   2 ☐ 5-10   3 ☐ 11-20   4 ☐ 21 +

11 What type of mortgage do you have?
1 ☐ Endowment   2 ☐ P.E.P.   3 ☐ Repayment   4 ☐ Pension   5 ☐ Other

12 If you have a mortgage or other loan commitments would you consider reducing your monthly payments?
1 ☐ Yes   2 ☐ Possibly   9 ☐ No

13 When does your Home Contents Insurance expire?
01 ☐ Jan   04 ☐ April   07 ☐ July   10 ☐ Oct
02 ☐ Feb   05 ☐ May   08 ☐ Aug   11 ☐ Nov
03 ☐ Mar   06 ☐ June   09 ☐ Sep   12 ☐ Dec

14 Please indicate if you renew your home contents insurance:
1 ☐ In the first half of the month   2 ☐ In the second half of the month

15 How long have you been with your existing Household Insurer?
1 ☐ Under 1 year   2 ☐ 1-2 years   3 ☐ 3-5 years   4 ☐ Over 5 years

16 When does your Buildings Insurance expire?
01 ☐ Jan   04 ☐ April   07 ☐ July   10 ☐ Oct
02 ☐ Feb   05 ☐ May   08 ☐ Aug   11 ☐ Nov
03 ☐ Mar   06 ☐ June   09 ☐ Sep   12 ☐ Dec

17 Please indicate if you renew your buildings insurance:
1 ☐ In the first half of the month   2 ☐ In the second half of the month

18 Are you considering any of the following home improvements?

	Yes	Possibly	No	Already Have
Fitted Bathroom	01 ☐	08 ☐	15 ☐	22 ☐
Double Glazing	02 ☐	09 ☐	16 ☐	23 ☐
UPVC Fascia & Bargeboards	03 ☐	10 ☐	17 ☐	24 ☐
Rewiring	04 ☐	11 ☐	18 ☐	25 ☐
Fitted Kitchen	05 ☐	12 ☐	19 ☐	26 ☐
Home Security	06 ☐	13 ☐	20 ☐	27 ☐
Loft Conversion	07 ☐	14 ☐	21 ☐	28 ☐

19 Are you considering purchasing any of the following? (Please tick all that apply)
1 ☐ Satellite TV   2 ☐ Cable TV   3 ☐ Mobile Phone

9. YOU AND YOUR FAMILY

In order for manufacturers to really understand what consumers want, it is important for them to know more than simply how much of a product is sold. They need to have a clear picture of who is buying and why they are buying. This survey can help.

The following questions are being asked as a means to place you and your family into sub-groups. This makes it easier for us to understand your preferences and attitudes.

If you are still uncomfortable for any reason with answering any of the following questions, please feel free to leave them blank. I would much rather have your survey returned to me without these facts, than not receive your survey at all.

Thank you, *Linda*

1 What are the dates of birth for:

You: |　| |　| 19 |　|　Partner: |　| |　| 19 |　|
　　Day　Month　Year　　　　　Day　Month　Year

2 Are you?　1 ☐ Married　3 ☐ Divorced/Separated　5 ☐ Living together
　　　　　　2 ☐ Single　4 ☐ Widowed

3 What is your partner's first name?

|　|　|　|　|　|　|　|　|　|　|　|

4 What is your partner's surname?

|　|　|　|　|　|　|　|　|　|　|　|

5 What is your partner's title?
1 ☐ Mr.　　2 ☐ Mrs.　　3 ☐ Miss　　4 ☐ Ms.

6 Please tell us the age and sex of all the children living at home:　99 ☐ None

	Girl	Boy		Girl	Boy		Girl	Boy
0-12 Ms	00 ☐	30 ☐	7 Yrs	07 ☐	37 ☐	14 Yrs	14 ☐	44 ☐
1 Yr	01 ☐	31 ☐	8 Yrs	08 ☐	38 ☐	15 Yrs	15 ☐	45 ☐
2 Yrs	02 ☐	32 ☐	9 Yrs	09 ☐	39 ☐	16 Yrs	16 ☐	46 ☐
3 Yrs	03 ☐	33 ☐	10 Yrs	10 ☐	40 ☐	17 Yrs	17 ☐	47 ☐
4 Yrs	04 ☐	34 ☐	11 Yrs	11 ☐	41 ☐	18 Yrs	18 ☐	48 ☐
5 Yrs	05 ☐	35 ☐	12 Yrs	12 ☐	42 ☐	19 Yrs	19 ☐	49 ☐
6 Yrs	06 ☐	36 ☐	13 Yrs	13 ☐	43 ☐	20 plus	20 ☐	50 ☐

7 Please state the date of birth of your youngest child:

| D | D | | M | M | | Y | Y |

8 If you or your partner are trade union members, would you like information on tailored financial products?　1 ☐ You　2 ☐ Partner

9 What are the occupations of you and your partner?

	You	Partner
Craftsman/Tradesman	01 ☐	11 ☐
Education/Medical Services	02 ☐	12 ☐
Housewife	03 ☐	13 ☐
Manual/Factory Worker	04 ☐	14 ☐
Middle Management	05 ☐	15 ☐
Office/Clerical	06 ☐	16 ☐
Professional/Senior Management	07 ☐	17 ☐
Retired	08 ☐	18 ☐
Shopworker	09 ☐	19 ☐
Student	10 ☐	20 ☐

10 Are you/your partner?

	You	Partner
Self-Employed/Business Owner	1 ☐	3 ☐
Running own in-home business	2 ☐	4 ☐

11 If you work, what is your work postcode? |　|　|　|　|

12 Has anyone in your home had an accident in the last 2 years which resulted in an injury or a condition lasting for 2 weeks or more? If so, would you like free information on possible compensation?　1 ☐ Yes

13 Do you or your partner have any of the following?
(Please tick all that apply)

01 ☐ Pension Plan - Private　　09 ☐ Savings Plan
02 ☐ Pension Plan - Via Employer　10 ☐ Accident Insurance
03 ☐ Health Care (BUPA, etc)　11 ☐ Critical Illness Insurance
04 ☐ Shares Privatisations (e.g. Gas/BT)　12 ☐ Mortgage
05 ☐ Shares General　　　13 ☐ Unit Trusts
06 ☐ Cheque Guarantee Card　14 ☐ Building Society Account
07 ☐ High Interest Investments　15 ☐ Life Insurance
08 ☐ Switch/Delta/Connect　16 ☐ A Will

14 If you have a need for, or if you would consider, any of the above, please write the number from the list above:

1 |　|　　2 |　|　　3 |　|　　4 |　|

15 Which of the following would you or your partner consider for the future?

	Life Assurance	Savings Plan	PEP
You:	1 ☐	2 ☐	3 ☐
Partner:	4 ☐	5 ☐	6 ☐

16 Does anyone in your home have a:
01 ☐ CD Player　04 ☐ Satellite TV　07 ☐ Tumble Dryer
02 ☐ Personal Computer　05 ☐ Microwave　08 ☐ Dishwasher
03 ☐ Cable TV　06 ☐ Video　09 ☐ Washing Machine
　　　　　　　　　　　　　10 ☐ Mobile Phone

---

17 Which group best describes your COMBINED annual household income?

1 ☐ Up to £5,000 (£96 per week)　　4 ☐ £15,000-£19,999
2 ☐ £5,000-£9,999 (£96-£192 per week)　5 ☐ £20,000-£24,999
　　　　　　　　　　　　　6 ☐ £25,000-£29,999
3 ☐ £10,000-£14,999　　　7 ☐ £30,000-£34,999
　　　　　　　　　　　　　8 ☐ £35,000 plus

18 Who do you currently bank with? (Please tick all that apply)

	You	Partner		You	Partner
Lloyds	01 ☐	17 ☐	Bank of Scotland	09 ☐	25 ☐
Barclays	02 ☐	18 ☐	Royal Bank of Scotland	10 ☐	26 ☐
TSB	03 ☐	19 ☐	Alliance & Leicester	11 ☐	27 ☐
NatWest	04 ☐	20 ☐	Nationwide	12 ☐	28 ☐
Co-operative Bank	05 ☐	21 ☐	Halifax	13 ☐	29 ☐
Midland	06 ☐	22 ☐	Other Bank	14 ☐	30 ☐
First Direct	07 ☐	23 ☐	Other Building Society	15 ☐	31 ☐
Abbey National	08 ☐	24 ☐	Other Financial Organisation	16 ☐	32 ☐

19 How long have you held your current main bank/building society cheque account?　Years |Y|Y|　Months |M|M|

20 Would you or your partner consider applying for another credit card in addition to your existing facility?
You:　　1 ☐ Yes　2 ☐ Possibly　9 ☐ No
Partner:　1 ☐ Yes　2 ☐ Possibly　9 ☐ No

21 Do you/your partner pay your monthly credit card balance in full?
You:　　1 ☐ Always　2 ☐ Sometimes　3 ☐ Rarely　9 ☐ Never
Partner:　1 ☐ Always　2 ☐ Sometimes　3 ☐ Rarely　9 ☐ Never

22 Which Cards do you or your partner have? (Please tick all that apply)

	You	Partner		You	Partner
Barclaycard	01 ☐	17 ☐	TSB Trustcard	09 ☐	25 ☐
American Express/Diners	02 ☐	18 ☐	Store Credit Card	10 ☐	26 ☐
Co-operative Bank Visa	03 ☐	19 ☐	GM Card	11 ☐	27 ☐
MBNA Credit Card	04 ☐	20 ☐	Visa Credit Card	12 ☐	28 ☐
Access	05 ☐	21 ☐	Bank of Scotland	13 ☐	29 ☐
Gold Card	06 ☐	22 ☐	GoldFish	14 ☐	30 ☐
Royal Bank of Scotland/Advanta	07 ☐	23 ☐	Other Credit Card	15 ☐	31 ☐
Peoples Bank	08 ☐	24 ☐	None	16 ☐	32 ☐

23 If you are not satisfied with your current bank/building society, would you consider banking by telephone or PC?
You:　　1 ☐ Yes　2 ☐ Possibly　9 ☐ No
Partner:　1 ☐ Yes　2 ☐ Possibly　9 ☐ No

24 Would you or your partner consider taking up a new credit card or changing your existing one?
You:　　1 ☐ Yes　2 ☐ Possibly　9 ☐ No
Partner:　1 ☐ Yes　2 ☐ Possibly　9 ☐ No

25 If yes, would you or your partner consider taking up a Gold Card?
You:　　1 ☐ Yes　2 ☐ Possibly　9 ☐ No
Partner:　1 ☐ Yes　2 ☐ Possibly　9 ☐ No

26 Would you consider professional help in arranging your personal finances?　1 ☐ Yes　2 ☐ Possibly　9 ☐ No

27 Are you likely to spend over £1000 on any of the following in the next 12 months?
1 ☐ Home Improvement　3 ☐ Car　　5 ☐ Wedding
2 ☐ Paying off Debt　4 ☐ Holiday　6 ☐ Consumer Durables (e.g. TV, Hi-Fi)

28 How do you intend to finance your purchases?
1 ☐ Loan　　　3 ☐ Credit Card　5 ☐ Other Credit
2 ☐ Overdraft　4 ☐ Savings

29 Do you or your family have Medical Cover?　9 ☐ No
1 ☐ Yes (Company)　　2 ☐ Yes (Private)　3 ☐ Considering

30 If yes, with which organisations?
1 ☐ BUPA　3 ☐ Private Patients Plan　5 ☐ Prime Health　7 ☐ Sun Alliance
2 ☐ WPA　4 ☐ Norwich Union Healthcare　6 ☐ Orion　8 ☐ Other

31 When will you renew your health cover?
01 ☐ Jan　04 ☐ April　07 ☐ July　10 ☐ Oct
02 ☐ Feb　05 ☐ May　08 ☐ Aug　11 ☐ Nov
03 ☐ Mar　06 ☐ June　09 ☐ Sep　12 ☐ Dec

32 Do you or your partner work in the local authority/public sector?
You:　1 ☐ Yes　9 ☐ No　Partner:　1 ☐ Yes　9 ☐ No

33 Please write your phone number here:

| 0 | 1 | | | | | | | | | |

Thank you for taking the time to complete this questionnaire. I hope you found it interesting.

One last thing - please CHECK to see if your name and address details on the first page of this questionnaire are correct. If any of the information is wrong, please correct it where appropriate. Please allow 6-16 weeks for the delivery of coupons, depending on how soon we receive your response. If you are moving house in the next 6-16 weeks, please write in your new address on the first page so we can make sure your coupons reach you.

Please return your completed survey within 7 days in the enclosed pre-paid envelope - No stamp required.

Kind regards, *Linda*

N　　　　　　　　　　5

Figure 26.6

1　Broadly outline the purpose of the questionnaire.
2　How would you describe the questions, i.e. are they 'open' or 'closed'?
3　Working in small groups describe how at least five areas in which information is obtained from this questionnaire might be used.

Administering the questionnaire

There are three different ways of administering a questionnaire:

- with a personal interview
- by telephone
- through the post.

Personal interviews allow direct two-way communication to take place between the researcher and the respondent. Although such interviews are more expensive than postal or telephone surveys, they enable an experienced interviewer to gather more sensitive and detailed information.

Telephone interviews tend to be unpopular with the public as they are perceived to be intrusive and also are regarded as a selling device. They are, however, more appropriate for business surveys and can be a cost-effective way of analysing an organisational market.

Postal questionnaires are a useful way of reaching a closed market, particularly if a mailing list is available. They are easy to administer but tend to yield a poor response, which can often be as low as 2 per cent.

Other primary research techniques

There are a range of other methods of collecting information which may be used in the market research process. For example:

- **Observation techniques** may be used to analyse how customers behave in buying situations.
- **Discussion groups** are a useful and inexpensive method of collecting qualitative information.
- **Focus groups** have become an increasingly popular method of obtaining information in recent years.
- **Opinion polls** are often used to assess consumer awareness and attitudes. Questions are usually short and attempt to find out how consumers react to issues such as product or image changes.
- **Electronic interviewing** is a technique based upon interactive communications using phone lines.

Chapter summary

- Market research helps to reduce the risks associated with business decision making.
- It involves the systematic gathering, recording and analysing of data about problems relating to the marketing of goods and services.
- Research may be basic or applied, proactive or reactive, quantitative or qualitative.
- There are three broad areas from which information may be extracted.

- Internal information will already be held within an organisation.
- External information or 'desk research' is found in published materials.
- Primary information is collected for a specific purpose.

---

27 An introduction to marketing strategy

We can only understand fully how marketing operates in the real world if we try to understand what marketing sets out to achieve. In 1985 the Chartered Institute of Marketing adopted a new slogan:

MARKETING MEANS BUSINESS

The implication is that it is marketing that directs and drives successful business.

Marketing is now accepted in most well-run businesses as a strategic discipline or general management function. In this respect, it cares for the future health of the business – especially enabling the organisation to deal with competition. This is because it is increasingly realised that although making a profit is important, an organisation should also develop its market share and search for brand leadership as well. So, the marketer must monitor the profitability of the business and attempt to anticipate the likely trends. At the same time, rival companies should be monitored and examined for vulnerable points.

> ### SYNTHESIS
>
> *What do managers seek? Scan the business pages of a 'broadsheet' newspaper. Many news stories refer to either evidence of 'success' or of 'failure' from various types of organisations. But, how are successes or failures determined. Is it just profitability or does market share, new orders, leadership, entry into new markets, etc, come into the equation? Are some of these more important than others?*

Marketing objectives

The first question that any organisation must answer is 'Where are we going'? Rather than seeking maximum profits, an organisation may seek to be the **brand leader** or otherwise to dominate a particular market – this may give it a dominant long-term position. **Corporate growth** is another common objective. Taking over other companies through **acquisition**, the **diversification** of activities or the introduction of **new products** may not in the short-term increase profitability, but they will provide managers with a range of new opportunities to develop a more successful business unit. Other organisations may take great pride in the way they are **viewed by the public**, and may be prepared to sacrifice profit but never reputation. At the centre of this process of planning lies the need to match marketing objectives with corporate objectives.

At the heart of marketing lies the degree to which an organisation becomes market-orientated. The more committed an organisation is to its marketing activities, the more it will be able to pursue is corporate and marketing objectives in developing and retaining its customers. Every business in existence relies on its customers for survival, and those who best meet customer needs will always survive a period of change.

The marketing function is therefore an essential ingredient of corporate strategy and this marketing focus should be communicated through marketing planning into all aspects of an organisation's activities.

Marketing planning

So far we have set out to understand the preliminary processes an organisation has to go through in order to satisfy customer needs. This has involved an understanding of the marketing environment, the nature of the marketplace, customer behaviour and the processes of market research. All of these activities are part of the research phase of the marketing plan. They are, therefore, more concerned with preparation than with implementation.

From this chapter onwards, both in this section on Marketing and in the other section on Marketing Strategy in Unit 9, we seek to broaden your understanding of the marketing process by looking at and developing the framework in which key marketing decisions are made.

Marketing planning is often described as 'anticipatory decision-making'. It involves planning today what has to be done tomorrow. This process of forward planning will help to:

- focus the organisation upon its business objectives (both marketing and corporate)
- provide all parts of the organisation with clear guidelines about what they are expected to achieve

- co-ordinate the activities of various parts of the organisation
- provide a mechanism against which the performance can be checked, modified and controlled.

Marketing planning should be viewed as a continuous cycle (see Figure 27.1). Collecting and sorting information from the research process will help to develop plans and identify alternative courses of action. Plans can then be modified and controlled in the light of performance.

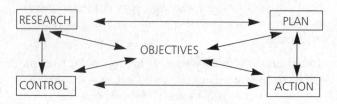

Figure 27.1   The marketing planning cycle

Research

The research phase, largely covered in the previous chapter, is concerned primarily with diagnosis and prognosis. As a result of the research it has undertaken, an organisation should be able to answer questions such as: 'Where are we and why'?; and 'Where are we going'?

Research is part of the **strategic audit** which finds out what has been achieved in the past. It also helps to predict what can be achieved in the future. One technique that is frequently used to match an organisation's strengths and weaknesses with the external forces in the business environment is a **SWOT analysis**. SWOT stands for:

- **S**trengths
- **W**eaknesses
- **O**pportunities
- **T**hreats.

The **internal** audit element of the SWOT analysis is the organisation's strengths and weaknesses; opportunities and threats reflect influences **external** to the organisation which exist in the business environment (see Figure 27.2). For example, a small business may have the following SWOT elements:

- Strengths   good product
                            good relationship with customers
                            strong management team
- Weaknesses   few economies of scale
                            liquidity problems
                            little experience of other markets
- Opportunities   new markets
                            changing tastes
                            diversification
- Threats   actions of competitors
                            recession
                            new legislation

SWOT analysis	
Within the organisation	In the environment
Strengths + Weaknesses −	Opportunities + Threats −

Figure 27.2

A SWOT analysis will help an organisation to complete a strategic audit and place itself in a better position to compile a marketing plan and make decisions about the marketplace.

The marketing plan

The marketing plan itself will comprise a number of plans drawn up by various parts of the organisation. In this way, it will both match and co-ordinate longer-term corporate goals with shorter-term plans. At the centre of the marketing plan will be each of the ingredients of the marketing mix (see Figure 27.3).

The **marketing mix** is often referred to as the Four Ps, i.e. Product, Price, Place and Promotion.

The marketing mix

Figure 27.3   The ingredients of the marketing mix

To meet customers' needs, an organisation must develop the **products** to satisfy them, charge the right **price**, get the goods to the right **place** (i.e. ensure that the product is available when needed), and make the existence of the product known through **promotion** (see Figure 27.4).

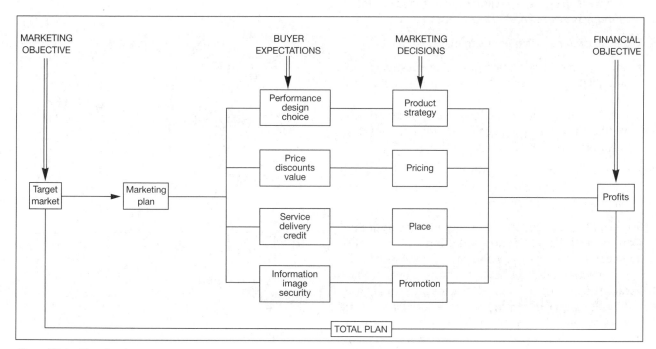

Figure 27.4   The planning process

Choosing a market in which to operate

In almost any market, market research will reveal that not all customers have the same needs. For example, they do not all have the same tastes or want the same things. An organisation has to look at what it is supplying and then instead of thinking about the market as a whole, to divide

the market into segments, rather like dividing an orange into segments.

For example, think about the market for jeans. Levi makes jeans, but the jeans market is split into a number of segments all catered for by Levi. One way of looking at the segmentation of this market is sex, while another is to look at the type of jeans – loose-fit, regular fit, stone-washed, pre-washed, etc (see Figure 27.5).

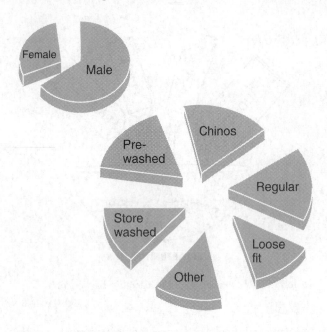

Figure 27.5   Segmentation of the jeans market

Segmentation is the strategy whereby an organisation partitions a market into submarkets (segments) which will respond in similar ways to marketing inputs.

There are two important points to make:

● each segment will contain groups of customers with 'roughly' similar needs or tastes than the market as a whole
● the part of the market represented by each segment will be reachable by a specific and different marketing mix from that used for other segments.

Segmentation, therefore, enables an organisation to develop a marketing mix which satisfies the requirements of different groups of customers.

Segmentation can be contrasted with **market aggregation** or **undifferentiated marketing**. With market aggregation a single marketing mix is developed for a whole market. Hence the term 'mass marketing'. Today, because of the increasing trend towards segmentation, it is difficult to think of a market which is not differentiated in any way through the process of segmentation. There are even many different types of flour, salt, sugar!

IT'S A FACT

That the only national newspaper read by more women than men (adult readership profile) is the *Mail on Sunday* which is taken by 51 per cent of women and 49 per cent of men. In stark contrast, the readership of the *Financial Times* is read by 72 per cent of men and 28 per cent of women.

Reasons for market segmentation

There are many different reasons for the movement towards differentiated marketing and segmentation. Segmentation helps an organisation to identify marketing opportunities which might include:

● **market penetration** – to increase the value/volume of their products in current markets
● **product development** – offering a wider product range to existing markets and segments
● **market development** – developing existing products in segments identified in new markets
● **diversification opportunities** – involving entry into new markets with new products.

Market segmentation enables an organisation to maximise the efficiency of its marketing efforts by using a different marketing mix for each segment. Undifferentiated marketing is said to be like firing a blunderbuss to pepper the whole marketplace, whereas segmentation is like hitting a target – which in this instance is a carefully specified market segment.

Segmentation is like hitting a target

Another reason for market segmentation is that it enables an organisation to develop a better understanding of **customer needs and requirements**. In doing this it can make fine adjustments to the marketing mix of each segment, enabling it to respond more quickly to any changes which need to take place. Segmentation also allows resources to be used more efficiently. For example, the efficiency of activities is likely to improve when they are concentrated on those sectors most likely to respond to such activities.

There are generally accepted to be three phases in the market segmentation process:

- **phase 1** – segmentation
- **phase 2** – targeting
- **phase 3** – positioning.

Segmentation

There are a number of different bases for segmentation. These may include the following.

Demographic segmentation

Demographic figures can be measured with relative precision and have helped many organisations to define a base for their market. Demographic segmentation may involve dividing the population by discrete segments, for example, by age for clothes retailing, by sex and age for the sale of cosmetics, by family size for different sized packages for breakfast cereals, as well as in many other ways.

TASK 27.1

Look at the UK population projections in Figure 27.6.

1 Comment upon how such information might be useful for:

  a a manufacturer of training shoes

  b a life assurance company

  c a local authority.

2 When looking at such information, explain the importance of looking at specific age groups in parts of the market rather than at population projections for the total population as a whole.

Population projections, UK						Thousands
	Projections					
	1992	**1996**	**2001**	**2011**	**2021**	**2031**
0–14	11,198	11,456	11,636	11,002	10,666	10,591
15–29	12,773	11,855	11,135	11,717	11,395	10,649
30–44	12,213	12,859	13,584	11,952	11,335	11,648
45–59	9,813	10,565	11,206	12,558	12,763	10,875
60–74	7,970	7,822	7,733	9,224	10,496	11,771
75+	4,034	4,224	4,505	4,803	5,491	6,707
Males	28,358	28,855	29,475	30,380	30,883	30,900
Females	29,640	29,930	30,325	30,878	31,263	31,314
Total	**57,998**	**58,784**	**59,800**	**61,257**	**62,146**	**62,241**

Figure 27.6   Population projections

Segmentation by age is widely applied. A good example is the way in which banks and building societies develop products for students, young children and elderly customers. Many products are also segmented by gender – clothing, alcohol, cosmetics and cars are all segmented in such a way. (Note that levels of education may also be a segmentation variable. For example, it would be expected that higher achievers at school, college and university would be more likely to buy broadsheet newspapers.)

Socio-economic segmentation

Income, occupation and social class are fundamental determinants of the pattern of segmentation adopted within certain markets. Income is a particularly useful way of dividing a market as it directly affects people's purchases. In Chapter 25 we looked at socio-economic grouping. Assigning people to social classes according to income is called **social stratification**. Each class or group has a certain pattern of behaviour which serves to reinforce consumption patterns. See for example the profile of drinkers in Figure 27.7.

Percent of Population	All Adults (18+)	Sex		Age				Social Grade			
		M	F	18–24	25–34	35–49	50+	AB	C1	C2	DE
Any Alc. Drink	**62.1**	**73.2**	**51.9**	**70.2**	**65.9**	**65.9**	**55.5**	**72.6**	**65.3**	**63.5**	**51.1**
Any Beer	40.9	62.2	21.2	55.0	49.3	43.6	30.9	43.0	41.4	45.4	35.6
Any Cider	6.7	7.2	6.1	15.6	9.2	6.4	2.9	5.5	7.0	7.5	6.4
Wine	29.0	27.5	30.4	22.3	30.9	36.1	25.3	47.8	34.8	24.1	14.9
Sherry	4.6	3.5	5.6	1.1	1.5	3.5	7.8	7.9	5.0	2.7	3.5
Vermouth	1.9	0.9	2.8	2.9	1.2	1.8	1.9	2.6	2.1	1.5	1.3
Any Spirit	20.3	23.5	17.2	21.2	14.9	19.0	23.5	25.5	21.5	20.4	15.5
Whisky	10.8	15.4	6.5	8.0	5.2	8.9	15.7	15.0	10.8	10.7	8.0
Brandy	3.2	3.5	3.0	1.8	2.1	3.0	4.3	4.1	3.2	3.3	2.6
Gin	4.0	3.7	4.3	2.7	3.2	4.0	4.9	8.3	4.9	2.3	1.8
Vodka	4.2	4.0	4.3	10.4	5.2	4.1	2.0	3.7	4.6	4.7	3.8
White Rum	2.0	1.9	2.1	4.6	2.4	2.1	1.1	1.6	2.2	2.4	1.8
Dark Rum	1.3	1.9	0.7	1.4	1.0	1.3	1.4	1.4	1.3	1.5	0.9
Liqueurs	2.1	1.8	2.4	4.2	2.7	1.7	1.5	2.9	2.3	2.2	1.3
Teetotallers*16		**12**	**19**	**11**	**12**	**13**	**21**	–	–	–	–

Profile of Alcohol Drinkers, GB: 1995   Alcoholic drinks drunk weekly or more often

Note:Proportion of people who never drink alcohol.
Source: PAS Drinks Market Survey 1995 (sample 20,000+).

Figure 27.7   Profile of alcohol drinkers

Lifestyle segmentation

Lifestyle is another variable. It has links with family, income, occupation, culture and education. It deals with people and not the product and attempts to relate lifestyle patterns to purchasing behaviour. Organisations have paid increasing heed to lifestyles over recent years. Many businesses now try to design and position products to appeal to groups with similar lifestyles.

Sagacity lifestyle groupings

This works on the principle that people have different behaviour patterns and aspirations as they go through life. Four main stages of the life-cycle are thus identified, and then further defined according to income and occupation groups (white-collar or blue collar occupations) – see Figure 27.8.

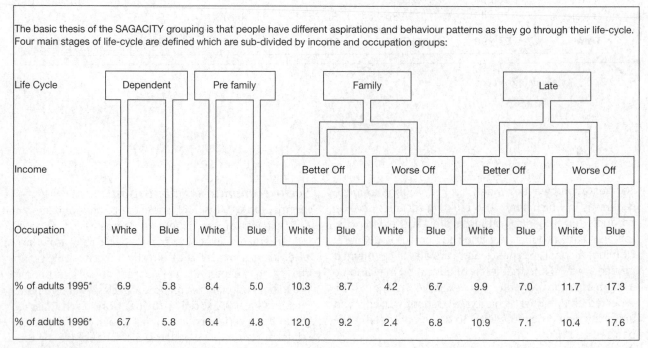

Figure 27.8   The sagacity life-cycle groupings

The life-cycle stages are defined as follows:

- dependent – mainly under-24s, living at home or full-time students
- pre-family – under 35s, who have established their own household but have no children
- family – parents, under 65, with one or more children in the household
- late – includes all adults whose children have left home, or who are over 35 and childless.

The occupation groups are:

- white – head of household in the ABC1 occupation group
- blue – head of household in the C2DE occupation group.

Geographic segmentation

This assumes that consumers in different regions may be affected by climate, natural factors, population density, different levels of income and consumption, etc. By dividing markets into regions it is possible to recognise and cater for the needs of customers in regions. Figure 27.9 identifies different spending patterns by marketplace in selected regions in the UK. Note that on average a person will spend £188.2 each year on cigarettes and tobacco in Greater London compared with £233.1 each year in Greater Manchester.

Geo-demographic segmentation

This newest method of segmentation combines both geographic and demographic principles. These are based upon the premise that households in a particular locality will have similar spending patterns. The best known of these methods is that provided by ACORN, which stands for A Classification of Residential Neighbourhoods (see Figure 27.10 overleaf).

Behaviouristic segmentation

This segments a market according to consumer behaviour patterns. For example, frequency of purchase, loyalty to a product, etc. This type of segmentation might be used to identify users who are more likely to switch brands.

Segmentation by use

Usage rate is another factor to consider when segmenting a market. A small number of consumers may be responsible for the bulk of purchases in a market. Certain products may be used in different ways. The same software may be used differently between various types of users.

	Greater London	South Manchester	Merseyside	South Yorkshire	Tyne and Wear	West Midlands	West Yorkshire	Central Clydeside
CONVENIENCE GOODS								
Cigarettes, tobacco	188.2	233.1	245.7	221.2	221.7	187.1	202.7	252.6
Food	831.1	818.5	820.5	806.6	832.9	793.1	787.3	826.6
Household goods	158.6	161.1	159.6	161.2	150.1	155.6	158.3	141.8
Newspaper, magazines, etc.	74.6	72.3	73.3	69.3	70.6	69.7	68.6	74.2
Alcohol (off licence)	116.2	121.6	125.0	111.0	116.0	118.4	109.7	119.7
COMPARISON GOODS								
Personal Goods								
Children's, infantswear	43.3	45.2	45.7	48.7	45.8	44.9	48.6	48.3
Footwear	67.5	64.7	65.7	63.1	59.8	60.0	63.9	70.3
Menswear	92.7	85.8	84.0	92.6	76.2	85.0	93.8	96.4
Womenswear	160.1	159.2	164.7	152.3	154.6	156.1	154.9	170.3
Home Goods								
Brown goods	59.3	58.7	57.1	60.6	56.0	58.7	61.4	60.2
White goods	72.3	75.0	78.7	70.4	63.2	71.2	70.3	80.6
Furniture, floorcoverings	148.6	144.3	146.1	133.9	135.1	126.0	134.1	135.5
H'hold textiles, soft furnishings	46.2	46.6	46.3	46.6	38.4	39.2	47.2	44.0
Leisure Goods								
Books	37.1	28.3	29.4	27.1	25.6	27.7	27.6	26.7
DIY, gardening	128.1	134.6	134.9	136.5	117.9	127.6	136.1	127.2
Eating out	218.5	183.3	180.6	158.9	170.1	158.4	160.7	202.3
Photographic	32.9	29.6	28.9	18.5	22.6	24.0	18.5	22.6
Records, tapes, CDs, videos	38.4	33.5	33.1	34.0	31.0	35.1	34.4	34.5
Sports equipment	10.6	10.5	10.0	9.8	10.4	10.3	9.9	11.4
Toys, games, cycles, prams	24.2	30.7	32.6	33.1	28.4	29.4	32.1	30.4

Actual personal expenditure (£)

Figure 27.9   Spending patterns

CACI's ACORN classification profiles customers in a trading area or on a database into 6 Categories, 17 Groups and 57 Types (plus 1 unclassified), so that marketers can understand more about their likely consumer characteristics. The table below shows the ACORN profile of CACI's 1997 population projections for Great Britain.

ACORN Types		Pop. Proj. 1997 %	ACORN Groups	
	ACORN Category A: THRIVING	**19.8**		1
1.1	Wealthy suburbs, large detached houses	2.6	15.1 Wealthy Achievers	
1.2	Villages with wealthy commuters	3.2	Suburban Areas	
1.3	Mature affluent home owning areas	2.7		
1.4	Affluent suburbs, older families	3.0		
2.6	Agricultural villages, home based workers	1.6	2.3 Affluent Greys	2
2.7	Holiday retreats, older people, home based workers	0.7	Rural Communities	
3.8	Home owning areas, well-off older residents	1.4	2.4 Prosperous Pensioners,	3
3.9	Private flats, elderly people	0.9	Retirement Areas	
	ACORN Category B: EXPANDING	**11.6**		
4.10	Affluent working families with mortgages	2.1	3.8 Affluent Executives	4
4.11	Affluent working couples with mortgages, new homes	1.3	Family Areas	
4.12	Transient workforces, living at their place of work	0.3		
5.13	Home owning family areas	2.6	7.8 Well-Off Workers,	5
5.14	Home owning family areas, older children	3.0	Family Areas	
5.15	Families with mortgages, younger children	2.2		
	ACORN Category C: RISING	**7.8**		
6.16	Well-off towns & city areas	1.1	2.3 Affluent Urbanites	6
6.17	Flats & Mortgages, singles & young working couples	0.7	Town & City Areas	
6.18	Furnished flats & bedsits, younger single people	0.4		
7.19	Apartments, young professional singles & couples	1.1	2.1 Prosperous Professionals,	7
7.20	Gentrified multi-ethnic areas	1.0	Metropolitan Areas	
8.21	Prosperous enclaves, highly qualified executives	0.7	3.4 Better-Off Executives,	8
8.22	Academic centres, students & young professionals	0.6	Inner City Areas	
8.23	Affluent city centre areas, tenements & flats	0.4		
8.24	Partially gentrified multi-ethnic areas	0.7		
8.25	Converted flats & bedsits, single people	0.9		
	ACORN Category D: SETTLING	**24.0**		
9.26	Mature established home owning areas	3.3	13.4 Comfortable Middle Agers,	9
9.27	Rural areas, mixed occupations	3.5	Mature Home Owning Areas	
9.28	Established home owning areas	4.0		
9.29	Home owning areas, council tenants, retired people	2.7		
10.30	Established home owning areas, skilled workers	4.5	10.6 Skilled Workers,	10
10.31	Home owners in older properties, younger workers	3.0	Home Owning Areas	
10.32	Home owning areas with skilled workers	3.1		
	ACORN Category E: ASPIRING	**13.7**		
11.33	Council areas, some new home owners	3.8	9.7 New Home Owners,	11
11.34	Mature home owning areas, skilled workers	3.1	Mature Communities	
11.35	Low rise estates, older workers, new home owners	2.8		
12.36	Home owning multi-ethnic areas, young families	1.1	4.0 White Collar Workers,	12
12.37	Multi-occupied town centres, mixed occupations	1.8	Better-Off Multi-Ethnic Areas	
12.38	Multi-ethnic areas, white collar workers	1.1		
	ACORN Category F: STRIVING	**22.6**		
13.39	Home owners, small council flats, single pensioners	1.9	3.6 Older People, Less	13
13.40	Council areas, older people, health problems	1.7	Prosperous Areas	
14.41	Better-off council areas, new home owners	2.4	11.5 Council Estate Residents,	14
14.42	Council areas, young families, some new home owners	3.0	Better-Off Homes	
14.43	Council areas, young families, many lone parents	1.6		
14.44	Multi-occupied terraces, mutli-ethnic areas	0.8		
14.45	Low rise council housing, less well-off families	1.8		
14.46	Council areas, residents with health problems	1.9		
15.47	Estates with high unemployment	1.1	2.7 Council Estate Residents	15
15.48	Council flats, elderly people, health problems	0.7	High Unemployment	
15.49	Council flats, very high unemployment, singles	0.9		
16.50	Council areas, high unemployment, lone parents	1.8	2.7 Council Estates Residents,	16
16.51	Council flats, greatest hardship, many lone parents	0.9	Greatest Hardship	
17.52	Multi-ethnic, large families, overcrowding	0.6	2.2 People in Multi-Ethnic,	17
17.53	Multi-ethnic, severe unemployment, lone parents	1.0	Low-income Areas	
17.54	Multi-ethnic, high unemployment, overcrowding	0.5		
	Unclassified	**0.5**		

Figure 27.10   CACI ACORN profile of Great Britain

Segmentation by type of organisation

Different organisations require different types of products. It may be possible to concentrate upon users from certain industries. One way of doing this is to use the **Standard Industrial Classification (SIC)**.

Benefit segmentation

With this method of segmentation a market is divided according to the benefits which customers seek. In other words, segmentation follows customer needs and requirements. For example, in the market for cars one group of buyers might seek space and comfort while others may wish for versatility.

Segmentation by customer size

Larger customers may have different needs to others. For example, banks cater for both small and large businesses.

Targeting

Segmentation helps an organisation to understand the market and to break it up into segments which match consumer needs and requirements. The next step is to classify one or more segments which has a need that can be met by the organisation. This process is known as **targeting**.

Concentration strategy

This involves targeting a single segment with a single product. The organisation's resources are thus concentrated on a very small part of the overall market. This is sometimes called **niche marketing**. For example, Porche targets a very exclusive segment of the market for cars. The main benefit of this targeting strategy is that it allows for a high degree of **specialisation** with the development of a marketing mix focused upon the needs of a distinctive group of customers.

Mass marketing strategy

If a single product is targeted at the whole market, this is known as **mass** or **undifferentiated marketing**. Probably the most famous example of mass marketing was the Model T Ford.

Selective marketing

This involves the use of a differentiated approach to marketing to target a number of products at a number of segments in the market by tailoring a separate marketing mix for each segment. A good example of selective marketing is the market for cars, where the larger manufacturers target products at a whole range of segments. For example, the Vauxhall Corsa, Tigra, Astra, Vectra, Calibra, Omega, Frontera, etc.

CASE STUDY CASE STUDY CASE STUDY CASE STUDY CASE STUDY CASE

TARGETING STUDENTS

There are more than a million students in the UK. They are generally considered difficult to target. This is because student behaviour is influenced by rapidly changing fashions. Students also lead a relatively insular life which centres upon their social habits and their work. However, as students have an estimated spending power of £4 billion, many companies are trying to target these consumers of tomorrow.

One such company is Beatwax. It began by organising promotions for record companies and this quickly expanded into video and film production. As other companies became aware of the student market, the Beatwax client base expanded.

In recent years there has been a 20 per cent rise in enrolment in universities and colleges of higher education. The market for students is growing faster than at any other time.

Chris Ward, who set up Beatwax, is keen to dispel the notion that students have little money:

'With student loans, they have as much money to spend as they ever did. They are just further in debt when they leave higher education. But it doesn't stop them spending money on the clichéd things that students have always spent money on – drink, music, cigarettes and convenience foods.'

One of Beatwax's most recent campaigns was for the tea producer Twinings. It has distributed 20,000 herbal tea sachets around universities and colleges in the expectation that, if students try the product and like it, they will buy it on a regular basis and continue to do so after graduation. Golden Wonder has also run a promotional campaign for its Pots of the World brand – an exotic version of traditional student fare!

Beatwax targets students on their home territory, through university or student publications. Such publications are read by 86 per cent of students. Beatwax also has access to campus radio stations and poster sites, and there are growing opportunities to use video. As campaigns are directed solely at students they can be more daring and often use outrageous humour.

1 Identify the factors which clearly distinguish students as a separate market segment.
2 Using the case, describe how students are targeted. Think of alternative ways of targeting students.
3 How would it be possible to target either students in further education or sixth formers in schools?

CASE STUDY CASE STUDY CASE STUDY CASE STUDY CASE STUDY CASE

Positioning

Even though parts of the market might have been divided into segments, within each segment buyers will not all have identical needs. **Positioning** takes into account the thoughts and perceptions of customers, to place a product relative to other products and brands. The position is, therefore, how the product is perceived in the minds of customers. Targeted customers will then create an image of the product which helps them to think about how it stands out against competitors.

Positioning a product involves identifying the key variables considered to be important for customers. For example, price is a key variable for groceries, quality for furniture and taste for wine.

One visual tool used by marketers to develop a picture of customer perceptions is **perceptual mapping** (see Figure 27.11). This can be used to help to show how a customer views brands and their attributes. Positioning may involve introducing a product into a position where it competes head-on with other products in that position. Alternatively, it may involve moving into a position where there is a gap in the map, where consumers do not perceive products with similar attributes.

Repositioning involves moving the product away from its current market position. For example, a repositioning may take the product to another part of the market which helps to emphasise attributes and strengths over those of its nearest competitors.

So, what are the stages in the positioning plan? After an organisation has segmented its market and target the appropriate segments it must:

- find out about the perceptions of targeted customers
- develop a product which caters for their needs
- use customer perceptions and image to identify the market position
- use the marketing mix to develop attributes and image for the chosen position
- communicate attributes and image to customers.

Figure 27.11 *An example of perceptual mapping of sports shops*

Chapter summary

- Marketing is generally accepted as a strategic discipline.
- Organisations must establish marketing objectives.
- Strategies match marketing objectives with corporate objectives.
- Marketing planning involves planning today what has to be done tomorrow.
- Planning is cyclical.
- A SWOT analysis can be used as part of a strategic audit.

- The marketing mix comprises product, price, place and promotion.
- Marketing strategy involves identifying a market in which to operate.
- Market segmentation enables an organisation to maximise the efficiency of its marketing efforts.
- The three phases of the segmentation process are segmentation, targeting and positioning.

28 Using the marketing mix: consumer protection

When organisations make decisions about how and when to market their goods and services they take on a responsibility for the consequences of their actions. In Chapter 11 we looked at stakeholders priorities and conflicts within the wider business environment. In this chapter, we develop this area further by looking directly at two key areas which interact with each other in the world of marketing.

First, we observe the operation of the marketing mix. In doing so we look at the mix and the use of the product life-cycle. Marketing decisions by their very nature have consequences. By marketing products there are ramifications both for consumers and the business environment. It is not so many years ago that consumers were simply expected to rely upon their own common sense. The Latin expression *caveat emptor* held true. Though you may feel consumers should exert greater responsibility in some instances, they need some protection from organisations and individuals who may breach a contract, provide dangerous and faulty goods or who use their marketing activities to deliberately mislead the consumer. For this reason the second part of this chapter focuses upon the key role of consumer protection.

The marketing mix

In Chapter 27 we saw that the marketing mix comprised of:

- product
- price
- place
- promotion.

The marketing mix is made up of a complex set of variables which an organisation can combine in order to ensure that marketing and corporate objectives are achieved. It will include strategic, tactical and operational elements and techniques.

'Mix' is an appropriate word to describe the marketing process. A **mix** is a composition of ingredients blended together to fulfil a common purpose. Every ingredient is vitally important and each depends upon the others for its contribution. Just as with a cake, each ingredient is not sufficient on its own but with all blended together it is possible to produce something very special. In the same way that there are a variety of cakes to suit various tastes, a marketing mix can be designed to suit the precise requirements of a market.

As a result the marketing mix must have:

- **A time-scale** In an organisation's plan it must identify when it expects to achieve its objectives. Some objectives will be set to be attained in the near future, while others may be medium term (one to five years) or visionary objectives for the long-term.
- **Strategic elements** These will involve the overall strategy of the organisation. They require considerable use of judgement and expertise and are only decided by senior managers. Such decisions may involve the development of new products or a new marketing strategy.
- **Tactical or medium-term elements** The business environment has to be constantly monitored and decisions have to be taken according to whatever changes take place. External events might affect pricing strategies, product modifications or amendments for marketing plans.
- **Short-term operational elements** These involve predictable everyday decisions such as contacts with customers, analysis of advertising copy and minor decisions about packaging.

The product

The product is the central point on which all marketing energies must converge. The product is more fully discussed in Chapter 52. Finding out how to make the product, setting up the production line, providing the finance and manufacturing the product are not the responsibility of the marketing function. However, it is concerned with what the product means to the customer. People buy goods and services for a variety of reasons and a wide range of characteristics will influence their decision to buy:

- **Appearance** Often the way a product looks is considered to be as important as what it can do. Carpets, furniture and jewellery are goods which must be designed to appeal to the tastes of the customer.
- **Function** Consumers will want to know what a product can do and how well it can do it. When you buy a car you might want it to accelerate quickly or last a long time. The functions of a care which are necessary to a taxi driver may be radically different from the functions for a motorist who wants a vehicle for recreational use.
- **Status** Consumers often associate products with a particular life-style. Organisations then try to emphasis the association to create an image for the product. For example, certain car badges and designer labels encourage consumers to make the purchase because of the status they portray.

The product range and how it is used is a function of the marketing mix. The range may be broadened or a brand may be extended for tactical reasons, such as matching competition or catering for seasons fluctuations. Alternatively, a product may be repositioned to make it more acceptable for a new group of consumers as part of a long-term strategic plan.

The price

Of all the aspects of the marketing mix, price is the one which creates sales revenue – all the others are costs. The price of an item is clearly an important determinant of the value of sales made (see Chapter 53). In theory, price is really determined by the discover of what customers perceive is the value of the item on sale. Researching consumers? opinion about pricing is important as it indicates how they value what they are looking for as well as what they want to pay. An organisation's pricing policy will vary according to time and circumstances. Crudely speaking, the value of water in the Lake District will be considerably different from the value of water in a desert!

The place

Though figures vary widely from product to product, roughly a fifth of the cost of a product goes on getting it to the customer. 'Place' is concerned with various methods of transporting and storing goods, and then making them available for the customer. Getting the product to the right place at the right time involves the distribution system (see Chapter 54). The choice of distribution method will depend on a variety of circumstances. It will be more convenient for some manufacturers to sell to wholesales who then sell to retailers, while others prefer to sell directly to retailers or customers.

As the distribution system is constantly changing, organisations need to update their plans frequently. The type of distribution network chosen for each product should be compatible with other elements in the mix and will help to reinforce the overall nature of the marketing mix.

The promotion

Promotion is the business of communicating with customers. It will provide information that will assist them in making a decision to purchase a product or service (see Chapter 55). The razzmatazz, pace and creativity of some promotional activities are almost alien to normal business activities.

The cost associated with promotion or advertising goods and services often represents a sizeable proportion of the overall cost of producing an item. However, successful promotion increases sales so that advertising and other costs are spread over a larger output. Though increased promotional activity is often a sign of a response to a problem such as competitive activity, it enables an organisation to develop and build up a succession of messages and can be extremely cost-effective.

The importance of the mix

The marketing mix is a carefully constructed combination of techniques, resources and tactics which form the basis of a marketing plan geared to achieve and match both marketing and corporate objectives. Whenever objectives or external influences change, so the blend of ingredients change. The effective solution to any problem will involve the careful scrutiny of every element. Changes to the mix have to be carefully considered and implications have to be assessed. Often timing is of crucial importance.

The product life-cycle

To help with the process of planning and shaping the marketing mix, marketers use the product life-cycle. Markets are in a constant state of change. Over a period of time tastes and fashions alter and the technology used to produce goods and services moves on. As a result, there will always be demand for new products and old products will become redundant.

The **product life-cycle** is a useful mechanism for planning changes in the marketing mix. It recognises that products have a finite market life which it charts through various phases. The sales performance of any product introduced to a market will rise from nothing, reach a peak and then, at some stage, start to decline. The life-cycle can be further broken down into distinct phases, as illustrated in Figure 28.1.

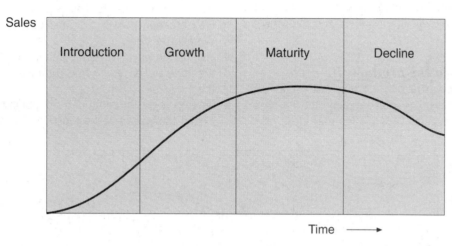

Figure 28.1   The classic life-cycle

- **The introductory phase** – During this period it is necessary to create demand. Growth is slow and volume is low because of limited awareness of the product's existence.
- The growth phase – Sales then rise more quickly. It is during this period that the profit per unit sold usually reaches a maximum. Towards the end of this phase, competitors enter the market which reduces the rate of growth.
- Maturity – In this period most of the potential customers have been reached. However, there will still be plenty of scope for repeat purchases. Competition from sellers in the market becomes stronger and new firms enter the market.
- Decline – The product becomes 'old' and sales start to fall. Perhaps a new or improved product will have entered the market.

The concept of the product life-cycle is perhaps best understood when related to real products. For example, what happened to the sales of long-play records (LPs)? Students used to pride themselves on their collections of LPs. Even by September 1989 they still accounted for a quarter of album sales in the UK. But today, that has all changed.

Students used to pride themselves on their LP collections

In terms of the product life-cycle we could say that:

- LPs are in decline
- cassettes are between maturity and decline
- CDs are between growth and maturity.

The market for albums exemplifies the importance of applying the concept of the product life-cycle to real situations. While LPs were the staple diet for many British consumers in the 1960s, 1970s and 1980s, they have rapidly declined in sales in the face of the onslaught of new sound technology. In fact, more recently the pace of change has quickened with the MiniDisc and the Digital Compact Cassette.

Injecting life into the product life-cycle

The product life-cycle of a product may last for a few months or for hundreds of years. To prolong the life-cycle of a brand or a product, an organisation may inject new life into the growth period by readjusting the ingredients of its marketing mix (see Figure 28.2).

A readjustment of the marketing mix might involve one or several of the following activities:

- a change or modification of a product to keep up with or ahead of the competition – for example, in 1996 Ford revamped the Mondeo
- alter distribution patterns to provide a more suitable place for consumers to make a purchase – for example, B&Q broadened their customer base by opening B&Q Warehouse stores
- change prices to reflect competitive activities – for example, the price of home computers was slashed in the mid-1990s.
- develop new promotional campaigns designed to extend the lives of well-established products.

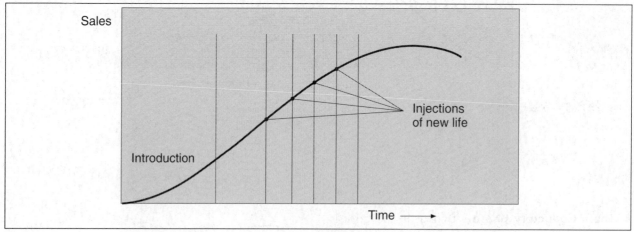

Figure 28.2   Injecting new life into a product

EXTENSION MATERIAL

Alternative product life-cycles

To a large extent the classic life-cycle of a product is a gross simplification. There are, in fact, many alternative explanations which help to illustrate the life-cycles of products.

In their French text on business, *Economie D'Enterprise*, J.L. Cordon and J.P. Raybaud suggest a series of different life-cycles as illustrated in Figure 28.3.

a *Apprentissage long* (long introductory period) – For example, some novels are available in bookshops for a long period before the public starts to buy them in significant numbers.

b *Pas d'apprentissage* (virtually no introductory period) – Some new 'wonderdrugs' became stars straight away.

c *Feu de paille* (straw on fire) – These are products that rise quickly in popularity and are burnt out quickly in a very short period. This has been the case with many children's toys, such as trolls, for example.

d *Feu de paille avec marché résiduel* (straw on fire but with a reasonable residual market) – Some products boom quickly but in decline still leave a sizeable market. Though the skateboard craze came and went you will still see some skateboards in the shops. There is usually scope for some of the more efficient first to stay in the market.

e *Echec* (flop) – Many new products flop. Oft quoted is the marketing classic, Clive Sinclair's C5 road vehicle, a sort of motorised tricycle.

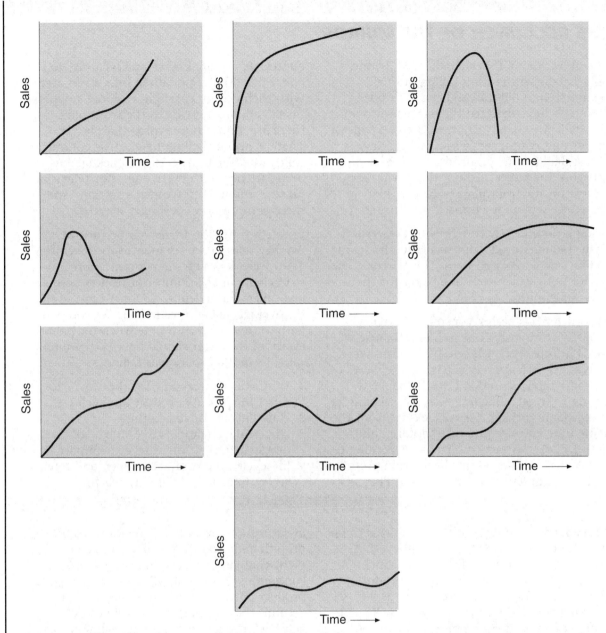

Figure 28.3   Different life-cycles suggested by Cordon and Raybaud

f *Cycle long* (long cycle) – Many products continue to go from strength to strength, such as potato crisps and chocolate bars.

g *Relances successives* (periodic rejuvenations) – Many products are frequently injected with new life.

h *Nouveau départ* (relaunch) – Some products need to be relaunched to bring them out of decline. To do this a product may need to be redesigned or have its image substantially altered. For example, in recent years the Babycham drink was relaunched.

i *Introduction manquée* (false start) – Sometimes the launch and introductory phase of a product fails to catch the public imagination. Seven Up was launched with six different names before Seven Up took off.

j *Mode* (fashion) – Some products have booms and slumps in sales according to fashion or season. The sales of swimwear or fireworks are examples.

TASK 28.1

Identify one product to match each of the life-cycle alternatives suggested by Cordon and Raybaud.

THE RELAUNCH OF THE MIRROR

The quest for more readers has led Britain's only Labour-supporting tabloid into a relaunch. In a bid to woo back the under 45s, who have deserted the paper in droves, the *Daily Mirror* has emptied its front page of words and redesigned it as a poster, New York tabloid style. According to Piers Morgan, the paper's editor, there will rarely be text on the front page in future. Instead the paper will go for impact and image!

Being economical with words has started with the 'masthead'. Out has gone the word 'Daily', to be replaced with 'The Mirror'. The *Mirror* now styles itself 'the paper for the new millennium'.

The *Mirror* has been reconstituted after months of intensive research and the use of focus groups in which selected readers were canvassed. Attention was paid to the views of younger readers. In doing so the paper was trying to tread a fine line between keeping its traditional working class readers while at the same time encouraging their children and grandchildren to read the paper. According to Piers Morgan, they wanted something more vibrant, aggressive and attitudinal. They also

appreciate regional news and weather, so the paper has been regionalised into seven areas with each edition carrying regional snippets. Inside, and in contrast to the front page, there are many more words than before. There is also a sizzling new music column called Mad for It. The *Mirror* package has been fattened with extra pages for television, puzzles and a daily women's section. And there is more news at longer lengths.

In recent times the *Mirror* has performed badly. Average sales in the six months to November 1996 were down by 5.6 per cent. More worrying was the number of readers aged 45 and under had fallen by 15.9 per cent, so that the average age of a reader was 46, compared with the *Sun*'s 42. At a time when the political legacy of the paper should have been winning sales, its market share was falling.

1 Why was it necessary for the *Mirror* to inject life into its product life-cycle?
2 How did the *Mirror* do this?
3 Undertake a comparative survey of newspapers. In your survey, compare the life-cycle phases of each paper, and refer to recent injections of life into each.

Many large organisations will produce a range of products, each with its own life-cycle. As old products go into decline new products come on-stream. The collection of products that a company produces is known as its **product portfolio**. In Figure 28.4 the line T1 represents a particular moment in time. At that point, product 1 is in decline, product 2 is

in saturation, product 3 is about to enter growth and product 4 is about to be launched. If the company is going to benefit from continuous growth, it will need to arrange its product portfolio in a way which takes into account these timings. This will be best achieved by the creation of appealing new products at regular intervals (see Figure 28.5).

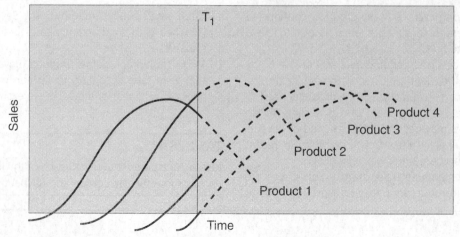

Figure 28.4   *A portfolio of products at different stages in their life cycle*

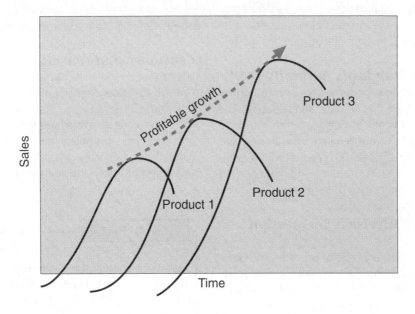

Figure 28.5   Planning for profitable growth

Consumer protection

Laws provide a framework within which transactions can take place and also serve to provide a means of settling disputes. The legal basis of the contract which exists between a buyer and a seller sets out the obligations that individuals and organisations have to each other every time they enter into an agreement.

Over the years, governments have responded to consumerism with successive Acts of Parliament designed to protect and increase the powers of buyers in relation to sellers. Such laws cover unfair business practices, poor quality of goods and services and the provision of credit. For example:

- **The Sale of Goods Act** – This states that sellers must provide goods that of 'merchantable quality', i.e. they must not be damaged or broken. Goods sold must also be fit for the purpose intended. If you bought a pair of shoes and they fell apart at the seams within a week, they would not have been fit for the purposes for which they were sold. Under this law you can ask for replacements if goods do not meet the requirements you specified to the seller.
- **The Trades Descriptions Act** – The description given of the goods forms part of the contract that the buyer makes with the seller. This Act makes it a criminal offence for a trader to describe goods falsely.
- **The Weights and Measures Act** – The aim of this Act is to ensure that consumers receive the actual quantity of a product that they believe they are buying.

- **The Food and Drugs Act** – This Act is concerned with the content of foodstuffs and medicines. This area of trading is controlled to avoid the public from buying harmful substances.

EXAM TIP:

Though you may be required to know about consumer protection and the framework within which it exists, it is unlikely that you will be expected to do much more than have to refer to the broad guidelines of any piece of legislation, as an example you can use to reinforce any argument you may wish to make. What is more important is that you can think about the importance of consumer legislation, its needs, requirements and applications within a business environment.

The Office of Fair Trading (OFT)

The OFT was set up by government to investigate monopolies and mergers, collect information on unfair consumer practices, and play a key role in developing consumer legislation. The Director General of Fair Trading:

- analyses information affecting the well-being of consumers
- refers matters where consumers' rights may be violated to the Consumer Protection Advisory Committee
- encourages the publication of 'codes of practice' for dealing with consumers

- takes action against organisations which persist in conduct which is against the interests of consumers
- produces consumer protection literature.

The Advertising Standards Authority (ASA)

The ASA is an independent body which exercises control over all advertising except that on radio and television. The ASA draws up its own codes of practice which it uses to ensure that advertisements are 'legal, decent, honest and truthful'. Advertisements should be prepared with a sense of responsibility to both consumers and society and should conform to the principles of fair competition.

The Independent Television Commission (ITC)

The ITC has a strong voluntary code of practice which covers all terrestrial broadcasting (i.e. not satellite broadcasting). As a statutory body the ITC has a remit to develop such a code for advertisers and, like the ASA code, this constantly changes to meet changing attitudes and expectations.

The British Standards Institution (BSI)

The BSI was incorporated by Royal Charter as a voluntary non-profit-making organisation to prepare and publish standards for safety, performance, size and testing. The BSI is identified by the now-famous kitemark displayed on packaging to denote that a product meets BSI requirements.

The Monopolies and Mergers Commission (MMC)

The MMC investigates possible monopolies and proposed company mergers referred to it by the Director General of Fair Trading. The Commission's role is to assess whether such monopolies and mergers are likely to be against the public interest.

Trading standards and consumer protection departments

These are departments of local authorities which work with the Office of Fair Trading and help to enforce laws, offer advice for shoppers and traders and watch for unfair trade practices. There is also an extensive network of Citizens' Advice Bureaux (CABs) in the UK which provide advice on consumer complaints and queries.

The National Consumer Council (NCC)

The NCC was set up in 1975 to provide independent advice to government and business organisations. It also seeks to further consumer interests by representation on public and other bodies, as well as to oversee the development of voluntary codes of practice.

Consumer and consultative councils

Nationalised industries have consumer and consultative councils to influence their policies and ensure that they do not abuse their powers. Privatised industries also have consumer councils which are set up to serve consumers' interests. For example, the Office of Water Services (Ofwat) has a director-general response for the economic regulation of water and sewage services.

IT'S A FACT

That when competition in domestic gas supply was first offered to households in the South West it met with a mixed response. Despite generous discounts from gas suppliers and much public criticism of the gas industry, only 18 per cent of domestic consumers chose alternative suppliers irrespective of the cost savings!

Pressure groups

Consumerism has also led to the formation of a number of influential pressure groups and movements. The Consumers Association has over 800,000 members and is the largest consumer organisation in the country. *Which?*, its magazine, carries the results of extensive product tests and scrutinises services.

Trade associations

In response to consumer pressures and increasing concern about the quality of goods and services, organisations in a number of industries have formed trade associations which have established codes of practices which go beyond the basic legal requirements and so provide the highest possible level of consumer satisfaction.

The European dimension of consumer protection

Consumer protection takes place today within a local, national and European framework. Over the years, the European Commission has set out to create a climate of competition between organisations in the European Union. Agreements between organisations are forbidden if they set out to prevent or distort competition within the common market. For example, fixing prices, sharing markets or discriminating against third parties are all forbidden.

Chapter summary

- This chapter focuses upon marketing decisions in a market environment.
- Each marketing mix is designed to suit the precise requirements of its market.
- The product is the central point upon which all marketing activities converge.
- The price is the area of the marketing mix which generates revenue.

- Roughly a fifth of the cost of a product goes on getting it to the consumer.
- Marketers use the product life-cycle to help with the process of planning and shaping the marketing mix.
- There are many different shaped life-cycles.
- There are many laws designed to protect consumers.
- Consumers are protected at a number of levels.

5 Accounting and finance

INTRODUCTION

The aim of this unit is to provide a basic introduction to accounting and finance. In every organisation people need to make judgements about the financial aspect of their activities. At the same time, individuals have to make decisions which help them to exercise some element of financial control over their areas of operation. Earlier in this book we saw that organisations have a range of aims and objectives. Although some of the may be broad, the successful achievement of such objectives frequently depends upon one overriding financial objective – financial success in terms of profits (the bottom line). Achieving this objective depends largely upon financial planning and control throughout the organisation.

In Chapter 29 we try to emphasise the importance of the accounting process. Accounting information is probably used by more groups of people than you think, with a different meaning for each group. The distinctions between financial and management accounting are drawn. Emphasis is placed upon the use of standards and regulation for the benefit of accounting users. Extension material in this section mentions the new form of financial report – the value-added statement.

All organisations require finance. In Chapter 30 the various routes for the provision of finance are explored. These vary widely starting from an owner's capital to finance from the Loan Guarantee Scheme. Borrowing money is one thing but what does it do for the business? Extension material for Chapter 30 adds perspective for the borrowing process by looking at the process of 'gearing'.

In business, decision makers frequently ask themselves questions about what they can afford. In answering such questions they have to engage in some form of financial planning. The biggest single cause of business failure is cash-flow problems caused by an inability to plan. In Chapter 31 we look at the process of cash-flow planning and the management of working capital.

Management accountants make decisions which help to improve planning, control and decision-making while at the same time providing some performance appraisal. In Chapter 32 we look at costs. There are various methods of analysing costs and these are described. The chapter uses a simple exercise to show how knowledge of costs would be useful in a working environment.

Contribution and break-even analysis is a useful and important costing technique which enables an organisation to make key decisions about pricing and profitability. In Chapter 33 the process of break-even is explained and then supported with some practical applications of break-even analysis and the construction of break-even charts.

At an early stage in any business course it is important that you can broadly distinguish between the various financial accounting statements, derive information from them and show what the information means. This is essentially the purpose of Chapter 34. In this chapter we start by looking at the importance of keeping accounting records. These records are then related to the stages in an accounting system. The chapter then looks at key accounting statements including profit and loss accounts, balance sheets and the cash flow statements. The statements are then followed with a description of basic accounting ratios which can be used for interpreting and analysing the statements.

29 An introduction to accounting and finance

Earlier in the book we saw that all organisations have a range of aims and objectives. Although this range might be broad, some objectives may be considered to be more important than others. For example, the successful achievement of all objectives will often depend upon meeting the overriding financial objective, in terms of profits – 'the bottom line'.

For example, consider the following which appeared in the press in 1997:

> 'Shares of Apple Computer plunged yesterday after a profit warning as the company prepared to outline its strategy ... The troubled computer manufacturer said that it would incur an operating loss of between $100 and $150 million in the last quarter because of weak retail demand over Christmas. The news sent shares down about $4 to $18, a third of their level a year ago. Mr Amelio, chief executive, said that Apple will have to reduce its expense by a further £1 billion to about £8 billion a year. This will require another round of redundancies on top of the 1,300 job losses announced last year. The weak sales and poor profit performance is likely to further damage Apple's image with customers and software programmers who are already worried that the company may not survive, i.e. the company has difficulty persuading programmers to write software for them as it works towards developing a new generation of computers.'

On the face of it, the short extract adapted from a newspaper article simply indicates that Apple is not doing very well. However, if you look closely you can see that the ramifications are much broader than simply not making profits. As a result of the fall in profits, important decisions are having to be made throughout the business. These decisions might affect key projects and investments, staffing and their security of tenure. In fact, as it implies, many programmers might not even write for them. As a profit objective has not been met other objectives are clearly affected.

The nature and role of accounting

In order to make judgements about business activities, individuals require information. Accounting acts as an information system by processing business data so that interested parties can be provided with the means to understand how well or badly the organisation is performing.

For example, the advertisement shown in Figure 29.1 was placed in the national press by General Accident. It summarises performance in the third quarter of 1996 and is presented as a series of financial highlights with a sup-

porting statement from the Group Chief Executive. A number of interested parties would appreciate this sort of news. Accounting is concerned with the collection, analysis and interpretation of such important information.

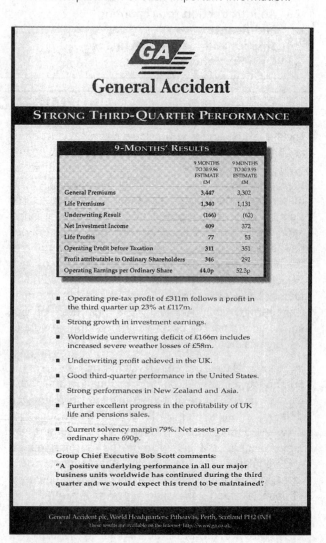

Figure 29.1   Communicating financial information

Business data are the inputs for an accounting system. The output is financial information. Financial information can then be fed to those who require such information for recording-keeping and decision-making purposes. This is particularly important as accounting is useful for those who need to make decisions within the business. However, there are other parties who are interested in accounting information. Accounting information will also satisfy many other users of information (see Figure 29.2).

Users	Use
Managers	Need information in order to improve their decision-making capabilities and to run the business more efficiently.
Shareholders	Want to assess the performance of managers and will also want to know what they are getting from their investment.
Suppliers	Are concerned about the organisation's ability to pay for materials or services supplied.
Employees	Are concerned about the tenure of their jobs as well as the prospects of any wage/salary rise.
Customers	Need to know that their supplies are secure not just in the short-term but perhaps also in the longer term.
Government	The Inland Revenue needs information about profitability in order to make an accurate tax assessment.
Lenders	They need to assess the organisation's ability to pay back a loan as well as their ability to pay interest.
Community	Areas depend upon the success of local businesses. If a business is doing well it is helping the local community to prosper not just by providing employment but by paying people who spend money in the community which then provides employment for others. Many organisations also become involved in a wide range of community projects.
Advisers and brokers	Need to know about company performance so that they can advise clients accurately.

Figure 29.2   The other users of accounting information

Accounting information is, therefore, used both within and outside an organisation. It involves providing key information which forms the basis for decisions to be made. In doing this it is possible to identify four key phases:

- identification of information
- recording of information
- analysis of information
- reporting of information.

One way of viewing the success of an accounting process is simply to find out how well accounting information has met the needs and requirements of the users. Accounting information needs to be:

- **reliable** – free from errors or bias
- **comparable** – accounting information should be comparable with information from other organisations
- **relevant** – accounting information should relate to

many of the decisions which have to be made about the business
- **understandable** – information should be capable of being understood by those for whom it is targeted.

Financial and management accounting

The process of accounting can be divided into two broad areas. The simple distinction between these two areas is that:

Management accounting is concerned with providing managers with the information they require for the day-to-day running of the business, while financial accounting is concerned with providing a range of financial information to many groups of users.

The differences between financial accounting and management accounting are as follows:

Financial accounting	Management accounting
Subject to accounting regulations to ensure that reports/statements are following a standard approach	Reports are only for internal use so no restrictions are necessary.
Provides a broad overview of the whole business using totals.	Information extracted relates to parts of the the organisation where it is used to help with a particular decision.
Provides information to a particular date	Will look at future performance as well as past performance.
Produces general statements and reports	Produces reports with a specific decision in mind.
Quantifies information in monetary terms and values.	May have non-financial information such as stocks.

IT'S A FACT

One of the most enduring statistics about accountants is the one that proves that at the profession's current rate of growth the entire nation will be accountants by the end of the next century.

Standards and regulation

If a number of accountants were presented with the same data and asked to prepare the accounts of an organisation, they might well come up with different figures or arrive at different conclusions. This is because estimates have to be made about future events and this involves an element of opinion or guesswork. For example, in calculating depreciation – how something a organisation owns loses is value over time – estimates have to be made for the useful life of each asset, and different accountants may have different estimates of an asset's lifetime.

The regulation of the accounting profession comes from two primary sources:

- **Legislation** in the form of the Companies Act 1985 as modified by the Companies Act 1989.
- **Statements of best accountancy practice** issued by the Accounting Standards Board.

Companies Acts

The Companies Act 1985 lays down requirements concerning financial statements prepared by limited companies. Members of the main accountancy bodies such as the Institute of Chartered Accountants in England and Wales, are under an obligation to use **best accounting practice** in the preparation of all accounts intended to give a 'true and fair view' of a business's trading performance and financial position. In practice, this means that all business accounts are prepared according to generally accepted accounting concepts and valuation rules.

The following information is required within ten months of the end of an accounting period (normally one year) for a private limited company, and within seven months for a public limited company:

- balance sheet (see page 204)
- profit-and-loss account (see page 202)
- cash flow statement (see page 207)
- notes to the accounts (describing the company's accounting policies and also to provide an analysis of certain items contained in the financial reports)
- auditor's report confirming that the financial reports are consistent with the company's trading records and that they provide a true and fair view of its trading performance and financial affairs.
- director's report providing details of the non-financial aspects of the business, such as principal activities and employee policies.

This information is filed with the Registrar of Companies where it is available for public inspection. Failure to conform to these reporting requirements may lead to financial penalties or the risk of criminal prosecution for the company's directors.

Accounting standards

The preparation of accounts is also subject to the influence of accounting guidelines designed to influence accounting standards.

In the 1960s, the accounting profession came under pressure to impose standard procedures on its members to avoid inconsistencies between the accounts of companies and to improve the quality and usefulness of financial statements.

An example of varying practice occurred in 1967 when AEI was taken over by GEC. AEI had forecast a profit for that year of £10 million, but when the figures were published they showed a loss of £4.5 million. At the time it was argued that such diversity of practice brought the accountancy profession into disrepute. Financial accountants try to ensure that a company's accounts bear a 'true and fair' view of business activities. The question is, can they do this? In recent years many questionable practices have come to light in accounting statements, and often frauds have failed to be discovered by the audit. Although auditors probe the inner depths of a company's affairs, they frequently deal just with totals, each of which reflect millions of financial transactions. Detecting a fraud can be very difficult.

The 1970s saw the introduction of a number of accounting standards. In 1970, the first **Statement of Standard Accounting Practice (SSAP)** was introduced with the aim of limiting the ability of accountants to use diverse accounting procedures. SSAPs were created by the Accounting Standards Committee, a sub-committee of the Consultative Committee of Accounting Bodies which linked the six major accounting bodies.

IT'S A FACT

For someone to call him or herself a qualified accountant, he or she must have passed examinations to have become a full member of one of the following accounting bodies:

- Institute of Chartered Accountants in England and Wales
- Institute of Chartered Accountants in Ireland
- Institute of Chartered Accountants in Scotland
- Chartered Institute of Certified Accountants
- Chartered Institute of Management Accountants
- Chartered Institute of Public Finance and Accountancy.

On 1 August 1990 the Accounting Standards Board took over from the Accounting Standards Committee. Unlike the ASC, which was a joint committee of the six major accounting bodies, the new Board is independent of the professional institutes and can set accounting standards in its own right. The ASB reports to the Financial Reporting Council (FRC) which oversees the accounting standards process. Its members are appointed by the Governor of the Bank of England, Secretary of State for Trade and Industry and various interested organisations, including the users and preparers of company accounts.

Whereas the extinct ASC produced SSAPs, the ASB issues accounting standards in the form of **Financial Reporting Statements (FRSs)**. Accounting standards indicate current best accounting practice which should be applied to all accounting statements. There is an obligation on the part of members of the main professional accounting bodies to comply with the accounting standards in cases where they prepare accounts or are required to audit them.

Examples of FRSs and SSAPs are as follows:

FRS 1   Cash Flow Statements
FRS 5   Reporting the Substance of Transactions
FRS 7   Fair Values in Acquisition Accounting
SSAP 1   Accounting for the Results of Associated Companies
SSAP 9   Stocks and Long-term Contracts
SSAP 22 Accounting for Goodwill.

While some of the accounting standards are quite specialised and affect only a few companies, others affect either all or most companies.

Accounting principles

The Companies Act 1985 specifies that certain basic concepts should be applied when preparing a set of financial reports. SSAP 2 Disclosure of Accounting Policies provides guidance upon the application of these concepts. These four fundamental concepts are as follows.

The going concern concept
This assumes that the business will persist with its business activities in the foreseeable future; therefore the accountant will not assume that there is a desire to cut back on business operations or an intention to liquidate. The significance of this concept is that goods should be valued not at their break-up value but at their net book value, based on the estimation of the cost of depreciation provision.

The accruals or matching concept
This recognises that revenues and costs are incurred when their liability is taken on and not as money is received or paid. Thus, at the end of a trading period all transactions relating to that period will appear in the accounts whether payments have been made or not. Revenues and profits earned in that period are 'matched' with the costs and expenses associated with these business activities.

The consistency concept
This concept indicates that the accounting treatment of similar items should be consistently applied with each accounting period and from one period to the next.

The concept of prudence or conservatism
This maintains that businesses should not lay claim to profits unless they are sure that they have been earned. Accountants will therefore tend to underestimate profits and overstate losses. As a result, profits are included in accounts only if it is certain that they have been made.

Accounting standards accepted and issued by the ASB are not enforced directly by law. However, a number of mechanisms exert pressure upon the preparers of accounts to comply with such standards. The Companies Act 1989 requires public and large private companies to state whether their accounts have been prepared in accordance with them. Non-compliance with an accounting standard must be highlighted and an explanation must be provided.

The role of auditors

The accounts of limited companies must be audited by a firm of accountants who are **registered auditors**.

Auditors are asked to verify the accuracy of financial records and to ensure that the accounts are consistent with such records.

If auditors have difficulty confirming that the financial reports do not provide a true and fair view, they may issue a qualified audit report. An audit report may have been written because of:

- **uncertainty** – the accounting records may be inadequate to carry out a full audit
- **disagreement** – the accounting records may not be factual or the non-compliance of accounting standards and legislation may cause disagreement.

Public limited companies listed on the London Stock Exchange have to disclose additional information in accordance with its *Yellow Book*. This includes the issuing of an interim financial report of performance, including details of turnover, profit and shareholder dividends.

SYNTHESIS

Is it reasonable to complain that accounting information as presented in accounts simply provides information mainly for people who own the business and that it does not provide enough information for other stakeholders? In thinking about this, look at the final published accounts of a limited company. How far do they cater for other stakeholders to a business?

EXTENSION MATERIAL
Value-added statements

A new form of financial report has recently been developed in order to address the bias of financial reporting towards business owners. This alternative is called a **value-added statement**. These identify 'value added' as the difference between the value of sales charged to customers and the cost of goods and services purchased from other businesses. The value added is then shown as being shared between employees, the government and those who provide the capital.

CASE STUDY CASE STUDY CASE STUDY CASE STUDY CASE STUDY CASE

A CHANGING PROFESSION

Over the ten years to 1995, the worldwide membership of the UK's six accounting bodies rose 45 per cent to 234,000, while within the UK membership rose by 40 per cent to 179,000. By 2005 the number within the UK is expected to rise to 250,000.

The reason that accountancy is the dominant profession today is that accountants have adapted and expanded the profession's circle of influence until it covers almost all areas of business activity. An increase in financial reporting is one reason for the expansion in their activities. Another reason is that accountants have changing work patterns. Many accountants are spending more time on non-financial matters, many of which are strategic rather than line functions.

The public sector is expected to be one area of

expansion in years to come. As this world becomes more business-orientated, it is increasingly expected to need accountants. At the same time the whole area of risk management and control within companies will continue to expand.

The average career path for accountants will also change over the next few years. They will no longer seek the security of a job for life as they did in more stable times. They will not expect to stay with the firms in which they trained but instead will develop a portfolio career, catering for a range of clients and interests.

1 Why have the numbers of accountants expanded so rapidly over recent years?
2 How will the careers of accountants differ from those of the past?

CASE STUDY CASE STUDY CASE STUDY CASE STUDY CASE STUDY CASE

Chapter summary

- The financial objective is often known as the 'bottom line'.
- The process of accounting acts as an information system.
- Business data is the input into the accounting system while financial information is the output.
- There are many users of accounting information.
- There are four key phases of an accounting system.
- Management accounting provides managers with information they require for the day-to-day running of the business.
- Financial accounting is concerned with providing a range of information for many groups of users.
- There are two areas of regulation of the accounting profession.
- The Companies Act lays down requirements con-

cerning financial statements prepared by limited companies.
- The preparation of accounts are also subject to the influence of accounting guidelines called accounting standards – SSAPs and FRSs.
- There are six professional accounting bodies within the UK.
- The four fundamental concepts of accounting practice are the going concern concept, the accruals or matching concept, the consistency concept and the concept of prudence or conservatism.
- The accounts of limited companies must be audited by a firm of accountants.
- A new form of accounting is developing using a value-added statement.

30 Sources and methods of finance

This chapter explores the various methods and sources of finance that are available to organisations. Reading the chapter should enable you to see that all organisations require funds and that intelligent organisations will seek to match the best sources and methods of finance with their funding requirements.

Every modern organisation needs to draw on sources of finance. It needs to have funds to carry out its activities. The finance problem for an organisation is very similar to that of an individual. If I want to visit the cinema then I will need to have cash in my pocket. If I want to buy a relatively more expensive item like a CD player then I will probably need to be able to draw on my bank account through a cheque book and cheque card. At other times I buy goods on credit – for example, I don't settle up my milk account until the end of the month. At other times I may borrow money to purchase a car, and I still owe a large sum on my mortgage which is for 25 years.

> *Sources of finance are the people and organisations that provide finance to an individual or organisation. Methods of finance are the form in which the funds are provided.*

For example, if I borrow money to buy a house:

the source of funds is a **building society**, and the method of finance is a **mortgage**.

If I pay to go into a cinema:

the source of funds is my own **savings**, and the method of finance is **cash**, etc.

SYNTHESIS

Think about the methods of finance that your household draws on. Rank these in order of the length of time that these funds are required for. Why is it that some methods of finance are required for longer periods than others? What are the sources of finance for each of the types of finance that you have listed?

Sources of finance

Organisations have available to them a number of sources of finance. In particular these include:

- individuals
- organisations providing venture capital
- banks and other financial institutions
- suppliers
- government
- profits retained in the business.

By drawing on these sources of finance organisations have available to them a number of methods of finance. In choosing what type of finance to draw on organisations need to consider:

- the length of time for which they need the finance
- the cost of raising the finance in one way rather than another

- the flexibility of the finance, i.e. how easy is it to change one form of finance into another, for example, by transferring a long-term loan into a short-term one.

Methods of finance can be ranked in order of the length of the term which they are typically used for. Going from the shortest term to the longest term we have: trade credit; overdraft; leasing and hiring; borrowing (loans); profit retention; organisational capital.

Methods of finance

Owner's capital
The business owners are the ultimate risk-takers, as they provide the business with capital and only expect a return if the business proves profitable. Providers of owners' capital benefit most when the firm is successful, but stand to lose the most if it fails. The form these funds take depends on the legal form of the business.

Unincorporated businesses

Corporations are organisations that have been legally recognised as companies with all the rights and obligations that come with such a form of business organisation.

Unincorporated businesses are made up of individuals acting as sole traders and groups of individuals who set up in partnership. The business is simple to set up but it is not recognised in law as being separate from its owners. The assets (what the business owns or is owed) and liabilities (what the business owes) of the business belong directly to the owners or partners. This means, therefore, that when a partner leaves or joins the business, the inconvenient situation arises of one partnership ceasing and another commencing. In addition, the owner may be forced to transfer more personal wealth into the firm if the business cannot generate enough funds to pay its debts. Generally speaking, unincorporated businesses are relatively small and are only able to raise limited amounts of capital. However, there are some very big partnerships which have access to vast sums of capital such as accountancy partnerships and major city law firms.

> **EXAM TIP:**
>
> Figure 30.1 may prove helpful to you in showing the methods of finance most commonly used by different forms of organisations.

> **IT'S A FACT**
>
> That when Tom Spencer joined Michael Marks to create Marks and Spencer, Spencer only had to put £300 into the business to form a partnership. Today that £300 has been multiplied many times over as M&S is one of the best known and biggest business organisations in this country.

Incorporated businesses
Unlike sole traders and partnerships, companies are legal identities quite separate from that of their owners. This enables easier exit for investors who only wish to tie up their money for a limited period of time, as the company's ability to trade is unaffected by changes in its ownership. The capital contributed by the owners of the business is divided into shares. Hence an owner is called a **shareholder**.

	Sole traders	Partnership	Private limited companies	Public limited companies	Non-profit making
Personal funds	*	*	*	*	*
Shares			*	*	
Mortgage	*	*	*	*	
Grants	*	*	*	*	*
Gifts					*
Loans	*	*	*	*	*
Profit retention	*	*	*	*	*
Trade credit	*	*	*	*	*
Overdraft	*	*	*	*	*
Leasing and Hire Purchase	*	*	*	*	*
Trade credit	*	*	*	*	*
Factoring	*	*	*	*	

Figure 30.1   Methods of finance used by different forms of organisations

Shareholders enjoy limited liability as the maximum amount they can lose in the business venture is the amount they paid for the shares they hold. Shareholders receive benefits from profits earned in the form of cash dividends and an increase in the value of their shares.

A private limited company is one that restricts the rights of members to transfer their shares and limits the ability of the public to subscribe for its shares. Membership of the Alternative Investment Market (AIM) is often seen as a halfway stage between a small company and a fully listed company on the Stock Exchange.

A fully listed public company on the Stock Exchange has almost limitless opportunities to raise fresh capital from the market as long as it abides by its rules. For example, a public company has a number of methods open to it for the issue of shares:

- It can create a public issue by prospectus. An issuing house will organise the issue by compiling a prospectus, accompanied by an advertisement and an invitation to buy shares. This can be an expensive method, and up to 7 per cent of the money raised by the issue can go to meet the costs.
- An offer for sale exists where a public company issues shares directly to an issuing house which then offers them for sale at a fixed price. This is also an expensive method and is best used when the size of the issue is too small to need a public issue by prospectus.
- A rights issue is a cheaper method, whereby existing shareholders are offered further shares at an advantageous price.
- A placing avoids the expense of going to the market by placing shares with a number of investors through an intermediary. Since this method avoids the market, the Stock Exchange keeps a close eye on these transactions.
- With an offer by tender, an offer is made to the public but the company states a minimum price below which shares will not be offered. Buyers then have to indicate the price they are willing to offer for the shares.

Ordinary shares (equities)

Most capital is normally raised through the issue of ordinary shares. An ordinary share is a fixed unit of ownership giving the holder the opportunity to share in the profits or losses. Ordinary shares carry voting rights at shareholders' meetings. Shareholders elect the board and can sanction the level of dividends proposed. **Authorised capital** is the amount of share capital a company is empowered by its shareholders to issue. **Issued capital** is the actual amount of share capital that has been issued. In other words, a company may hold back part of its authorised capital to issue at a later date.

Deferred shares

Another class of shares is deferred shares or **founders** shares. These are issued to the people who originally set up the business. Sometimes these shares have superior voting rights relative to other shares to ensure that the founders keep a substantial part of the power and influence in a company.

Preference shares

A less flexible class of share is the preference share. Owners of these share are not, strictly speaking, owners of the company. Their exact rights are set out in the company articles of association. Holders of these share have preferential rights to receive dividends if profits exist and, in the event of a company winding up, will receive the face value of their shares before the ordinary shareholders are paid. However, dividends on preference shares are limited to a fixed percentage of par value (i.e. the face value of the share).

Some companies issue **cumulative preference shares** and this avoids the difficulty of having to pay preference shareholders if profits are too small. The holder of a cumulative preference share will receive arrears of dividends accumulated from the past in later years. With **redeemable preference shares** the company can buy back the shares from the shareholders; redemption can be made from profits or reserves or it may be financed by a fresh issue of shares. **Participating preference shareholders** receive dividends above the fixed rate when ordinary shareholders have been paid if the company has done well in a particular year.

Advantages of risk capital

There are many benefits of using risk capital instead of alternative sources of finance, including the following:

- If the business has had a bad year, the company is under no legal obligation to pay shareholders.
- Unlike loans, whereby the principal has to be returned at the end of a period on a contracted date, the company does not have to pay the share capital back.
- Interest on loan capital is an overhead which reduces profits, whereas share capital does not create overheads.

Disadvantages of risk capital

However, there are several disadvantages of issuing risk capital. These include:

- It can be expensive to issue shares.
- Companies have to undergo the rigorous financial requirements of the Stock Exchange to be listed, and then demands for shares are subject to the uncertainties of the marketplace.
- The creation of more shareholders may dilute the influence of the founders of the company and affect their ability to make decisions.

GOING FOR EXPANSION

In an earlier unit we saw how, in April 1996, Spillers Petfoods acquired Quaker European Petfoods for £465 million to create Europe's second largest petfood supplier:

Spillers + Quaker European = Europe's Number 2

This was an important strategic move for Dalgety which like many other key UK companies has realised the importance of building up a branded business with a global dimension. The European market is very important to many UK companies. Lifestyles and buying patterns in many European countries have similarities with those in the UK.

Today, there can be no doubt that UK trade is closely tied to the EU. For example, over half of our exports by value go to EU countries.

In 1996, therefore, Dalgety put into effect a major strategic decision by focusing a key part of its activities on European petfoods. An important move in this direction was for the company to divest itself of its Golden Wonder and Homepride food businesses in order to acquire Quaker European Petfoods.

The sale of Golden Wonder and Homepride raised £300 million.

A rights issue raised £186 million.

1 What is a rights issue? Why is this a relatively cheap way of raising fresh capital?
2 Comment on the appropriateness of the way in which Dalgety decided to raise its capital.
3 How did shareholders stand to gain from the rights issue?

Venture capital

Another form of capital for business is venture capital. Venture capital companies provide finance in return for an equity (ordinary) shareholding in the company and an element of control. 3i is the largest venture capital company of this type. In recent years, the law has changed to allow companies to buy back their capital if certain safeguards have been met.

Profit retention

One of the most important sources of finance for business are profits that have been ploughed back. Initially, profits are subject to corporation tax, payable to the Department of Inland Revenue. Then a proportion of what is left is allocated to shareholders as dividends. The directors will recommend how much profit should be distributed in this way. The board needs to satisfy shareholders while at the same time ensuring that sufficient funds are available for reinvestment.

Borrowing

Borrowing is an important part of business activity. The charge for borrowing is interest and a crucial element in calculating the interest charge is the amount of risk involved with the loan. For example, longer-term loans tend to carry higher rates, as will loans made to small businesses with an unproven track record.

Bank loans

Bank loans are taken out for a fixed period, repayment either being in instalments or in full at the end of the term. Banks generally provide funds on a short- to medium-term basis, with relatively few loans over more than ten years' duration. Details of bank loans are as follows:

● **Source** – main clearing banks and merchant banks.
● **Cost** – in addition to interest charges levied at so many percentage points over base rate (e.g. 3 per cent over base), there may be arrangement fees and a security fee.
● **Limit** – banks are unlikely to lend more than the owners are putting into the business. In particular, the banks need to be convinced of the owner's commitment to the enterprise before they will pledge their own funds.

Debentures

Large, publicly quoted organisations may borrow money by issuing debentures. A debenture is a certificate issued by a company acknowledging a debt. The debt is paid at a fixed rate of interest and the certificate states the terms of repayment at the end of the period of debt. It is thus a long-term loan which can be traded on the Stock Exchange, i.e. the holder of a debenture can sell it on to someone else. A debenture holder is not a shareholder but a creditor. This means that interest payments are an expense to the company and are allowable against profits.

Although holding debentures is much less risky than holding shares, their value in the marketplace will vary according to interest rates. For example, a debenture that pays a 10 per cent rate of interest will be worth 10/8 or 1.25 per cent of its face value when interest rates are 8 per cent; if interest rates rise to 15 per cent it would only be worth 10/15 or 0.66 of its face value. Thus, if interest rates rise the value of the loan falls and vice versa.

Bank overdraft

An overdraft is the most frequently used form of short-term bank finance and is used to ease cash flow problems. Arrangements are made between the customer and the bank to include an agreed limit on an account beyond with the customer will not draw. Interest is calculated on the level of the overdraft on a daily basis. Often a bank will make a special charge for arranging an overdraft and committing the bank's money, whether the withdrawal facilities are used or not. After an agreed period, the bank will examine the account and make a decision about whether to revise or reinstate the limit.

Whereas the account of a personal customer will show a regular input of income per month and a regular pattern of expenditure, this does not happen with a business customer who is dependent upon debtors paying their bills. As a result, it is easy to understand why business customers often slip into an overdraft situation and need this flexible form of short-term finance.

Hire purchase

Hire Purchase (HP) allows the business to use an asset without having to find the money immediately. A finance house buys the asset from the supplier and retains ownership of it during the period of the hire-purchase agreement. The business pays a deposit and then further payments to the finance house, as stipulated in the agreement. At the end of the HP agreement, ownership of the asset is passed to the business. Details are as follows:

- **Source** – finance houses that are often subsidiaries of the clearing banks and equipment suppliers, e.g. Lombard Tricity Finance, RoyScot Trust etc.
- **Cost** – the payments made by the business under the HP agreement are in excess of the cash price of the asset. The difference is the finance charge required by the finance house.
- **Limit** – the finance house will want to be sure the company's profits will be well in excess of the planned repayments, and that it has a good payment record on the existing HP agreements and other debt arrangements.

Leasing

Leasing an asset provides similar benefits to hire purchase, in that a leasing agreement with a finance house (lessor) allows the business (lessee) to use an asset without having to buy it outright. The real distinction between the two forms of finance is that leasing does not confer an automatic right to eventual ownership of the asset. It is a very popular form of finance for company vehicles, office equipment and factory machinery.

The benefits of leasing are that:

- It enables a business to have complete use of an asset without having to use risk or loan capital to finance it.
- Leasing payments are an expense and are charged to the profit and loss account before tax is assessed.

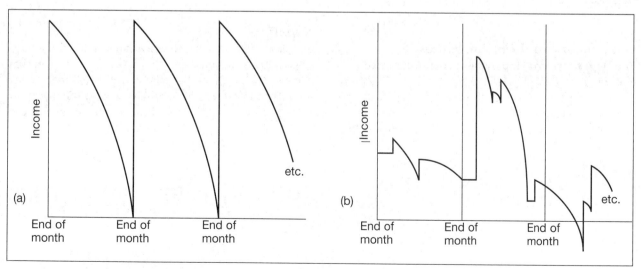

Figure 30.2   (a) Personal account   *(b) Business account*

- Leasing enables businesses to change their equipment more often and thereby to keep up-to-date with modern technology.
- Tax allowances can be claimed by the lessor and be filtered through to the lessee in lower lease payments.

Although leasing enables the lessee to manage expenditure more easily, the lessee does not own the equipment. If income falters, lease payments may impose a considerable burden on a business; furthermore, loans cannot be secured on assets that are leased.

Factoring

Trade debts mean that money can often be tied up for as much as six months. For a business requiring cash quickly this can be a real problem. A factoring company may offer immediate payment of part of the amount owed to a business – normally around 80 per cent – with the balance being paid when the debt is settled. This provides an immediate way for a business to improve its cash flow. In return the factoring company will charge a fee which includes interest and administration charges.

Commercial mortgages

A mortgage is a loan secured on land and buildings and can either be used to finance the purchase of the property, or to provide security for a loan applied to some other purpose. It is a long-term financing arrangement of typically 10 to 30 years. Details are as follows:

- **Source** – financial institutions, such as insurance companies and pension funds, as well as the banks.
- **Cost** – interest on amount outstanding.
- **Limit** – that values of the property is the basis for determining the maximum mortgage permissible.

Sale and lease-back

This involves a firm selling its freehold property to an investment company and then leasing it back over a long period of time. This releases funds for other purposes in the business.

Government and similar bodies

The Department of Employment Loan Guarantee Scheme

The government guarantees the repayment of 70–85 per cent of a medium-term bank loan (2–7 years) in return for a 2.5 per cent per annum premium. The scheme enables banks to lend money to businesses of less than 200 employees for projects that would otherwise be thought too risky.

IT'S A FACT

That some companies qualify for government grants or other concessions – such as 'tax holidays'!

Private Finance Initiative (PFI)

Over recent years, the government has forced its departments and local authorities to look for finance for capital projects. By doing this it has created a new industry – the PFI industry. The aim of this initiative is simply to use the private sector to manage and run projects or institutions which have traditionally been associated with the public sector. Others have criticised the initiative because they feel it is a smoke screen behind which the government reduces the amount it makes available for a capital project by encouraging the private sector to take on such responsibility.

For example, a PFI initiative might be to run a build a new school. Instead of the local authority paying for building it, under PFI it would be built by the private sector and then leased back. (The question would then perhaps be what control the investor would have over the running and maintenance of the school.) The Channel Tunnel rail link is a PFI and is set for completion in 2003. It is claimed that PFI provides a different way of looking at investments in the public sector with opportunities existing for new prisons, colleges and public buildings as well as for roads, light-rail systems and bridges.

The European Union

The European Union provides a range of finance for business, for example, loans or loan guarantees for investment projects.

Suppliers

Suppliers are a valuable source of finance for many businesses. Just as the business may give credit to its own customers, the firm may be able to negotiate credit terms with its suppliers. Credit terms are typically 30 days from date of supply or the end of the month following the month of delivery, i.e. 30 to 60 days.

CASE STUDY CASE STUDY CASE STUDY CASE STUDY CASE STUDY CASE

FINANCE FOR A NEW PETROL STATION

You have been asked to advise on the most appropriate methods of finance for an entrepreneur who wishes to open a petrol station on a new city by-pass.

Needs:

- Land and Buildings: £250,000
- Shopfittings: £25,000
- Petrol pumps: £50,000
- Stocks of petrol and other retail items: £10,000
- Computer terminal: £5,000
- First few weeks' wages: £5,000

Possible sources of finance:

- Hire purchase or leasing
- Bank loan for two years
- Commercial mortgage (limited to 80 per cent of the asset's value)
- Bank overdraft
- Trade credit
- Owner's equity: £75,000

Match the entrepreneur's needs with the possible sources of finance available to him or her.

CASE STUDY CASE STUDY CASE STUDY CASE STUDY CASE STUDY CASE

CASE STUDY CASE STUDY CASE STUDY CASE STUDY CASE STUDY CASE

MATCHING

Companies use a range of methods of finance, including:

- Owner's equity (in a limited company this is called share capital)
- Long-term loans, often in the form of debentures
- commercial mortgages
- bank loans and overdrafts
- hire purchase (HP) or leasing
- trade credit from suppliers
- retained earnings.

For each of the following organisations, identify the most relevant sources of finance.

1 A school wishes to replace its existing photocopier with a more elaborate version which they want to pay for over a period of time.

2 The Queens' Medical Centre wishes to build a new hospital wing on vacant land close to its existing site.

3 Prakesh Patel needs a new computer system costing £5,000 for his business. Identify two ways of financing the purchase and state the circumstances in which either would be more appropriate.

4 A medium-sized company wants to expand its factory building. The cost will be £500,000. Identify two ways of financing the expansion and state the circumstances in which either would be more appropriate.

5 A small firm is having temporary problems with its cash flow. Identify two ways of financing any shortfall it might currently have in its cash requirements and state the circumstances in which either would be more appropriate.

CASE STUDY CASE STUDY CASE STUDY CASE STUDY CASE STUDY CASE

EXTENSION BOX

Gearing

Financial gearing is the proportion of fixed return borrowing to shareholders' investment. Shareholders' investment is also known as equity capital and dividends on those shares depends on the organisation's success. Fixed return finance includes loans, preference shares and debentures.

The **gearing ratio** is therefore:

$$Gearing\ ratio = \frac{Fixed\ return\ borrowing}{Equity\ capital}$$

Ratios in excess of 1 indicate highly-geared companies. High gearing is not normally considered desirable.

Illustration of the effects of gearing

Johnson and Co Ltd employs £100,000 of capital, and generates profits in the range £5,000 to £20,000 per annum before paying out interest.

	High gearing	Medium gearing	Low gearing
Capital structure			
Ordinary shares	10,000	50,000	90,000
Debentures at 10 per cent pa	90,000	50,000	10,000

If the company makes a profit of £5,000, then investors are entitled to the following:

	High gearing	Medium gearing	Low gearing
Ordinary shareholders	(£4,000)*	nil	£4,000
Debenture holders (10 per cent)	£9,000	£5,000	£1,000
	£5,000	£5,000	£5,000

If the company makes profits of £20,000, then investors are entitled to the following:

	High gearing	Medium gearing	Low gearing
Ordinary shareholders	£11,000	£15,000	£19,000
Debenture holders (10 per cent)	£9,000	£5,000	£1,000
	£20,000	£20,000	£20,000

*   This is a 'debit' figure – i.e. the shareholders have to contribute £4,000 towards the £9,000 which must be paid to the debenture holders.

Whatever the level of profits, debenture holders will always receive 10 per cent of the value of their debentures. However, the percentage return enjoyed by ordinary shareholders varies widely, depending on the level of profits and financial gearing.

From this analysis, we can summarise ordinary shareholders' return on their investment.

	High gearing	Medium gearing	Low gearing
On profits of £5,000	(40%)*	0%	4.4%
On profits of £20,000	110%	30%	21.1%
Range of returns	150%	30%	16.7%

*   This is a 'debit' figure – i.e. the shareholders have to contribute a sum equal to 40 per cent of their nominal shareholding to the debenture holders.

The range of returns to ordinary shareholders increases as gearing increases. In addition, as can be seen from this illustration, there is a risk that interest paid on fixed capital may result in losses for ordinary shareholders. Business losses are eventually bad news all round, so the level of gearing is of interest to providers of any type of finance.

CASE STUDY CASE STUDY CASE STUDY CASE STUDY CASE STUDY CASE

FINANCIAL ADVICE

You are an investment adviser and have to advise a personal client on the relative strengths of the following companies from the same industry. The client has the opportunity to buy shares in each of the limited companies in the table below.

Forecasts indicate that profits may fall by 20 per cent for all three firms during the next year.

	Rock Ltd	Midway Ltd	Rise Ltd
Profits before interests	£80,000	£80,000	£80,000
Capital structure			
Ordinary share capital:	£600,000	£400,000	£200,000
Debentures @ 10 per cent	£200,000	£400,000	£600,000

1 Calculate the current year's gearing ratio for each company.
2 Calculate (i) the profit after interest for each company for this year and (ii) the amount forecast for next year.
3 What rate of return have shareholders obtained this year and what are the prospects for next?

4 Which proposal would you recommend investing in if the long-term prospects for the industry are good despite experiencing quite volatile business cycles? Give your reasons and the assumptions you have made.

CASE STUDY CASE STUDY CASE STUDY CASE STUDY CASE STUDY CASE

Chapter summary

- All organisation need to raise finance.
- Sources of finance are the people and organisations that provide funds.
- Methods of finance are the types of finance provided (e.g. loans or mortgages).
- In deciding on the best methods of finance it is necessary to consider the time finance is required for, the cost of finance, and the flexibility of different methods of finance.
- Incorporated businesses have the advantage of being able to raise share capital.

- Ordinary shareholders are the real owners of business organisations, but there are several other types of shares.
- Debentures are a form of loan to a company.
- Profit retention is a major form of finance.
- It is important to carefully balance the proportion of fixed return borrowing to shareholder's investment, i.e. the gearing ratio. High gearing is not normally considered desirable.

31 Cash flow and budgeting

In all organisations, money comes in and then flows out. From time to time managers might pose questions such as:

- Can we afford X?
- Are we going to be able to pay our workforce this month?
- We seem to be profitable and have plenty of work, but we don't we seem to have any money?
- If we borrow money to buy a new machine, can we meet the repayments?

To answer such questions and to make critical decisions, an organisation has to engage in financial planning.

Financial planning involves defining objectives and then developing ways of achieving them.

To plan ahead, a financial manager must have a realistic understanding of what is happening and what is likely to happen within the organisation: for example, when is money going to come in, what is it needed for, and would it be possible to use some of it for expansion and development. In the 'money-go-round' (Figure 31.1), capital and sales revenue come into a business, but is there

enough left over, after paying all of the costs, for expansion and development?

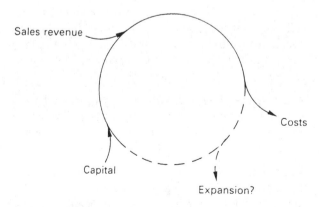

Figure 31.1   The money-go-round

Different organisations have, from time-to-time, produced different statistics to show why business organisations fail. The diagram in Figure 31.2 was based upon a report by the Society of Practitioners in Insolvency. It shows that the biggest single cause of business failure are financial problems, which accounted for 36 per cent of business failures: 20 per cent because of cash flow problems, 5 per cent because of loss of finance when lenders in the market became cautious about who they lent to, and 11 per cent because of bad debts when businesses failed to pay their bills.

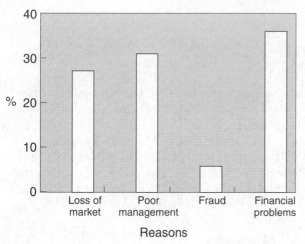

Figure 31.2   Causes of business failure

Purposes of budgets

We all budget to a greater or lesser extent. Out short-term budget may relate to how we are going to get through the forthcoming week and be able to do all of the things we have planned to do. Our slightly longer-term budget may involve being able to afford Christmas presents in several months time. Longer still, we may be thinking about how we can afford the car tax, MOT and motor insurance next year, all of which fall in the same month! Also, when can we afford to replace the car?

In exactly the same way, business organisations have to look into the future. The problem always is that the further you look into the future the more difficult it is to see accurately!

A budget is a financial plan which has been developed for the future. Many business organisations appoint a budget controller whose sole task is to co-ordinate budgetary activities.

- A short-term budget would be for up to one year.
- A medium-term budget would be for anything from one to five years.
- A budget for a longer period would be a longer-term budget.

Budgeting is an important function for almost every type of organisation. Wherever budgeting takes place it is important to draw upon the collective experience of people throughout the business. A budgeting team might consist of representatives from various areas of activity. The team will consider the objectives of the budgeting process, obtain and provide relevant information, make decisions, prepare budgets and then use these budgets to help to control the business.

So, what are the purposes of budgeting?

- Budgeting helps to predict what the organisation thinks will happen. Given the experience within the organisation, they help to show what is likely to take place in the future.
- Budgets create opportunities to appraise alternative courses of action. Information created for budgeting purposes forms of the basis of decisions which have to be taken. The research necessary for budgeting will look at alternative ways of achieving the organisation's objectives.
- Budgets set targets. If communicated to people throughout the organisation, the budgets will help them to work towards the targets which have been set up.
- Budgets help to monitor and control performance. This can be done by studying actual results, comparing this to budgeting results and then finding out why differences may have taken place.
- Budgets are fundamental to the process of business planning. They provide a series of quantitative guidelines which can be used for co-ordination and then followed in order to achieve the organisation's business objectives.

Budgeting may also have some useful spin-offs. Every year the business is reviewed and this gives members of the various departments a better understanding of the working of the organisation as a whole. In fact, by participating in the budgetary process they feel that their experience is contributing to policy decisions. The process may also highlight areas of concern.

Budgeting also increases co-operation between departments and lowers departmental barriers. In this way, members of one department can become aware of the difficulties facing another department. By being involved in the budgetary process, non-accountants also appreciate the importance of costs.

In reality, budgeting may take place in almost all parts of an organisation. Budgeting should also be viewed as something which is going on all the time and as a source of useful information and guidance for managers. However, for the purpose of this chapter we are only going to look at one type of budget known as cash flow forecasting.

Profit v cash

Whereas **cash** is a liquid asset owned by a business which enables it to buy goods and services, **profit** is a surplus arising from trading. It is therefore possible for a business to be selling goods at a higher price than they cost and to be making a profit but, if creditors have not been paid, for it to be having cash flow problems. A business must look carefully at its cash flow to ensure that the use of its most liquid asset resource is economically utilised. For example, if a business holds too much cash it could be sacrificing profits, and if it holds too little it could run out! The solution to the problem involves getting the balance just about right.

IT'S A FACT

According to economic theory there are three motives for holding cash:

- **The transactionary motive** In order to meet commitments such as wages, materials and other payments, a business requires cash. Cash is the 'life blood' of the organisation which circulates and enables it to meet obligations as and when they arise.
- **The precautionary motive** If cash flows are uncertain in the future it would be sensible to hold a sufficient large balance of cash to deal with any problems that may arise.
- **The speculative motive** Sometimes it might be worth holding cash just in case any profitable opportunities arise.

Cash flow

An organisation must ensure that it has sufficient cash to carry out its plans, and ensure that cash coming in is sufficient to cover cash going out. At the same time it must take into account any cash surpluses it might have in the bank.

Looking carefully at the availability of liquid funds is essential to the smooth running of any organisation. With cash planning or budgeting it is possible to forecast the flows into and out of an organisation's bank account so that any surpluses or deficits can be highlighted and any necessary action can be taken promptly. For example, overdraft facilities may be arranged in good time so that funds are available when required.

IT'S A FACT

It has been said that bankers are more concerned about an organisation's cash flow than the profits generated by trading activities!

The cash flow forecast is an extremely important tool within an organisation. It has a number of clear purposes. These are:

- **to highlight the timing consequences** for when machinery of other capital items need to be replaced
- **to help to compile the business plan** thus showing whether the organisation is capable of achieving its objectives. (This is very important if the business is applying for finance. The lender will almost certainly want to know about the ability of the applicant to keep on top of cash flow so that the proposed payment schedules can be met
- **to improve the lender's confidence and the owner's confidence** – by looking into the future it will provide them with the reassurance they require that their plans will go according to schedule
- **to monitor the performance of the business** – the cash flow forecast sets benchmarks against which the business can be expected to perform. (If the organisation performs differently from these benchmarks, then the cash flow forecast may have highlighted key areas which need to be looked at. Investigating differences between forecast figures and actual figures is known as 'variance analysis' – see Part 2, Chapter 60.)

Significance of timing

In order to prepare a cash flow forecast it is important to know what receipts and payments are likely to take place in the future and exactly when they will occur. It is also important to know the length of the lead time between incurring an expense and paying for it, as well as the time lag between making a sale and collecting the money from debtors. The art of successful forecasting is being able to calculate receipts and expenditures accurately.

Most business transactions take place on credit. As a result most payments are made either weeks or months after documentation has been sent.

For example, suppose a business sells goods on credit. Assume that the cash for these sales is received three months after the sale. This means that in April the cash will be received for January, in May the cash will be received for February and so on. From the other viewpoint, if you have been given three months' credit you would pay for goods bought in January during April and so on.

When working through a cash flow it is important to look at the timing of every entry.

Cash flow headings

Cash flow headings may vary according to the nature of the business and the complexity of the exercise as well as the range of possible in-flows and out-flows which it's possible for a business organisation to have.

Some of the more likely cash in-flow headings are as follows:

- **Start-up capital** This would be capital put into the business when trading activities began.
- **Loan receipts** If a business receives monies from a loan it would appear as a receipt.
- **Miscellaneous receipts** A business organisation may have a number of miscellaneous receipts which could inject finance into the cash flow forecast.
- **Sales receipts** Clearly the most important form of receipt, this is simply income from sales.
- **VAT recoveries** If more VAT is paid on purchases than is received on sales, then the VAT recovered from Customs and Excise would be an in-flow.

Some of the more likely cash out-flow headings are as follows:

- **Payments for assets** Asset purchase will be predictable and the amounts used for each purchase should be deducted from the cash flow forecast.
- **Raw materials** This is likely to be a regular out-flow which may relate to a production schedule or the volume of sales.
- **Expenses** These might include water rates, telephone bills as well as the many other running costs. They will not include depreciation as this is not a movement of funds.
- **Interest payments/loan repayments** These may appear as regular payments for the use of capital.
- **VAT payments** VAT is usually charged for three monthly periods.

An example of cash-flow headings is shown in Figure 31.3.

	Jan	Feb £	Mar £	Apr £	May £	June £
Receipts						
Start-up capital						
Loan receipts						
Miscellaneous receipts						
Sales receipts						
VAT recoveries						
TOTAL						
Payments						
Assets						
Raw materials						
Expenses						
Interest payments						
Loan repayments						
VAT payments						
TOTAL						
Receipts – payments						
Balance B/F						
Balance C/F						

Figure 31.3   Cash flow headings

CASE STUDY CASE STUDY CASE STUDY CASE STUDY CASE STUDY CASE

GUIDELINES FOR IMPROVING CASH FLOW

According to Paul Hancock, the sales and marketing director at International Factors, small businesses can follow simple guidelines to improve their cash flow. His tips include:

- consider credit insurance against customers who cannot pay
- plan purchases from suppliers to coincide with payments from customers
- buy new equipment on finance leasing. (This provides medium-term funding which allows new technology to be introduced within a structured plan.)

- try to pace new orders so that the business is not overstretched
- keep your bank manager informed
- finance assets over the life of the assets; for example, leasing for plant and machinery
- if you use factors or insurers, ask them to vet new buyers for creditworthiness.

1 What problems might be involved in planning payments from customers with purchases from suppliers?
2 Think of and then list other tips to add to those already provided.

CASE STUDY CASE STUDY CASE STUDY CASE STUDY CASE STUDY CASE

EXAMPLE

A cash flow forecast for the six months ended 31 December 1997 can be drafted from the following information:

- Cash balance 1 July 1997: £4,500
- Sales are £15 per unit and cash is received three months after the sale. For the period in question, the sale of units is:

1997
Mar	Apr	May	Jun	Jul	Aug
60	60	75	90	55	140

				1998	
Sep	Oct	Nov	Dec	Jan	Feb
130	150	150	160	170	150

- Production in units:

1997
Mar	Apr	May	Jun	Jul	Aug
40	50	80	70	80	130

				1998	
Sep	Oct	Nov	Dec	Jan	Feb
130	150	145	160	170	160

- Raw materials cost £4 per unit and these are paid for two months *before* being used in production.
- Wages are £5 per unit and this is paid for the same month as the unit produced.
- Running costs are £4 per unit. 50 per cent of the cost is paid in the same month of production while the other 50 per cent is paid for in the month after production.
- Sundry expenses of £50 are paid monthly.

Receipts from sales

					£
July	60 (April)	x	15	=	900
August	75 (May)	x	15	=	1,125
September	90 (June)	x	15	=	1,350
October	55 (July)	x	15	=	825
November	140 (August)	x	15	=	2,100
December	130 (September)	x	15	=	1,950

Payments

July
					£
Raw materials	130 (Sept)	x	4	=	520
Wages	80 (July)	x	5	=	400
Running costs	80 (July)	x	2	=	160
	70 (June)	x	2	=	140
Sundry expenses				=	50
					1,270

August
					£
Raw materials	150 (October)	x	4	=	600
Wages	130 (August)	x	5	=	650
Running costs	130 (August)	x	2	=	260
	80 (July)	x	2	=	160
Sundry expenses				=	50
					1,720

September
					£
Raw materials	145 (November)	x	4	=	580
Wages	130 (September)	x	5	=	650
Running costs	130 (September)	x	2	=	260
	130 (August)	x	2	=	260
Sundry expenses				=	50
					1,800

October
					£
Raw materials	160 (December)	x	4	=	640
Wages	150 (October)	x	5	=	750
Running costs	150 (October)	x	2	=	300
	130 (September)	x	2	=	260
Sundry expenses				=	50
					2,000

November
					£
Raw materials	170 (January)	x	4	=	680
Wages	145 (November)	x	5	=	725
Running costs	145 (November)	x	2	=	290
	150 (October)	x	2	=	300
Sundry expenses				=	50
					2,045

December
					£
Raw materials	160 (February)	x	4	=	640
Wages	160 (December)	x	5	=	800
Running costs	160 (December)	x	2	=	320
	145 (November)	x	2	=	290
Sundry expenses				=	50
					2,100

	July	Aug	Sept	Oct	Nov	Dec
Receipts						
Sales	900	1,125	1,350	825	2,100	1,950
Total receipts	900	1,125	1,350	825	2,100	1,950
Payments						
Raw materials	520	600	580	640	680	640
Direct labour	400	650	650	750	725	800
Variable expenses	300	420	520	560	590	610
Fixed expenses	50	50	50	50	50	50
Total payments	1,270	1,720	1,800	2,000	2,045	2,100
Receipts – payments	(370)	(595)	(450)	(1175)	55	(150)
Balance B/F	4,500	4,130	3,535	3,085	1,910	1,965
Balance C/F	4,130	3,535	3,085	1,910	1,965	1,815

TASK 31.1

Robin Williams sets up in business as a manufacturer of wheel nuts by putting £14,400 into a business bank account on 1 January. For the first six months of the year he anticipates the following situations:

- His forecasts for the purchase of raw materials and sales receipts for finished goods based upon extensive market research are as follows:

	Purchases(£)	Sales(£)
January	6,500	5,500
February	7,000	7,100
March	7,300	8,000
April	7,500	14,000
May	6,100	17,000
June	6,500	14,300

- Robin Williams has arrange one month's credit from suppliers, so raw materials purchased in January will have to be paid for in February.
- He expects one-half of sales to be for cash and the other half on credit. He anticipates two months on average to be taken by credit customers, i.e. sales made in January on credit will not be settled until March.
- Wages are expected to be £1,000 per month, paid for in the same month.
- Machinery must be purchased for £15,500 on 1 January and paid for in the same month.
- Rent for his factory is £6,000 per annum, payable in equal instalments at the start of each month.
- Other costs (overheads) are £1,500 per month, and these are to be paid in the month following that in which they were incurred.
- In April he expects to receive an inheritance from his Great Uncle Timothy of £8,000, which he will put into thebusiness bank account.

Prepare Robin Williams' cash flow forecast for the first six months.

Managing working capital

Working capital is the difference between current assets and current liabilities. Current assets are either in the form of cash or in a form that can soon lead to cash, and current liabilities will soon have to be paid for with cash. A prudent ratio of current assets to current liabilities is considered to be 2:1 although most businesses operate with a slightly lower ratio than this. It is now more commonly thought that a satisfactory working capital ratio will depend upon the company concerned, the type of business operations, stock levels and other factors.

Working capital is often considered to be the portion of capital that 'oils the wheels' of business. Funds employed in fixed assets are concerned with producing goods and services. Working capital provides stocks from which the fixed assets may produce. It allows the salesforce to offer trade credit and create debtors. Firms with insufficient working capital are in a financial straitjacket. They lack the funds to buy stocks, and to produce and create debtors. In these circumstances, providers of finance may well call a meeting of creditors and appoint a liquidator. Clearly, a business must always have adequate short-term funds to ensure the continuation of its activities.

The **operating cycle** expresses the connection between working capital and movements of cash. It can measure the period of time between:

- the purchase of raw materials and the receipt of cash from debtors
- the time when cash is paid out for raw materials and the time when cash is received from sales (see Figure 31.4).

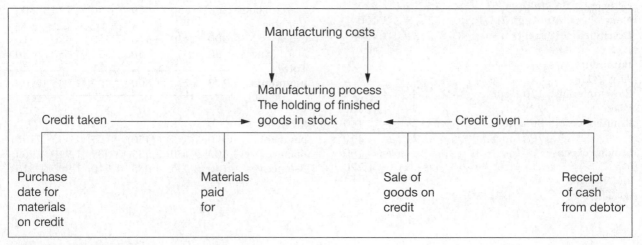

Figure 31.4   Managing the credit cycle

EXAMPLE

A firm buys raw materials on two months' credit and holds them in stock for half a month before issuing them to the production department from which they emerge as finished goods. These are held on average for one and a half months before sale. Debtors take three months to pay. The cash cycle would be:

	Months
Raw materials credit from suppliers	(2)
Turnover of stock of raw materials	0.5
Turnover of stock of finished goods	1.5
Debtors' payment period	3.0
Cash cycle	3.0

Not only does this cycle show the time ingredient; it also shows that income from debtors should be more than enough to cover any manufacturing costs and overheads encountered.

The dangers of insufficient working capital are clear to see:

- A company with limited working capital will not be able to buy in bulk and could miss out on any opportunities to obtain trade discounts.
- Cash discounts will be lost as the business will avoid paying creditors until the last possible opportunity.
- It will become more difficult to offer extensive credit facilities for customers. By shortening the credit period, customers may well go to alternative suppliers.
- The business will be unable to innovate. Limited finances will hinder its ability to develop new products or improve production techniques.
- The business's financial reputation as a good payer may be lost.
- Creditors may well take action. As capital becomes squeezed, a business will be forced to finance its activities by overdrafts and trade credit. A point could well be reached where its future is dependent upon the actions of creditors.
- Overtrading can take place. This would involve financing a large volume of production with inadequate working capital, often from short-term loans. This can lead to a complete imbalance in the working capital ratio.

Accountants will constantly review an organisation's asset structure to ensure that resources are utilised efficiently. Depending on the review, it might be necessary to increase working capital. This might take place in a number of ways:

- Reducing the period between the time cash is paid out for raw materials and the time cash is received from sales will provide funds for regeneration. Although the improved efficiency of the cash cycle will help working capital, it might be unpopular with creditors.
- Fixed assets such as land and buildings might not be fully utilised, or space might be used for unprofitable purposes. Space could be rented, sold or allowed to house a more profitable operation so that cash flow could be improved. A business's cash flow might be improved by selling assets and leasing them back, although this may commit an organisation to heavy leasing fees.
- A company could review its stock levels to see if these could be the subject of economy measures. If the stock of raw materials is divided by the average weekly issue, the number of week's raw materials held in stock can be calculated. Some companies attempt to maximise liquidity by using 'just-in-time' to hold the minimum stocks possible. Although this might save on expenses associated with running and large store and looking after stocks, the company might lose out on trade discounts or be susceptible to inconsistent supplies.
- Many businesses employ a credit controller to reduce debtors. A credit controller will vet new customers and set them a credit limit, ensure that credit limits are not exceeded and encourage debtors to pay on time. Credit controllers are often caught in a conflict with the sales department, whose staff wish to extend credit limits, and the accounts department who want debtors to pay quickly and so increase their working capital.
- As we have seen, cash budgeting can be used as an important control mechanism to predict the effects of future transactions on the cash balance of a company. Cash flow forecasting or cash budgeting can help an organisation take actions to ensure that cash is available when required.
- A number of short-term solutions are available to increase working capital. Companies might extend their overdraft or bring in a factoring company. It might be possible to delay the payment of bills, although this obviously displeases creditors.

What might happen if things go wrong?

Liquidation occurs when it is considered that an organisation can no longer pay its debts. This will be ordered by a court, usually on behalf of a creditor. This may then be followed by **receivership**, where independent accountants supervise the sale of the business. But, sometimes, while struggling to survive and meet the demands of creditors a **white knight** appears on the scene to launch a rescue bid and save the business.

Chapter summary

- Financial planning involves developing ways of achieving objectives.
- The biggest single cause of business failure is cash flow problems.
- A budget is a financial plan developed for the future.
- Budgeting affects all areas of business activity.
- Cash and profit are very different things.
- Cash flow forecasts have a number of clear purposes.
- Timing is very important for cash flow forecasts.
- There are a number of ways which can be used to improve cash flow.
- Working capital is the difference between current assets and current liabilities.
- There are many dangers of insufficient working capital.

32 The nature of costs

Almost all business activities involve some element of cost and most managers have to deal with costs on a day-to-day basis. Costs are fundamental – from the early development of business plans through to the controlling and monitoring of expenditure. Costing techniques help managers to work out what they should be doing and to develop measures that help them to control their activities. Cost accounting and the use of costing techniques also provide a useful source of information for management accountants, who use information from costs to try to guide their organisation in a particular direction in order to achieve objectives.

Information about costs will help to:

- create short-term, medium-term and long-term plans
- control the organisation's activities
- decide between alternative strategies
- appraise performance at strategic, departmental and operational levels.

Management accounting therefore involves collecting data and processing them so that decisions to control operations can be more efficient.

Accountants can use knowledge of costs to predict future events. In doing so, they will try to anticipate changes in taxation, interest rates, actions of competitors and also markets. They will also look at past events, and at information recorded about these events, in order to guide future decision making.

Over the past 20 years the nature of industry has changed dramatically. Information technology has revolutionised the ways in which information is being provided as well as the ways in which costs are calculated, measured and monitored. Managers have to be adaptable to changing disciplines so that they can provide the right information when required. In order to do this they must be constantly aware of new concepts, principles and techniques designed to help them to meet their objectives.

Costs

The word 'cost' has several meanings, even in everyday language. The cost of items we purchase is something we think about daily; for us it is a money sacrifice we have to make for goods or services that we require. Cost also implies some form of measurement as we automatically attach value to many of the products that we see. It can be an unwelcome word, particularly if we come across hidden costs which we had not anticipated having to pay.

People in organisations frequently talk about calculating the cost of an event, activity or product. Within this context, they are using a knowledge of costs together with a knowledge of revenues and income flows to determine whether or not something they are planning will ultimately reap the rewards they desire.

Nearly all business activities involve some sort of cost. A good knowledge of costs and their influences is fundamental in assessing their profitability, as profits are only a reflection of income over these costs. Costs from the past, which have already been incurred, should provide a guide to costs in the future. However, they have to be critically examined, discussed and often adjusted to be of use to the accountant for predicting future profitability. At a later stage, accountants will make informed comparisons between actual events and standards that have been set.

GETTING THE COST WRONG

The Channel Tunnel, when it opened at a cost of around £10 billion, was more than twice the original estimate. 'Refinancing' become a popular word, with the latest deal increasing the interests of banks, often at the expense of shareholders, with swaps of debt for equity. And, of course, the 'fire' in the Tunnel did not help.

In the gas industry, when the price of a product is low, the strongest player is the one with the deepest pockets. British Gas has recently signed a new deal with BP which BP regards as an excellent investment. Whereas companies like BP and Shell have plenty of money because of high oil prices and low costs, British Gas is not in quite the same position. By signing deals in the early 1990s

with huge volumes of gas at agreed prices before delivery, it committed itself too early. When competitors entered the market oil companies offered them lower discounted prices and with a succession of warm winters British Gas has been forced to leave much of the expensive gas in the ground.

1 How important is it to try to forecast the future cost of a business venture?
2 Why do you think that Eurotunnel's and British Gas's estimates were so wildly inaccurate?
3 What factors had they perhaps not taken into account?
4 How important is research and planning for this process?

There are two broad approaches to the classification of business costs:

- One method categorises costs by their type and identifies whether they can be directly related to the final product or service of the business.
- The other approach is to analyse costs according to whether they remain fixed with changes in output levels. This forms the foundation for decision making as we will see when we look at 'contribution' and 'break-even analysis' in the next chapter.

Direct and indirect costs

Direct costs

Direct costs are those costs that can be clearly identified with the product or service being provided. Typical examples include:

- **Direct labour** – payments made to workers who make products or provide services. An engineering firm may incur direct wages paid to machine operators and an office-cleaning firm will pay direct wages to cleaners.
- **Direct materials** – the cost incurred for materials used to make specific products or provide specific services. An engineering firm may require materials in the form of base metals and ready-made components; the cleaning firm will require chemicals and materials for specific cleaning contracts.

- **Direct expenses** – other costs may be incurred specifically for the final product or service. These may include payments to the product's designer (in the form of royalties), payments made to other businesses for work they have done as sub-contractors to help provide the finished product or service for the consumer. Sometimes also power and depreciation, *but only if there is a direct link* between the cost unit, the use of power or the depreciation taking place.

Indirect costs

Indirect costs are those that cannot be classified as direct costs. Wherever possible, costs incurred by businesses are identified with specific products or services, as this provides the most accurate costing of a firm's output.

However, many costs incurred by businesses cannot be easily related to specific units of production or service. For example, it is usually very difficult and time-consuming to relate precise amounts of electricity used and property rents incurred to specific units of output.

Indirect costs can be classified as follows:

- **Indirect labour** – this would include the cost of management, administration and marketing personnel. Even the cost of many 'blue-collar' workers may need to be classified as indirect labour if they are not doing work that results directly in a product or service. Examples are maintenance workers and stores personnel.
- **Indirect materials** – these include small items which are difficult to relate directly to items of output. In fact,

the costs of relating them to specific items of output would outweigh the benefits of slightly more accurate product costs. Examples of indirect materials include lubricating materials, rages for cleaning and small nuts and bolts.

● **Indirect expenses** – these include a wide range of costs such as property rents, power, stationery, rates, telephone and other running expenses as well as depreciation of fixed assets. Total indirect costs are often called overheads.

TASK 32.1

Make a list of the direct costs of the school or college you attend. Compare these with its indirect costs. How do they differ?

Variable and fixed costs

Another method of classifying costs, as we mentioned earlier, is according to their relationship with changes in output levels. This identifies costs as either **fixed** or **variable**.

Fixed costs

These are costs that do not increase as total output increases. For example, if an organisation has the capacity needed it might increase its production from 25,000 units to 30,000 units. Its rent, rates and heating bills will be the same, since they also had to be paid when the organisation was producing 25,000 units.

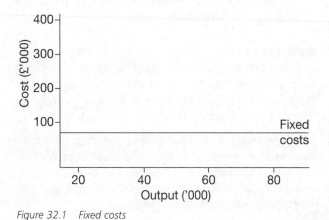

Figure 32.1   Fixed costs

Variable costs

These are those that increase as the total output increases because more of these factors need to be employed as inputs in order to increase outputs. For example, if you produce more items you need more raw materials.

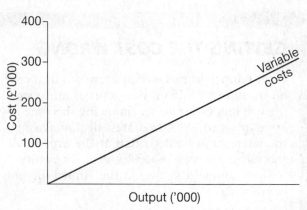

Figure 32.2   Variable costs

As output increases, total variable costs will increase but the variable cost per unit will stay the same (unless the levels of output are moving towards maximum capacity – see the case study on page 193). For example, if the only variable costs are direct materials and direct labour and these are 50p for every unit of output produced we can see that:

	100 units	200 units	300 units
Total variable costs	£50	£250	£500
Variable costs per unit	50p	50p	50p

Total costs

You have been introduced to two different classifications of cost. One describes the nature of costs incurred (direct and indirect costs) and the other how these vary with the level of production (variable and fixed costs). You may find it useful to related these two different classifications as follows:

● Direct costs can be generally considered as variable costs.
● Indirect costs can be generally considered as fixed costs.

Although this is in some ways a simplification, these statements should help your basic understanding of business costs. We can now identify total business costs using the two classification methods:

Total costs =   Direct costs   +   Indirect costs
Total costs =   Variable costs   +   Fixed costs.

TAYLOUR COATS PLC

Taylour Coats manufactures high-class country jackets. Business has developed well over recent years, particularly in their export markets to the USA, where English country clothing has become increasingly popular.

The company is managed and owned by Manjit Gill, the Managing Director, and Rosemary Williams, who supervises the operations. They own a factory unit on a trading estate in Gosforth and employ 20 full-time employees: a foreman, 15 machine operators who cut out the materials for the part-time workers, and 4 dispatchers. The part-time workers are employed as subcontractors, using their own sewing machines at home to make up the jackets from the cut-out pieces that have been sent to them.

The foreman is paid £400 per week, the machine operators £230 per week and the dispatchers £180 per week. The part-timers are paid £10 for each jacket they make up. Other business costs include:

- electricity at £100 per week
- rent and rates at £500 per week
- loan repayments, including interest at £200 per week
- other fixed costs at £120 per week
- directors' salaries for Manjit and Rosemary of £600 per week each
- material costs for each jacket of £5.

The existing capacity for Taylour Coats is 400 jackets per week. If it needs to produce more than this, it has to pay higher rates to cover overtime put in by part-time workers, which results in an increase in part-time rates from £10 for each jacket to £15, up to a maximum capacity of 500 jackets. At present jackets are priced at £35 and Taylour has a consistent weekly turnover of 350 jackets.

Taylour has been approached by two American chain stores who have tested samples and wish to purchase some jackets on a regular basis. Austin Stores Inc. wishes to purchase 100 jackets per week and is willing to pay £28 per jacket. NMAUSA wishes to purchase 50 jackets per week and is willing to pay £32 per jacket. As a personal friend of the directors and an adviser to the business, these figures have been left with you for further analysis.

1 Construct a table to show the fixed, variable and total weekly costs at each 50 units of production up to a maximum of 500 jackets.
2 Present the fixed, variable and total costs in a graphical form for the week.
3 Calculate the profit the company is generating at its present level of sales of 350 jackets per week.
4 Advise the directors as to whether they should accept:
   a the Austin Stores order
   b the NMAUSA order
   c both
   d neither.

Support your answer with figures and explanations.

Marginal cost

Marginal cost is the cost of producing one extra unit of production or service – because it is the cost of producing one extra unit of production or service it comprises the variable cost per unit.

We have seen that as output varies, some costs also vary but others remain fixed. It is because of this fact that average cost will change as product varies. The cost of producing more output or the saving in producing less output is the marginal cost per unit (variable cost), which is not the same as total cost per unit.

EXAMPLE

Roadrunners & Co operates a courier service for documents and parcels using small motor vans. The business charges its customers on the basis of the number of miles to be travelled. Fixed costs are £2,000 per month and variable costs 20 pence per mile. During March, the business's vehicles travelled 5,000 miles and in April they travelled 7,000 miles. Calculate the total costs and cost per mile for both months.

	March	April	Marginal cost
	£	£	£
Fixed costs	2,000	2,000	0
Variable costs at 20p/mile	1,000	1,400	400
Total costs	3,000	3,400	400
Number of miles	5,000	7,000	2,000
Cost per mile	0.60	0.49	0.20

The marginal cost simply comprises the variable cost of travelling the additional 2,000 miles during the second month.

TASK 32.2

The Rilton Hotel measures its output in terms of number of guest nights. It provides food and drinks only to overnight customers. It has incurred the following costs over the last two trading quarters:

	To June £	To September £
Food	4,500	6,000
Rent	5,000	5,000
Casual staff	3,600	4,800
Permanent staff	6,000	6,000
Drinks	900	1,200
Laundry	1,350	1,800
Power	2,650	2,650
Depreciation	3,000	3,000

The number of guest nights in the June to September quarters were 900 and 1,200 respectively.

1 Analyse costs into fixed and variable.
2 Calculate total costs for each quarter.
3 Calculate total cost per guest night.
4 Calculate the marginal cost for one guest to stay one night at the hotel.

Chapter summary

- An introduction to the nature and purpose of costing activities is provided.
- The role of the management accountant in respect of costs is discussed.
- The meanings of the word 'cost' are given.
- An understanding of the importance of costs for decision making activities is provided.
- A description of the two broad approaches to cost classification is given.
- Types of direct cost are shown.
- Types of indirect cost are shown.
- Distinctions are drawn between fixed and variable costs.
- You should understand the alternative methods of calculating total costs.
- You should apply your understanding of costs to a series of practical examples.
- You should understand the principles of marginal cost.

33 Contribution and break-even analysis

In the previous chapter, we looked at the nature of costs. In doing so we looked at two broad approaches to their classification. Having looked at costs we are now going to look at how one method of cost classification, that of fixed and variable costs, can be used within a working context.

If you look at Figure 33.1 you can see that fixed costs remain the same over a range of output. As we saw in the earlier chapter total cost is simply fixed costs plus variable costs. Variable costs, if added to the fixed cost line, represent total costs. When no units are produced the total cost is simply the level of fixed costs, but as more units are produced the wedge on top of the fixed costs (i.e. variable costs) not only shows how variable costs relate to increasing output but also gives the total costs of production.

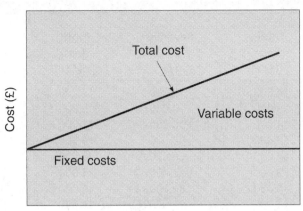

Figure 33.1

Contribution

The notion of contribution is an important ingredient in **marginal costing**. Think about what a business requires if it wishes to make a profit. First, it must be necessary for sales revenues to exceed total costs.

Sales revenue exceeds total costs = Profits

Secondly, it must be considered how far each individual sale helps with the accumulation of profits or the ability to pay off some of the fixed costs. With this form of costing, provided the value of each individual sale to a customer covers the variable costs incurred, then the sale makes a **contribution** towards fixed costs and profits.

Sales revenue per unit minus variable cost per unit is known as the contribution per unit.

Marginal or contribution cost pricing can be particularly useful when making pricing decisions (see Part 2, Chapter 53). It involves separating out the different products within an organisation's product portfolio in order to charge appropriate prices so that each product contributes towards fixed costs and profitability. If when the contributions of all products that an organisation produces are added together they more than cover fixed costs, then profits are made. However, if the contributions do not cover the fixed costs, then losses will be incurred. One way of looking at this is through break-even analysis.

EXAM TIP:

The notion of contribution and the process of break-even analysis is a key area for almost any business course. In developing your understanding of this area you must remember that as break-even analysis is a key decision-making technique for decision makers you need to understand the dynamics of this process in relation to pricing and profitability. Get as much practice as you can of examples and exercises so that you can develop your break-even techniques.

Break-even point

The break-even point is the point at which sales levels are high enough not to make a loss, but not high enough to make a profit.

Another way of describing this is to say that break-even is the unique point at which a business makes no profit and no loss. The concept of break-even is a development from the principles of marginal costing. Marginal costing is a commonly used technique which uses costs to forecast profits from the production and sales levels expected in future periods. The great benefit of marginal costing over other costing methods is that it overcomes the problem of allocating fixed costs – only variable costs are allocated, as we shall see.

The difference between an item's selling price and the variable costs needed to produce that item is known as the **contribution**.

Contribution = selling price per unit less variable costs per unit

By producing and selling enough units to produce a total contribution that is in excess of fixed costs, an organisation will make a profit.

EXAMPLE

Performance Sport Ltd manufactures leather footballs. It anticipates that next year it will sell 8,000 units at £12 per unit. Its variable costs are £5 per unit and its fixed costs are £9,000. From this we can deduce that the contribution is £12 minus £5, which is £7 per unit. Therefore £7 will go towards paying off the fixed costs and towards profits. We can also show this using totals to show how much profit will be made if the business sells 8,000 units(see Figure 33.2).

	£
Sales revenue (8,000 x £12)	96,000
Less marginal costs (8,000 x £5)	40,000
Total contribution	56,000
Less fixed costs	9,000
Net profit	47,000

Figure 33.2   Profit statement from Performance Sport Ltd

The problem can also be looked at by constructing a table as in Figure 33.3.

Units of production	Fixed costs (£)	Variable costs (£)	Total costs (£)	Revenue (£)	Profit (loss) (£)
1,000	9,000	5,000	14,000	12,000	(2,000)
2,000	9,000	10,000	19,000	24,000	5,000
3,000	9,000	15,000	24,000	36,000	12,000
4,000	9,000	20,000	29,000	48,000	19,000
5,000	9,000	25,000	34,000	60,000	26,000
6,000	9,000	30,000	39,000	72,000	33,000
7,000	9,000	35,000	44,000	84,000	40,000
8,000	9,000	40,000	49,000	96,000	47,000
9,000	9,000	45,000	54,000	108,000	54,000
10,000	9,000	50,000	59,000	120,000	61,000

Figure 33.3   Profit table for Performance Sport Ltd

TASK 33.1

Triumph Medallions produces a standard size trophy for sports shops and clubs. It hopes to sell 2,000 trophies next year at £9 per unit. Its variable costs are £5 per unit and its fixed costs are £4,000. Draw up a profit statement to show how much profit it will make for the year. Also construct a table to show how much profit it will make at each 500 units of production up to 3,000 units.

To take this analysis further we need to look at break-even analysis. To calculate the break-even point for Performance Sport Ltd there are two stages:

- Calculate the unit contribution (selling price less variable cost per unit).
- Divide the fixed costs by the unit contribution:

$$\text{Break-even point} = \frac{\text{Fixed costs}}{\text{Unit contribution}}$$

Taking the example of Performance Sport again, the contribution is £7 per unit and the fixed costs are £9,000. The break-even point would therefore be:

$$\frac{9,000}{7} = 1,286 \text{ units (to the nearest unit)}$$

The **sales value** at the break-even point can be calculated by multiplying the number of units by the selling price per unit. For Performance Sport this would be:

$$1,286 \times £12 = £15,432$$

Performance Sport has covered its costs (fixed and variable) and broken even with a sales value of £15,432. Anything sold in excess of this will provide it with profits.

If an organisation has a profit target or selected operating point to aim at, break even analysis can be used to calculate the number of units that need to be sold and the value of sales required to achieve that target.

Returning to the example, we can image that Performance Sport wishes to achieve a target of £15,000 profit. By adding this to the fixed costs and dividing by the contribution, the number of units can be found which need to be sold to meet this target. Thus:

$$\frac{9,000 + £15,000}{£7} = 3,429 \text{ units (to nearest unit)}$$

The difference between the break-even point and the selected level of activity to achieve the profit target is known as the **margin of safety**.

TASK 33.2

Garden Gates is a small business selling garden gates locally. Each gate is sold on average for £25. Fixed costs are £18,000 and variable costs are £13 per unit. The company wishes to achieve a profit of £18,000.

1 Calculate the break-even point both in terms of units and sales value.
2 Calculate the units and sales value necessary to achieve the selected operating point.

IT'S A FACT

Fixed costs are impossible to alter in the short term.

Drawing a break-even chart

A break-even chart can be used to show changes in the relationship between costs, production volumes and various levels of sales activity. The following is the procedure to construct a break-even chart like that drawn in Figure 33.5.

- Label the horizontal axis for units of production and sales.
- Label the vertical axis to represent the values of sales and costs.
- Plot fixed costs. Fixed costs remain the same over all levels of production, so plot this as a straight line parallel to the horizontal axis.
- Plot the total costs (variable costs + fixed costs). This will be a line rising from where the fixed cost line touches the vertical axis. It is plotted by calculating the total costs at two or three random levels of production.
- Sales are then plotted by taking two or three random levels of turnover. The line will rise from the intersection of the two axes.

The break-even point will be where the total-cost line and sales line intersect. The area to the left of the break-even point between the sales and total-cost lines will represent losses, and the area to the right of the break-even point between these lines will represent profit.

We can use an example to help make this more clear.

EXAMPLE

Elaine Welsh plans to set up a small restaurant. In doing so she knows that she will immediately incur annual fixed costs of £10,000. She is concerned about how many meals she will have to sell to break-even.

Extensive market research indicates that a typical customer will pay £8 for a meal, and Elaine knows that variable costs such as cooking ingredients and the cost of serving customers, will amount to about £3. Elaine has set herself a profit target of £14,000 for the first year of operation. Our task is to advise Elaine on the number of meals she has to sell and to show her the margin of safety.

Elaine's unit contribution is:

£8 – £3 (selling price – variable costs) = £5 per meal.

Her break-even point in units will be:

$$\frac{£10,000 \text{ (fixed costs)}}{5 \text{ (unit contribution)}} = 2,000 \text{ meals}$$

The sales value of the meals will be:

2,000 meals x £8 (selling price) = £16,000

Her profit target will be achieved by:

$$\frac{£10,000 \text{ (fixed costs)} + £14,000 \text{ (profit target)}}{£5 \text{ (unit contribution)}} = 4,800 \text{ meals}$$

The margin of safety will be the difference between the selected level of activity and the break-even point. It will be between 4,800 meals with a turnover of £38,400 and 2,000 meals with a turnover of £16,000.

The three random levels of variable costs and sales chosen for the purpose of plotting the break-even chart are at 1,000 meals, 3,000 meals and 5,000 meals (see Figure 33.4).

	1,000 meals £	3,000 meals £	5,000 meals £
Variable costs (£3/meal)	3,000	9,000	15,000
Fixed cost	10,000	10,000	10,000
Total cost	13,000	19,000	25,000
Sales	8000	24,000	40,000

Figure 33.4

We can now plot the break-even chart (Figure 33.5) which shows graphically the break-even point of 2,000 meals with a sale revenue of £16,000. The margin of safety can be seen on the chart if we identify the selected level of profit (4,800 meals) and the targeted turnover (£38,400), and compare this with the break-even point.

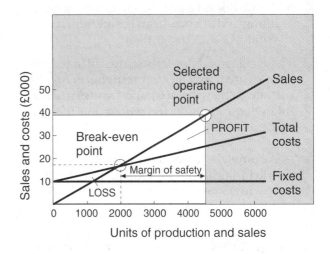

Figure 33.5 Elaine Welsh's break-even chart

The break-even chart is a simple visual tool enabling managers to anticipate the effects of changes in production and sales upon the profitability of an organisation's activities. It emphasises the importance of earning revenue and is particularly helpful for those who are unused to interpreting accounting information.

Analysing the break-even chart

The break-even chart can be used to explore changes in a number of key variables. These may include:

- **Sales volume and value** By looking at the chart if is possible to predict the effects of any changes in sales trends. For example, a sudden fall in sales may lead to a loss and a sudden increase may improve profitability.

- **Profits or losses at a given level of production** The break-even chart enables a business to monitor levels of production. By doing this important decisions can be made if changes take place.
- **Prices** It is possible to use the break-even chart to analyse different business scenarios. For example, given market research information, what would happen if we reduced the price by £2?
- **Costs** The effects of any sudden changes in costs can be plotted on the break-even chart.

Any of the above may affect an organisation's ability to achieve its selected operating point and margin of safety. The break-even chart is a useful management technique upon which to base action and which enables an organisation to achieve and develop its plans.

CASE STUDY CASE STUDY CASE STUDY CASE STUDY CASE STUDY CASE

UNCLE JOHN'S COTTAGE

Your Uncle John, a local farmer, has come to you for some advice. He is considering the future use of a recently vacated tied cottage on his farm as a holiday cottage.

The property has been allowed to deteriorate over the years and it is obvious that considerable internal improvements will be necessary before the cottage can be used as a holiday let. The house is, however, full of character with extensive views over North Yorkshire, extending to the Pennines on a clear day. There is easy access to Teesside, Northallerton and Thirsk.

The accommodation comprises:

- upstairs: three double bedrooms, large bathroom/toilet
- downstairs: large kitchen/diner, large lounge with open hearth and french windows into the garden.

The legal aspects of letting the cottage have been cleared, and all that remains is for the cottage to be renovated and furnished. The following quotation for renovation has been received:

	£
Complete redecoration	1,895
Refit bathroom and kitchen	2,800
Central heating	2,200
Wash basins in bedrooms	200

The quotation has been supplied by Pennine Rose Builders, a fairly large local business with a reputation for doing work of a reasonable quality.

Your uncle decides to fit the cottage out with items of reasonable quality and some durable furniture. These cost:

	£
Furniture and fittings	3,000
Kitchen equipment and household items	750

The finance for the renovation and for the purchase of the furnishings and fittings is obtained by means of a five-year bank loan with a fixed annual interest rate of 10 per cent payable each calendar month, and based upon the original sum. The loan principal is to be paid in five equal instalments.

Your uncle anticipates the following costs:

Fixed costs
- Annual loan repayment
- Annual interest on loan
- Community charge: £215 per half year
- Water rates: £80 per half year
- Insurance: £150 per annum
- Electricity: £17.50 per quarter

Variable costs
- Cleaner: £3 per hour for 5 hours per week
- Electricity and heating: £5 per week

The suggested scale of charges is as follows:
April–September £170 per week
October–March £110 per week.

1 How many weeks would it take for Uncle John to break even in:

a the summer season?
b the winter season?

2 If variable costs and rental prices both increase by 10 per cent in the second year, what would the new break-even point be? (Your answer should be supported by the appropriate break-even chart.)

Limitations of break-even analysis

It has been said that the process of identifying a contribution and break-even analysis presents an over-simplification of business behaviour by reducing it simply to an equation; how to generate enough contribution to cover fixed costs and provide a surplus for profit. Its limitations are as follows.

- It can be argued that, in reality, fixed costs are likely to change at different activity levels and that a stepped fixed-cost line would provide a more accurate representation.
- The business might be restricted by a limiting factor restricting its ability to break even or meet a profit target, such as lack of space, shortage of labour, shortage of orders, etc.
- Variable costs and sales are unlikely to be linear. Discounts, special contracts and overtime payments mean that the total cost line should really be a curve.
- Break-even charts depict short-term relationships and forecasts and are therefore unrealistic where the time scale covers several years.
- Break-even analysis is dependent upon the accuracy of forecasts made about costs and revenues. Changes in the market and in the cost of raw materials could affect the success of the technique.

SYNTHESIS

If 'break-even' is simply a formula based upon prediction, what strains might using this process put upon senior managers who use it within the working environment?

Reasons for using a break-even chart

The principal use of a break-even chart is to be able to find a **break-even** point given certain important information about sales and costs. Decisions may be then taken to select levels of operating activity which will provide required profits and also create a margin of safety.

As a tool, one of the great benefits of using a break-even chart is the ability to change and manipulate information so that predictions can be made about a range of different situations. This is knows as 'What if?' analysis. For example, if we could reduce variable costs by 10 per cent, how would this affect profitability? What would happen if we reduced prices by £3 in order to achieve a predicted 15 per cent increase in sales? All these situations can be plotted on a break-even chart. As a result, the chart is a useful device for quickly manipulating information so that outcomes can be anticipated.

The break-even chart is also a useful way of **anticipating and measuring** profits and losses. This is particularly important because, even though it reduces business to a diagrammatic equation, it is an important tool for predicting various levels of activity and then following actual levels of activity to see if plans are met.

Break-even analysis can also be used to work out how easily fixed costs can be covered from contributions made from sales. In a range of circumstances, break-even analysis can provide help with increasing profitability by providing information which enables a business to provide different services at different prices in order to make most of a business's ability to use all its capacity or as much as possible. For example, an hotel might be profitable with a 40 per cent occupancy rate, and bookings may always be around 50 per cent. The owner, however, knows that by providing cheaper beds by taking bookings after six o'clock at night, the occupancy rate is increasing, and although he or she is not getting as much to contribute to fixed costs and profitability as earlier bookings, the hotel is receiving something towards those costs and, of course, increasing its profitability.

Chapter summary

- The use of fixed and variable costs within a business scenario for forecasting is discussed.
- A description of the nature and purpose of contribution and marginal costing is provided.
- A definition of contribution is given.
- A definition of break-even analysis is given.
- The use of profit statements using fixed, variable and total costs is illustrated.

- The practical application of break-even analysis, using profit targets and margin of safety is shown.
- Break-even charts are constructed.
- The limitations of break-even analysis is discussed.
- The reasons for using a break-even chart are given.

34 Preparing financial statements from accounting records

In Chapter 29 we saw that there are many users of financial information. It is the recording of business transactions using a basic accounting system that provides such information. A useful definition of accounting is:

The art of preparing accounting reports from book-keeping records in accordance with acknowledged methods and conventions.

Let us look at the components of this definition:

- **Book-keeping records** – Traditionally records of accounts have been kept in books or ledgers. These records have been kept in a systematic way. Today, of course, most book-keeping and accountancy procedures are carried out using computers.
- **Preparing accounting reports** – It is necessary to summarise the entries which appear in book-keeping records in such a way that they can be presented for analysis and examination. Accounting reports summarise the entries that have been made in the books.
- **Acknowledged methods and conventions** – There are set ways of recording accounts which have been acknowledged over a period of time. Records needs to be set out to meet these methods and conventions. This is so that people can look at these records in order that comparison and analysis can take place between one period and another.

The accounting process can be seen as consisting of three parts:

- developing and keeping an accurate, full and useful record of the business's financial activities (this is normally referred to as book-keeping)
- the preparation of statements
- the interpretation of these records, for example, from accounting reports and statements.

There are a number of stages involved in putting together and keeping a basic accounting system:

- preparing, keeping and using documents
- transferring information from documents to records in books
- setting out a trial balance, i.e. a list of balances on all accounts
- producing financial statements (sometimes known as final accounts).

Accounting records

Accounting records have traditionally been associated with ledgers and clerks toiling long hours in dark gloomy offices making entries into musty books with quill pens. Today, happily, this picture has long since disappeared and most accounting staff work in bright and airy offices using computers.

Ledgers are often referred to as the **books of prime entry** because this is the first place book-keeping records will be kept. Ledgers are the subdivisions of the complete records kept by a business.

The **sales ledger** is used for making records of all the sales transactions carried out by a business. It contains the accounts of **debtors** – customers to whom goods or services have been supplied on credit.

The **purchases ledger** is used for making records of all the purchase transactions carried out by a business. It contains the accounts of **creditors** – suppliers to whom the organisation owes money.

The **cash book** is a very useful record of all the cash and bank transactions of a business.

The **general or nominal ledger** is used for recording all the other records of a business, for example:

- an **asset account** records the business's assets such as machinery, fixtures and fittings, etc.
- an **expenses account** shows all day-to-day expenses

of running the business

- an owner's **capital account** shows what the owner has put into the business.
- a **drawings account** shows money drawn out of the business by the owner or owners.

In ledgers, transactions are recorded using the **double-entry system** whereby, with each transaction, one account is debited and another is credited. This means that for every debit entry into one account there is always a corresponding credit entry into another account. Such as system assumes that all entries into an accounting system reflect a process of exchange. In other words, every transaction involves two parts which need to be recorded in the books of account. For example, if we buy equipment for cash we lose cash but gain equipment.

We would therefore record the loss of cash in a cash account and the gain of equipment in an equipment account. This dual element is carried through to the trial balance and then on to the final accounts.

The use of information technology has meant that today's integrated software packages contain the books of first entry and these are linked to a system which updates all records whenever a transaction takes place.

The **trial balance** is a list of all the accounts from all the ledgers. Is should balance because for every debit entry into one account there should have been a corresponding entry into another. This list of balances (as follows) provides the raw material for accountants to draw up the final accounts:

- sales ledger (containing numerous accounts of customers and businesses to whom goods are sold)
- purchases ledger (containing numerous accounts of customers and businesses from whom goods have been bought)
- cash book (contains bank and cash accounts)
- general ledger (contains all other accounts).

All these balances are transferred to the trial balance.

Financial statements or final accounts

Accountants provide valuable information to answer critical questions such as:

- How is the business doing?
- What sort of return on investments will the owners receive?

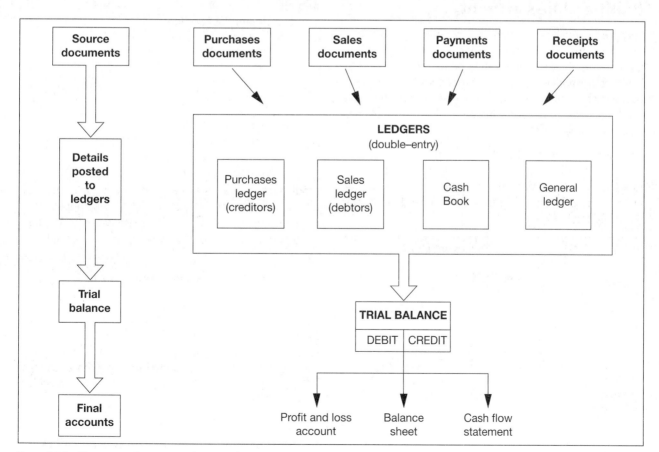

Figure 34.1   The process from accounting records to accounting statements

- Can the business meet its short- and long-term debts?
- Is the business in a position to expand?
- How much taxation is the business liable to pay?
- What are the financial prospects for the business?

IT'S A FACT

1997 saw the publication of the first set of auditor's accounts ever audited by another auditor. With auditors auditing auditors could anything happen or will they look at each other's books and fall asleep? The first audited report was for accountants KPMG and they were produced by auditors Grant Thornton who addressed their report 'to the partners of KPMG UK'.

Much of the information that accountants provide appears in the form of final accounts. These are drawn up regularly by each organisation's auditors and are used to assess performance.

Final accounts are made up of the following three elements:

- profit and loss account
- balance sheet
- cash flow statement.

Profit and loss account

The profit and loss account is a profitability statement which compares a business's income with outgoings (expenditures) over an accounting period. In other words, it values in money terms the transactions of a business over a specified time period of normally one year. It is a bit like a video which has recorded everything a business has done over a period of time.

The format of the profit and loss account may vary both in how it may be presented for you and also for a wide range of business organisations. For example, the layout and the descriptions of entries may depend upon the nature of the business (see Figure 34.2).

		Turnover/Sales
TRADING	Less	Cost of sales
	=	Gross Profit
ACCOUNT	Less	Expenses
	=	Operating profit
PROFIT AND	Plus	Non-operating income
LOSS ACCOUNT	Less	Interest payable
	=	Profit on ordinary activities
APPROPRIATION	Less	Corporation tax
	=	Profit after tax
ACCOUNT	Less	Dividends
	=	Retained profit

Figure 34.2   A layout for a profit and loss account

EXAM TIP:

It is important to understand that the profit and loss account is not just representing cash received and paid over a period. For example:

- the profit and loss account will indicate sales which have been made whether or not money has been received (see the accruals or matching concept in Chapter 29)
- similarly, if a business has used resources or purchased stock which has not yet been paid for, these figures will be included in the profit and loss account
- certain items in the profit and loss account may have been purchased but not used in the accounting period. For example, stocks at the end of an accounting period should be deducted from purchases over a period
- fixed assets have to be depreciated. The cost of these are itemised in expenses and spread over the lifetime of an asset. When an asset is depreciated no money changes hands.

A profit and loss account can be divided into three distinct sections. These are:

- the trading account
- the profit and loss account
- the appropriation account.

The trading account

For many businesses, trading involves buying and selling stock. The difference between the value of the stock sold (sales) and the cost of producing those sales – which is the production costs of manufactured goods for a manufacturing company, or the cost of purchasing supplies for a trading company – is known as the **gross profit**. The trading account simply shows how gross profit is arrived at:

Sales – Cost of sales = Gross profit

'Cost of sales' has to take into account the value of stocks. 'Opening stocks' are effectively a purchase as these will be sold in the current trading period. On the other hand, 'closing stock' must be deducted from purchases as these will be sold next year. The true cost of sales is therefore found by applying the formula:

Cost of sales = Opening stocks + Purchases – Closing stocks

EXAMPLE

Opening stocks	£25,000
Add purchases	£125,000
	£150,000
Less closing stocks	£40,000
= Cost of sales	£110,000

TASK 34.1

TT Trailers Ltd has 20 caravans in stock which cost the business £5,000 each. They sell 8 for £7,000 each and buy three more for a total of £18,000. Calculate the gross profit. If three of these sales had been on credit, how would profits be affected?

Remember the trading account appears at the top of the 'profit and loss' account. It starts with sales less cost of sales resulting in the calculation of gross profit.

The profit and loss account

The profit and loss section of the profit and loss statement is drawn beneath the trading account and covers the same period of trading. The gross profit figure from the trading account becomes the starting point for the profit and loss account.

Every organisation incurs expenses and a range of overheads, and these are deducted to show the true operating profit for the business. The expenses might include:

rent of premises	depreciation
gas	bad debts
electricity	interest on loans
stationery	advertising costs
cleaning costs	sundry expenses
insurances	motor expenses
business rates	accountancy and legal fees.

Some organisations receive income from sources other than sales. This is known as **non-operating income**. These may be rents received, profits on the sale of assets, etc. As these represent extra income they are added to the equation.

Figure 34.3 shows how the final account might look. The part of the account up to and including the gross profit is the trading account, while the remainder is the profit and loss account. Net profit is the final profit in the business which will belong to the owner.

An alternative way of looking at the same trading and profit and loss account is shown in Figure 34.4.

Blyth's Trading and Profit and Loss account for the year ended 31 May 1997

	£	£
Sales		27,500
Less cost of sales;		
Opening stock	9,000	
Add purchases	15,000	
	24,000	
Less closing stock	3,750	
		20,250
Gross profit		7,250
Add other income:		
Profit on sale of plant		2,000
		9,250
Less expenses:		
Electricity	510	
Stationery	125	
Business rate	756	
Interest on loans	159	
Advertising	745	
Depreciation of motor vehicles	1,000	
Insurances	545	
Sundry expenses	124	
		3,964
Net profit		5,286

Figure 34.3

Blyth's Trading and Profit and Loss account for the year ended 31 May 1997

		£
	Turnover	27,500
(less)	Cost of sales	20,250
	Gross profit	7,250
(less)	Expenses	3,805
	Operating profit	3,445
(plus)	Non operating income	2,000
		5,445
(less)	Interest payable	159
	Profit on ordinary activities	5,286

Figure 34.4

The appropriation account

The appropriation account is the section of the profit and loss account detailing how profit is shared between the owners. From this section the Inland Revenue will require is statutory levy in the form of corporation tax on a company's profits. Also in this section, companies set aside funds for reserves. Reserves are set up either as capital reserves from the balance sheet or as revenue reserves from the appropriation account. Revenue reserves represent tied-up, retained profits which are unlikely to be distributed. Retained profits generally increase from year to year as most companies do not distribute all of their profits as dividends. A full appropriation account would include:

Profit on ordinary activities/net profit
    less corporation tax
    less dividends for shareholders
    less any transfer to a reserve
    plus the balance of profit from the previous year.

The final balance from the appropriation account is then transferred to the balance sheet. *It appears in the reserves where it is added to share capital.* If a loss is made, then the reduced figure in the balance sheet will be added to share capital.

Remember the four stages:

- tax
- dividends
- reserves
- last year's balance.

In Figure 34.5, which shows a complete profit and loss account, we can see how these four stages are combined.

Balance sheet

Whereas the profit and loss account provides an ongoing picture, a balance sheet is a snapshot of what an organisation owns and owes on a particular date.

A balance sheet is a clear statement of the assets, liabilities and capital of a business at a particular time (normally the end of an accounting period).

Looking at the balance sheet can thus provide valuable information because it summarises a business's financial position at that instant.

The balance sheet balances simply because the accounts record every transaction twice. For example, if you give me £100 we can say that:

- I owe you £100 (a liability or a debt)
- I now have £100 (an asset, something I own).

Makemore Ltd: Profit and loss account for the year ending 31 December 1997

	£000	£000	£000
Sales			2,300
Less Cost of sales			
Opening stock		150	
Purchases		1,700	
		1,850	
Closing stock		200	
			1,650
Gross profit			650
add Profit on disposal of plant			50
			700
Overheads			
Wages and salaries		250	
Sundry expenses		105	
Light and heat		5	
Depreciation: buildings	12		
: plant	8	20	
Debenture interest		4	
Bad debts		2	
Advertising and distribution		4	
			390
Net profit			310
less corporation tax			108
Profit after taxation			202
less dividends: preference shares		18	
: ordinary shares		20	38
			164
less Transfer to general reserve			64
			100
add Retained profit brought forward			40
Retained profit carried forward			140

Figure 34.5

Assets are what an organisation OWNS or is OWED.

Liabilities or capital are what an organisation OWES.

lar time. The horizontal balance sheet has assets on one side with capital and liabilities on the other. The accounting process ensures that the total value of one half will equal the total value of the other half. We can now look at the balance sheet in more detail.

TASK 34.2

Make a list of six probable assets and six probable liabilities of a public house.

As with the profit and loss account there are a number of different ways of producing and presenting a balance sheet.

A horizontal balance sheet has two sides – an assets side representing uses of funds and a liabilities side showing the sources of funds (see Figure 34.6).

As you can see the balance sheet is a clear statement of liabilities, assets and the capital of a business at a particu-

In business accounts we always treat the business owner (or owners, in the case of partnerships and companies) as a separate legal entity to the business itself. The capital provided by the owner is therefore deemed to be owned by the business to the owner. The balance sheet therefore keeps an updated record of the amount owed by the business to the owner.

During a year's trading, the owner's capital will be increased by inflows of **profits** and decreased by outflows of **drawings** (money/assets taken out of the business for personal use). Having taken these into consideration, a new capital figure will exist at the end of the year.

The balance sheet of A Sole Trader as at 31 December 1997

(Assets side)	£	£	(Liabilities side)	£	£
FIXED ASSETS			Capital as at 1/1/97		23,000
Freehold premises	35,000		add Profit for the year		7,000
Fixtures & fittings	4,000				30,000
Motor vehicles	1,500		less Drawings		4,100
		40,500	Capital as at 31/12/97		25,900
FIXED ASSETS			LONG-TERM LIABILITIES		
Stock of goods	4,000		Loan		20,000
Debtors	1,500		CURRENT LIABILITES		
Prepayments	500		Creditors	1,500	
Bank	1,000		Accrued costs	500	2,000
Cash	400				
		£47,900			£47,900

Figure 34.6

Other liabilities are classified as current liabilities or long-term liabilities, depending on their duration.

Current liabilities

Current liabilities are debts of the business which need to be paid in a fairly short period of time (normally within one year). Creditors are normally suppliers of goods on trade credit for which the business has been invoiced but has not yet provided payment. Accrued charges are bills, often for expenses, that are outstanding at the end of an accounting period. They must be included in the accounts as they are a debt, often for a service that has been provided (e.g. a gas or electricity bill). Other short-term liabilities could include a bank overdraft, short-term loans and any taxes owed to the Department of Inland Revenue.

Long-term liabilities

A long-term liability is sometimes called a 'deferred liability' as it is not due for payment until some time in the

future; by convention, this means longer than one year in a set of accounts. Examples, would include long-term loans (e.g. bank loans), mortgages (loans secured against a freehold property) and debentures. Debentures are sometimes issued by companies at fixed rates of interest which have to be repaid on a specific date in the future. Those who hold debentures are therefore lenders of money.

Assets

Assets are items that are owned by a business and other items that are *owed to* the business. The asset side of a balance sheet will normally be set out in what is called an inverse order of liquidity. This means that items that are difficult to convert to cash quickly (i.e. are illiquid) appear at the top of the list. By examining the order in which they are listed, you can gauge the ease with which successive assets can be converted to cash until you come to the most liquid asset of all, cash.

A useful way of classifying assets is to use two classes:
- Fixed assets
  - tangible fixed assets
  - intangible fixed assets
  - investments (long-term)
- Current assets.

Fixed assets

The simple distinction is that all fixed assets must have a lifespan of more than one year. (Therefore all current assetswill have a lifespan of less than one year.) A **tangible fixed asset** is one that can be touched and seen (e.g. machinery, buildings, vehicles). An **intangible fixed asset** is one that does not have a physical existence and therefore cannot be touched. For example, the 'goodwill' of a business is an intangible fixed asset. Over a period of time a business builds up a client base and a reputation; this is a real asset to the business and can be valued when the business transfers ownership. (The goodwill of a business will normally appear in the books only if the business is taken over or transferred to new owners.)

Investments are also counted as fixed assets. A company might invest in the shares of another business or purchase debentures. These are investments that are usually made with a view to retaining the assets for more than 12 months.

Fixed assets might be held for a number of years, but they will eventually wear out. The accounts of a business try to recognise this gradual erosion of value and **depreciation** is written off against profits so that the value of fixed assets should be at their net book value after depreciation has been accounted for.

Current assets

Current assets are sometimes called 'circulating assets' because the form they take is constantly changing. A business will hold stocks of finished goods in readiness to satisfy the demands of the market. When a credit transaction takes place stocks will be reduced and the company will incur debtors. Debtors will have bought goods on credit and therefore will owe the business money. After a reasonable credit period, payment will be expected. After this inflow, payments will be made for further stock. Thus, the business has a cash cycle consisting of stocks, debtors, cash and further supplies.

Current assets might also include short-term investments. Although these may be in the form of stocks and shares in other businesses, it would be the company's intention to sell them in the near future. They could also include pre-payments; these are sums paid for goods or services that have not yet been received (e.g. business rates paid in advance).

It is now possible to show how the double-entry system affects the balance sheet. In the following example a businesswoman, Annie Box, sets up a business on 1 January by putting £25,000 into a business bank account. The business then owes Annie Box the amount she had invested but, at the same time, it will have received £25,000. Both the asset side and the liability side of the balance sheet will have an entry:

Balance sheet of Annie Box as at 1 January

	£		£
Bank	25,000	Capital	25,000
	£25,000		£25,000

On 2 January the business purchases a motor vehicle for £5,000 by cheque. This transaction involves a transfer from one asset to another:

Balance sheet of Annie Box as at 2 January

	£		£
Motor vehicles	5,000	Capital	25,000
Bank	20,000		
	£25,000		£25,000

On 3 January the business purchases stocks for resale for £15,000 on credit. Therefore liabilities increase as creditors are created and assets increase as stocks are now owed:

Balance sheet of Annie Box as at 3 January

	£		£
Motor vehicles	5,000	Capital	25,000
Stocks	15,000	Creditors	15,000
Bank	20,000		
	£40,000		£40,000

On 4 January, stocks valued at £10,000 are sold for £13,000 on credit. Clearly there is a profit element here. Stocks will decrease by the value sold (not by the sale price), i.e. by £10,000, but debtors will now have been created and so liabilities will be increased by £13,000. Assets have, therefore, increased by £3,000 in total. The profit element of £3,000 made on the sale of the stock items will be added to capital and as a result liabilities will also arise:

Balance sheet of Annie Box as at 4 January

	£		£
Motor vehicles	5,000	Capital	25,000
Stocks	5,000	add profits	3,000
Debtors	13,000	Creditors	15,000
Bank	20,000		
	£43,000		£43,000

On 5 January Annie Box's business pays the creditors off and the debtors all pay up. Both liabilities and assets will decrease when the creditors are paid. One asset disappears and another increases when the debtors pay up.

Balance sheet of Annie Box as at 5 January

	£		£
Motor vehicles		5,000	Capital	28,000
Stocks		5,000		
Bank	20,000			
15,000(-)				
13,000(+) =	18,000			
	£28,000		£28,000

On 6 January, Annie Box's business pays rent, rates and electricity totalling £1,000 by cheque. As we saw in the profit and loss account, business expenses are deducted from the gross profit to leave the net profit. In this example, expenses will be treated as a negative item and carried forward from the profit and loss account by reducing capital by £1,000 and bank by £1,000.

Balance sheet of Annie Box as at 6 January

	£		£
Motor vehicles	5,000	Capital	27,000
Stocks	5,000		
Bank	17,000		
	£27,000		£27,000

We could continue this process and record many more transactions. It is important for you to appreciate that all business transactions affect the balance sheet in some way of other. Because of the double-entry system, transactions will influence both sides of a horizontal balance sheet.

Although it is common practice to use horizontal balance sheets for demonstration purposes, the majority of businesses today present their balance sheets in vertical form. Vertical balance sheets are often thought to be easier to interpret; for example, working capital or net current assets can be identified at a glance (see Figure 34.7).

General Election Ltd: balance sheet as at 31 December 1997

	£	£	£
Fixed assets	Cost	Depreciation	
Freehold premises	50,000	5,000	45,000
Machinery	10,000	4,000	6,000
Fixtures and fittings	5,000	2,000	3,000
Motor vehicles	7,000	2,000	5,000
	72,000	13,000	59,000
Current assets			
Stocks		14,000	
Debtors		3,000	
Prepayments		500	
Cash		100	
		17,600	
Less current liabilities			
Bank overdraft	1,300		
Creditors	1,200		
Accrued costs	100		
Taxation payable	1,000	3,600	
Net current assets (working capital)			14,000
Assets less current liabilities			73,000
Less long-term liabilities			
Bank loan			18,000
Net assets			£55,000
Financed by:			
Share capital			
Ordinary shares			20,000
Preference shares			20,000
			40,000
Reserves			15,000
			£55,000

Figure 34.7

TASK 34.3

Where would you expect to find the following items:

- money owed to the business for supplies
- an item of stock sitting in a warehouse
- a piece of equipment used to make products
- electricity consumed
- rent paid in advance for the next three months?

Cash flow statement

In September 1991, the Accounting Standards Board set out the first Financial Reporting Standard (FRS 1) on cash flow statements. The standard supersedes SSAP 10 on sources and applications of funds. The new standard FRS 1 has changed the nature of the third statement in a company's accounts. The aim is for the cash flow statement to be viewed as important as the profit and loss account and balance sheet.

The problem with funds flow statements were that:

- companies drew up their statements in different ways
- they were difficult to use to compare one business to another
- they looked at funds or profit rather than at cash
- the meaning of funds was not very clear.

The new cash flow statements focus on something with which managers can identify – the need for a steady cash flow. Figure 34.8 shows an example. The key element is the change in what is called 'cash and equivalents'. The cash flow statement explains the movement by placing all cash flows into five categories. Note that in this example we have adopted the more unusual convention of putting outflows in parentheses.

Cash flow statement of for the year ended 31 December 1997

	(£m)	(£m)
Net cash inflow from operating activities		6
Returns on investments and servicing of finance		
Interest received	2	
Interest paid	(4)	
Dividends paid	(4)	
Net cash outflow from returns on investment and servicing of finance		(6)
Taxation		
UK Corporation tax paid	(4)	
Investing activities		
Purchases of tangible fixed assets	(4)	
Purchases of subsidiary undertakings (net of cash and cash equivalents acquired)	(18)	
Sale of plant and machinery	4	
Net cash outflow from investing activities		(18)
Net cash outflow before financing		(22)
Financing		
New secured loan repayable in 1998	17	
Repayment of amounts borrowed	(2)	
Net cash inflow from financing		15
Decrease in cash and cash equivalents		7

Figure 34.8

The idea is that the user can see at a glance the extent to which, for example, cash flow from operations has or has not paid for dividends, tax and new investments, or the extent to which those items had to be financed by the raising of new capital. The statement should expose more quickly than before those companies that are not generating cash – even thought they may be reporting profits.

You should be familiar with the following terminology:

Net cash inflow (outflow) from operating activities

The net cash flow from the operating activities of a company represents the actual cash receipts from customers less cash payments to employees and suppliers of goods and services. It excludes payments for fixed assets.

Returns on investment and servicing of finance

The returns on investments and the payments made to those who financed the business are analysed here:

- Cash coming into the business as a result of making investments that generate receipts of dividends and interest.
- Cash going out of the business as a result of payments of interest and dividends to those who have financed the business, e.g. the business owners, debenture holders and banks.

Taxation

Payment of taxes on profits to the Inland Revenue are separately disclosed here. Mainstream corporation tax paid will relate to the previous period's liability.

Investing activities

Cash goes out of the business on the purchase of fixed assets and cash flows in when fixed assets are sold. This section shows the extent to which cash has been invested to maintain and expand the future earnings capacity of the business.

Financing

This section shows how the financing needs of the business have been met. Cash flows into the business on new share and loan stock issues. Cash flows out of the business on loan repayments and the redemption of shares.

Increase/decrease in cash equivalents

The total of all the above cash flows results in a movement on cash holdings or cash equivalents.

The statement in Figure 34.8 shows that:

- the operations provided cash inflow of only £6 million
- £6 million was used up in dividends and interest
- £4 million was used in paying tax
- £18 million was used up in new investment
- to make all of this possible, £15 million had to be obtained by way of new finance.

It is clear immediately from the example that the operations were not even supporting the dividends and tax payment. The company is using up cash without even considering further investment. This is exactly the kind of situation a cash flow statement is intended to bring out. For example, this sort of information should help to provide readers of accounts with clearer warnings of business failures.

SYNTHESIS

If you were an investor in a business, what sort of information would you require about your investment? Make a list.

Interpretation of accounts

Under the Companies Acts, all limited liability companies are required to file copies of their accounts with the Registrar of Companies. The Acts specify the information that should be included in the profit and loss, balance sheet and cash flow statement and indicate that these accounts must provide a true and fair record of the affairs of the company for the period concerned. Additional information required with the accounts includes:

- details of subsidiaries
- group accounts if there is a group of companies
- a directors' report
- an auditor's report.

Accounts are a useful source of information about the conditions of that business. Final accounts can be carefully analysed, often by using ratios, which enable comparisons to be made between financial data. Financial ratios enable:

- comparisons to be made for the same business over different time periods in a useful way in order to detect favourable or adverse trends
- comparisons to be made with comparable businesses to indicate whether the organisation is operating efficiently in terms of profitability and how it uses the capital tied up in the business.

The following ratios are grouped into:

- profitability
- liquidity
- asset usage
- capital structure.

Profitability

The profitability of a business could be assessed on the basis of profits it is making on sales and the general profitability of the investment made in the business.

Gross profit to sales

$$\text{Gross profit to sales} = \frac{\text{Gross profit}}{\text{Sales}} \times 100$$

This will indicate the percentage gross profit made on sales. It is sometimes called profit percentage. Changes in this might reflect increases in the cost of raw materials, stock losses, changes in pricing policy, etc. A percentage of 40–60 per cent is common if businesses wish to make a profit after paying expenses.

Net profit to sales

$$\text{net profit to sales} = \frac{\text{Net profit}}{\text{Sales}} \times 100$$

This indicates final profit as a percentage of sales. If the gross profit percentage is consistent, then any changes in net profit percentage would indicate an increase in overheads as a proportion of sales which could signal a need to make economies.

Return on capital employed (ROCE)

Return on capital employed (ROCE) =

$$\frac{\text{Operating profit}}{\text{Total net asets}} \times 100$$

ROCE indicates how well the business has used the financial resources invested in it.

Return on equity (ROE)

Return on equity =

$$\frac{\text{Net profit (after tax and preference dividend)}}{\text{Ordinary shares and reserves}} \times 100$$

The ROE indicates how well the business has used the financial resources invested in it by the ordinary shareholders.

Earnings per share

$$\text{Earnings per share} = \frac{\text{Profit (after tax and preference dividend)}}{\text{Number of ordinary shares}}$$

This is an important determinant of the value of each share. This ratio indicates the amount that each share is earning. It provides the ordinary shareholder with key information about the earning capacity of each share.

Price/earnings (P/E) ratio

$$\text{Price earnings ratio} = \frac{\text{Market price per share}}{\text{Earnings per share}}$$

This is a comparison of the current market value of a share with the earnings per share. It is a measure of confidence in the growth potential of the company as well of the business sector.

Dividend yield

$$\text{Dividend yield} = \frac{\text{Dividend per share}}{\text{Market price per share}} \times 100$$

This relates the shareholder's dividend to the market price of the shares.

Liquidity

This refers to the ability of an organisation to convert short-term or current assets into cash to cover payments as and when they arise. Stocks are the least liquid of the current assets because they must first be sold (usually on credit) and the customer is provided with a credit period. As a result, there is a time lag before stocks can be converted to cash.

Current or working capital ratio

This is the ratio of current assets to current liabilities.

Current ratio = current assets: current liabilities

A prudent ratio is usually 2:1, though this might not necessarily be the case if stocks form the bulk of the value of current assets.

Acid-test ratio/quick ratio/liquidity ratio

This is the ratio of current assets less stocks to current liabilities.

Acid-test ratio =
current assets less stocks: current liabilities

This assesses how well a business can meet its current liabilities without stocks. Stocks are ignored as they are the least liquid current asset. A prudent ratio is often thought to be 1:1.

Debt collection period

$$\text{Debt collection period} = \frac{\text{Debtors}}{\text{Average daily sales}}$$

Average daily sales are calculated by dividing sales by 365. The normally accepted level of period is about 60 days.

Period of credit taken from suppliers

$$\text{Period of credit from suppliers} = \frac{\text{Creditors}}{\text{Average daily purchases}}$$

It can be useful to look at the average period of time taken from suppliers.

Asset usage

Asset usage ratios make it possible to assess the efficiency of certain areas of business activity. Use of these ratios, for example, in the analysis of stock turnover, enables comparisons to be made with other industries and previous periods.

Stock turnover

$$\text{Stock turnover} = \frac{\text{Cost of sales}}{\text{Average stock}}$$

where

$$\text{Average stock} = \frac{\text{Opening stock} + \text{closing stock}}{2}$$

This is an average length of time an item is held in stock before it is used or sold. The adequacy of this ratio depends upon the type of industry a business is in.

Asset utilisation

$$\text{Asset utilisation} = \frac{\text{Sales}}{\text{Fixed assets}}$$

This ratio indicates how efficiently fixed assets are being used in order to generate sales.

Capital structure

Businesses are financed by share capital, loans and other sources (see Chapter 30). Both the investors and the suppliers of finance will wish to ensure that their incomes are maintained and that the future of their money looks secure.

Gearing ratio

$$\text{Gearing ratio} = \frac{\text{Fixed return capital}}{\text{Ordinary shareholder funds}}$$

Fixed return capital normally refers to long-term debt, including debentures plus preference share capital. Gearing makes a direct comparison between the long-term capital in a business provided by ordinary shareholders and that provided through long-term loans and preference shares. Using the above we can say that a company is:

- low-geared if the gearing is less than 100 per cent
- high-geared if the gearing is more than 100 per cent.

Interest cover

$$\text{Interest cover} = \frac{\text{Profit before interest and tax}}{\text{Interest paid in the year}}$$

This refers to the risk of gearing. If the ratio is less than 1, a company has not earned enough to cover interest charges. A ratio of 3 would provide the minimum level of safety required.

Chapter summary

- The importance of keeping book-keeping records is discussed.
- The stages in an accounting system are shown.
- The processes from accounting records to accounting statements are shown.
- The trial discussed.
- Profit and loss accounts, balance sheets and cash flow statements are considered.
- A basic interpretation of accounts and accounting ratios is provided.

6 People in business

INTRODUCTION

Today, it is generally recognised that people are the most important resource of organisations. Increasingly, they are seen to be more important than machinery, land, finance and other resources in creating value for organisations. Indeed, business writers have played a great emphasis on 'knowledge workers' and 'information-based organisations' – i.e. people as the brainpower and the creator of human contacts which give organisations their distinctive edge over rivals.

Organisations therefore need to think carefully about how they organise their people at work. The term used to describe organisation is 'business structure'. Today, we have moved away from the old top-down command and control organisations based on layers of managers, sub-managers, supervisors and operatives. Increasingly, the emphasis has moved towards creating teams of employees whose prime function is to take responsibility for decision making, and to build their own relationships with customers rather than to wait to be told what to do by those higher up the chain.

Organisations have moved to new theories of building up human relations in the workplace and of motivating people. Early management theory was concerned with trying to get the most out of people almost as if they were machines. How was it possible to cut down their movements? How could the time they spent on a job be reduced? etc. However, later researchers found that people responded best when they were treated as people rather than as bits of machinery. In recent times, we have seen an increasing emphasis on Japanese working practices based on teams operating quality circles and total quality management approaches. Here the emphasis is on encouraging ground level employees to come up with their own solutions to work-based problems.

Human resource planning (HRP) is an important aspect of managing people at work. This involves trying to develop a balance between the needs of an organisation for people, and the existing and potential future supply of people available to work in the organisation. The organisation needs to identify future requirements and then to develop the policies and practices to meet these requirements, for example, by developing training schemes where a shortage of skilled employees may arise in the future. HRP is therefore about having the right people in the right place at the right time.

Managing people involves getting the most out of them as well as meeting their individual needs. Increasing emphasis is therefore placed on management styles today. Management style is concerned with the way managers go about managing and dealing with people. Autocratic managers are ones that like to make the decisions for themselves and others, whereas democratic managers are far more concerned to support their team members.

The pattern of communication within an organisation is crucial to its success. Today, the emphasis is more on open communication channels in a variety of directions rather than old style, top-down communication patterns.

35 Organising people in business: business structure

All businesses need to have a structure which enables them to work effectively towards meeting their goals and objectives.It is through this structure that people will be organised in an organisation. So what then do we mean by the structure of an organisation?

March and Simon have defined 'structure' as:

> *'Those aspects of the pattern of behaviour in the organisation that are relatively stable and that change only slowly'.*

While Child has defined 'structure' as:

> *'The relatively enduring allocation of work roles and administrative mechanisms that creates a pattern of interrelated work activities and allows the organisation to conduct, co-ordinate and control its work activities.'*

Both of these definitions focus on relative stability and enduring relationships within an organisation. However, as we shall see later a key feature of modern organisations is that they have a lot of flexibility to survive and adjust to changes that are taking place in the business environment. As Tom Peters has stated in his book *The Pursuit of Wow!*, 'crazy times call for crazy organisations'. In a period in which the business environment is changing rapidly it is essential for organisations to have the structural flexibility to respond to these changes.

It is interesting to note how far Peters' views on the importance of flexibility have moved on from those of earlier writers. For example a group of researchers called The Aston Group who examined 46 firms in the Birmingham area in the late 1960s identified the following key aspects of structure in organisations:

- **Specialisation** – the division of labour within the organisation, the distribution of official duties among a number of positions.
- **Standardisation** – procedures that are continually repeated and are acknowledged as part of standardised activities of an organisation.
- **Formalisation** – the extent to which rules, procedures, instructions, and communications are written down.
- **Centralisation** – where is the decision-making located in the organisation. (Who is the latest person that would need to sanction or approve a particular decision?)
- **Traditionalism** – the extent to which there is a customary way of doing things (often this will not be written down).

- **Configuration** – the shape of the structure of roles within an organisation, i.e. a pattern or chart setting out 'who does what'.

In looking at the structures of organisations it is therefore helpful to look at highly-organised and stable structures, before moving on to more modern flexible structures.

Organisation charts

In a very small organisation you are unlikely to find a formal structure. For example, in a one-person business the entrepreneur carries out most of the various business functions personally.

As a small firm grows, a formal organisational structure starts to develop based on functional specialisms. The firm may then be divided up into hierarchical functional divisions. In other words, the firm is divided up into a number of sub-sections each with a chain of command or offices.

EXAMPLE

In a school the teaching functions (specialisms) may be:
a science faculty; an arts faculty; and a humanities faculty. The hierarchy in each faculty might be:

- head of faculty (e.g. head of humanities)
- head of department (e.g. head of geography)
- subject teacher (e.g. geography teacher).

We could then illustrate this functional hierarchy in an organisation chart as follows:

- headteacher
- heads of faculties
- heads of department
- subject teachers.

Nearly all organisational structures can be charted to show the departments, how they link together, and the principal lines of authority. This gives a snapshot view of how the organisation is made up. It shows lines of decision making and levels of responsibility. Looking at a chart may expose any weaknesses in an organisation.

Formal and informal structures

The formal structure of an organisation is based on employees' official roles. If you asked the headteacher of a school or a hospital administrator to draw an organisation chart they would almost certainly set down the formal structure based on official definitions of what everyone should be doing.

However, concentration of formal structure may disguise what really happens.

To continue with the school example, it may be that the head of the science faculty is frequently away, so that many of the managerial decisions in science are made by one or two of the heads of department. There may be a number of teachers who regularly socialise together by frequenting the same leisure and sports club, and these teachers (whatever their ranks) could possibly be the major determinants of curriculum policy. In other words, decisions are made not only in staff meetings but also during recreational activities at the sports club. At the same time, a number of teachers will be university graduates, and these may have a major say when it comes to making academic decisions about the curriculum. The reality of decision making might therefore be that real power and influence lies within the informal structure of the organisation.

It is always important therefore to keep an eye on the informal structure of an organisation.

Levels within an organisation

When drawing an organisation chart, it is usual to show posts which have roughly equal amounts of responsibility on the same level. In Figure 35.1, the managing director and the senior management team are at the top level. At the next level are the middle managers. Then there are junior managers, superiors, and finally operatives at the bottom level.

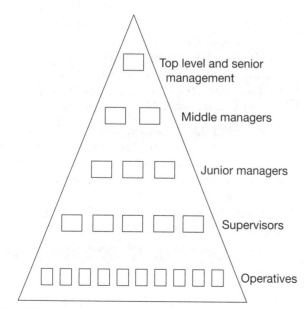

Figure 35.1   *Levels of responsibility*

Span of control

The span of control of an individual is the number of people he or she manages or supervises directly. Figure 35.2 shows an organisation with a narrow span of control. No one member of this organisation is directly responsible for more than two subordinates.

There is a limit to the number of people who can be supervised well by one person. Choosing the best span of control means striking a balance between having control over people below you (subordinates) and being able to trust them.

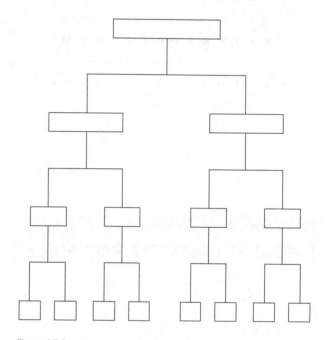

Figure 35.2   *A narrow span of control*

Tall and flat organisations

A narrow span of control makes it possible to control people and to communicate with them closely. However, the disadvantage is that this may lead to too many levels of management. This kind of **tall organisation**, as it is called, can be difficult to run (see Figure 35.3).

Having a wider span means managers must have far more trust in subordinate staff. Fewer managers are needed, and this gives a hierarchy with fewer levels, i.e. a **flat organisation** (see Figure 35.4).

How many people should managers have within their span of control? It is hard to say. Generally speaking, the higher up an organisation an individual is, the fewer people he or she should have in their direct span of control.

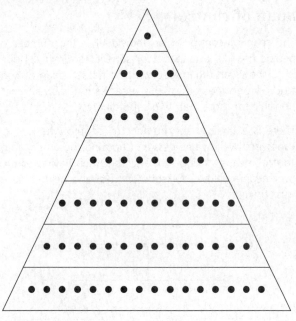

Figure 35.3   A tall organisation

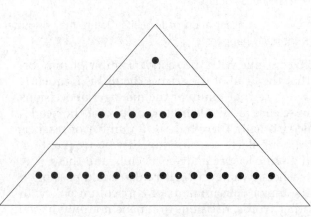

Figure 35.4   A flat organisation

ROBERT MAXWELL AND MOSES

Robert Maxwell, who was a major figure in British business in the 1980s and early 1990s was notoriously unable to delegate. He insisted on making most of the key and many of the minor decisions in his business empire himself. This meant that at times he would be conducting two or three meetings at the same time while also fielding telephone calls and handling other urgent business.

In this respect he shared some common characteristics with Moses at the time of the Exodus of the Israelites. Exodus 18: 17–25 tell us that when Moses' father-in-law noticed that he was spending too much time organising the Exodus of the Israelites he gave the following advice.

'The thing thou doest is not good. Thou wilt surely wear away, both thou and this people that is with thee, for this thing is too heavy for thee; thou art not able to perform it thyself alone. Harken now unto my voice.

I will give thee counsel ... Thou shalt provide out of the people able men ... and place such over them, to be rulers of thousands, and rulers of hundreds, rulers of fifties, and rulers of tens. And let them judge the people at all seasons; and it shall be, that every great matter they shall bring unto thee, but every small matter they shall judge; so shall it be easier for thyself, and they shall bear the burden with thee. If thou shall do this thing, and God commands thee so, then thou shalt be able to endure, and all this people shall also go to their place in peace.'

1 How sound do you think Moses' father-in-law's advice was? Could it equally have been applied to Maxwell?
2 In what types of situation can the theory of delegation be applied?
3 Are there situations in which delegation would be inappropriate?

The pattern of authority in an organisation

An important distinction is made in structuring organisations between line and staff authority.

Line organisation

Line organisation is the typical structure of a hierarchical body. Decisions pass down the 'line', for example, from senior line manager, to junior line manager, to supervisor and finally to operatives. People in an organisation are very aware of who their 'line manager' is.

Each member of the organisation will have a clear understanding of the chain of command within the organisation and to whom he or she is responsible. This type of structure can be very effective because of its clarity. There are set rules and procedures which can be referred to.

Line management is typically used to organise a firm's key activities such as the making and selling of products. In these areas there will be a clear hierarchical framework. Larger organisations will tend to have more rigid and bureaucratic structures than smaller ones. Although agreed and clear procedures will be necessary in such organisations, it will also be important to have an element of flexibility. Formal structures will frequently be subject to informal changes in the course of time as new situations arise.

Staff organisation

Staff organisation primarily services the various line departments of an organisation. Typical staff areas could include personnel, corporate affairs, data processing and office administration.

Staff departments typically cut across an organisation providing a range of specialist services and consultancy skills. For example, any line department of a company might require specialist legal help from time to time, might want to have data processed or might need help with recruiting new staff. Figure 35.5 illustrates the way in which various staff areas can be made available to all line departments within an organisation.

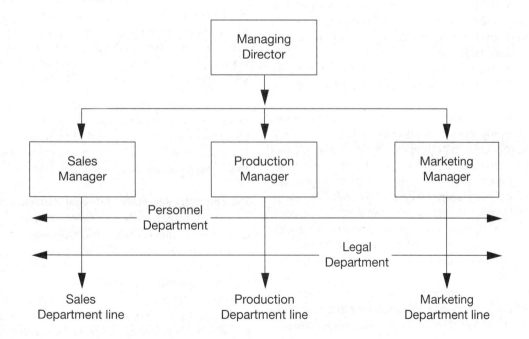

Figure 35.5   Combining line and staff organisation

Staff areas thus play an important role throughout an organisation. However, a staff department itself might be organised on hierarchical lines. For example, the personnel department may have several tiers below the personnel manager.

Combined line and staff organisation

Most medium and large business organisations will combine elements of line and staff organisation. There will be a number of advantages to having this blend:

- Line departments are able to concentrate on achieving the central objectives of a business, i.e. marketing, making, selling. At the same time, they are complemented in the achievement of these objectives by specialist service departments. Line departments can thus concentrate on their core function without the clutter of organisation activities that are secondary to their main purpose.
- Line managers need to familiarise themselves only with information related to their core activity.
- Staff groupings can be called in to provide specialist information and advice in a number of key areas.

However, there will also be a number of disadvantages to combining the two areas:

- A major disadvantage is that it can lead to confusion within an organisation. There will be less clarity over departmental responsibility and lines of authority. 'Unity of command' is often regarded to be the mark of an effective organisation. When there is more than one centre of responsibility confusion can arise; one section can blame another for failure to carry out work effectively or for a breakdown in communication. Where department managers compete with each other to secure high-status work, or where they try to avoid less prestigious work, numerous problems can occur.
- Often, line managers rise to a particular position through many years of hard work. This is particularly true in production departments, where it is not uncommon for managers to have worked their way up from the shop-floor. In contrast, many staff managers are 'academics' with a university background. Line managers may resent staff managers' rapid rise to managerial status, while staff managers may regard themselves to be better than those who have worked their way up. Such clashes can be detrimental to the smooth running of an organisation.
- Line managers may resent having to listen to the opinions of staff managers who may have different priorities from their own. For example, a corporate affairs or personnel manager might try to push a company into employing more youth trainees in order to project a certain image for a company within the community. In contrast, a production manager may be more concerned with using older, more experienced labour.

In order to overcome difficulties that may arise from combining line and staff organisation, it is essential for a company to devise a clear strategy to co-ordinate staff and line groupings. This strategy will involve setting out the goals of the company and then deciding on the responsibilities of line and staff groupings. These responsibilities need to be set out in a clear statement of company policy. Some companies even have an 'organisation and methods' department with the responsibility for clarifying such issues.

The superstructure of an organisation

The **superstructure** of an organisation is the way in which employees are grouped into various departments or sections. There are various ways of grouping employees depending on the needs and aims of a company.

The main methods of grouping employees are by:

- function
- product
- process
- geographical area
- type of customer.

We will also see later that a matrix structure can be used to combine grouping methods.

Grouping by function

This is probably the most important way of grouping employees in a company. **Functional organisation** means that a company is divided into broad sectors, each with its own particular specialism or function, for example, marketing, accounts, personnel – see Figure 35.6.

Every organisation will have its own way of structuring its functions. However, there are a number of common functional areas that will be typical of many large companies. These functions are referred to in outline here, and are deal with in greater detail in related chapters.

The company secretary and legal department

By law it is necessary for every company to have a Company Secretary. The Company Secretary is responsible for all the legal matters of the company. If paperwork is not done in the correct fashion, the Company Secretary can end up in court. He or she must fill in the documents that set up the company, including the Memorandum and Articles of Association, and must also keep the share register, which is a record of shareholders and any transfers in shareholding that take place.

The Company Secretary is regarded as a key link between the shareholders of a company and the directors. He or she will handle correspondence to and from shareholders

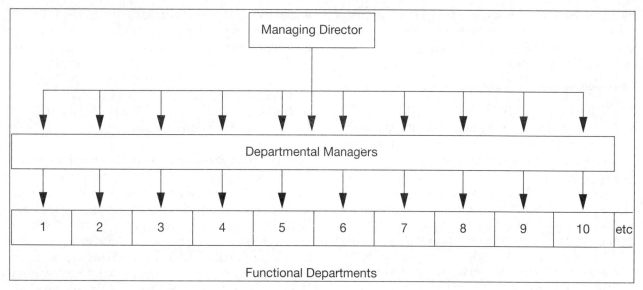

Figure 35.6   Grouping by function

informing them of company meetings and other important matters. In some companies, a Registrar will be appointed as a subordinate to the Company Secretary with the responsibility of keeping the share register.

The Administration Officer and administration department

Many large firms have a central office, or administration department, which is responsible for controlling the general paperwork of the firm. This department might handle the filing of materials and the company's mail, word-processing and data-handling facilities. The modern office is based on extensive use of information technology (IT) applications.

In many companies, each department will have its own clerical and support staff. However, it is common practice to have an Office Services Manager, or Administration Officer, with the responsibility for co-ordinating office services and offering expert advice to departmental managers.

The work of the Office Manager will include:

- Taking responsibility for an organising clerical training.
- Advising departments on office layout, office equipment, working practices and staff development.
- Co-ordinating the supply of office equipment and stationery.
- Studying and analysing office practice within the company in order to develop an overall strategy for administration.
- Ensuring the standardisation of office practice, the layout of forms, invoices and other documents.
- Providing and maintaining a communications system within a company including phones, mailing systems, computer hardware and other data-processing facilities.

- Reporting to, and providing statistics for, the board of directors about the effectiveness of existing office practice.

The Information and Computing Manager and the IT department

In a modern company a large proportion of the staff are likely to work directly with, or have access to computer terminals.

The role of the information and computing function will be to promote effective exploitation of IT in a company and to provide the guidance, support and co-ordination necessary to accomplish this objective.

Information is vital to decision-making in both commerce and industry. The quality of any decision depends on the relevance, accuracy and timeliness of the information available. The main task for the Information Manager will therefore be to identify the decision makers' information needs, to decide how best they can be met, and to develop the systems for meeting them.

Very rapid improvements in computing technology are providing opportunities for supporting businesses in ways that were not dreamed of a few years ago. For example, in many companies a computer work-station on the desks of all management and professional staff, as well as those of many support staff, is a fact of life. Increasingly, employees are able to work with extensive in-company databases and to access the Internet.

The Chief Accountant and the accounts office

The Chief Accountant is responsible for supervising the accounts department. The accounts section must keep a detailed record of all money paid in an out and must present the final balance sheet, source and use of funds, the profit and loss account and other financial records at regular intervals. Modern accounts are stored on computer files, and accounting procedures are greatly simplified by the use of computers.

Within the accounts department there will be two main sub-divisions:

- The **financial accounting department** is responsible for keeping records of financial events as they occur. Accounts need to be kept of all money paid to or by a company, and records must be kept of all debtor and creditor transactions. The payment of wages will also require calculations involving deductions for national insurance, pensions and other factors. As well as keeping day-to-day records, the financial accounting department will also be responsible for producing periodic records such as the annual account and interim figures for discussion at meetings of directors.
- The **management accounting department** has the responsibility for nudging the company in certain directions as a result of its analysis of figures for the present and predictions for the future. Management accountants will break down figures in order to extract information about a company's present performance and the sorts of improvements that can be made in the future. Using systems of budgetary control, it will set targets for achievement and limits for spending to the various parts of a business.

Within the accounts department, other sub-functions (i.e. functions within functions) might include a cashier's department and a wages department. The cashier's department will be concerned with handling all cash transactions as well as cheques and other payments through a bank account. These records will be kept on a computerised cash book system.

The wages department will be responsible for supervising the payroll and calculating and paying wages. The data for these calculations will be generated by the works department or other department responsible for recording the amount of work carried out by employees.

The Production Manager and the production department

The Production Manager is responsible for making sure that raw materials are provided and made into finished goods effectively. He or she must make sure that work is carried out smoothly, and must supervise procedures for making work more efficient and enjoyable.

The production function in a manufacturing company can be split into five sub-functions:

- **Production and planning** Set standards and targets for each part of the production process.
- **Purchasing** Responsible for providing the materials, components and equipment required for smooth production.

- **Stores** Stocks all necessary tools, spares, raw materials, and equipment needed.
- **Design and technical support** Researches new products and changes to existing ones. Estimates costs of producing goods in different ways. Designs, produces prototypes and tries out new products.
- **Works** Concerned with actual manufacture of a product including maintenance and repairs.

The Marketing Manager and marketing department

The marketing department is responsible for identifying, anticipating and satisfying customer requirements profitably. Marketing and sales are sometimes combined in a single department, but there is an important distinction between the two. Marketing is concerned with getting the company to produce what the customer wants; selling tries to get the customer to want what the company has. The marketing department, then, will be concerned primarily with investigating consumers' needs and wants. This will involve carrying out market research to find out who comprises a particular market, what they want, where they want it, how they like it and at what price. Marketing and production should go hand in hand.

The Sales Manager and the sales department

The sales department is responsible with creating orders for a good or service. Some companies will employ a large sales force operating in the field on a regional basis. Sales representatives will visit businesses and other customers in order to win orders for products. Other firms will sell their product by means of advertising and publicity (e.g. catalogue selling with few field sales staff).

The Publicity Manager and the publicity department

The publicity department will be responsible for areas such as advertising, promotions and public relations.

The Distribution Manager and the distribution department

The distribution department will be responsible for warehousing, dispatch and transport. Goods will need to be sent out on time, to the right locations, in the right quantities, and to the right standards.

The Customer Relations Manager and the customer relations department

The customer relations department will be concerned with handling customer complaints and feeding back suggestions and problems to other functional areas.

The Personnel Manager and the personnel department

The personnel function has three main areas of responsibility:

- Recruiting, training, developing and deploying people within a business.

- Ensuring that the terms and conditions of employment are appropriate, competitive and effectively administered.
- Employee relations policy and practice.

The Labour Relations Manager and the labour relations department

A specialist in labour relations may be employed to handle the interface between management and employees.

The Health and Safety Officer

Makes sure that organisations comply with health and safety regulations and laws.

Community Projects Manager and community projects department

A community projects manager may handle many projects ranging from help for small businesses, educational activities and environmental concern projects.

> ## SYNTHESIS
>
> *An advantage of organising an organisation on functional lines is that the organisation is able to concentrate activity on its key areas, for example, finance, production, marketing etc.*
>
> *A disadvantage is that narrow specialism will restrict individuals' and departments' abilities to develop a global view of the total organisation.*
>
> *What other advantages and disadvantages can you think of?*

Grouping by product

When a large organisation produces a range of different products, it might find it convenient to create an organisation structure based on product lines. For example, a firm in the publishing industry might have a newspaper division, a magazine and periodicals division and a book publishing division. Each division will then contain a mixture of all the specialist ingredients required for it to work independently.

Northern Food's divisional structure is based on product lines with the Dairy Group, Convenience Foods Group, Grocery Group and Meat Group as divisions of the main group.

A great advantage of this form of structure is that divisions can concentrate on their own market areas. It also becomes possible to assess the profitability and effectiveness of each sector. At the same time, it is still possible to share expertise between divisions and to share services such as a combined transport fleet. By isolating the various parts of a business organisation, it becomes possible to cut out loss-making divisions and to amalgamated divisions by merging them with similar divisions in other companies. It also becomes possible to generate competition within a company and to allow greater scope to create an internal promotion ladder.

Grouping by process

Where the manufacturer of a product requires a series of processes, departments will be set up to perform each process. To take the example of the publishing company, within each of the divisions, departments will be responsible for carrying out stages of production, for example, editing of copy, page layout and design, printing.

> ## SYNTHESIS
>
> *An advantage of grouping by process is that it becomes easy to identify points in production where things are going well or badly. A disadvantage is that a weakness at one stage can cause hold ups for other processes.*
>
> *What other advantages and disadvantages can you think of?*

Grouping by geographical area

Many companies will have branches spread throughout the country and sometimes overseas. Multiple retailing companies are a good example. A company like Marks and Spencer will have shops on every major high street in the UK. Groups of shops will be organised into a regional division which will have overall supervision of such features as training of staff and distribution policy.

> ## SYNTHESIS
>
> *What advantages and disadvantages can you think of that will result from grouping an organisation into geographical areas?*

Grouping by type of customer

Organisations will often set up different structures to deal with different sets of customers. This is because they will often give some groups more time and attention than others. An obvious example would be in a hospital, where casualty patients require a different type of attention from patients requiring a routine x-ray. In a department store, the restaurant department will operate in a different way and have different procedures from those of a department selling underwear, etc.

Matrix structure

So far, we have looked at the internal organisation of a business as if there is a single pattern of organisation. However, many large businesses combine two or more patterns in a matrix structure; for example, they might combine functional and geographical lines.

In a matrix structure each member of the organisation will belong to two or more groups. This is illustrated in Figure 35.7 where groups of employees are organised into regions (e.g. North and South) as well as functions (e.g. marketing or sales). In this example a particular group of employees (marketing section A) will be accountable to both the Northern manager and the marketing manager. Each member of the organisation (below managerial level) will be accountable to two or more managers. Marketing, sales and other key functional managers will have a global responsibility for their function within the organisation, while divisional managers have responsibility for these functions on a divisional basis.

Advantages of a matrix structure

The advantages to be gained from using a matrix structure are that:

- A matrix makes it possible to structure an organisation in such a way as to focus on a number of objectives at the same time (e.g. servicing different types of customers, servicing different regions, producing different types of product).
- A matrix structure gives an organisation extra flexibility to respond to new situations where there is an increase in demand for its resources.

- The system makes it possible to draw groups from specific departments in the required numbers.
- There can be cross-fertilisation of ideas across departments.

Disadvantages of a matrix structure

The disadvantages to be gained from using a matrix structure are that:

- A complex matrix may be difficult to understand, and employees can lose sight of the major organisational aims.
- The system will often require extra administrative resources to make it work.
- Power struggles can arise because there are several chains of command.

A matrix structure can be very effective. However, it must be clearly laid out, and clearly explained to all those involved.

> **EXAM TIP:**
>
> In case study examinations students are frequently asked to make suggestions as to how organisational structures can be improved. Very often the focus is on identifying ways in which powerful individuals within an organisation can create new structures which enable them to better delegate authority.

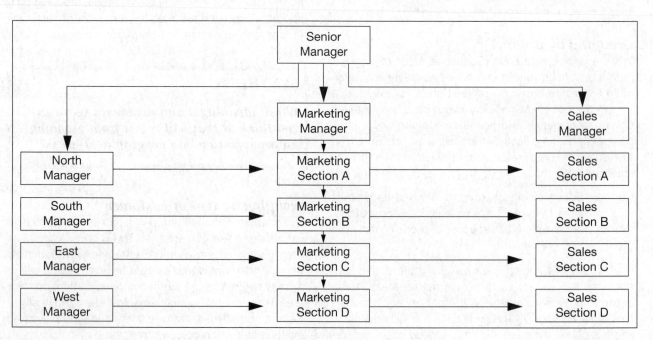

Figure 35.7   An example of a matrix structure

Moving on to more flexible structures

The types of organisational structures that we have outlined above are fairly typical of many UK organisations. However, in recent years many researchers and commentators have argued that organisational structures need to be more flexible and better able to respond to change.

Increasingly organisations have moved towards developing relatively small self-contained teams which are responsible for a specific part of the business or for a particular project. They work to set targets set by central management. They take advice and assistance from the specialist departments such as Research and Development, Finance, Personnel and Public Relations, although sometimes they may have their own specialists.

Intrapreneurship

A number of experts have argued that the key to being competitive and entrepreneurial in today's harsh environment is to be big, but non-bureaucratic. This has been termed **intrapreneurship**.

The challenge for large organisations is to devise ways of becoming intrapreneurial. Enterprise arises through innovation, particularly in developing new products and through process innovation, i.e. finding improvements to existing systems to enhance quality, reduce costs, and so on.

It has been suggested that intrapreneurial organisations should be structured in such a way that the following features are encouraged:

- Innovation is encouraged and rewarded frequently.
- There is free access to information within the organisation. Employees have the ability to tap into information from any part of the organisation using advanced IT.
- Individuals are encouraged to talk to each other and to share experiences.
- Individuals are encouraged to look outside the organisation, to attend courses, and to meet freely with other experts in the field.
- The organisation is relatively flat and highly adaptable to a changing environment.
- There is a strong emphasis on the internal and external consumer and on servicing their needs.
- Managers have had experience in innovation and they know what it feels like, enabling them to encourage others. Managers need to 'champion' innovation, helping the innovators to push through their ideas.

It is interesting to note that many large companies today have changed the way in which they set out their organisation charts. Instead of putting the managing director at the top of the diagram, they now place the customer at the top, and below that are a range of customer focused teams whose key objective is to satisfy customer needs and requirements.

Chapter summary

- It is possible to define structure as those patterns of behaviour in an organisation that are relatively stable.
- However, in modern organisations it may be necessary to have more flexible structures.
- An organisation chart is a helpful way to outline the formal structure of an organisation.
- The informal structure of an organisation may be just as important as the formal one.
- Organisations today are flattening out.
- Many organisations have both a line and a staff organisation.

- The superstructure of an organisation can be used to group employees by function, product, process, geographical area or type of customer.
- A matrix pattern is helpful for combining more than one method of grouping.
- Today, organisations are looking for more flexible structures so that they are more adaptable to change.
- Organisations can be big and non-bureaucratic by adopting intrapreneurial approaches.

36 Structure and organisations

In Chapter 35 we identified a number of ways in which organisations are typically organised, for example, by function or by geographical area. At the end of the chapter we examined ways in which organisations are changing and emphasised the importance of teamwork to modern organisations. In this chapter we want to build on this knowledge by exploring ways in which organisations are managed, and the various patterns of decision making by making comparison between a range of organisational types. For example, there is a clear contrast between patterns of decision making in a centralised and a decentralised organisation. In some organisations, most important decisions will be made from the centre whereas in others there is considerable delegation of decision-making powers.

The importance of the operating environment

All organisations operate within the framework of an environment. For some organisations the environment may be relative stable with few changes taking place. However, the reality for many organisations is that they operate within a turbulent and frequently changing environment.

The environment in which an organisation operates is made up of all of the following:

- **A physical place** – for example the centre of Nottingham, Nottingham, Nottinghamshire, the East Midlands, the Midlands, the UK, the European Union, or the global marketplace.
- **A set of conditions** – for example a competitive retailing market involving organised buying and selling conditions and trading rules.
- **A collection of individuals and other groups** – suppliers, customers, local council officials, VAT inspectors, competing organisations, etc.

Today's business environment is a change environment. Many commentators refer to the **Three Cs** as providing the 'basic facts of business life'. These are customers, competition and costs. Each of these three factors can be seen as existing within the external environment in which the business operates.

Customers are free to choose who they purchase from. Customers are notoriously fickle. They seek to further their own interests. If you cannot meet their requirements effectively they are likely to turn to a rival supplier. Customers are always seeking better offers and product improvements.

Competition is often the greatest environmental threat to an organisation. In most modern industries new technology provides a major driving force for change. Businesses that can effectively ride the wave of new technology can steal a competitive edge on rivals. Those that fall behind quickly lose that competitive edge.

Costs can be controlled within a business but there are many factors affecting the size of costs which are beyond the firms' control and therefore are determined within the external environment. For example, costs are influenced by international supply conditions – climate conditions can influence the supply of agricultural food products, wars can restrict the supplies of minerals and fuels such as oil and coal. As the world industrialises and there are increasingly strong demands for resources from growing populations then costs inevitably move in an upward direction.

As we shall see in this chapter it is important for organisations to match their organisational structures to the environment in which they operate. Today, as the environment becomes increasingly complex and changeable it has become necessary for organisations to develop increasingly flexible structures.

The nature of management

A popular definition of management is 'getting things done through or with other people'. Of course, experience tells us that some managers are able to get things done in this way, and there are some that cannot. And of course, there are many different factors determining whether the manager will be successful or not including the personality of the manager, the approach employed by the manager, the personality of those being managed, the expectations and values of those involved in the interaction, the type of setting and so on. The implication is that there is no one 'best' way of managing which will be effective whatever the setting and group of individuals involved.

Managers have the job of deploying an organisation's resources and making policy decisions. Managers use and develop systems for 'organising the organisation'. In the past, students used to learn the functions of management by learning the mnemonic:

POSDCORB
This stood for:
Planning
Organising
Staffing (i.e. getting the right people for the right posts)

Directing

CO-ordinating

Budgeting.

Indeed, much of management theory for a number of years was built around Henri Fayol's description of management functions which appeared in his classic work *General and Industrial Management* (Pitman, 1949). Fayol saw the traditional role of the manager as consisting of:

- **Planning** i.e. creating a framework for future decisions.
- **Organising** i.e. getting the right resources together and developing an appropriate organisational structure to divide up tasks.
- **Directing** i.e. achieving tasks either individually or through delegation to others.
- **Controlling** i.e. keeping up performance levels by monitoring and evaluation.

Indeed, this is the way that many managers continue to see their role. However, there is a lot of research into management which shows this is far from the way in which managers actually behave in practice, for example, Rosemary Stewart's famous book *Managers and their Jobs* (Macmillan, 1967). This and other research has indicated that managers typically:

- **Work long hours.** The number of hours worked increases with seniority and with more general rather than specific functional responsibilities.
- **Are highly interactive**. A typical day contains several hundred brief interactions. Working on one item for more than half an hour is very rare. As rank increases, the number of interactions increases, but the fragmented nature of the job remains.
- **Have to cope with highly variable tasks**. Managers have to cope equally well with paperwork, meetings, telephone calls, visits, ceremonial functions and managing by walking about.
- **Communicate mostly by word of mouth**. About three-quarters of communication is verbal. Many managers actually prefer verbal data such as hearsay, gossip or general feelings. Such data are immediate, accessible and can be acted upon before it is too late and gossip becomes fact. Information by post, or by written reports, comes very much in second place in informing the manager about what is going on.
- **Use lots of contact points to gather information**. Managers continually exchange verbal information with others. Most of this occurs within the organisation although as rank increases the number of verbal information points outside the organisation also increases. Information is traded across all levels of the hierarchy, with superiors, peers and subordinates.

CASE STUDY CASE STUDY CASE STUDY CASE STUDY CASE STUDY CASE

THE TRUTH ABOUT MANAGEMENT

People sometimes think that management is a very precise science. However, research has shown that this idealistic picture is often quite different from the reality.

In the real world, managers operate in a whirl of activity, constantly having to switch their attention from one subject, problem or person to another. They live in an uncertain world, where relevant and useful information is often mixed up with gossip and speculation.

It is often thought that a tidy desk, neat charts, colour coding and an appearance of organisation are signs of a good manager. However, inspirational managers are quite often scatty people who enjoy juggling lots of projects and ideas at the same time.

Good managers are able to get on with and motivate other people. Above all, they are good at making the best use of resources – whether human, physical or financial. Some of these management skills come naturally, others need to be learnt.

1 What traditionally are regarded as the main elements of effective management?
2 How might this view contrast with the way in which managers operate in the real world?
3 What do you feel are the most important characteristics of a good manager?
4 Why are people skills a key feature of effective management?

CASE STUDY CASE STUDY CASE STUDY CASE STUDY CASE STUDY CASE

Levels of management

Within a traditional organisation there will be several levels of management. However, in a modern organisation many of the traditional distinctions have become blurred or disappeared. Before examining these changes it is worth outlining traditional levels. Indeed if you talk to most British managers they are able to place themselves in one of the categories outlined below.

Strategic (senior) managers

Strategic managers make top-level decisions concerning the scope of an organisation's activities.These decisions set out what the managers want an organisation to be like and to be about. Strategic decisions are therefore vital for the development and welfare of an organisation. They require detailed analysis and considerable use of skilled judgement.

Examples of strategic decisions include deciding to develop a new product, to open up new markets, or to carry out major investment projects. Of course, many of these strategic decisions will need to be approved at Board of Directors level. Some top managers will have a dual role as Directors.

In a college, the Principal and Vice-Principals would be examples of senior managers. In a school the Head and Deputies would be good examples.

Middle managers

Middle managers organise and control the resources of an organisation within established guidelines. Middle managers do, however, usually have considerable scope for using their own judgement and for bringing in new ideas after consultation with senior management.

Examples of middle management decisions include setting out and controlling a departmental budget, organising a sales forces, and changing prices of products in response to changes in the market.

In a college, a Head of School or Department would be an example of a middle manager. In a school this would be a Head of Department.

Junior/supervisory management

Junior managers are concerned with short-term operational decisions, as well as longer term ones. Operational decisions are routine and frequently recurring tasks that can be carried out following straightforward rules. Examples include managing stock, arranging schedules for the delivery of goods, and organising hours worked by staff.

Management implies a level of responsibility in an organisation. In a college, lecturers can in some ways be looked at as junior managers – looking after day-to-day lectures, organisation of stock, management of the temperature in the classroom, etc. However, they will also be involved in some middle management decisions – planning of courses, and course development in conjunction with team leaders.

Unfortunately, the title 'junior manager' or 'trainee manager' is sometimes used by organisations to encourage people to work hard for relatively low pay because the title 'manager' seems to give a certain status. Anyone taking on a job described as a junior manager should check on the opportunities for promotion.

Supervisors

Supervisors are quite often the backbone of an organisation. They are people who know how things should be done at 'ground level'. They work with middle and junior managers to put plans into practice at an operational level. Supervisors know the capabilities of all the resources (machines, people, and materials) because they work in among them every day.

Supervision is a skilled and demanding job. The supervisor is like a sergeant major in the army giving orders to the ground troops. He or she will be first in line to deal with day-to-day problems as and when they occur.

Organisations therefore look for people with good qualifications to fill supervisory roles. They are likely to have mathematical and communication skills as well as a good knowledge of the technology of their industry. (Today this will almost certainly involve information technology.)

Supervisors may have risen 'through the ranks' of their organisation by hard work and the ability to cope with responsibility, so they need to have their skills periodically upgraded through training courses.

Teamworking

Increasingly, the emphasis today in UK industry is on teamworking. This involves giving increasing responsibility to members of a team. As a result, there is less of a hierarchical management structure. Instead there will be a team leader and a number of team members who share joint responsibility for meeting team goals and objectives. Team members require training both for job specific skills and teamwork skills. There will be regular team briefings at which team members are informed about overall business plans and developments by their team leader. Also there will be consultation procedures to encourage team members to make their own contributions to decision making. The team is therefore able to have more ownership of work-related decision making and hence builds a greater commitment to work activities. A teamworking structure would look more like that shown in Figure 36.1.

Top level	Objectives for the organisation
Level 2	Objectives for the divisions that make up the organisation
Level 3	Objectives for the departments that make up each division
Bottom level	Objectives for each individual team member.

Figure 36.2

The beauty of this approach is that it should lead to all members of the organisation working to meet the same clear objectives.

Principles of setting objectives/targets

Objectives or targets should be relevant, attainable and agreed rather than imposed and specific.

Relevant

Objectives should be relevant to the needs and priorities of the organisation. Setting objectives, and subsequently monitoring their achievement, absorbs time and resources. Therefore it needs to be done selectively. Not every activity is worth monitoring closely.

It is simpler to set targets for some activities than others because some activities are easier to measure than others. For example, it might be easier to measure the costs of medical supplies used in a hospital ward than the quality of patient care. Priority should not be distorted by the difficulty of setting a measurable target. The objectives should be relevant to the judged priorities.

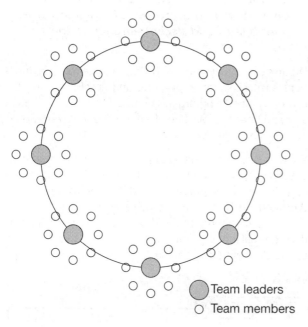

Figure 36.1   A teamworking structure

⬤ Team leaders
○ Team members

Attainable

Objectives should be attainable. To try hard and still fail is demoralising. Whether or not objectives are attainable depends, in the first place, on the provision of adequate resources. For example, if you have been asked at work, with the help of two staff, to complete a special project by a given date, it would not be surprising to fail should the two staff not be provided.

Agreed

Commitment is greater to objectives that have been agreed, than to those which have been imposed. It is better, therefore, to develop objectives for improvement through discussion between the job holder and the boss. Objective setting is then the logical consequence of an agreed need, rather than the exercise of arbitrary power. Unilateral imposition by the senior can cause resentment.

Management by objectives (MBO)

Management by objectives is one method of focusing and co-ordinating the activities of departments and individuals that make up an organisation. The approach was used as early as the 1920s before being popularised by Peter Drucker and others more recently. In the 1960s and 1970s, consultants like Urwick Orr and Partners advised companies on the use of MBO. The popularity as a consultancy technique has since diminished, although the approach has had a lasting influence on the use of objectives in management.

The idea of a an MBO approach is that you can set overall objectives for an organisation and then translate these objectives down through the various levels of the organisation, right down to objectives for individuals (see Figure 36.2).

Specific

There should be no ambiguity in the expression of an objective. Vagueness in definition can cause different interpretations of what actions are needed. Wherever possible, objectives should be expressed in numbers and the time period specified.

For example, 'to increase the sales of product X' is meaningless. Is the target increase 5 per cent, 10 per cent, or what? 'To increase sales of product X by 10 per cent' is still not clear. What is the base? Is it value or quantity of sales? By when is the increase to be achieved? Within a year? Within two years?

A meaningful target might read: 'To increase the value of annual sales by 10 per cent on the value of the 1996 sales valued by December 1997'.

Once an organisation has decided to go down the route of operating according to management by objectives it will need to establish clear plans for developing organisational objectives, and then objectives for each of the sub-components of the organisation.

Once the unit or departmental objectives have been fixed, each manager within the unit must then know what contribution he or she is expected to make. This is detailed in a document called a **management guide**.

The management guide document is designed to record agreement reached on:

- **the key result areas** i.e. the current priorities of the job
- **the performance standards** i.e. what outcomes are expected in the key result areas
- **control information** i.e. feedback on performance that will be supplied routinely to the job holder.
- **job improvement plans** i.e. plans to deal with identified problems.

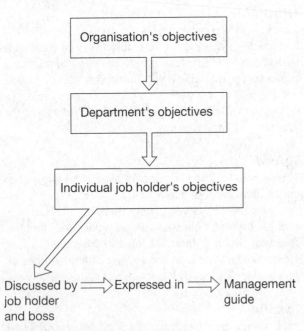

Figure 36.3   Management by objectives

Centralisation and decentralisation

Centralisation means keeping major responsibilities in an organisation within sections or units of the central headquarters or other central decision making groupings (e.g. a senior management team).

Decentralisation describes a situation in which many specific responsibilities have been delegated to branches, sub-groupings or individuals within an organisation. Delegation is the process of assigning responsibilities and decentralisation is the end result.

Organisations may choose to centralise certain key functions such as strategic planning and accounts, and purchasing in a retailing organisation. Other functions – such as recruitment – may be decentralised (i.e. left up to branches or departments).

While many firms are geographically centralised with major decisions being taken at the head office, others are organisationally centralised with decision-making being in the hands of a small group or section of management. When a centralised firm decides to push out new areas of decision-making to its middle or lower managers, or to its branches, then it is engaging in decentralisation.

IT'S A FACT

That in recent years decentralisation has become a management 'fad' although usually for very good reasons. For any company, but particularly one with a wide geographical spread and a huge range of product types, decentralisation of one kind or another is essential. Decisions need to be made at ground level by people who are in the know and have the information to hand – rather than by head office which may be thousands of miles or even continents away.

Reasons for decentralisation

1 Not all situations can be understood in depth by the small number of people at the top of an organisation. The information may be very complex, varied and specialised, and it may be difficult to transfer information accurately from the edges to the top of an organisation.
2 Decentralisation allows a swift response to local needs and conditions.
3 Decentralisation can encourage employee motivation. Giving local staff more responsibilities is likely to result in their feeling involved in the organisational decision-making process.

4 An organisation that is strongly centralised needs to be highly regimented with little scope for individual initiative. This is what characterised Eastern Bloc, centrally-planned economies prior to *perestroika*. There is inflexibility and the need for constant supervision of subordinates.

Vertical and horizontal decentralisation

Vertical decentralisation exists when decision-making authority is pushed down through the layers of the organisation so that several layers of management and supervisory workers are allowed to make decisions.

Horizontal decentralisation occurs when decision-making authority is pushed sideways across an organisation so that at any one level decisions can be made at a number of points rather than just by a few key individuals.

Delegation and consultation

Delegation (sometimes called **subsidiarity**) is the principle of pushing decision-making authority down to the smallest possible unit compatible with efficiency and cost-effectiveness in an organisation.

In general, the smaller the unit, the greater the capacity to respond to change, and the higher the morale within the unit.

Delegation is increasingly popular in modern companies, in contrast with how things were done in the past.

IT'S A FACT

That some major companies, like ICI, take groups of production level workers to meetings with customers so that the two groups can talk about what current perceptions are of products and discuss any problems that are occurring. By meeting customers, production line employees have a better understanding of their requirements, and can often come up with new solutions and ways of better meeting customer needs.

Employee participation

An organisation may want its employees to participate in the business. The purposes of introducing such a scheme include:

- to increase motivation
- to increase loyalty
- to increase commitment to the organisations goals,

particularly quality, productivity and competitiveness
- to benefit from employee's ideas
- to provide a degree of business democracy.

The Employment Act 1982 requires companies covered by the Companies Act and employing more than 250 people to report annually on action taken to introduce, monitor and develop employee involvement. It does not, however, require companies to do more than just report. No action is required by the Act.

There is a range of staff participation schemes. They can be classified as **direct** and **indirect**.

Direct participation

These involve individual employees directly. Examples are team briefings, quality circles and financial schemes, like profit sharing and share ownership, as well as team working. These are dealt with in detail in Chapter 38.

Indirect participation

This involves employees participating indirectly through representatives. Examples, are joint consultation and workers' representatives on the board of directors.

The importance of trust and accountability

Increasingly, organisations today talk about the importance of having trust in your employees. If individuals are going to be entrusted with the power to make decisions then they can't have someone looking over their shoulder all the time. Clearly this increases the risk element in running a business. However, without such trust organisations will not have the flexibility which is required to make them competitive.

Many organisations combine trust with accountability. Accountability means making sure that teamworkers are held jointly accountable for their actions. They therefore take on responsibility for their actions and regularly report back to the organisation on their performance. Accountability is an essential ingredient of trust.

IT'S A FACT

That one of the major merchant banks in this country, Barings, trusted one of its employees, Nick Leeson, to speculate on its behalf in the Far Eastern markets. Unfortunately, Leeson got out of his depth and gambled away millions of pounds leaving the bank with record debts. In this case, the company had extended trust a little too far. The bank collapsed as a result.

Chapter summary

- The pattern of management and organisation of an organisation is a key part of its structure.
- The way in which an organisation is managed and organised will reflect the environment in which it operates.
- In a placid and static environment an organisation will usually be structured in a hierarchical and mechanical way.
- In a turbulent/change environment an organisation will adopt more flexible structures.
- Three key elements of the organisational environment are costs, competition and the customers.
- The traditional view of management was that of a highly-structured activity involving planning, organising, directing and controlling.
- The reality is that management is a much less structured activity requiring flexibility and constant change of activity.
- There are a number of levels of management from senior to middle and junior levels.
- Increasingly, organisations today have moved to more flexible teamwork structures with considerable personal responsibility for individual team members.
- Management by objectives is one way of managing the organisation of an organisation. This involves establishing a hierarchy of inter-linking objectives from corporate down to individual level objectives.
- Increasingly, modern organisations are moving from a centralised to a decentralised pattern of working.
- Delegation and consultation are major ways of working in decentralised organisations and can be seen as logical responses to increasingly turbulent business environments.
- Employee participation makes it possible to transfer decision-making responsibility and accountability to all levels in an organisation.
- For employees to work effectively for an organisation they need to be given 'trust'. However, in order to ensure that employees do not take advantage of this situation they should also be made 'accountable' for their actions.

37 Motivation and demotivation

Motivation is the strength of commitment that individuals have to what they are doing. **Workplace motivation** is concerned with commitment to an organisation and its objectives and targets. In this chapter, we have set out to explore a range of factors influencing motivation at work and approaches managers can use to motivate employees. The chapter draws heavily on research that has taken place in this field over the years.

The experience which an individual has of work will depend on a complex mix of factors including:

- the individual
- the group
- the nature of the work
- the organisation of the business
- the economic climate.

IT'S A FACT

That the American writer Studs Terkel suggested in his book *Working*:

'It (work) is about a search, too, for daily meaning as well as daily bread, for recognition as well as cash, for astonishment rather than torpor; in short, for a sort of life rather than a Monday-through-Friday sort of dying.'

Human needs and work

People have a wide range of attitudes towards work. Many people see work simply as a means of earning money; others find that work is tremendously rewarding. Some of the things different people might look for in a job include:

- a good rate of pay
- good opportunities for promotion
- long breaks and holidays
- prestige
- the opportunity to combine work and family life
- job security
- friendship with work mates
- opportunities to be creative
- a degree of independence
- responsibility.

Generally, satisfaction will be greatest for individuals who have the greatest freedom to choose a job, and this will be those who have had the opportunity to acquire the most widely accepted range of qualifications and skills. Most jobs have some disadvantages, but workers will enjoy work if these disadvantages can be minimised.

The ingredients of a 'good job'

It would be very difficult to agree on the 'commonly accepted' ingredients of a good job. One person likes the freedom to work when and how she wants, another feels secure only when there is someone there telling him what to do; one person likes variety and change, another wants a good steady job. There are an infinite number of variations on this theme.

Job satisfaction therefore results from a complex mix of factors, including:

- the individual employee
- the work
- the nature of the business
- the rewards
- the working environment.

Individual employees bring their attitudes into the workplace and these attitudes are also shaped by the workplace. Some employees come to work looking for challenge and excitement, and place little emphasis on monetary rewards; others might see work as a means to enjoying a good life outside of the workplace and will not be too bothered about the nature of the work provided the pay is high.

The **nature of the work performed** will inevitably influence employees' perceptions of the pleasure involved. At one end of the spectrum will be the job that involves endless repetition of a simple and tedious operation, where there are only a few seconds in which to perform the task before it has to be repeated. Employees will get little sense of achievement from producing a very small part of an end-product which they may never see. There may be very little time for conversation with work mates because of noise and the urgency to perform the next operation.

At the other extreme, there will be jobs involving personal involvement and individual contributions to production methods. These jobs may require high levels of training and expertise and will give the employee prestige as well as meaning to his or her working life.

SYNTHESIS

To what extent are students' attitudes to school and college work determined outside of the school or college? Are there any parallels with workplace attitudes?

The nature of the business organisation is also of importance. Some organisations try and create an atmosphere of employee involvement. For example, Toshiba UK holds a daily five-minute communication meeting between workers and management. Organisations that directly involve employees in decision making help to foster a feeling of shared involvement in the success or failure of the enterprise. Some organisations such as co-operatives deliberately set out to share the decision making process. In contrast, large

---

CASE STUDY CASE STUDY CASE STUDY CASE STUDY CASE STUDY CASE

WEDDERBURN AND CROMPTON'S RESEARCH

Dorothy Wedderburn and Rosemary Crompton investigated work attitudes in a large chemical plant in Northeast England which they called Seagrass. They found that 'different attitudes and behaviour within the work situation could be manifested by different groups of workers largely in response to the differences in the prevailing technologies and control systems'. For example, the process workers in the plant (which was mainly automated) found their jobs interesting, and felt that they had enough scope to try out their own ideas and sufficient freedom to organise their own work tasks. In contrast, workers in the machine shop felt that their work was boring and gave them little freedom to organise their own work tasks. Attitudes produced by the job situation tended to be reflected in attitudes to supervisors. Workers who found their jobs interesting and enjoyable tended to have a favourable view of their supervisors, while employees who found work boring tended to resent supervision.

While finding that within the work situation attitudes were influenced by technology, Wedderburn and Crompton went on to conclude that workers still had an instrumental general attitude towards work itself. For example, in the assessment of their jobs the Seagrass workers listed four major considerations: 'the level of pay, the security of the job, the good welfare benefits and the good working conditions'. 'Job interest' was regarded as relatively less important.

CASE STUDY CASE STUDY CASE STUDY CASE STUDY CASE STUDY CASE

companies based on hierarchical lines can foster feelings of alienation.

The way in which employment is rewarded is another factor in determining attitudes to work. Some methods of payments, such as piece-rate (where employees are paid according to the number of items produced), can add to a feeling of alienation (e.g. workers rushing to produce given targets in order to increase pay). In the past 15 years there has been a dramatic rise in the number of British companies introducing incentive schemes to motivate staff. The range of incentives offered by companies are diverse, ranging from school fees, pensions, executive cars and private telephones to merit awards, life assurance bonuses and profit-sharing schemes.

IT'S A FACT

That Rank Xerox, for example, recognises the importance of praising and acknowledging individuals within the organisation. A recognition programme has therefore been introduced in its personnel department. It is called 'You Deserve an X Today' (X being a positive letter at Xerox). Anyone in the department, whether an executive or not, can give an X certificate (redeemable for $50) to anyone else for 'excellent support, excellent attendance, extra work or excellent co-operation'. This means that any member of the organisation can reward any other colleague for a quality contribution.

The working environment covers a range of factors, including lighting, heating, ventilation, the state of furnishings and equipment and recreation facilities. For example, recent reports have pointed out some of the dangers of the high-tech office; reports indicate that typists and computer operators nationwide are suffering from increasing problems caused by repetitive strain injury (RSI). Fast keyboard work can lead to the overuse of muscles, making it impossible to sleep, work or do ordinary household tasks.

We shall now consider the views of a number of leading researchers who have carried out detailed work looking at individual needs in the workplace.

Maslow

Maslow identified a hierarchy of needs split into five broad categories. He suggested that, although it is difficult, if not impossible, to analyse individual needs, it is possible to develop a hierarchical picture of needs, split into:

- self-fulfilment needs
- self-esteem needs
- group needs
- security needs
- basic needs.

Basic needs are for reasonable standards of food, shelter and clothing and those other items that are considered the norm to meet the needs of the body and for physical survival. This base level of need will typically be met in modern industrial society by the exchange of labour for a wage packet or salary.

Security needs are also concerned with physical survival. In the context of the workplace, these needs could include physical safety, security of employment, adequate rest periods, pension and sick schemes and protection from arbitrary actions.

Group needs are concerned with an individual's need for love and affection. Within groups there are always some people who are strong enough and happy to keep apart; however, the majority of people want to feel that they belong to a group. In small and medium-sized organisations (up to 200 people) it is relatively easy to give each member of the group a feeling of belonging. However, in large organisations individuals can lose their group identity, becoming just another number, a face in the crowd. As we shall see later in this chapter, there are ways of dealing with this problem, for example, by putting groups of workers into smaller work units with a common productive interest.

Self-esteem needs are based on an individual's desire for self-respect and the respect of others. Employees have a need to be recognised as individuals of some importance, to receive praise for their work and to have their efforts noticed.

Maslow placed **self-fulfilment** at the top of his hierarchy of needs. Self-fulfilment is concerned with full personal development and individual creativity. In order to meet this need, it is important for individuals to be able to use their talents and abilities fully.

Maslow argued that individuals first have to have their lower-level needs met; however, if they are not to experience frustration it is also important for their higher-level needs to be met. Frustrated employees are likely either to develop a 'couldn't care less' approach or to become antagonistic to working life. Maslow felt that in modern industrial settings, if employees are to feel a greater commitment to work and to become more effective workers, it is necessary to meet these higher-level needs. Self-fulfilment at work creates the 'complete' employee, the person who enjoys work and feels a direct involvement in it.

TASK 37.1

Applying theory to practical examples

Set out a table like the one shown below. Fill in the table using ticks to show where you think each of the characteristics in the left-hand column fits into Maslow's hierarchy of needs. (Often you will need to tick more than one box.)

Herzberg

Herzberg identified dissatisfiers associated with the context of the job, and satisfiers associated with the content of the job.

The research work of Herzberg in many ways complements the findings of Maslow. Herzberg argued that different factors in the work situation act in different ways to motivate people to work well or badly. His original work looked at the good and bad working experiences of 200 engineers. He drew a distinction between what he called 'hygiene' factors (which potentially could act as dissatisfiers) and 'motivating' factors or 'satisfiers'.

The dissatisfiers relate to the **context** of jobs which may easily provide sources of dissatisfaction.

Herzberg set out nine dissatisfiers:

- autocratic or arbitrary company policy and administration
- low pay
- poor working conditions
- antagonistic relationships between different levels in the hierarchy
- unfriendly relationships within the hierarchy
- unfair management and supervisory practices
- unfair treatment of employees
- feelings of inadequacy
- impossibility of growth and development.

Herzberg suggested that if these factors did not reach an acceptable standard it could lead to employee dissatisfaction, which might be expressed by absenteeism, poor levels of output, resistance to change, obstruction and/or other negative work practices.

In contrast, Herzberg pointed to five motivating factors, which relate to the **content** of jobs. These were called 'satisfiers' and are factors which can increase the motivation to work better and harder. They are:

- recognition of effort and performance
- the nature of the job itself – does it provide the employee with the appropriate degree of challenge?

	Physiological	Safety and security	Love	Esteem	Self-actualisation
Being given the opportunity at work to use your full creative talents to the full in a safe, secure and rewarding environment.					
Working part-time, for a pittance, with no job security, or job satisfaction.					
Doing monotonous, repetitive tasks, for a high rate of pay, in a well-organised and secure working environment.					
Working very long hours in a risky job with high rewards, and an exciting work atmosphere.					
Working in an atmosphere in which you are highly respected, but with little opportunity for promotion and with poor job prospects.					

- sense of achievement
- assumption of responsibility
- opportunity for promotion and responsibility.

On the basis of his research, Herzberg went on to suggest that jobs could be given more meaning if they incorporated elements of responsibility and a more creative use of abilities and opportunities, enabling employees to feel a sense of achievement.

Vroom

An alternative way of looking at motivation is presented in Vroom's expectancy theory. This theory puts forward the notion that the key ingredients in motivation are:

- an individual's wants
- his or her estimation of the likelihood of meeting these wants.

This theory is also known as the path–goal (P–G) concept. Vroom argued that performance is a multiplicative function of motivation (M) and ability (A):

$$Performance = f(M,A).$$

An individual's wants at work may include promotion, a high salary, a particular job, a company car and so on. Vroom used the measure valency to describe the level of a particular want, which can be placed on a scale of high to low. However, if high valency for a particular target is going to act as a motivator, the individual concerned must believe that the target is attainable. For example, an individual who want to work up to the position in which he or she is entitled to run a company car, or manage a department at work, must believe that this goal will be met in the course of time. The implications of the theory are that working life should offer opportunities for the goals of employees to be met, and at the same time provide clear evidence that these targets are attainable.

Vroom showed that valence and expectancy are the two key ingredients in motivation. The x sign indicates the multiplier effect created by the interaction of valence and expectancy.

Valence x Expectancy
creates
Motivation
which leads to
Action
which achieves
Results
from which stems
Satisfaction.

Schein

Theories related to motivation are all based on assumptions about the underlying nature of people. Ed Schein has classified these assumptions under three main headings.

- **Socio-economic drives** The assumption here is that people are driven by material urges alone. Satisfaction can be created by meeting these basic needs in the workplace.
- **Social drives**. Here the assumption is that people have a basic need to feel part of a group, and to be accepted.
- **Complex drives** A much broader perspective of motivation is that people are driven by a host of different factors which change over time and in different circumstances.

Schein believes that simplistic explanations of motivation should be avoided.

McGregor

McGregor's Theory X managers believe that they are in charge of employees who need to be directed and controlled. His Theory Y managers believe more in involving workers and creating opportunities for them to make positive contributions through motivating them.

The traditional theory of management as set out by Fayol (see Chapter 36) is based on the assumption that the organisation is controlled and directed by management. Certain other basic assumptions are made in traditional theory, which Douglas McGregor characterises as 'Theory X'. These are:

- The average person has an inherent dislike of work and will avoid it if possible. So management needs to emphasise productivity, incentive schemes and a fair day's work, and to denounce restrictions on output.
- Because people naturally dislike work, most people must be coerced, controlled, directed and/or threatened with punishment to get them to work towards business objectives.
- The average person likes to be directed, wishes to avoid responsibility, has little ambition and above all seeks security.

Against this view of human motivation and its implications for management of an organisation, McGregor proposed an alternative 'Theory Y'. The underlying emphasis here is on 'integration' to replace direction and control. The assumptions about human motivation of Theory Y are:

- Physical and mental effort in work is as natural as play or rest. The ordinary person does not dislike work: it all depends on the conditions under which work takes place – it can be enjoyable or not.

- External control is not the only way to get people to work. If they are committed to objectives, then they will be motivated to work towards achieving them.
- The most significant reward that will motivate people to work is the satisfaction of an individual's self-actualisation needs. This can be the result of working towards an organisation's objectives.
- The average human being learns, when given the opportunity, to accept – and more importantly, to seek – responsibility.
- Many people can contribute to a business's objectives when given the chance.
- Currently, the potentialities of the average person are not being fully used.

McGregor sees the potential to make organisations far more effective by unleashing the people that work for them. Organisations need to see themselves as interacting groups of people enjoying 'supportive relationships' with each other. Ideally, members of an organisation will see its objectives as being personally significant to them.

McClelland

McClelland believed that you should find out what drives people – nAch, nAff or NPow. Find this out and act accordingly. He argues that people have three basic needs, the need:

- for achievement (nAch)
- for affiliation, i.e. belonging (nAff), and
- for power (nPow)

He found that individuals with a high achievement factor display a number of characteristics. For example, they enjoy taking on responsibility, they like tasks which present and challenge and seek feedback on their performance. People with high affiliation or power factors will display other characteristics. Although each person has all of the three needs in some measure, one of them tends to motivate an individual at any given time.

A business would therefore need to know how these three needs affect individual employees. McClelland's ideas have been used in the selection of managers, where tests are used to identify attributes associated with achievement, affiliation and power. If particular attributes can be matched to particular jobs, then a person with high affiliation needs, for example, may be identified as being particularly suitable for a particular job.

Putting theory into practice

Having outlined a number of theories of motivation it is important to see how these can and have been put into practice. This can be done by taking a broadly historical approach to look at changing perspectives on putting motivation theory into practice.

We can illustrate this in the form of three major stages.

Stage 1: scientific management
Scientific management is associated with Speedy Taylor and Fordism.

The aim of the scientific management approach was to increase efficiency by carefully planning workers' movements in efficient ways. The most famous exponent of scientific management was Frederick W. Taylor (nicknamed Speedy Taylor) who stated that:

'The principal object of management should be to secure the maximum prosperity for the employer coupled with the maximum prosperity for each employee.'

Taylor set out to find ways of maximising the efficiency of labour using the stopwatch and 'time-and-motion' studies. He studied the movements made by production line workers in order to reduce the movements and tasks performed to the minimum for maximum efficiency. Labour tasks were thus reduced to machine-like efficiency. He felt that operatives would be prepared to work in this way in order to gain greater rewards in the form of higher pay.

In his book *Scientific Management* (1947), Taylor outlined four principles of management:

- The development of a science of work to replace the old rule-of-thumb methods by which working people operated. Fulfilling optimum goals would earn higher wages; failure to do so would result in loss of earnings.
- Scientific selection and progressive development of the worker – training each to be 'first class' at some task.
- Bringing together the science of work and the scientifically selected and trained workers for best results.
- Equal division of work and responsibility between workers and management, co-operating together in closer interdependence.

Henry Ford the car manufacturer was closely associated with this Scientific Management approach.

Flywheel production at Ford, 1914

The term 'Fordism' came to be associated with mass manufacturing organisations producing high-volume output of standardised products with specialist machinery and extensive stocks of spare parts. Ford employed a very strict form of work discipline based on the Theory X approach. Ford's workers were generally better paid than others, but working conditions were very strict and people had to work very hard. The term 'machine company' is associated with Fordism, because people were treated as part of the machinery and the organisation operated with machine-like efficiency.

Taylor's and Ford's ideas were based heavily on the assumption that high wages are the key motivator.

Stage 2: Human relations approach
The human relations approach identified by Elton Mayo's team showed that employees respond to interest taken in their work by others.

Taylor's scientific management approach can be contrasted with the human relations school of thought. Elton Mayo and a team of researchers from the Harvard Business School carried out a series of experiments from 1927 to 1932 at the Western Electric Company in Chicago. Initially, Mayo had taken on board some of the assumptions of the scientific management school, believing that physical conditions in the working environment, the aptitudes of workers and financial incentives were the key ingredients in motivation.

To this end, Mayo had experimented with different levels of heating, lighting, lengths and frequencies of rest periods and other variables. However, the results of the experiments were inconclusive; for example, Mayo and his team were surprised to find that wide variations in the level of lighting had little or no effect on output.

During the course of the experiments, Mayo found that the productivity of the group studied kept climbing, irrespective of various changes. Mayo came to the conclusion that, as a result of the experiment, a great deal of attention had been given to the group and members of the group had come to feel much closer ties with each other. Mayo felt that this was the important factor, and his work led to an appreciation of the importance of the informal group in industry.

Mayo's studies moved the emphasis from the individual worker to the worker as a member of a social group. Mayo suggested that managers should establish and maintain a sense of group purpose in industry. A famous example of this is the Volvo car assembly plant, where the traditional assembly line has been scrapped and small teams of workers build virtually the whole car. Not only do the workers build up a sense of group solidarity, but also they are able to identify with the production process from start to finish.

Stage 3: Modern 'empowerment' based approaches
Empowerment means the increased participation by employees in decision making.

The term 'empowerment' in an organisational context is used to mean the increased participation by employees in their organisation. Empowerment is regarded in management theory as a means of encouraging initiatives and entrepreneurialism in organisation members. In particular, it may have an important part to play in helping women to rise above the invisible barriers that until recently kept them in low-status roles within an organisation.

Rosabeth Moss Kanter, in her widely acclaimed book *Men and Women of the Corporation*, argued that organisations needed to make fundamental changes to improve the quality of working life, and to create equal opportunities for all groups, as well as to enable all members of an organisation to use their talents to the benefit of the corporation. This would involve opening up management positions to individuals by promotion from a wide range of more junior positions, by changing systems such as appraisal and career development plans. Intermediate jobs might need to be created as a stepping stone to senior management. All this would involve developing empowerment strategies – such as autonomous work-groups, with decentralised authority and flatter hierarchies.

Empowering others in an organisation involves giving them the responsibility to use their talents and express themselves. Rosabeth Moss Kanter argues forcibly that:

> *'By empowering others, a leader does not decrease his power; instead, he may increase it – especially if the whole organisation performs better'.*

An organisation prospers best when everyone in it believes that success depends on the excellence of his or her contribution. Short-term decisions made many times a day by individuals determine the quality of that day's work. Long-term decisions, again made by individuals, about their own career, training and ambitions, also affect the quality of their contribution

The governing principle, whether recognised or not, is that everybody has a customer – either outside the company (the traditional 'customer') or inside the company (the 'internal' customer). Both kinds of customer expect to be supplied with the product or service they need, on time and as specified.

The principle holds good for everyone in the company, whatever their level of skill and experience, whether their 'product' is answering a telephone in a helpful way or masterminding a major new project. It works to everyone's benefit. It gives the individual genuine responsibility and scope for initiative. And it virtually guarantees that the organisation's performance will be improved.

For any organisation, but particularly one with a wide

geographical spread and a wide range of product types, decentralisation of one kind or another is essential. Most decisions, especially tactical decisions, cannot be taken effectively at the centre – which may be miles or continents away. They have to be taken quickly, on the spot, by people who know all the circumstance. There is often no time for referral back to central office, even if central office had complete understanding of that particular problem.

The information technology revolution, by putting massive computer power into devices that can be carried around like notebooks and which can communicate instantly with other devices and their databases anywhere in the world, has made decentralisation even easier to handle and even more efficient in its effect.

In place of the specialist department, companies have begun to organise themselves into empowered multi-skilled teams responsible for a whole product. Such teams can more easily focus on customer needs, and so direct and combine their specialist skills to meet those needs more effectively. They are also better at judging what effort and expenditure are needed to do that.

Other important benefits follow from such an empowerment process. Individuals feel that their worth is valued. They can often make useful suggestions outside their specific area of expertise. They are no longer required simply to carry out orders, but to take responsibility for improving their own work and dovetailing it with the work of other specialists.

Tom Peters emphasises the important of trust in your employees if you are going to enable them to make a success of your organisation.

Empowerment is a way of thinking and working designed to enable everyone who has a good idea for improvement to carry the idea through, taking ownership of the idea themselves or in a team. In *The Pursuit of Wow!*, Tom Peters argues that:

'Hierarchies are going, going, gone. The average Mike or Mary is being asked to take on extraordinary responsibility. He or she may be on the payroll or, at least as likely, an independent contractor. In any event, the hyperfast-moving, wired-up, re-engineered, quality-obsessed organisation – virtual or not – will succeed or fail on the strength of the trust that the remaining, tiny cadre of managers places in the folks working on the front line.'

CASE STUDY CASE STUDY CASE STUDY CASE STUDY CASE STUDY CASE

DEMOTIVATION THROUGH HARASSMENT

Effective managers will set out to create an atmosphere and working environment which is conducive to genuine motivation. At the start of the chapter we asked you to consider what the effects of harassment in the workplace were likely to be on motivation. In recent times, many cases of such behaviour have been documented. The overwhelming evidence is that such a climate destroys motivation. For example, a woman executive made a claim in an Industrial Tribunal in York in September 1996 alleging that her line manager

patronised women who dared to argue back, labelling them as 'cheeky madams'. She told the tribunal how she had been terrified by the line manager's shouting fits alleging that this behaviour had a devastating effect on her character. She stated that, 'Before this I would have described myself as bubbly and assertive, perfectly able to work under pressure and to tight deadlines. I was capable of standing up for myself. I have changed dramatically. I have lost my self-confidence and become severely depressed.'

CASE STUDY CASE STUDY CASE STUDY CASE STUDY CASE STUDY CASE

DEMOTIVATION THROUGH STRESS

In May 1995, the Health and Safety Executive defined stress in the following way:

> *'The reaction people have to excessive pressure or other types of demands.'*

Stress is a disease which has increasingly affected individuals in modern industrial societies and has become particularly prevalent since the 1950s. A number of people argue that it became increasingly widespread in the 1990s. A number of commentators have identified recent industrial history as being one in which there are an increasing number of stressors (causes of stress) in the working environment. For example the Management Consultant Peter Drucker called our times *The Age of Discontinuity* (1968), and John Kenneth Galbraith referred to *The Age of Uncertainty* (1977); in the 1990s Tom Peters has simply referred to *Crazy Time* and *The Nano-Second Nineties*.

In the workplace, research has shown that employees feel stress is caused by factors such as performance related pay, increasing workload, new management techniques and a fear of unemployment, lack of time to do their jobs, poor relationships with immediate managers, exclusion from decision making, and pressures involved in decision making.

The effects stress is having on business and industry is widespread. A number of surveys have highlighted the impact of stress including one in 1994 which showed that in 65 leading companies over 40 per cent of employees believed that stress in their lives was caused by an excessive workload. Other common complaints involved a lack of sympathy and help given to staff relocating and travelling long distances to work. Moving house into a new area, and long hours spent behind the wheel were frequently cited. The criticism was that organisations often seem uncaring and lack thought and consideration for employees in these situations.

Another piece of research indicated that, on average, employees take about five or six sick days a year due to stress-related illness. In recent times, insurance companies have prepared themselves for a boom in claims from people suffering stress-related illnesses.

1 Why do you think that more emphasis has been given to stress in recent years?
2 What factors do you feel have been most significant in giving rise to work-related stress?
3 To what extent do you think that stress may have resulted from misguided motivation theories?
4 What practical measures could organisations take to reduce stress while maintaining high levels of motivation in the workplace?

Non-monetary methods of motivating

Pay as we have seen is only one means of motivating people at work. For example, if we look back at Maslow's hierarchy of human needs it immediately becomes clear that approaches such as providing opportunities for personal fulfilment in the workplace provide alternative avenues. The creation of empowered teams creates avenues to releasing individual creativity.

The notion that positive experiences lead to motivation is known as reinforcement theory. Positive reinforcement involves pleasant experiences while negative reinforcement involves unpleasant experiences.

There are four main kinds of reinforcement:

- **Positive reinforcement** involves giving pleasurable rewards for desirable behaviour.
- **Negative reinforcement** involves encouraging people to do things in the desired way in order to avoid negative sanctions and criticism.
- **Extinction** involves withdrawing reinforcement which was previously employed to encourage certain behaviours. For example, if a supervisor regularly praised employees for good work and then withdrew this praise – the result might be a fall off in the amount of 'good work' produced.
- **Punishment** involves sanction and unpleasant consequences as a result of certain actions.

SYNTHESIS

Can your provide real examples of the four types of reinforcement outlined above in actual situations in which you were involved? How effective were these approaches?

This type of case highlights the importance of managers being sensitive to the thoughts, feelings and aspirations of people they work with. Careful consideration needs to be given to creating working environments that get the best from people and which create a commitment model of working. Increasingly, the emphasis today is on empowering employees in the workplace. However, in creating such a model it is important to ensure that the right structures are created to support empowered employees so that they are not left in a state of uncertainty which can only lead to increased stress.

Some books of interest

A Maslow, *Motivation and Personality*, 1954, Harper, New York

F Herzberg, *Work and the Nature of Man*, 1966, World Publishing, Cleveland

V H Vroom, *Work and Motivation*, 1964, Wiley, New York

E H Schein, *Career Dynamics*, 1978, Addison-Wesley, Reading, Mass

D McClelland, *The Achieving Society*, 1961, Free Press, New York

Tom Peters, *The Pursuit of Wow!*, 1995, Macmillan Press

Chapter summary

- Motivation is the strength of commitment that individuals have to what they are doing.
- The experience which an individual has of work will depend on: the individual, the group, the nature of the work, the organisation of the business, and the economic climate.
- People go into the workplace with widely different needs and aptitudes. As a result their attitudes to work, and approaches to motivating them will vary enormously.
- Some people have an instrumental approach to work, i.e. work is seen as a means to an end rather than an end in itself.
- Wedderburn and Crompton found that people's attitudes to work could be strongly influenced by the technology and the work conditions with which they are faced.
- Maslow identified a hierarchy of needs in people. Successful managers and organisations will seek to satisfy people's higher level needs not just the lower ones.
- Herzberg identified a range of dissatisfiers associated with the context of a particular job, such as low pay and poor working conditions, and a range of satisfiers associated with the content of the job such as recognition for effort and performance. Herzberg argued that employees could be given more res-ponsibility and recognition in the workplace in order to increase motivation.
- Vroom argued that performance is a multiplicative function of motivation and ability. He argued that work should offer opportunities for the goals of employees to be met while providing targets which are clearly attainable.
- McGregor divided managers into Theory X managers who have a very directive approach to their subordinates and Theory Y managers who believe in motivating employees through giving them more responsibility and encouraging their efforts. McGregor believed in the importance of developing supportive relationships.
- McClelland believed that managers should find out what drives people and respond accordingly.
- Management theories of motivation have developed from the early scientific management/Fordist days, to a human relations approach, and more recently to an empowerment approach.
- Tom Peters as an example of recent empowerment theory argues that you need to put trust in your employees to achieve the best results.
- In recent times, employees have met with a number of demotivating forces at work such as rising levels of stress, and negative working relationships (e.g. harassment).

38 Human resource planning

Organisations today need to take particular care of their human resources, i.e. the people that work for the organisation. An organisation will best achieve its business objectives if it uses its human resources properly.

Increasingly in modern organisations, people have become the most productive asset. Today we talk about 'intelligent organisations' in which 'intelligence' is at a premium. We frequently hear references to 'knowledge' workers. Of course, people cannot be treated like other resources, for example, a piece of machinery, or a building. People have human needs and aspirations. They have a range of drives and motivations. They therefore need to be treated in a specialist way. Human resource planning is therefore a key aspect of organisational activity.

Human resource planning has taken over from the old fashioned 'manpower planning'. The change in wording is no accident. On the one hand it represents a move away from 'sexist' terminology, and on the other it represents a softening in attitudes and a realisation that people need to be nurtured and valued.

A useful definition of human resource planning (HRP) is:

> *The comparison of an organisation's existing human resources with forecast labour demand, and hence the scheduling of activities for acquiring, training, redeploying and possibly discarding employees. The purpose is to ensure that an adequate supply of labour is available precisely when required.*

In simple terms HRP can be defined as:

> *Having the right people, in the right place, at the right time.*

IT'S A FACT

That football managers need to be good human resource planners. They need to make sure that they have a good blend of players all the time. The manager who did not buy any new young players might suddenly find him or herself with an ageing playing staff with nobody prepared to chase the ball in midfield.

HRP can be seen as having a 'soft' and a 'hard' side. The harder side is what we traditionally associate with manpower planning – the softer side is associated with the new switch to human resource management (HRM).

The **hard side** consists of:

- analysing the current need for labour of the organisation
- creating a forecast of labour requirements for the organisation in the future
- creating a forecast for the likely supply of labour that will be available to the organisation in the future
- estimating likely future levels of labour turnover – i.e. the extent to which employees will leave the business.

The **soft side** will consist of:

- planning ways of motivating and satisfying employees
- planning ways to create an effective organisational culture – i.e. the general pattern of doing things in an organisation including the atmosphere within the organisation (e.g. relationships between people)
- planning ways of supporting and developing employees so that their needs and requirements are met.

SYNTHESIS

To what extent do you think that a 'soft' approach is more appropriate than a 'hard' approach at the end of the 20th century?

Planning can be both of a short- and long-term nature. Longer-term planning will involve the future needs and requirements of the organisation and of the people in the organisation. Short-term planning will be considered with more immediate concerns such as how to fill vacancies and meet current requirements of the organisation and its people.

In the past, manpower planning was seen as the responsibility of a specialist personnel department in an organisation with the responsibility for 'hiring and firing' employees. Today, many organisations still have personnel departments although a number have changed their names to 'human resource' departments. Human resource managers today work alongside other managers in an organisation to help other managers to take on increasing responsibility for creating frameworks for HRP and supporting people in the workplace. The human resources department, however, still retains an important responsibility for specialist 'people work' in an organisation. For example, human resource managers will create recruitment policies and codes of practice for an organisation and they will establish an overall training programme for the organisation, amongst other things.

MANAGING HUMAN RESOURCES IN NATIONAL WESTMINISTER BANK

The Banking industry in the 1990s has changed dramatically. Levels of competition in banking services have increased. The application of IT is widespread, and the numbers employed in banking have declined with all banks undertaking a shake out of employees. This has meant that the banks have switched from tall organisations with many layers to flatter organisations.

This delayering is nowhere more apparent than in the area of human resource management at NatWest. In the past nearly all training was carried out centrally by a large training department. Recruitment, selection and the development of individuals were the responsibility of a centralised human resources department. Now that has changed. There is still some training undertaken by the head office but the organisation now has human resource directors with a team of field managers.

The emphasis today is on encouraging bank managers and bank staff to take

responsibility for human resource management concerns, such as recruitment, selection, appraisal, training and development. The Field Managers work from home covering a geographical area. Their main job is to support bank managers in the branches in order to assist them in carrying out their human resource functions.

In recent years, there has been very little recruitment in the banking sector. The emphasis therefore is on the development of current employees. There is much less movement than in the past. Employees are expected to train to be multi-skilled. Today training and development of the individual is emphasised.

1 Why do you think that National Westminster Bank has adopted a new approach to human resource management?
2 What advantages are there in the new approach, and what disadvantages might there be?

The right place at the right time

People represent the most flexible resource available to an organisation and therefore making sure that they are in the right place at the right time with the right skills is essential to the success of any organisation. Human resource planning then is concerned with the acquisition, utilisation and development of human resources in order to meet an organisation's goals.

HRM contributes to the formulation of business strategy by identifying opportunities for the more effective use of staff and by analysing how human resource constraints may affect the implementation of a proposed strategy. The HRP process attempts to analyse the factors affecting the supply of and the demand for human resources with a view to maximising the organisation's future performance.

For example, a UK retailing chain may make a decision to expand in to the European market. It will then need to

consider what sort of skills and competences staff will need. How many current staff have those skills, e.g. fluency in key European languages? What new staff may have to be recruited? What training will be needed for current staff?

Figure 38.1 identifies, in general terms, the various stages of the HRP process.

Matching demand and supply

In creating the HRP the organisation will need to carefully examine its financial resource base and its long-term business plan (corporate strategy). Clearly, these plans will be in some measure based on market research into the future demand patterns for products made by the organisation. Demand for human resources is therefore a function of demand for the product or service. The other side of the equation will be the supply of labour, both already within the organisation and that which can be acquired from outside.

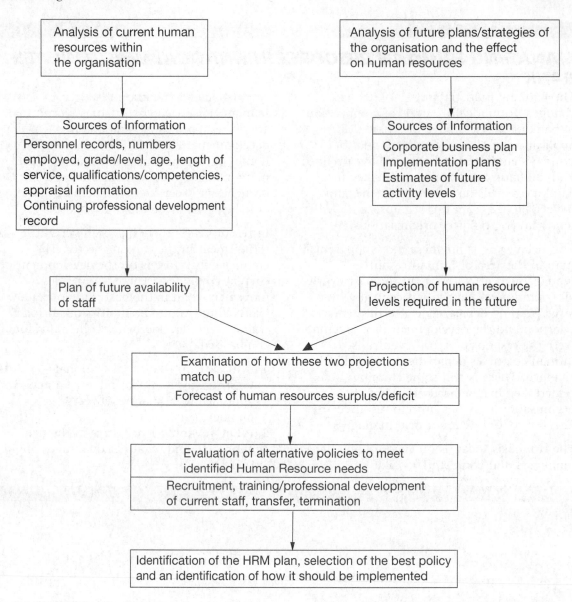

Figure 38.1   Human resource planning process

Methods of forecasting demand for human resources

These include:

- **Managerial estimates** Many small companies estimate their demand for human resources by asking managers to estimate their needs on the basis of likely future workloads and past resourcing levels. Managerial estimate can also be based on a variety of information including work study.
- **Work study techniques** These techniques can be used where it is possible to calculate how long operations should take and the amount of labour required. For example, in a manufacturing organisation it would be possible to forecast the volume of output and identify the time per unit which it takes to produce the product. Then by taking into account the average hours of

work a member of staff would put in each week it is possible to calculate staff requirements for annual production.

The supply of human resources

If an organisation is to assess the supply of labour available to it then it must examine not only how many people are available to do particular jobs but a range of other factors. An organisation will need to consider:

- the internal employee supply (the existing labour force)
  - the number of existing employees
  - the numbers in particular jobs
  - the skills of existing employees
  - the performance of employees

- promotion potential
- age distribution and length of service
- staff turnover
- the **external employee supply** (the external labour market)
  - the local labour market
  - the regional labour market
  - the national labour market.

The existing labour force

The following factors would have to be taken into consideration.

Numbers of employees in particular jobs

The aim is to identify groups of employees with similar skills for which forecasts of supply can be made. For example, in a hotel you would want to know how many kitchen staff, front-house staff, etc. you currently have.

Skills available

You would want to assess current skills of your employees and the extent to which the skills are transferable (e.g. could a kitchen worker become a porter?).

Skills analysis

The organisation needs to identify the skills that its labour force will require in the future compared with the skills they currently have.

Performance results

The organisation will need to examine the current performance of its staff.

Promotion potential

Internal promotions will change the availability of existing resources. It is therefore useful to an organisation to know how many employees have the skills and aptitude for promotion to more demanding roles.

Age distribution and length of service

Analysis of staff by age helps to identify possible problem areas. For example, is there an imbalance between experienced and inexperienced staff?

Staff turnover

This should be analysed in order to help an organisation to forecast future losses and to identify the reasons that people leave the organisation. A degree of staff turnover may be advantageous to an organisation as fresh staff can be recruited and promotion channels opened up. It may allow natural wastage when an organisation is trying to reduce its workforce. Too high a level of staff turnover, however, will mean that there will be high additional costs of replacement recruitment, additional training costs, and disruption to the quality of service or to production.

The labour turnover index

It is possible to calculate the number of staff who leave an organisation as a percentage of the total workforce. We call this a labour turnover index.

The labour turnover index is measured by:

$$\frac{\text{Number of staff leaving over a specified period}}{\text{Average number of staff employed over the period}} \times \frac{100}{1}$$

For example, if a college employed 200 lecturers but found that 50 of them left during the year the labour turnover index would be:

$$\frac{50}{200} \times \frac{100}{1} = 25\%$$

This sort of information is used to predict likely turnover in the future and to establish the need to examine in detail reasons for a high or rising turnover and to establish the need to recruit new staff to replace those leaving. In a large organisation, it would make sense to work out labour turnover index for different sections of the organisation.

TASK 38.1

The table below shows the average number of warders employed in a prison during the 1990s and the number that left each year.

Year	Average number employed	Warders leaving
1990	84	4
1991	83	3
1992	75	7
1993	70	10
1994	68	10
1995	66	10
1996	62	15

Calculate the labour turnover index for each year. Can you put forward any ideas which might help to explain the changes that took place in the index over the period in question?

That human resource planners often use Markov Models in examining internal factors relevant in setting out their HRP. A Markov Model sets out to model the flow of individuals within an organisation. It states that organisations have predictable wastage patterns (i.e. people leaving jobs) according to the lengths of service, and that this pattern can be picked out early in an individual's career. Once 'survival' rates have been calculated, a fairly stable pattern of regression and replacement needs over time can be worked out. It then becomes possible to predict future recruitment on the basis of stable patterns of wastage and promotion. The model can then be used not only for planning recruitment but also for training and development activities within the organisation.

The external labour market

The external labour market for any particular organisation is made up of potential employees – locally, regionally or nationally – who possess the skills and experience required at a particular time.

Important ingredients affecting the size and quality of this labour force will include:

- the number of people currently available for work
- numbers that will be available in the future
- the skills, experience and aptitudes of potential employees
- the extent of the competition from other organisations for these potential employees
- the age structure of the population (e.g. how many are in appropriate age ranges)
- the existing and future levels of education and training for potential employees.

Steps in the HRP process

In creating a human resources plan, organisations will need to consider the demand and supply of labour as outlined above. It is then possible to create a plan establishing how many and what kind of employees will be required in the future. Key steps in this planning process will be:

- Setting up a HRP Group in the organisation including key managers from across the organisation.
- Setting out human resources objectives for the organisation. These will be determined by such factors as the corporate plans for the organisation, the financial resources available for the organisation, likely future products and production levels, etc.
- A detailed analysis of the present use of human resources in the organisation.
- A detailed analysis of the external environment in which the organisation operates (e.g. government policies with regards to education and training, the availability of local housing, transport routes).
- The potential supply of labour.

A human resource audit

A human resource audit is a discrete part of the HRP which will set out the abilities, performance records and apparent potential of each of the organisation's departments and its employees. The aim of the audit is to match up the organisation's current and future human resources against current and forecast requirements. By carrying out this exercise the organisation is able to set out an HRP which sets out in detail, for each unit and sub-unit of the organisation, how many employees and what types of employees it is practicable to employ at various stages in the future.

Long- and short-term plans

Large organisations will want to create both long- and short-term plans for human resourcing. However, smaller organisations may not have the resources or capability to do this. Small organisations may therefore simply produce short-term plans, for example, for the next 12 month period.

HRP in a changing environment

HRP is not an easy discipline. It is very difficult to anticipate and forecast future changes in the supply of labour. Some factors are relatively predictable, for example, forecasting future demographics. There is a mass of information about population trends and once a baby has been born it grows older in a predictable way. However, other factors are more complex. For example, a new large firm may move into your area and employ large numbers of people. Changes in European Union legislation may have an impact for the UK economy in terms of the numbers of hours that people can work. An upturn in economic activity in a region or nationally may lead to surplus labour being taken up quickly. Changes in technology may mean that a training programme that your organisation has carefully built up becomes obsolete overnight and so on.

Balancing the needs of employees and organisation

In the past manpower planning was very much a discipline which was carried out for the purposes of organisational efficiency. It prevented the embarrassment of finding that you were faced with some departments that were overstaffed with others being badly understaffed. It was often a logistical and numerical exercise that could be carried out in a number crunching way.

More recently, HRP has developed a softer side in which an emphasis is placed on individual employee needs.

John Bramham, in a highly-regarded IPM text on HRP, has suggested that the human resource planner should aim:

> 'to develop with his or her colleagues co-ordinated personnel policies for the organisation which enable it to meet its economic objectives while fulfilling its social responsibilities.'

This perspective establishes that at times employees may have interests which are different or opposed to those of their employers or managers. Human resource managers then have a key mediating role to ensure that the organisation meets a plurality of interests including the very important needs of all employees. This is the essential difference between manpower planning and HRP.

Human resource planners must create frameworks which recognise and facilitate the reconciliation of the interests of different groups, for example, the desire of employees for shorter hours and more pay with those of managers for longer hours and less pay for employees.

Bramham and others argue that it is important to recognise the legitimacy of different views and perspectives in an organisation and that HRP should seek to create a framework for harmonious discussion of issues and moves towards mutual understanding rather than a conflict-based 'them and us' approach.

Importantly, many organisations have given greater status to HRP. In the 'old days' organisations often created a plan focusing on sales, profit and other targets. The manpower plan was then expected to follow on from the corporate plan.

Today, the HRP in many organisations is an integral part of the corporate plan. Human resource planners are expected to inform organisational planning rather than to follow others' leads.

Chapter summary

- Organisations will best meet their objectives if they use their human resources properly.
- Human resource planning (HRP) can be defined as having the right people, in the right place, at the right time.
- HRP can be seen as having a hard or a soft side. The hard side is associated with old fashioned manpower planning. The soft side emphasises a focus on employees as people and their needs.
- In the past manpower planning was seen as being the province of a specialist personnel department. Today HRP is a discipline which works across the organisation while being the particular specialism of the human resources department.
- Human resource planners need to enable organisations to match the demand with the supply of labour for the organisation.
- Demand for human resources can be calculated by analysing the future demand for an organisation's products and likely levels of future activity.
- To calculate supply an organisation needs to look at both the internal supply of labour and supply from external sources.
- The internal supply depends on a range of factors including the numbers of employees with particular skills and abilities.
- The external labour market depends on local, regional and national conditions.
- Organisations need to carefully construct a HRP which will include an audit of existing human resources as well as forecasts of future needs and available supply.
- Modern HRP involves trying to strike a balance between the needs of the organisation and those of individual employees.

39 Leadership and management styles

Introduction

A popular definition of **management** is 'getting things done through or with people'.

As we have already seen, managers operate in a whirl of activity, rushing from meeting to meeting and handling a range of projects and activities at the same time. What is required is the ability to juggle several schemes and ideas while managing and motivating people to create the best results. Managers need to be flexible and innovative as well as being organised and decisive.

Leadership is an important part of management. It is the process of motivating other people to act in particular ways to meet an organisation's objectives. The word 'leader' is derived from words meaning a path or road, and identifies the role of leader as giving direction to others and enabling them to follow the chosen path.

Leadership, power and position are not always the same thing in an organisation. Just because an individual appears to have a high position in an organisation does not necessarily mean that they possess a commensurate amount of power and influence. Sometimes, seniority and power do go hand in hand. More often, power is also to be found elsewhere in the organisation, sometimes in the most surprising places.

IT'S A FACT

That Tom Peters in his book *The Pursuit of Wow* has argued that successful organisations need to have a healthy share of 'crazies', i.e. people who are dynamic and innovative and are prepared to take a few risks and challenge existing assumptions. A dynamic business environment requires dynamic organisations staffed by dynamic people.

SYNTHESIS

Can you think of a situation in which a person has a high position in an organisation but has little power and influence? Can you think of a situation where a person has a low position in an organisation but a lot of power and influence? How would you explain this?

A useful definition of power is:

> **the ability of one social unit to influence the behaviour of another social unit and to achieve preferred situations or outcomes.**

A social unit can be an individual, a group, an organisation, or group of organisations.

The exercise of power will usually arise over specific issues, for example, in making a particular decision or series of decisions.

Managers in most organisations spend some of their time in a leadership role. This being the case, it can be seen that part of the role of a manager is to exercise power, often as part of the decision-making process. Effective leaders are able to exercise influence and bring about change.

A manager will often lead and guide others in an organisation. Henry Mintzberg regards the most important part of managerial activity as that which is concerned with decision making. He identifies four classes of decisions, depending on the role that a manager is playing:

- entrepreneur
- disturbance handler
- resource allocator
- negotiator.

As **entrepreneurs**, managers will make decisions about changing what is happening in an organisation. They may have to introduce change and also to take part in deciding what actually is to be done. In principle, they are acting voluntarily. For example, a sales manager might identify opportunities that would result from diversifying into new countries and new brands.

As **disturbance handlers** managers have to deal with situations in which problems have occurred which are beyond their immediate control – they have to calm things down, sort things out, and move the organisation forward. For example, when an overseas country in which your company sells products suddenly raises import restrictions, managers need to have the skills to make appropriate responses to such disturbances. When a supplier changes the terms on which they are prepared to supply then you need to come up with an appropriate response.

The **resource allocation** role of the manager is a key part of organisational management. Managers need to make decisions about how to allocate finance, people, equipment, time and other resources. Mintzberg points out that in the resource allocation role the manager schedules time, programmes work and authorises action.

In the **negotiator role** the manager has to negotiate with others, and in the process be able to create working relationships which are motivating and rewarding for all concerned. Wherever possible the good manager will help people to feel that they are involved in the decision-making process rather than having ready made decisions thrust upon them.

TASK 39.1

Nina Mistri owns her own business making engineering components. Which of the four roles outlined above is she exhibiting in each of the following examples.

1 Nina regularly meets with work teams in the organisation to share the results of current performance in meeting operating targets and in establishing new targets which can be agreed upon by all concerned.

2 Nina has identified an opportunity to produce a new component which will involve the company rapidly changing its production lines to accommodate the new line.

3 Nina is involved in planning an ongoing budget establishing how finance will be used within the organisation in the next time period.

4 Nina decides to purchase a rival outfit which is particularly successful.

5 Nina decides that employees will spend less time on producing smaller engineering parts and more time on producing larger ones.

6 Recently, Nina had to steer the company through a sudden shock when it lost a major order from a long-standing customer.

7 Nina helps to decide which employees will carry out particular tasks for important activities.

8 Nina has to respond to a new government law limiting the number of hours that her employees can work.

Management behaviour

A person's management style is shown in their behaviour in performing a management role over a period of time. There are four major types of management style.

Dominant

The dominant style involves making things happen by exercising control and influence. In order to be dominant, managers need to be forceful and dynamic. They therefore need to be assertive and push forward their ideas in order to get people to follow their lead. This type of manager is in charge, guiding and leading others through their actions.

Submissive

Submissive managers let things happen rather than taking control of events. They take a back seat and follow the lead of others rather than standing up for their own ideas. They give in easily, and quickly accept the superiority of other people's ideas.

Warm

Warm managers are sensitive to the needs of others and responsive to these needs. They show open and caring behaviour with a high regard for other people's ideas and feelings. This does not mean that they are affectionate or gushing, but that they have a genuine and caring approach.

Hostile

Hostile managers, in contrast, are insensitive to the needs of others and are therefore unresponsive to human needs at work. They have a selfish approach in which they put their own needs and requirements above those of everyone else. They can be hostile without letting this spill over in open anger.

A continuum of leadership styles

Good management alone will not ensure the success of organisation or of the people that run them. Good management needs to be complemented by good leadership. Leadership involves drawing together the various parts of an organisation in order to help them to work together to achieve the objectives of the organisation. It goes beyond the creation of systems and procedures; it must also involve the creation of a drive and momentum for change and a dynamism within the organisation.

However, there is not necessarily one best style of leadership. What is best for a particular situation depends on many factors such as cultural climate, time available for decision making and the personality of the individuals concerned.

Tannenbaum and Schmidt (1973) described the factors which influence a manager's choice of leadership style. Their research led them to argue that there are three main forces influencing the style adopted:

- Personal forces, including the manager's own background, personality, confidence and preference for a leadership style.
- Characteristics of others involved in the decision-makingprocess (e.g. subordinates) – including the subordinate's background, personality, confidence and preferred management style, and the willingness of subordinates to take responsibility.
- The situation, including the existing culture of the organisation, the nature of the decision that needs to be made, the time available to make the decisions, and the existing way of working in the organisation.

Tannenbaum and Schmidt set out a continuum of leadership styles which is shown in Figure 39.1.

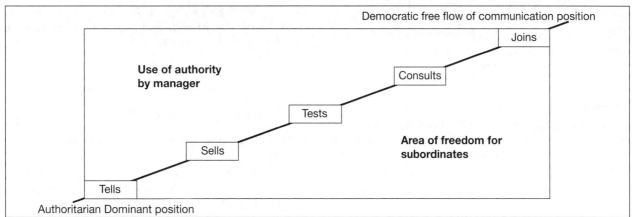

Figure 39.1   Continuum of leadership styles

In Figure 39.1, as we move upwards to the right the manager is using less authority and is instead allowing a greater amount of democratic decision making.

The '**best**' style of management depends on the situation and the people involved. In an emergency situation you will certainly need a manager that tells people what to do rather than the one who tries to set up a committee. In contrast, when a group of people come together to share ideas they may resent someone who takes on the role of leader and tries to tell everyone else what to do.

A **telling style** is best when subordinates are not prepared to take responsibility for themselves. They want the leader to 'tell' them what to do. They may be unable and/or unwilling to take responsibility and therefore need to be directed.

A **selling style** is best when subordinates are only moderately ready to take responsibility themselves. This approach offers both direction about what to do and support to those who are unwilling or unable to take responsibility. The manager will direct subordinates but also explain to them what they need to do and give them feedback on their performance in order to maintain motivation. Managers therefore go out to 'sell' new ideas and decisions to employees, e.g. by saying 'look this is a great idea – if you buy it you will reap the benefits'.

A **testing style** involves allowing subordinates to try out decision-making processes for themselves. The manager may test out new ideas on subordinates, encouraging them to start to take some of the responsibility for carrying out the decision and seeing it through themselves. They begin to take on more responsibility and ownership for the decision themselves, knowing that if things do not work out there is still scope for managers to take back full responsibility for the decision.

A **consulting style** involves giving even more freedom to subordinates to make decisions. This style is best when there is a fair amount of readiness among subordinates to carry out and make decisions for themselves. By enabling others to make decisions, the manager is able to motivate them by giving them clear ownership of large parts of the decision. Subordinates are in a position to consult managers about decisions that they want to make. This gives them the sense of security that their ideas have been screened by someone with more responsibility than themselves.

A **joint style** is at the democratic end of the continuum. The manager does not use authority over others. This would be the case in a self-managing team in which each individual has a key contribution to make to the decision-making process. Everyone is broadly at the same level and therefore takes an equal share of responsibility.

We can set out the range of leadership styles as follows:

- The manager imposes a decision which the team accepts.
- The manager 'sells' a decision in order to gain acceptance for it from the team.
- The manager presents a decision but responds to questions from the team.
- The manager puts forward a tentative decision which he or she is willing to modify after input from and discussion with the team.
- The manager presents the problem, gets input from the team, then makes the decision.
- The manager sets the boundaries within which a team is able to make a decision.
- The manager and the team jointly make decisions.

SYNTHESIS

Can you think of situations in which each of the above would be most appropriate for decision making?

Task orientation and people orientation

The task of a group within an organisation or the organisation as a whole is to ensure that certain targets or outputs are met. Some leaders become wrapped up in the task and forget about the people that are involved in carrying out the tasks. The problem with this approach is that the leaders may find that they fail to meet targets and objectives because they have not been able to carry the people with them. Employees may feel demotivated by working with leaders who just concentrate on meeting targets.

In contrast, a person-oriented style will show itself in a strong concern for employees. This type of manager sets out to boost morale and encourage employees to work together to get tasks completed.

The management grid

Blake and Mouton devised a matrix model comparing aspects of management style. They set out a contrast between managers whose prime concern is with production (getting things made and meeting production targets) and concern for people within the organisation.

This is easier to understand by looking at a Figure 39.2.

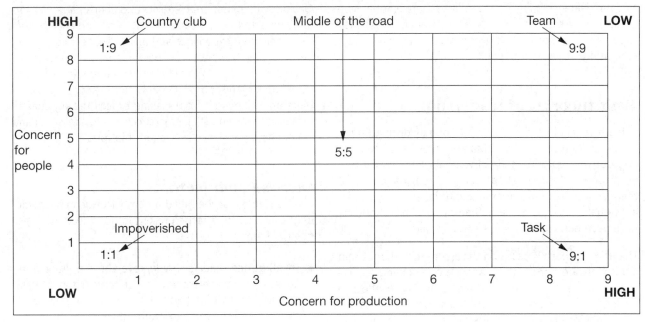

Figure 39.2   The management grid

The management grid is made up of 81 squares representing different combinations of emphasis on production orientation and people orientation. A number of positions can be identified in the grid:

- 1:1 shows a very low emphasis on both production in the workplace and on looking after people. It seems unlikely that such a situation would exist in the real world. Blake and Mouton refer to such a situation as **impoverished**.
- 1:9 shows a situation in which there is a maximum emphasis on looking after the needs of people in the workplace but only a very little emphasis on production. Clearly, such a situation would be unsuitable because very little would get done. The researchers call this the **country club** position.
- 9:1 shows a strong emphasis on production and very little emphasis on people. This is referred to as a **task** position. This approach could lead to considerable job dissatisfaction and tension among the workforce.
- 9:9 is the ideal position and shows a strong emphasis on both people and output. This situation is typified by the 'high-performance team' in which everyone works flat out to meet shared goals and objectives. There is considerable satisfaction for all concerned in such a situation. The researchers call this the **team** position.

Clearly, there are also many other intermediate positions such as position 5:5 which is referred to as middle of the road. Unfortunately, there are too many middle-of-the-road organisations in the UK today. Perhaps as a group you can identify a number of positions in organisations that you are familiar with.

Management as task orientation

Richard Varey of the Sheffield Business School draws a distinction between management and leadership in the following way. He argues that management tends to be 'task oriented'. It is concerned with getting things done with a particular interest in administering resources and budgets, maintaining performance and productivity standards, and achieving efficiency in operations. This is generally done by imitating 'good practice' observed elsewhere with the focus firmly on trying to motivate people to meet a company's objectives in the 'here and now'.

In contrast, leadership is concerned with the long-term viability of an organisation or part of an organisation and focuses attention on creating a vision of 'what could be' in the future. This will involve challenging existing practices, and motivating people to create and follow new objectives.

Varey argues that it is possible to distinguish two different styles of management in this respect. 'Old style' managers are largely task-oriented emphasising the setting of goals and meeting of targets using directives and formalised power structures.

'New style' managers are more people centred focusing on interpersonal skills and two-way communication in order to create a more democratic approach.

Positive and negative management

Managers may adopt a positive or negative style. A positive manager will emphasise rewards, for example, in the form of money, benefits, or better working relationships.

Negative leadership, in contrast, places more emphasis on punishments and sanctions. Negative leaders stress their superiority and domination over others – they play a boss role, using power as a threat.

Trait theories of leadership

A **trait** is a characteristic feature or quality distinguishing a particular person or thing. Many studies have been carried out that purport to identify certain traits which predominantly found in good leaders or managers. Trait theories may be used, for example, to explain why certain individuals, such as Richard Branson or Anita Roddick, have been particularly good leadership material.

The trait approach is based on the assumption that certain individuals are born with or acquire outstanding leadership qualities which enable them to be more effective leaders or managers. Desirable traits for strong leaders have traditionally been seen as self-assurance, dominance, intelligence, determination, and a desire to work hard to achieve targets. However, the traits which are appropriate for a modern organisation based on teamwork may be quite different (see Figure 39.3 below).

Strong leadership	Teamwork
• Self-assurance	• Self-assurance
• Dominance	• Sensitivity to others
• Intelligence	• Intelligence and interpersonal skills
• Determination	• Perseverance
• Desire to work hard	• Desire to work hard to create to achieve targets team goals, co-operation and team success

Figure 39.3   Leadership traits

It is not too difficult to think of individuals who are intelligent, self-assured and decisive. However, these people may lack the sort of sensitivity and interpersonal consideration that is so essential in the modern workplace.

A number of writers have argued that it is important to identify the traits necessary for leadership in a particular area of work. Management can turn on matters of process and experience, and many people in a profession can become good managers. Leadership requires very special personal qualities which fewer people in a profession have or are able to develop. However, it is possible to enable people to develop more of these qualities, although it is important to first pin down what these qualities are and to set out how they can be developed.

Obviously imagination, creativity and charisma are important characteristics of leadership. Passion and energy need to complement experience and ability. Leadership training become possible once you have identified the sorts of characteristics that are required by leaders in particular types of organisations. Organisations and professions therefore will benefit from making explicit the key characteristics of those most likely to succeed in establishing and maintaining excellence in a leadership role.

Charles Handy on traits

Charles Handy has identified a number of general characteristics which tend to be present in good leaders. These traits include:

- **Intelligence** Leaders should have above average intelligence but not necessarily be geniuses. Often a 'down to earth' sort of intelligence may be required if someone is going to work well with others.
- **Initiative** Leaders need to be able to take responsibility on themselves and show a certain amount of willingness to follow unexpected paths rather than wait for approval from others. They need to have that spark of creativity which will enable them to identify avenues for opportunity that others may see or not have the courage to pursue.
- **Self-assurance** Leaders need to have a good self-image which will give them the confidence to take others with them. However, leaders should also show respect for other people with whom they work. It has been suggested that good leaders will adopt an 'I'm OK you're OK' position when dealing with others rather than a rather disdainful 'I'm OK, you're not OK'.

Handy also identified a **helicopter factor** as being important for leaders. In other words, they need the ability to rise above a situation rather than being bogged down in minute details. In addition, good leaders also need to be generalists. They need to be able to build up an understanding of new situations quickly and apply broad-based experience of other fields and organisations.

In general, good leaders tend to be healthy, of above average height or well below it, and from privileged sectors of society.

Of course, there are many criticisms of trait approaches. For example, you may be able to think of leaders that do not have the traits outlined above. Also, the traits which are often identified by researchers are rather general and not clearly outlined. In any case, the traits in themselves are not sufficient to describe the characteristics of effective leaders. Perhaps it would be more helpful to identify the sorts of leadership qualities that are useful in a specific context in order to identify the sorts of people who will best be able to lead in such a context.

KEVIN KEEGAN AT NEWCASTLE UNITED

In January 1997, the footballing world was rocked on its heels by the resignations of Kevin Keegan as manager of Newcastle United. At the time Newcastle United were strongly placed in the Premier League, and in the European Cup, they had record attendance figures, and some of the best footballers in the world on their books – Alan Shearer, Faustino Asprilla, and David Ginola.

However, it seems likely that the pressure imposed by the responsibility of massive investment proved intolerable.

Keegan had a reputation for being thoroughly honest, to be a superb motivator, while at the same time being volatile with the inability to conceal his innermost feelings which led to a number of emotional outbursts. He was also dedicated to playing attractive and entertaining football – 'If we can only win the championship by changing the way we try to play, I'll get out' he said in 1996 after a 4–3 defeat by Liverpool.

As a manager, Keegan inherited the expectations of some of the most demanding fans in the country and a Chairman, Sir John Hall, with a long track record of success. Keegan and Sir John Hall had an excellent working relationship, although right from the start Keegan emphasised that he needed to have his own way if the partnership was to be a success.

In 1996 and 1997, Newcastle proved to be the most exciting of the UK Premier League teams but they failed to win any trophies. Increasingly, the pressure mounted to show a return in the form of a trophy as well as the millions of pounds that were earned through the clubs sale of tickets, shirts and all sorts of merchandise. Keegan created a style of football at Newcastle which had the supporters gushing with enthusiasm as well as the critics. However, it is possible that this style was not going to secure the points that would have won a Premiership title. Keegan was not willing to compromise on this approach, and when the team conceded goals was reluctant to alter the style of play from one based on the attacking flair of forwards to a defensive formation. With his players and staff Keegan proved to be a brilliant motivator who praised his team to the heights when they did well, showed a minute attention to detail and a detailed consideration for individuals. Above all Keegan was regarded to be scrupulously honest and fair minded.

1 What sort of management style did Kevin Keegan employ?
2 What traits did Keegan possess which made him an effective manager?
3 How effective a manager do you think Keegan was?
4 Compare and contrast the management style employed by Keegan with another manager that you are familiar with.

Contingency theories

Another approach to looking at management and leadership is based on contingency theories. These set out to account for the range of variables that may be relevant in a particular situation.

These variables would include:

● the task
● the nature of the work group
● the position of the leader in the group, etc.

The contingency approach can produce valuable insights and clues about appropriate management and leadership in particular situation. For example, Fielder (1967) suggested that the appropriateness of using an authoritarian or democratic management style depends upon whether the situation facing management is 'favourable' or 'unfavourable'. A favourable situation would exist when:

● the leader is popular and trusted by members of the group
● the task is well-defined
● the power of the leader is high.

Fielder felt that the first of these is the most significant. His findings led him to suggest that authoritarian approaches are most suitable in circumstances where (a) the task is well defined and the leader is strong and highly respected; or (b) the task is ambiguous and the leader is not in a strong position relative to the group. In the first case, decision making will be effective because subordinates will support a respected leader. In the second case, leadership must assert itself and clarify its aims for the organisation or go under.

In contrast, where a task is ambiguous and the leader is well-respected, the leader can afford to draw in the whole expertise of the group while still retaining power and authority.

The 'best fit approach' can be used as an extension to Fielder's work. It is based on the assumption that managers need to take account of four factors if they are to operate effectively.

● the leader
● the subordinates
● the task
● the environment.

The **leader** will have a given set of views about how things should be done and what is important. The **subordinates** will have a given set of views about how they should be led and how things should be done. They will relate to tasks in different ways, and will have varying levels of commitment to group tasks. The **task** will vary in nature, complexity, time scale and importance. Finally, the **environment** will vary according to the nature of the group, the position of the manager within the group, what the group or organisation is trying to achieve and the structure and technology of the organisation.

The 'best fit' approach argues that there is no single best style of leadership. Different styles are appropriate to different circumstances. The best style in a given group will be the style that most closely matches the requirements of leader, subordinate and task. The degree of fit can be measured on a scale running from 'tight' to 'flexible'. The three factors are then placed along the scale.

In Figure 39.4 we have a situation in which the task is highly unstructured, but both leader and subordinates are comfortable in operating with a flexible approach. Clearly, there is a 'fit' between each of the key elements. However, in Figure 39.5 we have a leader whose preferred management style is relatively authoritarian, working with a group whose members feel happier with a more flexible style, on a task which is fairly ambiguous. Because of this lack of fit, problems and difficulties are likely to arise. In the real world, it is likely that either the three elements will move some way towards each other, or the job will not get done.

IT'S A FACT

That being friendly, consultative, recognising, encouraging open communications, supporting, and representing subordinate interests have been shown to produce a high degree of subordinate satisfaction, but a link to higher output has yet to be conclusively proven.

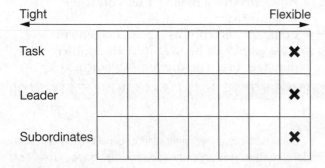

Figure 39.4   A 'good fit'

Figure 39.5   A 'poor fit'

Chapter summary

● Management is about getting things done through or with people, whereas leadership is concerned with motivating others to act in particular ways in order to meet the objectives of the organisation.
● Just because a person holds a senior position in an organisation does not mean that they have the power which is commensurate with the position – there is an important difference between leadership, position and power.

- The most important part of management is its involvement in decision making. Mintzberg identifies the four key roles of managers as being those of disturbance handler, entrepreneur, resource allocator and negotiator.
- Management behaviour depends on the style employed. Four key styles are those of the dominant, submissive, warm and the hostile manager.
- It is possible to set out a continuum of management styles from the authoritarian dominant position to the democratic one. The styles on this continuum range from tells, sells, tests, consults to joins.
- Another important distinction is between a task orientation and a people orientation depending on whether managers focus on getting 'things' done, or on making sure that human relations are effective within the organisation. A task-oriented manager will tend to focus on production targets rather than people targets.
- The management grid indicates that where there is both a high concern for people and for production you are likely to get the greatest 'team' efforts coupled with team satisfaction.
- Another way of looking at leadership is to identify various 'traits' which seem to appear in effective managers. However, as organisations change these traits are likely to change. The authoritarian leader is less relevant in a modern flexible organisation based on a teamwork approach.
- Handy and others have identified a number of leadership traits such as intelligence, initiative and self-assurance as well as a 'helicopter factor', i.e. the ability to rise above a situation. However, these indicators are not regarded to be 'necessary' conditions of good leadership.
- Contingency theories set out to account for the range of variables that may be relevant in a particular situation including the task, the nature of the work group, the position of the leader in the work group, and so on. It is important to have a 'good fit' between the leader's preferred style, subordinates' preferred styles of working and being led, the task, and the environment.
- Success in leadership and management depends on many factors.
- There is no single way to lead or manage that is always best.

40 Communication

The Advisory, Conciliation and Arbitration Services (ACAS) define communication in the following way:

> *'The provision and passing of information and instructions which enable a company or any employing organisation to function efficiently and employees to be properly informed about developments. It covers information of all kinds which can be provided; the channels along which it passes; and the means of passing it.'*

At the heart of management at all levels of responsibility lies a fundamental requirement to be able to communicate effectively with all people within his or her span of control. In fact, managers and administrators tend to spend by far the majority of their time communicating with others. Because communication is so important it is an essential skill required by all organisational members and particularly those with management responsibilities.

The importance of clarity

Effective communication requires not only the development of the basic skills of speaking, listening, reading and writing, but also an awareness and an understanding of the subject, the audience and the environment.

For communication to be successful, not only must information be transmitted, but it must be fully received and understood. Listening and reading skills are therefore just as important as speaking and writing skills.

The passage of information can be seen as a flow from the sender to the receiver (see Figure 40.1).

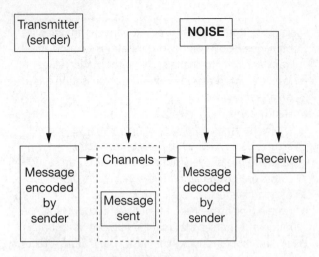

Figure 40.1   *The communication process*

Communication problems are known as **noise** and may lead to a message not being adequately communicated. They may include:

- **Situations where the language is not properly understood**. This may occur if the language is too technical or if the receiver comes from a different background from the sender.
- **Situations in which the receiver does not want to listen to the content of the message**. In these situations the message has to be redesigned to appeal to the receiver.
- **The use of a poor channel of communication**. Effective communication will be hampered if the means of passing the message is poor.
- **Too many steps in the message**. If there are too many stages in the message, or if it is too complicated, it may not be properly understood.
- **Message badly set out or ambiguous**.
- **The competing environment**. Background activities or interference from other activities in the working environment may interfere with the message, particularly if it is long or complicated and requires concentration by the receiver.
- **Cultural differences**. Our cultural backgrounds and differences may influence how we interpret the message.

TASK 40.1

What other barriers to communication can you add to the list above?

The basic communication skills

The five basic communication skills are:

- listening
- speaking
- reading

- writing
- using information technology (IT).

	Listening	Speaking
Learned	1st	2nd
Used	Most (45%)	Next most (30%)
Taught	Least	Next least

	Reading	Writing
Learned	3rd	4th
Used	Next least (16%)	Least (9%)
Taught	Next most	Most

Figure 40.2   *The flow of information from sender to receiver*

Speaking and listening

In most businesses, the most frequently used method of communication is speech. Speech takes place between people in direct contact with each other and, provided the listener is attentive, ambiguity in discussion can be removed by questioning. Questioning is a very important process because it can clarify meetings and points of view.

For speech to be an effective means of communication, it is important that individuals are aware of:

- their own role as communicators
- the receptiveness of the listener
- the listener's own knowledge of the subject.

We tend to assume that listening is an easy skill. However, people often forget what they have heard. Listening involves:

- physically hearing the message
- interpreting the message
- evaluating the message, which entails deciding how to use the information
- reacting to the message.

It is therefore hardly surprising that many verbal messages are quickly forgotten, misunderstood or not followed up. As a result, it is particularly important, after a meeting involving a lot of verbal discussion, that conclusions, recommendations and plans for further action are written down and circulated.

Writing and reading

Written communication varies from the very simple to the very complex. Written communications tend to be used in situations where:

- the receiver of the information is remote from the sender
- information is highly-complex, requiring extensive study
- information needs to be referred to over a period of time so that a clear record is kept in writing.

The written word in some circumstances can be open to ambiguity if the receiver is not immediately able to question the sender. For this reason, even informal notes need to be accurate, clear in their meaning and easy to read. Documentation systems are widely used in industry to reduce elements of ambiguity; very often drawings and sketches are used to support the written text.

Some forms of written communication are more easily read than others. The target audience and the nature of the information are important factors in deciding how to present data.

Information technology (IT)

The revolution in IT has completely transformed the way in which people and organisations handle the availability, processing and distribution of information. The result is that the quality of information is much improved; it can be accessed more quickly and sent more effectively and, by improving the quality of decision making, can create a competitive advantage for the organisation.

Body language

It is possible for some messages to be transmitted without the use of the spoken or written word. Non-verbal communication or body language can be used either on its own or to reinforce the spoken word. Physical gestures and facial expressions can often say as much as a written or spoken message. Being able to observe such signs is an important communication skill.

Facial expressions can also support physical gestures

Feedback

Most messages generate some form of response, or feedback. Some responses may be verbal while others might require a written answer. Feedback will indicate how a message has been interpreted and whether the information has been understood.

Direction of communication

Communication within an organisation can flow in a number of direction. They may flow:

- downwards from higher to lower levels
- upwards from lower to higher levels
- horizontally between people and departments at the same level
- multi-directionally.

Downward communication (top-down) communication

Top-down communication flows down the hierarchy often from higher level managers, to middle and junior managers, to supervisors and subordinates. Useful channels for communicating information downwards, include company magazine (house journals) and newspapers, reports to employees, and team briefing sessions.

IT'S A FACT

That sometimes people will cross their arms in a defensive position if they feel threatened or unsure in a social interaction. Rapid jabbing movements may indicate hostility. When someone rubs their eye this may indicate embarrassment or that what they are saying is not quite truthful. When people are relaxed in each other's company they will tend to mirror each other's movements and body poses.

Team briefings

Team briefings are particularly popular in the late 1990s. Teams are usually based round a common production or service area, and are made up of between five and 20 people. The team leader is usually the manager or supervisor of a particular section, and part of their personal development programme in the organisation will have involved training in team leadership skills.

Team briefings are called at regular intervals, sometimes every day (but more frequently one a week, fortnight or month), and may last up to half an hour with opportunities for questions from team members.

Research indicates a general level of satisfaction with such meetings. However, if meetings are cancelled or if there is a feeling that team members' views and questions are not taken into account then cynicism may set in.

House publications

House magazines, journals and company newspapers can be used to share information inside an organisation. They are particularly important in large organisations for communicating information to employees.

The quality of such publications varies from organisation to organisation. Some are glossy colourful publications while others are rather amateurish, poor quality newsletters. Some are very useful in that they provide clear information about company objectives and policies while others are nothing more than glossy justifications of company actions which may be regarded with considerable cynicism by staff. Effective publications will involve staff input and feedback on how employees are contributing to the success of the organisation.

SYNTHESIS

Do you think that top-down communication is still appropriate in the 21st century? Explain your views.

Upward communication

The purpose of upward communication is to draw on the skills and expertise of employees. This may involve individual employees or small groups. Typical forms of communication include suggestion schemes and attitude surveys.

Upward communication can be described more accurately as involving two-way communications so that there is communication both upwards and downwards.

Suggestion schemes

Suggestion schemes have been familiar in business for a long time. A well-known example is the suggestion box enabling employees to suggest improvements to working practice. Today, they have to a certain extent been replaced by more open communications such as quality circles enabling teams to sit down together to talk over ideas in an open and relaxed way.

Suggestion schemes can be tremendously beneficial to companies. 'Grass roots' employees can often see things far more clearly than higher officials. Their suggestions may save thousands or millions of pounds. Companies will frequently publicise 'good' suggestions that have been taken up in order to encourage further support for the scheme.

Attitude surveys

Attitude surveys have been particularly popular in the late 1990s. They are usually set out in the form of a questionnaire, but can also be carried out through face-to-face interviewing or telephone questionnaires. They will cover a range of issues but perhaps are most frequently used when managers are considering making a change and want to see what employees feelings are about existing or potential future working conditions.

Horizontal communication

Horizontal communication takes place within teams and between individuals and groups/teams within an organisation. Examples would include quality circles and IT link-ups for the sharing of information.

Horizontal communication is based on a more democratic form of decision making in organisations in which decisions are owned by a variety of individuals in a teamwork approach.

Quality circles

Quality circles are small groups of employees (about five to 20) in the same area of work who meet regularly to study and solve work related problems. In addition, such groups are intended to motivate and involve employees in decision making. A more detailed coverage of quality circles can be found in Chapter 44.

The idea of quality circles was originated in America but was then taken over to Japan by the American management consultants W Edwards Deming and J M Duran. The idea gained in popularity in Japan in the 1960s and 1970s, and was taken up by Western businesses in the late 1970s, although at first the idea was slow to spread.

The benefits of effective quality circles are that they:

- improve the quality and reliability of products and services
- make suggestions leading to cost savings
- increase employees' interest and commitment in jobs
- encourage a flexible response to problems
- improve supervisory authority and leadership skills.

While UK managers were enthusiastic about quality circles in the early 1980s they then began to lose popularity.

QUALITY TIME AT BRENT COUNCIL

Quality Time is an initiative that was introduced by Brent Council in 1994 for all of its staff. Each workplace holds a monthly two hour Quality Time Session led by someone drawn from that workplace (a Quality Facilitator). Each session is devoted to a topic related to improving the quality of services. In the first 18 months, these were determined centrally, based on customer research on what mattered most to Brent residents, with Quality Packs being produced to help the facilitators structure their sessions.

Features

The initiative had a number of features which at the time were unique in local government but which have been taken up in the late 1990s. These included:

- The right for all staff to two hours per month away from their day-to-day duties to create space for improving communication and the quality of service.
- The use of non-professional trainers as facilitators.
- The pursuit of a policy of 'training ourselves to do it ourselves' in a period of dramatic reduction in financial resources.
- The value of Quality Time in cascading important messages across a large organisation.

Practical benefits for the organisation's employees and customers

The Quality Time initiative produced a number of benefits, some planned and some as a consequence of the process. These are:

- considerable increased awareness of the importance of quality amongst staff, as shown in a number of surveys
- improved communication throughout the organisation
- the smoother introduction of new major initiatives (e.g. preparing the council's workforce for the Audit Commission's Citizens' Charter Indicators)
- tapping the previously unrecognised potential of over 300 members of staff who were trained as Quality Facilitators.

Resources

The concept of Quality Time – the making available of time in all employees' working patterns – is one which is readily adaptable to any organisation. As a proportion of the total budget of the organisation, the cost is negligible. In Brent, the cost of the launch, the training of quality facilitators, and the production of packs for the first 18 months of Quality Time sessions amounted to less than 0.04 per cent of its gross revenue budget.

1 What do you understand by EI?
2 How effective do you think the Quality Time Programme is as a form of EI?
3 Explain who benefits from this scheme and how they stand to benefit?
4 What other approaches to EI are you familiar with? Briefly describe three of these.

Researchers have indicated that in the UK many such initiatives were hampered by a lack of commitment from managers and employees.

Team working

Team working is another approach stemming from Japan. It focuses on problem-solving in team-working situations. A team will vary in size from five to ten members, although teams can be larger. To make sure that teams are successful it is necessary to train team leaders, managers and team-members to operate in a team situation. Clearly, the focus needs to be on developing interpersonal skills and ways of communicating effectively in a close working relationship based on mutual trust.

Total quality management (TQM)

We look at TQM in greater depth in the chapters on operations management. In this chapter we are concerned with TQM in terms of its implications for communications particularly in respect to employee involvement (EI).

TQM is an approach to management and to organising an organisation in order to create a planned approach to achieving continuous business improvement. 'Quality' is much the same as 'excellence' and the test of quality management is its ability to satisfy customers in the marketplace. Total quality management assumes that quality is the outcome of all activities that take place within an organisation and that all employees will participate in this improvement process. A crucial part of effective TQM will therefore be regular training for all employees in total quality practices.

While TQM may be very effective in some circumstances, in others it may be met with hostility and distrust. Where employees see the approach as encouraging EI they may be favourable to it. However, if they see it as a top-down attempt to impose management standards and controls they may be hostile.

Multi-directional communication

Involves a mixture of the above methods.

Forms of communication in an organisation

Internal communications are those that take place within an organisation – for example, between a manager and a supervisor or between two employees. External communication is concerned with how an organisation communicates with and is viewed by people and organisations outside the business.

Written communications

Written communications are used to pass on information and ideas. They can also be used to confirm verbal messages.

IT'S A FACT

That the word **memo** comes from the Latin *memorandum*, meaning 'a thing to be remembered'.

Internal written communications
Memos

One of the most often used forms of internal communication is the memorandum, or memo for short.

Today memos are used to pass on information, instructions and enquiries, and are like letters sent within an organisation.

The organisation's name does not normally appear on a memo and there is no need to start with 'Dear Sir', or finish 'Yours faithfully', as with a letter.

Memos are often sent to several people at the same time, although they are also sent to individuals. Most large organisations have pre-printed memo pads for their employees. Memos should be concise and to the point (see Figure 40.3).

MEMO

To:Advertising Director
From: Marketing Manager
Date: 26.5.1998

Successful results of market research

We have now completed our detailed market research for the new product 'Light and Bouncy'. The results have proved a complete success. Please draft a series of ideas for an advertising campaign to be presented to the marketing meeting 10.6.98.

Figure 40.3

Reports

A report is a written communication from someone who has collected and studied some facts or issues. It is usually sent to someone who has asked for it for a particular purpose. The report will often form the basis for a decision that needs to be taken.

Typical examples of situations in which reports would be sent include:

- to supply information for legal purposes, perhaps as a result of an accident
- to supply information to be given to shareholders
- to present the results of some research and to recommend action
- to weigh up the possible results of changing a policy.

Reports should be well-written, concise and to the point. They should not contain anything the reader does not need to know. They should be clear and arranged in a logical order. A suggested form of presentation for a written report is:

1. Title page
2. List of contents
3. Terms of reference
4. Procedure
5. Findings
6. Conclusion
7. Recommendations
8. Signature

The **terms of reference** explain why the report is being written, by stating the group or persons for whom it is being prepared.

The **procedure section** described how the report has been put together. What letters have been sent? Who has been interviewed? How were samples taken and what other research procedures were employed?

The **findings** indicate what has been discovered as a result of the investigations which have been carried out.

The **conclusions** contain a summary of the findings.

Recommendations may be included where appropriate. For example, you may be trying to look at ways of solving a problem through your research. If so, you may want to suggest some form of action as a result of your report.

Agendas and minutes

An **agenda** is a written outline of the issues to be discussed at a meeting. It is set out under a number of headings, and must contain the date, time and place of the meeting. It should be sent in advance to all the people who will attend the meeting so that they have the chance to prepare their contributions.

Minutes are a written record of a meeting. Sometimes they may be placed on a noticeboard so that more people can read them. Minutes should be clear, concise and accurate (see Figure 40.4).

Southtown Hospital Board

Minutes

of the meeting of members of the Hospital Board at 7.30 p.m. on Thursday 8th July 1999 in the Board Room, Southtown Hospital.

Present:
P.Patel (Chair)
H.Oliver
M.Khan
J.Obeng
D.Lee
D.Spencer

1. **Apologies for absence**
   Received from B.Head-Rapson, P.Shaw, K. Onion, D.Williamson.

2. **Minutes of previous meeting**
   The minutes of the previous meeting held on the 15th June, 1999 were accepted as an accurate record of the meeting.

3. **Proposal to put cleaning of hospital out to tender**........etc.

Figure 40.4   A layout for minutes

Notices and house publications
Notices are written displays placed in obvious places in order to give out information. They can be used to set out instructions, advertise future events, set out policies and so on. They can be a useful way of motivating staff. Notices should be designed and presented so as to attract people's attention.

House magazines, journals and company newspapers help to involve employees in decision making.

External written communications

The business letter
The business letter is still the most widely used form of external communications. It provides a written record and can be used to send almost any type of information. A well-written business letter may convey a favourable impression of an organisation. Its greatest benefit is its reasonable cost. Business letters are usually typed on headed A4 or A5 paper. Fully blocked layout is the most common form of display (see Figure 40.5).

Letters should be presented in a logical sequence and written in a style that lacks ambiguity. They should be concise and yet not leave out any relevant information. A typical business letter will contain the following features:

- heading or letterhead
- Reference, enabling the letter to be filed and later traced
- date
- inside address of the recipient
- salutation ('Dear...')
- subject heading
- body of the letter
- complimentary close ('Yours sincerely...').

Any enclosure will be noted by the letters 'Enc(s)'

There is a convention about the pairings of salutations and complimentary close. 'Dear Sir', 'Madam', should be paired with 'Yours faithfully' and 'Dear Mr/Mrs/Ms' should be paired with 'Yours sincerely'.

Other forms of external written communication
Advertising is a form of external communication. At the heart of advertising lies the need to understand how consumers will respond to both advertising copy and visual images. The effectiveness of an advertising campaign goes beyond the sale of products.

An **annual report** is a form of external communication produced by all limited companies. In addition to information required by the Companies Acts, many will also contain a range of non-financial information covering areas such as operations, business strategies, social and environmental objectives, etc.

Lighthouse Books Ltd

Token Court
Gorston
GN6 4PJ
Telephone: 01112 12345
Fax: 01112 67890

Our ref: MN/JW

15 June 199-

Mr P Wilde
Marketing Manager
Simpson Publishers
Beaverbrooke Broadway
Birmston
West Midlands
B3 2JB

Dear Mr Wilde

Thank you for sending me the photographs we requested so quickly.
They match the requirements of the manuscript perfectly and will
help to enhance the copy.

At some stage in the near future we must arrange a meeting and
discuss our future specialist photographic needs.

Could you please send us a copy of your new photographic brochure
when it is released.

Yours sincerely

Mark Newton
Editorial Assistant

Lighthouse International (UK) Ltd.   Registered no. 60127 England   Registered office: as above

Figure 40.5   An open-punctuated, fully blocked business letter

Magazines, publicity literature and educational services can provide strong informed links between organisations and their various publics. **Corporate videotapes**, although they constitute a visual rather than a written resource, have become an increasingly popular way of providing interested parties with information about an organisation's activities. **Visits, open days, exhibitions and demonstrations** can also be effectively used to generate interest, provide information and improve people's understanding and perception of an organisation's activities.

Verbal communications

Verbal communication involves direct word-of-mouth contact, either face to face or on the telephone, with the aim of giving messages, providing advice, personal discussion, instructions and guidance.

The telephone

The telephone is one of the most commonly-used forms of verbal communication in businesses both internally and externally. It is often the first point of contact an outsider has with an organisation, and if a bad impression is created through the first call, this may be difficult to correct.

> ### IT'S A FACT
>
> That there is a well used saying that 'You only get one chance to make a first impression.'

Many companies now have a **voice mail** system which allows callers to leave a message if the person they are calling is not there.

> ### IT'S A FACT
>
> That a study of motorists found that those who used a telephone in their car were 34 per cent more likely to have an accident.

Meetings

Nearly all employees at all levels in an organisation will spend some time at meetings. Meetings are held to discuss issues and problems, to come up with new ideas and to develop plans.

In a meeting you are able to draw on the specialist skills of a group of people, all of whom will be able to make a useful contribution.

A notice of a meeting will be accompanied by an **agenda** setting out the order of the meeting. Some meetings will be **informal** discussions between groups of people. Other meetings will be more organised or **formal**.

A **chairperson** has certain duties and powers in any type of meeting. He or she has the task of making sure that the meeting concentrates on the tasks in hand, and seeking the views of those who are involved. The chair makes sure that decisions are taken properly, and corrects anyone who wastes time or disrupts the meeting.

During a meeting someone, often a secretary, takes minutes which are later distributed to those attending the meeting.

The chairperson works through the items on the agenda. The final item is called any other business (AOB). This allows people at the meeting to bring up minor matters for discussion. It should not be allowed to go on for too long.

Visual communications

Visual communications is often the best way of getting a message across. If people can see what is expected of them, or how something works, they are more likely to remember it. Visual communication techniques are being used more and more within organisations. Examples are the use of overhead projectors, television and multimedia. For instance, medical specialists are able to view a patient's injuries from hundreds or thousands of miles away by means of television screens and virtual reality systems.

> ### IT'S A FACT
>
> That car crash repair claims are being revolutionised by the use of video cameras and computer technology. Instead of the long wait for insurance engineers to assess damages, within a few hours of a car being taken to a crash repairer, engineers can be looking at the damaged vehicle on a computer screen.

Modern companies, like Shell UK, use visual communications at their annual general meetings. These might include a video showing highlights of the year's performance, or a slide presentation using computer-generated graphics.

Information technology (IT)

IT has revolutionised communications both within and between organisations. Today, many employees are networked together and are able to share vast information systems. Increasingly, large numbers of employees are able to work from home and many people work with shared information systems such as the World Wide Web (WWW).

That a survey by the University of Leeds in 1996 found that 99 per cent of Britons have TVs, 80 per cent have video recorders, 20 per cent have mobile phones, but under 10 per cent are on the Internet!

Fax and e-mail

Instead of sending letters in the post and distributing paper copies of memos, many companies now use electronic methods of delivering written communications, both internal and external. **Facsimile** (fax) machines and **electronic mail** (e-mail) are both used to send information electronically over telephone lines.

The **fax** machine scans a document and sends it over telephone lines to be printed out on paper by the receiving fax machine. **E-mail** uses a 'mail-box' which is a computer terminal linked to the telephone network. It can put messages into the system and store messages that have been sent through the system. Every user has a password to allow him or her to use the system. A message can be sent to several mail-boxes at once, so the system can be used for internal memos in a company with several branches. The message will be stored in a terminal's memory until the 'mail-box' is 'opened'.

There are now a number of subscriber-based electronic mail services such as Telecom Gold. To use such a system, a subscriber sends a message using the telephone line. The advantage over ordinary mail is speed, low costs and time savings.

That voice mail was voted 'most useless' communications technology in a survey of British businesses and was condemned as 'robotic'; e- mail was voted the most useful in 1997.

Chapter summary

- Communication is the passing of information and instructions in an effective way.
- Communication needs to be clear, i.e. involve the minimum of noise.
- The basic communication skills are listening, speaking, reading, writing and using IT.
- The revolution in IT in recent years has greatly enhanced communications within organisations and enabled new forms of organisation.
- Communications can travel in a downward, upward or horizontal direction.
- Increasingly, organisations are replacing top-down communication with more democratic communications channels.
- Quality circles and total quality management approaches are examples of new forms of democratic communications. They represent a move towards greater employee involvement (EI).
- Organisations can employ a range of internal communications including written communications such as memos, and reports; verbal communications such as meetings; visual communications such as virtual reality systems; and IT.
- External communications include visual (e.g. the telephone), written (e.g. business letters), fax and e-mail.

41   Recruitment, selection, training, appraisal, transfers and termination

Personnel is a key function in all but the smallest business organisations. Traditionally, personnel was associated with the 'employment procession' of recruitment: selection – induction – training – transfers – termination of employment (see Figure 41.2).

In modern business organisation, however, personnel is also responsible for many areas related to employment, such as:

- appraisal, a key part of monitoring and helping an employee to develop a clear career path
- the administration of disciplinary procedures
- workplace bargaining with unions
- developing and supervising payment systems for employees
- supervising health and safety
- equal opportunities.

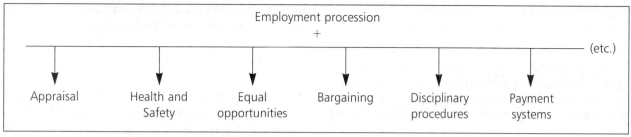

Figure 41.1 *The work of personnel*

Figure 41.2 *The employment procession*

In some companies employing as many as 100 workers, you will find a lone personnel manager working him or herself to the bone. By contrast, in some larger modern companies you will find personnel departments comprising a range of specialists housed in an extensive suite of offices.

Recruitment

Recruitment (and selection) is the process of filling a vacancy within an organisation by selecting the most appropriate candidate for the job. This is a very important task. Organisations will only be as successful as the resources they put into the job. Gaining the best pos-

sible human resources is done through recruitment and selection.

Personnel needs to have a clear view of:

● what jobs entail
● what qualities are required to do particular jobs
● what incentives are required to attract and motivate the right employees.

There are a number of stages that can be used to describe and set out the nature of particular jobs. Readers should note that the pattern shown in Figure 41.3 is most likely to relate to the creation of new jobs rather than to recruitment for existing jobs.

Figure 41.3 *Stages in organisational recruitment*

Job analysis

Job analysis is the process of studying what a job involves in order to identify its key requirements. A number of important questions need to be explored:

● What tasks have to be performed?
● What skills and qualities are required to perform these tasks?
● How can these skills be acquired?

Job analysis is used in order to:

1 Choose employees either from the ranks of existing staff (redeployment) or by recruiting new staff.
2 Set out the training requirements of a particular job.
3 Provide information that will help in decision-making about the type of equipment and materials to be employed with the job.
4 Identify and profile the experiences of employees in their work tasks (information that can be used as evidence for staff development and promotion).

5 Identify areas of risk and danger at work.
6 Help in setting rates of pay for job tasks.

Job analysis can be conducted by direct observation of employees at work, by information obtained from interviewing job holders or by referring to documents such as training manuals. Information can be gleaned directly from the person carrying out a task and/or from his or her supervisory staff. Some large organisations employ job analysts specifically to do this. In most companies, however, job analysis is expected to be part of the general skills of a training or personnel officer.

Four different areas of job analysis can be identified:

1 **Task analysis** involves the study of a particular task which is aimed at achieving a particular objective or end-product. For example, a particular employee may have the task of ensuring that all the assemblers in an electronics factory are supplied with a steady flow of components. Task analysis will therefore identify the tasks that will need to be completed as part of a job.
2 **Activity analysis** is the study of the elements involved in a given task. For example, one of the activities involved in circulating components in the electronics factory may be taking them down from the shelves in the stock room. Activities can be subdivided into physical (for example lifting, sorting) and mental (for example exercising judgement).
3 **Skills analysis** is the study of the ability needed to carry out a given task effectively. A wide range of skills may be identified, such as the ability to work in groups, to work independently, to perform manual operations, to make calculations, to communicate, to follow written instructions and many more.
4 **Performance analysis** involves setting out the criteria that will be used to evaluate how well a job holder carries out the job. Standards and expectations will be established in order to monitor performance.

Job analysis is not an easy task. There are a number of major difficulties to be overcome. It can be a very slow process, and the outside observer will not always be fully aware of what is going on. This is particularly true of jobs that require both mental and physical skills, because it is difficult to appreciate what is going on in the mind of the skilled operative. Individuals will often develop styles of work that suit their own particular aptitudes and may not be appropriate for other employees. When you ask a person to describe a particular job, they may miss out important steps which they have come to take for granted.

TASK 41.1

Set out a job analysis for either a newspaper deliverer, a shop assistant, or a person working in a bar or pub. The analysis should set out:

● what tasks need to be performed

● what skills and qualities are required
● how these skills can be acquired.

Job description

A job description is a simple word picture of a job. Note that it is not a description of a person; many individuals may have the same or very similar job descriptions. The description will set out how a particular employee is to fit into an organisation and will therefore need to set out:

● the title of the job
● to whom the employee is responsible
● for whom the employee is responsible
● a simple description of the role and duties of the employee within the organisation.

Job descriptions can be used by organisations to provide information for use in drafting a situations vacant advertisement and for briefing interviewers.

Job title

When looking through job advertisements, the first thing that job applicants will look for (apart from the salary) will be the job title. (From time to time titles will change, often to give a slightly different feel to some jobs or to confer new status, so the principal of a college may become chief executive or a dustbinman may become a disposal services officer.)

The job title is one of the most important parts of a job description. It should give a good indication of what the job entails. For example, you may hear people in organisations make statements such as: 'She's supposed to be the managing director, let her make the decisions,' or 'Leave the word-processing of letters to the secretary, that's not your job'. I heard a conversation between a lecturer and a porter concerning the carrying of boxes which ended up with the remark: 'You're supposed to be a porter – get porting.'

Responsibilities

A job description could be used as a job indicator for job applicants. Alternatively, it could be used as a guideline for an employee and/or line manager as to his or her role within the organisation. (It is not, however, a contract of employment). It will often establish where an individual stands in a particular organisational structure. This will mean that it can be clearly set out who the post-holder is accountable to, and who is accountable to him or her.

The position within an organisation will also give a clear idea of duties and responsibilities. Job applicants will be interested to locate their position so as to find out whether their previous experience will be extensive enough, and to assess the kind of commitment they will be expected to make to the organisation.

Person specifications

A job specification often goes beyond a simple description of the job, by highlighting the mental and physical attributes required of the job holder. For example, a recent Prison Service advertisement specified the following: 'At every level your task will call for a lot more than simple efficiency. It takes humanity, flexibility, enthusiasm, total commitment and, of course, a sense of humour'. The personnel department may therefore set out a person specification such as the following, which uses Rodger's seven-point plan:

A person specification is concerned with identifying those people who have the right qualities to fit the jobs being offered. Personal attributes for a member of the Paratroop Regiment, for example, might include physical toughness and alertness. The personal attributes of a shop assistant might include punctuality and smartness of appearance.

Qualifications are another important ingredient in person specifications. When recruiting a new Human Resources lecturer, for example, it would be essential to appoint someone with formal teaching qualifications and some form of academic qualification such as a degree in Business Studies.

There is a well-known saying that there is no substitute for experience. Someone with experience in carrying out a particular post or who has had particular responsibilities should be able to draw on that experience in new situations. For example, an experienced lecturer has already taught, assessed, administered, and carried out a variety of other duties in a college. A new lecturer does not have the same advantages.

Job requisition (recruitment profiles)

The person responsible for interviewing and recruiting is not always the person with a specialist knowledge of the job in question. For example, the personnel department may be given the responsibility of recruiting staff for all the functional areas within a company. Personnel will therefore ask for a recruitment profile giving the nature of the skills required, the type of person sought and a description of the job. The job requisition will therefore provide the specialist knowledge required to enable personnel to recruit the appropriate individuals. Job requisitions are also used to give advertising agencies and specialist recruitment companies more information from

Feature sought	Essential	Desirable
1 Physical makeup	Ability to lift and move boxes and equipment Ability to communicate effectively and to follow instructions.	Good general level of health and mobility
2 Attainments	Good level of general education	GNVQ Intermediate or beyond.
3 Intelligence	–	Able to understand quickly firm's way of working
4 Aptitudes	Positive approach to work	Ability to contribute to a team
5 Interests	–	General level of interest in life outside work
6 Disposition	Able to relate well with others	Can cope with routine activities in a team setting
7 Circumstances	–	Lives locally or has access to transport facilities

Figure 41.4   Personnel specification for a warehouse assistant

which to create recruitment advertisements (A business might employ a specialist recruitment firm to carry out a national recruitment campaign.)

Avenues for recruitment

Recruiting individuals to fill particular posts within a business can be done:

- internally, by recruiting within the firm
- externally, by recruiting people from outside.

Internal recruitment

The advantages of recruiting from within are that:

1 Considerable savings can be made. Individuals with inside knowledge of how a business operates will need shorter periods of training and time for fitting in.
2 The organisation is unlikely to be 'disrupted' by someone who is used to working with others in the firm.
3 Internal promotion acts as an incentive to all staff to work harder within the organisation.
4 From the firm's point of view, the personnel staff should already have been able to assess the strengths and weaknesses of an insider. There is always a risk attached to employing an outsider who may prove to be desirable only on paper.

The disadvantages of recruiting from within are that:

1 You will have to replace the person who has been promoted.
2 An insider may be less likely to make the essential criticisms required to get the company working more effectively.
3 Promotion of one person in a company may upset someone else.

External recruitment

> **IT'S A FACT**
>
> In the UK, the most common way of finding a job is by directly contacting a firm or place of employment; sometimes people apply for a job as a result of a personal contact, such as a relative already working for a firm.

There are many other channels than those outlined above and more formal approaches are usually required for jobs in larger organisations (not least because of Equal Opportunities considerations).

Figure 41.5   Some sources of external recruitment

Recruiting through newspaper and magazine advertisements

Newspaper advertisements are an obvious place for employees to place job advertisements. A good newspaper advert gives a substantial amount of information. Personnel managers place adverts in the most suitable medium for their target audience: jobs demanding limited skills can often be advertised locally, whereas jobs requiring specialist skills need to be advertised in specialist papers and journals. Advertisements for marketing specialists, for example, may be placed in *Marketing Week* or in the recruitment section of the *Sunday Times*.

When recruiting labour, the personnel manager will therefore do the following:

1 Target the recruiting campaign at the most suitable audience.
2 Advertise in the most cost-effective way i.e. the method that will have the greatest response per pound spent on the campaign.

> **IT'S A FACT**
>
> If you are seeking specialist work, it is sensible to look in the right media on the right day. Figure 41.6 shows where to look for specific jobs.

Area of employment	Widest choice	Daily Telegraph	Guardian	Independent	Financial Times	Daily Mail	Daily Express	Times
Arts and communication	Guardian	Mon	M/Thu	Fi/Wed	–	–	Tues	Wed
Academics and teachers	Guardian	Thu	Tues	Thu	–	–	T/Thu	Mon
Accounts and finance	Financial Times	Mon	Thu	Tue	W/Thu	Wed	Tue	Thu
Civil service & local government	Guardian	Mon	W/Fri	Thu	–	Wed	Tue	Thu
Computing	Daily Telegraph	Mon	Thu	Mon	–	Thu	Thu	Tue
Economics and statisticians	Financial Times	Thu	Wed	Tue	Wed	–	Tue	Thu
Engineers	Daily Telegraph	T/Thu	Thu	Mon		Thu	M/Tue	Thu
Management services	Daily Telegraph	Thu	M/Thu	Thu	Wed	Thu	–	Thu
Production, operations and works management	Daily Telegraph	Thu	Mon	M/Thu	–	Thu	Thu	Thu
Professional	Times	Thu	Thu	Thu	Wed	Thu	Wed	Thu
Sales representatives	Daily Telegraph	W/Thu	M/Thu	Wed	Wed	Tue	Wed	Thu
Sales, and marketing management	Daily Telegraph	M/Thu	Mon	Wed	Wed	Thu	Wed	Thu
Scientists and technologists	Daily Telegraph	M/Thu	Thu	Mon	–	Thu	Thu	Thu
Top management	Sunday Times	T/Sat	M/W/Thu	Sun	Wed	Thu	M/W/Thu	Thu
Secretarial/clerical	Daily Telegraph	–	–	–	–	Tue	Tue	M/T/Wed

Figure 41.6   Likely areas for specific job advertisements

To ensure that a newspaper advert gets the right response, at least some of the following points will have to be made clear:

- where the job is
- how much the job pays
- what qualifications are required to do the job
- what the job entails
- what fringe benefits are available
- how to go about applying for the job.

The managers responsible for recruitment will then sift through the replies, looking for applications from candidates who seem to have the required qualities.

IT'S A FACT

Surveys indicate that up to two thirds of potential job applicants will not apply for managerial posts if the salary is not indicated in the job advertisement.

Job Centres

Job Centres are run by the Employment Service, which is part of the government-run Employment Department, to offer employers' an effective source of recruitment and potential employees an indication of what they need to find a job. Job Centres are designed to help people to find their first job or to get back into the job market. Job vacancies are clearly displayed on cards. If people have been unemployed for a while, there are a range of services offered by Job Centres to help them in their job search, such as seminars and Job clubs to boost their confidence, help brush up on interview techniques, prepare CVs, etc. People using the centre will be given a client adviser to talk about the kind of work they want and give advice about the benefits that they can receive while looking.

The Careers Service

The Careers Service is the best source of careers guidance for young people, as well as helping adults too. In addition it collects lists and details of local vacancies which it distributes to schools, colleges, etc. The Careers Service is particularly effective in matching the demand for and supply of labour in a local area, although it will also provide detailed guidance about jobs further afield and career opportunities. It helps young people to think about their aptitudes and skills and how these can be gainfully employed.

Careers fairs

Organisations such as the Careers Service and local TECs sometimes arrange careers fairs where employers will set up display stands in a local college, school, shopping centre or other venue to talk to people who are or will shortly be seeking work about job opportunities. Employers also make annual visits to universities and other higher educational institutions ('the milk round') specifically to recruit graduate level employees for managerial or management training posts.

Employment/recruitment agencies

There is a wide variety of private employment agencies that help businesses to recruit staff. Fields in which these agencies are particularly common are professional staff agencies, secretarial work, high-technology areas, nursing and casual work. A business looking for staff will approach an agency, which will either undertake to interview applicants itself or will send suitable applicants to the firm to be interviewed.

The agency will take a commission based on the salary of the employee. The employment agency does not therefore charge a job seeker a fee, although it may charge for helping them to create a CV or for giving careers advice.

Recruitment consultancies and agencies are in business to supply people to companies who have slots to fill. They will be most interested in job seekers who have a good chance of finding employment.

Head-hunting

Head-hunting involves specialist agencies approaching individuals who are already known for their competence and skill in a particular area of work. They will find such individuals for firms seeking individuals with particular specialist skills. This is often a more cost-effective way of filling a specialist vacancy than blanket advertising which may not come up with the right person. Head-hunting usually takes place for senior management positions, and for specialist technical posts.

CASE STUDY CASE STUDY CASE STUDY CASE STUDY CASE STUDY CASE

RECRUITING EMPLOYEES FOR POSTS IN A SUPERSTORE

Opening up a new superstore is an important occasion for chains such as Tesco, Safeway, Sainsbury, etc. They will want to ensure that they recruit the best possible staff within the competitive local economy. Because stores tend to be of a standard design, the recruitment managers of a national chain will already have an outline of the jobs that they want to recruit for in the new store. Job analysis will therefore not be imperative. Instead there will be a selection of job descriptions which provide pictures of the employees that will be recruited.

The recruitment schedule will take about a year and follows a pattern similar to that described below.

RECRUITMENT SCHEDULE

Countdown 12 months before store opens:

1 Recruit senior management
2 Initial research into area
3 Advertising agency researches media and area
4 Advertising agency presents campaign package
5 Recruitment centre opens
6 Advertisements for supervisory staff appear
7 Advertisements for general staff go out
8 Interviews take place
9 Store opens

Staff and store managers will usually be recruited internally by the organisation. Research is then carried out in the area to assess the competition, find out what the standard wage is for similar employees, and terms and conditions of work, to examine the availability of labour, the available transport, housing facilities, and effectiveness of the local Job Centre.

An advertising agency will often be used to help with the campaign. The advertising agency will examine the local media, including daily and weekly newspapers and local radio. Typically advertisements will take place in the local press rather than national newspapers. A budget is then agreed on for the recruitment campaign.

Supermarket chains will rarely use local Job Centres when opening a new store because the centres will not be large enough. Instead they will hire their own premises for the period that recruitment takes place. Before recruitment begins in earnest the chain will advertise an open day at which potential employees can find out more information about the jobs that will be available and the nature of the work. Advertisements are then placed in local papers with benefits and salary being clearly indicated.

Supervisory and skilled vacancies are advertised about 20 weeks, and general vacancies up to 10 weeks before a store opens.

CASE STUDY CASE STUDY CASE STUDY CASE STUDY CASE STUDY CASE

TASK 41.2

1 Why is the emphasis placed on job description rather than job analysis when opening a new store to a national standard?
2 Why is it important that job descriptions are clear and unambiguous? What uses will job descriptions be put to?
3 Why is it necessary to carry out research before opening a store in a new location?
4 Why might a store hire an advertising agency to create its job advertisements?
5 What details would you expect to find in these job advertisements?
6 If you were going to open up a new superstore in your local town, what are the key labour recruitment questions you would need to answer?

Job evaluation

Organisations can use job evaluation to compare the value of different jobs. This will involve a detailed analysis of jobs in order to weigh up their relative worth.

Selection

Recruitment involves job analysis, description and specification. Selection involves creating the procedures and carrying out the actions necessary to place the most appropriate candidate in each post available in an organisation. An effective selection procedure will take the following into consideration:

● keeping the costs of selection down
● making sure that the required skills and qualities have been specified, and developing a process for identifying them in candidates
● making sure that the candidate selected will want the

job, and will stay with the organisation.

Keeping the costs of selection down will involve such factors as holding the interviews in a location that is accessible to the interviewing panel and to those being interviewed, ensuring that the interviewing panel has available all the necessary documentation, such as application forms, that should be studied before the interviews take place and also that a short-list is made up of suitable candidates, so that the interviews do not have to take place a second time, with new job advertisements being placed.

The skills required for the job should have been identified through the process of job analysis, description and specification. It is important then to devise ways of testing whether candidates meet these requirements. One way of doing this is to study applicants' application forms and to interview the most suitable people. Some employers go further and give applicants aptitude tests, putting them through a number of real-life situations to see how they cope with given business situations.

To gauge whether applicants will stay with the firm, it is important to ask them about their future intentions, and to familiarise them with the working environment into which they will be placed. There is no point in attracting a first-class candidate only to find that he or she does not like the firm's working conditions.

It is important to monitor the job selection process continually to see how effective it is. Ratios can be a useful method of appraising a selection process. These may include:

● Number of interviews: number of offers made. The most effective ratios would minimise the number of interviews relative to offers made that fill the posts as required.

- Number starting work: number of suitable employees. If a high number of applicants offered employment prove to be unsuitable or to turn down a job offer, there is something clearly wrong with the interviewing procedure.

Selection tests

In selecting candidates for employment many large organisations use a battery of selection tests in addition to formal interviews. Such tests are designed to test objectively a candidate's likely success in specific job situations and are used to measure personality and ability. They are often called psychometric tests. Candidates for jobs in organisations using these tests may be expected to attend a selection centre for a number of days.

IT'S A FACT

The term psychometric means measuring and testing of mental states and processes.

The main categories of psychometric tests used in selection are:

- ability tests
- personality questionnaires
- interest inventories.

Ability tests

Ability tests can be used to look at attainment, intelligence and aptitude. Attainment tests verify skills already acquired. For example, a secretary may be required to take a word processing test in order to demonstrate previously acquired keyboard skills. Intelligence tests are designed to give an indication of overall mental capacity. Aptitude tests aim to assess the candidate's potential to acquire further knowledge and skills. There are many aptitude tests which may be used as part of the selection procedure, depending upon the nature of the vacancy.

Personality questionnaires

Personality questionnaires are designed to give a more objective assessment of personality to supplement the rather subjective interpretation gained during the interview.

IT'S A FACT

Personality tests often build in questions which check whether candidates have been honest in carrying out the questionnaire.

Interest inventories

Interest inventories involve wide samples of questions which might cover hobbies, school work or general life experiences which seek to measure the direction in which an individual wants to develop.

Choosing the candidate

The final stage in selection is to make a decision on who to appoint. The selection process can be a very costly exercise. It is therefore essential to get an accurate picture of candidates and their likelihood of performing the job well. The selection process must be:

- fair: every candidate must have an equal chance
- legal: it must adhere to the requirements of equal opportunities and employment law
- honest: interviewer and assessors must give a true reflection of the candidate's performance
- objectives: the decision must be based on objective criteria
- quick: decisions should be made as soon as possible and communicated to candidate in a professional way.

Induction and training

Induction and training is another key area of human resource management. New employees in a firm are usually given an induction programme in which they meet other employees and are shown the skills they must learn. Generally the first few days at work will simply involve observation, with an experienced working showing the ropes. Many large organisations have detailed training schemes which are conducted on an in-house basis; this is particularly true of larger public companies such as banks and insurance companies. In conjunction with this, staff may be encouraged to attend college courses to learn new skills and gain new qualifications. As well as sending staff to local colleges and universities the firm may use the facilities of a training centre.

Training therefore takes place in the following ways:

- on the job: learning through experience at work
- off the job: learning through attending courses.

Promotion within a firm depends on acquiring qualifications to do a more advanced job; in banking, for instance, staff are expected to pass banking examinations. At the same time, a candidate for promotion must show a flair for the job. It is the responsibility of the training department within a business to make sure that staff with the right skills are coming up through the firm or being recruited from outside.

Appraisal

Most organisations today operate some form of staff appraisal or development scheme.

Common stages of staff appraisal are as follows:

1 The line manager meets with the job holder to discuss

what is expected. The agreed expectations might be expressed in terms of targets, performance standards or required job behaviours: attributes, skills and attitudes.

2 The outcome of the meeting is recorded and usually signed by both parties.

3 The job holder performs the job for a period of six months or a year.

4 At the end of the period, the job holder and line manager meet again to review and discuss progress made. They draw up new action plans to deal with identified problems and agree targets and standards for the next period.

There are three broad approaches to staff appraisal, based on personal attributes, skills or performance. They are not necessarily mutually exclusive. Schemes may contain elements of each. A large organisation may use different schemes for different groups of employees.

Personal attributes

The designers of the scheme identify the personal attributes that affect job performance. These are used as the basis for appraisal. Some examples are:

- reliability
- judgement
- application
- initiative
- adaptability
- disposition.

There are several criticisms of this approach. For example, the attributes are open to wide interpretation by the many managers undertaking appraisal in different parts of the organisation. The system is also not consistent and therefore potentially unjust.

Skills

Appraisal focuses on the employee's proficiency in the skills relevant to the particular job. Depending on the job, these might include technical competence, such as operating particular equipment, communication skills, such as report writing, and interpersonal skills needed to deal with customers. The person doing the appraisal, usually the manager, observes the employee over a period of time and records his or her judgement of the employee's competence. The standard could be a company's own, or it could be the performance standard of a relevant National Vocational Qualification.

Performance

The basis of appraisal is the achievement of agreed performance standards or targets. Advocates of this approach point to its objectivity. However, it is difficult in some jobs to find a satisfactory measure of individual performance. The outcome of a nurse's performance, is for

example, patient care. One way of assessing the success rate of patient care could be the discharge rate: how soon the patients are fit to go home. However, there are many variables affecting this outcome: the quality of resources, the performance of the rest of the team, changes in policy and practice relating to discharge, the home conditions of the patients, and so on. To isolate the effects of an individual's performance may be difficult and expensive to achieve. Where close teamwork is desirable, assessment and grading of individual performance could be divisive.

IT'S A FACT

Some organisations use peer group rather than top-down appraisal. Instead of being appraised by a line manager you would be appraised by someone at your own level in the organisation. The results of the appraisal would then be passed on to senior managers.

Transfers and termination of employment

The human resources department of an organisation has a responsibility for negotiating the smooth transfer of employees between departments. This may be necessary if employees are not able to get on together, or if it is felt necessary to give an employee a change. Some organisations believe that frequent changing of roles is helpful for the development of individuals so that they build up a broader range of transferable skills and competencies and gain a fuller understanding of how an organisation functions.

Termination of employment may be the result of a number of factors including retirement, dismissal and redundancy.

When employees retire after a long period of service to a business, they will need some recognition for their service. Companies such as the John Lewis Partnership keep in regular contact with retired employees, and arrange regular reunions.

The procedure for dismissal must follow strict legal guidelines.

Redundancy occurs when a business or firm closes down, when part of a business closes down, or when particular types of jobs are no longer required. It will usually be the responsibility of the human resources department to supervise and administer the redundancy procedures.

Chapter summary

- Traditionally personnel managers were responsible for the recruitment procession. Today this responsibility has been extended to include appraisal, the administration of disciplinary procedures, workplace bargaining, equal opportunities and a range of other concerns.
- Recruitment and selection is the process of filling a vacancy within an organisation by selecting the most appropriate candidate for the job.
- The key stages in recruitment are job analysis, job description, job specification, and the creation of a recruitment profile.

  Job analysis is the process of studying what a job involves in order to identify the key requirements of each job.

  A job description is a simple word picture of a job.

  A person specification is more detailed than a job description in that it highlights the mental and physical attributes required of the job holder.
- A recruitment profile needs to be produced to outline the nature of the skills required, the type of person sought and a description of the job. This recruitment profile can then be used by personnel and other managers to recruit the right people for jobs.
- Recruitment can be carried out internally or externally to the organisation.
- Internal recruitment enables an organisation to build on its existing human resources. External recruitment enables the organisation to bring fresh blood and ideas into the organisation.
- Selection involves creating the procedures and carrying out the actions necessary to place the most appropriate candidate in each post available in an organisation.
- Induction is the process of helping new employees to fit into an organisation and learn its ways of working.
- Training is concerned with enabling individuals to acquire the skills and abilities required by the organisation.
- Appraisal enables an organisation to communicate its objectives to individuals, and for individuals to clarify their aims and aspirations to the organisation.
- Personnel work is also concerned with transfers within an organisation and termination of individuals' employment.

7 Business operations

INTRODUCTION

Operations are the processes and acts which an organisation performs to satisfy its customers. For example, the person that visits a health farm may expect to be massaged, to be introduced to and follow through an exercise programme, to sit in front of a sun lamp and other processes which will help to make them fitter (thus meeting their desire to become healthier). When you buy a loaf of bread, the bakery will have carried out a number of processes from buying in the ingredients, to mixing and blending the ingredients, to baking and wrapping the finished loaves.

Operations lie therefore at the heart of the success of all businesses. Production involves the skilful bringing together of a number of resources such as management, finance, buildings, and people to create finished goods through a series of operations. Effective organisations will be able to add most value through the series of operations, i.e. making each stage of production effective in order to create customer satisfaction. The nature and type of operations will vary considerably from one type of good or service to another.

Key decisions in producing goods are 'where to produce?' – locations, and 'how much to produce' – scale. Location is one of the most important decisions a business has to make. For example, it may choose to be near to its market, or perhaps it may prefer to be nearer to its sources of raw materials.

Scale of production is important because by producing on a large scale organisations are able to reduce their unit costs of production. However, there is little point in producing on a large scale unless you have a large market to sell to. Organisations are most likely to benefit from technological innovations that enable bulk production (e.g. factory robots) if they have a sizeable market.

Production efficiency is essential if organisations are to be competitive. Efficiency involves making the best possible use of the resources used in an organisation. To be efficient organisations need to consider the ways in which they organise production, and the layout of plant and equipment. Efficiency is most likely to be achieved if the organisation regularly reviews its existing practice in order to identify opportunities for improvements.

The term 'quality' is used to refer to a situation in which the producer satisfies the consumer by producing goods and services which are 'fit for the purpose' required. It is therefore essential to find out what customers want and then to gear operations to meeting these needs. Quality should be seen as a continuous cycle of improvements so that an organisation continually seeks to improve on its existing standards.

42 Principles of operation

Every organisation from the multinational news corporations (e.g. News International owned by Rupert Murdoch), the public corporation such as the British Broadcasting Corporation (BBC), to the small local free paper exists to satisfy the needs and wants of its customers. This is the purpose of your local hairdresser, cinema or shop where you buy fruit and vegetables. It is through its operations that an organisation is able to satisfy the needs and wants of consumers.

Operations are the processes and acts which an organisation performs (often of a practical nature) to satisfy customers.

For example, your hairdresser may wash, dye, cut and shape your hair, while holding an entertaining conversation with you – all of the above are operations. These operations will take place in a particular physical location, for example, in the hairdressing salon or perhaps at your house in the case of a mobile hairdresser.

In order to meet customer requirements, an organisation must organise its methods of production so as to meet these needs efficiently. The organisation is acting as a **satisfier**.

Operations need to be designed to use available resources in the 'best' possible way. Operations management is therefore crucial to the success of an organisation.

The nature of the operations depend on the good or service being produced. Operations in schools and colleges, for example, take place in classrooms, assembly halls, on the playing fields or in the college office, and include such operations as teaching and learning, the organisation and running of sports fixtures, etc.

Operations in restaurants take place in the kitchens and in service at the tables and include operations like the preparation and construction of menus, the blending and cooking of food dishes, etc.

The production function

Production is the process of using resources to add value to a product or a service and so meet the customers' needs. In a manufacturing company, this will involve buying in raw materials and then transforming them into finished products which can be distributed to the market.

In service industries, the production function involves organising resources efficiently to offer the final consumer the best value and quality. The finished good may be a Premier League football match, a visit to the manicurist, having your funds looked after securely in a bank and so on.

Adding value

All businesses operating in a free market prosper in direct proportion to their ability to add value to their 'input' materials. The more value they add, especially in comparison with competitors, the better they do – provided always that the value is added in a way that does not conflict with the organisation's duties as a good citizen.

The key decisions therefore, whether technical or commercial, are all concerned with 'adding value responsibly'.

The notion of adding value is simple as the following example shows.

EXAMPLE

Ashok Patel has a small retailing outlet in Manchester selling vegetarian meals. On a typical day he purchases £400 worth of ingredients. He then performs a number of operations with the materials, for example, blending spices and condiments, cooking and preparing food, and packing the final meals for a take-away service. On a typical day he is able to sell £700 worth of vegetarian meals from the ingredients supplied.

Ashok is therefore able to add £300 worth of value to his ingredients each day.

Buying in price of inputs	Selling price of outputs	Value added
£400	£700	£300

Businesses constantly seek ways of adding value to products. Value can be added to products by making them more desirable so that more people are prepared to buy them and at higher prices. For example, value is added to motor cars by creating desirable additional features such as mobile phones, automatic route finders, increased safety features and economy fuel consumption.

SYNTHESIS

Can you identify at least five ways in which Ashok could add value to his vegetarian meals?

One of the most important ways of adding value to products in today's competitive market conditions is through service – personal attention to customers' requirements, friendly relationships with customers, etc.

The value added by a business to its input materials is thus more than simple physical improvement – it also involves non-tangible considerations such as service and 'image'. There is an essential human dimension. A business has to benefit not only the people who buy the products and services, but also its own employees, its suppliers and community at large.

Benefits, whether tangible, in the form of scientifically measurable product differences, or intangible, in the form of 'image' or service, are comparatively easy to add. However, the key is to add benefits which go above and beyond those being offered by competitors.

ADDING VALUE IN THE AIRLINE BUSINESS

When you travel with a major airline, like British Airways, passengers have a choice of where they want to sit and hence the price they have to pay for tickets. Passengers can travel ordinary standard class, business class, or first/club class. There are a range of benefits associated with each class but essentially the level and quality of benefit rises with the amount that passengers are prepared to pay.

When staff are trained at British Airways they will progressively develop skills which enable them to earn higher pay. The most highly-paid staff will be those that serve first-class passengers. They will be those who are most able to pamper the passengers and thus add value through the service that they offer.

By travelling first class, passengers will have a lot more leg room, and more spacious and comfortable chairs so that they feel as if they are in a large hotel lounge with access to newspapers and magazines. They will also have far more privacy and room to sleep.

Throughout the journey their every need will be met by smiling staff who are always helpful. These passengers receive the most value.

Business-class passengers will also have their needs met regularly in the form of drinks, food and access to facilities. However, they won't have quite as much space as first-class passengers. These passengers receive the second most value.

Finally, standard-class passengers will receive a good service, but will not benefit from as many services or from such highly trained staff as the other passengers. Their seats and accommodation are less comfortable.

Of course, British Airways' ability to create value for each class of passenger is important. The success of British Airways will rest with its value position when compared with rival companies – and, of course, price will be part of the equation. Passengers choosing to travel by a particular airline weigh up the benefits they receive in relation to the price they pay. The more value organisations can add to their service the more competitive they are. It is not surprising therefore that organisations pay such attention to staff training and development.

1 What does the term value added mean?
2 How does an airline add value in the process of production?
3 Explain how another service organisation that you are familiar with adds value.
4 Why is value added so important in creating competitive advantage?

IT'S A FACT

That oil, trapped in the rock thousands of metres below the surface, is worthless. Oil companies make a major addition to its value simply by bringing it up to the light of day. Then there are a thousand-and-one operations required to turn the product into that monochrome liquid that you hardly ever see because it goes straight into your tank or engine. Operations management is a highly complex but important process.

What can we learn from studying operations management?

Studying operations management is useful because similar organisations face similar problems. By studying how one organisation manages its operations you can learn how to better manage your own operations. Not only can a Head Teacher learn from studying the operations of other schools, he or she can also learn from studying other organisations like hospitals, and factories.

There are a variety of different types of producers. In each category there will be a number of common threads to the production process. Some organisations are mainly goods producers, others focus on services, and a third group combine the two. Here are a few examples:

Mainly goods producers
Chemical factories, engineering works, oil drilling and refinery installations. These installations may have little contact with final consumers.

Mainly service producers
Schools and colleges, banks and management consultants. These institutions primarily focus on providing a service.

Mixed producers
Most manufacturing companies, insurance companies and fast-food outlets mix production with a service. Manufacturing organisations often sell guarantees and provide repairs and after-sales service.

Responding to the customer

Organisations that fail to gear their production to the needs of customers have little chance of success. Production can therefore be seen as a response to market research. In meeting the needs of a market, businesses need to consider the Six Os:

- occupants
- object
- occasions
- organisations
- objectives
- operations.

Occupants
Who makes up (occupies) your market? For example, are you concerned with a limited market for a small band of customers (e.g. left-handed golfers or Braille readers), or are you concerned with a mass market such as those for the utilities like household gas and water?

Object
Here we are concerned with answering the questions: 'What do consumers wish to buy?', and 'What benefits are they looking for?'

Occasions
The questions to be answered here is: 'When will consumers purchase your product?' Will it be every week, every month, once a year? 'What time of the day are they most likely to make a purchase?' By finding the answers to these questions the organisation should be able to provide goods at the right time for customers.

Organisations
The question here is 'Who is involved in the decision to purchase'? An organisation that is selling goods need to aim its sales pitch at the purchasers. For example, in selling carpets to a department store you need to target the person in that organisation who makes the decisions about carpet buying. In dealing with a large organisation you need to identify the part of the organisation that makes these decisions.

Objectives
A key question is: 'Why do consumers buy particular goods or services?' In other words, you are trying to focus on the benefits that they are seeking. If you can find out why people make a purchasing decision, then you will be best placed to provide a solution to their buying problem.

Operations
This is concerned with 'How do consumers buy products and services?' For example, do they pay cash or use some form of credit? If you know their preferred method, you can make it easier for them to make a purchase. If you know people are most likely to buy a car in hire-purchase instalments over three years, then you can make sure the right credit terms are available.

The chain of production
For every product there is a chain of production. Some products go through many stages in the chain of production, while for others the chain is a lot shorter. Figure 42.1 shows the complexity of the chain of production for oil

and gas. At each stage, value is added. The stages need to be very closely linked together to avoid wastage and ensure that maximum value is added.

Other products may have a much shorter chain of production – for example, when apples are grown by a farmer and sold over the farm gate.

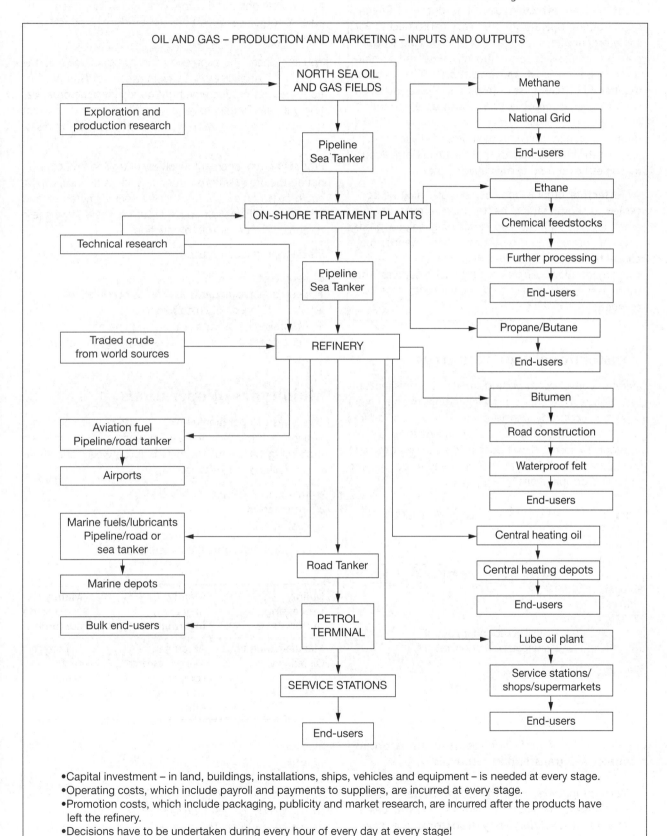

OIL AND GAS – PRODUCTION AND MARKETING – INPUTS AND OUTPUTS

- Capital investment – in land, buildings, installations, ships, vehicles and equipment – is needed at every stage.
- Operating costs, which include payroll and payments to suppliers, are incurred at every stage.
- Promotion costs, which include packaging, publicity and market research, are incurred after the products have left the refinery.
- Decisions have to be undertaken during every hour of every day at every stage!

Figure 42.1   The chain of production for oil and gas (courtesy of Shell Education Service)

Transforming your resources

Operations involves converting inputs into finished outputs. Figure 42.2 shows how operations management involves successfully transforming inputs into desired goods and services. (Note that there needs to be a feedback loop to ensure that if outputs do not conform with the required standards that changes need to be made to inputs and or operations.)

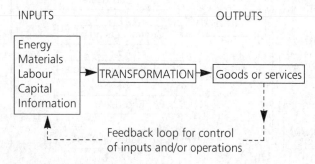

Figure 42.2   Transforming resources

We can make a distinction between **transforming resources** and **transformed resources**.

> *Your managers, employees, machinery and equipment are your transforming resources. The resources that they transform are the materials, and information which they process.*

Operations management

Organisations depend upon the management skills of their operations (production) managers. They need to be able to organise operations to produce products that satisfy consumers.

You may hear the expression that production is at the 'sharp end' of business activity. In other words, if production does not produce the right goods then the organisation will fail. Targets have to be met and standards kept up. Failure to meet targets and standards can be disastrous.

Production management involves controlling and co-ordinating the organisations resources such as finance, capital equipment, labour and other factors. Timetables and schedules will need to be set out to show how these resources will be used in production.

Efficient production sets out to:

- Keep costs to a minimum.
- Keep quality standards as high as possible.
- Meet the needs of customers.
- Maximise the use of plant and equipment.
- Keep down the level of stocks to the minimum requirement.

Main types of operations

The types of operations which an organisation carry out depend in a number of ways on what it is that they are processing. A useful distinction is between operations which focus on processing:

- materials
- information
- customers.

Figure 42.3 highlights this classification.

Mainly processing materials	Mainly processing information	Mainly processing customers
Manufacturing firms	Accountant	Hairdresser
Oil refinery	Market research company	Leisure centre
Post Office	Government statistical office	Hospital

Figure 42.3

You can see that the first two type of organisation would focus heavily on the logistics of efficiently converting inputs to outputs. This is a very technical process. The third type of organisation is far more likely to place most emphasis on service and face-to-face customer relations.

The Stadium at Twickenham, a finished example of job production

Methods of production

There are four production options for an organisation:

- **Job production** One job is completed at a time before moving on to the next. An example, might be the completion of an exclusive wedding dress for the Princess of Wales.
- **Batch production** This involves dividing the work into a number of different operations. Each operation is completed on the whole batch before moving on to the next. An example would be a batch of iced buns where each batch goes through several different baking stages.
- **Flow production** This involves mass production. Once work has been completed on one operation, the job moves on to the next without stopping. The production of bottled beer on a production line might be one example.
- **Just-in-time production** Just-in-time approaches involve producing and delivering goods just in time to be sold, partly-finished goods just in time to be assembled into finished goods, parts just in time to go into partly finished goods, and materials just in time to be made into parts.

Job production

Job, or 'make complete', production is the manufacture of single individual items by either one operative or a team of operatives. Ships and bridges are built this way. It is possible for a number of identical units to be produced in parallel under job production – for example, several ships of the same type. Smaller jobs can also be seen as a form of job production (e.g. writing this book, hand-knitting a sweater, rewiring a house). Job production is unique in that the project is considered to be a single operation which requires the complete attention of the operative before he or she passes on to the next job.

The benefits of job production are as follows:

- The job is a unique product which exactly matches the requirements of the customer, often from as early as the design stage. It will therefore tend to be specific to a customer's order and not in anticipation of a sale. For example, someone doing a customised spray job on a motorcycle will first discuss with a customer the sort of design he or she would like. A detailed sketch will then be produced on a piece of paper. Once the sketch has been approved, the back of the sketch will be traced on to the relevant piece of the motorbike. The background work will then be sprayed on with an airbrush before the fine detail is painted on. Finally, the finished work is handed over to the customer, who will pay for a unique product.
- As the work is concentrated on a specific unit, supervision and inspection of work are relatively simple.
- Specifications for the job can change during the course of production, depending on the customer's inspection, to meet his or her changing needs. For example, when a printing company is asked to produce a catalogue for a grocery chain, it is relatively simple to change the prices of some of the goods described in the catalogue.
- Working on a single unit job, coping with a variety of tasks and being part of a small team working towards the same aim provides employees with a greater sense of purpose.

There are however a number of problems:

- Labour, plant and machinery need to be versatile in order to adjust to a range of relatively specialised tasks associated with the same job. Trying to provide the right type of tools, equipment and labour to cope with such a range of specialised operations may be expensive.

- As job production is unique, costing is based on uncertain predictions of future costs and not on the experience of past events – for example, the Channel Tunnel project cost twice as much as originally forecast.
- Unit costs tend to be high, for example, there will be fewer economies such as bulk purchasing and the division of labour.

Batch production

The term 'batch' refers to a specific group of components which go through a production process together. As one batch finishes the next one starts. For example, on Monday machine A produces a type 1 engine part (for an aircraft engine), on Tuesday it produces a type 2 engine part, on Wednesday a type 3 engine part, and so on. All engine parts will then go forward to the final assembly of different categories of engine parts.

Batches are continually processed through each machine before moving on to the next operation. This method is sometimes referred to as 'intermittent' production, as different types of job are held as work-in progress between the various stages of production.

The benefits of batch production are:

- It is particularly suitable for a wide range of nearly similar goods which can use the same machinery on different settings.
- It economises on the range of machinery needed and reduces the need for a flexible workforce.
- Units can respond quickly to customer orders by moving buffer stocks, work-in-progress or partly-completed goods through the final production stages.
- It makes possible economies of scale in techniques of production, bulk purchasing and areas of organisation.
- It makes costing easy and provides a better information service for management.

Problems associated with batch production include:

- There are considerable organisational difficulties associated with batch production – for example, sequencing batches from one job to another to avoid building up excessive or idle stocks of work-in-progress is difficult in terms of routeing and scheduling.
- There is a time lag between an initial investment in material and its eventual transfer into cash upon the sale of a product.
- The time spent by staff on problems of paperwork, stock control and effective plant utilisation can be lengthy.

- Part of a batch has to be held waiting until the rest is completed before moving on to another stage.

Flow production

Batch production is described as 'intermittent' production and is characterised by irregularity. If the rest period in batch production disappeared, it would then become flow production. Flow production is a continuous process of parts passing on from one stage to another until completion. Units are worked on in each operation and then passed straight on to the next work stage without waiting for the batch to be completed. To make sure that the production line can work smoothly, each operation must be of equal length and there should be no movements or leakages from the line, for example, hold-ups to work-in-progress.

For flow production to be successful, there needs to be a continuity of demand. If demand is varied this will lead to a constant overstocking of finished goods (or periodic shortages, if the flow is kept at a low level). Apart from minor differences, all flow products need to be standardised as flow lines cannot deal with variations in the product.

Achieving a smooth flow of production requires considerable pre-production planning to ensure that raw materials are purchased and delivered on time, that sufficient labour is employed, that inspection procedures fit in with the process and that all operations take the required time.

Continuous flow production is an extension of line production. Today, in many organisations, the production line works 24 hours a day for six or more days a week, perhaps with one day being allocated to maintenance. Examples are food processing, and oil refineries. Maximum use is made of plant and operatives work shifts to ensure the continuous flow of products.

CASE STUDY CASE STUDY CASE

READY MEALS MANUFACTURE

Assume that on the lasagne line in a food factory a production level of 800 units per hour is required and that there are three stages in the process, requiring the use of machine A for stage 1, which can process 200 units per hour, machine B for stage 2, which can process 100 units per hour, and machine C for stage 3, which can process 400 units per hour. How can a balanced flow be established?

STUDY CASE STUDY CASE STUDY

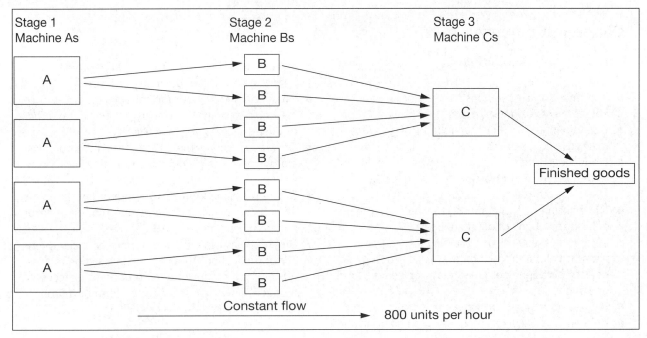

Figure 42.4   Flows in production

The benefits of flow production are:

- Labour costs will tend to be reduced as comprehensive planning and often investment will generate economies in both the type and numbers of those employed.
- Deviations in the line can be quickly identified.
- As there is no rest between operations, work-in-progress levels can be kept low.
- The need for storage space is minimal as there is no waiting period between processes.
- The physical handling of items is reduced.
- Investments in raw materials are more quickly converted into sales.

- As material and line requirements are easy to assess, weaknesses are highlighted and control is more effective.

There are, however, a number of problems:

- It is sometimes difficult to balance the output of one stage with the input of another, and operations may function at different speeds.
- Flow production requires constant work study.
- Providing a workforce with diverse skills to cater for circumstances such as cover for absence may be difficult and expensive, and regular absences can have far-reaching effects.
- Parts and raw materials need to arrive on time.
- Maintenance must be preventive to ensure that emergencies do not cause the flow to stop.
- If demand falters, over-stocking may occur.

Just-in-time manufacture

It is possible to argue that just-in-time manufacturing (JIT) should be regarded as a method of production in its own right. The authors certainly feel that it should be given this importance. We look at this method in greater detail in Chapter 43.

Chapter summary

- Every organisation exists to satisfy the needs of its customers.
- It is through its operations that the organisation is able to meet customers' needs.
- Operations involve the organisation of production methods and processes.
- Production is the process of using resources to add value to a product or a service in such a way as to effectively provide customers with benefits.
- The principles of operations management can be applied to a range of organisations.
- In meeting the needs of customers through production it is helpful to focus on the Six Os – occupants, object, occasions, organisations, objectives, and operations.
- Every product goes through a chain of production.
- Links in the chain of production are crucial and include links with suppliers, with customers and between activities inside an organisation.
- Organisations employ transforming resources such as employees and machinery to transform other resources such as raw materials.
- Operations management is concerned with organising operations to produce products that satisfy consumers.
- Different organisations place more or less emphasis on processing materials, processing information or processing customers.
- Organisations can employ a number of major methods of production. These are job production for 'one offs', batch production for groups or batches of products, flow production in the form of a production line, and just-in-time production.

43 The location and scale of production

One of the most important decisions affecting the success of a business organisation is its location:

- Local businesses need to decide on the best location within a particular town or area.
- National businesses need to decide on the best spot in a country.
- International companies often search all over the world for the right location.

In the late 1990s, we live in a world in which the revolutions in communications and information technology (IT) have transformed the ways in which organisations think about their marketplaces and what, when and where they will produce. We have moved into the global economy. Major multinationals can establish their production bases in those economies where relative costs are lowest. Today, it is relatively easy to set up a large-scale automated plant using all the latest technology, for example to produce garments, or components for cars. It makes little difference to the way the product is made whether it is located in Manchester, Milan, or Manila. The organisation therefore will seek to set up in locations where there is a ready supply of highly skilled and relatively cheap labour. Increasingly, areas such as the Pacific Rim provide suitable locations for setting up manufacturing operations. Not only do they provide a suitable production base, they are also close to a massive and growing market.

We have seen the growth of global corporations such as Tate and Lyle which operates nearly everywhere. Tate and Lyle has operations in Europe, Asia, Africa, North America, Australia and many other locations, producing not only sugar cane, but rum and corn, and engages in corn milling. From its roots in the heyday of British imperialism, the company has close ties with many emerging markets, which has allowed it to steal a lead on much of the competition. Wherever you find sugar production you are almost certain to find Tate and Lyle and of course its interests spill out into many related fields, for example, producing sticky syrups for drinks like Coca-Cola.

In 1991, Tate and Lyle made the decision to expand into industrialising countries. The rationale was simple (and mirrors that for many other major companies). The main markets – North America and Europe – were maturing and left little room for growth (particularly for a company like Tate and Lyle with a dominant market share). In contrast, newly-industrialised countries have younger populations, where, as national income grows, more money will fall into consumer pockets and then satisfy the local sweet tooth. For example, in Mexico 50 per cent of the population is under 15 years of age. It also has the highest per capita consumption of soft drinks in the world. Therefore Tate and Lyle has focused on producing sugar based syrups for Coca-Cola in Mexico. In a similar way, the company has moved in a big way into Vietnam and Zambia.

Most UK business could choose to be globally minded from the earliest days of the industrial revolution. (The British Empire helped!) Today, there is no choice. Businesses must be internationally minded or die. The market is global, there is virtually no other. Even small businesses serving a local community are measured by customers against the standards set internationally. In addition, key legislation on industry matters comes increasingly from Brussels rather than Westminster.

The location of the organisation

The location of the organisation will undoubtedly have a major effect on its performance. The problems of location are long-term and, clearly, decisions taken today have implications for tomorrow. For many smaller businesses, the problem is not so much one of location but of finding a site. For example, an owner who lives in one area may not wish to set up a business away from that locality. The local area may provide the entire market for a small local business such as that of a plumber, electrician or fast-food retailer. In contrast, large companies may have the world as their market, and numerous factors when taken together are capable of influencing any decision.

Whatever the type of business, the aim will be to locate in an area where the difference between benefits and costs is maximised. Important considerations will be the minimising of unit costs and maximising of outputs from given quantities of resources. Some of the important factors influencing the choice of location are considered below.

Transport costs

In situations where raw materials or finished goods are bulky, the transport costs are more significant. If the output of an industry is more expensive to transport than its input, it is a **bulk-increasing industry**, and is more likely to locate near to the market. For example, brewing tends to take place close to the market because of the expense of transporting the finished product.

However, if the raw materials are bulky and expensive to transport and the industry is a **bulk-decreasing industry**, it would be beneficial to locate near to raw materials. For example, historically the steel industry has located near to sources of coal, iron ore and limestone.

SYNTHESIS

Would you classify the following as bulk-increasing, or bulk-decreasing:

- *furniture manufacture*
- *food processing*
- *manufacture of heavy chemicals such as sulphuric acid*
- *soft drinks manufacture*
- *lavender distilling*
- *mustard manufacture?*

In practice, decisions are not as clear-cut as theory would indicate. Markets tend to be spread out and raw materials tend to come from a number of suppliers. The type of industry, the spread of the market, the availability of raw materials and their influence upon the costs of transport all have to be weighed against each other.

Integration with group companies

To **integrate** means to join together. A large organisation will wish to locate a factory where its work can be integrated with the work of other units in the same group. The ease with which it can integrate will influence its location. For example, if a large company is thinking about taking over a supplier of raw materials then it is far more likely to integrate with a supplier to which it is connected by fast and effective transport links than one which is remote and inaccessible.

Labour/housing

Labour and skills are more readily available in some areas than in others. Providing labour with incentives to move can be expensive and has had little success. Variations in house costs may also inhibit he mobility of labour. Often organisation will find it easier to move work to the workers than to try to encourage workers to move to the work.

Amenities

There are five standard amenities to be considered:

- gas
- electricity
- water
- waste disposal
- drainage.

For example, certain industries use considerable reserves of water such as for food preparation, metal plating and paper making; their use of water could exert considerable pressures on a local system. In the same way, the disposal of waste can be an expensive business. An assessment must be made of all these requirements, as underestimating the cost of amenities can be costly.

Land

Land costs will vary from area to area. In some circumstances the geology of the area needs to be considered (e.g. whether the land can support heavy buildings and plant). Climate may also affect the manufacturing process. For example, the Mars confectionery company occasionally has to shut down its Mars Bar production line in a very hot summer – it would not be wise to produce such a product in very high temperatures.

Local regulations may also affect certain types of activity and may need to be checked. Moreover, it would be unwise to build a factory that used up all the land available on a given site with no room for expansion. A large employer will also require parking spaces and have investigated access to land, etc.

Regional advantages

Locating in an area that contains similar businesses, suppliers and markets may be a considerable advantage. Local research facilities and commercial expertise may be of some use.

Safety requirements

Certain types of industry may be considered to be a danger or a nuisance to the local environment, for example, nuclear power stations, munitions factories or chemical plants. Locating such plants away from high-density population levels may be considered desirable.

Communications

Accessibility of ports, airports, and motorways has become an increasingly important factor over recent years. A good infrastructure will encourage industry to move to a region.

Government influences

High levels of unemployment in certain areas of the country have been a feature of the 1990s and are likely to continue into the next century. Governments look towards balanced economic and regional growth and provide incentives for organisations to move to identified areas.

CASE STUDY CASE STUDY CASE STUDY CASE STUDY CASE STUDY CASE

HIGH TECH OPERATIONS LTD

High Tech Operations Ltd is a company in the electrical components industry which is in the process of reviewing its present location at site D in Figure 43.1. A, B and C are three possible alternative locations for an electrical components factory.

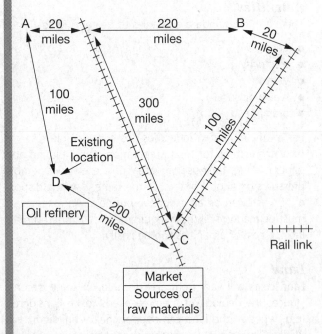

Figure 43.1   Alternative locations for an electrical components factory

The management at High Tech understands the need to take many factors into consideration when deciding on the most appropriate location. These factors include:

- cost of transporting finished goods to the market
- cost of transporting raw materials and oil supplies to the plant
- grants and other inducements available from the government
- labour costs
- removal costs.

The company will locate its plant at the point where all of these costs are minimised. Production costs are constant wherever the factory is located. The High Tech management needs to compare the costs involved, and then provide a recommendation. This can be done by calculating the costs of providing electrical components at each of the three alternative locations and comparing these with the costs of staying at the existing location. The preferred location will be the one with the lowest costs.

The market for components exists at location C, and locations A and B are eligible for government grants. For each 1,000 electrical components:

- Transporting oil costs £2 per mile by road and 50p per mile by rail.
- Transporting raw materials from C costs £4 per mile by road and 70p per mile by rail.
- Labour costs are £1,300 at A, £1,400 at B, £1,300 at C and £1,500 at D.
- Transporting finished goods to the market at C costs £5 per mile by road and £1 per mile by rail.

- Removal costs would be spread over 10 years and would be £1,000 per 1,000 units per annum.
- Government grants reduce costs by 20 per cent.

1 Work out the costs by copying out and filling in the table shown below:

	A £	B £	C £	D £
Oil transport costs				
Raw material transport costs				
Labour costs				
Finished goods transport costs				
Removal costs				
Effects of government grants				
Total cost per 1,000 units				

2 Find the lowest-cost location.
3 Production is forecast at 492,000 units for the next year. How much would moving to the lowest-cost location save in the first 12 months?
4 What additional information do you think would help the company in making a locational decision?
5 What factors are likely to alter, and thereby upset the calculations you have made?

CASE STUDY CASE STUDY CASE STUDY CASE STUDY CASE STUDY CASE

Wherever a factory locates, there will be certain limiting factors to the choice of site. For example, a chemical plant needs to be near vast sources of water; a large engineering workshop will need to be close to its labour force; an ice cream seller needs to be close to customers. Choosing a site means taking a number of relevant factors into consideration and attempting to weigh them in relation to each other. Sometimes a ranking technique which gives appropriate weights to relevant factors can be helpful. Using this technique, factors affecting location are assigned weight relative to their importance and each location is examined and ranked in terms of the factors. When ranks have been multiplied by the weighting factor and the scores totalled, the desirably of locations can be compared.

An example, of such a comparison is given in Figure 43.2. The rank attached to the relative importance of each locational factor for each location appears in the top left-hand corner of each cell, and the rank multiplied by the weight appears underneath the diagonal. Location D is shown as the most desirable location using the method.

Factor	Weight	Possible location			
		A	B	C	D
Transport	7	1 / 7	2 / 14	3 / 21	4 / 28
Integration with group	2	4 / 8	3 / 6	1 / 2	2 / 4
Amenities	4	1 / 4	2 / 8	3 / 12	4 / 16
Land	2	1 / 2	3 / 6	2 / 4	4 / 8
Regional advantages	3	2 / 6	3 / 9	1 / 3	4 / 12
Communications	6	4 / 24	2 / 12	3 / 18	1 / 6
Government grants	2	1 / 2	2 / 4	3 / 6	4 / 8
Totals		53	59	66	82

Figure 43.2   Possible factory location by rank and weight (Note that for each criteria the most favourable location is given a ranking of 4.)

CASE STUDY CASE STUDY CASE STUDY CASE STUDY CASE STUDY CASE

FORD SET TO IMPOSE HUGE JOB CUTS AT HALEWOOD

For many years Ford's Halewood plant was at the centre of its European operations. In particular, the plant was associated with the production of the Ford Escort which until the mid-1990s was the UK's most popular car. However, in 1997 Ford decided to cut back on production at Ford with the likelihood that the long-term future of the plant is in jeopardy.

With the rise of new car manufacturers and products throughout the world Ford's share of the market has been falling. Currently, it has three plants in Europe – Halewood, Saarlouis in Germany and Valencia in Spain. However, it is the latter two that have been assured that they will be producing the new Escort due to be launched in 1998.

On recent figures, Ford is only in a position to sustain two of its plants in Europe and the Spanish and German plants are closer to the core European markets. In addition, the cost of transporting components to Halewood (Liverpool) are higher than to the other two locations. Moreover, the plant and equipment at Halewood are less up-to-date so that productivity per labour hour is lower than in the other two European locations. Moreover, sales have been particularly badly hit in the UK which has increasingly become the base for Japanese and other Far Eastern manufacturers.

Ford's vehicle production in Britain has

declined from 635,000 in 1979 to less than 400,000 in 1996, while employment at the company's plants in the UK dropped in the same period from 75,000 to 30,000. Employment levels in Germany have remained level at around 50,000.

1 What factors do you see as being most significant in locating a car plant?
2 Why have Japanese car manufacturers located their production in the UK in recent times?
3 Why has Halewood become progressively less attractive as the site for a Ford car plant?

CASE STUDY CASE STUDY CASE STUDY CASE STUDY CASE STUDY CASE

The size of the organisation

Organisations can gain many operational benefits from producing goods on a large scale. Whereas bridges and submarines will never be mass produced, the vast majority of everyday consumer goods can be.

The scale or size of production is usually measured by the number of units produced over a period of time. If the scale of production increases, average unit costs over most production ranges are likely to fall because the company will benefit from **economies of scale** (the advantages gained from being larger). All businesses will aim for the scale of production that suits their line of work best, and this will be achieved when unit costs are at their lowest for the output produced. Beyond this point a company will start to find that inefficiencies push average costs up, and **diseconomies of scale** (i.e. the advantages of growing too large) set in.

If output increases faster than the rate of inputs, average unit costs will be falling and a company is said to be benefiting from increasing returns to scale. Beyond the point at which average unit costs are at their lowest, the increase in output will be less than the increase in input, so that average unit costs are pushed up and the company is suffering from decreasing returns to scale (see Figure 43.3).

If, as the organisation becomes larger, it manages to organise its production more efficiently, it is benefiting from **internal economies of scale**. If the company is a member of an industry that is growing, benefits will be felt outside the individual organisation, i.e. by all the companies in an industry, and these are known as **external economies of scale**.

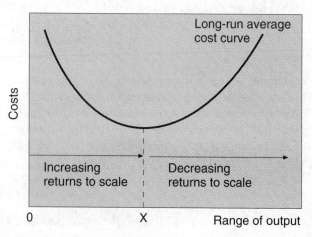

Figure 43.3   *Returns to scale*

In recent years in this country there has been a move away from very large-scale organisations. Instead there is a move to leaner more flexible organisations. Of course some people have always believed that 'small is beautiful'.

Alfred Schumacher in his book *Small is Beautiful* (Abacus, 1973) argued that:

> *'What is the meaning of democracy, freedom, human dignity, standard of living, self-realisation, fulfilment? Is it a matter of goods or of people? Of course, it is a matter of people. But people can only be themselves in small comprehensive groups. Therefore we must learn to think in terms of an articulate culture that can cope with a multiplicity of small scale units. If economic thinking cannot grasp that, it is useless. If it cannot get beyond its vast abstractions, the national income, the rate of growth, capital-output ratios, input/output analysis, labour mobility, capital accumulation, if it cannot get behind all of this and make contact with human realities, of poverty, frustration, alienation, despair, breakdown, crime, escapism, stress, congestion, ugliness and spiritual death, then let us scrap economics and start afresh.'*

Internal economies

Technical economies

Large organisations use techniques and equipment that cannot be adopted by small-scale producers. For example, a company might have four machines each producing 1,000 units per week at a unit cost of £2; as the company becomes larger these could be replaced by one machine that can produce 5,000 units per week at the lower unit cost of £1.75. If small companies tried to use such specialised machinery their costs would be excessive, and the machines might become obsolete before the end of their physical life.

That the economic lifespan of a machine may be shorter than its physical life because demand for the goods produced by the machine can diminish before the machine wears out.

An essential by-product of higher-tech operations is that processes are simplified and standardised so that cost reductions can be made in other areas, for example, labour.

Labour and managerial economies

In larger organisations, highly-skilled workers can be employed in jobs that fully utilise their specialised skills, whereas in a small business unit they may have to be 'Jacks of all trades'. The division of labour possible in a larger organisation therefore avoids the time-wasting element caused by the constant need to switch from one type of job to another. In the same way, a larger company can employ a number of highly specialised members on its management team, such as accountants, marketing managers and personnel managers, in the hope that the improved quality of work and of decisions made by this more qualified workforce will reduce overall unit costs.

Commercial economies

Larger organisations obtain considerable benefits in the commercial world. They can gain enormously by devoting more resources to market research and the development of new products. Raw materials can be purchased in bulk so that large discounts and extended credit periods can be negotiated. Larger companies may be able to organise their retail outlets or to have a financial stake in their suppliers, and thus can collect profit at the various stages of production. Overheads such as rent and rates can be spread over a larger output. Goods can be distributed via a network of warehouses rather than at one central store, and carefully targeted advertising can be spread over a wider marketplace.

Financial economies

As larger companies tend to present a more secure investment, they find it easier to raise finance, are frequently treated more favourably by the banks and are in a better position to negotiate loans with preferential interest rates. For example, during the last recession many small businesses complained at the treatment they were receiving from the banks. A further financial advantage to large companies is their ability to raise capital by issuing new shares on the Stock Exchange.

BRITISH BOOK PUBLISHING PLC

In recent years, British Book Publishing PLC has grown through a rapid expansion programme to become one of the biggest book publishers in London and the South-East of England. The figures shown in Figure 43.4 have been extracted from its most recent financial statements. How do these figures illustrate economies of scale?

	1994	1995	1996	1997
Yearly output ('000)	300.00	450.00	525.00	615.00
Number of machines	8.00	10.00	12.00	13.00
Number of employees	175.00	182.00	190.00	194.00
Number of products	14.00	27.00	38.00	51.00
Cost of manufacture per publication (£)	3.20	3.10	2.90	2.00

Figure 43.4   Extract from financial statement

External economies

In many industries, the reduction of average unit costs and the benefits of internal economies of scale will depend upon the ability of a company to increase the length of production runs, introduce mass production and standardisation techniques, and increase the output capacity of the industry as a whole. This could lead to the following economies of scale.

Concentration

A concentration of special benefits builds up as companies within an industry concentrate in a particular area. These benefits may include: a skilled workforce, the reputation of an area for high-quality work, local college courses tailored to the needs of that particular industry, and better social amenities.

Information

Larger industries often set up information services designed to benefit all producers in that industry, such as the Motor Industry Research Association.

Disintegration

Companies producing components or supplying specialist machinery might well be attracted to areas of specialised industries, along with companies that are able to help with maintenance and processes.

EXAM TIP:

Internal economies take place within a company or organisation, external economies take place within a whole industry or region including benefiting a number of companies or organisations.

Organic growth

Organisations can obtain the benefits of economies of scale through a gradual build-up of their business, through acquiring assets, developing products and/or expanding sales. Organic growth of this kind, however, is often a slow process.

Mergers or take-overs

A quicker and more dynamic form of growth is through mergers or takeovers, which involve the integration of a number of business units under a single umbrella organisation. In addition to enjoying the benefits of being larger, the new organisation will have a larger market share, will probably be more competitive in export markets and, depending on the type of merger, could be in a position to control raw material supplies or the sales of finished products.

Sometimes the easiest way to achieve larger scale production is to merge. This brings financial and marketing economies of scale. First, the many small producers which set up the motor industry in the UK amalgamated, more recently Ford took over Jaguar and BMW took over Rover.

A **horizontal merger** takes place when two companies producing goods of a similar type at the same stage of production join together. A **vertical merger** takes place when two companies producing goods of a similar type at different stages of production join together. **Backward vertical integration** involves the take-over of a supplier, and **forward vertical integration** involves joining with a company at a later stage of production.

It is common practice today for organisations in industries that are only loosely connected to join together in order to maximise risk-bearing economies. For example, a company producing toothpaste may join together with a soap manufacturer in order to benefit from similar channels of distribution (e.g. supermarkets and chemists).

TASK 43.1

Study the financial pages of newspapers and professional business magazines and make a list of some of the recent mergers and acquisitions of larger companies. Find out about the main trading activities of the companies involved and comment on whether the mergers were horizontal, vertical or lateral. What motivations would you expect to lie behind each merger?

Diseconomies of scale

IT'S A FACT

That one of the major failings of businesses is over-trading. In other words, they try to get too big too quickly. People who have experienced modest success see themselves as the next Richard Branson or Anita Roddick. They therefore try to expand their businesses too quickly. They over-trade and quickly run into cash flow and organisation problems.

One of the dangers that companies face when they become large is that the optimum size for the business could be exceeded. Large organisations are considerably more difficult to manage, and these inefficiencies are known as **diseconomies of scale**.

Diseconomies include the following:

- **Human relations** Larger numbers of employees are always more difficult to organise. It can be difficult to communicate information, and instructions that need to be passed down long chains of command reduce the personal contact between decision makers and staff. This can lead to a low level of morale, lack of motivation and ultimately industrial relations problems. Larger organisations tend to have more industrial disputes than smaller organisations.

- **Decisions and co-ordination** The sheer scale of production may limit the management's ability to respond to change and make good decisions. With a large hierarchy, both the quality of the information reaching the decision maker and the quality of the instructions passed on could be affected. Difficulties arising from discussions could involve considerable paperwork and many meetings.

- **External diseconomies** In recent years, many consumers have become more discerning about both the quality of product they purchase and the activities of certain organisations. Public displeasure can ultimately lead to some form of consumer boycott. For example, some consumers boycotted tuna fish unless it was 'dolphin-friendly'. Consumers sometimes form groups to represent their interests such as CAMRA, the CAMpaign for Real Ale.

Not only is the existence of small businesses necessary because of diseconomies of scale, they also obtain many separate and vital economic advantages. Small businesses have the flexibility to respond quickly to market opportunities. Small companies often specialise and so contribute towards divisions of labour within the wider productive process. Relations with both employers and customers tend to be good and, although specialists may not be employed on a full-time basis, consultants may be called in as and when required.

Clearly, some industries will suit a larger-scale organisation better than others. A business needs to look carefully at the effects of size upon its cost structure before deciding on the most appropriate scale. There may be little scope for economies of scale because of limited demand (the small corner shop, for example, may cater for a very local demand); or the product may be highly specialised, as in the case of the market for 'customised' motor bikes.

Chapter summary

- One of the most important decisions affecting a business is its location. Organisations will seek their most effective location taking a number of factors into account such as transport and labour costs.
- Increasingly, large multinational organisations are choosing to set up where labour costs are relatively low. It is relatively easy to set up a large modern automated plant anywhere in the world.
- Bulk-increasing industries tend to set up close to their markets, whereas bulk-reducing industries will set up closer to their raw material supplies.
- The government plays a role in influencing some locational decisions. For example, government incentives have helped to attract some foreign multinationals to the UK.
- Organisations can gain many operational advantages from producing on a large scale.
- Economies of scale enable a company to spread its costs over a large output making possible the production of large outputs at low unit costs.
- Diseconomies of scale set in when companies are too large leading to a rise in costs.

- In today's competitive environment, companies are downsizing because the optimum scale of production is getting smaller. The use of IT enables companies to operate efficiently at a smaller size than in the past.
- Internal economies are advantages from the growth of an individual company or plant to a large scale.
- Technical economies enable large companies to use better techniques and methods to produce goods.
- Other internal economies of scale are marketing, commercial, financial and managerial economies.
- External economies benefit all the companies in a particular industry or region from the growth of that industry or region.
- Companies can grow organically, i.e. by the natural growth of the company, for example, by ploughing back profits into expansion and the purchase of new plant and equipment.
- Companies can also grow by merger and acquisition.
- Companies can grow too big too quickly. Diseconomies of scale can set in raising the unit cost of production.

44 Production efficiency

All organisations seek to be productive. Being productive means using resources efficiently and effectively in order to add value in the production process in the best way possible. The organisation that is not particularly good at adding value will quickly lose any competitive edge that it might have.

Measuring efficiency

It is important to be able to measure productive efficiency. By doing so you are able to:

- Identify inefficiencies and cut them back.
- Identify areas for improvement.
- Analyse how effectively you are using your resources.
- Make comparisons of productivity within an organisation.
- Make comparisons between organisations.
- Establish clear plans and targets for improving efficiency.

Productivity can be looked at as the relationship between costs or inputs (e.g. people, marketing, materials, finance, distribution) and the revenue from outputs (e.g. income from sales, repeat sales, continuity of sales).

A productive system can be thought of a whole economy (e.g. the UK economic system) or other systems (e.g. an organisation or plant), or sub-systems (e.g. units in a plant). The productivity of the system is the amount of output that can be produced from a given set of inputs:

$$\text{Productivity} = \frac{\text{Output}}{\text{Input}} \quad \text{or} \quad \frac{\text{Results achieved}}{\text{Resources consumed}}$$

The productivity ratio therefore measures how efficient a system is in converting inputs of resources into useful outputs.

IT'S A FACT

That in the 1970s, the UK car industry was notorious for inefficiency because efficiency was not monitored in a systematic way. For example, there were numerous stories in the press of employees playing cards or sleeping through complete night shifts without anyone finding out. There was a failure to monitor the efficiency of particular units.

Increases in productivity can be gained by:

- Output increasing while input remains the same.
- Output increasing while input increases at a slower rate.

- Output staying the same while input decreases.
- Output falling while input falls at a faster rate.

Measuring the productivity of labour

If we wanted to find out how productive the employees in a food-processing plant were, we could do so by studying the following ratio:

Productivity =

$$\frac{\text{Number of units of goods produced per month}}{\text{Average number of people employed per month}}$$

TASK 44.1

Figure 44.1 shows changes in the productivity of labour in a car factory during a particular year.

	Jan	Feb	Mar	Apr	May	June	July	Aug	Sept	Oct	Nov	Dec
Total output (000s)	5.2	5.3	5.4	5.4	5.4	5.3	5.3	5.2	5.2	5.1	5.0	5.0
Average number of employees	110	120	120	115	100	100	98	98	95	95	90	85

Figure 44.1

PRODUCTION EFFICIENCY IN OIL REFINING

An oil refinery, where crude oil is turned into the products that people want

The oil industry provides a good example of the importance of production efficiency. The refinery is the oil company's 'factory' where the crude oil is turned into the products that people want – fuels, greases, waxes, bitumen, base oils for lubricants, and chemical feedstocks for use by companies manufacturing paint detergents, pharmaceuticals and plastics. In other words, 'refining' to an oil company is what 'manufacturing' is to most others.

Refinery = Factory

The basic aim is to turn the crude oil into the most valuable product as efficiently as possible and with minimum waste.

The refinery must convert more of each barrel of crude oil into the lighter 'whiter' oil products – such as petrol and aviation fuel – for which the market is prepared to pay more, rather than the 'black' products, such as fuel oils.

1 How could you measure production efficiency in an oil refinery?
2 How could this efficiency be increased?

1 Set out a graph which shows changes in labour productivity during the period.
2 Explain and analyse the changes that you can observe in productivity over the period.

Multifactor productivity ratios

Outputs are not produced by labour alone; we also need to take account of machinery and raw materials. A **multifactor productivity ratio** like the one shown below takes into account other inputs:

$$\text{Productivity} = \frac{\text{Output}}{\text{Labour} + \text{Materials} + \text{Fixed assets}}$$

In the real world, the most common calculation made is for labour productivity. This is because labour is the most commonly used factor of production. Industries that use a great deal of labour are said to be **labour-intensive**.

Today, however, with the introduction of new technology, capital is becoming more and more intensive. Many new industries are employing more and more capital – that is, they are becoming increasingly **capital-intensive**. Value can be added to products by switching to high-tech capital equipment which is far more productive than traditional methods. High outputs can be produced at much lower unit costs.

Figure 44.2 shows how the breakdown of manufacturing costs has altered between the year 1930 and 1997.

FIG 42.2

Factor	Weight	Possible location			
		A	B	C	D
Transport	7	1 / 7	2 / 14	3 / 21	4 / 28
Integration with group	2	4 / 8	3 / 6	1 / 2	2 / 4
Amenities	4	1 / 4	2 / 8	3 / 12	4 / 16
Land	2	1 / 2	3 / 6	2 / 4	4 / 8
Regional advantages	3	2 / 6	3 / 9	1 / 3	4 / 12
Communications	6	4 / 24	2 / 12	3 / 18	1 / 6
Government grants	2	1 / 2	2 / 4	3 / 6	4 / 8
	Totals	53	59	66	82

Figure 44.2   The breakdown of manufacturing costs

Measuring productivity over time

It is important to be able to monitor productivity trends over a time period to see whether an organisation is becoming more efficient or less efficient. Clearly, if a company increases the training of its workforce, increases the automation of its plant, or successfully reorganises the production process, it will expect to see an increasing productivity ratio. This can be tracked over time. Value is thus added through increasing productivity because revenues can be added to at a quicker rate than costs rise.

$$\text{Productivity index} = \frac{\text{Productivity ratio in time period}}{\text{Productivity ratio in base year}} \times 100$$

Measuring productivity of inputs by value

As we have already seen, it is possible to measure productivity by value. For example, we can use a multifactor measure of productivity:

$$\text{Productivity} = \frac{\text{Sales revenue}}{\text{Labour} + \text{Materials} + \text{Overheads}}$$

This can be broken down further to measure the productivity of particular inputs:

$$\text{Labour productivity} = \frac{\text{Sales revenue}}{\text{Wages}}$$

Alternatively:

$$\text{Labour productivity} = \frac{\text{Output (£ value)}}{\text{Labour hours (or costs)}}$$

$$\text{Capital productivity} = \frac{\text{Sales revenue}}{\text{Value of capital items}}$$

$$\text{Materials productivity} = \frac{\text{Sales Revenue}}{\text{Value of materials used}}$$

Recently, another measure of performance has become popular which is based on added value. **Added value** can be calculated by deducting material and outside service costs from sales revenue. You can then create an added value index:

$$\begin{array}{c}\text{Added value index} \\ \text{(AVI)}\end{array} = \frac{\text{Total employment costs}}{\text{Added value}}$$

New ways of measuring efficiency

The student will be aware that in recent times organisations have created a whole range of new efficiency measures, for example, in privatised industries, private sector companies, and even in the health service and education.

A team of researchers headed by Slack (*Operations Management*, Pitman, 1995) has identified the following as five major performance objectives:

Doing things fast – the speed advantage
Doing things on time – the dependability advantage
Doing things cheap – the cost advantage
Changing what you do – the flexibility advantage
Doing things right – the quality advantage.

The speed advantage

This can be measured in a variety of ways, for example, the speed with which customer complaints are handled or the speed with which customer orders are handled. We will explore the just-in-time approach below; this is one way of ensuring that the steps in the production process are put into place at just the right time.

> ## SYNTHESIS
>
> **What indicators of speed could be used to measure the success of:**
> **a a transport system**
> **b a department store**

The dependability advantage

This is concerned with making sure that things are done in time for the customer. If a customer's requirements are met in a dependable way then there will be less room for error and time wasting in sorting out mistakes. For example, in a supermarket dependability would consist of making sure that the supermarket opens and closes on time, that staff are at the check-outs when required and that goods are not out of stock.

The cost advantage

This is perhaps the most important advantage in that all the other types of advantages will help to drive down costs. Key areas of cost advantage relate to:

- employee costs
- technology, facilities and equipment costs
- materials and bought-in services costs.

The flexibility advantage

Flexibility is concerned with the ability to change operations, for example:

- by offering different products or services
- by offering a wider range of products or services
- by offering different volumes of products or services
- by altering delivery patterns and times.

The quality advantage

Quality is concerned with ensuring that products and services conform with customer requirements so that customers are delighted with what they receive. Quality can be measured by such indicators as customer satisfaction levels.

The five Ps of production

Production activities vary considerably depending on the product, but there are a number of components which are common to all forms of production. Together these make up the so-called 'five Ps of production':

- product
- plant
- people
- process
- programme.

The product

It is essential to provide a good or service that clearly meets the needs of consumers and that can be provided for them at the right place, at the right time and for the most attractive price.

The plant

In order to add value to a product or service, companies nearly always needs some form of plant or base.

The location, size, design, safety and layout of the plant are all very important. Managers need to think carefully about how parts and materials are to be delivered, and how finished goods will be transported away from the plant. The layout should make it easy to co-ordinate the various activities that will take place there. Time and costs involved in transferring goods, materials, information and people should be kept to a minimum.

Managers must also make sure that plant and equipment are properly maintained. A maintenance department may include electricians, plumbers and joiners, as well as many other skilled workers. The effectiveness of the maintenance department can be judged by the number of breakdowns and accidents at work. Safety is vitally important.

The process

The process is very important. Different organisations will have different sets of operations depending on the nature of the product they make, the type of plant and equipment employed and many other factors. Process management sets out to:

- Identify the key processes of business activity. If these are carried out properly it will be possible to maximise customer satisfaction thus leading to better financial performance.
- Develop a detailed understanding of how processes work.
- Identify who in the organisation is involved in these processes.
- Seek ongoing improvements in the management of these processes.
- Set in motion an ongoing cycle of continuous process improvement.

The programme

Programming is mainly concerned with timetabling the use of resources. To meet orders successfully, the organisation will need to plan and control activities carefully. Successful programming involves purchasing, stock control and quality control.

The people

The success of any production process will depend on the people involved. The quality of people depends on how much is invested in them. Training and development are vital.

The design and layout of plant and equipment

An important aspect of efficient production is the organisation of plant. The design of a plant and the positioning of equipment should enable it to function smoothly. Although designing the layout is normally a work-study problem, it needs to be carried out with specialist engineers who are concerned with factors such as the structure of the plant, power availability, maintenance requirements and so on.

Plant layout tends to follow one of a number of basic designs. But whatever techniques are used in setting up a layout, the aim must be to maximise flexibility and ease of co-ordination so that process time and costs will be minimised.

Product or line layout

Plant is laid out according to the requirements of the product in a line of production. Products 'flow' from one machine or stage to another. Control is simplified as paper work, material handling and inspection procedures are reduced (see Figure 44.3).

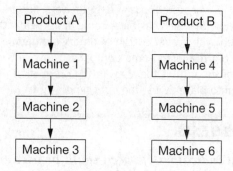

Figure 44.3   Product layout

Function or process layout

All operations of the same type are performed in the same area; for example, spot welding may be in one location, riveting in another and stapling in a third. It is rather like the provision of a centralised print service or word-processing pool. Although this system is flexible, considerable pre-production planning is necessary to ensure that machines are neither overloaded nor idle (see Figure 44.4).

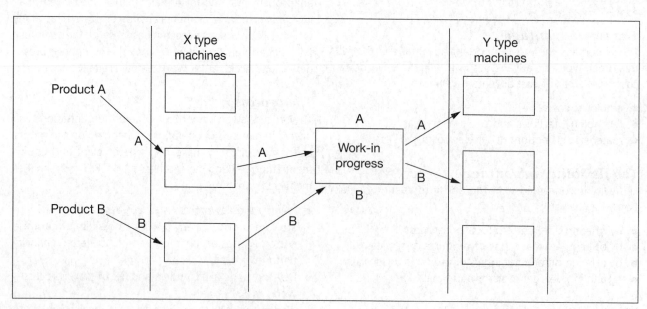

Figure 44.4   Process layout

Layout by fixed position

Operations are performed with the material or part-finished good returning to a fixed position after each process (see Figure 44.5).

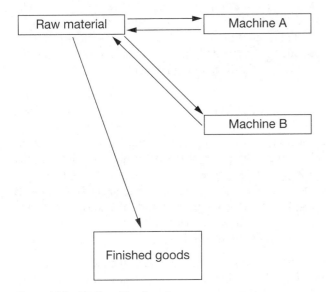

Figure 44.5   Fixed position layout

Performance, maintenance and safety of the plant

The justification for expenditure on new equipment is that it contributes towards the quality of goods and services being provided. Before equipment is bought, the general effects upon the organisation have to be evaluated and standard capital appraisal techniques have to be applied to find out if such changes will be worthwhile.

It is the duty of an employer to remove all possible causes of accidents. Accident can cause time to be lost by the unfortunate employee, other employees and supervisory staff. An accident can damage equipment, interfere with production schedules and lead to compensation payments. Employers need to anticipate circumstances likely to lead to such accidents, to try and eliminate hazards and to train staff in good production practices.

The importance of process management

Organisations should seek to identify those processes which are central to customer satisfaction and to the success of the organisation. It is helpful to identify a relatively short list.

The sorts of processes which an organisation might identify as being essential will include:

- identifying consumer needs and requirements
- finding new business

- developing new products
- invoicing customers
- processing orders
- developing an efficient value chain
- developing managers.

IT'S A FACT

That IBM has identified 13 key processes which are central to its success.

Traditionally organisations tended to allocate responsibilities for each of these areas to specialist functions. For example, identifying customer requirements and needs would have been the province of the marketing department; invoicing of customers would have been the responsibility of finance, and so on.

The problem with such an approach is that accountability rests with particular functional specialists. The reality, however, is that the process is often carried out by a range of people across the organisation. If people are only working hard at those things that they are accountable for then they may neglect other areas. Elements of a 'blame culture' may develop – for example, 'that's not my responsibility it's yours'.

Effective process management therefore might involve identifying processes, who is involved in the process, and then ensuring that there is a shared accountability for making sure that the process is carried out effectively. Instead of people in an organisation being responsible for a functional specialism they become responsible for processes. This is the heart of successful process management.

Process management involves identifying who is involved in the process and drawing out a detailed picture of events from start to finish. It is then necessary to bring together all the participants in the process so that they can work together to outline ways of making the process more efficient.

TASK 44.2

Can you identify a process, or set of processes in an organisation that you are familiar with? Describe this process and who is involved in the process. How would you go about making sure that everyone involved in the process is accountable for its success?

Simplification, standardisation and specialisation

Production variety is inevitable within all industrial units. While variety is clearly sometimes desirable, increases in variety are bound to add to organisational problems. For example, an increase in the number of component types will require more space in the stores. Control of variety is essential in reducing storage space, the number of production runs, types of machines and production aids, and in making production control easier.

As firms move towards specialisation, opportunities exist for mass production. **Mass production** is the production of goods on a large scale. It usually follows that the greater the volume of mass production, the greater the benefits of economies of scale as the company moves towards its lowest unit cost size.

The operations planning and control department

Operations managers are frequently responsible for a major part of an organisation's assets, and thus have responsibility for a substantial budget. It is important therefore for operations managers to have a good understanding of finance and financial control.

Operations managers make important decisions about:

- the process, and how processes will be organised (e.g. technology employed, layout)
- capacity – forecasting demand, and how demand will

be met using plant; this will involve project planning
- inventories – making sure that there is a steady flow of stocks of the right type to ensure a steady flow of production
- people – making sure that there are the right people, in the right place at the right time with the right skills and motivation
- quality – ensuring continuous improvement and satisfaction of consumer requirements.

Much of production planning and control will be concerned with the organisation's plans for the future and needs to be carefully tied in with marketing planning. Decision making ranges from long-term issues, such as making sure that the organisation has the right capacity next year and in five years' time, through to medium-term issues such as having the right machinery and materials supplies, to short-range and current issues such as the organisation of labour and other resources to carry out current production schedules.

The operations controller has one of the most difficult jobs in any organisation. He or she needs to understand fully the organisation of production processes and costing and administrative procedures, and will need to use mathematical techniques to solve problems.

CASE STUDY CASE STUDY CASE STUDY CASE STUDY CASE STUDY CASE

JUST-IN-TIME PRODUCTION

Just-in-time (JIT) can be seen as an important modern method of production. JIT manufacturing is one of the strengths of the Japanese production system and is one which enabled Japan to have a highly-productive economy. It is not surprising that it has been so widely copied by modern manufacturers.

JIT is a very simple idea:

- Finished goods are produced just in time for them to be sold, rather than weeks or months ahead.
- The parts that go into a finished product arrive just in time to be put together to make the final product, rather than being stored (at some cost) in a warehouse.

The idea is to run a company with the smallest possible levels of stock and work-in-progress. Clearly this needs careful planning:

- All sources of uncertainty must be removed from the manufacturing process. There must be absolute reliability of

production targets, supplies, and levels of output achieved.
- The time to set up machines must be reduced to a minimum so that components and finished products can be produced in small batches as and when required.
- Bottlenecks must be eliminated.

Using a JIT system requires a complete re-organisation of the traditional factory. Factories have traditionally been organised into 'shops', each working at a particular stage in producing a final product. With a JIT system the factory is re-organised so that people are grouped together around the products they produce. They may need to have access to a family of machines (e.g. a lathe, a milling machine, a drill and a grinder) – see Figure 44.6.

A recent survey has shown that two-thirds of Western manufacturing companies are trying to use JIT. However, the ability to make JIT successful may depend on the organisation and environment in which the idea is applied.

1 What do you see as being the major strengths of the JIT system?
2 What do you see as being its major weaknesses?
3 The Kobe earthquake in 1995 led some Japanese to question over-reliance on JIT. Why do you think they might have had these reservations?
4 How applicable do you think that JIT is to UK industry?

Factory using old methods

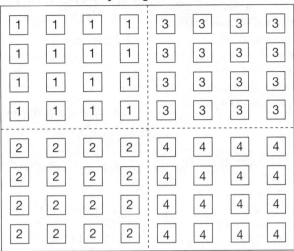

Factory using JIT

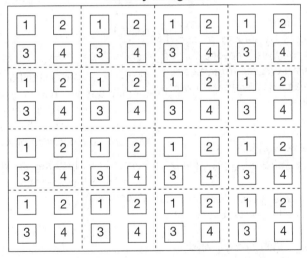

1=Lathe 2=Milling machine 3=Drill 4=Grinder

Figure 44.6   Adopting the JIT system

The programme

Programming is essentially concerned with timetabling the resources used by the production department. Much of its success will depend on the abilities of the production planning and control department, whose staff will set dates and timetables for the delivery of finished products and will plan operations to meet these targets. Delivery timetables will require further timetables in areas such as purchasing, stock control and quality control.

Purchasing

Procuring materials is a key management function for any type of business.

The purchasing department will aim to provide the company with a steady flow of materials and services while at the same time ensuring a continuity of supplies. It will aim to obtain the best value for money and will try to provide the best service for a low cost. The use of value analysis often makes it possible for considerable savings to be made, though a particular danger is that quality could be sacrificed to cost considerations.

For example, if designers were left free to operate without cost control guidelines, they would be sure to produce components of a higher quality than were needed for a particular task. This would be costly and fail to give consumers value for money. A team is therefore drawn together to create 'value for money'.

The team could consist of:

- a designer – for knowledge of the product
- a member of the sales team – for knowledge of the market
- a production engineer – for knowledge of operations
- a member of the work-study staff – for experience of efficient working procedures
- a financial specialist – for knowledge of cost analysis
- a buyer – for knowledge of sources of supply.

A successful purchasing department will keep its costs down, produce a fast stock turnover, reduce obsolescence, ensure a continuity of supplies and reduce lead times (the interval between the identification of a need and its ultimate fulfilment upon delivery).

Stock control

In an ideal world, in which businesses know demand well in advance and suppliers always meet delivery dates, there would be little need for stocks. In practice, demand varies and suppliers are often late, so stocks act as a protection against unpredictable events.

Organisations hold stocks in a variety of forms:

- raw materials

- work-in-progress
- finished goods
- consumables
- plant and machinery spares.

The aim of any stock control system is to provide stocks that cater for uncertainties but are at minimum levels, thus making sure that costs are kept low without reducing service to customers.

Balancing stock levels is essential. Having too few or too much stock can be harmful to a business. High stock levels represent money lying idle, whereas low stock levels might mean that the business can't fulfil its orders.

Figure 44.7 shows the impact of having the wrong stock levels.

Problems of low stocks	Problems of high stocks
Difficult to satisfy consumer requirements. Potential loss of business. Potential loss of goodwill. Ordering needs to be frequent and handling costs rise.	Increased risk of stock becoming obsolete. Increased risk of stock losses. High storage costs. Stocks tie up working capital.

Figure 44.7

Buffer stocks can be built up as a protection against stocks running out owing to unexpected variations in demand. A minimum level will be set below which it will be hoped that stocks will not fall, although this may depend upon the lead time between placing an order and its receipt.

Figure 44.8 illustrates an ideal situation in which stocks never fall below the set minimum level or go above the set maximum level.

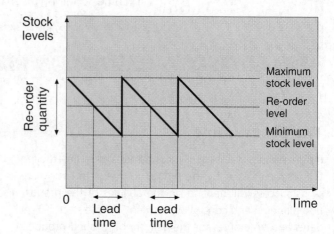

Figure 44.8   Managing stock level

Stocks are replenished just at the point at which the minimum stock level is about to be breached. In reality, delivery times, re-order quantities and rates of usage will vary, and either a continuous or periodic review system will monitor and control the levels.

At regular intervals, stock is counted and accurately recorded so that trading results can be calculated. The physical counting of stock can be time-consuming and it is inevitable that inaccuracies will creep in. After stock is counted it is checked against records so that discrepancies can be investigated.

CASE STUDY CASE STUDY CASE STUDY CASE STUDY CASE STUDY CASE

CREATING EFFICIENCY – LEAN PRODUCTION

The notion of lean production has been popularised in the late 1990s. Its chief exponents are James P Womack and Daniel T Jones (*Lean Thinking*, Simon and Schuster, 1996). The emphasis is on getting more from less and cutting down on waste. Much of the approach draws on the experience of Japanese business organisations such as Toyota, but the authors feel that the general principles can be applied to all types of organisations.

Womack and Jones start from the position that organisations must offer customers value of some sort. The objective is not just to shake out cost by paring down all the process. It is to focus on what the customer needs 'at a specific price at a specific time'.

Having decided that 'the critical starting point for lean thinking is value' the writers go on to set out other key principles.

The next step is to identify the 'value stream' or set of all the actions required to bring a particular product from concept to completion. When this is done properly all sorts of 'muda' (waste) will be discovered.

Once you have decided on how to cut out 'muda', the third step is to get the value-creating steps that are left after this reappraisal to flow. This will involve re-thinking the way in which organisations are currently organised.

Organisations need to be re-organised into product teams which focus on the customer. This enables companies to let customers pull the product from them as they need it, rather than pushing products on to a market that does not necessarily want them. From this stage it is a small step forward to mass customisation, i.e. mass producing products which at the same time meet individual customer needs through subtle yet clear differences.

When companies have all of these steps in action they realise 'that there is no end to the process of reducing effort, time, space, costs and mistakes while offering a product which is ever more nearly what the customer actually wants. Suddenly, perfection, the fifth and final principle of lean thinking does not seem like a crazy idea.'

1 What is the central focus of lean production?
2 Why do you think it is termed 'lean production'?
3 How does lean production enable organisations to become more competitive?
4 Why is it a continuous process?

CASE STUDY CASE STUDY CASE STUDY CASE STUDY CASE STUDY CASE

Resource management, waste minimisation and pollution control

Today, there is increasing emphasis placed on businesses to use resources in the best way possible – by minimising waste and controlling pollution. In making this change, organisations have been prodded by government strategy, by the actions of competitors and of course by consumer pressure.

Organisations need to:

● reduce the amount of waste that is produced
● make the best use of what waste is produced
● to choose waste management practices which minimise the risk of immediate and future environmental pollution and harm to human health.

IT'S A FACT

That households, commerce and industry in the UK currently generate about 240 million tonnes of controlled waste and a further 190 million tonnes of non-controlled waste each year. This means every nine months we produce enough waste to fill Lake Windermere.

There are many ways of managing our waste in a more sustainable way. The different waste management options can be ranked in a hierarchy:

REDUCTION
RE-USE
RECOVERY
  recycling
  composting
  energy
DISPOSAL

The important thing is that if organisations are going to move in a sustainable direction then they need to move the management of waste further up this waste hierarchy.

Of course, while the waste hierarchy represents overall priorities for waste, it will not hold true for all types, and waste producers will still want to recover or dispose of their waste in a cost-effective way.

For example, some types of waste cannot be reduced or re-used, others cannot be composted, and for some hazardous wastes, disposal is the only option. So organisations need to establish what is the Best Practicable Environmental Option (BPEO) for any particular type of waste. In working out the BPEO, the organisations should take into account the environmental and economic costs and the benefits of the different waste management options. The above hierarchy provides a checklist:

● Can the waste be reduced?
● Can it be re-used?
● Can some value be recovered from it?

Organisations and individuals have to recognise that in a sustainable waste strategy all the waste hierarchy options have a place.

Better waste management is an opportunity for all organisations to be more competitive. Industry and commerce are by far the biggest waste producers. However, a mounting body of evidence from demonstration projects and case studies makes it clear that substantial cost savings can be made when businesses adopt waste reduction strategies. This can be achieved by adopting better waste management practices which are sustainable.

As well as adding to its own waste, manufacturing industry also contributes to the waste of others through its products. To limit this waste: industry can ensure that is products are designed to take into account the objective of sustainable waste management.

To encourage businesses to consider these issues, the government challenged business in 1995 to meet the targets of:

● 75 per cent of companies with more than 200 employees to have published environmental policies covering waste issues by the end of 1999
● 50 per cent of companies with more than 200 employees to have management systems in place to give effect to their environmental policies by 1999

Chapter summary

● Being productive means using resources effectively.
● It is important to find accurate ways of measuring productive efficiency in order to make comparisons and improvements.
● A productivity ratio measures how efficient a system is in converting inputs of resources into useful outputs.
● It is helpful to measure productivity over time.
● In addition to productivity measures other measures of performance include: speed, dependability, cost, quality, and flexibility.
● The five Ps of production are the product, process, programme, plant, and the people involved.
● The design and layout of plant and equipment is essential in ensuring efficient operations.
● Increasingly today, the emphasis in operations is on process management. It is important to identify those processes which are central to consumer satisfaction and then to make sure that these are done well by all those involved in these processes. There

needs to be a shared accountability for processes.
● Operations planning is a key area of any organisation and involves decisions about processes, capacity, inventories, people and quality.
● Just-in-time is an important new way of organising production.
● Programming is concerned with the timetabling of resources used in operations.
● Stock control needs to ensure just the right level of inventories for an organisation.
● Lean production is a modern way of giving consumers what they want while minimising wastes and costs in an organisation.
● There is an increasing emphasis placed on businesses today to use resources to the best of their abilities in order to minimise waste and control pollution.
● This involves organisations in placing more importance on the management of waste.
● Better waste management is an opportunity for all organisations to be more competitive.

45 Quality

Tim Hannagan has suggested that quality can be defined as:

> **'continually meeting agreed customer needs'**
> **or 'what it takes to satisfy the customer', or**
> **simply 'fitness for purpose'.**

In his widely acclaimed book, *Thriving on Chaos*, Tom Peters argued that consumers' perception of the quality of a product or service is the most important factor in determining its success.

Quality as defined by the consumer, he argued, is more important than price in determining demand for most goods and services. Consumers will be prepared to pay for the best quality. Value is thus added by creating those quality standards required by consumers.

Figure 45.1 shows what is meant by quality from the consumer's point of view.

Figure 45.1   Consumer quality standards

Peters emphasises the importance of total quality management (TQM), which involves taking quality to new heights. Peters identifies three stages in the development of quality:

- quality control
- quality assurance
- total quality management.

Quality control

Quality control is an old idea. It is concerned with detecting and cutting out components or final products which fall below set standards. This process takes place after these products have been produced. It may involve considerable waste as defect products are scrapped. Quality control is carried out by Quality Control Inspectors. Inspection and testing are the most common methods of carrying out quality control.

Quality assurance

Quality assurance occurs both during and after the event, and is concerned with trying to stop faults from happening in the first place. Quality assurance is concerned to make sure that products are produced to predetermined standards. The aim is to produce goods with 'zero defects'.

Quality assurance is the responsibility of the workforce, working in cells or teams, rather than an inspector (although inspection will take place). Quality standards should be maintained by following steps set out in a quality assurance system.

Total quality management (TQM)

Total quality management (TQM) goes beyond quality assurance. It is concerned with creating a quality culture, so that every employee will seek to delight customers. The customer is at the centre of the production process.

Companies like Marks & Spencer and Sainsbury's have been following this policy for a long time. It involves providing customers with what they want, when they want it and how they want it. It involves moving with changing customer requirements and fashions to design products and services which meet and exceed their requirements. Delighted customers will pass the message on to their friends.

Figure 45.2 shows the move along the path to total quality management.

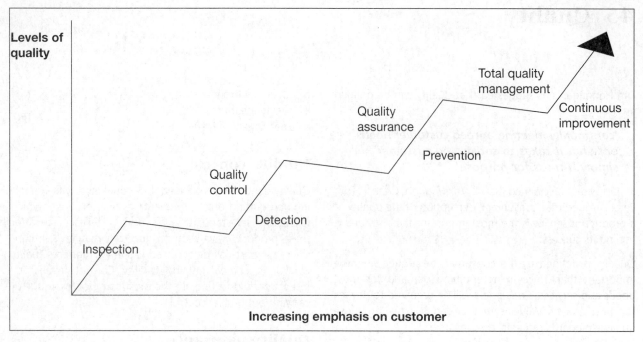

Figure 45.2   *Moving to total quality management*

JAPANESE EMPHASIS ON QUALITY STANDARDS

The emphasis in Japan is on providing the right products at the right price. This is achieved by strong marketing programmes in which products are designed to meet consumer requirements. There is also a continuing emphasis on lowering costs while maintain the quality of products. Factory automation has been a major weapon in making this possible, for example, by using robots and computer numerical machine tools coupled with automated warehouses and unmanned vehicles.

We have already seen that 'just-in-time' is central to the Japanese system. All ingredients in the production process are carefully planned so that they arrive just in time and in just the right sequence to enable smooth production.

Quality control circles are organised so that small groups of grass-root level employees meet together regularly to discover and analyse daily problems in order to come up with the most effective solutions.

The aim of Japanese industry is total quality management. TQM is seen as the prime way of achieving competitive advantage.

In recent times we have come to talk about the 'Japanisation' of British industry. Not only have British companies been able to benefit by learning from the increasing number of Japanese companies operating in this country, but they have also been able to benefit from taking on board the overall approach used by industry in Japan.

1 What do you see as being the main benefits of the 'Japanese' approach outlined above?
2 To what extent do you see it as being applicable to UK organisations?
3 Why is quality management seen as a continuous cycle of improvement?

A continuous cycle of improvement

Quality management should be seen as a continuous cycle of improvement. It seeks to search for ongoing improvement as a natural part of organisational life. Improvements should be focused at the consumer and involve everything that an organisation does from the market research that identifies customer needs to the establishment of specifications and standards set out to ensure that the product or service delivered meets customer requirements.

Quality circles

Making the most of what employees have to offer and valuing their contribution is becoming increasingly important for businesses wishing to remain competitive.

The old-fashioned idea that employee involvement was just about collective bargaining through trade unions is steadily disappearing. Today's ideal form of consultation tends to be by means of groups or teams of employees.

Quality circles are made up of small groups of employees engaged on any sort of problem affecting their working environment, for example, safety, quality assurance and efficiency. They are a means for employees to improve their working life by putting forward their points of view on day-to-day issues. They are therefore a form of indirect consultation designed to meet both employee and management needs. They also allow employees to identify their actions more closely with the success of the organisation and this increases their degree of job satisfaction.

Quality circles may meet once a week, usually during working hours. Each circle has a leader. Figure 45.3 identifies what a quality circle does.

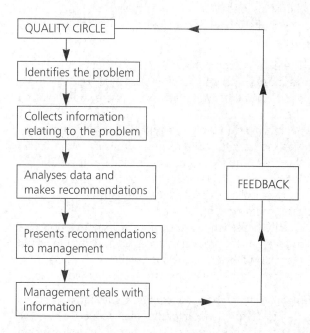

Figure 45.3   Functions of a quality circle

Benefits of quality circles

A great benefit of quality circles is that an organisation can use line specialists, who know and understand their jobs, to resolve problems without having to call in management consultants. Furthermore, the management's support of quality circles implies that the employees are trusted to solve problems and their contributions are valued. This helps to develop stronger links between managers and employees and improves morale, as well as quality of performance.

Drawbacks of quality circles

There is evidence that while quality circles boomed in the early 1980s they have now gone into decline. Many organisations have found it difficult to maintain the early momentum of support that was built up for these initiatives, they have not always fitted into the organisation's way of working, and total quality management (TQM) has in many cases replaced them. In an article entitled 'Why quality circles failed but total quality management might succeed' (S Hill, *British Journal of Industrial Relations*, 1991) the author argued that quality circles developed in this country:

- As a response to industrial relations in the UK in the late 1970s and early 1980s which were seen as being based on conflict between management and unions. A new way forward was needed.
- In the face of Japanese competition it was becoming obvious that UK manufacturing industry could not compete in terms of costs and quality.

Quality circles were seen as a way to transform working relationships and standards of quality in this country. However, these high hopes did not lead to the expected results:

- There was a comparatively low participation in circles (at most 25 per cent, and at least 2 per cent, of those eligible joined). Most employees were indifferent to these circles.
- Surveys indicated very little difference in job satisfaction and motivation between those employees who joined the circles and those who didn't. Nor was there any difference in employees long-term commitment to a company or feeling of trust in the company. 'Us and them' differences were maintained.
- Quality circles tended to confuse working relationships in an organisation as employees often had to maintain a set of working relationships within their circle, with another set of relationships in their other work roles.

Companies that chose to continue with quality circles tended to do so for 'social' rather than economic reasons. They felt that they improved working relationships within the organisation.

Hill's overall assessment was that:

> *'The dominant impression, conveyed by companies with and without circles alike, was of fragility. Every programme needed constant stimulus to keep it alive. (One) company … had been forced to relaunch its programme once before, after it collapsed in the mid-1980s. Facilitators in two other firms gave identical accounts of how, after they had been on sick leave for several months, they returned to find that more than three-quarters of the circles had not met in their absence. Every company experienced a continued ebb and flow as circles went into suspension or collapsed and others started. The continued flux meant that companies were never certain how many circles were in operation at any moment … Thus, all the evidence points to the widespread failure of circles to become institutionalised. The rhetoric of the early days of the boom, that circles would become a normal way of doing business, was hollow. Circles never really took hold in the great majority of these firms, remaining both experimental and marginal throughout their lives.'*

However, Hill and others have argued that the success of quality circles should be measured in that they provided a half-way house towards TQM. TQM has been far more successful because it provides a total **system** rather than piecemeal sub-parts.

SYNTHESIS

Do you think that there was anything particular about UK working practices or people's attitudes that led to the failure of many quality circles?

TQM principles

The gurus of TQM are the Americans Dr W Edwards Deming and J M Juran. It was these two writers, thinkers and consultants who provided the basis of much of the thinking that went into Japan's rise as an economic power after the Second World War.

In a total quality system, TQM takes place at every stage of an organisation's operations, and is the responsibility of all employees. It is therefore a business philosophy as well as a set of guiding principles.

Emphasis is placed on **quality chains**, i.e. links between groups and individuals involved in operations. Quality chains exist both within an organisation and between the organisation and other stages in the value chain.

The concept of 'customer' extends to include the **internal customer**. Internal customers are people inside the company receiving products (usually unfinished) or services from their colleagues also in the company. This extended concept is useful for several reasons:

- It enables people inside the company to realise the importance of what they are doing.
- It makes the point that the quality of the products and services sold to the external customer depends on the quality of products (perhaps only half-finished products) and services provided to colleagues within the company.
- Perhaps most usefully it helps people to realise their own significance – each person is an expert with something unique and essential to contribute.

TQM will only be as successful as the links that exist within the quality chain.

TQM must be led by senior managers within an organisation. Deming put this in the following way:

> *'There is so much talk about involvement of employees, quality of work life, communications and other poetic words. What is needed is involvement of management: get the management involved. Employees will become involved, the quality of life will improve, once management takes on the job of restoring dignity to the hourly worker.'*
>
> (quoted from *Quality, Productivity and Competitive Position*)

Organisations therefore need to establish quality policies. These policies need to be put into practice in order to create total commitment throughout the organisation. An important word is **accountability**. Individuals within the TQM system must be accountable for their actions and must take on responsibility. In return management should put **trust** in individuals and groups. Without trust the system cannot work.

Another important ingredient of a TQM system is **control**. Control mechanisms need to be in place to ensure that quality standards are being achieved. If an error occurs it should be instantly identifiable so that immediate actions can be taken to put things right. Under a TQM system, control is an ongoing part of the production system rather than an afterthought.

TQM involves high levels of **delegation** and **empowerment** of employees. Many areas of decision making and accountability are pushed down the organisation to be near the point where the decision takes effect. The operational units are the closest group to their markets and they know best the requirements of the consumer. They also have the clearest understanding of relevant operations.

Tim Hannagan has set out a number of principles which maximise the involvement and creativity of employees in TQM systems involving high levels of delegation. These are:

> '● *Make certain that each individual understands what is expected from them in terms of their time at work;*
> ● *Set the limits of delegation so that everyone knows the extent of their responsibility;*
> ● *Train individuals so that they understand the aims and objectives of the delegated systems and are technically able to cope with it;*
> ● *Communicate effectively the corporate business goals so that everyone understands how these relate to them;*
> ● *Enable a reverse flow of information to take place, from the shopfloor upwards so that each manager knows the attitudes and aspirations of each person reporting to him or her.'*

Once a TQM system is up an running it is essential to monitor the system in order to identify possible improvements. There are a number of methods and processes for doing this including a technique known as **statistical process control (SPC)**. This involves collecting data relating to the performance of a process to check on its effectiveness and to identify scope for improvement.

Benefits to organisations of using TQM

There are a number of benefits to be reaped from TQM:

● It enables the organisation to focus on the customer.
● It enables the organisation to focus on quality.
● The emphasis is on continuous improvement.
● All operations and activities are thoroughly scrutinised on an ongoing basis to identify scope for improvement.
● Teamwork is emphasised.
● Team members feel that they have ownership over the improvement process.
● TQM can lead to motivation of all concerned. They are trusted and empowered.
● The system builds in control mechanisms and accountability.
● TQM is a total system involving everybody involved in the consumption and production of products.

Potential drawbacks of using TQM

The downside is that:

● The system requires considerable planning and organisation, and is initially costly to introduce (e.g. training costs can be high).
● TQM requires a commitment from all those involved in the process.
● Setting up quality systems involves considerable paperwork and bureaucracy. At times the volume of paperwork can be very frustrating.
● Stress may arise from establishing TQM processes.
● At times TQM is based more on rhetoric rather than on practice. This can be tremendously wasteful.

CASE STUDY CASE STUDY CASE STUDY CASE STUDY CASE STUDY CASE

KAIZEN

On 1 February 1984, Nissan and the UK government signed an agreement to build a car plant near Sunderland in the North East of England. Within months the company had appointed its first British employee, the personnel director. Since then its time in the UK has been a success.

Nissan's aim is to build profitably the highest-quality car sold in Europe. The company also wants to achieve the maximum possible customer satisfaction and ensure the prosperity of its enterprise and the staff. To assist in this, Nissan aims to achieve mutual trust and co-operation between all people in the company and to make Nissan a place where long-term job satisfaction can be achieved.

Nowadays, *kaizen* is a word much used in Sunderland. It is Japanese, the literal translation being simply 'continuous improvement'. The improvement is gained by slow and steady change, and once achieved it is maintained at that level until such time as the next improvement step takes place.

During the 1950s, Japanese industry made great efforts to improve the image of its product quality. These efforts were assisted by Deeming and Juran. Their influence caused Japanese industry to take a fresh look at its strategy, and in 1962 the first quality circles were formed and registered. By the mid-1960s most of the larger Japanese companies were supporting a great many quality circles, and currently Nissan in Japan has over 4,000 active circles.

In the whole of Japan there are over 10 million members of some 1.2 million quality circles covering manufacturing industries, service industries and commerce. Such circles have been viewed as a powerful force for promoting a company-wide quality awareness and for encouraging contributions from an organisation's greatest resource – the workforce.

At Nissan's UK plant, the kaizen programme has been developed as a replacement for periodic quality circle activity. It encourages constant quality awareness and is better suited to the needs and aspirations of the British workforce. Kaizen assumes the total involvement of all employees but recognises that participation depends on individuals genuinely feeling part of the Nissan team.

The company policy is that:

- All staff have a valuable contribution to make as individuals, and this contribution can be most effective within a team environment.

- *Kaizen* team activity helps develop leadership and presentation skills as well as enabling people to understand, acknowledge and learn from others.

Kaizen is one way in which employees may participate in issues that affect their workforce. The *kaizen* philosophy may be applied anywhere at any time. Everyone is encouraged to participate in the activity, and, as members of a team, learn how to analyse situations logically and factually, and discuss issues meaningfully and efficiently. People who contribute to the activity include:

- **Leaders** who receive special training in the *kaizen* process and then apply these skills to team activities.
- **Members** who participate in the activities, often from the same work unit or area.
- **Specialists** who assist a team with a particular project.

A steering committee develops the policies and guidelines under which the activity operates.

The *kaizen* process is designed to enable a team to move on from the stage of dealing with current problems or areas in need of improvement to a stage where sources of concern are dealt with in advance of their actual occurrence.

1 Explain how and why *kaizen* activity or the process of participation through quality circles might motivate employees.
2 Explain how the *kaizen* approach is based on 'total quality'.
3 What difficulties would you anticipate in introducing *kaizen* approaches to UK manufacturing plant?
4 What organisational benefits can you see arising from adopting a *kaizen* approach?

CASE STUDY CASE STUDY CASE STUDY CASE STUDY CASE STUDY CASE

IT'S A FACT

That *kaizen* involves small projects that seek to build success and confidence, and develop a base for further ventures in improvement. By way of illustration, Joseph Juran talks of 'elephant sized' and 'bite-sized' projects. He argued that the best way to tackle the 'elephant-sized' projects is to divide them up into manageable 'bite-sized' assignments. He recommends assigning one team the task of 'cutting up the elephant'.

ISO 9000

The increasing demands for quality from customers and suppliers alike in the late 1990s have meant that more and more organisations today are creating quality standards that match ISO 9000. BS 5750 literature stated that:

> 'The supplier's management shall define and document its policy and objectives for, and commitment to, quality.'

Once the system is set up:

> 'The supplier shall carry out internal audits to verify whether quality activities comply with planned arrangements and to determine the effectiveness of the quality system.'

BS 5750 was introduced in 1979 and has been updated recently to become ISO 9000 which brings it into line with European and International Standards. It is made up of a series of national standards that can be used by any organisation, whether it employs 10 or 10,000 people.

Such standards identify basic procedures and criteria that help to ensure that organisations provide goods or services that meet customer requirements.

Achieving ISO 9000 standards may take an organisation between one and two years, and the costs will vary. Many organisations employ an adviser to help them reach the standards.

The great benefit of ISO 9000 is the economies it helps to create. For example, systems are improved, customer needs are identified and then satisfied, and overall product requirements provide genuine market and competitive benefits.

TASK 45.1

1 Explain how ISO 9000 would be useful to an organisation that you are familiar with.
2 What drawbacks can you see that an organisation would face in going for ISO 9000?

Benchmarking

Benchmarking is an approach which has become increasingly popular in recent times for organisations to improve the quality of their goods and services. Benchmarking involves identifying 'best practice' in a particular sector, industry, or group of firms and then seeking to employ this practice in your own organisation. Benchmarking therefore involves looking outside your own organisation in order to ensure that you utilise the best current practice.

Once you have identified best practice you should seek to make sure that you match or exceed this practice in order to lead the field. The first step is to identify exactly what your organisation wants to benchmark, for example, responding to customer complaints, time taken to deliver goods, quality of customer care or number of rejects in the production process.

The next step involves choosing the companies that you want to benchmark against, i.e. identifying those companies that have the very best practice in your field (e.g. the high flyers like Shell and Marks & Spencer).

The third stage involves finding out as much as you can about the operations and practices employed by the organisations you are benchmarking against. Some of this information will appear in published sources such as specialist journal articles and the press. Some of the information may be found by talking to people at the company you are benchmarking against (although understandably they may want to hold on to their secrets).

The fourth stage is to make sense of, i.e. analyse, the information that you have found out about the organisation you are benchmarking against.

The final stage is to use this information to make the improvements in your own organisation. Hopefully, you will be able to move one step ahead of your rivals by innovative improvements on the benchmark standard.

Chapter summary

- Quality can be defined as 'continually meeting agree customer needs'.
- Today, total quality management is regarded to be a desired goal for organisations.
- TQM is a progression for quality assurance, and quality control.
- TQM is concerned with creating a quality culture, so that every employee will seek to delight customers, and the customer becomes the centre of the production process.
- Quality management should be seen as a continuous cycle of improvement.
- Quality circles were popular in the early 1980s. They were made up of small groups of employees engaged in problem-solving activities. However, they had a poor level of commitment in this country and have since been superseded by TQM.
- TQM originally developed in the USA but is most widely associated with the development of the Japanese economy.
- TQM is based on a series of quality chains.
- Effective TQM stresses accountability, trust, control, delegation and empowerment.
- Every employee in a TQM system is responsible for maintaining and enhancing quality at every stage of operations.
- The *kaizen* approach is a variation of TQM that has been used by Japanese companies operating in the UK. The word means 'continuous improvement'.
- The increasing demands for quality from customer and suppliers in recent times has led to the creation of ISO 9000 for quality management.
- Benchmarking is widely used by leading UK companies to bring their standards up to and beyond the best in their industry or sphere of operations.

Question bank

Case study questions

1 Prices unveiled for Eurostar Channel Service

The railways of Britain, France and Belgium yesterday announced the start of their high-speed Eurostar passenger service through the Channel Tunnel with prices for a return ticket from London to Paris or Brussels starting at £95.

European Passenger Services, the British partner in the three-country project, said the prices did not seek to undercut airline fares because Eurostar aims to sell tickets on the basis of more convenient travel. Mr Richard Edgley, managing director, said 'We will run a city centre to city centre service with less hassle. We will also offer better and more interesting meals'.

He said Eurostar would gain 'a major share' of the market for journeys between the three capitals and a significant, though probably smaller, share of longer distance journeys between Manchester and Paris.

Fares for what Eurostar calls its Discovery service start at £95 return between London and Paris or Brussels if the traveller books 14 days in advance. They rise to £155 for a standard ticket, without pre-booking, and £195 for first-class travel which includes a hot three-course meal.

The service starts on November 14 with tickets on sale from October 24. British Airways said the Eurostar fares were higher than expected, making its own cheap flights look competitive. BA said air travellers could buy return flights from London to Paris for £83, provided they travelled in mid-week and stayed in the French capital over a Saturday night.

However, Mr Chris Rees, commercial manager at Thomas Cook, the travel agents, said Eurostar could probably afford to charge a small premium because it offered a convenient route from the centre of London to the centres of Paris and Brussels, cutting out travel to and from airports. Mr Rees said travelling by rail for the weekend would also be more appealing for families than flying.

American Express, the financial services and travel group, said it welcomed the added competition for London–Paris travel, the world's busiest air route. The company said it expected Eurostar to win over travellers who found it easier to travel to Waterloo station than to Heathrow airport. American Express said: 'Commuters to Waterloo will just have to change platforms to travel to Paris'. They would also be able to work more comfortably on the trains than on an aircraft, the company said.

Tickets will go on sale through Eurostar's telesales office, at main railway stations and through travel agents.

The journey time between London and Paris is three hours and between London and Brussels $3\frac{1}{4}$ hours. These times will fall when the Belgian and British high-speed-links have been completed.

Source: The Financial Times, 18 October 1994)

(a) (i) What do you understand by the term 'market segmentation'?

(2 marks)

(ii) According to the article, in what ways is Eurostar trying to segment its market?

(2 marks)

(b) What effects might the introduction of Eurostar as a new competitor have on the market for cross-Channel travel? Use supply and demand analysis to illustrate your answer.

(5 marks)

(c) The capital cost of digging the tunnel and laying the rail line was considerable. In view of this, use the concepts of contribution costing, fixed cost and variable cost to explain why the prices of Eurostar journeys were set between £95 and £195.

(6 marks)

(d) (i) What does the phrase 'injections into the circular flow' mean?

(2 marks)

(ii) What economic arguments could be used to explain why the building of the high-speed rail link was welcomed in the relatively depressed region of North-East France but opposed in the more prosperous South-East of England?

(8 marks)

(EDEXCEL June 1996)

2 Body Shop profits up despite ethics row

Body Shop International, the cosmetics retailer, said yesterday that recent criticism of its 'green' credentials had had little impact on sales, as it reported a 23% increase in interim pre-tax profits from £10m to £12.3m.

Mr Gordon Roddick, chairman, said there was a 'very small, almost unnoticeable, drop in [UK] customer numbers at one point, but the recovery was almost immediate'. In the US, sales had not been affected.

The controversy was sparked by a US magazine article which questioned Body Shop's treatment of franchisees, its ethical trading and animal testing policies, and product ingredients. Body Shop rejects the criticisms but said it was not planning to take legal action.

Mr Roddick added that the company stood by its animal testing policies but was bringing in an unnamed 'European organisation' to carry out an independent assessment of its policies.

It is also bringing in consultants to carry out a 'social audit', examining such issues as human resources, relations with franchisees, and third world trade activities.

Mr Roddick said he hoped criticism of the company, which last year won a libel case against the makers of a Channel 4 television documentary, would now die.

Mr Stuart Rose, managing director, said Body Shop's results for the half year to August 31 – which were towards the top of market expectations – reflected the 'stability' provided by having operations in 45 countries. Total sales increased 18% to £208.1m, while sales through Body Shop's directly owned shops increased 13% to £93.5m. Second half trading was following a similar trend.

Total UK sales increased 7% to £60.7m, with US sales up 31% at £38.1m. Turnover elsewhere increased 21% to £109.3m. Year-on-year sales, which exclude new store openings, increased 5% in the UK but fell 1% in the US. Year-on-year sales in the rest of the economy increased 14%.

Body Shop plans to increase customer awareness in the US through 'documercials', or paid-for information films during off-peak periods on cable television. It has hired its first advertising agency, Chiat Day, which is to investigate new forms of media advertising for the company, including using the Internet.

Some 83 new shops were opened in the period, taking the total to 1136, with 80 more planned for the second half. The interim dividend was increased from 0.75p to 0.9p, with earnings up from 3.4p to 4.2p per share.

Source: The Financial Times, October 1994

(a) (i) Briefly explain the difference between turnover and profit.

(3 marks)

    (ii) What proportion of the Body Shop's turnover is profit?

(2 marks)

(b) Part of a social audit is an examination of a company's human resources. What are the key areas of human resource management that the 'consultants' may be examining as part of their 'social audit' of the Body Shop?

(6 marks)

(c) (i) Distinguish between informative and persuasive advertising.

(2 marks)

    (ii) Why do you think that the Body Shop is planning to use 'documercials or paid-for information films during off-peak periods on cable television'?

(4 marks)

(d) 'Businesses do not have a natural propensity to do good. What is natural for them is to minimise costs and maximise profits' (*The Economist*, June 1995).

To what extent is this view compatible with the policies adopted by the Body Shop?

(8 marks)

3 The Daily Speaker, July 31st, 1991

'We told you so,' said critics of Britain's membership of the European Monetary System at last night's Economists Benevolent Fund dinner in Cambridge. Two of the five speakers claimed credit for showing wisdom before the event when back in 1990 they predicted the country's current decline in house sales. Even as they tucked into the truffle salad, house prices continued to fall throughout the country. The problem, as the critics see it, is that the Government cannot reduce interest rates, to get the market moving, without threatening the value of the pound. As the pound is now bouncing on the bottom of its permitted range against the other European currencies, any fall in interest rates would be followed by a run on the pound – beyond anything which the Bank of England would support. Given the lack of enthusiasm for devaluation, the Government appears to have few devices for getting the house market stoked up.

The fall-out from the housing market collapse has spread beyond the armies of building sub-contractors into less closely related sectors of the market. Widespread bankruptcy among those businesses which rely upon the regular sale of new and used houses was predicted by some experts at Cambridge last night. Doubt was cast as to whether the nation's stock of 22 million houses would ever again be added to at the average rate of the last decade: 200,000 per year.

(a) By what percentage has the country's housing stock increased on average in recent years?

(2 marks)

(b) Explain **three** factors affecting the demand for private housing.

(6 marks)

(c) Why do some building firms use sub-contractors for such work as, bricklaying, electrics and plumbing?

(5 marks)

(d) How would a slowdown of housing sales affect businesses outside the construction industry?

(6 marks)

(e) Why might British membership of the European Monetary System have a depressing effect on the British housing market?

(6 marks)

(AEB June 1993)

4 The following information refers to the accounts of HTV Supermarkets, a small privately owned chain of supermarkets which specialises in frozen food.

	1992	**1993**
Current ratio	2.0	2.0
Acid test ratio	0.7	0.7
Sales	12.75m	£12m
Operating profit	£1.23m	£1.02m

Graph to show the depreciation of HTV's standard freezer.

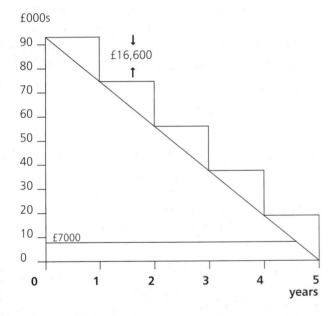

£000s

(a) (i) What is meant by the terms 'current ratio' and 'acid test ratio'?

(4 marks)

(ii) Comment on their significance for HTV Supermarkets.

(4 marks)

(b) Calculate the profit ratio for 1992 and 1993.

(3 marks)

(c) List and explain **four** possible reasons for the decreased profit margin.

(8 marks)

(d) What method of depreciation is employed by the HTV accountants?

(1 mark)

(e) What is the forecast residual value of the freezer?

(1 mark)

(f) (i) State **one** other method of depreciating fixed assets.

(1 mark)

(ii) Compare the advantages and disadvantages of HTV's chosen depreciation method with your suggested alternative method.

(6 marks)

(AEB June 1993)

5 Read the following material and answer **all** the questions which follow.

The information relates to Gento plc. The ratios have been calculated from figures provided in its published accounts.

	1995	**1994**		**1995**	**1994**
Current ratio	2.2	2.1	Gearing ratio	45%	22%
Acid test ratio	0.4	0.4	Days' sales in debtors	95	63
Profit margin	12%	18%	Earnings per share	6p	10p

(a) Explain **one** action which could be taken by the company to reduce its 'days' sales in debtors'

(2 marks)

(b) If Gento's sales in 1995 were £2 million, calculate its gross profit for that year.

(2 marks)

(c) Explain **two** limitations of using ratio analysis when deciding whether to invest in a company.

(4 marks)

(d) Explain and analyse the liquidity position of the company in 1994 if it were:

(i) a high street supermarket;

(ii) a fashion clothing manufacturer.

(9 marks)

(e) Discuss the significance of the changed gearing ratio.

(7 marks)

(AEB June 1996)

6 Read the following material and answer **all** the questions which follow.

The Nomina Pharmaceuticals Company has succeeded in developing a drug (code named Placebo) which can help prevent the spread of cancer. To produce this drug commercially, however, demands a massive investment in plant as the process is highly complex. The board of directors is enthusiastic to see the product developed, as they want Nomina Pharmaceuticals to be associated with medical drugs rather than the more cosmetic products which currently dominate its product portfolio. They have therefore secured a twenty year patent on Placebo.

(a) In the context of the material, what is the meaning and significance of 'product portfolio'?

(3 marks)

(b) Sketch the likely life cycle of Placebo using an appropriately labelled diagram. Give reasons for the curve you have drawn.

(6 marks)

(c) Analyse why the pricing policy for Placebo may vary at different stages in its life cycle.

(6 marks)

(d) Explain how Nomina Pharmaceuticals securing a patent benefits society.

(4 marks)

(e) Analyse the market research methods which would be appropriate to this type of product in this kind of market.

(7 marks)

(AEB June 1996)

7   Read the memo below and answer **all** the questions which follow.

PLACARD MAGAZINES GROUP

Memo:

To: Personnel Director

From: Managing Director

Subject: Recruitment

Date: 23/3/94

We have now lost our third Features Editor in eight months. Could you please start the recruitment process again? We also need a Music Columnist and we will need an updated job description and specification for that post. Do please make sure that the selection processes are above criticism; we narrowly missed a tribunal last time. I'll leave you to sort out the salaries and packages.

(a) Why do most firms have a personnel department?

(5 marks)

(b) What is the difference between a job description and a job specification?

(4 marks)

(c) How far should staff turnover be a cause of concern to an employer?

(6 marks)

(d) Name **two** legal considerations which affect the recruitment process.

(2 marks)

(e) Examine the role of money in the motivation of people at work.

(8 marks)

(AEB June 1994)

8   Read the following information and answer the questions which follow.

Recently, Benetton, a well-known Italian fashion house, ran an advertising campaign in which large posters were placed in prominent locations. One particular poster showed a newborn baby in the hands of a midwife still connected by its umbilical cord. The only writing on the poster was the words 'United Colors of Benetton.' This poster proved to be controversial and following protests, in which some described the campaign as a breach of ethics, it was withdrawn.

(a) In what ways might a poster of this kind meet the purposes of advertising?

(6 marks)

(b) Explain an advantage that poster advertising has over television advertising.

(3 marks)

(c) A controversial poster campaign may be good and/or bad for a company. Give **one** reason why controversy may be

(i)   good for a company;

(1 mark)

(ii) bad for a company.

(1 mark)

(d) To what extent might a firm have ethical standards as one of its objectives?

(9 marks)

(e) A firm may spend thousands of pounds on advertising. Outline the effect of this expenditure on the price of the goods advertised.

(5 marks)

(AEB June 1994)

9   Read the following extract from the 'Blesford Chronicle', a local paper serving an area of the West Midlands, and answer the questions which follow.

Wallpaper Business folds

Hiren Singh's business ceased trading on 18 March 1994. Ironically his order book for the wallpapers he produced had never been as full and his projected turnover for the full financial year was £1.7m. Hiren was one more victim of a cash flow crisis. So were the 32 people he employed. So were the retailers who bought his specialised silk products and who saw no prospect of persuading the large wallpaper manufacturers to supply the demand in such a small market segment. Several retailers telephoned Hiren to express their disappointment and to offer sympathy. The closure of another small business meant a personal disaster for a producer they respected and a blow to the local and national economy.

(a) In the context of the article, what is meant by 'segment'?

(3 marks)

(b) What measures could you use to decide whether a firm was small, medium or large? Give reasons for your choices.

(6 marks)

(c) Give reasons which might explain the continued existence of small firms despite high levels of failure.

(8 marks)

(d) What contribution do small firms make to the UK economy?

(8 marks)

(AEB June 1995)

10 Study the information below and answer the questions which follow.

Extracts from a management consultant's report commissioned by Interiors PLC concerning its wholly-owned subsidiary R.K. Barkworth Associates.

'Communications within R.K. Barkworth Associates as measured by such performance indicators as workforce morale, speed of decision taking, sickness and labour turnover rates, etc, appeared to be very good.'

'Senior personnel had a highly developed understanding of the functions of management and were particularly expert at controlling the organisation through meticulous attention to detail. Monitoring was relentless and delegation proved effective.'

'We commend recent moves within the organisation to create a flatter organisational structure. The care which has been taken to construct an effective formal organisation is mirrored by the attempts made to use the informal organisation to its best advantage.'

'We are concerned that new communications technology was embraced with an enthusiasm which perhaps blinded its promoters to the disadvantages of the technology.'

(a) In the context of the consultant's report, what is meant by 'delegation' (line 6)?

(3 marks)

(b) (i) Sketch a typical organisation chart.

(2 marks)

(ii) Explain the likely effect on communication of a 'flatter organisational structure'.

(4 marks)

(c) (i) Explain **two** advantages of new communications technology.

(4 marks)

(ii) Explain **two** disadvantages of new communications technology.

(4 marks)

(d) All organisations have managers. What functions does a manager fulfil?

(8 marks)

(AEB June 1995)

11 The following is a summary of the balance sheet for G White Ltd as at 31 May 1995.

	£	£
Fixed Assets at cost		65,000
Less depreciation to date		14,000
		51,000
Current Assets		
Stock	60,000	
Trade Debtors	35,000	
Bank	14,300	
	109,300	
Current Liabilities		
Trade Creditors	30,000	
		79,300
		130,300
Capital and Reserves		130,300

The company is in the process of preparing budgets for the three months ending 31 August 1995, and the following information is available.

(i) Budgeted sales (which provide a gross profit of 25% on cost) are:

	£
May	**70,000**
June	**75,000**
July	**65,000**
August	**100,000**
September	**90,000**

Half the sales are paid for in the month in which the sales are made and attract a 2% cash discount. The remainder are paid net the following month.

(ii) It has been company policy since January 1995 to arrange purchases, such that stock at the end of each month exactly covers sales for the following month. Half of the purchases are paid in the month received and the company have negotiated a 2.5% discount for prompt payment, the remainder are paid net the following month.

(iii) Expenses (excluding depreciation) are £8,400 per month, payable in the month they are incurred.

(iv) The company will be purchasing additional fixed

assets costing £17,000 on 1 June 1995, with 50% payable in July and the balance in October 1995. Depreciation on all fixed assets is at the rate of 10% p.a. on cost (rates being charged from the date of purchase).

REQUIRED

(A) A Cash Budget for the three months ending 31 August 1995.

(12 marks)

(B) A Budgeted Trading and Profit and Loss account for the three months ending 31 August 1995, together with a Balance Sheet as at that date.

(13 marks)

(Oxford Delegacy of Examiners, Specimen Paper 1996)

12 Turning the Tide for Tyneside Jobs

Interconnection Systems, one of Tyneside's most successful businesses, keeps a list of people wanting to join the company. The list contains more than a thousand names. The company is an interface between the old and the new Tynesides. It has been recruiting men from Tyneside's last, now closed, coal-mine and from Swan Hunter, its last, dying shipbuilding firm, to join a workforce of 850.

Among the lucky ones is George Cook from Jarrow, a former Swan Hunter boiler-maker. Mr Cook is delighted with his new job after 19 years in shipbuilding. The production line work is clean and his weekly flat wage for a permanent night-shift is £250 gross, £31 more than at Swan's. But, he says, some former Swan recruits at the factory would return to shipbuilding tomorrow.

Tyneside's traditional industries offered regular wages for men, a sense of identity and a formidable world role. Between 1970 and 1990, Tyne and Wear, a county with a labour force of 523,000, lost 100,000 manufacturing jobs – half the total – and 25,000 of its primary sector jobs (two-thirds), mostly in mining and energy. It gained 50,000 service sector jobs.

According to a recent research report, mid-1990s prospects for Tyne and Wear's manufacturing sector look good. These prospects are under-pinned by a growing motor industry centred on Nissan's £900 million Sunderland plant. Inward investment has been vital in diversifying the local economy, broadening the industrial base and offsetting the decline of traditional industries. Tyne and Wear companies are also strong performers in world export markets. Yet, in spite of decades of effort, Tyne and Wear still has the fourth highest county unemployment rate in mainland Britain with 65,400 people (12%) unemployed.

There are other worrying trends. Key firms in the Tyneside economy such as turbine generator maker Parsons, tank builder Vickers, Northern Electric and British Gas, have all recently announced significant redundancies. Newcastle University's Centre for Urban and Regional Development Studies, points out that the job losses are in the managerial, professional and R & D area. In a region already lacking substantial locally controlled companies, Newcastle has also suffered a number of losses of regional offices to the Yorkshire area. Big companies and decision-makers in a local economy are vital to the success of small and medium-sized enterprises (SMEs).

Tyne and Wear is also fighting to improve low levels of entrepreneurship and the low post-16 rates of staying on in education – both legacies of its heavy-industrial past. It is estimated that the number of new jobs created locally by SMEs, high technology companies and inward investors is equalling the losses from traditional companies. However, they are not equal jobs. For many former Swan Hunter employees this means they are job-hunting house-husbands while their wives go out to work. 'It's total role reversal' says 38-year-old Mr Graham Gibson, whose typist wife works a 6-day week in two jobs. Mr Gibson was made redundant from Swan's after receivership. He is now a better qualified unemployment statistic, thanks to a college computer course. 'I can do Cvs for other lads now on my word-processor'.

Source: adapted from: *Financial Times*, 6 November 1994

(a) (i) Using evidence from the article, describe and explain the economic changes which have taken place in Tyne and Wear since 1970.

(12 marks)

(ii) Discuss how changes in technology since 1970 might have affected employment in this region.

(6 marks)

(b) Nissan is a Japanese company which has set up a plant in Sunderland.

(i) Describe the possible differences in business attitudes and practices Japanese firms might encounter when setting up a plant in the United Kingdom.

(8 marks)

(ii) Explain why it is important that '… diversifying the local economy and broadening the industrial base (paragraph four) …' takes place in Tyne and Wear.

(4 marks)

(c) There are a number of different factors which influence business activity in Tyne and Wear which are mentioned in the article.

Evaluate the **relative** importance of these factors in leading to the 1994 situation described in the article.

(20 marks)

(Oxford Delegacy of Examiners)

13 High-rise Confectionery plc. is a large manufacturer of packaged cakes. In addition to their own brand of products, the company makes products for 'own brands' supermarket chains. All the products have a limited shelf-life.

Production is carried out on three production lines, which operate on two, eight-hour shifts per day for five days per week. The product range is extensive, and a change of product takes place on average once per shift. At each change there is a period of downtime during which equipment is cleaned and re-set for the next product. Downtime between runs averages two hours and the average run length is six hours. The production plan for each line is worked out for the next four weeks and updated every two weeks. The aim of the plan is to ensure that the production lines are as fully utilised as possible and to allow appropriate supplies of raw materials and packaging to be ordered. Preparation of the plan is difficult, complex, and time-consuming.

The production process is split into four stages each linked by motor-driven conveyors. The production process is as follows.

Stage 1   Weigh and mix the ingredients and put into moulds
↓
Stage 2   Bake in ovens
↓
Stage 3   Decorate (by hand or machine)
↓
Stage 4   Package and store (ready for distribution)

Each product can require different ingredients and weights of ingredients, and a different temperature profile for baking in the ovens. Finished cakes are dispatched within three days.

A major operating cost is that of the energy used in the ovens. These are kept hot overnight, but allowed to cool at weekends. The oven temperature profiles are set manually and controlled by thermostats. The ovens account for 75% of the company's energy bill, the other 25% is accounted for by other equipment on the production lines.

The costs for the firm comprise the following items:

Raw materials and packaging	10%
Energy costs	20%
Labour costs	40%
	(20% Stages 1 and 2,
	20% Stages 3 and 4)
Depreciation	15%
Overheads	15%
	(includes administration
	and management salaries)

Production Stages 1 and 2 (mixing and baking) are capital intensive. They employ some unskilled people, but mainly skilled operatives and technicians: 30% of the workforce. Production Stages 3 and 4 are labour intensive and employ essentially unskilled people: 60% of the workforce. Two-thirds of this group are women and part-time working is common. Managers, supervisors and administrative staff comprise 10% of the workforce. Overall, there are about 2,000 employees.

(a) The Sales department has received an emergency order from a major customer of long standing. The delivery date is four days from the receipt of the order and the customer will accept a small premium on the normal price.

Explain the factors the firm would have to consider before accepting or declining the order.

(10 marks)

(b) (i) Using percentages, show the allocation of costs into fixed and variable, which could be used as a basis for calculating unit cost. State and justify any assumption made in the allocation of costs.

(6 marks)

(b) Outline the difficulties in calculating the cost of making a cake.

(4 marks)

(c) The Company only uses computers in the accounts department, where a bought-in package is used to calculate wages and prepare invoices.

Describe other ways in which computers might be used in this firm to increase efficiency.

(10 marks)

(d) In the past two years, certain of High-rise confectionery brands have experienced a serious decline in sales. The Board of Directors are concerned about this situation.

Describe and evaluate possible solutions the firm could consider which might solve this problem.

(20 marks)

(Oxford Delegacy of Examiners, Specimen Paper, 1996)

14 Smalley Excavators Ltd

Richard and Ann Smalley have built up Smalley Excavators into a business with an annual turnover of over £4 million.

Richard comes from a farming family, and it was his familiarity with agriculture and farm machinery, coupled with mechanical engineering talent, that enabled him to find a profitable niche in the market for his specialised form of excavator. Always inventive by nature, he had trained as an agricultural engineer before gaining experience with hydraulics at Lucas and Massey Ferguson, developing and testing hydraulic pumps.

In 1960 Richard started his first company, making a mechanical ditcher that sold for £69. A year later, while he and Ann were on honeymoon, he designed the first of his excavators. This was a hydraulic, portable grave digger, to which he later added wheels and 360° slewing, making it into a walking excavator. The usual practice of using four strong men to dig a grave was excessively labour-intensive, and the new product, launched in 1963 after a year's development, was an immediate success. He sold 50 all over the world in the first year.

Since then, he and Ann have always worked together. Today she is the publicity director with additional responsibility for equipment and transport purchasing. But 25 years ago she was a fully fledged working member of the production line, drilling holes and painting the finished units which were being turned out at a rate of four or five a week from their farm workshop. She was also sending out letters and typing invoices, preparing the publicity, and chasing around agricultural shows and exhibitions to boost sales.

Richard's early ideas proved to be effective. He had put a cab on an engine on a chassis. He knew that by pushing the load down into the feet, all the weight was going into the bucket and imparting a very substantial tearout force. It was an elementary principle of common-sense engineering that was very effective, and it is one that has been retained in his machines for a quarter of a century.

Richard continued developing two-wheeled excavators up to about 5 tonnes in weight. Ann says that, up to the size of small conventional excavators, the customer is not really interested in saving money. She realised that when the purchaser of their first machine walked away saying 'I can throw away my spade! I have always been a navvy but now I have an excavator.' In the boom days of the 1960s, the capital outlay on such a machine would be written down on the first contract and the operators didn't have to worry about saving money.

When the Smalleys began looking to other possibilities, the Waterway Authorities of England provided the biggest stimulus. The old canals were beginning to be used as leisure facilities and maintenance was essential. The authorities provided the boats, and Smalley mounted machines on them that could dredge and clear weed, working in shallow waterways under low, narrow bridges, unhindered by a counterweight tailswing.

At the same time, the firm started making peat excavators and more grave diggers. It was the peat machines that led the firm into producing low-ground-pressure crawler machines, which brought about the Smalley rubber-band type of track.

To a large extent, the Smalley success formula has been based on the flexibility of his designs. The units are all made from standard units produced by a variety of companies. These units can be mixed and matched to meet most customers' requirements without involving a lot of expensive specialised one-off production.

Another important ingredient in the formula is the

Smally's belief in personal contact with customers. The company has now spread its business over about ten different markets, and diversification is the name of the game.

(a) Where did the original business idea come from?

(b) What would have been the main problems in developing the idea into a finished product?

(c) Could either Richard or Ann have run the business on their own?

(d) Describe the most important stages in the growth of the business.

(e) What were the key functional areas of the business?

(f) What have been the main reasons for the success of the business?

(g) What major problems can you possibly foresee for Smalley?

15 The market for tea

Tea is Britain's traditional drink; its use is ingrained upon our culture. As a nation, Britain imports approximately 22 per cent of the major tea growing countries' exports. Tea accounts for more than 43 per cent of everything we drink with the exception of tap water. The main organisations in the tea market are Lyons, Tetley, Brooke Bond and Premier Brands. These firms compete not only in terms of taste, flavour and price but also in terms of packaging, convenience, innovation, value for money, quality and distribution.

The British consume an average of 3.56 cups per person per day, which adds up to some 178 million cups of tea daily. More than 80 per cent of the nation's inhabitants drink tea, and there are some 1,500 varieties and blends from which to choose. The information given in Figs 15.1, 15.2 and 15.3 was supplied on a specific date by several market research organisations.

(a) Comment on the personality of teabag drinkers. In you profile, refer to groups of consumers (a) most and (b) least likely to use teabags.

(b) Explain why, in your opinion, teabag sales vary regionally.

(c) How might the information shown in Figs 15.1, 15.2and 15.3 be used by tea producers?

16 Savoury Snacks

Over the last ten years the savoury snack market in the United Kingdom has undergone a fourfold increase in value, from roughly £100 million to more than £400 million. The previous top flavours of Hula Hoops, Quavers and Discos are being seriously challenged by new

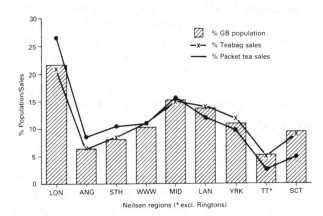

Figure 15.1   Regionality of total tea sales.

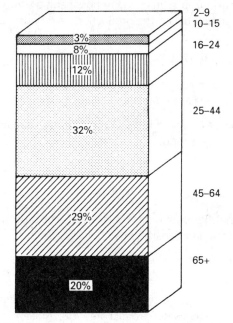

Figure 15.2   Age-group breakdown: teabag drinkers.

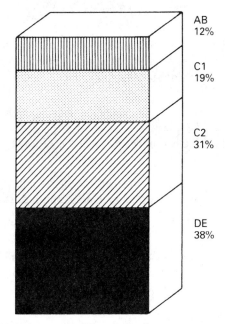

Figure 15.3 Social class breakdown: teabag drinkers

contenders in the market whose innovation in shapes, flavours, textures and branding contribute significantly to the growth of the snacks industry.

The growth in the size of this market reflects the changes in snack eating habits. Snacks are today an integral part of children's diets, and adults nibble snacks with drinks more than they have ever done.

One of the main developments in the snacks market is that children who have grown up on snacks have now become adults who *still* consume snacks. This demand from an older generation has led to the introduction of more sophisticated snacks, such as Tortilla Chips, Kettle Chips and Indian Poppadoms. Snacks packaged with dips have also made a remarkable impact upon the market.

For children's products, shapes have had an enormous impact. Improved technology has meant that the shape and the texture of products have changed significantly. The ingredients of the products have also changed, with greater emphasis on healthy eating and the elimination of artificial colours and preservatives. Packaging has also changed; metallized film bags extend the shelf-life of products by up to 50 per cent.

In the snacks market, marketing has taken on a new meaning. Investment in product innovation and research into market needs has added considerable value to product portfolios. Competition will, however, continue to be fierce as many small independent companies enter this sector looking for a share of the growth.

(a)   Identify two market segments in the savoury snacks market. For each market segment, draw up a profile of a typical consumer.

(b)   Explain how the consumer has benefited from the growth of the savoury snacks market.

(c)   Have any groups/individuals been adversely affected by the growth of this market? Give reasons with your answer.

(d)   To what extent does this short report emphasise the various parts of the definition of marketing?

17   The birth of mass production

A new era began when in 1913 Henry Ford opened up a moving final assembly plant at his car factory in Michigan. This development represented the birth of mass production with the Model T Ford.

Henry Ford's ambition was to manufacture the simplest car possible in large numbers at low cost. His aim was to create mass consumption by making cars available for everybody; to achieve this he had to create mass production. As a result of both this and other developments, Ford guided the evolution of car manufacture from the primitive methods of the early 1900s towards some of the advanced techniques we see today.

In the early days Ford workers built cars in the same way as everybody else. They started with the chassis. Helpers and stock runners brought parts to mechanics who assembled the car while it was left standing in one place. Later cars were assembled on stands which could be moved from one team of workers to another. This speeded up production a little, but cars were still largely hand-made.

The production of interchangeable parts in quantity was introduced by Eli Whitney in 1798 when the US government gave him a rush order for 10,000 muskets. Instead of making these weapons by hand, Whitney built machines that duplicated parts so accurately that assembling them into muskets was comparatively simple.

A second antecedent of mass production was the development of conveyors, an invention of Oliver Evans in 1738, who used them in his automatic grain mill. This technique was developed further in the 1860s when Chicago meatpackers hung hog carcasses from an overhead rail. The carcasses were carried past a series of workers who each performed a single operation on the carcass.

The principle of dividing work to multiply output was given a boost by Elihu Root, one of the great production geniuses. While working for Samuel Colt, Root proceeded to accelerate the production of six-shooters by further dividing steps in manufacture and inventing machines to perform each step. Another great innovator whose methods led towards mass production was Frederick Winslow Taylor, a contemporary of Ford, who was the original efficiency expert.

Mass production as we know it today was the result of Henry Ford's combining into a single manufacturing process the principles of Whitney, Evans, Root and Taylor and then refining them. For example, he made extensive use of interchangeable parts and experimented with different types of conveyors in order to gain maximum efficiency. By breaking each manufacturing operation into various parts, he multiplied the production of products often by the factor of four.

(a) What is mass production?

(b) Comment on the methods Henry Ford used to introduce mass production.

(c) Name (a) two advantages and (b) two disadvantages of mass production.

Short questions

1 (a) Analyse the reasons for companies undertaking market research.

(12 marks)

(b) Discuss the various methods of market research, showing their advantages and disadvantages, which are open to a company which is considering the introduction of a newspaper aimed at 16–25 year olds.

(13 marks)
(Oxford Delegacy)

2 (a) Define the term 'marketing mix'.

(4 marks)

(b) Define the term 'market segmentation', explaining how it might be used by a business.

(9 marks)

(c) How might market segmentation and the marketing mix be best used for the following products?

(6 marks)

(i) A new tabloid newspaper competing with the 'Sun' and 'Mirror'.

(6 marks)

(ii) A new, sophisticated, digital Hi-Fi system.

(6 marks)
(Oxford Delegacy)

3 The 'Product Life Cycle' is a concept used by Marketing departments.

(a) Define and explain the term 'Product Life Cycle'.

(5 marks)

(b) Using the example of a firm producing goods with a short product life cycle, explain the importance of the product life cycle in the management of the marketing function.

(10 marks)

(c) Discuss the tactics which a firm may use to extend the life cycle of a product which is in the decline stage of its product life cycle.

(10 marks)
(Oxford Delegacy)

4 (a) Briefly outline the functions of trade unions.

(6 marks)

(b) Analyse the reasons for the decline in the membership and bargaining strength of trade unions since 1979.

(9 marks)

(c) Discuss the argument that trade unions are outdated institutions with little relevance to the modern world.

(10 marks)
(Oxford Delegacy)

5 In recent years, more companies have become concerned with the need to motivate their workforce more effectively.

(a) By reference to some of the theoretical work which has been done in this field, discuss the ways in which employees may become more motivated.

(12 marks)

(b) Evaluate the ways in which companies can re-design or re-arrange work so as to encourage greater motivation in the workforce.

(13 marks)

(Oxford Delegacy)

Essay questions

1 Explain in detail the main features of two organizations with which you are familiar. Compare and contrast aspects of these organisations.

2 'The business of business is business!' To what extent do you agree with this statement?

3 Any business that we set out to study operates in a complex environment of changing forces that are interdependent. Discuss this statement with reference to specific organisations.

4 Business life is based on conflicting interests. Discuss.

5 Use examples from industries with which you are familiar to show how specialisation operates in the real world. Explain why such specialisation occurs.

6 People will always have needs and wants. Business has a role to play in satisfying these needs and wants. Discuss.

7 Why does the structure of industry change over time? Illustrate your answer by reference to an economy of your choice.

8 Britain will never be competitive so long as the importance of manufacturing is ignored.

Discuss.

9 There is no clearly charted route to the market economy.

Discuss this assertion.

10 How does the economic system turn inputs into finished outputs?

11 Consumers know best how to spend their own money. There is therefore no need for a benevolent government! Discuss.

12 Compare and contrast different forms of business organizations in the private sector of the economy.

13 Every year approximately 50,000 businesses are started in the United Kingdom and in the same year over 10,000 fail. What do these statistics indicate to you?

14 What are the key features of an effective organisation? Illustrate your answer by drawing on examples from the real world.

15 What procedures need to be carried out to set up a company? What protection does company status provide?

16 In what ways does business activity involve

(a) competition for and

(b) co-operation in the use of scarce resources?

17 Reconcile the following statements:

(a) A decrease in demand leads to a decrease in price.

(b) A decrease in price leads to a rise in the quantity demanded.

18 Explain how the demand for a particular product depends on a complex interdependence of factors.

19 How important is market research to the marketing and production strategies of a business?

20 Explain why it is essential to have a clear picture of your target market.

21 To what extent is a successful organisation one that is close to its customers?

22 Why might a firm wish to:

(a) change the position of a product in a particular market?

(b) relaunch an existing product?

Explain your answer by using actual examples.

23 Why does the emphasis on different elements of the marketing mix vary between products?

24 Describe the part played by the marketing function in business.

25 (a) Why are changes in the structure of the population of interest to producers?

(b) In what ways will these changes be viewed by:

(i) builders of old people's residences?

(ii) manufacturers of school uniforms?

(c) Distinguish between the production system that might be used in producing (i) white shirts and (ii) school ties.

(Cambridge)

26 Discuss how systems of wage payments may sometimes conflict with quality standards.

(Cambridge)

27 How far do the marketing and production functions have to compromise their objectives in order to accommodate each other.

(Cambridge)

28 Company financial statements are used by a variety of individuals and institutions for a variety of purposes. Specify six different types of users of financial statements and in each case describe the aspects of performance in which they would be interested.

29 (a) State three items that might appear as current

liabilities in the balance sheet of a company.

(b) Define the terms 'dividend per share' and 'earnings per share' and explain the difference between them.

(AEB)

30 State the reasons why companies prepare financial statements and accounts. Comment on their usefulness.

(AEB)

31 Explain how cash flow statements operate. Why are cash flow statements a useful further analysis of a company's position?

32 What are the essential human needs that must be met if work is to be carried out willingly?

33 What is the relationship between technology and job satisfaction?

34 What methods are available to motivate employees other than pay?

35 Personnel is the most vital of all company functions because it deals with the human resource. Discuss this statement.

36 What are the most important stages involved in recruiting and selecting skilled managers?

37 What are the most important steps in interviewing candidates for a job?

Part 2

BUSINESS STRATEGY AND APPLICATION

8

The changing business context

INTRODUCTION

In this unit we return to two of the main areas introduced in the earlier units of this book: the nature of continual change facing business, and the importance of environmental influences.

Many organisations today expect to change their structure and ownership pattern on a regular basis. Change can take many forms: small companies can get bigger; mutual organisations (e.g. building societies) can change to PLCs, and large public corporations can be taken into private ownership.

Twenty years ago the logic of business growth pointed towards larger and larger units. At the time, large-scale producers could benefit from producing high outputs at low unit costs. Today, the situation is less clear. In a competitive environment most organisations seek flexibility, preferring to avoid high operating costs by contracting out activities to satellite organisations. Businesses are also more market-focused than ever before, and need to be able to adapt quickly to changing market conditions.

Business writers have observed a cycle in the pattern of merger activity. At certain periods organisations seek to merge with others to develop more of a global presence, fight off competition, benefit from shared technologies, and for a number of other reasons. At other times organisations seek to split by the process of demerger – perhaps to create greater flexibility or market focus. Organisations continually seek the 'right size'. But the right size depends on the market in which the firm operates and on the economic climate which exists at a particular moment in time.

In Chapter 47 we examine the nature of organisational culture – i.e. the typical patterns of behaviour and values within organisations. Today's managers are particularly aware of the importance of creating the 'right' culture within an organisation, as well as 'rightsizing'. An organisation needs to create a 'positive' rather than a 'negative' culture. It is essential that individuals who make up an organisation are able to identify with its objectives and that each member of the team pulls in the same direction. Cultures do not arise of their own accord, and positive cultures especially need to be created and nurtured. Management therefore need to take careful account of the culture within the company, and of the way that change is perceived and managed.

No organisation is wholly in control of its own destiny. It must learn to manage its relationships with the external environment effectively. Key influences on organisational activity are that of government and the legal framework. Governments by their very nature are interventionist. Today the government continues to take responsibility for a very large percentage of overall spending in the economy. In addition, its policies on inflation, employment, the exchange rate, interest rates and many other areas impact directly on business activity.

It is essential for students to have a broad understanding of the nature of government economic policy and its impact on the economy and organisations. It is also necessary to have a broad knowledge of legal requirements in the field of employment, health and safety, consumer protection and other significant areas.

46 Changing ownership

The business environment is one of change. In order to respond to that environment, organisations must change with it.

Businesses in the UK are in a constant process of change. Some organisations are growing internally in order to benefit from economies of scale. Others are acquiring new outside concerns to expand their operations or to increase the scope of their activities. By contrast, some organisations are rapidly divesting themselves of businesses in order to slim down. Others are disappearing completely as they are swallowed up or forced out of business by rival concerns. At the same time new organisations are entering the market. Some are spin-offs of existing organisations, while others are completely new entrants to a market, perhaps carried along by enthusiasm for a new product or idea or a recently-spotted 'gap in the market'.

Through this process of transition the ownership of companies may change several times over. An organisation that starts as a sole trader may become a partnership, and then a company. The company may be bought up by new groups of shareholders who take a controlling interest in the company. After a period of time, they may become bored with the company, or feel that it is not offering a sufficient rate of return. They will then sell up and move on to fresh pastures.

The trend towards merger

Out of this background of change, certain trends and patterns can be identified. For example, during much of the 1980s (until 1988) there was a tendency for business organisations to merge in order to take advantage of economies of scale and other benefits. During the first few years of the 1990s this declined as firms started to **downsize** – i.e. become smaller by focusing on smaller core units – and to contract-out many of their non-core functions. In the present climate, size is less relevant than in the past and organisations are increasingly focusing on smaller work teams, customers and processes.

The need for change

The Case Study on page 325 opposite gives some useful lessons as to how intelligent organisations operate today. Companies recognise the need for change. They move into new areas when they are led by the market and when they can meet the needs and requirements of customers in a profitable way. They do not allow loss-making or difficult-to-manage businesses to become a drain on resources. Increasingly they take a European and a global perspective, looking out for growth opportunities and synergies with organisations in other countries. This will often involve mergers and take-overs. At the same time they have to be careful to avoid being taken over by predators.

What is a merger?

Mark Cook and Craig Meredith have defined a merger as a situation in which two or more enterprises (business activities of any kind) 'cease to be distinct'.

This can occur in two ways:

1 They are brought under common ownership and control;
2 There is an agreement between the enterprises that one of them ceases to trade. For example, Company X may agree with Company Y that the latter will close down operations which compete with those of X.

A **take-over** is a form of merger. It occurs where one company buys a majority shareholding in another company.

Legal mergers

It is possible to distinguish at a general level between full legal mergers and mergers involving only changes in the ownership of the companies concerned. A l**egal merger** transfers the assets and liabilities of two or more companies to a single new or existing company. Companies whose assets are merged may all disappear into a new company, or one of the companies involved may absorb the other, i.e. X takes over Y.

Figure 46.1 indicates trends in UK merger activity in recent times:

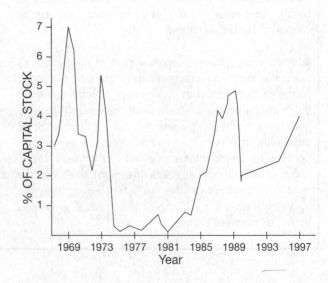

Figure 46.1 UK merger activity, 1969–1997

GÉNÉRALE DES EAUX IN TRANSITION

Générale des Eaux is France's largest private employer. Figure 46.2 shows that between 1981 and 1995, Générale des Eaux comprehensively transformed the nature and scale of its operations to respond to different market conditions and make best use of its resources.

In the early 1990s the company's focus was on water, waterworks, energy and building/public works. In recent times the organisation has moved out of the catering and private hospital business altogether, embarking on a root-and branch restructuring of its property, building and public works operations and focusing on communications and environmental services as key engines of future growth.

Compagnie Générale des Eaux needs careful management as it owns a bewildering array of holdings – for example, as well as owning 27% of *Parc Astérix*, it is the largest car park operator in France.

In recent times (1997) the organisation has decided to simplify its organisation and holdings. The President of Générale des Eaux, Jean-Marie Messier, has recently stated that all the company's 'minority participations are earmarked to leave the group.'

Today the organisation recognises that its main sources of income and profits are its environmental services – water, energy, waste and transport. These will be relied on to provide half of the group's turnover in years to come. The organisation therefore sees its future in these main lines and its new areas of growth. Anything that is a drain on the organisation's resources will be sold when the time is right.

In recent times Compagnie Générale des Eaux has made increasing inroads into the UK market. In just ten years it has bought or set up 53 companies covering 11 industries in the UK. Through General Utilities, its UK subsidiary, it operates in such sectors as water supply, waste management, transport, telecoms, healthcare and construction. Générale des Eaux looks carefully at the rate of return and growth prospects of each of the activities and businesses that it engages in. Inevitably this involves change, as new sectors become more attractive and some old sectors show falling rates of return.

1 How does Compagnie Générale des Eaux respond to the environment in which it operates?

2 How does it decide which lines of business to focus on?

3 What major changes have taken place between 1981 and 1995?

4 How are these changes likely to continue into the future?

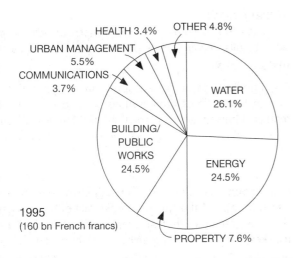

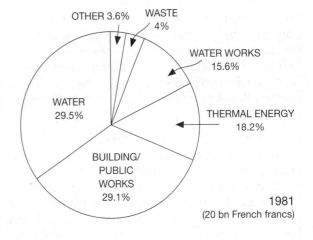

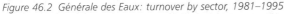

Figure 46.2 Générale des Eaux: turnover by sector, 1981–1995

Reasons for merger activity

A number of explanations have been put forward for increasing merger activity in the UK and in Europe in recent times.

1 **The spread of the global activities of companies** For example, in the global soft drinks and confectionery markets there is considerable pressure on companies such as Cadbury Schweppes to seek a bigger share of the market. Market size usually leads to competitive advantage. For Cadbury Schweppes this involves taking on huge corporations like Coca-Cola, PepsiCo, Nestlé and Mars.

   On a European level, the creation of the single market has opened the door to the creation of huge pan-European corporations.

2 **Pressure from shareholders** Today's shareholders, particularly the large corporate investors, are keenly aware of the relative earnings of different parts of their portfolio. They will switch finance towards successful organisations and divert finance away from those which are less successful.

3 **Undervaluing of companies** When the market undervalues the real value of a company and real interest rates are high (e.g. in the UK in the 1980s and early 1990s), profits are heavily discounted. It therefore is cheaper to buy existing companies than to expand new ones.

4 **Flexibility** Acquisitions allow established companies to change direction quickly and to reposition themselves – as in the case of Générale des Eaux moving into rail companies and telecommunications.

5 **Filling gaps** Acquisitions help companies to plug gaps in their current portfolio of assets.

6 **Converging technologies** Mergers can help to integrate organisations with converging technologies – for example, manufacturers using continuous flow production methods or companies using new forms of information technology, as in telecommunications and the media.

7 **Greater influence** Acquisitions help organisations to spread their sphere of influence – for example, when a French utilities company buys into the UK utilities market.

8 **Greater synergy** Synergy is usually explained through simple mathematics in the form of $2 + 2 = 5$. In other words, the sum of the parts working together in an effective merger is greater than the individual components involved.

According to Cook and Meredith, there are four main motives behind mergers:

1 Diversification;
2 The addition of new and profitable products;
3 The acquisition of management or technical personnel to overcome poor operating performance in the main business;
4 The acquisition of currently underperforming businesses which can be made profitable.

They also argue that **opportunism** is a factor – for example, when a company purchases others at a knock-down price and sells off their assets for a profit. This practice, known as **asset-stripping**, can lead to large-scale waste of resources.

Merger cycles

Mergers tend to come in waves. Periods of activity give way to lulls, leading to a phenomenon known as the **merger cycle**.

An important reason for an upturn in merger activity is that in boom times organisations seek to expand their market dominance and market share. Merger is a quick way to achieve market growth, whereas in a downturn organisations are more concerned with cutting costs.

During a merger boom, shareholders receive a relatively good return on capital, giving managers more funds with which to expand the sphere of influence of the business. A further factor is that at times when there is a **bull market** for shares, companies tend to be overvalued. Recognising that their companies are overvalued on paper, managers seek to acquire more physical assets to justify the paper valuation.

IT'S A FACT

A number of newspaper columnists and financial analysts hailed 1996 as a return to the heady days of 1986. It was a year that started and finished with successful hostile take-over bids, and one in which house prices increased and retail sales sky-rocketed. 1996 saw the largest take-over bid by a British company for an American company, when British Telecom and MCI agreed to merge for around $20bn, a deal which would create the world's fourth-largest telecoms operator by revenue. The merger followed BA's proposed strategic alliance with American Airline. On a no less ambitious scale, car-part maker Lucas merged with American competitor, Varity, after surviving a potentially hostile intervention from British engineering group BBA.

Predators were pouncing in all directions. Three British regional electricity companies fell victim to US companies, leaving two independents in the sector. East Midlands agreed to a £1.3bn take-over by Dominion Resources of Virginia, and London Electric succumbed to Energy's £1.3bn offer in December. In Europe there were many take-overs and mergers, including Ciba's merger with Swiss pharmaceutical giant Sandoz to form Novatis.

Demergers

Despite their many attractions and benefits at certain times, mergers are not always the answer – as ICI found in 1993 when the company came to plan its strategy for the future. Recognising that their business fell into two distinct sectors, the company made an unexpected decision to **demerge** (see Case Study).

Not all splits are as straightforward. To achieve greater efficiency, a company may have to divest itself of large numbers of subsidiaries in order to concentrate on its core business and gain competitive advantage over its rivals.

'Downsizing' and UK business

As companies develop, they tend to carry their previous structures with them. This is not always beneficial. An organisational structure which is suitable for a small company may not be able to cope with the more complex planning and decision-making of a larger company.

It is also true that as markets become increasingly competitive, companies may not be able to afford the luxury of a large staff with many administrators. The euphemism **downsizing** is popularly used to describe the process of reducing staffing levels. Many companies from Unilever to Shell have undergone downsizing or restructuring schemes in recent times.

CASE STUDY CASE STUDY CASE STUDY CASE STUDY CASE STUDY

ICI AND ZENECA: THE GREAT DIVIDE

Sixty-six years after its formation in 1926, the chemicals giant ICI made a dramatic decision. From now on, the company would be divided into two groups: bulk chemical production, which would continue to be known as ICI, and the bio-science sector which took the name Zeneca.

The logic behind the division was that these two sectors required very different strategies, so by functioning as separate companies each would pursue its own priorities.

The chemical industry is, in part, an undifferentiated bulk business. One tanker-full of sulphuric acid is much the same as another, so competition can only be on price. Chemical companies must drive down costs in order to be competitive.

At ICI much of this process had already taken place. Two years before the demerger, the company had taken 20% out of the cost base of the chemicals and plastics side of the company in order to reduce concentration in certain parts of its portfolio. The highly competitive bulk chemicals sector was to be scaled down by selling some of the businesses and concentrating on higher-value-added products. The whole organisation and management structure of the company was to be streamlined.

The changes were required because Dow Chemicals in the US achieved sales of £222,000 per employee, whereas the equivalent in ICI was only £99,000. The company planned to become 'performance-orientated, cost-conscious with no frills.'

The bio-science sector, Zeneca, produces drugs and other products in a high-margin industry where R & D are essential for success. The sector had been too dependent on one drug, which had produced 50% of sales but was rapidly losing its place in the market because its patent had expired. The new company needed investment if it was to re-establish itself as a leading drug company. The new strategy aimed to produce one new drug every year. Investment in research and development was therefore crucial.

The company's chief executive did not rule out the possibility of a merger between Zeneca and another pharmaceutical firm. The pressure for research and the costs involved, combined with the increasing pressure on healthcare costs throughout the world, means that companies need to be large and concentrated to have any degree of success in the industry.

1 What were the main reasons behind the demerger?

2 Why does demerger provide a suitable way forward for the two parts of the company?

3 Can you think of other cases where organisations might benefit from demerger? Why?

STUDY CASE STUDY CASE STUDY CASE STUDY CASE STUDY CASE STUDY

The example of Ford, which faced heavy losses and which was reorganised from top to bottom, shows how it can be necessary to make such changes in order to remain competitive.

Rightsizing

In his influential book *The New Realities* (Butterworth Heinemann,1994) Peter Drucker argues as follows:

> *'Greater performance in a mechanical system is obtained by scaling up. Greater power means greater output. Bigger is better. But this does not hold for biological systems. There size follows function. It would surely be counterproductive for the cockroach to be big. It would equally be counterproductive for the elephant to be small. As biologists are fond of saying, the rat knows everything it needs to be successful as a rat.'*

Today there is considerable debate as to what is the 'right size' for an organisation. For fifty years from the early days of the Great Depression to the 1970s, the trend ran towards centralisation and bigness. Yet today the era of the big battalions seems to be over, as more and more organisations seek flexible structures which will enable them to be more responsive to customers and to take advantage of new communications technologies.

It is now widely recognised that smaller process teams are more effective than big bureaucracies. But the way in which these teams are created is very important. It is not enough for a company to simply reduce its numbers: the important social relationships that exist within it must be considered too.

IT'S A FACT

Workplace stress has caused a 90 per cent increase in insurance claims for mental and psychological illness over the period 1992–1997, with the medical profession and teachers hardest hit, according to a report published by UNUM (one of the biggest insurers providing protection for employees against loss of income) in March 1997.

The study found that one in five of its claimants had been off work for at least six months because of severe anxiety and depression. The report said that employers were becoming more demanding as working methods changed and staff numbers were cut back. Another study found that British employees were reporting higher stress levels than colleagues in continental countries. The poll of 5,000 workers by the Harris Research Centre said that half of British respondents reported increasing stress levels, compared with 41 per cent in France, 38 per cent in Germany, 33 per cent in Italy and 22 per cent in Spain.

All too often businesses have stripped out layers of management, only to realise that in the process they have lost some of their most valuable and experienced members of staff. Effective organisations take years to build – they cannot simply be re-engineered as if they were Lego building blocks.

As Drucker has pointed out, 'the right size' for an organisation is whatever enables it to perform its chosen function efficiently. Where the traditional organisation was held together by command and control, the 'skeleton' of the information-based organisation will be the optimal structure for the modern company. But such a system will only work if it is built on solid interpersonal relationships. People need to have genuine relationships if they are to be motivated and loyal to an organisation. They need to be part of a team and not to feel 'put upon' and overloaded with work by the organisation.

The 'satellite business'

The 1980s saw an increasing number of small business start-ups. This was partly as a result of government support for such ventures, but more directly as a result of the changing nature of business structures.

When the 'big battalions' were broken down, the result was widespread redundancies. Those who lost their jobs were often highly skilled people with extensive business knowledge and contacts. In particular, they often had good relationships with their previous employers, and with the company's customers and suppliers.

In many cases, groups of ex-employees teamed up to establish new businesses focused around their previous employer, building on their existing contacts but winning new customers as well. These **satellite businesses** were flexible, versatile and small enough to make rapid and effective decisions.

Flexible structures

An entrepreneurial organisation does not simply analyse the past in order to predict the future; it looks for opportunities to use all its resources more effectively as an ongoing part of its development.

An organisation with an entrepreneurial culture actively seeks change and is quick to respond. It may be a relatively small independent organisation, or it may be an independent process team within a larger organisation.

An effective organisation will be market-led and prepared to take risks, but in order to succeed it must have a flexible structure that can be adjusted rapidly to meet changing circumstances.

Kenyon Green has used the term 'adaptive organisation' in modern organisational theory. He writes:

'The highest-level property of the adaptive organisation is the ability to change purposely the structure, function and behaviour of the organisation in keeping with experience and with the actual and dynamic demands imposed by the environment – that is, the higher-level property is the ability to learn. Top-level learning is itself a function of structure, including the degree to which learning ability is distributed throughout the various levels and parts of the organisation.'

Greene argues that the adaptive organisation should have a modular structure. At each level there should be functionally overlapping units, so that breakdown or malfunction of any one unit does not create a crisis. Each unit should be semi-autonomous and built on a culture of local problem-solving, decision-making and control. This decentralisation and empowerment create both a flexible and a resilient organisation.

Risks and rewards

Today, individuals and institutions are increasingly involved in a variety of business activities. For example, because of the number of privatisations that have taken place since 1979, as well as the transformation of building societies from mutual societies to PLCs, more and more people have become shareholders. Organisations and individuals therefore have portfolios of assets including shares, investments in banks and building societies, properties which yield rents etc.

All organisations take risks as part of their business activities. Some are prepared to take large risks and stand or fall by their ability to choose the right outcome. Many fail. More typical organisations will take **calculated risks**. For example, insurance companies calculate insurance premiums on the basis of detailed statistical tables.

Business organisations therefore have to create a careful balance between **risk** and **reward**. There are a number of options open to them.

1 For example, an organisation may decide to take a 'safe and sure' position which more or less guarantees them a given return on their capital. Such organisations are likely to be successful, but may be overtaken by rivals with a greater willingness to take risks;

2 Other organisations may maintain a core of safe 'banker' lines and businesses, and 'spin off' around these a range of more risky ventures. This may be a sensible option for growing a business in a prudent way;

3 Other organisations may go for a 'high risk' strategy which has inherent dangers but could yield very high rates of return.

SYNTHESIS

Which of the three approaches outlined above do you think is most suitable for running a business? To what extent would your choice depend on factors such as the type of market, the type of people you employ, your customers, the nature of the product, the nature of the providers of capital, etc.?

Chapter summary

- In a changing business environment organisations need to adapt in order to compete effectively.
- A merger is a situation in which two or more enterprises cease to be distinct. This may be either because they are brought under common ownership and control, or because it is agreed that one enterprise will cease to exist.
- A take-over occurs when one company buys a majority shareholding in another.
- A legal merger involves the transfer of the assets and liabilities of one company to a new and single company.
- The trend towards globalisation and internationalisation of markets has given fresh impetus to mergers in recent times.
- The merger cycle is an important aspect of business activity. In boom times organisations look for expansion; in periods of recession and slump they tend to contract.
- Demerger involves the breaking down of organisations into smaller components.
- Downsizing is the process whereby organisations reorganise their structures to become leaner and more efficient.
- The 'right size' of an organisation is a matter for debate. Ultimately the decision must depend on the nature of individual organisations and the specific contexts in which they operate.
- Today there is an emphasis on organisations operating as process teams.
- The breakdown of large companies has led to the creation of smaller satellite companies.
- Successful organisations today need to look to creating flexible structures.

47 Corporate culture

Organisational culture is one of the most frequently talked-about aspects of modern business. In simple terms, the culture of an organisation is its established pattern of working. Visit any organisation for the first time and you immediately begin to get a feel for the way it works.

For example, at one school, pupils may be well dressed, polite, eager to get on and hardworking. At another school pupils may be demotivated, uninterested in study, and lacking in respect for authority. These different cultures will have developed over time as a result of the the attitude of staff, the patterns of behaviour and rules that have been established, and many other factors.

Changing organisational culture

An organisation's culture can be changed – in some cases, fairly quickly. For example, in 1996 The Ridings School in Halifax hit the national headlines following reports of violence and indiscipline among pupils. The school had to be closed and the existing head teacher resigned. A new head teacher was appointed for a six-month period with a mandate to make sweeping changes.

Immediately, the new head set about changing patterns of behaviour in the school. A number of pupils were expelled, and extra funds and equipment were provided by the local authority. New staff were recruited and guidelines drawn up for encouraging pupils. The school began to make positive steps forward, new ways of going about things began to develop and standards began to improve. The result was that the culture of the school was dramatically altered.

Definitions of organisational culture

Because so much has been written about organisational culture there are many definitions of what it is. Here are three which may be helpful:

'The culture of the factory is its customary and traditional way of thinking and of doing things, which is shared to a greater or lesser degree by all its members, and which new members must learn, and at least partially accept, in order to be accepted into service in the firm. Culture in this sense covers a wide range of behaviour: the methods of production; job skills and technical knowledge; attitudes towards discipline and punishment; the customs and habits of managerial behaviour; the objectives of the concern; its way of doing business; the methods of payment; the values placed on different types of work; beliefs in democratic living and joint consultation; and the less conscious conventions and taboos.'

E. Jaques
The Changing Culture of a Factory

'Culture is "how things are done around here". It is what is typical of the organisation, the habits, the prevailing attitudes, the grown-up pattern of accepted and expected behaviour.'

D. Drennan
Transforming Company Cultures

'Culture is the commonly held and relatively stable beliefs, attitudes and values that exist within the organisation.'

A. Williams *et al.*
Changing Culture, New Organisational Approaches

These definitions should give you a feel of what culture is. This culture is very important because it can act either as a constraining or a liberating force. In some organisations, individuals are able to put their dreams to the test, to innovate and to be creative. In others there is no scope for individuality and employees feel de-motivated and frustrated.

All organisations have their own distinctive cultures and these are very important in business life. In particular, the culture of an organisation must match the environment in which it operates, the styles of working of those who make up the organisation and generally accord with the organisation's declared aims and objectives.

Creating the culture

There are a number of aspects of the way in which organisations function and operate that help to create their culture.

The legends of the organisation

Many organisations have stories and legends which are often retold to give outsiders, newcomers to an organisation or existing members of an organisation a feel for how it operates.

For example, in an organisation that values the 'work ethic' there may be stories about how the founder of the company used to get up at five o'clock in the morning to start work and never went home before midnight. These legends help to strengthen and perpetuate the culture of the organisation.

The rituals of the organisation

Many organisations have 'rituals' or ceremonies which highlight and reflect their particular corporate culture.

In Japanese companies it is customary for employees to sing the company song and perform exercises to music in

THE BRANSON STYLE

Richard Branson, founder of Virgin

Richard Branson has sought ideas, generated ideas and he has made creative use of other people's bright ideas. He employs a good team, often promoting them from within, rather than head-hunting from outside. His own housekeeper became a managing director and he motivates his staff by his energy and determination. His staff may not always have been among the best-paid employees, but he always claims that they are his first consideration, above shareholders and customers. Many of those who worked for Virgin Music from the start recall the excitement of the early days, when the company was prepared to hire keen musicians who had not yet made a name for themselves with a recording company. Staff were encouraged to think for themselves and to work together as a team. They were encouraged to take decisions and learned a great deal. One managing director described Branson as 'more likely to praise than to criticise'.

The staff have always dressed informally, and any managing director who preferred to dress formally was referred to as 'a suit'. Virgin used to bank with Coutts, the Queen's bank in the Strand. After Her Majesty, Virgin was their biggest customer. The staff at the bank all wear black morning coats and striped trousers. Imagine how they received the hippies from Virgin in the early days – bedraggled, sometimes bare-footed – as they brought in the takings from the record shops!

1 According to the Case Study, what type of culture was Richard Branson trying to develop at Virgin?

2 What do you see as being the advantages and disadvantages of this sort of culture?

the morning to symbolise the solidarity of the workforce and management. In other organisations there are 'away days' for staff members in order to strengthen teamwork and encourage 'bonding'. Again, these rituals help to strengthen and perpetuate the existing culture.

Language of the organisation

In the course of time, organisations develop their own language to describe people, parts of the organisation, routines, rituals etc. For example, people within the organisation may be referred to as 'the boss', 'the shrink', 'the number cruncher' and so on. Because those who use the language are seen to be 'in the know', the language has the effect of reinforcing the official values of the organisation.

Organisational norms

Within organisations there can often be intense pressure to conform to established patterns or **norms** of behaviour. These patterns can vary widely from one organisation to the next. In some companies, it may be the norm for everyone to arrive at their desks well before work starts. In others it may be the norm for nobody to arrive on time!

Values of the organisation

Every organisation establishes a set of values which need to be reinforced by senior managers. These values will cover the way in which members of an organisation relate to each other and to people outside the organisation.

These values need to be clear and easy to communicate. They need to be shared and continually made clear through the company's mission and vision. They also need to be translated down into operating activities and regularly made explicit within the organisation.

Andrew Brown in his book *Organisational Culture* has set out the following selection of beliefs/values commonly found in commercial organisations:

Belief/value	Definition
Adaptability	Ability to change in response to new stimuli
Autonomy	Ability to work independently
Co-operation	To be able to work well with others
Creativity	Ability to generate new ideas and develop innovative approaches
Equality	Equal rights and opportunities for all
Honesty	Being open, candid and ethical in work activities
Rationality	Being analytical and logical

Types of organisational culture

The culture of an organisation develops and changes over a period of time to reflect the values and aspirations of the dominant groups within it. We shall consider four main types of corporate culture: power, role, task and person.

1 The power culture

Centralisation of power is the key feature of this type of culture. It is frequently found in small entrepreneurial organisations where control rests with a single individual or a small group of individuals.

The structure of the power culture can be illustrated as a web. There is a central power source and rays of influence spread out from the centre. Decisions are made by high-status individuals rather than by the group. This speeds the process of decision-making.

The weakness is that people in the organisation may feel demotivated by the lack of challenge and suppressed by those who have power. Size is also a problem: the 'web' can break if it has to support too many activities.

2 The role culture

The role culture is typical of bureaucratic organisations made up of layers of offices and officials. This type of organisation is divided into sets of functions that are determined by rules and procedures. It operates by logic and reason.

A role culture can be illustrated by a neatly organised arrangement in a formal tight pattern.

Some role-culture organisations are arranged according to functions such as marketing, human relations, finance etc. The work of the organisation is organised along these functionally distinct spheres of operation, each focusing on specific areas of competence.

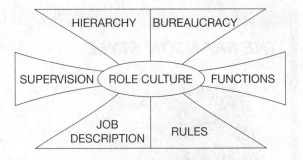

Figure 47.1 A role culture

In a role culture, power is hierarchical and depends on the employee's position in the organisation (e.g. field marshal, general, colonel, major). The relationship between the various roles is determined by job descriptions and set communication procedures. The system of supervision and the role set out in a job description should make sure that job-holders carry out their allocated tasks – performance beyond this is not required or expected. Position is the main source of power, and rules and procedures are the main source of influence.

A major disadvantage of the role culture is that there is little scope for individual initiative. Job-holders can feel cramped by their position, as there is little scope for individual growth and development.

3 The task culture

A task culture is job- or project-orientated and emphasis is placed on completing a specific task. It is a team culture. The task determines the way in which the work is organised, rather than individuals or the rules of the organisation.

A task culture can be illustrated by a net, with some strands being thicker and stronger than others. Much of the power and influence lies at the interstices of the net.

Task cultures are based on bringing together work-teams for particular projects. The success of the team depends on the unifying power of the group to complete a specific task.

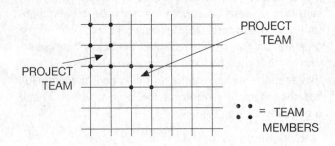

Figure 47.2 The net-shaped task culture

In task cultures, employees can have considerable freedom, and this makes them rewarding environments to work in. However, lack of formal authority and the considerable number of 'strands' can make management and control difficult.

4 The person culture

In a person culture individuals are central. The organisation exists only to serve the interests of those within it. Not surprisingly, person cultures are more likely to be found in communities such as kibbutzim than in profit-motivated enterprises. Other examples may include co-operatives, barristers' chambers and architects' partnerships, where there is a cluster of individuals or a galaxy of 'stars' all operating at the same level.

In a person culture, hierarchies are impossible except by mutual consent. Given a choice, many people would opt for this type of culture.

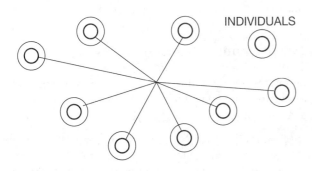

INDIVIDUALS

Figure 47.3 The person culture

Positive and negative cultures

Some organisations have **positive cultures**. They are places where employees (and often external stakeholders) can identify with the culture of the organisation. They are effective organisations because people are pulling in the same direction.

In other organisations there are **negative cultures** in which there is tension and disagreement about the objectives and activities of the organisation and people pull in different directions.

Backward-facing and forward-looking cultures

One important aspect of organisational culture is the emphasis on tradition. Some organisations are heavily influenced by previous practice. Other organisations are innovative and entrepreneurial with little respect for previous patterns or methods. Anita Roddick, for example, has stated that 'running in the opposite direction and breaking the rules has always been part of the culture of The Body Shop.'

A company with a backward-facing culture is likely to be:

- Product- or procedure-led;
- Controlled by traditional managers who have worked their way up 'through the ranks';
- Conservative in attitude;
- Resistant to change;
- Inward-looking;
- A risk avoider.

Such organisations are becoming fewer in a modern dynamic, business environment. In contrast, entrepreneurial organisations are likely to be:

- Market-led;
- Inclined to trust individual employees to make decisions at ground level;
- Keen to introduce talented managers who will bring in new ideas;
- Enthusiastic about change;
- Keenly aware of changes in the external environment, with the capacity to choose appropriate strategic options to make a response;
- Prepared to take risks.

> ### *SYNTHESIS*
>
> *Can you think of organisations where there appears to be a positive culture? Why has this culture come about?*
>
> *Can you think of organisations with a negative culture? How has this come about?*

Sub-cultures within organisations

A sub-culture is a 'culture within a culture'. For example, in a departmentalised organisation there may be different sub-cultures in each department.

Members of a particular sub-culture share a common set of values, expectations, beliefs and assumptions which differ from those of other sub-cultural groups. They may dress differently, speak differently, act differently, and tend to associate primarily with people in their own grouping.

The existence of sub-cultures is not necessarily a bad thing. Within an organisation it may be important to have different groupings of people, e.g. researchers with a research-driven culture, accountants with a finance-driven culture, marketers with a sales culture etc.

Some groupings may need to be risk-orientated, others more people-orientated, more flamboyant, more conventional, etc. The important thing is that these cultural groupings are all working towards the same organisational goals.

Changing cultures

Many organisations start with power cultures. Then, as they mature and become less dependent on their founders, they tend to become role cultures. When the role culture needs greater flexibility, there can be a further change towards a task culture to fit the requirements and needs of each part of the organisation.

In a dynamic environment it is important that organisations are able to change their culture as and when appropriate. Particularly over the last fifteen years, many organisations have changed from top-down multi-layered structures, to much flatter and democratic ones. There has also been a distinct move away from the confrontational 'them-and-us' approach to employee relations, and towards an approach based upon teamwork, team briefings, consultation and shared decision-making.

For the members of an organisation this has required considerable change. Clearly such changes cannot be introduced overnight. People who are used to telling others what to do will find it difficult suddenly to start asking others for their opinions and making decisions jointly. Similarly those who are used to being told what to do may not always welcome the stress and responsibility of being empowered decision-makers.

'Unfreezing' a culture

Cultural change within any organisation requires care and consideration. Business writers talk about 'unfreezing an existing culture', changing it, and then refreezing it in a new and desired way (see Figure 47.4).

Being SMART

When implementing change in an organisation, it has been suggested that managers should be 'SMART'. Being SMART involves setting clear objectives that are:

S **S**pecific about what needs to be achieved;
M **M**easurable – so that clear differences can be identified;
A **A**ttainable – so that targets can actually be achieved;
R **R**esult – leading to a clear and measurable result;
T **T**ime-limited – a clear time framework should be established.

IT'S A FACT

In some organisations introducing change involves 'rites of degradation'. This involves certain individuals being publicly identified with problems and failures and then stripped of their position and status. The procedure recalls scenes in Eastern bloc countries when discredited leaders were publicly humiliated following the collapse of communism.

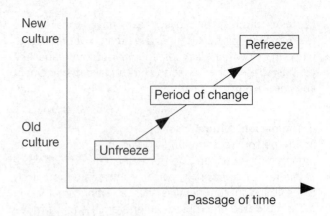

Figure 47.4 Unfreezing an existing culture

All organisations should prepare themselves to manage change. Peter Drucker in *The Coming Of The New Organisation* (1988) talks about: 'a shift from the command and control organisation, to the information-based organisation – the organisation of the knowledge specialist. It is the management challenge of the future.'

Driving and restraining forces

Before implementing organisational change it is important to carry out what is called a **force field analysis** to ascertain the relative strengths of the driving and restraining forces for change.

For example, the figure below shows a rough representation of some of the driving forces and restraining forces in an organisation that is seeking to 'delayer'. In the diagram the arrows going from left to right represent the driving forces; the arrows going from right to left represent the restraining forces, and the length of an arrow represents the intensity of the driving or restraining forces:

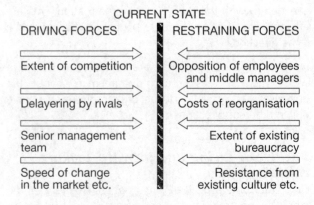

Figure 47.5 Force field for the flattening of an organisation

Clearly those with most power in an organisation can exert a strong driving force for change. Implementing new procedures and practices will depend on securing the approval of these individuals. However, the strength of resistance at grass-roots level should not be underestimated. If commitment is required for the change to be successful, it may be better to use participative approaches and bring in people from across the organisation.

Changes in organisations are strongly influenced by the magnitude, direction, and/or number of factors that encourage and support change and those that discourage change. Equilibrium exists when driving forces are balanced by restraining forces.

Managing organisational change

A number of steps need to be carried out in preparing for organisational change:

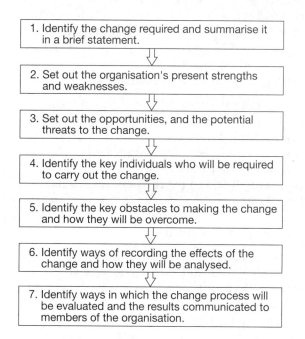

1. Identify the change required and summarise it in a brief statement.

2. Set out the organisation's present strengths and weaknesses.

3. Set out the opportunities, and the potential threats to the change.

4. Identify the key individuals who will be required to carry out the change.

5. Identify the key obstacles to making the change and how they will be overcome.

6. Identify ways of recording the effects of the change and how they will be analysed.

7. Identify ways in which the change process will be evaluated and the results communicated to members of the organisation.

Figure 47.6 Preparing for change

1 Identify the change required

This can be done through a diagnostic approach. The organisation will need to communicate the nature of the change to all concerned, so a clear, concise statement will need to be prepared.

2 Set out strengths and weaknesses

The key question is whether the organisation is ready for change. There will be existing strengths (e.g. departments that will benefit from the change and who may have already had similar experience of making changes), but it is important to show how the change fits with existing practices as well as identifying necessary improvements. Where weaknesses are identified, extra resources and time may be needed to make sure that the change works.

3 Environmental analysis

Alterations to the organisational environment are likely to have played a major part in necessitating the change. These need to be identified so that people within the organisation do not perceive the change as being purely a management whim. Changes to the environment provide opportunities to be grasped. Threats should be highlighted as real dangers to the organisation and its employees.

4 Identify key individuals

It is essential to win support from those with most power in the organisation, in particular paying close attention to formal and informal power structures. The more people who can be made to take 'ownership' of structural changes the better.

5 Identify obstacles

In particular it is necessary to explore the concerns of individuals and groups. Time spent building up trust and support and explaining the positive benefits, is not wasted. Clear objectives and a timetable should be communicated to all those involved. People can be prepared for change through training courses and development programmes.

6 Record change

Methods should be identified at the outset rather than waiting until the change is in place.

7 Evaluate

It is vital to evaluate the results in order to show how successful the change has been. At first, people may not be convinced that the change was worthwhile, so concrete evidence is helpful. The results should be communicated in a newsletter or in meetings.

Establishing a framework of objectives

In order for an organisation to move forward in an appropriate direction, it needs to have a sense of where it is going and **a framework of objectives**.

In a modern business setting these objectives will need to involve more flexibility than in the past. Organisations need to be able to adapt to a change environment. Their objectives should not be 'cast in stone'.

Organisations should establish objectives and make sure that these are communicated to the various parts of the organisation. However, it is important to regularly update the principles and practices on which the organisation is based in order to successfully accommodate change in the organisation.

CHANGING PRACTICES IN LOCAL GOVERNMENT*

Rapid and radical changes in technology, the economy, social attitudes, customer expectations and political agendas have presented a major challenge to local government in recent times. This Case Study explores how one such authority has set about changing its culture in recent times. We shall call this area Midshire.

Changes in the environment and leadership were the main trigger for changes in the late 1990s. The authority set about a programme which it called *Midshire for the Millennium*.

Prior to this change, the management style was autocratic, and creativity and innovation were not encouraged as they were perceived to involve risk, which could lead to mistakes. The established procedures had worked for years, so why change?

The premium placed on conformity and compliance was reflected in the control procedures which were followed, and by the stories told about individuals who had 'come a cropper' by 'overstepping the mark'.

A hierarchical structure was operated and information was controlled and limited to the powerful few at the top. The authority was task-focused. Behaviour was internally biased and introspective. It was assumed that little could be learned from the external market.

Objectives for change

The main objectives of the change process were to reduce levels of hierarchy, to expand departmental functions, to introduce a new management style, and to make the organisation more flexible and customer-driven.

The existing hierarchical structure required managers to obtain approval from senior management for trivial decisions and expenditure. It was therefore decided to reduce the number of levels in the organisation.

The organisation was split up into smaller units which would focus on particular groups of customers. The new structure opened up new information channels.

The dissemination of information was to be carried out through team briefings and departmental newsletters. Ground-level employees were to take far more responsibility for developing good relationships with their customers.

Changing attitudes, values and behaviour

Although the change in structure was a helpful starting point, it was not enough to change the organisation. What was needed was a change in attitudes, values and behaviour. Staff were not immediately comfortable with taking responsibility and exercising initiative. The change caused anxiety and resentment. Changes in structure were imposed, but the behaviour of management needed to change as well.

The initiative was not fully accepted by the Chief Officers and senior managers of each department, as there were not enough extra resources to make the changes work. The result was that senior managers did not lead by example and failed to show enthusiasm for the changes.

The need for consultation

Whilst greater consultation was hoped for, the reality was that managers were still making decisions, or asking for reports from subordinates with little or no time for consultation or discussion. Individuals were told how they needed to change without any consultation. Middle managers were told to make the changes work rather than being involved in the decision to implement change. They therefore felt little ownership of the change initiative.

1 What problems can you identify in the change process outlined above?

2 How could the change process be handled more effectively?

3 What do you see as being the major requirements needed to make a change process work effectively?

* *Source:* Helen Robinson

Chapter summary

- The culture of an organisation is often summarised as 'the way we do things around here'.
- Culture is very important because it can act as a barrier or an opening to the organisation and the individuals who work for it.
- All organisations have their own distinctive cultures.
- The culture of an organisation is expressed through its legends, rituals, language, norms and values.
- Common types of organisational culture are:
  - a power culture dependent on one or a small number of powerful individuals;
  - a role culture in which organisational members have clearly defined roles;
  - a task culture based on work teams or processes designed to meet specific purposes;
  - a person culture which places individuals at the heart of the organisation.
- An organisational culture may be positive or negative.
- Some organisations are backward-facing, while others are more dynamic, innovative and forward-looking.

- Although an organisation may have a formal or official culture, it may also contain a range of distinctive sub-cultures within it.
- In modern societies it is frequently necessary to change the culture of organisations to keep abreast of the times. This will involve 'unfreezing' the existing pattern, introducing change, and then 'refreezing' the culture in a new and more desirable state.
- A key aspect of management is being able to manage successful change in an organisation.
- When preparing for change it is first necessary to identify the forces for and against change, and their relative strengths.
- Preparing for change involves identifying the strengths and weaknesses of the organisation, the individuals required to make the change, and approaches to making change effective.
- Organisations need to have a clear framework of objectives for change. These objectives should not be cast in stone, but be flexible according to the need for change in the organisation.

48 State influence on business activities

By their nature, governments intervene on a regular basis in many areas of life, from imposing a tax on a packet of cigarettes to determining the appropriate sentence for mugging an old-age pensioner. In the period since 1979, Britain had a government that publicly claimed to be against intervention in industry, and the present Labour government has declared itself to be less interventionist than at any time in the past.

The reality is that governments of all political persuasions have intervened in industry for years, from Macmillan's decision in the 1950s to erect the Ravenscraig steelworks in Motherwell, to the Thatcher government's repeated intervention in the aviation industry in preparation for British Airways' privatisation.

> ### SYNTHESIS
>
> *Why do you think that governments interfere so much in the economy?*

Michael Heseltine, during the Conservative administration of 1979–1997 stated that 'The government, like all its predecessors for at least the last fifty years, is up to its neck in the business life of this country, stimulating one enterprise here, stifling another there and interfering everywhere.'

It is to be expected that New Labour will continue this trend.

Working together

By working together co-operatively, societies can seek common solutions to common problems.

For example, imagine that two cars are heading for each other on a collision course. Each driver can veer either to the left or the right. If both veer to the right or both veer to the left, a collision is avoided. There must be some form of co-ordination of the decisions if disaster is to be avoided.

GOVERNMENT SPENDING AS A PERCENTAGE OF ALL SPENDING

Figure 48.1 (right) shows government spending as a percentage of all spending during the years 1974–1996

1 Describe the major changes shown in the illustration. Why do you think that expenditure has changed in the way indicated?

2 Can you find some more recent information which outlines how government spending as a percentage of all spending has altered since 1996?

3 How would you explain the causes of changes since 1996?

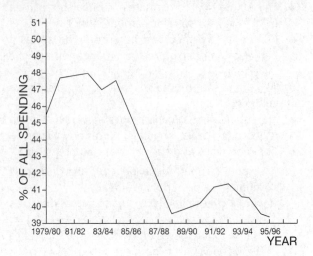

Figure 48.1 Government spending as a percentage of all spending, 1974-96

One way to ensure co-operation is to establish conventions or ground rules – in this case, rules about driving on the left- or right-hand side of the road. These 'rules of the road' are formalised in the UK Highway Code. The resulting co-operation minimises the risk of accidents and works to the benefit of all.

If people simply pursue their own interests, this may be harmful to society as a whole. 'What is best for me alone' may not be best for the rest of the community. For example, fishing communities who have no interest but their own survival may quickly deplete an essential national and international resource by overfishing. Individuals who use aerosols may make their hair look attractive, but in doing so they damage the ozone layer and endanger the whole of society.

To achieve the benefits of co-operation it is essential to have a **referee** or umpire who makes sure that all parties in society keep to rules that are of benefit to the community as a whole.

Market failure

Markets working on their own are unlikely to create economic efficiency. There will be a tendency for businesses to produce too much of some goods and too little of others. In the extreme case of complete market failure, the market will fail to exist, so that certain goods will not be produced at all. The chief cause of market failure is the inability of individuals to work co-operatively on their own unless they are forced to. Other causes include:

1 **Poor information** Buyers and sellers are not clear about what goods are available in the marketplace and at what prices.

2 **Externalities** The act of producing some goods and services has knock-on harmful effects such as noise, waste, dereliction, etc. Externalities exist when the actions of consumers and producer also affect third parties. In a completely free market, it can be very difficult to make people pay for the costs created by such externalities.

3 **Public goods** Public goods are goods which are provided in the same quantity regardless of levels of consumption. Examples include the peace and security of a community; national defence; the law; air pollution control; fire protection; street lighting; weather forecasts and public television. If we take the example of peace and security, it would be very difficult to make people pay privately for a police service which benefits the entire community.

4 **Imperfect competition** Competition in the marketplace does not take place on a 'level playing field'. Some firms are much larger and more powerful than others and are able to sell goods in bulk at low prices. Because of their size they are able to 'see off' competitors and may use their power to exploit consumers unless restrained.

5 **Uncertainty** In the marketplace, consumers and producers may be unwilling to make products or to carry out transactions when they cannot see into the future.

The public purse

In all modern economies the government plays a key role in running and manipulating the economy. Nearly half of all government expenditure is on health and social security. To finance this expenditure, the government has available to it a very large proportion of national resources, raised mainly through taxation.

The growth of public expenditure has to be financed either by increased taxation or by borrowing. Taxation in the UK as a percentage of national income (roughly, money earned by all citizens) has risen from about one-third in 1955 to about one-half in the mid-1990s. The Conservative government claimed to be a tax-cutting government. Generally speaking, however, while it reduced taxes on income (e.g. income tax) it increased taxes on expenditure (e.g. VAT).

There are a number of reasons why the government plays such a prominent part in the economy:

1 Some goods and services are provided by the government because it is felt that all citizens are entitled to a share in the public provision of such items. For example, most UK citizens believe that all children should have some form of healthcare and education.

2 Some goods and services which are of benefit to the community as a whole can only be provided effectively by the government. The police force is one example.

3 Some people believe that the government should try to reduce inequality. This can involve taxing some people at a higher rate than others, and giving benefits to those who are worse off. (Of course, there are others who believe that inequality is not a bad thing because it gives people a motive to try to better themselves; they would argue that the government should remove any obstacles that prevent people from bettering themselves by working harder.)

4 The government can also try to make the economic system run more smoothly. For example, it passes laws against monopolies and acts to protect consumers and prevent pollution and other anti-social practices.

The government's role

There are a number of possible roles for the government in a modern economy.

Enabling effective use of resources

Given the existence of market failure, the government has an important part to play in enabling the effective use of resources. For example, it can subsidise activities which are poorly provided for by the market. It can also restrict or ration the use of certain resources. For example, if everyone visited Stonehenge at the Summer Solstice it would rapidly deteriorate from over-use. The government therefore limits access to the site on this day, and makes people pay a charge on other days to restrict entry, as well as to raise revenue. This ensures that future generations are able to benefit from the site.

Redistributing income and wealth

The government helps to redistribute income and wealth in society by raising taxes and awarding benefits.

Redistributing income and wealth is often seen as a means of promoting **social justice**. Yet there are many views as to what social justice actually means. The problem that faces society is to decide which particular distribution of incomes and welfare it prefers, and what measures it is prepared to accept in order to achieve it.

Stabilising the economy

Economies periodically suffer from inflation, unemployment, lack of real growth, balance of payments problems, etc. The government's role includes the use of economic policies to stabilise the economy – for example, introducing measures to reduce spending when prices rise too quickly.

Regulating social behaviour

The government administers a general system of law and justice which regulates the behaviour of individuals and organisations.

The illustration below shows some of the ways in which the activities of government, consumers and businesses are intertwined in a mixed economy:

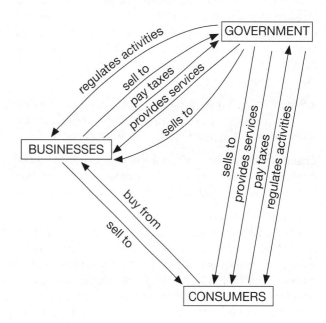

Figure 48.2 Links between businesses, consumers and government

- The government regulates the activities of producers and consumers by setting out health and safety standards for the production of goods and by setting down legal requirements controlling the way in which finance companies manage hire purchase agreements with their customers;
- The government sells goods and services **directly** to businesses and consumers – for example, consultancy services to exporters, and goods and services produced by nationalised industries;
- It also provides services **indirectly** to business and consumers – e.g. the disposal of waste, the provision of street lighting, repairs to roads, all of which are paid for indirectly from taxes.

The government also has a role in buying commercially produced goods and services and producing goods and services for sale to individual consumers and to business.

Government control of the economy

Government control of the economy focuses on five main variables:

- Inflation;
- Growth;
- The balance of payments;
- The international exchange rate;
- Unemployment.

It is never easy to get a balance of policies which is just right for the economy.

Inflation

Governments normally set **target rates** for controlling inflation. Usually, the target rate is lower than that of competing countries. By keeping price rises at a lower level than those in competing countries, it should be possible for an economy to increase its share of international markets.

Inflation occurs when the general price level persistently moves upwards. (An alternative definition used by monetarists is 'Too much money chasing too few goods.')

Creeping inflation is a condition experienced by most developed countries since 1945, whereby continued but not excessive rises take place in average price levels.

If people's expectations are based on the past, when inflation rates were low, then increases in the inflation rate will be unforeseen but low; however, as inflation rates increase, consumers will start to anticipate higher increases and will adjust their behaviour accordingly. If inflation then really begins to accelerate and dramatic rises in prices take place at hundreds or thousands of per cent, the result is **galloping** or **hyperinflation.**

Demand-pull inflation

'Demand-pull' refers to a situation in which aggregate demand persistently exceeds aggregate supply, and prices are constantly being pulled upwards. In Figure 48.4 you can see that an economy can initially increase output without causing prices to rise. There then follows a zone in which both price and output rise along the aggregate supply curve. Finally, the aggregate supply curve is represented by a vertical line whereby it is impossible to increase output further, and only prices will rise.

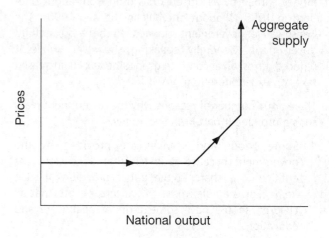

Figure 48.3 The aggregate supply curve

Under demand-pull inflation the aggregate demand curve moves upwards and to the right, leading to an increase in prices. Demand-pull inflation occurs when supply in the economy responds poorly to increases in demand. (Hence the emphasis in supply-side economics is to extend the range over which the aggregate supply curve represents rising real output.)

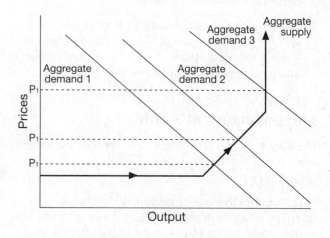

Figure 48.4 Demand-pull inflation

Cost-push inflation

Cost-push inflation occurs where rising costs provide better rewards to the factors of production, leading to rising prices. The **wage-price spiral** is the most dangerous feature of this type of inflation. In a wage-price spiral, increasing prices cause increases in wage demands from employees. If these increased wage demands are not matched by increases in productivity, this leads to a further rise in costs and therefore prices, and then further rises in wage demands – and so on. Many attribute the rise in inflation rates in the 1970s largely to increasing oil prices and inflationary pay settlements.

Monetarism

Monetarists argue that increases in the money supply are a cause of inflation and that inflation can be brought under control by reducing the rate of growth of the money supply.

IT'S A FACT

Milton Friedman

Milton and Rose Friedman, the most famous advocates of monetarism, list what they call 'five simple truths':

1   Inflation arises from a more rapid increase in the quantity of money than of output.
2   Governments can determine the quantity of money.
3   A slower rate of increase in the quantity of money is the only cure for inflation.
4   Inflation develops over years and can only be cured over years.
5   Side-effects are unavoidable.

The effects of inflation

Inflation has a number of effects which are significant to business organisations.

Distribution of income

Inflation influences different types of income groups in different ways. Those who lose tend to have fixed incomes in money terms, while those who gain tend to have commission-based incomes related to sales values. Inflation tends to encourage borrowing, as loans are repaid in money that is now worth less, while those who lend are concerned about whether it is worth their while to do so. Debtors therefore gain and creditors lose. Those whose bargaining power is strong are able to ensure that their salaries keep up or move ahead of inflation, while those with weaker bargaining power tend to see their salaries fall behind.

Expectations

If inflation persists it will distort expectations. A society used to inflation will try to stay ahead by anticipating price rises, and this can lead to a wage-price spiral.

Investment

Because inflation makes it difficult to predict the future, it can seriously disrupt the investment plans of businesses. As a result of government policies, interest rates tend to be high in order to allow lenders to earn a real rate of interest. This also discourages investment. The falling value of money may encourage spending rather than saving/lending and so may reduce funds for investment.

External effects

If other countries are not experiencing similar high rates of inflation and there is no compensating adjustment in foreign exchange rates, home-produced goods will be more expensive to foreign buyers, and this will dampen export sales. At the same time, imports will be more competitive with home-produced goods and this can lead to balance of payments difficulties.

Unemployment

There can be no doubt that the level of unemployment in an economy is a key test of the success of government economic policies. Immediately after the Second World War, the emphasis was on creating a situation of full employment in which everyone who wanted to work had a job. In recent years, the Conservative government appeared to step back from this commitment, with the result that in 1996 the jobless total topped 3 million.

Some commentators see some measure of unemployment as being 'beneficial' to an economy in that it helps to keep the lid on inflation. However, there comes a point at which levels of unemployment are 'unacceptable' because of the waste of resources and the affront to human dignity involved. New Labour has shown an increased commitment to full employment.

Growth

Growth is complex. Everyone appears to want more growth, but they are unclear about what they mean by growth. In recent years many commentators have seen growth as a process in which national income, or income per capita, steadily rises over a period of time. However, many refuse to accept this definition. Critics argue that the quality of life is more important than the quantity of goods produced, and that factors such as leisure time, the quality of the environment and healthcare also need to be taken into account.

An important requirement of growth is that it should be 'sustainable'. Again, the term is difficult to define. To some, it simply means an increasing national income, enabling greater than ever consumption.

But for others, sustainable development means creating a social and economic system that ensures that the goals set by society as a whole are achieved. These goals are usually broken down into two categories:

- An improved standard of living;
- An improved quality of life.

An improved standard of living is generally defined in terms of real income per head. An improved quality of life is reflected in raised educational standards, an improvement in the general health of the population, and in a general increase in the social well-being of mankind. For this broader version of sustainability to be achieved, it is necessary to value the environment around us and look to both the long and short term when planning for the future, in order to safeguard the needs of our own generation and of those who will come after us.

Balance of payments

International trade involves making payments overseas for goods and services received and receiving payments for goods and services supplied.

As this trade proceeds, capital movements take place between countries. The **balance of payments** is a statistical way of recording both a country's international trade and its movements of capital over a particular period. Balance of payments accounts always balance, as they are based on a double-entry format, i.e. for every plus item there will always be a corresponding minus one.

In recent years the method of presenting balance of payments accounts has changed as there is less need to highlight changes in reserves. Today the broad classification of transactions in the accounts are:

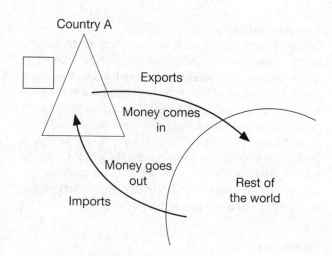

Figure 48.5 International trade

1 The current account

The current account is made up of the **visible balance**, sometimes referred to as the 'balance of trade', and the **invisible balance**. The visible balance is the difference between the sale of exported goods from the UK and the purchase of imported goods to the UK. As Britain depends on raw materials and foodstuffs, it usually runs a deficit on visibles. Although a surplus developed from 1980 to 1982 because of North Sea oil and gas, it soon disappeared because of the glut in the supply of oil and increased import penetration.

The invisible balance consists of services. Services sold abroad are known as **invisible exports**, and services bought abroad are referred to as **invisible imports**. Invisibles include the interest, profits and dividends earned as a result of investment overseas, the selling of financial services such as banking and insurance overseas, transfers by private individuals, and transfers by governments for areas such as overseas aid and embassies as well as tourism.

2 Changes in UK external assets and liabilities

This involves capital movements by individuals, firms and governments. Assets purchased abroad by UK residents are considered to be an outflow of capital and are given a negative sign. Also included are any increases in gold and foreign currency reserves. Investments in the UK by foreigners are considered to be liabilities and are shown by a plus sign.

Visible exports	500	Invisible exports	400	Total exports	900
Visible imports	650	Invisible imports	200	Total imports	850
Visible balance	−150	Invisible balance	+200	Current balance	+50

Figure 48.6 Examples of a simplified trading balance

UNEMPLOYMENT AND THE SOCIAL CHAPTER

Over-regulation of economies doesn't work. And, as a result, nor do millions of Europeans. This was the case put forward by John Major in Brussels in February 1997 when he argued that signing the Social Chapter would put 500,000 Britons out of work.

In setting out this agenda, John Major put the link between unemployment, Europe, and 'socialist' legislation at the centre of his election strategy. He argued that social protection for Continental workers has bogged Europe down and reduced its ability to compete.

Under EU social legislation it is difficult and expensive to fire and hire. Holiday and sick-pay entitlements, pension deals and the tax system, plus strong trade unions make it difficult for European firms to create large numbers of new jobs.

'It may sound responsible and caring. But the European social model is, in fact, fundamentally flawed,' Mr Major argued. As unemployment continues to rise in Germany and other heartland EU nations, it is an argument which Europe's business leaders and politicians increasingly accept. John Major argued that Britain, because of its flexible labour market, has escaped this economic trap, creating 900,000 jobs between 1993 and 1997.

1 How can government help to keep down the level of unemployment in an economy?

2 What measures can the government take to influence levels of employment?

3 Why might the government want to maximise employment opportunities in an economy? Why might a government not want to create full employment?

While it is acceptable for a country to run a short-term deficit on trading, this is undesirable in the longer term. If British goods are not selling in international markets this means that UK firms are losing out; they will therefore produce less and may eventually lay off employees.

Exchange rates

The **exchange rate** is another key variable for government policy control. In the foreign exchange market, buyers and sellers come together and prices are determined by supply and demand. In theory, this provides an automatic mechanism for keeping the balance of payments in equilibrium. For example, with an adverse balance of payments, the exchange rate would fall, enabling exports to become cheaper and more competitive and imports to become more expensive. This will change the imbalance and cause the deficit to subside. If the government does not intervene and allows its currency to find its own value, it will not be necessary to use up foreign exchange reserves in order to support it.

In practice this tends not to work. Falling exchange rates increase the price of imports and severe inflationary pressures can result. In effect, it means importing cost-push inflation. The costs of home manufacturers would then rise, so the increasing competitiveness resulting from

a fall in the exchange rate would be offset by the imported inflation. For this reason, governments seldom allow exchange rates to be determined solely by forces of supply and demand. If currencies threaten to vary too much, authorities intervene to ensure that variations do not harm economic objectives.

EMU

A key issue facing the UK government today is whether or not to tie the UK in with the **European Monetary Union** with a single currency, the Euro. Many business people are in favour of such a move as it would ensure a steady price for imports and exports so that it would be much easier to take long-term business decisions.

Fiscal policy

We have already seen that monetary policy can be an important method for the government to control the economy. The other major approach is that of **fiscal policy**.

Fiscal policy is the government's policy with regard to public spending, taxes and borrowing. The government can try to influence the level of demand in the economy through directly altering the amount of its own spending in relation to its total tax revenues:

A **deficit budget** arises when the government spends more than it takes in taxes. The government can then borrow money from banks and other sources or sell government stocks in order to carry out its own expenditure policies.

The difference between government spending and tax revenue is known as the **Public Sector Borrowing Requirement (PSBR)**.

The logic of the deficit budget is simple: if there is not enough spending in the economy to create enough demand for goods to give everyone a job who wants one, then the government can itself boost spending. However, this may have inflationary effects. In a balanced budget the government matches its spending with taxes. The idea behind the balanced budget is that the government should not encourage price increase. There is also a belief that the government itself should spend as little as possible, because private individuals and groups are in a better position to make their own spending decisions.

A **surplus budget** arises when the government takes in more revenue than it spends. This is known as a deflationary policy because one outcome is a cut in inflation.

Any form of government – whether at local, national or European level – needs to raise revenue in order to carry out its expenditure policies. Many economists feel that the smaller the role that the government plays in the economy the more efficient the system is likely to be. The larger the part that government plays in running things, the more employees it will need to carry out purely administrative tasks. For example, in 1993 the Scottish Office, which looks after the interests of 5 million people, employed over 6,240 officials. On a wider front, there has been widespread criticism of the bureaucracy of the European Union at Brussels.

Since 1994 the British government has announced its plans for both expenditure and revenue-raising at the same time (in the autumn). Prior to this, different government departments put in bids for budgeted expenditure during the coming year. It is up to the Chancellor of the Exchequer to decide how a global

> ### IT'S A FACT
>
> The Brundtland Commission defined the term 'sustainable development' as follows
>
> *'Development which meets the needs of the present without compromising the ability of future generations to meet their own needs'*
>
> Gro Haarlem Brundtland,
> *Our Common Future*,1987

budget figure will be divided between individual departments. The decision will depend on politics and which budget headings are seen as priority in a given year.

Taxation rates

Taxation rates are an important aspect of fiscal policy. For example, the government has the power to increase the rate of income tax, so that people are expected to pay standard income tax at 35p in the pound rather than 25p.

The main criticism of high taxation rates is that they discourage effort and enterprise. For example, a number of people argued that the taxation rates levied by the Labour government in the 1970s were too high, particularly for those on higher incomes. This led to a so called 'brain drain' whereby top people moved to countries with less punitive tax regimes.

In a similar way it is argued that over-high tax rates on business profits (corporation tax) discourage businesses from declaring profits, leading to a decline in capital spending and investment. The Conservative government of 1979-1997 claimed to be a low-tax government.

Incomes policies

A further control available to government is that of incomes policy. In the past, governments have imposed **wage freezes** to control price rises caused by rising wages. More recently, the present Labour government has threatened to impose a freeze on 'top people's pay' to set an example for everyone.

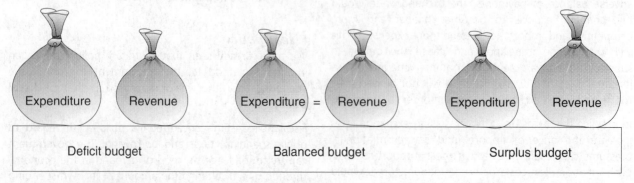

Figure 48.7 Types of budget

Industrial policy

Industrial policy is aimed at supporting particular industries. This is an area of policy for which the Japanese are famous. The Japanese government ministry, MITI, supports industries which are essential to the development of the economy such as micro-electronics and new technology-based industries.

Regional policy

Regional policy is concerned with providing selective assistance and support to particular areas of the country – typically, those of high unemployment and decline. Policies have also been put in place to provide tax and other incentives for a given period of time in order to encourage to firms to set up in these areas.

Labour market policy

A key aspect of government economic policy in recent times has been its approach to the labour market (see Chapter 67).

Throughout most of the 1990s, the Conservative government set out to create flexible labour markets in which there were as few artificial barriers such as minimum wages as possible to prevent the free flow of labour according to the laws of demand and supply. Today's Labour government is committed to creating a minimum wage, but it is also keen on flexibility.

Chapter summary

- Governments intervene in many areas of business activity. This is particularly true today.
- During the 1980s the government deliberately set about reducing its own spending as a percentage of total spending.
- Co-operation is an important part of the activities of modern communities. The government can help to co-ordinate the co-operative activities of communities.
- Market failure is a common feature of modern markets. The government can step in where markets fail.
- The government finances public expenditure through taxation and borrowing.
- The government plays a number of roles in the economy: allocating, distributing and re-distributing, stabilising and regulating.
- Governments set out to control inflation, to create sustainable growth, to reduce unemployment to an acceptable level, to ensure that the balance of payments does not get out of control, and to help to establish an exchange rate which enables UK businesses to be competitive on the world stage.

- Inflation can be caused by cost-push and demand-pull factors.
- The government can use monetary policy to control the quantity and price of money in the economy. When monetary conditions are too loose, this can cause or add to inflationary pressures.
- There can be no doubt that the level of unemployment is a key test of the success of government economic policies.
- Growth can be measured by rises in the national income. However, it is also important to measure the quality of life, both now and for future generations.
- The balance of payments outlines trading activities and capital movements that affect external assets and liabilities.
- Fiscal policy involves the deliberate manipulation of government expenditures and revenues in order to influence the economy.

49 The law

Every business faces a minefield of legal requirements. Some, like the need to pay taxes or to seek planning permission, are fairly obvious. Others, like the requirement for managers of pop groups to register as employment agents, are rather more obscure.

Ignorance of the law, however, is no an excuse for failure to comply. This section outlines some of the laws which businesses need to observe. It is however only a very brief outline and students should bear in mind that business law is a specialist subject which requires separate study in its own right.

Contracts of employment

As soon as a person agrees to work for an employer and the employer agrees to pay wages, a **contract** exists. The Employment Protection (Consolidation) Act 1978 requires an employer to give all employees who work for 16 or more hours per week written details of their main terms of service.

```
┌─────────────────────────────────────────┐
│  Employer makes an offer and employee accepts  │
│        (Contract exists in law)           │
└─────────────────────────────────────────┘
```

```
┌─────────────────────────────────────────┐
│   Employer provides employee with written │
│        contract of employment             │
│   (Confirms and gives details of contract)│
└─────────────────────────────────────────┘
```

```
┌─────────────────────────────────────────┐
│  Latest possible time that contract must be received │
│  by employee is 13 weeks after verbal agreement is │
│                 made                      │
└─────────────────────────────────────────┘
```

Figure 49.1 Stages in creating a contract of employment

The details of the contract are known as the **terms and conditions**, and an employer must give each employee a written statement setting out the main particulars of the employment within 13 weeks of the date of engagement. The written statement simply sets out the details of a contract that has already been made between the two parties.

Many rights depend upon an employee's period of continuous employment with an employer. These include entitlement to the minimum statutory notice period and written particulars of employment, protection from unfair dismissal, probation, redundancy pay and maternity rights. In order to qualify for these, an employee has to have worked for an employer for a minimum period of time.

Unfair dismissal

In 1971, a new employment law gave employees the legal right not to be unfairly dismissed from their job. Prior to this, organisations had been able to hire and fire people as and when they pleased. This situation, of course, meant that individual employees had limited security in their jobs.

Under the **Employment Protection (Consolidation) Act 1978**, the law now states that employees have a right not to be unfairly dismissed and that those who believe they have been unfairly dismissed may seek a remedy by taking a complaint to an industrial tribunal.

Dismissal: information and procedures

Employees are treated as **dismissed** if:

● Their contract of employment is terminated with or without notice;
● A fixed-term contract expires without being renewed;
● They leave their employment due to their employer's conduct, such that they are justified in terminating their employment without notice (constructive dismissal).

Under the Employment Protection (Consolidation) Act 1978 only those employees who have been continuously employed for 16 or more hours per week for 2 years or more or part-timers working between 8 and 16 hours per week for 5 years or more, can claim unfair dismissal. The extra limitation on part-timers' rights was amended by the Employment Protection (Part-time Employees) Regulations 1995. This was after a House of Lords ruling that the limitation on part-timers was not compatible with the European Union Equal Treatment Directive since most part-timers were women and therefore suffered disproportionately from the limitation.

If an employee is entitled to make a claim for unfair dismissal, it must be lodged with an industrial tribunal within three months. The employer must then prove that

---

IT'S A FACT

Many young people are not aware of their right to a contract of employment. As a result they do not know about many of the protections that they have in the workplace. If you are in employment you should always insist on receiving a copy of your contract.

THE EMPLOYMENT PROTECTION (CONSOLIDATION) ACT 1978

Below is an extract from the Employment Protection (Consolidation) Act 1978, as amended by the Trade Union Reform and Employment Rights Act 1993, and Statutory Sick Pay scheme. Read it through carefully then complete the tasks:

(1)   Not later than two months after the beginning of an employee's employment with an employer, the employer shall give a written statement to the employee which may, subject to s.2(3), be given in instalments before the end of the period.

(2)   The statement shall contain particulars of:

a. The names of the employer and the employee;

b. The date when the employment began, and

c. The date on which the employee's period of continuous employment began (taking into account any employment with a previous employer which counts towards that period)

(3) The statement shall also contain particulars, as at a specified date not more than seven days before the statements or instalment of the statement containing them is given, of:

a. The scale or rate of remuneration or the method of calculating remuneration

b. The intervals at which remuneration is paid (that is, weekly, monthly or other specified intervals).

c. Any terms and conditions relating to hours of work (including any terms and conditions relating to normal working hours).

d. Any terms and conditions relating to any of the following:

i.   entitlement to holidays, including public holidays, and holiday pay (the particulars given being sufficient to enable the employee's entitlement, including any entitlement to accrued holiday pay on the termination of employment, to be precisely calculated).

ii. Incapacity for work due to sickness or injury, including any provisions for sick pay, and

iii. pensions and pension schemes.

In addition the Statutory Sick Pay scheme (1983 onwards) requires employers to give details in writing of the 'qualifying days' for calculation of sickness payments, and the rules of notification of absence. These details should be given in this section.

e. The length of notice which the employee is obliged to give and entitled to receive to determine his or her contract of employment.

f. The title of the job which the employee is employed to do, or a brief description of the work.

g. Where the employment is not intended to be permanent, the period for which it is expected to continue or, if it is for a fixed term, the date when it is to end.

h. Either the place of work or, where the employee is required or permitted to work at various places, an indication of that and of the address of the employer.

i.   Any collective agreements which directly affect the terms and conditions of the employment, including, where the employer is not a party, the persons by whom they were made.

1   What do you see as being the key aspects of the legislation outlined above? Set out a brief description.

2   What do you see as being the primary purpose of this legislation?

3   Who do you see as being the prime beneficiaries? How do they benefit?

the employee was dismissed for one of the potentially fair reasons laid down in law. These reasons are:

1 **Capability or qualifications** for the work which the employee must do. This covers employee incompetence, short and long-term sickness, and lack of qualification to do the job;
2 **Conduct** A wide range of employee misconduct can lead to justifiable dismissal. If an offence entails **gross misconduct** – e.g. damage to company property, insubordination or acts of violence – dismissal can take place without notice;
3 **Redundancy** Here the law is concerned with whether the employed acted reasonably in selecting employees for redundancy;
4 Situations where continued employment of a worker would be **illegal**. For example, a driver who is disqualified from driving could be fairly dismissed;
5 Some other **substantial reason**. This covers justifiable reasons which do not come under the above categories.

IT'S A FACT

The right not to be unfairly dismissed applies to all full-time employees (persons normally employed for 16 hours or more a week, or for 8 hours per week or more for 5 years or more), who have the required period of service (2 years full time, or 5 years if working between 8–16 hours per week) and are under retirement age.

The ACAS code of practice

As a guide to fairness in determining claims of unfair dismissal, the tribunal will use the code of practice issued by the Advisory, Conciliation and Arbitration Service (ACAS), namely **Disciplinary Practices and Procedures in Employment**. The code of practice recommends that:

● Individuals should be informed of the complaints against them;
● Employees should be given the opportunity to state their case;
● Individuals should have the right to be accompanied by a trade union representative or a fellow employee when interviewed by management;
● For minor offences, an employee should be given a formal oral warning or a written warning, making it clear that the warning is the first formal stage of the procedure;
● Further misconduct warrants a final written warning, prior to suspension or dismissal; a written statement of the reasons for dismissal should also be given.

Failure to follow this code is likely to make it difficult for employers to argue that they acted fairly. Employees who successfully bring a claim of unfair dismissal against their employers are entitled to:

● **Reinstatement** The employer must treat the employee as if the employment had not been terminated. Tribunals rarely order reinstatement because this would often result in difficult situations; they prefer to take into account the employee's wishes and the practicalities involved;
● **Re-engagement** In this case the employee must be re-employed, but not necessarily in the same job;
● **Compensation** This is often required in cases where an employer is not ordered to re-employ the dismissed employee, or if such an order is ignored. The basic award is the equivalent of a redundancy payment award. A compensatory award is based on an assessment of the employee's loss arising out of dismissal, e.g. loss of earnings, loss of expected wage increases and increments, loss of pension rights and the expense of looking for a new job;

If an employer has failed to comply with an order to re-employ an employee, an additional award may be given. Such awards may be reduced if the tribunal believes that the employee's conduct contributed to his or her dismissal.

Automatic unfair dismissal

In three situations, a tribunal will always find a dismissal unfair. These are:

1 Unfair selection for redundancy;
2 Dismissal of a woman for pregnancy;
3 Dismissal for union membership or activities, or for refusal to join a union.

Health and safety legislation

The employer has a duty to create a safe and healthy workplace. Health and safety affects all key aspects of human resource work.

There are a number of laws and regulations which affect Health and Safety at work in the UK.

1 The Health and Safety at Work Act 1974

This Act covers all workers except domestic servants in private households. Sets of regulations under the Act deal with different kinds of work in various places. All those receiving training or work experience in the workplace are covered by the Act.

Under the Act, both employers and employees are responsible for providing safe conditions at work. Part of the Act sets out that:

(1) It shall be the duty of every employer to ensure, so far as is reasonably practicable, the health, safety and welfare at work of all his or her employees.

(2) Without prejudice to the generality of the above, the matters to which that duty extends include in particular:

a. the provision and maintenance of plant and systems of work that are, so far as is reasonably practicable, safe and without risks to health;

b. arrangements for ensuring, so far as is reasonably practicable, safety and absence of risks to health in connection with the use, handling, storage and transport of articles and substances;

c. the provision of such information, instruction, training and supervision as is necessary to ensure, so far as is reasonably practicable, the health and safety at work of his or her employees;

d. so far as is reasonably practicable as regards any place of work under the employer's control, the maintenance of it in a condition that is safe and without risks to health and the provision and maintenance of means of access to and egress from it that are safe and without such risks;

e. the provision and maintenance of a working environment for his or her employees that is, so far as is reasonably practicable, safe, without risks to health and adequate as regards facilities and arrangements for their welfare at work.

(3) Except in such cases as may be prescribed, it shall be the duty of every employer to prepare and as often as may be appropriate revise a written statement of this general policy with respect to the health and safety at work of his employees and the organisation and arrangements for the time being in force for carrying out that policy and to bring the statement and any revision of it to the notice of all his employees.

EXAM TIP

In your reading you may find references to **The Factories Act, 1961**, and **The Offices, Shops and Railway Premises Act, 1963**. These Acts have now been included in an updated, all-embracing **Health and Safety at Work Act**.

Failure to issue a safety policy statement to employees is a criminal offence which can lead to a maximum fine on conviction of £2,000 if the case is heard in a Magistrate's Court, or an unlimited fine and/or up to two years' imprisonment if heard in a Crown Court.

The Act also imposes duties on those who design, manufacture and import articles and substances for use at work to make sure that they are safe when used properly, and that sufficient information is provided with the product to enable it to be used properly. The employer has a duty to pass on this information to employees.

The Health and Safety at Work Act also places a responsibility on employees. The employee's duty is to take reasonable care to ensure both their own safety and the safety of others who may be affected by what they do or do not do.

The Act is backed up by a **Health and Safety Executive** which includes representatives of employers, employees and local authorities. Health and safety inspectors are appointed with responsibility for making sure that the law is observed.

There are also laws and codes applying to specific industries, for example, mining, the explosives industry and textiles. Many industries set their own additional safety regulations. Personnel officers normally attend conferences and refresher courses on safety as a regular feature of their duties.

CASE STUDY CASE STUDY CASE STUDY CASE STUDY CASE STUDY

WHO IS TO BLAME?

In June 1996 John Smith was employed by Midtown County Council to cut the grass verges on council-maintained highways. He had recently left school, where he had been studying a range of vocational subjects including technology.

In his first week at work John's supervisor had been absent so he had not received any training in using the mechanical equipment required to cut grass verges. On the third morning, the strimmer he was using hit a stone, part of which flew up and lodged in his eye. He had not been wearing protective goggles at the time.

John took the case to court, claiming that he had not been given any safety training, that he did not know he needed to wear protective goggles and had not been shown how to use the machinery.

Who do you think would have won the court case? Why?

STUDY CASE STUDY CASE STUDY CASE STUDY CASE STUDY CASE STUDY

Other requirements of current (1997) health and safety legislation are as follows:

- Adequate toilet and washing facilities must be provided;
- The inside of buildings must be properly heated and ventilated. Temperatures must not fall below 16°C in places where people work for any length of time;
- There must be adequate supplies of fresh or purified air;
- Suitable lighting must be provided wherever people walk or work;
- The minimum amount of floor space per person is 12 square metres;
- Floors must not have slippery surfaces;
- Machinery such as presses must have fenced screens to prevent serious injury;
- Fire escapes must be provided and kept in good order;
- Fire doors should not be locked or obstructed.

2 Reporting of Injuries, Diseases and Dangerous Occurrences Regulations, 1985

Injuries that result from accidents at work where an employee is incapacitated for three or more days must be reported to the authorities within seven days. Injuries involving fatalities must be notified immediately by the most practical means. Listed diseases must also be reported.

3 Control of Substances Hazardous to Health (COSHH) Regulations 1988

Employers must carry out an assessment of work tasks that are likely to create risks for the health and safety of employees. Following on from the assessment, decisions must be made on how to prevent or limit risks of exposure to such substances. Employees should be given appropriate information and training, and measures taken to meet the regulations should be continually monitored. All substances that are potentially harmful to health are covered by the Act, whether in solid or liquid form or in the form of a gas or vapour.

Enforcement of the laws and regulations is carried out by the Health and Safety Executive, backed up by local authority inspections. Inspectors' powers include the right to enter premises, to obtain information and to take possession of articles and substances. Offending organisations can be taken to court and may be fined or in some cases have prison sentences imposed on them.

Negligence at Common Law

An employee can claim for damages arising from an employer's negligence if the employer fails 'to abide by the duty of care to the employee so that the employee suffers injury or damage to health'. The employer has a duty of reasonable care for the safety of employees, and

this extends to cases where employees are sent to the premises of third parties. Negligence occurs when there is a breach in the duty of care which applies to:

- Safe premises;
- A safe system of work;
- Safe plant, equipment and tools;
- Safe fellow workers.

Health and safety: the European dimension

Today, EU directives under Article 189 of the Treaty of Rome, and more recently under the Maastricht Treaty, are an important part of health and safety laws. Directives are binding, although member states can decide how to give them legal and administrative effect. In the UK this is usually in the form of regulations. For example, the **Noise at Work Regulations** mentioned earlier are an example of a European directive that has been enacted in the UK.

Health and safety is an important part of the **Single European Act**, which lays emphasis on providing safe working conditions in all member states. The emphasis is on harmonising working conditions.

In addition, new directives have been established about the technical requirements and safety standards of products.

The **Working Time Directive** which has implications for health and safety, was adopted in 1994. The main provisions of the directive are:

- A minimum daily rest period of 11 consecutive hours;
- At least 1 day off a week;
- Mandatory daily rest breaks after 6 hours;
- Four weeks' annual paid holiday;
- No more than 8 hours per shift for nightwork averaged over a period to be determined by each member state.

This directive, which is now likely to be enforced by all EU members, will have a significant impact in Britain, which has the longest working hours and the most shift work of any European country. In the past, the UK abstained from voting on the directive; under the present Labour government, the UK is expected to rapidly move into line.

Consumer protection law

Every good or service that is bought or sold must meet certain standards. Some of these standards are laid down in law, some in voluntary codes of practice within an industry, and others are set by individual businesses.

Businesses supply goods or services for consumers in return for payment. The legal system sets out a fair framework for trading and for the settlement of disputes that may arise.

- The **Sale of Goods Act** says that goods must be:

  – *'Of merchantable quality'*, i.e. free from significant faults, except defects which are drawn to the buyer's attention by the seller (for instance, if goods are declared to be 'shop soiled').

  – *'Fit for the purpose'*, including any particular purpose mentioned by the buyer to the seller. For example, if the customer asks for a jumper that is machine-washable, they should not be sold one that has to be hand-washed.

  – *'As described'*, i.e. on the package or sales literature, or verbally by the seller. If the customer is told that a shirt is 100% cotton, then it should not turn out to be a mixture of cotton and polyester.

  The Sale of Goods Act also states that products must reach a reasonable level of safety.

- The **Trades Descriptions Act** states that the description given of the goods forms part of the contract between the buyer and the seller. This Act makes it a criminal offence for a trader to describe goods falsely. A type of case frequently prosecuted under this Act is the turning back of the 'clock' on a used car to disguise the mileage.

- The **Consumer Credit Act** states that if a business plans to hire out equipment for longer than three months, it must apply for a licence. It is a criminal offence to trade without a licence. The Act sets out to protect the rights of consumers when they purchase goods on credit, e.g. through hire purchase.

  It states for example that consumers must be given a copy of any credit agreements into which they enter. It also prevents credit firms from sending their representatives to people's homes to persuade them to take on credit agreements which have high interest rates. It also allows consumers a 'cooling-off period' in which they can cancel any credit agreement which they may have entered into in haste.

- The **Data Protection Act** requires businesses which hold personal data about individuals on computer to register with the Data Protection Registrar.

- The **Financial Services Act** states that businesses that provide financial advice or any related services must meet certain requirements.

  For example, they must make sure that customers are given full advice on the range of alternative ways of investing their money and the likely rewards from such investments.

- The **Supply of Goods and Services Act** requires that suppliers of services should carry out their task with reasonable care and skill and within a reasonable timescale.

IT'S A FACT

In America insurance claims under product liability can cost firms millions of dollars. One woman successfully sued a company that supplied her with a microwave oven. She had placed her pet dog in the microwave to dry it off after a bath without realising how quickly the microwave would have a cooking effect. She argued that the microwave should have come with clearer instructions about its use. She won several million dollars in compensation from the manufacturers.

- The **Weights and Measures Act** aims to ensure that consumers receive the quantity of goods that they believe they are buying. For example, pre-packed items must display details of the quantity contained within the pack. It is an offence to give 'short weight'.

- The **Food and Drugs Act** covers the contents of food and medicines. The government needs to control this area of trading so that the public is not led into buying anything that might be harmful. Some items have to carry warnings – tins of kidney beans, for example, must clearly state that they need to be boiled thoroughly before eating. The Act also lays down minimum standards for certain food products. For example, a sausage can only be called a sausage if it contains a certain amount of meat.

- The **Food Safety Act**. This gives Environmental Health Officers powers to shut down premises where food is not being prepared in a hygienic way. Regulations cover such things as refrigeration temperatures.

- The **Prices Act** covers the way prices are displayed in restaurants, pubs, cafés and petrol stations.

- The **Unsolicited Goods and Services Act** prevents businesses from sending customers unsolicited goods in the hope that the recipient will buy them.

- The **Unfair Contract Terms Act** prevents businesses from evading their responsibilities by using unfair disclosure clauses or disclaimers.

TASK 49.1

Set out a table showing which of the above laws has been broken in each of the following examples:

1 A householder receives goods that they have not ordered through the post. Shortly afterwards they receive a bill for the goods.

2 A customer buys sausages from the local butcher which on inspection are found to consist almost entirely of bread paste.

3 A consumer is visited at home by a 'high-pressure salesperson' who persuades them to buy living-room furniture costing several thousand pounds.

4 A businessman signs a deal to hire a photocopier. After six months he finds that the photocopying charges are too expensive and decides to return it. He is then informed that there is an obscure clause in tiny print on the original agreement, to the effect that he must keep up the hire for a minimum of five years.

5 A motorist visits a garage and buys ten litres of petrol. She is shocked to find that the price of petrol is 50% higher than elsewhere. This is not displayed anywhere on the forecourt.

6 A shopper buys apples in the local market. On returning home he discovers that he has been sold short weight.

7 A consumer buys a watch which is described as being waterproof. After swimming with the watch on, the consumer discovers that the watch has stopped.

8 A customer visits a supermarket bakery and notices that the people working in the bakery are not wearing protective hair coverings.

Trading Standards Departments of local authorities (also known as **Consumer Protection Departments**) have powers to investigate complaints about false or misleading descriptions or prices, inaccurate weights and measures, consumer credit and the safety of consumer goods. They will often advise on everyday shopping problems.

Environmental Health Departments deal with health matters such as sub-standard food and drinks and dirty shops and restaurants.

Compulsory insurance

Many business activities involve a considerable amount of risk, including risk to members of the public. When accidents occur businesses stand to be sued in courts of law. There are therefore a number of types of business insurance which are **compulsory** in law. Businesses need to take out insurance against these risks, and their insurance premiums are an important part of their overheads.

Public liability

Public liability insurance covers an organisation's legal liability to pay compensation for bodily injury, illness or disease to third parties, or for loss or damage to their property caused through activities of the business (including the ownership or occupation of premises used in connection with the business).

£1 million of public liability insurance is generally regarded to be the minimum level of indemnity required by even a small business.

IT'S A FACT

For owners and managers of sporting facilities, public liability insurance is essential, particularly in the case of spectator sports. Teams entering the football league must have grounds which meet minimum safety requirements, and in the higher divisions all-seater stadiums are a legal requirement.

Product liability

Product liability must be taken out in conjunction with public liability. This will cover an organisation against legal liability to pay compensation for bodily injury, illness or disease to third parties, or for loss or damage to their property, caused by goods sold, supplied, repaired, serviced, tested, altered, installed, processed or delivered by or through the organisation.

Organisations should only deal with suppliers that have product liability.

Employer's liability

This covers employers against claims by employees arising out of employment. Under the **Employers' Liability (Compulsory) Insurance Act**, most employers are legally required to take out a minimum indemnity of £2 million and most will take out an indemnity for at least £10 million. A copy of the insurance certificate must be prominently displayed in the workplace.

Motor Insurance

It is a compulsory requirement for business organisations to insure against accidents caused by their vehicles. Accidents may lead to death, bodily injury or damage to other people or their property. The minimum insurance required is **third party** i.e. insurance to cover vehicles, property, and lives other than your own.

For business purposes, organisations should take out comprehensive insurance to cover all parties involved in accidents.

Chapter summary

- Every business operates within a legal environment which is a key influence on its activities. Key areas are contracts of employment, employment rights, health and safety and consumer protection.
- A contract of employment comes into being once an employer has made an offer of employment, and the employee has accepted this offer.
- Many rights depend upon an employee's period of continuous employment with an employer.
- In 1971 a new law gave employees protection against unfair dismissal.
- Claims for unfair dismissal must be lodged with an industrial tribunal within three months. The employer must then prove that the dismissal was for a fair reason.
- Both the employer and the employee have a duty in law to provide safe working conditions.
- The Health and Safety at Work Act is the most important piece of legislation covering health and safety in the workplace.

- An organisation must issue a safety policy statement to its employees.
- An employee can claim for damages arising from an employer's negligence if the employer fails 'to abide by the duty of care to the employee so that the employee suffers injury or damage to health'.
- UK working practices are increasingly governed by European Union legislation, directives and regulation. The Single European Act places emphasis on providing safe working conditions in all member states.
- Organisations need to be familiar with a range of consumer protection laws governing aspects of business activity such as credit agreements, the supply of goods, the pricing of goods etc.
- Organisations are required by law to take out various forms of insurance, including employer's liability, public liability, and product liability, as well as taking out a minimum of third-party motor insurance.

9 Marketing strategy

INTRODUCTION

In Unit 4 of this book we looked at the process of marketing and gave a brief description of the nature of the marketplace and the marketing mix. Much of this earlier unit was about the marketing process and the preparation for action rather than the action itself. Unit 9 takes this a stage further, exploring in detail the design of the marketing process and its strategic orientation towards customer needs.

We begin this unit by looking in some detail at how firms make sense of marketing information. As we show, there must be a clear link between market research and the decision-making process. Much of this research will generate both quantitative and qualitative information,

both of which are valuable. The unit then analyses marketing strategies such as the Boston Matrix and the theories of Ansoff. This is followed by a detailed analysis of the four generally identified ingredients of the marketing mix, Product, Price, Place and Promotion, emphasising the importance of each element.

Chapter 56 deals with marketing planning, a critical process which brings together the ingredients of the marketing mix and the process of strategic marketing in a blueprint which keeps the organisation focused on its key objectives. This is followed by a short chapter on the development and importance of international marketing.

50 Making sense of marketing information

In Part 1 we saw that market research was concerned with the *'systematic gathering, recording and analysing of data about problems relating to the marketing of goods and services'*. This definition makes a clear link between market research information and the decisions which are made about goods or services. It is **market research information** that provides the basis for these decisions.

A key point to remember is that what comes out of market research is only as good as what goes in. The structure of the questions, the sample size and type and the nature of the questioning should all be carefully considered before any project proceeds.

All market research generates some form of **data**. Data is the *product* of market research. Data might include sales figures for the last few years, stated area by area. This information can be very useful. Comparisons can be made between areas; changes in sales trends and also changes over time can be analysed. In other words, the figures lend themselves to comparison and interpretation. A single piece of data such as a sales figure on a particular date is not very useful unless it can be used to make comparisons.

Qualitative information
As we saw earlier, there are two broad types of data: **qualitative** and **quantitative** information.

Qualitative information will usually consist of some form of narrative which may be spoken or written. Where words are spoken, it may be necessary to record or transcribe what is being said. Most qualitative information arises from some form of detailed interview with a respondent or through focus group activity.

The 'what do you think about x?' approach allows people to offer a variety of opinions, reasons, motivations and influencing factors. A group discussion allows different opinions to be offered. This will frequently lead to a consensus, which in turn will reflect the popular view.

In general, people enjoy giving their opinions, and this helps researchers. But it is vital that the audience is carefully selected to provide relevant replies. For instance, if you are sounding out large-scale cereal farmers' opinions of their advisory body with particular reference to grain-drying techniques, the sample chosen for the research must be composed of cereal farmers with appropriate acreage.

Quantitative information
Quantitative research yields numbers. These provide a measurable record or a series of values from which analysis can proceed. For example, a piece of quantitative data might refer to whether people watch TV on a Friday between 7.00 pm and 9.00 pm. As some will watch TV between these times and some will not, there will be two values or categories of respondents. These two values are referred to as **dichotomies**.

Sometimes there are more categories or values which form a **scale**. There are a number of different types of scale. Some, known as **ordinal scales**, are presented in order – for example, 0–15, 16–35, 36–50, etc. But it may be that the scale is not in any form of order. For example, research may ask individuals how they cook potatoes. Respondents may refer to frying, roasting, boiling and other alternatives. The term used to describe scales which list categories in any order is **nominal scales**.

Elements of quantitative measurement are said to have four components. These are:

1 **A case** – the object, person, situation or organisation being measured and recorded;
2 **A variable** – the characteristic which is being measured and classified;
3 **A scale** – as we have seen, this is a series of values/outcomes which the research measures;
4 **A value** – what is actually recorded by the process, usually as a series of numbers or measures.

The uses of qualitative and quantitative data
Market research helps an organisation to develop a clear picture of the effectiveness of its strategies and to assess the size and shape of its markets. Quantitative information should help to provide a clear indication of:

● The relative success of different products and brands;
● The influence and timing of strategies;
● Quarterly and annual sales and trends;
● Market potential;
● Current and potential market share.

Qualitative data provides:

● Information to enable organisations to identify the reasons behind trends;
● Opportunities for further market development;
● First-hand ideas that might influence the development of products and strategies;
● Opportunities to assess and evaluate the effectiveness of strategies.

In summary, **quantitative** data helps to produce an idea of the size and overall shape of markets and the effects of strategies on the demand for goods and services.

Qualitative data helps to take this process further. It shows how goods or services meet the needs of current and potential customers.

	Theatre	Classical Concerts	Jazz Concerts	Pop & Rock Concerts	Opera	Ballet	Contemporary Dance
				Percentage of adults			
Adults	37.6	12.0	6.4	22.1	6.6	7.2	3.6
Male	33.8	11.6	7.6	24.5	5.8	5.0	2.6
Females	41.2	12.4	6.3	19.8	7.3	9.3	4.4
15–24	33.3	8.7	7.9	40.1	4.3	5.7	5.8
25–34	39.0	9.2	8.4	40.2	6.0	6.9	4.2
35–44	41.4	12.9	5.9	27.7	6.3	7.7	4.0
45–54	44.8	16.0	8.0	16.1	7.7	8.9	3.5
55–64	40.1	16.1	6.9	3.1	9.4	9.0	2.7
65+	29.3	11.0	2.3	1.1	6.5	5.9	1.3
AB	57.2	26.0	11.3	24.9	14.3	14.3	6.2
C1	46.4	14.2	8.3	28.7	7.3	9.2	4.2
C2	28.9	6.1	4.2	22.0	3.5	3.5	2.2
D	22.4	3.9	2.4	16.4	2.1	2.6	1.9
E	19.2	5.5	3.2	9.6	2.9	3.2	2.1

Figure 50.1 Profile of theatre- and concert-goers

A useful perspective can be provided by a **control group**. This is a second non-target group added to the sample to allow comparisons to be made. A control group will often provide direction for more precise quantitative research to support qualitative work which has already been done.

TASK 50.1

Imagine that you have been asked to introduce a new magazine which targets potential opera-goers aged under 44. How might you use the information in Figure 50.1? What other data might you require? Would this data be quantitative or qualitative? In what way would the two forms of data be complementary?

Analysing market research data

Having collected data, the market researcher must decide upon the analysis techniques to be used. The choice will depend on the aims of the research. Statistical analysis of the data will allow decisions to be taken with greater precision and probability of success.

Central tendency
One way of analysing a collection of values is to use **measures of central tendency** – middle values. When we talk about middle values we normally think of an 'average' but a more correct term is the **arithmetic mean**. Two other measures of average or central tendency are the **median** and the **mode.**

The mean
This is quite simply the sum of a set of numbers divided by the number of items. For example, if sales figures (in pounds) over a six-day period are 165, 190, 185, 190, 180 and 170, the mean would be:

$$\frac{165 + 190 + 185 + 190 + 180 + 170}{6}$$

$$= \frac{1,080}{6} = £180$$

Therefore we can say that:

$$\textit{Arithmetic mean} = \frac{\textit{Sum of observations}}{\textit{Number of observations}}$$

If data such as daily sales figures are collected over a long period, adding up all the levels and dividing by the number of days may be time-consuming and prone to error. In these circumstances, it can be useful to derive a **frequency distribution table**.

For example, assume that a business's sales figures (in units) over 50 days are as follows:

5	6	2	6	5	2	6	4	6	5
5	6	4	5	3	5	6	5	6	5
6	5	3	3	2	4	3	2	3	5
4	3	5	2	1	4	2	5	1	4
5	4	4	4	5	3	5	2	4	5

These can be presented as shown in the frequency distribution table below ('Σ', the Greek character 'sigma', stands for 'sum of'):

Daily sales levels in units (x)	Frequency of occurrence (f)	Level x frequency (fx)
1	2	2
2	7	14
3	7	21
4	10	40
5	16	80
6	8	48
	$\Sigma f = 50$	$\Sigma(fx) = 205$

On multiplying each value or daily sales figure (x) by the frequency with which it occurs (f), a total is achieved – $\Sigma(fx)$. This can then be divided by the number of days to derive the arithmetic mean.

The arithmetic mean is usually shown as $\bar{x}$ and the formula by which it is calculated is:

$$\bar{x} = \frac{\Sigma(fx)}{\Sigma f}$$

In our example, the arithmetic mean is $\frac{205}{50}$, or 4.1 units per day.

The median

When figures are arranged in numerical order, the median is the value in the middle. For example, data ordered into the array 2, 7, 9, 12 and 15 would have the number 9 in the middle, so 9 would be the median value.

In our previous example, there was an even number of figures (50). When calculating the median for a frequency distribution it is usual to say that the middle value is:

- $\frac{(n + 1)}{2}$ if the total frequency (n) is an odd number;

- $\frac{n}{2}$ if the total frequency (n) is an even number.

In this example, the 25th number reflects a daily sales figure of 4 units.

The mode

The mode is simply the value that occurs more frequently than any other. If sales over four days are 15, 12, 15 and 17, the mode is 15 because that number occurs more frequently than any other. If two or more frequencies occur the same number of times, the distribution is **multimodal**. When there is only one mode the distribution is said to be **unimodal**.

Finding the mode is more complicated when the values are not known precisely but have been found to be in definite ranges. In the example below there are five ranges:

Range		Frequency
At least	**Less than**	
10	20	5
20	30	12
30	40	18
40	50	10
50	60	4

The mode is now calculated approximately from the formula:

$$\text{Mode} = L + \left[\frac{(F - F_{m-1}) \times c}{2F - F_{m-1} - F_{m+1}} \right]$$

where L is the lower limit of the modal class (30), F_{m-1} is the frequency of the class below the modal class (12), F is the frequency of the modal class itself (18), F_{m+1} is the frequency of the class above the modal class (10), and C is the class interval (10). Our estimate of the mode in this case would therefore be:

$$\text{Mode} = 30 + \left[\frac{(18 - 12) \times 10}{(2 \times 18) - 12 - 10} \right]$$

$$= 34.28$$

The mode, calculated in this way from a frequency distribution, is only an estimated figure.

Time series

A time series is a set of values recorded over time. It may be plotted daily, weekly or monthly, and it is usual for the horizontal axis to be used to denote the time dimension. If there is a clear trend, the historical figures can be used to predict what will happen in the near future.

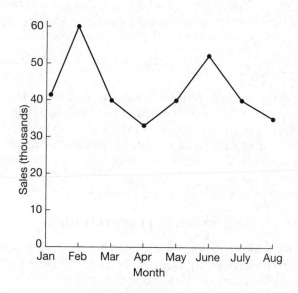

Figure 50.2: Time series showing monthly sales

In Figure 50.2, the fluctuation in sales figures from trough to trough and from peak to peak is called a **cycle**. However, what we need to know is whether the sales are steadily increasing in the longer term. Somehow, we need to separate the trend from the short-term fluctuations.

Calculating a moving average

To separate out a trend from a cycle we can use a statistical technique known as a **moving average**. Imagine that a business which sells financial services wants to keep a weekly moving average of sales in order to identify a trend. Its sales tend to peak every four weeks. The moving average smoothes out the peaks so that the

CASE STUDY CASE STUDY CASE STUDY CASE STUDY CASE STUDY

UK POPULATION PROJECTIONS

You work as a market researcher for a business producing a range of white goods such as washing machines mainly for the home market. Look through the population projections below and consider:

1 How you might use measures of central tendency to analyse this information;

2 How this information could be used to help make marketing decisions.

		1992	1995	2000	2010	2020
Home population	Millions	58.0	58.6	59.6	61.1	62.1
	Index	100.0	101.0	102.8	105.4	107.0
Sex distribution	% Males	48.9	49.0	49.3	49.6	49.7
	% Females	51.1	51.0	50.7	50.4	50.3
Age distribution	% aged 0–14	19.3	19.5	19.5	18.1	17.2
	% aged 15–29	22.0	20.6	18.9	19.1	18.5
	% aged 30–44	21.1	21.6	22.6	19.9	18.1
	% aged 45–59	16.9	17.8	18.5	20.2	20.9
	% aged 60–74	13.7	13.5	13.0	14.9	16.6
	% aged 75+	7.0	7.0	7.5	7.8	8.7

Population projections for the UK

STUDY CASE STUDY CASE STUDY CASE STUDY CASE STUDY CASE STUDY

underlying trend can be followed. Figure 50.3 shows how this is done, and Figure 50.4 shows the data plotted as a graph. The moving average is calculated in three stages.

- *Stage 1:* Calculate the four-week moving totals using the sales figures from the second column. For example, 25 + 28 + 33 + 38 = 124. The total then moves by deleting the first week and adding the following (fifth) week. The second total is 28 + 33 + 38 + 34 = 133.

- *Stage 2:* Calculate the four-week moving averages by dividing the four-week moving totals by 4. For example, 124 divided by 4 is 31, 133 divided is 4 is 33.25, etc.

- *Stage 3:* The four-week moving averages show the trend. If the trend line in the graph is extended to the right, this process of extrapolation will help to provide a forecast of sales activity in the coming weeks.

Week	Sales (thousands)	Four-week moving totals	Four-week moving averages
1	25		
2	28		
3	33		
4	38	124	31.00
5	34	133	33.25
6	37	142	35.50
7	42	151	37.75
8	43	156	39.00
9	39	161	40.25
10	42	166	41.50
11	45	169	42.25
12	48	174	43.50
13	43	178	44.50
14	47	183	45.75
15	50	188	47.00
16	52	192	48.00

Figure 50.3 Weekly sales of financial services

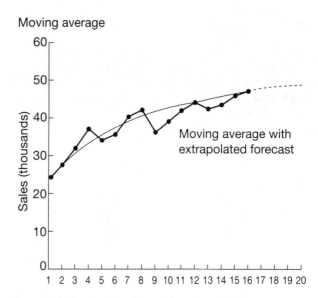

Figure 50.4 Weekly sales of financial services, showing a moving average

Week	Sales (thousands)	Four-week moving totals	Four-week moving averages	Weighting	After exponential smoothing
10	42	166	41.50	1.0	41.50
			NEW SHOPPING CENTRE OPENS		
11	45	169	42.25	1.1	46.48
12	48	174	43.50	1.1	47.85
13	43	178	44.50	1.1	48.95
14	47	183	45.75	1.1	50.33 etc.

Figure 50.5

One criticism of the moving average is that it tends to disguise the most recent changes to figures, as these are counterbalanced by figures from earlier weeks. The moving average, therefore, may not adequately identify any sudden changes in trends. To compensate for this, **exponential smoothing** can be used. This uses a weighting technique to emphasise the importance of the most recent figures. The weighting is chosen at the discretion of a manager, depending on how much emphasis he or she wishes to place on the later figures.

For example, imagine a business in a typical high street. If a new shopping centre opens, the business owners will naturally expect to see more shoppers in the town and the later figures would then take on more importance. Figure 50.5 above shows that the weighting was increased from 1.0 to 1.1 when the new shopping centre opens. As a result the exponential smoothing provides a more optimistic forecast than the moving average.

Correlation and regression

Correlation analysis is concerned with the relationship or correlation between two sets of variables. For example, it can be used to analyse the relationship between the use of a variable in the marketing mix such as advertising, and its influence on the sales of a particular brand.

The closer the relationship or correlation between two variables, the better and more accurate predictions are likely to be. For example, Figures 50.6 and 50.7 show the relationship between advertising expenditure and the sales of Brand A.

Advertising expenditure (£000s)	Brand A (sales units)
12	284
18	325
27	376
39	447
47	499
55	530
64	602

Figure 50.6

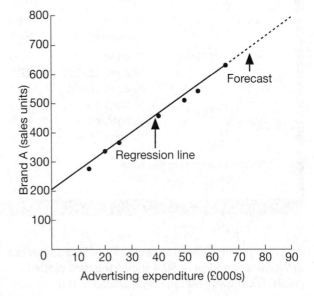

Figure 50.7

A scattergraph may be used to illustrate the relationship between two variables. It shows the **independent variable** on the horizontal axis and the **dependent variable** on the vertical axis.

If both variables rise, as in this case, then this is known as **positive correlation**. The straight line or 'line of best fit' is called the **regression line** (the closer the points lie to the line, the stronger the linear correlation). Beyond the end of the regression line it is possible to use extrapolation to forecast future sales.

In other circumstances there can exist what is called a **negative correlation**. Here, as one variable gets bigger, the other gets smaller. This produces a scattergraph in which, although the points may again be close to a straight line, the line slopes downhill from the top left to the bottom right. Figure 50.8 on page 361 opposite shows what might happen to the sales of *The Sun* if advertising expenditure on *The Daily Mirror* was substantially increased.

There are some situations where virtually no relationship can be identified between two variables. In such a case there is said to be **zero correlation** (Figure 50.9).

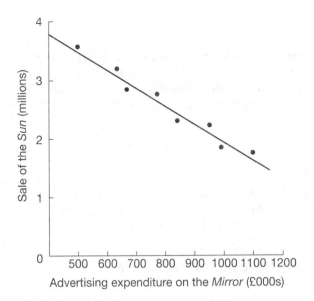

Figure 50.8 Scattergraph showing negative correlation

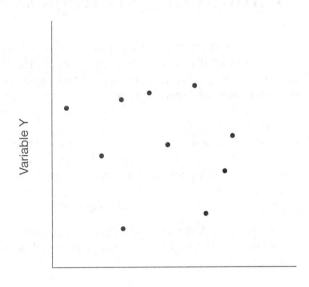

Figure 50.9 Zero correlation

The marketing information system

When undertaken properly, market research creates a considerable flow of information throughout an organisation. In order to co-ordinate this information and ensure that data is collected and used properly, it is important to set up some form of **marketing information system**.

A well-constructed marketing information system should be able to identify sales levels, together with stock and output figures, and then analyse these together with market share details, trend data and information on profitability. The system should regularly generate:

- Internal weekly or monthly operating data, such as sales trends, price information, production targets and budgets;
- External data such as sales performance, information on consumer behaviour, lifestyles and attitudes, and the needs of consumers for products.

The marketing information system helps an organisation to develop in response to its research objectives, and provides information in a usable form for a range of management purposes. This database of knowledge and supporting statistical analysis will help managers to ensure that they supply goods and services effectively for their customers.

Chapter summary

- Marketing research data forms the basis for marketing decisions.
- There are two broad types of data, qualitative data and quantitative data.
- Elements of quantitative measurement are said to have four components: a case, a variable, a scale and a value.
- Central tendency is a way of analysing middle values.
- The mean is the sum of a set of numbers divided by the number of items.
- When figures are arranged into numerical order, the median is the value in the middle.
- The mode is the value that occurs more frequently than any other.

- A time series records a set of figures as they occur over time.
- To separate out a trend from a cycle, a statistical technique known as a moving average is used.
- If a trend is extended, this is known as extrapolation.
- Exponential smoothing uses a weighting technique to emphasise the importance of recent figures.
- Correlation analysis is concerned with the relationship between two sets of variables.
- A marketing information system is used to co-ordinate data and to ensure that data is used properly.

51 Marketing strategies

The first question any organisation must ask is 'What are our objectives?' Rather than seeking maximum profits, an organisation may wish to become a brand leader or otherwise dominate a specific market. This may yield more benefits in the long term. Corporate growth is another common objective. Taking over companies, diversifying and introducing new products may not help profitability, but it will provide managers with control over a larger corporate unit. Other organisations may take great pride in the way they are viewed by the public; they may be prepared to sacrifice profit, but never reputation.

All of these activities are a function of marketing strategies. Such strategies are firmly intertwined with corporate strategy.

The essence of corporate planning is to match marketing objectives with corporate objectives. This enables an organisation to develop marketing strategies which focus upon the consumer in achieving their goals.

Differentiation
Earlier in this book we saw that there are two main components in a marketing strategy. These are:

1 Identifying and targeting customers in a market which an organisation wishes to reach;
2 Creating and maintaining a marketing mix for customers in that market.

In using this marketing mix, an organisation has to decide whether to use an undifferentiated or total market strategy based on providing a single mix for the whole market, or to use a differentiated approach based upon segmentation.

Injecting life into the product life-cycle
In Chapter 5 we looked at the stages of the product life-cycle and how the marketing mix can be used to inject new life into the product. We saw that this can be done by:

● Changing or modifying the product to keep ahead of the competition;
● Changing prices in line with competition from rivals;
● Altering distribution patterns to make it more convenient for consumers to make a purchase;
● Running promotional campaigns.

Using the product life-cycle
Businesses with a single product are always likely to be vulnerable in the marketplace. By spreading investments across a range of products an organisation is able to spread its risks.

The Boston matrix

A common method used by organisations when developing a marketing strategy is based on the **market share/market growth matrix**. This was devised by the **Boston Consultancy Group (BCG)**.

The 'Boston matrix' identifies four main types of product:

1 **Prospects/stars**
   These products compete in rapidly expanding markets. They take up large sums for investment purposes but they also yield high cash returns. On balance they provide a neutral cash flow, but generally they will go on to become the yielders/cash cows of the future.

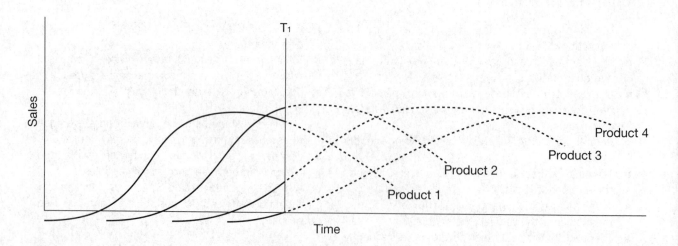

Figure 51.1 A portfolio of products at different stages in their life-cycles

FIG 51.4

Market growth \ Relative market share	High	Low
High	Prospects/ Stars	Question marks/ Problem children
Low	Yielders/Cash Cows	Dogs

Figure 51.2 Growth/share matrix

2 Yielders/cash cows

These have a high market share in markets that are no longer expanding. Because the market is relatively static they need few fresh injections of capital. Advertising and promotion may be required to inject fresh life from time to time. However, the net effect is positive cash flow. Cash cows often provide the 'bread and butter' of a business.

3 Question marks/problem children

These have a low market share in fast-growing markets. The question is, can they be turned into market leaders? Though they may go on to be powerful earners, they can be a drain on resources.

4 Dogs

These products have a low market share in low-growth markets and generate negative cash flows.

In terms of cash flow, the matrix may be redrawn as in Figure 51.3 below. Cash generated by the yielders is used to help with the development of question marks. The aim is to increase the market share of the question marks in order to move them into the 'prospect' category, with the expectation that they will eventually become yielders.

In order to manage the development of products effectively, it is important to have a balanced portfolio. For example, an organisation may require a number of yielders, as well as prospects, at any one time.

SYNTHESIS

How might the various product categories from the Boston Matrix relate to the various phases of the product life-cycle?

Use a product known to you to see if you can match the two.

Reviewing the product portfolio

What happens when a question mark fails to become a star, or a cash cow goes into decline? These are questions that need to be constantly reviewed. Marketers need to consider a number of factors:

- **Expected sales and profits**

  A product's performance can be evaluated against its previous performance. Once the indicators start to dip, then it is clear that remedial action is needed.

- **Relative market share**

  This is always important. Once market share starts to fall, the product may lose its competitive edge.

- **Threats**

  The development of threats in the marketplace needs to be carefully monitored. These can include:

  – The emergence of new technology;
  – the arrival of competition;
  – Changes in consumer expenditure patterns, etc.

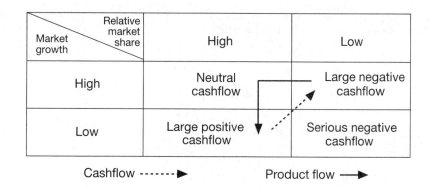

Figure 51.3 Cash flow in the Boston Matrix

COMPETING IN THE PETROL WAR

As the petrol industry continues its vicious contraction, motorists are becoming used to the sight of empty forecourts, padlocks on pumps and shutters on kiosks. During 1996, more than 1,500 petrol stations closed in the UK, a decline of 10 per cent and more than double the rate of the previous year.

Petrol station numbers have been shrinking for more than a decade. Big oil companies like Esso have been discounting the price of petrol for long periods, often selling the product at a loss in order to restore market share lost to the hypermarkets. BP recently disclosed that the price war in the UK had cost its downstream business some £85 million.

Overall, it is thought that petrol retailers in the UK have lost around £1 billion. According to an oil consultant, the average gross margin earned from selling petrol has fallen by 3p a litre since 1994. Whereas major oil companies can stand losses as the UK represents only a small part of their global marketplace, independent dealers suffer.

The irony is that the underlying petrol marketplace is healthy. During 1996, the volume of road fuel sales grew by 4 per cent. The reason for all this activity is the hypermarkets. Huge volumes and low overheads allow superstores to sell petrol at tiny gross margins – 3p a litre – without suffering losses. Most service stations which

pay rent and rates and have lower-volume business need margins of 6 or 7p to stay in business.

Esso claims that its marketing strategy has succeeded in restoring its market share. But at whose expense? The hypermarkets continue to expand. The contraction has come from the independent dealers – sites owned and managed by private operators who have an agreement with an oil company to supply their brand of petrol. Lacking huge volume sales, the independents cannot afford to run at the tight margins imposed by the discounters.

The biggest reduction in dealer network during 1996 came from the Frost Group, which saw its chain shrink from 1,144 sites to 614. Other smaller dealer networks have continued to suffer.

1 Why are hypermarkets able to discount petrol at low prices?

2 What strategies have the oil companies used to compete with the hypermarkets? Refer in your answer not just to prices, but also to the changing role of the service station.

3 Is there any future for independent petrol retailers? If you were an independent retailer, what strategies would you adopt to inject life into your product?

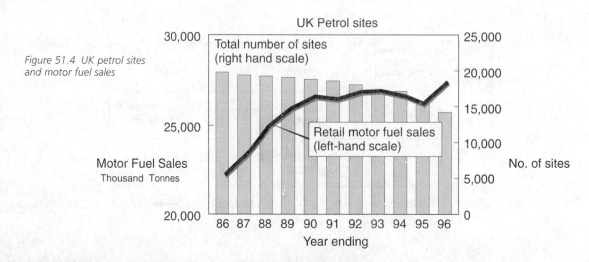

Figure 51.4 UK petrol sites and motor fuel sales

The product/market matrix

Another way of analysing a marketing strategy is to look at the product/market matrix. This theory was developed by H Igor Ansoff. It looks not just at the management of the product portfolio but also more widely at market developments and opportunities. Ansoff's matrix matches existing and new product strategies with existing and new markets.

PRODUCTS

		Existing products	New products
M A R K E T S	Existing markets	Consolidation Market penetration	Product development
	New markets	Market development	Diversification

Figure 51.5 Ansoff's product/market matrix

The matrix suggests five alternative marketing strategies which hinge on whether the market and the product are new or existing:

- **Consolidation** implies a positive and active defence of existing products in existing markets;

- **Market penetration** suggests a further penetration of existing markets with existing products. This will involve a strategy of increasing market share within existing segments and markets;

- **Product development** involves developing new products for existing markets;

- **Market development** will use existing products and find new markets for them. These new markets will be identified by better customer targeting, market research and further segmentation;

- **Diversification** will lead to a movement away from core activities. This might involve some form of integration or diversification into related activities.

EXTENSION MATERIAL

The 'experience curve'

The Boston Consultancy Group's work is based upon the concept of the 'experience curve' which shows that unit costs of adding value fall as production increases.

Efficiency stems from greater experience. The BCG argue that the principle has general currency, and that average cost per unit falls by roughly 20–30 per cent with each doubling of experience. Greater experience leads to:

- Economies of scale;
- Elimination of less efficient factors of production;
- Increased productivity
- Improvements in product design.

The key lesson is that the benefits of experience do not just happen. Companies must act positively to ensure that they reap the benefits.

An important implication is that 'experience' is a key asset. Companies that have a high market share should be able to accumulate more experience. Therefore companies should strive for a high market share. The best indicator of market share is relative – that is, the ratio of a company's market share to that of its largest competitor:

Relative market share of A =

   Market share of company A
   ——————————————————
   Market share of nearest competitor

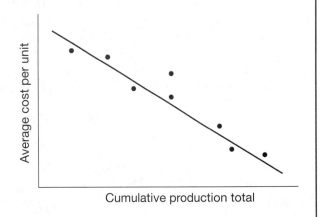

Figure 51.6 An 'experience curve'

This indicator gives a clear measure of comparative strength. The Boston Consultancy Group used statistical evidence to argue that a ratio of 2:1 is likely to give a 20 per cent cost advantage.

With regard to market growth, the Boston Consultancy Group argues that the faster the growth of a particular market, the greater the costs necessary to maintain market share. In a rapidly growing market, firms need to invest heavily in developing product lines and combatting the threat posed by new firms and brands.

Strategies in markets

Inevitably, in any one market there is only room for one market leader. The market leader is simply the organisation or product with the highest market share. In some markets, market leaders may have a large slice of market share, but in most, market leaders have a share of between 10 and 20 per cent.

Challengers, followers and nichers

Organisations which follow market leaders and which seek to become market leaders are known as **market challengers**. Their aim is to win market share. They may be the second, third or fourth companies in a market.

In most markets there will also be **market followers**. These organisations will have little market share. Their commitment to research and development may be poor. For these businesses, survival is often the main aim.

Markets will also contain **market nichers** – companies which target a single segment and specialise in a narrow range of products.

SYNTHESIS

Pareto's rule states that 20 per cent of time and effort produces 80 per cent of the results. An extension of this idea would be to suggest that 20 per cent of customers account for 80 per cent of an organisation's sales. Is there any truth in this? If so, what implications might this have for an organisation's marketing strategies?

IT'S A FACT

The end of the road is nearing for the Ford Escort. More than 30 years after it first rolled off the production line, Ford is seeking to rename the humble family saloon whose drivers have included Princess Diana and Kenneth Clarke.

Chapter summary

- Market strategy is a plan of action designed to target customers in a way which provides an organisation with a series of benefits over its competitors.
- Corporate growth is a common objective of organisations.
- Marketing strategies are intertwined with corporate strategies.
- The two components of a marketing strategy are the identification and targeting of customers and the creation of a marketing mix for that market.

- A common marketing strategy is to inject life into the product life-cycle in order to extend the growth period.
- The market share/market growth matrix is commonly used to help develop marketing strategies.
- The BCG's work is based upon the 'experience curve'.
- Another way of analysing the alternative marketing strategies available is to use the product/market matrix.

52 Product

Probably the most important decision for any organisation is how to develop an effective **product strategy**. The product is at the heart of any exchange or transaction.

The product provides a range of physical or functional characteristics which accompany the good or service being offered.

Product issues

For any product there are always a range of issues to be decided. For example:

- How long are products going to last?
- Which products require support?
- How can products be improved?
- How well do products perform against competitors?

In solving product issues, organisations have to analyse what their products mean to people who buy them. Customers buy goods for a number of reasons and are influenced by a number of factors when making their purchasing decisions.

For example, to buy a morning paper, most of us go to a local newspaper shop. The shop may or may not be conveniently located on the way to work or college. There may or may not be parking spaces outside. The shop itself may or may not be well laid out; it may or may not be possible to buy other products at the same time, and the service may or may not be polite and attentive. There may be the opportunity not only to buy the tangible goods on sale, but to benefit from an intangible service as well.

Product benefits

A starting point for product issues is to think about what benefits a product provides for customers. For example, many products have clear, tangible benefits such as:

- Shape
- Colour
- Size
- Design
- Packaging
- Taste

Intangible benefits are not so obvious. They may include the reputation of a business. For example, the closure of branches has clearly had a negative effect on NatWest's reputation amongst customers. Similarly, the personal vitality of someone such as Richard Branson can enhance a company's reputation and encourage people to buy its products. Brand image is also important. Many customers are willing to pay more (i.e .a premium price) for a product which has a recognisable brand name.

The product concept

Have you ever thought about why you buy products? At a simple level you may buy a coat to keep you warm, or a newspaper to read. However, as we have seen, consumer buying behaviour is a complex process. We all have a range of different motives for making our buying decisions.

For example, think about the sort of clothes you wear and then contrast them with the sort of clothes you would definitely not want to wear. A product for many of us is something which fits with our perception or self-image. Products are not just purchased to meet a single need; the ownership and use of a product involves a whole range of factors that make up the **product concept**.

For example, if a couple choose to holiday in the West Indies, it may be because they are attracted to sand, sun and surf. However, holidaying in the West Indies is associated with a particular lifestyle. In the public imagination it may represent being rich and able to afford exotic things. The couple may therefore see a holiday in the West Indies as a means of enhancing their status among friends and associates.

The purchaser of an expensive modern car will probably be interested in the quality and reliability of the vehicle. He or she may be attracted by `state of the art' technology and other features. However, a significant motivation may also be the desire to show the world they have 'arrived'.

Product dimensions

Products include a number of important dimensions. These include:

- Generic dimensions;
- Sensual dimensions;
- Extended dimensions.

Generic dimensions are the key benefits of a particular product which relate to its functions. Shoe polish cleans shoes. Freezers store frozen food. Deckchairs provide a comfortable seat on a sunny day. Hairdressers cut and style hair.

SYNTHESIS

What is a product? Cite one example from your own experience – for example, going to a football match or visiting a pub. Is the product simply the match itself or is it something more? If so, what is it?

CLIPPING THE PUFFIN'S WINGS

The Puffin biscuit became an endangered species after having its wings clipped in a fight for nesting rights on the shelves of supermarkets. At stake was a multi-million-pound chocolate biscuit business. After consulting ornithological handbooks, a High Court judge ruled that Asda was guilty of 'passing off' its own cheaper biscuit brand Puffin, in a way which implied a connection with United Biscuits' 60-year-old best-selling Penguin brand.

'Passing off'

The judge granted an injunction against continued passing-off by Asda after concluding that the Puffin's 'packaging and get-up was deceptively similar to those of Penguin', although he did not believe this was intentional. Had the Asda product, for example, been called `Bison', with a cartoon picture of a brown woolly bison, he felt that the proceedings brought by United Biscuits could not have succeeded.

Asda plan to appeal against the ruling and have made it clear that the Puffin will not vanish forever. Outside the High Court, the battle lines were drawn again, as two lifesize costumed figures of the rival birds shook hands for the television cameras before both sides flew off to prepare to do battle again!

1 How important do you think that the Penguin brand is for United Biscuits?

2 Why might customers buy Penguin in preference to other chocolate biscuits?

3 How or why might the Puffin brand confuse customers?

4 What does this case illustrate about intangible product features?

The **sensual dimensions** of a product are those that have an effect on the senses – design, colour, taste, smell and texture. A ring donut has a shape, appearance, texture, taste and smell all of its own. The sensual benefits of a product are frequently highlighted by advertisers. This is clearly true of advertisements for food and drink, e.g. `The cream of Manchester' (Boddingtons bitter), `The amber nectar' (Fosters lager).

The **extended dimensions** of a product include a wide range of additional benefits. Examples are servicing arrangements, credit facilities, guarantees and maintenance contracts.

The product portfolio

Product development requires planning. Part of this process is often an **audit** of the product portfolio to find out how far the product mix matches marketing objectives. An audit involves a thorough evaluation of all the products offered by an organisation. It enables marketers to focus not only on the positive elements of performance, but also on where the organisation may be going wrong.

Auditing the product portfolio

For example, an internal audit of a product mix may involve listing products, evaluating their types and classifications and examining their performance over a period of time to identify trends. It is important to examine various market segments and the relationships between them. Useful ratios are the net profit made per product and per region; the net profit as a percentage of sales, and the market share per region and country. Important elements may be cashflow and risk. Helpful tools of analysis may be the product life-cycle (see page 362) and the Boston Matrix (see page 363).

The **width** of a range refers to the number of different products sold or made by an organisation – for example, detergents, bleaches and washing-up liquids. The depth of a range concerns the number of different sizes or versions of each product on offer; for example, Smarties come in a range of sizes, tubes and boxes, and even appear in packets.

IT'S A FACT

The most popular tourist attraction in the UK is Alton Towers, with more than 3 million visitors a year. Kew Gardens attracts less than a million visitors!

SYNTHESIS

Identify an area for blue-sky investigation in an industry of your choice. If you were put in a position of having to justify such research, how would you do it?

New products

The product life-cycle and the Boston Matrix help to show that products do not last forever. Consumer preferences are constantly changing, and organisations need to be continually involved in developments and innovations to meet the needs of tomorrow's customers. In any well-run organisation, **research and development (R&D)** plays a vital commercial role:

- It furthers the organisation's business objectives by creating better products;
- It improves operational processes;
- It helps the rest of the business and its customers.

Not all research will pay for itself in the short term. Large companies may allocate as much as one-tenth of their research budget to blue-sky investigations – research which may only lead to the development of new products and a possible payoff in the distant future.

A new product may be one which:

- Replaces an old product;
- Opens up a new market;
- Broadens an existing market.

It may involve a major innovation or simply be a line extension, reflecting a change in a range strategy. It is often said that only about 10 per cent of newly launched products are really 'new'. In fact, it is possible to turn old products into new products simply by finding a different market for them and packaging them in a different way.

Product development may be **proactive** or **reactive**. Proactive development involves taking the lead in a market with the launch of innovative new products that are completely different to those of competitors. For example, Mercedes used airbags in their cars several years before other car manufacturers. Reactive developments follow innovations made by others. Developing a reactive approach to marketing new products can reduce the risks of being the first into a market.

New product development

There are a number of distinct stages in new product development. These are:

1 Ideas;
2 Screening of ideas;
3 Marketing analysis;
4 Product development;
5 Testing;
6 Launch and commercialisation.

As products go through each stage, crucial decisions have to be made about whether to go forward with the project or abandon it. There is, therefore, a mortality rate throughout the product development process.

Ideas

New products start from ideas. These may be completely new and unrelated to past experiences or they may simply be on-going developments based on existing products. It may help if organisations encourage ideas from within. Sources of ideas may be:

- **Research and development (R&D)** Product research and development goes hand-in-hand with market research and development (see Chapter 26). Considerable research is required between these areas, and processes need to be standardised;

NEW DRUGS FUEL GROWTH

As new drugs gain momentum, SmithKline Beecham (SB), the UK's second-largest pharmaceutical group, are promising high growth. According to SB, drugs introduced over the last five years have increased sales by 37% over the last twelve months. The star performer was Seroxat/Paxil, the depression and panic disorder treatment. Five other drugs recently entered Phase 3 trials - the final tests before commercial production. SB will not lose any drug patents until 2002.

1 Is it possible for pharmaceutical businesses to be 'reactive'?

2 How important is it for such organisations to invest in blue-sky research?

3 What phases are new drug developments likely to go through before being launched?

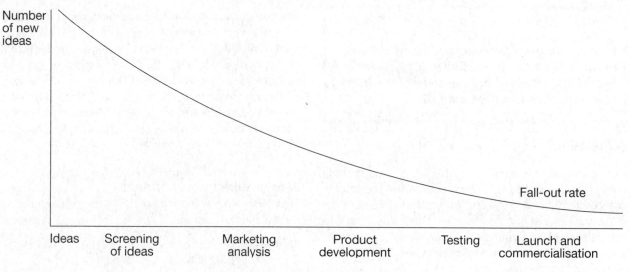

Figure 52.1 The product development process

- **Brainstorming sessions** These involve a number of people working together in a relaxed, non-judgemental atmosphere. A leader introduces key words and concepts in order to encourage participants to contribute ideas;
- **Suggestions box** Financial incentives may be used to encourage people at every level of the organisation to offer their ideas;
- **Sales force** As the sales force works in the marketplace, it is close to customers and in a strong position to understand their needs and requirements. Ideas from the sales force may be particularly useful;
- **Forced relationships** One or more products may be 'joined' or 'forced' together to form a single product – for example, shampoo and conditioner or a radio and a cassette player;
- **Competitors** If competitors seem to be doing well, it may be possible to use their ideas to develop other successful new products.

Screening of ideas

Once ideas have been generated, the next step is to screen them. Those most likely to succeed will pass through to the next phase, while others will be rejected. At this stage an organisation may consider:

- Whether the product idea matches the organisation's capabilities, e.g. in terms of technology and ease of manufacture;
- How well the product fits in with other products in the organisation's portfolio;
- What unique elements the idea offers, so that any competitive advantage can be identified;
- Practical testing of the concept before any financial investment takes place;
- The likely demand for the product.

Marketing analysis

Once ideas have been screened, marketing analysis begins. This involves a thorough analysis of the product's potential market as well as the product's place within that market.

Marketing analysis attempts to provide more detailed information about the commercial aspects of the project and may involve both primary and secondary research (see Chapter 26). For example, it may help to answer the following questions:

- How will consumers react to the product?
- What is the likely size of the market?
- Will the market sustain its size?
- Who are the competitors?
- How should the product be packaged?
- What additional features should be developed?

This type of research also helps to identify the market volume (the number of units which could be sold) as well as market value (the value of expected sales).

Product development

If the idea has survived marketing analysis, the next step is to translate it into a product. Marketing information is used to develop a suitable design.

Product design involves understanding consumer needs to develop style and functions within a product in a way which makes it safe, attractive, easy to use and economic to produce.

Testing

Testing is a vital stage in the development process. It provides valuable information that can often be used to fine-tune the product and minimise the risks of the venture.

Test-marketing involves testing the product in a consumer market which is thought to be typical of the market as a whole. By putting the product into the marketplace, even on a small scale, it is possible to assess consumer reaction to the product and also to monitor its performance. Test-marketing is usually carried out in a television region. For industrial markets, where firms are likely to have fewer customers, test-marketing may not be feasible. In these circumstances, more rigorous product testing, as well as a series of trials, may ensure that the product meets the standards required.

Launch and commercialisation

At the **launch** stage, the product is finally revealed to the customer in the marketplace. It can be launched nationwide on one day, or the launch may 'roll' from TV region to TV region and be spread over a period of time.

In recent years the launch of new products has become something of an art. For example, one technique is to provide 'sneak glimpses' and to 'leak' information to whet the appetite of customers. The success of a launch and the development of a product for full-scale commercialisation will depend on how well marketing programmes and systems have been developed.

Product branding

As consumers, we identify products in many different ways. A **brand image** comprises a range of features which identify the products of a particular organisation, e.g. a name, sign, term, symbol or other creative element.

There are many reasons for branding. The reputation of a brand may encourage a consumer to buy its newly launched product without first considering other brands. Branding is itself a form of product differentiation, and

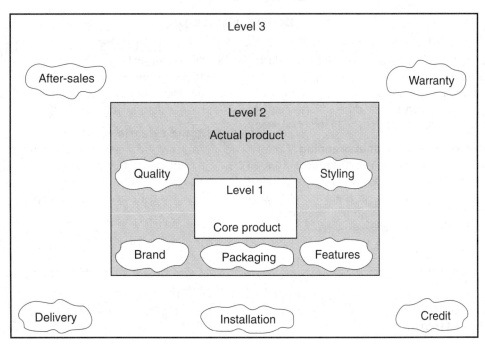

EXTENSION MATERIAL

Product planning

Figure 52.2 The three levels of a product

Kotler and Armstrong in *Principles of Marketing* perceive three different levels of a product for planning purposes.

- **Level 1: The core product**
  This consists of the benefits customers are provided with when they purchase and use a good or service.

- **Level 2: The actual product**
  This consists of five elements: the brand, quality, styling, features and packaging.

- **Level 3: The augmented product**
  This includes support issues which are important to the customer and help to enhance the product's attractiveness and competitive advantage.

quickly and effectively communicates a great deal of information about a product range. For example, the name 'Levi's' instantly conjures up an image of the qualities we associate with jeans.

A brand does not have to be identified by words alone. For example, a brand of teabags may be recognised by a picture of its `Tea Folk'. As we saw earlier in the chapter, an image of a cartoon penguin immediately provides an association with the best-selling chocolate bar.

It is argued that branding provides consumers with an assurance that they are purchasing a product that they like and can rely upon. It also reduces price competition and helps to foster loyalty. This provides the producer with a stable market,and enables popular or 'premium brands' to be sold at higher prices than those of competitors.

For the producer, branding will lead to wider acceptability of products by both wholesalers and retailers. This helps the personal selling process and also makes it possible for manufacturers to obtain display space in larger stores. Branding also helps to provide **unique selling propositions (USPs)** which help to differentiate products from their competitors.

There are three different types of brands:

- **Manufacturer brands** These associate the producer with the product. Where this happens, the producer may be involved with the promotion, distribution and, to some extent, the pricing of the product.
- **Own-label brands** These brands are owned by resellers who may also be the wholesalers or retailers. Manufacturers are, therefore, not associated with the products.
- **Generic brands** These brands only show the product category and will not include the company name or any identifying terms. An example is bin liners. Though these brands are sold at vastly reduced prices, they only account for a small proportion of retail turnover.

EXTENSION MATERIAL

Brand strategy

Organisations have to think carefully before introducing any form of brand strategy. For example, products may be difficult to brand, like nails or milk. It is also important to understand how consumers differentiate between brands. There are three main types of branding strategy.

- **Multi-branding or individual branding**
  This is a strategy of naming each product from an organisation differently, even though it might cater for similar consumer tastes. For example, both Lever Brothers and Proctor & Gamble use individual branding for their washing detergents.

- **Family branding**
  This uses the power of the family name to brand products. For example, Vauxhall, Kraft and John West have wide product portfolios.

- **Brand extensions**
  This involves extending a product line to take advantage of a brand which is already well known, e.g. the use of confectionery names such as Mars and Opal Fruits to create ice-cream products.

Chapter summary

- A product involves a range of physical or functional characteristics which accompany the good or service being offered.
- A product will provide a range of benefits.
- A number of factors make up the product concept.
- The product has three dimensions, generic, sensual and extended.

- The product life-cycle and Boston Matrix can be used to manage a product portfolio.
- Products may be proactive or reactive.
- There are six distinct stages in new product development.
- A product brand comprises a range of features which identify the products of a particular organisation.

53 Pricing

The *Oxford English Dictionary* defines price as the 'sum or consideration or sacrifice for which a thing may be bought or attained'. This has different meanings for different groups of people. For example:

- **Buyers** For buyers, price may be regarded as an unwelcome cost. Price involves sacrificing the next-best alternative that could be bought (sometimes referred to as **opportunity cost**). Price also provide buyers with a measure of value;
- **Sellers** For sellers, price is a key element in the marketing mix. It is an important selling point. Getting the price 'right' is an important tactical decision and a key factor influencing revenue and profit. A business can make wonderful products, but if they are just a little too expensive, it will go bust! Similarly, if it sells them too cheaply, it will not generate enough revenue to cover costs;
- **Government** The price of individual products is an influence on the general price level – and hence votes!

It is also important to be aware of the international impact of prices. The price of a country's products alters with the exchange rate. When the price of the pound increases against other currencies British goods become less competitive abroad. Fewer goods will be sold abroad, leading to falling order books at home.

These contrasting viewpoints about prices often conflict. Each perspective needs to be considered when setting prices.

Price and the marketing mix

The importance of price within the marketing mix varies from one market to another and between different segments in the same market. In low-cost, non-fashion markets, price can be critical (e.g. in the sale of white emulsion and gloss paint for decorating). In fashion markets, such as fashion clothing, it can be one of the least relevant factors.

Certain products are designed to suit a particular price segment (e.g. economy family cars), whilst others perform a specific function regardless of cost (e.g. sports cars). For consumers with limited budgets, price is a key purchasing criterion, whilst for others for whom 'money is no object', price is less important.

PRICE CUTS AND REVENUE

One of 20th-century America's most potent cultural forces is in trouble. Amid reports of an unexpected slump in sales, the McDonald's Corporation of Illinois has encouraged its distributors to slash prices. The head of the company's US restaurants has made an urgent plea to franchises to drop the price of a Big Mac from $1.90 to 55 cents and to give free burgers to customers who do not receive brisk service. Many franchise-holders are expected to refuse as this will mean substantial cuts in revenue.

This dramatic strategy could wreck profits and lead to a price war at America's fast-food counters. It could decide not only the future of a company that was once regarded as unstoppable, but also seal the fate of the traditional American hamburger itself.

Since the 1970s, McDonald's has been the undisputed leader of the world. But a recent rise in chicken sandwiches and tacos plus the rejuvenation of Burger King under British ownership have challenged McDonald's domination of the market. McDonald's operates 15,000 sites around the world, 12,200 of which are in America. Its international outlets are not in trouble; in fact, the company recently unveiled a major investment programme in new restaurants in Britain. But at home the problems are serious. The market has reached saturation point.

1 With McDonald's in trouble in the US, how far might cutting prices help them to overcome problems in sales?

2 How would it be possible to assess whether a price-cutting strategy would be successful?

3 Using another example, explain what is meant by a 'price war'. Who, if anybody, benefits from a price war?

Pricing decisions

It is possible to identify a number of key situations when pricing decisions have to be made:

- **When a price needs to be set for the first time** This can happen when a new product is launched on the market, when new outlets are used, when new contracts are made, or when businesses move into new markets;
- **When it becomes necessary to make a change in the pricing structure** This may be because of the development of competition, a movement along the product life-cycle, or a change in demand or cost conditions.

In selecting an appropriate price for each of these situations, an organisation has to consider its objectives, strategies and techniques.

```
┌─────────────────────────────┐
│        OBJECTIVES           │
│  (e.g. to maximise profits) │
└─────────────────────────────┘
              ▼
┌─────────────────────────────┐
│        STRATEGIES           │
│ (e.g. to charge a low price)│
└─────────────────────────────┘
              ▼
┌─────────────────────────────┐
│        TECHNIQUES           │
│  (e.g. to charge a very low │
│   mark-up cost, which will  │
│     maximise unit sales)    │
└─────────────────────────────┘
```

Figure 53.1 Objectives, strategies and techniques

The starting point is to be clear about pricing objectives. These might include the following:

1 **Profit maximisation** A key assumption of many business theories is that profit maximisation is the most important pricing target. While it is true that unless businesses can make profits in the long run their futures will be uncertain, studies of actual business behaviour reveal a wide range of objectives other than simple short-term profit maximisation.

2 **Price competition** A competitive price is one that gives a competitive edge in the marketplace. It is not necessarily the one that is lower than that of a rival, because other elements of the marketing mix also have to be taken into account.

SYNTHESIS

To what extent does the importance of pricing depend upon the nature and type of product being offered? Can you think of any examples to support your observations?

3 **Yield on investment** Any money that is allocated to a particular use has an opportunity cost. Could this money be spent in a better way? What are the alternatives that have to be sacrificed? Investors will usually have expectations of what they regard to be an appropriate rate of return on their investment. This will be an important factor in determining the pricing decision.

4 **Sales maximisation** Sometimes organisations pursue the objective of generating high sales figures rather than high profits, because it makes them look good. For example, it may lead to a larger market share, a bigger sales team and a range of bonuses.

5 **'Satisficing'** H.A. Simon put forward the view in *New Developments In The Theory Of The Firm* that businesses sometimes choose to 'satisfice', that is, to achieve given targets for market share and profits from sales that may not necessarily maximise profits but will inflate boardroom egos. This can be the case when the managers of a company are clearly different from the owners. Provided that the managers can produce sufficient profits to keep the shareholders satisfied, a proportion of the profits can be diverted to provide more perks for managers and larger departments.

  'Satisficing' policies are most likely to be associated with industries where there is only a limited degree of competition. They are fairly common in organisations such as schools or oil companies, where managers readily produce long lists of achievements which are not necessarily profit-related.

6 **Other objectives** There are many other possible objectives in establishing prices. For example, a company may want to maximise sales to create brand leadership, or it may want to establish a high price in order to establish a reputation for quality.

When organisations set the objectives outlined above, it is essential to remember that it is not only customers who may respond unfavourably:

- **Competitors** may choose to match price cuts or not to match price increases;
- **Distributors** may insist on high margins and thus resist price-cutting;
- **Employees** may ask for wage increases – one of the most important components of costs;
- **Government bodies** may withhold contracts, certificates or grants;
- **Shareholders** may demand higher dividends.

Factors affecting pricing decisions

There are a number of factors to be considered before arriving at a pricing decision. They include the following:

Costs

Many organisations relate prices to costs in the following way. They first calculate fixed costs such as rent, interest repayments and salaries. They then add variable costs, i.e. costs that increase with the level of output (see Chapter 32).

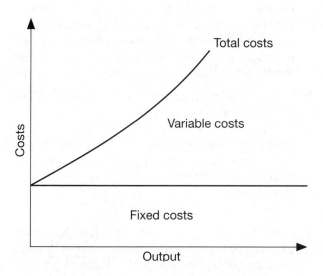

Figure 53.2 Components of total cost

A break-even chart can show the relationship between costs, profits and revenues at different levels of output. Using this information, an organisation can then establish a **revenue target**. The revenue target will coincide with a given level of output and will establish the price charged

per unit. In Figure 53.3 below, the revenue line crosses the fixed cost line at A. At this point, the business would just be covering its fixed costs. As output increases, the revenue line rises to the point B, at which total revenue covers total cost (comprising fixed and variable costs).

Above point B (i.e. to the right of it) the firm moves into a profit position. Point X represents the chosen target revenue and the line XY indicates the profit margin.

The amount of sales that an organisation makes will depend, among other things, on the price charged. If prices are too low, the revenue line will be less steep and revenues may not cover costs or profit margins may be too low. If prices are too high, the revenue line could be very short.

Pricing policies are crucial to the success of a business. In the long run, a firm will continue in business if it can cover its total costs. In the short run, it needs to cover at least its variable costs if it is going to be worth producing an output. If it closes down in the short run, it will still need to cover its fixed costs. By staying open and covering its variable costs, it may still be able to pay off some of its fixed costs, keep its staff and equipment working and preserve the good name of the business.

In the long term it is likely that the costs of producing units of output will fall. This is because, as time goes on,

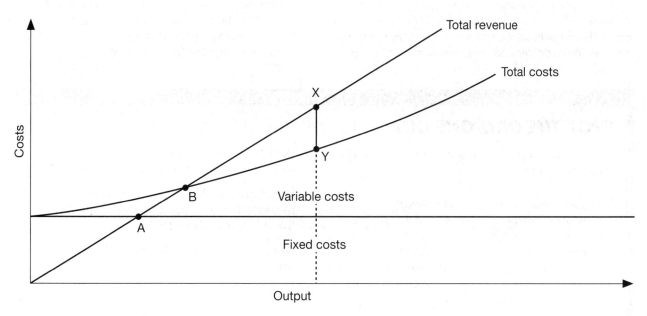

Figure 53.3 Establishing a revenue target from a break-even chart

businesses become more experienced in all aspects of producing goods or services. Technology improves, waste is reduced and distribution channels become more effective. In addition, a firm only has to pay its setting up costs once; tool and equipment costs therefore become less important until the firm needs to modernise its existing lines. When products are sold in a competitive environment, falling costs are often matched by falling prices. This type of relationship, illustrated in Figure 53.4, can be related to a wide range of products, from personal computers to package holidays:

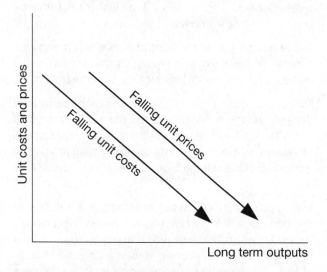

Figure 53.4 Falling costs and falling prices

Price sensitivity
Elasticity of demand is used to calculate the way in which the demand for product alters as price changes. Some products are highly sensitive to price changes so demand is said to be **elastic**; the demand for a product with many competitors, such as a brand of tinned tomatoes, is likely to be highly elastic. In contrast, a product with little competition such as a distinctive luxury car may show an **inelastic** demand curve over a range of prices.

There are a number of factors influencing elasticity:

1 It depends whether the good is a **necessity** or a **luxury.** By definition necessities such as food, shelter or clothing will be needed by purchasers. When the price of a necessity increases, consumers will be reluctant to reduce their purchases. In contrast, it is easier to give up or postpone the purchase of a luxury item. Of course, with the passage of time, individuals' perceptions of what is a necessity or a luxury can alter. Today, for example, many people regard central heating in winter to be a necessity. If consumers perceive an item to be necessary, they will continue to purchase more or less the same quantity as the price increases. For example, the demand for petrol is seen to be highly inelastic over a considerable price range.

2 There may be many **substitutes** for a product or just a few. Goods and services offered by a large number of competitors tend to experience elastic demand conditions. Examples include brands of fish fingers, tabloid newspapers and various tinned groceries. Inelastic demand is most likely to occur where there is little competition, such as when there is only one service station on a long stretch of motorway.

3 There is a variable proportion of household income that may be spent on an individual product. If only a small proportion of a household's income is spent on a product, then demand is more likely to be inelastic. The reason for this is that if a household spends only a small fraction of its income on an item, e.g. salt, shoe polish or mustard, then a rise in the price of the item will hardly be felt. In contrast, items that make up a sizeable proportion of total expenditure such as heating or a new motor car will have a more dramatic impact when their prices change. The items representing small fractions of income will tend to have inelastic demand curves over a particular price range, whereas items making up large fractions of income will tend to have greater elasticity.

SPOT THE ODD ONE OUT

In 1995 the top 12 grocery brands in the UK were as follows:

1	Coca-Cola	2	Nescafé
3	Walkers Crisps	4	Ariel
5	Persil	6	Andrex
7	Pampers	8	Whiskas
9	Robinsons Squash	10	Flora
11	Silver Spoon Granulated Sugar	12	Muller Yoghurt

1 Which of the 12 brands would you describe as **inelastic** at the current price?

2 What are the differences between the markets for that brand and the markets for other brands in the list?

3 How might these differences affect pricing decisions?

4 A product may have a large or small number of **different uses**. If a product has many uses there will be many different markets in which price changes can exert their effect. There is therefore a greater possibility that in some markets substitutes may be readily available. Electricity and gas, for example, have many uses – cooking, heating, lighting etc. A rise in the price of electricity therefore might cause people not only to make economies in these areas, but also to substitute gas for electric heating and cooking.

5 The **length of the time period** under consideration is another factor. Following a change in price, the elasticity of demand will tend to be greater in the long run than in the short run.

For example, if the price of a product becomes relatively cheaper it will take consumers time to adjust. Let us assume that Kiwi fruit fall in price by 50 per cent compared with other fruits. In the shorter period this will lead some consumers to switch to Kiwi fruit. In the longer term an even greater number of consumers are likely to make the switch as tastes alter and awareness increases.

6 If the price of **durable items** increases, consumers will try and make the product last longer. This applies to a whole host of consumer durables and factory machinery. For example, if car prices rise, purchasers may want to make their existing car last one year longer before trading it in. This is impossible with non-durable items such as cream cakes, eggs and bread.

Consumers' responses to price changes are an important ingredient of price determination. Businesses have more scope for charging high prices in markets where consumers are insensitive to price increases (i.e. where demand is inelastic).

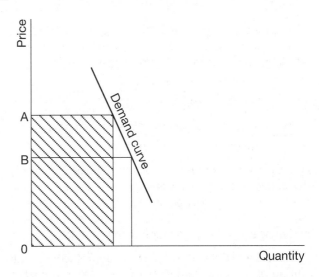

Figure 53.5 *Comparing revenues at different prices (demand-inelastic)*

In Figure 53.5, a firm has a choice of charging a high price, A, or a lower price, B. The demand curve for the product is relatively steep, indicating inelastic demand. The firm's total revenue is calculated by the formula:

Total revenue = Quantity sold x price

The shaded area represents total revenue at Price A. This is larger than the rectangle under Price B, so the firm will gain most revenue from charging the higher price.

In contrast, if consumers are sensitive to price changes, firms may adopt a low-price strategy. In Figure 53.6 the demand curve is relatively flat and the firm gains most revenue from charging Price B rather than Price A. (But note that costs are an important factor in determining price and output. If the extra cost of expanding output exceeds extra revenues, it may pay to produce a smaller output, even when demand is elastic.)

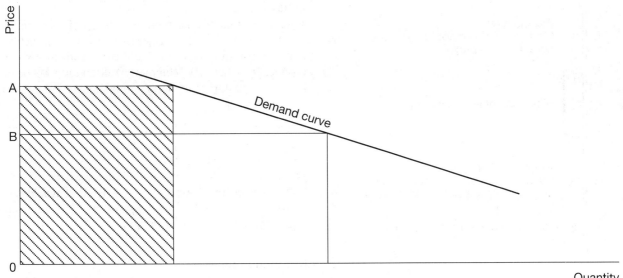

Figure 53.6 *Comparing revenues at different prices (demand-elastic)*

Price elasticity is measured by taking the percentage increase or decrease in the quantity demanded (or sales) resulting from a change in price, and dividing it by the percentage change in price:

Price elasticity of demand =

$$\frac{Percentage\ change\ in\ quantity\ demanded\ of\ A}{Percentage\ change\ in\ price\ of\ A}$$

Elastic markets are those in which the change in quantity demanded is a higher percentage than the percentage change in price. Conversely, inelastic markets are those in which the change in quantity demanded is a lower percentage than the percentage change in price.

In the real world it is very difficult to apply theory to the making of price decisions. Firstly, firms rarely possess the empirical data required to construct actual demand or revenue curves for their products – in other words, realistic figures showing how much would be demanded at different prices. They are often unable to distinguish costs sufficiently clearly to construct cost curves. Secondly, the goals that firms set themselves are rarely easy to build into theories such as 'profit maximisation'.

Customers' perceptions of price

Customers generally have views about what constitutes value for money. If prices are thought to be too high they may feel they are not getting their money's worth. If prices are too low, they will begin to question the quality and value of a product. (This is illustrated by the story of the expensive designer coat reduced to £20 in a department store window: nobody bought it because, at that price, they thought there must be something wrong with it!)

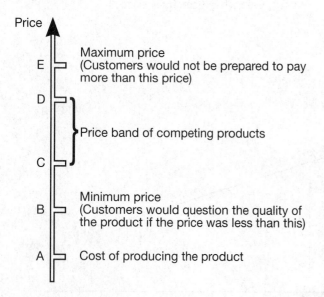

Figure 53.7 Price bands

Figure 53.7 shows that a product costs A to produce. The business cannot sell the product for less than B without quality being questioned. Competing products are selling for prices between C and D, and the maximum chargeable price is E. If the product is not very exciting, the business will need to pitch its price between B and D; if, however, the product is a market leader and has some novel features, then it can pitch the price between C and E.

Competition

The nature and extent of competition is often an important influence on price. If a product is faced by **direct competition** then it will compete against other highly similar products in the marketplace. This will often constrain pricing decisions so that price-setting will need to be kept closely in line with rivals' actions.

In contrast, when a product is faced by **indirect competition** (i.e. competition with products in different sectors of the market), there will be more scope to vary price. This opens up the possibility of a number of strategies. For example, a firm may choose a high-price strategy to give their product a 'quality' feel. In contrast, it may charge a low price so that consumers see the product as a 'bargain'.

Because price is only one factor in the equation, it is not always necessary to charge the lowest price in the market. For example, in a recent annual report, Shell stressed that price is considerably less important than other factors. It stated that: *'The Company's marketing strategy is based on establishing a differentiation between Shell and its competitors through quality in its facilities, products and services.'* This policy is based on the belief that customers are more interested in performance and reliability than cost.

Product range

A number of companies produce a range of products in which each product is specifically geared to a particular market segment or position. This is particularly true in car production, where it is common to distinguish between 'middle-' and 'top-of-the-range' models.

A manufacturer will aim to cater for either as many sectors of the market as possible, or a specific market segment. When the former strategy is applied, careful consideration has to be given to the product range. When new products are introduced, the price of existing products will set boundaries on the price that can be asked. It would not be wise for a firm to compete against itself by producing two models in the same price range.

Distribution costs

The cost of distribution is another important consideration in setting prices, particularly when producers use third-party transport, wholesaling and retailing services. Each of these services will need to be provided at a profit, and the costs to the business must be considered in terms of the price strategy.

Until 1967 manufacturers were able to control the prices at which their goods were resold. The 1967 Resale Price Maintenance Act put an end to this. Today the retail price of items can vary considerably. The implication for producers is that, if retail outlets compete extensively with each other, inefficient units will be forced out of the market. As a result, producers might be faced with fewer sales outlets. Some producers control retail prices by owning their own selling outlets – for example, breweries, shoe manufacturers and some bakeries.

Pricing strategies

In this section we look at a range of pricing strategies.

1 Cost-plus pricing

Information about costs is often easier to collect than information about other variables such as revenues. Many organisations therefore make pricing decisions by adding a margin to unit cost. (The **unit cost** is the average cost of each item produced – e.g. if a business produces 1,000 units at a total cost of £2,000, the unit cost will be £2.) Similarly, many small business owners set their prices by costing each hour worked and then adding a margin for their profits.

The process of cost-plus pricing can best be illustrated in relation to large firms where economies of scale can be spread over a sizeable output. As we have seen, large firms are often characterised by flat-bottomed average cost curves, where average cost is constant over a large range of output. It is a relatively simple calculation to add a fixed margin, e.g. 10 per cent, to average costs. The firm is therefore able to select an output to produce and set a price that will be 10 per cent higher than unit costs of production (see Figure 53.8).

The dangers of applying this pricing method are that if the price is too high, sales may fall considerably short of expectations, but if the price is too low, potential revenue can be sacrificed.

If a firm applies average cost pricing too rigidly, it can cause problems in the marketplace. For example, if demand is lower than expected, average costs may be slightly higher. (Bear in mind that although we refer to 'flat-bottomed curves', there will inevitably be a slight downward slope.) In this situation the company accountant may press for price increases. This will make it even more difficult to make sales.

Conversely, if demand is higher than expected, average costs may fall slightly, leading to a demand for a price reduction. This may result in a potential loss of revenue.

2 Contribution pricing

Contribution pricing involves separating out the different products that make up a company's portfolio, in order to charge individual prices appropriate to a product's share of total costs. As we have seen (page 191), two broad categories of costs can be identified:

- **Direct** costs, which vary directly with the level of output;
- **Indirect** costs, which have to be paid irrespective of the level of output.

Contribution is the sum remaining after the direct costs of producing individual products have been subtracted from revenues. When the contributions of all the individual products that a business produces have been added together, this should more than cover their indirect costs.

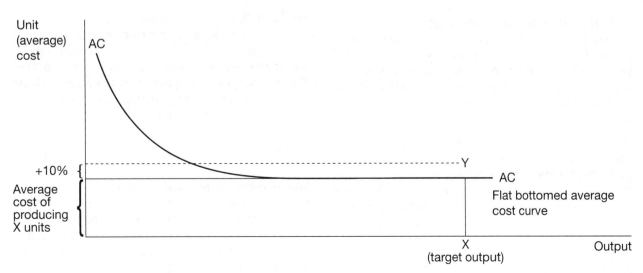

Figure 53.8 Cost-plus pricing

There are strong arguments in favour of contribution pricing because of the way it separates out individual products and analyses them in terms of their individual profitability. A new product may be brought 'on-stream' because it can be shown that it will more than cover its direct costs and make a contribution towards the company's total indirect costs.

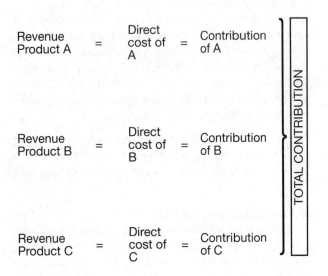

Figure 53.9 *Contribution pricing*

In contrast, if we analyse individual prices in terms of the relationship between total revenue and total cost, the calculations might show a loss. For example, if two products use the same distribution facilities, it would not make sense to expect both products to cover their own distribution costs individually. Contribution pricing enables a more rational analysis of individual products because prices can be set in relation to each product's individual direct costs.

3 Demand-orientated pricing

Market research is essential to establish and monitor consumer perceptions of price. Demand-orientated pricing involves reacting to the intensity of demand for a product, so that high demand leads to high prices and weak demand to low prices, even though unit costs may be similar.

When an organisation can split up the market in which it operates into different sections, it can carry out a policy of **price discrimination**. This involves selling at high prices in a section of the market where demand is intense (where demand is inelastic), and a relatively low price where demand is elastic – i.e. where there is a more than proportionate response in quantity demanded as a result of a fall in price. Price discrimination can be carried out in a number of situations (see Figure 53.10).

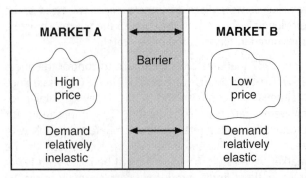

Figure 53.10 *Price discrimination*

Customer-orientated discrimination

Some customers may have an intense demand for a product, while others may only have a weak demand. Discrimination involves selling the product at a high price to the first type of customer and at a lower price to the second. However, firms can only do this if they can physically divide up their market in such a way that the customer with the intense demand cannot get hold of the same item at the lower price.

It is common practice to introduce some products at a high price and then later to reduce it. For example, many books are initially sold in hardback at a high price. When that segment of customers has been satisfied, the cheaper paperback is produced.

Product-orientated discrimination

Slight modifications can be made to a product to allow high and low price strategies. For example, many models of car have additional extras (two- and four-door versions, ABS, 16V, etc.). Customers have the choice of the cheaper or more expensive version.

Time-orientated discrimination

Sellers are also able to discriminate when demand varies by season or time of day. In high season, a product can be sold at a high price. At other times, prices can be reduced. This applies to a wide range of items, from fashion clothes to river cruises. Some products experience varying intensities of demand during the course of a single day – for example, telephone calls are charged at a higher rate during peak hours.

Situation-orientated discrimination

A good example of situation-orientated discrimination occurs in the property market, where the same type of house will sell for one price in the centre of town and for another price in a quiet suburban area. House prices also vary widely from one region to another. Cinema and theatre seats may be priced according to their proximity to the screen or stage. Although production costs are similar, demand varies according to the situation.

There is frequently price discrimination between countries which have different average incomes and other factors influencing demand. Products are therefore sold at different prices according to the elasticity of demand in individual countries and regions. For example, cars are cheaper in continental Europe than in the UK.

5 Competition-orientated pricing

In Chapter 21 we looked at competitive and non-competitive markets. Here we focus specifically on the effects of competition on pricing strategies.

In extremely competitive situations, cost has to be treated as a secondary consideration in short-term price determination. This is particularly true in markets where:

- Competing products are almost identical;
- Customers are well informed;
- There are few suppliers.

The nature and extent of competition is often an important influence on price. If a product is faced by direct competition it will compete against other very similar products in the marketplace. This will constrain pricing decisions so that price-setting will need to be kept closely in line with rivals' actions. In contrast, when a product is faced by indirect competition (i.e. competition with products in different sectors of the market), there will be more scope to vary price.

An individual firm may try to insulate itself against price sensitivity by differentiating its products from those of its rivals. Markets are sometimes classified according to the level of competition within them. An extreme level of competition is termed **perfect competition** and tends to exists in theory rather than practice. At the other extreme is **monopoly**, where a single organisation dominates a market. In the real world, most markets lie between these extremes and involve some level of imperfection.

In a perfect market there would be no limitations to new organisations entering the market, and buyers would know exactly what was on offer and would incur no costs in buying from one seller rather than another. Products would be almost identical. By contrast, in a monopoly situation, only one firm exists and barriers are put up to prevent new firms entering the market (e.g. a very high cost of setting up, patent and copyright restrictions, etc). The seller therefore has power to control the market.

In imperfect markets as we know them, there may be few or many sellers. Products are usually differentiated and consumers do not have perfect information about the differences between products.

In the real world, businesses naturally strive to give themselves the protection of monopolistic powers. They seek to reduce competition and to make their products seem 'better' than those of rivals. Monopolistic powers enable firms to push up prices and hence make larger profits. However, larger profits should not always be viewed as a cost to consumers. Profits can be ploughed back into research and development, into advanced technology and the production of larger outputs at lower average costs. This may ultimately benefit consumers.

Short-term pricing policies

Price can be an effective means for an organisation to pursue short-term marketing and selling objectives. Typical 'attack-based' policies include:

- Skimming pricing
- Penetration pricing
- Destroyer pricing
- Promotional pricing

1 Skimming pricing

At the launch of a new product, there will frequently be little competition in the market, so that demand for the product may be somewhat inelastic. Consumers will have little knowledge of the product. Skimming involves setting a reasonably high initial price in order to yield high initial returns from those consumers willing to buy the new product. Once the first customers have been satisfied, the seller can then lower prices in order to make sales to new groups of customers. This process can be continued until a larger section of the total market has been catered for. By operating in this way, the business removes the risk of underpricing the product.

2 Penetration pricing

Whilst skimming may be an appropriate policy when a seller is not sure of the elasticity of demand for the product, penetration pricing is appropriate when the seller knows that demand is likely to be elastic. A low price is therefore required to attract consumers to the product.

Penetration pricing is normally associated with the launch of a new product for which the market is untried. Because the price starts low, the product may initially make a loss until consumer awareness develops. A typical example is a new breakfast cereal.

Penetration pricing is particularly appropriate for products where economies of scale can be employed to produce large volumes at low unit costs.

3 Destroyer pricing

A policy of destroyer pricing can be used to undermine the sales of rivals or to warn potential new rivals not to enter a particular market. Destroyer pricing involves reducing the price of an existing product or selling a new product at an artificially low price in order to destroy competitors' sales. This type of policy is based on short-term considerations and is likely to lead to short-term losses.

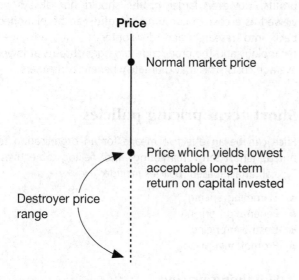

Figure 53.11 Destroyer pricing

4 Promotional pricing

From time to time prices can be lowered to promote a product. Promotional pricing can be used to inject fresh life into an existing product or to create interest in a new product. Promotional pricing can be employed to increase the rate at which a product turns over and this can reduce levels of stock or increase the rate of activity of a business. A form of promotional pricing is the use of **loss-leaders** These are products offered at lower than cost price in order to attract the attention of customers to a business's activities.

Pricing decisions and the marketing mix

In this chapter we have focused upon the importance of pricing decisions. However, remember that pricing must be used to complement other ingredients of the marketing mix.

For example, pricing decisions need to be accompanied by:

- **Product differentiation** to produce the required benefits for customers;
- Careful **segmentation** so that benefits are promoted to those who appreciate them most;
- **Development of valid non-product features**, such as better delivery, after-sales service, etc.
- Improvement of **product strength**;
- Attention to **company and product image**.

<table>
<tr><td colspan="2">

Chapter summary

- Prices have different meanings for different people;
- The prices of a country's products alter with the exchange rate;
- A number of situations can be identified when pricing decisions have to be made;
- There are a range of pricing objectives;
- Factors affecting pricing include costs, price

sensitivity, customers' perceptions of price, competition, the product range and distribution costs;
- Marketers can choose from a range of pricing strategies;
- Pricing strategies should fit in with other elements of the marketing mix.
</td></tr>
</table>

54 Place/distribution

Distribution (or **place** according to the 'Four Ps' of the marketing mix) is the process of making goods or services available to those who want to buy them. It includes:

- The process of moving goods and services to the places where they are wanted;
- The **channels** through which the products are available (e.g. shops, mail order, wholesalers).

Distribution may involve a single step, or any number of steps. For example, a local baker may make the bread and then supply it direct to his or her customers. In contrast, a furniture store may supply chairs and tables that have been manufactured in Scandinavia, exported through various intermediaries and stored two or three times before arriving at their destination.

A number of key decisions have to be made about distribution. Managers must try to ensure that goods are moved efficiently to meet customer needs on time. They will also be concerned about choosing the best channel of distribution so that efficiency and sales can be maximised. The importance of these decisions should not be underestimated. Many organisations such as Avon, Amway and Reader's Digest have built and developed their organisations around their ability to use this element of the marketing mix to reach customers.

One important element in distribution is **timing**. Many goods are seasonal and have to reach customers at a particular time in order to meet their needs. For example, fireworks which reached retailers on 6th November would be of little use. In fact, any distributor who sends goods late, or at a time when customer needs have already been satisfied, will be at a competitive disadvantage. Establishing an efficient distribution system is particularly important for perishable products.

Physical distribution management

Physical distribution includes all the activities concerned with moving products, both inwards to manufacturers and outwards to customers. **Physical distribution management (PDM)** describes the role of managers in developing, administering and operating systems to control the movement of raw materials and finished goods.

Physical distribution is an important part of the marketing mix. It helps an organisation to meet customer needs profitably and efficiently and enables manufacturers to provide goods for customers at the right time, in the right place and in the condition required. It may also reduce the **lead time** – i.e. the period between the customer first placing an order and the fulfilment of the order.

Transport is a key component in physical distribution. Choosing the best possible transport system involves weighing up and trading off a number of key factors. What forms of transport should be used? Can they be integrated? Should the firm use its own fleet or outside carriers?

Different methods of transport may prove to be more or less cost-effective in different situations, depending on the cost of transport relative to the type of good being transported, the value and the urgency of the order.

CASE STUDY CASE STUDY CASE STUDY CASE STUDY CASE STUDY

REDUCING TRANSPORT COSTS

Improving cost-effectiveness is a continuous effort for any successful business. Over the last few years Shell Transport has reduced the cost of oil product transported by 20 per cent. This increased efficiency is based on a number of factors:

- Improvements in the UK road network;
- Larger, more efficient road tankers;
- Non-rush-hour deliveries;
- Better planning systems;
- Better information systems;
- More efficient handling of customer orders and payments;
- Investment in depots;
- Use of contracts;
- Use of salaried drivers;
- Maintenance of safety at all times;
- Working closely with refineries.

1 Which of the above benefits are (a) internal economies of scale, and (b) external economies of scale?

2 Which groups of stakeholders benefit from improved efficiency of distribution?

3 What future developments could take place which might improve the distribution process still further?

STUDY CASE STUDY CASE STUDY CASE STUDY CASE STUDY CASE STUDY

The physical distribution system balances the need for customer service against the need to minimise costs. Maximising customer service implies increasing stock levels and warehousing space, and employing large numbers of distribution staff and rapid transport systems. But minimising costs implies the reverse: minimum storage space, skeleton staff and slow transport. Designing a physical distribution system therefore involves trading off costs against service, or inputs against outputs.

Evaluating distribution channels

The **channel of distribution** is the system by which goods are transferred from producer to end-user. Every business must constantly appraise its existing channels and reorganise them from time to time.

When looking at how to develop a channel to reach customers, firms need to establish their major objectives. But they also need to explore the constraints in achieving these objectives and look at possible alternatives. The alternatives then need to be evaluated before a decision can be made as to how to plan the channels.

The distribution channel is the route to the customers. In defining the objectives, it is necessary to consider:

● The customers' needs;
● The nature of the competition;
● The nature of other services and intermediaries involved.

For example, a firm's overriding objective may be to supply customers the day after the product has been manufactured, at the lowest price on the market. If so, it will need to look at how its rivals are operating and what they are offering, and choose the quickest and most effective channels with the least delays.

Some alternative channels are shown in Figure 54.1. To reach a mass market a product may be distributed through more than one channel. Alternatively, a company may give exclusive rights to certain dealers or middlemen. It is essential to specify who does what at each stage of the distribution map. If a particular channel of distribution looks as if it may cause problems, it may have to be scrapped in favour of another.

The three main criteria in evaluating channel alternatives are:

● Cost
● Control
● Flexibility

In evaluating the economic performance of alternative routes, costs must be weighed against revenues in order to make profit calculations. Control is also a major consideration because customers will often blame the producer for breakdowns and problems in distribution.

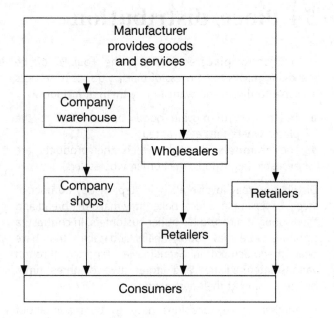

Figure 54.1 Alternative channels of distribution

A distribution channel should also be capable of being adapted to changing circumstances.

A business operating a single plant and selling in several scattered markets can choose whether to distribute directly from the plant or through a range of localised intermediaries. On the other hand, a firm with several plants and several markets must weigh up a range of distribution channels. Should it use the same distribution channels for all its products, or should it set up specialised routes? In this situation, choosing the correct channels of distribution is very important.

Industrial products such as machines, bulldozers, expensive computer systems etc. are commonly sold by the maker direct to the user. Consumer goods such as clothing, food, games and sports equipment are more usually distributed through retail shops. Here the maker can supply the shops directly, but to do this, a company needs a large salesforce. An alternative is to use **wholesalers** who buy in bulk and who can be served by a smaller salesforce. The wholesaler is part of the chain of distribution and is a link between the manufacturer and the retailer.

The choice of distribution channel can have a marked effect on other areas of the marketing mix such as price, promotion or product. For example, if it is decided to distribute through a chain of readily accessible cut-price stores, this will have obvious implications for the public perception of the product.

Some manufacturers require tight distribution schedules. Nowhere is this more true than in the distribution of fresh food. This limits the number of intermediaries who can sensibly be involved in the distribution process.

Though it is usual to accept one of the available distribution arrangements, in certain markets it is possible to set up a new one from scratch, such as door-to-door selling or the 'parties' used by Tupperware or Avon.

Other types of channel flow

Physical distribution is about getting the product or service to the consumer. But several other flows take place at the same time. For example, the title of ownership of goods needs to pass from the purchaser, and this may be in the form of a receipt or invoice. Payment will flow from the purchaser to the seller. Information will need to flow both ways between the buyer and the seller. The seller must make clear what the terms of the offer are, and the buyer needs to specify his or her requirements.

Why use intermediaries?

Given the cost of distribution, it may be asked why more firms do not simply sell direct to the public. The answer is that most manufacturers lack the financial resources to carry out their own direct marketing operations. By contracting-out the process of distribution they can concentrate upon their core functions.

The expense of direct marketing also often requires that several similar or complementary products are promoted at the same time in order to spread the cost.

The intermediary is a specialist. When an organisation sells its products in this way it benefits from the specialist's expertise in a wide range of areas, including packaging, pricing and where to sell. An author may be able to write a good story but is unlikely to have the time, know-how, contacts and finance to publish the book as well.

The roles of a wholesaler

Though it is possible to argue that intermediaries add to the cost of a producer's goods, it is important to emphasise the many valuable functions which a wholesaler performs. For example:

1 **Breaking bulk** Manufacturers like to produce goods in bulk but do not generally want to store goods themselves or have the task of selling them to many thousands of customers. A wholesaler will help them by buying a large amount of stock and storing the goods on their premises, where they can be ordered in smaller quantities by retailers.

2 **Simplifying the distribution process** Without the wholesaler, the chain of distribution would be as shown in Figure 54.2. As you can see, even with only 4 customers, each manufacturer has to make 4 journeys and send out four sets of paperwork. In total, 16 journeys are made with 16 sets of paperwork.

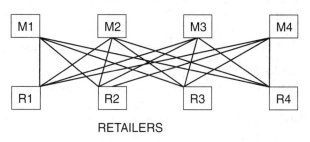

Figure 54.2 The distribution chain without the wholesaler

By contrast, the wholesaler can cut down on journey costs, paperwork and other costs. With the wholesaler, everything is simplified.

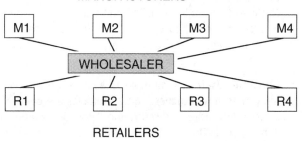

Figure 54.3 The distribution chain with the wholesaler

Retailing

The French word *retailler* means to 'cut again'. We have already seen that the wholesaler breaks down bulk supplies from the manufacturer. The retailer cuts the bulk once again to sell individual items to customers.

There are a number of different ways of categorising retailers. One way is by type of ownership. For example, who owns the retail unit? Is it independently owned or a large multiple unit with shareholders? Another way is to look at the range of merchandise. Does it specialise in a narrow range of goods or does it have a spread of

---

IT'S A FACT

Booker Cash & Carry has 160 depots in the UK, followed by Today's Supergroup with 103, Landmark Cash & Carry with 74 and Nurdin and Peacock with 55. In the grocery trade Spar convenience stores have 2,427 outlets, followed by over 2,200 Happy Shoppers, 1,400 Londis and 1,270 Family Choice.

interests? Examples of specialist outlets include furniture stores or fast-food outlets. Woolworths is an example of a more generalised outlet. Some retailers concentrate at the bottom of the price range, for example, Aldi or Netto, while others such as Binns and Harrods emphasise quality.

Another key distinction between retail outlets is location. Small corner shops tend to be located in communities. City centres have large shopping malls. Out-of-town sites have recently become increasingly popular, notable examples being the Metro Centre in Gateshead and MeadowHall in Sheffield.

Types of retailers

There are many different types of retailer. They include:

1 **Independent traders** The *Census of Distribution* classifies an independent trader as a retail organisation with fewer than ten branches. The average number is one or two branches. Many small shops in the UK are owned by one person whose business interests are confined to a single shop. The number of independent retailers has declined over the last few decades. For many retailers, joining a voluntary group has become a route for survival.

2 **Multiple chains** A multiple is a store group with more than ten branches. Some multiples are counted as specialist stores concentrating upon one range of items such as Dorothy Perkins, while others are variety chains like Marks & Spencer and Boots. It can be argued that there has been a convergence of retailing interests. A high street in York may be very similar to high street in Camberley, and many familiar retailing names will be the same.

3 **Supermarkets** A supermarket is a store with at least 2,000 square feet of selling area, using mostly self-service methods and having a number of check-out points. In recent decades, supermarkets have become a key feature of the way we shop.

4 **Department stores** A department store is a store with a range of departments located in a city centre. The store will provide high standards of service and comfort with carpeted floors, cafés and other facilities. Despite changes in shopping trends and the loss of some famous names, department stores are still a potent force in the marketplace with a good reputation for service and quality.

5 **Discount stores** Many specialist stores such as Argos and Comet concentrate upon selling large quantities of consumer durables at discount prices, using their own retailing techniques. Many of such stores have also moved to out-of-town sites.

6 **Co-operative retail societies** Originally several hundred strong, today there are fewer than 30 retail societies operating in the UK. Traditionally, co-ops aimed to do more than just run a business and were firmly based on principles of community self-help dating back to the beginnings of the co-operative movement.

7 **Mail order** Mail-order firms sell goods either through agents or through catalogues distributed free to the public. Agents receive a commission on sales.

8 **Franchising** This method for developing retail outlets has become increasingly popular within the UK (for example, The Body Shop). A franchise is a permission to market a product in a specified area. The person taking out the franchise puts up a sum of money and is issued with equipment and other forms of central support by a franchising company.

9 **Direct selling** The most commonly quoted examples of direct selling are mail order and direct response advertising, but more often than not these involve some form of intermediary. Television selling as a form of direct selling has become big business in the US and Australia.

It is important to remember that of all areas of business, retailing patterns change the most frequently. Looking at the technology used for retailing today, it is hard to predict what changes may come next.

Chapter summary

- Distribution involves moving goods to where they are required.
- There are a range of channels through which products may be made available.
- It is important to choose the best channel of distribution.
- Physical distribution involves all the activities concerned with moving products both inwards to manufacturers and outwards to customers.
- There are a number of ways of evaluating distribution channels.
- The wholesaler provides a range of functions to benefit the manufacturer or supplier.
- Retailing patterns are constantly changing.

55 Promotion

It could be said that **promotion** is about communicating with others. In the marketing context, the term usually refers to activities used to inform one or more groups of people about an organisation's products. There are many different forms of promotion. For example, it may simply involve creating awareness of a range of activities, or it may involve using sales staff to talk to customers and, in doing so, to promote their products.

Communication and promotion methods

The promotional mix consists of all the marketing and promotional communication methods used to achieve the promotional objectives of the marketing mix. These methods can be broken down into two distinct areas:

1 **Non-controllable communication** consists of marketing messages which are conveyed by word-of-mouth, via personal recommendation, or by means of consumers' overall perceptions of a particular product or service. In the short term these messages are outside the domain of a marketing strategy. In the long term, however, they may include a brand heritage, or the reputation of a company and its products – good or otherwise.

2 **Controllable communication** consists of marketing messages which are carefully directed to achieve the promotional objectives of an organisation. These fall into four main areas:

  – **Advertisements** are messages sent via the media which are intended to inform or influence the people who receive them.

  – **Sales promotions** are techniques designed to increase sales, such as money-off coupons, free samples and competitions.

  – **Personal selling** involves the making of sales and depends on the skills of the individual salesperson.

  – **Publicity** is non-personal communication via the media. However, unlike advertising, its success is not measured by the sales of any particular product. Its key component is public relations.

IT'S A FACT

In 1995 the top five advertisers in the UK were:

1 Procter & Gamble
2 British Telecommunications
3 Vauxhall Motors
4 Ford Motor Company
5 Dixons Stores Group

Promotional requirements will vary according to the size of the market, demographic dispersion and market segmentation. As we saw earlier (page 157), the more precisely an organisation can define its market segment, the better the targeting of the promotional mix.

A common mnemonic used to summarise the operation of the controllable methods of promotion is '**AIDA**':

A A customer's **attention** is captured and he or she is made **aware** of the product;

I The **impact** of the promotion stimulates the customer's **interest**;

D The customer is persuaded that he or she is **deprived** by not having the product, and this creates a **desire** for it;

A **Action** involves the purchase of the product.

The promotional mix must match the various stages of the product life-cycle. For example, consumer awareness must be developed during the introductory stage. As the product experiences growth, promotions must be introduced into the cycle from time to time. As the brand reaches maturity, its heritage must be emphasised in order to sustain consumer loyalty.

Advertising

When we think about promotion we immediately think of advertising. But advertising is only one part of the controllable promotional mix.

Few adverts simply set out to inform. For example, a soap powder advert does not simply give information about the product: its aim is to convey a **persuasive message**.

A persuasive message is one that promises a desirable and believable benefit to the people to whom it is addressed.

For example, persuasive adverts might:

● Show a famous personality using a product;
● Compare one product with another;
● Use sex appeal to make the product seem desirable and attractive.

In their literature the car manufacturers Vauxhall state the following:

'It is not sufficient for a manufacturer to produce the best products in its field if few people know about them. First and foremost, advertising is essential in letting purchasers know that a specific product exists and in keeping its brand name uppermost in their mind. Advertising fulfils a number of important functions by:

– *Creating or building an image for the product. This 'targets' the particular model so that the consumer is made aware of who the product is aimed at.*

– *Encouraging a desire to own the product. Effective advertising should be persuasive. Its prime function is to **sell**.*

– *Providing information about the product. Initially, it will let many people as possible know that the product exists, as well as providing relevant details.'*

For advertising to be effective it must:

- **Reach the right audience** This means selecting appropriate media and particular areas of the media. For example, if you want to reach socio-economic group B, you will need to research the media slots that are most likely to reach that sector of the population.

    Test-marketing may be employed to gauge how a sample of the population is likely to react to a particular product or promotion. For example, when a new biscuit is prepared for a market 'launch', members of the public may be tested to find out what they think of various possible ways of presenting or packaging the product;

- **Be attractive and appealing to the reader or viewer** The starting point in any campaign is to arouse interest and capture the attention of the public;

- **Cost little in relation to the extra sales made** The extra sales made as a result of an advertising campaign should bring in far more revenue than the cost of the advertising. Advertising will only be effective if consumers respond to the message.

An acronym frequently used to assess how well money is spent on advertising is **DAGMAR**. It stands for:

- **D** – **D**efining
- **A** – **A**dvertising
- **G** – **G**oals for
- **M** – **M**easured
- **A** – **A**dvertising
- **R** – **R**esults

The advertising campaign

To plan an advertising campaign, a company will first consult an advertising agency. The agency will act as a link between themselves and the consumer, creating, developing and implementing an advertising campaign on behalf of the client. Some agencies offer all kinds of advertising services, while others specialise in buying media or in particular types of creative work.

Within the agency, each client is looked after by a team of experts who collectively manage their **account**. An

account executive mediates between the client and the agency and, together with the **account director**, will attempt to meet the objectives of the campaign. The **account group** consists of representatives from various departments within the agency.

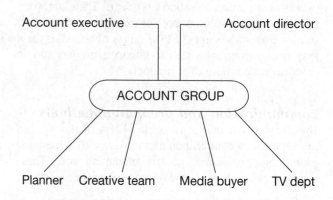

Figure 55.1 The account group

The **planner** assists the account executive, timetabling events and activities and assessing the reactions of the public to the campaign. The **creative team** usually consists of an **art director**, who will develop and create 'rough' drawings or visuals for a **copywriter**, who produces the words or **copy**. Ideas are discussed with the client. The message may be a combination of words, symbols, gimmicks, colours and sounds. For example, buzzwords or straplines may be used. Sometimes a character is used to help consumers to identify the brand. Good artwork and effective use of colour may also help to develop a distinctive identity for the product or service.

Media selection

A key element in advertising is **media selection**. Media selection depends upon the required **coverage** – i.e. the number of potential customers the advertiser wishes to reach – as well as the number of times the advertiser wishes the message to be transmitted (**frequency**).

In order to plan a campaign, the company or advertising agency must gather information about members of the target audience. Media choice will be made on the basis of cost-effectiveness. For an advertisement to be cost-effective, it must not only have good coverage but also have the required impact on the target audience.

According to the 'threshold concept', unless a brand reaches a certain level of awareness, any expenditure will be wasted. An advertisement's effectiveness is therefore closely related to advertising expenditure – the more times people are exposed to a message the more likely they are to remember it.

Types of media include:

WHAT'S IN A NAME?

Visitors to the headquarters of Interbrand, a business which helps companies name new products, gain a rare insight into the pitfalls of naming products for a worldwide audience. They are shown the `black museum', a display cabinet crammed with tins, sachets and aerosols. All the products on display bear names which are perfectly acceptable in their home market but which seem ludicrous to foreign consumers.

`Plopp' chocolate, for example, may go down well in Scandinavia but is unlikely to catch on in the UK. The Japanese sports drink `Sweat' hardly conjures up the right image, nor does France's `Dribly' lemonade or `Krapp', the toilet paper from Sweden!

More than 28,000 new products and company names are registered with the UK trademarks register each year. This gives their owners intellectual property rights and prevents competitors from using the same or similar names. As the museum shows, a lot can go wrong.

Creating a product name

Arriving at a new product name involves four stages:

1 Generating a large number of potential names;
2 Cutting down the possibilities to a manageable shortlist;
3 Selecting the final name;
4 Registering the name.

Although name consultants like Interbrand are experts, even they bring in outsiders to help build the initial list. The aim is to cut the list down to around 10 possibles. The list is then cut down further through trialling and mock-ups of packages and advertisements so that the names can be viewed in context. Consumer research is also used in the process.

When Pickfords Travel merged with the retail travel business Hogg Robinson, they consulted The Brandnaming Company to help them find a name for the new company. Consumer groups favoured 'Destinations', but it was 'Going Places' that was eventually chosen. It was felt that `Destinations' implied a long haul and had too much of a premium feel, whereas 'Going Places' was more appropriate for a mass market.

Choosing a name is part of the product branding process. Getting it wrong it can damage a business.

1 Work in small groups to brainstorm names for (a) a new cereal and (b) a new chocolate bar.

2 Provide two examples of what you consider to be good names and two examples of bad names.

3 Why might firms use agencies to help them choose product names?

4 Describe the consequences of coming up with the wrong brand name. If you can, use examples to support your arguments.

- **Printed materials** These make up by far the largest group of media. They include newspapers, periodicals, magazines and journals as well as the trade press. There are about 9,000 regular publications in the UK which can be used by advertisers. Printed media allow accurate targeting since each publication has its own distinct readership profile;
- **Broadcast media** This includes commercial television and commercial radio. TV is the most powerful of all media, reaching 98 per cent of households with viewing figures that can exceed 20 million;
- **Outdoor media** This includes fixed posters and hoardings, advertising on buses, taxis, underground trains and other forms of transport, as well as neon signs and electronic screens;
- **Direct mail** This is personalised advertising sent through the post. Every month each British household receives on average six and a half direct mail items;
- **Cinema** Though this has been declining as an advertising medium, it remains popular with the young and is a good way of targeting a younger audience.

SYNTHESIS

Have you ever thought about how the readership profiles of The Sun and The Daily Telegraph might compare?

	Circulation 000s	Men %	Women %	15–34 %	35–54 %	55+ %	ABC1 %	C2DE %
The Sun	3,926	55	45	44	32	24	30	7
The Daily Telegraph	1,013	55	45	23	35	42	85	13

Figure 55.2 Comparison of Sun *and* Telegraph *readers*

Controls in advertising

There are many restrictions governing the content of advertisements, and advertisers must keep within the law. The **Trades Descriptions Act** requires that goods advertised for sale must be as described. The advertising industry also has its own code of practice. The **British Code of Advertising Practice** is a voluntary agreement by organisations in the advertising industry to maintain certain standards. For example, when advertising slimming aids, the advertiser must state that these should be taken in addition to a balanced diet. These restrictions cover newspapers, magazines, cinema adverts, leaflets, brochures, posters and commercials, but not TV and radio adverts.

The **Advertising Standards Authority (ASA)** is an independent body which monitors all advertising except on radio and television. The authority draws up its own codes which it uses to ensure that advertisements are 'legal, decent, honest and truthful'. A number of other agencies are involved with consumer protection, including monitoring misleading adverts. These include the Independent Television Commission, the Office of Fair Trading, consumer groups, the Chartered Institute of Marketing and other professional bodies.

Sales promotion

The term **sales promotion** describes techniques designed to encourage customers to make a purchase. These are essentially short-term and may be used to:

- Increase sales;
- Fight off competition;
- Help with the task of personal selling;
- Provide an alternative to media advertising.

The Institute of Sales Promotion defines sales promotion as follows:

'Sales promotion is the function of marketing which seeks to achieve given objectives by the adding of intrinsic, tangible value to a product or service.'

Sales promotions can include point-of-sale materials, competitions, demonstrations and exhibitions. The essential feature of a sales promotion is that it is a short-term inducement to customers to buy, whereas advertising is usually a more long-term process involving the building and developing of a brand.

Sales promotions can be divided into two broad areas:

- Those which are designed to enhance the sales of a product to the trade;
- Those which assist the trade in promoting and selling the products to the final customer.

Selling into the pipeline describes promotions which move products from the manufacturer into the distribution system, or 'to the trade'. **Selling out of the pipeline** describes promotions aimed at the final consumer.

Although distributors may be influenced by materials designed for final consumers, they may also be persuaded by techniques addressed at themselves. Sales promotions of this type might include:

- **Dealer loaders** – e.g. a free case with every so many bought (an offer of '13 for the price of 12' is known as a 'baker's dozen');
- **Point of sale (POS) materials** – e.g. displays, posters and racks;
- **Dealer competitions** with attractive prizes;
- **Offers of staff training** – e.g. if the handling or servicing of the product needs special expertise;
- **Sale or return** – can be used to encourage a dealer to stock an untried product;
- **Promotional gifts** – e.g. bottles of spirits, clocks, watches etc.

Promotions out of the pipeline help the trade to promote and sell goods to the end-user. Such promotions require a creative approach and may have an 'impulse' element.

Out-of-the-pipeline promotions may include:

- **Free samples or trial packs** – either given to customers or available for a low price;
- **Bonus packs** – beer and lager cans frequently offer extra volume for the same price;
- **Coupon offers** – e.g. money off the next purchase;
- **Price reductions** – these are always popular with customers and are useful as part of a short-term pricing policy;
- **Competitions** – e.g. scratch cards, free draws and bingo;
- **Premium offers** – may provide an extra product for the same price or a free gift with a pack

TASK 55.1

Analyse the effectiveness of at least two sales promotions you have come across recently.

Personal selling

Although we may not realise it, probably every one of us is involved in some form of personal selling activity every day of our life. It can be persuading a friend to accompany us to a sports event, or asking a parent or relative to buy something for us. What we are doing is using a relationship to 'sell' our ideas to someone else.

Personal selling involves persuasive communication between a seller and a buyer which is designed to convince a consumer to purchase the products or services on offer. The objective of personal selling is therefore to make a sale. It is the culmination of all the marketing activities that have taken place beforehand.

TASK 55.2

Make a list of the number of times you try to persuade other people to do something or follow a particular course of action in an average day.

The importance of personal selling varies from business to business. For some organisations, the high cost of salaries, commissions, travel expenses and hotels can make it a very expensive process. In the organisational and business-to-business sector, the sales force **push** products into markets, whereas in consumer goods markets, advertising tends to **pull** products into the distribution network.

The sequence of events used in the personal selling process is often summarised as **The Five Ps**.

1 **Preparation** Sales staff should be well trained and familiar with the products they are selling. Equally important, they should have a good knowledge of customers, the competition and the market;
2 **Prospecting** This involves identifying prospects or potential customers before selling takes place;
3 **Pre-approach** This involves learning about customers, finding out about their previous purchases and generally trying to identify their needs and aspirations;
4 **Presentation** This involves active use of selling skills using **AIDA** (see page 387). The process starts with probing in order to identify customers' needs and finishes with the salesperson recognising the buying signals which will enable him or her to close the sale;
5 **Post-sale support** It is important to follow up a sale as this helps to generate repeat business.

Public relations

The purpose of **public relations (PR)** is to project a positive image of the organisation to the outside world through planned communications and activities. The PR process embraces every aspect of an organisation's actions and communications, and can include:

- Hospitality at sporting events;
- Press releases;
- Press conferences;
- Visits and open days;
- Event sponsorship;
- Corporate videotapes;
- Magazines, publicity, educational services.

Whereas other areas of the promotional mix are essentially short-term, public relations is a long-term process which sends messages to outside bodies and attempts to build and develop the reputation and image of an organisation over an extended period.

By reacting to a range of social, political, economic, local and environmental forces, an organisation can build a positive image which may influence a variety of groups such as shareholders, local residents, employees and special interest groups. Building goodwill in this way requires sound organisational behaviour and the communication of such behaviour to a range of different groups.

According to Frank Jefkins in his book *Public Relations,* PR involves a 'transfer process' which helps to convert the negative feelings of an organisation's many 'publics' into positive ones. By identifying unfavourable feeling of bodies external to an organisation, the company can use PR to create a more favourable environment.

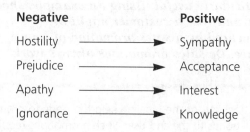

Negative		Positive
Hostility	⟶	Sympathy
Prejudice	⟶	Acceptance
Apathy	⟶	Interest
Ignorance	⟶	Knowledge

Figure 55.4 The PR transfer process

EXTENSION MATERIAL
The salesperson's role

Sales staff form an important link between suppliers and their customers. Personal selling takes place at the boundary between the supplying organisation and the customer, allowing information to flow in both directions. Often the salesperson's role is not only to sell but also to interpret the activities and policies of the organisation to the customer, and vice versa.

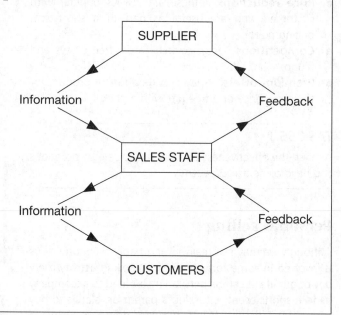

55.5 The link between customer and suppliers

Chapter summary

- Promotion is about communicating with others.
- There are four main areas of controllable communications. These include advertisements, sales promotions, personal selling and publicity.
- The acronym AIDA is often used to describe how the controllable methods are used.
- Advertisements are messages sent through the media to inform or influence people who receive them.

- Sales promotion is the function of marketing which seeks to achieve given objectives by the adding of intrinsic, tangible value to a product or service.
- Personal selling involves persuasive communication between a seller and a buyer designed to convince the consumer to purchase products or services on offer.
- Public relations involves projecting a positive image of an organisation to the outside world through planned communications and activities.

56 Marketing planning

Marketing planning is concerned with identifying clear objectives and setting out how they can be achieved. Marketing objectives govern the way in which an organisation operates and need to be built into every aspect of its strategic and tactical thinking.

Marketing planning involves:

- Establishing objectives and goals, allocating resources to meet them and setting out a clear plan of action;
- Setting out ways of evaluating performance against targets;
- Assessing the position and performance of the organisation in the various markets in which it operates, and its strengths and weaknesses.

Planning is fundamental to the marketing process. The purpose of planning is to develop a competitive advantage so that the organisation can outperform its rivals. It is a key process which ensures that an organisation's actions are focused on stated goals and objectives.

Models of planning

It has been said that 'If you don't know where you are going, any road will take you there'.

The point is that without clear planning you may achieve something, but it is unlikely to amount to much. If an organisation's objectives are well defined, individual departments have clear guidelines and it is possible for them all to work in a co-ordinated way.

Planning also makes it possible for management to evaluate performance. Without evaluation, there can be no control. Of course, plans are unlikely to be met in every detail. However, they establish guidelines against which performance can be checked and if necessary modified.

Model 1
A useful model is set out in Figure 56.1. The first step is to establish objectives. This is followed by clarifying the planning assumptions that are being made, collecting and sorting out useful data, evaluating alternative courses of action, selecting an appropriate course of action, and re-evaluating the chosen course. Finally plans are modified in the light of the results.

Model 2
Another approach to planning is as follows:

- **Diagnosis** *Where are we and why?* This usually involves some form of audit of company performance which can then be analysed.

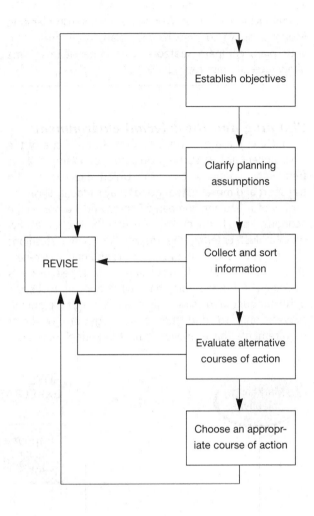

Figure 56.1 A model for planning

- **Prognosis** *Where are we going?* This involves looking at possible future scenarios in the light of present performance and trends.
- **Objectives** *Where do we want to go?*
- **Strategy** *What is the best possible way of achieving our objectives?*
- **Tactics** *What specific actions will enable us to meet our day-to-day targets?*
- **Control** *How far have we progressed?* A company will need to establish performance indicators against which it can measure its success.

SYNTHESIS

Is a good dose of marketing planning a solution for every product or business, or are some ventures doomed to failure regardless of how carefully they plan?

TASK 56.1

You have been given the task of relaunching Scalextric, the model racing car game. Working in teams, use planning Model 2 above to prepare your plan. After presenting your plan, compare strategies with other teams. Time allowance: 30 minutes.

Planning and the external environment

In marketing, it is important for firms to be aware of the environment in which they operate. For example, laws frequently change. A European Union directive on the transport and movement of goods may suddenly slash the profits of a haulage company. Booms and slumps in the economy may harm or improve the chances of a new product just entering the market. Tastes and fashions change with social attitudes. Environmental awareness changes the ways in which consumers like to see products packaged. A business may have what appears to be the right product and have made all the right planning moves, only to find that technology or consumer requirements have moved on. Marketing planning, therefore, takes place within a constantly changing political, social, economic, legal and technological environment. Businesses ignore it at their peril.

Strategic marketing planning

Any organisation that takes strategic marketing to heart will be involved in three interrelated activities:

- **Strategic analysis** involves building up a view of factors which are likely to influence the short-term and the long-term well-being of an organisation;
- This analysis helps planners to develop a menu of choices for strategic **development**;
- One or more of these choices must be selected for **implementation**, and this will lead to a further cycle of analysis, choice and implementation.

The process of strategic marketing analysis and choice clarifies the objectives that the organisation is working towards. Today most large and many small organisations express their overall objectives in a **mission statement** setting out their key goals and aspirations.

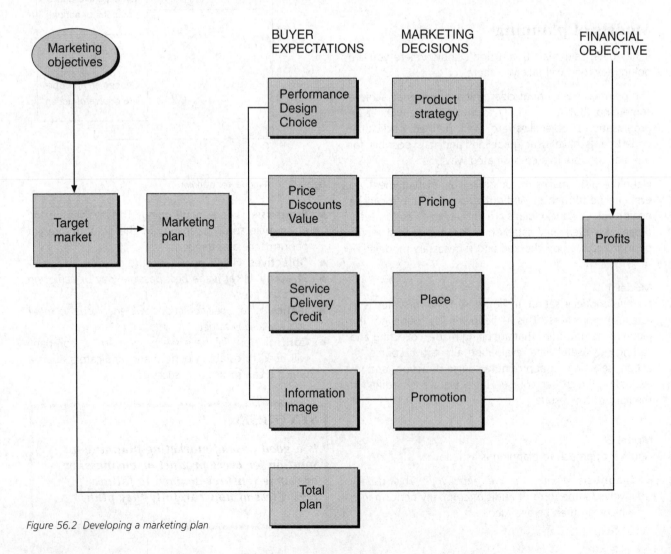

Figure 56.2 Developing a marketing plan

The corporate objectives of an organisation are often expressed in measurable terms and may be translated into financial targets. These are formulated by senior managers. They are also likely to reflect the expectations of stakeholders.

Marketing and financial objectives are brought together in a **total marketing plan**. The financial objectives of an organisation are usually tied up with the strategic objectives, which may, for example, be described in terms of profit-making and growth. However, there are many possible objectives depending on the vision and relative influence of different groups of stakeholders.

Developing an effective marketing plan involves investigating buyer expectations in order to make decisions about Product, Price, Place and Promotion. If the plan is effective, not only will consumers be satisfied, but so too will other strategic objectives of the organisation such as those which relate to financial targets.

Tactical marketing planning

An organisation's marketing plan must be grounded in strategic marketing. At the same time, it is important to plan carefully the tools and tactics of marketing. **Tactical marketing** will involve:

- The product mix plan;
- The pricing plan;
- The physical distribution plan;
- The promotional plan.

The product mix plan

An internal audit of the product mix involves listing the products and examining their performance over a period of years in order to identify trends. It is important to examine not only market segments but also the relationships between them. This process helps the organisation to identify products which need to be phased out and those which require modification, and to decide which products should enter the portfolio and at what time.

The pricing plan

Pricing is important for every organisation. A starting point is to evaluate the quality of pricing decisions that have been taken in the past and the effect of competitors' pricing policies.

The business may wish to explore the degree of price elasticity in the various markets which it serves. The pricing plan should set out the principles that cover pricing and discounting of products. Lower prices do not always mean

---

CASE STUDY CASE STUDY CASE STUDY CASE STUDY CASE STUDY

A TRANSFORMING INDUSTRY

It has been said that Japanese motor manufacturers have done more for the UK car industry than Alex Issigoni's Mini. You are probably asking, what *was* Issigoni's Mini?

The unveiling of the new Honda Civic recently marked another change of gear as Japanese manufacturers Honda, Toyota and Nissan accelerate car production within the UK. The new Civic will raise output from Honda's plant at Swindon by a third within two years, to more than 150,000 cars per year.

As we move towards the Millennium, it is the Japanese who have been responsible for the huge growth of investment and production in the British motor industry. Over the last ten years, they have helped to push production and export earnings to levels not seen in this country for 25 years. No longer is car manufacturing dominated

by the Big Three of Rover, Ford and Vauxhall: the Big Three have become the Big Six with the inclusion of the Japanese manufacturers.

Ten years ago, 9 in every 100 cars made in Europe came from the UK. Last year that figure was 12 in every 100. As we approach the year 2000, the figure will increase again. The British are back... with a little help from their Japanese friends!

1 What would be the key ingredients in the marketing plan for a motor manufacturer like Honda?

2 Explain how Japanese manufacturers have transformed the British motor industry.

3 What tactical decisions might the Japanese have made to support their marketing strategy?

4 Why do you think that the Japanese decided to locate production in the UK in preference to other countries?

STUDY CASE STUDY CASE STUDY CASE STUDY CASE STUDY CASE STUDY

SYNTHESIS

It is virtually impossible to draw a boundary around 'marketing'. Perhaps all an organisation's activities should be classified as 'marketing'. Do you agree?

more or better business. It may be better to build a sound long-term business than to lower prices in the short term in order to attract orders. The pricing plan should answer questions such as 'Do we need big volume turnover and can we manage it?' and 'Do we need to aim for lower volume but with a bigger margin?'

The physical distribution plan

Efficient distribution can help organisations to build competitive advantage. Where physical distribution costs are high, it is important to use the most effective channels. A useful ratio to compare distribution performance over a number of years is:

$$\text{Distribution effectiveness ratio} = \frac{\text{Distribution costs}}{\text{Sales}}$$

The promotional plan

In many large companies, promotions are tied to the **life-cycle** of a product. Promotional activity is required at launch and periodically to inject new life into a product. Promotional activity will also be closely tied to seasonal fluctuations and other short-term influences on demand. Advertising is a key ingredient of the promotional plan, but is only one element in the promotional mix.

Monitoring effectiveness

In a market-conscious company the cost of marketing will be high. A major problem faced by many organisations is that it is very difficult to apportion costs to marketing activities and also to monitor their effectiveness. For example, how can you tell what effect advertising at sports grounds is having on the performance of a company's products? It is difficult to ascertain how marketing activities translate into profitability.

A rough-and-ready ratio that can be used to measure marketing performance is:

$$\text{Marketing performance} = \frac{\text{Marketing cost}}{\text{Sales}}$$

In this chapter we have set out to show that marketing planning is crucial to the success of an organisation because it underpins the whole process of corporate planning. Marketing activities are carried out to meet the organisational objectives shaped by the marketplace. The pursuit of marketing objectives should lead to an effective and efficient use of resources, both for individual organisations and for society. They should also maximise returns in terms of objectives set.

The marketplace moves on. An organisation should know where it is going, while always being prepared to shift rapidly in response to changing patterns of consumer demand. For example, a marketing survey recently revealed that the over-50s have a total disposable income higher than the entire contents of the nation's building societies and double that of the 16-34 age group. This particular age group is know as the 'grey market'. Stylish clothes for fuller figures are becoming a new area for clothes designers. Both trends have important implications for any businesses catering to these market sectors.

So what of the future? Marketing planning is about looking ahead. By forcing organisations to think strategically and focus on corporate objectives, it helps them to foresee future trends and to plan for them.

Chapter summary

- Marketing planning involves setting clear objectives and working out how to achieve them.
- Planning is fundamental to the marketing process.
- Planning involves the use of the 'Four Ps'.
- There are various models of planning.
- Planning has to take into account the external environment.
- The process of strategic marketing helps to clarify the objectives an organisation is working towards.

- Marketing and financial objectives are brought together in a total marketing plan.
- Tactical marketing planning involves the marketing mix.
- It is difficult to measure the success of a marketing plan.
- Planning helps an organisation to foresee future trends and plan for them.

57 International marketing

When you buy goods, do you ever look to see where they were made? Have you ever thought about who made them, why they have been brought to your country and about all the distribution procedures that have taken place before the goods arrive in your high street?

This complex process of exchange is made possible through **international marketing**.

International marketing involves the marketing of products in two or more countries.

At one end of the spectrum, international marketing can simply involve trade between a company and customers in one other country. At the other extreme, a company may both sell and manufacture in a variety of countries.

The key element in international marketing is that it requires companies to take account of **differences** between domestic and overseas markets. They must not only understand the differences in customer requirements, but develop and tailor the marketing mix of their products accordingly.

Why trade internationally?

Imagine what it would be like to live in a country which did not trade with its neighbours. Many of the goods and services we take for granted today simply would not be available. Domestic companies would be small because they would not be able to specialise and export their wares overseas. Measured in terms of the variety of goods and services in the marketplace, our standard of living would be poor.

There are many other reasons for international marketing:

1 In an increasingly interdependent world, international trade is an **economic necessity**. Because we are not self-sufficient, we depend upon imports of raw materials and products from other countries;
2 Trading overseas helps organisations to **grow.** This is particularly useful if the domestic market is limited in size or nature. It also allows companies to use up surplus capacity;
3 Expanding into overseas markets enables organisations to benefit from **economies of scale**. This means that over a larger output, unit costs are reduced;
4 Trading overseas enables organisations to **react to competition**. For example, intense competition in the home market can be combatted by trading overseas;
5 International marketing also enables companies to produce goods overseas where they are in **demand**. There may be a number of cost advantages associated with locating units of manufacture overseas;
6 Many companies trade overseas so that they can sell **discontinued products or seconds** without having to dispose of them cheaply in the home market;
7 Often **rules, regulations and economic conditions** provide a favourable climate for overseas trade.

Domestic v. international marketing

International marketing involves recognising that people all over the world have different needs. Organisations have to accept that, because of differences in values, customs, languages and currencies, many products will

---

CASE STUDY CASE STUDY CASE STUDY CASE STUDY CASE STUDY

DELL SEEKS A COMPETITIVE ADVANTAGE

As profit margins in the tough computer (PC) market have become slimmer over recent years, manufacturers such as Dell have been seeking imaginative ways to trim costs and gain competitive advantage. Competition in the small office/home sector of the market has been fierce, with many manufacturers only making around £50 for each computer sold. Sales and support costs are also high as many buyers initially need help to run their computers. The solution for Dell, the American manufacturer, was to centralise its operations in Europe.

The personal computers sold by Dell throughout Europe are already manufactured in the Irish Republic. Now the company has located its support staff and telesales there too. All this has helped Dell to make huge cost savings and enabled the company to compete more effectively in the European marketplace.

1 What benefits does Dell receive from manufacturing overseas?

2 Explain how the marketing of products in Europe may differ from the marketing of products in the US.

STUDY CASE STUDY CASE STUDY CASE STUDY CASE STUDY CASE STUDY

only suit certain countries. The fact is that there is rarely such a thing as a global market – rather, a number of different foreign markets.

Catering for such differences involves greater risks. Developing products for different overseas markets and also being aware of the changes in currency prices requires careful planning and research.

Consumer behaviour, customs and culture vary throughout the world. Patterns of demand are determined by factors such as lifestyle, income, use of credit, family and religion. For example, exporting alcohol-based products to Islamic countries would be totally inappropriate.

Communication systems also vary from one market to another. It may be possible to contact representatives easily in the capital of another country, but not necessarily in other cities and towns. Communications problems may make it difficult to track goods in transit or keep in touch with representatives and channels of distribution.

Language can also present a problem, particularly in countries where several different languages or dialects are spoken.

Economic factors

A number of economic factors can also influence trade overseas. One important issue is whether customers can afford to pay for the goods or services they require. A country's stability and the guarantees of payment which it can offer play an important role in its ability to trade. The use of different currencies makes the whole process more complicated. Transactions overseas also depend upon the value of the currency involved.

Currencies fluctuate in value against one another. For example, the relationship of the yen to the dollar may vary from one day to another because of the changes in the demand and supply of the two currencies. If the pound falls in value, this makes British goods cheaper overseas, and this will determine an organisation's income and therefore the profitability of its transactions overseas.

Political risks

Trading overseas also carries political risks. There may be protocols to follow, such as diplomatic channels or negotiations between senior managers and directors. Catering for an overseas market and the demands it presents can involve considerable organisation.

Marketing goods and services in other countries is rarely an easy process. Shipping costs, tariffs and legal regulations, credit risks and the high cost of adapting goods to suit the needs of different groups of consumers can all cause problems. At the same time, there may be a preference for home-produced products, and this can

make it difficult for foreign firms to enter the market and develop their business.

Despite the problems and risks, however, many firms continue to market their products internationally. For the successful ones, the rewards can be considerable.

TASK 57.1

Consider why businesses market their goods overseas. Either scan the press (use periodicals or journals), take the case of an organisation known to you (e.g. MacDonald's) or use a case study from *The Times 100*.

Try to identify:

a) How the organisation markets its goods or services in the UK;
b) The problems it faces;
c) Why it markets its goods overseas;
d) The benefits it gains from doing so.

Entering overseas markets

Before entering an overseas market, particularly for the first time, an organisation has to consider its mode of entry into that market. There are three main methods of market entry:

1 **Indirect exporting**, where sales are made to an intermediary who then proceeds to resell to customers overseas;
2 **Direct exporting**, where the company sells direct to customers overseas;
3 **Overseas manufacture** This might be in the form of a joint venture or the establishment of a wholly-owned subsidiary.

1 Indirect exporting

Many organisations first venture into the field of international marketing through an **export house**. This is an organisation whose main activity is handling or financing overseas trade.

The export house has links throughout the world and plays a key role in promoting exports, providing valuable

> **IT'S A FACT**
>
> Until recently the Soviet Union and its Eastern European satellites limited their operations in overseas markets. So did China. India closed its doors to trade on a large scale. The same was true of many other countries. Today, many of these countries, totalling more than 3 billion people, are opening up their markets, providing enormous opportunities for international marketing.

experience for manufacturers and suppliers. It may act as a merchant by buying in the home market and selling in the export market. It can act as an agent and hold the sole rights for the promotion and sale of products. It can also perform the role of an export department and market overseas on behalf of the manufacturer or supplier, even sometimes bearing the credit risk. The export house helps to provide a link in the chain of distribution between the UK supplier and the foreign buyer.

2 Direct exporting

This involves manufacturers or suppliers shipping their products overseas and selling their wares directly to customers using their own personnel. The drawback is that they have to set up offices abroad, employ staff to monitor operations and constantly monitor the overseas trading restrictions. This takes considerable time, money and staff as even on a limited scale, direct exporting calls for specialised administration.

3 Overseas manufacture

Many companies, particularly those who produce bulky products, choose to manufacture overseas. By locating plant overseas they can establish themselves in the overseas market and in the process gain a better understanding of the needs of foreign customers. Secondly, in many overseas countries costs are lower. Manufacture overseas may overcome the effects of any barriers to market entry, such as tariffs.

There are a number of different types of overseas manufacture. **Joint ventures** exist where two or more firms join forces to make products overseas. Sometimes joint ventures involve **licensing** or **franchising**. For example, Pepsi-Cola is produced under franchise agreements in different countries.

Establishing a **wholly-owned production facility** demonstrates a firm commitment to an overseas market. Toyota and Nissan in the UK are two examples. The benefit for these organisations is that they retain their independence.

Standardisation or adaptation?

Before becoming involved in exporting, an organisation must answer two questions:

IT'S A FACT

When Cadbury Schweppes decided to enter the Polish market they were faced with three options. After considering direct exporting and joint ventures, they decided to go for local manufacture which led to the building of a factory at Wroclaw.

1 Is there a market for the products or services on offer?
2 Will the product need to be adapted for overseas markets?

The product must have characteristics that are acceptable for the market – features like size, shape, design, performance, even colour. For example, red is a popular colour in Chinese-speaking areas.

The marketing of a product which is undifferentiated between any of the markets is referred to as **standardisation**. In most markets, however, there are many barriers to standardisation. It is not difficult to imagine a standard marketing mix for a product and how this might vary from one country to another. For example:

- **Product** Tastes and habits vary between markets
- **Price** Consumers have different incomes;
- **Place** Systems of distribution vary widely;
- **Promotion** Consumers' media habits vary widely, as do languages and levels of literacy.

With **differentiated marketing** on the other hand, an organisation segments its overseas markets, offering a different marketing mix to suit each one.

The great benefit of standardisation is that costs are lowered, profitability is increased and the task of supplying different markets becomes much easier. However, some would argue that the success of many products in international markets has only come about because marketers have successfully adapted their marketing mix to meet local needs.

Delivery, paperwork and getting paid

When delivering goods overseas it is usually best to use the services of a **freight forwarding agency**. The freight forwarder will take responsibility for arranging the paperwork and transport of the goods. It is essential to work with a reliable freight forwarder. The choice of transport used depends on speed, cost, reliability and product requirements.

- **Paperwork** is a perennial problem for exporters. With the arrival of the Single Market, paperwork in the EU has been considerably reduced. The **Single Administrative Document (SAD)** was introduced in January 1988 to replace over 100 documents previously used;
- **Payment** Before selling goods overseas it is important to check that they can be paid for. Major banks and other specialist agencies can provide reports on the creditworthiness of potential customers. Also, insurance, called **credit insurance**, can be taken out against non-payment. Insurance can be obtained from banks, insurance companies and the government's Export Credit Guarantee Department.

Firms that export abroad are not paid immediately. There are two main ways of financing exports:

1 **A bank finance scheme** Most large banks offer export finance, including credit insurance:
2 **Factoring** This involves selling your invoices to a factoring company (often owned by a major bank) in exchange for money you are owed.

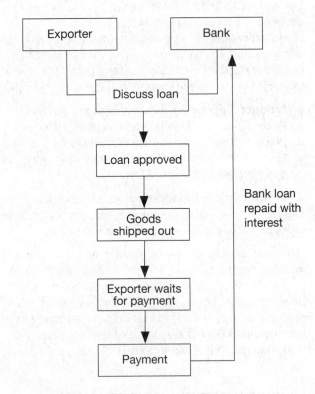

Figure 57.1 Bank finance scheme

Businesses need to negotiate a **credit period** when making deals. Within the European Union, 30 days' credit is a common credit period. About 70 per cent of UK exports are sold on an open account basis, i.e. payment is made by settling up within a given credit period through bank payment. About 20 per cent of UK exports are sold using bankers' letters of credit, whereby a reputable bank guarantees to make the payment at the end of the credit period. Letters of credit guarantee that customers get the goods they want and that the exporter is paid promptly. Exporters must give proof of delivery by submitting documents listed in the credit to the bank. If these documents are accurate and show that the goods are correct, then payment will be made within a few days.

Planning and control in international markets

Planning for international markets is a much more complex process than for domestic markets. However, as international marketing is only one part of an organisation's total marketing efforts, planning is likely to be more tactical and operational than strategic. Good planning is important as it allows decision-makers to analyse the effectiveness of policies.

As well as containing the usual ingredients of a marketing plan, an international marketing plan should:

● Constantly analyse developments in the international marketing environment;
● Review overseas performance by market, parts of market and region;
● Analyse how strengths have been utilised and opportunities developed, as well as how threats have been minimised and weaknesses corrected;
● Relate decisions made to marketing objectives;
● Indicate how marketing programmes have been co-ordinated and show budgeted costs.

IT'S A FACT

In a recent survey across Europe, IBM – an American company – was judged to have the most successful pan-European identity, ahead of Mercedes-Benz and Shell.

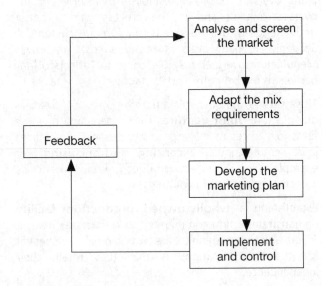

Figure 57.2 A model for international marketing planning

In the model above, the screening process enables an organisation to analyse how it will benefit from entry into each market. Adapting the mix requirements involves adaptation of the mix for each market. However, it is important to note that if the mix requires too much adaptation, it may not be profitable for a firm to enter a market.

Finally the planning process has to include a stage where the plan is implemented. **Control** is a way of checking that the plan meets the goals and objectives identified.

EXTENSION MATERIAL

To standardardise or not to standardise?

To a large extent the standardisation/adaptation dilemma depends on an organisation's view of its overseas markets and the degree to which it is prepared to commit itself to meeting the needs of overseas customers. Three different types of approach are usually quoted:

- **Polycentrism** With this approach, organisations usually establish subsidiaries with their own objectives and marketing policies which are decentralised from the parent company. Adaptation takes place in every market and different mixes are chosen to satisfy different customer requirements.

- **Ethnocentrism** Overseas operations are considered to be of little importance. Plans for overseas markets are developed at home. There is little research. The marketing mix is standardised and there is no real attention to different customer needs in each market.

- **Geocentrism** Standardisation takes place wherever possible. Adaptation takes place where necessary.

Chapter summary

- International marketing involves the marketing of products in two or more markets overseas.
- International marketing focuses upon the differences between selling domestically and selling overseas.
- There are many reasons why organisations market overseas.
- There is rarely such as thing as a global market.
- Marketing goods overseas involves greater risk.
- Consumer behaviour, culture and customs vary throughout the world.

- A number of economic factors may influence trading conditions, particularly currency fluctuations.
- The three modes of entry into overseas markets are through indirect exporting, direct exporting and overseas manufacture.
- Organisations need to find out whether there is a market for their goods or services and how far they have to adapt the ingredients of their marketing mix.
- Planning for international marketing is more complex than for domestic markets.

10 *Financial planning*

INTRODUCTION

All organisations require resources. These may be tangible such as property, equipment and materials, or less tangible, such as human resources. Using any of these resources requires financial planning. The management of finance is therefore inseparable from the management of the organisation as a whole. In this section we build upon the accounting and finance section earlier in the book to provide a detailed understanding of the role of finance in business.

Chapter 58 looks at accounting information and its users. It starts by looking at the development of management information systems and the nature of the information generated by such systems. It also looks at information flows as well as the changes brought about by new technology.

In Chapter 59 we look at the use of budgeting for planning and control. Throughout the chapter it is emphasised that budgeting is a form of responsibility accounting which works alongside other management initiatives. The process of setting up budgets is analysed, together with all the main features of budgeting

processes. Chapter 60 takes the budgeting process one stage further, covering standard costing and variance analysis.

Chapter 61 looks at investment appraisal and the importance of understanding such techniques when making key business decisions. It provides an analysis of the four main methods of appraising capital investment projects.

Chapter 62 explores accounting statements and policies and looks at the problems of stewardship of accounts. It outlines the legal requirements for the accounting statements of companies as well as the policies which accompany them.

Finally, the purpose of any system of costing is to find out the unit cost of a product. Chapter 63 explores the processes of allocation and apportionment and then looks at overhead cost absorption.

58 Accounting information

In order to make decisions, managers need the right information. When we asked the question 'What is accounting?' in Chapter 00, we saw that accounting is an information system. The objective of accounting, therefore, is to provide the right sort of information for making business decisions. It serves a variety of users by providing them with information through a series of well-defined processes.

Financial accounting information

Financial accounting serves both **external** and **internal** users. Some users, such as Inland Revenue and Customs and Excise, have the authority to require certain information by law, while other users, such as creditors and shareholders, will rely upon information which is translated into accounting reports published in final accounts.

Users may be interested in:

- The effects of investment or credit decisions;
- The cash flow position of an organisation;
- An organisation's profitability;
- The solvency or stability of an organisation;
- Its growth potential;
- The quality of decisions made by an organisation.

Management accounting

Management accounting is concerned with generating information for decision-making within an organisation. It identifies the areas where accounting information is required and then develops the information needed using various techniques of analysis. Finally, it reports the results of its analysis.

The National Association of Accountants (NAA) defines management accounting as:

> 'the process of identification, measurement, accumulation, analysis, preparation, interpretation, and communication of financial information used by management to plan, evaluate and control within an organisation and to assure appropriate use of and accountability for its resources.'

Management Information Systems

In order to be of use, accounting reports must be both relevant and reliable.

Relevance is likely to be measured in terms of the user's situation. For example, if they are looking at the liquidity position of an enterprise, relevant data would include information on current assets and liabilities. Accounting

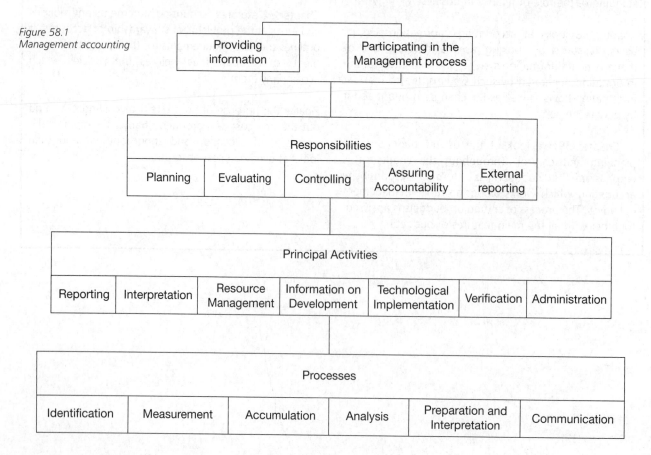

Figure 58.1
Management accounting

Type of business	External information	Internal information
Car manufacturer	Industry-wide innovations Economic information Trade regulations Market share Political changes	Production figures Quality tests Waste figures Output per worker Lead times
Supermarket chain	Market shares Competitors' prices Demographic changes Competitors' innovations	Sales per employee Stock levels Product lines Number of stock-outs

Figure 58.2 Types of management information system

information must also be reliable. **Reliability** helps to ensure that information is constant and trustworthy.

A small business may be run by one person. That person may know the business inside out and may have no need for a formal accounting system. But as soon as a business grows, the management function is performed by people who are more specialised and may be removed from day-to-day activities. In this case some form of **management information system (MIS)** is required.

Management information systems are sometimes referred to as **accounting information systems (AIS)**. The distinction between the two is not always clear. Some say that AIS systems are a subset of MIS systems, while others argue that MIS systems are a subset of AIS systems. Others argue that MIS and AIS both work together to provide the information required by managers and end-users. For the purpose of this text, we will assume that AIS and MIS work and interact together.

A management information system uses data to provide meaningful information to enable its users to make appropriate decisions in pursuit of business objectives.

Lucey in *Management Information Systems* defines a management information system as:

> *'a system using formalised procedures to provide management at all levels in all functions with appropriate information, based upon data from both internal and external sources, to enable them to make timely and effective decisions for planning, directing and controlling the activities for which they are responsible.'*

The nature and type of business has a bearing upon the sort of information generated by its MIS system. Information may be internal information generated within the business, or external information generated outside the business but relevant for the business (see Figure 58.2).

Anthony identifies three levels of management information:

1 **Strategic planning** The strategic planning process uses both internal and external sources of information. In a dynamic and changing business environment information is geared towards helping an organisation to use strategic planning in order to adapt.

2 **Management control** Management control is the 'process by which managers ensure that resources are obtained and used effectively and efficiently in the accomplishment of the organisation's objectives.' Control involves planning. Questions might Include: 'Are sales ahead of budget?', 'Does cost data support costing estimates?' and 'Are policies in line with predictions?' Most of the information for management control is generated internally.

3 **Operational control** Operational control ensures that tasks are carried out efficiently. At this level, tasks have been specified and methods determined. Information for operations involves providing those involved with the responsibility of executing tasks with the minimum of expenditure on resources.

Features of MIS systems

Management information systems consist of:

- **Physical resources:** computers, telephone lines and manual records;
- **Personnel:** human resources necessary to operate the system;
- **Methods:** how the physical and human resources are brought together to produce a coherent system.

Management information systems have developed rapidly over recent years. Modern management information systems have been influenced by three main factors:

1 The rapid growth in the use of information technology;
2 The increasing complexity of business organisations;
3 The changing business environment.

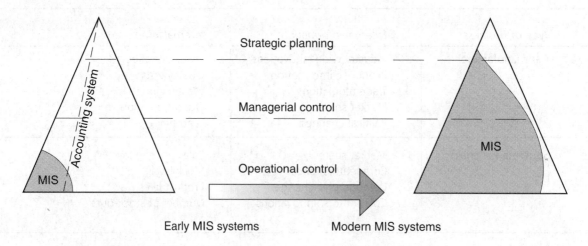

Figure 58.3 The rapid growth of MIS systems

It is important to understand that the term 'MIS' does not simply mean computers. Computers are merely tools in the wider information process.

Control systems

For organisations to be efficient, management need to monitor and control performance. There are broadly three different types of control systems:

1 **Closed-loop systems** With some business activities the desired outcome is known with a fair degree of precision, for example, tolerance in production processes, or departmental expenses and budgets. Where an outcome can be compared with a previous or expected value, a closed-loop system can be developed. The essential feature of the system is a feedback loop to allow the monitoring of output on the basis of expected values.

2 **Automatic loop systems** Some businesses provide automatic control without further involvement by management or staff. A prime example is the automatic ordering of stock once a given re-order level has been passed. The comparison of stock balances with control totals and the automatic printing of purchase orders means that a time-consuming management function has been largely eliminated.

3 **Open-loop systems** Open-loop systems do not have a feedback loop and so it could be argued are not

control systems at all. Though many systems, particularly at operational level, are best served with a control mechanism, it can be argued that other systems, particularly for higher managers at a strategic level, require information for decisions which cannot be programmed. The main requirement is that the management mechanism and the information required to support it are appropriate to the circumstances.

TASK 58.1

Working in groups, find out more about the MIS system in your school or college. Who is the system designed to serve and who are the decision-makers? How is data captured? Which decisions are closed-loop, automatic or open-loop? What are the aims and objectives of the system? How is data captured, stored and used?

SYNTHESIS

Identify three situations in which a closed-loop system might exist. How might a closed-loop information system related to certain activities help managers to make judgements about key control decision-making areas?

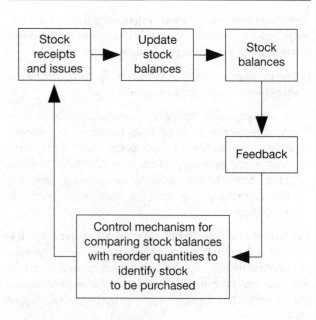

Figure 58.4 A closed loop system

CASE STUDY CASE STUDY CASE STUDY CASE STUDY CASE STUDY

THE NEED FOR INFORMATION

The two examples below both describe situations in which companies are faced with the need for information. Read them carefully then complete the tasks:

1 RJB Mining, England's main coal producer, has teamed up with National Power, the electricity generator, to pioneer a 'clean coal' power station. Together with Texaco, the US oil group, the two companies will spend several million pounds to study the feasibility of building the 400-megawatt station adjacent to RJB's Kellingley colliery in Yorkshire.

2 Seventeen of the world's most famous hotels will be up for grabs as Granada clears out assets which it acquired as a result of the takeover of Forte in 1996 and which are now deemed superfluous. Granada maintains it wishes to concentrate upon economies of scale and branding of the mid-market hotels such as Posthouse, Crest and Heritage chains, and that hotels such as the Grosvenor House in London and Ritz in Madrid cannot be justified in terms of returns on capital.

1 In the two cases above, what sort of information would help to make the key decisions required?

2 Who would benefit from the availability of such information?

3 What form might that information take?

STUDY CASE STUDY CASE STUDY CASE STUDY CASE STUDY CASE STUDY

Information flows

MIS systems start with the collection of data from data sources, with data flowing through certain processes before being transformed into information for managers.

Data capture

Much of the information flowing through a business comes from the recording of financial transactions. Other information comes from procedures set up to control business activities, such as machine logs, workers' timesheets and work progress reports. Examples include:

- **Accounting systems** – processing financial information with customers and suppliers, financial reporting, including budgetary control, credit control, payroll and the costing of jobs;
- **Personnel systems** – databases of employees' details including current skills and training needs;
- **Engineering** – computer-aided design and production of bills and materials;
- **Manufacturing** – computer-aided manufacturing, production planning, the monitoring of production efficiency, throughput volumes, machine utilisation and quality rejection rates;
- **Resource procurement** – purchase order systems and stock control;
- **Service functions** – allocation of work, e.g. maintenance programmes and measures of productivity;
- **Distribution** – sales order processing, planning physical distribution, sales analysis, analysis of response to promotions, etc.

IT'S A FACT

Computer downtime costs British industry more than £1 billion per year.

The methods adopted for the capture of data depend upon the transactions and the relative costs of manual procedures and computer systems. They might include:

- Manual recording on standard forms;
- Keying-in to a computer system;
- **Electronic Data Interchange (EDI)**: this enables data to be transferred from one computer system to another. Problems of compatibility between systems have so far restricted use of EDI, although it is widely used in the retail sector where large retailers can pass stock requirements to suppliers without manual intermediate steps;
- **Electronic input,** with transactions recorded by scanning equipment. Examples include the use of bar codes on sales at supermarkets **(EPOS)**, bar codes on college enrolment forms to track student attendance, and optical character recognition by banks for clearing cheques.

Processing information

Businesses can accumulate large quantities of data from the recording of financial transactions.

Though important for the monitoring of balances, individual pieces of data such as the sale of a single item are not sufficient in themselves for running a business. If

CASE STUDY CASE STUDY CASE STUDY CASE STUDY CASE STUDY

PROTECTING INFORMATION SYSTEMS

It is easy to take information held on computers for granted. There is a famous story of a disgruntled employee working out her notice who set off the sprinkler system in her office. As staff fled they forgot to turn off their computers. The water damage proved to be minor, but the damage to information systems was beyond repair.

Unfortunately the company had failed to realise how dependent they were on computers and had neglected to develop a disaster recovery plan for this type of situation. The net result was months of chaos and lost business. In fact, the company never fully recovered from the incident.

This year British industry will buy around 3 million PCs, yet under 5 per cent of firms

have a disaster recovery plan. There are a number of providers of recovery packages. For example, Hewlett Packard provides three levels of business protection. The back-up service is designed for customers who require protection within hours of a computer disaster. The stand-by service rescues customers whose hardware has failed because of a disaster. The company also offer a full-scale mobile service which brings a large van containing a specially designed computer room to the clients' door.

1 Why do organisations need a disaster recovery plan?

2 Provide an example of the sort of problems which might be caused by the loss of information from a MIS.

STUDY CASE STUDY CASE STUDY CASE STUDY CASE STUDY CASE STUDY

managers were presented with every piece of data collected, they would have no time to interpret its meaning and make appropriate decisions. Data collecting needs to be transformed by management information systems into information which management can act upon. This involves sorting, analysing and summarising.

Communicating information
Management information systems can communicate information to end-users in a number of different ways:

1 **Verbally**: by telephone, meeting, audio tape and video conferencing;
2 **In writing**: via memoranda, newsletters, printed reports;
3 **Via presentation media**: videos, slides, overhead projector, black/white boards;
4 **Via electronic systems**: E-mail, computer disks, teletext, viewdata, fax;
5 **Other**: microfiche (sheet film) or microfilm.

The choice of medium should reflect the nature of information, the audience it is required to reach and the use to which the information is to be put.

Data storage

Data stores may be **manual** records or **computer files**. Most organisations use both. Manual records include:

● Documents in a filing system such as filing cabinets or documents recorded on microfiche or microfilm;

● Written entries in registers, ledgers and diaries;
● Card indexes.

Data records stored in computers are known as **databases**. They can be used as a basis for sharing data between different applications.

The Chartered Institute of Management Accountants defines a database as:

'a file of data structured in such as way that it may serve a number of applications without its structure being dictated by any one of those applications, the concept being that programs are written round the database rather than files being structured to meet the needs of particular programs.'

Processed data is normally stored in two types of file:

● **Master files** for permanent data concerning the data entry, such as a stock part or customer;
● **Transaction files** for details of individual transactions such as date, description, quantities and value. The transaction history will dictate how often the transaction files are erased.

Design and implementation of a MIS
How information systems are designed and implemented is of crucial significance to their efficiency and effectiveness. A MIS system must not be designed upon the needs of one department but should relate to the needs of employees and managers throughout the organisation.

The starting point for the design of a management information system is to develop a general overview of the organisation and its needs. The implementation and development of a system usually goes through five main processes:

1 **Feasibility study** to determine whether the system will produce net benefits to the business;
2 **System design** to explore the logic of the system;
3 **Physical design**, involving writing the programs, training the user and obtaining the hardware;
4 **System testing;**
5 **Implementation.**

After implementation, systems have to be maintained and evaluated to ensure that the organisation's needs continue to be met. System improvements may have to go through the same stages as initial implementation to address new problems or needs.

Advances in computer technology and software tools have contributed greatly to the development of management information systems. However, management information systems are not just about the development of applications for computers. They are about using the processing of data to support decision-making.

Chapter summary

- Managers require information to form the basis for decision-making.
- Decision-making information can come either from the process of financial accounting or from management accounting.
- Accounting reports must be relevant and reliable.
- A management information system uses data to provide meaningful information to enable its users to make appropriate decisions in pursuit of business objectives.
- Information for decision-making may be internal or external.
- Information may be used for strategic planning, management control and operational control.
- Computers are merely a tool of the information process.

- Control systems may be closed-loop, automatic-loop or open-loop.
- Data for information systems may be captured in a variety of ways.
- Management information systems will sort, analyse and summarise data.
- Systems will communicate data in a variety of forms.
- Databases help to provide a basis for sharing information between a variety of different applications.
- Management information systems are about the processing of data to support decision-making systems.

59 Budgeting: using information for planning and control

Wherever there is a need for control, there has to be a plan. In this chapter we look at the process of budgeting and the uses of budgets for monitoring not only the organisation's progress towards its objectives, but also the performance of different parts of the organisation. In Chapter 60, we will look at another form of plan through the process of standard costing and variance analysis.

Budgetary control is the technique of looking at an organisation's future in order to anticipate what is going to happen and then trying to make it happen. Budgeting is sometimes described as a system of **responsibility**

accounting because it puts an onus upon budgeted areas to perform in a predetermined way.

Lucey in *Management Information Systems* defines responsibility accounting as:

> *'a system of accounting in which costs and revenues are analysed in accordance with areas of personal responsibilities so that the performance of the budget holders can be monitored in financial terms.'*

We all budget to a greater or lesser extent. For example, our short-term budget might describe how we are going to get through the coming week and do all of the things we want to do. Our slightly longer-term budget might enable us to afford Christmas presents in two months' time. Our longest-term budget could take into account future expenses such as car tax, MOT and motor insurance, all of which fall due ten months from now.

In the same way, businesses try to see far into the future. Although a detailed budget is prepared only for the year ahead, it can be part of a five-year plan. The problem is that the further one looks into the future, the more difficult it is to see accurately.

```
IT'S A FACT
```

A charity called TAXAID provides free advice for people who cannot afford professional help with self-assessment and their accounts.

Budgeting

The aim of budgeting is provide a system of control which enables the organisation to work towards its objectives. It has been said that 'the preparation of a budget depends critically upon its purpose.' In fact, there are two kinds of purpose for budgets. These are:

1 To provide 'a map' of an organisation and all of the parts of the organisation which go into that map;
2 To form a basis for financial management and control.

A budget can be a defined as a **'quantitative economic plan for a period of time'**. Let us look at these terms more closely:

● **Quantitative** A budget involves values expressed as quantities. An organisation may produce a number of household brand names. It would only be through quantification that a worth could be attributed to these brands;
● **Economic** A budget is expressed in economic terms. Though a business may be a market leader, its budgets are expressed in financial rather than market terms;
● **Plan** A budget is a plan designed to achieve a range of objectives. It is not a forecast in the sense of a prediction, but an intention – i.e. something which is *intended* to happen;
● **Time** Budgets have to be expressed over a specific time period.

Functions of budgets

Budgets have many different functions. These include:

● To provide all managers within an organisation with a financial responsibility;
● To control an organisation and its activities as it works towards achieving its business goals;
● To map a way forward for an organisation and the steps it has to take;
● To co-ordinate the various activities of an organisation;
● To instruct managers/section leaders on how to manage their part of the organisation;
● To provide a benchmark against which performance can be measured;
● To motivate members of the organisation;
● To aid decision-making.

Setting up budgetary activities

Organisations often appoint a **budget controller** whose job is to co-ordinate budgetary activities. The **budgeting team** will consist of representatives from various areas of the organisation. The team should be involved in every stage of the budgetary process:

CASE STUDY CASE STUDY CASE STUDY CASE STUDY CASE STUDY

WIDGET SUPPLY CO LTD

You have been appointed to the board of Widget Supply Ltd. The business has successfully supplied widgets to light engineering companies for the last 30 years.

The present managing director has recently taken up post. In the past, the only financial information available for management was a copy of the previous year's final accounts. These were always presented on traditional lines. In your role as an accountant, you feel that you could improve decision-making

with a better control structure. You think that budgeting could go a long way towards providing the right solution.

1 What would be the advantages of introducing a budgetary system?

2 What steps would you take to introduce it?

3 How might this information improve the quality of decision-making?

STUDY CASE STUDY CASE STUDY CASE STUDY CASE STUDY CASE STUDY

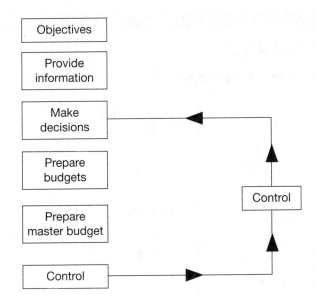

Figure 59.1 The budgetary process

1 **Considering objectives** All decisions should enable an organisation to work towards achieving its objective, be it maximising profit, improving product quality or increasing output.

2 **Providing information** Managers often look at figures from the past so that budgets are based on the results of the previous year. **Zero-based budgeting** is a technique that starts each year afresh, so the performance of the whole organisation is re-appraised. A clear knowledge of the predicted performance of the industry in general and the political and economic climate are of benefit here.

3 **Making decisions** Forward planning and co-ordination of departmental activities will inevitably require decisions to be made – for example, how much to spend on advertising, whether to put off the purchase of capital equipment, etc.

4 **Preparing budgets** Detailed budgets are prepared for all of the necessary areas of business activity.

5 **Preparing a master budget** Various budgets can be linked together to produce a master budget which will show a forecast set of final accounts.

6 **Control** Even though a plan is outlined in the form of a budget, this does not necessarily mean that it will take place as planned. Managers try to use budgets as a guide to achieving certain results. If actual performance is different from budgeted performance at the end of the year, action will need to be taken.

IT'S A FACT

A senior accountant was recently asked 'what side the debit balances appeared upon'. His reply was simply 'the side by the window'!

The control hierarchy

Setting up a system of responsibility accounting involves breaking an organisation down into a series of 'control centres'. Each individual manager then has the responsibility for managing the budget relating to their particular control centre.

Budgetary reports reflect the assigned responsibility at each area of the organisation. As all organisations have a structure of control, it is important that the budgetary system fits around this. The reports should be designed to reflect the different levels within the organisation and the responsibilities of each of the managers concerned.

If the budgeting process reflects the different levels of control, managers will be kept informed not just of their own performance, but also of that of other budget holders for whom they are responsible. They will also know that managers above them will be assessing *their* performance. This system will be regularly reviewed at meetings attended by all the individual managers concerned.

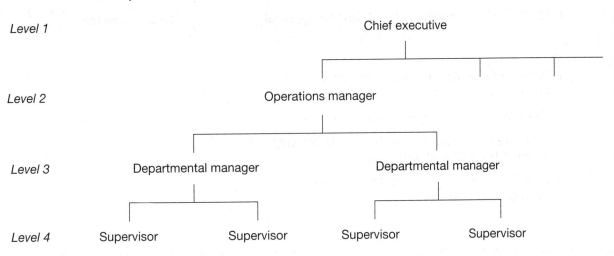

Figure 59.2 A reporting hierarchy

BUDGET TIMETABLE

for year 1st April 1997 to 31st March 1998

Date	Narrative	Responsibility
1/9/96	Board of Directors review long-term objectives and specify short-term goals for the year.	Directors
22/9/96	Budget guidelines and standard forms issued to line managers.	Accounts
6/10/96	Actual results to September 96 are issued to line management with comparisons to current budget and last year's actual results.	Accounts
20/10/96	Budget submissions to the management accountant.	Accounts
27/10/96	First draft of master budget is issued.	Accounts
3/11/96	First draft of the budget is reviewed for results and consistency – line managers to justify their submissions.	Managing director and individual directors
6/11/96	New assumptions and guidelines to line management.	Accounts
10/11/96	Budgets revised and submitted.	Line management
27/11/96	Second draft of master budget issued.	Accounts
28/11/96	Final review of the draft budget.	Managing director and accounts director
30/11/96	Final amendments.	Accounts
1/12/96	Submission to board for approval.	Finance director

1 What individuals and managers are involved in the budgetary process?

2 Describe the purpose of a budget timetable.

3 Why might 'actual results' be compared with 'current budget' and 'last year's' results?

4 What short-term goals might influence the budgetary process?

Benefits of a budgetary system

The budgetary process has a number of important advantages to organisations:

1 Annual budgetary reviews give members of different departments a better understanding of the working of the organisation as a whole. Often by participating in the budgetary process they feel that their experience is contributing to policy decisions. The process also provides targets and highlights areas of concern;

2 Budgeting increases co-operation between departments and lowers departmental barriers. This helps members of one department to be aware of the difficulties facing other departments;

3 By being involved in the budgetary process, non-accountants become aware of the importance of costs. Their increasing awareness may encourage them to work harder to meet budgeted targets;

4 Budgeting encourages participants to think more about profitability and their role in helping the organisation to achieve its objectives.

Problems with the budgetary process

There can, however, be inherent dangers in budgeting, particularly if the budgetary system is rigid:

1 If actual results are dramatically different from budget, the whole process can lose its credibility as a means of control. Whereas a fixed budget is unable to adapt to changes, a flexible budget will recognise changes in the behaviour of its variables and can be amended each control period in line with changing activities;

2 Following a budget too rigidly can restrict a business's activities. For example, if the budget for entertainment has been exceeded and subsequent visiting customers are not treated with the usual hospitality, orders may be lost; on the other hand, if managers realisetowards the end of the year that the department has underspent, they may decide to go on a spending spree;

3 If senior managers impose budgets without consultation, departmental staff and middle managers may either ignore them or make no effort to keep to them.

The main objective of budgetary control is to allow management to plan ahead and exercise some control over future events. This allows them to develop an insight into areas of concern and take action to avoid any problems. The process is sometimes called **goal congruence**, because it enables individuals and groups to be developed to match higher organisational goals.

Budgets provide an opportunity for everybody to play a part in either the strategic or tactical development of the organisation. As the activities following the budgetary process unfold, they provide a benchmark against which actual performance can be measured and judged.

> ### SYNTHESIS
>
> *Can you imagine a situation in which a budget affects the flexibility of empowered managers to make key decisions? How could steps be taken to avoid this?*

Budgeting exercise: Randle & Hopkins

Randle & Hopkins manufacture and sell one design of filing cabinet. It is the start of 1997 and the company wishes to budget for the coming year.

You have been given the following information from which to draw up a budget:

1 The company anticipates selling 8,800 cabinets at a price of £50.

2 Each cabinet requires 10 sq. m. of materials costing £0.75 per sq. m. and 3 hours of direct labour at £4 per hour.

3 Other factory costs include variable indirect labour of £0.50 per unit and expenses including power and paint at £1.00 per unit. Fixed overheads comprise £40,000 and depreciation on plant calculated at 10 per cent on cost.

4 Halfway through 1997 the partners intend to purchase additional plant at a cost of £20,000.

5 Stock levels at the end of 1996 were 300 finished cabinets and 7,000 sq. m. of raw materials.

6 Stock levels at the end of 1997 are forecast to be 500 finished cabinets and 5,000 sq. m. of raw materials. Finished goods stock is valued to include the costs of direct labour and materials and factory overheads.

7 Each cabinet incurs distribution costs of £2 and salesperson's commission of £3. Selling and distribution fixed costs are forecast at £40,000.

8 Administration costs are forecast at £54,000 for salaries, £8,000 for stationery and telephone and £20,000 for other expenses.

9 Trade debtors are currently historically low, so Randle suggests it may be prudent to assume they will increase by £10,000 over the coming year.

10 Trade creditors are forecast to end the year at one month's worth of raw material purchases. Unless otherwise stated, all other transactions are on a case basis.

11 The balance sheet for the end of 1996 is as shown on page 414.

Randle & Hopkins – Budgeted balance sheet
as at 31st December 1996

	Cost £	Depreciation £	Net £
Fixed assets			
Plant	100,000	50,000	50,000
Current assets			
Raw materials stock		5,250	
Finished goods stock		7,380	
Debtors		65,000	
		77,630	
Current liabilities			
Creditors	12,000		
Bank	10,000	22,000	
Net current assets			55,630
			£105,630
Capital b/f			95,000
Profit			10,630
Capital c/f			£105,630

You are required to prepare the following budget statements for 1997:

1 Sales budget
2 Production budget
3 Raw materials usage budget
4 Raw materials purchases budget
5 Direct labour budget
6 Factory overhead budget
7 Selling and distribution budget
8 Administration budget
9 Debtors budget
10 Creditors budget
11 Cash budget
12 Budget profit and loss account
13 Budget balance sheet

1 Sales budget

Forecast number of units	8,800
Selling price (£)	50
Sales turnover (£)	440,000

2 Production and finished goods budget

Stocks of finished goods are budgeted to increase by 200 units. Production therefore has to be in excess of sales.

	Units
Forecast sales units	8,800
Add required closing stock to start the next year	500
	9,300
Less opening stock from this year	300
Production required	9,000

3 Raw materials usage budget

	Sq. m.
Forecast production units	9,000
Material per unit	x 10
Total	90,000
Price per sq. m.	£0.75
Total value	£67,500

4 Raw materials purchases budget

Stocks of raw materials are budgeted to fall over the coming year, so purchases will be less than production requirements. We know the opening and closing balances and the production requirements, so by deduction we can arrive at purchases.

	Sq. m.	£
Opening stock	7,000	5,250
Add purchases at 75p	88,000	66,000
Less production usage	90,000	67,500
Closing stock	5,000	3,750

5 Direct labour budget

Forecast production units	9,000
Direct labour hours per cabinet	3
Total direct hours	27,000
Wage rate per hour	£4
Total wages	£108,000

6 Factory overhead budget

For factory overhead we need to identify expenses that will vary with the level of business activity and those which are fixed costs.

Variable overhead per unit	£
Labour	0.50
Expenses – power and paint	1.00
Total variable overhead per unit	1.50
Forecast production units	9,000
Total variable overhead	13,500

Fixed overhead	
Depreciation	11,000
Other	40,000
Total fixed overhead	51,000
Total factory overhead	64,500

7 Selling and distribution budget

As with production overhead budget, we have to identify both fixed and variable elements of the various indirect expenses charged to the profit and loss account.

	£
Variable costs	2
Distribution per cabinet	3
Commission per cabinet	5
Total variable costs for 8,800 cabinets	44,000
Total fixed costs	40,000
Total selling and distribution cost	84,000

8 Administration budget

	£
Salaries	54,000
Stationery and telephone	8,000
Other	20,000
	82,000

9 Debtors budget

Debtors are forecast to increase over the year, so we know that the amounts received from customers will be less than the level of sales included in the profit and loss account.

	£
Opening debtors balance	65,000
Sales	440,000
Cash received (balancing figures)	430,000
Closing debtors balance	75,000

10 Creditors budget

As with debtors, if we know the level of creditors at the beginning and end of the year, together with the purchase figure, we can calculate the amount to be paid to suppliers in the year.

	£
Opening creditors balance	12,000
Purchases	66,000
Cash payments (balancing figure)	72,500
Closing creditors balance (£66,000/12)	5,500

11 Cash flow forecast (cash budget)

In the subsidiary budgets we have identified all of the cash to be received and paid out, so we are in a position to prepare the cash budget.

Randle & Hopkins
Cash budget for the year ended
31st December 1997

Receipts	£
Sales	430,000
Payments	
Raw material suppliers	72,500
Direct labour	108,000
Factory overhead	53,500
Selling and distribution	84,000
Administration	82,000
New machinery	20,000
Total payments	420,000
Receipts less payments	10,000
Opening cash balance	−10,000
Closing cash balance	0

Remember that when preparing cash flow statements, we are only interested in items that relate to actual cash transactions. The factory overhead budget included a depreciation charge of £11,000 which is not a cash flow so should be excluded from the cash flow forecast (£64,000 – £11,000 = £53,500). The cash flow forecast shows that the bank overdraft has been paid off by the end of 1997.

However, care should taken when interpreting these in practice, as wide variations can occur.

12 Budget profit and loss account

Randle & Hopkins' budgeted trading and profit and loss statement and budgeted balance sheet are shown below. It is usual to call the budget profit and loss account and the balance sheet the **master budget**.

Budgeted trading and profit and loss statement for the year ended 31st December 1997

	Units	£	£
Sales	8,800		440,000
Opening stock	300	7,380	
Raw material usage	9,000	67,500	
Direct wages		108,000	
Factory overheads		64,500	
	9,300	247,380	
Closing Stock at £26.60 per unit (£247,380/9,300)	500	13,300	
Cost of sales	8,800		234,080
Gross profit			205,920
Less expenses:			
Selling and distribution		84,000	
Administration		82,000	
			166,000
Net profit			£39,920

Budgeted balance sheet as at 31st December 1997

	£ Cost	£ Depreciation	£ Net
Fixed Assets			
Plant	120,000	61,000	59,000
Current assets			
Raw materials		3,750	
Finished goods		13,300	
Debtors		75,000	
Bank		0	
		92,050	
Current liabilities			
Creditors		5,500	
Net current assets			86,550
			145,550
Capital b/f			105,630
Profit			39,920
Capital c/f			145,550

TASK 59.1

The Premier Christmas Pudding Company requires you to prepare its budget statements for the seven months to January 1998. You have been given the following forecast information:

a) The sales forecast for 1 kg. puddings is as follows:

Jul.	Aug.	Sept.	Oct.	Nov.	Dec.	Total
100	100	500	1,300	10,000	20,000	32,000

b) No sales of puddings have been made in the previous six months.
c) Each 1 kg. pudding sells for £2.50.
d) Customers are mainly retailers and wholesalers who take one month to pay for puddings received.
e) It is company policy to hold a minimum stock of puddings each month that is equivalent to the next month's forecast sales. After December, sales are not forecast until July of the next year. The requisite minimum stock would be held at the end of June, valued at £1.20 per pudding.
f) Sufficient dry fruits are held in stock to cover the next month's forecast production. Other ingredients are purchased in the month of use.
g) All suppliers are paid on delivery.
h) Production capacity is limited to 10,000 kg. per month.
i) Direct labour is employed on a piece-work rate of £0.20 per kilo of pudding.
j) Costs for a 100 kg. batch are as follows:

	Kg.	£
Dried fruit	50	60
Other	50	30
Packaging	10	
Distribution	20	

k) The whole period's packaging materials will be received from the printers at the beginning of July. The packaging is of a special design to celebrate the firm's 50th anniversary. In case sales exceed forecast, sufficient packaging for 35,000 puddings has been ordered. Excess packaging is to be disposed of in December.
l) Administration overhead is fixed at £3,000 per month and is payable up to the end of January 1998.
m) The bank balance at the end of June 1997 is forecast to be £15,930.
n) No losses are assumed in the production process.

Prepare for each of the seven months to 31st January:

1 Sales budget
2 Finished stock and production budget
3 Raw materials stock and purchases budget (separate for mixed fruit, packaging and other)
4 Direct labour budget
5 Cash budget
6 Forecast trading and profit and loss account

Chapter summary

- Budgeting is used to monitor all parts of an organisation.
- Budgetary control is a method of looking at an organisation's future in order to anticipate what is going to happen and then trying to make it happen.
- Budgeting is a form of responsibility accounting.
- We are all engaged in some form of budgeting.
- The aim of a budgetary system is to provide a control system which enables an organisation to work towards its objectives.
- Budgets have many functions such as financial responsibility, control of activities, mapping a way forward, co-ordination, the setting of benchmarks for motivation and also for decision-making purposes.
- A budget controller co-ordinates budgetary activities.
- When setting up a system of responsibility accounting an organisation must be broken down into control centres.
- Budgeting gives members of an organisation a better understanding of the operation of the organisation as a whole.
- Budgeting increases co-operation between departments.
- Flexible budgets can help an organisation to adapt to changes as and when they occur.

60 Budgeting: control, standard costing and variances

A key feature of the budgeting process is the feedback it provides for individuals and groups throughout an organisation. Feedback should reflect the information needs of each level of the organisation, with each level of reporting being interrelated with levels below and above. For example, a budget-holder will wish to be informed of his or her own performance as well as that of budget-holders for whom they are responsible.

In this chapter we look at the process of feedback and control through **variance analysis** and **standard costing**. The key feature of this chapter is the use of information for control and decision-making purposes.

Budgets and control

In the previous chapter we looked at the construction of budgets related to functional aspects of an organisation for the control and monitoring of performance. The key benefit of the budgeting process is to analyse how closely actual performance relates to budgeted performance. Wherever actual differs from budgeted performance a **variance** takes place. The process of analysing the difference between actual performance and budgeted performance is called **variance analysis**.

Variances are recorded as being either **adverse (A)** or **favourable (F)**, depending upon whether actual expenditure is more or less than budget. For example, if actual expenditure is *less* than budgeted expenditure then the variance would be favourable. On the other hand, if actual expenditure is *more* than budgeted expenditure, then the variance would be adverse.

Figure 60.1 below shows that managers cannot be answerable for cost overruns if they occur in areas where they have no control. For example, whereas expenditure on machine maintenance may be controlled, this is not true of depreciation which is outside the control of any manager.

Understanding variances

Variances may arise for a number of reasons. These include:

1 **Random deviations** which are uncontrollable. As we saw above, these are outside the control of individual managers;
2 **An incorrectly set budget** This may require further research and management action;
3 The failure by a manager to meet an agreed budget.

Problems of the budgetary process

Budgetary and control systems vary from one organisation to another. They are found both in the private sector and the public sector, and in all sorts of organisations from the very small to the very large. Given the different aims of organisations, budgetary systems reflect the context in which they are put to use. There are, however, certain

---

Machine shop overhead report for October 1997

	Budget £	Actual £	Variance £
Controllable costs			
Indirect wages	8,000	8,200	200A
Machine maintenance	2,250	1,900	350F
Consumable materials	500	550	50A
Total controllable	10,750	10,650	100F
Uncontrollable costs			
Depreciation	5,700	6,000	300A
Property cost apportionment	8,500	9,000	500A
Total uncontrollable costs	14,200	15,000	800A
Total cost centre overheads	24,950	25,650	700A

A = Adverse
F = Favourable

Figure 60.1 Controllable and uncontrollable costs

problems associated with budgeting processes which have to be recognised.

Firstly, reliance upon budgeting and its processes is no substitute for good management. Budgeting should simply be viewed as one tool among many for managers to use. If forecasting is poor or inadequate allowances are made, the process may create unnecessary pressure upon managers to perform in a particular way. This may be stressful and cause antagonism and resentment within the organisation.

The creation of rigid financial plans which are 'cast in stone' may cause inertia in certain parts of a business and reduce its ability to adapt to change. Budgets may also not reflect the realities of the business environment and act simply as a straitjacket upon the performance of managers and decision-makers.

It has also been argued that delays and timelags can make it very difficult to compare budgeted and actual results.

TASK 60.1

Which of the following costs could be controlled by a marketing manager? Give reasons for your answers:

a) Depreciation of furniture
b) Insurance of the building
c) Wages paid to staff
d) Advertising
e) Stationery
f) Office redecorations
g) Training costs

Standard costing

Standard costing is another key method for budgetary control. Standard costing establishes predetermined estimates of costs and sales and then compares them with actual costs and sales achieved. The predetermined costs are known as **standard costs**. As we have already seen, the difference between standard and actual costs is known as a **variance**.

There are a number of objectives of standard costing:

- To control costs by establishing a range of standards from which variances can be analysed;
- To assist with the setting of budgets;
- To provide a basis for measuring performance;
- To assist with the process of responsibility accounting (see page 409);
- To motivate staff and managers;
- To provide a basis for evaluating and improving upon current performances.

Setting standards

According to Lucey in *Management Information Systems*, standard cost can be defined as:

'A standard expressed in money. It is built up from an assessment of the value of cost elements. Its main uses are providing a basis for performance measurement, control by exception reporting, valuing stock and establishing selling prices.'

Based on this interpretation, a standard must be set at a planned cost per unit from whatever is being costed. A standard cost may include use of materials, the price or other standard upon which cost is based, the planned hours to be worked and the hourly labour rate as well as the overheads incurred.

Setting standards is the critical part of the standard costing process. Line managers are clearly involved here, assisted by work study staff, engineering specialists, accountants and many other specialists, all of whom can provide an input into the standard-setting process.

The four key elements in the standard costing process are:

1 **Materials;**
2 **Labour;**
3 **Overheads;**
4 **Sales price and margin.**

Materials

Standards are set for the quality and the quantity of materials used for a specific volume of production and the price to be paid per unit of direct material. The amount of materials used for a product will be derived from some form of bill of materials, based upon the specifications for the assembly or provision of a product. Standard quantities should make an allowance for losses in production, returns and breakages. The purchasing department has a responsibility for material prices. Costs will be based upon expected forecast costs for the budgeted period.

Labour

It is sometimes difficult to set standard labour times, although work study and work measurements help to provide a basis upon which a standard can be developed. Labour standard costs will specify the grades of labour to be used as well as the times involved. For example, they will identify the grades of labour, the direct labour hours and the standard rate per hour. The standard rate per hour will be the quantity of work which can be achieved at standard performance over an hourly period.

Overheads

It is difficult to associate overheads with a given product in the same way as labour and materials. Instead, an

overhead absorption rate creates the standards for overheads for each cost centre. This usually involves developing a rate based upon the estimated overheads for the cost centre and the expected number of direct labour hours or machine hours which are needed in order for a product to be completed.

Overheads are analysed into **fixed** and **variable** rates. These are:

Standard variable overhead rate =

Budgeted variable overheads for cost centre

Budgeted standard labour hours for cost centre

and:

Standard fixed overhead rate =

Budgeted fixed overheads for cost centre

Budgeted standard labour hours for cost centre

Sales price and margin

The setting of a **selling price** involves a number of factors. In Chapter 00 we looked at the process of pricing and discussed many of these factors. Once a selling price has been set, this becomes the **standard selling price**. The **standard sales margin** is the difference between the standard cost and the standard selling price. Normally where total standard cost is identified, cost-plus absorption principles are involved. These incorporate a unit fixed and variable cost, to which the margin is added in order to achieve the price.

The standard cost card

The net effect of developing standard costs for materials, labour and overheads is the setting of a standard cost for each product. This may be recorded on a **standard cost card** (see Figure 60.2 below).

Standard cost variance analysis

A key element in the process of standard costing is the ability to monitor the performance of the organisation through the use of variance analysis. Although the principles of variances which we examined earlier in relation to the control of the budgetary process still apply, the analysis of variances in the standard costing process is more detailed.

Part No. G459 per 100	Description Ball joint	Work study ref. B345		
Cost type/quantity	Standard price/rate	Dept. 3 £	Dept. 6 £	Total £
Direct materials 2 kg. P10	£10 kg.		20.00	20.00
Direct labour Machine operation 3 hrs.	£4.50 hr. 13.50			13.50
Assembly 4 hrs.	£3.50 hr.		14.00	14.00
Overheads Machine hour rate	£10 hr. (x 3 hrs.)	30.00		30.00
Assembly rate	£9 hr. (x 4 hrs.)		36.00	36.00
		43.50	70.00	113.50
Standard cost summary	£			
Direct materials	20.00			
Direct labour	27.50			
Overheads	66.00			
Standard cost per 100	113.50			

Figure 60.2 Standard cost card

TAKING BUDGETING TOO SERIOUSLY?

MBB Tools Ltd recently appointed a young accountant, with a brief to set up a budgetary control system which could be used to co-ordinate activities across the business. Budgets were drawn up for all departments based upon actual results over the last five years.

Shortly after the system started, it was noted that total expenditure was considerably higher than anticipated. Certain departments such as production and marketing had expenditure higher than planned, while other departments such as personnel and administration had favourable variances.

On receiving the results, the chief executive threatened to dismiss the managers of the production and marketing departments for exceeding their budgeted costs. The production manager resigned and has since joined a competitor.

1 What problems have arisen at MBB Tools?

2 How could these problems have been avoided?

The purpose of variance analysis is to provide an understanding of any causes of performances which are not standard. This enables managers to diagnose problems quickly and take appropriate action.

There are essentially three ways of analysing standard cost variances:

1 Direct material variances

Direct material variances can be divided into **usage variances** and **price variances**:

- **Usage variance** This is defined as the difference between the standard quantity of material specified for actual production and the actual quantity used as a standard purchase price.

  Usage variance = (Standard quantity for actual production x standard price) – (Actual quantity x standard price)

  The usage variance can be affected by the efficiency of those employees responsible for purchasing resources. There could also be a greater or lower yield from materials used than planned, or a higher or lower scrap rate than anticipated.

- **Price variance** This is the difference between the standard and actual purchase price for the actual quantity of materials purchased or used in production.

  Price variance = (Actual quantity x standard price) – (Actual quantity x actual price)

  One of the causes of a price variance may be that the purchasing department are not choosing the lower cost supplier. Prices may therefore be higher than planned. Other reasons may be the loss of discounts, the buying of lower or higher quality materials than planned, or the buying of other materials due to lack of availability.

SYNTHESIS

Would it be easier to calculate the standard cost for some items than others? For which items might it be difficult to calculate a standard cost?

2 Direct labour variances

- **Efficiency variance** This variance is defined as the difference between the actual production achieved measured in standard hours and the actual hours worked, valued at the standard labour rate.

  Efficiency variance = (Standard hours produced x standard rate per hour) – (Actual hours worked x standard rate per hour)

  There are a number of causes of changes in the efficiency variance. For example, the use of poor quality labour, poor levels of supervision or the use of incorrect materials will affect labour efficiency.

- **Rate variance** This is the difference between the standard and actual direct labour rate per hour for the actual hours worked.

  Rate variance = (Standard rate x actual hours) – (Actual rate x actual hours)

  Direct labour rate variances may change because of pay awards, the use of higher grade workers in the production process, or due to unplanned bonus arrangements.

3 Overhead variances

There are three overhead variances: efficiency, volume and expenditure. Each forms a part of the overhead total variance.

- **Overhead total variance** is the difference between the standard cost specified for the production achieved and the actual cost incurred;
- **Overhead efficiency variance** is the variance of actual hours from the standard usage specified for the actual activity level specified;
- **Overhead volume variance** is the variance caused by changes in the level of activity from that budgeted;
- **Overhead expenditure variance** is the difference between budgeted and actual overhead expenditure.

TASK 60.1

Paula Green runs a small company manufacturing office desks. She produces a single product which has the following data for each standard batch of 100 made:

Wood	800 m. at £4.50 per metre
Metal plate	10 kg. at £8.00 per kg.
Labour	800 hrs. at £5.00 per hour
Overhead	£5 per labour hour

During the month of May, two batches were produced and the actual data was as follows:

Wood	1,500 m. at £4.25 per metre
Metal plate	24 kg. at £8.50 per kg.
Labour	1,700 hrs. at £5.50 per hour
Overhead for the month	£5,200

1 Calculate the standard and actual costs for each desk and also the standard and actual costs for a batch.

2 Calculate the following variances from standard and suggest reasons for them:

   i)   labour rate variance
   ii)   labour efficiency variance
   iii) material price variances
   iv)   material usage variances
   v)   overhead variance

Criticisms of standard cost variance analysis

The system for standard costing depends upon how well standards have been set. If the standard setting process is flawed, then comparing actual performance with the standard will have little value. Another criticism is that standard costing does not compare like with like. Changes may occur because conditions have altered. It is important that standards are reviewed to take this into account.

If variances are regularly adverse this can have an affect upon the motivation of employees. They may see their role as an uphill struggle to meet standards which have been set. For this reason standards used to monitor performance should always be realistic and attainable.

Standard costing can only exist within the framework of a budgeting system. It should only be employed when appropriate and cost-effective. It provides another form of responsibility accounting as managers are held responsible for the control of a variance.

Chapter summary

- Budgeting provides feedback for individuals and groups throughout an organisation.
- The aim of budgeting is to analyse how closely actual performance relates to budgeted performance.
- The process of analysing the difference between actual performance and budgeted performance is called variance analysis.
- Variances may be adverse or favourable.
- Budgetary and control systems vary from one organisation to another.
- Reliance upon budgeting is no substitute for good management.
- Standard costing establishes predetermined estimates of costs and sales and compares them with actual costs and sales achieved.
- A standard has to be a planned cost per unit.
- Four key elements in the standard costing process are: materials, labour, overheads and sales price and margin.
- Standards are set for the quality and quantity of materials used for a specific volume of production.
- Labour standard costs will specify the grades of labour as well as the times involved.
- Standard costs may be represented on a standard cost card.
- Variance analysis is used to monitor the performance of the organisation.
- The variance is the difference between the standard and actual cost.
- Direct materials variances are divided into usage and price variances.
- Direct labour variances are divided into efficiency and rate variances.
- Overhead variances may relate to efficiency, volume and expenditure.

61 Investment and decision-making

All organisations have to plan not just for the short term but also for the long term. The difference between the two is simply that long-term outcomes are much more difficult to predict. Because of this, there are also increased risks associated with the long term.

Investment involves the immediate risk of funds in the hope of securing returns later. There are often more investment options than finance available to back them up. It is therefore important to be able to compare projects in order to assess the degree of risk. A good decision will provide a high return, while a poor decision may result in fewer benefits. Managers must try to make decisions that maximise returns and provide shareholders and other stakeholders with the best possible result.

Investment planning should try to highlight the risks associated with a project. Though this can be difficult with a long-term investment, it is important to ensure that the expected financial return adequately compensates for the risks involved. This rate must therefore be related to the cost of capital for the project.

There are two key questions faced by any manager having to make a long-term investment decision. These are:

1 **What** projects should the organisation invest in?
2 **How much** should they be prepared to invest?

For the purposes of the long term, these questions will be based upon the overall business strategy of the organisation. Strategic planning and long-term investment decision-making will involve managers in bridging the gap between the results the organisation would achieve *without* the investment, and the business's long-term objectives.

What is risk?

Risk occurs where future outcomes of current actions are unknown. Though it can be argued that the future outcome of *any* decision is unknown, the probabilities of most future outcomes can be estimated, based upon knowledge of both past and current events. Uncertainty exists where probabilities cannot be used for prediction because there is no past or current evidence.

Using the notion of probability, we can define risk as the gap between what an organisation realistically plans to achieve, given the probabilities of success within the business environment, and the actual outcome.

Wherever there are risks, there is a need to compensate those who take the risks, be they lenders, managers or investors.

The relationship between a company's business risk and their financial risk is an interesting one:

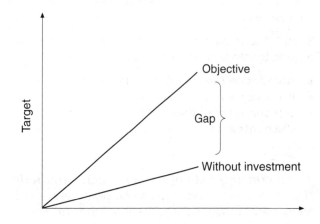

Figure 61.1 Gap analysis

- A company's **business risk** is determined by what projects it undertakes. Market share and competitive position may all be influenced by business risk;
- A company's **financial risk** is determined by how it finances these projects. Financial risk may be influenced by level of gearing and liquidity ratios.

The relationship between financial and business risk is illustrated in Figure 61.2 below.

As can be seen, companies in the top right-hand box face high levels of total risk because both business and financial risks are high. Investors would demand high returns from such risks. In the bottom left-hand box the combination of low financial and low business risk is simply not rewarding. Over the long term investments of this kind could reduce the value of the business.

Investments in the top left-hand box represent a prudent strategy: although they carry a high business risk, the financial risk is low.

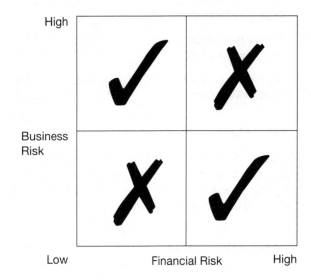

Figure 61.2 The relationship between business and financial risk

Finally, the box in the bottom right-hand corner shows that an aggressive financial risk may be acceptable if the business risk is low.

In this chapter we will look at four ways of appraising projects for capital investment. These are:

- **Accounting rate of return (ARR)** method;
- **Payback** method;
- **Discounted cash flow (DCF)** – net present value;
- **Discounted cash flow (DCF)** – internal rate of return.

1 *Accounting rate of return (ARR) method*

This method is concerned simply with expressing profitability as an **average rate of return** on an investment. It is generally considered to be a quick and convenient guide for assessing the profitability of alternative projects. Profit is expressed as an **average** over the life of the project, and capital is considered to be the initial outlay or the capital invested. It is therefore calculated by dividing the average annual profit by the initial investment:

$$ARR = \frac{Average\ annual\ profit\ \times\ 100}{Initial\ investment}$$

For example, if we had two projects we could select an alternative as shown in Figure 61.3. Project A provides an accounting rate of return of 20 per cent and project B an accounting rate of return of 25 per cent. Using this form of appraisal, project B would be a better investment.

	Project A £	Project B £
Initial cost	−10,000	−20,000
Year 1 cash receipts	+4,000	+9,000
Year 2 cash receipts	+5,000	+9,000
Year 3 cash receipts	+5,000	+12,000
Year 4 cash receipts	+4,000	+10,000
Total cash receipts	+18,000	+40,000
Profit over 4 years	+8,000	+20,000
Average annual profit	+2,000	+5,000
Initial investment	10,000	20,000
	20%	25%

Figure 61.3

The accounting rate of return method can be criticised for being based upon book values and therefore failing to take heed of changing price levels. It also fails to consider the timing of cash receipts.

2 *Payback method*

The purpose of this method is to establish how quickly the investment cost can be repaid. The shorter the payback period, the better the project.

SYNTHESIS

Why would it be considered prudent to go for the shortest possible payback? Should other factors come into the equation?

Using this method, for example, if we had two investment possibilities that both cost £15,000, we could select an alternative as shown in Figure 61.4. Project A repays the initial cost by the end of Year 4, whereas Project B does not repay until the end of Year 5. On this basis, we would choose Project A.

	Project A £	Project B £
Initial cost	−15,000	−15,000
Year 1 cash receipts	+3,000	+1,000
Year 2 cash receipts	+3,000	+3,000
Year 3 cash receipts	+4,000	+3,000
Year 4 cash receipts	+5,000	+3,000
Year 5 cash receipts	+3,000	+5,000

Figure 61.4

The essential feature of the payback form of capital appraisal is that it takes timing into consideration. This can be of special value to firms with liquidity problems, where early return of funds is of primary importance. For businesses where capital equipment is constantly being changed, the payback method can provide a rough guide to the extent of the risk.

The main criticism is that it does not take into account cash flows (see Figure 61.5). Also it does not differentiate between Project A and Project B because both methods pay back in three years. In the same way, it ignores cash receipts expected after the payback period. No attention is given to subsequent years. It does not, therefore, take into account the profitability of the two alternatives.

	Project A £	Project B £
Initial cost	−15,000	−15,000
Year 1 cash receipts	+5,000	+1,000
Year 2 cash receipts	+5,000	+2,000
Year 3 cash receipts	+5,000	+12,000

Figure 61.5

Not only does the payback method fail to account for the timing of cash flows, it also fails to relate the value of future returns to immediate investments. In money terms, an investment made today should have a higher value in the future. Discounted cash flow relates the expected value of future cash receipts and expenditures to a common date.

3 DCF (net present value)

This method of weighing up investment decisions relies heavily on the theory of **opportunity cost**. Before managers commit an organisation to an investment decision, the benefits of which will be reaped over a number of years, the real value of future returns needs to be assessed. Because the value of money alters with time, it is helpful to look at future flows in terms of their present value.

Interest payments compensate for:

- Cost of time (i.e. not having the money available now);
- Cost of inflation (price rises erode the real value of money);
- Risk of investment.

The interest rate gives a guide to the future value of investment. Alternatively, the current value of the investment can be compared with its past value.

If an investor has £1,000 in a bank account where it is earning 10 per cent interest, the balance will stand at £1,100 at the end of the first year. By compounding this annually,

- At the end of Year 2, it will be worth £1,210 (£1,100 + £110)
- At the end of Year 3 it will be worth £1,331 (£1,210 + £121); etc.

At the end of this time the investor can say that £1,331 was worth £1,000 three years earlier. This calculation can also be performed the other way round, by asking what an investment of £1,000 *now* would have been worth three years ago at a 10 per cent rate of interest. For example:

$$\frac{£1,000}{£1,331} \times £1,000 = £751.3$$

Two years ago?

$$\frac{£1,000}{£1,210} \times £1,000 = £826.4$$

One year ago?

$$\frac{£1,000}{£1,100} \times £1,000 = £909.1$$

Thus, assuming a constant rate of interest of 10 per cent, £1,000 now was worth £751.30 three years ago, and will be worth £1,331 in three years' time. The time element has now been taken into account. DCF tables are available relating rates of interest to a period of time in years (see Figure 61.6 below).

Looking at the net surplus returns for two projects that have an initial capital investment of £200,000 (see Figure 61.7 on page 426), it is clear that at today's value, returns will be higher for Project A than Project B. If net present value comes out at less than the original investment, it is not worth considering the project at all.

Advantages and disadvantages

The clear advantage of the net present value method is that it takes into account the time element of money and is also easy to calculate. The drawback is that both interest rates and cash flows are subject to uncertainty.

SYNTHESIS

Is it always possible to identify the costs of an investment project?

Future years	*Percentage rate of discount*									
	1	*2*	*3*	*4*	*5*	*6*	*7*	*8*	*9*	*10*
1	0.990	0.980	0.971	0.962	0.952	0.943	0.935	0.926	0.917	0.909
2	0.980	0.961	0.943	0.925	0.907	0.890	0.873	0.857	0.842	0.826
3	0.971	0.942	0.915	0.889	0.864	0.840	0.816	0.794	0.772	0.751
4	0.961	0.924	0.888	0.855	0.823	0.792	0.763	0.735	0.708	0.683
5	0.951	0.906	0.863	0.822	0.784	0.747	0.713	0..681	0.650	0.621
6	0.942	0.888	0.837	0.790	0.746	0.705	0.666	0.630	0.596	0.564

Figure 61.6 DCF tables

	Project A	Project B
	£	£
Earnings Year 1	100,000	80,000
Earnings Year 2	110,000	100,000
Earnings Year 3	100,000	100,000
Earnings Year 4	80,000	100,000
Earnings Year 5	20,000	30,000
Total return	410,000	410,000

Project A

Year	Earnings £	NPV* £
0		200,000
1	100,000	90,900
2	110,000	90,860
3	100,000	75,100
4	80,000	54,640
5	20,000	12,420
		323,920

Project B

Discount factor	Earnings £	NPV* £
		200,000
0.909	80,000	72,720
0.826	100,000	82,600
0.751	100,000	75,100
0.683	100,000	683,300
0.621	30,000	18,630
		317,350

* Net present value

Figure 61.7 Discounted cash flow at a rate of 10 per cent

4 DCF (*internal rate of return*)

This method aims to find out the average return of an investment throughout its lifespan. This 'internal rate of return' is then compared with the criteria for the project to see if it is worthwhile. This method is therefore concerned with percentage returns, and not with cash figures.

	£
Year 0	– 20,000
Year 1	+ 8,000
Year 2	+ 5,000
Year 3	+ 5,000
Year 4	+ 5,000
	£23,000

To find out the internal rate of return we use trial and error. At 10 per cent it would be:

$$
\begin{aligned}
-20,000 + 8,000 \times 0.909 &= 7,272 \\
+ 5,000 \times 0.826 &= 4,130 \\
+ 5,000 \times 0.751 &= 3,755 \\
+ 5,000 \times 0.683 &= 3,415 \\
&\ \overline{18,572}
\end{aligned}
$$

$-20,000 + 18,572 = -1,428$

Discounted at 10 per cent, the return is less than the level of investment. The return is clearly not 10 per cent, and so we need to try a lower rate. At 6 per cent it would be:

$$
\begin{aligned}
-20,000 + 8,000 \times 0.943 &= 7,544 \\
+ 5,000 \times 0.890 &= 4,450 \\
+ 5,000 \times 0.840 &= 4,200 \\
+ 5,000 \times 0.792 &= 3,960 \\
&\ \overline{20,154}
\end{aligned}
$$

$-20,000 + 20,154 = 154$

We have shown that the internal rate of return lies between 6 and 10 per cent. To obtain the exact internal rate of return, we:

1 Take the lower rate (6);
2 Add the difference between the two interest rates (4) multiplied by the difference at the lower rate (154), divided by the total difference between the two rates (1,582):

$$
6 + \frac{(4 \times 154)}{1,582} = 6.39\%
$$

As long as the firm can borrow at less than 6.39 per cent, the project is worthwhile.

SUTTON COLDFIELD PLC

Sutton Coldfield Plc is considering two alternative projects to develop its profitability. Until recently the company has always appraised projects on the basis that any investment should pay back within four years. After extensive discussions at board level, it has been decided to use a DCF method of project appraisal (net present value) with a target rate of return of 10 per cent.

Project A

This involves setting up a production line to fully automate the productive process. It will cost £120,000 and provide a saving of £30,000 each year for the first six years.

Project B

This involves spending £100,000 on a prolonged advertising campaign. Evidence suggests that this will increase revenues by:

	£
Year 1	20,000
Year 2	30,000
Year 3	30,000
Year 4	40,000
Year 5	10,000
Year 6	10,000

Both projects are to be evaluated using the payback and DCF (net present value) methods.

For **Project A**, as the initial investment is £120,000 and the annual saving is £30,000, the investment will be paid back in four years. This only just meets the criterion that the payback period should be reached within four years. Clearly, the returns are greater than the initial investment, and the project provides a net present value of £10,620 with a discount factor of 10 per cent.

Year	Earnings £	DCF (NPV) £	Discount factor
0	120,000		
1	30,000	27,270	0.909
2	30,000	24,780	0.826
3	30,000	22,530	0.751
4	30,000	20,490	0.683
5	30,000	18,630	0.621
6	30,000	16,920	0.564
		130,620	

Figure 61.8 Project A: DCF (net present value)

Year	Earnings £	DCF (NPV) £	Discount factor
0	100,000		
1	20,000	18,180	0.909
2	30,000	24,780	0.826
3	30,000	22,530	0.751
4	40,000	27,320	0.683
5	10,000	6,210	0.621
6	10,000	5,640	0.564
		104,660	

Figure 61.9 Project B: DCF (net present value)

For **Project B**, the initial investment of £100,000 can be paid back in three and a half years. This is an improvement on the payback period for Project A. The returns are, again, greater than the investment and provide a net present value of £4,660.

1 Given the information provided, which project would you recommend and why?

2 What other information might you require before reaching a final decision?

Cost–benefit analysis

Cost-benefit analysis is normally associated with the evaluation of large-scale, government-backed investment projects. The siting of an airport or the building of a new underground rail link are thought of as typical examples of projects for which cost-benefit analysis would be used.

However, cost-benefit analysis is a much more widely applied technique than this. It can, in fact, be used to weigh up any policy decision, although it is not a magic solution to problem-solving.

Carrying out a cost-benefit analysis involves organising all the relevant information involved in a particular decision in such a way as to focus on the key issues and to concentrate on the real choices to be made. It is an attempt to put a money value on all the costs and benefits of a particular decision – including intangible factors.

Although it is often very difficult to measure intangibles in money terms, Johnson and Scholes in *Exploring Corporate Strategy* provide a framework in which intangibles can be identified. For example, in Figure 61.10, a local authority is considering whether to construct a new town-centre car park on the site of existing public gardens. The main costs and benefits are shown in the left-hand column. Clearly the basis on which costs and benefits are measured needs to be justified. Different people will have different ideas about the values given. For example, if the town centre is felt by some people to be 'spoilt' by the creation of a car park, they may want to place a high value on the cost of the amenity which is to be sacrificed – the garden.

To take another example, the first task in preparing an analysis of building a new training centre for unemployed people is to find out who would benefit and who would lose out by its construction. This needs to be converted into measurements in money terms. One way of doing this is to ask the people who will benefit from the centre

Costs/benefits	Bases of quantification
Costs	
1 Acquiring site	Already owned, market value known.
2 Construction costs	Tenders obtained.
3 Loss of amenity (gardens) (if privately owned).	Known usage of gardens and notional entry charge
4 Increased transport costs	Known usage of private travel (car).
Benefits	
1 Revenue	Demand and price forecasts.
2 Reduced congestion in streets	Incremental increase in consumer spending due to easier access.

Figure 61.10 Benefits and costs incurred in constructing a new town-centre car park (from Johnson, G, and Scholes, K: Exploring Corporate Strategy)

how much they are prepared to pay to see the project carried out. A person who will lose out from the building of the centre could be asked the minimum amount he or she would be prepared to accept as compensation for the project taking place. Then the gains and losses need to be added up. If the gains outweigh the losses, the project passes the test.

Although cost-benefit analysis has a number of problems when it comes to ascribing money values to costs and benefits, it does at least force decision-makers to focus on the main issues and interest groups involved in the decision. Weights can then be attached to the costs and benefits identified.

Chapter summary

- Long-term outcomes are more difficult to predict than short-term ones.
- Investment involves the immediate risk of funds in the hope of securing returns later.
- Long-term decisions have to fit in with the strategy of the organisation.
- Risk occurs where the outcomes of current actions are unknown.
- Wherever there are risks there is a need to compensate those who are taking the risks.
- There is a relationship between a company's business risk and their financial risk.
- Accounting rate of return (ARR) expresses profitability as an average rate of return on an investment.
- The payback method establishes how quickly the investment cost can be repaid.
- DCF (net present value) takes into account the real value of future returns.
- DCF (internal rate of return) aims to find out the average return of an investment throughout its lifespan. It expresses this as a percentage return on an investment.
- Cost-benefit analysis helps to evaluate large-scale government-backed investment projects.

62 Accounting statements and policies

The activities of businesses affect a wide range of individuals and organisations, each with their own particular areas of concern and each with their own demands for information. In order to satisfy these needs, the government and other regulatory bodies impose **reporting requirements** on businesses. In practice many organisations regularly go beyond these statutory information requirements to keep stakeholders informed of their activities.

In Chapter 11 we identified a range of stakeholders who have different information needs about organisations, including managers, shareholders, suppliers, employees, customers, the government and its departments, lenders and the community affected by the actions of any organisation. All these groups are concerned about the quality and accuracy of the information they receive.

One area of particular concern is **comparability**. Users may want to compare the financial results of a business organisation with its past results to establish trends, and with the results of similar organisations to monitor performance. Without any guiding framework for the preparer of accounting information, there would be no consistency between these financial statements and they would be of little use for comparative purposes.

It is also more difficult for business organisations to deceive interested parties if there are rules laid down concerning how accounts must be prepared and presented. Users of financial statements need to know the assumptions made when preparing accounts. If they use the same conventions this facilitates comparisons and meaningful conclusions.

Understanding financial statements

In Chapter 34 we looked at the three key elements of financial statements. These were the profit and loss account, the balance sheet and the cash flow statement. We went on to emphasise that under the Companies Acts, companies are required to file copies of their accounts together with an annual report with the Registrar of Companies. Finally, we provided a series of ratios which can be used to interpret and analyse the information contained in the accounts.

The aim of this chapter is to further develop an understanding of these financial statements and the policies supporting them. Remember that the balance sheet is concerned with balances *at a point in time,* and that the profit and loss account and the cash flow statement are concerned with describing how two of these balances, profit and cash, have changed over a period of time.

The annual report and accounts is probably the most important document issued by a company. You can obtain an annual report and accounts by writing directly to a company or by visiting a business library.

Annual report contents

It is possible to divide the contents of an annual report into three key areas of information. These are:

1   **Information which is required by law** Under the 1985 Companies Act as modified by the Companies Act 1989, the following information is required within 10 months of the end of an accounting period (normally one year) for a private limited company, and within seven months for a public limited company:

- – Profit and loss account;
- – Balance sheet;
- – Cash flow statement;
- – Notes supporting the accounts;
- – Directors' report;
- – Auditors' report.

Members of the main accountancy bodies are under an obligation to use best accounting practice in the preparation of all accounts and to give a 'true and fair view' of a business's trading performance and financial position.

2   Many public companies will also include:

- – A description of the business;
- – A statement from the Chairman or Chairwoman;
- – Details about the directors;
- – A review of business activities for the year;
- – A summary of the company's results;
- – Notice of the annual general meeting.

3   **Other information** Producing an annual report and accounts is a huge public relations exercise. It provides information about the company not just for shareholders but for many other stakeholders who may be interested in the activities of the organisation. The annual report can contain information about community links, training initiatives, donations to charities and also investment in energy efficiency and other environmental initiatives.

An annual report and accounts is more than just a set of figures: it is a statement about how the organisation has performed over a period of time and the business strategies and key decisions taken by its managers. As a practical example, the Case Study on pages 430–431 investigates the accounts of United Biscuits, highlighting some of the key decisions taken by the company's directors during the recent financial year.

UNITED BISCUITS

United Biscuits is an international foods business marketing a wide range of biscuits, savoury snacks and frozen and chilled products. It has a market-leading position in the UK, continental Europe and Australia and is building its presence in Asia. It operates in 22 countries, has 40 manufacturing sites worldwide and its products are available in over 90 countries.

The information below comes from the United Biscuits Annual Report and Accounts 1996. Read it through carefully then complete the tasks on page 431.

In 1996 we did all that we set out to do.

We continued to concentrate our efforts on markets where we could build most value for shareholders. We became a more focused organisation and we began the promised steady improvement in financial performance.

Profit before tax and exceptionals increased from £49.7m to £109.1m; earnings per share increased from 4.8p to 14.8p; return on capital employed increased from 7.9% to 15.9%; the group generated cash and reduced borrowings to push gearing down from 97% to 35%. The proposed final dividend is increased by 3%.

We now have a stronger balance sheet and a healthier, more coherent portfolio of businesses, brands and products.

And we're clear about what remains to be done.

We are building a business that will deliver sustained, superior performance.

	1996 £m	1995 Restated £
Turnover	1,987	3,001
Operating profit before exceptionals	137.0	98.6
Profit before tax and exceptionals	109.1	49.7
Profit (loss) before tax	24.4	(100.6)
Profit/(loss) attributable to shareholders	17.0	(126.2)

Figure 62.1 United Biscuits trading results 1996

We are not there yet. Steady, progressive growth and consistent attainment of world-class standards in all that we do will depend upon:

- Continuing to focus on activities that create value for shareholders;

- Exploiting the full potential of our businesses by making better use of all our assets; highly skilled people, powerful brands, strong market positions, excellent technology and efficient facilities.

Sharpening our focus and improving profitability

We have simplified our portfolio, managed it more rigorously and continued to focus our resources to drive for profitable growth.

After withdrawing from the US early in the year, we sold Ross Vegetable products, our Portuguese and Italian businesses and closed our Hungarian snack operation. We also withdrew from our minority partnerships in Turkey and Brazil. Total group sales are lower than last year but profitability is considerably improved.

UB is now a focused food business with a snackfood emphasis that trades from strength in the UK, Continental Europe and Australia and is building rapidly in Asia. We will compete only where we can win and where we can achieve profitable sales.

We have worked hard to reposition those businesses with potential that were underperforming. In 1996, we achieved some quite dramatic turnarounds – for example, Verkade, our biscuit business in the Netherlands, achieved a 40% profit improvement under new management.

As well as simplifying our portfolio, we have focused on improving shareholder returns through more rigorous financial management and improved targeting of marketing investment. Our return on average capital employed from continuing operations improved from 14.8% to 15.5% during the year, with a particularly encouraging improvement in the UK.

Reshaping the portfolio

We have classified our business portfolio into three categories: those to 'drive' for growth, those to 'develop' for the future prosperity of the group and those that we need to 'fix' to deliver acceptable returns.

We aim to move businesses out of the 'fix' category and Figure 62.2 shows how our portfolio has changed in the last 12 months.

Performance indicators

Rigorous financial management has been critical to improving shareholder returns. Figure 62.3 shows significant progress in key financial indicators.

- *Average working capital:* Average level of net stocks, trade debtors and trade creditors held by the group throughout the year.

- *Cash flow before acquisitions and disposals:* Net cash generated before the benefit of proceeds from the sale of businesses or the cash cost of acquisitions

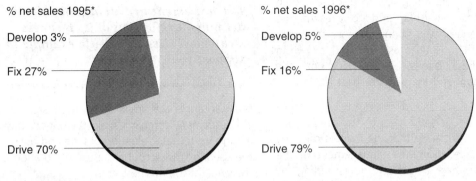

% net sales 1995*

Develop 3%

Fix 27%

Drive 70%

% net sales 1996*

Develop 5%

Fix 16%

Drive 79%

Figure 62.2 Percentage net sales 1995-1996

- *Gearing:* Net borrowings divided by shareholders' equity.
- *Interest cover:* Operating profit before all exceptional items divided by the interest charge.

Making better use of our assets

As a more focused business, we are concentrating on working our assets harder to generate growth.

Our portfolio of established brands provides excellent growth opportunities. For example, in 1996 brand extensions and well-targeted promotion boosted sales of Penguin by 24% and Skips by 25%. We have the skills and technology to create innovative new brands - like the McVitie's Go Ahead! range.

We have strong market positions and we have the resources to support them. In Australia and Benelux we have regained market share lost to aggressive competitive campaigns. We are making increasingly good use of our international network – sharing recipes, technology and best practice and cross-sourcing to profitable effect.

And we are ever more determined to make better use of our strong trade relationships to meet our customers' needs.

We recognise that our concentration on return on capital employed as a short-term driver of shareholder value could adversely effect the longer-term health of our business. Accordingly, our management processes aim to provide a balance between short-term financial performance and the need for investment in our brands, customers and employees for the longer term.

Figure 62.3 Performance indicators

Tasks

1 Provide a brief analysis of United Biscuits results and comment upon the changes between 1995 and 1996.

2 What did UB decide to do between 1995 and 1996 in order to improve the performance of their business?

3 What does this tell us about the relationship between business strategy and performance?

4 How did UB improve the performance of Verkade?

5 Comment upon how UB have reshaped their business portfolio.

6 How has the new business strategy affected average working capital, cash flow, gearing and interest cover? In each instance explain the meaning of the terms you use.

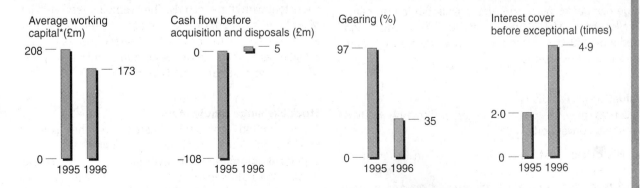

Average working capital*(£m)

208

173

0

1995 1996

Cash flow before acquisition and disposals (£m)

0 — 5

−108

1995 1996

Gearing (%)

97

35

0

1995 1996

Interest cover before exceptional (times)

4·9

2·0

0

1995 1996

Content of published accounts

Limited companies are bound by law to disclose certain information in their accounts, and to present the information in a certain way. Although more than one format is specified, it is usual to use Format 1 shown in Figures 62.4 and 62.5 (pages 433–434) for both the profit and loss account and the balance sheet.

Stewardship

The Companies Acts recognise that the owners of many companies are divorced from the management of the organisations. To ensure a better understanding by shareholders of the directors' stewardship the following information is required:

- Directors' emoluments and benefits;
- Transactions in which the directors have a personal interest.

Social issues

To provide information on social issues, the directors' report which accompanies the various financial statements is required to provide details of:

- Worker participation;
- The employment of disabled workers;
- Donations to charities and political organisations.

IT'S A FACT

As well as being subject to the Companies Act, charities have to file accounts with the Charities Commission if their gross income or expenditure exceeds £10,000 a year.

Business size

Many of the reporting requirements for business organisations are the same irrespective of the size of company. However, there has been a realisation that reporting requirements which may be appropriate for large companies place an unreasonable burden on many smaller ones. Under the Companies Acts, small and medium-sized businesses are therefore relieved of some reporting requirements.

Valuation

Accounts may be prepared according to one or two valuation conventions:

- **Historical cost**: the value placed on an item or transaction at the time it arose.
- **Alternative cost:** a valuation based on current cost after making adjustments to allow for the changing value of money.

SYNTHESIS

To what extent are an organisation's accounts a reflection of its business strategies? Use a real-life example to support your arguments.

Most accounts are prepared on the historical cost basis, although many companies take the opportunity to include a more up-to-date valuation of land and buildings to give the users of the accounts better information concerning the value of the business.

Accounting standards

The preparation of accounts is subject to the influence of the accounting guidelines issued by the **Accounting Standards Board (ASB)**. The ASB reports to the **Financial Reporting Council (FRC)** which oversees the accounting standards process. These accounting standards indicate current best accounting practice and should be applied to all financial statements.

Accounting bases

These are generally accepted methods of applying accounting concepts to practical situations. Different bases have evolved in response to the needs of a diverse range of business activities.

Accounting policies

These are specific accounting bases adopted as being the most appropriate to an organisation's circumstances. There is a requirement that these accounting policies are disclosed in a note to the accounts.

The role of auditors

Accounts of a limited company must be registered by a firm of independent accountants known as **registered auditors**. The auditors are asked to verify the accuracy of financial records and to ensure that the accounts are consistent with these records. The overriding responsibility of auditors is to confirm that the accounts provide a 'true and fair' view, or to confirm the valuation of assets and liabilities as at the date of the accounts and of the profit or loss up to that date (usually one year).

Stock Exchange requirements

Public limited companies listed on the London International Stock Exchange are required to disclose additional information in accordance with its **Yellow Book**. One requirement is to issue an interim financial report of performance, including details of turnover, profit and shareholder dividends.

	Note	Year 97	Year 96	Guidance
1 Turnover	1			
2 Cost of sales	2			
3 Gross Profit or loss				Item 1 minus item 2
4 Distribution costs	2			Less
5 Administration expenses	2			Less
6 Other operating income				Add
7 income from shares in group companies				Add
8 Income from shares in related companies				Add
9 Income from other fixed asset investments				Add
10 Other interest receivable and similar income	4			Add
11 Amounts written off from investments				Less
12 Interest payable and similar charges				Less
13 Tax in profit or loss on ordinary activities				Less
14 Profit or loss on ordinary activities after taxation				Item 3 add/less items 4–13
15 Extraordinary income				Add
16 Extraordinary charges				Less
17 Extraordinary profit or loss				Add or less
18 Tax on extraordinary profit or loss				Add or less
19 Other taxes not shown under the above items				Less
20 Profit or loss for the financial year				Item 14 add/less items 15–19

Notes

1 Although the standard format does specify some profit sub-total, the accounts should be prepared with additional sub-totals to facilitate clear presentation. For example, it would be normal practice to insert a sub-total after item 6 to give a clear indication of profit from operating activities only.

2 The line numbers need not be disclosed although items should appear in the order listed. Items 1 to 20 not disclosed on the face of the profit-and-loss account should be disclosed in 'notes to the accounts'.

3 The current period's figures should be compared with the previous period's.

4 Items with a nil value for both years need not be detailed.

Figure 62.4 Profit and loss account (Format 1)

	Notes	1997 £	1997 £	1996 £	1996 £
A Called-up share capital not paid	*1*				
B Fixed assets					
i Intangible assets					
ii Tangible assets					
iii Investments					
C Current assets					
i Stocks					
ii Debtors					
iii Investments					
iv Cash at bank and in hand					
D Prepayments and accrued income	*2*				
E Creditors: Amounts falling due within one year					
F Net current assets (liabilities)					
G Total assets less current liabilities					
H Creditors: Amounts falling due after more than one year					
I Provisions for liabilities and charges					
J Accruals and deferred income	3				
K Capital and reserves					
i Called-up share capital					
ii Share premium account					
iii Revaluation reserve					
iv Other reserves					
v Profit and loss account					

Notes

1   Called-up share capital not paid may be disclosed as a sub-heading of debtors.
2   Prepayments and accrued income may be disclosed as a sub-heading of debtors.
3   Accruals and deferred income may be disclosed as a sub-heading of creditors, either within one year or after more that one year as appropriate.
4   The letters and numbers for each line do not have to be shown.
5   The current period's figures should be compared with the previous period's.
6   Items with nil values for both years need not be disclosed.

Figure 62.5 Balance Sheet (Format 1)

Sole traders and partnerships

No requirement exists for sole traders and partnerships (unincorporated businesses) to file accounts for public scrutiny. Government departments, particularly those concerned with taxation, require financial statements in sufficient detail to allow for computation of tax according to tax regulations.

Two key accounting policies

Two key accounting policies which will be mentioned in the 'notes to the accounts' are **depreciation** and **stock valuation**.

Depreciation

Fixed assets are acquired in order to earn profits. But although their use is not limited to a single accounting period, they do not last forever. Most companies have expectations about the lifetime of their assets. They will wish to show a true asset value in the balance sheet and to charge the cost of its depreciation to the profit and loss account.

SSAP 12 (see Chapter 29) defines depreciation as:

> 'the measure of the wearing out, consumption or other reduction in the useful economic life of a fixed asset, whether arising from use, time or obsolescence through technological or market changes.'

There are a number of different methods of allowing for depreciation. The most common are:

- The **straight-line** method
- The **reducing balance** method
- The **machine hour** method
- The **sum-of-digits** method.

Straight-line method

The most frequently used method is the straight-line or equal-instalment method, which charges an equal amount of depreciation to each accounting period for the life of an asset. The instalment is calculated by:

$$\frac{Cost\ of\ asset\ -\ residual\ value}{Expected\ useful\ life\ of\ asset}$$

For example, a machine which is expected to last five years costs £20,000; at the end of that time its residual value will be £5,000.

$$Depreciation\ charge\ =\ \frac{£20,000 - £5,000}{5\ years}$$

$$=\ £3,000$$

Reducing balance method

The reducing balance method calculates the depreciation charge as a fixed percentage of net book value from the previous period. This method allocates higher depreciation costs to the earlier years of an asset. It can be argued that this system is more realistic, as it caters for the increased expense of repairs and running costs as machinery becomes older.

For example, a machine is purchased by a business for £20,000 and its expected useful life is three years. The business anticipates a residual value of £4,320 and thus wishes to depreciate it at 40 per cent.

	£	Accumulated depreciation £
Machine at cost	20,000	
Depreciation Year 1	8,000	8,000
Net book value	12,000	
Depreciation Year 2	4,800	12,800
Net book value	7,200	
Depreciation Year 3	2,880	15,680
Residual value	4,320	

Figure 62.7 Reducing balance method

Machine hour method

The machine hour method relates depreciation to use rather than time; therefore depreciation is calculated on the basis of the number of hours a machine has been worked. The depreciation charge per hour is calculated by:

$$\frac{Cost\ of\ asset\ -\ residual\ value}{Estimated\ lifetime\ of\ asset\ in\ machine\ hours}$$

	Year 1 £	Year 2 £	Year 3 £	Year 4 £	Year 5 £
Cost	20,000	20,000	20,000	20,000	20,000
Accumulated depreciation	3,000	6,000	9,000	12,000	15,000
Net book value	17,000	14,000	11,000	8,000	5,000

Figure 62.6 Straight-line or equal instalment method

	Depreciation charge £	Accumulated depreciation £	Cost of asset £	Net book value £
Year 1: 2,000 x £3	6,000	6,000	34,000	28,000
Year 2: 3,000 x £3	9,000	15,000	34,000	19,000
Year 3: 1,000 x £3	3,000	18,000	34,000	16,000

Figure 62.8 Machine hour method

For example, a machine is purchased for £34,000 with an estimated useful life of 10,000 machine hours and a residual value of £4,000. The depreciation rate would be:

$$\frac{34,000 - 4,000}{10,000} = \text{£3 per machine hour}$$

Therefore, if the machine was used for 2,000 hours in Year 1, 3,000 hours in Year 2 and 1,000 hours in Year 3, depreciation would be charged as shown in Figure 62.8.

Sum-of-the-digits method

The sum of the digits method is similar to the reducing balance method in that higher levels of depreciation are charged in earlier years. However, it uses digits rather than percentages as a simplified way of working out the depreciation charge. Digits are allocated in a descending order to each year of the life of an asset and a charge is worked out for each digit used.

For example, a machine is purchased for £15,000 and is expected to last for three years, after which it will be sold for £3,000:

Year	Digits
1	3
2	2
3	1
Sum-of-the-digits =	6

A weighted charge is then calculated as follows:

$$\frac{\text{Cost of asset} - \text{residual value}}{\text{Sum-of-the-digits}}$$

$$\frac{15,000 - 3,000}{6} = \text{£2,000 per digit}$$

	Digits	Depreciation charge £	Accumulated depreciation £
Year 1	3 x 2,000	6,000	6,000
Year 2	2 x 2,000	4,000	10,000
Year 3	1 x 2,000	2,000	12,000

Figure 62.9 Sum-of-digits method

Depreciation is treated as an expense, and for each period it will be charged to the profit and loss account. The accumulated depreciation is added together to form a provision for depreciation which is deducted from the cost price of the fixed asset which it represents in the balance sheet.

Stock valuation

Controlling stocks is nearly always a headache. An organisation has to balance the danger of running out of stock against the risk of overstocking.

Business activities are continuous, but accounting statements must be drawn up on a particular date. Stocktaking, therefore has to take place in such a way that:

● The quantity of stock held on the balance sheet is verified;

● A monetary amount can be allocated to each stock unit.

Stock valuation has a direct influence upon profits:

	High valuation £	£	Low valuation £	£
Sales		5,000		5,000
Less cost of sales				
Opening stock	2,000	2,000		
Add purchases	4,000		4,000	
	6,000		6,000	
Less closing stock				
	5,000		3,000	
		1,000		3,000
		4,000		2,000

Figure 62.10 Stock valuation

Including a higher stock valuation in the accounts has an obvious implication for the profit declared, as higher stock valuations as illustrated above, lead to higher profits.

The **prudence concept** rules out the use of selling prices in stock valuation, as it declares that profits should be recognised only when they are actually made and after the goods are sold. SSAP 9 indicates that stocks should be valued either at cost or at their **net realisable value**, whichever is the lower. Net realisable value is the selling price of the stocks, less the costs incurred in getting them ready for sales and selling them.

Stock item	Cost £	NRV £	Lower of cost/NRV £
No. 1	15	17	15
No. 2	21	18	18
	£36	£35	£33

Figure 62.11

It would be wrong to state stocks at £36 (Column 1), as the cost total would be ignoring a loss on Item 2. The prudent valuation would be £33, which values Item 2 at the lower or cost, or NRV.

A major problem of stock valuation is allocating the **purchase cost**. Businesses continually purchase items, and newer items are often mixed with older items in a bin. Accountants are not concerned with physically identifying the older items so that they are always used first. However, they are concerned with developing a pricing technique that allocates a cost to each component in the stores.

Three of the principal methods of stock valuation are:

- **FIFO** (First In, First Out)
- **LIFO** (Last In, First Out)
- **Cumulative weighted average cost** (AvCo)

We will look at each of these methods in turn and relate them to the following transactions:

January:	balance 100 units at cost of £2.90 each
February:	received 100 units at £3.00 each
March:	issued 80 units
April:	received 70 units at £3.80 each
May:	issued 50 units

FIFO

The FIFO method of stock valuation makes the assumption that stocks are issued in the order in which they were delivered, so that the stocks that have been held the longest will be issued first. This means that issues are priced at the cost of the earlier stocks, while the stocks remaining are priced at a level nearer the replacement cost.

FIFO provides a slightly higher valuation than some of the other methods we shall illustrate (see Figure 62.12).

Date	Receipt and price	Issue and price	Running stock valuation (£)	
		Balance		
January			100 @ £2.90	= 290
			100 units	290
February	100 @ £3.00		100 @ £2.90	= 290
			100 @ £3.00	= 300
			200 units	590
March		80 @ £2.90	20 @ £2.90	= 58
			100 @ £3.00	= 300
			120 units	358
April	70 @ £3.80		20 @ £2.90	= 58
			100 @ £3.00	= 300
			70 @ £3.80	= 266
			190 units	624
May		20 @ £2.90	70 @ £3.00	=210
		30 @ £3.00	70 @ £3.80	= 266
			140 units	476

Figure 62.12 The FIFO method of stock valuation

Date	Receipt and price	Issue and price	Running stock valuation (£)	
		Balance		
January			100 @ £2.90	= 290
			100 units	290
February	100 @ £300		100 @ £2.90	= 290
			100 @ £3.00	= 300
			200 units	590
March		80 @ £3.00	100 @ £2.90	= 290
			20 @ £3.00	= 60
			120 units	350
April	70 @ £3.80		100 @ £2.90	= 290
			20 @ £3.00	= 60
			70 @ £3.80	= 266
			190 units	616
May		50 @ £3.80	100 @ £2.90	= 290
			20 @ £3.00	= 60
			20 @ £3.80	= 60
			140 units	426

Figure 62.13 The LIFO method of stock valuation

LIFO

The LIFO method of stock valuation assumes that recent deliveries are issued before the earlier ones. This means that stock issued is close to the replacement price while remaining stock is kept at the older and probably lower price.

The tendency with this method is to undervalue stocks in relation to current market values (see Figure 62.13).

Cumulative weighted average pricing

With cumulative weighted average pricing (AvCo), every time a new consignment arrives the average cost of stock is calculated. Each unit is assumed to have been purchased at the average price of all components (see Figure 62.14). The average unit cost of stock is a weighted average price and is calculated in the following way:

$$\frac{Existing\ stock\ value\ +\ value\ of\ latest\ purchase}{Number\ of\ units\ then\ in\ stock}$$

The final valuation using AvCo is 140 units at £456.40 which falls between the FIFO and LIFO stock valuations.

Date	Receipts	Issues	Weighted average unit cost (£)	No. of stock units	Running stock valuation (£)
January		Balance	2.90	100	290.00
February	100 @ £3.00		£2.95	200	590.00
March		80	2.95	120	354.00
April	70 @ £3.80		3.26	190	619.40
May		50	3.26	140	456.40

Figure 62.14 The AVCO method of stock valuation

UNITED BISCUITS ACCOUNTING POLICIES

Look at the accounting policies of United Biscuits as set out in their 1996 Report and Accounts, then answer the questions which follow the Case Study on page 440.

Basis of accounting

The accounts are prepared on the historical cost basis of accounting and in accordance with applicable accounting standards.

Changes in accounts presentation

Changes in the presentation of the group's cash flow statement have been made following adoption of the revised *Financial Reporting Standard 1 – Cash Flow Statements*. Comparative figures have been restated in accordance with the revised presentation.

Basis of consolidation

The group accounts consolidate the results of United Biscuits (Holdings) Plc (the company) and its subsidiaries, all of which are subsidiary undertakings as defined by Section 258 of the Companies Act 1985. The results of subsidiaries acquired or sold are consolidated for the periods from the effective date of acquisition or to the effective date of sale.

Turnover

Turnover consists of sales to third parties after trade discounts, and excludes sales-related taxes. This represents a change from prior years when turnover was defined as sales to third parties before trade discounts.

Research and development

Expenditure on research and development is written off as incurred.

Foreign currency translation

Company: Monetary assets and liabilities denominated in foreign currencies are translated at the rate of exchange ruling at the balance sheet date. Transactions in foreign currencies are recorded at the rate ruling at the date of the transaction, all differences being taken to the profit and loss account.

Group: The profit and loss accounts of overseas subsidiaries are translated at weighted average rates of exchange, taking into account the effect of currency hedge transactions. The balance sheets are translated at the rates of exchange ruling at the year end. Exchange differences arising are taken directly to reserves. All other translation differences are taken to the profit and loss account, with the exception of differences arising on the translation of foreign currency borrowings to the extent that they are used to finance, or provide a hedge against, group equity investments in foreign enterprises. These are taken directly to reserves together with the exchange difference arising on the translation of the net assets of the related investments.

Commodity purchases

Certain commodities are purchased on the futures market in order to reduce exposure to changes in the cost of ingredients. When contracts are closed, the realised surpluses and deficits are applied against the cost of the related ingredients in the year of delivery.

Taxation

Deferred taxation is provided on all timing differences of material amount, except where no liability is likely to arise in the foreseeable future. Advance corporation tax is carried forward provided that it is expected to be offset against corporation tax liabilities on the profits of the next accounting period.

Exceptional items

Items which are of an exceptional nature by virtue of their size or incidence are included within operating profit unless they represent profits or losses on the sale or termination of a business, costs of fundamental reorganisation or restructuring having a material effect on the nature and focus of the group, or profits or losses on the disposal of fixed assets. In these cases, separate disclosure is provided in the profit and loss account after operating profit.

Goodwill

On the acquisition of a subsidiary, business or associated undertaking, fair values are attributed to the net tangible assets and significant brands acquired. Where the fair value of the consideration exceeds the aggregate value of these assets, the difference is treated as goodwill and is charged directly to reserves. When a business is sold, goodwill which had been written off through reserves on acquisition is shown as a charge against profit. A credit of equal amount to reserves ensures that there is no effect on shareholders' funds.

Intangible assets

A fair value is attributed to acquired brands at the date of acquisition by the group. They are accounted for as intangible assets. The value is calculated by multiplying the earnings of the brand by a factor based on the brand's strength. No depreciation is provided on these assets, but the directors review their value each year and the cost will be written down if, in their opinion, there has been a permanent diminution in value.

Tangible assets

Depreciation is calculated to write off the cost of tangible fixed assets over their expected useful lives by equal annual instalments, principally at the following rates:

Land and buildings:	1.5% unless short leasehold
Short leaseholds:	Over the life of the lease
Plant:	3% to 15% p.a.
Vehicles:	20% to 30% p.a.
Fixtures and fittings:	10% to 33% p.a.

Government grants

Capital grants received in respect of any fixed assets are credited to deferred income and amortised to the profit and loss account over the economic useful lives of the assets to which they relate.

(Continued on page 440)

UNITED BISCUITS ACCOUNTING POLICIES

(Continued from page 439)

Employee Share Ownership Plan (ESOP) Shares of the Company held to the order of the ESOP Trust are shown on the balance sheet as investments held at directors' valuation based on their market value at the balance sheet date. Any losses, and any gains to the extent that they represent the reversal of previous revelation losses, are taken to the profit and loss account as exceptional items. The corresponding borrowings used to finance the share purchases are recorded as borrowings of the group. Dividend income, interest expense and costs of the Trust are recorded within the appropriate captions in the profit and loss account.

Stocks Stocks are valued at the lower of cost and net realisable value. Cost in the case of raw materials and goods for resale is determined on a first-in, first-out basis. Cost in the case of products manufactured by group companies comprises direct material and labour costs together with appropriate factory overheads.

Leasing and hire purchase commitments Assets obtained under finance leases and hire purchase contracts are capitalised and depreciated over their useful lives. The interest element of the rental obligations is charged to the profit and loss account over the period of the primary lease and represents a constant proportion of the balance of capital repayments outstanding. Rentals paid under operating leases are charged to income on a straight-line basis over the term of the lease.

Adjustments to comparative figures Comparative figures in the accounts and the notes thereto, in respect of continuing and discontinued operations, have been adjusted to reflect the disposals made in 1996.

Tasks

1 What are the purposes of accounting policies?

2 How might users of accounts use information from accounting policies?

3 Comment upon the following:

   – The basis of accounting;
   – The depreciation of tangible assets;
   – Valuation of stocks.

4 Use the accounting policies to explain what is meant by 'goodwill'.

STUDY CASE STUDY CASE STUDY CASE STUDY CASE STUDY CASE STUDY

Chapter summary

- Information from accounts is required by a number of individuals and organisations who serve as stakeholders.
- Users of accounts require information for comparability, and to establish trends and evaluate performance.
- Three key areas of information appear in an annual report: information required by law, information usually included with accounts, and other information.
- Annual reports contain information relating to stewardship, social issues and valuation.
- The reporting requirements for small businesses are not the same as for larger businesses.
- Accounts may be prepared according to one of two valuations, historical cost or alternative cost.
- The preparation of accounts is subject to the influence of accounting guidelines issued by the Accounting Standards Board (ASB).
- Accounting bases are generally accepted methods of applying accounting concepts.
- Accounting policies are specific accounting bases adopted as is most appropriate to an organisation's circumstances.
- Accounts of limited companies must be registered by a firm of independent accountants known as registered auditors.
- The most common methods of calculating depreciation are the straight-line method, reducing balance method, machine-hour method and sum-of-digits method.
- The three principal methods of stock valuation are FIFO (First In, First Out), LIFO (Last In, First Out) and cumulative weighted average cost (AvCo).

63 Costs for total costing

In Chapter 33 we looked at contribution and break-even analysis. We saw that a limitation of marginal costing is that it reduces accounting behaviour to an equation – how to generate sufficient contribution to cover fixed costs and provide a surplus in the form of profits.

An alternative approach is to look at all of the costs incurred in producing a single product. This is known as **absorption costing**. With this method, all costs are absorbed into the cost of the product. The absorption unit is calculated by dividing total costs by the total production in order to obtain a **unit cost**. In order to price the product, a **profit margin** is added to the cost to obtain a **selling price**.

Cost allocation and apportionment

Cost units
The aim of any form of costing is to build up a system which provides a cost of production for each of the units produced or supplied. The starting point is to identify what the cost unit is. Usually the cost unit is the final product produced by an organisation. For example, in the aircraft industry the cost unit might be an aeroplane; for a tobacco company it might be a packet of cigarettes; for a pen manufacturer the cost unit might be 1,000 pens; for a motor car manufacturer it would be a car – and so on. The cost unit need not necessarily be the final product; it may be part of a product. For example, for an aeroplane manufacturer it might be a wing or an engine.

Cost centres
In addition to collecting costs by cost units relating to something produced by the organisation, it is quite likely that an organisation may wish to determine the costs of specific departments or sections. For example, they may wish to know the cost of running something as large as a factory, or as small as a machine. These areas are known as **cost centres**. A cost centre is, therefore, any part of a business organisation for which costs are collected. There are two types of cost centre. These are:

- **Production cost centres** In these, parts of the production process are carried out. For example, in a dog biscuit factory cost centres might include preparation, baking, cutting and packaging.
- **Service cost centres** These represent areas outside the main production processes, for example, maintenance, staff canteen or quality control. Though these cost centres are not directly involved in producing products or cost units, they may be just as important as the production cost centres themselves.

The important role of service cost centres and the costs they incur cannot be ignored. The question is, where will these costs go? The costs must be apportioned to production cost centres so that they can be incorporated in the cost of the product produced.

Cost allocation
Cost allocation is carried out if a cost can be easily identified with, and charged to, a particular cost unit or cost centre.

Allocation is the allotment of complete overhead items to cost centres. For example, if there was a quality inspector in each of five departments, the wages of each inspector would be allocated to the department in which he or she worked.

Direct costs
These can usually be allocated to the cost unit, as they can be identified with it. For example, time sheets and clock cards would help identify direct wages; invoices and materials requisition forms would help identify direct materials and invoices might help to identify direct expenses.

Production overheads
It is not possible to allocate production overheads to products or cost units in the same way as direct costs. However, it may be possible to allocate some production overheads to a cost centre. For example, if a maintenance facility existed for the sole use of a plant, this would be a cost centre direct cost. Where overheads cannot be treated as cost centre direct costs, they will require **apportionment**.

Cost apportionment
Cost apportionment is the allotment of only part or a proportion of an overhead item to cost centres. For example, if only one quality inspector supervised the work of five departments, then a way would have to be found to apportion the overhead – perhaps on the basis of the time spent by the inspector in each department.

Methods of overhead apportionment
There are several ways of apportioning overheads:

- By actual time spent;
- By usage;
- By number of direct workers;
- By area or volume of building;
- By cost of machinery;
- By number of stores requisitions.

Basis of overhead apportionment	Overhead	Ratios for each production department		
		Dept. 1	Dept. 2	Dept. 3
Time spent (hours)	Maintenance	2,000	2,000	1,000
Area (sq. m.)	Rent	500	300	200
Usage (machine hours)	Power	8,000	5,000	7,000
Direct workers	Canteen	12	10	10
Machine cost (£)	Depreciation	20,000	15,000	5,000
Requisitions	Storekeeping	10	20	20

Figure 63.1 Apportioning overheads

Overhead	Total Cost	Dept. 1	Dept. 2	Dept. 3
	£	£	£	£
Maintenance	2,500	1,000	1,000	500
Rent	3,000	1,500	900	600
Power	2,000	800	500	700
Canteen	1,200	450	375	375
Depreciation	4,000	2,000	1,500	500
Storekeeping	1,500	300	600	600

Figure 63.2 Apportioning overheads between departments

It is important to choose the most appropriate form of apportionment. The best form of apportionment should:

- Relate closely to the ways in which costs are incurred;
- Be easily obtainable from records of the organisation;
- Reflect the use of resources by each cost centre;
- Be fair in sharing costs between cost centres.

The basis for apportionment can be arrived at using simple ratios. In Figures 63.1 and 63.2 above, overheads are apportioned using each of the above methods. By looking at the total cost for each overhead the overhead can be apportioned between departments.

TASK 63.1

Using the information given in Figure 62.3 below, apportion overheads to each department.

The total costs of each overhead was as follows:

Quality control	= £5,400
Power	= £5,000
Maintenance	= £6,000
Wages office	= £7,500

Dept. 1	Dept. 2	Dept. 3	Overhead	Basis for apportionment
60	90	90	Quality control	Hours spent
140	70	70	Maintenance	Hours spent
600	1,200	600	Power	Machine hours
4	5	11	Wages office	Direct workers

Figure 63.3

To summarise: the aim of any form of costing is to develop a system which provides a cost of production for any product supplied. The cost unit is the final product produced by the organisation and the cost centre may be a specific department or section. The principles of allocation and apportionment help to charge overhead costs to different parts of the business. They help to work out the cost of operating each cost centre and the production overhead for each product or cost unit worked on by each cost centre.

Overhead cost absorption

The next stage is to take the process further and look at how overhead costs are transferred from production cost centres to products or cost units in those cost centres. This method is known as **overhead cost absorption**.

In order to charge the total cost units of a production cost centre to the cost units, we need to calculate a rate for each cost centre. This is known as the **overhead absorption rate**. The formula for calculating the overhead absorption rate is:

$$\frac{Total\ budgeted\ cost\ centre\ overheads}{Total\ budgeted\ production}$$

Remember that the techniques of apportionment and allocation will have been used to calculate the budgeted totals for each production cost centre.

There have to be a number of ways of working out the unit cost of a product in absorption costing. This is because a single cost centre within an organisation may produce a range of different types of units. For example, if a production cost centre is makes tables and chairs, then it is producing two types of products. It would be unreasonable to assume that the cost value added to each by that centre would be the same. There are, therefore, a number of ways of calculating an overhead cost absorption rate.

1 Rate per unit of production
In some cost centres it is possible to express production in units of production if all items of output are similar in terms of size, time spent on them and other features.

For example, KP Joiners make headboards for beds. Assembly Department A only make one type of standard headboard. For next year they have budgeted to produce 50 headboards a day over 300 working days. The year's budgeted overhead for the department is £90,000.

Therefore:

$$\frac{Total\ budgeted\ cost\ centre\ overheads}{Total\ budgeted\ production} = \frac{£90,000}{50 \times 300}$$

$$= £6.00$$

In Assembly Department A, each headboard must have £6 added to it to ensure that each unit has a fair share of assembly department overheads.

2 Rate per direct labour hour
If the assembly department in the previous example had produced several different types of headboards instead of one standard type, it would not have been possible to use a rate per unit of production. A method of measuring production is therefore required which can be applied to different sizes of headboard or headboards with different characteristics. As the assembly department uses labour-intensive activities, it might be decided to use direct labour hours as a more useful method for measuring the value of output.

For example, suppose that Assembly Department A at KP Joiners now make *two* types of headboard:

1 A single headboard for single beds;
2 A double headboard for double beds.

The budgeted production overhead is still £90,000 but the budgeted production is expected to be 8,000 single headboards and 8,000 double headboards. It takes 3 hours to produce a single headboard and 4 hours to produce a double headboard.

The rate per direct labour hour =

$$\frac{Total\ budgeted\ cost\ centre\ production\ overheads}{Total\ production\ direct\ labour\ hours}$$

$$= \frac{£90,000}{(8,000 \times 3) + (8,000 \times 4)}$$

$$= \frac{£90,000}{56,000\ direct\ labour\ hours}$$

$$= £1.6\ per\ direct\ labour\ hour$$

So, each single headboard produced by the assembly department must have 3 hours added to it. This would be 3 x 1.6 = £4.80. Each double headboard would have 4 hours added to it. This would be 4 x 1.6 = £6.40.

Other methods
So far, in order to identify the amount to be charged to a cost unit, we have looked at the rate per unit of production where items of output are similar in terms of size and time spent on them, and at the rate per direct labour hour method.

Where the method of production is intensive it is possible to measure production in machine hours by calculating a production overhead absorption rate per machine hour. It is also possible to use a percentage of direct material cost as a basis for absorbing production overhead costs into the product or cost unit.

PETERLEE PINE

Peterlee Pine produce three different types of standard pine products, including wardrobes, tables and chairs. The finishing department is labour-intensive. It has been decided to use the rate per direct labour hour method for measuring the value of output. The budgeted overheads for the department are £240,000. For the year, the budgeted production is expected to be 5,000 wardrobes, 1,000 tables and 14,000 chairs. It takes 8 hours to produce a wardrobe, 6 hours to produce a table and 2 hours to produce a chair.

1 Calculate the overhead absorption rate per direct labour hour and the overhead cost of a wardrobe, a table and a chair.

Over- and under-absorption

As absorption rates are based upon budgeted figures which involve forecasts of overheads and units of output or direct labour hours, they are pre-set for the forthcoming accounting period. However, it is quite likely that during the year – for example, because of seasonal variations in demand – actual output or actual direct labour hours may differ from planned rates. Where this happens, a variance takes place with some degree of over- or under-absorption. If there is a difference in actual production, this is described as a **volume variance**. The difference between the overhead budgeted and the overhead incurred is an **expenditure variance**.

Chapter summary

- An alternative to marginal costing is to look at all the costs incurred in producing a single product. This is known as absorption costing.
- The aim of any form of costing is to build up a system which provides a cost of production for each of the units produced or supplied.
- The cost unit is the final product produced by an organisation.
- A cost centre is part of an organisation for which costs are collected.
- Cost allocation is carried out if a cost can be easily identified with and charged to a particular cost unit or centre.
- Apportionment is the allotment of only parts or proportions or an overhead item to cost centres.
- There are several ways of apportioning overheads.

- Overhead costs can be transferred from production cost centres to products or cost units in cost centres. This is known as overhead cost absorption.
- The formula for calculating the overhead absorption rate if all of the units are the same is total budgeted cost centre overheads divided by total budgeted production.
- The direct labour hours method provides a way of measuring production for different types of products.
- The rate per direct labour hours is total budgeted cost centre production overheads divided by total production direct labour hours.
- Other methods include production in machine hours or a percentage of direct material cost.
- Variances can be used to measure differences either in production or in overheads.

11 Human Resource Management

INTRODUCTION

In this unit we explore and examine the nature of Human Resource Management and its growing influence on modern business organisations.

The term **Human Resource Management (HRM)** has come to be associated with a range of new initiatives aimed at giving a higher priority to individuals and their needs in organisations. Some people are cynical about such initiatives, particularly in the mid-1990s, when many organisations who claimed to regard people as their 'most precious resource' were in fact downsizing (i.e. making employees redundant).

This unit begins by examining the nature of teamwork and the importance of creating high-performance teams in which people feel a genuine commitment to each other and to shared goals. It also examines a number of roles that individuals can play in teams. It goes on to examine the nature of HRM and a range of initiatives associated with **employee involvement (EI)** in the workplace.

The move towards EI has often involved building a new relationship with employees. In the 1960s and 1970s the UK had a poor reputation for industrial relations, which were characterised by a confrontational approach between managers and trade unions. In recent times organisations have set out to create a new industrial relations climate based on empowering employees to make more decisions for themselves. This involves giving more responsibility (accountability) to ground-level employees, rather than the traditional 'top-down' approach. By developing new work practices, organisations have been able to develop more flexible work practices such as **multi-skilling** where employees are expected to do a range of jobs and tasks, often working in process teams.

The unit goes on to examine the nature of the labour market in which organisations purchase the services of employees. Key changes taking place in this labour market are highlighted, including the increased emphasis on part-time employment at the expense of full-time work and the increasing emphasis on female employment.

Finally the unit examines the role of the Human Resources department within the modern organisation, from traditional areas such as recruitment, selection, training and termination of employment to newer areas such as appraisal and the personal development of employees. Personnel are also responsible for payment and benefits in an organisation, and so we examine a variety of payment systems and their respective merits. Finally we examine the key area of equal opportunities, exploring a range of legislation relevant to gender, race, disability and other areas and examining their implications for business organisations.

64 Teams in organisations

Increasingly in modern workplaces, people need to be able to work together co-operatively as a team.

This requires increased levels of interpersonal skills. Team members are expected to make a contribution to the activities, tasks and well-being of their team.

Modern employees are no longer simply expected to 'take' instructions which have come down the line to them. Rather, they are expected to make decisions for themselves and to help others to make effective decisions.

Becoming a team

Jon Katzenbach and Doug Smith, in their book *The Wisdom of Teams* (1993), argue that there is a threshold that a group must cross before it becomes a team.

They define a team as:

> *'A small number of people with complementary skills who are committed to a common purpose, performance goals and an approach for which they hold themselves accountable.'*

Katzenbach and Smith argue that managers need to be able to understand the ingredients of a team if they are to operate a successful organisation. They set out a simple framework for the development of teams, and show a team performance curve:

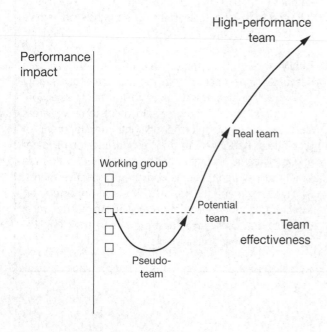

Figure 64.1: A team performance curve

1 **The working group** This is a collection of individuals who have no real opportunity or need to become a team. Each working group member produces something that helps the task to be completed but belonging to the working group places no more demand on them than if they worked independently.

2 **The pseudo-team** In this situation there is no benefit in being a part of the team. Indeed, members' individual performances are worse than if they were working alone. This is because there is no focus or common sense of purpose. The group members are confused as to what they should be doing and how they should be working together. This generates antagonism, and the team quickly falls apart.

3 **The potential team** This is a collection of individuals with a clear performance need who are seriously seeking to improve their impact as a group. They are aware that there is a need for something to be done in order to improve their performance and they want to do it. Unfortunately they lack clarity about their aims, as well as the discipline needed for a common working approach. Also, they have not established the final criterion – mutual accountability. Many organisations contain potential teams. This provides a real opportunity and a challenge for management.

4 **The real team** It is worth repeating that a real team is 'a small number of people with complementary skills who are committed to a common purpose, performance goals, and an approach for which they hold themselves mutually accountable'.

5 **The high-performance team** As well as meeting the criteria for a real team, this group will also be deeply committed to the personal growth of its members. It will significantly out-perform other teams.

Teams come in many different forms and guises. Dumaine (1994) identifies five common types:

1 **The management team** Managers representing various functions, such as production and sales, co-ordinate work among the teams;

2 **The problem-solving team** A group of employees who work together as a team to solve a specific problem and then disband;

3 **The work team** An increasingly popular type of team, undertaking the daily work of the organisation. When empowered, the work team is known as a **self-managed** team;

4 **The quality circle** A group of workers and supervisors meeting from time to time to discuss workplace problems and suggest solutions;

5 Virtual team A characteristic of this new type of teamwork is that members communicate and participate by computer.

Dumaine suggests that a common problem with teams is that organisations do not think carefully enough about what sort of team will be most effective for the job. In some cases teams are over-used. Does the task in hand really require interaction in a team or would it be more effectively undertaken by an individual?

In recent years downsizing in organisations has meant that many middle-management responsibilities have been shifted down onto teams of employees who have also taken on the authority to make decisions.

The emphasis on teamwork suggests that well-organised teams will outperform the same group of individuals operating in isolation. It is therefore important to identify the processes involved in team working and some of the characteristics of an effective team.

IT'S A FACT

The focus on teams which surfaced in the 1980s was partly influenced by Japanese working methods and also by a need to compete. Quality circles were used to discuss improvements in quality, often resulting in greatly improved production standards.

Team processes

Whenever a group is required to work together there will be three strands involved in the team process:

- **Identifying the task** This is the content of the work. For example, the task of a management meeting may be to decide on the location of a new factory; the task of an interview is to select the best candidate to take up a particular post. The task represents the conversion of information and opinions from group members into decisions or recommendations. In general terms this covers what has to be done by the team and why. Most groups give a lot of attention to the task.

- **Drawing up the action schedule** The action schedule is concerned with how a group will be organised to do a given task. The schedule will cover such questions as who will fill the necessary roles, how progress will be checked and monitored, how the group will keep to the time schedule, etc. It will also deal with the procedures of decision-making: how to ensure that everyone gets a say, how conflict will be dealt with, etc. In general, the action schedule will cover the where and how of decision-making. Most groups will give some attention to their action schedule.

- **Managing the process** The process is the interaction that takes place between members of a group. It is about how people work together, their relationships and the feelings created by their behaviour within the group. It involves interpersonal skills such as listening to others and helping others to join in a discussion, recognising feelings and giving and receiving feedback. In general it covers who does what and when. Many groups pay little attention to process.

These three threads of group working are all important in group decision-making. It will be apparent that a group that concentrates on its action schedules and its process entirely may have a wonderful time but is unlikely to achieve the task since morale will suffer and the group will disintegrate. In contrast, concentration purely on the task is likely to lead to arguments about how things should be organised, and inattention to group members' thoughts and feelings will lead to mishandled resources and to misunderstandings.

Factors affecting group effectiveness

There are a number of important factors influencing the effectiveness of a group, including the size of the group, the flow of communication within the group and the style of management.

1 The size of the group

There are a number of reasons why it is easier to make decisions within small (i.e. five or six people) groups rather than larger ones. The more people are drawn into the decision-making process, the more difficult it is to involve everyone, the more difficult it is to get everyone to agree, and the higher the level of dissatisfaction with the way the group operates. Individuals find it more difficult to identify with the group, and sub-groups start to form. In order to prevent a group from becoming fragmented, it is increasingly likely that a leader will need to take centralised control over decision-making as the size of the group grows.

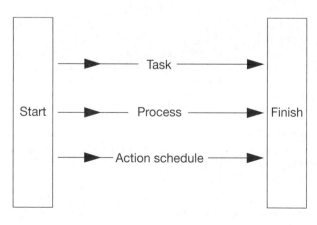

Figure 64.2 Stages in group working

However, large groups also have a number of clear advantages. A large group will be able to call upon a greater pool of skills, energy and resources. If a larger number of members of an organisation feel they are involved in the decision-making process, they may also be more willing to implement policies.

2 Communication within the group

The main factors influencing the flow of communication within a group are the formal organisation of the group, the informal organisation and the means of communication employed.

Research carried out by Bavelas (1948) and Leavitt (1951) suggests that there are four main types of communication network. These are illustrated in Figure 64.3.

The wheel and chain networks are typified by a centralisation of the flow of information. Effective decision-making thus depends to a great extent on those in key central positions and on the quality of the information channelled towards them.

Bavelas and Leavitt saw these centralised forms as exhibiting the following characteristics:

1 They are highly effective at making and carrying out straightforward, well structured and predictable activities;
2 Levels of satisfaction for group members are relatively low compared with those for members of less centralised groups;
3 The centralised form helps to strengthen the leadership position in such groups;
4 A stable structure rapidly emerges in the group;
5 The group becomes dependent on those with greatest access to relevant information.

In terms of our previous analysis, such a group structure lends itself to short-term operating control decisions.

In contrast, the circle network and the completely connected network lend themselves to a more open, decentralised form of decision-making. Members of these groups are mutually interdependent, and share the decision-making process. The group is not so dependent on key individuals, and levels of satisfaction are usually greater. Disadvantages are that, because responsibility is shared, there may not be an effective mechanism for pushing decisions through. There may be a lot of talk about action without the mechanisms required to create action and see it through.

Style of management

The way in which an organisation is managed will have an important effect on how well its groups operate (see Chapter 65).

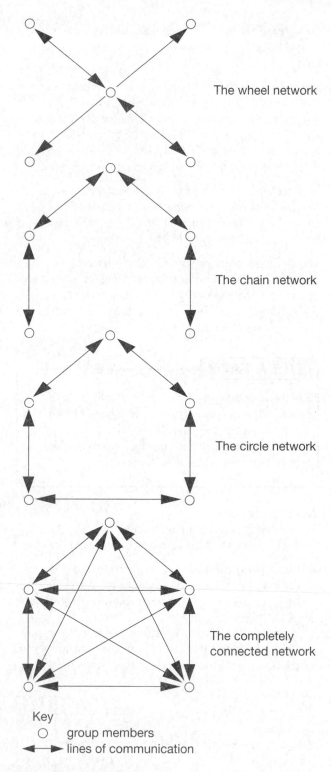

The wheel network

The chain network

The circle network

The completely connected network

Key

○ group members
◄──► lines of communication

Figure 64.3: Types of communication network

Roles within teams

When people work together in a team, the members of the team usually adopt particular roles. For example, one person may have the role of monitoring progress, checking the time-keeping or acting as leader. There is a tendency for one member of a group to take on the **task functions** and for others to adopt a **maintenance** role.

APPROACHES TO TEAMWORK

A group of individuals were brought together as an experiment to work together on a project. Half of the group had previously worked for charities and social service organisations; the other half came from large business organisations. They were given four days to plan the delivery of a consignment of materials in Africa. The members of the group with commercial business experience wanted to immediately set targets, plan schedules and get the project organised. In contrast, the members of the group with

voluntary sector experience wanted to start off by carrying out activities designed to weld the group together into a bonded team.

1 Why do you think that the two groups set about the project in different ways?

2 How did their approaches vary?

3 Which of the approaches do you feel would have been the most appropriate in the situation?

Task functions are those which will help the group to get the task done as effectively and efficiently as possible. Task functions include:

- Proposing objectives and clarifying goals;
- Seeking information and opinions;
- Keeping the group on track;
- Summarising ideas;
- Suggesting ways forward;
- Evaluating contributions.

Team members who take on the **maintenance** role offer encouragement, for example, by:

- Supporting other group members;
- Ensuring all members of the group are included;
- Reconciling disagreements and reducing tension;
- Making suggestions for compromise;
- Monitoring the group.

The effectiveness of a team will, to some extent, depend upon the mix of roles which team members take on. Successful teams will tend to have a range of appropriate personalities and qualities. Belbin (1981) identifies eight roles required within a well-functioning team:

1 The **chairperson** co-ordinates the efforts of the group and makes sure the team makes best use of its resources in achieving its goals;

2 The **shaper** sets objectives and priorities and drives the team towards successful completion of the task;

3 The **plant** comes up with new ideas and strategies;

4 The **monitor/evaluator** is able to analyse problems and evaluate progress;

5 The **resource investigator** is outgoing and will explore and report on ideas and developments from outside the group;

6 The **company worker** is an administrator rather than a leader and good at carrying out agreed plans;

7 The **team worker** supports the team, helps to keep it together and tries to improve communication between members;

8 The **finisher** maintains momentum in the team and plays an important part in getting the task finished.

Belbin suggests that, although team members may tend towards one of these roles, most people are also able to undertake a second role.

If people have particular attributes and ways of working which suggest that they will tend to take up particular roles within teams, it is obviously important that there is a balance of roles in order to produce an effective team.

Team-mapping

Research has shown that individuals like to organise their work in different ways. This involves the way in which they plan, organise and communicate.

Management consultants have tried to devise techniques for identifying people's work preferences in order to be able to identify the sort of roles which people are likely to take on in a team situation.

SYNTHESIS

Think about groups and teams which you have joined in order to do a specific work-related task, e.g. a combined class-related project, a workplace project as part of a part-time job etc. Can you identify particular individuals who played any of the roles outlined above? Which of the roles came most naturally to you?

For example, the **Margerison McCann Team Management Index** can be used to find out information about people's work preferences. These preferences are then used to place individuals on a **Team Management Indicator**.

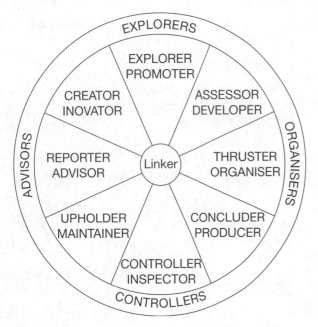

Figure 64.4: The Team Management Indicator

McCann identifies nine key team roles:

- **Reporter-advisers** are good at generating information and gathering it together so that it can be understood. They are usually patient, and prepared to delay making a decision until they know as much as they can about the work to be done. Some people feel that they procrastinate and put things off, but reporter-advisers prefer to be accurate than to put forward advice which later might turn out to be wrong. Such people are invaluable as 'support' members of the team, but they are not likely to be the ones who will get things organised. Indeed, their concern is to make sure that the job is done correctly.

- **Creator-innovators** are people who have a number of ideas which may well contradict and upset the existing way of doing things. They can be very independent and often want to experiment and pursue their ideas regardless of the present systems and methods. They need to be allowed to pursue their ideas without disrupting the present way of working until their new approaches have been proved.

- **Explorer-promoters** are usually excellent at taking up an idea and generating enthusiasm for it. They will find out what is happening outside the organisation and compare new ideas with what is being done by other people. They are also good at bringing back contacts and information and resources which can help the innovation move forward. They may not necessarily be good at controlling details, but are excellent at seeing the 'bigger picture'. They are very capable of pushing an idea forward, even if they are not always the best people to organise and control it.

- **Assessor-developers** look for ways to make an idea work in a practical way. Their concern is to see if the market wants the innovation and to test it against some practical criteria. Very often they will produce a prototype or do a market research study. However, once they have done this, they may lose interest, preferring to move on to another project.

- **Thruster-organisers** are the people who get things done. Once they have been convinced that an idea is of interest, they will set up procedures and systems and make the task into a work reality. They push people and systems to the limit to ensure deadlines are met. They can be impatient, but they get results, even if 'feathers are ruffled' in the process.

- **Concluder-producers** take great pride in producing a product or service to a particular standard. They like working to set procedures and doing things in a regular way. The fact that they produced something yesterday does not mean that they will be bored with producing it again tomorrow. This is in contrast to the creator-innovators who dislike doing similar things day after day. For the concluder-producer the important thing is to use existing skills rather than to continually change and learn new ways of doing things. They therefore enjoy reproducing things and achieving the plans that they have set.

- **Controller-Inspectors** enjoy doing detailed work and making sure that facts and figures are correct. They are careful and meticulous. Indeed, one of their great strengths is that they concentrate for long periods on a particular task. This contrasts with explorer-promoters who continually need a wide variety of tasks. Controller-inspectors like to pursue issues in depth and make sure that work is done accurately and according to plan. They are extremely valuable in financial and quality issues.

- **Upholder-maintainers** are very good at making sure the team operates on a sound basis. They take pride in maintaining both the physical and social side of work and can easily become the 'conscience' of the team, giving a lot of support and help to team members. They usually have strong views on the way the team should be run, based on their convictions and beliefs. If upset, they can become rather obstinate and difficult, but when convinced that what the team is doing is of value, they can be a tremendous source of strength and energy and often make excellent negotiators.

The importance of linking

In the middle of all these work functions are the **linkers**. These are people close to the centre of the team whose main skill is in co-ordinating. All the other roles mentioned involve some aspects of linking, but those closer to the 'hub' of the team are more able to co-ordinate and integrate the work of others.

In theory, all managers should aim to develop linking skills; in practice, not all managers are good at linking and many prefer to have someone on their team who can perform this role for them.

Group decision-making

It is generally accepted that group decision-making is better than individual decision-making because the quantity and quality of input tends to be higher. But it is also true that the cost to the organisation is greater. It is important therefore that teams operate effectively and make quality decisions and that their work is more effective than work which could be produced by an individual working alone.

Vroom and Yetton (1973) identified three criteria essential for measuring good decision-making:

- The **quality** of the decision reached;
- The **time** it takes to reach the decision;
- The extent to which the decision is **accepted** by those whom it affects and who have to work with it.

One of the advantages of team decisions is that there should be a higher commitment to the decision and its implementation since a group of people have shared in the decision-making process.

Effective group performance

According to Gilligan, Neale and Murray in *Business Decision Making* the following should lead to effective group performance:

1. The structure of the group and the status of group members should be stable and well formed;
2. The group should be large enough to fulfil the tasks, but not so large as to encourage the formation of sub-groups;
3. The group members should have appropriate skills;
4. The atmosphere should be informal and relaxed;
5. Objectives should be understood and accepted by group members;
6. Discussion should be encouraged and members should be willing to listen to each other;
7. Decisions should be reached by consensus;
8. The leader of the group should not dominate, nor should there be power struggles among group members;
9. The group should operate with mild or moderate levels of stress;
10. Disagreements should not be overridden; the reasons for disagreements should be examined and an attempt made to resolve them;
11. The allocation of tasks to members should be clear and accepted;
12. The group should act in a cohesive way.

EXAM TIP

You should be able to:

1. Explain why teams are more effective than individuals at making decisions;
2. Describe the 'types' of individual skills that are required for an effective team;
3. Give examples from real organisations of effective teamwork in action.

SYNTHESIS

Which of the above roles do you see as being most essential for a well-functioning team? Is it possible to rank them in any way? To what extent does the importance of each role depend on the situation?

Phases of team development

Tuckman and Jensen have identified four distinct phases of team development:

1. **'Forming'** A number of individuals come together. They start to exchange ideas and gather information about the nature of the task. They also explore how other members of the group operate and what behaviour is acceptable.

2. **'Storming'** The group begins to exchange ideas as they try to reach agreement on objectives and strategy. There is often conflict and disagreement.

3. **'Norming'** The group begins to share ideas. Group cohesion starts to develop and members start to act collaboratively.

4. **'Performing'** The group is able to turn its attention to the task. A pattern of working is established. Members may assume particular roles or functions. Every member of the group is able to make the best possible contribution to the team.

CASE STUDY CASE STUDY CASE STUDY CASE STUDY CASE STUDY

A CASE FOR TEAMWORK

Until recently, the plant at Top Cement operated on the basis of an old-fashioned relationship between managers and employees. The managers made the decisions, which they then passed on to employees with lists of instructions and a tightly-written rule book. This worked well for a number of years. Employees were used to 'doing what they were told' and their work was highly routine.

However, over the years the cement industry changed and became a lot more competitive. As a result, Top Cement replaced many of their large plants with new automated ones requiring a smaller workforce and based around equipment which was more reliant on computer control and other types of automation. This meant that a lot more responsibility needed to be given to ground-level employees. In addition it was essential for employees to work in teams and to pool skills and knowledge. These teams needed to be highly 'bonded' together to ensure maximum success.

1 Why would the old top-down approach be no longer appropriate at Top Cement?

2 What teamwork skills do you think that the 'new type' of employee at Top Cement needs to learn?

3 How should Top Cement go about making sure that its employees develop these 'new skills'?

STUDY CASE STUDY CASE STUDY CASE STUDY CASE STUDY CASE STUDY

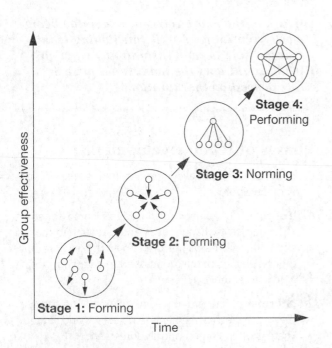

Fig: 64.5 Phases of team development

Different groups will go through this cycle at different rates and face different problems at each stage. The early stage of group formation, when there is no leader, may be dominated by particular individuals. At this point quieter members of the group may not be heard. If a group is very task-focused short-term progress may be rapid, but the group may face difficulties in the longer term. Social rela-

tionships in the group may be so poor that no team spirit is evident. On the other hand an over-emphasis on team processes may mean that the task is never completed.

Groups may well go through these phases in a non-linear way, repeating earlier phases in the cycle. A change in group membership, for example, may cause the group to revert to an earlier phase.

Team building

Most organisations introduce teamwork in order to improve the motivation of personnel and benefit from reduced costs due to more effective working practices and decision-making.

Teamwork is most likely to be successful when it operates in a supportive environment. The atmosphere within the organisation therefore needs to support co-operation and trust. The development of teamworking skills may include exercises and sessions to explore and develop relevant skills. Tasks may be devised for groups to help them develop consensus decision-making or listening skills.

Chapter summary

- Teamwork is an increasingly important requirement of modern organisations.
- A team is a small number of people whose skills complement each other and who are committed to a common purpose, goals and an approach for which they feel accountable.
- There are a number of stages required to turn a loose collection of individuals into a real team.
- Team process involves three strands: task, process and action schedule.
- Factors influencing group effectiveness include the size of the group, communications within the group and the style of management employed.

- Research has indicated a number of key roles within teams – for example, studies by Belbin and the very useful Margerison Mcann Team Management Index.
- It is generally agreed that group or team decision-making is better than individual decision-making.
- Teams can develop through a number of stages including forming, storming, norming and performing.
- Team building is an important exercise to make teams stronger and more effective.

65 Principles of Human Resource Management

In the fast-moving business world, new terms and descriptions are constantly appearing as ideas change and evolve. Often these are simply examples of jargon or 'buzzwords' which come and go. But when, during the 1980s, the term 'personnel management' gave way to **Human Resource Management**, it was clear that a fundamental change was taking place.

Human Resource Management aims to focus on people and their needs, as well as on the needs of the organisation. It marked a new way of managing based on a new set of values and brought with it a battery of approaches to increase human involvement in the workplace.

HRM can be seen as part of an ongoing effort to raise awareness of the 'human side' of the workplace. In simplified terms, this process has involved three main stages:

1 A 'command and control' stage, characterised by rigid hierarchical structures, with workers regarded as being little different from tools and machinery;

2 A 'human relations' stage, drawing on the study of industrial psychology and based on the belief that productivity can be increased by attending to employees' motivation and general welfare;

3 The 'HRM' stage, where organisations seek to 'get more out of people' by addressing their need for fulfilment at work, giving them greater responsibility and responding to their human needs and motivation – for example, by regular appraisal.

What is Human Resource Management?
Human Resource Management is concerned with:

1 **Commitment to employees**
   HRM organisations view their employees as one of their most important assets. This is reflected in their corporate strategy and 'values statements' and in their objectives, policies and ways of working.

2 **Recognising employee aspirations and needs**
   Human Resource Management requires organisations to develop policies and ways of working which recognise the aspirations and needs of their employees and allow them to satisfy their needs and aspirations through their work.

Enlightened Human Resource Management is based on the belief that *organisations work for their employees as well as employees working for the organisation*. This approach has material benefts for employers:

- Employees who are contented and well-motivated are more likely to help the organisation to meet its objectives;

- Committed employees are most likely to enable organisations to develop a competitive edge;

- Employees who are fulfilled in their work are also most likely to project a positive image of the organisation to the public – an important factor for the growing number of firms who operate in the service sector.

In practical terms, HRM involves:

- Making commitments to people in terms of defining the mission and goals of the whole organisation;
- Considering the implications for human resources of any major decision made by the organisation;
- Designing the structure of the organisation in such a way as to meet the needs of the employees;
- Having the Director of Human Resources working at Board level in the organisation;
- Ensuring that management actions and decisions within the organisation continually focus on human resource considerations.

Human resources: from cost to asset

Perhaps one of the biggest shifts in approach has been the change in the perceived value of people at work, from *cost* to *asset*.

This transformation can be illustrated as follows:

People as cost	People as asset
Employees are a key cost of production.	People create the value added that makes the organisation successful.
Employees are just one of a number of resources that need managing.	People are the key resource of the organisation, and therefore a prime management responsibility.

HRM as a strategic discipline

Properly understood, Human Resource Management is the concern of the whole organisation, and decisions should be seen as an integral part of corporate strategy.

Human resource strategy will filter down into every aspect of activity in the organisation. This does not mean that the strategy is imposed on people lower down the organisation by those higher up (although in some organisations this happens) – rather, that decision-making is **devolved** so that top-level strategy fully reflects the needs and wishes of all levels within the organisation.

HRM requires ground-level employees to be **empowered** to make decisions for themselves – for example, through the creation of self-managing teams and project teams involving considerable levels of autonomy.

This can be achieved in two principal ways:

- **Direct participation schemes** These engage individual staff directly. Examples are team briefings, quality circles and financial schemes such as profit-sharing and share ownership. Some schemes hand responsibility directly to individual working teams.
- **Indirect participation schemes** Here employees participate indirectly through representatives. Examples are joint consultation and representation of workers on the board of directors.

A company's choice of participation scheme is influenced by its views on industrial relations, the legal requirements prevailing in the industry and its experience of previous schemes. The Employment Act 1982 requires companies covered by the Companies Act and employing more than 250 people to report annually on action taken to introduce, monitor and develop employee involvement. It does not, however, require companies to do anything other than report their activities.

Employee Involvement (EI)

Over the years there have been many attempts to encourage greater employee involvement in organisational activity. According to Ian Beardwell and Len Holden in *Human Resource Management: A Contemporary Perspective*, the Second World War saw a strong move towards increasing EI:

'The need for huge productivity increases to meet the war effort led workers to demand something in return – a greater say in the operation of the workplace. Works committees and joint consultative committees (JCCs) were set up in many factories.'

However, interest fell off during the 1950s when the emphasis switched to collective bargaining between trade unions and employers.

During the 1960s and 70s there was a revival of interest in the concept of industrial democracy which found expression in the 1977 Bullock Committee Report. Particular interest was shown in models of co-determination which had been successful in Germany and Sweden.

With the return of the Thatcher government in 1979 this interest declined. However, in the 1990s there has been a considerable revival in interest in Employee Involvement.

There are two main reasons for this:

1 **The increasing importance of the European Union** As a member of the European Union, the UK is increasingly affected by European social and employment policy, particularly the European Social Chapter which upholds:

> '...the right to freedom of association and collective bargaining, including the right to strike as well as encouraging measures to enhance dialogue between "social partners", i.e. employers and employees at all levels.'

2 **The influence of 'management gurus'** – writers and communicators such as Tom Peters and Rosbeth Kanter have consistently argued that people are an organisation's most valuable resource, and that training and developing them, adequately rewarding their performance and involving them in policy-making enhance motivation and performance.

A further important driving force behind the rise of Human Resource Management was the remarkable industrial success of Japan. There was considerable evidence that a key to the Japanese success lay in the involvement of employees in work groups such as quality circles.

Another particularly influential model in the 1980s was the **Harvard Human Resource Management programme**, which identified employees as major stakeholders in the organisation. The creators of this framework argued that 'it is critical that managers design and administer various mechanisms for employee influence.'

Methods of involving and motivating employees

There are many ways of motivating employees besides the more obvious incentives of pay and conditions.

Experience has shown that motivation can be improved by:

- Making work more varied and stimulating;
- Giving employees greater responsibility;
- Recognising and praising employees' efforts;
- Encouraging employees to work as a team.

Organisations can choose from a number of different strategies to raise motivation:

- **Job enrichment** involves giving employees an increase in responsibility/and or recognition. The aim is to make them feel that their contribution has been upgraded and is more highly appreciated. Ways of doing this vary from simply giving them a new title to extending the perks associated with a particular job.

- **Job enlargement** involves giving employees a greater range of responsibilities. An employee who feels that a job is going 'stale' and is losing interest in it, may feel rejuvenated when asked to take on additional tasks.

For example, an employee who has been used to handling routine mail and answering telephone calls may gain fresh motivation from being asked to meet clients, take them out to dinner and perform a public relations role.

- **Employee participation in decision-making** can also be a great motivator. The 'flattened' organisation chart in which decisions can be made at all levels of an organisation helps employees to feel important and valued. But effective employee participation must go beyond the factory 'suggestion box', to actually giving a wider number of people the responsibility for making decisions.

Other methods of employee participation include:

- **Team briefing**
  Employers encourage and train supervisors to hold regular meetings of their teams. The Industrial Society's guidelines on team briefings are:

  - They should be held regularly, at least monthly, on a pre-arranged basis. Each meeting should last no longer than 30 minutes;
  - Teams should have no more than 15 members;
  - The composition of teams should be decided by area of work rather than by occupation;
  - Ideas for the central message at a meeting should come from senior management;
  - There should be time for questions at the end of each meeting;
  - The meeting should be led by the immediate manager or supervisor.

SYNTHESIS

How effective do you think team briefings will be in encouraging employees to feel genuinely involved in organisational decision-making?

- **Quality circles**
  These were popular in the 1980s but have recently lost ground to **Total Quality Management (TQM)** approaches. In the UK, quality circles are typically made up of small groups of seven or eight people who voluntarily meet on a regular basis to investigate quality-related matters or other work-related arrangements using problem-solving techniques. Members tend to be from the same work area and do similar work.

  Quality circles have been particularly effective in Japanese industry and can be an effective means of creating group loyalty and raising productivity.

However, there have been reservations about their value in recent times. In many cases they have not worked because support has not been maintained from the top. For quality circles to be effective, the culture of an organisation has to be based on participation. (Further information on quality circles can be found in Chapter 45.)

- **Profit-sharing and employee share ownership**
Supporters argue that these help employees to link their interests to the success of the company and educate them in the need for efficiency and competitiveness. The employer sets aside a proportion of the profits to be shared between the employees according to an agreed formula. This can take into account basic pay and in some cases length of service. Alternatively, the bonus may be in the form of shares in the company which can be held or sold. There are tax advantages in this form of payment.

Critics of the schemes point out that there is little direct link between employees' efforts and the bonus payments or shares. The values of both are affected by factors outside the control of the employees – their own executives' decisions, the competition and the market for products and for shares. The schemes were designed in rising markets. Some critics warn that in falling markets employees could lose both their jobs and their savings.

- **Joint consultation**
Joint consultation is an indirect form of participation in which management representatives meet regularly with elected representatives of the employees to hear their views. A central problem is how this fits in with collective bargaining. Trade Unions sometimes see joint consultation as a method of undermining their function of representing the workers. It is usual therefore to exclude issues of pay, working hours and other substantive issues from the agendas of JCCs. This avoids friction with the unions but can result in a one-way flow of management information and in agendas being dominated by minor complaints.

IT'S A FACT

Cynics have dubbed Joint Consultative Committee agenda as 'the three T's': tea, toilets and trivia.

- **Worker directors and works councils** The concept here is that representation at Board level brings employees closer to strategic decision-making. In Europe, employees of firms with more than 1,000 workers can request the formation of a works council. However, the UK is exempt from this EU directive (1997).

The experience of two public sector organisations who have used worker directors suggest that the idea is not popular in this country for the following reasons.

- Worker directors have difficulty in handling the information provided. They are disadvantaged by not being present at prior discussions in management committees before the Board meeting, and lack the training and background to interpret the disclosed information;
- Management are often opposed to trade union representation at Board level;
- Trade unions have reservations. Some feel that it inhibits their freedom to act in the workers' interests;
- Workers in general are indifferent to the proposal.

How widespread are Human Resource Management approaches?

The answer to this question is not clear. Some people argue that HRM has been 'talked up'. During the first half of the 1990s many organisations publicly stressed their commitment to 'people', yet at the same time carried out delayering programmes in which large numbers of employees lost their jobs, particularly in middle management. It was also a time of increased job insecurity. Instead of being employed for life on a full-time contract, many people were switched to short-term and temporary contracts. Many people therefore became cynical about 'HRM', some even seeing it as a cost-cutting exercise.

Frequently, large, overstaffed 'command and control' organisations were restructured to create a much leaner organisation in which employees were empowered to make far more decisions for themselves, often working in teams. For those who were lucky enough to win a place in the team, there were obvious rewards: higher pay, higher status, more freedom to make decisions for themselves. For others it was a period of considerable uncertainty.

Some critics argue that the whole of the delayering process in this country was handled very badly indeed. Many employees felt that organisations no longer deserved their loyalty and that in future they were entitled to put their own interests first.

Building positive relationships

Recent commentators argue that, in order to succeed in the long term, organisations need to build on their people rather than use them. To achieve this, they need to find out what their employees' hopes and aspirations actually are and give them the means to realise them.

A key part of this process is regular **appraisal** and the sharing of information. It may also require that employees work in small, self-managed teams.

THE LOSS OF JOB SECURITY

Psychologists have argued that organisations have failed to understand their employees' basic need for security. Just as a child needs to feel secure in the family, the individual needs to feel secure in the organisation.

In an effort to become more responsive to customer needs, many organisations have moved from paternalism to 'survival of the fittest'. Almost overnight, job security has been replaced by the cut-and-thrust of the open market. To continue the family metaphor, this is the same as asking a five-year-old to take over the wheel of the family car at a busy junction. The 'adolescent phase' of development – i.e. the stage in which individuals are prepared to cope with change – has been completely by-passed.

For many, this rapid, forced change will scar rather than steel. The process of 'steeling' is the 'sadder-but-wiser' phenomenon, whereby people emerge from period of change with a deeper understanding of themselves and a more extensive range of strategies for coping with change in future. This is good, and should be an objective of any change initiative.

'Scarring' is when the experience is so severe that people are permanently damaged. Their self-esteem is harmed and they will avoid further change at almost any cost. The exploratory, creative behaviour which every organisation claims to seek is at best inhibited, and possibly eliminated.

There is evidence that for some people, change is so painful that their relationship with the organisation breaks down completely. The consequence is a shift to a more transactional relationship, in which loyalty and commitment are replaced by 'a fair day's work for a fair day's pay' and forms of avoidance behaviour such as sickness and absenteeism.

Measuring employee loyalty

A recent 'resilience audit' of a major UK company showed that while those with less than one year's service have an almost 70 per cent chance of 'being attached' to the organisation, those with between three and five years' service – most of the senior management team – have a zero probability of attachment. The company was in the process of losing its middle management. Some had asked to leave, while others had been asked to do so. The result would have been the loss of the skills and knowledge base of the organisation – a potentially terminal case of organisational amnesia.

1 Why do you think organisations have adopted an HRM approach in recent years?

2 Why have organisations adopted a 'downsizing' approach in recent years?

3 Are the two initiatives compatible?

4 How can organisations develop a better relationship with employees?

'Creative compartments'

HRM approaches have focused on the individual at a time when organisations are increasingly looking to build smaller 'working teams'. Often these are project teams that come together to work collaboratively on a specific assignment. Team members may be working in several teams at the same time.

Gerard Fairtlough, the chief executive of the Biotechnology company Celltech, has proposed a new way of working based on the biological cell. In his book *Creative Compartments: A Design for the Future* Fairtlough argues that organisations should organise themselves into **creative compartments** which can compete against each other. He argues that within ten years there will be very few construction or manufacturing activities that require more than a few hundred people.

Creative compartments should be made up of people who share certain skills, aims and concerns and who communicate effectively and non-hierarchically. These properties give creative compartments certain intrinsic qualities. For example, it is the creative compartments within organisations who set the prevailing standards of excellence. Fairtlought's Celltech succeeded in part because it facilitated easy communication between scientists and managers and between scientists of different disciplines. In the youthful field of biotechnology, old rules and hierarchies were invalid. The same is undoubtedly true for many other innovative companies.

Just as nature overproduces in order to guarantee survival, so a happily constituted creative compartment will generate a plethora of ideas – many more , in fact than can realistically be used.

New organisations which operate in this way provide considerable motivation for their members. They also provide a fertile ground for effective Human Resource Management initiatives. Indeed they are driven by the logic of an HRM approach. However, it is important to remember that these creative and innovative organisations represent only the leading edge of development. There still remain a large number of organisations which are very much tied in with the models of the past.

Hard and soft approaches to HRM

The reality is that different organisations employ HRM for different reasons. At a simple level it is possible to identify two main schools of thought:

1 The hard approach

This is concerned with treating people as a vital resource, but in a calculating, profits-driven way. Employees are encouraged to see their interests as being linked to those of the organisation. Recruitment is concerned with taking on those employees who best fit in with the styles and practices of the organisation, and are thus likely to be most productive. The reality that the organisation's needs take precedence over individual needs.

IT'S A FACT

Richard Branson bases his business practice on a number of key principles. Firstly, he favours small units of about 50 people because he believes that a unit ought to be just large enough for everyone to know each other. The centre of Branson's empire is a large house near Marble Arch with no more than twelve employees. There are separate headquarters for each of Branson's groups, a much more sociable arrangement than a great tower block. His organisation is frequently described as being the least hierarchical, the least élitist.

---

2 The soft approach

The soft approach is people-centred and recognises that people are different from all other resources. It recognises that people need to be nurtured, motivated and made to feel important.

A soft approach emphasises involving employees in the management of work – for example, by creating self-managing teams – and is concerned to build commitment to the organisation by informing employees about the organisation's purposes and values. In such an organisation, employees will ask 'How can we help?' Appraisal and other employee involvement schemes will lie at the heart of organisations that use the soft approach.

Critics of both the hard and soft approaches are cynical. They argue that HRM approaches are more often talked about than practised and that in many UK organisations today the emphasis is still on traditional personnel management. It is these aspects of personnel management that we will go on to look at in Chapter 66.

Chapter summary

- In recent years, many organisations have switched from traditional personnel management to Human Resource Management (HRM).
- A key reason for the switch has been the need for organisations to become more competitive. Today the key resource of most organisations is the 'intelligence' of its people rather than its physical plant and machinery.
- HRM manifests itself both through the strategy of the organisation and through operational details such as team working, appraisal procedures etc.
- HRM treats people as an asset rather than as a cost.
- Employee Involvement (EI) is part and parcel of the HRM approach. It involves a range of policies and practices to empower and involve employees in decision-making.

- Job enrichment, job enlargement, employee participation, and quality circles are some of the measures developed to involve and motivate employees.
- Some people argue that Human Resource Management has been 'talked up'. The reality is that many organisations exploit their workforce just as they exploit many other resources.
- A distinction is sometimes made between a 'hard' and a 'soft' approach to HRM. Soft approaches genuinely focus on the development of individuals within an organisation.
- HRM is perhaps most likely to succeed in small compartments of organisations or small organisations where it is possible to have a democratic form of organisation.

66 Employer/employee relations

Many organisations today are concerned with developing employee involvement in the workplace and in decision-making. This represents a considerable move from the 'them and us' approach to employer/employee relations which often existed in the past. Increasingly, employees are being seen as key stakeholders in the organisation. Businesses realise that the more employees are involved in decision-making, the more likely they are to identify with their workplace, and the more committed they will feel to organisational objectives.

In many ways this approach has been borrowed from successful Japanese corporations such as Komatsu, Nissan, Hitachi, Honda and Toyota. The adoption of Japanese practices has grown as major Japanese corporations such as Toyota and Nissan have sited their manufacturing plants in the UK.

Pascale and Athos in *The Art of Japanese Management* (1982) have shown that the work group is the central pillar of Japanese business:

> *'Owing to the central importance of group efforts in their thinking, the Japanese are extremely sensitive to and concerned about group interactions and relationships.'*

They go on to argue that the Japanese employee's view of the group can be likened to a marriage which is based on commitment, trust, sharing and loyalty. While power ultimately rests with management, the group leader must handle the interaction within the group carefully.

In this chapter we examine the development of employer/employee relations in the UK. In particular we focus on the role of trade unions and their declining relevance in the modern workplace.

The role of trade unions

There are two broadly opposing views on the role of trade unions: the **unitary** and the **pluralist**.

1 The unitary perspective

The unitary perspective is based on the belief that organisations should be based on a single dominant set of values. This leaves little room for trade unions which may oppose the dominant value system. The unitary view can be summarised as follows:

- To achieve success, members in an organisation must share common goals. Organisations measure their success by their achievements of these goals. Trade unions may weaken or subvert the organisation's unity of purpose. They are therefore a threat to the values of the organisation.

- There is one source of authority in an organisation: the appointed management hierarchy. Management should be the one focus of loyalty. Trade unions may undermine management authority and divide loyalties within the organisation.

- The development of factions in an organisation is bad. Employees should accept their place in the hierarchy, work to the best of their ability and support the appointed leader. Unions do not have the necessary expertise to be involved in management decisions.

- Conflict is disruptive and destructive and should be prevented.

2 The pluralist perspective

In contrast, the pluralist view recognises that there are a number of stakeholders in an organisation with different views and perspectives. These differences cannot be ignored. The successful organisation will recognise diversity and seek ways of managing this diversity in an effective and productive way.

The pluralist perspective can be summarised as follows:

- The individuals and sub-groups that make up organisations have related but different interests and expectations. For example, they might all want a prosperous organisation, but have different views on how that prosperity should be achieved and shared.

- Where there is diversity of interest, it is natural that there should be rival sources of leadership. The existence of informal leaders or trade union leaders is not subversive, it is normal.

- Rival interests cannot be ignored. They need to be acknowledged and negotiated into a working arrangement.

- Conflict is normal. It is therefore important to have channels and procedures for handling it constructively.

What is a trade union?

Trade unions are made up of groups of employees who have joined together to further their common interests. These employees may share a skill, a trade, an industry, an employer or an occupation. Trade unions are formed, financed and run by their members, and a number of unions have existed for over a century. As well as bargaining with employers, trade unions seek to:

- Obtain good levels of pay for members;
- Ensure adequate working conditions and opportunities, etc.
- Negotiate bonuses for achieving targets;
- Obtain job security for their members;
- Establish appropriate ways of handling grievances;
- Provide a safety net of benefits including pension support for their members.

Trade unions in a changing environment

Like other organisations in the business world, trade unions in the last decade of the twentieth century have had to adapt to a rapidly changing environment in order to survive. Some of the important changes in the external environment include:

1 The development of new jobs and skills requiring greater flexibility of working practices and attitudes;
2 The growing role of women in the workplace;
3 The growth of part-time jobs;
4 The hiving-off of non-core service functions and the contracting-out of work by large businesses to smaller organisations (the development of the 'flexible firm');
5 The growing affluence of many employees;
6 The growth of the service sector of the economy at the expense of manufacturing;
7 The development of new business practices related to Human Resource Management.

These changes and others have necessitated widespread changes in union practice. In the late 1970s there were 12 million trade union members; in the late 1990s there are nearer 8 million. With prodding from the Trades Union Council, unions have begun to develop new strategies for attracting members and updating their image.

Declining trade union 'density'

Trade union 'density' is a statistic which shows actual trade union membership as a percentage of potential union membership. Since 1979 this figure has declined from over 55 per cent to less than 40 per cent by 1995.

Rising employment in the 1990s was experienced mainly in the service industry, where unions tended to be weak. The recession in the early 1990s made it difficult for unions to win back members as the numbers of people in employment fell. When employment picked up again in 1996, people were reluctant to return to trade unions. Many of the larger unions have continued to lose members. As a result there have been a number of mergers, leading to the formation of some very large unions. For example, the GMB (General, Municipal, Boilermakers and Allied Trade Union) was created in the early 1980s, and a series of mergers between print unions led to the creation of the GPMU in 1991.

> ### IT'S A FACT
>
> Unions in traditional manufacturing industries such as the NUM (coalmining) and the ISTC (iron and steel-making) now have memberships of less than 50,000. The engineering union AEU lost 10 per cent of its members in 1991. Public service unions have also seen a decline in their numbers with cutbacks in the public sector.

Responding to a changing environment

Today the trade union movement is facing the challenge of a rapidly changing world of work. Many of the old jobs are disappearing, to be replaced by jobs requiring new skills and working practices. Increasingly, employers are seeking 'single-union deals' with only one union operating in an industrial unit. With the decline of manufacturing, the dominance of the blue-collar workers (i.e. manual operatives) has been whittled away and the influence of white-collar services (i.e. people who work with paper and pen) has grown. With women now making up 52 per cent of the total population, the percentage of male union members has consistently fallen. In 1980 the number of men in full-time and part-time employment exceeded the number of women by more than 45 per cent – 13.1 million against 9.4 million. By the late 1970s the balance between the sexes was almost equal. This trend is likely to continue.

A growth in skilled jobs has led to more people being considered in the A/B/C1 social groups. Higher incomes have enabled more people to buy their own houses and to purchase shares in publicly listed companies. All these factors have helped to change public attitudes to trade unions and have reduced the relative size and importance of the various trade union groups.

> ### SYNTHESIS
>
> *Why do you think that the adoption of new technologies might have led to a decline in unionisation?*

Throughout the 1960s and 1970s, the numbers of employees who were members of trade unions continued to grow. During the 1980s, however, when the adoption of new technology in industry greatly increased, this trend was reversed.

Unions have not been seen as natural players in some of the key growth industries and services. As a result a number of trade unions have become increasingly 'image-conscious' and have adopted modern marketing techniques such as advertising and market research in an attempt to update their public image. For example, the General, Municipal, Boilermakers and Allied Trade Union spent £35,000 on hiring the Jenkins Design Group, which

> ### SYNTHESIS
>
> *Why do you think that trade unions have sought to make their image more 'upbeat'? Do you think that this move is likely to be successful?*

has worked for WHSmith and Next, to help improve their image. A number of changes were made, including shortening the initials of the union to the 'GMB' and changing its motto from 'Unity is Strength' to the softer 'Working Together'. Other unions have followed the GMB's lead.

Union consolidation

Another way in which trade unions have responded to a changing environment is by **merger**. Most of the major trade unions have been involved in merger discussions during the late 1980s (e.g. the AEU with the EETPU, and NUPE with NALGO). At the root of the merger talks was the loss of members and the sharp reduction in union incomes, coupled with the growth of what many held to be anti-union legislation, all of which magnified the appeal of the economies of scale to be gained from merger.

The result of the mergers was to create at least five mega-unions with memberships of over 750,000. Large unions have more resources, enabling them to offer more benefits and services to their members.

Flexible working practices

Trade unions have also adapted to a rapidly changing economic environment by allowing and encouraging more flexible working practices. Today the UK has a far more flexible workforce than in the recent past. Decades of demarcation between skilled and unskilled workers have been swept away, and there is a growing tendency for production workers to carry out routine maintenance tasks which were previously the preserve of skilled craft workers.

The increasing use of new technologies also means that the demarcation lines between manual, technical and clerical workers are fast disappearing. More people work flexi-time and part-time, and companies are increasingly turning to contract or temporary staff rather than hiring full-time employees.

Single-union deals

A further important development in trade union practice has been the growth of **single-union deals** with companies. The UK has tended to have a more complicated union structure than some of its major competitors at plant level. It is not unknown for a UK car plant to have ten or more separate unions, each

---

CASE STUDY CASE STUDY CASE STUDY CASE STUDY CASE STUDY

THE CREATION OF EUROPE-WIDE UNIONS

In March 1997, a deal was struck between the biggest employees' organisations in Britain and Germany, bringing Pan-European trade unions a step nearer.

The British GMB general union and the German IG Chemie made an agreement that will give nearly two million workers in both countries dual membership.

Senior union leaders believe that the single European currency is inevitable, that wages and conditions will eventually be determined at single bargaining tables throughout the continent, and that the future for workers now lies in international organisations. The union deal was signed simultaneously in London by John Edmonds, leader of the GMB and in Hanover by Hubertus Schmodt, president of IG Chemie-Papier-Keramic. The agreement means that British workers employed in the process industry in Germany will have the protection of IG

Chemie, and vice-versa.

Mr Edmonds saw this as an important step towards a 'con-federal' relationship with German unions, with the doors open for the creation of a single group to represent employees throughout the sector in Europe. Mr Edmonds argued that unions had to respond to the Europeanisation of companies.

'The long-term intention is to develop collective bargaining at European level. This is just one stage in that direction.'

1 What arguments would you put forward in favour of unions developing a pan-European structure?

2 What would be the benefits and drawbacks of such a move?

3 How would employers and employees view such a development?

STUDY CASE STUDY CASE STUDY CASE STUDY CASE STUDY CASE STUDY

negotiating separately with management. This process can waste a lot of time and effort and lead to continual instability. Increasingly, unions are coming to recognise the advantages of having a single union operating within a plant and opting for single-union deals with management.

Trade unions have also been active in creating better opportunities for women at work.

Strategies for survival

A number of possible strategies have been put forward for helping trade unions to adapt to changing times.

1 **Work for a Labour government**
   During the Conservative period of office (1979–97) a number of laws were passed which commentators felt weakened the position of trade unions. In particular the 1982 Employment Act made unions liable for any action which was not in furtherance of an industrial dispute. This meant that a union could be liable to pay civil damages to an organisation which suffered as a result of a dispute to which they were not a party. A result of this was that courts started to grant **injunctions** restraining unions from taking action while judicial hearings of disputes were in progress. Judges were able to grant injunctions if they felt that businesses would suffer if the action went ahead.

   Following this, the 1990 Employment Act also made unions liable for damages to customers or suppliers as a result of action not in furtherance of an industrial dispute.

   In the run-up to the 1997 General Election, trade union leaders were careful to play down their role under a future Labour government in the hope that this would improve the Labour Party's electoral prospects. They certainly succeeded!

2 **Merge unions**
   Merger or absorption is often seen as a route to survival as well as to increased influence. For example, in July 1993 NALGO, NUPE and COHSE formed UNISON, a union of 1.5 million members.

3 **Recruit new members in the fastest-growing industries**
   Women workers (who now represent over one-third of all union members) are a popular target for many unions. The GMB for example has reserved 10 out of 40 places on its National Executive Committee for women.

4 **Improve services to members**
   In recent years blue-collar unions have set the pace in extending the benefits of union membership, offering advisory and financial services in insurance, savings and share ownership, as well as private health insurance.

5 **Change trade union purposes**
   There is debate among trade unions about their primary purpose. One view, put forward by the **new realists**, is that the primary purpose of trade unions is to further the needs and interests of their members in terms of pay and conditions and to get the best deal for them. This view is supported by unions made up largely of core workers whose jobs are guaranteed.

   An alternative view is put forward by the **new traditionalists**, which tend to represent the groupings of peripheral and part-time workers. These unions concentrate on wider social issues such as a community-based approach to women's issues, the needs of the disabled and other disadvantaged groups. The GMB talks about extending its membership to the new 'servant class', such as people on low incomes in low-status jobs.

6 **Develop firm links with the European Union**
   A number of trade unionists see EU membership as providing a real opportunity for developing the strength and influence of unions through the Social Charter and Resultant Social Chapter of the Maastricht Treaty. The current Labour government has already made rapid steps to bring the UK into line with other EU countries.

Developing working relationships

At the heart of the human resources debate in the UK is the extent to which employees should feel loyalty and commitment to the organisation. Other countries such as Japan and Sweden have developed models in which employees are encouraged to operate as part of a team and to work together with management to arrive at common solutions. The European Union through its Social Chapter has also sought ways of creating a shared-ownership, consensus approach to management-employee relations.

Over the years, the EU has moved increasingly towards creating a framework for joint decision-making. More recently, the 1980 **Vredeling Directive** aimed to introduce formal employee information and consultation procedures into organisations with more than 1,000 employees. The directive requires organisations to disclose to employee representatives a considerable amount of information concerning its activities, including the financial position of the company, expected production and sales targets, likely numbers of employees planned for in the near future and so on.

In 1985 the **VAl Duchesse Meetings** between employers and employee organisations agreed that information should be provided and consultation carried out in organisations that were employing new technologies. Many of these provisions came to be incorporated in the Social Charter, particularly in the following cases:

PROTESTS AT PLANNED RENAULT CLOSURE IN BELGIUM

In March 1997, Renault faced legal action and threats of stoppages across Europe as a result of its plans to close its Belgian car factory with the loss of 3,100 jobs.

As more than 4,000 workers protested in the streets of Brussels, the Belgian government said it was likely to take the French car-maker to court over its failure to consult workers about the closure.

Unions called for one-hour stoppages in Renault's French and Spanish plants to coincide with a day of action by Belgian workers, with Portuguese and Slovenia workers also being asked to join in.

The Belgian prime minister Jean-Luc Dehaene described Renault's decision as 'brutal and unacceptable' and backed calls for court action against the car-maker from Mr Karel Van Miert, the European competition commissioner.

Van Miert claimed that Renault had failed to respect two European Union directives.

A 1975 EU directive on collective redundancies, revised in 1992, states that employers planning cuts must consult workers 'in good time with a view to reaching an agreement'.

The 1994 EU works council directive reinforced the obligations for companies, such as Renault, which have set up worker consultation bodies.

Immediately, employees in Belgium took a number of industrial actions. In Brussels 3,500 workers from Vilvoorde and Renault showrooms marched past EU institutions calling for the plant to be saved. They were joined by workers from Forges de Clabecq, the bankrupt southern Belgian steelworks where 1,800 jobs may be lost. Staff blockaded the Vilvoorde factory to prevent shipment of almost 5,000 cars and threatened to hold 'hostage' some 2,000 partly finished models.

1 Describe how the Renault dispute went beyond international frontiers and industrial boundaries.

2 Why do you think that Renault might want to close its Belgian plant?

3 How does the case indicate that Renault must abide by EU requirements for relationships between employers and employees?

4 How could Renault have handled this case better?

- When technological changes are introduced which have major implications for working conditions and working practices;
- During restructuring operations in organisations or in the event of mergers having an impact on the employment of workers;
- During collective redundancy procedures;
- When trans-frontier workers in particular are affected by the employment policies pursued by the organisations where they are employed.

After considerable pressure from the UK government, the adoption of the 1989 version of the Social Charter allowed the process of **subsidiarity** to replace enforcement and obligations on these issues. This in effect meant that each member country was permitted to interpret the rulings in their own way. Inevitably this gave far more involvement to employees in countries like Germany, the Netherlands and France than in the UK.

However, the Labour government is likely to introduce measures which encourage greater employee participation, and at the time of writing (1997) it seems likely that we shall see the UK signing up to the Social Charter in due course.

Industrial relations

Industrial relations is concerned with communication between representatives of employers and employees.

Successful industrial relations involves striking a balance of interests. From the employer's point of view, it is important to retain the right to manage and to plan for the future so that the company can continue to be a success, to make profits for its shareholders and keep its employees motivated. From the employee's point of view, industrial relations is about securing the best possible living and working standards for employees.

Who is involved in industrial relations?

Industrial relations involves employer and employee representation. There are many different organisations representing employers and employees.

Employer's organisations

Like trade unions, the main function of employers' organisations is collective bargaining. Faced by large and powerful trade unions, small employers would be at a disadvantage if they had to stand alone. An employers' association may bargain on behalf of all firms in an industry. Other functions include:

● Pooling ideas and funds for industrial research;
● Collectively setting up training centres;
● Discussing common interests such as the threat of foreign competition;
● Providing a collective voice to raise industry-wide problems with government and other bodies.

In the UK, the mouthpiece for the business community is the **Confederation of British Industry (CBI)**. It exists primarily to voice the views of its members and ensure that government and society understand the needs of British business and the contribution it makes to the well-being of the nation.

Professional associations

Many employees, particularly better-paid white-collar workers, belong to a **professional association**. These organisations do many of the same things as trade unions but are not registered as trade unions. An example is the British Medical Association, which negotiates on behalf of doctors. Professional associations also try to establish standards for members and to insist on a high level of competence for membership.

Staff associations

Staff associations are very similar to trade unions. Cynics would argue that the term is simply a posh name for a trade union. Staff associations tend to exist in middle-class occupations such as teaching and insurance. Most insurance companies have a staff association. In a number of cases staff associations eventually form into trade unions – e.g. the National Union of Teachers (NUT).

Day-to-day industrial relations

Evidence from the UK suggests that employee relations increasingly involves new HRM approaches instigated by management, rather than old confrontational models. However, trade unions are still important in many industries and organisations.

On a day-to-day basis, the main industrial relations bargaining usually takes place between the personnel department and a **shop stewards' committee**. Normally these groups would meet regularly once a week and thrash out issues such as:

● Pay
● Bonuses
● The working environment
● Disputes
● Work schedules
● Grievances
● Health and safety at work
● Hours
● Production targets

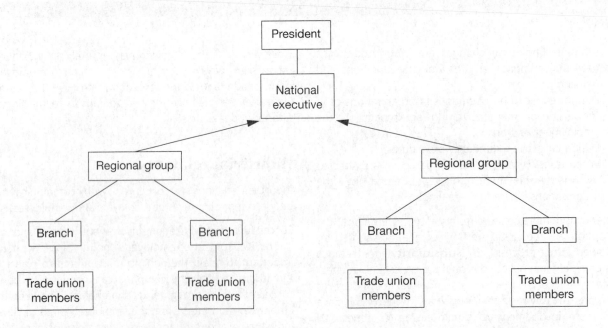

Figure 66.1: A typical union structure

Major industrial relations issues

In addition to local bargaining, which is concerned with small-scale industrial relations, larger issues may be thrashed out on an industry-wide scale. Wages for state employees, for example, are usually agreed at an **annual pay award**. The parties involved would normally be the central executive of a union and employers' leaders. However, in the 1990s we have increasingly seen the fragmentation of this process, so that negotiation is carried out at a local or unit level, e.g. between an individual hospital and its employees.

Trade union structure

Figure 66.1 opposite shows the structure of a typical trade union.

Groups of employees are members of a **union branch** and elect branch officials to represent them. The branches also choose members to represent them at a **regional committee**. Regional groups then choose representatives to go to an **annual conference**. The annual conference makes decisions relating to the industry and choose a full-time body of officials known as the **national executive**. The top official in the union is the **President**.

A good example of union industrial structure is the National Union of Mineworkers (NUM). The local branch is based on the colliery, the unit of operation in mining, and branch personnel deal with day-to-day problems, disputes, grievances and many minor issues that can arise. Shop stewards as such are not found in the mining industry.

The branch is based on the pit and includes in its membership all manual and craft grades. Branch officers undertake the duties allotted to shop stewards in other industries. (Factories in many trades are traditionally divided into 'shops', e.g. the cutting shop, the sewing shop, etc. Each shop chooses at least one **steward** to represent it in the workplace. The leading shop steward is called the **convenor**, and is responsible for calling together and organising meetings of stewards.) There is a single line of communication, from the branch up through the area coalfield office to the national centre, and similarly from centre to branch.

Unofficial trade union activity

While much trade union activity takes place on a day-to-day basis through the official union structure, it is important not to overlook *un*official union activity. This takes place when members carry out actions which are not approved by the union – for example when local stewards call out workers in a lightning strike. In fact, most industrial action in the UK is unofficial and short-lived. This was particularly true in the late 1970s in industries like car manufacture, in which shop stewards

had a great deal of local influence. Union funds cannot be used for unofficial action, because it is not officially approved. Unofficial action generally takes place when local union members feel that the national union is out of touch with grass-roots feeling, or if they want to take prompt action.

> ### IT'S A FACT
>
> During the mid-1990s the UK was noted for the lack of official and unofficial strike action by union members. Generally speaking, the UK has been a strike-free zone.

The Advisory, Conciliation and Arbitration Service (ACAS)

ACAS has been particularly successful in helping to create better industrial relations in the UK.

ACAS was set up by the government in 1974 in order to improve industrial relations. It is managed by a council of nine members: three chosen by the TUC, three by the CBI and three who are independent.

In an industrial dispute where there is deadlock, the parties may ask ACAS to help. Sometimes they may allow ACAS to look at the issue and come up with a solution that is 'binding'; at other times ACAS can simply be asked to make recommendations.

- **Conciliation** takes the form of attempts to persuade the parties to reach, by negotiation, a settlement of their dispute;
- **Arbitration** consists of an award made after the arbitrator has heard the cases of all parties involved in the dispute. In general, arbitration is more appropriate to disputes of rights (i.e. disputes over the interpretation of an existing agreement) than to disputes over new terms and conditions of employment. In the former case the arbitrator can simply clarify existing rules, but with disputes of interest, the two sides may be reluctant to entrust the proposal of new ideas or fundamental changes to an outsider.

The media and public tend to view ACAS as ambulance chasers and fire-fighters in situation of conflict. Although this sort of emergency work is an important part of the work of ACAS, it is only a small part of their overall workload. ACAS deals with over 20 new collective disputes a week.

The negotiation process

The first stage of union communication with management prior to industrial action should be through the negotiation process. Ramsumair Singh has illustrated the process of negotiation in diagrammatic form as shown in Figure 66.2 below.

Singh points out that in negotiations, management and unions tend to choose positions that favour their own interests. The starting point in a wage dispute would be the union's initial demand **(TID)** and the employer's initial offer **(EIO).** One party is unlikely to be able to persuade the other to accept its starting position; therefore there has to be a movement towards a central, compromise position. There is, however, a limit to this process, which can be called the **break-point** or **fall-back point**. Neither party is prepared to go beyond its own break-point.

In the illustration the employer's break-point **(EBP)** overlaps with the union's break point **(TBP).** There is therefore a **zone of agreement** in which a settlement can be made. The point at which the final settlement is made, **Point X**, depends on the bargaining strength and skill of the two parties.

The Trades Union Congress (TUC)

This is the annual meeting of the trade union movement. All the major trade unions are members of the TUC and send a number of delegates to the conference, depending on the size of their membership. The annual congress takes place in September every year, traditionally at seaside resorts like Scarborough and Blackpool.

The conference lasts for a week and during this time a number of motions are passed. It is a mistake to assume that the TUC is concerned simply with wages. The congress discusses matters as far-ranging as education, the health service, privatisation, AIDS and the environment.

The TUC appoints full-time officials including a president and vice-president, and has its own substantial headquarters in London. The TUC is an important organisation because it reflects the general feelings of the trade union movement. It is particularly active in the field of negotiation in industrial disputes. It offers advice and assistance to unions with problems and tries to iron out difficulties that arise between unions. It also acts as a pressure group, trying to influence government and employers on a range of issues.

Getting employees involved

At the start of this chapter we emphasised the importance of Employee Involvement, i.e. getting employees involved in workplace decisions so that they feel an increased ownership of these decisions. While many organisations would see this as a desirable goal, there is considerable evidence that UK businesses still have a long way to go in this direction.

For example, a survey carried out by the Institute of Management in March 1997 reported that of the 1,800 people they had surveyed, only 15% said that their firms encouraged staff participation, while one in three complained that their organisations were too bureaucratic!

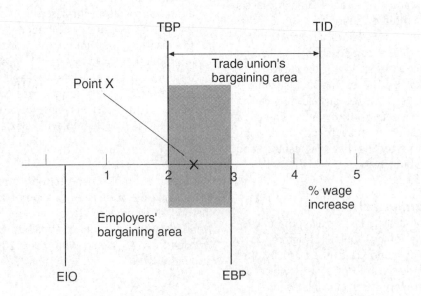

Figure 66.2: The negotiation process

Chapter summary

- Today many organisations have sought to increase employee involvement in decision-making processes. This involves breaking away from 'them and us' approaches. In particular UK businesses have learnt from Japanese approaches to teamworking.

- There are two broad perspectives on the role of trade unions.

  - The **unitary** view is based on the belief that the organisation should have a dominant set of values and that factions who do not share this should be excluded.

  - The **pluralist** view regards conflict as normal and favours a diversity of views including those of employees and their representatives.

- A trade union is made of groups of employees who have joined together in an organisation which seeks to further their common interests.

- Today's unions operate in a rapidly changing environment which has forced them to adapt in order to survive.

- Since the 1970s the number of trade union members has fallen considerably. Patterns of union membership have also changed, with for example a significant increase in the number of female union members.

- In recent times a number of unions have changed the way they operate, e.g. by supporting moves to single union deals, multi-skilling arrangements and increased flexibility.

- Unions are beginning to amalgamate into larger pan-European groupings.

- The Social Chapter of the European Union's Maastricht Treaty set up a number of arrangements for increased employee involvement in decision-making in organisations.

- Industrial relations are the communications between employer and employee representatives.

- In addition to trade unions, employees may also be represented by professional associations and staff associations. Groups of employers form themselves into employers' organisations such as the CBI.

- Major industrial relations issues tend to be negotiated by national bodies, e.g. the national executive of a union meeting with employers' leaders. Local issues can be resolved at local level.

- ACAS plays an important role in trying to smooth the path of industrial relations and to take the sting out of disputes.

- The Trades Union Congress (TUC) is the representative body of all trade unions in this country.

67 The labour market

Like any other market, the labour market involves buyers and sellers. In this case the buyers are employers and the sellers are those people who are prepared to sell their labour services.

Although we talk about the labour market as a generality it is really split up into several sub-markets. For example, there is a market for skilled labour, for semi-skilled labour and for unskilled labour. There is a market for computer programmers, another for food technologists and another for teachers. If we examine the market for teachers in greater depth we will find that there is a market for head teachers, another for middle managers and another for new teachers. Then of course there are science teachers, maths teachers, teachers of business; permanent teachers, temporary teachers and supply teachers. However, for all these markets there is a general set of principles that apply. This is that *the higher the level of demand relative to supply, then the higher the price of labour, i.e. wages, will be.*

Labour supply and demand

We can illustrate some of the changes that might occur in the labour market by a series of illustrations.

In Figure 67.1 below, the demand for teachers has increased because of a rise in the number of children at school (i.e. demand has moved from **DD** to **D₁D₁**). As a result, the wages of teachers increase.

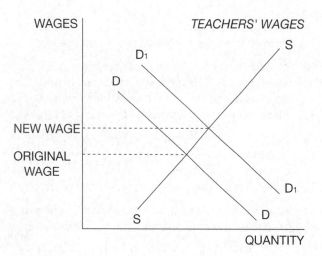

Figure 67.1

In Figure 67.2, the supply of science teachers falls because there is full employment in the economy and scientists are attracted to higher-paid jobs in private industry. As a result the price of science teachers increases.

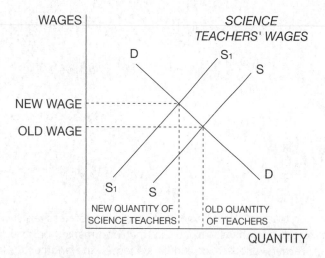

Figure 67.2

In Figure 67.3 the demand for Latin teachers falls because it has become a minority subject in the curriculum. The wages of Latin teachers fall.

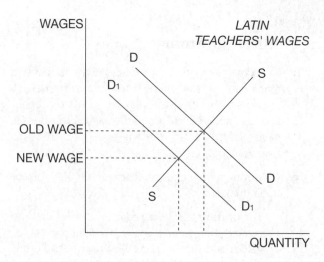

Figure 67.3

In Figure 67.4 the supply of business teachers rises because there is an increasing number of business teachers being trained as more and more people have Business Studies degrees. The price of business teachers therefore falls.

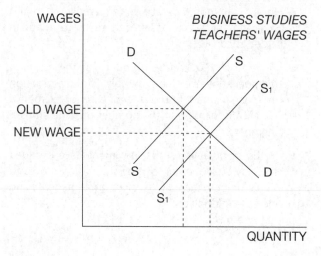

Figure 67.4

IT'S A FACT

The importance of labour market flexibility has been recognised by governments for some time. A 1985 White Paper, *Employment: The Challenge for the Nation*, included references to flexible hours, job-sharing, home-working and self-employment.

Mobility in the labour market

It is very important to have **mobility** in a labour market. This is because the supply of labour needs to respond quickly to changes in demand. This means that:

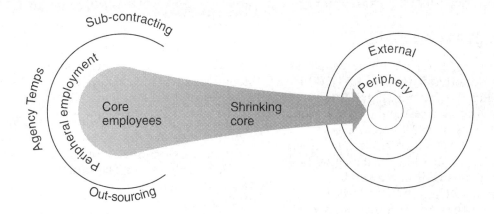

Fig 67.5: The shrinking core

- If demand for labour increases then supply will quickly follow:
- If demand for labour falls, supply will be reduced.

Similarly, if the demand for labour falls, wages will fall, and if demand rises, wages will rise in line with the new conditions.

Unfortunately in the real world, mobility of labour is limited. Often, when demand for a particular type of labour increases, supply is slow in responding. This may be because of the length of time and scale of resources required to train employees to develop the new skills.

Another restriction to mobility is the fact that often employees are resistant to wage decreases when the demand for their particular type of labour goes into decline. This often leads to rising unemployment as labour prices itself out of a job.

The classical and neo-classical economists see lack of mobility in the labour market as a major cause of business inefficiency. They argue, for instance, that the chronic unemployment of the 1920s and 30s was caused by trade unions preventing wages from falling when the demand for the products of certain industries went into decline.

Between 1979 and 1997, the Conservative government set out to address this problem by creating 'flexible' labour markets, i.e. markets which enabled the smooth operation of the forces of demand and supply.

Changes in working conditions

The working world today is dramatically different from the 1960s and 1970s when job security was taken for granted. Let us look at some of the changes which have taken place and the more important reasons behind them.

In 1984, Charles Handy warned in *The Future Of Work* that the old patterns of work were breaking down and

that 'the new patterns are on their way, whether we welcome them or not.' Handy claimed that in the future there were simply not going to be enough jobs to go round, and that this would be true whatever government was in power over the next twenty years. What was needed was a new notion of work, to be adopted not only by those seeking employment, but also by those currently employed. If there were not going to be enough full-time jobs to go round, the alternative was to give everyone a job for part of their lives, or a 'part-job' for most of their lives.

> **IT'S A FACT**
>
> Large supermarket chains commonly vary the number of hours they allocate to employees each week, depending on the profit figures recorded in the previous week.

New patterns of working

The principle of **work-sharing** is increasingly put forward as a possible solution to the problem identified by Handy and others. But the extent to which this is feasible depends not only on the nature of the job (not all jobs are suitable for job-sharing), but also on the willingness of those involved to accept lower incomes.

A shorter working week and a reduction in overtime work might be one way of reducing the supply of labour – but it is unlikely to increase the number of full-time jobs.

Early retirement has become increasingly common in recent years. But the reality is that many employers offer employees early retirement in order to slim down their labour force, cut costs and increase productivity, without taking on new staff to replace them.

DOWNSIZING AT SHELL

At the beginning of April 1995, Royal Dutch Shell announced that it was to cut 1,200 jobs at its headquarters in London and The Hague as part of a dramatic reshaping of the group. Instead of having over 100 regional organisations – Shell UK, Shell Ireland, Shell Denmark, etc. – it would now have five large business units answering to a small corporate centre. The key to the process was to cut back on the large administrative core and to create self-managing businesses.

Simplified structure

Cor Herkstroter, the group's Chair, argued that Shell's structure must become simpler, less costly and more responsive to customers. The business environment in the late 1990s is characterised by low oil prices with flat profit margins. The market is highly competitive with major firms striving for higher productivity, innovation, quality and effectiveness.

The redundancies were programmed for the second half of 1995, taking out 1,200 of the 4,000 jobs at the company's head office.

At one time Shell employees would have expected a job for life. Today this is a thing of the past. In 1990 Shell employed 135,000 people worldwide; in 1995 they employed 106,000. Today the number is below 100,000.

What is happening at Shell is mirrored in many other large organisations today. Jobs are being shaken out in a relentless drive for efficiency and competitive advantage.

1 What do you understand by the terms 'downsizing' and 'flexibility'?

2 Why do you think that organisations like Shell have been cutting their numbers in the way indicated?

3 What do you see as being the major benefits and the major drawbacks of downsizing?

Flexible working

One of the major changes in working conditions in recent times has been the growth of **flexible working**.

There are a number of definitions of flexibility. **Numerical flexibility** refers to the ability of firms to adjust the number of workers or the number of hours worked in line with changes in the level of demand for their goods and services. Typically this refers to the use of part-time, temporary and sub-contracted workers.

Temporal or **working-time flexibility** can be seen as a particular form of numerical flexibility, relating to changes in the number and timing of hours worked from day to day or week to week, for example, through flexitime or annual hours contracts.

The use of more temporary and contract workers and other methods of flexible working will permanently change the UK's employment patterns. These changes are due to the need for increased productivity, flexibility and cost control.

In the first half of the 1990s the vast majority of the UK's largest organisations were restructured, leading to job losses at all levels.

The flexible firm

A business concept that has been growing in importance has been that of the **flexible firm**.

In the past many large organisations had a large core of full-time workers who expected a job for life. Throughout the country, school-leavers would join firms such as Boots or Raleigh and remain with them for the rest of their working life. It was common for whole families to work for the same employer.

Today, the pool of **core workers** in organisations has been severely slimmed down. Instead:

- Core workers tend to be multi-skilled, full-time, enjoying good pay conditions and benefits;
- Peripheral workers are short-term, temporary, part-time and receive less favourable pay, conditions and benefits;
- External workers are not employees of the firm at all but are agency temps, workers in contracted-out services and self-employed suppliers.

The flexible firm sets out to cut its labour costs to a minimum by limiting the number of core workers relative to peripheral and external workers.

	Total	Men	Women
Total in employment	25,381	13,934	11,446
Full-time permanent employees	15,685	10,204	5,480
As percentage of total in employment	61.8	73.2	47.9
All other workers	9,693	3,729	5,964
As percentage of total in employment	38.2	26.8	52.1

Figure 67.6: UK employment 1993/4 (000s and %)

TASK 67.1

Can you identify the core, peripheral and external workers in an organisation that you are familiar with?

Figure 67.6 sets out in a fairly dramatic way the impact of the flexible workforce on today's labour market. The figures show that, of the 25 million-plus workers in employment today, 38.2% are not in full-time employment. Both men and women contribute significantly to the flexible workforce.

Clearly, firms find it increasingly convenient to take on flexible workers.

> ## SYNTHESIS
>
> *What in your view are the most important trends outlined above? What do you see as being the major causes of these changes? Are the changes beneficial for (a) organisations and (b) individuals?*

Types of employment

A range of different types of employment and conditions exist in organisations today, including:

- Self-employed
- Skilled/unskilled
- Home-working
- Contract/non-contract
- Permanent/temporary
- Full-time/part-time
- Permanent
- Full-time/temporary

Self-employment

Self-employment grew significantly in the 1980s and an upward trend has now reappeared following a fall during the recession in the early 1990s. At the end of 1994, 13% of those in employment were self-employed compared with 11% in 1983.

The term **self-employment** simply indicates that an individual works for himself or herself rather than for a larger organisation. The classic example of the self-employed person is the window-cleaner, plumber or cornershop-owner.

Nowadays there are also many self-employed people in dynamic sectors of the economy, such as IT specialists (e.g. providing desktop publishing services), business consultants and designers.

Full-time

In 1850 the normal working week in the UK was 60 hours spread over 6 days at 10 hours each. By the 1960s this had been reduced to 40 hours spread over 5 days. Today the average full-time working week is between 35 and 40 hours, still spread over 5 days.

It is difficult to give a hard-and-fast definition of **full-time** work. A dictionary defines it as work carried on 'for the entire time appropriate to an activity'.

For example, a full-time teacher would work to the full contractual time established by the school – e.g. from 8.30 am until 4.00 pm each day for 180 days a year. A full-time lecturer in a college might work a set number of contractual hours, e.g. 800 hours of contact and preparation time a year.

In its statistical work the *Labour Force Quarterly Survey* accepts respondents' definitions of whether they are full-time or part-time. It is interesting to note that the number of hours worked has risen in recent years.

> ## SYNTHESIS
>
> *Recently European Union regulations have set out that part-time employees have entitlements to pensions, redundancy pay and other employment rights.*

SOCIAL TRENDS SURVEY – JANUARY 1997

The survey *Social Trends* provides us with an interesting picture of changes which have recently taken place in the labour market.

The survey indicates that by the year 2006 women are expected to account for 46% of the workforce. Over the 10 years from 1995, economic activity rates are expected to fall by 2% for men but rise by 3% for women. The biggest losers are likely to be men aged between 55 and 59; those who gain the most will be women between 25 and 34. More than 3 in 10 of these older men are likely to be economically inactive by 2006 against just over a quarter in 1995. The economic activity rate for the younger women is expected to rise by 10 percentage points to 81%.

Of the 1.4m extra people expected in the labour force by 2006, it is projected that 1m will be women, although the number of full-time jobs is not expected to change much.

Instead, existing trends for more part-time and self-employed workers are likely to be reinforced. The number of part-time workers is set to rise by a tenth; those in self-employment by almost a quarter.

The research also indicates that the labour market may not be as flexible as we are often led to believe. It would appear that the length of job tenure and turnover among full-time employees has 'changed very little over the past 10 years; falling for men from 9.4 to 8.9 years but increasing for women from 6.5 to 7.1 years.

The proportion of workers in 'temporary' jobs in 1995 was 7% or about 1.5m (6% for males and 8% for females). Within the European Union only Austria and Belgium have a lower number in temporary employment. About 40% of UK temporary workers said that they had a temporary job because they could not find a permanent one.

A quarter of workers were in part-time jobs in 1996, only 8% of men and 45% of women. The number of women in part-time work rose by 18% between 1986 and 1996 to 5.3m and the number of men doubled to 1.2m.

Full-time employees are working longer hours than 10 years ago. In March 1996 the average number of hours worked a week by men was 45.8 hours compared with 44.5 hours in April 1978. The increase for full-time women was from 37.5 hours to 40.6 hours. The longest hours worked last year were by full-time managers and administrators (48.4 hours). British employees work more hours than any other in the European Union.

Part-time employment

Part-time employees are those who do *not* 'work for the entire time appropriate to an activity'.

Traditionally, people performing jobs which do not require more than a few hours a day to complete, such as school cleaner or dinner supervisor, have been employed on part-time contracts. The number of part-time employees has increased dramatically in recent years and is directly linked to the rise in the proportion of women in the labour force.

The *Labour Force Survey* for autumn 1994 revealed that, on average, part-time employees worked 15.4 hours a week.

In 1994, 24% of those employed had part-time jobs, compared with 20% in 1983.

TASK 67.2

The following figures relate to changes in the numbers of part-time and full-time employees, 1981–2001. The figure for 2001 is based on a projection.

Year	Numbers working part-time (millions)	Numbers working full-time (millions)
1981	4.5	18.0
1991	6.0	16.5
2001	7.0	15.0

Use a computer graphics plotting package to set out these results in the form of a bar chart. Work out the percentage of employees working part-time and full-time and set this out in a pie chart. What do the figures show?

EXTENSION MATERIAL

The minimum wage

An important source of debate in recent times has been over the **minimum wage**. Some argue that by guaranteeing everyone a minimum wage it is possible to protect them from unscrupulous employers. There has also been much discussion about how much the minimum wage should be – for example, £4 an hour?

Critics of the minimum wage say that it will lead to unemployment, whereas supporters claim there is no evidence for this.

We can illustrate the case against the minimum wage by using demand and supply diagrams.

In Figure 67.8 the market wage is shown where demand cuts supply – say, at £3.50 per hour. At this wage everyone who wants to work for £3.50 is able to get a job.

However, when the wage is put up to £4.00 per hour (a minimum wage) some people can no longer get jobs because there is no demand for their services from employers.

OZ people want to work at £4.00 per hour. However, employers are only prepared to employ OX people. This means that ZX people are frustrated.

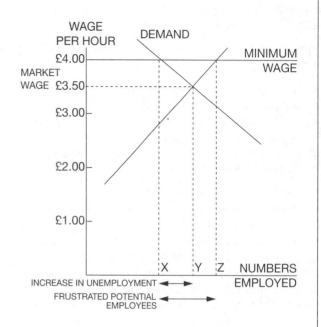

Figure 67.8 Effects of the minimum wage

Also it is clear that fewer people are employed at £4.00 than at £3.50. Therefore XY people lose their jobs.

Advantages of part-time working

The reasons why employees may choose to work part-time are:

- They have greater flexibility in working hours;
- They can use part-time employment as a supplement to other income, e.g. their student grant;
- It enables them to enjoy more leisure time;
- They can use it as a 'hobby' job, rather than doing nothing during the day;
- Full-time work is not available.

The reasons why employers may want part-time employees are as follows:

- Part-time workers offer greater flexibility. It is easier to recruit part-time staff to work evenings and weekends, for example. This is particularly useful in retailing;
- Part-time employees are generally lower paid;
- Part-time employees do not have the same legal rights as full-time employees, although EU legislation has somewhat reduced this imbalance.

Permanent employment

Permanent employees are those who have a contractual commitment from their employees to continue employment, irrespective of whether they work full-time or part-time. A simpler definition is that employees have an **open-ended** rather than a **fixed-term** contract. This can be ended only when either party gives **notice of termination**. The period of notice will depend on the employee's length of service and will be specified in the contract of employment.

IT'S A FACT

Professional footballers usually work to fixed-term contracts.

Temporary employment

Temporary employees have a work contract for a limited time period only. They can be employed on a full-time or part-time basis. Many factories, for example, take on temporary packers before Christmas to cope with increased orders.

When employees have worked for an organisation for a given period of time, often three years, they may legally come to be regarded as full-time employees. Organisations often get round this by employing staff for less than three years and then replacing them with another employee.

Reasons why organisations employ temporary staff include:

● To cover staff sickness or holidays;
● To assist with exceptionally large orders;
● To cope with seasonal changes in demand, e.g. in the hotel and tourism industry;
● To work on special projects for a limited timespan;
● To clear backlogs of work.

Contracted and non-contracted employees

Today short-term contracts are becoming more and more common. In times of economic uncertainty, employers find greater flexibility in giving short-term contracts for one or two years to new employees, e.g. in teaching or lecturing. This gives them the option to renew or not to renew at the end of the period. Computer programming is another example of an area where short-term contracts are commonplace.

The term **contracted worker** refers either to a fixed-term contract worker, employed for a specific period of time, or to a **subcontractor**. A subcontractor is hired to do work that someone else has been contracted to do. Subcontractors are very common in the construction industry where builders will contract other companies or individuals to do electrical, plumbing and other work.

A fixed-term contract could be one-off or renewed on a periodic basis. Many of the catering staff in schools are on fixed-term contracts which are reviewed annually.

Skilled/unskilled employment

A skilled job is one which requires special ability or special training. It is no longer enough to think simply of the specific skills needed for specific jobs. Change within jobs, and demands for greater flexibility between jobs, mean that employees need broad vocational skills which can provide a foundation for other, more specific skills to be acquired at a later date. Increasingly workers need to be **multi-skilled**.

Skills can be acquired through practice, experience and by detailed study and training. Employees who are properly prepared for skilled jobs are likely to be the most effective.

Some people have more natural aptitude for particular skilled occupations than others. However, it is unlikely that someone could become skilled without training or practice. The New Zealander Zinzan Brooke is one of the most skilled rugby forwards that we are ever likely to see,

Zinzan Brooke

Steffi Graf

and the German Steffi Graf is a world-class tennis player. However both got where they are today through many hours of practice as well as natural aptitude.

Home-working

Home-working is simply work that is done at home for pay. This type of work was common in the days of cottage industries prior to the Industrial Revolution, and in recent times has again become popular. For example, many sales representatives and professionals (accountants, consultants) are based at home. This is possible because of improved communications and technology. Some business organisations encourage home-working to reduce overheads and there is the additional benefit to many people of reducing the stress of commuting.

The drive to flexibility

If UK organisations are to develop a competitive edge, the UK labour market must be based on mobility. There is a saying that productivity leads to performance which leads to profits. But the reverse is also true. Poor productivity leads to poor performance and to losses. On a national scale this leads to decline and rising unemployment.

Today labour is far more mobile in modern Britain than it was in the past. There are two main types of labour mobility: geographical mobility and occupational mobility.

Geographical mobility

Geographical mobility occurs when employees are prepared to move around the country or within a region in search of jobs. If people are not prepared to move, this accentuates the depressed conditions that exist in a particular area.

Norman Tebbit (then a government minister in the Thatcher era) achieved notoriety by suggesting that people should 'get on their bikes' to where jobs were available. This is not as easy as it sounds. Many people have strong social bonds with a particular area: they may have an aged grandparent living in an old people's home there; their children may be attending local schools, or they may simply feel a strong historical and emotional attachment to a particular area and its people.

The Conservatives throughout their term of office progressively reduced the state benefits that enabled unemployed people to stay put. However, changing patterns of employment in recent years mean that people are often reluctant to uproot themselves in search of work, particularly when there is no certainty that conditions will be any better elsewhere.

Occupational mobility

Occupational mobility involves changing from one job to another. Increasingly, individuals need to become more flexible in their skills in order to be able to adjust to new job requirements. Individuals may retrain to take on new jobs and responsibilities with an existing employer or with a new employer.

The benefits of flexible labour

Although the decline in job security places added pressure on employees, flexible labour markets in the UK seem to be delivering a number of benefits:

- There was less productivity decline in the recession in the early 1990s;
- There was a more rapid decline in unemployment after the recession;
- Flexibility allowed employees to combine employment with other responsibilities.

A past feature of the British industrial scene was **demarcation disputes**. These were arguments over who should do what. The trade union movement insisted that only members of a relevant union could be asked to do particular tasks (e.g. mend a broken machine). This led to a great waste of time and other resources.

Multiskilling involves training employees to do a range of tasks in the workplace, so that for example a machine operative can be trained in the art of performing routine maintenance work and in doing straightforward repairs. This can be a great motivator because it increases job variety and provides opportunities for higher pay. It means that a plant can be continuously productive, more competitive, and therefore better able to provide good wages and conditions for those who work there.

Chapter summary

- The labour market is the market for the buying and selling of labour by employers and employees.
- Wages are determined by the interaction of demand and supply.
- Flexible labour markets encourage the smooth exchange of labour in the marketplace.
- Working conditions in the late twentieth century have changed dramatically. There are far fewer full-time jobs available and more part-time and other types of jobs.
- Many organisations have been downsizing in an attempt to become more flexible and competitive.
- The flexible firm is one in which the core has been shrinking, and there has been a growth in peripheral and external employment.
- Today there are as many males as females in employment, but females tend to dominate the part-time sector.
- By the year 2006 women are expected to account for 46% of the workforce. Opportunities for women in the 25–34 age bracket have been improving, while for men in the 55–59 age bracket they have been deteriorating.
- There are a variety of different types of employment today, ranging from full-time to temporary work, from skilled to unskilled. There is also a growing emphasis on home-working, facilitated by the development of Information Technology and telecommunications.
- The introduction of a minimum wage may distort the free working of the labour market and possibly increase the level of unemployment.

68 Remuneration and benefits

The principal means of 'compensating' or 'rewarding' employees for work done is through **pay**. There are many different types of jobs, and there are many reasons why people receive different levels of payment. In this chapter we look at a variety of different approaches to remuneration and benefits.

Organisations are continually seeking better ways of increasing the 'value added' by employees. A key way of doing this is to encourage employees to increase their effort and performance in order to raise productivity. Designing effective reward systems is therefore an important way to add value to production.

Designing a payment system

In creating a payment system it is essential to ensure that it is not only fair, but is seen to be fair. There are two key sets of criteria which managers and employees can use to check whether a payment system is fair. These are:

1 **Internal criteria** These involve measuring rewards to employees against the amount of effort, qualifications, skills and aptitudes that they put into their work. In simple terms it can be argued that managers and employees make a 'wage-for-effort bargain'. Clearly it is unfair for employees to receive rewards which are not in proportion to their qualifications, skills and efforts. For example, until relatively recently it could have been argued that large numbers of women and ethnic minority workers did not receive 'fair' pay.
2 **External criteria** This involves assessing pay by making comparisons with the incomes of other individuals or groups – e.g. by comparing the wages of a similar employees in other plants or firms, or even in different but comparable industries.

   If these criteria were applied in an honest way then it would be possible to carry out **job evaluation** schemes to calculate the rewards that employees should receive for carrying out particular jobs. In other words, job evaluation would be based on a wage-for-effort bargain, and by making comparisons with other employees' wage-for-effort bargains.

It is essential that employees feel that they are receiving a fair day's reward for a fair day's work. If they feel that they are being underpaid they are likely to reduce their efforts, seek employment elsewhere or fail to co-operate in order to meet organisational objectives.

It is also essential that managers establish equitable remuneration packages if they are going to be able to attract and retain the right sort of employees, and not lose them to competitors.

Objectives of payment systems

In his book *Human Resource Management: A Contemporary Perspective* (1995), Ian Beardwell suggests that in any payment system there will always be a tension between simplicity and rigidity, complexity and flexibility. He states that:

> 'There is an inherent tension between designing a differentiated payment system which reflects diversity in needs, motivation, expectations and performance of individuals and encourages career advancements, and the objective of maintaining simplicity, predictability, and control through a standardised system.'

It will therefore always be difficult for managers to get the balance right, particularly in large organisations in which many different jobs are carried out.

Wages and salaries

Many organisations draw a distinction between those employees who are paid in the form of **wages** and those who receive a **salary**. There are a number of differences between the two:

1 Wages are normally expressed as an hourly rate, whereas salaries are expressed as an annual figure;
2 Wages are normally paid a week in arrears (i.e. the wage you earn at the end of the week is for that week's work), whereas salaries are paid at the end of the month;
3 Salaries are normally paid on the basis of an annual rate divided by 12; a salary is thus expressed in terms of an annual figure. Wages are calculated in several different ways including **piece-rates** and **time-rates** (see below).
4 In many organisations benefits packages are different for salaried and waged employees;
5 Salaries are typically paid automatically into an employee's bank account by credit transfer; wages are paid either in cash or by credit transfer.

Harmonisation

In recent times there have been moves towards creating what is called **harmonisation** of working conditions and payment schemes in many UK companies. However, this can mean different things in different organisations. Depending on the context, the term can be used to describe:

● The gradual breakdown and elimination of differences between blue-collar and white-collar employees (e.g. by having one canteen for all staff, all employees clocking in at the same time, standardising holiday arrangements and sick pay etc.);

- Working towards single status, i.e. treating all employees alike in every respect except pay;
- Enhancing staff status by placing employees who previously had non-staff status on staff grades.

Harmonisation has become possible because 'blue-collar' workers are increasingly using skills and technology which previously were the preserve of white-collar workers. Harmonisation is also felt to enhance employee motivation by giving employees a feeling of worth and value. It encourages flexibility if employees are to be expected to carry out a range of tasks and activities in a multi-skilling framework.

IT'S A FACT

A number of UK companies have followed the Japanese example of requiring managers and employees to wear a company uniform in order to get away from the traditional 'them and us' approach. In some companies employees and managers exercise together before the start of the day. However, the idea of singing a company song has never really caught on in the UK!

Fees

Fees are an alternative system of payment to wages and salaries. In the UK today they are becoming increasingly common as employees are hired indirectly to carry out service contracts for businesses.

The fee is payment for work done, but the employee is not taken directly on to the firm's payroll. A fee may be paid for a short-term contract (e.g. to a photographer making a film about a company) or on a longer-term basis – for example, a financial consultant may receive regular fee payments over a period of time. Fees may be paid on the basis of time worked, quantity of output, completion of a particular contract or on some other basis.

Objectives of systems of payment

Payment systems are usually arrived at through a process of collective bargaining between unions and management. In setting out the objectives of such a system, we therefore need to explore the aims and purposes of both sides.

Management's objectives

From the management point of view, a payment system should:

1 Be effective in recruiting the right quantity and quality of labour;
2 Be effective in retaining labour over the required period of time – it is expensive to have to keep advertising for and training new employees;

3 Keep unit labour costs as low as possible. The unit labour cost is the proportion of output cost that can be attributed to labour. Reducing labour costs is one of the key factors in maintaining competitiveness in local, national and international markets;
4 Help to motivate staff and encourage effort. Careful thought needs to be applied to structuring pay systems in a way that encourages motivation and performance;
5 Be aimed at maximising output per unit of factor of production employed – i.e. maximising productivity;
6 Be designed in such a way as to effectively incorporate fringe benefits.

Trade union's objectives

From the union point of view, the payment system should:

1 Maximise the growth of members' real earnings;
2 Be consistent with working practices that best suit trade union members' needs, taking into account issues such as fatigue, boredom, safety etc.;
3 Balance monetary rewards with issues such as hours worked, breaks and holidays;
4 Offer the best long-term benefits for trade union members, consistent with maintaining the company's competitiveness;
5 Avoid being linked to unattainable performance targets.

Clearly, different groups within an organisation will have different perceptions of what makes an effective system of payment. What works in one company or for one type of production may be inappropriate in another. What is needed is a system that creates the 'best fit' given the type of company, employee, technology, production methods, state of the market etc.

Calculating pay

The amount paid for a normal working week is referred to as a **basic** wage or salary. Many employees receive other benefits in addition to their basic wage, either in a money or non-money form. The main ways of calculating pay are outlined below. Sometimes elements of these methods are combined.

Flat rate

This is a set rate of weekly or monthly pay, based on a set number of hours. It is easy to calculate and administer but does not provide an incentive to employees to work harder.

Time rate

Under this scheme, workers receive a set rate per hour. Any hours worked above a set number are paid at an 'overtime' rate.

Piece-rate

This system is sometimes used in the textile and electronics industries, among others. Payment is made for each item produced that meets given quality standards. The advantage of this is that it encourages effort. However, it is not suitable for jobs that require time and care. Also, many jobs particularly in the service sector produce 'outputs' that are impossible to measure.

Bonus

A bonus is paid as an added encouragement to employees. It can be paid out of additional profits earned by the employer as a result of the employee's effort and hard work, or as an incentive to workers at times when they might be inclined to slacken effort, e.g. at Christmas and summer holiday times.

Commission

This is a payment made as a percentage of the sales a salesperson has made.

Output-related payment schemes

Output-related schemes are the most common method used to reward manual workers. Most schemes involve an element of time-rates plus a bonus or other incentive.

Standards are set in many ways, varying from casual assessment to detailed **work study** based on method study and work measurement.

- **Method study** sets out to determine what is the most effective way of carrying out particular tasks.

- **Work measurement** takes place in three stages:

1 The time taken to perform a task is measured;
2 The effort of an individual worker or work-group is rated;
3 The work carried out is assessed and compared with the standard rate.

A standard allowable time or price is set according to the first two stages. The worker's pay is then determined according to success at the third stage.

Variations in output-related schemes

There are many different types of output-related schemes, for example based on individual or group performance, or time period covered (day/week/month etc.). There are also schemes relating earnings to changes in performance as shown in Figure 68.1.

The type of scheme used depends on whether it is intended to encourage workers to meet a set standard, to encourage learners, or even to prevent too high a performance being achieved. The alternatives are as follows:

1 **Straight proportional** Earnings and performance vary in the same proportion (this can be represented in a line which slopes at 45°;
2 **Geared** The rate of change of earnings (although constant) is greater than the rate of change of performance;
3 **Stabilised** The rate of change of earnings (although constant) is less than the change in performance.

The above three approaches can all be represented by linear relationship (i.e. straight lines). Two further possibilities are:

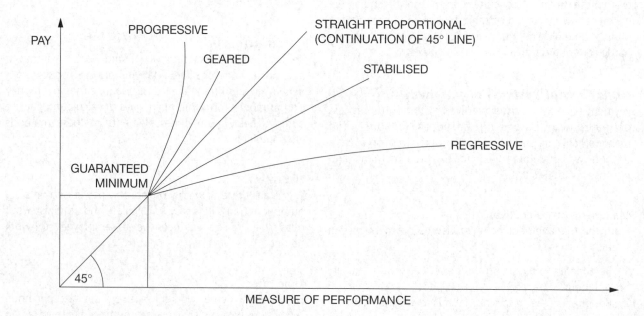

Figure 68.1: Variations in output-related schemes

4 Progressive The rate of change of earnings gradually changes with performance;

5 Regressive The rate of change of earnings gradually falls with performance.

These two approaches are non-linear; the bonus rate varies with performance.

Job evaluation

Job evaluation is the process of assessing the value of one job in relation to another, without regard to the abilities or personality of the individuals currently holding the jobs. The aim is to decide the differentials in the basic pay or salary of jobs. Job evaluation results in a pay range for each job. An individual's personal worth is recognised by awarding increments within a fixed range for that job.

When introducing a job evaluation scheme, it is normal to go through the following stages:

1 Consult with employees Employees need to agree on the results of the job evaluation and should be consulted from the earliest stage.

2 Form a job evaluation team Relevant managers, supervisors and employee representatives will need to be included.

3 Choose the job-evaluation method There are a number of ways of evaluating jobs. One way is by ranking the job according to its importance to the organisation. Another method is **paired comparison** in which one job is compared with another. A third approach is that of classification or **grading**. The evaluators will decide on a number of classifying factors, e.g. the level of responsibility, the level of decision-making etc. They will then look at each job to see where it fits against each of the classifications that have been chosen. A fourth approach is a **points rating** scheme. This is the most popular method in the UK. The evaluating committee decides which factors will be taken into account when grading jobs. Factors might include mental effort required, physical effort, skills, experience etc. The evaluation committee then weights the selected factors according to what they judge to be their relative importance. For example, if they feel that experience is the most important factor then it will be given the highest weight. The effect of weighting is illustrated in the Case Study below.

In choosing an evaluation scheme, important considerations will include:

– The number and complexity of the jobs;
– The nature of the jobs;
– The views of the employees and their representatives.

4 Train the evaluators Evaluators need training if a scheme is to be applied fairly and consistently.

5 Obtain job descriptions In large organisations evaluators will not be familiar with all the jobs to be covered in the scheme. Therefore it will be necessary to get hold of and study the relevant job descriptions.

6 Select and evaluate key jobs In a very large organisation it will be sensible to start with a selection of 15–20 key jobs which represent a sample from across the organisation.

7 Evaluate the remaining jobs Once the team has graded the initial sample, they go on to evaluate the rest of the jobs and gain acceptance of the gradings.

8 Install and maintain the new system Once installed, the job evaluation scheme will need regular review to take account of changing job requirements.

CASE STUDY CASE STUDY CASE STUDY CASE STUDY CASE STUDY

JOB EVALUATION: THE POINTS RATING METHOD

Assume that there are five factors in an evaluation scheme, and that the maximum possible points awarded is 100. A straight average would give a maximum of 20 points for each factor. Applying weighting, the most important factor might have a maximum of 30 points and the least important a maximum of 10 points.

The committee defines the criteria for awarding the available points in each factor. For example, in the case of experience the criteria might be months or years. In the case of skills it might be levels of qualifications.

1 Can you establish a points weighting scheme for a job that you are familiar with?

Decide on **five** factors to be taken into consideration when grading the job. Attach weights to each of these factors so that the combined weight adds up to 100 (e.g. 30, 25, 20, 15 and 10). Then define the criteria for awarding available points for each of the five factors (e.g. in the case of experience, years and months).

STUDY CASE STUDY CASE STUDY CASE STUDY CASE STUDY CASE STUDY

Performance-related pay

In recent years the emphasis in a number of organisations has shifted towards **performance-related pay**. Based on performance appraisal techniques, such schemes have been adopted in a wide range of occupations, including the police force, universities, insurance and banking. Evidence indicates that up to three-quarters of all employers are now using some form of performance appraisal to set pay levels.

Managerial jobs are most affected by performance-related pay. Today managers' performance is increasingly assessed against working objectives. Individual objectives can be set by reference to company goals. An individual may be set broad objectives known as **accountabilities**. Shorter-term goals may be attached to each objective. Scoring systems are then worked out to assess performance against objectives, and these distinguish levels of attainment, e.g. high, medium or low.

One way of rewarding performance is to give a **bonus** if certain targets are met. Another is to give **increments** as targets are met, with the employee progressing up an incremental ladder each year (see Figure 68.2).

A third method is a **salary range scheme**. Here, a 'rate for the job' is set against the mid-point scale of a salary range; for example, in a salary range of £20,000–£25,000 the mid-point would be £22,500. The salary would then depend on performance against the 'rate for the job'. Employees who equalled the rate for the job would receive £22,500; those who exceeded the rate for the job might receive, say, 110 per cent of £22,500 and so on.

While performance-related pay has become increasingly popular, it has attracted a number of criticisms:

1 Too much emphasis has been placed on performance as a way of calculating pay and rewards and too little on employee development ;
2 Performance objectives have often been too vague;
3 Subjective elements of performance-related pay give rise to criticisms of favouritism. A typical complaint is, 'Why has that person's performance been graded in that way when we all know that she is a waster and the boss's favourite?'
4 Complex schemes tend to be misunderstood by employees;
5 The scheme tends to benefit 'high flyers' who do not stay long in the organisation;
6 Teamwork can be undermined when some individuals are rewarded and others are not;
7 Trade unions are often resistant to such schemes.

Incentive schemes

Most employees are paid a salary or a weekly wage that is fixed, but many also belong to an **incentive scheme**. The aim of financial incentive schemes is to improve productivity. There are a number of types of incentive schemes:

1 **Individual payment by results (PBR)** Payment is calculated either on the number of acceptable units of work completed – i.e. on a piece-work basis – or on the basis of time saved by working faster than the standard;
2 **Group payment by results** A bonus can be calculated for a team of workers and then shared either equally or in proportion to their basic pay. This is often employed where it is difficult or expensive to identify individual efforts;
3 **Measured day work** Work measurement is used to establish the number of staff needed to complete a given volume of work at standard performance. If the staff agree to work consistently at a higher pace of work – i.e. a bonus pace – they move on to a higher rate of pay known as the **measured day rate**. This system is used in the health service for services like catering and gardens maintenance.
4 **Plant and enterprise schemes** Plant and enterprise schemes share bonus benefits with all employees. There are different bases used for calculating the bonus according to the nature of the work. Some examples of the different bases are:

    – Increase in the value of sales over the period, excluding price increases;
    – Increase in the ratio of sales value (excluding price increases) to total wage costs over the period;
    – Increase in the volume of production, where a single product is made;
    – Increase in added value over the period, excluding price increases.

Figure 68.2: Performance-related pay

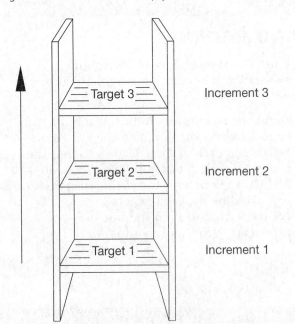

Profit-sharing

During the 1980s there were substantial increases in profit-based methods of pay. There are two main types of scheme:

1 **Cash-based systems** in which a bonus in cash is paid on profits;

2 **Share-based systems** in which employees receive a profit bonus in the form of shares, or are given incentives to acquire shares in the business. In this way, cash flow is not affected; at the same time, employees are given a stake in the ownership of the enterprise.

A survey carried out in the mid-1980s found that as many as 65% of companies operated at least one type of profit-related scheme. The Conservative government of the time encouraged profit-sharing schemes by giving tax incentives to employers and employees who adopted such schemes. The aim was twofold: to create both an enterprise culture and a share-owning democracy.

However, recent evidence suggests that such schemes have had only limited success. In 1993 the proportion of adults owning shares in their companies was only 4 per cent. Reasons for this relative lack of success include:

1 Failure on the part of employers to consult employees about whether to adopt or participate in such schemes;

2 Lack of trust by employees that employers will run such schemes to their benefit;

3 Unequal status and outcomes. In recent years many jobs have become less secure, and there are widespread inequalities in earnings. Profit-related schemes are seen to do little to reduce worsening conditions.

4 Lack of institutional support. Top management support for such schemes has been perceived to have been lukewarm and detached from the interests of ordinary employees.

Non-pay benefits

In addition to pay benefits in the workplace many jobs also include a range of **fringe benefits** including:

- Pension schemes;
- Subsidised meals or canteen services;
- Educational courses;
- Opportunities for foreign travel;
- Holiday entitlements;
- Crêches;
- Assistance with housing and relocation packages;
- Discount and company purchase plans (i.e. cheap purchases of company products);
- Telephone costs;
- Discounts on insurance costs;
- Private healthcare, dental treatment, etc.;
- Time off (sabbaticals);
- Sports, leisure and social facilities.

EXAM TIP

Don't mix up **profit-related pay** and **performance-related pay**. Profit-related pay is tied to changes in an organisation's profit figure, and could for example involve employees owning shares in the company. Performance-related pay is tied to particular performance indicators and objectives being met. For example, under the latter scheme an individual's pay may be linked to their productivity.

Advantages of fringe benefits

There are a number of reasons for offering employees fringe benefits:

1 They can often be provided to employees free of tax, which benefits both the employer and the employee;

2 Some benefits can be provided cheaply through economies of scale, e.g. a works canteen offering cheap meals;

3 Some benefits are needed to improve employee performance e.g. healthcare and haircuts on site;

4 Some companies may be able to offer discounts on their own products and thus at the same time increase their sales;

5 The provision of certain benefits may help to create long-term commitment to the company e.g. a crêche on site, a company pension scheme, company cars etc.

Chapter summary

- Pay can be seen as a way of compensating or rewarding employees for work done.
- In designing a payment scheme it is essential to create a scheme which is fair and seen to be fair. Employees will compare their rewards to those of other employees in their own company and in other workplaces. They will want to be paid 'a fair day's wage for a fair day's work'.
- In devising a payment system there is often a tension between simplicity and rigidity and complexity and flexibility.
- Waged workers used to be rigidly differentiated from salaried ones. Increasingly the emphasis today is on 'harmonisation' of conditions.
- A payment system should be seen from both the perspective of management and that of employees and their representatives.
- There are a number of ways of calculating pay in addition to the standard flat rate, e.g. time-rates, piece-rates and bonuses.
- If output-related methods are to be used, it is essential to develop effective techniques for work measurement.
- Job evaluation is the process of assessing the value of one job in relation to another, without regard to the abilities or personality of the individuals currently holding the jobs.
- A points rating scheme is the most widely employed approach to job evaluation in the UK today.
- Most medium and large organisations in the UK have adopted some form of performance-related pay scheme.
- A number of different types of incentive schemes are used to improve productivity in organisations.
- Profit-sharing was popular in the early 1980s but many schemes have fallen by the wayside.
- Fringe benefits can be used to motivate and reward employees in addition to the traditional payments system.

69 Equal opportunities

Most people today have an idea of what is meant by 'equal opportunities', but not everyone feels that equal opportunity in itself is a good thing. To some people it means giving everyone the same access to opportunities on equal terms. Of course, those that have the most skills, qualifications, etc. will be best placed to take advantage of these opportunities. A rather different approach involves trying to help the disadvantaged to catch up with those who have been relatively more advantaged by giving them more access to training, etc.

In an important piece of writing on the subject published by the Institute of Personnel Management, Jack Straw identifies three key approaches to equal opportunity which can be summarised as follows:

1 Equal opportunity as equal chance

When applying for a job, everyone should have the same opportunities and be considered equally. The theory is that everyone will have the same chance, but unfortunately in practice, discrimination (legal and illegal) will inevitably occur.

2 Equal opportunity as equal access

Having passed the hurdle of recruitment and entry to a job or profession, all individuals should be given equal access to training, chances of promotion etc. The reality however, may be that discrimination and inequality continue to occur.

3 Equal opportunity as equal share

This according to Straw is the ideal situation. All groups are represented at every level within an organisation. If this ideal state occurs, then only lawful, justifiable and necessary criteria are used to discriminate for recruitment, selection and promotion decisions.

The management team of an organisation has the responsibility to implement and publicise equal opportunities policies, to train and issue guidelines and to ensure that policies are being carried out.

Statutory provisions are designed to regulate discrimination in a number of areas.

Discrimination in employment

Under the Sex Discrimination Act 1975 and the Race Relations Act 1976, discrimination in employment is illegal. This affects the processes and procedures adopted in the recruitment process. These two Acts make it unlawful to discriminate against individuals on the grounds of sex, marital status, race, colour, or ethnic or national origin. Discrimination can occur either directly or indirectly.

Direct discrimination

This relates to how individuals are treated. No individual should be treated less favourably than another on the grounds of their race, sex or marital status. For example, the following are clear cases of **direct discrimination**:

- **Not shortlisting or appointing applicants because of their sex, marital status or ethnic origin**

  Example: In *Whitehouse v Highland Regional Council (Industrial Tribunal)*, the defendant unlawfully refused to employ a married woman, in the belief that it was wrong that both husband and wife should have jobs during a period of high unemployment.

- **Giving less favourable terms and conditions of employment because of a person's sex, marital status or ethnic origin**

  Example: In *McEvans and Others v Associated Biscuits (Industrial Tribunal)*, temporary, part-time but qualified women were discriminated against when the employer recruited redundant men with less previous service for temporary, full-time work.

- **Recruiting to a post on the assumption that it is unsuitable for applicants of one particular sex or ethnic group**

  Example: In *Gordon and Murray and East Felin Ltd (Industrial Tribunal)*, the employer unlawfully refused men jobs on the assumption that they would not want to do 'boring' work.

Indirect discrimination

This takes place where a requirement or condition is specified with which few people in a particular group will be able to comply. The following are examples of indirect discrimination.

- **Asking applicants for information on marital status, child care and family responsibilities, which may be used in a discriminatory way**

  Example: In *Elliott v Buttler (Industrial Tribunal)* a candidate's domestic responsibilities were unlawfully assumed to be likely to conflict with the job requirement.

- **Enforcing an organisational rule on dress which would have an adverse effect on some women due to their cultural or religious beliefs**

- **Advertising a post, stating that there is a need for certain physical attributes (e.g. the ability to lift heavy weights) when this is not essential to the position and with the intention of discouraging female applicants.**

Genuine occupational qualifications (GOCs)

In certain cases where sex and race constitute a genuine occupational qualification, it is lawful specifically to recruit women, men or members of ethnic groups to a particular post.

For example, belonging to a particular racial group is a *genuine* occupational qualification where the job involves:

- Participation in a dramatic performance or other group entertainment for which a person of a particular racial groups is required for reasons of authenticity;
- Participation as an artist or photographic model in the production of a work of art, visual image or sequence of images for which a person of a particular racial group is required for reasons of authenticity;
- Providing food and drink to members of the public in a particular setting where a person of a particular racial group is required for reasons of authenticity;
- Providing personal services to, or promoting the welfare of, people belonging to a particular racial group, where those services can most effectively be provided by a person of that racial group.

Being a man or woman is a *genuine* occupational qualification where:

- The nature of the job calls for a man for reasons of physiology (excluding physical strength or stamina) or in a dramatic performance or other entertainment for reasons of authenticity;
- The job needs to be held by a man to preserve decency or privacy;
- The nature or location of the establishment makes it impractical for the holder of the post to live elsewhere than in the premises provided by the employer;
- The work is concerned only with men and requires special care, supervision or attention (as in hospitals or prisons);
- The job provides individuals with personal services in welfare and education which can most effectively be provided by a man;
- The job is likely to involve the performance of duties outside the UK in a country whose laws and customs are such that the duties could not effectively be performed by a woman;
- The job is one of two to be held by a married couple.

Equal opportunities in recruitment and selection

The requirements of Human Resource Management are such that the issue of discrimination must be considered throughout many standard personnel procedures. Selection procedures for recruitment, promotion or transfers should be unbiased and objective.

An examination of these procedures will enable us to highlight good and bad practices at various stages.

SYNTHESIS

Which of the following questions asked in an interview situation would you consider to be legal and which illegal/discriminatory? Explain why.

- *'Mrs _____ I see you are married. Do you intend to start a family soon?'*

- *'What will happen when your children are ill or on school holidays? Who will look after them?'*

- *'Your hair is very long, Mr_____. If offered the job are you prepared to have it cut?'*

- *'Mr _____, as you are 55, do you think it's worth our employing you?'*

- *'Miss _____, as a woman do you think you are capable of doing the job?'*

- *'Do you think your disability will affect your performance in the job?'*

- *'How do you feel about working with people from a different ethnic background from yourself?'*

- *'As a woman returner, Mrs _____, do you feel you will be able to cope with the new technology in the office?'*

- *'As a man, Mr _____, you will be working in a department consisting mainly of women. Are you easily distracted?'*

- *'Miss _____, don't you think your skirt is rather short?'*

The job description

As the document which defines a post in terms of major tasks, duties and responsibilities, the **job description** should be written in clear straightforward language, avoiding unnecessary jargon or complex terminology. In practice, job descriptions are often overstated, leading to

the person specification setting unnecessarily exacting requirements. For example, conditions relating to length of service or experience may have a disproportionate impact on women and thus be indirectly discriminatory.

The person specification

This should contain details of the attributes that applicants need to have for a particular job. Care must be taken when writing a person specification to avoid bad practice such as using criteria of age, gender or physical ability to determine suitability. Where work is heavy, it is common to set physical standards which are higher than necessary and which exclude more women than men. This amounts to indirect discrimination.

Obtaining candidates

Advertisements should not indicate any intention to discriminate. Care must also be taken with wording and illustrations.

Bias may occur if posts are advertised only in specific journals or papers intended primarily for one particular group. Care must also be taken when advertising internally, where particular groups may not have access. Such limited advertising potentially involves indirect discrimination.

Shortlisting

The Equal Opportunities Commission and the Commission for Racial Equality strongly recommend that organisations adopt a procedure for recording reasons why applicants have been rejected at each stage of the selection process. The criteria used for shortlisting must be job-related and applied consistently to all applicants.

Interviews

Appointments should be based on factors determined from the job description and person specification. A candidate's ethnic origin, gender, personal circumstances or disability must not be used in appointment decisions.

Oral or written fluency in English language should not be used as a selection factor unless it is a legitimate job requirement and identified on the person specification. Many interviews which are conducted according to the principles of equal opportunities will involve asking all candidates the same standard set of questions.

Monitoring

This is the process of checking whether unfair discrimination is happening and whether the organisation's equal opportunities policy is being carried out. Monitoring which employees are in which grade in an organisation will allow any instances of under-representation of a particular group to be identified and investigated. For example, if women employees are heavily concentrated in the lower grades and men dominate the higher grades, further investigation will need to include consideration of whether factors such as age, marital status, child-related responsibilities and working arrangements are influencing recruitment and promotion decisions.

Codes of practice to promote Equal Opportunities

Both the **Commission for Racial Equality (CRE)** and the **Equal Opportunities Commission (EOC)** have developed codes of practice in order to monitor and promote equal opportunities

Both codes require careful monitoring of employees. Employers are also required to check and record the sex and marital status and ethnic origin of job applicants. This information then feeds into a review of selection criteria and personnel procedures. An organisation may find, for example, that women, married people or individuals from a particular ethnic group are not being promoted within the organisation. This may be due to practices which are indirectly discriminatory.

Although codes of practice are not law, failure to comply with them can be used against an employer in proceedings taken against them, for example, at an industrial tribunal.

IT'S A FACT

The Sex Discrimination Act lays down that single-sex words such as 'waiter', 'postman', 'stewardess' shall be taken as evidence of an intention to discriminate unless there is a specific indication to the contrary.

Positive action

If an organisation's monitoring procedure shows that women or individuals from a particular ethnic group are not being promoted, the organisation cannot use 'positive discrimination' to redress the situation – for example, making sure that the next three promotions are all women. Under the Race Relations Act and the Sex Discrimination Act, it is unlawful to use a quota system based on sex and racial origin. It *could* however take positive steps to encourage women to apply, for example, by setting up a training scheme for women employees to encourage them into management posts.

Positive action provides a way of encouraging applicants of a particular racial group or sex to apply for specific posts if they have been under-represented in that area of work at any time during the previous twelve months. Applicants can be encouraged by including a

---

SYNTHESIS

In the following examples, state whether discrimination has taken place or not and whether this is direct or indirect discrimination. Some cases may involve a 'genuine occupational qualification'.

- *A local prison hospital advertises in the press for 'male nurses to work with potentially dangerous patients'.*

- *A vicar places an advert in The Church Times for a young male curate.*

- *The managers of a health farm are seeking a female sauna and changing room assistant.*

- *A school insists on maintaining a policy that female staff are not allowed to wear trousers at work.*

- *A television company advertises for actors of West Indian origin.*

---

statement in the advertisement and in the particulars for a post, making it clear that applications from under-represented groups are welcome. Appointments, however, must always be made on the basis of merit.

Other positive measures which may help under-represented groups to increase their representation in particular areas of employment include:

- Job advertisements and outreach work to encourage applications from women, people from black and ethnic minority groups, people with disabilities and lesbian and gay men;
- Encouraging women, people from black and ethnic minority communities and people with disabilities to apply for promotion and transfer opportunities, through career counselling or training schemes;
- Special training schemes for women, people from black and ethnic minority groups and people with disabilities who show potential for promotion or skills training but lack the necessary qualifications;
- Job advertisements aimed at ethnic groups, and encouragement of applications through the use of the ethnic minority press as well as other newspapers.

Equal pay

In addition to legislation covering discrimination in employment matters, the **Equal Pay Act 1970** established the right of men and women to receive equal treatment with regard to the terms and conditions of employment when engaged in the same, or broadly similar work, or work of equal value.

EMPLOYEE RECRUITMENT POLICY STATEMENT FOR MELTON COLLEGE

What do you consider to be the major strengths and weaknesses of the employee recruitment policy statement set out below?

1 Recruitment, promotion and training decisions

All decisions in relation to the above will be taken, having regard only to the requirements of the job (or of the training proposed).

Promotion and training opportunities will be available to all employees, irrespective of race, ethnic origin, religion, sex, marital status or possible family commitments, sexual orientation or disability.

2 Shortlising, interview and appointment procedures

Interview and appointment procedures shall be adopted so as to minimise any disadvantage suffered by the handicapped or members of ethnic minority groups of either sex.

Accordingly, except in so far as it is necessary for particular appointments, questions will not be asked at interview regarding the following: prospects of marriage, future family plans, religion or sexual orientation.

Application for all posts will be by standard job application forms. A copy of this statement shall accompany every application form issued. All members of the interviewing panel should receive appropriate training, be familiar with this policy and be aware of the guidelines to be followed.

3 Induction

Induction procedures will include arrangements to ensure that such procedures are clearly understood by everyone. (This particularly applies to instruction and notices in respect of the Health and Safety at Work Policy.)

For disabled people with mobility difficulties, special attention will be paid to emergency evacuation procedures.

4 Other decisions

It is implicit in this policy that employees should not be treated more favourably or less favourably in any matters of employment (except where an exception is necessary and is allowed under the law) because of race, ethnic origin, religion, sex, marital status or possible family commitments, sexual orientation or disability.

It is possible that discrimination can be implicit in unnecessary job requirements of experience and qualifications, the arrangements and timing of training courses and any other unnecessary aspects of the structure and conditions of the work which are, or may be, difficult for members of certain groups to comply with.

5 Monitoring

Monitoring of this policy in relation to employee recruitment will be by the Senior Management Team together with the Curriculum and Employment Committee of Governors.

The Act therefore requires employers to give equal pay to men and women if they are doing the same work or work regarded as equivalent, or if they are undertaking work of equal value. In order to claim equal pay, employees must meet one of these three conditions, and be able to compare themselves directly with a person of the opposite sex. If a claim is successful, a tribunal can award up to two years' back pay and damages.

Disabled persons

The **Disabled Persons (Employment) Acts 1944** and **1958** require firms of more than 20 people to employ a quota of disabled persons. At present the quota is set at three per cent of the workforce. It is not an offence for an employer to be below this figure, but an employer has a duty to engage suitable registered disabled people if anyone is available and when vacancies arise.

| IT'S A FACT |

Many business organisations have produced their own codes of conduct which go beyond the bare essentials of statutory obligations regarding Equal Opportunities.

For example, 'Littlewoods Equal Opportunities Code of Practice' is a 21-page booklet covering policy on the company's recruitment and advertising; selection processes; training; career development; job satisfaction; terms and conditions; part-time employment; responsibilities of managers and supervisors; ethnic minorities and religious beliefs; and employees with domestic responsibilities. It states that no job applicant or employee should receive less favourable treatment on grounds of gender, marital status, social class, colour, race, ethnic origin, creed or disability, or be disadvantaged by conditions or requirements that cannot be shown to be relevant to performance.

The company's aspirations, at least so far as employees are concerned, are backed up by an Equal Opportunities internal appeals procedure, to be 'invoked in cases of alleged sexual or racial harassment'. Where this process fails to resolve a problem, the employee can then use the company's formal grievance procedure.

The rehabilitation of offenders

The **Rehabilitation of Offenders Act 1974** was designed to wipe clean the record of offences, so that people who have had a previous police conviction but have managed to keep out of trouble for a specified length of time should not be discriminated against on grounds of their past conviction.

The rehabilitation period runs from the time of the conviction and depends on the sentence imposed. The idea is that for some offences the conviction could eventually be discounted.

Union members' rights

Until the 1970s, the law gave no rights to union members to protect them against victimisation by employers. Under the **Trade Union and Labour Relations (Consolidation) Act 1992**, it is unlawful to refuse employment because someone is, or is not, a member of a trade union.

Women in the workplace

The position of women in the labour market today is changing. However, it is not easy to predict the course these changes will take in the future.

Some people argue that there are definite signs that 'the future is female'. By this they mean that women are increasingly taking the major share of new jobs that are becoming available and that women are coming to be represented in large numbers in professions such as accountancy and law. The argument runs that women have the sort of skills that are increasingly in demand in modern organisations, e.g. communication, interpersonal and teamworking skills.

Proponents of this theory argue that a critical mass for change is increasingly building up as women go on to take more and more middle management positions in organisations such as banks and the financial and services sector of the economy. Organisations that depend on competitive advantage will increasingly see the wisdom of promoting and developing women in the workplace.

However, other commentators argue that the above scenario is somewhat over-optimistic. For example, the *Social Trends Survey* published in February 1997 indicated that while half of women now have female bosses, only 10 per cent of men do.

The future for women

Over the next ten years the labour force is predicted to rise by 1.4 million, of which 1 million will be female. But the statistics are not the success story for women they might appear.

The difference between the number of men and women with female bosses shows that many women are still in junior positions. There are more women in supervisory positions than in managerial ones. It is a success story in that there are now more women in junior management jobs, but there is still damning evidence that few women are reaching senior management level. Statistics from the *Labour Force Survey* indicate that in 1995 half the female workforce were in clerical, secretarial, sales and personal service jobs, compared with only 16 per cent of employed men.

Two-thirds of managers and administrators are men, and 84% of part-time workers are female. Women still only receive 79% of men's hourly earnings (1997).

| IT'S A FACT |

Some commentators argue that there is a 'glass ceiling' – an invisible barrier which prevents women from rising beyond a certain level in the senior management hierarchy.

Others dispute this, claiming that dominant or 'alpha' people can be drawn from either sex. 'Alpha females' are often better at managing organisations because they are more socialised. They are better at manipulating covertly. To put it another way, 'Men tell, women influence.'

SUPPORTING WOMEN TO RETURN TO THE WORKPLACE

Opportunity 2000 is a business-led campaign launched in October 1991 with the objective 'to increase the quality and quantity of women's employment opportunities in private and public sector organisations. Opportunity 2000 recognises that in an increasingly insecure working culture, employees work best when they feel supported.

For women returners to work, it is often difficult to balance work with family responsibilities. It is not just childcare that can cause a problem: the rapid increase in the elderly population means that an increasing proportion of the workforce are having to look after elderly or disabled dependants. Family–friendly employment practices are needed to make the best possible use of human resources in the workplace.

Restoring confidence

Women who return to work after a career break often lack confidence in their abilities. Some employers realise this and try to convince women returners that they have a lot to offer. For example, Tesco, B&Q, Pizza Hut and Thorn EMI joined together with the Dow-Stoker Consultancy to design a women returners' training course with the aim of 'offering help to those who need to update their skills and gain more confidence before they feel able to start work again'.

Littlewoods provide a loan pack, *Returning without Fears*, for women employees who are returning to work following maternity leave. Amongst the useful information it contains is a guide to reviewing their personal qualities aimed at restoring their confidence in their own abilities.

Juggling work and family

Flexible working practices make it easier for employees to combine work and family. There are a variety of possible options to choose from, for example, part-time employment; job sharing; term-time working; working from home; flexible working hours; annual hours contracts. Other practices that encourage flexibility are career breaks, flexible leave arrangements and childcare facilities.

- Job-sharing enables women to share the work, benefits and security of a full-time job while working part time;

- Term-time working helps parents who are unable to make childcare arrangements over the school holiday periods, or just prefer to spend time with their children. Examples of firms who offer this kind of employment are Boots and B&Q;

- Home working enables women to combine a career with family responsibilities. New technology makes working from home easier;

- Flexible working hours mean that employees can structure their working day to accommodate domestic commitments.

Many women choose to work part-time so that they can combine work with family responsibilities. Some employers look at this type of work positively, as part of an equal opportunity package and as a means of recruiting and attracting top-quality staff.

Career break schemes

Career-break schemes are a good way of attracting new recruits and retaining existing staff. Women can lose out in terms of pay, status, and confidence when they break employment to have children. Organisations who offer the best maternity and career-break schemes are more likely to retain their high-quality employees. Shell UK, for example, offers benefits well above the legal minimum. Women employees get six months' maternity pay, and the whole period of maternity leave is counted as pensionable service. At Shell more than 80% of women taking maternity leave return to work.

For many working mothers, finding and paying childminders for out-of-school and holiday care is a major headache.

Tasks

1. Why should organisations encourage women returners to resume work with them?

2. What are the main obstacles to women returners?

3. How can organisations best help women to return to work?

Chapter summary

- There are different interpretations of the term 'Equal Opportunities' ranging from 'equal chances' and 'equal access' to 'equal shares'.
- There are legally established frameworks for controlling discrimination in areas including race, sex and disability.
- Discrimination in employment is illegal.
- Direct discrimination occurs when individuals are treated less favourably than others.
- Indirect discrimination occurs when a requirement or condition is specified with which few people in a particular group will be able to comply.
- In certain cases, sex and race may constitute a genuine occupational qualification.
- The principles of Human Resource Management require that the issue of discrimination is considered throughout personnel procedures.
- The Commission for Racial Equality and The Equal Opportunities Commission have produced codes of practice in order to monitor and promote equal opportunities.
- In addition to laws covering discrimination in employment matters, the Equal Pay Act 1970 established the right of men and women to receive equal treatment with regard to the terms and conditions of employment when engaged in the same or broadly similar work, or work of equal value.
- The position of women in the labour force is changing. Women are taking most of the new jobs created in the economy. Some people argue that we are seeing a critical mass developing in which women are rapidly catching up with men and are increasingly taking on new management responsibilities. Other commentators are less optimistic and point to the fact that women are still mainly confined to junior management positions.

12 *Operations management*

INTRODUCTION

Managing activities successfully depends on creating an effective system for production and operations management. Once an organisation has identified clear objectives it must think about how they should be achieved. This is as true for services as for manufacturing organisations: both are involved in transforming inputs through a range of processes in order to produce outputs. Control and planning are key elements in business performance. It has been said that without two blades the scissors will not cut!

This unit starts by looking at the processes involved in new product development and design. Production planning and control is never an easy process for an organisation and involves a lot of thought and co-ordination. Efficiency and effectiveness are key ingredients in the operations process. Technological change is a key issue in production control, and the processes involved are analysed. An understanding of quantitative information is equally important for this area.

To conclude this unit, we look at understanding data, decision-making techniques using data and some of the processes involved in analysing data. We explore the key role of information technology, evaluating its use both within an organisation for operational purposes and as a decision-making tool. Finally, this is followed by a key chapter which analyses productive efficiency and how it can be improved.

70 New products

In today's marketplace It is essential for companies to come up with new products to meet the constantly changing needs of consumers. Today's success story may be forgotten tomorrow. Organisations therefore need to develop a 'stream' of products as shown in Figure 70.1.

Today we expect to see new products appearing on the market at regular intervals. Some will change our lifestyles. For example, in the near future we can expect to see the wider development and use of solar-powered cars, Internet shopping, and many other new products and services.

We can illustrate this by looking at British pharmaceutical companies. The UK has an excellent record in pharmaceuticals. However, firms who produce a new drug only have the patent for a limited amount of time. A **patent** is a government grant to an inventor, giving them the sole right to make, use and sell the invention for a period of time. Once the patent runs out anyone can copy the product.

Today, British companies need new products to replace their top sellers – drugs such as Zantac, an anti-ulcer treatment and the best-selling drug in the world, whose patent ran out in 1997. They are desperately seeking new 'wonder cures' that will prevent and cure AIDS or 'flu. The aim is to create a a regular supply of new products that will replace those whose shelf-life is coming to an end.

Major breakthroughs

New products change our lives. Create a brilliant breakthrough and you should be able to generate an excellent business from it.

Some new ideas are simple and some are extraordinarily complex. Major breakthroughs include the development of non-stick frying pans, 'cat's eyes' on roads, cordless kettles, CD-ROMs, the Sony Walkman, and many others. At any given time, huge numbers of people will be putting time and effort into finding new ways of taking a product a little bit further.

Research and development

A great deal of planning needs to take place before a good or service is launched. This involves knowing the market and the way it is changing. **Research and development (R&D)** is a very important business process that relies on market research information.

Setting up a production line can be very expensive. Organisations therefore need to be sure that the product is right before going into production on any large scale. Careful work in the early stages will help to ensure that the launch will be successful and that consumers get the benefits that they want.

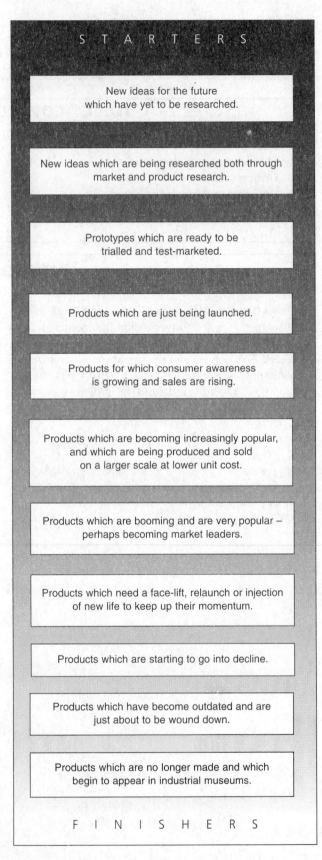

Figure 70.1 A 'stream' of products

CASE STUDY CASE STUDY CASE STUDY CASE STUDY CASE STUDY

RESEARCH AND DEVELOPMENT IN JAPAN

Many major Japanese corporations invest considerable parts of their profits on research and development because they are seeking longer-term growth. This was particularly obvious in the mid-1980s when Japanese companies made their biggest inroads into world markets:

	% of sales	% of pre-tax profit
Canon	3.3	150
Fuji Film	6.2	30
NEC	10.5	80
Sharp	5.8	90
TDK	3.9	25

Figure 70.3 R&D spending by major Japanese companies, 1985

The researcher Samuel Ho has shown that the most significant Japanese achievements in R&D have been in the electronic, new materials and biotechnology areas. Japanese R&D departments are not stand-alone. They work closely with other departments and are given clear targets for the creation and timing of new ideas and products.

1 Why is research and development such a key function of the companies listed above?

2 How can money spent on R&D in Japan enable these organisations to build up a competitive advantage?

3 What are the long-term benefits of R&D?

4 Why might UK companies not be able to set so much money available for R&D?

STUDY CASE STUDY CASE STUDY CASE STUDY CASE STUDY CASE STUDY

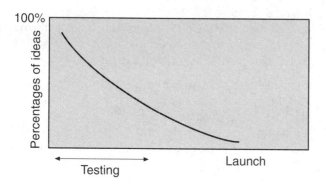

Figure 70.2 Product test and launch

Once it has been established that there is a suitable market for a product, research and development must find out the best way of meeting demand.

The design must be attractive to consumers and meet their needs. Designers need to bear in mind the treatment products will receive; for example, garden tools must be weather-resistant, while kitchen appliances need to be safe and easy to keep clean.

Today designers often build in 'planned obsolescence' so that the product will need replacing after a particular period. Many cars are only built to last a limited number of years, and today we even have 'throw-away cameras'. Product designers may also want to incorporate certain familiar features in their products, particularly if it provides some form of status or helps to give a good image of the

organisation – for example, the radiator grille of a BMW or the lettering on a Coca-Cola can.

Once a design has been developed, the researchers will either build a prototype which can then be tested, or trial the service on offer. Many prototypes will be tried and later discarded, while others may be altered and improved.

It is essential to look at the likely profits that a new product is likely to generate. This involves estimating how many units it is likely to sell in a given period and how much costs will be.

Sometimes a **test market** is set up, where the product or prototypes are tested with a sample of consumers. This provides useful feedback which reduces the risk of a failure at the time of the launch.

The **launch** is the final stage and involves presenting the product to the real market for the first time.

The business of 'R&D'

In any well-run company, research and development has a strictly commercial function – to further the company's business aims by creating new and better products, improving operational processes and developing new ones, and providing expert advice to the rest of the company and to customers. The functions centre on two imperatives:

1 To make the best possible use of resources

2 To take maximum care for the environment.

The continued commercial success of the company depends on these imperatives being followed in full.

The R&D department therefore has to respond to a very great number and variety of complex requirements and must endeavour to measure the costs of their work against the value of their output.

'Blue-sky' research

The value of research output is difficult to assess. How much of the financial success of a new product is attributable to research and how much to packaging and promotion?

What is certain is that without a flow of new improved products and processes, no company can hope to remain successful.

Some research cannot be expected to pay for itself in any foreseeable time span. Many companies allocate a

---

IT'S A FACT

In the petroleum business, the on-going costs of research can be considerable – £1 million to carry out engine tests for a new lubricant formulation, for example. The capital costs of laboratories and equipment are similarly huge: a new laboratory on a greenfield site costs upwards of £20 million. One major oil company spends something like £70 million a year in the UK on research and development – and of course has access to the work of its other laboratories either in this country or in other parts of the world.

---

proportion of their research budgets – as much as 5–10% in some cases – to so-called 'blue-sky' investigations. These are projects which may produce spectacular commercial results in the shortish term, but whose more likely contribution is to the long-term understanding of scientific, technical and operational processes, with a possible pay-off in the far distant future.

This kind of research has the unquantifiable benefit of stretching the minds of the scientists undertaking it or reading about it, and so helping them to achieve a deeper understanding of their own more practical work. It also sometimes has unexpected 'spin-off' benefits when researchers make chance discoveries that could not have been predicted.

In addition, many companies devote part of their research budgets to general and exploratory work which may not have an immediate application but has the practical effect of keeping future business options open.

Finding a 'research customer'

Generally, R&D is carried out according to the principle of the 'internal customer'. Unless there is a knowledgeable customer for R&D results somewhere within the organisation, the R&D process will be most unlikely to succeed.

In other words, most R&D work is aimed at tightly defined business objectives. Organisations identify their most important priorities for research and development, then R&D efforts are channelled into meeting those priorities.

All good commercial laboratories maintain close links with other research institutions, particularly universities and colleges. Their objectives remain commercial, but the exchange of knowledge and expertise is stimulating to everyone involved and contributes to the long-term vitality of scientific research everywhere.

A trade-off between risk and return

Research and development offers a range of returns varying from high risk with potentially high returns to low risk accompanied usually by low returns. The returns can be financial or environmental.

For any organisation, it is important to achieve the right blend of risk in the way money and effort are invested. No one can forecast with certainty what the right blend is. Business history is littered with expensive research ventures that failed. On the other hand, a company that never takes risks by making a major investment in an R&D project may never achieve major success.

Companies are more likely to achieve the right balance in R&D if they encourage all parts of the business to become involved. In particular, the people who would be responsible for selling the end-result of the research should have a decisive say in the way the research is carried out.

The importance of design

'Designing' a good or service involves far more than simply creating products which look and feel good: it means creating goods which meet the requirements of end-users.

For example, when Damon Hill started his 1997 motor racing world championship in his new Arrows Yamaha car he was far from impressed when the car failed to leave the starting-grid. Although the car looked the part, there were considerable faults in its technical design.

Designers themselves have widely diverging views on their role in product development. Some argue that their job is to come up with new ideas which consumers are not aware of, and that consumers then need to be educated to follow their lead. Others argue that their function is to create new products which best meet a design brief presented by a client.

Aspects of product design

In the real world many designers have to follow the brief. It is usually the client who comes up with funds for new design. However, there are many designers who continue to follow their own ideas and interest and then seek sources of funding once they have come up with new designs.

Good product design involves taking account of a number of important issues:

1 **Financial viability** Most businesses are driven by the 'bottom line' i.e. profitability. This is an important design consideration. Designers need to balance the cost of materials and other factors that go into design against the likely revenues. Sometimes adding an extra feature to a product can lead to a considerable increase in its perceived value to the consumer – e.g. a designer label on a fashion item. At other times consumers resent having to pay for extra features which add to costs.

2 **Ease of use** In the age of 'convenience' goods, most consumers will opt for goods which are convenient and easy to use. For example, we have seen the increasing use of 'automatic cars' by motorists. The multiplex cinema has become increasingly popular because people find it easy to 'pop in and pop out'. In fast-food restaurants people no longer have to wait to be served. Most people state a preference for cars with central rather than manual locking, etc.

3 **Ease of manufacture** In designing goods it is important to consider how they will be manufactured. This is particularly true in food processing – e.g. the sorts of 'ready meals' available from Marks & Spencer. Producing a recipe in a small kitchen is quite different from mass-producing it in a factory. Food technologists and designers need to design new products which are easy to manufacture in bulk while retaining their distinctive quality.

4 **Safety** Today one of the biggest 'value-addeds' in design is extra safety features. Nowhere is this more true than in car design, where buyers are increasingly concerned about the availability of drivers' airbags, side bumpers and so on. Designers also have to ensure their products comply with European Union and UK safety standards.

5 **Reliability** Reliability is a key design feature. Many consumer products such as cars, computer, television sets, vacuum cleaners etc. are far more reliable than they were 10 years ago. The emphasis today is on high standards of quality. There is no way that products from the past could compete with their modern counterparts.

IT'S A FACT

The European Commission has put forward a draft Directive which aims to harmonise legislation concerning the transfer of corpses across the EU. It requires that coffins should:

a) be watertight;

b) be built sufficiently strongly to be able to withstand shocks and prevent deterioration in transit;

c) meet the quality standards for each of the different materials used in its construction;

d) be of guaranteed quality.

---

6 **Environmental impact** A key aspect of current design is 'environment- friendliness'. Designers are required to take this into account both to comply with EU and UK government regulations and also to meet the expectations of consumers. One of the first questions that many buyers ask is about the impact of a product on the environment.

7 **Legality** Designers must ensure that their products comply with all of the legal requirements relevant to their particular area of production.

8 **Maintenance** In product design it is essential to consider the ongoing maintenance of the product. A product that is difficult or costly to maintain will lose custom in the longer term.

9 **Consumer focus** It is essential at all times to make sure that products are consumer-focused and to consider the 'Four P's'. For example, how easy is it to deliver the product to the final consumer given the chosen packaging? How easy is it to promote the good, etc.

10 **Aesthetics** The aesthetics of a product are what it looks like, feels like, smells like, tastes like etc. For a number of products aesthetics are all–important, e.g. evening fashion wear, swimsuits, a restaurant meal, etc. It is the aesthetics which often lead to the greatest value added, although the design features mentioned above are also important.

SYNTHESIS

Explain how the aspects of design outlined above relate to two or three goods or services that you are familiar with.

The design process

The design process involves a number of stages:

1 **Identify the problem or need** In a large organisation this may come about as a result of market research or by a realisation in the organisation that there is an opportunity to produce a new good or service to fill a gap in the market;

2 **Draw up the design brief** After much discussion, an initial design brief will be created, and presented to the design team. The design brief will be created by whoever is the 'customer' for the new design – for example, the production or sales department in the organisation;

3 **Draw up the design specification** The next stage is to produce a design specification and analysis giving a clear description of the purpose of the product, the functions the product must have, and constraints such as size, quality, cost, etc.;

4 **Investigation/research** The next stage is for the design team to carry out investigations and research, drawing in the expertise of researchers, designers, the sales department, the costings specialists, as well as potential customers;

5 **Ideas and solutions** Ideas and possible solutions can be considered by the organisation's own design team or by outside specialist design consultants;

6 **Select the best ideas** The most successful ideas can be developed in more detail. Prototypes can be built of the whole product or parts of it;

7 **Production plans** Now is the time to start planning how to produce the finished good or service. This will involve the use of detailed drawings and models to determine when, where and how the finished item will be produced;

8 **Testing and evaluation** Before the end product can be sold, it will need to be tested to check that it does its job properly. It is also necessary to find out whether the product meets the customer's requirements. Often alterations need to be made before the item goes into mass production.

Patenting a new idea

When designers or inventors create a new idea they can register the idea with the patent office for a period of fifteen years. This protects the creator of a new idea from patent infringement. However, to register a patent and have it approved can take quite a long time. There are two important requirements for a patent to be granted:

- The idea must be new;
- It must contain an 'inventive step' (i.e. it should be more than just a development of an older idea).

The existence of legal protection for new ideas encourages inventors and organisations to spend money on research and development. It also enables them to benefit from the protection of their patent for a period of time. Once the patent expires, other firms are able to copy the idea and the price often falls as a result.

IT'S A FACT

In 1977 Andreas Pavel filed a patent for an invention which consisted of a belt with a battery-powered cassette recorder attached to it connected to a headset.

The Sony Walkman became available in shops in 1979 and in 1982 Pavel took Sony to court for infringement of his patent. However, he did not win the case because Sony argued that they had arrived at the idea independently.

Innovation and change

There is a difference between **innovation** and **invention**. An invention occurs when a new product or technology is created. For example, one of the most famous inventions was the steam engine.

Innovation involves producing new solutions to problems. It should involve the whole organisation and occur at every stage of business activity.

Innovative steps

Innovation should be seen as a staircase to progress. In nearly every field, innovation is going on all the time.

Often it proceeds in small steps. For example, a car manufacturer with a range of models might gradually add new features such as side-impact bars, power-steering, etc. Each successful innovation will be included in all the future models produced by the company.

But sometimes businesses seem to take a great leap forward, often following some new invention or technological breakthrough.

For example, for years tabloid newspapers kept adding new features to the way they presented the news. Then suddenly the *Today* newspaper pioneered the use of computer technology and colour printing. Very soon all the other national newspapers were following suit.

In practice, a great deal of what appears to be innovation comes from borrowing ideas, imitating what other organisations are already doing, or from firms employing people from outside with new ideas.

Chapter summary

- Organisations today need to continually come up with streams of new products to replace ones which are out-dated.
- New products can change people's lifestyles, and this creates an ongoing impetus to further change.
- Research and development drives the engine of change. Research and development should be market-led.
- Many of the results of research and development may take a long time to filter through to the market.
- The Japanese spend a considerable percentage of their profits on research and development.
- Research and development in organisations is largely concerned with generating further profitability.
- It is important to find an 'internal research customer' in an organisation to secure the place of R&D.
- It is possible to outline a simple trade-off between risk and return.
- Design is the process of creating products which meet the needs of customers.
- A key aspect of design is financial viability, but it is not the only consideration.
- Other key aspects of design are the ease of use and ease of manufacture of products, safety, reliability, environmental impact, legality, maintenance, customer focus and aesthetics.
- The design process involves arriving at final solutions from an original brief and specification.
- Patenting new ideas enables them to be legally protected from being copied for a fifteen-year period.
- Invention occurs when a new product or technology is created. Innovation involves finding new solutions to problems.

71 Technology and operations

In order for organisations to become globally competitive, they must be able to manage their production and operations efficiently. The way they manage their operations will actively influence their success in the marketplace. With the advent of new technologies, manufacturing and operational decisions have today become the major factor in determining a company's competitiveness. The organisation which delivers high-quality products at reasonable cost will quickly eliminate less successful rivals.

The breathtaking pace of technological advance in the 1980s and 1990s has placed an enormous onus upon managers to adapt to change. Companies such as Ford, General Motors, IBM and Kodak have embarked upon extensive overhauls of their production systems in recent years in order to deliver a more competitive product. This has involved closing down inefficient plants and restructuring others, often through downsizing. Using new technologies, these and other companies have extensively 'refixtured' plants with new equipment and technologies designed to meet the global competitive challenge.

But it would be wrong to regard production and operations as being simply about the manufacture of goods. In the past, the term 'production' referred to manufacturing, while 'operations' referred to services. However, over time, manufacturing companies have not only become increasingly dependent upon the provision of services: they have also had to learn to function more like service organisations.

Similarly, service organisations have become more like factories in the way they synchronise people, technologies and products. As this process represents a convergence of manufacturing and service organisations, it would be wrong to focus upon one sector and not include the other.

IT'S A FACT

According to Peter Drucker 'We do have a choice and must learn to become aggressive managers of technology by choosing certain technologies and rejecting others.'

Phases of production and operations

There are three distinct phases of production and operations which apply to all goods and services:

1 **Planning** the operations process;
2 **Starting up** the operations process;
3 **Controlling**, or running, the process.

In this chapter we are going to look at operations and technology. Technology today touches almost every aspect of life and work. Technology can be defined as 'the process of applying science and knowledge to human affairs, especially in transformations, processes, and products used to solve problems.' Essentially the term 'technology' refers to equipment or tools which are designed to help us to do things better.

It is usual to divide technology into two distinct areas:

1 **Material** technology consists of tangible tools, devices and equipment;
2 **Non-material** technology consists of knowledge, processes and methods.

IT'S A FACT

The word 'robot' is derived from the Slavic word *robotnik* which means 'worker'.

Types of new technology

Much has been said and written about the 'factory of the future'. **Numerical-controlled (NC)** machines and **computer numerical-controlled machines (CNC)** have been around since the 1960s. More recently we have seen:

● **Computer Aided Design (CAD)**
This assists the designer with the use of computer graphics and computer-based structural analysis. It helps design to be responsive to changing specifications.

● **Computer Aided Manufacture (CAM)**
This converts the CAD design into instructions for manufacturing equipment. As CAM follows CAD, the result is often called **CADCAM**. CADCAM has been described as the greatest boon for manufacturing productivity since electricity. One of the benefits is the way it can be integrated with the use of robots. Whereas skilled labour might require £8 per hour, a robot may perform the same task at a cost of £2 per hour over a range of output. Another benefit of robots is that they perform work which is otherwise considered dull, dreary or dirty. Robots are frequently used in spot and arc welding, materials handling, coating and painting as well as in assembly and parts finishing.

CASE STUDY CASE STUDY CASE STUDY CASE STUDY CASE STUDY

THE 'SEVEN AGES OF FACTORY MAN'*

* This Case Study is based upon an analysis by David Pearson of the Strathclyde Institute.

Not many years ago, Japanese goods were automatically associated with cheap or shoddy copies of British goods. How things have changed! Today, the Japanese approach to quality has overwhelmed us. Japanese manufacturing has moved from a position of low competence to one of supremacy over European and US manufacturers.

Japan's first success in the battle for markets was won on quality. Today, quality is taken for granted and Japanese manufacturers are working to improve flexibility and customer response.

In order to understand how the Japanese have achieved quality we need to look at the 'seven ages of factory man'. When looking at this evolutionary scale the best and most capable of British producers tend to exist towards the top. However, many still lie around the middle and some are in the early stages of development. The stages are:

1 **Fordian man** This organisation is characterised by long flow-lines, lengthy change time and large batch sizes. Fordian man provides low variety, lacks flexibility and has high direct labour and inventory costs.

2 **Automation man** In this age, organisations became obsessed with automation, mainly to reduce direct labour costs. The weaknesses stem from a change of focus from manufacturing to systems issues instead and include poor labour relations, high capital and white-collar investment and, often, poor product quality.

3 **Low inventory man** In this stage, managers begin to realise that equipment and people should be driven by market demand, and increasingly understand the importance of developing employees. The negative tendency at this stage is to reduce market flexibility and limit the number of suppliers.

(Continued on page 499)

THE 'SEVEN AGES OF FACTORY MAN'

(Continued from page 498)

4 Balanced man This stage focuses upon eliminating 'bottlenecks'. The result is higher-throughput operations. The negative consequences include high levels of capital investment.

5 Integrated man This age is heralded by the understanding that marketing, research and development and production departments are all part of the same company rather than deadly warring enemies. The growing strengths in this stage include sharing of information and systems, better customer delivery and service, higher-quality products and more choice, while the weaknesses include a growing dependency on expert systems.

6 Low-overhead man In this stage, IT is used as a primary vehicle in the displacement of administrative and middle management jobs. Strengths include improving cost structures and margins, a clearer vision of the strategic role of IT and shorter decision and information structures. The weakness is that organisations becomes much flatter and stress-laden, with a heavy dependency on expensive 'knowledge' workers.

7 Quality man This age is characterised by organisations producing quality goods and services in the marketplace, where faults are measured in one or two parts per million. Quality, service to the customer and internal communication are excellent. Weaknesses include a belief that quality is the ultimate business goal, a cost structure that becomes inflexible and an inability to make production compromises.

Improving competitive advantage

Though UK electronics companies tend to be towards the top of this scale, many traditional British industries, such as chemicals, plastics, pharmaceuticals, textiles and food processing, tend to be stuck at around stages two to four.

Japanese companies, however, not complacent about their present success, are moving further ahead with three more strategies to improve their competitive advantage. These appear to be:

- **Flexible man** This represents the major challenge from Japan over the next decade. 'Flexible factories' will be designed to give short delivery times, have high levels of demand change[?] and will be optimised to provide maximum product variety and choice.

- **Service man** Customer response will be taken a step further. The factory will be opened up directly to the consumer, enabling them to take part in a direct dialogue with the production line. Production capability will become the key element in market penetration, and the customer will have more control over the making, timing and features of the product order.

- **Enterprise man** This development carries the mantra: *'To make is to be'*. By this stage, manufacturing capability becomes so significant as a competitive force that it influences all other elements of corporate strategy.

Tasks

1 What are the 'seven ages of factory man'?

2 What role might technology have in each of the stages?

3 Compare and contrast the operations of Fordian man with those of Quality man.

4 Why do you think that many British companies are floundering between stages two and four?

5 Discuss the seven ages of factory man with an employee in a large organisation in either the manufacturing or services sector. Find out which 'age' they feel their organisation belongs to and why.

6 Explain why the consumer benefits as organisations work beyond each stage.

7 Explain what is meant by the following terms:

flexibility	*customer response*
large batch sizes	*direct labour*
inventory costs	*labour relations*
white collar	*market flexibility*
bottlenecks	*expert systems*

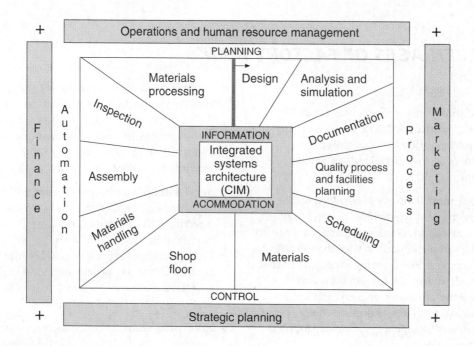

Figure 71.1 Computer-integrated manufacture

- **Computer Aided Engineering (CAE)**
  This involves using sophisticated computer equipment to aid engineers. Though for many organisations this is still experimental, the aim of CAE is to provide rapid engineering responses and solutions to problems.

It has been argued that with the development of new factory technologies we are undergoing a 'second industrial revolution'. With global competitors using such technologies, it is almost impossible to ignore them.

Donald Schoen has identified three stages in the process of change:

1 **Invention** The creation of a new product or process;
2 **Innovation** The introduction of that product or process into use;
3 **Diffusion** The spread of the product or process beyond first use.

SYNTHESIS

Is it possible to relate Schoen's stages of change to a product life-cycle for technologies? Should there be a fourth stage?

Towards the flexible factory

The word 'flexibility' is often used in operations management. In the operations context it is really about **responsiveness** and how well an organisation is able to meet changing needs. Perhaps the best way to understand it as a concept is to think of a small factory. In order to explore how flexible the factory is, the following questions would be relevant:

- *How many products do you make and how many do you promote in your catalogue?*
- *How quickly can you change from making one type of product to making another?*
- *How soon could you make a product which is not in your catalogue but is required by your customers?*

Though these questions relate to output for the customer, they are also about the organisation's internal ability to change in order to meet customer requirements.

At present, two leading concepts which are associated with flexibility are:

1 **Flexible manufacturing systems (FMS)**
  FMS systems apply computer technology to drive machines to produce high-quality goods and services at low cost. The basic elements of FMS are computer-driven workstations which are operated entirely through remote-entry terminals. The transfer of work between workstations is also computerised. There is a hierarchy of groupings of equipment, starting with numerically-controlled (NC) machines. Several NC machines are grouped together, with an automatic transfer system between them. The result is an **FMS cell**.

2 **Computer-integrated manufacturing (CIM)**
  Whereas FMS may simply consist of a few machines which are linked together, CIM looks at a manufacturing system as an entity. CIM involves co-ordinating people with their machines, materials, computers and

design for the process of manufacture. It involves integrating all parts of an organisation through 'systems architecture' (see Figure 71.1).

Classifying flexible systems

There are generally considered to be four main levels of flexible systems:

1 **Stand-alones** These exhibit **machine flexibility** (see Extension Material, page 502). NCs and CNCs are improved versions of basic machines – in other words, they do the same job but without a machine operator;

2 **Machine cells** These are groups of flexible machines with operators transferring work between them. There is an integration of facilities between the machines;

3 **Islands of automation** With this flexible route, automatic transfer is built into the system. There is also routing flexibility.

4 **Flexible factories** These are complete organisations or units which use integrated automation systems to respond to orders and to produce products from start to finish. For example, Toyota has flexible factories producing motor cars.

Effects of flexible systems

The Boston Consultancy Group have identified five effects of increased flexibility in the process of automation:

1 Scale effects will be reduced. Increased flexibility will mean that smaller-scale operations will be able to compete with larger organisations;

2 Labour rate differences will lose importance. Location choices will depend more on the proximity of the market and the customer rather than on the price of labour;

3 Suppliers will have closer contact with customers. If organisations become flexible this will lead to more one-to-one relationships (customisation);

4 There will be more price differentiation. As products are tailored for more specific customer needs with faster delivery times, this will lead to premium prices for both consumer and industrial goods;

5 Organisations will have to be more flexible. Short delivery times will require better co-ordination between manufacturing and distribution.

BENETTON

The clothing company Benetton provides an example of the fusing together of manufacturing, service, design and office operations using technology as the key ingredient. The company was formed in 1965 and is based upon a network of manufacturing subcontractors and franchised outlets. Benetton itself only employs around 10 per cent of the workforce needed to make and distribute its products.

Benetton uses an integrated production planning and distribution system to eliminate any form of warehousing. Stock is displayed on the shelves of outlets and is replenished through a complex demand forecasting and ordering exercise based on IT networking. IT is a key source of competitive advantage – essential in the world of fashion.

CADCAM is used to design new product automatically allowing for a range of sizes. Designs are downloaded to machinery in appropriate factories, followed by automated despatch and distribution instructions. IT enables technology to respond to short development cycles. In these ways Benetton provides an example of a computer-integrated business which is allied to providing competitive advantage through the process of flexibility.

1 How important is flexibility for an organisation like Benetton?

2 What role does technology play in providing Benetton with the flexibility it requires?

3 In what other product areas is flexibility important?

EXTENSION MATERIAL
Types of flexibility

The authors of a paper entitled 'Classification of Flexible Manufacturing Systems' identify eight different types of flexibility. These are:

1 **Machine flexibility** This is the ease of making the changes required to produce a given set of part types. Flexibility may be measured by the time taken to make changes in tools or to insert different parts;

2 **Process flexibility** Also called 'job flexibility'. The ability to use different part types and materials;

3 **Product flexibility** The ability to change over to producing a different type of product;

4 **Routing flexibility** The ability to handle breakdowns while continuing to produce parts;

5 **Volume flexibility** The ability to operate profitably at different production volumes;

6 **Expansion flexibility** The ability of a system to expand as necessary;

7 **Operation flexibility** The ability to interchange the ordering of several operations for each part of the system;

8 **Production flexibility** This flexibility is reflected by existing technologies and includes all of the parts which can be added to the Flexible Manufacturing System.

Chapter summary

- The ability to efficiently manage production and operations will affect an organisation's competitiveness.
- Technology is the key to delivering a more competitive product.
- There is a convergence in the operation of manufacturing and service organisations.
- Technology is often divided into material technology and non-material technology.
- New technologies include CAD, CAM and CAE.
- The three stages in the process of change are invention, innovation and diffusion.

- Flexibility refers to how well an organisation can meet changing needs.
- The two areas associated with flexibility are flexible manufacturing systems (FMS) and computer-integrated manufacture (CIM).
- The four-level structure for classifying flexibility consists of stand-alones, machine cells, islands of automation and flexible factories.
- The Boston Consultancy Group have identified five effects of increased flexibility.

72 Understanding data

Every organisation has to make decisions. Often decisions are influenced by a host of both internal and external factors which can make decision-making very difficult. In an uncertain world, organisations require information on which to base their decisions. **Statistics** fulfil this role by providing a management tool for making estimates or comparisons of previous or current events, so that decisions about the future can be made.

Much of the information used by organisations on a day-to-day basis is quantitative in nature – i.e. it involves figures. Interpreting these figures requires common sense,

problem-solving skills and the ability to communicate. The results of decisions are never entirely predictable, but by understanding and using statistics, it is possible to keep the uncertainty to a minimum. Knowledge of statistics is therefore an essential tool of business management.

The word 'statistics' contains three fundamental elements: first, it can be used as a blanket term for describing facts and figures; second, it enables a mass of information to be presented according to a particular pattern; third, it provides a method of interpreting business data.

Information for simple problems

The first question any manager in any organisation will ask is, 'What information do I need? Managers at all levels will from time to time need to have information at their fingertips. It may be derived from the market; it may relate to the activities of competitors, or it may relate to their own output or productivity. The more accurate and complete the information is, the more successful decision-making is likely to be; the more inaccurate or misleading the information, the worse the decision. Information must wherever possible be accurate and complete. Where it is vague or lacks reliability, it may mislead managers into making key decisions which turn out badly for the organisation – and for them!

Internal data is information extracted from within an organisation. **External data** is found outside the business in the environment in which it operates (see Figure 72.1).

Before gathering information, a number of key questions need to be asked:

1 **What are the precise objectives of the exercise?**
   It is important to consider the aims of the exercise to ensure that time is not spent upon collecting unnecessary information.

2 **What units of measurement are to be used?**
   For example, if you are collecting sales figures, do you require the information to be in pounds, volume or both?

3 **What degree of accuracy is required?**
   To obtain a high degree of accuracy you will have to spend more time and effort gathering information. However, an investigation of a sample of the total may be just as revealing.

4 **Is obtaining this information cost-effective?**
   If the point of the exercise is to collect information, it must be worth spending the time and money to do so.

Levels of decision-making

Each level of management will have different information needs.

For example:

1 **Strategic-level** managers deal with policy decisions and matters concerning the future of the organisation. They need to use carefully prepared information, not only from within the business but also from outside;

2 **Tactical-level** managers tend to make decisions based on strategic policy decisions. They are concerned with analysing issues within the organisation and will often require information relating to a particular period;

3 **Organisational** decision-makers will need information for grass-roots problems associated with the day-to-day running of the organisation. The information required should help to resolve practical operational problems.

As we saw earlier, **qualitative** data typically consists of attitudes, opinions, reactions, suggestions or subjective descriptions, often given in response to surveys or questionnaires. **Quantitative** data involves *amounts*, such as the average number of customers who come into a shop during a day. Qualitative data often helps to provide the context within which quantitative facts operate.

Different individuals have different styles of decision-making and therefore tend to require different types of data. For example, the analytical decision-maker may be inclined to use statistical information before arriving at a decision. In contrast, the directive decision-maker may prefer to make an intuitive decision based on what 'feels right'. This decision-maker may not consciously weigh up the advantages and disadvantages of the alternatives, but may simply make a decision based on a 'hunch'.

Research shows that senior managers often have to rely on intuitive judgement when making decisions simply because there is insufficient data available. Many of the most exciting decisions made by entrepreneurial organisations may be based on intuition rather than calculated analysis. However, basing managerial decisions solely on intuition is unwise. Organisations operate in complex environments requiring sound judgement. The more that chance can be removed from the equation, the more successful the decision is likely to be.

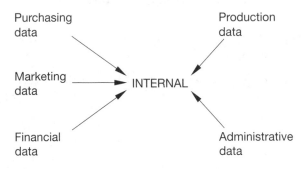
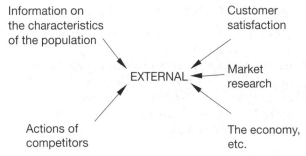

Figure 72.1 Examples of internal and external data

Managers who say, "I've been in the industry for 30 years" as if that alone provided the basis for making decisions are deluding themselves. But those who have no practical experience on which to base their decisions are equally at a disadvantage. Decision-making should be based on a combination of practice, observation and theory.

Quantitative approaches to decision-making are often helpful in that they allow alternatives to be measured in terms of a common denominator. For example, if a company wished to maximise its return on a £10,000 investment over a three-year period, the quantitative comparison in Figure 72.2 would show that Project A was the best long-term investment:

Initial investment	Year 1	Year 2	Year 3
£10,000 – Project A	£3,000	£5,000	£8,000
£10,000 – Project B	£2,000	£3,000	£4,000
£10,000 – Project C	£3,000	£4,000	£4,000

Figure 72.2 *Comparing return on investment*

Those in favour of quantification argue that without it, resources may be wasted, because decisions tend to based on subjective qualitative procedures. But many decisions cannot be reduced to such simple mathematical calculations. Often decisions involve variables which cannot be quantified (except perhaps by very dubious 'guestimates').

Collecting primary data

In order to meet an organisation's specific needs, it is necessary to collect **primary data** through a process of field research. This data is first-hand knowledge – i.e. information 'straight from the horse's mouth'.

As we saw in Chapter 26, when collecting primary data it is simply not possible to collect information from everybody, so in most cases it is necessary to **sample**. How the sample is taken determines how reliable the results are likely to be. Chapter 26 highlights the various sampling techniques.

The design of the questionnaire is fundamental to the success of any survey. A badly constructed questionnaire will irritate respondents and compromise the quality of their input. It is important that respondents know what they are being asked to do, and why, and that they are happy to co-operate. A good questionnaire should obtain the information required and exclude anything that is unnecessary or irrelevant.

Questions should be brief, functional and to the point. The aim must be to obtain the maximum information possible with the greatest ease. Testing questions on a pilot group is an essential step in questionnaire design: no matter how carefully you try to anticipate the reactions of respondents, it is difficult to judge how they will react.

CASE STUDY CASE STUDY CASE STUDY CASE STUDY CASE STUDY

INFORMATION NEEDS

'Have you ever had the feeling that the information you are giving managers isn't exactly what they wanted? Have you ever tried to find out what they do want?

'If you have, then you may well have reached – or at least approached – a state of despair! For years, no matter what variations and improvements I made to the information I gave to managers, I just never seemed able to satisfy their exact needs. I even went through the stage of believing it was some kind of plot to make management accountants feel inadequate.

'Then one day I discovered – some people might say stumbled on – a solution to the problem of defining management's information needs. My amazing discovery was that information is the raw material of decision-making and that, in order to know what information managers need, we have to know what decisions they

take. This pretty obvious statement led to the development of a process which I have appropriately named "decision information analysis". This requires a careful analysis of the decisions that managers make and then, for each decision, assessing the information needed.'

(From *Management Accounting*)

1 Explain why managers require information.

2 Why is it important to give managers the information that they want?

3 What solution is suggested by this case?

STUDY CASE STUDY CASE STUDY CASE STUDY CASE STUDY CASE STUDY

Collecting secondary data

Cost and circumstances dictate that it is not always possible to collect primary data. Sometimes **secondary data** which is collected elsewhere by others can be just as useful, as it provides a different and broader perspective on specific issues.

The problem with secondary data is that it may not necessarily give the whole picture. For example, the information could be out of date, or it may not be clear how or why it was originally collected.

Sources of secondary data

Sources of secondary data are numerous and wide-ranging (see Chapter 26). Published statistics are a form of secondary data, and these can be used by a wide range of organisations. Useful information may be picked up from any of the following:

- Company reports;
- Business publications;
- Newspapers;
- Trade periodicals and professional magazines;
- Reports from professional research agencies.

Presentation of data

Imagine that you have been asked by your manager to obtain information for a report. After collecting armfuls of facts and figures from every possible source, you deposit the results of your on his desk. He complains: 'You can't expect me to read all this. I'm *busy*!'

The fact is that people find it difficult to look at a sea of information. It can be time-consuming and it may be difficult to establish what it all means, particularly for those who are not experienced in interpreting figures.

Once statistical data has been obtained, it needs to be broken down and presented in a way that reveals its significance. Information can be displayed in the form of a frequency distribution or table, or as a chart or a graph. The nature of the data collected and use to which it is to be put will determine the way in which it is presented.

Arrays and frequency distributions

When raw data is first assembled, it is unlikely to be in any kind of order. By imposing order on it, it is possible to draw out and interpret the values and concentrations of values contained within it.

An **array** is a simple arrangement of figures into ascending or descending values. For example, suppose that the number of days' credit for 20 customers is varied as follows:

```
12  21  32  65  18  20  14  51  81  32
31  45  16  51  71  40  24  32  18  33
```

This could be arranged in ascending order as follows:

```
12  14  16  18  18  20  21  24  31  32
32  32  33  40  45  51  51  65  71  81
```

In the past, tally marks were a quick and useful method of counting totals by displaying them in the form of match-sticks. After every four marks, the fifth crossed out the previous four so that totals could be easily counted. Using tally marks, the average age of a company's employees could be presented in tabular form as show in Figure 72.3 below.

Age range	Tally marks	Number of employees
Under 20	II	2
21–30	IIII IIII I	11
31–40	IIII IIII II	12
41–50	IIII III	8
51–60	IIII	5
Over 60	III	3
Total Employees		41

Figure 72.3

The table shows various age bands, but does not show the individual age of each employee. Within each band, some measurements of the 'age variable' appear more than once – for example, the table shows that there are two employees in the 'under 20' age band. Since the table records how many times a value occurs, it can be described as a **frequency distribution**. As groups have been used, it can also be described as a **grouped frequency distribution**.

TASK 72.1

In a factory the following number of machine breakdowns have occurred each hour over a 40-hour week:

```
8   15  43  12  51   2   4  19
4   18  39  56  12  23  27  28
11   2   5  25  18  51  19  50
12   5   6  29  16  57  19  33
24  37  18   3  12   6  60  39
```

Construct a grouped frequency distribution from this data using:

- Six class intervals of equal width;
- Class intervals of ten.

Tables

After data has been broken down, it can be organised in a table. A **table** is a matrix of rows and columns demonstrating the relationship between two variables. It summarises information in a form that is clear and easy to read.

CASE STUDY CASE STUDY CASE STUDY CASE STUDY CASE STUDY

EUROPEAN POPULATION FORECASTS

1 What are the variables shown in Figure 72.4?

2 Identify two countries that are forecast to experience a decline in population.

3 Explain why a table is useful for making comparisons.

4 State one other method of showing this information.

			Year		
	2000	2005	2010	2015	2020
Austria	8,091	8,162	8,201	8,221	8,172
Belgium	9,893	9,820	9,713	9,580	9,423
Denmark	5,233	5,224	5,172	5,095	5,019
Finland	5,096	–	5,076	–	4,984
France	57,883	58,451	58,766	58,821	58,664
Germany	81,126	80,224	78,858	77,065	74,964
Greece	10,335	10,448	10,554	10,571	10,594
Ireland	3,486	3,456	3,466	3,461	3,463
Italy	57,611	57,257	56,411	55,089	53,484
Luxemburg	394	399	403	406	410
Netherlands	16,020	16,419	16,688	16,857	16,979
Norway	4,373	4,414	4,437	4,455	4,470
Portugal	10,577	10,639	10,703	10,612	10,460
Spain	39,381	39,333	38,940	38,200	37,231
Sweden	8,950	–	9,167	–	9,507
Switzerland	7,380	7,546	7,591	–	7,533
Turkey	70,440	79,420	–	–	–
United Kingdom	59,039	59,599	59,966	60,306	60,674

Figure 72.4 European population forecasts (000s)   *Source: National statistical offices*

STUDY CASE STUDY CASE STUDY CASE STUDY CASE STUDY CASE STUDY

Charts

For many people a table is simply a sea of figures. They need time to think about it, analyse the figures and draw meaningful conclusions. Charts are eye-catching and enable information to be presented in a form that can be readily understood. A chart may succeed in making the information more meaningful.

A **pictogram** is a diagramatic form of display which uses pictures or symbols as well as numbers. The symbols used are explained in a key (see Figure 72.5).

One form of statistical representation commonly used in newspapers, articles and other publications is that of the **pie chart**. In a pie chart, each 'slice' represents a component's contribution to the total amount. The 360° of the circle are divided up in proportion to the figures obtained. If you are using a computer spreadsheet or graphing program it will automatically convert a table into

Barker's Pet Shop

Sale of dogs

Figure 72.5 Example of a pictogram

a pie chart. If you need to do it by hand in an exam, you will need a protractor. The following method can be used to convert each relative proportion to degrees:

$$\frac{Proportion}{Total} \times 360°$$

For example, suppose that a company's export figures are as follows:

Exports	Size (£m)
USA	5
Europe	3
Australia	4
Canada	2
Others	6
Total exports	20

$$\text{Exports to the USA} = \frac{5}{20} \times 360^{\circ} = 90^{\circ}$$

$$\text{Exports to Europe} = \frac{3}{20} \times 360^{\circ} = 54^{\circ}$$

$$\text{Exports to Australia} = \frac{4}{20} \times 360^{\circ} = 72^{\circ}$$

$$\text{Exports to Canada} = \frac{2}{20} \times 360^{\circ} = 36^{\circ}$$

$$\text{Exports to others} = \frac{6}{20} \times 360^{\circ} = 108^{\circ}$$

The pie chart can then be presented as in Figure 72.6 below:

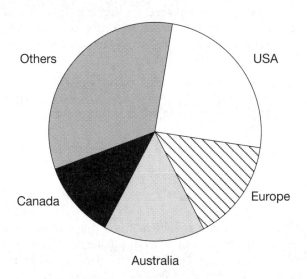

Figure 72.6 *Example of a pie chart*

Bar charts

Although pie charts provide a simple form of display, they show only limited information, and it can be difficult to make accurate comparisons of segment sizes.

In **bar charts**, the areas of comparison are represented by bars which can be drawn either vertically or horizontally. The length of the bar indicates the relative importance of the data.

For example, suppose a company's production figures over the last five years are as shown below. The data from this table could be shown in either of the ways depicted in Fig 72.7.

Year	Units produced
1993	4,300
1994	4,500
1995	3,900
1996	4,100
1997	4,600

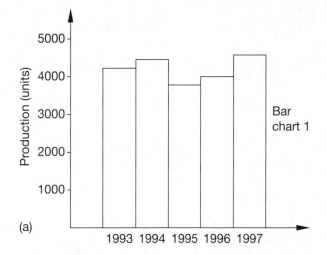

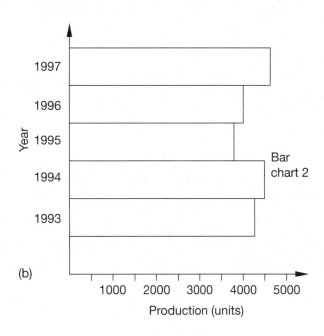

Figure 72.7 *Bar charts illustrating a company's production figures*

A **component bar chart** enables component areas to be subdivided. Individual component lengths represent actual figures (see Fig 72.8 – chart 1). With **percentage component bar charts** individual component lengths represent the percentages that each component forms of the overall total; all bars will therefore be at the full height of 100 per cent (see chart 2).

A company's sales of products A, B and C in value from 1995 to 1997 are shown below. Component and percentage component bar charts drawn from the figures in the table are shown in Figure 72.8 .

	1992		1993		1994	
	£	%	£	%	£	%
Product A	2,200	36	2,400	38	2,500	37
Product B	800	13	700	11	800	12
Product C	3,100	51	3,200	51	3,500	51
Total	6,100	100	6,300	100	6,800	100

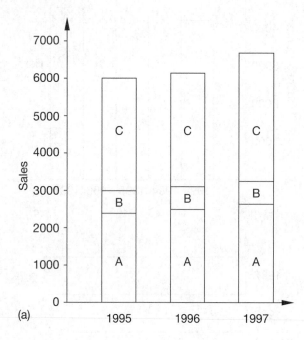

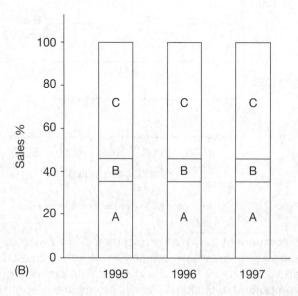

Figure 72.8 Component and percentage component bar charts

TASK 72.2

Over the last four years, the sales of three products for ASAP plc are as shown below:

(£000s)				
	1994	*1995*	*1996*	*1997*
Product 1	4,100	4,500	4,400	2,100
Product 2	5,300	5,400	5,700	6,300
Product 3	2,200	4,100	4,300	4,700
Totals	11,600	14,000	14,400	13,100

1 Prepare a percentage component bar chart from these figures.
2 Explain why bar charts are better for making comparisons than pie charts.

A **histogram** is a form of bar chart that has certain unique features. It represents grouped frequency distributions using bar chart techniques. The key difference between a bar chart and a histogram is that the width of each bar on a histogram relates to a numerical scale, and the width of each block reflects this. The number of observations relating to each variable may now be represented by the area covered by the bar on the chart, and not necessarily by the height of the bar.

In the example given below, the first three bars will be normal height; the fourth and fifth bars will need to be twice as high to compensate for the fact that 1,000 is only half the standard class interval.

Sales per salesperson (units)	No. of salespersons
Up to 2,000	2
2,000 – 4,000	5
4,000 – 6,000	10
6,000 – 7,000	10
7,000 – 8,000	8
8,000 – 10,000	2

If the class intervals are different, the height of each bar needs to be worked out. In many situations, however, it is more likely that the class intervals of each bar will be the same and that this procedure will not be necessary, so that the histogram can be drawn straight from the frequency distribution. Histograms are a variation of the bar chart in which it is the area, and not necessarily the height, of the bar that represents the frequency.

Whereas a histogram is a stepped graph, it might be desirable to show this information in the form of a single curve. Such a curve is known as a **frequency polygon**. It is drawn by constructing a histogram, marking off the mid-point of the top of each rectangle and then joining the mid-points with straight lines. An example of a frequency polygon is shown in Figure 72.10

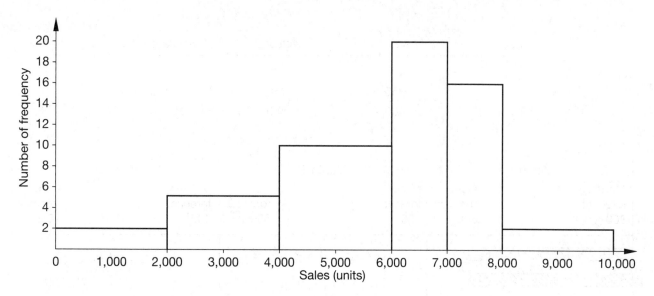

Figure 72.9 *Example of a histogram*

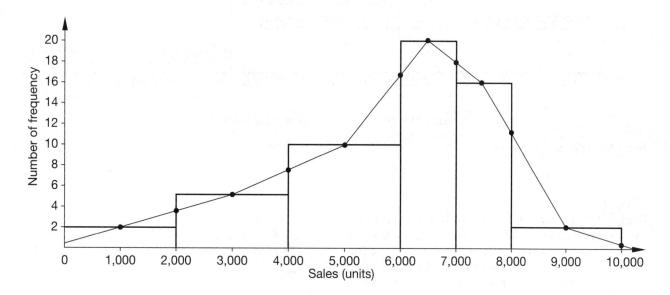

Figure 72.10 *Frequency polygon and histogram*

The curve of a frequency polygon is extended at both ends so that it cuts the axis at points half a class interval beyond the outside limits of the end-classes. The area of the frequency polygon is exactly the same as that of a histogram, since the area lost as each rectangle is cut by the polygon has the same area as each triangle added. If the frequency polygon is smoothed out, it is known as a **frequency curve**.

Gantt charts were named after Henry Gantt, a management scientist who lived during the early years of this century. They are a useful form of bar/line chart for comparing actual progress with forecast progress and can be used as a visual tool to indicate whether performances are on schedule. An example is shown in Figure 72.11 on page 510.

An example is shown in Figure 72.11 on page 510.

SYNTHESIS

What are the limitations of a histogram? Could they cause confusion if users mistake them for bar charts?

> **IT'S A FACT**
>
> Gantt was a master chartmaker. His expertise was in developing charts which helped to formalise sequencing problems.

Month	Forecast	Actual	Percentage
1	300	240	80
2	350	350	100
3	400	440	110

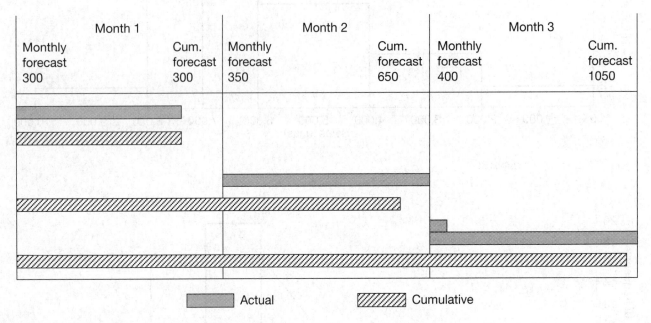

Month 1		Month 2		Month 3	
Monthly forecast 300	Cum. forecast 300	Monthly forecast 350	Cum. forecast 650	Monthly forecast 400	Cum. forecast 1050

Actual   Cumulative

Figure 72.11 Example of a Gantt chart

Graphs

Graphs show the relationships between two variables and can be presented in the form of either a straight line or a curve. Whereas frequency polygons show frequency distribution, the **ogive** is the name given to the curve when cumulative frequencies of a distribution are presented in the form of a graph.

The table below depicts a firm's sales totals over 40 weeks. Points on the graph will not relate sales achievements directly to output in the same way as an ordinary graph, but will indicate how many times the number of sales units (or less than that number) was achieved.

Output (units)	No. of times sales realised (weeks)	Cumulative frequency
0–400	3	3
401–800	9	3+9 = 12
801–1,200	13	3+9+13 = 25
1,201–1,600	11	3+9+13+11 = 36
1,601–2,000	4	3+9+13+11+4 = 40
	40	

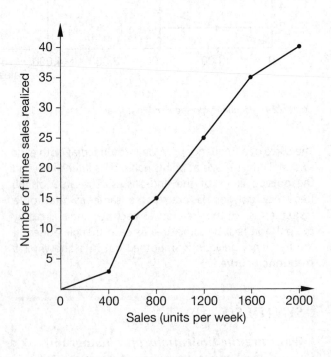

Figure 72.12 Example of an ogive

TASK 72.3

You work for a building society and have been asked by your employer to arrange the following information in a graphical form as part of a presentation of your branch's activities to a group of local fifth-formers:

Percentage of loans granted

House prices (£)	Buyers
Under 20,000	3
20,000 – 39,999	7
40,000 – 59,999	11
60,000 – 79,999	13
80,000 – 99,999	14
100,000 – 119,999	21
120,000 – 139,999	13
140,000 – 159,999	18
	100

1 Draw a histogram and frequency polygon from the table.
2 Construct a cumulative frequency table and use it to draw an ogive.

TASK 72.4

A market research agency is undertaking a survey on behalf of a company concerned about falling sales in a town in Scotland. The company is particularly concerned about changes in the distribution of wealth caused by recent factory closures and increasing unemployment levels.

After an extensive survey involving a carefully worded questionnaire, the agency has extracted the figures shown below to illustrate the spread of wealth in the area:

Wealth (£ per adult)	No. of people	Total wealth (£m)
Under 10,000	1,200	9.5
10,000–49,999	1,500	52.5
50,000–99,999	1,300	97.0
100,000–149,999	400	50.0
Over 150,000	100	20.0
	4,500	229.0

1 Construct a Lorenz curve.
2 Comment upon the distribution shown by the graph.

EXTENSION MATERIAL

The Lorenz curve

A Lorenz curve is a form of cumulative frequency curve which can be used to demonstrate the disparity between a range of actual distribution and a line of equal distribution, thus highlighting the equality or inequality of any range of distribution.

Probably the most common application is to highlight the distribution of wealth within a society. By glancing at a Lorenz curve (see Figure 72.13), you can quickly pick out levels of equality or inequality within a society.

If the distribution is completely even, this shows that wealth is spread evenly between members of a society (i.e. there is no concentration of wealth).

If the distribution is uneven (a feature of all societies!), then this will appear as a difference between the line showing the actual distribution of wealth and a line of equal distribution. In Figure 72.13 we can quickly see that the distribution of wealth in country A is a lot more even than in country B.

(Continued on page 512)

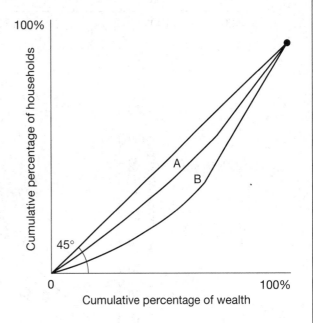

Figure 72.13 Lorenz curve illustrating the difference in wealth between two countries

The Lorenz curve (Contd.)

It is also possible to draw a Lorenz curve to show the relationship between the size of the firm and the output of an industry. For example, the table below shows the size of firms measured by the number of employees:

No .of employees	No of firms	Output (tonnes)
Under 50	50	3,000
50 – 99	80	12,000
100 – 199	120	21,000
200 – 299	135	48,000
300 and over	25	36,000
	400	120,000

In order to construct a Lorenz curve, these figures need to be broken down further. Figure 72.14 below includes a column that calculates each figure as a percentage of its column total, as well as a column that lists the cumulative total percentages. The cumulative total percentages are the figures required to construct the curve.

If all firms were of equal size, then 25% of output would have been produced by 25% of the firms. The curve that would be expected to be obtained if all firms were of equal size is therefore the line of equal distribution.

The extent to which a Lorenz curve deviates away from the line of equal distribution reflects the degree of inequality.

The Lorenz curve in Figure 72.15 shows that, as we would expect, larger firms generate more output. By looking at the curve at its furthest point from the equal distribution line, we can see that 60% of firms control 30% of output, and so it is not equally shared.

No. of firms			Output (tonnes)		
No.	%	Cumulative %	No.	%	Cumulative %
40	10	10	3,000	2.5	2.5
80	20	30	12,000	10	12.5
120	30	60	21,000	17.5	30
135	34	94	48,000	40	70
25	6	100	36,000	30	100
400	100		120,000	100	

Figure 72.14

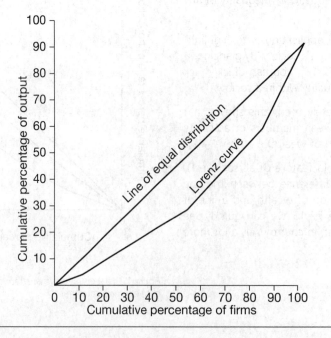

Figure 72.15 Lorenz curve showing the distribution of production between firms

Chapter summary

- If information is neither accurate or complete it will lack reliability.
- Internal data is from within the organisation while external data is from outside the organisation.
- Qualitative data involves descriptions, views, attitudes and opinions.
- Quantitative data involves numbers and figures.
- Primary data is collected by an organisation for its own requirements.
- Secondary data is collected by others.
- There are a number of rules and guidelines for drawing up questionnaires.
- An array is a simple arrangement of figures into ascending or descending order.
- Tally marks are a quick and useful way of counting totals.
- When you group bands you obtain frequency and grouped frequency distributions.

- A pictogram uses pictures instead of numbers.
- Pie charts are a simple form of display using circles.
- In bar charts comparisons are made of bars which may be drawn vertically or horizontally.
- A component bar chart enables component areas of a bar chart to be subdivided.
- A histogram takes the bar chart concept further by taking into account grouped frequency distributions.
- Gantt charts are a useful form of bar/line chart.
- Graphs show the relationships between two variables.
- A Lorenz curve is a cumulative frequency curve which shows the difference between a range of actual distribution and equal distribution.

73 Decision-making techniques

Decision-making, or choosing between different options, is perhaps the most important of all organisational activities. Taking decisions inevitably involves risk because the outcome of most decisions cannot be predicted with any certainty. The level of risk depends on the amount of information available and the quality of the decision-making techniques employed. In this chapter therefore we outline a range of key decision-making techniques that can be used by managers and other decision-makers in an organisation.

Defining the problem

In any decision-making activity the first step is to identify the problem or area requiring the decision to be made.

Brainstorming

Brainstorming involves defining a question and then suggesting a range of possible answers through group activity. In the first instance, all 'answers' which are brainstormed are recorded without judgement being passed on their usefulness or accuracy. Later this range of options are pared down to those that are most appropriate. In the case of decision-making, the first questions will be 'What is the problem?', and 'What is causing it? These provide a starting-point for the decision-making cycle.

Force field analysis

Force field analysis is a simple technique to help decision-makers identify where they currently are and where they want to be. It involves identifying the forces which are helping towards achieving the goal (positive forces) and the forces which are working against it (negative forces).

Value analysis

Having identified the major relationships involved in decision-making and the nature of the key problems, the next step is to identify a technique which will enable the decision-maker to focus on the main issues.

The aim of **value analysis** is to check that organisational activities are giving best value for money, particularly in relation to satisfying customers as economically as possible. Value analysis involves examining all the elements of organisational activity in order to eliminate any unnecessary or wasteful expenditure and exploring how value is added in order to identify better ways of creating value.

Pareto analysis

Pareto developed a simple piece of analysis known as the **80:20 rule**. In simple terms, this states that in organisational activity, 20% of activities or products will generate 80% of sales/profits and that 20% of an organisation's customers will create 80% of customer complaints – and so on. Pareto analysis involves establishing who or what constitutes the 20% of your problems or results and then taking appropriate action to make sure that efforts are effectively targeted.

Statistical/mathematical techniques

There are many mathematical techniques which can be used to aid decision-making. We shall look at some of the more commonly used of these below. However, it is important to bear in mind that most techniques today involve the use of computer programs, which do most of the calculations for the decision-maker. It is therefore only necessary to develop an overall appreciation of what the techniques involve rather than to waste time doing pointless exercises and detailed calculations which can be done in seconds by a computer.

Modelling

Mathematical models are used for a whole range of tasks, from planning which sequence of numbers to aim for in a game of darts, to planning journeys, when the two variables of speed and distance are combined to work out how long a journey will take. Modelling enables us to make more precise calculations than relying on instinct, experience or 'gut feeling'. Today's manager needs to understand a range of mathematical modelling tools, many of which are available as computer programs.

Types of model

Highly-structured situations and decisions lend themselves to **quantitative** models. These involve clear logical patterns and precision, often at the expense of realism. Data is fed into a mathematical model and the output is a fairly 'closed' solution.

Qualitative models are more realistic but less neat than quantitative ones. The way this type of model operates is less clear-cut and predictable and more like real life.

Models can be used for a range of different purposes and at a number of different levels within an organisation:

- At a **strategic** level, models can be used for planning corporate objectives and top-level policy-making;

- At a **tactical** level, models can be used for financial and manpower planning, designing plant and factory layout etc.;

- At an **operational** level, models can be used for customer credit ratings, media selection, production scheduling etc.

Mathematical techniques can be summarised under four headings:

1 **Statistical decision theory** sets out to optimise decision-making by identifying the statistically 'best' option;
2 **Mathematical programming** sets out to calculate the best solution with given conditions;
3 **Game theory** sets out to work out the best solution where several decision-makers or groups of decision-makers are involved;
4 **Multiple criteria decision-making** sets out to find the best solution where many criteria are involved.

In developing a model, it is necessary to:

- Define and express quantitatively the key variables involved in a decision;
- Set out the main components and limits of a model in numerical terms;
- Make sure that the problem can be tackled using mathematical tools.

The time taken to work out the problem in this way needs to be reasonable. The results also need to be easy to understand and of practical use.

Network analysis

When co-ordinating a business project, it is important to map out the tasks that must be carried out and perform them in a planned sequence. For instance, in building a house the walls are assembled before the roof is put on; the layers of a sponge cake are made before the icing is applied, etc. These events can be linked diagrammatically as shown in the illustration below, where A must be completed before B can be started:

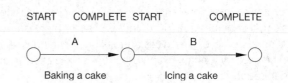

However, in many cases, activities do not have to take place in sequence; they can be carried out simultaneously. For example, the icing could be prepared at the same time as the cake is being baked. The diagram below shows that before you bake the cake and/or prepare the icing, you need to mix the ingredients for each, but the latter stages of production can be carried out simultaneously:

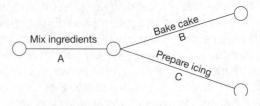

Network analysis can be used to map out programmes of activities in such a way as to create the most effective planning.

TASK 73.1

Set out a network diagram to indicate the performance of the following activities:

Activity	Relationship to other activities
A	Must be done first
B	Can be started only when A is finished
C	Can be started only when A is finished
D	Requires completion of B
E	Requires completion of C and D
F	Completes project and must await completion of all other activities

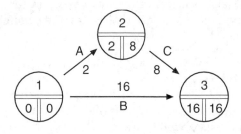

Figure 73.1 An example of critical path analysis

Critical path analysis

Critical path analysis is an important decision-making technique used in project planning. It involves setting out in a diagram:

- The sequence of activities involved in carrying out an activity;
- The time taken to carry out each activity;
- The **critical path** – i.e. the sequence of activities which are most crucial because delays to them will delay the completion of the project as a whole.

Once the critical path has been identified, it becomes possible for project managers to keep a close eye on this sequence of activities to make sure that tasks are being completed on time. If problems arise it may be possible to plough extra resources into activities along this path.

The network in Figure 73.1 above shows the relationship between the individual tasks. Each task is represented by a circle and is identified by a letter. Arrows drawn from left to right show the order in which the tasks must take place. The circles are the **nodes**, i.e. points in time when one or more activities finish or start.

A **network** links together a series of nodes showing the sequence of activities and timescale involved. Each of the circles can be broken down into two components:

1. The top semi-circle gives the number of the activity;
2. The bottom semi-circle can be used to show the earliest and the latest times for finishing the activity.

For example, in the set of activities in Figure 73.1 above, the earliest time to complete Activity C is 16 days. This is because although activities A and C can be completed in 10 days, it takes 16 days to complete activity B and so the earliest time to arrive at node 3 is 16 days.

The latest time to finish an activity is calculated by working backwards from the end of a project.

Figure 73.2 below shows the number of days required to finish a project with 12 nodes. Latest times are calculated by working backwards. Note that the two activities drawn in dotted lines are 'dummy activities' which do not use up time or resources. The critical path is shown by the line of grey arrows.

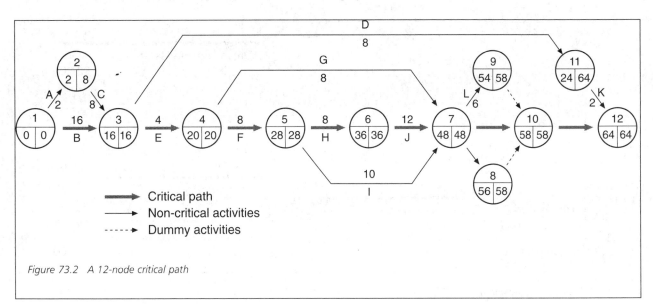

Figure 73.2 A 12-node critical path

For planning exercises that require critical path analysis, software packages such as Microsoft *Project* can be invaluable. They highlight the times certain resources need to be employed, including the specific responsibility of the project team members. As well as helping to solve the problem, the software facilitates the effective communication of the plan.

Probability analysis

In the previous chapter we briefly discussed the nature of probability. Probability analysis is often used in business in the form of **probability trees**. Probability tree analysis can be useful in cases where it is possible to obtain fair estimates of the probability of various eventualities.

A **decision tree** is a particular way of setting out the results of decision-making alternatives. Examining the tree enables the decision-maker to weigh up alternatives, compare the likely financial implication of each, adjust the figures according to their probability and then make a comparison. The steps involved are set out in a simple sequence.

Organisations can also reduce risk by using statistical techniques, as shown in the Case Study on page 517 opposite.

Using decision trees

Decision trees are another useful technique to help managers choose between two or more options. A decision tree consists of:

- **Decision points** These are represented by squares placed at points at which decisions have to be made;

- **Chance nodes** These are represented by circles. At these points there are different possible outcomes resulting from decisions that have been made – for example, the decision may lead to success or failure.

- **Probability** The probability of a certain event occurring is expressed as a numerical value on the decision tree. The values used are between 0 and 1. E.g. if there is a 0.7 chance of success, there is a 0.3 chance of failure.

- **Expected values** These are the financial outcomes of the decisions that have been made. E.g. if a firm is faced with a decision that has a 0.5 chance of making a £50,000 profit and a 0.5 chance of making a £20,000 loss, then:

Expected value $= 0.5 \; x \; 50,000 + 0.5 \; x - 20,000$

$= 25,000 - 10,000$

$= £15,000$

For example, using the information contained in the Case Study about John Sebastien opposite, a decision tree could be constructed as shown in Figure 73.3 below.

When making a decision, it is necessary to work out the expected values of each decision, taking into account the expected profit (or loss) and the probabilities.

In practice, decision tree analysis today is done almost exclusively using computer software. Many decisions will be very complicated, involving many decision points and probabilities. Decision trees are therefore most useful in solving technical problems when there are clear and easily calculated probabilities.

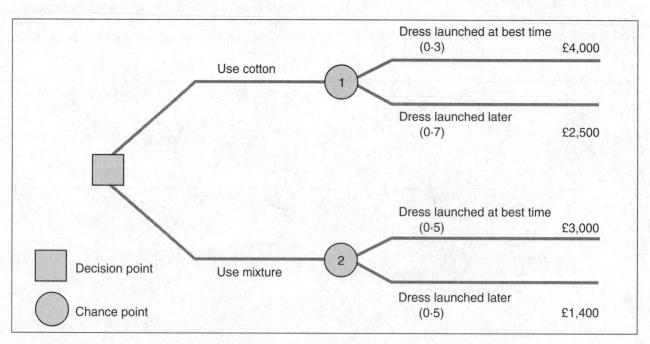

Figure 73.3 Example of a decision tree

DECISION-MAKING IN THE FASHION INDUSTRY

John Sebastien is in the business of producing fashion clothes. As important as the quality and design of John's garments is the timing of their launch on the market.

John believes that if he launches one of his new cotton dress designs this year it will yield a monthly gross profit figure of £4,000.

He could reduce his costs by making the dress in a cotton and synthetic mixture which would yield £3,000. However, this might extend the production time, which will cause him to come to market too late and the value of his sales might only yield a profit of £2,500 a month. Similarly, using the synthetic materials could cause technical problems which would lead to a delay, and profits of only £1,400 a month.

How can John choose from these alternative courses of action? The answer is to use a simple set of mathematical techniques:

1 The maximum payoff

This shows the *best possible result* from the four options. Clearly this would be to make the dresses out of cotton *and* get them to market on time. This would yield a gross profit of £4,000.

2 The minimum payoff

If we then look at the *worst possible scenario* we can see that this would arise as a result of not getting the dresses onto the market at the right time.

John should therefore try to make the best out of a bad situation – what we call the **maximin** situation. This would be to make the dresses out of cotton with a possible delay. This would yield a gross profit of £2,000.

Maximum regret

We can now introduce the notion of **regret** into our considerations. Regret is a measure of the possible loss incurred as a result of choosing a particular option. We can set out the 'regret' for each of the four eventualities in a simple diagram:

	Dresses on time	*Dresses are late*
Use cotton	0	1,500
Use cotton/ synthetic mix	0	1,600

John Sebastien can then compare the eventualities and choose the option which exposes him to least regret – i.e. use cotton (and of course do everything possible to get the product to market on time).

Calculating the odds

Simple mathematics can also be used in other ways to help managers make logical decisions. Because business activity usually follows a regular pattern it is possible to calculate the likelihood of particular events happening. These probabilities can be built into calculations in order to work out likely profits or **expected monetary values**.

For example, from previous evidence, John Sebastien is able to come up with figures for the probability of delays occurring if he uses cotton or cotton/synthetic mix, as follows:

- He knows that the probability of the hold-ups occurring if he uses cotton are 7 chances in 10, i.e. 0.7 : 0.3;
- He also knows that the probability of the hold-ups occurring if he uses the cotton/synthetic mix are 5 chances in 10, i.e. 0.5 : 0.5;
- The expected profits would therefore be:

For producing dresses in cotton:

(profit when on time x probability on time)
+ (profit when late x probability late)

= (4,000 x 0.3) + (2,500 x 0.7)

= 1,200 + 1,750

= 2,950

The same procedure can be followed for the cotton/synthetics mixture, i.e.:

- (profit when on time x probability on time)
+ (profit when late x probability late)

= (3,000 x 0.5) + (1,400 x 0.5)

= 1,500 + 700

= 2,200

It is clear therefore that if John goes for the cotton dresses option his profits are likely to be in the region of £2,950 per month compared with £2,200 for the mixtures option. Of course, in the real world it might not quite turn out like this, but the technique outlined above at least provides an opportunity to plan ahead logically.

Linear programming

Linear programming (LP) can be a useful decision-making tool where there is a linear (straight line) relationship between variables – for example, when choosing whether to make loaves of bread or cakes when there is a direct relationship between oven capacity and the number of items that can be made.

For a problem to be solved by linear programming, it needs to satisfy all four requirements below:

1 The problem must be capable of being stated in numeric terms;
2 All factors involved in the relationship must have linear relationships;
3 The problem must permit a choice, or choices, between alternative courses of action;
4 There must be at least one restriction on the factors involved. This may be on resources (e.g. a bakery can only bake bread for 72 hours in a week) or on particular characteristics (e.g. fertiliser used in a particular process must contain 15% phosphates and 10% nitrogen).

Linear programming is used mainly for short-term operating control decisions – for example, to identify ways of minimising the costs of production given certain minimum production rates, or to find the best ratio of processes to produce certain goods.

Specifying the constraints

To start a linear programming activity the first step is normally to specify the **constraints**. This is because the physical resources available are likely to be limited – for example, there may be restrictions on access to machines, working hours or other resources.

The problem therefore becomes one of 'constrained optimisation' – i.e. you want to achieve maximum results but you are limited by the constraints.

In producing items, a business may be able to produce a given number with its existing resources, e.g. 10,000 garden gnomes. However, the optimal solution may be to produce less than 10,000 garden gnomes because some of the resources will be better used for producing other items (e.g. birdbaths).

Therefore the constraint can be expressed as:

Production of garden gnomes ≤ 10,000

In this case the constraint involves a 'no greater than' situation. However, a constraint may also involve a 'no less than' situation. For example, the firm may have a regular order to supply to a retailer *at least* 500 birdbaths.

In this case the constraint would be set out as:

Production of birdbaths ≥ 500

Linear constraints

Constraints in LP must be linear. For example, suppose that a firm producing gnomes and birdbaths has 1,200 hours of labour available per month. Each garden gnome requires 1 hour of labour and each birdbath requires 2 hours of labour.

This means that the firm can produce *either* 1,200 garden gnomes *or* 600 birdbaths, *or* a combination of the two. This combination would be represented as a straight line on a graph involving a rate of exchange of production of 2:1. For every birdbath made, the firm sacrifices the production of two garden gnomes.

CASE STUDY CASE STUDY CASE STUDY CASE STUDY CASE STUDY

SOLVING A PROBLEM USING LINEAR PROGRAMMING

There are many ways of using LP, most today involving the use of computers. In order to learn how to use LP, you only need to concern yourself with problems involving two variables. For example:

Better Books Ltd produces two types of expensive book - **information books** and **atlases**. Its objective is to maximise its profit.

For each information book that it produces, it makes a profit of £10, and for each atlas it makes a profit of £10. This means that when the firm produces both items, total profit is represented by the equation:

Profit (P) = £10I + £10A

where 'I' is information books and 'A' is atlases.

The total profit will be:

£10I x number of information books produced + £10A x number of atlases produced

The functional relationship which represents the objective of the firm is therefore:

Maximum profit = £10I + £10A

(Continued on page 519)

SOLVING A PROBLEM USING LINEAR PROGRAMMING (Contd.)

We now need to look at the capacity restrictions facing the firm. For simplicity's sake we will say that there are two of these:

1 In the firm's warehouse there are only 15,000 cubic metres available;
2 Per month, there are only 2,400 machine hours available to produce the books.

By calculating the storage space for the books and the machine hours required to make them we will be able to present these restrictions in a linear form.

The warehousing constraint

Let us assume that each information book requires 1 cubic metre of warehouse space and each atlas requires half a cubic metre.

Because the total storage space is 15,000 cubic metres, Better Books could store 15,000 information books, or 30,000 atlases, or a combination of the two. However, the amount of books stored should not exceed the constraint of 15,000 cubic metres. This constraint can be written as:

$$1I + \tfrac{1}{2}A \leq 15,000$$

This can then be shown on a graph as in Figure 73.4. Note that the area above the curve is shaded to show that it is infeasible.

The feasible areas in terms of the storage constraint is OAB.

The machine hours constraint

We have seen that there are 2,400 machine hours available in a month to make the books.

We can assume that each information book takes 6 minutes of machine time, and each atlas requires 8 minutes of machine time (since atlases involve more colour printing).

This means that if available machine time was wholly dedicated to information book manufacture, it would be possible to produce 24,000 books in a month. If the time was allocated purely to atlases, 18,000 could be produced in a month.

Alternatively, it would be possible to produce a combination of the two books which lies somewhere along a straight line. All points on this line or to the left of it are feasible. Points to the right are infeasible.

We can then represent the linear constraint as:

$$6I + 8A \leq 2,400$$

This relationship is shown in Figure 73.5.

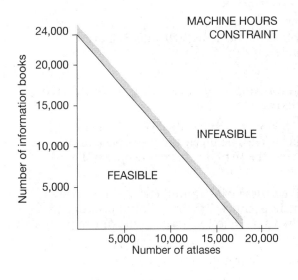

Figure 73.5 Machine hours constraint

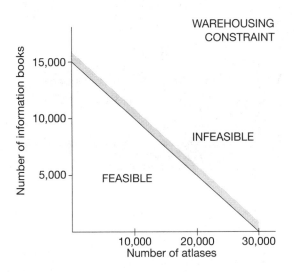

Figure 73.4 Warehousing constraint

(Continued on page 520)

SOLVING A PROBLEM USING LINEAR PROGRAMMING

(Continued from page 519)

The next step is to add the two constraints - i.e. the warehouse constraint and the machine hours constraint – onto a single diagram. The result is shown in Figure 73.6 below.

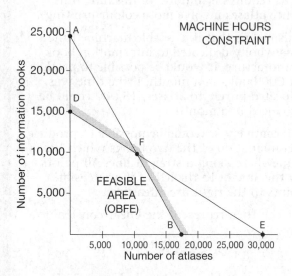

Figure 73.6 Graph showing machine hours and warehousing constraint combined

Note that the areas ADF and BFE are infeasible.

Maximising profits working within existing constraints

So far we have identified the production area that is feasible given the two constraints facing the firm, i.e. warehousing and machine hours.

Given these constraints, we can now work out how much the firm should produce to achieve its objective - i.e. to maximise profits.

We can do this by adding another ingredient to our diagram - an *iso-profit line*.

An iso-profit line will show combinations of atlas and information book production which will yield equal levels of profit.

Drawing iso-profit lines

At the start of this case we established that each book produced yielded a profit of £10, whether it was an atlas or an information book. Therefore we could draw an illustration setting out a series of iso-profit lines depending on the amount of profit made.

For example, if a £50,000 profit was made, this could be from producing 5,000 information books only, or 5,000 atlases only, or a combination of the two which would yield £50,000, e.g. 4,000 information books and 1,000 atlases.

Because Better Books is seeking to maximise profits, it will want to be on the highest possible iso-profit line that it can reach. We can therefore show the combination of two products that a firm will produce, given its objectives and constraints.

The *profit-maximising point* will be the feasible combination of products that touches the highest possible iso-profit line – Point J in Figure 73.7 below:

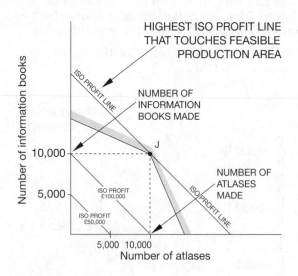

Figure 73.7 The profit-maximising point

Simulation

Simulations are often used when creating models of repetitive processes. Many business systems involve regular patterns which become routines – for example, ordering materials, taking delivery, making up finished goods, delivering finished goods, etc. It is essential to find out the best possible systems and methods for performing these routine functions.

Organisations are forever seeking ways of improving processes – usually by speeding them up. It is possible to study what happens by monitoring an activity under various conditions. Statistical techniques can also be used to simulate what might happen under a number of different conditions in order to make comparisons – e.g. working with more or fewer machines, working with machines in a different order, etc.

Simulating a queuing problem

Simulation can be a useful technique for making decisions about something we all dislike – queues! It is possible to simulate the size of queues that form given different numbers of 'stations' or service points. The same technique can be applied to loading bays, shop assistants, counter clerks, docking bays, etc.

The advantage of simulation is that the effects can be analysed without the expense of actually creating a queue and testing out the changes in real life.

There are four factors that contribute to the formation of a queue:

- The pattern of arrivals;
- The length of service time;
- The number of service points available;
- The queue discipline, e.g. first in, first out (FIFO), or last in, first out (LIFO), etc.

All four factors must be known before the simulation technique can be used.

Random numbers

Simulation involves imitating a real-life queue by sampling the rate of arrivals and the service times. **Random numbers** are used to reflect the fact that arrivals and service time will vary randomly over a short period of time. For this reason the technique is sometimes called the **Monte Carlo** method.

The procedure is as follows:

1 Identify the problem;
2 Gather the information concerning the four factors listed above;
3 Allocate the random numbers and simulate the imaginary event;
4 Analyse the results.

The Case Study below illustrates this process.

CASE STUDY CASE STUDY CASE STUDY CASE STUDY CASE STUDY

SOLVING A QUEUING PROBLEM

A sweetshop owner wanted to know if the addition of another assistant would reduce his queues significantly.

One morning he took a sample of the rate of arrivals:

Mins.:	0	1	2	3	4	5	6
Nos.:	6	15	23	24	16	10	8

The service time averaged out at 4 minutes per person.

The following calculations could then be made. First, the frequencies (f) are turned into cumulative frequencies (cf), and these are then used to determine the range of random numbers that will represent each arrival interval.

As can be seen from the table, a larger range proportionally represents the more frequent intervals.

Arrivals (min.)	%f	%cf	Random numbers
0	6	6	01–06
1	15	21	07–21
2	23	44	22–44
3	24	68	45–68
4	16	84	69–84
5	10	94	85–94
6	6	100	95–00

Figure 73.8

(Continued on page 522)

SOLVING A QUEUING PROBLEM

(Continued from page 521)

The random numbers in Figure 73.8 are taken from a **random number table**. Each number in the table has an equal (1 in 100) chance of appearing as long as the numbers are read from the table in a systematic order, i.e. top to bottom or left to right. The random numbers (**R nos.**) are used to represent the random nature of people arriving at the shop over a short period of time.

The shop opened at 9.00 a.m. and the first half-hour's activity is recorded in Figure 73.9 below. The 'Queue' column increases as customers are kept waiting.

The table could then be drawn to show the effect of employing two assistants in order to see if the queue would be eliminated. However, the sweetshop owner would have to take care that the two assistants were not idle for too long.

Random number	Mins.	Arrival time	Served at	Mins.	Free at	Queue no.	Idle
20	1	9.01	9.01	4	9.05	0	1
35	2	9.03	9.06	4	9.10	3	0
98	6	9.09	9.10	4	9.14	1	0
94	5	9.14	9.14	4	9.18	0	0
04	0	9.14	9.18	4	9.22	4	0
11	1	9.15	9.22	4	9.26	7	0
00	6	9.21	9.26	4	9.30	3	0
51	3	9.24	9.30	4	9.29	6	0

Figure 73.9 *Effect of employing two assistants*

Table A

20	84	27	38	66	19	60	10	51	20
35	16	74	58	72	79	98	09	47	07
98	82	69	63	23	70	80	88	86	23
94	67	94	34	03	77	89	30	49	51
04	54	32	55	94	82	08	19	20	73
11	25	66	08	79	68	19	37	82	73
00	63	79	77	41	17	06	67	18	33
51	51	54	44	64	13	51	92	10	37
49	72	73	93	29	39	37	94	42	66
77	09	20	05	20	77	47	58	96	05

Table B

16	45	77	65	20	11	65	65	56	36
51	63	28	55	12	23	72	99	04	41
64	46	55	58	78	96	52	43	23	05
37	75	41	57	02	14	88	79	97	09
55	36	70	34	66	58	63	90	06	37
99	10	23	74	53	13	59	59	36	71
53	80	84	57	47	60	60	70	69	95
99	29	37	69	30	83	48	05	88	91
21	41	63	90	85	65	07	46	75	42
01	97	45	05	95	88	19	78	14	32

Figure 73.10 *Random number tables*

Chapter summary

- The function of decision-making techniques is to help managers and others to make more accurate decisions.

- The starting point is to define the problem.

- Once the nature of the problem has been established, there are a range of techniques for analysing and finding the 'best' solutions.

- Statistical and mathematical techniques produce clear-cut answers. However, they are only relevant if there are clear-cut relationships between variables.

- Network analysis makes it possible to outline a sequence of stages involved in carrying out an activity.

- Critical path analysis is a technique used in project planning. The purpose is to identify the most crucial sequence of activities in the project. It is then possible to focus efforts and resources into making sure that tasks on the critical path are completed on time.

- Probability analysis involves setting out the probability of events occurring in order to come up with a solution to a problem that is most likely to be successful. This can take the risk out of decision-making provided it is possible to predict the likely success or failure of particular events, activities, etc.

- Probability analysis makes it possible to calculate such things as maximum and minimum pay-offs, and maximum regret. A decision tree sets out a series of decisions involving chance in a sequence of activities on paper.

- Linear programming is an important mathematical technique that can be used in making calculations for short-term operational decisions. In particular it is helpful in calculating the best ways of combining resources, and what products to concentrate on given limited resources and other production constraints.

- Simulations can be used to create models of repetitive or routine processes. Simulation makes it possible to study routines in order to identify the best way of carrying out tasks and sequences of activities.

74 Analysing data

In Chapter 72 we looked at the importance of data collection for decision-making purposes. We examined the collection techniques themselves and also some of the presentation methods for data. But presentation is not an end in itself. For example, a report might contain histograms or even Lorenz curves, but what does this data mean and how should it be interpreted? In order to be able to draw some meaningful conclusions from the figures which have been collected and presented, it is important to understand the principles and techniques of **data analysis**.

Central tendency

In Chapter 50 we looked at central tendency in order to analyse market research data. Central tendency, or the use of averages, is a useful way of comparing one set of data with another. This is then used to represent that data set. As we saw, there are three methods of calculating an average from a set of data: mean, median and mode.

Figure 74.1 shows the prices of wine cases sold by Red and White Ltd. during a particular week. We shall use it to demonstrate the calculation of various statistical measures.

CASES

		A	B	C	D	E	F	G	H	I	J
	1	41	35	36	48	52	41	60	32	33	34
D	2	37	44	53	46	49	29	28	31	30	46
A											
Y	3	51	42	28	26	27	34	35	26	42	65
S	4	46	48	37	39	42	31	30	56	29	54
	5	46	42	81	31	35	34	39	41	35	68
	6	24	90	35	36	43	44	52	46	42	33

Fig 74.1 Red and White Ltd: one week's sales of wine cases (£s)

Mean

As we saw in Chapter 50, the **mean** is the average of all the values in the table. The average is calculated by summing all of the case prices (which in this case equals £2,490), and dividing by the number of cases, giving £41.50. The change in average price over time may indicate to Red and White the extent to which people have changed their spending priorities.

Median

The **median** is the middle set of numbers. To find the median manually, we have to place all the case prices in order and find the middle value. In this example, as we have two middle values, we would have to average the thirtieth and thirty-first prices. This comes to £40.00.

Mode

The **mode** is the value that occurs most frequently in a set of numbers. In this example, customers buy cases priced at £46 five times – more often than any other value – so the mode is £46. Where there are two values with the same frequency, the set of numbers is said to be **bimodal**.

If Red and White were to analyse their wine sales by country of origin, the mode would indicate which was the most popular (and also the country to which it could justify travelling in search of new wine suppliers).

Dispersion

Although averages are important in providing information about the middle of a distribution, they do not tell us how other figures in the distribution are spread. Some data might be tight around the mean, while other values might be well dispersed.

A **range** represents the difference between the highest and lowest values in a set of data. It is easy to find and provides information about a spread of figures:

Range = Highest value – lowest value

The problem with looking at a range is that it can be distorted by one extreme value and it provides no indication of the spread *between* values. The range for the figures 4, 4, 4, 4, 4 and 20,000 is '4 to 20,000'. This is misleading in terms of both values and the spread

between the extremes. This disadvantage can be overcome and extreme values can be ignored by slicing away the top and bottom quarters and then analysing what is left.

Whereas the median is the middle number of an array of figures and represents 50 per cent, a **quartile** represents a quarter or 25 per cent of a range. The lower or first quartile is the area below which 25 per cent of observations fall, and the upper or fourth quartile is the value above which 25 per cent of observations fall:

Inter-quartile range = Upper quartile – lower quartile

From this, conclusions can be drawn about the middle 50 per cent of the data analysed.

For example, the lower quartile, median, upper quartile and inter-quartile range can be extracted from the array of 20 numbers below as follows:

4	5	8	9	15	18	20	22	24	29
32	35	37	40	44	44	48	52	58	60

- The **lower quartile** will be the value below which 25 per cent of the numbers will fall and therefore will be 25 per cent of 20 and the fifth value of 15. Using $n/2$, the median will be 20/2, giving the tenth value, 29.
- The **upper quartile** will be the value above which 25 per cent of the numbers fall. As there are 20 values in the array, it will be 75 per cent of 20, i.e. the fifteenth value which is 44. Whereas the range for this set of figures is 54 and extends from 4 to 60, the **inter-quartile range** will be the upper quartile of 44 less the lower quartile of 15, i.e. 29.

Although the inter-quartile range, or quartile deviation, is easy to understand and is unaffected by extreme values, it might not be precise enough for a large sample. In these instances it could be necessary to use **deciles** or **percentiles**.

A decile represents a tenth of a given distribution. From our example, the first decile will be 10 per cent of 20, i.e. the second value, 5; the second decile will be the fourth value, 9; and so on. A percentile represents a hundredth part of a given distribution. The 95th percentile of our values will be 95 per cent of the 20 values and so will be the nineteenth value, 58.

> ## IT'S A FACT
>
> The monthly mean daily maximum temperatures in August in various parts of the UK are:
>
> | Northern Ireland | Northern Scotland | Western Scotland | Eastern Scotland | NW England | NE England | Midlands | East Anglia | SW England | SE England |
> |---|---|---|---|---|---|---|---|---|---|
> | 21.9 | 19.6 | 21.7 | 21.6 | 23.4 | 22.3 | 25.1 | 24.4 | 23.8 | 25.3 |

Mean deviation

A measure of dispersion that further analyses a group of values and makes use of all observations is the **mean deviation**. This simply measures the average deviation of all values in a distribution from the actual mean. It averages the differences between the actual values in a distribution and the mean, while at the same time ignoring the negative signs of differences. For the figures of 5, 6, 13, 20 and 26, the arithmetical mean ($\bar{x}$) is:

$$\bar{x} = \frac{5 + 6 + 13 + 20 + 26}{5} = \frac{70}{5} = 14$$

The differences from the arithmetic mean are:

$$5 - 14, \ 6 - 14, \ 13 - 14, \ 26 - 14$$
$$= -9, -8, -1, 6, 12$$

If we ignore the negative signs, we can find the mean deviation as follows:

$$\frac{9 + 8 + 1 + 6 + 12}{5} = \frac{36}{5} = 7.2$$

The mean deviation, or average difference, from the mean is therefore 7.2. It is usual to express this in the following way:

$$\text{Mean deviation} = \frac{\Sigma|x - \bar{x}|}{n}$$

where $|x - \bar{x}|$ represents the difference between the mean and the actual value but ignoring negative signs.

Variance and standard deviation

The major problem of all methods of dispersion looked at so far is that they have limited uses for further analysing data. Having worked out a quartile or a decile, you know more about a distribution, but there are few further uses to which this information can be put. As the mean deviation ignores the plus and minus differences, it also has limited uses for further statistical processing. This is not so in the case of the **variance** and **standard deviation**, which are widely used in statistical analysis and are the most important measures of dispersion.

Variance

Instead of ignoring the minuses and differences from the mean, the variance and standard deviation square the differences, instantly eliminating the negative signs. When the squared differences have been averaged, a variance is created and the square root of this variance provides the standard deviation.

For example, if the output of a machine over five days were 4, 5, 5, 7 and 9 units, the arithmetical mean would be 6. The variance measures the extent of the dispersion around the mean by:

1 Calculating the difference between the number of units produced each day and the arithmetic mean: this is shown as x − $\bar{x}$;
2 Squaring the difference: $(x - \bar{x})^2$;
3 Finding the average of the total of these squared differences. This is shown as:

$$\frac{[\Sigma(x - x)^2]}{n}$$

where *n* is the number of values. For example, in the table below:

Outputs

x	x − $\bar{x}$	$(x - x)^2$
4	−2	4
5	−1	1
5	−1	1
7	1	1
9	3	9
	0	16

the variance would be

$$\frac{16}{5} = 3.2 \text{ units}$$

Standard deviation

The standard deviation is the square root of the variance. In our example, this will be:

$$\sqrt{3.2} = 1.79 \text{ units}$$

Thus we have an arithmetic mean of 6 units, a variance of 3.2 and a standard deviation of 1.79 units. By taking into account frequency (*f*) and denoting standard deviation as *s*, we can show its formula as follows:

$$s = \sqrt{\frac{\Sigma f(x - \bar{x})^2}{n}} \text{ or } \sqrt{\frac{\Sigma f(x - \bar{x})^2}{\Sigma f}}$$

Value x	Frequency f	x − $\bar{x}$	$(x - x)^2$	$f(x - x)^2$
4	4	−2	4	16
5	6	−1	1	6
6	9	0	0	0
7	8	1	1	8
8	3	2	4	12
	30			42

The example given in the table takes into consideration frequency and has an arithmetic mean ($\bar{x}$) of 6. The standard deviation will be 1.4 = 1.18.

Although it is sometimes difficult to understand the significance of the standard deviation, it can be said that the greater the dispersion, the larger the standard deviation. As all values in the distribution are taken into account, it is a comprehensive measure of dispersion capable of being developed further.

Distribution curves

Any frequency distribution may either be **symmetrical** or **skewed**. A symmetrical frequency curve will be divided into two equal halves so that the arithmetic mean, median and mode will all have the same value. Such distributions create a normal curve with a symmetrical bell shape and represent a continuous variable in frequency distribution.

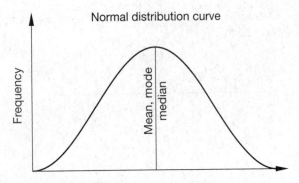

Figure 74.2 Normal distribution curve

The normal distribution curve represents all possible outcomes and the frequency with which they will take place. As the curve is symmetrical, 50 per cent of events will take place above the mean and 50 per cent below the mean value (see Figure 74.3). This can be used to find probabilities of certain events taking place.

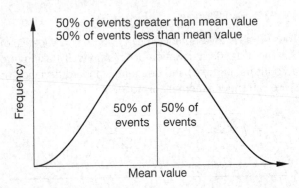

Figure 74.3

Normal distribution tables can be used to find these probabilities, as they measure the area from the mean to a fixed number of standard deviation away from the mean. The letter Z represents the number of standard deviations a value is above or below the mean. It is calculated by:

$$Z = \frac{x - m}{s}$$

where:

Z = number of standard deviations above or below the mean

x = the value

m = the mean

s = the standard deviation

For example, suppose that a frequency has a normal distribution, a mean of 50 and a standard deviation of 10. We can use this process to find out what proportion of the total frequencies will be:

- Above 30
- Above 60
- Below 45
- Below 75

To calculate the proportion of frequencies above a value, it must be remembered that:

1   Fifty per cent of the values are above the mean and so the proportion calculated as being between the mean and the value must be added to the 50 per cent.

For frequencies above 30, we can see that:

$$Z = \frac{50 - 30}{10} = \frac{20}{10} = 2 \text{ standard deviations}$$

By referring to the normal distribution tables (see Figure 74.5 opposite), the number of frequencies above 30 is therefore:

$$0.5 + 0.4772 = 0.9772 \text{ or } 97.72\%$$

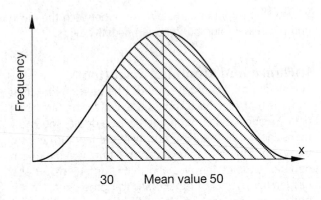

Figure 74.4 Frequencies above 30

The shaded area in Figure 74.4 represents 97.72 per cent of the frequencies above the value of 30.

2   If the value is above the mean, the total proportion is 50 per cent minus the area between the value and the mean.

With frequencies above 60:

$$Z = \frac{60 - 50}{10} = \frac{10}{10}$$

= 1 standard deviation above the mean

The number of frequencies above 60 is therefore 0.5 − 0.3413, or 15.87%

Z	0.00	0.01	0.02	0.03	0.04	0.05	0.06	0.07	0.08	0.09
0.0	0.0000	0.0040	0.0080	0.0120	0.0160	0.0199	0.0239	0.0279	0.0319	0.0359
0.1	0.0398	0.0438	0.0478	0.0517	0.0557	0.0596	0.0636	0.0675	0.0714	0.0753
0.2	0.0793	0.0832	0.0871	0.0910	0.0948	0.0987	0.1026	0.1064	0.1103	0.1141
0.3	0.1179	0.1217	0.1255	0.1293	0.1331	0.1368	0.1406	0.1443	0.1480	0.1517
0.4	0.1554	0.1591	0.1628	0.1664	0.1700	0.1736	0.1772	0.1808	0.1844	0.1879
0.5	0.1915	0.1950	0.1985	0.2019	0.2054	0.2088	0.2123	0.2157	0.2190	0.2224
0.6	0.2257	0.2291	0.2324	0.2357	0.2389	0.2422	0.2454	0.2486	0.2517	0.2549
0.7	0.2580	0.2611	0.2642	0.2673	0.2704	0.2734	0.2764	0.2794	0.2823	0.2852
0.8	0.2881	0.2910	0.2939	0.2967	0.2995	0.3023	0.3051	0.3078	0.3106	0.3133
0.9	0.3159	0.3186	0.3212	0.3238	0.3264	0.3289	0.3315	0.3340	0.3365	0.3389
1.0	0.3413	0.3438	0.3461	0.3485	0.3508	0.3531	0.3554	0.3577	0.3599	0.3621
1.1	0.3643	0.3665	0.3686	0.3708	0.3729	0.3749	0.3770	0.3790	0.3810	0.3830
1.2	0.3849	0.3869	0.3888	0.3907	0.3925	0.3944	0.3962	0.3980	0.3997	0.4015
1.3	0.4032	0.4049	0.4066	0.4082	0.4099	0.4115	0.4131	0.4147	0.4162	0.4177
1.4	0.4192	0.4207	0.4222	0.4236	0.4251	0.4265	0.4279	0.4292	0.4306	0.4319
1.5	0.4332	0.4345	0.4357	0.4370	0.4382	0.4394	0.4406	0.4418	0.4429	0.4441
1.6	0.4452	0.4463	0.4474	0.4484	0.4495	0.4505	0.4515	0.4525	0.4535	0.4545
1.7	0.4554	0.4564	0.4573	0.4582	0.4591	0.4599	0.4608	0.4616	0.4625	0.4633
1.8	0.4641	0.4649	0.4656	0.4664	0.4671	0.4678	0.4686	0.4693	0.4699	0.4706
1.9	0.4713	0.4719	0.4726	0.4732	0.4738	0.4744	0.4750	0.4756	0.4761	0.4767
2.0	0.4772	0.4778	0.4783	0.4788	0.4793	0.4798	0.4803	0.4808	0.4812	0.4817
2.1	0.4821	0.4826	0.4830	0.4834	0.4838	0.4842	0.4846	0.4850	0.4854	0.4857
2.2	0.4861	0.4864	0.4868	0.4871	0.4875	0.4878	0.4881	0.4884	0.4887	0.4890
2.3	0.4893	0.4896	0.4898	0.4901	0.4904	0.4906	0.4909	0.4911	0.4913	0.4916
2.4	0.4918	0.4920	0.4922	0.4925	0.4927	0.4929	0.4931	0.4932	0.4934	0.4936
2.5	0.4938	0.4940	0.4941	0.4943	0.4945	0.4946	0.4948	0.4949	0.4951	0.4952
2.6	0.4953	0.4955	0.4956	0.4957	0.4959	0.4960	0.4961	0.4962	0.4963	0.4964
2.7	0.4965	0.4966	0.4967	0.4968	0.4969	0.4970	0.4971	0.4972	0.4973	0.4974
2.8	0.4974	0.4975	0.4976	0.4977	0.4977	0.4978	0.4979	0.4979	0.4980	0.4981
2.9	0.4981	0.4982	0.4982	0.4983	0.4984	0.4984	0.4985	0.4985	0.4986	0.4986
3.0	0.4987	0.4987	0.4987	0.4988	0.4988	0.4989	0.4989	0.4989	0.4990	0.4990

Figure 74.5 Normal distribution tables

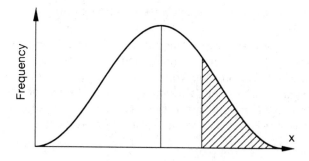

Figure 74.6 Frequencies above 60

The shaded area in Figure 74.6 represents 15.87 per cent of the frequencies above the value of 60.

To calculate the proportion of frequencies below a certain value:

1 If the value is below the mean, the proportion is 50 per cent minus the area between the value and the mean.

For example, to calculate frequencies below 45:

$$Z = \frac{50 - 45}{10} = \frac{5}{10}$$

$$= 0.5 \text{ standard deviation below the mean}$$

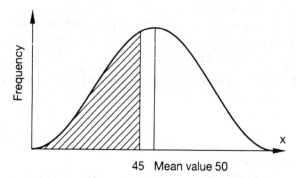

Figure 74.7 Frequencies below 45

The number of frequencies below 45 are therefore $0.5 - 0.1915 = 0.3085$ or 30.85%

The shaded area in Figure 74.7 represents 30.85 per cent of the frequencies below the value of 45.

2 If the value is above the mean, the proportion to be obtained is 50 per cent plus the area between the value and the mean.

For example, to calculate frequencies below 75:

$$Z = \frac{75 - 50}{10} = \frac{25}{10}$$

= 2.5 standard deviations above the mean

The number of frequencies below 75 are therefore:

0.5 + 0.4938 = 0.9938 or 99.38%

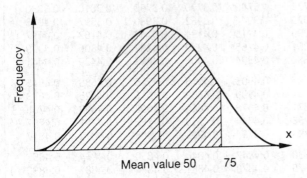

Figure 74.8 Frequencies below 75

The shaded area in Figure 74.8 represents 99.38% of the frequencies below the value of 75.

Binomial distribution

The name 'binomial' refers to another method of analysing probability from a distribution and describes any situation where there are two possible alternatives. For example, you might change your car, or you might not change your car: there are two possible courses of action. For any situation to fit the binomial pattern, one of the following conditions must apply:

1 It must be an 'either/or' situation with only two possible outcomes;
2 It must consist of a number of trials denoted by *n*.
3 It must have a known probability of success on each trial, denoted by *p*.

Probability may be measured with some accuracy. If a die is rolled, there is a 0.167 probability (i.e. 1 in 6) that a 4 will turn up; when a coin is tossed, there is a 0.5 probability (one in two) that it will turn up heads. Probability may be measured from past experiences, from information such as weather records, analyses of machine breakdowns, faulty goods, working days lost, etc. It may also be estimated from surveys or trials in the market.

For example, if a sample contained five green products, two yellow products and three purple products, and if stocks were not replenished after being sold, we can work out the probability of a customer picking out the two

yellow products. On the first occasion the chances of picking out two yellow products are 2 in 10, so *p* = 1 in 5. As there is only 1 yellow left, the changes of picking it from the 9 remaining products are 1 in 9. By multiplying the two probabilities together, we can work out the chances of picking two yellow products as follows:

$$\frac{1}{9} \times \frac{1}{5} = \frac{1}{45}$$

With a knowledge of probabilities, using the binomial model enables management to predict more precisely the outcome of future events.

Skewness

Skewness is used to describe a non-symmetrical frequency distribution curve. A **positively skewed** frequency distribution curve will have a bias towards the left-hand side of a graph and will have a long tail sloping out to the right (see Figure 74.9 below). With a positively skewed distribution the mode will have a lower value than the median and the mean will have a higher value than the median.

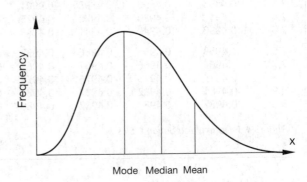

Figure 74.9 Positively skewed frequency distribution curve

A **negatively skewed** frequency distribution curve will have a bias towards the right-hand side of the graph and will have a long tail sloping out towards the left (see Figure 74.10). With a negatively skewed distribution the mode will have a higher value than the median and the mean will have a lower value than the median.

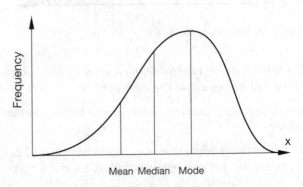

Figure 74.10 Negatively skewed frequency distribution curve

STATISTICAL PROCESS CONTROL

Statistical process control (SPC) is a quality system which uses simple statistics to assist in the control of manufacturing processes. All manufacturing processes combine 'the four M's' – Men (people), Materials, Machines and Methods – which, together with the environment, affect output.

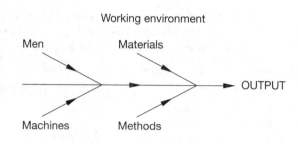

Figure 74.11 *The manufacturing process*

When output is in statistical process control, any variation is solely due what are known as **common causes,** and even these can be reduced. Common causes are inherent to the process and therefore stable over time. They are always predictable and present. **Special causes** are not inherent to the process and are due to a few **major causes.** These are unpredictable and will recur if no action is taken.

The lower part of the diagram shows that when special causes are present the distribution of products is skewed. When special causes are eliminated the distribution becomes normal, and when common causes are reduced, more products are centred around the mean, median and mode.

Statistical process control should be viewed as part of a never-ending search to improve product quality. A process is in statistical control when all of the points are within control limits and there are no abnormal patterns or trends present.

Tasks

1 Explain how statistics can support manufacturing quality procedures.

2 Why do 'special causes' lead to skewed frequency distributions?

3 When is a process in statistical control?

Figure 74.12 *Statistical process control and the many causes*

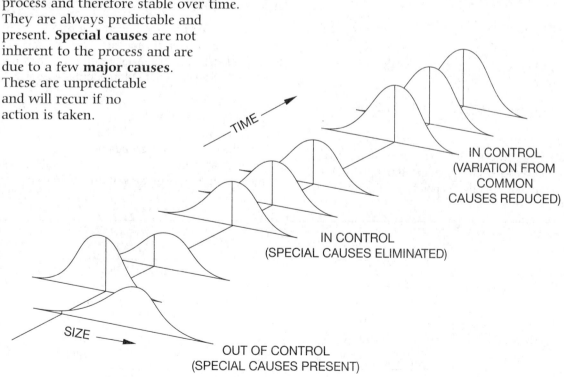

Index numbers

It is sometimes difficult to make comparisons between sets of figures. Often the complexity and size of the units being measured can make direct comparisons meaningless. Instead of trying to make sense of complicated technical figures based upon a mass of information, it can be better to strive for a single figure which shows a direct comparison between one time period and another. **Index numbers** provide a way to do this by taking a typical year as a base and expressing figures for other years as percentages of it.

For example, suppose an organisation's sales figures are as shown in the table below:

Year	Sales (000)
19X0	458
19X1	535
19X2	573
19X3	584

We decide to use 19X0 as a base year against which all others are to be compared. It is usual to use 100 as a base, as in everyday life we are used to making comparisons based on percentages, so the index for 19X0 is 100. In order to work out the index for the other years, we must now divide each year's sales figures by the base year and multiply this by 100 as follows:

$$\frac{\text{Figures for other years}}{\text{Base year's figures}} \times 100$$

For 19X1 this will be $\frac{535}{458} \times 100 = 116.81$

For 19X1 this will be $\frac{573}{458} \times 100 = 125.11$

For 19X1 this will be $\frac{5843}{458} \times 100 = 127.51$

We can see from these figures that sales have increased by nearly 28% from 19X0 to 19X3. We can work out annual percentage increases from the index. Between 19X2 and 19X3 the index has risen by 2.4 points. By dividing this by the sales index figure for 19X2 and converting the result to a percentage, we can find the percentage increase in sales for 19X3:

$$\frac{2.4}{125.11} \times 100 = 1.92\% \text{ increase in sales}$$

Index numbers are widely used to represent a variety of areas or items. A well-known example is the Retail Price Index, which is used as an indicator of domestic price inflation. Domestic prices cover a host of commodities, and clearly more than one item is taken into consideration when the Index is calculated.

As an example, let us produce a hypothetical index for country A. Over the period 19X0–19X1 prices of bread, cheese, meat and vegetables were as follows:

Item	19X0	19X1
Bread	50p per loaf	55p per loaf
Cheese	130p per kg.	125p per kg.
Meat	160p per kg.	180p per kg.
Vegetables	40p per kg.	50p per kg.

As we can see, in the year 19X0 to 19X1, prices for bread, meat and vegetables went up, but the price of cheese fell. We wish to produce a single index figure to reflect these changes, but the table gives no indication of how important each item is to the cost of living and also tries to compare different units. This can be overcome by **weighting** each item in proportion to its relative importance.

By selecting a weight, the importance of each item and the units in which it appears can be taken into consideration to produce a final figure which is directly comparable. The procedure for doing this is:

1 List all the items with their prices;
2 Select appropriate weights;
3 Multiply prices by their weights;
4 Add the weighted prices together;
5 Produce an index by comparing the total weighted prices from the base year with the other year.

			19X0		19X1
Item	Weight	Price	Price x weight	Price	Price x weight
Bread	80	50	4,000	35	4,400
Cheese	50	130	6,500	125	6,250
Meat	30	160	4,800	180	5,400
Vegetables	10	40	400	50	500
Total			15,700		16,550

Figure 74.13 Weighted cost of living index

Continuing our example, we allocate a weight of 80 to bread, 30 to meat and 10 to vegetables. By taking 19X0 as the base year and designating 100 to it, we can see that:

$$\frac{16,550}{15,700} \times 100 = 105.41$$

i.e. prices have risen during the year by 5.41 per cent.

Probably the best known of all UK official statistics is the **Consumer Price Index**, which is generally accepted as the official measure of price inflation. This measures inflation in real terms rather than just monetary terms and has important implications for pay negotiations and settlements.

Although indices are traditionally associated with prices, they can also be used for a multitude of commercial purposes such as insurance and index-linked schemes. Perhaps their greatest advantage is that they are easy to understand and provide a common scale by which to compare different types of information.

Chapter summary

- Data analysis helps managers to draw meaningful conclusions from data.
- Central tendency uses averages to compare one set of data with another.
- The range helps to provide information about the spread of data.
- A quartile represents a quarter of a range and a decile one-tenth.
- The mean deviation helps to analyse a group of values from the mean.
- The square root of the variance is the standard deviation.
- Any frequency distribution may be symmetrical or skewed.
- We can use the normal distribution curve to estimate probabilities.
- The binomial distribution is another method for analysing probability from a distribution.
- Index numbers help us to make comparisons between one time period and another.

75 Using information technology

Not long ago, many people were frightened by the idea of using a computer. The hardware seemed alien and prone to go wrong at the most inconvenient times, and manuals and documentation were often dauntingly complex. Since then, computers have become much more consumer-orientated, and a great deal of thought has gone into making them user-friendly and suitable for the needs of different people and organisations.

There are many different definitions of information technology, but as the field develops and IT becomes further ingrained in our society it is probably becoming easier to define. A modern definition is as follows:

'IT refers to technologies and applications developed through the recent combining of data-processing and storage powers of computers with the distance-transmission capabilities of telecommunications.'

As this definition implies, computers were originally used for storing data rather than for transmission. The definition also usefully reflects the increasing convergence of technologies between computing and tele-communications.

A further definition of IT is provided by The Macmillan Dictionary of IT:

'The acquisition, processing, storage and dissemination of vocal, pictorial, textual and numerical information by a microelectronics-based combination of computing and telecommunications.'

Information technology as we understand it today dates back to the 1960s when the satellite Telstar was launched to provide television and telephone services. The 1960s saw widespread development of the use of transistors, followed in the 1970s by digital technology in telecommunications and integrated circuits.

In the 80s we saw the beginning of convergence with the telecommunications industry using electronic switches in exchanges and the computer industry developing applications using telecommunications.

How will IT affect you?

There is no doubt that IT already affects many aspects of our daily lives both at home and in the workplace.

There are generally considered to be two approaches to IT.

1   **The utopia scenario**
    For the IT optimists, everything about information technology is wonderful. IT is seen as increasing productivity and improving lifestyles, helping to create wealth and leading to a better society with new levels of perfection. IT will also help to create social harmony, democracy and decentralisation, give power back to the people and provide the opportunity for limitless individual creativity and expression.

2   **The doom scenario**
    IT doom-merchants think that technology will irrevocably damage society. It will place power in the hands of faceless bureaucracies, divide society into information 'haves' and 'have-nots', and cause massive unemployment and de-skilling. Far from transforming society, IT will simply bolster existing commercial and political interests.

The more down-to-earth position is that certain aspects of information technology will have a positive effect, while others will not. The result is likely to be complex and not simply good or bad!

Michael Marien states [source] that two particular preconceptions about technology should be avoided:

1   The uncritically euphoric stance adopted by commercial interests, which invariably emphasise only the positive attributes of new technology;

2   The excessively negative and pessimistic stance that perceives all modern technology as a human disaster, or focuses solely on growing corporate or government control of information systems.

Marien himself admits some validity in both of these positions. He concludes that IT has the potential for both good *and* evil, centralisation *and* decentralisation, freedom *and* oppression, wealth *and* poverty. In contrast to the extreme views above, he states that the reality is likely to be complex and ambiguous, requiring many critical choices and bringing both euphoria and gloom.

TASK 75.1

Working in groups, comment upon how you feel about the following statements:

1   'Information technology is friendly; it offers a helping hand, and it should be embraced. We should think of it more like ET than IT.'

Margaret Thatcher

2   'The choice of technology and the way it is applied to work is a political issue because the purposes of employers are not necessarily consonant with those of employees.'

3   'Ultimately, the way that the world looks in the 21st century will be determined by the collective accumulated choices of ourselves as individuals and the directions taken by the corporate bodies whose actions determine the general shape of our society.'

CASE STUDY CASE STUDY CASE STUDY CASE STUDY CASE STUDY

INFORMATION OVERLOAD

A recent study by accountants Deloitte & Touche Consulting Group found that office workers are drowning in information from computer systems and the Internet – and that much of it has little value.

Around 40% of the 150 people questioned had major problems knowing where to look for information. Almost a third said that there were too many sources. Big organisations in particular waste a lot of time reinventing information which already exists. At the same time, nearly 40 per cent of them rarely have the information they need to do their jobs properly.

The usefulness of the Internet was not rated highly by office workers. Even so, most organisations are on the Net and are considering going live in the next two years.

1   What is meant by information overload?

2   Why might many managers have problems looking for information?

3   What might be the uses of the Internet for business organisations?

4   Why are many organisations going on the Net if they do not value its use? Is this a case of technology for technology's sake?

Information technology at work

A modern organisation can be seen of consisting of three sub-systems:

1 The **management sub-system** is concerned with all the people and activities involved in planning, controlling and decision-making;
2 The **operations sub-system** is concerned with all the activities, material flows and people directly involved with performing the primary function of the organisation such as manufacturing a product or providing a service;
3 The **information sub-system** is made up of the people, machines, ideas and activities that go into gathering and processing data. This may include the way the information is collected, stored and used.

It has been claimed that a significant element in modern society is the value it places upon information. Bell describes information as 'the characteristic technology of post-industrial society'. Similarly, Touraine argues that in post-industrial society, the treatment of information plays the same central role that the treatment of natural resources played at the beginning of industrialisation .

SYNTHESIS

Where do you stand between the 'utopia/doom' scenario? Outline your position, using examples to support your case.

Objectives of information processing

Information processing affects almost everybody within an organisation. The ability to process information efficiently provides organisations with many advantages in the markets in which they compete.

For example:

● It improves speed and response to customer demands and requests;
● It improves the accuracy and reliability of information being processed;
● It reduces costs and improves performance;
● It supports decision-making processes;
● It helps to provide organisations with advantages over their competitors.

CASE STUDY CASE STUDY CASE STUDY CASE STUDY CASE STUDY

ACCOUNT MANAGEMENT

Computers have transformed the way that businesses store and process information – and how they relate to their customers. Take the case of the electricity supply company and their customers, the Patel family from Reading...

The electricity supply company keeps a regular record of amounts owed by the Patels for electricity used, the amounts paid and the resulting balance. Every now and then it may want to check on this information - for example, if the Patels have a query on their account.

All the details relating to the Patel's account are stored on files and can be retrieved whenever required. They can be reproduced and printed out instantly when the Patels need to see a statement of their account.

The company can also classify the information about the Patel's account under various sub-headings - for example, under the totals of electricity used at peak and off-peak times.

Customer information held on file by the electricity company can be sorted in many ways - for example, date order to show how much electricity consumers used at different times of the year. The electricity company can also see at a glance which customers have unpaid balances; and at the end of a quarter, all the figures can be summarised to show the total amounts outstanding.

At any one moment, the company's accountants and senior managers can have a precise overall picture of the company's financial status.

1 How might this information have been handled before the advent of computers?

2 What advantages are created through the use of IT for the supervision and management of the Patels' account?

Data handling processes

In a modern office data is needed for a large number of different operations. One way of looking at an organisation is as a 'data/information processing system'.

As in any system, there will be a variety of processes for transforming inputs into outputs, many of which will be carried out with the support of IT.

The processes which take place within an organisation which involve data include:

1 **Capturing data** This involves recording information from invoices, sales slips, meters, counters, etc.

2 **Verifying data** Once captured, data needs to be checked to ensure that it is accurate. Employees will also need to check that instruments or recording procedures are working correctly;

3 **Classifying data** This entails putting different types of data into appropriate sections – for example, a company's sales data could be sorted according to which department made the sale;

4 **Sorting data** refers to the placing of data elements into a specified order; for example, an inventory file could be sorted into money-value order, code-number order, etc.

5 **Summarising data** Aggregates and totals can be presented in a number of ways. One method is to total up various figures, e.g. sales, or to draw up balancing figures for a balance sheet.

   Alternatively, summarising could be used to reduce data logically to a common form, e.g. by producing a list of all employees who worked a night shift on a particular date;

6 **Calculating** This involves performing mathematical functions such as adding or multiplying. For example, wages of employees can be calculated by multiplying hours by the wage rate and then subtracting the various deductions;

7 **Storing data** involves transferring data to an appropriate storage medium (see below);

8 **Retrieving data** involves calling up data from the place of storage;

9 **Reproducing data** is the process of transferring the same data from one medium to another. At a simple level this could involve photocopying material, or calling up data from one screen to another, as with Stock Exchange dealing;

10 **Communicating data** refers to the transfer of data from one place to another. The ultimate aim of information processing is to provide information for the final user.

Hardware and software

Wherever information processing takes place – within a telecommunications network or within a computer system – it will involve the use of **hardware** and **software**:

- 'Hardware' refers to the computer and any connected devices such as printers and scanners;
- 'Software' describes the coded programs which enable the computer to carry out the user's instructions.

Within an information processing system, each element performs a different function:

- **Input devices** transfer information to the system;
- **Storage devices** store programs and information;
- The **processor** uses information for processing;
- **Output devices** produce data in the form required by the user.

Let us look briefly at each of these elements:

1 **Input devices** There are many ways of inputting data to the system. For example:

   - **Keyboard** This is the most common input device;
   - **Mouse** Pointing device used when working with GUI screens (see Figure 75.1 opposite) and most standard software products;
   - **Keypad** This provides a means of entering data with one hand;
   - **Barcode reader** Supermarkets and libraries use bar code readers to decode price and other data;
   - **Optical mark reader** This is a device for reading marks on a card;
   - **Magnetic ink character recognition** These readers can capture data from large volumes of documents;
   - **Voice** Voice input is rapidly growing in popularity as it avoids the need to use a keyboard;
   - **Magnetic strip reader** This helps shops and stores to accept plastic credit cards, debit cards and cheque guarantee cards. Data is recorded by 'swiping' the card through a reader.

2 **Storage devices** Advancing technology has allowed computers to store ever greater amounts of data in the form of numbers, text, pictures and sound;

3 **The processor** The **central processing unit (CPU)** is the part of the system which controls computer operations. It receives data either from an input device or from the computer's internal memory. **Application software** then manipulates data to perform specific tasks such as accounting and other office functions;

4 **Output devices** These communicate information to end-users in the form they require. Users will use the information from the output to help them with their professional job roles.

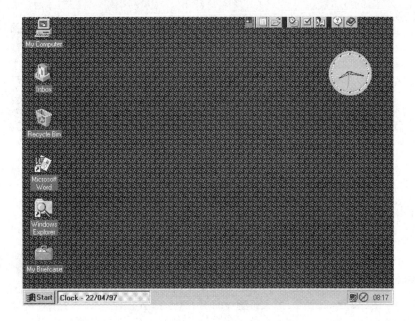

Figure 75.1 Example of a Graphical User Interface (GUI)

Communication technology and business

As we have seen, the success of a business enterprise depends in large measure on the efficient and accurate production of goods and services. But its survival also depends on the rapid and accurate processing and distribution of information. This process is increasingly being carried out with the help of new technology. A number of features make computer-aided communication vital to business:

1 The scale of many large organisations makes it impossible for every meeting to be conducted face-to-face;
2 Many organisations are geographically spread out, but require communication links between interrelated plants and offices;
3 Modern business decision-making frequently requires up-to-date information from a variety of sources;
4 Competition between organisations is more fierce;
5 The pace of industrial development has increased. Organisations must therefore be quicker in responding to factors such as technological change, market forces and competition from rivals.

Software applications

Word processing

The basic function of a word processor is to manipulate text. Its great advantage is that it allows the user to make unlimited changes to text on screen before the final document is printed out. Word processors make life easier for the writer in a number of ways:

- New text can be put on the screen while existing text moves to create space for it;
- Blocks of text can be moved around on the document that is being created;
- The text can be spaced out to fill the whole line;
- A word or phrase can be searched for, and can be removed or replaced by another word or phrase. A spelling mistake which is repeated throughout a document can be corrected 'globally' in a single operation;
- A header or footer can be added to the top or bottom of the page.

You will know from your own experience of word processors about some of the features they offer, e.g.:

- Use of different printing styles and fonts;
- The ability to insert graphics into text;
- The use of spell-checker, thesaurus, word count and auto-correct functions;
- Insertion of borders, tables, bullets and numbers.

Desktop publishing

Desktop publishing is the process of producing documents and printed matter with aid of computer software. Using DTP, it is possible to produce pages of combined text and graphics to a very high standard. Different graphics can be created, diagrams can be placed on pages with text flowing around them, and pictures can be introduced into the document and re-sized to fit the space available. DTP is used nowadays to produce an enormous variety of printed items, includings reports, newletters, training materials and advertisements.

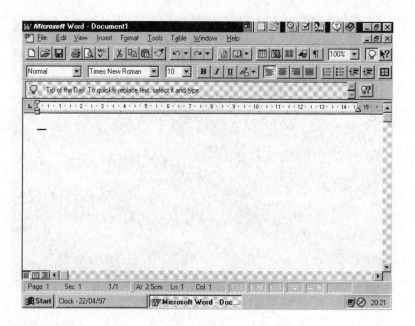

Figure 75.2 Example of a word-processing screen

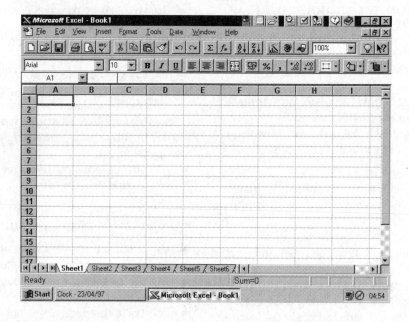

Figure 75.3 Example of a spreadsheet screen

Spreadsheets

A spreadsheet is a table of numbers which can be organised and altered on computer according to preset formulae. Spreadsheets are particularly useful for forecasting and financial modelling, as they can show the effects of financial decisions without the need to repeat calculations manually.

For instance, a firm will make a forecast of all the money coming in and going out over a twelve-month period. The spreadsheet user can alter the inputs to calculate the effect, for example, of lowering a heating bill by a certain amount each month. The computer will automatically recalculate the columns to change the heating figures, total cost figures and profits for each month.

In this way a manager, accountant or any other user of a spreadsheet can quickly carry out business calculations such as introducing and finding out the effect of minor changes of variables.

Databases

A database is a store of information held on computer. Examples might include anything from a list of customer accounts held by a bank or building society to a record of members of a church congregation and their addresses held by a parish priest or vicar. Another use might be to record tickets sold by a football club for various matches.

The essence of a database is that data can be accessed and analysed in a number of different ways, depending on the needs of the user. For example, suppose that Amin Stores wishes to record the account details of all its customers. It would store the information in a number of **fields** – address, value of goods supplied, payments received and balance of the account. If a customer rings up asking for the state of his account, Mr Amin can simply order the computer to produce the appropriate information and display it on the screen.

Planning a database

Any work with a database needs careful planning. Having decided broadly the purpose of the database, it is necessary to consider:

● What questions need to be asked to obtain the information;
● Under what headings the information needs to be collected and stored.

Project planning

Computers and computerised databases can be used to assist in project planning. Computer programs allow projects to be broken down into a number of interrelated stages called **activities**. First the activities are defined and the time taken by each is estimated. Then the way in which the activities depend on each other is defined. The computer calculates the total time for the project and shows the activities which must be completed on time in order for the project not to be delayed.

For example, in the case of a project to build a new office, the activities and times might be as follows:

1	Prepare land and build foundations	30 days
2	Build walls	30 days
3	Build roof	15 days
4	Install equipment	30 days
5	Equip office	20 days

Activity 1 must be done first, then Activity 2, then Activity 3. However, Activities 4 and 5 – although they come *after* Activity 3 has finished – can be done at the same time. Therefore the total time for the project is only 105 days (30 + 30 + 15 + 30), not 125 days. The computer output will also show that Activity 5 is not critical; that is, it can start late or take longer than planned without delaying the project.

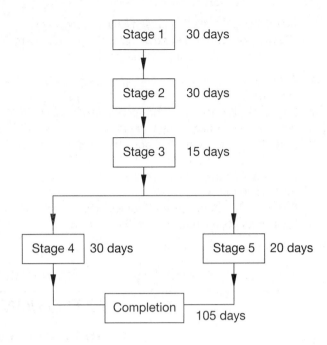

Figure 75.4 Planning the building of a new office

Expert systems

Expert systems are growing in popularity. An **expert system** is a computer program consisting of a set of rules based upon the knowledge of experts. These rules can be used to form conclusions on information the program is given.

Imagine, for example, that you feed into the computer all the rules that experts know about a particular field – say, geology. Geologists could feed in all the information they have about the conditions in which particular minerals are found. The program could be used to support researchers looking for new mineral fields.

Expert systems are of particular use where a human expert is not available. One interesting use is in medicine where programs are currently being developed to aid diagnosis. The program is designed to be used by the patient, not the doctor – the idea being that for personal and intimate problems a patient may answer questions more easily from a machine than from a person. It may also mean that minor problems can be diagnosed without taking up the doctor's time.

Data Protection Act

The purpose of the **Data Protection Act** is to regulate the use of computerised information which relates to 'individuals and the provision of services in respect of such information'.

The Act covers the holding of computer records only, and *not* manual records.

The Act requires those using personal data to register with the **Data Protection Registrar**. Registered data users must then follow the eight principles of the Act:

1 Data must be obtained and processed fairly and lawfully;
2 Data must be held only for specific lawful purposes which are described in the entry in the register;
3 Data should not be used in any other way than those related to such purposes;
4 Data should be adequate, relevant and not excessive for those purposes;
5 Personal data should be accurate and kept up-to-date;
6 Data should be held no longer than is required;
7 Individuals should be entitled to access their data and, if necessary, have it corrected or erased;
8 Data must be protected with appropriate security against unauthorised access or alteration.

There are a number of exemptions to the Act, including information kept by government departments for reasons of national security.

To ensure that data is held only for legitimate purposes, many organisations appoint a Data Protection Officer whose job is to monitor the use of computerised information within the company.

EXTENSION MATERIAL
IT and management strategies

It has been argued that managers and business strategists have a vested interest in the use of technology in order to reduce unit costs, increase the flexibility of the organisation, improve quality and also to enable them to improve their control.

Any consideration of new technologies in the workplace must be looked at within the context of the organisation and the status and position of employees in the workplace.

It is possible to relate the development of new technologies with four management-initiated processes:

1 The virtual elimination of direct labour;
2 The spread of contracting;
3 Dissolution of traditional job/skill demarcations;
4 Degradation of jobs through de-skilling.

The virtual elimination of direct labour

Many management missionaries have dreamed of eliminating direct labour. It is predicted that the 'fully automated factory' with virtually no direct labour will be running in the next few years.

There are two main technological routes:

● Integrated production flows using computer controls linked to micro-electronic sensors and intelligent data gathering equipment;

● Flexible manufacturing systems (FMS) which are computer-controlled and programmed integrated production systems.

The spread of contracting

This refers to an arrangement whereby the employer pays for an agreed period of labour time but leaves the precise scheduling to the workers concerned. Contracting arrangements are becoming increasingly popular, not just in production but also for office and managerial workers.

Dissolution of traditional job/skill demarcations

This is sometimes called **polyvalence**. The removal of skill demarcations has often involved the enlarging of the competences of workers by giving them additional tasks and providing them with more autonomy and responsibility through job enrichment.

This strategy offers the employer cost advantages and flexibility.

Degradation of jobs

It is argued that a consequence of new technologies is de-skilling – i.e. it is possible to use technology to avoid reliance on the skills and judgements of workers, and to use technology to regulate their performance.

Chapter summary

- IT consists of technologies and applications developed through the combining of data-processing and storage powers of computers with the distance-transmission capabilities of telecommunications.
- IT impinges upon almost all aspects of our lives.
- Attitudes to IT range from the 'utopia' to the 'doom' scenario.
- A modern organisation consists of a number of sub-systems.
- IT may help may people within an organisation.
- IT creates outputs from inputs.
- Data processing involves the use of input devices, storage devices, a processor and output devices.

- There are many different management strategies for IT.
- Word processing is used to manipulate text.
- DTP combines text and graphics to produce high-quality documents.
- A spreadsheet is a table of numbers which can be altered and manipulated on a computer.
- A database is a computerised store of facts or information.
- Computers can be used to aid project planning.
- Expert systems are based on a series of rules reflecting the knowledge of experts.
- The Data Protection Act regulates the use of computerised information about individuals.

76 Improving productive efficiency

The 20th century has seen many dramatic changes in our way of life. The basis of the production of food, clothing, shelter, housing, communications, leisure equipment and consumer and durable goods has moved from workshops and basic mechanised systems to highly developed technological systems. In fact, there are few places today, even in the developing world, where production processes remain in the hands of artisans.

As we move towards globalisation, production and operations systems have become significantly more complex. Knowing how to manage such systems in a world experiencing increasing change is becoming a major challenge.

In an increasingly competitive world, the concept of **productivity** – the measure of a country's efficiency in converting inputs to outputs – is therefore a crucial one. Over recent years, a great deal of attention has been focused upon why some people, organisations and countries are better at producing certain goods or services than others.

We looked at the basic elements of productivity and how to measure them in Chapter 43. In this chapter we will cover some of the specific strategies which companies can use in order to improve their productive efficiency.

Relating price elasticity to production planning

The concept of price elasticity relates prices to demand.

Elasticity is the way in which demand changes as price goes up or down (see Chapter 53).

This has important implications for the process of **production planning**. Quality also has a bearing on the relationship. By looking at different systems and the levels of quality and cost they offer, we can see how strategic productivities and cost structures.

For example, when demand is price-elastic in a market with a lot of competition, a low price is required in order to generate enough demand to consume all the production output. Figure 76.1 shows why a high volume of output is need to keep production costs low and productivity high.

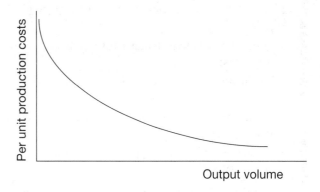

Figure 76.1 Per unit production costs decrease with increasing output volume

It is important to think about the concept of elasticity and plan output with volume and price in mind. For example, a possible sequence might be:

1   Select a production process and output volume;
2   Determine the per unit production costs, which are a function of the process and output volume;
3   From the costs, determine a satisfactory selling price, plus a required profit;
4   Estimate the demand determined by the selling price and the perceived quality required by customers;
5   If demand is likely to be too low, consider at what price and quality demand would match capacity.

Going back and forth between output volume, per unit production costs, selling price and demand using elasticities, helps to identify the best possible match with the lowest per unit production costs for a given volume of output.

Cost leverage

A key aspect in improving productivity is **cost leverage**. The price charged for goods or services must either be equal to or exceed the costs of producing the goods or providing the services. Therefore costs form a base upon which all price structures are built and upon which productive systems can be analysed. The design of a productive system must be developed in a way which minimises costs and avoids unnecessary expenses. If an organisation fails to minimise costs in designing its production system, it then provides cost leverage for its competitors. Cost leverage accrues to organisations which are sharp enough in developing their systems to identify low-cost opportunities.

The importance of experience

In their study of learning and experience, the Boston Consulting Group found that unit cost tends to decrease as more product is manufactured. They pointed out the **learning effect**, whereby efficiency is improved as experience is accumulated. This finding is consistent with many current ideas about 'continuing improvement' and now occupies a central role in operations strategy. On the basis of this work, a link has been established between continual improvement through learning and the use of cost advantages as a key competitive tool.

IT'S A FACT

Since its inception the USA has been the most productive nation on earth. However, now other nations are catching up.

CASE STUDY CASE STUDY CASE STUDY CASE STUDY CASE STUDY

FALLING PRODUCTIVITY

In 1982 the US Department of Labor reported that 42 of 69 industries surveyed experienced a fall in productivity. The American Productivity Institute suggested:

1   Falling productivity yields rising labour costs;
2   Unit labour cost increases lead to higher prices;
3   Higher prices lead to declining sales volumes;
4   Declining sales volumes lead to reduced employment and reduced plant capacity;
5   Reducing capital utilisation leads to lower productivity;
6   Lower productivity leads to reduced competitive ability.

A number of others sources and reasons for the slowdown in productivity were identified:

• Insufficient capital investment;
• Slowdown in research and development;
• Growth in government regulation;
• Labour and management inattention;
• Ageing industrial plant;
• Increases in energy costs;
• Growth of the service sector;
• The age-sex mix of the workforce.

1   What lessons, if any, can we draw from this survey?

2   In what way does falling productivity lead to a downward spiral?

3   Working in groups, look at the reasons for falling productivity and suggest ways in which an organisation can avoid falling productivity.

STUDY CASE STUDY CASE STUDY CASE STUDY CASE STUDY CASE STUDY

Improving productivity

The starting point is to understand *why* global competitiveness is so intimately related to production and operations. In global markets where trade takes place, customers are sensitive to price, quality and speed of delivery. Each of these different values is the outcome of the production process and operations systems used.

For example, prices are a reflection of production costs; quality is a feature of production processes, and delivery is responsive to production scheduling and inventory policies. Service is another aspect of the mix of elements included within the broad term 'quality'.

Flexibility

Flexibility is often thought of as a means to an end – a way of improving productivity and delivering performance. In Chapter 71 we saw that flexibility is also about response. The term is often used in managing operations to refer to productivity, cost-effectiveness and high quality.

Similarly, the phrase **'flexible manufacturing systems' (FMS)** refers not only to the range of products provided but also the to response of the organisation to the needs of customers.

Just-in-time production

Just-in-time (JIT) systems became widely adopted following the success of Japanese production in the 1970s and 1980s. Shonberger, in his book *Japanese Manufacturing Techniques*, described JIT in the following way:

> 'The JIT ideas is very simple; produce and deliver finished goods just in time to be sold, sub-assemblies just in time to be assembled into finished goods, fabricated parts just in time to go into the sub-assemblies, and purchased materials just in time to be transformed into fabricated parts.'

The JIT system is geared to ensuring that a plant has just enough resources – human and material – to meet its current production and distribution requirements. There are no stocks kept in reserve to protect against delivery problems.

Just-in-time production has a number of advantages:

- It is highly flexible and encourages flexible attitudes within the organisation;
- It requires lower levels of stocks;
- There is a continuous flow of new stocks into the organisation;
- Human and other resources become respectively multi-skilled and multi-purpose;
- Costs are minimised;
- There is a continuous emphasis upon improvement.

IT'S A FACT

The following dates represent key landmarks in the history of operations management:

1500	Birth of Benvenuto Cellini (craftsman/apprenticeship)
1780	Eli Whitney (interchangeable parts)
1890	Frederick W Taylor (scientific management)
1910	Henry Ford (sequenced assembly)
1920	Walter Shewhart (statistical quality control)
1940–60s	Successful job shops
1950–80s	Global changes (flow) and growth of computer technology
1980–2000	Growth of flexible manufacturing

However, it also has some disadvantages:

- It depends upon a continuous supply of new components and raw materials. If these are not forthcoming, the plant will grind to a halt;
- The system depends upon flexible attitudes and flexible practices;
- Because an organisation purchases many of its ingredients from outside, it is at the mercy of the quality-control and inspection standards of suppliers.

Scientific stock control

Scientific stock control (SSC) has as its basic unit of analysis an item of stock held at a particular location. It involves setting up an elaborate system for forecasting demand, often based upon a statistical analysis of past usage, and then attempting to control inputs in terms of amount and frequency, with the objective of cost-minimisation. Costs are seen as those involved in holding stock and those incurred in buying stock.

Optimised production technology

Optimised production technology (OPT) is sometimes known as **synchronised manufacturing**. The approach was associated with E.M. Goldratt who popularised it through a book he wrote which focused on the life of the production manager. OPT links together a number of useful ideas for materials flow with a clear view of how such improvements could affect a company's financial performance. OPT sets objectives through the concepts of throughput, inventory and operating expense.

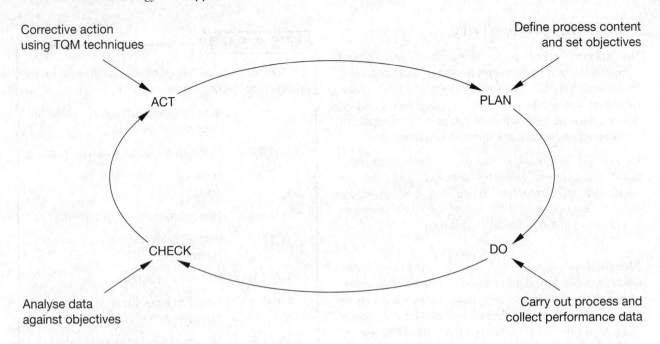

Corrective action
using TQM techniques

ACT

Define process content
and set objectives

PLAN

CHECK

Analyse data
against objectives

DO

Carry out process and
collect performance data

Figure 76.2 Plan–do–check–act cycle

Total Quality Management

In Chapter 44 we looked at the concept of **Total Quality Management (TQM)**, underlining the fact that TQM takes place at every place at every stage of an organisation's operations, and is the responsibility of all employees. It is a business philosophy as well as a series of guiding principles.

Kanji defines TQM in the following terms:

- **Quality** is to satisfy customer's requirements continually;
- **Total quality** is to achieve quality at low cost;
- **Total Quality Management** is to obtain total quality by involving everyone's daily commitment.

Kanji then describes quality as a process of continuous improvement, or **Kaizen**. This is embodied in the **plan–do–check–act cycle** (see Figure 76.2 above) which may be applied either for the solution of specific problems or to the organisation as a whole.

ISO 9000

In Chapter 44 we looked at **BS 5750**, the recognised standard for quality management in the UK. In the past, when an organisation achieved BS 5750 it was also able to claim **EN 29000** and **ISO 9000**, which were identical in content. However, in mid-'94 the British Standards Institution revised its standards in line with changes in ISO 9000, and BS 5750 is now no more.

The concept of quality underlying ISO 9000 is that of meeting requirements. A product or service, therefore, is defined as having quality when it satisfies the needs of users and meets customer requirements. Quality assurance involves the planning and management of activities in a way which has a bearing upon the quality of the final output. ISO 9000 is therefore both a set of principles or framework upon which quality is to be evaluated and a statement about how quality should be managed and achieved.

Other methods for improving productivity

Over recent years, we have heard of many other methods for improving productivity. These include:

- Job redesign such as enlarging jobs and eliminating unneeded tasks;
- Teamwork and job rotation;
- Employee participation programmes;
- Improved communications;
- Better training;
- Improvements in technology and wider use of technological applications;
- Cost-reduction programmes;
- increased expenditure upon research and development;
- Better management.

Chapter summary

- Productivity helps to explain the relationship between inputs and outputs.
- Productivity involves comparing the quantity of goods and services produced and the quantity of resources employed in turning out these goods and services.
- Productivity may be increased by raising the quality or quantity of output or by reducing the inputs applied.
- Efficiency of technology + efficiency of labour + efficiency of capital + effectiveness of management = productivity.
- Productivity assessment is usually based upon simple statistics.
- Labour productivity is based on assessing the number of man-hour inputs required to achieve a certain level of output.
- Total productivity is the combination of worker and machine hours required to achieve a level of output.
- The interaction of output volume, per-unit production costs, selling price and demand elasticities helps to identify the best possible match with the lowest per-unit production costs for a given volume of output.
- Cost leverage accrues to organisations which are sharp enough to develop low-cost opportunities which provide them with advantages over their competitors.
- The Boston Consulting Group found that learning and experience reduced unit costs as more product is manufactured.
- Flexible manufacturing systems (FMS) refer not just to the process of manufacturing and the products on offer, but also the response needs of customers.
- Just-in-time (JIT) production involves holding few stocks in reserve and ensuring that an organisation has just enough resources to meet production and distribution requirements.
- Scientific stock control (SSC) is an elaborate system for forecasting demand based upon statistical analysis of past usage.
- Optimised production technology (OPT) sets objectives for throughput, inventory and operating expense.
- Total Quality Management (TQM) takes place at every stage in operations and is the responsibility of all employees.
- Kaizen involves continuous improvement.
- ISO 9000 is the recognised standard for quality management in the UK.

13

The wider business environment

INTRODUCTION

This unit provides an in-depth analysis of key features of the broader organisational environment, including economic influences, the nature of the international business environment, the importance and significance of the European Union, government influences on the competitive environment and social and ethical constraints on business activities.

Today we live in an environment in which global and international forces increasingly impact on all organisational activity. Business organisations no longer have to respond simply to changes at local and national level: far more powerful forces are at work throughout the global economy. In particular, all organisations are influenced by the upturns and downturns of the trade cycle. In a period of upturn, all organisations can expect to prosper, while in the downturn everyone may feel the pinch.

In this unit we explore some of the explanations given for the trade cycle and the ways in which it impacts on the economy and organisations, in particular by exploring the nature of unemployment and inflation. We also examine macro-economic variables, including exchange and interest rates, particularly focusing on how these affect business. This leads to an examination of a number of key economic theories, in which the views of free-market thinkers such as Milton Friedman are contrasted with those who see an important role for the government in the economy – most notably John Maynard Keynes.

We then move on to examine the nature of international trade and identify the nature of major trading patterns in the world today, showing how these provide both opportunities and threats to UK organisations. We identify some of the key processes which are involved when UK organisations sell abroad.

Today it is essential for all students to have a firm grasp of the nature of the European Union and its major institutions and policies. Increasingly, the European Union and the ramifications of EU membership are encroaching on all our lives. Students needs to have a clear understanding of the nature of current issues and developments, including European Monetary Union and the Social Chapter of the Maastricht Treaty.

In Part 1 of this book students were introduced to the nature and importance of competition. It is now necessary to build on this knowledge by examining the role the government plays in creating the 'rules of the game' of competition and in setting out a framework for organisations to operate in a competitive environment.

For many students, the most important part of this unit will be that concerned with the nature of the social and ethical framework within which organisational activity takes place. We therefore conclude by outlining a range of social and ethical constraints on business activity and discussing how organisations can and should respond to these influences.

77 Macro-economic issues

In this chapter we return to examine the macro-economy in greater depth. The wider economy is an environment which presents both opportunities and threats to businesses and other organisations. When macro-economic conditions are favourable, businesses as a general rule will flourish. When macro-economic conditions are unfavourable, this will create a climate which is generally unfavourable to most organisations.

However, while this general rule applies it is not set in stone. For example, the Case Study below presents a useful picture of the macro-economy. Major changes in total national spending, national income, and national output have an influence on the economy and people in general. However, they may not necessarily give an accurate picture of the impact of change on particular individuals and organisations. The business that is just about to close down because its debtors have not paid up on time may take little comfort from press reports announcing an imminent improvement in the economy as a whole.

In this section we examine a number of macro-economic issues which are particularly significant to business at a general level. These are:

● The trade cycle;
● Unemployment;
● Inflation;
● Interest rates;
● Exchange rates.

The trade cycle
It would be comforting to think that economies could experience a steady upward path to growth. The conditions we would all like to see would be a general rise in living standards, jobs for all who wanted one, prices staying constant or at the worst rising very slowly, a stable exchange rate, and the development of an increasingly healthy living environment, with improved standards of education, health and social welfare.

Unfortunately, in the real world, we rarely (if ever) experience these desirable conditions at the same time.

The reality is that economic growth appears in a series of fits and starts and that often we have to make trade-offs between pleasure and pain – e.g. between falling levels of unemployment and rising prices.

Part of this disjointed process of economic development is a process referred to as the **trade cycle**. This affects individual countries, and also often has a global dimension because of the interrelated nature of international economies.

For example, many countries sell quantities of exports to the USA. If the United States economy 'catches a cold' the effect is likely to be felt by other countries.

The trade cycle can be represented in the following way:

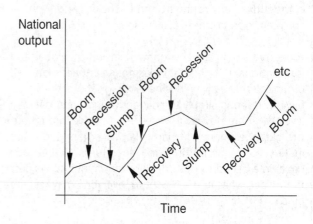

Figure 77.1 The trade cycle

HALEWOOD IN THE COLD

On Friday 16th January 1997, the day before the the announcement of the lowest unemployment total for six years, Ford announced 1,300 job losses at its Halewood factory in Merseyside. The timing of these two events should be a useful reminder that generally cheering overall news will often conceal particular stories of despair.

In terms of crude numbers, the loss of jobs at Halewood was small by comparison with the creation of jobs elsewhere – for example (to take another big story of that week) the building of the new runway at Manchester airport. But it was small comfort to those individuals who lost their jobs.

In a **boom** period, output, incomes and employment are increasing. In a period of **recession** this growth begins to slow down. In a **slump**, output, incomes and employment may fall, before picking up in a **recovery**.

Picking up from a slump

Following a slump, the economy may be in the 'doldrums' for up to a year or two. During this period businesses are very negative. It is this very negativism which tends to perpetuate the slump. A firm is unlikely to expand if it feels that there will not be a market for its new output. Collectively, this attitude results in falling production, falling order books, laying-off of employees, etc.

However, there will be some encouraging signs. For example, prices will have been falling through lack of demand, so that the cost of materials, labour, etc. will be relatively low. An important cost will be that of money, i.e. interest rates. As with other prices, this will have fallen, making it relatively more attractive to borrow money. Also, inventors and innovators are forever coming up with new ideas and ways of improving production processes. During the slump their ideas will not have been taken up – but they are there, ready and waiting.

'Green shoots' of recovery

Eventually, the slump reaches its **nadir** (low point). Unnoticed at first, one or two adventurous souls begin to borrow money to try out an exciting new idea. Perhaps they buy some new capital and equipment and employ a few people to build their new business premises. Fresh spending therefore starts to move into the economy – first in a trickle, then in larger and larger quantities. The recovery has begun.

Soon people begin to sit up and notice. People who have become net savers in the slump now start to draw out these savings. Perhaps they purchase a new Hoover, a new car or a dishwasher. They have become more optimistic and are prepared to take bigger risks.

The same sort of development is visible in the firms and organisations section of the economy. The hospital that had put its spending plans on hold decides to build a new wing… The local authority that had cut back its expenditure decides to improve road facilities which have fallen into disrepair… Manchester Airport gets the go-ahead for a second runway. And so on. A critical mass for change has occurred. The recovery is now well and truly underway.

Full steam ahead

As the economy moves forward into a boom, consumer spending begins to rise substantially, as does output and employment. There is a general feeling of confidence in the economy. Prices start to increase, and the best spare resources in the economy start to be used up. Increasingly, less effective resources start to be employed and the economy starts to 'suck in' imports from overseas. We are now in a boom, but we are heading for a situation which is called 'overheating'. If we are not careful we will soon find that prices will rise too fast, and that we will run into a balance of payments deficit on trading. Moreover, most of the best new inventions and innovations have been put into practice and there are relatively few new ideas to draw upon. It is at this stage that the government tries to 'damp down' demand in the economy by using a range of measures such as raising interest rates and taxation.

Meltdown

A boom is not sustainable in the longer term. There comes a point at which confidence starts to ebb and organisations and individuals begin to 'tighten their belts'.

Once demand falls from a peak, business people begin to feel pessimistic about the future and start to make cutbacks in production. Because of this, they invest less in capital equipment. This means that people earn less and spend less. The whole process is a vicious circle:

- Consumer demand falls;
- Producers make less;
- Producers invest less;
- Employees are laid off;
- People have less money to spend.

A multiplier effect

A small fall in consumer demand can therefore lead to a much bigger overall change in incomes and spending. This is known as a **multiplier effect** because the original fall in demand is multiplied. For example, if consumers reduce spending by £1m and this leads eventually to an overall fall in demand of £3m, we can see that the multiplier is 3.

$$Multiplier\ (k) = \frac{Overall\ change\ in\ demand}{Original\ change\ in\ demand}$$

$$= \frac{£3m}{£1m} = 3$$

We can illustrate the multiplier effect in a town with a large college or university. When students arrive in October with plenty of spending money, the economy begins to boom. Shops, cafés and bookshops take on more part-time staff who receive wages for their work. These wages are spent in the town and the multiplier effect continues as the original increase in spending by students is multiplied around the local economy.

However, in the summer holidays, the reverse happens as students leave town and lots of part-time jobs disappear, leading to a localised recession.

We shall return to look at ways of managing a recession in the notes at the end of this chapter.

Unemployment

For approximately 20 years prior to the Second World War, unemployment averaged at least 10%. The war effort fully employed all our resources, and in 1944 the government published a White Paper pledging the maintenance of full employment after the war. As the White Paper stated, the will to provide this was matched by the means:

'The government accepts as one of their primary aims and responsibilities the maintenance of a high and stable level of employment after the war... total expenditure must be prevented from falling to a level where general unemployment appears.'

For the next 25 years, unemployment averaged only 1.8%. However, a major concern over the policy of maintaining full employment was that it was accompanied by inflation. When the Conservative government came to power in 1979 they gave a high priority to trying to cut back on price increases.

In recent years, we have seen the resurgence of high unemployment. The first six years of the 1990s were characterised by unemployment at well over 2 million. In 1997 the figure started to fall, but at the time of writing it remains to be seen whether this is merely part of a pre-election boom, or part of a more healthy longer-term trend. Today, unemployment is a problem confronting most industrialised countries. It is interesting to note that in 1997 while unemployment in the UK was at 6.7 per cent of the population, in Germany the figure was almost double, at 4.2 million unemployed.

Interpreting unemployment figures

When we look in detail at unemployment figures we are presented with some interesting findings. For example:

- Unskilled and semi-skilled manufacturing workers are twice as likely to be unemployed as skilled manual workers;
- Manual workers on the whole are twice as likely as non-manual workers to be unemployed. For example, in 1991 unemployment for the latter stood as 3.1% compared with 16.3% for general labourers;
- For the 50+ age group in 1992, 39% of those unemployed had been out of work for over a year, compared with 24% of 18–25-year-olds.

There is always disagreement over the exact number of unemployed people in the UK at any time, because only those receiving state benefits and registered for work are counted in the official statistics. This misses out some married women who, if their husbands are working, cannot receive benefit. People on some training schemes are also not included, nor are men over 60 who have been unemployed for a long time. The total unemployed therefore depends on the way the figures are collected.

Causes of unemployment

There are many explanations of how unemployment is caused.

1   Cyclical unemployment

One cause of unemployment may be downswings in the trade cycle, i.e. periods of recession. In a period of recession, with a downward multiplier, spending, income, outputs and thus employment will all fall. The term **cyclical unemployment** is used to describe unemployment resulting from this downturn.

2   Structural unemployment

Another explanation of large-scale unemployment is that of structural unemployment. This arises from longer-term changes in the economy affecting specific industries, regions and occupations.

For example, the coal industry in regions such as Central Scotland, South Yorkshire and East Midlands has been in decline for a number of years because of the development of new substitute fuels such as gas, oil and electricity, and the importing of cheap coal from Australia, Nigeria, Russia and other places. The changes in demand for products like coal, steel, shipbuilding, textiles, shoes, etc., also led to structural unemployment as old industries declined. A further factor was the Conservative governments' deliberate attempt to destroy the National Union of Mineworkers, which was for many years a major source of opposition to what was effectively during the 1980s a one-party state.

The effect of structural unemployment would be less if people moved away from declining industries and areas and into new, expanding areas. However, changes do not occur smoothly, and people are often understandably reluctant to move to other parts of the country where they have no connections or family, particularly if there is no guarantee that conditions there will be any better in the long run.

3   'Technological unemployment'

It is sometimes claimed that new technology is a cause of unemployment. The argument is that the introduction of new technology destroys jobs and trade while at the same time imports from low-wage developing countries are undercutting goods produced in this country.

However, a number of studies contradict this. For example, the OECD *Job Study* for June 1994 argued that 'history has shown that when technological progress accelerates, so do growth, living standards and employment.'

New technology generates new products, new services and therefore new jobs. Fewer workers may be required in some production processes where specific tasks are taken over, but rising productivity boosts incomes and the demand for new jobs in the economy as a whole.

INFLATION IN THE UK IN RECENT TIMES

The illustration below shows inflation trends in the UK since 1959. Briefly describe the trends that you can see. Which periods do you think would have caused the most concern to governments? What problems do you think inflation caused in the economy during these periods?

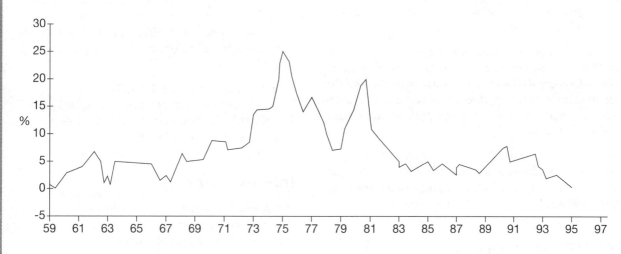

Figure 77.2 Underlying inflation in the UK 1959–1995

The arguments for and against technology reflect considerable differences in opinion about the causes of unemployment. However, it can be seen that the government has a major role to play in ensuring that unemployment does not rise to an 'unacceptable' level. What that level is is a matter for debate.

4 'Real wage' unemployment

Some commentators argue that the UK has much lower rates of unemployment than other EU countries because it has 'flexible labour markets' – unlike other countries of the EU, where labour is protected by 'social' measures. The number of people employed by an organisation depends on **wage costs**. If wage costs are artificially raised, e.g. by the European Union's Social Chapter, then some employees will be too expensive and unemployment will result.

The **real wage rate** is the wage rate that determines the supply of labour. Unemployment occurs where the real wage rate is above that needed to employ all workers. If wages are higher than this, unemployment will occur. There is strong evidence to support this view. Flexibility may be required if unemployment is not to reach unacceptably high levels, but higher insecurity may be the price of low unemployment.

Inflation

Unemployment and inflation are economic problems which have repercussions for a large number of individuals and organisations. When unemployment is at a high level, the population as a whole has less money to spend and this affects many firms and industries. In a period of inflation, rising prices are likely to affect everybody.

Inflation is measured in several different ways. To the government, inflation means a general increase in the level of prices. Statisticians use the **Retail Price Index (RPI)**, which is an average of price changes and shows the general change over a period of time. Some items in the Index will rise, some will remain the same and others will fall. The RPI is a very useful in picking out general changes in inflation.

Calculating the Retail Price Index

The **Retail Price Index (RPI)** is calculated in the following way.

About 7,000 households throughout the UK keep a record of all their spending over a two-week period. This gives a picture of the 'typical items' bought by an 'average household'. The items are recorded in the Index. Each month, government officers make a record of about 150,000 prices of some 350 different items up and down the country. The average price of each of these items is calculated.

Using this data, the average inflation rate can be calculated. Each individual price change is given a 'weight' which depends on how important it is in the typical household's spending pattern. For example, food makes up about one-fifth of a typical household's spending, so that a 10% rise in the price of food would raise average prices by one-fifth of this – i.e. 2%.

Price changes are measured over a definite period of time so that it is possible to compare the changes from one period to another. The choice of a starting (or 'base') date for an index is important, the aim being to choose a time which is 'normal' – that is, when nothing abnormal or unusual is happening.

The base date is given an index of up to 100. It is then possible to say, for example, that if in 1985 the RPI stood at 100 and today it is 350, prices on average have risen three and a half times over that time period.

Indexing: an example

Suppose that in an imaginary country, Averageland, the Average family spend half their income on food, a quarter on clothing and the remaining quarter on entertainment. These items are given 'weightings' out of 10: food 5, clothing 2.5, entertainment 2.5.

In 1991 (the base year), food cost on average £1 per unit, clothing £5 per unit, and entertainment £2 per unit.

In 1997, food in Averageland cost £5 per unit, clothing £7.50 per unit, and entertainment £3 per unit. We can analyse these changes in prices as shown in Figure 77.3 below.

The total of the last column is 1,750. In order to find out the new RPI in Averageland we must divide this total by the total number of weights (10), so:

$$\text{New RPI} = \frac{1,750}{10} = 175$$

This shows that, on average, prices rose by 75%. Food doubled in price, while the other two items increased by one and a half times. Food was the most significant item in the index because the average family spends as much on food as on clothing and entertainment combined.

TASK 77.1

In Redland, consumers spend on average seven-tenths of their income on wine, two-tenths on bread and one-tenth on cheese. In 1993 (the base year) the price of all these items was £1 per unit. In 1997, wine has fallen to 50p per unit, bread has gone up to £2 per unit and cheese has risen to £4 per unit.

1   What is the new index for 1997?
2   Has it risen, fallen or remained the same?
3   Give at least three reasons why the weighting might need to be changed in 1997.

Interest rates

The **interest rate** is the cost of borrowing money. As with all prices, an important determinant of the interest rate is the demand and supply of money.

In 1997, under new measures introduced by the Labour Chancellor Gordon Brown, the Bank of England took over responsibility for managing interest rates from the government.

The effect of changes in interest rates

The main effect of changes in interest rates is on spending decisions by firms and by individuals.

IT'S A FACT

One of the easiest ways for firms to save money is to cut down on labour and training. Therefore when interest rates rise this may lead to immediate cutbacks in employment (rising unemployment) and in training budgets.

	Original index	New index	Expenditure weighting	New index x weighting
Food	100	200	5	1,000
Clothing	100	150	2.5	375
Entertainment	100	150	2.5	375

Figure 77.3 Increases in household spending in Averageland

1 A rise in interest rates means an increase in the cost of credit, thus raising the cost of all financial operations (including both short-term overdrafts and long-term loans and mortgages).

When the cost of credit increases, profits are reduced and firms are left with less ready cash. Organisations therefore become more reluctant to borrow and will often postpone or cancel their investment plans. A rise in interest rates has a dampening effect on the economy. This is why the Bank of England uses changes in interest rates as a macro-economic tool.

When interest rates rise, this will make firms with higher gearing ratios more risky as investments. Since costs of production also increase, firms will seek to make economies elsewhere.

2 Changes in interest rates also have an impact for net lenders (i.e. people who lend more money than they borrow). A rise in interest rates will lead to a rise in their incomes, and a fall in interest rates will reduce their incomes.

If interest rates rise, this will lead to an increase in spending by net lenders (because they are better off). If interest rates fall, the reverse is likely to happen. Net lenders tend to be people in the older age brackets. As a result, changes in interest rates may have a relatively big impact on firms that produce goods and services aimed at older people.

When interest rates rise, this will hurt net borrowers, e.g. people with large mortgages to repay or people whose mortgage repayments are high in proportion to their incomes. High interest rates are likely to handicap net borrowers, and this may lead to a substantial fall in the amount of their spending, which in turn will have a considerable impact on the economy.

Interest rates and loans

Because small businesses are often dependent on banks, building societies and other lenders for start-up capital, they will be particularly hard hit by rises in interest rates.

An increase of as little as 1% or 2% could completely wipe out a small businesses profit margin. In a period of economic slump and pessimism, far fewer new businesses are likely to start up, helping to dampen down the economy. Many new businesses start up on the crest of a wave of booming conditions. However, they may feel the pinch when demand conditions start to dampen down.

The Chancellor of the Exchequer will use interest rate policy as a means of managing the economy. In a boom period the Chancellor will worry that demand is increasing too much, sucking in imports and encouraging inflation. The Chancellor will therefore try to dampen down this excess spending by raising interest rates. For people who have borrowed a lot of money this can be a disaster. As demand dampens down they are burdened with high rates of interest and may not be able to survive. Large companies too must avoid borrowing too much if interest rates are likely to rise.

In May 1997 the incoming Labour Chancellor Gordon Brown handed over control of interest rates to the Bank of England. This meant that the Bank could keep a very tight rein on inflation by raising interest rates when required.

Exchange rates

Whenever international trade takes place, there is a need for foreign exchange by at least one of the parties to the transaction. The foreign exchange market is a global mechanism for the buying and selling of foreign currencies.

A country's **foreign exchange rate** is the price at which its own currency exchanges for that of others. Every currency has many rates, to reflect all the currencies that are traded. In the UK the sterling exchange rate is matched against the US dollar, the yen and the deutschmark.

Who is affected by exchange rates?

Many different groups of people are interested in exchange rates. For example, when you go on holiday to another country, you will want to know how much foreign currency you will receive in exchange for the pounds that you have saved up. You might be disappointed if the value of your money has recently fallen against the value of the currency of the country you are visiting.

But it is not just tourists who are directly affected by movements in exchange rates. We all regularly purchase goods and services that are imported or which have an import content – for example, oranges, petrol, wine and paper.

At the same time, many of the goods and services that we produce are exported to other countries.

▓ IT'S A FACT

The classic example of an organisation that is vulnerable to fluctuations in the exchange rate is Jaguar.

In the mid-1980s the pound was weak against the dollar. This made British goods attractive in the USA and increased sales of British cars in North America, giving Jaguar a boost to its profits.

When, from the mid-1980s, the dollar weakened against the pound, British exports became less attractive in the US and Jaguar's profits fell significantly.

Why are exchange rates important for business?

When it comes to trading in international markets, business people claim to be happiest in a period of stability. Most international transactions are carried out on a credit basis. If I sell whisky to a Japanese importer, then I will need to give the importer a period of credit (usually three months), during which they must sell the whisky in their domestic market in order to be able to make payment to me.

When a business sells goods on credit they make a sacrifice and take a risk. The sacrifice is that until payment takes place, they have invested time, effort and money in producing goods for nothing. The risk is:

- There is a possibility of non-payment;
- That when payment in foreign currency takes place, the value of the currency could turn out to be less than originally expected.

Linking the exchange rate to profitability

There are two ways in which the exchange rate may influence business activities.

- It may affect the price of goods and services which businesses buy in international markets;
- It may affect the price at which businesses sell goods and services in international markets.

Looking at Figure 77.4 below, we can see that changes in the exchange rate may create uncertainty in both instances:

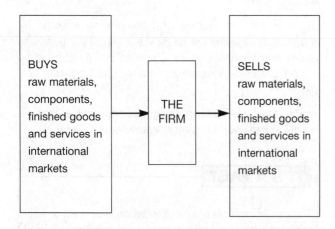

Figure 77.4 Buying and selling in international markets

For example, if a business *imports* goods or services, the exchange rate will influence the price of their purchases, and any changes will make pricing and costing more difficult. On the other hand, if they *sell* goods or services abroad, changes in the exchange rate will affect the amount of foreign currency coming in and this will either

earn them more or less than they had planned. Movements in the exchange rate will thus have a distinct bearing on profit margins, as well as a business's ability to sell overseas, i.e. its **export competitiveness**.

The situation is however a little more complicated than this, as the Case Study on page 553 opposite shows.

How is the value of the pound determined?

Consumers require money so that can they can spend it on goods and services. The price of the pound therefore depends on supply and demand.

Let us assume that one pound sterling is worth ten French francs (as was the case at the end of the 1980s). Demand for pounds may come from two sources:

1. When British producers sell goods in France they will want payment in pounds (but will often be paid in francs);
2. French citizens who want to buy shares in British firms, e.g. Laura Ashley or Marks & Spencer, must change their francs into pounds.

On the other side of the equation, a supply of pounds may arise in the foreign exchange market because UK firms and households want to purchase French goods, and because UK citizens want to purchase French assets. Figure 77.5 below illustrates the demand and supply for pounds in our simplified foreign exchange market.

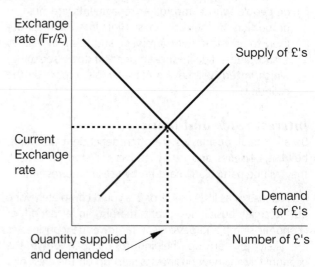

Figure 77.5 Determining the market exchange rate

If Marks & Spencer sells ties at £5 each, with an exchange rate of 10fr/£, each tie will cost 50 francs to a French consumer. However at 9fr/£ (the exchange rate during 1997) they will cost only 45 francs. We would therefore expect Marks & Spencer to sell more ties (and other goods) at the lower exchange rate. We can therefore make a generalisation that a larger quantity of pounds will be demanded at lower franc/sterling exchange rates. Hence, in Figure 77.5 the demand curve for the pound slopes downwards from left to right .

The supply curve for pounds depends on the number of francs that UK citizens will need in order to buy French imports or purchase French assets. For instance, if a trip to EuroDisney costs Fr 8,000 at 10fr/£, it costs £800; but at 9fr/£ it costs £900 for the British consumer. A lower fr/£ exchange rate raises the price in pounds, and lowers the quantity of trips to EuroDisney demanded by British holidaymakers.

Interest rates and the exchange rate

Exchange rates are affected directly by interest rates in the UK and abroad. An increase in the domestic interest rate relative to those in other countries causes our exchange rate to rise. An increased inflow of capital to the UK causes a bigger demand for pounds, causing the value to rise.

This means imports become less expensive, while export prices will be increased.

CASE STUDY CASE STUDY CASE STUDY CASE STUDY CASE STUDY

SELLING M & S UNDERWEAR TO FRANCE

Marks & Spencer are currently setting up a chain of stores in France where their goods have proved to be very popular. Interestingly, their best-selling line has been English-style white bread. In the UK, 'M & S' have a leading reputation for quality products, particularly in underwear. Walk into any room and you can be almost certain that there will be more people wearing M & S underwear than any other brand. M & S expect this trend to extend to their growing French operations.

Let us assume that M & S decide to price their underwear at a level which reflects the quality of their goods. It is at this point that we can see how the uncertainties of international trade may come into play.

For example, if the value of the pound weakens against the franc, M & S will find that their French earnings (when converted into pounds) are less than anticipated from the same volume of goods. Of course, one advantage of a falling pound is that UK exports become cheaper and it may be possible to sell more goods. However, this may not always be desirable – for example, if consumers associate a higher price with better quality.

Conversely, if the value of the pound rises against the franc, M & S may find that their earnings increase against the same volume of goods. However, this would depend upon whether the French would be still willing to buy British goods at higher prices.

1 Why are Marks and Spencer prepared to trade in France despite fluctuations in the exchange rate?

2 What could they do to cover themselves against such fluctuations?

3 What are the benefits to organisations like Marks and Spencer of setting up operations in France and other EU countries?

4 How might Marks and Spencer benefit from a Single European currency?

Marks & Spencer's shopfront in Paris

STUDY CASE STUDY CASE STUDY CASE STUDY CASE STUDY CASE STUDY

A key link between inflation and unemployment

In the next chapter we examine the link between unemployment and inflation in greater depth. It is important to stress the importance of this link. When unemployment rises, it tends to dampen down prices in the economy. Fewer people at work means fewer people spending money and a downward multiplier.

After the Second World War the government pledged itself to full employment. In recent years, however, successive governments have realised that there may be a benefit to having some unemployment in the economy because this keeps inflation down.

Everyone knows that if unemployment falls beyond a certain point, the shortage of labour pushes up wage rates and hence fuels inflation. This rate, called by economists the **non-accelerating inflation rate of unemployment**, or **NAIRU**, is currently reckoned to be about 6.5% in the UK.

In 1997 the UK economy was very close to this figure. The problem is that nobody knows what the exact number is until it is reached!

Chapter summary

- Businesses as a general rule will flourish in a positive macro-economic climate.
- Key aspects of that macro-economic climate are healthy levels of demand, output and income, relatively low levels of unemployment, steady prices, relatively low interest rates and stable exchange rates which favour the domestic economy.
- The trade cycle is characterised by a series of fluctuations in economic activity in which periods of recovery and boom are followed by a recession and sometimes slump conditions.
- The general level of pessimism or optimism in the economy is an important trigger for economic change.
- Once a recession sets in, it tends to feed on itself. However, once recovery gets underway it can often build up and sustain itself over a period of time.
- The multiplier effect is important in accentuating the 'up' and 'down' swings of the trade cycle. Initial changes in demand are multiplied as a result of the way they feed into fresh changes in demand.
- Today unemployment is an important feature of all European Union economies. In the UK the figure in 1997 was just under 2 million. Various reasons have been suggested for this figure including cyclical, structural and technological factors.

- A further explanation is that when real wages rise above the level that is justified in an economy, labour can price itself out of a job. One explanation of why the UK has a relatively low level of unemployment when compared for example with France and Germany is that we have far more flexible employment conditions.
- Inflation is a general rise in the level of prices, measured through the Retail Price Index. In recent years inflation in the UK has been at low levels.
- The interest rate is the price of borrowing money. It is detemined both through the market and by government interference.
- In the 1990s, interest rates have been used as a major measure to control the economy.
- High interest rates encourage saving and discourage borrowing. Businesses that have borrowed money will feel the pinch when interest rates rise. A rise in interest rates can be used as a measure to damp down spending.
- A country's foreign exchange rate is the price at which its own currency exchanges for that of others.
- Exchange rates are important to business because of their influence on the price at which goods are bought and sold in this country and abroad.
- Business people generally prefer stable exchange rates.

78 A more complex view of the economy

The previous chapter examined some key variables in the economic environment in which businesses operate. For students who are particularly interested in this field, this chapter provides an even more detailed view of the functioning of the economy. In examining the more complex economy, we will be building on some of the extension material about Adam Smith in Chapter 10 and John Maynard Keynes, whom we introduced in Chapter 22.

The school of economists that followed Smith and who were particularly influential in the 19th and early 20th century were called the **classical economists**. Classical economic thinking was again very popular between 1979 and 1997 when it was referred to as **neo-classical economics** ('neo' meaning new). Margaret Thatcher and Ronald Reagan were strong believers in neo-classical economics and gave rise to the terms **Thatcherism** and **Reaganomics**.

A central belief of classical economics is that optimum economic conditions are created by letting the market work freely with the minimum amount of government interference, e.g. by having very low taxes and government spending.

Another piece of classical economic theory is the simple idea known as **Say's Law**, after the economist Jean Baptiste Say, which states that 'Supply creates its own demand'.

The implication is that factors of production make their factor services available to the market in order to earn income to purchase goods for themselves.

IT'S A FACT

Milton Friedman, one of the leading exponents of classical economics today, argues that people will spend the dollar or pound in their pocket far more sensibly than if the government is allowed to spend it on their behalf. This idea has often been repeated by Conservative politicians. For example, in the months leading up to the 1997 general election, John Major echoed this tenet several times in party political broadcasts.

For example, an employee may go to work in an office (a **supply act**) to earn money to buy food, clothes, pay the mortgage etc. – all of which are **demand acts**.

If this is the case, in the longer term, demand will be sufficient to purchase outputs, so that unemployment will at the worst only be a temporary state of affairs.

Sometimes business organisations will make the wrong supply decisions and make goods that do not sell. However, very quickly they will be forced to alter their production to the requirements of the market or go under. Unemployment, and recession may appear in the short period, but are strictly a temporary occurrence. The economy will be forced to re-structure to produce goods for which consumers signal a preference.

Government 'meddling'

The classical economists believed that the only danger to their system was if the government started meddling in the economy, or if bodies like monopolists or trade unions started setting prices above the free market level. They regarded any government interference as 'Socialism', and felt that there was a very real danger in the 20th century of Socialist government policies destroying the free market. They also saw the growing power of Trade Unions as a major threat. Unions artificially raised the free market price of labour so that workers were pricing themselves out of jobs. This was to be the classical economists' explanation of the great slump which occurred in this country in the 1920s and 1930s.

IT'S A FACT

Neo-classical economists argue that the reason why the UK economy has been so successful in the 1980s and the 1990s is the return to free markets through privatisation and the creation of greater competition, e.g. between opticians, bus services, etc. The emphasis, particularly under Thatcherism, was on individual initiative.

The influence of Keynes

John Maynard Keynes who wrote *The General Theory of Employment, Interest and Money* in 1936 is the most influential economist of the 20th century. He provided an alternative explanation of economics to the classical view.

Keynes had witnessed the Great Depression of the 1920s and 1930s in which huge swathes of the economy had come to a standstill. His view was that the market was not as effective as classical economists liked to think. The problem was that business people became pessimistic when the economic cycle went into a downturn. This meant that the economy was stuck in a situation in which demand equalled supply, but there was large-scale unemployment. Keynes saw no evidence that the economy would naturally arrive at an equilibrium (where demand equals supply) at a full employment level.

ADAM SMITH AND THE 'DESIRE FOR BETTERMENT'

Adam Smith

Adam Smith, who wrote the influential book *The Wealth of Nations* in 1776, argued that there was a propulsive force which put society on an upward growth path and a self-correcting mechanisms that keeps it there.

The propulsive force was 'the desire for betterment' - or the profit motive. In Smith's words it 'impels every manufacturer to expand his business in order to increase his profits.' The main road to profit consists in equipping working people with machinery that will increase productivity. Thus the path to growth lies in what Smith called accumulation, or – in modern terms – investment. Because of increased productivity, society's output grows.

The rising demand for workers pushes up wages. As people become better off they become healthier and mortality rates fall. More people become available to swell the working population. As a result the demand for products increases and the rising working population prevents wages from rising and eating into profits. Because profits are sustained we have a self-correcting mechanism that enables growth to be maintained.

This form of market-led growth can be represented as an engine providing a propulsive force and a set of tracks that serve as a self-correcting mechanisms enabling growth to take place.

Smith believed that there was an 'invisible hand' which guided the economy into producing the best results through the market system (i.e. the operation of supply and demand).

1 Do you support the argument that the market system provides an impetus to growth?

   What evidence would you draw on to support your view?

2 What are the benefits and the drawbacks of the capitalist path to growth?

3 What do you think Adam Smith meant by 'the invisible hand'?

Market-led growth (the engine) provides the propulsive force for economic growth.

The tracks represent the self-correcting mechanisms of the market.

Keynes therefore felt that there was a clear role for government to play in helping to **manage** the economy. The government would need to try and boost demand if there was a high level of unemployment; if demand was rising too fast, it would need to put a brake on people's spending, e.g. by increasing taxes or by reducing its own spending.

According to Keynes, governments play a very important role in creating the conditions for sustainable growth. Growth will take place if there is sufficient demand in the economy to lead to increased supply. It will also take place if supply is becoming increasingly more efficient – for example, if labour productivity is improved as a result of training, or if machine output is increased through the use of better machines.

Booms and slumps arise almost inevitably from changes in market demand and market supply on a grand scale. On the demand side, changes in demand are likely to come from:

● Consumers **(C)**;
● Investment decisions **(I)**;
● Government spending **(G)**;
● Exports **(X)**.

● **Consumer demand** varies with income levels. When incomes are rising, people are likely to spend more – for example, when taxes are lowered. People are also likely to spend more when it is easier to borrow money, and the cost of borrowing (i.e. the interest rate) is low;
● **Investment demand** is likely to be high when the economy appears to be booming. At this time business people will be optimistic and will expect good returns on their investments. Investment by businesses will also be higher when interest rates fall, because loans are less expensive;
● **Government demand** is likely to be higher when the government is trying to encourage a boom. This may be to reduce unemployment or to make people feel better before an election. A government may also spend more simply because it believes this is the right thing to do – for example, in order to secure high standards of healthcare and education;
● **Export demand** is likely to be high when a country's products are relatively cheap on world markets. The volume of world trade is likely to be highest when there is a general world boom.

Demand will be lower in situations which are the opposite of those outlined above.

On the supply side, output is likely to increase when goods can be produced more efficiently. This may be because factors of production become more effective, there are fewer problems in the production process, or because technology improves.

TASK 78.1

Which of the following are (i) *most* likely, and (ii) *least* likely to lead to growth in the national economy?

● An increase in demand for consumer goods after a period of recession;
● An increase in demand for imports by home citizens;
● An increase in the use of more efficient investment goods in the domestic economy;
● An increase in the demand for a country's exports;
● A fall in the productivity of labour in the home market;
● A rise in government spending on capital equipment during a recession.

Injections and withdrawals in the economy

Keynes argued that demand and supply analysis could be applied to the economy as a whole.

At the centre of the economy is a **circular flow** of incomes, output and expenditure. Firms produce output, for which they pay rewards to factors of production in the form of incomes. The people who provide factor services spend their incomes in the form of consumer spending. The process can be represented as a simple flowchart as follows:

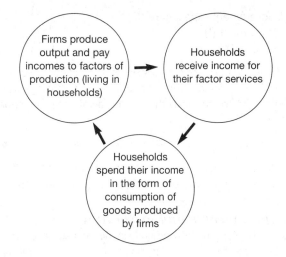

Figure 78.1 Circular flow of output, income and spending

If things were as simple as this, and if households were to spend all their income, then Say's law – that supply creates its own demand (i.e. output generates an equal amount of consumer spending) – would indeed hold true.

But this is not the case. We have to build a more complex model. Figure 78.2 on page 558 illustrates a more complex circular flow model indicating injections and withdrawals from the circular flow. For example, households give up part of their income in the form of taxes to the government, and so on.

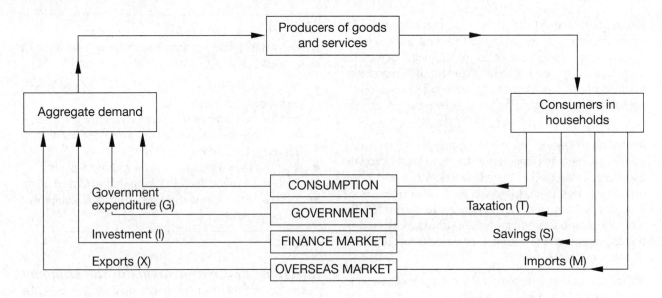

Figure 78.2 A complex circular flow model

Withdrawals from the circular flow of income include:

- Taxation **(T)**
- Savings **(S)**
- Imports **(M)**

Injections into the circular flow of income include:

- Government expenditure **(G)**
- Investment **(I)**
- Exports **(X)**

If an equilibrium state is to exist in the economy so that there is no tendency for national income to change from one period to the next, then withdrawals need to equal injections, i.e.:

Injections (G + I + X) = Withdrawals (T + S + M)

As Keynes argued, this state of equilibrium could just as easily exist with 5 million people unemployed as with 5.

Output, income and expenditure

As we have seen, households do not consume all their income because at various points money is withdrawn from the circular flow. Let us therefore look at withdrawals and injections in more detail.

Injections

1 Investment spending

Investment or capital goods are not immediately consumed; their purpose is to help in the production of further goods which may be for consumption – for example, an oven (capital good) makes bread (a consumption good). **Investment** refers to additions to the capital stock of the economy such as new factories, machinery and roads. It includes anything that adds to the physical stock of wealth.

2 Government spending

The government makes an important contribution to the overall level of spending in the economy. It spends money on goods which give immediate consumption value, for example by buying usable items such as chalk and felt-tip markers for use in schools, medicines for use in hospitals and so on. It also purchases major items of capital which go into further production, e.g. the construction of major bridges or hospitals. The government's spending also includes **transfer payments** such as child benefit, pensions, etc. These are so called because they are not made to people for work done, but are simple transfers from taxpayers to the receivers of benefits.

3 Exports

Exports are goods and services sold abroad, in return for which money enters the circular flow.

Withdrawals

1 Savings

Many people save a portion of their income rather than spending it. Over recent years the main savers have been the household and business sectors. Savings tend to depend on the level of a household's current income or likely future income. They are also influenced by interest rates. Saving and dis-saving can be illustrated by means of a **saving function diagram** (see Figure 78.3 on page 559 opposite).

The savings function shows that at low levels of income, dis-saving will occur, while at higher levels of income saving becomes possible.

This is true both for individual households (an individual's savings function) and for a national economy (national savings function).

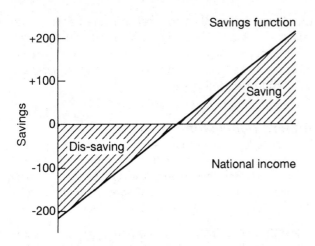

Figure 78.3 A simple savings function

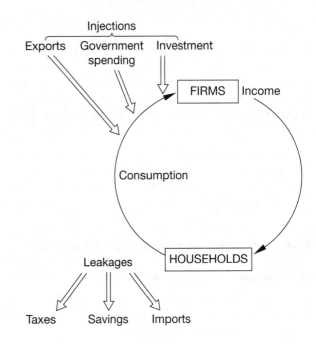

Figure 78.4 Withdrawals and injections

2 Taxes

Taxation helps to finance government activity. Fiscal policy is used by the government to alter the relationship between its spending and the taxes it imposes to meet particular objectives. For example, in a period of unemployment the government may want to spend more than it collects in taxes to pump extra aggregate demand into the economy; whereas in a period of inflation it may want to suck excess demand out of the economy by spending less than it takes in taxes. The government will adopt different budgetary strategies in different situations as shown in Figure 78.5 below.

Playing with the variables

Keynes argued that it was possible to interfere with the economic system to help the market to operate more effectively. In a situation where demand is insufficient to create full employment, there are a number of options available.

1 Encourage consumers to spend more by giving them more money in their pockets and by reducing incentives to save, for example by lowering interest rates;
2 Encourage investment, e.g. by giving tax incentives to businesses to invest more, or by lowering interest rates so that money becomes cheaper to borrow;
3 Increase the government's own expenditure, particularly on projects that will create jobs;
4 Encourage exports by subsidising them;
5 Discourage savings, perhaps by offering lower interest rates on government saving schemes;
6 Lower taxes;
7 Discourage imports, perhaps by putting restrictions on them.

Type of budget	Relationship between tax revenue and government spending	Purpose of budget
Surplus budget	Taxes greater than government spending	To 'suck' surplus spending out of the economy because it is overheating, i.e. inflation is high, and imports are being pulled in too quickly
Deficit budget	Government chooses to spend more than it earns in tax revenues	To 'kick-start' the economy into life and pump more demand into the economy to revive business, encourage investment, and reduce unemployment
Balanced budget	Government spending is matched by taxation	To play a neutral role in the economy – to encourage market forces and to limit inflation

Figure 78.5 Types of budget

TASK 78.2

Can you divide the following into consumer and capital goods? A taxi, a ham sandwich, a bacon slicing machine in a butcher's, a bottle of beer, a beer-bottling plant, a pot of salt, a pot of paint, confetti, a spanner, horseradish sauce, lipstick, a factory robot, an industrial cutting machine, a pineapple.

Which of these items when purchased would represent withdrawals from the circular flow of income, and which would consist of injections into the circular flow?

Demand-side and supply-side economics

A major distinction is drawn in economics between **demand-side** and **supply-side** economics.

Returning to our circular flow model, you will remember that two of its most important sections are **national output** and **national expenditure**:

1 Demand-side economics

Keynes concentrated on the demand-side policies as a means to influence the economy. In particular, he emphasised that investment demand is quite volatile and is the key to understanding the need for government interference in the economy. If business people are confident that the economy will boom for a period of time, they will be keen to invest. However, when they are gloomy they will cut back heavily on investment projects. If you watch business programmes on TV you will frequently hear references to 'business confidence'.

Changes in demand factors can also have a dramatic impact. For example, when a building contractor loses a contract to build a new plant, workers may have to be laid off. These workers then forgo their wage packets. They buy less in local shops. The local shops then 'feel the pinch'. They buy in fewer stocks and reduce the numbers of hours worked by staff. In turn, these shopworkers have smaller incomes and buy less.

A more complex multiplier

We have already seen that the multiplier effect measures the change in total demand in the economy as a result of an initial change in demand. The size of the multiplier depends on the size of the **leakages** from the circular flow ('leakage' is another word for withdrawal).

If leakages constitute a high proportion of income, the multiplier will be low, and if leakages make up a low proportion of income, the multiplier will be high. The multiplier can be measured mathematically in the following way:

$$\text{Multiplier } (k) = \frac{1}{\text{Marginal propensity to leak}}$$

The **marginal propensity to leak (MPL)** is the fraction of extra income earned by the average person that is leaked from the circular flow. For example, if my income increased by £1, how much of that income will I withdraw from the circular flow? The marginal propensity to leak is obtained by adding together the marginal propensity to save, the marginal propensity to be taxed and the marginal propensity to buy imports.

This sounds more complicated than it is. For example, if the typical citizen saves one-quarter of his or her extra income, is taxed one-eighth of his or her marginal income and spends one-eighth of marginal income on imports, then the marginal propensity to leak in the economy is one-half.

Demand-side economics:	Supply-side economics:
Concentrates on **national expenditure**	Concentrates on **national output**
Draws on the theories of Keynes and the neo-Keynesian economists	Draws on the theories of classical and neo-classical economists such as Friedrich Hayek and Milton Friedman
Is associated with Social Democratic Parties such as Tony Blair's Labour Party	Is associated with Free Market Parties such as Margaret Thatcher and John Major's Conservative Parties, and with Reaganomics
Argues that more government can be better government	Argues that 'best government is least government'
Gives priority to fiscal policy, i.e. taxation and government spending, as key instruments of economic management	Gives priority to control of the money supply and changes in interest rates as the key instruments of economic management

Figure 78.6 Demand- and supply-side economics

We can summarise this as follows:

Marginal propensity to leak = mps + mpt + mpm

Where:

- *mps* is the marginal propensity to save;
- *mpt* is the marginal propensity to tax; and
- *mpm* is the marginal propensity to import.

Therefore *mpl =*

$$\frac{1}{4} + \frac{1}{8} + \frac{1}{8} = \frac{1}{2}$$

The formula for the multiplier is therefore:

$$\text{Multiplier} = \frac{1}{\text{MPL}} = \frac{1}{\frac{1}{2}} = 2$$

The multiplier is a useful tool because it enables us to calculate the effect of an initial change in demand. For example, it will indicate to government that if government spending is increased by £x, the total effect on the economy once the multiplier has worked through will be £y.

TASK 78.3

Which of the following are (i) part of the circular flow, (ii) injections in the circular flow, and (iii) withdrawals from the circular flow?

- The purchase by a UK citizen of a Japanese radio;
- Consumption by a UK citizen of British beef;
- Wages paid to UK employees;
- Income tax paid by a UK employee;
- The purchase by BP of an oil rig manufactured in this country;
- The purchase by students of milk in their student canteen;
- The purchase by the UK government of British-made food for employees in a government installation;
- The purchase by French tourists of holidays in Hartlepool;
- Money which a UK citizen puts aside for a rainy day.

TASK 78.4

On average, UK citizens pay 25% of their income in taxes. Lately they have been saving 10% of their income, and have spent 10% of the income on imports. What is the size of the multiplier?

Assuming that the government spends an extra £10 million, what will be the overall impact of this increase in expenditure after the multiplier effect has come into play?

Assume that every £100,000 of expenditure in the economy creates 8 jobs. How much will unemployment fall as a result of the government's actions?

The accelerator

The accelerator is another simple but useful tool. It shows us that, even if consumer demand falls by just a little, this may have a much larger consequential effect on the machinery and capital goods industries.

One way of classifying industry is into companies that produce capital goods and those that produce consumer goods.

Consumer goods producers buy machinery from the capital goods industries. Each year they will need to replace machinery that is wearing out. For example, they may replace 10 per cent of their machinery on a regular basis each year.

Now, if the economy is in a slump, they may not buy any new machinery at all. Just imagine the effect if all consumer goods producers did the same thing. There would be little demand for capital goods, the capital goods industry would experience a massive downturn in orders and many capital goods companies would be crippled. We can therefore say that a relatively small downturn in orders for consumer goods will have a vastly **accelerated** effect on capital goods companies.

It is not surprising, therefore, that capital goods producers look carefully at the economic forecasts of booms and slumps. When the forecasts are gloomy, they will start to make cutbacks, and these cutbacks may be multiplied into a slump in consumption which feeds back into an accelerated slump in investment. The accelerator and multiplier effects work together.

The Phillips curve

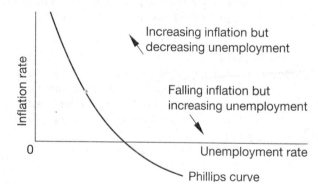

Figure 78.7 The Phillips curve

Most economists recognise that there is a trade-off between unemployment and inflation. If the government is worried about inflation, it will need to dampen down demand. It can do this by, for example, raising interest rates to reduce borrowing and cutting back its own spending. This will lead to a slow-down in the economy and to increasing unemployment figures.

The **Phillips curve** (see Figure 78.7) is an attempt to show a statistical relationship between unemployment and inflation. When inflation is rising, unemployment is falling, and when unemployment is rising, inflation is falling. The Phillips curve is used to describe this trade-off.

However, evidence indicates that the position of the Philips curve moves from one period to the next (and that at times it is possible for inflation and unemployment to rise or fall together).

2 Supply-side economics

During the 1980s there was a big switch in economic policy away from demand-side towards supply-side theories. While demand management had worked very well from 1945 until the 1970s, the policy eventually ran into trouble.

After the war most governments used Keynesian policies in managing their economies. To counteract unemployment, the government would use its own spending to pump up demand in the economy. However, a major fault of this policy was that outdated industries were artificially supported. Inefficient units, instead of being cut out, continued to survive on government subsidies. This meant that the UK lost its competitive edge in world markets.

The supply of goods (i.e. output) in the economy rose very slowly in the 1960s and 1970s. Because of this, an increase in demand led to both rising prices and an increased reliance on foreign imports. Too many imports led to a growth in the national debt, and the government was then forced to cut back on spending to reduce imports. Britain experienced **stagflation** – a stagnant economy that was not growing, coupled with inflation. Demand management did not seem to be working.

The cure was thought to lie in new policies that the Conservative government began to introduce in 1979 and continued to implement through to the election of 1997. Those policies concentrated on increasing supply rather than demand, i.e. focusing on making national output more efficient. A whole host of measures were introduced to stimulate supply, including:

- Reducing income tax to encourage people to work harder and for longer hours;
- Reducing benefits to those out of work;
- Reducing subsidies to loss-making industries;
- Privatising previously nationalised industries;
- Reducing the size of the civil service;
- Reducing government spending;
- Passing laws to reduce trade union powers;
- Taking measures against monopolies and restrictive practices;
- Encouraging competition among groups such as solicitors, opticians and even in the health service and schools;
- Emphasising the importance of education and training, e.g. through a National Curriculum that focused on areas such as numeracy and literacy for all children; and improving the status of vocational qualifications such as NVQs and GNVQs;
- Doing away with minimum wage laws.

Combining the demand and supply side.

When the Labour Party came to power in 1997 it was able to draw on the experience of both demand- and supply-side management. As a social democratic government, it has a leaning towards using government demand management to ensure a steady state of demand in the economy. However, it also appreciates the importance of having an effective supply side. Without effective production we will not be able to compete internationally. Therefore it is important to retain flexible labour and other factor markets without too much state interference. The government has also pledged itself to keeping to Conservative government targets for taxation and spending for the period 1997–1999. However, the Labour Party is committed to introducing European Union legislation which will give more social protection to employees, which in turn is certain to raise business costs.

The next few years will therefore see a tight balance being struck between demand- and supply-side management of the economy. Hopefully, the Millennium should create a boom period for the economy so that government spending will not need to rise at a faster rate than increases in national output.

Chapter summary

- Adam Smith described a market system in which the price system helps economic activity to be automatically regulated in a smooth pattern. Self-interest on the part of individuals lays the foundations for the growth of an economic system as a whole.
- Say's law sets out the simple theorem that supply creates its own demand.
- According to classical economists, unemployment can only be a temporary state of affairs. The only danger to the system occurs if external bodies and organisations, e.g. governments, monopolists and trade unionists, tamper with the system.
- Keynes was particularly influenced by the Great Depression of the 1920s and 30s. He argued that full employment was not a natural state of affairs: it might occur, but this was likely to be as a result of 'chance'.
- Keynes felt that the government should step into the market to pump up demand if there was insufficient demand in the system. The government could damp down demand if the economy was overheating.
- Aggregate Demand is made up of C + I + G + X.
- Investment demand (I) is particularly variable and depends on business optimism. In a period of pessimism it will fall and this will have a multiplier effect in the marketplace.
- There are three main leakages from the circular flow of income and three main injections.
- The government can pump up demand through increasing its own expenditure (G) or by lowering taxes (T).
- The government can run a deficit budget to boost spending in the economy.
- Demand-side economics concentrates on manipulating the components of aggregate expenditure, whereas supply-side economics focuses on making output more efficient.
- Between 1945 and 1979 the emphasis was on demand-side economics. Between 1979 and 1997 the focus then switched to the supply side. It is likely that over the next few years we will see a combination of these two approaches.
- The multiplier and accelerator effects provide helpful explanations of rapid variations in economic activity in an economy, causing upturns and downturns in the economic cycle.
- The Phillips curve outlines a trade-off between unemployment and inflation in the economy

79 The European Union

Throughout the course of European history, attempts have been made to bring the European nations together under a single (if dictatorial) order. The Roman and Napoleonic empires provide good examples of this. Although the European Union is the only successful example of a democratic attempt to unite (politically and economically) the European nations, European unity itself is not a new idea.

Origins of the European Union

The notion of a rebirth of the 'European ideal' was taken up by European and US leaders at the end of the Second World War. The aim was to bring lasting peace and prosperity to Europe through economic co-operation and integration. It was hoped that European economic integration would accomplish two specifically political objectives:

1 With the German experience in mind, the founding fathers of the European Union intended to make war amongst the European neighbours a practical impossibility. This was to be achieved by increased co-operation and understanding between the nations and by enmeshing their economies so closely together that war would become economic suicide;

2 By the end of the Second World War, the balance of world power had shifted; the USA and the Soviet Union were the new superpowers. It was hoped that a strengthened bloc of economically united and democratic western European nations would halt the spread of Communism from the East.

A supranational institution

The European Union is the prime example of a **supranational** institution, in that its power and authority are not confined to one state but are wielded over many. It has a common political structure which is authorised to make decisions within the prescribed areas for member states, but as a decision-making body, it supersedes or overrides the sovereign authority of individual states who are its constituent members.

The EU exists in order to foster increased intergovernmental co-operation among the European trading partners. This has been defined as the:

'... mutual adjustment of government policies through a process of policy coordination... Co-operation does not require that states confront no conflicts of interest, but addresses how they might be able to overcome these conflicts to their mutual benefit...'

(*The Oxford Companion To The Politics Of The World*, OUP 1993)

Main steps to unification

The European Union as it exists today has evolved through a number of stages:

1   The European Coal and Steel Community

The first step towards European integration was the creation of the European Coal and Steel Community (ECSC) in 1951. Jean Monnet (Planning Commissioner responsible for plans for the modernisation of France) and Robert Schumann (French Foreign Affairs minister) were the founding fathers of this scheme which aimed to 'pool' German and French coal and steel resources. The French and Germans were to give up sovereignty on policy issues relating to their respective coal and steel operations to an independent 'high authority' – a supranational body which would manage and co-ordinate policies in this field – thus linking two of their essential resources. Italy, Belgium, Luxembourg and the Netherlands also joined in this venture;

2   The European Economic Community

The next step came in 1956 when the six countries of the ECSC agreed plans to form a **European Economic Community**. For a number of years after the war, the countries of Western Europe had debated the benefits of adopting a **Free Trade Area (FTA)**. It was thought that an FTA would promote trade, increase prosperity and help the countries' economies in the processes of reconstruction and redevelopment. However, the European countries were divided as to how to achieve this:

- The six members of the ECSC felt that a Free Trade Area would not be sufficiently binding to deliver the security and economic benefits to which they aspired. They favoured a supranational model of organisation, in which countries would give up a portion of their decision-making powers to a higher authority (as in the ECSC). This was to be reinforced by the adoption of a common customs union and tariffs barrier;
- Britain and another group of European countries, (Denmark, Portugal, Switzerland, Norway, Austria and Sweden) objected to the idea of giving up a portion of their sovereignty and preferred an FTA based on intergovernmental co-operation.

In 1957, the ECSC six signed the **Treaty of Rome**, effectively creating both the **EEC** and **EURATOM** (The European Atomic Community). Together with the ECSC, these three organisations became known as the 'three communities'. Because of the objections outlined above, the other western European countries declined to join the organisation, although most of them became members later.

The Single European Act

The Single European Act was signed by the twelve members of the EC in 1986, with the aim of kick-starting the flagging process of European integration. With this purpose in mind, a deadline was set for the completion of the **Single Market** by 1992.

What is the Single Market?

The EEC created a European common market protected by a customs union and an external tariffs barrier. A **common market** involves the free movement of goods, trade, labour, services, capital and people between a group of countries.

The problem was that although the Treaties of Rome had removed the most obvious barriers to trade, (i.e. customs duties and tariff barriers) the member states had found other ways of protecting their home markets against their internal trading partners. Although they had promised to remove all barriers to trade, in practice, they used 'non-tarrif barriers' to give their home markets an unfair advantage. Examples included production subsidies, market-sharing cartels, use of different technical rules and standards (e.g. different specifications on packaging design or composition), refusal to recognise professional or educational qualifications, etc. Non-tariff barriers are generally harder to detect and the Community's practice of unanimous voting to make decisions meant that removing them was a slow process.

The intention of the Single European Market, therefore, was to create an internal European trading space, free from any national trading barriers. The aim of the Single European Act was to remove the hidden, non-tarrif barriers to trade – to harmonise inequalities in national law such as environmental law, or technical laws, which might otherwise prevent member states from trading with eachother on an equal basis.

Maastricht: the Treaty on European Union

Over the years, members of the EU have massively increased the scope for action at European level. Whole new swathes of policies have been introduced in addition to those appertaining to the original Common market and common customs union – the common fisheries policy, the environmental policy, to name but two.

SYNTHESIS

Can you think of examples for five more policy areas in addition to those already mentioned?

The new treaty significantly alters the shape of the European Union. Many of the new policies have been placed within the existing Treaty. This means that they operate within the normal framework of Community decision-making. They are given a 'supranational' character (i.e. the member states' governments no longer have direct control over what happens in those fields of policy). However, in addition to revising the existing European Community treaties, the treaty incorporates two new areas of policy co-operation – the **Common Foreign and Security Policy (CFSP)** and **Justice and Home Affairs**. The member states have promised to 'co-operate' on issues arising in these new areas and decisions will be made on 'intergovernmental' rather than on 'supranational' lines. This means that normal Community decision-making procedures will not apply in these two areas: the European Court of Justice will have no powers of jurisdiction, the Commission and the European Parliament will only have limited roles to play and the main sources of power will be the Council and the European Council, both of which are accountable to national parliaments.

The European Union 'temple'

Because the scope of European co-operation has been extended to include policies made on intergovernmental as well as supranational lines, the new structure of the European Union has been likened to a Greek temple (see Figure 79.2 on page 566). The overall 'building' (the EU) is now supported by three 'pillars':

1 The revised EEC treaties *(supranational)*;
2 The Common Foreign and Security Policy *(intergovernmental)*;
3 Justice and Home Affairs *(intergovernmental)*.

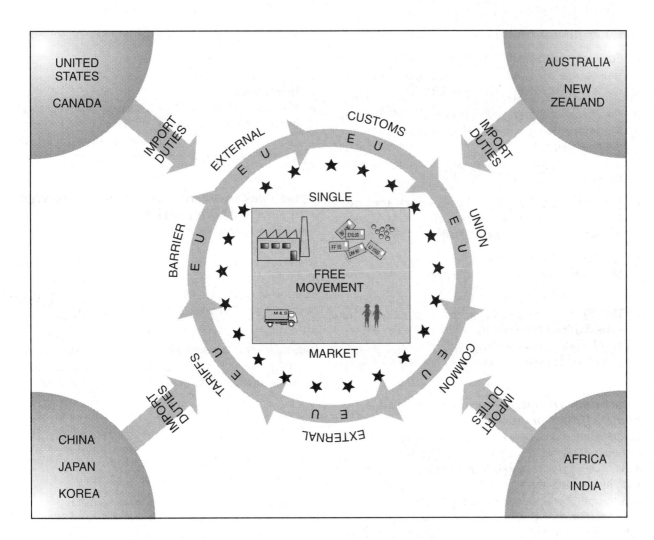

Figure 79.1 The Single European Market

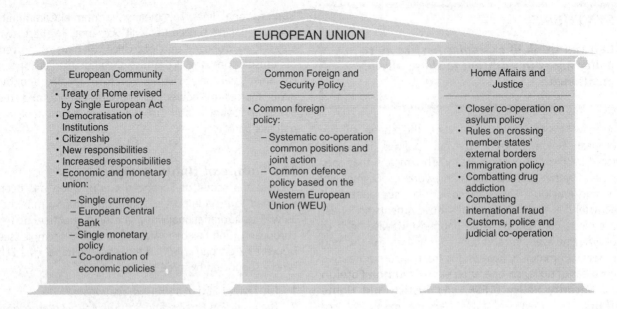

Figure 79.2 The European Union 'temple'

What is new in the revised EEC treaties?

- **European citizenship** Any national of a member state of the EU is now an EU citizen and may live, reside and move freely anywhere in the EU;

- The treaty includes new provisions in **European Monetary Policy** and sets 1999 as the deadline for the final stage of monetary union: the replacement of existing currencies by a common European currency, the Euro;

- The treaty includes some **institutional reforms**. Notably, it gives more power to the parliament, enabling it to block policies in some circumstances;

- The **Social Chapte**r aims to give the Union a 'human face' and prevent unfair competition in the Single Market;

- The Treaty also formally adopts the principle of **subsidiarity**. This means that action will only be taken at European level when action at state level is considered to be insufficient

What does co-operation in justice and home affairs mean?

Co-operation in justice and home affairs means that the member states will designate areas of common interest and concern in related issues such as crime, law and order, and immigration for 'joint action'. 'Joint action' means that the member states will decide upon common courses of action for the 'designated' areas and that they will subsequently promise to respect the agreements and act together in those areas.

Areas already designated for 'joint action' include:

- Customs co-operation;
- International fraud;
- Drug trafficking;
- Europol – an organisation set up to promote cross-border police co-operation to combat international crimes such as terrorism, fraud or drug trafficking. Europol includes a police information exchange centre.

What does co-operation in common foreign and security policy mean?

The CFSP works on the same principle as justice and home affairs: the member states designate areas of common concern for joint action. Alternatively – and depending upon the particular circumstances – they may choose to react to a particular event by adopting a 'common position' or by issuing a 'joint statement'.

For example; the members of the EU might collectively issue a statement condemning country 'X' for its poor record in human rights, or for its persecution of a particular section of its population. Under the CFSP, the member states have been able to deal with issues such as the war in former Yugoslavia, the Middle East peace process and stability in Central and Eastern Europe. Action in the field of the CFSP does not as yet include defence, although it does allow for the possibility of a common defence policy at some future point in time.

Actions taken by the member states in the fields of justice and home affairs are taken in the forum of the 'Union' but not within the decision-making processes of the 'Community' proper.

The Social Chapter

The Social Chapter is not actually part of the Treaty on European Union: it is a **protocol** (an agreement) attached to the Treaty. It was initially signed by eleven member states, not including Britain:

France	Germany	Italy,
Belgium	Netherlands	Luxembourg
Spain	Portugal	Greece
Ireland	Denmark	

The eleven signatories wanted to increase their joint co-operation in the field of social policy, using the aims set out in the **Social Charter** as their basis for doing so. This was a non-binding agreement which was adopted at the Strasbourg summit of December 1989. It laid down a number of social policy aims and objectives for the member states, including:

- Freedom of movement;
- Employment and remuneration;
- Improvement of living and working conditions;
- Social protection;
- Freedom of association and collective bargaining;
- Vocational training;
- Equal opportunities;
- Information, consultation and participation for workers;
- Health and safety in the workplace;
- Protection for children, elderly and disabled persons.

Originally the eleven wanted to incorporate the chapter into the Treaty. Britain, however, objected to this and consequently the eleven made a separate agreement on social policy – a protocol, which is attached to the Treaty, but not a part of it.

Other social policy provisions that were included in the original EEC Treaty and extended by the Single European Act, still apply to Britain, but Britain is exempt from any decisions made under the Social Chapter protocol.

Even though the protocol is not part of the Treaty and therefore not subject to normal Community decision-making, the Social Chapter protocol allows the signatories to 'borrow' the use of the Community institutions in order to make decisions agreed under the protocol legally and communally binding.

Article 1 of the Chapter outlines the Community's main aims in implementing a social policy:

> *'The Community and the Member States shall have as their objectives the promotion of employment, improved living and working conditions, proper social protection, dialogue between management and labour, the development of human resources with a view to lasting employment and the combatting of exclusion.'*
>
> Treaty on European Union, p197

The Social Chapter was created with two main purposes in mind:

1 **As part of an attempt to give the European Union a 'human face'**

   Those involved in shaping the Union, realised that it appeared bureaucratic and detached from ordinary people. They took account of the fact that European integration was not just an economic venture and that it needed the understanding and support of the people in order to succeed;

2 **In order to guard against 'social dumping'**

   As part of the attempt to run a fair Single European Market, the member states wanted to prevent countries with poorer social standards from reaping benefits over those with more stringent social standards.

   By maintaining differences in social standards – particularly with regard to employment (e.g. minimum pay, annual holiday entitlement, maternal leave, health and safety at work, etc.) one country could maintain an advantage over the others in attracting employment opportunities created by foreign investment.

TASK 79.1

Imagine that Toyota have just announced plans to establish a new plant in Birmingham. This will create around 600 new jobs in the region.

The other member states of the EU react angrily to this announcement.

Why have Toyota decided to invest in Britain? And why are the other states so angry?

Subsidiarity

The concept of **subsidiarity** first emerged in the 1989 Social Chapter and was subsequently incorporated into the 1992 Treaty on European Union.

The principle of subsidiarity is that action should only be taken at Community level when it is more effective and appropriate to do so than it would be at national level.

The intention was to attempt to clarify the blurred line of policy responsibility between the European Community and the member states, by adopting a general rule that decisions should be made at the lowest government level possible.

In practice, the principle of subsidiarity has been used by pro-Europeans in order to justify more decisions being made at European level and, paradoxically, by anti-Europeans to justify the reverse.

Enlargement

Since its creation, the EEC has progressed and developed enormously. The original nations in 1957 were France, Germany, Italy, Belgium, The Netherlands and Luxembourg. The organisation has been enlarged 5 times and now has 15 member states (possibly 21 in 1998):

1 Britain, Ireland and Denmark joined in 1973;
2 Greece joined in 1981;
3 Spain and Portugal joined in 1986;
4 East Germany joined in 1990 (following reunification);
5 Sweden, Finland and Austria joined in 1995.
6 Poland, Hungary, the Czech Republic, Slovenia, Estonia and Cyprus start negotiations for entry in 2002.

The institutions

In most democratic countries or states, governments are organised around a set of institutions which collectively combine to produce 'governance', i.e. policies, decisions and the implementation of policy. These institutions usually perform the following functions :

1 **Legislative** – passing laws and enacting policies;
2 **Executive** – translating policies into action;
3 **Democratic** – representing the wishes and views of the electorate and scrutinising the day-to-day work of the legislative and executive bodies;
4 **Judicial** – enforcing the law and safeguarding the country's constitution.

Although the European Union has no government as such, it has institutions (decision-making bodies) which collectively operate to provide the member states with 'governance'. There are five main institutions: the Commission, the Council, the Parliament, the European Court of Justice and the European Council.

The tasks of governance are shared out between the institutions so that each performs a separate function. Collectively the functions interlock, so that the whole system works interdependently.

Intergovernmental and supranational

The European Union is the product of a combination of different political approaches. These approaches are reflected in the make-up of its institutions. For example:

- The **Council of Ministers** and the **European Council** are organised along 'intergovernmental' lines, i.e. they mainly work on the basis of seeking co-operation, agreement and understanding between the representatives of the member states. Both these institutions are accountable to their national parliaments;
- The **Commission** and the **Parliament** have a more supranational and federal character respectively. They are more representative of the collective interests of the member states and they are not accountable to national parliaments.

The Commission

The Commission has a **president** (who is chosen by the heads of the member states) and a 'college' of 20 **commissioners**, who are similarly appointed by the member states. Each country appoints one commissioner and the five larger countries appoint two (generally one from the ruling government party and one from the main opposition party).

Each commissioner is given a 'portfolio', for example, the environment, agriculture, competition, etc. Each commissioner also has a **cabinet** – a small team of people (usually about six) who help the commissioner in his/her work, by giving advice, liaising, keeping in contact with other commissioners or interested parties, and by informing them about what is happening in the Commission and the Community.

The work of the Commission is organised into policy areas undertaken by the **Directorates General** (much in the same way that a government has ministries). There are more than 20 DGs, each responsible for a particular policy area. Because there are more DGs than there are either commissioners or portfolios, and because the responsibilities of commissioners and DGs do not always coincide, commissioners may have more than one DG in their portfolio and a DG's responsibilities may cover more than one commissioner. DGs usually control about 150–250 staff although numbers vary according to workload. DGs are responsible for much of the preparation and groundwork for policy proposals.

SYNTHESIS

Can you think of any organisations (not countries) with whom the Commission might have diplomatic relations?

Commission functions

The Commission has both an executive and a legislative role.

- In its **legislative** role, the Commission makes policy proposals which are sent to the Parliament and Council to be debated and decided upon. Although the Commission does not have a large legislative role, the ability to propose policies gives it some significant power in setting the Community's policy agenda. The Council also gives the Commission a role in making 'secondary' legislation. This means that the Commission can pass policies of a technical or administrative nature. These often help to smooth the path of the broader and more important policies that are passed by the Council.

- In its **executive** role, the Commission ensures that the policies passed by the Council are acted upon by the member states. The Commission sends out notices; regulations and directives which inform and direct the member states as to what (or what not) to do. The Commission depends on the member states' own civil services to help it in accomplishing this task, as the Commission itself has very few regulatory groups or officials actually enforcing Community regulations 'in the field'.

The Commission plays an important role in conducting the Community's external trade relations. It negotiates important agreements on behalf of the Community such as the **General Agreement on Tariffs and Trade (GATT)**.

The Commission also maintains diplomatic relations with organisations and countries outside the Community. This is done through small parties of permanent delegates which function rather like embassies.

TASK 79.2

The Community sets down what it considers to be acceptable levels of chemicals and nitrates in drinking water. The Commission informs the member states of the new laws.

1 Who makes sure that the new levels set by the Community are being observed?

2 Can you think of a reason why the new levels might not be observed?

3 If the levels are not being observed, how might the Commission find out?

The Council

The **Council of Ministers** is the main legislative arm of Community decision-making. Organised on intergovernmental lines, it is the Council that decides (always with the advice of, and sometimes in conjunction with the Parliament) which policy proposals become law and which do not.

The Council of Ministers is a generic name for an organisation which actually consists of several councils. Each council is responsible for a particular policy area and is attended by the appropriate national ministerial representatives (for example, the member states' environment ministers will meet in the Environment Council).

The most important council is the **General Council**, where the member states' foreign ministers meet. The General Council also deals with generally sensitive issues, or issues where the member states' representatives are

likely to disagree. There are also 'technical' councils for the whole range of policy areas: fisheries, the budget, transport, the environment, the internal market, etc. The regularity with which these councils meet reflects their workload, their status and the amount of interest that the Community has in their sector at any given moment.

The Council of Ministers has a presidency which rotates at six-monthly intervals among the member states. The president calls meetings and works to promote agreement between the Council members and to ensure the smooth and effective operation of the Council.

The Council reaches decisions by voting. There are three voting mechanisms:

1 **Unanimity** The Council must reach a unanimous decision. This is the most difficult agreement to gain and has been used by member states to stall agreements and to preserve their national interests at the expense of Community progress. In recent years, majority and qualified majority voting have been extended in order to speed up the decision-making process;

2 **Qualified majority voting** Each state is allocated a number of votes according to size of population; a winning majority constitutes 70% of all votes cast. The allocation of votes is weighted so that the smaller states are protected from 'bullying' tactics;

3 **Majority voting** A simple majority is required; all states have one vote each.

The EC treaties stipulate which voting mechanism should be used for each policy area.

Like the Commission, the Council is supported by a bureaucratic substructure which ensures the smooth running of the organisation by preparing much of the work intended for the top-level Councils.

The Parliament

The **European Parliament** has 626 members and provides democratic representation and control at European level. The Parliament sits in Strasbourg, although it has committee meetings in Brussels and officials based in Luxembourg. **MEPs** receive the same salary as MPs and sit in cross-national political groups rather than nationally. Members of the European Parliament were originally appointed by the member states. Direct elections to the Parliament began in 1979.

> ### IT'S A FACT
>
> 'Agenda 2000', produced in July 1997, opened the door to new members of the EU who had sufficiently proved their economic and democratic credentials.

Functions of the European Parliament

Parliament performs three basic functions:

- It has a role in Community decision-making;
- It has certain powers over the budget;
- It performs the task of a democratic watchdog over the other Community institutions.

1 Although traditionally the European Parliament does not have a strong role in Community decision-making, its scope for influencing legislation has increased in recent years. Originally, the Council only had to consult Parliament before making a final decision as to whether to adopt or reject a policy proposed by the Commission. It did not have to act upon Parliament's advice. This was called the **consultation** or **single reading** process and is still used in certain policy fields (notably the Common Foreign and Security Policy and Justice and Home Affairs). The 1986 Single European Act increased Parliamentary powers of decision-making by giving Parliament the right to a second reading of the proposed policy text: known as the **co-operation procedure**, this effectively made it harder for the Council to ignore the Parliament's advice and increased the likelihood of some of the Parliament's suggestions being incorporated into the Council's final decision.

   The 1992 Treaty on European Union gave the Parliament a **third reading (co-decision procedure)** which effectively allows the Parliament equal decision-making power with the Council. If the Council cannot demonstrate that it has taken Parliament's advice sufficiently into account, Parliament can reject the policy.

2 The Parliament has the power to adopt or reject the Union's budget plan. This is very important because unless Parliament approves the budget, the Union cannot implement its planned annual policy programme. Consequently, the Commission, whose task is to draw up plans for the budget, does so in consultation with the Parliament. This is done in order to ensure that Parliament will not reject the final draft.

3 The Parliament has certain powers of approval over the investiture of the Commission President and the Commissioners. The Parliament also has the power to force the entire college of commissioners to resign, although it cannot dismiss individual commissioners. (This effectively diminishes the Parliament's actual right of dismissal, as it is unlikely that the Parliament would ever want to sack the whole college, whilst it might well wish to rid the college of a particular individual from time to time.) In addition to this, the Parliament has some supervisory powers; it examines monthly and annual reports, submitted to it by the Commission and it can also set up committees of inquiry.

The European Court of Justice

The Court consists of 15 judges, each appointed by the member states for a six-year term (which is often renewed). The judges are assisted by nine advocates-general, who do much of the preparation work for the cases. The Court also employs about 650 staff, who perform administrative or language services tasks. In 1988 a **Court of First Instance** was created to rule on:

- Disputes between the Community and its staff;
- Actions filed against the Commission under provisions included in the ECSC Treaty;
- Aspects of competition rules.

The ECJ is not like a European version of a British court, nor should it be confused with the **European Court of Human Rights**. It does not deal with criminal or family law. It is a constitutional court, more akin to the United States Supreme Court and is mainly confined to economic and commercial law, such as ruling on questions appertaining to the Single Market. The court has two main functions:

1 It interprets the Community's written constitution (in other words, the Community's treaties) and tries to ensure that the law is upheld;
2 It upholds, interprets and rules on laws made by the Community institutions.

The Court rules in disputes between:

- The member states;
- The EU and the member states;
- The institutions (e.g. between the Council and the Parliament);
- Individuals and the Union.

The Court also gives opinions on international treaties and gives preliminary rulings when disputes waiting to go before national courts are referred by the national court to the Court of Justice.

All member states and their citizens are legally bound by Community law. Community law applies in fields where national law is deemed insufficient. Community law overrules national law except in circumstances where national law is tougher or when the memeber state's aim is simply to protect its home market at the expense of free trade rules in the Single European Market (for example, in the case of environmental law).

The Court constitutes one of the most supranational elements of the Community. Member states do not simply co-operate with each other; they have agreed to accept common laws (in many policy areas) ruled upon and interpreted by an independent body. It is not the member states who interpret how and when to apply Community law: it is the Court. If it were left to the member states there would probably be no effective common laws.

TASK 79.3

Can you think of two examples of cases that have been brought before the European Court of justice? Who was involved? What were the cases about?

The European Council

The **European Council** is the twice-yearly meeting of the heads of the member states of the European Union. Although inter-state summits had previously been called, the Council was not put on a formal statutory basis until the 1974 Paris Summit. The European Council was established at a time of 'Euro-sclerosis', when the European Community momentum was flagging. It was created to help give direction to, and breathe new life into, the project of integration. It was also seen as a way of promoting co-operation and co-ordination between the states and to promote understanding between the heads of government.

The Council is composed of the heads of state or of government and the President of the European Commission, 'assisted' by the Ministers for Foreign Affairs and a member of the Commission. The Presidency of the European Council is held concurrently with the presidency of the Council of ministers.

European Council meetings are held in the country of the Council president and it is his/her task to organise and chair meetings and to seek agreement amongst the other members.

The European Council deals with new projects for integration, (e.g. Monetary Union and the Single Currency), discusses sensitive issues that the Council of Ministers has not been able to resolve and responds to events which occur on the international scene.

EMU

EMU stands for **European Monetary Union**. It refers to that section of the Maastricht Treaty which provided for the creation of monetary union between EU members, such that, at an agreed date in the future, some, and in time maybe all member countries could enter a 'monetary union'. Individual currencies, such as the pound or the franc, the mark or the lira, would, in effect, cease to exist and would be replaced by a single currency, probably known as the 'Euro'.

If Britain were to join such a system, what would it mean in practical terms?

For the individual citizen it would mean being able to spend their domestic currency, 'the Euro', in any other country in the EMU. In principle, they would be able to move their personal assets – bank balances or other financial assets – much more easily from any part of the EMU to any other part, as they are, at present, able to do within the UK. From the monetary point of view, transactions with citizens of other members of the EMU would be little different from transactions at present with other

---

CASE STUDY CASE STUDY CASE STUDY CASE STUDY CASE STUDY

THE REFERENDUM PARTY MANIFESTO

The following statement appeared in the Referendum Party manifesto of 1997:

> 'Britain could be on the brink of surrendering all its powers to determine interest rates, the rate of inflation, levels of unemployment and the rate of growth. That is what will happen if, later this year, the government of the day commits the country to monetary union. The European Central Bank would take over these responsibilities in 1999.

> 'Sterling would be irrevocably fixed to the Euro, and Europe's new synthetic currency would take over from national currencies. The Treasury and the Bank of England will lose virtually all their powers over monetary policy. The Bank will be a sort of agent – an errand boy – for the ECB, which will control interest rates and credit

> throughout all participating countries. The same for all. It does not matter whether one country is suffering from a long slump and another is feeling the heat of incipient inflation – all and every one must be given the same medicine under the ECB. Monetary union is seen as the lynchpin of this greater union centred around Germany. The concentration of monetary power spawns the concentration of budgetary and political power, and ultimately of security and foreign policy.'

1 What do you see as being the main points of criticism of the Single Currency by the Referendum Party?

2 How valid do you think that these criticisms are?

STUDY CASE STUDY CASE STUDY CASE STUDY CASE STUDY CASE STUDY

citizens of the UK. We do not think of transactions across the borders of England, Scotland, Wales or Northern Ireland as in any way problematic. This could soon be true of transactions with other European countries, such as France, Germany, Holland or Belgium.

The implications for business

For companies, such a development could be even more significant. International trade does not consist of large numbers of 'one-off' transactions. By and large, it consists of well-established trading relationships between companies and individuals who know each other well and who have a substantial track-record of mutually beneficial commercial transactions. Some of these take place between different sections of the same international organisation – Ford Motors in the UK trading with Ford Motors in Belgium, for instance.

Very many of these relationships are enshrined in contracts, which specify products, prices and conditions of supply months, and sometimes years, ahead. Such arrangements offer security of service and a guarantee of essential components some way into the future. The production process is, of necessity, planned some time in advance of intended delivery dates. Clearly it is advantageous to companies if prices are also negotiated in advance, in order to secure future supplies of components or finished goods at a pre-determined prices.

Hazards of international trade

Where trade is conducted within a single country with a single currency, this presents little problem in principle. An agricultural co-operative in the Paris basin would not think twice about agreeing to buy a Renault tractor from a local supplier in three months' time, at a price fixed in advance. They may, however, think twice about importing a tractor from a supplier in the UK at a fixed price in three months' time. For instance, between August 1996 and November, the value of the franc fell by over 15% against the pound sterling. If the price of the tractor had been agreed in advance in sterling, the French co-operative would have had to pay at least 15% more francs in November than they expected when they signed the contract in August 1996.

In these circumstances, the exchange rate between currencies a can play havoc with perfectly sound commercial calculations and can make international trading a hazardous business. Naturally, companies try to build into their contracts safeguards against currency fluctuations, but no safeguard is foolproof or free of cost. Such fluctuations discourage medium and long-term trading relationships and make longer-term commitments riskier than domestic investment. It is clear, therefore, that for individuals, firms and investors, currency fluctuations add uncertainty and cost to cross-border trade.

Controlling currency fluctuations

It is possible to remove some of this uncertainty by establishing some sort of fixed-parity exchange level between two or more currencies. In 1944, the **Bretton Woods Agreement** sought to establish a post-war system of fixed international rates of exchange in which currencies were permitted to float only within narrow bands.

The disadvantage of this was that it could only operate if trade patterns were relatively stable and if international currency speculation was made very difficult. This was achieved by limiting capital transactions between currencies. This had the undesirable effect of restricting opportunities for real capital investment abroad.

The EC attempted to create a similar system in the form of the **ERM** or **Exchange Rate Mechanism**. This was designed to restrict currency fluctuations between European currencies by establishing large gold and foreign currency reserves which the central banks of Europe could use collaboratively to stem a 'run' on any currency – in effect preventing speculators from causing large short-term swings. However, the events leading up to the departure of the pound sterling from the mechanism, when Chancellor Norman Lamont took the pound out of the ERM after failing to stem speculation by changing the bank rate several times in the course of one afternoon, make it clear that, even with substantial resources, inter-bank co-operation and the willingness to take drastic action, speculators will not be discouraged if they feel that there are substantial profits to be made.

Pros and cons of a common currency

The advantage of a common currency as opposed simply to an ERM is that there is no opportunity for international currency speculation. This would produce as much medium or long-term certainty regarding impending price fluctuations as would be true of domestic trade. Thus an important element of risk would be eliminated.

Moreover, costs of international financial transactions should be substantially reduced, since all would be conducted in a single currency, obviating exchange commission charges by banks.

However, there are disadvantages to a single currency, and at the time of writing monetary union remains the subject of bitter political debate in the UK.

The Common Agricultural Policy

The main purpose of the Common Agricultural Policy is to guarantee future supplies of food in Europe. The experience of rural decay during the inter-war period and of food shortages during the Second World War caused by the strategic interruption of food imports to Europe prompted the European leaders in the post-war era to make plans for the revival and modernisation of the agricultural industry.

The intention of the CAP was therefore to make Europe self-sufficient in the production of food, so that food-shortages would never again be an issue in Europe. The CAP was adopted by the Community in the 1960s in order to realise these intentions.

Objectives of the CAP

The main objectives of the present policy are:

- To keep people on the land in order to ensure a viable agricultural sector;
- To prevent rural decay;
- To ensure reasonable incomes for farmers;
- To modernise the agricultural industry and make it more efficient.

The policy works on the two-fold principle of subsidising the farmers and protecting the price of their produce within the Common Market from directly competitive exposure to lower 'world prices'.

1 **Protecting prices** The CAP enables EU farmers to keep the price of their produce artificially higher than the price outside the Common Market (i.e. the flat price paid in the rest of the world, or 'world price'). This is achieved by placing an import tax on all cheaper foodstuffs entering the Common Market. This creates a 'threshold price', while also raising the price of cheaper imports up to the same level as that of the Common Market (and often higher).

2 **Subsidising the farmers** The farmers are subsidised:

- By EU citizens/consumers who pay an artificially high price for their food products;
- By the member states who pay large sums of money to the EC budget so that the EC can guarantee farmers a market for their produce. When they over-produce, the EC buys up the surplus and stores it (hence the notorious wine lakes and butter mountains). This ensures a stable price for foodstuffs and a good income for farmers.

In July 1997 the EU introduced a new policy to phase out subsidies to agriculture.

CASE STUDY CASE STUDY CASE STUDY CASE STUDY CASE STUDY

THE UK AND THE 48-HOUR WORKING WEEK

In November 1993, members of the Council of Ministers decided by majority vote to introduce a directive on working time under the Health and Safety article 118A of the EC Treaty. This enabled Council members to introduce a 48-hour maximum working week. The legislation stated that employees had a right to refuse to work longer than 48 hours, although they could work longer if they wished. The hours specified did not include paid overtime. The legislation also guaranteed workers:

- One day's holiday a week;
- A maximum working day of 13 hours;
- A minimum of 3 weeks' paid holiday a year.

The legislation did not apply to certain classes of workers such as junior doctors, transport workers or workers in some 'essential services'.

The British government objected to the measure on the grounds that, having opted out of the Social Chapter, Britain should not be affected by European decisions touching upon social issues. However, the decision on the 48-hour week was not introduced through the Social Chapter but through a health and safety provision to which Britain had formally agreed.

Britain's European partners consequently insisted that the decision should apply to Britain, whilst the British government complained that the other members were trying to force it to accept European social legislation 'by the back door'. The British government also objected to the decision on the grounds that the health and safety provision, which the member states used to introduce the 48-hour week, had been given too broad an interpretation and should not be used to legislate on working hours.

Subsequently, the British government referred the matter to the European Court of Justice. The Court ruled in autumn 1966 that Britain should adopt the 48-hour week.

(Continued on page 574)

THE UK AND THE 48-HOUR WORKING WEEK

(Continued from page 573)

Read the following extracts:

The business manager

Angela Horace, 38, manages Spotlight Multimedia Business Presentations. The business employs 11 people and organises conference staging and audiovisual presentations. Angela is deeply angry about the EU ruling on working hours (see page 573) and is concerned that her business will suffer as a consequence.

"When we organise a big conference, our chaps can do 48 hours in three days, working right through the night. With these new rules they will be able to refuse, so either we will have to pay them hefty overtime, which we can't afford, or we will take to employing freelances who will quote a set rate for getting the job done. The bottom line is that we cannot impose more charges on our clients and we will look for the cheapest option."

The restaurant manager

Martin Beale manages a restaurant in London's fashionable West End. He works an average of 65 hours a week and has been known to put in as much as 70 hours a week during particularly busy periods. He earns £19,000 a year. The EU directives do not apply to Martin, although he personally wishes that they did:

"In common with managers in most industries, I always work more than 48 hours a week. Most of that is voluntary, on the basis that the job needs doing and won't go away if I don't deal with it. I don't have any choice and I don't get paid overtime. I am paid a salary, so working fewer hours wouldn't affect me financially, but it would improve my quality of life."

The switchboard operator

Kirsty Fields works as a communications officer on the emergency switchboard for the West Midlands Police force. Her work is organised around a weekly shift pattern.

"We are trying to find out if the rulings include us, or if we are exempt because we work for the emergency services. I hope to God the rules do apply, because shiftwork like ours is a nightmare.

"We have a really ridiculous shift pattern. It effectively means 10-hour shifts which averages out to 37.25 hours per week over a month, but in practice you can do 70 hours one week and 20 the next. It's ridiculous, particularly when you are doing nights, as it exhausts you and messes up your system."

Tasks

1 Make a list of arguments for and against the adoption of a 48-hour week.

2 Can you think of any organisational problems or procedural problems that might arise through the implementation of the 48-hour week ruling?

3 Can we make any generalisations about which kind of jobs will benefit from the 48-hour week ruling, and which will not?

Chapter summary

- The European Union orginated for economic, political and social reasons. One of the earliest driving forces was to create co-operation and to end division and war.
- The European Union progressed through a number of stages. The initial step was the European Coal and Steel Community which was to form the basis for the European Economic Community.
- The six founding members were France, West Germany, Italy, The Netherlands, Luxembourg and Belgium.
- Over the years the union enlarged. Major steps were the Single European Act (involving 12 nations) in 1986 and the completion of the Single Market in 1992.
- The Single Market is an internal European trading space which is free from national trading barriers.
- The Maastricht Treaty went on to give a more supranational character to the European Union, basing it on the three pillars of Economic Community, Common Foreign and Security Policy and Home Affairs and Justice.
- The Social Chapter of 1997 is a protocol creating harmonised social rights within the European Union. It was not signed by the UK.
- Maastricht placed great emphasis on the principle of subsidiarity – that action should only be taken at Community level when it is effective and appropriate to do so.
- Today the EU has grown to 15 members and is likely to grow in the future with the incorporation of new members such as the Czech Republic.
- The EU has a number of key institutions including The Commission, The Council, The Parliament, The European Court of Justice, and The European Council.
- The prospect of full European Monetary Union based on a Single Currency, the Euro, is the subject of much bitter political debate in the UK.

80 International business

Business activity in the UK takes place against a wider background of world trade. Many UK businesses are owned by foreign companies. Similarly, many UK businesses have operations overseas.

Increasingly, UK firms buy and sell their products internationally. They also face greater competition than ever from foreign firms.

It is therefore essential for students of business to have a good working knowledge of the international environment in which business organisations operate.

The benefits of international trade

We can illustrate the benefits of international trade by means of a simple example.

Once there were two islands separated by a sea that was too dangerous to cross. On the first island, which was very flat, wheat could be grown in plenty, but the waters around the island contained few fish. The second island was very hilly and only a little wheat could be grown. However, around this second island, fish were plentiful. One day an explorer found a sea passage, to the south of the two islands, that was not dangerous to cross.

Let us suppose that before the trade route was discovered, half of the people in each island spent their time farming, and the other half spent their time fishing.

In a year, the amount of wheat and fish that could be produced was:

	Wheat	Fish
Hilly island	20 baskets	100 baskets
Flat island	100 baskets	20 baskets

Without trade links, the combined annual production of wheat was 120 baskets and the combined production of fish was 120 baskets. After trading, the combined totals could be 200 baskets of each:

	Wheat	Fish
Hilly island		200 baskets
Flat island	200 baskets	

Advantages of specialisation

In the two-island economy, we can see that with specialisation the two islands will be better off. Without trade links, the two countries cannot specialise in what they do best. When trade links are opened, both islands benefit.

Of course, this may be a simplification. For example, each island may want to produce some of its less plentiful products to avoid being dependent on the other (or to maintain employment). Also people on each island may have developed a diet which favours a particular product – e.g. many Japanese people favour a fish diet.

One possible limitation to trade is the rate at which the two islands are prepared to trade the two items. Another is the time taken to transport the goods, and the cost of transport (for example, fish may lose freshness if it takes a long time).

SYNTHESIS

1 *Explain how the people of these two islands could benefit from the opening up of the sea passage.*

2 *Are there any problems that could be caused by the opening up of this sea passage?*

3 *Supposing that all the people of the flat island now just grow wheat and the people of the hilly island just fish. Can you show how the people on the two islands could be better off than before?*

4 *Why might this not always be true?*

Geographical specialisation

As the 'two islands' example shows, different areas are endowed with different resources. Some districts, for example, have a climate particularly suitable for certain products (e.g. the highlands of Kenya for coffee-growing, the South of France for wine production, etc.). Other districts possess minerals, gases and oils which are not found elsewhere, e.g. the North Sea and the Falkland islands. It is easy to understand why Italy exports citrus fruits and Scotland whisky.

Different kinds of labour are also unevenly distributed between countries. For example, trained chemists are relatively abundant in the UK and Germany, so these countries are known for the export of chemical products. India is particularly well-endowed in highly-skilled IT specialists, so many companies have IT tasks processed for them in India.

A factor of production (i.e. land, labour, capital and enterprise) which is relatively abundant in a given district will be relatively cheap there. Goods requiring a relatively large proportion of that factor can therefore be produced more cheaply in that district than elsewhere.

The reasons for trade

We can therefore set out a list of reasons why countries trade as follows:

1 To gain products that they cannot produce in their own country;

2 To gain products that are very expensive to produce in their own country;

3 To increase the variety of goods available in their country;

4 To build up good relationships with other countries so that there is give and take, i.e. importing and exporting;

5 To create jobs by producing goods for export.

Barriers to trade

We do not live in a world in which goods and services are traded freely between countries. Often individual countries or groups of countries restrict imports from other countries. They do this for a number of reasons:

1 **To protect their own industries**
   Industries develop over time and involve considerable investment. Specialist machinery needs to be bought and the labour force needs to build up specialised skills. Countries are naturally reluctant to see domestic industries destroyed by cheap foreign imports;

2 **To protect firms and employment**
   Countries also protect industries in order to maintain a way of life. For example, some European countries have large farming communities. The farming community will live in rural villages and small towns, and maintain a distinct lifestyle. If cheap food imports force farms to close down, the result may be the destruction of the rural way of life, pushing unemployed agricultural workers into already overcrowded cities;

3 **To protect new or 'infant' industries**
   Once these new industries are established they may prove to be the lifeblood of an economy;

4 **To maintain security**
   Countries may also want to restrict the import of strategic goods, e.g. basic sources of energy, fuel, materials and defence goods.

Types of barrier

There are a number of methods countries can use to restrict imports from other countries or groups of countries:

1 Import duties (tariffs)
An import duty is a tax. The price of the taxed commodity will be higher inside the taxing country – by the full amount of the duty, plus transport charges – than on the world market.

2 Subsidies

A subsidy is the reverse of an import tax. A government can subsidise domestic producers by giving them a sum of money according to how much they produce. This gives domestic products an advantage in competing with imports.

3 Quotas

An import quota lays down the maximum amount – not value – of the commodity that may be imported during a given period. For example, the EU imposes quotas on the import of Japanese cars.

Why should businesses develop trade links?

When UK firms sell their goods in the UK they sell to a market which, at most, contains 60 million people. When the same firm extends its horizon to the European market immediately the opportunities are far greater – 80 million people in Germany, 56 million in France, etc.

The opening up of the Single European Market on 1st January 1993 created golden opportunities for capitalising on a huge 'domestic' market of 340 million consumers.

If a company can produce goods for a mass market, there are many benefits to be gained:

● On the demand side, it is faced with a much bigger target market;
● On the supply side, it has the opportunity of reducing the costs of production through massive economies of scale.

Market knowledge

Whenever firms export goods, they must achieve the right balance between price, quality and delivery. These are areas in which, in the past, some UK businesses have not been too successful. Exporters must also *know their market*.

Information about overseas markets can be obtained from two main sources: the government and banks. With their experience and contacts, both can play a major role in promoting overseas trade, helping to organise finance, giving advice, helping with insurance and assisting with foreign currency.

However, it is not altogether surprising that some businesses are reluctant to engage in international trade. Problems can include:

● Uncertainty in exchange rates;
● Language differences;
● Differences in tastes;
● Paperwork;
● Customs duties;
● Extra transport and insurance costs.

Patterns of world trade

The chart below shows world trading patterns in 1992. What immediately becomes clear from looking at the figures is that at the time there were three main trading areas, the EC, Asia (including Japan), and North America.

Country/region	Exports % of total trade	Imports % of total trade
USA	12.1	14.4
Canada	3.6	4.4
Mexico	1.2	1.6
North America	16.9	19.3
EC	39.5	39.6
Japan	10.8	6.1
Other Asia	15.5	16.0
Asia (incl. Japan)	24.8	22.1
All others	18.7	18.6

Figure 80.1 World trade, 1992

Today we are seeing the accentuating of the trend of countries to trade together in **blocs**. In particular we have seen the growth of the **North American Free Trade Area (NAFTA)** bloc which is increasingly developing links with the Pacific Rim group of countries, including Australia, China, Japan, South Korea, Indonesia etc., and the **European Union** which is increasingly developing trading alliances with rapidly growing Eastern European markets.

If we look at the growth of exports in recent years we can immediately see the importance of the East Asian and Pacific countries in contributing to this growth. The percentage increase in the volume of exports in the period 1980–1993 was:

East Asia and Pacific	11.4
US	4.0
Japan	4.0
European Union	5.0
World	4.3

Opportunities in new market economies

Until recently the world economy did not really exist. The former Soviet Union and its East European satellites opted out because of Communism, as did China. India also largely closed its doors to international trade and the same was true of many other smaller countries. Altogether, more than half the world's population was outside the market economy.

Today many of these countries, totalling some 3 billion people, are returning. They are doing so at different speeds, faced by differing problems and with differing chances of success. The potential gains from this process

IS EXPORTING FOR YOU?

The following Case Study has been adapted from a DTI publication Trading with Europe. *It highlights the questions that organisations need to face when deciding to trade internationally.*

With the whole of Europe as your home market, commitment to customers and consistency in meeting their requirements are no longer a luxury but a necessity.

You will need to give your product and your sales effort as much support as you would in the UK. Look, for example, at the number of sales representatives you employ to cover the UK, and then consider how many you would need to cover other parts of Europe properly. France, for example, is geographically two and a half times the size of the UK. Quite often a company expects big results from a small sales force. If you have limited resources, it may be better to choose one key market (or even key customer) and to concentrate your attention there.

Remember that you may also face increased competition in the British market as other European companies compete to seize their new opportunities.

To sell to other European countries involves four basic challenges:

1 Adequate management resources

Successful export marketing requires the near-constant involvement of senior management not just in making decisions, but in making contacts with representatives and customers.

2 Adequate staff resources

Exporting means more paperwork and more correspondence, much of it in foreign languages. Some of this can be contracted out but even these activities will need careful supervision.

3 Adequate production capacity and flexibility

The object of export marketing is to obtain extra orders. Have you the capacity to fulfil them and the flexibility to incorporate the modifications that may well be required in order to meet the needs of different markets?

4 Access to adequate finance

Laying in extra raw materials, extra packaging, insurance and freight charges, and the longer periods often required to realise payment for overseas orders will put extra strains on your cash flow. Can you obtain the necessary bridging finance? And can you support other extra activities such as research?

Tasks

1 What are the main costs outlined in the above article of extending a business's home market?

2 What are the costs of not extending your home market?

3 What are the main priorities that a business needs to consider in expanding into new European markets?

4 What types of business will be best placed to take up the opportunity of expanding into new areas of the Single Market?

are enormous. Trade and investment have the ability to revitalise the world economy and create a new period of growth. Already the Asian-Pacific area is the world's most dynamic economic area.

It has become so without the benefit of the huge markets of China and India. Japan and the Asian 'tiger economies' of South Korea, Hong Kong, Singapore and Taiwan became prosperous through trading with America and Europe, not with Asia. Today they have the opportunity to benefit from the huge new markets on their doorstep.

Links with Asian-Pacific countries

In 1989 Australia was instrumental in encouraging the development of a new trading organisation and alliance, the **Asian-Pacific Economic Co-operation (APEC)** and more recently the **Indian Ocean Rim Association**. This organisation is made up of Asian and Pacific Rim countries and includes the world's two largest economies, the US and Japan, and the fastest-growing, China. Also among APEC's members are East Asia's up-and-coming economic powers, South Korea, Taiwan, Malaysia, Thailand and Singapore. APEC accounts for more than half the world's economic output and two-fifths of its trade, but is only a relatively loose organisation of trading nations when compared with the European Union. However, its significance is that it presents new trading alliances.

Changes in Eastern Europe

The 1990s have seen massive changes in the economies of Eastern Europe. Eastern Europe is made up of numerous countries, many of which are quite distinct in character. The former Soviet Union was a massive area made up of many different types of peoples. The Czech Republic, Slovakia, Croatia, Hungary and Poland have a long tradition of economic and cultural ties with Western Europe, particularly with Germany and Austria. These countries have made extensive changes to their economies. Western countries have been able to develop joint ventures with companies and to invest capital in Poland, the Czech Republic, Hungary and, to a lesser extent, other Eastern bloc countries.

In the not-too-distant future, it is likely that a number of these countries will be invited to join the European Union. Already multinational organisations are investing heavily in a number of them – for example, Volkswagen/Skoda. Some commentators argue that once some of these nations have sorted out transitional problems of moving towards freer markets, they will experience faster rates of growth than many western European countries. A further incentive is the vast number of consumers in eastern Europe who are rapidly developing a taste for a wider range of consumer goods. Geographically, countries like Poland and Hungary are well placed to benefit from these developments.

The importance of the multinationals

For a number of years commentators have argued that in a global economy, multinational companies can often have more power and influence than some national governments.

A **multinational enterprise (MNE)** is a company with its headquarters in one country but with operations in other countries. Today there are over 12,000 MNEs. However, the largest 50 of these account for 80% of the world's foreign direct investment.

Of the world's top 500 multinationals, 434 are from what is referred to as the **Triad** blocs of the European Union, Japan and the United States.

An MNE has two major areas of concern: the home country of its headquarters and the host countries in which it operates. Its environment is a dynamic one in which there are a range of influences, including the actions of competitors, customers, suppliers, financial institutions and governments.

Another important characteristic of a multinational is that it is able to draw on a common pool of resources including assets, patents, trademarks, information and human resources. These resources can be shared within the organisation: for example, information can be pooled through organisation-wide databases, and patents and technologies can be exploited on a global scale.

A multinational will also have a **global strategy** so that all parts of the organisation pull in the same direction.

IT'S A FACT

Today United States trade across the Pacific is already over 60% higher than across the Atlantic. The USA is increasingly trading with the Asian-Pacific region rather than with the EU. The USA also intends to expand NAFTA to include all of North and South America.

The advantages of being a multinational

There are a number of advantages to organisations in being a multinational:

1 **To protect themselves from the risks and uncertainties of the trade cycle within their own economy.** Multinationals are able to spread risks by extending their sphere of influence;

2 **To benefit from the growing world market for goods and services.** This is part of the process of globalisation – the rapid growth of similar goods and services produced and distributed by MNEs on a world scale;

3 **As a response to increased foreign competition and to protect world market share.** When other foreign multinationals start to compete in a particular MNE's market, then it is time to expand into new markets;

4 **To reduce costs.** By setting up operating units close to foreign customers it is possible to reduce transport costs;

5 **To overcome tariff walls by serving a foreign market from within**. A major reason why so many Japanese car manufacturers have set up in the UK is to enable them to sell their goods inside the European Union;

6 **To take advantage of technological expertise by making goods directly rather than allowing others to do so under a licence.** A typical licensing contract lasts for about seven years, giving the licensee access to patents, trademarks, etc., in exchange for a fee or royalty. However, by producing goods directly instead, multinationals can keep more closely in touch with emerging technological development and be better placed to exploit and adapt new ideas.

'JUST DO IT' AND 'BIG ME' – THE WORLD MARKET IN 2020

In a speech in Melbourne, Australia in September 1996, C. A. J. Herkstroter, the President of Royal Dutch Shell, set out the following vision of globalisation, Asia and the 21st century and its implications for Shell.

'In the Shell Group, as a management tool and an intellectual aid, we prepare global scenarios looking at possible developments in the medium to long term – currently to the year 2020.

Our current scenarios are based on two ideas. The first is a global trading system of virtually unlimited competition - the model being the United States. We call that 'Just Do IT'.

The other is a system in which government plays a greater role, in which there is a network of rights and responsibilities – something similar to East Asian development today. We call that 'Da Wo' – 'Big Me' in Chinese.

Under Just Do It, free trade rules. Innovation is rapid and continuing, and those societies which are individualist, entrepreneurial and fast-moving prosper. Of course, the US is the exemplar in this scenario.

Under Da Wo, countries which are more cohesive, where social obligations are given more weight by business enterprises, grow faster. Japan, China and some other Asian nations fit here. With some variations many of the social welfare states of Europe also fit in.

What is striking about both these scenarios when they are applied to the Asia Pacific is that, while the outcome for individual countries varies, the central message of growth does not.

In both scenarios, barring unforeseen discontinuities, the message is growth – growing wealth, growing economic diversification and growing trade. Population growth will also continue, as will technological innovation.

As this growth develops, we expect regional demand for hydrocarbons - coal, gas and oil – to rise strongly.

A good example is the gas industry. The emergence of significant demand, primarily from a number of urban centres from Jakarta in the south to Tokyo in the past and Bombay in the west, is likely to create the need for the most extensive gas pipeline network yet seen in the world.

Under the Da Wo scenario, we forecast that this network could eventually link fields in Turkmenistan, Iran, Siberia, Sakhalin and the South China Sea, with almost as widely scattered, consumption centres. The scale of such a network is breathtaking. Many of its component parts are already being built and any energy company that sees itself as a global player - which Shell assuredly does - must take part.

A similar picture emerges in the oil market. Under Da Wo, we forecast that nearly half of new oil demand in the next 25 years will come from this region.

1 How can the development of the Asia Pacific region be seen as an opportunity for UK companies? How might it also be seen as a threat?

2 Which sectors of UK industry do you see as having the greatest potential to benefit from these developments?

Multinationals: good or bad?

There is considerable debate as to whether multinationals and their activities are good or bad for economies and their people.

1 **Job creation and employment** One argument put forward in favour of multinationals is that they create jobs. For example, the establishment of the Toyota plant near Derby created a lot of local jobs and was welcomed by many people in the area. The downside is that multinationals can just as easily pull out of a country as stay in. If they feel that it is more advantageous to set up elsewhere they can close down large plants at a moment's notice.

2 **The balance of payments** The UK has benefited from having a number of Japanese, American and European car manufacturers operating within its borders. Goods produced by these companies are sold abroad thus creating exports for the UK. However, this also means that many or all the raw materials, parts, etc., which go into the finished products have to be imported.

3 **Technology and expertise** Foreign multinationals may introduce new technology, production methods and ways of working into an economy and thus help to move it forward. For example, in recent years we have come to talk about the 'Japanisation' of UK

HOW POWERFUL ARE THE MULTINATIONALS?

In February 1997, the president of Toyota caused a considerable stir when he stated that if the UK failed to join the European Monetary Union, Toyota might consider leaving the UK.

Today goods and services can be delivered across immense distances at incredible speeds. This has dramatically changed the environment in which businesses and government operate. When considering his next European car plant, Mr Okuda could site it in Spain rather than Britain – indeed, wherever he considers he can make the most profit.

This would suggest that multinationals have considerable 'clout' politically. If they or any other major investors are dissatisfied with the way a government is running a country, they can switch their operations elsewhere.

This view contrasts with that put forward recently by Paul Hirst and Grahame Thompson writing in the magazine *Soundings* in January 1997. Hirst and

Thompson argue that the trend to globalisation has been overplayed. They support their argument by pointing out that trade is roughly the same proportion of national income for many industrialised countries today as it was at the beginning of the century, and that most businesses tend to stay close to home. Governments therefore have as much freedom to manoeuvre as they did a century ago.

1 Can you think of cases where multinationals have switched operations from one country to another?

2 How much power do you think that multinationals have relative to the power of national governments?

3 How easy do you think it is for multinationals:

   i) To switch the base of their operations?

   ii) To influence government policy?

industry – i.e. the large-scale adoption of factory robots, just-in-time working practices, teamwork and Total Quality Management. It is widely recognised that this has helped to improve the competitive edge of UK businesses. **Technology transfer** of this kind from one country to another is particularly effective in bringing less developed countries forward;

4 **Social responsibility** Multinationals have received the most scathing criticism for the social costs of some of their activities, e.g. destroying local communities, pollution, etc.

    In particular, a major criticism levelled at MNEs is that of employing double standards. It has been claimed that they transfer their manufacturing operations to economies which have less rigorous environmental standards than at home, and thus effectively 'export' pollution from richer to poorer countries. Economies which are desperate for income may be susceptible to the advances of unscrupulous multinationals.

5 **Government control** The size and financial power of multinationals can make it difficult for governments to control them. For example, MNEs may be able to win concessions as a result of their size and influence. Some corporations evade taxation by transferring profits from one country to another, declaring high profits in low-tax countries and low profits in high-tax countries.

    Some commentators argue that global trade and global business operations are rapidly becoming far more important than national governments and that the important decision-makers in the world today are the multinationals.

IT'S A FACT

Often multinationals will play down the fact that they are based in another country.

For example, did YOU know that Nestlé has its headquarters in Switzerland? Or that Phillips is a Dutch-based company? How many people realise that Jaguar, the former British car company, is owned by Ford and 25% of banks in California are Japanese-owned?

The World Trade Organisation

In recent years there has been a growing impetus to trade-between countries promoted through the efforts of the **World Trade Organisation (WTO)**.

The origins of the World Trade Organisation can be traced back to the creation of the **General Agreement on Tariffs and Trade (GATT)** in 1947. GATT operates on three levels:

- As a set of trading rules (the 'rules of the road' for trade);
- As an international agency for helping to resolve trade disputes between countries and groups of countries;
- As a means for countries to collaborate to create freer trade and to cut down existing barriers.

The growth in world trade during the 1980s was supported by a liberalising of trading conditions throughout the world. At the end of 1993 there were 112 members of GATT, accounting for 90 per cent of world economies. With China and Russia joining the new **Multilateral Trade Organisation** this was extended to include nearly all world trade.

With the completion of the **Uruguay Round** (a series of talks which started in 1986 – the eighth such round of reductions in barriers to trade since 1947 – the World Trade Organisation was created to replace GATT.

The WTO is a powerful umbrella organisation which has ratified agreements on trade in goods, services and intellectual property. If there is a consensus among most member states, the WTO is able to force terms even on members who do not want to make the changes. The WTO is in effect an international trade organisation.

Chapter summary

- Businesses today operate in an international environment. Increasingly the distinction between the domestic and the international market is becoming blurred.
- The process of specialisation at an international level provides mutual benefits to trading partners.
- Countries may seek to restrict trade in order to protect their own industries, firms and employment. They can do this by imposing tariffs and quotas and by subsidising their own industries.
- By developing trade links, UK firms are able to benefit from much larger markets. This enables them to sell larger outputs, and to produce at a lower unit cost.
- In order for firms to be successful in trading in international markets they must be able to offer the right price, quality and terms of delivery.
- World trade is dominated by the USA, the European Union and Asia including Japan.
- New players are increasingly entering the arena of international industrialisation and trade. Of particular significance is the growing importance of the Pacific Rim, the Tiger economies and China.

These developments provide both an opportunity and a threat for the UK.

- Eastern European markets are also of growing significance and provide plenty of opportunities for UK companies both through joint ventures and as markets for sales.
- Multinationals continue to dominate world trade. A multinational is a company with its headquarters in one country but with operations in others. Of the world's top 500 multinationals, 434 are based in the Triad bloc of countries.
- Being a multinational enables organisations to benefit from the synergy of an integrated group, from shared resources, and the ability to fight competition.
- Some argue that multinationals today are more powerful than national governments. Others claim that the powers of multinationals have been exaggerated.
- The creation of the World Trade Organisation has given added impetus to the expansion of world trade.

81 The government and the competitive environment

This chapter explores a key aspect of the wider business environment in which organisations operate, namely that of the **competitive environmen**t.

In a perfectly competitive environment there would be no restrictions or restraints on trade and buyers and sellers would be able take actions in the marketplace with no fear of being exploited by monopoly or restrictive practices. However, in the real world there is a need for an independent body to create the rules of the game for competition. This is the responsibility of the government.

Freedom is an essential ingredient of economic activity. For example, individuals and organisations must have the freedom to set up in business, to buy and sell goods, and to take part in business transactions. In this chapter we focus on just one aspect of economic and business freedom – the freedom to compete.

This freedom lies at the heart of fair business dealing. It is because of the existence of this freedom that organisations like The Body Shop, Virgin, and First Direct have been able to introduce new ideas into markets which were previously dominated by large companies.

The benefits of competition

Competition is an essential element in the efficient working of markets:

- It encourages enterprise and efficiency and widens choice;
- It enables consumers to buy the goods they want at the best possible price;
- By encouraging efficiency in industry, competition in the domestic market – whether between domestic firms alone or between domestic and overseas firms – also contributes to our national competitiveness.

The purposes of competition policy
Competition policy exists to encourage and improve the competitive enviornment. It shows no favours to individual firms but sets out to intervene to protect individuals and organisations against unfair practices. The law provides a number of ways of helping to create more effective competition, to punish those who act unfairly and protect those who have been wronged.

A case-by-case approach
Competition policy exists to protect the 'public interest'. Individual incidents are examined using a 'case-by-case' approach to decide whether the public interest is threatened or not.

Competition is not seen as an end in itself. In most cases the law makes no pre-judgement that actions which reduce competition are wrong in themselves. It needs to be proved that it would be against the public interest to reduce competition in a specific case:

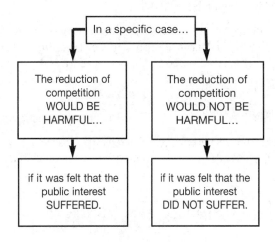

Figure 81.1 Competition and the law

Who is responsible for competition policy?

1 The Secretary of State for Trade and Industry has overall responsibility;
2 The Director General of Fair Trading is appointed by the Secretary of State, and is independent. He/she heads the **Office of Fair Trading** which is a government department. The Director General also has responsibilities for competition law enforcement and consumer protection;
3 The **Monopolies and Mergers Commission** is an independent tribunal whose chair and members are appointed by the Secretary of State. It carries out investigations into the behaviour of organisations and studies the way in which particular markets operate to see if the public interest is being maintained. It then makes recommendations to the Secretary of State.

IT'S A FACT

Currently in the UK there is considerable debate as to whether the Office of Fair Trading and the Monopolies and Mergers Commission should be separate or a single body. You will need to study the press to see what happens in the near future. An argument for bringing the two together would be that it enables more concerted and cohesive action. An argument against is that it would narrow the range of thought and criticism if the two powers were in a single body.

UK competition law

UK competition law is made up of four main Acts of Parliament, each dealing with separate aspects of competition policy:

● The Fair Trading Act 1973;
● The Restrictive Trade Practices Act 1976;
● The Resale Prices Act 1976;
● The Competition Act 1980.

The detail of these laws has been further amended recently by the **Deregulation and Contracting Out Act 1994**. The broad scope of the Acts is as follows:

Act	Deals with…
Fair Trading Act	Mergers and monopolies
Restrictive Trade Practices Act	Agreements between persons or companies that could limit their freedom to operate independently
Resale Prices Act	Attempts to impose minimum prices at which goods can be resold
Competition Act	Anti-competitive practice

These laws can be split into two categories:

● In the case of the Restrictive Trade Practices Act and the Resale Prices Act, action is taken in the courts;
● In the case of the Fair Trading Act and the Competition Act, practices are examined by the Director General, the Monopolies Commission and Secretary of State.

Monopolies

Where a company or group of companies has market power, there is potential for the market to be harmed in a number of ways. Excessive prices, reductions in the level of service and unfair restrictions on entry into the market are typical examples of what can happen in the absence of effective government regulation.

Monopolies are not necessarily a bad thing. The inventor of a revolutionary new device, for example, will inevitably be a monopolist to start with, even if the device provides a substantial benefit to the public. However, it is the responsibility of the Commission to determine when a monopolist is abusing their position and damaging the public interest.

The Director General keeps a constant eye on UK markets, looking at how major organisations are operating and at allegations and complaints. If the Director feels that there may be evidence of monopoly malpractice, a case can be referred to the Commission. At this stage no companies are named: it is simply suggested that aspects of competition – e.g. prices – need to be investigated in a specific

IT'S A FACT

Although we normally think of a monopoly as the domination of a market by a sole supplier, UK law uses a wider definition. Under the Fair Trading Act, a monopoly is defined as a situation where a company supplies or buys **25% or more** of all goods or services of a particular type in the whole country or in a particular area, e.g. the East Midlands.

The Act also defines a **complex monopoly** as a situation where a group of companies that together have 25% of the market all behave in a way that restricts competition.

market. The Commission then investigates and reports to the Secretary of State with suggestions for possible action, and the Secretary of State and the Director General decide what should be done. This might involve asking companies to make promises to change, or asking for promises backed up with measures to make sure that promises are kept.

Anti-competitive practices

In a competitive market, companies will naturally adopt policies that give them a competitive edge. This can lead to many benefits. However, sometimes firms use practices which may be harmful to competition. Practices that may be acceptable in a market where competition is strong may be unacceptable where competition is weak. Under the Competition Act, an **anti-competitive practice** is one that **has, is intended to have, or is likely to have, the effect of restricting competition**.

Market power

The ability of a firm to influence the market depends on its **market power**. Market power stems from having a large share of the market, a leading brand name, or being able in some way to prevent new firms from entering the industry (perhaps through the use of patent rights). Companies are covered by the Act if they have more than 25% of a market or a turnover of more than £10 million.

If an alleged anti-competition practice is identified, the Director can conduct an initial informal inquiry. If it is found that unacceptable practices have been taking place the Director can either:

● Accept binding undertakings from the parties concerned that the practice will stop;
● Refer the case to the Monopolies Commission, which must decide whether the case is against the public interest. Companies can be named immediately, and once the investigation is carried out, recommendations will be made to the Secretary of State.

POLICING ANTI-COMPETITIVE PRACTICES

1 Bryant & May meet their match

On the 5th March 1992, the Monopolies and Mergers Commission found that match-makers Bryant & May accounted for 78% by volume of retail sales of matches, while the company was also the largest supplier of disposable lighters.

It concluded that the company had been guilty of making excessive profits on sales of matches, and that prices were higher than they would have been under competitive conditions. In its report, the MMC recommended the imposition of price controls on certain brands supplied by the company. (These were later lifted when the market became more competitive.)

2 On the scent of monopoly

On 11th November 1993, the Commission published the results of its investigations into the 'fine fragrances' market in the UK.

It concluded that the selective retail distribution systems operated by the fine fragrances houses amounted to a complex monopoly.

Nevertheless the MMC also thought that there was strong competition between suppliers, that consumers had the option to

buy cheaper fragrances, and that selective distribution was no more than was required to preserve the up-market appeal on which fine fragrance brands rely. For these reasons the complex monopoly was found not to act against the public interest.

Tasks

1 Why do you think that the Monopolies and Mergers Commission made the two judgements outlined above?

2 Can you see any general rules behind its thinking or is it simply employing a case-by-case approach?

Resale price maintenance

Attempts by manufacturers or suppliers to enforce a minimum price at which their goods can be resold by dealers or retailers restrict competition and can keep prices higher than they would otherwise be. **Resale price maintenance** is unlawful under the Resale Prices Act, except for exempted goods such as books and certain pharmaceuticals.

Under the 1976 Act, it is unlawful to try to establish minimum prices. It is also unlawful to cut off supplies or to offer less favourable terms to dealers whom the supplier believes to be responsible for price-cutting. A supplier is, however, entitled to withhold goods from a dealer who is pricing them as **loss leaders** (that is, goods sold at a loss in order to attract customers towards more profitable items).

The Director General has the power to seek a court injunction to force the parties involved to scrap a retail price agreement. In recent years it has been typical for the Director General to receive about 30–40 complaints a year alleging foul play in this area.

Mergers

Under the Fair Trading Act, a merger is said to take place when two or more companies 'cease to be distinct' (see page 324). The aim of competition policy is not to pre-judge mergers but to examine the merits of individual mergers. The advantages in each case must be weighed against the disadvantages.

The Act sets out two tests to determine whether a particular merger should be investigated:

AN ACCEPTABLE MERGER?

Consider the following situation:

Two companies are hoping to merge. One company has 35% of the market and the other has 25%. The assets of each company are in excess of £100 million. Both companies manufacture finished clothing items for retail sale. Because of the perceived high quality of their product, they will only deal with selected retail outlets, and under the new (merged) company structure these outlets will only be allowed to sell the product if they agree to a mark-up of exactly 60%. In addition there will be a number of regulations as to how the product can be displayed and offered to customers. The companies are confident that the new company will shortly capture all of this exciting and rapidly developing market. Prices are expected to remain high, and the product performance and quality are currently better than any other textile garment in the world. Many new jobs will be created. UK prices compare favourably with those of the foreign competition.

1 List the facts making it likely that this proposed merger would be referred to the Commission.

2 What arguments can be put in favour of the merger?

3 Do you think that the merger is likely to be allowed to take place?

1 The **assets test** requires that the total gross assets of the company to be taken over exceed £70m in value;
2 The **'market share' test** requires that, as a result of the merger, 25% or more of the supply or purchase of goods or services of a particular description in the UK, or a substantial part of it, should come under the control of the merging enterprise, or a 25% share is increased.

The critical factor in deciding whether a merger should be allowed to take place is again the public interest. Those most likely to cause concern are **horizontal mergers**, where two companies supplying the same sort of product or service combine, e.g. to form large brewery groups.

Vertical mergers where companies are at different stages of producing the same product – e.g. a brewery merging with a chain of public houses – and **conglomerate mergers** where companies that produce quite different products, e.g. baked beans and toothpaste, may also be investigated.

Companies should notify the Director if they hope to merge. The Director General will then conduct an investigation before deciding whether to advise the Secretary of State to refer the merger to the Commission. Companies are not allowed to acquire eachothers' shares while the investigation is taking place. If they have already started to merge, they will be ordered not to join the operations together. The Commission reports to the Secretary of State, who decides, in consultation with the Director General, whether or not the merger is in the public interest.

Restrictive trade practices

All commerce is based on agreements of one form or another. The buying and selling of goods and services would be impossible without them. In such agreements, businesses agree to do certain things. However, some of the agreements may restrict competition. All arrangements made by two or more parties in business who accept specified restrictions on their freedom to compete must be registered with the Office of Fair Trading and entered in a public register.

Businesses may not always recognise that an agreement might be anti-competitive. Not only formal, written agreements must be registered. An agreement arising from a chat in a pub, or even an unspoken understanding, can be just as significant as a formal contract drawn up by lawyers. The most obvious cases are those involving the fixing of prices and the sharing of markets. A serious view is taken of deliberate evasion of the legal requirement to register agreements. The Director General refers these agreements to the Restrictive Practices Court to be struck down.

The **Restrictive Trade Practices Act** covers agreements affecting goods and services. Companies must register certain types of agreement they make, including:

● Restrictions on prices or charges;
● Conditions on which business is conducted ;
● Geographical divisions of business;
● People with whom business may take place;
● The quantity of goods to be produced;
● The manufacturing process to be used.

Any agreements which the Restrictive Practices Court find to be against the public interest are struck down. Parties to an agreement therefore need to be able to prove to the court that there are real benefits from their restrictive practices.

In arguing that a restrictive practice is in the public interest, organisations may be able to point to one or more of the so-called **seven gateways**. These are that the agreement:

- Protects the public against injury;
- Brings other substantial benefits to the public;
- Helps to fight anti-competitive practices by other firms;
- Enables the parties concerned to negotiate fair terms with dominant businesses;
- Helps to create jobs and/or to generate important export earnings;
- Supports other restrictive agreements which the court has already approved;
- Has very little impact in reducing competition.

European Union competition law

The main provisions of European Union law dealing with competition are dealt with in Articles 85 and 86 of the Treaty of Rome.

Together with a number of implementing regulations, these articles cover similar ground to the UK competition laws, including those parts that deal with monopolies and anti-competitive practices. Community law applies only where practices may have an effect on trade between member states.

Article 85 forbids agreements which may adversely affect trade between the 15 member states, and in particular which have as their object a limitation of competition. This includes price-fixing, market-sharing, restriction of production or technical development and the imposition of discriminatory terms of supply. Such agreements are automatically disallowed unless given an exemption by the European Commission.

A **European Merger Control Regulation** allows the European Commission to control mergers which have a 'community dimension', i.e. where:

- The combined aggregate worldwide turnover of all parties concerned is more than EURO 5 billion;
- At least two of the parties have a Union-wide turnover exceeding EURO 250 million, *unless...*
- Each of the parties achieves more than two-thirds of its total Community-wide turnover within one and the same member state.

The European Commission is directly responsible for the application of EU legislation in the UK. Before deciding that a law has been broken, the Commission issues a statement of objection to the two parties concerned, who then have the opportunity to reply to the Commission both in writing and orally.

For example, during the 1990s the Commission used this procedure to investigate exclusivity agreements whereby Unilever prevented small retailers from putting Mars ice cream into Unilever-supplied freezer cabinets.

Chapter summary

- Freedom, and especially freedom to compete, is an essential ingredient of the marketplace.
- Competition policy exists to encourage and improve the competitive process.
- Competition policy sets out to protect the public interest on a case-by-case approach.
- The Secretary of State for Trade and Industry has overall responsibility for competition policy. The Director General of Fair Trading heads the Office of Fair Trade and is appointed by the Minister.
- The Monopolies and Mergers Commission carries out investigations into the behaviour of organisations and makes recommendations to the Secretary of State.
- UK competition law consists of The Fair Trading Act, Restrictive Trade Practices Act, Resale Prices Act and Competition Act.

- A monopoly is defined as a situation where a company supplies or buys 25% or more of all goods or services of a particular type nationally or locally.
- An anti-competitive practice is defined as any practice that has, is intended to have, or is likely to have, the effect of restricting competition.
- Resale Price Maintenance involves businesses trying to impose a minimum price on retailers.
- A merger exists when two or more companies 'cease to be distinct'. If mergers fail an asset test or market share test, they can be subject to investigation and ultimately disallowed.
- Restrictive trade practices are practices which limit or restrain free trade and commerce.
- Articles 85 and 86 of the Treaty of Rome set out a legal framework for creating fair competition in the European Union.

82 Social constraints on business activity

Society is made up of a large number of individuals, groups and institutions, each with their own aims and views about the way in which scarce resources should be used. Because business activity is such an important part of social relations, it will often be the subject of conflicts of interest.

For example, a town may want a company to build a new factory because of the extra employment it will bring. The problem is that green fields have to be built on and the extra lorries will add to traffic in the area. This will inevitably be unwelcome to local residents.

It is important therefore to recognise that business exists within a social context and that society provides constraints on business activity, as well as providing opportunities (e.g. by providing a market for goods). Businesses have **social responsibilities** and they need to operate in an ethical way. Business activity also needs to be placed within a context of **sustainability.** It is necessary to create a balance between the needs of economic growth and those of environmental sustainability.

The social responsibilities of business

An organisation has responsibilities to a range of interested parties – people who have a **stake** in what the organisation does. So defined, a company's stakeholders include not only its customers and owners, its workforce and suppliers (and their families) but also those living near its sites, as well as special interest groups – and of course society as a whole, in its role as 'steward' of the environment.

Balancing these responsibilities is difficult but far from impossible. In fact, companies now realise that there is a **synergy** between the disciplined, innovative approaches needed to satisfy a purely commercial responsibility and those needed to satisfy, say, a problem of worker safety. In other words, they help each other.

Business ethics

Ethics are moral principles or rules of conduct which are generally accepted by most members of a society. They determine those actions individuals and groups believe to be right and those they consider to be wrong. An **ethic** is therefore a guide as to what should be done or what should not be done.

From an early age, parents, schools, religious institutions and society in general provide us with moral guidelines to help us to learn and form our ethical beliefs. Many ethics are reinforced in our legal system and thus provide a constraint to business activities, while others are not. In areas covered by law, there may well be social pressure to conform to a particular standard. Pressure groups often set out to force individuals or organisations to operate in an 'acceptable way'.

Newspapers and television regularly make us aware of business malpractice – for example, insider dealing, the failure of organisations to disclose information about the harmful nature of their products, false descriptions, lying and cheating in business dealings, and so on. Increasingly consumers have begun to exert pressure on business to behave in a moral and ethical way.

Today's citizens, consumers and employees are more concerned than ever before about what organisations stand for, who they trade with, what they do and whether or not they provide equal opportunities. In a recent *Which?* survey, 63% of those who responded were concerned about the activities of companies that they might invest in.

Benefits and costs

Business activity creates benefits and costs for those both directly and indirectly involved. Today it is recognised by many that industrial development can only be socially effective if it takes into consideration community losses as well as profits. Society as a whole has to decide what balance it wants to strike. How much pollution – even destruction of the environment – should we accept? Heavier lorries are more cost-effective in moving goods, but how heavy is too heavy? More factories and better roads can mean more jobs, but the price can be the loss of more farmland.

We therefore need to look at the **social benefits** and the **social costs** of business activity to get a clearer picture of net benefits.

1 **Private benefits** are all the benefits accruing to an individual or group as a result of a particular activity, e.g. the profits from a business that are earned by the shareholders, the wages earned by employees, etc.;
2 **Private costs** are all the costs to an individual or group resulting from a particular activity, e.g. the cost to a sole trader of building and running a cinema;
3 **Social benefits** are the private benefits *plus* all the beneficial effects for other members of the community resulting from a particular activity, e.g. the entertainment value received by cinema-goers, and the wages earned by the projectionist, cashier and ice-cream seller;
4 **Social costs** are the private costs *plus* all the detrimental effects for other members of the community, e.g. the extra traffic congestion, parking problems and litter left in the street by cinema-goers.

The benefits of business activity

Business organisations bring together productive resources to produce wealth. In so doing they yield the following major benefits:

1 Organisations provide **employment**. Millions of people work in industry and commerce. Some of them are doing enjoyable, creative work while others are in boring, unimaginative environments where work is a burden rather than a pleasure;

2 Industry creates **income**. The factors of production that produce goods earn factor incomes. Shareholders receive profits, landlords receive rent, lenders receive interest, workers receive wages, and so on;

3 Organisations create **products**. Value is added at each stage of production. For example, bringing petrol to the final consumer involves the addition of value at several stages: extracting oil from the geological reserves, refining and storing oil, transporting the fuel, and providing the petrol to consumers in an easy-to handle form;

4 Industry **improves living standards**. Materially, most people are better off today than ever before. Figure 82.1, for example, shows that real household disposable income has risen considerably between 1971 and 1997;

5 Industry makes it possible for people to enjoy more **leisure**. Because of industrial growth and the resulting technological innovations, people have more free time on their hands. Hospitals, schools, museums and many welfare functions which we have come to take for granted are all supported by the wealth created by businesses.

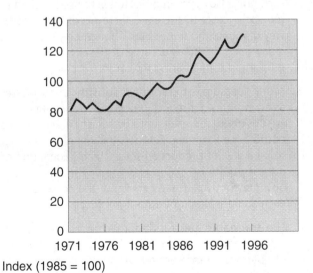

Index (1985 = 100)

Figure 82.1 Real household disposable income (for a married couple with husband only working 1971–1997)

The costs of business activity

When a firm produces something, it has to bear in mind a number of internal costs, including production, marketing, financial and administration.

In addition, there are external costs which go beyond the balance sheet of the firm. These are sometimes known as **externalities** or **spillover costs**:

Externalities = Social Costs – Private Costs

An individual business will be more interested in weighing up decisions in terms of private profits and losses than in accounting for externalities. However, when a firm applies to the planning authorities or other governmental bodies for permission to put into effect a business decision, the wider social implications will be an important consideration.

Society benefits if resources are used in a socially effective way. It is therefore vital for government agencies to employ social criteria in implementing decisions.

Cost-benefit analysis

Cost-benefit analysis is often used to weigh up the merits of government-sponsored projects such as building a new London Underground line, a third London airport, or schemes to subsidise firms in depressed regions.

In carrying out a cost-benefit analysis it is necessary to sum all the benefits of carrying out a particular project or course of action and all the costs, and then assess the net benefit.

For example, in planning a project to build a new motorway or by-pass on a greenfield site you would need to carry out the following calculation:

Benefits of carrying out the development – Benefits of leaving the land in its current use – Cost of carrying out the development

Or in mathematical form:

$B_d - B_o - C_d$ = Net Benefit or Net Loss

Suppose for example that:

● The benefits of creating the by-pass are estimated to be worth £100 million over five years, including the saving on travel time and fuel;

● The benefits of leaving the land in its present state are estimated at £30 million over five years, including the benefits to current users of the land for recreation purposes;

● The costs of carrying out the project over five years are calculated at £40 million, including the construction costs of the by-pass.

Then:

£100m – £30m – £40m = Net Benefit of £30m

Cost-benefit analysis seeks to attach a money value to costs and benefits, including those which are not traded through the marketplace in the conventional way. For example, in assessing the benefits of a greenfield site you would need to calculate (in money terms) the benefits to direct users such as birdwatchers, ramblers and others, and also people who simply benefit from the existence of the site – e.g. people who have seen it on television, or who attach a sentimental value to it because they once visited it as a child. A similar approach is used with costs.

Such approaches are increasingly used in modern industrialised countries. For example, in Germany calculations have been made of the costs of pollution damage as illustrated in the table in Figure 82.2 below.

The figures show a total of about $34 billion of damage, the major part of which was accounted for by the disamenity effects of air pollution, and the effects of noise nuisance on house values.

	US $ billion
Air pollution	
Health (respiratory disease)	0.8–1.9
Materials damage	0.8
Agriculture	0.1
Forestry loss	0.8–1.0
Forestry recreation	1.0–1.8
Forestry other	0.1–0.2
Disamenity	15.7
Water pollution	
Freshwater fishing	0.1
Groundwater damage	2.9
Recreation	n.a.
Noise	
Workplace noise	1.1
House price depreciation	9.8
Other	0.7
Total	3.9

Figure 82.2 Costs of pollution damage

The important point is that, if the estimates can be accepted as being broadly in the area of the true costs, pollution damage was costing an amount equal to 6% of Germany's GNP at the time.

EXAM TIP

The series of books produced by David Pearce, *Blueprint for a Green Economy* (Earthscan Publications, 1992–1997), provide a useful outline of economic thinking about sustainable development in the 1990s.

Pollution

The most obvious social cost of business activity is pollution. On page 594 we compare the private and the social perspective of pollution by looking at the case of a chemical firm that uses a nearby river as a convenient dumping ground for untreated waste products.

Government intervention to deal with the problems of pollution can take any of six forms:

1 **Education** can make individuals and groups more aware of the real costs of business activity and highlight the possible long-term effects;

2 **State provision** involves the state taking over activities that generate pollution and operating them so as to produce levels of output that are more socially acceptable and fair. However, this runs against the trend of privatisation in the 1980s and early 1990s.

3 **Regulation** is the most common way of controlling pollution. Most countries have regulations governing the disposal of waste and the control of smoke emissions and exhaust fumes. Given sufficient information, the government would be in a position to control waste-creating activities effectively. Unfortunately, the information to hand is often imperfect and contentious. Powerful producers provide convincing statistics to prove that their activities do not need control, while consumers' groups provide a strong lobby supporting the opposite view;

4 An alternative way is through **taxation**. Taxes can be levied either on the quantity of a product produced by a business, or on the quantity of effluent produced. Taxation makes it possible to control the output of such firms. However, in order to tax firms according to the social costs they create, there needs to be some way of measuring these costs. Though only rough and ready, such measures do at least penalisie polluters in proportion to the harm they cause.

5 A fifth measure is to provide a **subsidy** to businesses as an incentive for reducing pollution. A polluting firm is subsidised for each unit by which it reduces its output. The firm then considers the loss of the subsidy to be a cost of production for each additional unit of output that is produced. As with taxes, the government would need to know the social cost of each additional unit of output produced.

6 The **tradeable permits** approach uses the marketplace to control the level of pollution. A fixed number of permits, representing a specific amount of pollution, are allocated to each polluter. Firms then buy and sell them to each other if they have a shortage or surplus. In order for the system to work, a decision must be made as to how much pollution is acceptable. Permits are then issued to this level.

AN ORGANISATION AND ITS STAKEHOLDERS

United Utilities supplies water and electricity to millions of business and domestic customers in the North-West. The company was formed by the take-over of the regional electricity company Norweb by North West Water. It has a turnover of £1.5 billion.

Public expectations of such a multi-utility company are crucial. Many people are not happy with the idea of water being privately owned and supplied for profit. It doesn't take much for the public to take against the activities of such an organisation.

United Utilities has therefore set out to involve the community in an integrated approach to its social responsibilities. Research by the company confirmed a widespread view that the government's sale of the water industry was 'a privatisation too far'. Customers' concerns included:

● Reliability of supply;
● Management of drought;
● Investment in infrastructure;
● Pollution of beaches;
● Prices;
● How the benefits of privatisation were to be shared between consumers and shareholders.

However, many of those surveyed also saw a valuable opportunity to develop community links. As the largest company in the North West they felt that the company could champion local firms and vocational training as well as benefiting the environment by investing in research and education.

The organisation's planning uses a model developed by the European Foundation for Quality Management. This includes 'impact on society' (with an index weighting of 6 per cent) as one of the nine areas of assessment.

In United Utilities' first annual report (1997), the chief executive, Brian Staples, cited *Tomorrow's Company*, a report by a group of 25 major UK companies. The report posed the question: How can sustainable success be achieved 'in a world which is not only increasingly competitive, but also increasingly critical and vigilant of business standards'? It concluded: 'Only through deepened relationships with - and between - employees, customers, suppliers, investors and the community'.

1 What sort of concerns would you expect the public to have over the activities and operations of an integrated utility organisation like UU?

2 How might these concerns act as constraints on the activities and operations of the organisation?

3 How might taking account of 'impact on society' enable organisations to plan and operate in a more effective way?

4 How can organisations develop more effective relationships with employees, customers, suppliers, investors and the community?

The Environmental Protection Act 1990

This Act created two new systems for regulating industrial pollution in the UK:

● **Integrated pollution control (IPC)** applies to more than 5,000 industrial processes with serious pollution potential. It covers releases to land, water and air and is enforced by an **Inspectorate of Pollution**;

● A second system covers complex processes which involve emissions to air.

IPC extends the controls previously applied only to air pollutants to all the wastes, gases, solids and liquids generated by organisations. The Inspectorate ensures that the least environmentally damaging solution overall – the so-called **best practicable environmental option** or **BPEO** – is chosen to do this.

IT'S A FACT

When Shell decided to bury the Brent Spar platform at sea, they were supported by the UK government and by extensive research indicating that this was the 'best possible environmental option'. However, pressure groups argued that there might be better options.

THE 'DAY AND HODGSON MODEL'

John Day and David Hodgson have identified a number of considerations to take into account when deciding whether to use taxation or regulation to control pollution. In the table below, the form of pollution in question is sulphur dioxide emission. What do YOU think is the best method of controlling it? Explain your choice.

Taxation	Regulation
The cost of continuous monitoring of total emissions to assess how much tax is to be paid, is high.	Continuous monitoring is not necessary. Standards can specify some maximum limit not to be breached and can be monitored by spot checks at sample sites.
Law and enforcement can be aided by the monitor providing a cumulative record that can be checked. It is less susceptible to coercion.	Enforcement can be lax if it is too informal, with firms and enforcement agencies having too 'cosy' a relationship.
Firms are encouraged to seek new pollution control technologies to cut their tax bills.	This method provides little incentive to reduce sulphur emissions at source. Firms may think they have the right to pollute to the maximum standard set.
Setting the same rate of tax on sulphur emissions irrespective of where they occur is inefficient. Varying the tax rate is more efficient but is impractical to administer.	It is administratively easier to use.
It is difficult to take account of different meteorological conditions.	It can be used to restrict emissions under certain meteorological conditions or on days when pollution has already built up to danger levels.

Environmental audits

An **environmental audit** is an evaluation of a company's environmental performance carried out regularly, systematically and objectively.

This procedure began in the USA as an assessment of a company's conformance with official regulations on the environment. Now its role has been extended. Today, environmental auditing is a management tool to improve control of environment practices as well as ensuring that the company's and the government's policy on the environment is fulfilled. The audit should be carried out by personnel who are expert in the technologies used at the sites to be inspected.

For example, a typical environmental audit in the oil industry might consist of a visit to a refinery, a factory, an offshore oil production platform, a laboratory, or a distribution depot. During the visit, the team will interview staff and inspect records, facilities, equipment and the immediate surroundings of the site according to a systematic testing procedure. Following the visit, the team will prepare a detailed report. This is discussed and an action plan agreed. This in turn become a regular agenda item at management meetings to ensure that the action plan is effectively monitored.

Audits should be backed by top management and carried out at regular intervals. The benefits include:

- More effective compliance with company environmental goals and official regulations;
- Increased employee awareness of environmental requirements;
- Improved environmental training;
- Reduction of waste;
- Better environmental reporting to government and public.

CASE STUDY CASE STUDY CASE STUDY CASE STUDY CASE STUDY

BUSINESS AND THE NATURE OF 'HARM'

The philosopher Robert Frederick poses some important questions about the responsibility of businesses to the community. He presents his arguments as follows:

- A number of people take the view that businesses have a responsibility to protect the environment. This responsibility goes beyond what is required by law and regulation. Businesses often have the knowledge and resources to limit environmental damage from their actions. To refuse to take such action can be seen a a neglect of moral duty.

- A businessperson may reply that businesses have only a limited power to serve the economic needs of society and must operate within the bounds of law. A business has no moral obligation to try to solve other social problems which may be only partly caused by its activities. Businesses have no moral duty to do more than meet the requirements imposed on them by law and regulation.

- A basic ethical principle is that you should 'do no harm', because to do so violates the rights of another person not to be harmed. However, perhaps this should be limited to a statement that you should do no *'unwarranted'* harm. If a knowledgeable and competent investor loses money on the stock market, his or her rights have not been violated. However if the investor

were to be trampled underfoot in a rush by floor traders to sell on the announcement of bad news, then their rights *would* have been violated.

- The same principle can be applied to business. If individuals or groups are harmed by business activity, and the harm is unrewarded in that it is not offset by a balancing benefit, or if it is unnecessary and avoidable, then there has been a violation of the right not to be harmed.

Tasks

1 What is your view of the nature of harm as outlined by Robert Frederick?

2 How important is it for businesses to develop a set of principles related to the notion of harm?

3 How do you think the notion of harm would apply when:

   – A consumer buys baby food which is found to contain impurities?

   – A motorist buys a car which proves to have a steering fault?

   – A sports fan visits a stadium in which a fire breaks out?

4 Can you think of other examples which would be appropriate for a discussion of 'harm' in business activity?

STUDY CASE STUDY CASE STUDY CASE STUDY CASE STUDY CASE STUDY

The eco-industrial revolution

Corporate strategy involves planning ways of securing a competitive edge in the marketplace. Today a company's environmental performance will be increasingly central to its competitiveness and survival.

The term **eco-industrial revolution** was first given prominence by a group of Asian industrialists in the early 1990s. The eco-industrial revolution is concerned with developing competitive strategies based on the need to derive a key part of a firm's competitive advantage from superior environmental performance.

SYNTHESIS

What specific actions would you see as being involved in developing 'competitive advantage through environmental performance'?

Is it possible to reconcile the need of businesses to maximise competitive advantage with the ideal of conserving the environment?

THE SOCIAL EFFECT OF DUMPING

Amount of chemical produced (tons)	£ Price per ton (marginal revenue)	£ Cost to firm of producing an extra ton (marginal cost)
1	40	34
2	40	35
3	40	37
4	40	40
5	40	44

Figure 82.3 Costs and revenues from different levels of output

Let us assume that a chemicals firm sets out to maximise profits, and that it will carry on expanding output so long as the revenue from selling one extra unit is greater than the cost of producing that extra unit. The technical term used to describe an extra unit is a **marginal** unit.

Let us also assume that the costs and revenues from producing different levels of output are as shown in Figure 82.3 above. Given this schedule, the firm will produce 4 tons of chemical in the given period: the surplus of revenue over cost from producing the first ton would be £6; from the second ton, £5, and the third ton, £3.

However, suppose that discharge of chemicals into the river adjoining the factory kills a large proportion of the fish population of the river and that this seriously affects the business of a commercial fishery downstream. In order to simplify our example, we will also assume that the only way of reducing the pollution is to cut back on chemical production (in the real world an alternative would be for the firm to invest in pollution control equipment).

We can now draw up a new table which includes the cost of pollution in the figures already presented. Column 2 in the table shows the price the firm could get for each ton, given existing market conditions. Column 3 shows that it is more costly to produce larger outputs than smaller outputs, reflecting the fact that the firm has to bring into use older units of machinery to produce the larger quantities. Column 4 shows the damage to the downstream fishery's business

(Continued on page 595)

Amount of chemical produced (tons)	Price per ton (£)	Cost to firm of producing an extra ton (£)	Pollution damage to fishery of an extra ton of production (£)	Social cost of producing extra ton of production (£)
(1)	(2)	(3)	(4)	(5)
1	40	34	3	37
2	40	35	3	38
3	40	37	3	40
4	40	40	3	43
5	40	44	3	47

Figure 82.4 Costs and revenues including pollution costs

THE SOCIAL EFFECTS OF DUMPING

(Continued from page 594)

resulting from the dumping of each extra ton of waste. Column 5 shows the combined cost to the chemical firm and the fishery of producing extra units of output. If we assume that no one else is affected by the pollution, this final column will represent the marginal cost to society of additional units produced.

If we look at Figure 82.4, we can see that the most socially efficient output will be 3 tons, rather than the 4 tons that would have been the case if we considered only the chemical firm. The benefits to society can be measured by the price that consumers of chemicals are prepared to pay for each ton. These must then be weighed up against the private costs and externalities incurred in chemical production.

At the end of the day we still have pollution, but society will have traded off the benefits of chemical production against the social costs of chemical production.

STUDY CASE STUDY CASE STUDY CASE STUDY CASE STUDY CASE STUDY

Pressures on business

Externally, businesses have to contend with a number of pressures:

1 Perhaps the biggest is to sell their products. Consumers do not have to buy. The product has to meet their needs and requirements;
2 The business is under pressure from its competitors. Competition is often a spur to business efficiency.
3 The government and other regulatory bodies exert pressure on businesses to produce within certain standards;
4 Businesses also have to respond to the influence of organised 'pressure groups'.

Types of pressure group

Pressure groups come in many shapes and forms. Some are highly organised with paid officials, set subscriptions and planned meetings and may be active for many years. Others may be 'nine-day wonders', set up on the spur of the moment, lacking any real structure and vanishing as quickly as they arise.

However, two main types of pressure group are commonly recognised:

1 **Protection groups** These are set up to fight a specific issue such as danger on a local road caused by construction traffic. They consist primarily of people protecting their interests against an outside threat. Recent examples are environmental groups opposed to large-scale construction schemes such as the Newbury by-pass and the building of the second runway at Manchester airport.

Figure 82.5 The 'eco-warrior' Swampy (above) and fellow environmental protestors lived in trees and tunnelled underground in order to get their message across to the public.

2 **Promotional pressure groups** These are more formal groups which are often highly organised and fight campaigns on a wide range of issues. Examples include Greenpeace and Friends of the Earth. Such organisations have clearly defined long-term aims and strategies.

Today in the UK we have a number of important consumer pressure groups such as the **Consumers' Association** which publishes the magazine *Which?* The association is funded by subscriptions from members who buy the magazine. It uses its funds to test a wide variety of products on which it then produces reports in its monthly magazine. It also produces books on consumer-related matters.

Businesses response to pressure groups

There are a number of ways in which businesses can respond to pressure groups:

1　They can ignore them, using the argument that consumers can choose whether or not to buy the product. In the meantime they can make sure that production takes place within the bounds of legal requirements;

2　They can run a counter-campaign to win public support. This is the policy that has been used by British Nuclear Fuels PLC. 'Come to Sellafield. Look around the place. See for yourself how safe it is' – loosely paraphrased, this was the message of a multi-million-pound advertising campaign commissioned by BNF which appeared on television as well as in the press.

3　They can take advice from consumers in order to compromise and win public support.

Chapter summary

- Business needs to build up an effective relationship with a wide range of internal and external stakeholders. It has a particular responsibility to the community and the environment at a local, national and international level.
- Ethics are moral principles. It is essential that business operates in an ethical way.
- Individuals have a right not to be harmed by business activities.
- Businesses create both benefits and costs. The benefits should outweigh the costs.
- Benefits and costs are both private to the individual organisation and social when taken from the view of society as a whole.
- Externalities consist of social costs less private costs.
- In carrying out a development based on cost-benefit analysis it is essential that there is a net benefit to society and to the organisation carrying out the development.
- The most obvious social cost of business activity is pollution. Pollution can be controlled or reduced by means of education, state provision, regulation, subsidies, taxation or tradeable permits.
- Environmental audits enable organisations to closely monitor their impact on the environment. However, they require a commitment at all levels in the organisation.
- Today organisations are increasingly developing strategies which combine environmental considerations with the goal of maximising competitive advantage.
- Promotional and protection pressure groups impact on business activity.

INTRODUCTION

A key aspect of organisational activity is the ability to create effective plans which will enable an organisation to create its own future rather than simply respond to changes in the environment in which it operates. Business organisations need to be proactive rather than reactive.

We therefore start this unit with a Case Study which shows how every organisation needs to adopt careful and well organised planning structures. It highlights the sorts of problems that an organisation can get into if it fails to plan. All of the good intentions of the organisation and its creators can come to nothing if the organisation is not founded on clear thinking.

We then move on to identify the principles of planning by setting out a clear framework for developing a business strategy. Planning needs to build a bridge between where the organisation is coming from (its history), where it is now (the present), and where the organisation wants to go (the future). Corporate strategy is all about making the big decisions about what the organisation should and will be doing, and how this will be matched to its current resources and

future resources. The plans which the organisation is able to develop will depend on its environment and the way it seeks to steer its way through this environment. It will involve identifying the strengths and weaknesses of the organisation, and how strengths can be maximised and weaknesses minimised.

Organisational/corporate planning involves a series of stages, from creating overarching purposes and aims down to the details of day-to-day operation. We identify these stages and levels in our section on preparing a business/corporate plan.

Finally we conclude our text by revisiting the key theme of the book: living with change. Today many business writers focus on the Darwinian notion of 'survival' of organisms and organisations. Organisations need to be keenly in tune with the process of change which is continually taking place around them. It is then a case of responding to these changes in an appropriate way in order to survive and prosper.

83 The Homeless Trust:
A case study in good management[1]

This chapter is set out in the form of an extended case study. Its aim is to develop knowledge acquired from earlier units and to set the scene for planning frameworks which are outlined in the final chapters. The case is simple to understand, but it is of tremendous importance because it establishes the need for clear and well organised thought and planning.

The role of management is to plan, make decisions, and to control and co-ordinate organisational activities. Good managers use resources well and enable an organisation to meet its objectives. Bad managers, however well-intentioned, can lead organisations into all sorts of problems.

This case study shows how a poorly managed organisation almost collapsed. Fortunately, the organisation realised in time what was happening , and it has now moved to a position of strength. **Disorganised management** has been replaced by **focused management**.

The context

The case study examines the recent history of the **Homeless Trust**. The Homeless Trust is a voluntary sector charitable organisation which is the largest provider of emergency accommodation and support to single homeless people in a large city in the Midlands.

The Trust was set up by a group of committed Christians during the early 1970s who were concerned about the plight of the needy in large cities. They wanted to help those less fortunate than themselves, and felt that a project dedicated to the homeless would be a good way to put Christianity into action.

The group purchased a hostel with enough space to house 12 homeless people and successfully ran this project for ten years between the mid-1970s and 80s.

Initially they provided accommodation for men only. However, in the mid-1980s the organisation moved on to an 'open door' policy in which women were taken in and provision was expanded to take in more people.

The Trust began to open new hostels, renting premises from private landlords. It also extended its operations to cater for 60 homeless people in London as well as 300 in its home city in the Midlands.

Management

During the period of expansion the organisation increasingly came to rely on a charismatic director who took the major policy decisions. Management became focused on this individual. Unfortunately, whilst the director had considerable commitment to the mission of the organisation, he failed to introduce methods and procedures required to operate on a larger scale. In particular, there was increasingly poor control over resources such as finance, so that the Trust increasingly began to build up debts.

The 'open door' policy meant that demand for shelter considerably outstripped the ability of the organisation to fund the shelter it was providing. At the same time, the government had changed the way it assessed benefits for accommodation, leading to a substantial reduction in the income flowing into the Trust.

Drains on resources

In a period of expansion it is essential that any organisation keeps a tight check on the relationship between income and expenditure. At the same time it needs to have contingency funds to provide for a 'rainy day'. If expenditure exceeds income, over a period of time an organisation will become increasingly insolvent.

It soon became obvious that the Homeless Trust was living beyond its means. In particular, it was providing more housing shelter than it could afford, and was running an expensive fleet of cars. Any organisation that tries to operate on a larger scale than the resources available to it is likely to suffer a serious collapse.

When the media revealed that the Homeless Trust was in financial difficulty, this led to adverse publicity in the press, leading to a fall in public donations which had been a major source of income for the organisation.

Developing a managerial approach

In the early 1990s the director of the Trust was replaced, and the new management team quickly set about putting the organisation on a firmer footing in order to restore public confidence. Important steps included:

- Getting rid of the fleet of cars;
- Cutting back bed spaces to a manageable number;
- Making sure that the accommodation used was in houses that were safe. A number of the houses previously used had been found to infringe fire regulations.

1 Written by Andrew Heming and edited by Rob Dransfield, both of Nottingham Trent University. The 'Homeless Trust' is a fictional organisation and no resemblance to any actual organisation is intended.

Comparison of elements of the Homeless Trust's balance sheet at 31/3/91 and 31/3/95

	1991 £	1995 £	Difference £
Assets			
Fixed	439,892	252,486	(187,406)
Current	116,931	256,229	139,293
Total	556,823	608,715	(48,108)
Liabilities			
Current	398,453	197,584	201,169
Other	217,737	44,100	(175,637)
Total	616,190	241,031	(374,506)
Assets less Liabilities	**(59,367)**	**267,031**	**326,398**
Represented by:			
General Fund	(59,367)	223,405	
Permanent endowment	–	43,626	

Interpretation of changes in the balance sheet between 31/3/91 and 31/3/95

Some reduction in total assets, though broad similarity across the years.

- There is stability in financial size.

Significant change in the ratio of fixed to current assets. Reflecting:

- Reduction in bed spaces from around 320 in 1990/91 to 200 in 1994/95 and a reduction in the number of properties owned.
- The organisation moved away from direct ownership and towards managing housing association owned properties.
- Reduction in number of cars owned.
- Move towards larger cash 'buffer' in case of difficulties.

Liabilities significantly reduced, indicating:

- Improved financial control and budgeting.
- Move to balance need and what is possible with resources.

Increased general fund:

- There are legal requirements for charities to maintain a balance of assets and liabilities.
- The Trust is not incorporated which means that members of the management committee are ultimately liable for the liabilities of the organisation. Since the financial difficulties of the early 1990's they have required stronger financial controls and rigorous budgeting.

Income and expenditure accounts
for the years ending 31/3/91 and 31/3/95

	1991 £	1995 £	Difference £
Income			
Rents	790,873	585,990	(204,883)
Grants	55,498	332,751	277,253
Donations	156,045	117,579	(38,466)
Miscellaneous	28,896	881	(28,015)
Bank interest		10,144	10,144
Total Income	1,031,312	1,047,345	16,033
Expenditure			
Property (1)	580,316	413,212	(167,104)
Staff	350,875	526,524	175,649
Transport	98,280	17,676	(80,604)
Administration (2)	66,505	118,301	51,796
Discretionary (3)	19,066		(19,066)
Bank charges	23,241	5,558	(17,683)
Total Expenditure	1,138,283	1,081,271	(57,012)
Deficit/Surplus inyear	(106,238)	(33,926)	(72,312)
General Fund			
Balance at Year End	(59,367)	223,405	282,772

Notes

1 Property includes rents, service charges and upkeep costs.
2 Administration includes legal and professional fees and fund-raising costs.
3 Discretionary includes financial assistance given to residents.

Interpretation of changes in the
Income and Expenditure accounts between 31.3.91 and 31.3.95

Relatively small rise in total income and drop in total expenditure. Provides:

● Confirmation of relatively stable financial size.

Rental income and expenditure reduction. Reflects:

● Reduction in number of bed spaces.

Significant increase in grants at a time of reduction in public funding availability shows:

● Recognition within the organisation of the importance of statutory fund holders as possible sources of income.
● Willingness to engage with the statutory sector.
● Reflection of the change in how the organisation is perceived by the statutory sector.

(Continued on page 601 opposite)

Interpretation of changes Contd.

Donation reduction. Following:

- Drop in public confidence following the adverse publicity about the Trust's financial affairs. (When comparing the years between 1991 and 1995 there has actually been an increase in donation income from a low of £89,000 in 1991/1992.)

Bank interest rise and charges reduction:

- Reflects the asset balance ratio and changes in financial management.

Staff costs increase. Resulting from:

- Generally better wage levels and conditions of service.
- Introduction of specialist workers at higher rates of pay.

Transport cost reduction. Because:

- The transport department was disbanded.
- The Trust now owns no vehicles. Essential users now receive subsidised car loans.

Administration cost increase. resulting from:

- Introduction and maintenance of improved financial systems.
- Increased complexity of administration systems.
- Increased demands made by projects for administration support, particularly in the areas of monitoring of service delivery.
- Introduction of paid fund-raising team.

Deficit reduction

- There was a deficit in 94/95 but this was in the context of a brought forward surplus from the previous year. Unlike the 1990/91 deficit.

Important steps involved:

- Making sure that the correct accounting procedures were employed;
- Making sure that income more than exceeded expenditure;
- Making sure that the organisation operated at a level which did not exceed its resources;
- Making sure that there were enough spare funds to cover emergency requirements (a contingency fund);
- Making sure that only professionally qualified staff were employed;
- Making sure that public confidence was restored, so that donation funds once again began to flow back into the organisation.

An overview of the development of the Homeless Trust

If we take a broad overview of the development of the Homeless Trust we can see that it went through a number of phases of development:

- 10 stable years of providing a reasonable service to only a dozen people at a low cost;
- 6 years of rapid growth to a peak of providing a poor service to over 300 people at a relatively low cost per person;
- 5 years of providing improved quality of service to 200 people at a substantially increased cost per person.

Today, the Trust operates in a far more professional way. It recognises that in order to provide the service that homeless people need and deserve it will have to commit more resources to each of them. It has to be managed and run efficiently: it requires the right accommodation, and it requires the right people working for it. This costs money. But it is money well spent if it is to provide a quality service.

The Trust today is doing everything in its power to provide good-quality resources for those in need. It is not enough simply to have a 'mission': it is also essential to have the management and the procedures to put the mission into practice.

Analysing recent financial performance

Good managers should have a broad understanding of the major financial and accounting indicators which are used to highlight the performance of an organisation over a period of time.

In particular, it is important to look at the relationship between current assets and current liabilities.

- The **current assets** show those assets which the organisation can quickly turn into cash in the short term – e.g. money in the bank, money owed to the organisation which will shortly be repaid, etc.;
- **Current liabilities** show the organisation's pressing debts in the short term.

Common sense tells us that in the short term (e.g. the next few months) we need to have enough money coming in to meet money that will go out (any student will tell you that!).

In addition we need to look at the main items of income and expenditure so that we have a clear idea of changes over a period of time. For example, a charity may be worried to find that its donations are falling away, particularly if they are not being replaced by other forms of income.

Conclusion

The case study we have just looked at provides an excellent example of the way resources can and should be managed in an organisation.

All organisations have aims and objectives. However, the success or failure of an organisation depends on its ability to achieve those aims and objectives. It is all very well to have a mission and a vision of what things can be like. It is highly laudable to want to provide for the homeless. However, in order to give people the help they need it is vital to plan ahead and make use of resources in an organised way. Charitable trusts as much as any other organisations need to have purpose and direction and to be managed in a professional way.

TASKS AND QUESTIONS FOR DISCUSSION

1 At what stage in the development of the Homeless Trust did things start to go wrong? What exactly was the problem?
2 What do you think could have been done to stop these difficulties from arising?
3 What do you see as being the advantages and disadvantages of having a charismatic director?
4 Which of the changes that have taken place in the organisation of the Trust do you see as being most important in recent times? Explain why.

5 Looking at the financial and accounting records on pages 599–600, explain why the position for 1995 is far healthier than it was in 1991.
6 Why is it important for all organisations to have good management?
7 Why is it important for a charitable trust to be highly organised and professional in its approach?
8 What is the importance of planning? How should organisations like the Homeless Trust approach planning?

Chapter summary

- Whatever type of organisation you are dealing with, you need to have good management skills.
- Planning and organisation are at a premium.
- It is important to be guided by clear and realistic targets.

- It is important to establish budgets and financial targets.
- You will best meet the needs of your customers if you are well organised.

84 Developing a business strategy

In Part 1 of this book we saw how important it is to give a business a direction through the creation of a clear strategy.

With direction, it is possible to set out the detailed plans which will enable the organisation to move along its chosen path and to check progress on the way. If the organisation slips on some of its goals and objectives it is then possible to take action to put the organisation back on course.

Strategies are key planning processes for organisations through which they identify their futures. A strategy enables an organisation to build on its past, plan for its future and monitor progress towards its goals.

What is strategic management?

In simple terms strategic management involves creating a plan of action to enable an organisation to move from where it is now to where it wants to be at a future date.

It is essential that organisations are clear about how successful they are in meeting their desired goals. Organisations that fail to do this may suddenly find that they are failing to make best use of their potential. A gap opens up between potential and actual performance (see Figure 84.1 below).

Strategic planning should therefore begin with an analysis of the company's history. This includes its past markets, market shares and the record of its investments and profits, as well as those values and practices which give it its distinctive character.

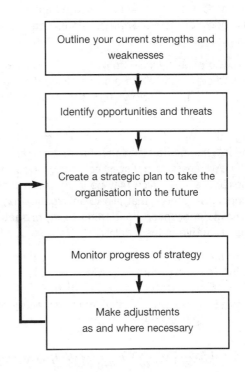

Figure 84.2 *The relationship between past, present and future in creating strategy*

The organisation needs to identify those areas which it is particularly successful at and why. It can then identify those areas in which it can be successful in the future. It will also need to identify those areas which are not profit-making but which at the same time are essential.

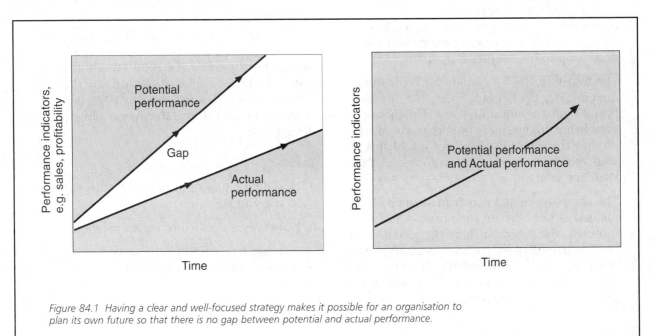

Figure 84.1 *Having a clear and well-focused strategy makes it possible for an organisation to plan its own future so that there is no gap between potential and actual performance.*

Looking outside the organisation

However, it is not enough simply to look within the organisation to identify direction. Kerry Napuk in his influential book *Corporate Strategy* [date?] quotes the following proverb from Sun Tzu:

> *'Those who understand strategy*
> *Move without delusion and progress without tiring.*
> *Hence the saying:"Know the other and know yourself."'*

'Knowing the other' requires knowledge of the organisation's competitors and the threats they pose, as well as an awareness of political, economic, social and technological changes which may be in the air. It is this understanding of 'others' that allows an organisation to convert threats into opportunities amd to be **proactive** rather than **reactive** in the market.

In order to identify its strengths and build on them, an organisation will also need to identify its weaknesses. By combining these with an investigation of the opportunities, threats and challenges it faces, the company can identify a range of possible outcomes and development potentials. One way of doing this is to carry out a **SWOT** analysis. A key part of this will be a **PEST** (Political, Social, Economic, Technological environments) analysis.

This process of 'knowing the other' is often referred to as **scanning the environment**. An advantage of this process is that it allows organisations to be aware of rivals in its own field and of the precise threat posed by new entrants into its key markets. Sometimes this can highlight a need for change. For example, Sainsburys acquired Texas in order to gain the major share of the DIY market; Coca-Cola and Macdonalds moved into Russia in order to extend their influence into new markets ahead of the opposition.

Scanning will also help to identify threats such as new substitutes – for example, Levintons peat products recognised the threat from the use of coconut husk products which are more environment-friendly but which had previously been regarded as a waste product.

CASE STUDY CASE STUDY CASE STUDY CASE STUDY CASE STUDY

CLOSING THE GAP

The Warehouse retail clothing store started in 1976. In 1987 it was bought by the catalogue giants Freemans who introduced Bymail and a menswear collection. However, these proved to be unsuccessful. Warehouse therefore had to think fast and review their market position. In 1992 they carried out extensive research from which they concluded that the brand had drifted into a younger market. A repositioning plan was drawn up to be completed by 1996.

The first step was to employ a new fashion director. Her brief was to inject life into the brand whilst maintaining key elements of its established image. New buyers were taken on, but the company also kept established staff who had a good understanding of the Warehouse brand.

The company image was transformed. The focus was not only on the brand but also on more specific details such as the actual shop fit. The overall objective was to create a light, spacious loft-like atmosphere. The individual fitting rooms were given plenty of hanging space, chairs and mirrors.

To follow up the introduction of the new image, Warehouse regularly carried out quantitative research. This involved communicating with the new target market through focus groups. The discussions were not only about the product but also the store design, customer service and visual campaigns.

By the end of 1993, major changes could be seen in the product, and public reaction proved very positive. In 1994 Warehouse was nominated for Retailer of the Year by the British Fashion Council, and in 1995 it received an award for effectiveness in store design.

Tasks

1 How had a gap in performance developed at Warehouse?

2 How was it decided to close this gap?

3 At what levels within the organisation did the gap need to be addressed?

STUDY CASE STUDY CASE STUDY CASE STUDY CASE STUDY CASE STUDY

Looking at past, present and future

As we saw earlier, in order to know themselves, organisations have to look at their past, present and future. The vision and strategy for the future must capitalise on the strengths and weaknesses of the organisation. This process involves asking questions such as:

- What is it that customers like about our company?
- What do they like about our products?
- What are our strengths that give us an edge?
- How can we build on our strengths?
- How can we minimise our weaknesses?
- How can we turn weaknesses into strengths?

The starting point in strategy is therefore to carry out a detailed analysis of the organisation and its environment.

We can illustrate the ingredients to creating a strategy in Figure 84.3 below:

When all of these are taken into account it is possible to create a focused strategic direction.

The purpose of planning

Planning is concerned with looking ahead. This purpose was expressed forcefully by Henry Fayol, when he stated in 1949 that

> The maxim 'managing means looking ahead' gives some idea of the importance attached to planning in the business world, and it is true that if foresight is not the whole of management at least it is an essential part of it.

Planning makes possible the co-ordination of decision-making, so that there is a clear focus and direction for the organisation. Lack of co-ordination means that people are pulling in different directions. Planning also means

IT'S A FACT

Many successful organisations have turned external threats into opportunities, and weaknesses into strengths.

For example, some organisations have responded to tougher new environmental regulations imposed by government (a possible threat) by building a reputation for being 'the most environmentally friendly' company in their field – for example, Tesco and its 'green' and organic lines.

Similarly, when Smarties were threatened by the arrival of M&Ms in the UK market they introduced a range of novel Smarties such as the 'blue' Smartie and 'gruesome greens' to build themselves a bigger market share rather than surrender it.

preparing for the future so that the organisation is can take contingency measures if the future turns out to be different from what was originally anticipated. Planning also enables managers to take more control over future development.

Kerry Napuk has defined strategic planning as 'a total concept of the whole business, involving a framework and a process that guides its future'.

You can see from this definition that strategic planning involves taking the organisation as a whole iin order to come up with 'holistic' plans. These plans then are put into action. They are not plans that are filed away in company records and forgotten – they are practical guides which provide an ongoing direction to action. The strategy needs to be shared among all members of the organisation so that everybody can work together towards common goals.

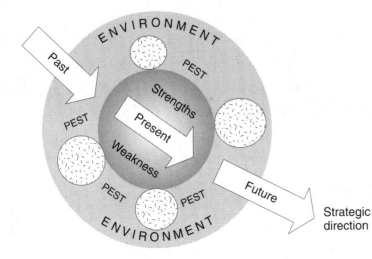

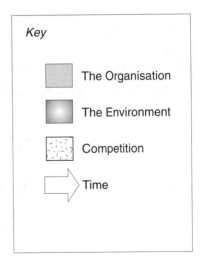

Figure 84.3 Ingredients in creating an organisational strategy

Who creates the strategic plans?

In a perfect world, the strategy for an organisation would be created by a detailed, democratic consultation of all members of an organisation. In this ideal world, the stakeholders would help to shape and thus own the strategy.

Although at the end of the day, the final creation of a strategy document and plan would be the responsibility of a small group of senior directors, those directors would have a good understanding of the issues involved. Through the process of consultation of stakeholders, they would create a commitment to the strategy. This would represent a **bottom-up approach** to strategy.

The reality is that in many cases some important stakeholders are consulted, but the major part of strategy is created at Board level by the most powerful directors of the organisation.

When are strategic plans reviewed?

Similarly, in an ideal world, strategy would be constantly reviewed, altered as necessary and made an ongoing area for improvement. Johnson and Scholes in *Corporate Strategy* have set out a tripartite model with three elements: strategic analysis, strategic choice and strategic implementation:

1 **Strategic analysis** is concerned with understanding the strategic position of an organisation, e.g. what sort of environment are we operating in? What is the scope of our operations? How can we match our activities to our environment? How can we match our activities to our resource capability? etc.

2 **Strategic choice** involves:

   – Setting out a menu of strategic options;
   – Comparing the options provided by the menu;
   – Choosing the best option from the menu.

3 **Strategic implementation** involves putting the chosen strategy into action.

Johnson and Scholes see this as a circular process. The organisation is therefore continually evaluating the strategy in order to make ongoing modifications.

In the real world the process may not be as effective as this. Managers may seek to implement strategic choices without really weighing up how effective they are – often until it is too late.

The key questions for strategic planning

The key questions in strategic planning and the processes that are associated with it are set out in Figure 84.5 opposite. These questions lie at the heart of effective business planning. They provide a framework for devising effective strategic management.

Once developed, a strategic plan has to shift into the everyday realm of tactics and operational decision-making. For example, if the organisation has set itself the target of being 'the best-known organisation for customer care in Europe' then it must develop the processes and practical actions in staff working behaviours to ensure that this becomes a reality. Strategy needs to be converted into operational activity. Tactics are required to ensure that the plan is believable, achievable and motivates all members of the workforce towards a common end.

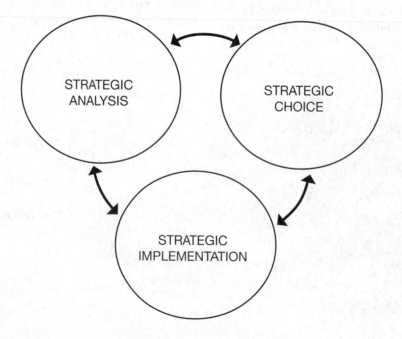

Figure 84.4 Strategic planning: a tripartite model

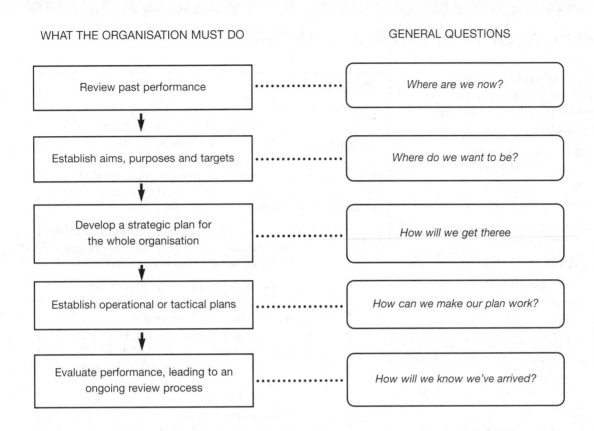

WHAT THE ORGANISATION MUST DO

GENERAL QUESTIONS

Review past performance ·············· *Where are we now?*

↓

Establish aims, purposes and targets ·············· *Where do we want to be?*

↓

Develop a strategic plan for the whole organisation ·············· *How will we get theree*

↓

Establish operational or tactical plans ·············· *How can we make our plan work?*

↓

Evaluate performance, leading to an ongoing review process ·············· *How will we know we've arrived?*

Figure 84.5 Key questions in strategic planning

Finally, the whole business of reviewing, specifying goals, drawing up a strategic plan and its tactical elements needs critical scrutiny through systematic monitoring and evaluation. The plan developed by the organisation should be easily measured against its performance.

The whole exercise can be described in the following way:

> *'To think, then act, then review and think and act again.'*

Strategic planning therefore is, or should be, part of a **continuous learning cycle**.

Action planning

Once a strategic plan has been formulated, managers need to agree on and outline the actions that will enable the plan to become a reality. This involves answering the question: 'How will we achieve our organisational objectives with the resources at our disposal?'

It is therefore necessary to create detailed guidelines and plans to cover all of the activities in an organisation so that everyone knows what is expected of them. **Performance indicators** will need to be established to measure performance.

Action plans are therefore the means by which an organisation converts its plans and priorities into actions. They create the guidelines to resource management in an organisation.

Tim Hannagan defines action plans as:

> *'Lists of actions to be carried out by particular managers or operatives in order to achieve the requirements of the business unit. They are often the responsibility of operating managers in order to ensure that those responsible for implementing a strategic plan are also involved in developing it. They are usually accompanied by detailed budgets, which may act as a means of control as well as a means of communicating an action plan.'*

IT'S A FACT

The Roman emperor Marcus Aurelius stated:

> *'It is planning, not gambling, that produces profit and security.'*

AN EXERCISE IN STRATEGIC PLANNING

This Case Study looks at a strategic planning exercise conducted by a manufacturer of soft drinks.

Read the details carefully then complete the tasks below.

PHASE 1
Strategic analysis

A manufacturer of soft drinks has two main lines, orange and lemon fizzy drinks, which it sells in the UK and Europe. Over the last ten years it has been making healthy profits. However, it has noticed that the world market for soft drinks is expanding at a very fast pace as real incomes rise in the Pacific Rim area in particular.

It has also noted that there are a number of other soft drinks manufacturers who are increasingly expanding and moving into new markets.

The organisation needs to think how it can compete in this new environment. It may be threatened by drinks manufacturers extending their share of the domestic market. One possibility is to extend the scope of its product lines – e.g. by adding a Cola drink to its existing orange and lemon drinks. If the organisation moves into the global marketplace there will be considerable resourcing implications in terms of investment in new plant.

PHASE 2
Strategic choice

This involves setting out options as follows:

1 Extend the scope of drinks on offer;
2 Expand in the domestic European market;
3 Expand into Eastern Europe;
4 Set up new plant in South-East Asia.

From this menu of choices the organisation decides to set up new plant in Malaysia and Indonesia to produce Cola, orange and lemon fizzy drinks.

PHASE 3
Strategic implementation

It is now necessary to create a series of action plans for opening up the new plant in Malaysia and Indonesia, and to plan distribution channels.

However, while the organisation is doing this they receive news that the world's major drinks manufacturer is also to expand its operations in Malaysia, opening up one of the world's largest plants producing Cola, orange and lemon drinks, as well as some new flavours. The organisation therefore decides to go ahead with the Indonesian operation and to use this as a base for a wider South-East Asian operation.

In addition it decided to set up a new bottling facility in Southern Spain. These plans are to be reviewed on a regular three-month cycle.

Tasks

1 What comes first? Strategic analysis, strategic choice or strategic implementation? Explain your answer?

2 Why should the strategic process be seen as a cycle?

3 Why is resource capability such an important ingredient of strategic planning?

4 What do you understand by the term the 'scope' of an organisation's activities?

5 What is the relationship between the scope of an organisation's activities and its resource capability?

6 Why is the external environment so important in strategic planning?

ACTION PLANNING AT BLUE CIRCLE

After the war, firms in this country employed a 'command and control' way of working. Decisions were made by senior managers and were passed vertically down the hierarchy. In recent years this has changed in many industries. Layers of employees have been stripped out and employees at the 'grass roots' have been empowered to make decisions for themselves.

As part of its corporate strategy, Blue Circle Cement has begun in recent years to introduce measures to encourage empowerment of employees. The programme of change involved a radical overhaul of working practices, reward systems and, not least, company culture.

To create these changes the organisation has had to put in place a range of action plans to make the vision a reality. At the heart of the change process has been a series of training programmes to get all employees used to adopting more of a teamwork approach.

At the same time 'nitty-gritty' measures have been introduced including:

- The **reduction of job categories** from 14 to 3. Jobs are now defined far more broadly than in the past and employees are expected to be multi-skilled;

- A new **teamworking approach**. The ability of everyone to work together and have mutual respect was considered essential to the new culture. The new teams have been helped to function together by extensive training in new approaches and methods of working;

- A **joint (management and union) review** of the system on a regular basis in order to seek continuous improvements. For the overall 'holistic' strategy to be successful, it is essential that the practical action plans are effective. Strategic planning therefore involves translating strategy down into operational planning.

Chapter summary

- Strategies are over-arching plans which enable an organisation to build on their past, plan for their future and monitor their progress.
- They are concerned with the big issues that face the whole of the organisation.
- Strategic management involves creating a plan to enable an organisation to move from where it is now to where it wants to be at a future date.
- Strategies help organisations to eliminate the gap between actual and potential performance.
- In creating a strategy it is essential to analyse the external environment and the nature of competition in the marketplace, and to identify opportunities and threats.
- Just as importantly, an organisation needs to identify its own strengths and weaknesses. Often weaknesses can be converted into opportunities and strengths.

- Foresight is an essential part of business management.
- Strategic plans need to involve the full range of stakeholder interests if there is to be a genuine commitment to strategy.
- Strategic plans should be constantly reviewed and adjusted in the light of experience.
- Strategy is an ongoing process involving analysis, choice and implementation.
- Strategic planning should be seen as part of a continuous learning cycle.
- Once a strategic plan has been formulated it is necessary for managers to agree on and outline the specific actions that will enable the plan to become a reality – i.e. the creation of action plans.

85 Preparing a business/corporate plan

In this book we have repeatedly stressed the importance of **planning** within an organisation. Planning involves thinking ahead and coming up with clearly thought-out proposals for the future. Planning takes the margin for error out of business activity. Every type of organisation needs to plan in order to make sure that the scarce resources which it controls are used effectively.

Large business organisations will set out detailed corporate plans. These will start from the overall mission and strategy of the organisation and filter down to operational action plans for individual units. But strategic planning is not simply the preserve of the major organisation. Small businesses will also produce a plans setting out details of:

● The business;
● The product or service;
● The market;
● Personnel to be employed and their responsibilities;
● Buying and production;
● Premises and equipment;
● Profit;
● Cash flow;
● Finance.

Figure 85.1 A hierarchy of plans

Organisational planning

Organisational planning takes place at a number of levels. It is particularly important that managers are aware of these different levels and that top-level planning provides clear direction for lower-level planning.

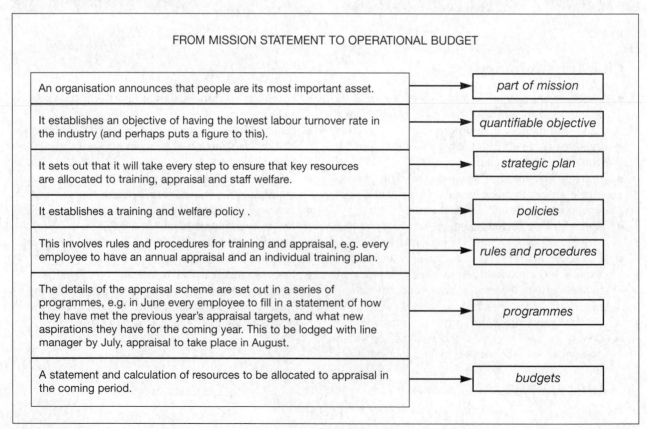

Figure 85.2 From mission statement to budgetary plan

An important starting point is to establish the purpose or **mission** of the organisation. Objectives and goals can then be formulated which direct the organisation and its activities towards the achievement of its mission.

Strategies can be formulated at a high level in the organisation, setting out key aspects of direction and focus. Once strategies are in place, policies can be established to put into practice **strategic** decisions, e.g. a recruitment policy, an equal opportunities policy, etc.

At a lower level it is essential for the organisation to plan procedures and rules which outline day-to-day operations as well as programmes for putting activities into action. An important part of operating activities will be working towards budgetary plans (see Figure 85.2 opposite).

Football 2000
An exercise in business planning

In this section we look at how the vision or mission of an organisation can be translated into a variety of individual activities which all pull towards the achievement of that mission.

Imagine that Ruud Gullitt *(left)* the new manager of Chelsea football club in 1996, makes the following statement.

"Over the next three years we are going to become the team that all other teams will want to emulate. We shall go on to head the Premier League and win European honours, as well as playing the most attractive football in England."

This manager is building up a big vision for his club. However, the vision will not materialise unless it can be translated into all the activities the club engages in, including the buying of players, training, youth development, sponsorship projects, ticket sales and supporter involvement. Effective planning therefore, involves creating a framework of plans from top to bottom.

For example, Ruud Gullitt knew that he wanted the players Le Boeuf from France, and Zola and Di Matteo from Italy to provide the heart of his new team. He also knew that he wanted them to play a particular brand of intelligent and attractive football.

Effective planning therefore involves creating a framework of plans from top to bottom.

- **Objectives** should provide the reference point upon which all decisions about the future of an organisation can be made. Corporate objectives are made for the company as a whole and sub-sets of objectives are created for each sub-section of the organisation;
- **Strategic plans** are concerned with the basic directions, broad intentions and the organisation's general approach to business planning;
- **Policies** are the general statements which guide thinking, action and decision-making. They define the area within which decisions have to be made and ensure that the decision contributes to the meeting of objectives. Organisational policies will normally be set out in writing;
- **Rules and procedures** set out a required method of handling particular activities;
- **Programmes** are sets of policies, procedures, rules and tasks which make up a particular course of action, e.g. a factory expansion programme, or a staff development programme;
- Money is always one of the key resources required for any series of programmes. A **budget** sets out the financial requirements for the plan. The financial operating budget is often called the **profit plan**.

Contingency planning

All organisations need to make contingency plans. A **contingency plan** is what you hold 'up your sleeve' in case your original plans and intentions go wrong. Contingency plans are therefore 'what if?' plans.

Most of us think ahead and set down the groundwork of contingency plans: for example, we might ask ourselves, 'What would I do if I lost my present job?', or 'What would I do if my car broke down and I needed to pay an emergency repair bill?' etc.

At all times, organisations are faced with a broad spectrum of possible scenarios concerning future development in the external environment and in internal relationships. A multitude of variables are continually changing – for example, the prices of raw materials, consumers' demand for products, the actions of rivals. Planning for contingencies therefore involves imagining these scenarios.

Risk and uncertainty are everywhere in the business world. Managers do their best to make sure that their plans are well-prepared, but they can rarely hope to have certainty about the outcomes. They must estimate the **probability of success** of their plans. In this way 'uncertainty' is converted into an estimation of 'risk'. Forward-looking

CREATING A PLAN – POSTALCHOCS

We can illustrate the planning process by taking the fictional example, of Postalchocs to get a good picture of how planning works.

Postalchocs: a brief history

The idea of sending chocolates through the post was first developed in the United States in the 1970s.

In 1990 the idea first reached the UK.

During the 1990s a chain of confectioners was set up throughout the UK, trading under the name of **Postalchocs**. The organisation had recognised the popular demand for sending chocolates through the post – for example, for birthdays, to people in hospital, to make up for forgotten presents, etc. Postalchoc organised themselves into a highly organised group to compete with rival confectioners.

A woman with a mission

In 1996, Jane Stevenson became the new chief executive of Postalchocs. She recognised the need for change within the existing organisation in order to protect the market position and to build a competitive edge for the future.

Jane Stevenson and the directors helped Postalchocs to create the following mission statement:

> 'Our mission is to make sure that Postalchocs will always be the consumers' first choice for postal chocolates and appropriate confectionery.'

This mission statement is displayed in every office and the reception area of the company head office. Each Postalchocs shop also has a copy so that all employees are constantly reminded of it.

The aim is for the mission to be translated down through polices and programmes to create everyday operational activities. All staff are trained to understand its purpose and how the contents should be interpreted to guide their actions.

What makes a good mission statement?

There is a general feeling that mission statements need to make immediate sense to people who read them. They should also be brief.

In the Postalchocs 'values statement' brochure, the directors have set out a number of reasons why organisations need mission statements. They include:

- Allows everyone to share and understand the company's vision and goals;
- Good benchmark against which to judge our priorities and values;
- Understood by customers, investors and suppliers;
- Defines the critical difference between success and failure;

The mission statement sets out a generalised objective for the organisation. This then needs to be translated into practical objectives at each level in the organisation. This is normally done in two stages; firstly, the goals are set out from the mission (goals are a generalised statement of aim or purpose). Then objectives are set out. These are a 'quantification' (if possible) or a more precise statement of the goals.

Postalchocs' goals are:

- Recognising and responding to customers' changing needs;
- Providing a seamless service to customer;
- Leading the industry in innovation and design;
- Continuous improvement in quality, service, processes and costs;
- Enabling employees and associates to give of their best.

These goals can then be broken down into specific objectives. For example, in relation to quality, Postalchoc's objective is to 'operate an effective quality assurance programme covering all our goods and services. We will strive to get everything right, first time, every time.'

(Continued opposite)

CREATING A PLAN Contd.

Once you have established where your organisation is going and what its key objectives are, it is essential to create your action plans and detailed programmes for ground-level activities and decision-making. In the case of Postalchocs this can be illustrated by the way in which the organisations communication goals are translated down into a communication diary to enable the effective development of communication within the organisation.

The communication goals for Postalchocs under the culture change programme introduced by the directors are:

- Personnel to drive;
- Identify existing communication practice;
- Improve and develop;
- Introduce company-wide briefings;

- Monitor;
- Report to Executive Committee.

Figure 86.2 shows how this translates down into daily activities.

Tasks

1 What do you see as being the particular strengths of Postalchoc's approach to planning?

2 Why is it important to develop a match between the top level plans of an organisation and operational activity and detail?

3 How can an organisation ensure that its strategies are translated into everyday

Twice-yearly	*3-monthly*	*Monthly*	*Weekly*	*Daily*
Mass-meetings: 1) October pre-peak conference 2) May post-peak/mid-term convention – Held over two days; – *Location:* out-of-office; – Chaired by Jane Stevenson.	Executive Managers meeting	Team briefings with feedback: – Progress; – Profitability; – Plans; – Policies; – People.	Bulletin on board: – Visitors; – Leavers; – Starters; – New babies. 1-sheet staff newsletter: – No. of orders; – Complaints; – No. of phone calls; – Achievements; – Suggestions (e.g. Remember mission objectives); – departmental update.	5-minute briefings between staff and supervisor: – Good morning; – Previous day's good points and any other points to note; – Targets if appropriate; – Praise – Aim: TO MOTIVATE

Figure 86.2 Postalchocs: a communications diary

plans can be created in a meaningful way only if they are related to the best possible judgements based on reasonable assumptions about contingencies.

Most organisations have contingency funds to cater for unexpected costs.

Coping with risk

There is an element of risk in an activity when the outcome cannot be predicted with certainty, or where the outcome is known but its full consequences are not. Individuals and organisations vary in their attitude to taking a risk:

- The **risk lover** is a person (or organisation) who enjoys a gamble, even when mathematical analysis shows that the odds are unfavourable;
- The **risk-neutral** person or organisation will gamble only if the odds are favourable. The person will not be concerned with the range of possible outcomes, only with the odds being in their favour;
- The **risk-averse** person or organisation will gamble only if the odds are strongly favourable.

Organisational activity is fraught with risk. For example, when organisations use resources for a particular purpose, there is always the chance that they could be used to better effect or that stakeholder objectives would be better met by an alternative policy. So taking any decision or course of action involves the risk of missing out on a more appropriate choice.

Risks are an ever-present part of planning, but planners try to minimise them by weighing them up and looking at the probabilities of different events occurring. Contingency planning is about making the unknowable as knowable as possible.

SYNTHESIS

What type of attitude to risk do you have? How does this influence your day-to-day decision-making?

Making contingency plans

Routine organisational planning involves managers and others in setting out, in detail, ways of meeting objectives in an orderly manner. Contingency planning uses many of the same processes and procedures, but also needs to take account of a variety of new factors. Managers sometimes say that Action B is **contingent** on the results of Action A, or that plan C is contingent on the successful completion of plan D, etc. Of course, many plans are also contingent on unpredictable factors which appear 'out of the blue'.

Thus, contingency planning is based necessarily on forecasts and projections. The relationship between planning variables can also be uncertain. The process is a bit like trying to plan a network of activities, without knowing fully what each activity will entail, its outcome, or exactly how it will influence the following activity. There has to be a flexible approach to meeting contingencies. This approach is reflected in a recent observation by an English rugby international just before a key match:

> "Dynamism is more a state of mind. Previously we have, perhaps, been guilty of taking to the field stuck on playing to a single game-plan. What (the coach) is looking for is a rather more flexible strategy whereby should Plan A fail, then we have the mental and physical capacity to change to Plan B, and so on... What this requires is an altogether greater contribution from all involved so that from 1 to 15 we all have a role to play, whether we are taking the ball up through the forwards, the backs or through a combination of both. If all 15 play these roles as expected, then our decision-makers are left free to use the complete armoury at their disposal."

IT'S A FACT

In a sense, the National Lottery has converted many people in the UK into contingency planners. Nowadays, nearly everybody has their own contingency plan for what they would do 'if they won the lottery'.

Identifying contingencies

In making plans we have to ask: 'How probable is it that a particular event will occur?' This probability can be assessed by guesswork, or by using statistics and mathematics. Guesswork depends on wisdom (from previous experience), hunch and intuition.

The first step in identifying contingencies is to clarify the conditions which enable the organisation to operate as it currently does. These are the **primary conditions**. We need then to ascertain the **secondary conditions** which enable the primary conditions to exist. It may then be possible to imagine future conditions that could inhibit or enhance the secondary conditions. Armed with the results of this analysis, it becomes easier to draw up contingency plans that respond to the events that work for or against the organisation. Thus, the key questions are as follows:

- What primary conditions enable us to operate in the way we do?

- What secondary conditions support or restrain the primary conditions?

- What possible future events may act to inhibit or enhance the secondary (and primary) conditions?

There are a number of ways in which contingencies can be identified, including the following:

- By using experience and/or research;
- By forecasting and projecting;
- By imagining a worst-case scenario;
- From intuition and/or guesswork;
- By acknowledging rumours.

Experience and/or research

It may be possible to predict contingencies if the same situation has been faced before. For example, organisations that have been dealing in credit for a considerable period of time are likely to have developed detailed statistics of how many customers are likely to become bad debtors and the likely extent of these debts. They are then able to protect themselves against debts in future.

Imagining a worst-case scenario

This involves developing a picture of all the things that could go wrong in the future. The emphasis is on coping with the worst possible conditions. The process sounds pessimistic, but in fact it can be a very useful way of forcing people to think about future events, and to be prepared for them. Shell's scenario planning procedure involves identifying the worst case as well as the best, and a number of other scenarios (see Case Study below).

CASE STUDY CASE STUDY CASE STUDY CASE STUDY CASE STUDY

SCENARIO PLANNING AT SHELL

Shell is particularly proud of one scenario set out in 1984. At the time, oil was $28 a barrel; one scenario envisaged oil falling to $16 a barrel by April 1986. With some pushing, Shell executives devised plans to deal with this eventuality. In the event, the price of oil *did* fall: from $27 in January 1986 to $17 in February and just $10 in April. The fact that Shell had already considered what it would do helped it to successfully manage this period of difficulty

Peter Schwartz, in his book *The Art of the Long View* (1991) tells another story of how scenario planning was used effectively at Shell. In 1983, there was still considerable tension between the Soviet Union and the West, and it would have been difficult to predict the changes that have taken place since in Russia and its satellites. At the time, Shell was reviewing demand for North Sea gas and considering whether to develop the Troll gas field. The platform and associated equipment was calculated to cost over $6 billion, although it would make it possible to sell gas throughout Europe.

The other potential supplier of natural gas was the Soviet Union, which could provide it far cheaper. The Western European states had agreed informally to limit supplies from the Soviet Union to 35% of the market. Shell was concerned, however, that it would take a long time and a great deal of money to develop this new gas field. To be worthwhile, Shell needed a decent return on its investment, and to get that return it needed good sales. It therefore needed to identify all the factors that would determine the size of those sales.

In particular, Shell were interested to identify factors which might lead to other European countries relaxing their 35% limit of gas supplies from the Soviet Union. The planners felt that the failing Soviet economy might force the Soviet Union to abandon its existing Communist system. They could see that it was possible that this failure would come about.

One of the scenarios the planners developed was based on Gorbachev achieving power, massive economic and political changes, opening up to the West, declining tension in the West, and major shifts in international relationships. This was one of a series of scenarios that Shell developed. Although the situation was an imaginary one, it was invaluable in helping them to understand the environment in which they operated and to cope with changes when they actually materialised.

Tasks

1 What is scenario planning?

2 Explain why scenario planning is vital to a large organisation like Shell.

3 Do you think that all organisations should analyse their environments in this way?

STUDY CASE STUDY CASE STUDY CASE STUDY CASE STUDY CASE STUDY

Forecasting and projecting

Forecasts and projections can be put together in many ways, including using computer-based and other models. A good example is a weather forecast, which nowadays may be the result of highly complex computer simulations based on present and past conditions.

Intuition and/or guesswork

Intuition is always an important part of the repertoire of successful managers, enabling them to identify possible contingencies and ways of dealing with them. Many would argue that intuition is simply experience coupled with business acumen and intelligence. Inspired guesswork, too, is often an important factor in contingency planning.

Listening to rumours

Rumours can sometimes genuinely predict change within an organisation and in the wider business environment. Planners should take account of the possible implications of rumours rather than brushing them aside.

For example, there may be a rumour that the organisation will lose an important contract. Remember the adage: no smoke without fire!

Chapter summary

- Planning helps to take the margin of error out of business activity.
- Larger business organisations set out corporate plans which then filter down to the operational activities of the organisation.
- Corporate planning involves setting out a mission, objectives, strategic plans, policies, rules and procedures, programmes, and budgets.
- The Postalchocs example provides us with a good case study of how an organisation has created a mission which then works down into operational frameworks.

- All organisations need to set out contingency plans. These are plans which can be put into effect if original plans and intentions do not materialise.
- Individuals and organisations have different approaches to coping with risk. These range from the risk-lover, to the risk-neutral, to the risk-averse.
- There are various ways of identifying contingencies including experience and/or research, forecasting and projecting, imagining a 'worst-case' scenario, intuition and/or guesswork and listening to rumours.

86 Living with change

From reading and working with this book students should have a wider understanding of the importance of change and the tremendous impact that it has on business activity. Perhaps the greatest challenge for any business today is the ability to live with change.

At one time it was common practice to distinguish between businesses that operated in a static environment and those that operated in a dynamic environment. Today most if not all businesses operate in a dynamic environment. It is the ability to cope with the pace of change in the environment that distinguishes the successful from the less successful business. In this chapter we set out to identify some of the key changes that affect business and some of the approaches that businesses can adopt to cope with change.

The evolutionary approach to coping with change

Darwin emphasised the importance of the survival of the fittest and the adaptation of organisms to their environments. A number of business writers argue that the prime aim of modern organisations is that of 'survival' in this Darwinian sense. By careful adaptation to changes in the external environment, the intelligent organisation will anticipate and identify changes and make adjustments to the way in which it operates. These changes will then have a knock-on effect for the environment in which the organisation operates.

There is therefore a two-way relationship between the organisation and its environment.

Steady change and rapid shock

All organisations today are faced by changes in their environment. The organisation that operates in a strategic fashion will scan its environment as an ongoing process to identify changes and to make sure that it is ahead of change, rather than merely responding to change.

However, as well as incremental, ongoing change, society is subject to a series of ongoing shocks. These can have an enormous impact on business activity. Some shocks are beneficial and help a range of organisations, while others are plainly harmful.

Shocks include the crumbling of political systems in Eastern Europe, or events such as sudden collapse in the worldwide financial markets. The effect of such shocks can be dramatic and can take even the most skilful of business pundits and speculators by surprise. Businesses should be prepared for shocks as well as for more predictable change – although some of the biggest shocks will take us all by surprise.

A good example occured in the early 1990s when one of Britain's best known merchant banks, Barings, was virtually wiped out overnight as a result of the activities of one of its traders on the Far East Futures market. Nick Leeson had speculated away billions of pounds of the company's money. It is tempting to draw a parallel with the dinosaurs, faced by an asteroid winging down towards them at millions of miles an hour (see Case Study on page 618).

Organisations need to protect themselves by making sure that they are sufficiently forward-thinking and flexible enough to cope with shock. Inevitably, many will not be able to and will have to go the way of the dinosaurs.

SYNTHESIS

What shocks can you think of that have had a major impact on organisations in recent times? Is there any way in which organisations could have prepared themselves to cope with these shocks?

Managing change

Today the emphasis in most organisations is on successfully managing change. Some writers argue that this involves continually 'unfreezing' and then 'refreezing' the ways in which organisations operate (see page 000).

CASE STUDY CASE STUDY CASE STUDY CASE STUDY CASE STUDY

DARWIN AND THE SURVIVAL OF THE FITTEST

In this book, *The Origin of Species*, published in 1859, Charles Darwin wrote:

'We shall best understand the probable course of natural selection by taking the case of a country undergoing some slight physical change, for instance, of climate. The proportional numbers of its inhabitants will almost immediately undergo a change, and some species will probably become extinct. We may conclude, from what we have seen of the intimate and complex manner in which the inhabitants of each country are bound together, that any change in the numerical proportions of the inhabitants, independently of the change of climate itself, would seriously affect the others. If the country were open on its borders, new forms would certainly immigrate, and this would likewise seriously disturb the relations of some of the former inhabitants. Let it be remembered how powerful the influence of a single introduced tree or mammal has been shown to be.'

And on the struggle for life between individuals and varieties of the same species:

'As the species of the same genus usually have, though by no means invariably, much similarity in habits and constitution, and always in structure, the struggle will generally be more severe between them, if they come into competition with each other, than between the species of distinct genera. We see this in the recent extension over parts of the United States of one species of swallow, which have caused the decrease of another species. The recent increase of the missel-thrush in parts of Scotland has caused the decrease of the song-thrush.'

1 What parallels can you draw between the above and recent business and organisational development in the UK?

2 What implications can you see for UK businesses?

STUDY CASE STUDY CASE STUDY CASE STUDY CASE STUDY CASE STUDY

THE DAY THE DINOSAURS DIED

In mid-February 1997, scientists announced that they had definite proof that a massive asteroid impact on Earth killed off the dinosaurs. To some this was hailed as the most significant discovery in geosciences in 20 years.

According to the asteroid theory, the impact point was a huge submerged crater in the Yucatan Peninsula, Mexico. Scientists involved in the investigations believed the violence of the impact would have been unlikely to leave clear samples. However, the resulting waves would have washed across Florida and deposited debris in the Atlantic – which was what they found when they drilled 300 feet beneath the seabed. The deepest, oldest layers contained fossil remains of many animals which may have been living in the ocean before the impact.

Just above this was a layer with material from the bottom of the sea which was believed to have melted in the giant energy release of the impact. Next was a rusty brown layer which scientists believe to be the vaporised remains of the asteroid itself. Above these were two inches of grey clay with barely anything in it, which scientists believe shows the asteroid wiped life out. Because of the force of the impact of the asteroid 70% of all species on earth, including the dinosaurs, perished.

What are the implications for business organisations of the type of shock described above?

Organisations and their employees get used to operating in a certain way as a result of adapting to their existing environment. However, as the environment alters, it is important to develop flexibility in the organisation – i.e. to unfreeze its patterns and systems and the expectations of its people. In particular, effective leadership is needed to identify new possibilities and new ways of working which will enable the organisation to adapt to its new environment. The organisation can then temporarily 'refreeze' in new patterns and systems of working.

For change to be successful, it will involve consultation right across the organisation, and beyond the organisation. Today, successful organisations have developed **value chains** which involve close working with customers and suppliers.

As we have seen, the emphasis in many organisations is on Total Quality Management based on continuous improvement. The organisation that is able to keep ahead of the competition is best placed to respond to continuous change and to shocks in its environment.

The 'right time' to change

Many writers today argue that the right time to change is 'all the time'.

Charles Handy in his influential book *The Empty Raincoat* (1995) has identified the **Sigmoid curve** as a useful illustration of when organisations should make changes. The Sigmoid curve is simply an 'S' shape on its side.

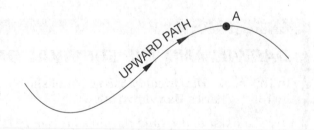

Figure 86.1 The Sigmoid curve

The upward path of the 'S' curve indicates the time when the organisation appears to be most successful. Everyone is given a pat on the back. Sales and profits are increasing, as is market share.

The organisation appears to be leading the field. However, Handy argues that it is at this point that things may already have started to go wrong. He argues that at Point A on the curve the organisation may have peaked and be on the edge of a downswing.

SYNTHESIS

How should an organisation decide on the appropriate time to make significant changes?

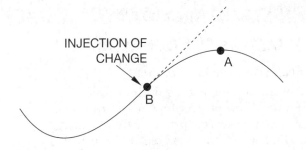

Figure 86.2 Introducing change at the 'right' time

Therefore at Point B on the curve, the organisation should make key strategic and structural changes. If it does this in an intelligent way it can create an ongoing and sustained period of growth.

The importance of scenario planning

At one time 'futurology', i.e. the science of predicting future trends, was treated with a certain amount of mirth and disdain. However, in recent times it has been given a lot more credibility. As we have already seen, the Shell organisation has placed serious emphasis on what it calls 'scenario planning' (see Case Study, page 615). This discipline has been widely copied by other organisations.

Preparing for the future

It is imperative that people in business understand the changes they will face in the near future. The business student needs to be an avid reader of newspapers and forms of communication such as the Internet.

Our world is being shaped by powerful forces:

- **Economic liberalisation** within and between countries;
- **Accelerating technological advance**, particularly the enabling power of the information revolution;
- **Globalisation**, as capital, information, technology and tastes are disseminated increasingly quickly and easily.

New technology

It is not just the falling cost of communications that has had a dramatic impact on the world in which we live in recent times. In addition we have seen tremendous falls in the price of computers and computer applications. This has had a major impact on our lives, and a number of commentators argue that we have not taken this sufficiently into account in measuring aspects of standard of living such as inflation and economic growth.

Today computers are used in a wide variety of ways from education to the office and the factory. Today's computers are very cheap and very powerful compared with the computers of the past.

Serving the customer

Another key change which has been of enormous import in recent times has been the emphasis on marketing and serving the needs of customers. Today the customer is right at top of the organisation chart, instead of at the bottom, as with the old hierarchical 'top-down' management structure.

Organisations can only remain effective by developing close personal links with their customers. This involves giving considerable powers to team members to build effective relationships with customers, often in direct face-to-face meetings.

The importance of flexibility

Increasingly in Europe there has been a rising tide of opinion in favour of flexible labour markets. The UK has followed the USA down the road to flexibility whereas countries like Germany and France have sought to provide protection for employees, e.g. in the form of minimum wage legislation, maximum hours, etc. At a time when continental European countries have rising numbers of pensioners this has led to problems of dependency. For many in the UK this poses a real dilemma. New Labour and other social democratic parties are in favour of greater social protection, but this is not easy to reconcile with the need of the economy to be competitive.

In February 1997, the European Commission and the Paris-based Organisation for Economic Co-operation and Development (OECD) both joined the call for further deregulation in European labour markets. In its annual economic report, the European Commission went further than before in calling on European Union (EU) governments to embrace worker flexibility as the key to casting off the millstone of persistently high unemployment.

The Commission stopped short of advocating the American economic model which for 'social and political reasons' could not, it says, be emulated in Europe. According to the report, the US approach to job-creation had caused a 'significant' drop in real wage income for the low-skilled.

Nevertheless, the Commission called for 'pragmatic solutions', including below-minimum wages for the low-skilled, for young people or the long-term unemployed, more flexibility in working time and greater use of voluntary part-time work.

Flexibility will continue to be a major business issue as we enter the next century. Currently unemployment tends to be lowest in those countries with the greatest labour market flexibility. Flexibility provides competitive advantage. Tampering with it immediately reduces competitive advantage, so that the survival of organisations within the economic system is put at risk.

SCENARIO PLANNING FOR ENERGY DEMAND 1995–2020

As a management tool and an intellectual aid, the Shell Group has prepared a number of global scenarios looking at possible developments in the medium-to-long term – currently up to the year 2020.

Two contrasting scenarios recently developed by Shell planners are:

- A world driven by individualism, flexibility and hyper-competition;
- A world which – while necessarily responding to those global forces – continues to emphasise cohesion, relationships, long-term vision and a role for government.

Different countries would obviously respond in different ways, and with varying success, to these alternatives. The United States would be most comfortable in an individualist world. Cohesion and strong government would fit East Asian cultures. For this reason, Shell envisage that Asian economic growth would be strongest under the second scenario, leading to higher overall global growth and energy demand. Shell have termed these two scenarios **low growth** and **high growth**.

Protecting the environment

Another theme is how an increasing emphasis on protecting the environment may shape the future - particularly for energy industries. It seems increasingly probable that man-made carbon dioxide, produced largely from burning fossil fuels, may have an impact on global climate. So it is clearly prudent for the international community to consider possible precautions. Shell believe that it is vital that any measures should not inhibit the economic and technological progress on which people depend for higher living standards and a better environment. These concerns will certainly lead to an increasing focus on improving energy efficiency and developing renewable energy sources so that new technologies will emerge.

Shell have developed complex scenarios using these broad basic themes to outline the future state of demand for energy up to the year 2020. In this way they have been able to prepare detailed plans which will enable them to respond to whatever scenario unfolds.

The technological imperative

New technology has transformed our lives and will continue to do so in the future. But long-established technologies also offer considerable scope for improvement. For example, the use of unleaded petrol has made the internal combustion engine much more environment-friendly, removing 90% of harmful emissions such as carbon monoxide.

In spite of its phenomenal developments in recent years, information technology still has immense potential. We quickly become frustrated with current technology, yet five years ago we would have been astounded at the speed and power of today's computers. Information technology will continue to astound us and to transform our lives. The corporation of the future will have to continually change and upgrade its technology if it is to survive. The way in which it does this will be determined both by consumer preference and by the availability of new ideas, methods bund processes. Business success involves a continual process of preparing for tomorrow. Businesses cannot rest on their past successes. They need to build for the future.

The importance of the environment

Concern for the environment has become one of the most important business issues today. No company can survive and prosper if it neglects the developing needs of the customer and the increasingly insistent needs of the environment.In practice, the two sets of needs go together:

- Customers will not want to buy products and services from companies with a bad environmental record;
- In addition, government regulation and taxation will put greater financial burdens than ever on companies who do not meet agreed environmental standards.

The net result is that business policies will have to become environmentally efficient to survive.

A SHRINKING WORLD FOR BUSINESS

One of the most significant changes in recent times was the agreement signed in February 1997 to liberalise the world telecommunications market. The United States representative at the talks, Charlene Bashefsky, estimated that this would lead to international phone charges falling by 80 per cent.

This will have a dramatic impact on the world economy. Customers will be able to telephone suppliers in far-flung corners of the world almost as cheaply as ringing their local supplier.

The chart below shows the falling cost of four communications technologies over the last 80 years. The two mechanical technologies, ocean freight and air-transport, have had enormous economic and social consequences over a number of years.

For example, consider the impact on our diet of the falling costs of ocean transport (the average item purchased in our supermarkets today has come from 1,500 miles away!).

With telecommunications the fall has been much faster. The latest change will have a significant impact. Hamish Macrae has identified a number of possible consequences of the latest change:

● In five years most businesses will have global 0800 numbers. The cost of a call to a business from anywhere in the world will normally be carried by the business itself. In the US, half the calls to businesses are on an 0800 basis. The attraction of a business having a single free number for use from anywhere in the world is enormous. With low-cost calls, the business will be able to have much greater access to global sales;

● There will no longer be 'fringe countries'. Any country, anywhere in the world, will be able to communicate with any other at zero marginal cost. Global communications networks will be able to deliver any screen-based service at zero marginal cost, with the result that we will find financial or entertainment services coming from anywhere in the world. Location of industries which can deliver their output over the wires – software, computer games, audio-visual entertainment, financial services, etc. - will therefore migrate to places where there is the best-value human capital available. With manufacturing, people have to move to the jobs; with screen-based services, the jobs can move to the people. But the jobs will only come if the people have appropriate skills.

(Continued on page 622)

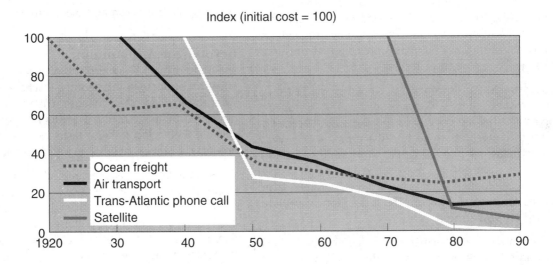

Figure 86.3 The falling cost of transport and communications

A SHRINKING WORLD FOR BUSINESS

(Continued from page 621)

- The low cost of phone links enables even small businesses to keep open lines for its computers. In the developed world at least, organisations will be able to have computers continuously connected to networks;

- Trading blocs may become less popular. Present popular wisdom is that the world is gradually moving towards three trading blocs, American, European and East Asian, and that trade will tend to be ordered by negotiation between these. But if any country can communicate with any other virtually for free and an increasing proportion of trade is simply shot down the wires, these blocs are irrelevant. As countries become richer, an increasing proportion of their trade is 'weightless', in areas like information technology;

- If very cheap telecommunications level the field between countries, they also level it between companies. If size and location are less important for the former, they will also become less important for the latter. Small businesses and sole traders will be able to enjoy many of the advantages of the larger ones, just as small businesses can at present use the Internet just as effectively as large.

Tasks

1 What are the major implications of the falling costs of communications for world trading patterns?

2 What are the major implications for UK organisations?

STUDY CASE STUDY CASE STUDY CASE STUDY CASE STUDY CASE STUDY CASE STUDY

Smaller businesses

Today there is more scope for small business than in the past. Because large organisations are 'downsizing' and streamlining, they need to buy in many of their 'non-core' requirements from outside. This is called **outsourcing**.

At the same time, people have more leisure. As incomes increase, they want to buy in a wide range of personal services. There are therefore plenty of opportunities for people to set up small businesses providing hairdressing, massage, gardening, cleaning, etc.

Rigidly-structured, slow-moving companies will not only not prosper, they will not survive. The European companies that are doing well today are not necessarily going to do well as we go into the new century. What organisations must ensure is that they provide a culture and an environment in which their highly skilled people respond appropriately to external stimuli, rather than waiting for external direction. This is the process we have termed **empowerment**.

Increasingly in the global marketplace, large organisations are transferring their points of production closer to final consumers. There is already an observable trend towards manufacturing networks – they are known as **virtual factories** – closely tied to localised demand patterns. As the cost of transferring the intellectual component of production sinks ever nearer to zero, we may find that smaller factories closer to the final point of consumption gain a significant advantage over more distant facilities.

Beyond the Millennium

The onset of the Millennium is already having a profound effect on business in this country. Psychologically, people want to see widespread changes. The new century offers new opportunities. There is a groundswell of demand for change, embracing fashion, taste, popular culture, new products, and ways of working and enjoying leisure.

We cannot be sure where these changes will take us. However, we can be sure that some people and firms will reap tremendous rewards from surfing this wave of change. In Darwinian terms these will be the organisational 'species' that are best able to adapt to a new environment and new conditions.

Chapter summary

- Organisations operate in a dynamic environment. They need to be able to adapt to this environment in order to survive and flourish.
- Organisations are influenced by their environment and they help to change their environment.
- Change can occur in regular dynamic pulses, or it can appear in the form of 'shocks'.
- Organisations need to be able to live with both types of change.
- Organisations need to be able to develop mechanisms and processes for managing change.
- Often the best time to change is when you have a winning formula and are 'ahead of the game'. A downturn may be just around the corner.
- Scenario planning is an important way of preparing yourself for a range of possible eventualities. You then reduce the number of possible surprises to a minimum.
- Our world is being transformed by economic liberalisation, accelerating technological advances and globalisation. Communication costs are about to drop dramatically.
- By being customer-focused, organisations are able to respond to perhaps the most importance change – that of customer requirements and needs.
- On the supply side, organisations also need to be responsive. Today, flexible organisations can develop a competitive edge. Inflexible organisations are likely to go under.
- Organisations must keep up to date with the latest technology and show a keen understanding of environmental imperatives.
- Organisations are becoming smaller and responsive to local requirements and conditions.
- The Millennium provides all organisations with a threat and an opportunity

Question bank

Case study questions

1 Study the information and answer all parts of the questions which follow.

IMPERIAL LIGHTS UP IN FAR EAST MARKET

Imperial Tobacco has responded to the Chancellor raising taxes on cigarettes by looking to expand in overseas markets, notably the Far East.

Imperial Tobacco has successfully increased its market share in the domestic market. The government is aiming to reduce cigarette consumption and Imperial Tobacco estimates that cigarette consumption, totalling 84 billion in 1995, could fall to 59 billion by the end of the century. However, it recognises its social responsibility to maintain UK production and anticipates exporting greater quantities from its Nottingham factory.

Imperial Tobacco is developing a new brand to be produced using new technology at a factory in the Hunan province in China. Other deals are expected in China which accounts for 33% of world cigarette sales. Imperial Tobacco also aims to export the new brand to other parts of South East Asia and even to the former Soviet Union.

Source: adapted from *The Sunday Times,* 4 December 1994

(a) What is meant by the term 'social responsibility'?
(2 marks)

(b) (i) Outline two problems that Imperial Tobacco might encounter when increasing exports from its Nottingham factory.
(4 marks)

(ii) Explain one form of assistance given by the government to exporters.
(2 marks)

(c) Discuss the possible effects on the domestic cigarette market of the increased taxation.
(7 marks)

(d) Evaluate the arguments for and against Imperial Tobacco's decision to produce cigarettes in China.
(10 marks)

(AEB , January 1996)

2 Study the information and answer the questions which follow.

MUSCLE PUMP HEALTH CLUB

The Muscle Pump opened twelve months ago near the centre of town and is trading as a private limited company. The premises are held on a 29-year lease and include a large entrance lounge currently being used as a reception area. The owners are concerned about health issues and believe that fitness is vital for a person's well-being. They have provided a comprehensive range of services designed to enhance physical fitness. The club is open to anyone over 18 for a monthly fee of £80 which includes all facilities and full insurance. The services of the trained staff are also included unless specialist training programmes are requested. The town has seven other health/fitness clubs trading commercially, as well as local authority provision at leisure centres. There is a range of sports clubs offering the chance to engage in sporting activity. All these have been established for some time and public interest in leisure pursuits has been increasing. This widening market has enabled the industry to expand. In general, the commercial concerns have fixed prices at a level which suggests they are not aiming at higher income groups. They have also been offering a range of services to cater for wider leisure time use than fitness or bodybuilding. Partly as a result of these policies, all the available space in their premises is being used. Four of the local competitors are now acting in conjunction with travel agents in the promotion of foreign holidays.

(Continued on page 626)

THE MUSCLE PUMP HEALTH CLUB

* Fitness for the 1990s   * Fully equipped weights room
* Qualified supervision   * Individual fitness plans
* Sauna and showers   * Workouts and Aerobics
* Healthy light food   * Luxurious lounge area
* Parking   * Body building

Open 9:30 – 21:30
Corton Street   Tel.: (01289) 6349

'Be fit for Everything – Business or Pleasure'

Figure 1: Muscle Pump as advertised in Yellow Pages

2 *Contd.*

Muscle Pump was launched with a promotional day involving a TV celebrity, media coverage and a leaflet drop in selected areas of the town. Reminder adverts are run occasionally in local papers and there is an entry in Yellow Pages (see Figure 1, page 625).

The club has deliberately tried to present itself as 'more exclusive'. It looks for clients who prefer luxurious surroundings and personal attention. This approach is reflected in sumptuous décor, furnishings and carpeting.

Muscle Pump needs 120 members to break even. The owners are prepared to wait before seeing large returns on their investment. However, they are concerned enough to think about developing the facilities and have put together a report on possible changes. Suggestions for new business are:

● Books, sportswear and equipment;
● Diet and slimming programmes;
● Lectures and filmshows;
● Wider food and drinks range;
● Beauty and health care services.

Many of these are offered by their competitors. If Muscle Pump pursues any of them, the owners wish this to be carried out sensitively so as to not lose sight of their original objectives. They are aware that current policy may appeal to only a limited target market and they would require an assurance that changes will lead to an increase in profit. They are certain that some finance for further investment is available and there is sufficient space in the premises for development. Before taking any decision they intent to consult a friend in banking about national economic prospects, including relevant government policies.

A graph showing fluctuation in Muscle Pump membership during its first year of operation is shown in Figure 5 below. In months 7 and 8, Muscle Pump's competitors increased their prices by an average of 10%. Further information on Muscle Pump's membership is given below:

	Muscle Pump	Competitors
A	5	5
B	35	20
C1	35	35
C2	15	20
D	10	15
E	–	5

Figure 2 Muscle Pump client profile: socio-economic group

	Muscle Pump		Competitors	
	F	M	F	M
18–23	3	14	16	23
24–29	14	12	16	19
30–34	8	17	6	7
35–39	3	15	5	6
40–49	–	9	2	–
50+	–	5	–	–

Figure 3 Muscle Pump client profile: age/sex profile – nearest %

	%
Only Muscle Pump	82.00
Other club member	18.00
No previous club	38.00

Figure 4 Club membership: % of Muscle Pump members

1 (a) Comment on the marketing objectives of Muscle Pump.

(9 marks)

(b) Assess the extent to which the company is succeeding in achieving these.

(16 marks)

FIG 5

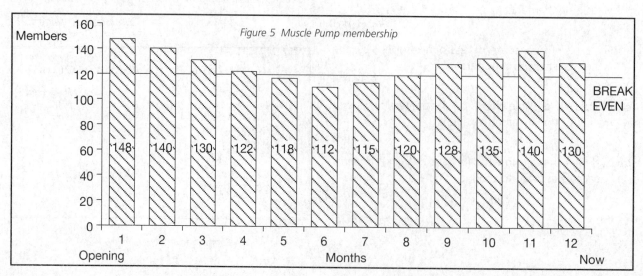

Figure 5 Muscle Pump membership

Members: 148, 140, 130, 122, 118, 112, 115, 120, 128, 135, 140, 130

BREAK EVEN

Months — Opening ... Now

2 *Contd.*

2 The owners need to satisfy themselves that any change in services offered will be profitable.

(a) In carrying out a survey, what sampling frames could they use?

(10 marks)

(b) Consider the relative merits of the sampling frames you have described, and recommend one as the most appropriate.

(10 marks)

3 (a) Calculate, for Muscle Pump's first year of operation:

(i) Total revenue

(2 marks)

(ii) Profit. (Assume all costs incurred can be treated as fixed costs.)

(2 marks)

Following its market research, Muscle Pump has calculated average charges made by its competitors and has estimated the average use made of facilities. These are set out below:

Facility	Average charge per session (£)	Average use sessions/member/year
Weights	2.50	36
Aerobics	2.00	25
Sauna	2.00	42
Solarium	3.00	22

The average annual membership fee charged is £95.

(b) (i) Demonstrate that the annual cost of individual membership of Muscle Pump is greater than that of a typical competitor. State your assumptions

(4 marks)

(ii) What conclusions can you draw from this?

(2 marks)

(c) Would you advise Muscle Pump to change its pricing policy? Justify your answer.

(10 marks)

(d) Explain how the other elements of Muscle Pump's marketing strategy may need to be modified if the suggested shift to a more market-led product is made.

(15 marks)

4 Comment on the risk to Muscle Pump of introducing any two of the suggestions for new business.

(20 marks)

(University of Cambridge LES, May 1992)

3 This question is specifically about market research. You will be expected to include knowledge relevant to this aspect of business studies in your answers.

Read the following extract from a newspaper article then answer the questions which follow it. You may draw on evidence from the article to support your answers.

The European Union Tax Commissioner has pledged to abolish tax-free shopping for European citizens travelling between member states. In response, the managing director of United Distillers pointed out that 'duty-free sales are to a great extent impulse-driven' and 'lost duty-free sales are unlikely to be recovered in domestic markets'. A similar message was delivered by the managing director of Pringle [*the Scottish knitwear firm*]: 'This will mean our firm will have to face new problems and adopt new strategies to remain competitive.'

Source: The European, November 4 1994

Before Pringle can begin to adopt new strategies, the firm must commission some market research.

(a) (i) Identify and explain a major marketing aim for Pringle.

(ii) Explain how this might determine the kind of market research commissioned by the firm.

(4 marks)

(b) The market research agency employed by Pringle is considering primary research. Explain with reasons which methods would be most suitable.

(8 marks)

(c) Explain what you would expect this market research to find and how such information could influence Pringle's marketing of its products.

(8 marks)

(d) Identify which secondary data would help Pringle's market research and explain how this would help with a marketing strategy.

(4 marks)

(e) Pringle requires a questionnaire suited to its market research aim. The questionnaire must be designed to collect information which can be collated using a database.

Explain, with examples:

● How the use of such software will influence the questionnaire;

● How the database should be structured;

● How the database would be used to search and sort the information gathered.

(16 marks)

(London Examinations, June 1996)

Lichfield Holdings Plc
Balance Sheet as at 3 January 1993

	1992 £000s	1991 £000s
Fixed Assets		
Tangible Assets	47,234	46,629
Investments	20	13
	47,254	46,642
Current Assets		
Stocks	26,678	23,717
Debtors	20,652	15,775
Cash at bank and in hand	2,632	5,626
	49,962	45,118
Current Liabilities		
Creditors due within one year	30,547	24,164
Net Current Assets	19,415	20,954
Total Assets less Current Liabilities	66,669	67,596
Long-term Liabilities	33	14
Net Assets	66,636	67,582
Capital and Reserves		
Capital	31,025	31,163
Reserves	5,726	5,588
Profit and Loss Account	29,885	30,831
Shareholders' Funds	66,636	67,582

Figure 6 Lichfield Holdings Plc: balance sheet

Lichfield Holdings Plc:
Profit and loss account
for the year ended 3 January 1993

	1992 £000s	1991 £000s
Turnover	144,235	148,379
Profit on operations	3,912	13,281
Share of profit of associated undertaking	9	19
Interest	(583)	(110)
Profit before taxation	3,338	13,190
Taxation	1,302	4,510
Profit after taxation	2,036	8,680
Dividends	2,792	5,609
Retained (loss)/profit for the period	(756)	3,071
Earnings per share	1.64p	6.95p

Figure 7 Lichfield Holdings Plc: profit and loss account

4 Study the accounts shown in Figures 6 and 7 opposite and answer the questions below:

a) Explain the difference between Fixed Assets and Current Assets.

(2 marks)

b) What alternative name might be given to Net Current Assets?

(1 mark)

c) Using data from the accounts for 1991 and 1992:

(i) Calculate the current ratios;

(3 marks)

(ii) Calculate the returns on equity;

(3 marks)

(iii) Comment on your findings.

(4 marks)

d) Explain why the Profit and Loss Account shows a retained loss in 1992.

(3 marks)

e) Assess the importance of three non-financial factors that an investor may consider before buying shares in a company such as Lichfield Holdings Plc.

(9 marks)

(AEB, Winter 1995)

5 Read the material below carefully, then answer the questions.

Evidence A:

WHAT PRICE WAR?

Thanks to a buoyant Christmas season, Sainsbury announced it would be cutting prices on a selected range of goods. The cuts would be considerable – as much as 50% on some lines – and the product range would be bigger than ever. Within minutes, its shares started to slide, dragging Tesco and Kwik Save with them as brokers feared a damaging price war that would hurt the industry's profits.

It was a classic marketing coup. Publicly Sainsbury directors played down the price war – it was just another promotion, part of a 52-week war – in an effort to reassure the stock market. The reality is that there is no price war. Sainsbury's loudly trumpeted price cuts will affect less than 5% of the goods the company sells every day.

In the last real price war of 1977–78, all of the giants slashed prices on a fortnightly basis. It became difficult to get off the treadmill and it all got out of control.

In a recession that has taken a savage toll of the retailing sector, food retailers have stood out from the pack, so much so that their profits have proved politically embarrassing and have sparked repeated calls for the government to intervene. Far from cutting each others' throats in a vicious price war, many industry commentators contend that the big three – Sainsbury, Tesco and Argyll's Safeway – have been enriching themselves at the expense of their customers and suppliers.

Sainsbury's success has been built around talented management, the creation of an exceptionally strong brand, an enviable reputation for quality, and never losing sight of the real profit centre, selling food.

The company has ploughed hundreds of millions of pounds into expanding its network of superstores in Britain, and its profits rose from £375m in 1989 to £628m last year. This year, the City expects profits of about £740m: Tesco will make £570, and Argyll £415m.

Sainsbury's and Tesco's dominance and profitability have swung the pendulum of power firmly and irrevocably away from suppliers into the hands of the retailers.

(*Source: The Sunday Times*, 3 January 1993)

Evidence B:

SUPERMARKETS GIVE MANUFACTURERS FRIGHT WITH OWN BRAND OF SUCCESS

There are some things that Britain is good at. One of them is supermarketing, and as part of that, the management of retailers' brands – own brands or private labels, are very important. The supermarket chains have steadily eroded manufacturers' brands in many areas, and are now poised to attack the few remaining sectors such as detergents, where own labels have remained in the shadows.

Private labels are a particularly British phenomenon reflecting the food retailers' power, which is greater in the UK that in most other countries. The private label share of each retailer's product range has not changed dramatically. It is therefore profitable even at a lower revenue than branded production.

BZW analyst Bill Currie says own label is also a powerful competitive weapon for the supermarkets.

> "It is a marketing weapon, because it allows differentiation. And because it breaks down barriers to entry into food manufacturing it allows them to create excess capacity."

That helps to prevent the branded manufacturers pushing up their own margins.

Source: The Grocer's Review, June 1995

5 *Contd.*

Evidence C: Retail and own brand concentrations

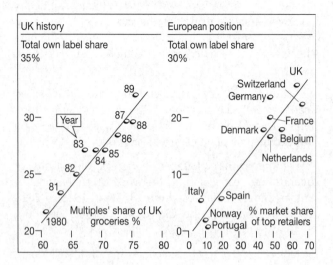

Source: Adapted from *The Guardian*, November 1992

(a) Using the information contained in Evidence A, explain why a 'price war' between supermarkets might be damaging to them all.

(4 marks)

(b) It appears that, despite a recession, the major supermarkets have succeeded in raising profits. Give possible reasons why this may have occurred.

(6 marks)

(c) Describe the circumstances in which own brand products develop a significant role in retailing.

(10 marks)

(d) Discuss the effects of own brand products on producers, retailers and consumers.

(10 marks)

(London Examinations, specimen paper)

6 Read the description below and answer the questions which follow:

FRANCIS DALE AND CO. LTD

Francis Dale and Co Ltd is a family business which was founded by Francis Dale in 1900. The largest shareholder now is Frank Dale, a grandson of the founder, who owns 60% of the equity. A further 20% is owned by Janice Penrose, Frank's sister. The remainder of the shares are held by cousins of these two, none of whom holds more than 5% of the shares or takes any active interest in the management of the business.

The company produces a range of food products with a 'home-made' image which sell, mainly locally, at premium prices. It has grown over the years by ploughing back a substantial proportion of its profits. Profits have grown, although not spectacularly, but measured as a return on capital they have tended, in the long term, to fall. An investment analyst has recently advised the Board that, although unquoted, the company's shares are worth about 15p each. As this is below the balance sheet value there has been some concern.

Until recently the Board of Directors consisted of Frank (Chairman), Janice (Managing Director) and five other salaried executive directors, none of whom owns any shares in the company. It has recently been joined by David Dale, son of Frank Dale, who has just completed a degree in business studies.

Wishing to create a good initial impression, David has placed before the Board his proposals for expanding the output of the company's products and thus improving both its short term profits and its longer term prospects. In order demonstrably to maintain existing standards he proposes that existing productive capacity should continue to serve the traditional market in the way that it always has. This part of the business would continue to yield results in line with those experienced in the past. The new capacity would be designed to produce the same quality but, by replacing many manual processes by machine processes, it would do so more efficiently, saving 15% on the current variable cost of sales for its part of the output. The whole of cost of sales may be treated as variable except for depreciation amounting to £100,000.

Under the plan 50% can be added to output. To realise the full potential, sales would also have to increase by that proportion. This would be achieved by a programme of advertising and promotion aimed at more distant, as yet untapped, markets.

The new capacity would involve capital expenditure of £800,000 and would require an additional amount of working capital of £200,000. Funds would be raised by means of a fixed-term bank loan for this total amount for which interest at the fixed rate of 12% per annum would be paid. Depreciation of the investment in the new capacity would be on a straight-line basis over its expected useful life of 10 years. Corporation tax is at the small companies rate of 25%. This is to be applied to the figure of profit before taxation as shown by the accounts, to which no significant adjustment would be required. The plan envisages that a dividend would be paid such that it would be 1.5 times covered by available profit.

If the project went ahead there would be additional administrative costs (in addition to the interest charges arising from the bank loan) of £50,000 per annum and there would be additional selling costs of £100,000 per annum.

The most recent set of accounts are set out in summary form below:

Francis Dale & Co. Ltd.
Profit and loss account for the year ended
31 December 1991

	£000s	£000s
Sales		2,000
Less Cost of Sales		1, 300
Gross profit		700
Less Administrative costs	300	
Selling costs	200	500
Profit before taxation		200
Less Corporation tax		50
Profit after taxation		150
Less Dividends paid		50
Retained profit		100

Balance sheet at 31 December 1991

	£000s
Fixed assets	2,000
Net current assets	500
	2,500
Financed by:	
12 million ordinary shares of 10p each	1,200
Profit and loss account	1,300
	2,500

1 (a) On the assumption that the investment in new capacity is made and that all expectations are fulfilled, draft a pro forma profit and loss account for the subsequent year and a pro forma balance sheet at the end of the year in as much detail as the information available allows.

(15 marks)

(b) Calculate the existing gross profit rate and the rate which would exist after the new investment had been made.

(10 marks)

(c) Calculate the after-tax return on shareholders' equity before and after the new investment.

(10 marks)

2 (a) What is the minimum level of increased sales revenue which must be achieved for the new capacity just to cover the costs directly associated with it?

(17 marks)

(b) What is the minimum term of the bank loan on the assumption that the whole of the cash flow generated by the company's activities (after taxation and dividends) is accumulated to repay the bank loan?

(5 marks)

(c) What accounting information would you expect to be of prime concern to the bank manager when making the decision as to whether to lend the money?

(12 marks)

(d) The company has never before borrowed money to finance its operations. Explain the main advantages and the main disadvantages of this method of finance.

(11 marks)

3 (a) Assuming that the price/earnings ratio of the shares is unchanged, predict the value of a share in the company after the new investment has been undertaken. Compare this with the balance sheet value of the share and comment on any difference.

(10 marks)

(b) Advise Frank Dale on how he might value his holding in the company.

(10 marks)

(UCLES, May 1992)

6 Read carefully the material provided in Evidence A, B and C and then answer the questions which follow.

Evidence A

Pettipont is a small, family-run business that makes quality door furniture, i.e. handles, locks, door knobs etc. It sells mainly to interior designers via a catalogue and a large proportion of its output is for special runs, which are produced to order in batches.

Rick Hoburn, a newly-appointed business manager, proposed that the company buy new production line equipment and move into mass production. He wanted the firm to widen its channels of distribution. The Board had agreed to buy a new machine and Rick hoped this would be Machine 1 (see Evidence B). However, it had not agreed to a wholesale change in production techniques, but Rick felt time would change that. Rick felt he had moved the decision-making process away from a non-scientific style and into an era of modern, rational, clear-minded business techniques.

Matt Harvey, Production Manager, was already worried, but when the shop steward, Angie Tallent, walked in he was more so.

"I've heard that you're putting in new machinery. I suppose that means redundancies. You know the law!"

"Hang on," said Matt. "It's just *one* machine, no redundancies, and we mean to concentrate on job enlargement and enrichment for production workers."

6 *Contd.*

Evidence B

Extract from Rick Hoburn's presentation to the Board of Pettipont Ltd.

The capital outlay for 1 is less than for 2, and with interest rates likely to rise, we can't afford too much borrowing. Machine 1 has a significant reject rate, but with average order sizes of 200–300, customers should tolerate some rejects. Someone checking returns, altering invoices and smoothing over any problems should suffice. Indeed, for someone on the shop floor this would be a chance for training and job enlargement and enrichment.

PROPOSAL

Machine 1:

Initial Cash Outflow: £15,000

Cash inflows	£	Discounted Cash Flows (6%)
Year 1	6,000	5,660
Year 2	8,000	7,120
Year 3	10,000	8,396
Year 4	12,000	9,505

Present Value at 6%: £30,682
Net Present Value at 6%: £15,682

Machine 2:

Initial Cash Outflow: £20,000

Cash inflows	£	Discounted Cash Flows (6%)
Year 1	6,000	5,660
Year 2	8,000	7,120
Year 3	10,000	8,396
Year 4	12,000	9,505

Present Value at 6%: £30,682
Net Present Value at 6%: £10,682

Recommendation: Purchase Machine 1.

Why?

● Broaden us away from niche market;
● Update production process and increase automation;
● Widen our channels of distribution, so reducing our reliance on interior design market;
● Use as Pilot Project, ready for further introduction of automation.

(*Note:* All figures are rounded to the nearest whole number.)

Evidence C

Extract of a conversation between John Pettit (Managing Director) and Sally Barnes (Financial Controller)

John Pettit: Well, I liked Rick's presentation. Pity you could not be there – the ideas are both financially sound and good for our workforce. Let's hope the delivery date is soon. These are exciting times at Pettitpont!

Sally Barnes: Yes, I wish I had been there. I have some serious concerns regarding both the financial and non-financial aspects.

John Pettit: Surely not. It was rational and scientific. I'll give you until tomorrow morning to produce something that makes us change our minds.

Sally Barnes: Rising inflation is just one of my concerns, but I'll put the rest on paper by tomorrow.

1 Rick Hoburn used the Net Present Value method of investment appraisal in his report.

   (a) Suggest reasons why Rick might have chosen to use Net Present Value.

   (4 marks)

   (b) Name two other methods of investment appraisal that Rick could have used.

   (2 marks)

2 Sally Barnes has to write a report to the Board in response to Rick Hoburn's proposal. How might she criticise:

   (a) The financial aspects of the proposal;

   (4 marks)

   (b) The strategic implications of the proposal?

   (6 marks)

3 Discuss the possible effects on staff morale if Rick Hoburn's plan is put into operation at Pettipont.

   (6 marks)

4 Comment on the 'decision-making' processes illustrated by the Evidence.

   (8 marks)

   (London Examinations, June 1996)

7 The following question is specifically about investment and production. You will be expected to include knowledge relevant to this aspect of business studies in your answers.

Study the cash flow forecast in Figure 8, and the notes which accompany it on page 635. Read the information below and then answer the questions. Your answers should draw on evidence contained in the forecast. You may use a calculator.

AIMS

Agro-Industrial Machine Systems Ltd (AIMS) is a newly established private limited company. The firm manufactures farm equipment and the cash flow forecast for its first year of trading is illustrated in Figure 8 on page 634. Production began in April 1995 and AIMS currently manufactures only one product – a machine for harvesting crops on a large scale. Each harvester retails for £20,000 and sells to a specialised and limited market. There is a two-month period between the end of the manufacturing process and the day the firm receives payment from customers. Having studied the cash flow forecast provided for her finance department, the Managing Director of AIMS is unhappy about the predicted cash balance at the end of July.

(a) Suggest how AIMS might be able to improve its cash balance at the end of July without affecting its estimated output and sales revenue.

(4 marks)

(b) Explain how your suggestions for improving the July cash balance would affect the firm's operations.

(4 marks)

Magyar Pepper Growers Ltd will be approaching AIMS at the beginning of December wishing to place an order for three harvesters. It will want to take delivery of the machines in January, but will only be able to pay for them when it receives a Hungarian Government grant in March. To meet the order, AIMS would, in the month of December, have to:

- Increase output;
- Incur additional direct labour costs of £4,000 (as a result of taking on temporary labour);
- Purchase the necessary materials.

(c) Assume that AIMS accepts the order. Using all the information available, fill in the following blank cells on the Answer Sheet shown in Figure 9 on page 635.

Payments:	Materials for December
	Wages (Direct Labour) for December
Total Payments:	December, January, February and March
Net Cash Flow:	December, January, February and March
Balance at beginning of month:	December, January, February and March
Balance at end of month:	December, January, February and March
Receipts:	Sales for March

(8 marks)

(d) Discuss the operational implications of the firm accepting the order.

(8 marks)

One of the firm's primary objectives is to develop computer-based systems which will help it to manage finances and production. The managing director is particularly keen to use computers to help the firm to anticipate how changes in costs, sales revenue and external factors (e.g. interest rates) may affect its financial position.

(e) Using Figure 8 and drawing on your previous analysis, explain in detail how software could be used to evaluate the effect of any changes on cash flow

(8 marks)

A management training conference on 'Just-in-time' production techniques has been advertised. The production manager at AIMS has decided to go to the conference.

(f) How might a computerised productions system including JIT help the production manager to improve production methods and cash flow at AIMS?

(8 marks)

(London Examinations, June 1995)

(Continued on page 636)

CASH FLOW FORECAST: Financial Year 1995/96

	March	April	May	June	July	Aug	Sept	Oct	Nov	Dec	Jan	Feb	March
Receipts(£)													
Sales		0	0	20000	20000	40000	40000	40000	40000	40000	40000	40000	40000
Loans	20000												
Capital Introduced	10000												
Total Receipts	30000	0	0	20000	20000	40000	40000	40000	40000	40000	40000	40000	40000
Payments(£)													
Materials		6000	6000	12000	12000	12000	12000	12000	12000	12000	12000	12000	12000
Owner's payments		0	0	1000	1000	2000	2000	2000	2000	2000	2000	2000	2000
Wages (direct labour)		4000	4000	8000	8000	8000	8000	8000	8000	8000	8000	8000	8000
Wages (Admin)			1200	1200	1200	1200	1200	1200	1200	1200	1200	1200	1200
Capital items	25000												
Uniform Business rate		1400	1400	1400	1400	1400	1400	1400	1400	1400	1400	1400	1400
Water Rates		300			300			300			300		
Electricity		550			550			550			550		
Legal Fees	750												
Advertising	800												
Stationery	400						200						200
Telephone					450				450				450
Insurance	1200												1400
Premises	1500	1500	1500	1500	1500	1500	1500	1500	1500	1500	1500	1500	1500
Bank charges	600	600	600	600	600	600	600	600	600	600	600	600	600
Loan repayments	150	150	150	150	150	150	150	150	150	150	150	150	150
Total payments	30400	14500	14850	25850	27150	26850	27050	27700	27300	26850	27700	26850	28900
Net cash flow	-400	-14500	-14850	-5850	-7150	13150	12950	12300	12700	13150	12300	13150	11100
Balance beg month	0	-400	-14900	-29750	-35600	-42750	-29600	-16650	-4350	8350	21500	33800	46950
Balance end month	-400	-14900	-29750	-35600	-42750	-29600	-16650	-4350	8350	21500	33800	46950	58050

Figure 8 AIMS cash flow forecast

Notes to Figure 8 (AIMS cash flow forecast 1995/96)

1 Receipts:

- **Loans:** the owners borrowed start-up capital of £20,000 from their bank in the form of a business loan.
- **Capital introduced:** the three owners who formed the company put a total of £10,000 personal equity into the business.

2 Payments:

- 'Materials' are the raw materials and components needed to manufacture each machine. These are bought two months before production takes place. Monthly outlay on these is 30% of the retail price ('sales' on the cash flow forecast). Because AIMS is a new business, materials are paid for at the time of ordering and the purchaser usually buys more than is needed for each month's output, to enable the firm to build up a stock of materials during the year.
- Direct labour costs are 20% of the retail price.
- The owners of the firm receive 5% of each month's sales revenue as their income.
- Capital items – to set up the business the owners had to purchase £25,000 worth of Specialist equipment.
- Uniform Business Rate (UBR) is paid to the District Council for services and amenities. The amount is influenced by the location of the site.
- Premises: the firm leases a factory building on a prime site which is part of an industrial estate.
- Bank charges and loan repayments are the monthly amounts paid to the bank for the loan taken out at the beginning of the venture.

CASH FLOW FORECAST: Financial year 1995/96

	Sept	Oct	Nov	Dec	Jan	Feb	March
Receipts(£)							
Sales	40000	40000	40000	40000	40000	40000	
Loans							
Capital Introduced							
Total Receipts	40000	40000	40000	40000	40000	40000	
Payments(£)							
Materials	12000	12000	12000		12000	12000	12000
Owner's payments	2000	2000	2000	2000	2000	2000	2000
Wages (direct labour)	8000	8000	8000		8000	8000	8000
Wages (Admin)	1200	1200	1200	1200	1200	1200	1200
Capital items							
Uniform Business rate	1400	1400	1400	1400	1400	1400	1400
Water Rates		300			300		
Electricity		550			550		
Legal Fees							
Advertising							
Stationery	200						200
Telephone			450				450
Insurance							1400
Premises	1500	1500	1500	1500	1500	1500	1500
Bank charges	600	600	600	600	600	600	600
Loan repayments	150	150	150	150	150	150	150
Total payments	27050	27700	27300				
Net cash flow	12950	12300	12700				
Balance beg month	-29600	-16650	-4350				
Balance end month	-16650	-4350	8350				

Figure 9 Answer sheet for Question 7

8 Study the information and answer all parts of the questions which follows.

BANK CHIEF WARNS STAFF OF TOUGH YEAR

National Westminster Bank (NatWest) has written to its 55,700 staff saying that the past year has been 'difficult' and that parts of the business have failed to reach their targets. The letter has prompted concern that up to half the bank's staff will not receive a pay rise this year.

Dai Davies, Assistant General Secretary of the NatWest Staff Association, said the bank's performance-related pay scheme meant that 65% of staff would get an increase in pay of less than 1% and that a 'significant' number would not receive any pay rise at all.

A NatWest spokesperson said the offer would give rises of between 0 and 9%, depending upon a worker's performance. She added that the bank had designed a sophisticated remuneration system, and that 'pay should not be reviewed in isolation, but as part of a total reward package which includes basic pay, performance bonus, profit-sharing and other non-cash benefits'. The bank operates an appraisal system for all its employees.

The Staff Association hopes to continue negotiations with the bank later in the month, but has not ruled out the involvement of ACAS.

Source: adapted from *The Times*, 4 February 1995

(a) (i) Identify two types of non-cash benefit that an employee might receive.

(*2 marks*)

(ii) Examine the objectives the National Westminster Bank may have had when designing its remuneration system.

(*8 marks*)

(b) Discuss the role ACAS might play in bringing about the resolution of a dispute of this kind.

(*6 marks*)

(c) (i) Give three reasons why a business might operate an appraisal system.

(*3 marks*)

(ii) Discuss the dangers which might exist in using an appraisal system to determine awards of performance-related pay.

(*6 marks*)

9 Study the article and answer all the questions which follow.

IMPROVED RIGHTS FOR PART-TIME WORKERS

The Government yesterday granted improved rights to 750,000 part-time workers. This was as a result of an appeal to the House of Lords by the Equal Opportunities Commission on the grounds that 87% of part-time workers are female.

The Secretary of State for Employment warned jobs would be threatened by allowing part-time workers access to industrial tribunals and redundancy pay after two years. This would be the same as for full-timers, whereas before, part-timers had to wait five years.

Those working 16 hours per week or less will have the same unfair dismissal and redundancy rights as full-timers. About 750,000 people who have been in part-time employment for between two and five years are expected to benefit.

Yesterday's decision regarding part-timers still leaves them without parental leave, sick pay and pension rights. The Institute of Directors, however, warned that the decision would '...inevitably mean fewer jobs for women and young people'.

Source: adapted from *The Independent*, 21 December 1994

(a) Explain the following terms.

(i) Unfair dismissal

(*3 marks*)

(ii) Industrial tribunals

(*3 marks*)

(b) State three rights which the law grants to employees when they are made redundant.

(*3 marks*)

(c) For what reasons might the Institute of Directors warn that allowing part-time workers improved rights will '... inevitably mean fewer jobs for women and young people'?

(*6 marks*)

(d) Between 1979 and 1994 the number of part-time employees in the UK rose from 3.8 million to 6 million. Discuss the factors that may have led to the increase of part-time employment.

(*10 marks*)

(*NEAB*)

10 Study the information below and answer all the questions which follow.

MARKS AND SPENCER PLC: PERSONNEL

New operational structures have provided responsible and fulfilling jobs for our younger managers with better opportunities to develop skills early.

Our policy remains to uphold our position as the premier employer in the retail industry, attracting and retaining people of the highest calibre.

Both management and staff continue to respond well to the introduction of new systems and operating methods with a major focus on customer service. Many of our smaller stores are now run from our regional centres which has resulted in improved standards, better utilisation of resources and lower costs. This arrangement provides more responsible and fulfilling jobs for our best managers and in a number of cases it has allowed younger managers a better opportunity to develop their skills and talents at an earlier stage in their careers.

Management development continues to concentrate on programmes which emphasise the individual's responsibility for self development.

The National Vocational Qualifications (NVQs) are being made available to sales assistants in all stores as quickly as resources allow.

A renewed emphasis on communication within stores, through regular meetings of 'focus groups' composed of staff representatives, has enabled staff and management to work together to resolve store and business issues more effectively.

Source: adapted from Marks & Spencer Plc, Annual Report and Accounts, 1993

(a) How is the full-time equivalent calculated for a business such as Marks & Spencer?

(2 marks)

(b) What evidence is there in the text to illustrate Marks & Spencer's methods of employee motivation?

(5 marks)

(c) Use the ideas of either Herzberg or Maslow to explain the techniques employed by Marks & Spencer to motivate its employees.

(8 marks)

(d) Discuss reasons which might explain the changes in the number of staff of all types employed by Marks & Spencer over the period 1989 to 1993.

(10 marks)

(AEB, June 1995)

	1989	1990	1991	1992	1993
Average number of UK company employees	62,125	61,469	60,930	55,190	51,897
Full-time	20,382	20,538	20,083	19,522	16,555
Part-time	41,743	40,931	40,847	35,668	35,342
Full-time equivalent	40,003	39,875	38,119	34,957	33,251
Financial services full-time equivalent	473	506	507	501	514
UK annual salary cost *(£m)*	390.0	421.3	475.0	448.4	444.0
Profit sharing allocation *(£m)*	13.1	14.7	15.3	16.2	18.1
Number of employees eligible for profit-sharing	41,002	40,759	42,040	43,354	42,890

Figure 10 UK employee statistics, 1989–93

11 Study the information and answer all parts of the question which follows.

UK CAR COMPONENT INDUSTRY OUTCLASSED BY RIVALS

The UK's car component industry remains hugely outclassed by international rivals, despite a drive to improve productivity and quality. Productivity in France and Spain is nearly twice that in the UK, while only Italian manufacturers achieve lower quality standards.

All twelve UK companies examined were not internationally competitive and failed to reach acceptable levels of productivity, unit labour costs and customer satisfaction.

According to the researchers, the UK's component industry suffered from a fragmentation of both component suppliers and customers. Despite the efforts of car makers to encourage improvements by suppliers, the large number of car makers and variations in standards made such improvement difficult. However, rising volumes should provide some help in the future.

Source: adapted from The Times, *4 November 1994*

(a) How might the managers of a firm in the car component industry measure productivity?

(2 marks)

(b) Explain how 'rising volumes… in the future' might help the efficiency of the UK's car component industry.

(8 marks)

(c) Analyse the possible causes of the UK's low productivity in this industry.

(9 marks)

(d) Discuss two ways in which a quality assurance system might help to improve customer satisfaction.

(6 marks)

(AEB,1996)

12 This question is about implementing business decisions. You will be expected to include knowledge relevant to this aspect of business studies in your answers. Read the information carefully then answer the questions.

KILMINSTER ENGINEERING

Kilminster's is an engineering firm which produces flywheels and crankshafts using a shift system.

The daily production run is made up of three eight-hour shifts. During each shift the flywheels and crankshafts have to pass through an acid bath and also spend time on a special machine. It takes 1 hour and 20 minutes to prepare the acid bath for each shift. The special machine is only available for 5 hours per shift. The storage space available to the firm during any shift for the finished flywheels and crankshafts is 1,000 square feet.

The firm knows that during production each flywheel needs 4 minutes in the acid bath while each crankshaft needs 1 minute, and that both products need to spend 1 minute on the special machine. As finished products, each flywheel needs 2 square feet of storage while each crankshaft needs 5 square feet.

The firm knows that when sold, the flywheels will generate a unit profit of £20 while the crankshafts will generate a unit profit of £10.

Kilminster's is hoping to use linear programming to help it calculate the outputs of flywheels and crankshafts needed to maximise its profits.

(a) State a decision-making problem that CANNOT be solved using linear programming. Which operational research technique should be used to solve such a problem? What are the limitations of the technique you have identified?

(8 marks)

(b) The information above includes a number of production constraints that are present during each shift. List these as a set of inequalities and then show this information on a graph.

(8 marks)

(c) One corner of the feasible region on the graph is the origin. Label the other three corners, in a clockwise direction from the origin, A, B and C.

By analysing each of these points, state the outputs of flywheels and crankshafts Kilminster's should produce in order to maximise its profits.

(8 marks)

(d) Unfortunately these profit-maximising outputs do not result in the firm minimising its costs as the special machine is idle for approximately 66 minutes per shift. Calculate whether the firm would be able to increase its daily profit if the daily production run was changed to four 6-hour shifts, *and all other factors remained constant*.

(8 marks)

(e) The profit-maximisation problem above could be solved by computer. Name a software package that could be used, and describe how you would use it.

(8 marks)

(London Examinations, June 1995)

13 This question is about implementing business decisions. You will be expected to include knowledge relevant to this aspect of Business Studies in your answers.

Read the passages below and answer the questions that follow them.

BOOKSELLING IN THE UK

Traditionally, if a person wanted to buy a book they would do so from a newsagent or bookshop. Nowadays, most of the major supermarkets in the UK also sell books. Over the last two years some supermarkets have been able to negotiate directly with bestselling authors to sell their new books at a discount. This has given the supermarkets a competitive advantage over newsagents and bookshops. However, the new arrangements have also involved the supermarkets in a number of additional tasks in the week or so before a discounted title goes on sale.

The list of tasks that have to be undertaken by a particular supermarket might be as follows:

A Check with publishers that copies of the book have been printed;
B Check with printers that in-store advertising posters have been run off;
C Check with manufacturers that point-of-sale displays have been made up;
D Place newspaper advertisements;
E Have in-store advertising posters delivered to the store;
F Have the point-of-sale displays delivered to the store;
G Have copies of the book delivered to the store;
H Check that relevant newspaper advertisements have appeared;
I Put copies of the book into the point-of-sale displays;
J Sell first day copies.

The order of these tasks, their dependency upon one another, and the estimated time to complete each task is shown in Figure 11 below.

(a) Using the information in Figure 11, complete a network diagram for the project.

(16 marks)

(b) (i) Describe the critical path of the project and state the shortest time it will take to complete.

(2 marks)

(ii) Suggest why there might be lead time of four days between the end of Task D and the beginning of Task H.

(1 mark)

Note: There is some float on both Task E and Task F.

(iii) Suggest why the supermarket manager should use all of the time available on Task E.

(2 marks)

(iv) Explain why it would be inappropriate for the supermarket manager to employ two people to carry out Tasks B, C and D.

(3 marks)

The supermarket manager knows queues are likely to form on the day a new title goes on sale.

(c) (i) State FOUR factors that may contribute such queueing problems.

(4 marks)

Figure 12 on page 640 shows some information relating to customers arriving at a supermarket checkout.

If the supermarket manager wanted to run a simulation she could allocate random numbers between 01 and 100 to the data in Figure 12.

(ii) State the range of random numbers that would be allocated to the last row of data in Figure 12.

(1 mark)

(London Examinations, 1996)

Task	Order/dependency	Estimated time (days)
A	Must be done first	0.5
B	Must be done after A	0.5
C	Must be done after A	0.5
D	Must be done after A	0.5
E	Must be done after B, and before I	1
F	Must be done after C, and before I	1
G	Must be done after A, and before I	1
H	Must be done four days after D, and before I	1
I	Must be done after E, F, G and H	1
J	Must be done last	1

Figure 11 Task order and dependency

Time between arrivals (Mins)	Cumulative frequency	Time at checkout (Mins)	Cumulative frequency
0	6	1	4
1	20	2	15
2	37	3	30
3	56	4	48
4	70	5	70
5	82	6	86
6	92	7	94
7	100	8	100

Figure 12 Customers arriving at a supermarket checkout

14 You are advised to spend approximately 90 minutes on this question and to spend about 45 minutes in reading and studying the enclosed extract before attempting to answer the question.

40 marks are allocated to this question. You should treat each part of the question as being of approximately equal importance.

OUT OF THE ROUGH

Lawn-mower maker Ransomes is slowly emerging from the darkest period in its history – decades of neglect, misjudgement and extravagance which left it burdened by debt and almost ready for the scrapheap.

Every revolution leaves pockets of resistance: isolated communities which, for one reason or another, carry on with old, traditional practices long after they have been forgotten elsewhere. For industrial anthropologists, one example is Ransomes, the lawn-mower manufacturer nestling in the suburbs of Ipswich. To step into its plant is to step back in time, back into a pre-Thatcherite world of decaying and ugly factories, of poor management, and of fine old commercial dynasties humbled by world competition.

The place stretches as far as the eye can see. A vast, aircraft hangar of a building, looking as if it hasn't seen a lick of paint since the beginning of the century, lies next to a stout, redbrick head office. Inside, men in oil-soaked overalls gather around lathes, tooling out components, then passing them on to colleagues for the assembly of strange-looking green contraptions. There is little sign of mechanisation, nor of modernisation. 'Any colour you like, so long as it's green', jests the chief executive as he wanders past.

The sheer size of the place is evidence enough that the last five decades or so have not been kind to this place. At one stage some 10,000 people worked here, at the existing plant, and at another across the road, now shut down and redeveloped as a shopping-centre (a small sign of the 80s catching up with this forgotten community). It's like a wizened old creature whose body has shrunk too far to fit its skin. The folds and creases, the bagginess of the place are a mark of the toll age has taken – and of how little rejuvenation there has been.

Ransomes is a company with a long history. It was in at the beginning of the industrial revolution, founded by Robert Ransome, who began as an ironfounder with capital of £200 in Ipswich in 1789. In 1803, a patent was taken out for the chilled cast-iron ploughshare, an implement still widely used today, and one that turned out to be the foundation of the company's fortunes. By the end of the first decade of the 19th century, ploughs were being exported to Canada and South Africa. By 1832, Ransomes had manufactured the world's first lawn mower, a boon to gardeners, who had previously had to trim their lawns with scythes – skilled and time-consuming work which had restricted lawns to the houses of the very rich. The English love-affair with neatly trimmed lawns could now begin, and none would profit from it as handsomely at Ransomes. The company was an exhibitor at the Great Exhibition at Crystal Palace in 1851, and through the 19th century developed its lawn-mower business, while at the same time becoming one of the leading producers of mechanised farm equipment.

History counts for very little in business, however. Today Ransomes is a very different kind of company. Its workforce has shrunk, it is burdened down by massive debts, and it is barely profitable. Blinking slightly, it is starting to emerge from the darkness of its history, and cast its eye onto the glimmering lights of the modern world.

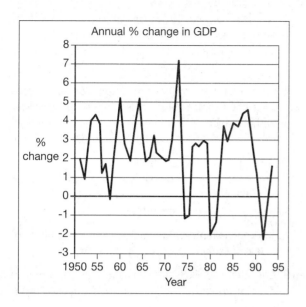

Figure 14 Post-war trade cycles   *Source: Business
Studies Update 1994*

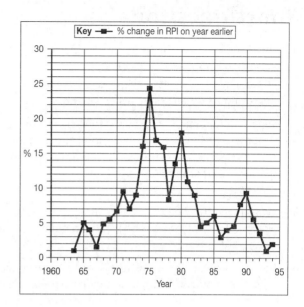

Figure 15 Headline rate of inflation   *Source: Economics
Update 1995*

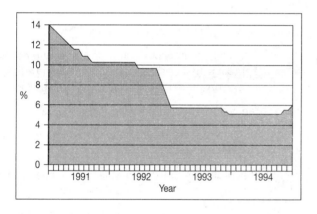

Figure 16 UK interest rates   *Source: MICS Update 1995*

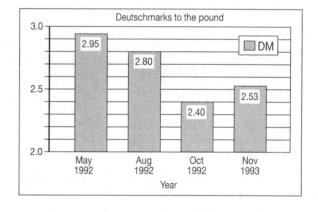

Figure 17 Exchange rates   *Source: Business Studies
Update 1995*

1 (a) What are Ransomes' strengths and weaknesses
        and what opportunities and threats does it face?

   (b) Outline the corporate strategy of Ransomes.
        What do you think are the principal objectives of
        the company?

   (c) 'Ransomes is in with a good chance of surviving
        into its next century.' How far is this appraisal
        supported by the facts given in the extract?

2 (a) What is meant by Gross Domestic Product?

                                             (*2 marks*)

   (b) With reference to Figure 14, in what phase of the
        trade cycle was the UK economy between 1989
        and 1991?

                                             (*1 mark*)

   (c) How might UK firms be affected by fluctuations
        within a trade cycle?

                                             (*6 marks*)

   (d) Referring to the data in Figures 15, 16 and 17, analyse
        the factors which might have aided the recovery of a
        UK-based manufacturer from 1990 onwards.

                                             (9 marks)

   (e) Evaluate the usefulness of the data in Figures 14 –17
        to a fast food retailer in the UK.

                                             (*7 marks*)

                                        (AEB, Summer 1996)

Short questions

1 What do you understand by (i) business process re-engineering/re-design and (ii) Total Quality Management? Assess their relative merits in improving an organisation's effectiveness.

2 What is productivity and how can it be measured? According to OECD figures, UK productivity is higher than that of Japan. How can this be reconciled with the relative performance of British and Japanese industry?

3 What is the function of a leader of an organisation? How, if at all, might leadership vary according to the nature of the task?

4 Recent developments in retailing have included television shopping and banking by telephone. What factors have been responsible for these developments and what are the likely consequences?

5 What is the function of a balance sheet? What information, besides a balance sheet, would be needed to evaluate the likely future performance of a company? Justify your answer.

6 Why have some British companies invested abroad rather than in the UK? What are the effects of this kind of investment on the various stakeholders in the company?

(NEAB, June 1996)

7 What is meant by performance-related pay? Can a seven-figure salary for a chief executive ever be justified?

8 Why have many firms recently reduced the number of middle managers? Evaluate the effect of this process on an organisation's employees and customers.

9 Over 90% of firms in the European Union are 'small'. Why are there so many small firms? To what extent should the UK government assist small firms?

10 In what ways might a firm's market share be measured? Is it always advantageous to a firm to increase its market share?

11 Outline the main determinants of a capital investment decision. What factors might a foreign company consider in deciding whether to invest in a region of the UK?

12 How has technology improved international communications in recent years? Discuss the effect these improvements have had on the strategies of international and national companies.

(NEAB, June 1995)

13 A crisis has led to a dramatic loss of confidence among the customers of a medium-sized company. Consider the effects this may have on the organisation and how it may respond.

14 Many companies make decisions on the basis of quantified data. Given the degree of uncertainty within which firms operate, to what extent should managers adopt this scientific approach to decision-making?

15 'Information technology has done more to bring about an increase in labour flexibility than any measures taken by government.'

To what extent do you believe this statement to be true or false?

16 Consider the likely impact upon British firms of a decision to withdraw this country from the European Union.

(AEB, June 1996)

17 Discuss the implications for a firm's marketing strategy of a decision to pursue the objective of short-term profit maximisation.

18 (a) Distinguish between consultation and delegation.

(b) Consider the impact upon a firm of changing its approach to decision-making from being based upon consultation to reliance upon delegation.

19 Softran is a British clothing manufacturer. Examine:

(a) the main factors determining its international competitiveness;

(b) the problems Softran may face if it needed to substantially boost its competitiveness.

20 Over recent years, the directors of many companies have been receiving substantial increases in pay and fringe benefits, while imposing small rises upon their workforces. Discuss the reasons why a business might pursue such policies.

21 A firm forecasts that it will make a £1 million loss on a £10 million turnover in the coming year. How might it respond?

22 'Although the number of business start-ups has boomed over the past 15 years, too few have developed to create more jobs.'

(a) Why may this be?

(b) To what extent should the government intervene to tackle this problem?

(AEB, June 1995)

Index